Nineteenth-Century Literature Criticism

Guide to Thomson Gale Literary Criticism Series

For criticism on	Consult these Thomson Gale series
Authors now living or who died after December 31, 1999	*CONTEMPORARY LITERARY CRITICISM (CLC)*
Authors who died between 1900 and 1999	*TWENTIETH-CENTURY LITERARY CRITICISM (TCLC)*
Authors who died between 1800 and 1899	*NINETEENTH-CENTURY LITERATURE CRITICISM (NCLC)*
Authors who died between 1400 and 1799	*LITERATURE CRITICISM FROM 1400 TO 1800 (LC)* *SHAKESPEAREAN CRITICISM (SC)*
Authors who died before 1400	*CLASSICAL AND MEDIEVAL LITERATURE CRITICISM (CMLC)*
Authors of books for children and young adults	*CHILDREN'S LITERATURE REVIEW (CLR)*
Dramatists	*DRAMA CRITICISM (DC)*
Poets	*POETRY CRITICISM (PC)*
Short story writers	*SHORT STORY CRITICISM (SSC)*
Literary topics and movements	*HARLEM RENAISSANCE: A GALE CRITICAL COMPANION (HR)* *THE BEAT GENERATION: A GALE CRITICAL COMPANION (BG)* *FEMINISM IN LITERATURE: A GALE CRITICAL COMPANION (FL)* *GOTHIC LITERATURE: A GALE CRITICAL COMPANION (GL)*
Asian American writers of the last two hundred years	*ASIAN AMERICAN LITERATURE (AAL)*
Black writers of the past two hundred years	*BLACK LITERATURE CRITICISM (BLC)* *BLACK LITERATURE CRITICISM SUPPLEMENT (BLCS)*
Hispanic writers of the late nineteenth and twentieth centuries	*HISPANIC LITERATURE CRITICISM (HLC)* *HISPANIC LITERATURE CRITICISM SUPPLEMENT (HLCS)*
Native North American writers and orators of the eighteenth, nineteenth, and twentieth centuries	*NATIVE NORTH AMERICAN LITERATURE (NNAL)*
Major authors from the Renaissance to the present	*WORLD LITERATURE CRITICISM, 1500 TO THE PRESENT (WLC)* *WORLD LITERATURE CRITICISM SUPPLEMENT (WLCS)*

ISSN 0732-1864

Volume 182

Nineteenth-Century Literature Criticism

Criticism of the
Works of Novelists, Philosophers, and Other
Creative Writers Who Died between 1800
and 1899, from the First Published Critical
Appraisals to Current Evaluations

Kathy D. Darrow
Russel Whitaker
Project Editors

THOMSON
GALE

Detroit • New York • San Francisco • New Haven, Conn. • Waterville, Maine • London

Nineteenth-Century Literature Criticism, Vol. 182

Project Editors
Kathy Darrow and Russel Whitaker

Editorial
Jeffrey W. Hunter, Jelena O. Krstović, Michelle Lee, Thomas J. Schoenberg, Noah Schusterbauer, Lawrence J. Trudeau

Data Capture
Frances Monroe, Gwen Tucker

Indexing Services
Factiva, Inc.

Rights and Acquisitions
Robert McCord, Sue Rudolph, Tim Sisler

Composition and Electronic Capture
Tracey L. Matthews

Manufacturing
Cynde Bishop

Associate Product Manager
Marc Cormier

LIBRARY OF CONGRESS CATALOG CARD NUMBER 84-643008

ISBN-13: 978-0-7876-9853-9
ISBN-10: 0-7876-9853-9
ISSN 0732-1864

Printed in the United States of America
10 9 8 7 6 5 4 3 2 1

Contents

Preface vii

Acknowledgments xi

Literary Criticism Series Advisory Board xiii

Preface

Since its inception in 1981, *Nineteenth-Century Literature Criticism* (*NCLC*) has been a valuable resource for students and librarians seeking critical commentary on writers of this transitional period in world history. Designated an "Outstanding Reference Source" by the American Library Association with the publication of is first volume, *NCLC* has since been purchased by over 6,000 school, public, and university libraries. The series has covered more than 500 authors representing 38 nationalities and over 28,000 titles. No other reference source has surveyed the critical reaction to nineteenth-century authors and literature as thoroughly as *NCLC*.

Scope of the Series

NCLC is designed to introduce students and advanced readers to the authors of the nineteenth century and to the most significant interpretations of these authors' works. The great poets, novelists, short story writers, playwrights, and philosophers of this period are frequently studied in high school and college literature courses. By organizing and reprinting commentary written on these authors, *NCLC* helps students develop valuable insight into literary history, promotes a better understanding of the texts, and sparks ideas for papers and assignments. Each entry in *NCLC* presents a comprehensive survey of an author's career or an individual work of literature and provides the user with a multiplicity of interpretations and assessments. Such variety allows students to pursue their own interests; furthermore, it fosters an awareness that literature is dynamic and responsive to many different opinions.

Every fourth volume of *NCLC* is devoted to literary topics that cannot be covered under the author approach used in the rest of the series. Such topics include literary movements, prominent themes in nineteenth-century literature, literary reaction to political and historical events, significant eras in literary history, prominent literary anniversaries, and the literatures of cultures that are often overlooked by English-speaking readers.

NCLC continues the survey of criticism of world literature begun by Thomson Gale's *Contemporary Literary Criticism* (*CLC*) and *Twentieth-Century Literary Criticism* (*TCLC*).

Organization of the Book

An *NCLC* entry consists of the following elements:

- The **Author Heading** cites the name under which the author most commonly wrote, followed by birth and death dates. Also located here are any name variations under which an author wrote, including transliterated forms for authors whose native languages use nonroman alphabets. If the author wrote consistently under a pseudonym, the pseudonym will be listed in the author heading and the author's actual name given in parenthesis on the first line of the biographical and critical information. Uncertain birth or death dates are indicated by question marks. Single-work entries are preceded by a heading that consists of the most common form of the title in English translation (if applicable) and the original date of composition.

- The **Introduction** contains background information that introduces the reader to the author, work, or topic that is the subject of the entry.

- The list of **Principal Works** is ordered chronologically by date of first publication and lists the most important works by the author. The genre and publication date of each work is given. In the case of foreign authors whose works have been translated into English, the list will focus primarily on twentieth-century translations, selecting those works most commonly considered the best by critics. Unless otherwise indicated, dramas are dated by first performance, not first publication. Lists of **Representative Works** by different authors appear with topic entries.

- Reprinted **Criticism** is arranged chronologically in each entry to provide a useful perspective on changes in critical evaluation over time. The critic's name and the date of composition or publication of the critical work are given at the beginning of each piece of criticism. Unsigned criticism is preceded by the title of the source in which it appeared. All titles by the author featured in the text are printed in boldface type. Footnotes are reprinted at the end of each essay or excerpt. In the case of excerpted criticism, only those footnotes that pertain to the excerpted texts are included. Criticism in topic entries is arranged chronologically under a variety of subheadings to facilitate the study of different aspects of the topic.

- A complete **Bibliographical Citation** of the original essay or book precedes each piece of criticism.

- Critical essays are prefaced by brief **Annotations** explicating each piece.

- An annotated bibliography of **Further Reading** appears at the end of each entry and suggests resources for additional study. In some cases, significant literary essays for which the editors could not obtain reprint rights are included here. Boxed material following the further reading list provides references to other biographical and critical sources on the author in series published by Thomson Gale.

Indexes

Each volume of *NCLC* contains a **Cumulative Author Index** listing all authors who have appeared in a wide variety of reference sources published by Thomson Gale, including *NCLC*. A complete list of these sources is found facing the first page of the Author Index. The index also includes birth and death dates and cross references between pseudonyms and actual names.

A **Cumulative Nationality Index** lists all authors featured in *NCLC* by nationality, followed by the number of the *NCLC* volume in which their entry appears.

A **Cumulative Topic Index** lists the literary themes and topics treated in the series as well as in *Classical and Medieval Literature Criticism, Literature Criticism from 1400 to 1800, Twentieth-Century Literary Criticism,* and the *Contemporary Literary Criticism* Yearbook, which was discontinued in 1998.

An alphabetical **Title Index** accompanies each volume of *NCLC*, with the exception of the Topics volumes. Listings of titles by authors covered in the given volume are followed by the author's name and the corresponding page numbers where the titles are discussed. English translations of foreign titles and variations of titles are cross-referenced to the title under which a work was originally published. Titles of novels, dramas, nonfiction books, and poetry, short story, or essay collections are printed in italics, while individual poems, short stories, and essays are printed in roman type within quotation marks.

In response to numerous suggestions from librarians, Thomson Gale also produces an annual paperbound edition of the *NCLC* cumulative title index. This annual cumulation, which alphabetically lists all titles reviewed in the series, is available to all customers. Additional copies of this index are available upon request. Librarians and patrons will welcome this separate index; it saves shelf space, is easy to use, and is recyclable upon receipt of the next edition.

Citing *Nineteenth-Century Literature Criticism*

When citing criticism reprinted in the Literary Criticism Series, students should provide complete bibliographic information so that the cited essay can be located in the original print or electronic source. Students who quote directly from reprinted criticism may use any accepted bibliographic format, such as University of Chicago Press style or Modern Language Association style.

The examples below follow recommendations for preparing a bibliography set forth in *The Chicago Manual of Style,* 14th ed. (Chicago: The University of Chicago Press, 1993); the first example pertains to material drawn from periodicals, the second to material reprinted from books:

Franklin, J. Jeffrey. "The Victorian Discourse of Gambling: Speculations on *Middlemarch* and *The Duke's Children.*" *ELH* 61, no. 4 (winter 1994): 899-921. Reprinted in *Nineteenth-Century Literature Criticism.* Vol. 168, edited by Jessica Bomarito and Russel Whitaker, 39-51. Detroit: Thomson Gale, 2006.

Frank, Joseph. "*The Gambler*: A Study in Ethnopsychology." In *Freedom and Responsibility in Russian Literature: Essays in Honor of Robert Louis Jackson,* edited by Elizabeth Cheresh Allen and Gary Saul Morson, 69-85. Evanston, Ill.: Northwestern University Press, 1995. Reprinted in *Nineteenth-Century Literature Criticism.* Vol. 168, edited by Jessica Bomarito and Russel Whitaker, 75-84. Detroit: Thomson Gale, 2006.

The examples below follow recommendations for preparing a works cited list set forth in the *MLA Handbook for Writers of Research Papers,* 6th ed. (New York: The Modern Language Association of America, 2003); the first example pertains to material drawn from periodicals, the second to material reprinted from books:

Franklin, J. Jeffrey. "The Victorian Discourse of Gambling: Speculations on *Middlemarch* and *The Duke's Children.*" *ELH* 61.4 (Winter 1994): 899-921. Reprinted in *Nineteenth-Century Literature Criticism.* Eds. Jessica Bomarito and Russel Whitaker. Vol. 168. Detroit: Thomson Gale, 2006. 39-51.

Frank, Joseph. "*The Gambler*: A Study in Ethnopsychology." *Freedom and Responsibility in Russian Literature: Essays in Honor of Robert Louis Jackson.* Eds. Elizabeth Cheresh Allen and Gary Saul Morson. Evanston, Ill.: Northwestern University Press, 1995. 69-85. Reprinted in *Nineteenth-Century Literature Criticism.* Eds. Jessica Bomarito and Russel Whitaker. Vol. 168. Detroit: Thomson Gale, 2006. 75-84.

Suggestions are Welcome

Readers who wish to suggest new features, topics, or authors to appear in future volumes, or who have other suggestions or comments are cordially invited to call, write, or fax the Associate Product Manager:

Associate Product Manager, Literary Criticism Series
Thomson Gale
27500 Drake Road
Farmington Hills, MI 48331-3535
1-800-347-4253 (GALE)
Fax: 248-699-8054

Acknowledgments

The editors wish to thank the copyright holders of the criticism included in this volume and the permissions managers of many book and magazine publishing companies for assisting us in securing reproduction rights. Following is a list of the copyright holders who have granted us permission to reproduce material in this volume of *NCLC*. Every effort has been made to trace copyright, but if omissions have been made, please let us know.

COPYRIGHTED MATERIAL IN *NCLC*, VOLUME 182, WAS REPRODUCED FROM THE FOLLOWING PERIODICALS:

American Literature, v. 63, June, 1991. Copyright, 1991 Duke University Press. All rights reserved. Used by permission of the publisher.—*Annales Benjamin Constant*, v. 26, 2002 for "Doux Commerce, Social Organization, and Modern Liberty in the Thought of Benjamin Constant" by James Mitchell Lee. Copyright © 2002 Editions Slatkine. Reproduced by permission of the publisher and the author.—*Arizona Quarterly,* v. 49, winter, 1993 for "Working Through the Frame: Charlotte Temple and the Poetics of Maternal Melancholia" by Julia Stern. Copyright © 1993 by the Regents of the University of Arizona. Reproduced by permission of the publisher and the author.—*The Dalhousie Review,* v. 82, autumn, 2002 for "'Seated on her Bags of Dollars': Representations of America in the English Jacobin Novel" by Nancy E. Johnson. Copyright © 2003. Reproduced by permission of the publisher and the author.—*Historical Reflections,* v. 28, fall, 2002. Copyright © 2002 Historical Reflections/Reflexions Historiques. All rights reserved. Reproduced by permission.—*Journal of American Culture,* v. 19, spring, 1996. Copyright © 1996 by Ray B. Browne. All rights reserved. Reproduced by permission of Blackwell Publishers.—*Journal of Narrative Technique,* v. 26, winter, 1996. Copyright © 1996 by *The Journal of Narrative Technique.* Reproduced by permission.—*Journal of the Australasian Universities Language and Literature Association,* no. 86, November, 1996. Reproduced by permission.—*Journal of the History of Ideas,* v. XLIII, January-March, 1982. Copyright 1982 Journal of the History of Ideas, Inc. Reprinted by permission of the University of Pennsylvania Press.—*The New Criterion,* v. 13, February, 1995 for "A Concept of Liberty: Benjamin Constant" by Renee Winegarten. Copyright © 1995 by Renee Winegarten. Reprinted by permission of Georges Borchardt, Inc., on behalf of Renee Winegarten.—*Nineteenth-Century French Studies,* v. 7, spring-summer, 1979. Copyright © 1979 by T. H. Goetz. Reproduced by permission./ v. 19, winter, 1991. Copyright © 1991 by *Nineteenth-Century French Studies.* Reproduced by permission.—*Stanford French Review,* v. XII, fall-winter, 1988 for "The Demystification of Rousseau: Benjamin Constant's Critique of Rhetoric, Abstraction, and Consequence in *Du contrat social*" by Robert Wilcocks. Copyright © 1988 by ANMA Libri & Co. All rights reserved. Reproduced by permission of the publisher and the author.—*Studies in Romanticism,* v. 38, spring, 1999. Copyright © 1999 by the Trustees of Boston University. Reproduced by permission.—*Studies in the Humanities,* v. 18, December, 1991. Copyright © 1991 by Indiana University Press of Pennsylvania. Reproduced by permission.—*The William and Mary Quarterly,* v. LX, January, 2003. Copyright © 2003, by the Omohundro Institute of Early American History and Culture. Reproduced by permission.—*Women & Language,* v. XXIII, spring, 2000. Reproduced by permission of the publisher.

COPYRIGHTED MATERIAL IN *NCLC*, VOLUME 182, WAS REPRODUCED FROM THE FOLLOWING BOOKS:

Alexander, Ian W. From *Benjamin Constant: Adolphe.* Edward Arnold, 1973. Copyright © Ian W. Alexander 1973. All rights reserved. Reproduced by permission of the publisher and the author.—Butler, Marilyn. From *Jane Austen and the War of Ideas.* Oxford At The Clarendon Press, 1975. Copyright © Oxford University Press 1975. All rights reserved. Reproduced by permission of Oxford University Press.—Cappadocia, E. From "Benjamin Constant and Restoration Liberalism," in *The Triumph of Culture: 18th Century Perspectives.* Edited by Paul Fritz and David Williams. A. M. Hakkert Ltd., 1972. Copyright © 1972 by A. M. Hakkert Ltd. All rights reserved. Reproduced by permission of the Literary Estate of Ezio Cappadocia.—Coleman, Patrick. From *Reparative Realism: Mourning and Modernity in the French Novel, 1730-1830.* Librairie Droz S. A., 1998. Copyright 1998 by Librairie Droz S.A., 11, rue Massot, Geneve. All rights reserved. Reproduced by permission.—Coleman, Patrick. From an Introduction to *Adolphe.* Edited by Patrick Coleman. Translated by Margaret Mauldon. Oxford University Press, 2001. Translation © Margaret Mauldon 2001. Editorial matter © Patrick Coleman 2001. All rights reserved. Reproduced by permission of Oxford University Press.—Dodge, Guy Howard. From *Benjamin Constant's Philosophy of Liberalism.* The University of North Carolina Press, 1980. Copyright © 1980 The Univer-

Thomson Gale Literature Product Advisory Board

Robert Bage
1728-1801

English novelist.

INTRODUCTION

Robert Bage, a relatively little-known novelist who published—anonymously—six works during the last two decades of the eighteenth century, is distinguished both in terms of his radical views and as a businessman who turned to writing at the age of fifty-three as a means of coping with financial difficulties. His works garnered wide critical attention among his contemporaries, but his liberal viewpoint was dismissed by the majority of conservative writers and critics of the nineteenth century. Modern scholars have tended to focus upon the similarities between Bage's works and those of such English Jacobin novelists as William Godwin and Thomas Holcroft, while noting various unique aspects of Bage's narrative approach, particularly his use of comedy and his characterization of women.

BIOGRAPHICAL INFORMATION

Bage was born on February 29, 1728 in Darley, England, a hamlet near the town of Derby. His father was a paper miller, and his mother died shortly after Bage's birth. Bage was subsequently cared for by three stepmothers and was educated in Derby, where he distinguished himself as able student at an early age. It has been speculated but not established that Bage's religious upbringing followed the Quaker tradition. Bage succeeded his father in the paper-milling trade, and was married at the age of twenty-three to Elizabeth Woolley. In 1753 Bage purchased his own paper mill in the village of Elford, Staffordshire. He enjoyed a quiet life in Elford, educated himself in music, French, and Italian, and traveled very little, with the exception of weekly visits to Birmingham between 1760 and 1772, where he augmented his three-hour daily study of mathematics with lessons from Thomas Hanson. In response to negative financial trends in the paper-milling business that necessitated Bage's selling and then leasing his factory during the 1760s, Bage expanded his pursuits to include iron manufacturing. Following substantial financial losses in the iron business in 1780, Bage became despondent, and turned to writing as a means of coping with his emotional distress. Bage's association with well-known liberal, political "radicals" of the time, including his close friend and business associate William Hutton, as well as Joseph Priestley, Josiah Wedgwood, Sir Brooke Boothby, and Erasmus Darwin, influenced his own views which were subsequently expressed in his novels. His first novel, *Mount Henneth,* was published in 1782 by Thomas Lowndes, to whom Bage sold the manuscript for thirty pounds. The popularity of the novel encouraged Bage to write more novels while he continued to operate his paper mill. In 1793 Bage's youngest son died, and the family moved to Tamworth, which was near Derby. Bage spent the rest of his life in Tamworth, where he wrote his last novel, *Hermsprong; or Man as He Is Not* (1796). He died in his home on September 1, 1801.

MAJOR WORKS

Bage's narrative approaches are informed by the epistolary novels of Samuel Richardson, as well as the comic novels of Henry Fielding, Tobias Smollett, and Laurence Sterne. His first novel, *Mount Henneth,* features an epistolary narrative that traces the journey of the altruistic, hard-working businessman James Foston as he attempts to search for people to occupy a utopian society at his rural estate, Henneth. In his search Foston encounters prejudice based on class, religion, social and moral views; prostitution, greed, and other social ills; and issues relating to English colonialism. The novel ends happily with the marriages of several of the members of the utopian society. In *Barham Downs* (1784), Bage treats the social and political decadence of the aristocracy in a narrative that features the plight of Annabelle Whitaker, who is being pressured by her father to submit to the sexual advances and marriage proposal of the villainous politician Lord Winterbottom. Henry Osmond, a young lawyer whose rejection by socialite Lucy Strode leads him to retreat from city life to live in seclusion in rural Barham Downs, serves as Annabelle's rescuer, and the morality of Barham Downs is thus juxtaposed against the corruption of society and the abuse of power. *The Fair Syrian* (1787), which is set in England, France, Turkey, and in Revolutionary War America, centers on the experiences of French aristocrat Marquis de St. Claur, who is captured by an English officer while he is on his way to assist the American forces in the war. St. Claur and the English officer, Sir John Amington, become friends, support the Americans, and tour America after the war. The two men fall in love with women from lower social classes: St. Claur flees to Turkey to avoid the marriage his mother has arranged for him in Paris, and he suffers many misfortunes. Amington's love interest, Honoria Warren, resides for a time in an Eastern harem, and Bage examines her many adventures as a means of deriding the French orientalism of the time, as well as comparing the traditions of the various nations that serve as settings in the novel. In the end the couples convene at Amington's estate, and America is portrayed by Bage as superior to other countries due to its democratic ideology. *James Wallace* (1788) features middle-class protagonists and a dual plot; the title character is an orphan whose experiences with both vice and virtue ultimately lead him to embrace the sensibilities and moral uprightness embodied by Paracelsus Holman, a pharmacist's son with whom Wallace corresponds. The novel's sub-plot centers on the struggles faced by virtuous Judith Lamounde and Pauline Edwards as they defend themselves against the unwanted advances of various men, including members of the aristocracy. *James Wallace* is noted as more politically and socially radical, and less humorous, than its predecessors.

Man as He Is (1792) and *Hermsprong; or, Man as He Is Not* have been widely regarded as Bage's best works. Both novels were written in the 1790s following the French Revolution, which Bage supported as an appropriate response to the abuse of power. Bage disagreed strongly with Edmund Burke's views in *Reflections on the Revolution in France,* and modeled the closing paragraphs of *Man as He Is* to serve as direct responses to passages from Burke's *Reflections.* The adventurous George Paradyne, son of Sir Jeffrey, serves as the protagonist of *Man as He Is,* and learns through trial and error to emulate his genteel father, who exemplifies Bage's ideal of nobility based on character rather than economic or social status. George's various reckless misadventures serve to disparage the frivolity and excess of the aristocracy, and Bage communicates his affirmation of radical political and economic positions on the slave trade, religious tolerance, progressiveness, and libertarianism, through lengthy discussions between the novel's characters. Bage also maintains that the British constitution asserts equal rights for all citizens within a system administered by law. *Hermsprong; or, Man as He Is Not,* Bage's best known novel, relates the tale of Caroline Campinet, daughter of the domineering Lord Grondale, who attempts to force Caroline to marry Sir Philip Chestrum, a feckless dandy. Caroline is saved after a riding accident by a mysterious stranger who disappears after performing his heroic deed. Following this incident, Caroline thinks often about her rescuer, who is ultimately revealed to be Hermsprong, a Native American with plans to found a utopian society along the banks of the Potomac River. Hermsprong embodies the American democratic ideals favored by Bage. He challenges the views of Lord Grondale and Dr. Blick, the orthodox Anglican parson with whom Grondale con-

trols the village, by speaking approvingly of American reformer Thomas Paine's radical work, *The Rights of Man,* and by questioning the ideals espoused by the British constitution. At the novel's end, Hermsprong is revealed to be Sir Charles Campinet, the rightful heir to Grondale's estate; he marries Caroline and established his utopian society at the family estate in Cornwall.

CRITICAL RECEPTION

Critics such as J. M. S. Tompkins have noted that Bage's use of humor in the service of advancing his social and political agenda not only set the author's novels apart from those of his contemporaries but renewed interest in a livelier approach to the English novel form in general. These qualities, critics hold, led to the popularity and critical approval of Bage's earliest works, even while the ideals espoused within them were often disparaged or dismissed. Sir Walter Scott, who strongly disapproved of Bage's political and social views, offered praise for his narrative skills and included three of Bage's novels in his collection *Ballantyne's Novelist's Library* in 1824. *The Fair Syrian* garnered Bage wide popular and critical attention, both in Europe and America, and Bage was lauded for skillfully managing a complex plot while representing and making comparisons between vastly differing cultures and locales.

Man as He Is earned Bage the praise of poet William Cowper, as well as several laudatory reviews, including one by Thomas Holcroft in 1793 and another by noted author Mary Wollstonecraft, who provided a highly favorable assessment of the novel in an unsigned review that appeared in *The Analytical Review* in 1796. *Hermsprong; or, Man as He Is Not* is regarded by most critics, past and present, as Bage's best novel, and it remains the work for which the author is best known. Commentators note that Bage fully realized his potential as an author with *Hermsprong* by achieving a cohesiveness and evenness of narrative style, plot, and tone that are lacking in various respects in his earlier works. William Godwin's admiration for *Hermsprong* inspired him to spend a day with Bage during his travels to the English countryside in 1797.

Bage's works fell out of favor during the Victorian Age, when the vast majority of critics adhered to a strict and conservative social and moral code that contrasted sharply with Bage's radical, liberal ideals. During the twentieth century, critics began to re-examine Bage's works alongside those of other authors who wrote during the tumultuous last quarter of the eighteenth century. Modern critics generally tend to focus on the valuable insights into late eighteenth-century life and thought that can be gained by studying Bage's works, rather than on their literary merits, and scholarly commentary on the author and his works is relatively scarce. Nevertheless, Bage is regarded by those scholars who have studied his works as an earnest, gifted thinker and a witty storyteller whose works retain their capacity to entertain readers as well as to inform them.

PRINCIPAL WORKS

Mount Henneth. 2 vols. (novel) 1782
Barham Downs (novel) 1784
The Fair Syrian (novel) 1787
James Wallace (novel) 1788
Man as He Is (novel) 1792
Hermsprong; or, Man as He Is Not (novel) 1796

*All of Bage's novels were published anonymously.

CRITICISM

Mary Wollstonecraft (review date October 1796)

SOURCE: Wollstonecraft, Mary. Review of *Man As He Is,* by Robert Bage. *The Analytical Review* (October 1796): 398-403.

[*In the following review, originally published anonymously but subsequently attributed to Mary Wollstonecraft, the critic offers praise for* Man as He Is.]

From the number of novels which yearly are brought forth, the spawn of idleness, the inconsiderate are apt to conclude, that a novel is one of the lowest order of literary productions; though a very different estimation seems to be suggested by the small number of good ones which appear.

The author of **Man as he is,** one of the favoured few destined to throw a lustre on the novelist's character, displays richness of mind, and acquired knowledge, blended with such felicity of association, that he starts from the crowd of competitors with easy gaiety, and curveting and frisking attains the goal.

But let us not be misunderstood, we mean merely to say, that the good humoured satire, and amiable playfulness exhibited in these volumes, prevent strength of mind, and soundness of thinking, from always appearing as the predominant features. The mode of instruc-

tion here adopted is indeed so graceful, that few people of sensibility, we suppose, can read this work without wishing to know more of a writer who thus steals on their affections.

But, in praising this novel, the history of a man of fashion, it is not so much the story, as the manner in which it is told, that interested us so warmly. It is rather a bundle of finely imagined incidents than a regular plot, which should open as we advance; and the conclusion is wrought up with so little art, as to call for censure, when it is evident, that the author could have executed it in a style much superiour, would he have taken the trouble.

The taste and judgment, conspicuous in the delineation of many of the characters, merits emphatic praise, because many original touches mark their inviduality, not in the least bordering on caricature; the vulgar mode of securing attention. Neither a monotony of phrase easily retained by the memory, nor a singularity of behaviour, only amusing because singularly ridiculous, is here laboriously adopted, because the author could do something better—seize the discriminating shades of nature.

We wish to notice, with peculiar approbation, the characters of Mr. Mowbray, lady Ann Brixworth, Mr. Bardoc, Mr. Lindsay, and miss Carlill.

The language does justice to the sentiments, and the dialogues are pointed. We shall select one, as independent as any of the story.

> P. 230.—I believe it is just as possible for English gentlemen to meet over a bottle without canvassing affairs of government, as for English ladies—or any ladies—to meet over a tea-table without canvassing fashions or reputations. Amongst other refractory matters, soluble only in wine, our company set seriously to work to decide upon the quantum of good or of evil produced in England by parties.
>
> Parties—according to Mr. Holford—were the bane of all government, which, to be strong and vigorous, ought to go on in a smooth, free, uninterrupted course; and best of all, when governed by a single will; for Mr. Holford was a sound tory, and would have been a jacobite, if that sect of isolaters had not vanished from amongst us for want of a deity. Mr. Holford said all that was to be said on that side the question, and was plyed with counter arguments by Mr. Ward, who not only thought parties useful in a state, but deviated from his subject to prove that kings—an individual here and there excepted—were a breed pernicious to man, and which mankind ought to extinguish or to muzzle.
>
> Irreverence to kings was blasphemy, in the opinion of Mr. Holford. His eyes sparkled with holy rage, and was scarce to be restrained by good manners from anathematizing the wretch who could maintain such opinions. The argument went into abuse, and very much into diffusion. Mr. Lindsay heard all with the calm

tranquillity of a philosopher. Sir George enjoyed the controversy; and if he spoke, it was with the mischievous view of animating the combatants.

Not so the stranger; he cared little indeed for the argument, but much for the peace of this small society. Twice he called to order, without effect; the third time with a voice and look that seemed to say, I will be heard, he said, "Gentlemen—anger may, breed contention, but cannot be productive of wisdom. A little reflection will convince you, that you are wasting words, and giving good sense to be scattered by the winds of heaven. What! has experience so little taught mankind the road to truth, that men will still seek it by ways in which it is not to be sound. Things not known, are to be sought for by the medium of things that are known; this is an axiom not less true in politics than in mathematics; but gentlemen—where are your data?"

Sir George and Mr. Lindsay, struck with the stranger's good sense as well as his manner, applauded what he had just said; Mr. Holford and Mr. Ward were reduced to silence, more by the commanding emphasis with which the gentleman spoke, than by his axiom.

"It is," continued he, "a rule in well ordered societies, that every person should say what he chuses without interruption; and this rule preserves decorum, and may gain attention; without it, gentlemen are too apt to attend to no ideas but their own. In such a case, Michael the archangel might speak, and speak in vain. Every man expects to be heard; every man then should be ready to hear.

"It is to be observed, gentlemen," continued the stranger, "that a good argument is nothing but a series of antecedents and consequents, of propositions, proofs, and deductions; the conclusions ought to be taken from the premises strictly, but perspicuously. I hope I have the honour of your assent to these particulars."

All bowed and were silent except Sir George, whose curiosity being highly raised by this exordium, said, "Certainly, sir; and I wish a gentleman who knows so well to give the precept, would also give the example."

"If," said the gentleman, "you will accept a feeble specimen of what may be done by your superior powers rightly directed, I will endeavour to satisfy you." They bowed assent.

"Government," the stranger proceeded, "whether of divine or human ordinance, has for its end the good of mankind.

"Man is carried by instinct, or something as strong as instinct, to the gratification of his appetites, and to the indulgence of his passions.

"Kings are men.

"When the love of power becomes a passion—and when does it not become a passion in kings? it seeks its own enlargement.

"Power may be directed to the increase of the general welfare; it may also be directed to its injury.

"If ten kings stretch it to the injury of mankind, for one who uses it for their benefit—and I fear the history of mankind will not lead us to deny the proposition—the reason for restraining it is ten times as great, as the reason for leaving it unlimited.

"Therefore it ought to be restrained. This argument being directed against Mr. Holford's principle position, I attend his reply."

Mr. Holford declined to answer—for says he, "Though perhaps I might find matter, I cannot, for want of practice, dispose of it by logical arrangement."

"May I be permitted," the stranger asked, "without offence, to endeavour it, as far as I have this day heard your argument."

Mr. Holford nodded an ungracious assent.

"Since," continued the speaker, "the powers that be, are ordained of God; government is of divine authority.

"Kings are therefore the delegates of heaven, and how can it be supposed that delegates of heaven can abuse their power?

"If men are ever unfortunate enough to think they do, it ought to be considered as permitted by heaven, and therefore a chastisement for the sins of a people.

"In such a case, resistance would be impious. We ought to bow down our heads before the Lord, and before his anointed,"

This was said with so imposing a tone of gravity and importance, that Mr. Holford cried out exultingly, "Yes, certainly, these are my elements, as I may call them; these are my fundamental propositions, and I think they will not be easily refuted."

"They may be denied, however." Mr. Ward answered.

"Any thing may be denied, sir," said Mr. Holford; "a man may deny the incarnation."

"That he may indeed," replied Mr. Ward. "Let us however return to our subject. I flatly and positively deny that kings are delegates of heaven."

"We must prove it then," said the stranger, with his accustomed gravity. "God governs the world; then all the active powers in it are his ministers. Kings are active powers. Then Kings are his ministers."

"I deny that he governs the world in any such sense," said Ward. "As we go on," said the stranger, "we must give up the argument for want of data on which we can build. Let us try again.

"God made the world, and all things in it." The speaker looked at Mr. Ward for his assent, who not answering, he added, "for the use of man."

"With that addition," replied the apothecary, "I deny the proposition."

"If so," resumed the stranger, "I must turn you over to the clergy; for," continued he, smiling, "when I think upon gnats, locusts, and mosquitoes, I dare not enter upon the proof."

Mr. Holford at this conclusion, happened to be in the midst of a pipe, sucked in the grateful perfume with double avidity; probably hoping amidst his other inspirations, a small blast of the spirit. As it was rather too long in coming, sir George asked the stranger, if he thought the question concerning parties was capable of logical decision?

"One might reason upon it," said the stranger, looking at the apothecary with complacency, "if the gentlemen of the faculty would not deny us our data thus:

"Laws are necessary for man, and require certain individuals to execute them.

"Generally—man will not take a trouble without expectation of any emolument. There are emoluments of ambition, of vanity, of pride, of revenge, as well as of avarice.

"Generally—for I would not absolutely deny the existence of pure patriotism, though I consider it as a rare virtue—contention for office, is a contention of these and other similar passions.

"Generally—the servants of the crown are desirous to preserve their emoluments; whilst they have upon their right hand and upon their left, those who desire to obtain them for themselves.

"In every proposition that comes from the part of government, their odds are to lay, that the ostensible is not the sole, and seldom the principle motive. That there is some cabal to gratify, some concealed interest to promote, some crooked politics which shun the face of day.

"The eye of the people is not that of a Lynx. The keen eye of opposition is alone competent to see the barbed hook, which too often lies concealed under the splendid baits of government. So far parties are good.

"If all were fair on the part of administration, still, disquisition is necessary for finding the good or the evil of an unknown object; and party is necessary for disquisition. Parties then are generally good."

It is true, that neither the antecedents or the consequents in these arguments, were indebted to their author for precision; but the mode was new, and as none of the gentlemen seemed disposed to follow it, sir George, after a compliment paid to the stranger, adroitly changed the subject.

After many diffusive turns and changes, in which the stranger took little share, the conversation fell upon the manners and morals of the age. Many good things were said which have been said before, and others not so good, and none deserving repetition.

After disputing long with little hope of concordance, the stranger was requested to give his opinion.

"We have," said he, "corrected many faults, and we have brought many into more general existence. The manly manners of our more immediate ancestors, we have exchanged for the manners of women, We have gained in gentleness and humanity; we have lost in firmness of nerve, and strength of constitution. The vices of our more remote ancestors were great and ferocious; ours are of softer temperament, but more diffused. In point of quantity, their follies bore but a small proportion to our frivolities; in short, we have lost tobacco; but we have made it up to the revenue in pomades, in essences, and in hair-powder."

This conclusion, seeming to descend into the bathos, drew a general smile from the company.

"But what shall I say," continued the stranger, his eyes sparkled with superior animation: "what shall I say of our women? heavens! what pen or tongue can enumerate the evils which arise from our connexions, our matrimonial connexions with this frail and feeble sex? which of our corruptions may we not trace to their vanities?"

It is with pleasure we inform our readers, that the author has published another work, entitled, *Man as he is not,* which we shall very soon notice.

Sir Walter Scott (essay date 1887)

SOURCE: Scott, Sir Walter. "Robert Bage." In *Lives of Eminent Novelists and Dramatists,* pp. 605-17. London: Frederick Warne and Co., 1887.

[*In the following essay, Scott offers biographical details on Bage's life, extracts from some of Bage's letters, a positive critical assessment of Bage's works, and a negative response to Bage's social, political, and theological views.*]

Robert Bage, a writer of no ordinary merit in the department of fictitious composition, was one of that class of men occurring in Britain alone, who unite successfully the cultivation of letters with those mechanical pursuits which, upon the continent, are considered as incompatible with the character of an author. The professors of letters are, in most nations, apt to form a *caste* of their own, into which they may admit men educated for the learned professions, on condition, generally speaking, that they surrender their pretensions to the lucrative practice of them; but from which mere burghers, occupied in ordinary commerce, are as severely excluded, as *roturiers* were of old from the society of the *noblesse*. The case of a paper-maker or a printer employing their own art upon their own publications, would be thought uncommon in France or Germany; yet such were the stations of Bage and Richardson.

The writer has been obliged by Miss Catherine Hutton, daughter of Mr. Hutton of Birmingham, well known as an ingenious and successful antiquary, with a memoir of the few incidents marking the life of Robert Bage, whom a kindred genius, as well as a close commercial intercourse, combined to unite in the bonds of strict friendship. The communication is extremely interesting, and the extracts from Bage's letters show, that amidst the bitterness of political prejudices, the embarrassment of commercial affairs, and all the teazing technicalities of business, the author of *Barham Downs* still maintained the good-humoured gaiety of his natural temper. One would almost think the author must have drawn from his own private letter-book and correspondence, the discriminating touches which mark the men of business in his novels.

The father of Robert Bage was a paper-maker at Darley, a hamlet on the river Derwent, adjoining the town of Derby, and was remarkable only for having had four wives. Robert was the son of the first, and was born at Darley on the 29th of February, 1728. His mother died soon after his birth; and his father, though he retained his mill, and continued to follow his occupation, removed to Derby, where his son received his education at a common school. His attainments here, however, were very remarkable, and such as excited the surprise and admiration of all who knew him. At seven years old he had made a proficiency in Latin. To a knowledge of the Latin language succeeded a knowledge of the art of making paper, which he acquired under the tuition of his father.

At the age of twenty-three, Robert Bage married a young woman who possessed beauty, good sense, good temper, and money. It may be presumed that the first of these was the first forgotten; the two following secured his happiness in domestic life; the last aided him in the manufacture of paper, which he commenced at Elford, four miles from Tamworth, and conducted to the end of his days.

Though no man was more attentive to business, and no one in the country made paper so good of its kind, yet the direction of a manufactory, combined with his present literary attainments, did not satisfy the comprehensive mind of Robert Bage. His manufactory, under his eye, went on with the regularity of a machine, and left him leisure to indulge his desire of knowledge. He acquired the French language from books alone, without any instructor; and his familiarity with it is evinced by his frequent, perhaps too frequent, use of it in the **Fair Syrian.** Nine years after his marriage he studied mathematics; and, as he makes one of his characters say, and as he probably thought respecting himself, "He was obliged to this science for a correct imagination, and a taste for uniformity in the common actions of life."

In the year 1765, Bage entered into partnership with three persons (one of them the celebrated Dr. Darwin), in an extensive manufactory of iron; and, at the end of fourteen years, when the partnership terminated, he found himself a loser, it is believed, of fifteen hundred pounds. The reason and philosophy of the paper-maker might have struggled long against so considerable a loss; the man of letters committed his cause to a better champion—literary occupation—the tried solace of misfortune, want, and imprisonment. He wrote the novel of **Mount Henneth,** in two volumes, which was sold to Lowndes for thirty pounds, and published in 1781. The strong mind, playful fancy, liberal sentiments, and extensive knowledge of the author, are everywhere apparent: but, as he says himself, "too great praise is a bad letter of recommendation"; and truth, which he wor-

shipped, demands the acknowledgment, that its sins against decorum are manifest.

The succeeding works of Bage were, **Barham Down,** two volumes, published 1784; **The Fair Syrian,** two volumes, published (about) 1787; **James Wallace,** three volumes, published 1788; **Man as he is,** four volumes, published 1792; **Hemsprong, or, Man as he is not,** three volumes, published 1796. It is, perhaps, without parallel in the annals of literature, that, of six different works, comprising a period of fifteen years, the last should be, as it unquestionably is, the best. Several of Bage's novels were translated into German, and published at Frankfort.

Whoever has read Hayley's *Life of Cowper* will not be sorry that an author should speak for himself, instead of his biographer speaking for him; on this principle are given some extracts from the letters of Robert Bage to his friend, William Hutton. Hutton purchased nearly all the paper which Bage made during forty-five years; and, though Bage's letters were letters of business, they were written in a manner peculiarly his own, and friendship was, more or less, interwoven in them; for trade did not, in him, extinguish, or contract, one finer feeling of the soul. Bage, in his ostensible character of a paper-maker, says—

March 28, 1785

I swear to thee I am one of the most cautious men in the world with regard to the excise; I constantly interpret against myself in doubtful points; and, if I knew a place where I was vulnerable, I would arm it with the armour of Achilles. I have already armed myself all over with the armour of righteousness, but that signifies nothing with our people of excise.

August 15, 1787

Oh how I wish thou wouldst bend all thy powers to write a history of Excise—with cases—showing the injustice, the inequality of clauses in Acts, and the eternal direction every new one takes towards the oppression of the subject: It might be the most useful book extant. Of whites and blues, blue demy only can come into thy magazine, and that at a great risk of contention with the Lords of the Exchequer; for I know not whether I have understood the sense of people who have seldom the good luck to understand themselves. The paper sent is charged at the lowest price at which a sober paper-maker can live, and drink small beer."

December 10, 1788

Authors, especially when they have acquired a certain degree of reputation, should be candid, and addicted to speak good as well as evil, of poor dumb things. The rope paper is too thin, I own; but why abuse it from the crown of the head to the sole of the foot? If I have eyes, it has many good qualities, and I hope the good people of Birmingham may find them out. But it is too thin—I am heartily and sincerely concerned for it: But, as I cannot make it thicker, all I can do is to reduce the price. Thou proposest threepence a ream—I agree to it. If thou really believest sixpence ought to be abated, do it. Combine together the qualities of justice and mercy, and to their united influence I leave thee."

February 23, 1789

The certainty that it cannot be afforded at the stipulated price, makes me run my rope paper too thin. Of this fault, however, I must mend, and will mend, whether thou canst, or canst not mend my price. I had rather lose some profit than sink a tolerable name into a bad one."

March 11, 1793

I make no bill-of-parcels. I do not see why I should give myself the trouble to make thee bills-of-parcels, as thou canst make them thyself; and, more especially, when it is probable thou wilt make them more to my liking than the issues of my own pen. If the paper is below the standard so far as to oblige thee to lower the price, I am willing to assist in bearing the loss. If the quantity overburthens thee, take off a shilling a bundle—or take off two: for thy disposition towards me—I see it with pleasure—is kindly.

June 30, 1795

Everything looks black and malignant upon me.—Men clamouring for wages which I cannot give—women threatening to pull down my mill—rags raised by freight and insurance—Excise officers depriving me of paper! Say, if thou canst, whether these gentlemen of the Excise-office can seize paper after it has left the maker's possession?—after it has been marked?—stamped?—signed with the officer's name?—Excise duty paid?—Do they these things?—Am I to hang myself?

June 6, 1799

Thou canst not think how teazing the excise-officers are about colour. They had nearly seized a quantity of common cap paper, because it was whitened by the frost. They have an antipathy to anything whiter than sackcloth.

Bage actually had paper seized by the excise-officers, and the same paper liberated, seized again, and again liberated. If his wisdom and integrity have been manifested in the foregoing extracts, the ignorance and folly of these men, or of their masters, must be obvious.

A few extracts, not so immediately connected with conduct in trade, may not be superfluous:—

I swear by Juno, dear William, that one man cannot be more desirous of dealing with another than I am with thee. The chain that connects us cannot be snapped asunder without giving me pain almost to torture. Thou art not so sure of having found the place where Henry the Seventh was lost, as thou mightst have been of finding Elford and a friend.

I received thy pamphlet,[1] and am not sure whether I have not read it with more pleasure than any of thy former works. It is lively, and the reasoning just. Only

remember, it is sometimes against the institutions of juries and county courts that thou hast directed thy satire, which, I think, ought to be confined to the abuses of them. But why abusest thou me? Didst thou not know of **Mount Henneth,** and **Barham Downs,** before publication? Yea, thou didst. I think thou didst also of the **Fair Syrian.** Of what, then, dost thou accuse me? Be just. And why dost thou call me an infidel? Do I not believe in everything thou sayest? And am I not impatient for thy *Derby*? I am such a scoundrel as to grumble at paying 30 per cent, *ad valorem,* which I really do, and more, on my boards, as if one could do too much for one's king and country. But I shall be rewarded when thy *History of Derby* comes forth.

Miss Hutton was the harbinger of peace and good-will from the Reviewers. I knew she had taste and judgment; I knew also that her encomium would go beyond the just and proper bounds; but I also believed she would not condescend to flatter without some foundation.

Eat my breakfast quietly, thou varlet! So I do when my house does not smoke, or my wife scold, or the newspapers do not tickle me into an irritation, or my men clamour for another increase of wages. But I must get my bread by eating as little of it as possible; for my Lord Pitt will want all I can screw of overplus. No matter. Ten years[2] hence, perhaps, I shall not care a farthing.

Another meeting among my men! Another (the third) raising of wages! What will all this end in? William Pitt seems playing off another of his alarming manœuvres—Invasion—against the meeting of Parliament, to scare us into a quiet parting with our money.

If thou hast been again into Wales, and hast not expired in ecstacy, I hope to hear from thee soon. In the interim, and always and evermore, I am thine.

I am afraid thy straggling mode of sending me anybody's bills, and everybody's bills, will subject me often to returned ones. But I have received good at thy hands, and shall I not receive evil? Everything in this finest, freest, best of all possible countries, grows worse and worse, and why not thou?

I looked for the anger thou talked'st of in thy last, but could not find it; and for what wouldst thou have been angry, if thou couldst? Turn thy wrath from me, and direct it against the winds and the fogs. In future I fear it will be directed against the collectors of dirty rags in London and in Germany, where the prices 'have increased, are increasing, and ought to be diminished'— but will not be so, because we begin the century by not doing what we ought to do. What we shall do at the end of it I neither know nor care.

In October, 1800, Bage had visited Hutton at Birmingham, where the latter still passed the hours of business, and had taken Bennett's Hill in his way home, to call on Catherine Hutton, the daughter of his friend. Both were alarmed at the alteration in Bage's countenance, which exhibited evident symptoms of declining health. They believed that they should see him no more; and he was probably impressed with the same idea, for, on quitting the house at Birmingham, he cordially shook hands with Samuel Hutton, the grand-nephew of his friend, and said, "Farewell, my dear lad, we shall meet again in heaven."

At home, Bage seems to have indulged the hope of another meeting in the present world; for two months after his letter of January, he says, in a letter to Hutton, "Tell Miss Hutton that I have thought of her some hundred times since I saw her; insomuch that I feared I was falling in love. I do love her as much as a man seventy-three years of age, and married, ought to love. I like the idea of paying her a visit, and will try to make it reality some time—but not yet." In April he was scarcely able to write a letter. In June he was again capable of attending to business; but in reply to his friend, who had mentioned paying him a visit, he said, "I should have been glad and sorry, dear William, to have seen thee at Tamworth." On the 1st of September, 1801, he died.

Bage had quitted Elford, and during the last eight years of his life he resided at Tamworth, where he ended his days. His wife survived him. He had three sons, one of whom died as he was approaching manhood, to the severe affliction of his father. Charles, the eldest son, settled at Shrewsbury, where he was the proprietor of a very extensive cotton manufactory. He died in 1822, at the age of seventy. Edward the younger son, was apprenticed to a surgeon and apothecary at Tamworth, where he afterwards followed his profession. He died many years before his brother. Both possessed a large portion of their father's talents, and equalled him in integrity and moral conduct.

In his person, Robert Bage was somewhat under the middle size, and rather slender, but well proportioned. His complexion was fair and ruddy; his hair light and curling; his countenance intelligent, mild, and placid. His manners were courteous, and his mind was firm. His integrity, his honour, his devotion to truth, were undeviating and incorruptible; his humanity, benevolence, and generosity, were not less conspicuous in private life than they were in the principal characters in his works. He supplied persons he never saw with money, because he heard they were in want. He kept his servants and his horses to old age, and both men and quadrupeds were attached to him. He behaved to his sons with the unremitting affection of a father; but, as they grew up, he treated them as men and equals, and allowed them that independence of mind and conduct which he claimed for himself.

On the subject of servants, Bage says, in **The Fair Syrian,** "I pity those unhappy masters, who, with unrelenting gravity, damp the effusions of a friendly heart, lest something too familiar for their lordly pride should issue from a servant's lip." Of a parent he says, in the same work, "Instead of the iron rod of parents, he used

only the authority of mild persuasion, and cultivated the affections of his children by social intercourse, and unremitting tenderness." It matters not into what month Robert Bage put these sentiments; they were his own, his practice was conformable to them, and their good effects were visible on all around him.

The following comparison between Robert Bage and his friend, William Hutton, was written by Charles Bage, son of the former, in a letter to Catherine Hutton, daughter of the latter, October 6, 1816.

> The contrast between your father's life and mine is curious. Both were distinguished by great natural talents; both were mild, benevolent, and affectionate, qualities which were impressed on their countenances; both were indignant at the wantonness of pride and power; both were industrious, and both had a strong attachment to literature: yet, with these resemblances, their success in life was very different; my father never had a strong passion for wealth, and he never rose into opulence. Your father's talents were continually excited by contact with 'the busy haunts of men;' my father's were repressed by a long residence in an unfrequented place, in which he shunned the little society he might have had, because he could not relish the conversation of those whose minds were less cultivated than his own. In time, such was the effect of habit, that, although when young he was lively and fond of company, he enjoyed nothing but his book and pen, and a pool at quadrille with ladies. He seems, almost always, to have been fonder of the company of ladies than of men.

After this satisfactory account of Bage's life and character, there remains nothing for the writer but to offer a few critical remarks upon his compositions.

The general object of Robert Bage's compositions, is rather to exhibit character than to compose a narrative; rather to extend and infuse his own political and philosophical opinions, in which a man of his character was no doubt sincere, than merely to amuse the reader with the wonders, or melt him with the sorrows of a fictitious tale. In this respect he resembled Voltaire and Diderot, who made their most formidable assaults on the system of religion and politics which they assailed, by embodying their objections in popular narratives. Even the quaint, facetious, ironical style of this author seems to be copied from the lesser political romances of the French school; and if Bage falls short of his prototypes in wit, he must be allowed to exhibit, upon several occasions, a rich and truly English vein of humour, which even Voltaire does not possess.

Respecting the tendency and motive of these works, it is not the writer's purpose to say much. Bage appears, from his peculiar style, to have been educated a Quaker; at least—for we may be wrong in the above inference—he has always painted the individuals of that primitive sect of Christians in amiable colours, when they are introduced as personages into his novels. If this was the case, however, he appears to have wandered from the tenets of the Friends into the wastes of scepticism; and a sectary, who had reasoned himself into an infidel, could be friend neither to the Church of England, nor the doctrines which she teaches. His opinions of State affairs were perhaps a little biased by the frequent visits of the excisemen, who levied taxes on his commodities, for the purpose of maintaining a war which he disapproved of. It was most natural that a person who considered tax-gatherers as extortioners, and the soldiers, paid by the taxes, as licensed murderers, should conceive the whole existing state of human affairs to be wrong; and if he was conscious of talent, and the power of composition, he might, at the same time, naturally fancy that he was called upon to put it to rights. No opinion was so prevalent in France, and none passed more current among the admirers of French philosophy in Britain, as that the power of framing governments, and of administering them, ought to remain with persons of literary attainments; or, in other words, that those who can most easily and readily write books, are therefore best qualified to govern states. Whoever peruses the writings of the ingenious Madame de Staël, will perceive that she (one of the most remarkable women certainly of her time) lived and died in the belief, that revolutions were to be effected, and countries governed, by a proper succession of clever pamphlets. A nation which has long enjoyed the benefit of a free press, does not furnish so many believers in the omnipotence of literary talent. Men are aware that every case may be argued on both sides, and seldom render their assent to any proposition merely on account of the skill with which it is advocated, or the art and humour with which it is illustrated. The writer was never one of those who think that a good cause can suffer much by free discussion, and though differing entirely both from his political and theological tenets, admitted Mr. Bage's novels into the collection which he superintended, as works of talent and genius.

The satirical novel is a species of composition more adapted to confirm those who hold similar opinions with the author, by affording them a triumph at the expense of their opponents, than to convince those who, their minds being yet undecided, may be disposed calmly to investigate the subject. They who are inclined to burn an obnoxious or unpopular person in effigy, care little how far his dress and external appearance are exaggerated; and, in the same way, it requires little address in an author, to draw broad caricatures of those whom he regards as foes, or to make specious and flattering representations of such as he considers as friends. They who look on the world with an impartial eye, will scarcely be of opinion, that Mr. Bage has seized the true features which distinguish either the upper or lower ranks. The highest and the lowest rank in society, are each indeed liable to temptations peculiarly their own,

and their relative situation serves to illustrate the wisdom of the prayer, "Give me neither poverty nor riches." But these peculiar propensities, we think, will in life be found considerably different from the attributes ascribed to the higher and lower classes by Mr. Bage. In most cases, the author's great man resembles the giant of the ancient romance of chivalry, whose evil qualities were presumed from his superior stature, and who was to be tilted at and cut to pieces, merely because he stood a few inches higher than his fellow-mortals. But the very vices and foibles of the higher classes in modern times are of a kind different from what Bage has frequently represented them. Men of rank, in the present day, are too indifferent, and too indolent, to indulge any of the stormy passions, and irregular but vehement desires, which create the petty tyrant, and perhaps formerly animated the feudal oppressor. Their general fault is a want of energy, or, to speak more accurately, an apathy, which is scarcely disturbed even by the feverish risks to which they expose their fortune, for the sole purpose, so far as can be discerned, of enjoying some momentary excitation. Amongst the numbers, both of rank and talent, who lie stranded upon the shore of Spenser's Lake of Idleness, are many who only want sufficient motives for exertion, to attract at once esteem and admiration; and among those, whom we rather despise than pity, a selfish apathy is the predominating attribute.

In like manner, the habits of the lower classes, as existing in Britain, are far from affording, exclusively, that rich fruit of virtue and generosity, which Mr. Bage's writings would teach us to expect. On the contrary, they are discontented, not unnaturally, with the hardships of their situation, occupied too often in seizing upon the transient enjoyments which chance throws in their way, and open to temptations which promise to mend their condition in life, or at least to extend the circle of their pleasures at the expense of their morals.

Those, therefore, who weigh equally, will be disposed to think that the state of society most favourable to virtue, may be most successfully sought amongst those who neither want nor abound, who are neither sufficiently raised above the necessity of labour and industry, to be satiated by the ready gratification of every wild wish as it arises, nor so much depressed below the general scale of society, as to be exasperated by struggles against indigence, or seduced by the violence of temptations which that indigence renders it difficult to resist.

Though we have thus endeavoured to draw a broad line of distinction between the vices proper to the conditions of the rich and the poor, the reader must be cautious to understand these words in a relative sense. For men are not rich or poor in relation to the general amount of their means, but in proportion to their wants and their wishes. He who can adjust his expenses within the limits of his income, how small soever that may be, must escape from the temptations which most easily beset indigence; and the rich man, who makes it his business, as it is his duty, to attend to the proper distribution of his wealth, will be equally emancipated from those to which opulence is peculiarly obnoxious.

This misrepresentation of the different classes in society, is not the only speculative error in which Bage has indulged during these poetic narratives. There is in his novels a dangerous tendency to slacken the reins of discipline upon a point, where, perhaps, of all others, society must be benefited by their curbing restraint.

Fielding, Smollett, and other novelists, have with very indifferent taste, brought forward their heroes as rakes and debauchees, and treated with great lightness those breaches of morals, which are too commonly considered as venial in the male sex; but Bage has extended, in some instances, that licence to the female sex, and seems at times even to sport with the ties of marriage, which is at once the institution of civil society most favourable to religion and good order, and that which, in its consequences, forms the most marked distinction between man and the lower animals. All the influence which women enjoy in society,—their right to the exercise of that maternal care which forms the first and most indelible species of education; the wholesome and mitigating restraint which they possess over the passions of mankind; their power of protecting us when young, and cheering us when old,—depend so entirely upon their personal purity, and the charm which it casts around them, that to insinuate a doubt of its real value, is wilfully to remove the broadest corner-stone on which civil society rests, with all its benefits, and with all its comforts. It is true, we can easily conceive that a female like Miss Ross, in **Barham Downs,** may fall under the arts of a seducer, under circumstances so peculiar as to excite great compassion; nor are we so rigid as to say, that such a person may not be restored to society, when her subsequent conduct shall have effaced recollection of her error. But she must return thither as a humble penitent, and has no title to sue out her pardon as a matter of right, and assume a place among the virtuous of her sex as if she had never fallen from her proper sphere. Her disgrace must not be considered as a trivial stain, which may be communicated by a husband as an exceeding good jest to his friend and correspondent; there must be, not penitence and reformation alone, but humiliation and abasement, in the recollection of her errors. This the laws of society demand even from the unfortunate; and to compromise further, would open a door to the most unbounded licentiousness. With this fault in principle is connected an indelicacy of expression frequently occurring in Bage's novels, but which, though a gross error in point of taste, we consider as a matter of much less consequence than the former.

Having adverted to this prominent error in Mr. Bage's theory of morals, we are compelled to remark, that his ideas respecting the male sex are not less inaccurate, considered as rules of mental government, than the over-indulgence with which he seems to regard female frailty. Hermsprong, whom he produces as the ideal perfection of humanity, is paraded as a man who, freed from all the nurse and all the priest has taught, steps forward on his path, without any religious or political restraint, as one who derives his own rules of conduct from his own breast, and avoids or resists all temptations of evil passions, because his reason teaches him that they are attended with evil consequences. In the expressive words of our moral poet, Wordsworth, he is

> A reasoning self-sufficient thing,
> An intellectual all-in-all.

But did such a man ever exist? or are we, in the fair construction of humanity, with all its temptations, its passions, and its frailties, entitled to expect such perfection from the mere force of practical philosophy? Let each reader ask his own bosom, whether it were possible for him to hold an unaltered tenor of moral and virtuous conduct, did he suppose that to himself alone he was responsible, and that his own reason, a judge so peculiarly subject to be bribed, blinded, and imposed upon by the sophistry with which the human mind can gloss over those actions to which human passions so strongly impel us, was the ultimate judge of his actions? Let each reader ask the question at his own conscience, and if he can honestly and conscientiously answer in the affirmative, he is either that faultless monster which the world never saw, or he deceives himself as grossly as the poor devotee, who, referring his course of conduct to the action of some supposed internal inspiration, conceives himself upon a different ground, incapable of crime, even when he is in the very act of committing it.

We are not treating this subject theologically; the nature of our present work excludes such serious reasoning. But we would remind, even in these slight sketches, those who stand up for the self-sufficient morality of modern philosophy, or rather sophistry, that the experiment has long since been tried on a large scale. Whatever may be the inferiority of the ancients in physical science, it will scarce be denied, that in moral science they possessed all the lights which the unassisted Reason, now referred to as the sufficient light of our paths, could possibly attain. Yet, when we survey what their system of Ethics did for the perfection of the human species, we shall see that but a very few even of the teachers themselves have left behind them such characters as tend to do honour to their doctrines. Some philosophers there were, who, as instructors in morality, showed a laudable example to their followers; and we will not individiously inquire how far these were supported in their self-denial, either by vanity, or the desire of preserving consistency, or the importance annexed to the founder of a sect; although the least of these motives afford great support to temperance, even in cases where it is not rendered easy by advanced age, which of itself calms the more stormy passions. But the satires of Juvenal, of Petronius, and, above all Lucian, show what slight effect the doctrines of Zeno, Epictetus, Plato, Socrates, and Epicurus, produced on their avowed followers; and how little influence the beard of the Stoic, the sophistry of the Academician, and the self-denied mortification of the Cynics, had upon the sects which derived their names from these distinguished philosophers. We shall find that these pretended despisers of sensual pleasure shared the worst vices of the grossest age of society, and added to them the detestable hypocrisy of pretending that they were all the while guided by the laws of true wisdom and of right reason.

If, in modern times, they who own the restraint of philosophical discipline alone have not given way to such grossness of conduct, it is because those principles of religion, which they affect to despise, have impressed on the public mind a system of moral feeling, unknown till the general prevalence of the Christian faith; but which, since its predominance, has so generally pervaded European society, that no pretender to innovation can directly disavow its influence, though he endeavours to show that the same results, which are recommended from the Christian pulpit, and practised by the Christian community, might be reached by the unassisted efforts of that human reason to which he counsels us to resign the sole regulation of our morals.

In short to oppose one authority in the same department to another, the reader is requested to compare the character of the philosophic Square in *Tom Jones,* with that of Bage's philosophical heroes; and to consider seriously whether a system of Ethics, founding an exclusive and paramount court in a man's own bosom for the regulation of his own conduct, is likely to form a noble, enlightened, and generous character, influencing others by superior energy and faultless example; or whether it is not more likely, as in the observer of the rule of right, to regulate morals according to temptation and to convenience, and to form a selfish, sophistical hypocrite, who, with morality always in his mouth, finds a perpetual apology for evading the practice of abstinence, when either passion or interest solicits him to indulgence.

We do not mean to say, that, because Bage entertained erroneous notions, he therefore acted viciously. The history of his life, so far as known to us, indicates a contrary course of conduct. It would seem, from his language, as we have already said, that he had been bred among the strict and benevolent sect of Friends; and if their doctrines carried him some length in speculative

error, he certainly could derive nothing from them to favour laxity of morals. In his fictitious works, the Quakers are always brought forward in an amiable point of view; and the characters of Arnold, and particularly of Miss Carlile, are admirable pictures of the union of talent, and even wit, with the peculiar manners and sentiments of these interesting and primitive persons. But if not vicious himself, Bage's leading principles are such as, if acted upon, would introduce vice into society; in men of a fiercer mould, they would lead to a very different line of conduct from his own; and, such being the case, it was the writer's duty to point out the sophistry on which they are founded.

The works of Bage, abstracted from the views against which we have endeavoured to caution the reader, are of high and decided merit. It is scarce possible to read him without being amused, and, to a certain degree, instructed. His whole efforts are turned to the development of human character; and, it must be owned, he possessed a ready key to it. The mere story of the novels seldom possesses much interest—it is the conduct of his personages, as thinking and speaking beings, in which we are interested; and, contrary to the general case, the reader is seldom or never tempted to pass over the dialogue in order to continue the narrative. The author deals occasionally in quick and improbable conversions, as in that of Sir George Osmond, from selfishness and avarice, to generosity and liberality, by the mere loveliness of virtue in his brother and his friends. And he does not appear to have possessed much knowledge of that species of character which is formed by profession or by nationality. His seamen are indifferent; his Irishmen not beyond those usually brought on the stage: his Scotchmen still more awkward caricatures, and the language which he puts in their mouths, not similar to any that has been spoken since the days of Babel. It is in detecting the internal working of a powerful understanding, like that of Paracelsus Holman, that Bage's power chiefly consists; and great that power must be, considering how much more difficult it is to trace those varieties of character which are formed by such working, than merely to point out such as the mind receives from the manners and customs of the country in which it has ripened.

A light, gay, pleasing air, carries us agreeably through Bage's novels; and when we are disposed to be angry at seeing the worse made to appear the better reason, we are reconciled to the author by the ease and good-humour of his style. We did not think it proper to reject the works of so eminent an author from this collection,[3] merely on account of speculative errors. We have done our best to place a mark on these; and, as we are far from being of opinion, that the youngest and most thoughtless derive their serious opinions from productions of this nature, we leave them for our reader's amusement, trusting that he will remember that a good jest is no argument; that a novelist, like the master of a puppet-show, has his drama under his absolute authority, and shapes the events to favour his own opinions; and that whether the Devil flies away with Punch, or Punch strangles the Devil, forms no real argument as to the comparative power of either one or other, but only indicates the special pleasure of the master of the motion.

Notes

1. *Dissertation on Juries.*

2. Bage lived eight months after the date of this letter, which was written Jan. 24, 1801.

3. The Novelists' Library.

Hermione Ramsden (essay date January 1897)

SOURCE: Ramsden, Hermione. "A Forgotten Novelist." *The Yellow Book* 12 (January 1897): 291-305.

[*In the following essay, Ramsden provides a survey of Bage's life and works.*]

There is no sufficient reason to account for the manner in which Robert Bage has been forgotten, while numbers of his contemporaries have been canonised among the classics. It may be true that his works have not the enduring qualities of Samuel Richardson's many-volumed novels, yet they are not without many of the attributes which go towards the making of popular romances, and in many respects they are better calculated to appeal to the reading public of our time. His style is brighter than Richardson's, less sentimental than Fielding's; his good men are less priggish, and his young women have more of nature in them; while, as regards his subjects, he may be said to have much in common with some modern authors, who would find it no easy matter to surpass him in the boldness with which he upholds his opinions.

Bage was born on the 29th of January, 1728, at Darley, where his father was a paper manufacturer, which profession he afterwards followed. In politics he was a Whig, while in religion it is said that, for a time at least, he was a Quaker, which would account for his peculiar way of writing; but if this was the case, he does not appear to have remained one long, for, to use the expression of a contemporary, he very soon "reasoned himself into infidelity," and all the traces that remained of his former religious persuasion were a sincere esteem for the Quakers and an unconquerable dislike for the clergy. The characters of Miss Carlill in *Man as He Is,* and of Arnold in *Barham Downs,* are delineated with a touch of sympathy which is quite unmistakeable, while Mr. Holford and the Rev. Dr. Blick, who differ so

little as to be virtually the same man, are both of them the *beau-idéal* of the sporting parson of the period, and are described as the toadies of a rich lord, for ever holding up the example of the patriarchs as an excuse for the behaviour of their wealthy patrons. Mr. Holford "was a sound divine, orthodox in preaching and eating, could bear a little infidelity and free-thinking, provided they were accompanied with good wine and good venison."

But to return to Bage's own life. Shortly after the death of his mother, his father removed to Derby, and Robert was sent to school, where it seems that he soon proved himself a distinguished scholar, for at the age of seven he was already proficient in Latin.

In 1765 he entered into partnership in an iron manufactory with three persons, one of whom was the then celebrated Dr. Darwin; but the business failed, and Bage lost a considerable portion of his fortune. It was partly as a distraction from these pecuniary troubles that he wrote his novels. Of these, *Mount Henneth* was the first, and it was written, as he informs his readers in the preface, in order that he might be able to present each of his daughters with a new silk gown. The fashions appear to have been as tyrannical in those days as they are now, for our author declares that it was with feelings approaching to dismay that he observed that his daughters' head-dresses were suffering "an amazing expansion."

This novel was written in the form of letters, and was published in 1781, when the copyright was sold for the sum of £30. It is filled with the most surprising and improbable situations, while many of the characters appear to have been introduced for the sole purpose of relating other peoples' histories, the result being awkward and unnatural. *Mount Henneth* was speedily followed by works of a similar nature: *Barham Downs,* two vols., published in 1784, which, by some, was considered his best; *The Fair Syrian,* two vols., 1787; *James Wallace,* three vols., 1788; and, finally, his two masterpieces: *Man as He Is,*[1] and *Hermsprong, or Man as He Is Not.*[2]

The epistolary style in which Richardson had succeeded so well was not suited to the lighter substance of Bage's novels, and it was not until he dropped it and developed a style of his own that he can be said to have achieved anything worthy of immortality. It was his careful studies of character, no less than the fidelity with which he pictured the manners and customs of the times, to which he owed the wide-spread reputation that he enjoyed in his life-time, when translations of his novels were published abroad, in France and Germany. In his own country, fresh editions were continually called for, and after his death in 1801, they were republished under the editorship of Mrs. Barbauld and Sir Walter Scott. The poet

Cowper may also be counted as one of his admirers, for, in a letter to William Hayley, dated May 21, 1793, he writes as follows:

> . . . There has been a book lately published, entitled **Man as He Is.** I have heard a high character of it, as admirably written, and am informed that for that reason, and because it inculcates Whig principles, it is, by many, imputed to you.

And the same year, in a letter to Samuel Rose, dated Dec. 8, he writes:

> We find it excellent; abounding with wit and just sentiment, and knowledge both of books and men.

According to his friend, William Hutton, Bage cared little for the world, although he seems to have resembled Richardson in the preference which he evinced for the society of ladies, and he undoubtedly surpassed the latter in his manner of describing some of them. Maria Fluart, for instance, in **Hermsprong,** is a woman of the same type as Charlotte Grandison, yet it cannot be denied that her character is better drawn and her frivolous moods more consistently sustained; for Charlotte, in spite of her flightiness, partakes too strongly of the Grandison temperament, and there are moments when she relapses into conversations worthy of her brother.

Of Bage's domestic life we know very little, beyond the fact that he had three step-mothers, and that he married, at the age of twenty-three, a lady possessed of beauty, good sense, good temper, and money. In a letter, written a few months before his death, we learn that his wife sometimes scolded him to the extent of spoiling his appetite at breakfast, but that he bore it patiently we may conclude from the following passage, quoted from **Man as He Is,** which seems likely to have been the result of personal experience:

> Every man whose education has not been very ill-conducted, has learned to bear the little agreeable asperities of the gentle sex, not merely as a necessary evil, but as a variety, vastly conducive to female embellishment, and consequently to man's felicity.

In Bage, as in almost all authors, the autobiographical note is not absent, and when we come upon sentences as astounding as the following, we cannot avoid the suggestion that one or other of those three step-mothers must have inspired it:

> "Ladies," said Sir George, "have no weapons but their tongues and their nails. . . ."

But Lady Mary Paradyne by no means confined herself to these, for when suffering from one of her periodical attacks of gout, a "slipper or a snuff-box thrown at the head of her nurse or her woman gave her tolerable ease." And on one occasion "she enforced her observations with a knife," and inflicted a wound on the nurse's arm which resulted in "an eloquence superior to her own."

Domestic happiness is decidedly not a characteristic of Bage's novels, and here, as elsewhere, it is the women who receive all the blame.

"What shall I say of our women?" exclaims Mr. Mowbray.

> Heavens! What pen or tongue can enumerate the evils which arise from our connections, our matrimonial connections, with this frail and feeble sex? Which of our corruptions may we not trace to their vanities?. . . . In every connection with woman, man seeks happiness and risques it—and the risque is great. It is so much the greater, because in the usual mode of connection, the laws come in to perpetuate it, and the misery is for life. Gentlemen endeavour to avoid this . . . and no doubt that 'as long as we love,' is a more advantageous formula than 'as long as we live.' Yet there are drawbacks.

Mr. Fielding, a friend of Sir George's, goes further still in maintaining that "matrimony kills love, as sure as foxes eat geese."

Sir George Paradyne was a model son, and always respectful in his behaviour towards his mother, although her complaints, poured forth over five glasses of Madeira in succession, must often have been a severe trial to his patience. It was Lady Mary's desire that he should be the most accomplished gentleman of his age, and in order that this wish might be realised, she was anxious to procure him a tutor who had studied manners under Lord Chesterfield, in place of the worthy Mr. Lindsay, whose views on education were the direct antithesis to her own. Of Lady Mary it is said that "her affections went to the whole duties of a mother. . . . It was she who regulated his taste in dress, who superintended the friseur in the important decoration of his head."

Poor Sir George! What a vision of powdered hair and pig-tail, flowered satin waistcoat and velvet coat, to say nothing of the shoes with diamond buckles! He was only just twenty when the story begins, and as yet quite unspoilt by the world; his chief delight at this period was to converse with Lindsay on Cicero and Demosthenes, Horace and Virgil, or to spend a quiet evening "in moralizing upon the various follies of mankind." It was not without reason that he had asked Lindsay to become his friend and guide, for he sadly needed some one to whom he could confide his love for Miss Cornelia Colerain. Mr. Lindsay was a man of parts; he had met with a variety of misfortunes, and was a philosopher, if, also, somewhat of a pessimist. His chief aim at this time seems to have been to warn his pupil against the dangers of matrimony, because, as he says:

> The love of women and the love of fame lead to differ-
> ent things; no one knows better than myself how fatal
> love, as a passion, is to manly exertion.

Even the worthy Lindsay does not seem to have held the ordinary views on the subject of marriage, for on one occasion he shocks the fair Quakeress by observing that:

> "If it was the law or usage of the country for men and
> women to make temporary contracts, no one would call
> it a vice."
>
> "According to thee, then," said Miss Carlill, "vice and
> virtue are mode and fashion?"
>
> "Not wholly so, perhaps," Mr. Lindsay said, "nor
> wholly otherwise. . . . It is a pity a tender mistake, as
> it often does, should involve two people in wretched-
> ness for life."

Yet he is not afraid to risk his happiness with Miss Carlill, and she condescends to marry him at last, in spite of their differences of opinion.

> "I like not the doings of thy steeple-house," she tells
> him; "there is much noise and little devotion. . . . If I
> take thee, it is out of pity to thy poor soul."

And with this reason he is obliged to be content.

Sir George, on the other hand, is no pessimist with regard to marriage; he feels assured that a good wife is the greatest blessing that Heaven can bestow; but when Miss Colerain will not accept him because she considers that their acquaintance has been too short, the effect upon his character is not all that could be desired. These circumstances result in a strained relationship with Lindsay, they part in anger, and Sir George is left to continue his "airy course." "Youth," he argued, "must have its follies; the season would be over soon; a few years œconomy would free him from their effects," . . . and for the time being he forgot Miss Colerain.

The author here excuses himself for his hero's conduct by saying that the rules of probability would be violated were he to depict the character of a young gentleman of quality in the reign of George III. with too many virtues.

Sir George goes to Paris, gets into debt, and is obliged to have recourse to Lindsay to help him out of his difficulties. Three years he intends to devote to the business of regeneration; the remainder of his life to his country, to friendship, and, if he can obtain her, to Miss Colerain. But the lady in question requires to be fully convinced of the sincerity of his repentance before she will marry him, and because of this delay "his spirits flagged; his appetite ceased; his bloom changed; and it was too apparent that he must soon be lost to his friends and to himself." His days were spent in the contempla-

tion of Miss Colerain's picture which he had hung in a temple in the garden, and so great was the depression of his spirits that he would most certainly have died but for the timely intervention of a certain Mr. Bardo, who thus addressed him:

> "Paradyne," said he, "you are a fool."

Thus roused, Sir George regained his courage, and before long the fair Cornelia consented to become his wife.

If we may trust the combined testimony of eighteenth century authors, *Man as He Is* may be studied as a faithful representation of a time when emotional natures were more common than they are now, when young men wept because their mothers scolded them, and turned dizzy at an unexpected meeting with the lady of their choice. Sir George, on one occasion, after he had been severely reprimanded by his mother for fighting one of the many duels in which he was constantly engaged, "withdrew to his library with his handkerchief at his eyes." With women, fainting was more than a fashion, it was an art, and Cornelia, like other fair ladies of her time, could faint at a moment's notice.

Another very interesting point in Bage's novels is the important part played by the lady's maid and the valet. That this was actually the case, and was not merely an invention of the author's, is proved by the frequency with which like incidents occur in the works of contemporary novelists; readers of Richardson will remember how a dishonest footman assisted the villainous Sir Hargrave Pollexfen in the abduction of Miss Harriet Byron, and how that that young lady herself sees no harm in cross-questioning her friend's maid on the subject of her mistress's love affairs. Miss Grandison's maid was the daughter of a clergyman, and it does not appear to have been at all unusual for young ladies in distressed circumstances to earn their living in this way, for even the learned Mrs. Bennet, in Fielding's *Amelia,* had some thoughts of going into service and was advised by her aunt to do so, in spite of her knowledge of Latin.

In *Man as He Is,* the ladies' "women" and gentlemen's "gentlemen" are persons of influence, and Sir George Paradyne, the first time that he is refused by Miss Colerain, drives off, leaving his purse in the hand of Susanna, her "woman," with the request that she shall pray for him three times a day to her mistress. And another time, whilst he is discussing the subject of his sister's matrimonial happiness with Mr. Lindsay, his "gentleman," who happens to be in waiting at the breakfast table, suddenly assumes the air of having something of importance to say, and, upon being pressed, he reads a love-letter which he has just received from the abovementioned lady's "woman," which serves to confirm Sir George's worst fears.

Bage's last and best work, ***Hermsprong, or Man as He Is Not,*** marks a new stage in contemporary thought, and this time the change is brought about by a woman. Nora realises that she is being treated like a doll! In other words, the "woman question," which had slumbered since the days of Mary Astell, had just made its re-appearance in the person and writings of Mary Wollstonecraft, whose *Vindication of the Rights of Woman* first saw the light in 1792. That Bage was strongly influenced by it is proved by the fact that his hero—who, it must be remembered, represents man as he is *not*—is very eloquent in his arguments in favour of the higher education of women. Women, he maintains, are allowed too little liberty of mind, and he adds:

> "Be not angry with me . . . be angry at Mrs. Wollstonecraft . . . who has presumed to say that the homage men pay to youth and beauty is insidious, that women for the sake of this evanescent, this pitiful dominion permit themselves to be persuaded that their highest glory is to submit to this inferiority of character, *and become the mere plaything of man.* Can this be so?"

> "Now, the devil take me," said Sumelin, "if I know what either you or this Mrs. Wollstonecraft would be at. But this I know, that the influence of women is too great; that it has increased, is increasing, and ought to be diminished."

> "Well then," Mr. Hermsprong answered, "let it be diminished on the side of charms; and let its future increase be on the side of mind."

> "To what purpose?" the banker asked. "To invade the provinces of men? Weaker bodies, you will allow, nature has given them, if not weaker minds."

> "Whatsoever may be the design of nature, respecting the sex, be her designs fulfilled. If she gave this bodily weakness, should education be brought in to increase it? But it is for mind I most contend; and if 'a firm mind in a firm body' be supposed the best prayer of man to the gods, why not of women? Would they be worse mothers for it? or more helpless widows?"

> "No," said the banker; "but they would be less charming figures."

> "Let us be more just, Mr. Sumelin. They are our equals in understanding, our superiors in virtue. They have foibles where men have faults, and faults where men have crimes."

Hermsprong is the necessary complement to Sir George Paradyne. He is the ideal, while the other is the real. Hermsprong is a native of America, and in many respects he resembles the Alien of Mr. Grant Allen's hilltop novel. In Bage's time, America was still sufficiently unknown to supply the novelist from Mrs. Aphra Behn[3] onwards with an original character for which now-a-days he is obliged to seek among the phantoms of the twenty-fifth century, or in the person of an angel visitant. Hermsprong, like the Alien, or Mr. H. G. Wells's angel, is a thoroughly unconventional being who finds

it impossible to accustom himself to the ways and habits of British barbarians. He is, according to his own description, a savage whose wish it is to return to nature, and who holds up the habits and customs of the American Red Indians as worthy of being imitated. He is in fact an Anarchist, who maintains that virtue is natural to man, and that a return to nature is a return to the primeval state of innocence before the laws had taught men how to sin.

Hermsprong's views, however, do not assume any very dangerous proportions. The utmost that he does to astonish the natives is to announce his intention of going to London on foot, a journey which is likely to occupy three days. But if he had suggested flying, the announcement could hardly have excited more surprise.

> "Surely, Mr. Hermsprong, you cannot think of walking?"

> "Oh, man of prejudice, why? In what other way can I travel with equal pleasure?"

> "Pleasure! Pleasure in England is not attached to the idea of walking. Your walks we perform in chaises."

> "I pity you for it. For myself, I chuse not to buy infirmity so dear. . . . I must be independent, so far as social man can be independent. In other words I must be free from the necessity of doing little things, or saying little words to any man. . . ."

It is said of him that his singularities of character unfit him for the society of English gentlemen; he eats only to live, instead of living to eat; he cares nothing for the pleasures of the bottle, nor for the still greater pleasures of cards and dice, yet his manners are such that he never fails to please. An English dinner he considers melancholy:

> "If to dine," says he, "were only to eat, twenty minutes would be ample. You sit usually a couple of hours, and you talk, and call it conversation. You make learned remarks on wind and weather; on roads; on dearness of provisions; and your essays on cookery are amazingly edifying. Not much less so are your histories of your catarrhs and toothaches. . . . It is said that physicians have much increased in your country; one great reason may be, because you dine."

He has, moreover, a secret, but deep-founded contempt for the forms of politeness, and is often found to err on the side of plain speaking, to the intense anxiety of those who are anxious to befriend him.

> "I have often been told," he says, "that in very, very civilised countries no man could hold up the mirror of truth to a lady's face, without ill-manners. I came to try."

In this experiment he is fairly successful, for the ladies do not resent his truthfulness as much as might have been expected. His mission, like the Alien's, is to rescue a lady from tyranny, only this time the tyrant is a father and not a husband. By degrees he overcomes her filial prejudices by bidding her lay aside all preconceived notions of duty, and declaring that "in vain would the reasoners of this polished country say everything is due to the authors of our existence. Merely for existence, I should have answered, I owe nothing. It is for rendering that existence a blessing, my filial gratitude is due."

The lady of his choice is a certain Miss Campinet, the daughter of Lord Grondale, but the latter does not favour his suit, which is the less surprising when we consider that it is one of the characteristics of the savage that he does not love lords. It will be remembered that the Alien did not love lords either, and that he, too, was equally contemptuous of rank and riches. The conversation which takes place between Hermsprong and his father-in-law elect is sufficiently original to be worth transcribing:

> "Before I condescend to give you my daughter," says Lord Grondale, "I must have a more particular account of your family, Sir; of its alliances, Sir; and of your rent roll."
>
> "Upon my word, my Lord; here is a great deal of difficulty in this country to bring two people together, who are unfortunate enough to have property. For my part I have thought little of what your lordship thinks so much. I have thought only that I was a man, and she, a woman—lovely, indeed, but still a woman. Nature has created a general affinity between these two species of beings; incident has made it particular between Miss Campinet and me. In such situations, people usually marry; so I consent to marry."

We must observe that it was a gross inconsistency on the part of Hermsprong that he should be guilty of one of the most barbarous customs of the times. When applying to Lord Grondale for permission to marry his daughter, he never contemplates the necessity of first consulting the wishes of the young lady herself; these he takes for granted, and when reproached for his lack of humility, he defends himself by saying:

> "I consider a woman as equal to a man; but . . . I consider a man also as equal to a woman. When we marry we give and we receive. Where is the necessity that man should take upon him this crouching mendicant spirit, this excess of humiliation?"

All this is very plausible, of course, but his notions of lovemaking were curious, to say the least, and it is difficult not to feel some compassion for Miss Campinet. In course of time, however, his arguments convince her, and his efforts on her behalf are crowned with the success they deserve. He turns out to be none other than her long-lost cousin, Sir Charles Campinet, the lawful heir to Lord Grondale's estate, and the son of his shipwrecked brother. A reconciliation takes place, Lord Grondale dies, and the young couple are happy ever after.

As an author, Robert Bage resembles Mr. Grant Allen in more than one respect, for in the first place his publisher was one named Lane, and in the second his object was to instruct women. Instruction intended for them can only be offered in the form of a novel as they are not likely to read works of a more serious nature, and *Man as He Is* is intended especially for the fair sex, amongst whom he hopes to find twenty thousand readers; in it he treats of the subjects which he thinks will be most agreeable to them, *i.e.*, love and fashion. In like manner, Mr. Grant Allen, in his *British Barbarians,* informs us that he writes not for wise men, because they are wise already, but that it is the boys and girls and women—women in particular—whom he desires to instruct.

The study of *Man as He Is* and *Is Not,* or rather, as he was and was not, in the years 1792 and 1796, is very instructive and also distinctly salutary, and as such it deserves to be recommended as an antidote to pessimism. Both these books prove in the most convincing manner that a great change for the better has taken place in the ways and customs of English men and women since the close of the eighteenth century. Men no longer fight duels at the smallest provocation, nor weep in public, and women have long ceased to cultivate the art of fainting, nor do they—in polite society—use their nails as weapons of defence, while even the art of writing fiction has made considerable progress since the days when Robert Bage first began to write his romances.

Notes

1. *Man as He Is.* A novel in four volumes. London: printed for William Lane, at the Minerva Press, Leadenhall Street. 1792.

2. *Hermsprong; or, Man as He Is Not.* A novel in two volumes. By the author of *Man as He Is.* Dublin: printed by Brett Smith, for P. Wogan, P. Byrne, J. Moore, and J. Rice. 1796.

3. *Oroonoko; or, the Royal Slave.* By the Ingenious Mrs. Behn. Seventh Edition. London, 1722.

J. M. S. Tompkins (essay date 1932)

SOURCE: Tompkins, J. M. S. "New Life in the Novel." In *The Popular Novel in England, 1770-1800,* 1932. Reprint edition, pp. 172-205. Lincoln: University of Nebraska Press, 1961.

[*In the following excerpt from an essay first published in 1932, Tompkins highlights Bage's expression of his views on social, political, and theological issues in his novels.*]

II

> While thou keepest always looking up at me, and I, down at thee, what horrid obliquities of vision may we not contract?
>
> —Bage, *Mount Henneth,* 1781.

> The greater number of human opinions seem to me to be swaddling clouts for children.
>
> —Bage, *Barham Downs,* 1784.

Robert Bage, paper-manufacturer in the Midlands, wrote six novels, which he published anonymously, *Mount Henneth* (1781), *Barham Downs* (1784), *The Fair Syrian* (1787), *James Wallace* (1788), *Man as he is* (1792) and *Hermsprong, or Man as he is not* (1796). He commenced novelist at the age of fifty-three, to take his mind off business losses, and persisted in the soothing occupation through years of commercial and political anxiety. He was warmly welcomed by the critics; they found in him something strong and unusual, a cheering exception to the general run of novels; they praised his characters, his humour and philosophy, and, admitting that his strokes were sometimes coarse and that he had more genius than taste, found it a cheap price to pay for the re-entry of a vigorous masculine mind into the novel. Later the note of praise dropped to a lower pitch; it had indeed been forced up by contrast with the insipid novels with which the Press overflowed, and a modern reader, though pleased and interested, looks in vain for that "thrilling, lambent fire" which the *Critical* detected in Bage's first two books. His lanterns shone bright in that murky dawn, and were quenched as the day widened.

What Bage brought to the novel was a great increase of intellectual content. His active, liberal and independent mind had ranged through a variety of subjects, and his books are full of thought. They are indeed, to use Mr. J. B. Priestley's classification of the far more finished but not wholly dissimilar work of Peacock, novels of opinion. In the house-parties which, like Peacock, he loves to assemble, from which his philosophers-errant go forth and to which they return, bearing their trophies of experience and philanthropy with them, the talk turns from government to religion, from democracy to sex. There is nothing ponderous about these debates and nothing dogmatic about the conclusions; Bage has no rigid system to compare with the moral stiffness of the woman's novel. Seeing that conduct must be to some extent experimental and spontaneous, the best we can do is not to choke spontaneity nor penalize experiment too heavily; to beware of submission, lest it engender the vices of a slave, and of power, lest it lead to tyranny; to be slow to anger; to look always to the points of similarity between men rather than to those of difference; and to follow reason without fear but without fanaticism, remembering that the suffering of others can

be too high a price for our own mental integrity.[1] This position he explains with cheerfulness and moderation, in a forthright, short-breathed style, broken with whimsy. Less solemn than the band of didactic novelists, he is, if not more convinced than they, at least, in right of the scope and frankness of his speculations, more honest; he will distinguish between ancient decencies and ancient follies, and whatever concessions he feels called upon to make, they will be no blind immolations to tradition. It is, however, necessary to understand just how far his seriousness went and to what extent it affected the structure of his novels. It was by no means the intense, the almost tyrannical seriousness of modern art. Unity of impression, a religious verisimilitude, meant nothing to Bage. The novel was still a pastime, and no novelist required austere endeavours on the part of his readers, or refused to indemnify them for such efforts as they did make by a liberal supply of providential coincidences and turns of fortune. Bage accepted the old framework without any misgivings, and set out to amuse. Patches of common novel-material lie beside pictures of real life, and he does not seem to have felt that one invalidated the other or disturbed its effect; they amused the reader in different ways, of which he must be trusted to distinguish the relative importance. In the case of Bage's first book, *Mount Henneth,* it is possible to maintain that the majority of the adventures, the kidnapping, imprisonments and the meeting with privateers, are illustrative of the author's opinions, that they are not there for the sake of their value as entertainment, but as they flow from a state of war, which he detests. In *Barham Downs,* also, while the story is not very significant, nearly all the characters reflect special moral ideas. But in the later books he tended more and more to express his opinions in conversation rather than in action, and except in *Hermsprong* the connection between opinions and story is very loose. He does not in his plots oppose two systems of ideas in sharp and sustained conflict, as Holcroft does in *Anna St. Ives* (1792); he seems to have felt that, unless one were an egoist, occasions for such a rigid opposition are not frequent. Action in his books, where it is relevant to opinions at all and is not simple storytelling, is less often an expression of these than an amused comment on them. Like Peacock again, if not to the same extent, he felt the disconnection between a man's ideas and his life, and nowhere is this more clear than in *Man as he is,* with its impulsive, convincible, blundering hero, and the tutor, who, having done his utmost on several occasions to persuade his charge of the criminal folly of duelling, himself makes ready to fight. Certain moral principles are exempt from this sceptical banter; circumstances do not imperil the value of benevolence or of independence.

Man as he is is Bage's best book. It is the most forward-looking. Where the other five are, at times, comparable to Peacock, but at times wholly of their age, this reads for whole chapters like a lighter-handed anticipation of Thackeray. There is Thackeray's scene— Spa, with its English visitors, its foreign noblemen, its adventurers and adventuresses—and, partaking somewhat too lavishly of its pleasures, there is the generous, dissipated young man, Sir George Paradyne, who is the pencilled outline of one of Thackeray's heroes. We move through Europe and back to England, losing and recovering our acquaintances as the crowds shift, aware, like Thackeray, of the irrational in society, though with less perturbation than he betrays. The story is slight, though natural enough, and variegated with the usual eighteenth-century insets. Sir George Paradyne, coming early into his inheritance, sets forth in life with the noblest intentions, chooses Mr. Lindsay as his travelling tutor in a tour through England, and, almost at the first stage, falls in love with Miss Colerain. She will not accept him until he has proved his worth in the world. Sir George takes his good intentions to London and the Continent, taints them with dissipation, is ashamed and sorry but cannot rally effectually. At last, ill and unhappy, he receives the reward he does not deserve, for Miss Colerain sees that she must supply the stabilizing power in his life, and that without her all his good qualities will go to waste. Round Sir George and Miss Colerain are grouped Bage's most interesting characters: Lady Mary Paradyne, Sir George's aggressive mother, who accosts her invalid son with the remark: "They say you are in a waste, Sir George"; Miss Carlill, the Quaker; Bardoe, the *nil admirari* Englishman; and Birimport, the returned "nabob," who will not discard his habits of autocratic command, but lives jealously secluded to avoid humiliations, re-establishing his sense of power by tyrannizing over his wife.[2] Birimport, particularly, with his perpetual *malaise* working out in a cruelty of which he is fundamentally ashamed, is finely imagined.

After the comedy and truth of ***Man as he is*** it is strange to turn to ***Hermsprong; or, Man as he is not,*** for here the natural development of Bage's art is suddenly checked, or rather reversed. Hitherto he has been evolving a novel of manners and character, stripped of improbable turns of fortune and strengthened by a strong speculative interest. Now, forsaking the natural fluidity of this form, he writes a book in which the tendencious elements have stiffened into a bizarre framework.[3] ***Hermsprong,*** in spite of its touches of humour and pathos and a fairly lively cast, really belongs to what one may call the diagrammatic type of novel, and the mental process behind it is akin to that behind allegory. The author is visibly coercing his human agents; they stand in symmetrical relations to one another, as representatives of this or the other system of ideas, and they pass through the action as through a formal dance, maintaining these relationships intact. They are ingredients in a pattern rather than individuals, and they are stripped of all complexities of character in order that the pattern

may not be disturbed. On one side stands Hermsprong, bred among the American Indians to physical hardihood and moderation and instructed by his reason in honesty and a proper independence of mind; on the other, the purple figure of Lord Grondale, swollen with tyranny and prejudice, supported by the sycophantic Doctor Blick. Between the two vibrates his lordship's daughter, Caroline Campinet, drawn to the side of unreason by what is good, not what is base in her, by an ideal delicacy of mind that yearns to render the most implicit filial duty and has to be tutored by Hermsprong and her friend Miss Fluart. There is a pleasant grotesqueness about this angularity; the persons of the story are never at a loss, never, even in moments of crisis, fail to support their characters. One delights equally in the brisk exchange between Hermsprong and Lord Grondale over the body of the rescued Miss Campinet,[4] and in Hermsprong's subscription to his letter to his antagonist: "Obedient to the forms of politeness, I am your lordship's obedient servant." Even in this book, however, there is much that overflows the formula. Bage's practical sense and observation are never long dormant, and he has no taste for the fantastic heights of consistency to which the diagrammatic method can sometimes climb.

To test the difference in climate between Bage and the true perfectibilian dreamer, one has only to turn to L. S. Mercier's *L'An Deux Mille Quatre Cent Quarante. Rêve s'il en fût jamais* (1770),[5] translated into English by W. Hooper, M.D., as *Memoirs of the Year Two Thousand Five Hundred* (1772). In this "consoling dream" of a future that Mercier believed, in its essence, possible, when the vast majority of the human race shall act with a uniform and enlightened nobility, the author, like Bacon in the *New Atlantis,* makes a fine use of symbol and ritual. His most elaborate scene is the public trial and execution of a murderer. The man is condemned to death, but his voluntary submission to the sentence is required before it can be executed; the alternative is a life of exile and shame. The head of the senate adjures him to do justice to society and condemn himself. He bows his head, and with that resolve his guilt is atoned. The pastors strip off his bloody shirt, clothe him in the white robe of reconciliation, and dismiss him to his death with the kiss of peace. The bells of the city toll for him, and the populace prays; he is shot beside the corpse of his victim, his body honourably bestowed, and his name re-inscribed on the roll of citizens, whence his crime had blotted it. Is not this a sort of sacred ballet? The critic[6] who complained of Mercier's "total ignorance of the principles of human conduct" was beside the point; the book was a dream, not a scientific forecast. Mercier had cast aside the burden of man's complex nature to design a pattern in the ideal. The same effect of lofty and bloodless beauty—for beauty it is— can at times be achieved in fairy tales; but neither Hermsprong, that philosophic Grandison, nor Miss

Campinet could figure in it, and the old innkeeper who had served with Marshall Keith would break the pattern to fragments.

It is certain that the French philosophic tale largely determined Bage's course in the novel. Not that he was the implicit disciple of Voltaire and Diderot; his French sympathies never obscured the sturdy English strain in his work; but they showed him what could be done in the way of marrying philosophy and fiction. He would probably not have written novels, he said, if he had had books and opportunity for more serious work; as it was he managed to say what he had to say in this form, and the English novel, which suffered as much from a paucity of ideas as the French novel from an overplus,[7] benefited exceedingly. His first reviewers praised his liberal philosophy, though later, when liberal philosophy was exploding violently into action across the Channel, it was found disquieting, and Scott, in his memoir of Bage, thought it necessary to include antidotes to his subject's morality. Bage's philosophy, in its connection with the common stock of progressive ideas that preceded and accompanied the French Revolution, has been studied by Miss Allene Gregory in her book *The French Revolution and the English Novel* (1915), and there is no need and no space to repeat the analysis here. It is enough to remember that a common creed is found, with individual variations, in the books of the English revolutionary group of whom Bage was the precursor; that all these writers believed that man could be, if not perfected, at least infinitely improved by the free use of reason in education and the abolition of crippling laws and customs; and that all of them saw in the novel a means of expressing this belief. It was not a new function for the novel, which had helped to disseminate one or two creeds already; it was the ideas that were new. For a few years they were given a sharp and challenging expression; then the menace of the reactionary forces became too formidable, and the prophetic voices, if they did not wholly cease, were content with a quieter and intermittent utterance. But though there is no need to rehearse the whole revolutionary testimony, it is worth while to glance at some of Bage's leading ideas, both as they illustrate the general quickening of thought in the 'eighties, and connect, by way of supplement or corrective, with the modes of thought and feeling already prevalent in the novel.

In the first place, he was no indiscriminate admirer of the attitude of submission. "Proud superiority" and "servile dependence" were ignoble bases, he felt, for human relationships. A man must be "free from the necessity of doing little things, or saying *little* words to any man." Moreover, humility is not always a grace; it can be "weak and enervating," and destroy the foundations of happiness, for "to be happy a man must think well of himself," and vanity is a great spur to virtuous action. The question of filial obedience occurs several times in

his books and is a subject of debate between James Wallace and his friend Paracelsus Holman. One notices that the young people, though boldly "philosophical" in their talk, are quite moderate in their behaviour; even Holman, who roundly declares that his father is a fool and that he cannot be expected to love him, finds that the fool has a claim on his compassion which he cannot deny.[8] Duty, however, is reciprocal. "Merely for existence . . . I owe nothing," Hermsprong tells Miss Campinet. "It is for rendering that existence a blessing, my filial gratitude is due." Authoritative control must, in any case, cease when the children reach maturity, but wise parents will by then have won their children's friendship, and can rely on this. Wifely duty too has its limits, and Lady Bembridge will not follow a weak, vicious and unrepentant man into misery. "Servile compliance is a crime when it violates rectitude, and imbecility, at least, when it is prostituted to folly."

Some allusion has already been made to Bage's fearless dealings with the virtue of his heroines. His books were full of shocks for the conventional. A girl who has been ravished becomes the happy wife of another man; militant Clarissas defend themselves with sarcastic and resolved vigour; another young woman, chaste in mind, yet determines out of gratitude to become the mistress of the man who has preserved her from death, while vivacious girls claim the right to think, talk, and even jest about sex, since it is their prime concern. Bage's moderation, however, does not desert him in this last instance; the claim is conceded, but with the caveat that it is easy to lose the modesty of the mind. Critics who cried haro at this relaxation of discipline, did not always notice that it is made possible by Bage's belief in the strength of will and faculty of mental growth in women. Kitty Ross is no Magdalen of the sensibility school, but a creature of "Amazonian goodness."[9] His liberal propaganda did not amount to a system. He felt that the custom of society punishes woman too much for an offence against chastity, and man too little, and in his books he redressed the balance a little. He pleaded also, through the mouth of Mr. Lindsay in *Man as he is,* for "a little more free-will to the sexes in the important article of their sexual conjunction"; but he is no theory-monger; others must find and invent new forms of life; he but testifies to the coming of a spirit that breaks the old.

Bage's tolerance, his readiness to live and let live, is marked in all his books. It is the necessary and far from exorbitant price paid by a man in order that he may enjoy to the full the company of his fellow-beings. Youth, however, from a mixture of high and low motives, often refuses to pay this price, and so we have in *Mount Henneth* Mr. Foston's story of his own development from a bigoted young man blinkered by religious prejudice, into the tolerant philanthropist of his mature years. This education in philosophy replaces in Bage the widely popular theme of the education in morals, and is probably one of the signs of French influence in his work. As for the good which tolerance purchases, the free and kindly intercourse with different types of men, the mind which does not find delight in this is in no healthy state. In **Barham Downs** we have two types of solitary, and the attack is launched against both Sir George Osmond's anti-social pride and his brother's flinching sensibility. Tolerance is particularly needful in religious matters; indeed, bigotry is not only foolish but arrogant, for the basis of all religions is the same, "the silent meditation of a contrite heart, lifting up its humble aspirations to the author and preserver of all being," and the dogmatic superstructure is unimportant, temporary and probably wrong. This community of aspiration among men of good-will is illustrated in **Mount Henneth** by the marriage of the Persian with the Jewish girls, and of his daughter with the Englishman. Bage liked these intermarriages, and liked too to trail his story through many lands, not for love of the varying background—he despatched the picturesque rather disdainfully—but in order to show reasonable men of all nations living in friendship together. The part of the merchant in furthering international amity was a source of pride to Bage, who regarded him as the prime civilizer, and is never tired of praising the mercantile virtues of keeping contracts and paying debts. One notes that the Utopia at **Mount Henneth** has a pronounced mercantile aspect, very different from the unsatisfactory feudalism of *Shenstone-Green,* and that it includes a dock and a glass-bottle manufactory. **James Wallace** is a novel of the trading and professional classes, and one of the most carefully wrought figures in it is that of Paul Lamounde, the Liverpool merchant, sound, gruff, shrewd and benevolent. The author was a democrat, who enjoyed giving gentlemen's daughters in marriage to honest merchants and lost a little of his usual serenity in contemplating the insolence of birth. A respectful treatment of the middle classes was, as we have seen, one of the things that the novel, stranded among night-cellars and the dimly realized drawing-rooms of the aristocracy, most required; a whole world of circumstance, hardly touched as yet except by the satiric quill, lay among the counting-houses and quays.

Bage's personal character as a novelist is something more than the sum of his opinions; it includes his unspoilt pleasure in the commonplaces of story-telling and his humorous gust in strokes of character. It is a vigorous character, uttering itself in a vigorous style. In the French translations of his work, his style is inevitably and deliberately flattened; the curt emphasis, the whimsical conceits, did not do in French and were smoothed out; his very strong vein of irony, on the other hand, tallied well with French taste and probably owed something to French examples. It is impossible to read in **The Fair Syrian** the Georgian Amine's account of her slavery without thinking of Voltaire.[10] Amine has cultivated apathy as the only means of bearing her fate, and her apathy, and the horrors and tyrannies through which she passes, are described with a high-wrought irony that obviously pleased Bage, as it threw up, like a varnish, the irrational absurdity of these tyrannies and of that apathy. In face of the generic sorrows of human kind, however, he drops his irony for a simpler speech. His deep sense of sorrow and the firmness with which he relegates it to its proper place in life, leading all his young tragedians back from their solitudes to the daily paths which must be travelled and are best travelled in company, are both the merits of a man who began novel-writing not in raw youth but in his full and wise maturity.

Notes

1. Cf. *Man as he is*; on the subject of compliments Bage says:

   > We owe to society . . . not to sacrifice the vanity of others at the shrine of our own.

2. *v.* also the pedantic Catherine Haubert, whose learning is a balm for mortification in love; and, in *James Wallace,* the family of the successful oilman, Gamidge, Sir Anthony Havely, the fop with the Parisian coat and the real, though pedantic, scientific knowledge, and Squire Thurl, the Tony Lumpkin, recognized by all his acquaintances as an anachronism.

3. The *Monthly* reviewer preferred it, however, on account of its greater unity and of the figure of the hero, "a prominent and fine delineation of the accomplished, firm, frank and generous man, worthy to be impressed as a model for imitation." v. *Monthly,* Sept. 1796.

4. Lord Grondale at once asks the rescuer his fortune and rank. "My fortune," answered the stranger, "Kings might envy; it is equal to my desires. As to rank—I have been taught to distinguish men by virtue."

5. Mercier published his book anonymously, but the authorship was known in England by 1781 (v. *Monthly,* Sept., p. 227). He published an enlarged edition in 1787. The book, which anticipates Mr. Wells's device in *When the Sleeper Wakes,* is full of interesting detail,—roof gardens and fountains in the streets of Paris, a literary censorship that forces the author of a noxious book to go about masked until he has retrieved his reputation, state-supported theatres, cheerful communal cremations, and the destruction of all that is pernicious in the world's literature, *e.g.* "Herodotus, Sappho, Anacreon and the vile Aristophanes." The first communion is replaced by a séance with the telescope and microscope, which is called the Communion of the Two Infinites. Observatories serve as

churches. "On the day consecrated to the praise of the Creator, it is an affecting sight to see on our observatory the numerous adorers of God falling on their knees, the eye applied to the telescope, and the spirit in prayer, sending forth their souls with their sight, towards the Fabricator of these stupendous miracles" (Chap. XXI). There is also the usual flaw of these Utopias,—butchers are foreigners.

6. v. *Monthly,* October 1772.

7. Cf. F. C. Green, *French Novelists, Manners and Ideas* (1928).

8. Cf. Holcroft's *Anna St. Ives,* where Frank Henley apologetically admits the "folly" that vice in his father grieves him more than vice in another.

9. Cf. Miss Wilmot in Holcroft's *Hugh Trevor,* whose intellect is awakened by her misfortunes and errors.

10. I have seen only the French translation of this book, *La Belle Syrienne. . . . Traduit de l'Anglois. A Londres,* 1788. The translation naturally emphasizes the likeness, but does not account for it.

Vaughan Wilkins (essay date 1951)

SOURCE: Wilkins, Vaughan. Introduction to *Hermsprong; or, Man as He Is Not,* by Robert Bage, edited by Vaughan Wilkins, pp. v-xiii. Bristol, England: Turnstile Press, 1951.

[*In the following essay, an introduction to an edition of Bage's* Hermsprong; or, Man as He Is Not, *Wilkins provides historical, social, and political context for Bage's composition of the novel, and surveys the critical response to the work.*]

Robert Bage, the author of **Hermsprong,** is remarkable apart from the fact that in this delightful, ironic, and whimsical novel he produced, in his old age, a book which should appeal to every reader with a palate for the dry wine of literature.

For not only is he one of the few distinctive writers in that drab era in the history of English fiction, the latter part of the eighteenth century; but he is also a stepping-stone from Voltaire to Thomas Love Peacock. Not only, also, was he so much in advance of his time as to believe in the equality of man, but as to believe, too, in the equality of woman with man; and this in a day when the first notion was held to be horridly unconstitutional, and the second horribly immoral.

If follows that a good many of his contemporaries considered him a subversive fellow—monstrously 'red,' odd in his ideas about women, and notoriously no

gentleman. This crusted opinion was succinctly expressed some twenty years after his death by the great *Quarterly Review,* which contemptuously declared that this 'paper-maker in a little country town' had not merely drawn a 'gross and senseless caricature' of 'the manners of English gentlemen and ladies', but had 'systematically made his novels the vehicle of all the anti-social, anti-moral, and anti-religious theories that were then but too much in vogue among the half-educated classes in this country.'

Sir Walter Scott rated Bage as a novelist of 'talent and genius,' but deplored his politics, his theology, and the manner in which he 'seems at times even to sport with the ties of marriage.' Nevertheless the satirist's skill in the delineation of character and the construction of amusing dialogue outweighed his offences, and Scott admitted no fewer than three of his unconventional works to the Valhalla of Ballantyne's *Novelists' Library.*

Hermsprong, oddly enough, was not one of the novels honoured, although Scott himself considered it to be Bage's best. Perhaps he thought it to be more anti-social than the others; for the worthy Mrs. Barbauld—Horace Walpole's 'Virago'—in prefacing the edition of 1810: gravely warned the reader that the book was 'democratical in its ten dency.' It need not be gathered from this, however, that Bage wished, with Messelier, to see 'the last king strangled with the entrails of the last priest.' He was a radical and not a revolutionary; like Peacock, a sarcastic commentator on events, a detached and cultured observer, writing for the sheer pleasure of self-expression and literary creation, rather than a propagandist. But it was unwise to be notably broad-minded in 1796, when **Hermsprong** first made its bow to the British public.

With the French Revolution the sunlight had faded from the august Georgian landscape, across which for so long the splendid figures of rank and privilege had lounged in silk and satin, as aloof, serene, as carelessly secure as though they were divine. Vast and appalling storms darkened every quarter of the horizon, and within that darkness the propertied classes heard the ravening noises of those heathen who would violate their Olympus. The word 'Revolution!' drummed itself insistently in their minds like the over-loud pulsation of blood-vessels.

They applauded that pattern of orthodoxy, Dr. Horsley, Bishop of Rochester, when he declared that 'the people had nothing to do with the laws but to obey them.' They concurred most heartily with the judge who burbled that 'the landed interest alone has a right to be represented in Parliament. The rabble has nothing but personal property; and what hold has the nation on them?'

Invigorated by such considerations, they made ready their thunderbolts. They hurled them at the humblest apostle of reform—even the bill-stickers who posted up placards asking for extension of the suffrage. They sentenced a poor wretch to fourteen years' transportation for the foul crime of circulating Tom Paine's *Rights of Man.* They banned all political meetings unless advertised beforehand. They turned a blind eye when true-blue mobs loyally rioted in Birmingham because 'jacobinical' philosophers had held a dinner to celebrate the anniversary of the fall of the Bastille.

In conditions such as these it is not surprising, perhaps, that Bage, the outspoken follower of Rousseau and Paine, should have been thought anti-social, anti-moral, and anti-religious by those—and they were many—who considered that the good things of this world were their exclusive prerogative.

If the political background to **Hermsprong** is lurid, the literary background, on the other hand, is arid; for Bage wrote during the long interregnum between the two great eras of fiction—the age of Fielding, Smollett, Sterne, Goldsmith, and Richardson, and the age of Jane Austen and Scott. There is a gap of forty years between the publication of *Humphrey Clinker* in 1771 and the appearance on the scene of *Sense and Sensibility*: during it no great light shone across the literary landscape.

The modern novel, born in the early days of the century but already adult, was still, however, the outstanding feature of contemporary letters. Hundreds upon hundreds of novels streamed from the presses during this period, most of them dreary rubbish like the *Henry* of Richard Cumberland, who was gibbeted by Sheridan as Sir Fretful Plagiary in *The Critic*; or junk of the sort for which Lydia Languish dredged the circulating libraries of Bath.

There are indeed only two novels that you are likely to pick up in modern editions at the bookseller's to-day—Fanny Burney's *Evelina* and Maria Edgeworth's *Castle Rackrent.* That is not to say that there is not a little good browsing among the lesser-known contemporaries of Bage upon the lower slopes of Parnassus—Graves's amusing and readable *Spiritual Quixote,* the preposterous Beckford's *Vathek,* Godwin's grim story of suspense, *Caleb Williams,* and that study in villainy, *Zeluco,* by Dr. John Moore, only remembered to-day—*if* he is remembered—as the father of the general who was buried darkly at dead of night.

I am not going to claim for Bage that he is a star of the first magnitude, but the light streams very brightly from his cottage window across the darkness that enshrouds late eighteenth-century fiction. That cottage is snug, the host amiable and amusing, the sherry dry, the supper savoury. Even with all the palatial establishments which

I have upon my visiting list, I still contemplate occasionally dropping in on friend Bage. I like him for his whimsicality, for his outspoken honesty, for his ironical philosophy, for his humanity, even for his discursiveness: I like him for the company to whom he has presented me.

One particularly realises in **Hermsprong** what Bage—individual though he be—owes to Voltaire, and that his book is in direct descent from those *romans philosophiques* of the Sage of Ferney, *Candide, Zadig,* and above all *L'Ingénu.* At the same time Bage does far more than merely inherit; he evolves his own formula for the palatable mixing of romance and satire—a formula unquestionably studied and, to an extent, followed by the author of *Melincourt* and *Nightmare Abbey.*

Peacock, that vivisector of statu-quo-ite and perfectibilian, however, regarded with scholarly aloofness his characters as mere instruments of his cynicism and erudition, as the weapons of his steely wit. Bage, on the other hand, quite clearly took the keenest possible interest in the warm-blooded people of his fancy and their multifarious adventures and funny ways: sometimes they even ran away with him.

Hermsprong, like all this writer's books, it will be realised, falls within the category of fiction generally given the rather uninviting label of 'Novels of doctrine or purpose.' In other words the story is not just told for the sake of the story, for the narration of incident and the unfolding of character: it is also made the platform from which abuses can be revealed, or doctrines and philosophies expounded.

The first English novel of this type was a rambling, Rousseauistical five-volume affair called *The Fool of Quality,* which came out between 1766 and 1770, and so impressed John Wesley that, with the author's permission, he blue-pencilled it down to two-thirds of its original length and re-issued it under a new title. Twenty years later there were at least three practitioners in this particular branch of fiction beside Bage: Godwin, the lovely and industrious Elizabeth Inchbald, and Thomas Holcroft.

Bage uses his platform to comment caustically on social inequalities and injustices—to tilt at the pretensions of the privileged; but he does not venture to suggest a remedy. He is no more a Jacobin than Peacock was the 'Rabelaisian pagan' that he has been termed. What he says in effect is: 'Look at what we have to put up with! Isn't it an abominable world we live in? . . . Let's withdraw from it, survey it from afar, and set up a private Utopia of our own, passing our time with books, in philosophical conversation, in discussion of the *Vindication of the Rights of Woman,* enjoying the pleasures of the table, and being thoroughly philoprogenitive!'

That idea runs through all his books. The hero of **Herm-sprong,** for example, as you will see, at one time contemplates retiring to America and constituting such a society of intimate friends within a two-mile ring on his 60,000-acre estate on the banks of the Potomac.

Well before Mary Wollstonecraft had published her famous *Vindication* Bage had championed the cause of sex equality. One of the characters in **James Wallace** is made to consider that 'daughters were the gift of God, as well as sons, and, in her judgment, to the full as deserving.' Hermsprong declares, 'I consider a woman as equal to a man,' but qualifies the remark cautiously with the codicil, 'I consider a man also as equal to a woman.' Elsewhere Bage's mouthpiece expresses the opinion that 'Parents, in their mode of education, must make less distinction of sex.' Fine words these at a time when woman's interests were supposed to be confined to dress, scandal, husband-hunting, child-bearing, and knotting genteelly in the drawing-room after tea!

But far more than this. Let me present the remainder of that sentence of Scott's apology from which I have already quoted a few words:

> Fielding, Smollett, and other novelists, have, with very indifferent tate, brought forward their heroes as rakes and debauchees, and treated with great lightness those breaches of morals, which are too commonly considered as venial in the male sex; but Bage has extended, in some instances, that licence to females.

The fact of the matter is that Bage—the disreputable Bohemian!—refused to believe that a young woman was damned for good and all, and must pass her life dripping with penitence if she had once slipped from the path of virtue. Kitty Ross in his novel, **Barham Down,** is none the less charming for all that she was seduced by a villain. The man who later falls in love with her is unconcerned by the lapse. He writes to a friend:

> 'She attempted to cure me by a frank confession of her original seduction. *It would not do.*'

> The italics are mine.

It stands to reason, therefore, that Bage was still less able to see why a girl who had 'suffered a fate worse than death' should not survive that horror to marry and lead a happy and normal life.

In **Mount Henneth** the beautiful Persian, Caralia, is raped by two Indian soldiers just before help arrives. Nevertheless she attracts the honourable attentions of Mr. Foston, a young volunteer in Clive's army. Discussing philosophically with her father the question of matrimony, she says:

> "Let it be remembered also . . . that though he saved my life, he came too late to save my honour."

> "Honour, Cara! Is there upon earth a man so absurd as to associate the idea of dishonour to thy sufferings?"

> "I know not, sir. In all these English books your goodness has procured for me, I find it is the leading idea: women who have suffered it, must die, or be immured for ever; ever after they are totally useless to all the purposes of society; it is the foundation of a hundred fabulous things called novels, which are said to paint exactly the reigning manners and opinions: all crimes but this may be expiated; no author has yet been so bold as to permit a lady to live and marry, and be a woman after this stain."

> "By heaven, a woman is more dishonoured by a wanton dream! What say you, Foston, is Cara a painter after truth?"

Mr. Foston is obliged to admit that that sort of nonsense may be found in novels, but expresses the hope that 'for the honour of the human intellect, little of it will be found anywhere else,' and sets out forthwith—and successfully—to vanquish the fears and scruples of the gentle Caralia.

It will be abundantly clear that though Bage wrote the *roman philosophique,* he liked plenty of incident and bright colour. His heroines are rescued from brothels, from cruel fathers, from the claws of debauched and hypnotic peers. I have, by the way, a strong feeling that Bage did not care for lords; but I also have a deep suspicion that he may never have met one to speak to in all his worthy middle-class life. Lord Grondale in **Hermsprong,** for instance, is twice as large as life, murky in character and sultry in behaviour—quite preposterously naughty.

Peerages, says the cynical Bage, speaking with the tongue of Mr. Glen who had had a passage or two with my lord, are 'charming things' that 'raise man far above man, and nearer to the divinity, since kings have once more become divine; and enable him to look down on the lesser inhabitants of this best of worlds, with a due sense of his great superiority.' 'As to rank,' avers Hermsprong, both for himself and his creator, 'I have been taught only to distinguish men by virtue.'

So far as the mechanics of this novel are concerned, Bage employs the self-same device that Voltaire used in *L'Ingénu,* Montesquieu in the *Lettres Persanes,* and Goldsmith in *The Citizen of the World* he displays the contemporary scene through the agency of a critical witness from another sphere. His Hermsprong surveys English society from the standpoint of one who was brought up to a simple, virtuous, and virile life amongst Red Indians—just like Voltaire's Huron. Incidentally he is, to the best of my belief, the first American-born hero in English fiction.

He is, indeed, a typically Bagian hero—very high-minded, devoted to the Rights of Man, and most magnificently forthright. He arrives in Cornwall from revolutionary France and the American backwoods, and immediately proceeds to give battle to the entrenched forces of privilege and exalted rank. There is much about him, which calls to mind that remarkable eccentric, Thomas Day, author of *Sandford and Merton,* whom Bage might very well have met in Lichfield through the medium of Dr. Erasmus Darwin, Charles Darwin's grandfather, his partner in an unprosperous ironworks.

The views of Mr. Hermsprong and Mr. Day on most subjects are very similar, although I cannot bring myself to believe that the former's notions of female education on philosophic principles would have included the firing of pistols (with blank charges) at young women in order to inculcate fortitude.

However that may be, Hermsprong is so busy being high-minded and forthright that he is not so truly alive as many of the other dramatis personae, who, not being compelled constantly to air the sublimest of views, can comfortably develop all sorts of amusing fads and foibles.

The ironical Mr. Sumelin, the Falmouth banker, is quite definitely related to Mr. Bennet of *Pride and Prejudice,* and views the elopement of his silly daughter with the same show of philosophical composure that was displayed by the latter gentleman when his Lydia vanished into the blue with young Wickham. No one, however, could possible imagine Mr. Bennet discussing before his daughters at breakfast the simultaneous *accouchement* of fifty ladies of the Grand Signior's seraglio. Mr. Sumelin did so.

Then there is a full-length portrait, painted with minute care, of the satirical and daring Miss Fluart. She is a perfect darling who would have graced and enlivened a Peacock novel, and yet has a Jane Austenish touch about her, even though Elizabeth Bennet or Emma Woodhouse would have been quite incapable of saying lightheartedly, 'A kiss! Lord bless me, I thought your lordship had wanted to undress me!' after a rather alarming little tussle with an amorous peer. I wish Bage had made her his heroine. I do indeed.

Another nice and careful study is that of young Mr. Glen, who plays commentator to the tale, and actually had the hardihood, one rainy day, to address Lord Grondale with his ill-bred hat fixed firmly upon his head. There is a delicious whimsicality about his luckless love affair with a young lady to whom he read *Cassandra* and *Cleopatra,* those tedious romances of De La Calprenède, and about the ignominious end of his youthful attempt at suicide.

But there are a host of people whom you will meet for yourself in a moment or so. Some of them (let us admit it) are as incredible as figures in transpontine melodrama or a Hollywood screen-play; like the ignoble nobleman; like Dr. Blick, the clerical yes-man—Bage would term him an exponent of 'the agreeable art of assentation'—of whose political doctrines Dr. Horsley would have greatly approved. Some of them are a little more than shadows, but many are delightful oddities. It is quite obvious that Bage enjoyed himself immensely when he felt that he could let himself go. The reader will share his relish.

The period of **Hermsprong** was one of transition, not only in the worlds of politics, economics, and literature, but also in the world of fashion. The rococo era was in process of transformation into the classical. Men no longer wore swords and three-cornered hats; women no longer dressed a towering edifice of hair with feathers and models of ships in blown glass. The days of powder and patches and hooped dresses had passed. The lovely Miss Campinet and her friends adorned gowns that were high-waisted and very full, fichus that made them look like pouter-pigeons, their ringleted heads crowned by Leghorn hats. Their male acquaintances displayed themselves in pantaloons reaching half-way down the leg, tailed coats and round hats.

They dined in the country at three in the afternoon; shot one another with flint-lock pistols; could buy a cloak in a London slop-shop for as little as four shillings and sixpence, or a pair of shoes for three shillings and ninepence; journeyed by mail-coach from London to York in thirty-one hours; could get a reasonable meal at an inn with brandy for eighteen pence; lost five hundred pounds an hour gambling at White's or Almack's; were hanged in droves at Newgate for any one of more than two hundred capital crimes; or, if girls, were suspended by the neck in female seminaries in order to draw out their muscles and increase their growth.

It is a sidelight on the times that two of the **Hermsprong** ladies are recorded as setting up house together on about five hundred pounds a year, on which they were able to maintain an establishment of three maids, two men-servants, a couple of horses, and a small pleasure-carriage!

The two most surprising things about Bage's literary life are, that he did not set up as author until he had reached the mature age of fifty-three, and that his last novel, **Hermsprong,** is beyond all argument, and contrary to all rule, his best—and far and away his best. It was published when he was sixty-eight, and was his sixth book. He died in 1801, five years later.

Bage was brought up under a succession of stepmothers—presumably as a Quaker—and educated at Derby, for his father owned a paper-mill just outside the town. He married at twenty-three, and established himself as a paper-manufacturer at Elford some five miles from

Tamworth in Staffordshire. In this remoteness he spent a lifetime, busied with his mill—the price of linen and cotton rag in London and Germany, the operations of pulping and bleaching and sizing, the sale of his products, the continual clamour of his men for higher wages, and, above all, the baffling iniquities of officialdom in the matter of taxation. For in those days—as Holyoake has recorded—'every paper-maker was regarded as a thief and the officers of the Excise dogged every step of his business with hampering, exacting, and humiliating suspicion.'

The social life of a small town clearly held no great interest for Bage, although he was obviously not a complete recluse. He was happy in the company of his books; found recreation in teaching himself modern languages, and later plunged into the study of higher mathematics, even going regularly once a week to Birmingham for instruction. He is manifestly voicing his own opinions when one of the personages of *Barham Downs* asserts that 'when my tutors presented algebra to me. I found it so agreeable to my appetite, that I might rather be said to devour than eat. It soon became the consoling power that recompensed me for all my mortifications. . . . The beauties of the divine Mathesis.'

This faculty for self-education was another characteristic he shared with Peacock, who left school when he was twelve years of age and yet became one of the finest classical scholars of his day.

Bage's first novel, *Mount Henneth,* was born soon after the failure of the business in which he had engaged in company with Erasmus Darwin. The writing of it may have diverted his attention from his losses, but it certainly could not have compensated him pecuniarily; for all he got for the work was thirty pounds! In a light-hearted introduction he explains:

> It is very easy to say I wrote it for my own amusement, and published it to satisfy the importunity of some very judicious friends, who could not bear that so many beauties should lie concealed in the drawer of a cabinet. But as I intend to be upon honour with my reader, in point of veracity, I must candidly confess, I have been determined by very different motives. In short, my daughters assure me, that I wrote in a very tasty manner; and that it is two years, bating two months, since I made each of them a present of a new silk gown.

It is really rather an odd sort of book, very chaotic and rambling, and told in a series of discursive letters. It had, however, a modest success, for it was published in Dublin in the following year, went into a second edition in 1788, and later received the honour of inclusion in the *Novelist's Library.*

Barham Downs, also in epistolary form, followed in 1784. It is a great technical improvement on the earlier novel, and not at all unamusing, although the effect it has on the mind is as of reading three serial stories simultaneously.

The Fair Syrian in 1787 was succeeded in the next year by *James Wallace.* The hero of the latter tale is a young lawyer who fails in his profession, 'being convicted of honesty,' and eventually becomes footman to the eminently desirable and intelligent Miss Lamounde. The end you can guess. The pungent commentator, Paracelsus Holman, and his father, the experimental chemist, are very well drawn. There are several nice vignettes, particularly of one oddity, a delicate exquisite who divided his interests between science and the extreme of foppery.

The immediate predecessor of *Hermsprong* was *Man As He Is,* in which Bage breaks away from the epistolary pattern of narration, and ambles through four volumes recounting the adventures and misadventures, the efforts at reform, and the back-slidings of a youthful baronet.

As for *Hermsprong,* it ran into two editions during its author's lifetime, and three more, possibly five, during the succeeding quarter of a century. Mr. E. A. Osborne in a recent bibliographical study of Bage does not record any foreign editions, although there had been French and German translations of the other novels, and *Man As He Is* had also been published in America.

So, pleasantly engaged with his pen, his books, and the business of his mill, Bage grew old, enjoying nothing more for relaxation than a game of cards with the ladies. He seems—like little Richardson, the bookseller creator of *Pamela*—to have preferred the society of women.

He would appear to have been comfortably off in a modest way. Why he was never opulent is probably explained in the following characteristic excerpts from letters of mixed business and friendship to his old crony, William Hutton, bookseller and antiquarian of Birmingham:

> The paper sent is charged at the lowest price at which a sober paper-maker can live and drink small beer.

> I had rather lose some profit than sink a tolerable name into a bad one.

> If the paper is below the standard so far as to oblige thee to lower the price, I am willing to assist in bearing the loss. If the quantity overburthens thee, take off a shilling a bundle—or take off two; for thy disposition towards me—I see it with pleasure—is kindly.

No one can read anything that Bage wrote without realising that his friendship would have been an honour to any man, and that there is no mere rhetorical flattery in the following tribute paid him by that other in whom the same bright virtues were so manifest—Scott:

His integrity, his honour, his devotion to truth, were undeviating and incorruptible; his humanity, benevolence, and generosity were not less conspicuous in private life, than they were in the principal characters of his works. He supplied persons he never saw with money, because he heard they were in want. He kept his servants and his horses to old age, and both men and quadrupeds were attached to him. He behaved to his sons with the unremitting affection of a father; but, as they grew up, he treated them as men and equals, and allowed them that independence of mind and conduct which he claimed for himself.

It remains but to add that the present edition of ***Hermsprong*** is based on the Chiswick Press edition of 1828. In its preparation I have been greatly assisted by the staff of the London Library, to whom I owe more thanks than I can adequately express for more favours on more occasions than I can reckon.

The only liberty that has been taken with the text has been an occasional modification of the punctuation in the interests of clarity, particularly with regard to the employment of quotation marks.

John H. Sutherland (essay date April 1957)

SOURCE: Sutherland, John H. "Robert Bage: Novelist of Ideas." *Philological Quarterly* 36, no. 2 (April 1957): 211-20.

[*In the following essay, Sutherland characterizes* Hermsprong; or, Man as He Is Not, *as a "novel of ideas" in the tradition of works by such authors as Thomas Love Peacock and Aldous Huxley.*]

In this paper the term "novel of ideas" will be used to refer to a sort of novel written by Thomas Love Peacock and by Aldous Huxley, among others: a sort of novel which is distinguished by its concern with the contrast and dramatic interplay of a number of ideas, rather than with the didactic recommendation of any single idea or point of view.[1] In terms of this definition it is something of an innovation to say that Robert Bage is primarily a novelist of ideas, since his work has usually been associated with that of liberal, didactic novelists of his time like Thomas Holcroft and William Godwin. The fact that Bage's last novel, ***Hermsprong, or Man As He Is Not*** (1796) is quite didactic, and is better known than his earlier, more characteristic work, may help to account for this misunderstanding (as I consider it). Another contributing factor may be the frequent critical neglect of the form of the novel of ideas, and the natural consequence of this—a tendency to try to fit practitioners of the form into other classifications. Thus, although Mr. Vaughan Wilkins, in his excellent recent edition of ***Hermsprong,*** relates Bage's work to that of Peacock, he goes on to classify all of Bage's books under the label "novels of doctrine or purpose."[2]

The novel of ideas, if it is to succeed, depends on the use of the technique of multiple point of view.[3] A typical Peacock novel, for example, usually reaches its high point in a country house, or—even more specifically—around a dinner table. Seven or eight characters, of violently contrasted natures and opinions, present their ideas as the claret or port circulates. The interest is focussed on the conflict of ideas rather than on the didactic recommendation of any one of them: in fact some of Peacock's pet theories (such as his opposition to the use of sugar produced by slave labor) are presented in as comic a light as ideas which he privately opposed, and might be presumed to be deliberately satirizing.

However, Peacock sets an unusually high standard; and even Peacock, in many instances, makes his own point of view quite apparent. In presenting a number of characters representing widely differing points of view, an author is almost certain to betray some bias or preference; nonetheless, he must preserve considerable structural balance and objectivity in his treatment of all of them if he does not want his book to develop—to a greater or lesser degree—into didacticism and propaganda. Thus it may even be an advantage for a writer of books of this sort to be without any very positive persuasions of his own. For example, Aldous Huxley's competence as a writer in this genre seems to have been seriously and adversely affected by his development of positive religious ideas.

The successful novelist of ideas need not be completely cynical, however; nor need he be contemptuous of the different points of view he represents. There is another way in which objectivity in the treatment of controversial subjects may be achieved, and that is by means of tolerance—a genuine conviction that different human beings may believe quite different things, and that each of these different beliefs may be proper (or at least inevitable) for the individual concerned. This seems to be the way in which Robert Bage reached a position from which he could represent and develop opposing ideas with considerable objectivity: because of, rather than in spite of, his liberal, democratic, deistic convictions.

There are several explicit statements in Bage's novels which seem to substantiate this interpretation. In ***Mount Henneth*** (1782), for example, one of the older protagonists, a Mr. Foston, tells of his experiences as a young man. Early in his career, while on board ship on his way out to India, he quarrelled with a fellow passenger over a matter of religious doctrine. The ship's captain prevented the two men from duelling, and then lectured Mr. Foston on the evils of dogmatism and the necessity of a free circulation of ideas. This speech seems to reflect Bage's own opinions, and thus serves to demonstrate his theoretical aptitude for writing the novel of ideas:

Under pretence of zeal for religion, you have insulted not Mr Lewis only, but all the company: you have indirectly supposed, that the faculty of perceiving truth is yours exclusively, and that other people have not an equal right with yourself to the free communication of their own ideas. A more general knowledge of the world will convince you of this equal right of mankind; and will shew you the folly of calling upon the civil magistrate, as you have often, in the warmth of argument, supposed just and necessary, to support the dogmas of any set of men whatever. Reflect that nothing, in itself indisputable, can be long disputed, and that in propositions not absolutely demonstrable, the degrees of probability on which they rest are best known by free and ample discussion; the more truth they contain, the more visible it will become by examination. Happily mankind is not in so deplorable a situation, as that its happiness should depend upon disputable dogmas.[4]

Unfortunately, Mr. Foston was not convinced by this speech; he had to learn by experience. Bage puts him through a series of adventures which serve to cure him of a great many of his prejudices. Finally this erstwhile religious enthusiast is so far converted to liberalism as to marry a girl most of whose qualities are opposite to those to be expected in a conventional heroine: she is not a virgin, she is of Jewish ancestry, and she has no religious beliefs at all.

The girl, whose name is Cara, continues to educate Foston in liberal ways. At one point she seems to speak for Bage as she points out to her husband the frequent lack of connection between a man's nature and a man's ideas. As Foston tells it:

> In spite of my better reflections I was still subject to little violences of temper when my opinions were contradicted. In order to cure me of these, Cara engaged me in a thousand little agreeable arguments concerning the origin of ideas, and their association; she taught me to consider how opinions were formed; how little share man himself could claim in the formation; and how unjust it was to attach the idea of turpitude to speculative notions, created or changed according to the disposition of external objects, and the sport of a thousand accidents. By these sweet means, she brought me to look upon a man's habits of thinking and acting, where the one does not necessarily lead or follow the other, as two distinct things; one altogether worthy of my esteem, although I might judge the other involved in a labyrinth of error.[5]

Because of these passages, and others like them, we know that Bage believed in the sort of objective and tolerant treatment of conflicting ideas which can serve as a basis for writing novels of ideas. However, his novels must be examined in more detail to see what success he actually achieved in the genre.

Bage's first four novels (*Mount Henneth,* 1782; *Barham Downs,* 1784; *The Fair Syrian,* 1787; and *James Wallace,* 1788) not only represent two-thirds of his

work—they also serve as better examples of his usual practices than do his last two novels (*Man As He Is,* 1792; and *Hermsprong,* 1796). Much in the first four novels is patterned after the work of the four great mid-century novelists. The epistolary form and some elements of the melodramatic plots are reminiscent of Richardson; however, many stylistic traits, and the arch, jesting, and yet half serious tone in which problems involving sensibility and female chastity are treated, remind the reader of Sterne. A number of themes and comic situations (involving practical jokes, country squires, and, again, the relationships of virtue and chastity) seem to owe something to the examples of Smollett and Fielding.

All these debts indicate that Bage was consciously making use of the tradition of the eighteenth-century novel. However, he was not trying to imitate any of these writers; rather, he was using any methods he could lay his hands on to treat the ideas in which he was interested. Godwin reports that Bage believed "he should not have written novels, but for want of books to assist him in any other literary undertaking."[6] Thus many of the techniques of the novel were put to uses unthought of by their originators. However, the patterns which served his purpose best were devised for reasons like his own. Examples of these include the following: the objective treatment of melodramatic incidents in order to illustrate general philosophical ideas (as in many of Voltaire's *contes philosophiques*); the use of the epistolary form as a device for the presentation of a number of different points of view (as in *Humphry Clinker*); and the use of multiple point of view in present scene as a source both for comedy and for serious comment on human nature (as in *Tristram Shandy*).

Because of the necessities of the epistolary form, Bage's many heroes are usually widely separated during the course of a novel. They can, and do, experience a great variety of violent adventures, which serve to illustrate the ideas they discuss in their letters. Most of them come together at the end of each novel to participate in the group weddings with which Bage, half-playfully, pleased and appeased his readers. Thus Bage was unable to make much use of Peacock's country house, or round-table discussion method of contrasting ideas. His usual technique was far more discursive: he would introduce a controversial problem, and then exhibit, both in words and in action, a variety of different human reactions to the problem.

In *Barham Downs,* for example, a number of characters are involved in what might be called a demonstration on duelling. One man, Sir George Osmond, refuses to duel because it is unreasonable. Another, Mr. Arnold, a Quaker, refuses from combined motives of reason, benevolence, and religious conviction. Yet another, Captain O'Donnel, an Irish mercenary soldier, is eager to fight at every hint of a proper opportunity.

On one occasion, O'Donnel is wounded in a duel which he undertook in an attempt to defend the "honor" of Sir George Osmond. (Sir George knew nothing about this particular duel until after it occurred.) After the duel, O'Donnel discusses the morality of the affair with Parry, his erstwhile antagonist—who is really a friend of his. O'Donnel speaks in the first person:

> All this is true, my dear, says I; but what of that? By Jasus, sentiment stinks, when it goes to persuade a brave fellow to pocket an affront.
>
> It ought to be an affront indeed, and a heavy one too, says Parry, to require a life for expiation; but any foolish thing serves the turn. What was it to you, O'Donnel, that I amused myself with a willing woman? You had refused her, you know.
>
> But she was Lady Osmond, says I, the wife of my friend; and I would as soon resent an affront done to him as to myself, and sooner too.
>
> And how, says Parry, did Sir George behave to you upon a similar occasion?
>
> By my soul, like a noble gentleman—like a man of sense; not like a man of modern fashion—like a fool—like a blockhead.
>
> O'Donnel, if his sentiments are right, yours are wrong.
>
> Oh, the devil burn me, says I, and why can't they be both right? and what is right and wrong at all but what a man thinks to be so?'

This is, of course, an Irish bull. But it is also intended more seriously, I think, as a climax to a long section in which a variety of points of view are presented. As the passages we examined earlier help to prove, Bage was convinced that right and wrong, for the individual, was determined in many instances by what that individual sincerely believed—that the duties of conscience took precedence over the pronouncements of any doctrinaire moralist.

Most of the problems investigated in Bage's novels center around four general subjects: war and duelling; politics and revolution; religion and philosophy; love and marriage. Illustrations of his treatment of various points of view on these subjects are hard to present concisely, since the rambling structure of the novels permits him to give extended treatment to each. For example, the two passages from *Mount Henneth* which were quoted above are part of a long demonstration on religion in which the ideas of a Hindu, a Methodist, an Episcopalian, a deist, an atheist, and a free-thinking Jew, are all represented. In addition, elsewhere in this book and in other books, Bage introduces the religious opinions of Catholics, Orthodox Jews, Quakers, Mohammedans, and American Indians. All of these positions (except that of the enthusiastic Methodist) are presented quite fairly and favorably. It should be said, however, that this is not the best possible example of

Bage's perception of the truth of multiplicity, since he tends to emphasize the deistic beliefs which, in his opinion, reasonable men of different religions have in common.

A better example may be found in his treatment of the question of violence and war. The quotation from *Barham Downs,* in which O'Donnel discusses duelling, gives some idea of the nature of the extended treatments of this subject to be found in several of the novels. A situation in *James Wallace* illustrates Bage's method even more neatly.

A Scots sea captain writes from Algiers, where he has touched on a trading expedition. He reports the conversation of a Moorish pirate, who, with great reason and ability, defends the practice of piracy as no more than a perpetual war on the Spaniards (and others), fought for the same reasons that Christians fight their intermittent wars—plunder and revenge. The captain is shocked, and attempts to preach "true" Christianity—which in this context amounts to Christian pacifism—to the Moor. In a witty reply, the Moor remarks on the paucity of sincere practitioners of such a doctrine, then says: "I laugh at your peaceable precepts. If a man smite thee on the right cheek, turn to him thy left. If he steal thy cloak, give him thy coat also. By Ismael! a community of *true* Christians must always be governed by the greatest scoundrel amongst them."[8] Almost immediately after this exchange, a report comes in of a corsair attack on a Spanish coasting vessel on which the gentle Christian, James Wallace, was a passenger. Wallace is said to have led the defense of the ship, with the result that all attacks were repulsed with "terrible havoc."

If this were a purely didactic novel, this episode would probably be intended as an illustration corroborating the cynical opinions of the Moorish pirate: that war and piracy are much the same thing, that both are justifiable, and that Christian pacifism is nonsense. The illiberality of such a moral, of course, makes it clear that Bage could not have intended it. The passage is ironic, and the irony is intended to serve as satire aimed both at warmongers and at unreasonable idealists. If Bage's personal views were presented, they probably would run about like this: that war and piracy are very much alike, that both are cruel and unreasonable, and that Christians are often tremendous hypocrites; that absolute pacifism is a praiseworthy, perhaps impractical, ideal; that violence is sometimes, but not always, justifiable in self-defense. (Earlier in the story, James Wallace uses pistols to defend himself from some ruffians who threaten him with indignities. He says of this incident: "I had not time to examine whether it was better one man should die, or another be dragged through a horse-pond.")[9] The whole presentation seems not complex, but muddled, if it is examined only in terms of satiric ironies; however, all becomes much clearer if it is realized that the author's purpose is not so much to present his own point of view as to compare a number of different points of view. Objectivity is not complete, since the author's opinions become clear in the course of the novel; however, the effect is not didactic, because most of the points of view are presented favorably, as being right for the persons holding them. In a didactic novel the Moorish pirate probably would be either a hero or a bloodstained villain. In *James Wallace* he is a reasonable man, worthy of respect, presenting an unorthodox point of view on a moral question.

The foregoing examples illustrate multiple point of view, but they also show how the author's own opinions find clear expression. Still better examples for our purpose may be found in the number of points of view Bage brings to bear on the question of the proper relations of the sexes. His opinions on this subject were not extreme by modern standards, but they brought him under mild censure from critics of his own age, and did much to cause his complete rejection by publishers and readers in the nineteenth century. Stated simply, in the words of a character in *Man As He Is,* he seems to have thought that ". . . there is still one desideratum in our happiest European societies. It is to preserve a little more free will to the sexes in their mutual conjunctions."[10]

This sort of opinion did not limit Bage, as his religious ideas limited him; rather it freed him to represent a number of different approaches to the subject. He does this candidly, and without apparent prejudice. In many of his novels he has at least two heroines of very different temperament and principles. In *Barham Downs,* for example, one heroine is seduced at an early age, while the other behaves in a proper and conventional manner. It shocked Sir Walter Scott a great deal that Bage represented both these women as being essentially admirable, and that he rewarded both of them with happy marriages at the end of the story.[11]

In *Mount Henneth,* one heroine, Laura Stanley, is arch and self-confident; she has common sense and a strong sense of humor. Another heroine, Julia Foston, is mild, meek, and virtuous. In a representative passage these two are in company with a number of friends, among whom is a Miss Caradoc. Miss Caradoc's brother is a member of the Antiquarian Society, and she is described as a sort of female virtuoso who "Minces snails to multiply the breed, kills cats in an air-pump, and generates eels in vinegar."

Bage represents Miss Caradoc, in perfect unembarrassed naivete, calling the attention of the whole group to the sexual activities of a donkey and a mare:

> In the beautiful hanging pastures beneath, amongst other quadrupeds, was your little roan mare, employed, as females sometimes are, in attending to the love of

an ass. This animal was in love *à la folie*; had broke through three several barriers, and was eager to reap the fruits of his bold enterprize. To the philosophic eye all things are equal. Miss Caradoc was first struck with the view, and drawing Julia and Laura to the wall, See, says she.—Julia, blushing rosy red, withdrew her arm, and walked gently on. Laura, in a few seconds followed, and bursting into a laugh, See! cries she.—Fie, Laura, said Miss Foston, walking on.—Brother, says the contemplative Miss Caradoc, you have constantly asserted that copulation between animals of different species is unnatural, and always committed by a rape of the female—see the contrary. . . .[12]

This passage, again, shows characters with different points of view reacting to a representative situation. Further reading in Bage can confirm the amused, objective tone of the presentation. This is not propaganda for free-thinking: the point of view of the modest girl is represented in as genuinely favorable a light as that of the bold one.

Another example may help to make Bage's position clearer. Miss Warren, in *The Fair Syrian,* is a virtuous and modest young lady. Bage never suggests that she should be anything different, and yet he has her, in a letter, report the following conversation with a harem girl named Amina:

> "But you say you are a christian, Amina—what then becomes of your principles?"
>
> "Principles?"
>
> "The christian religion condemns the life you lead."
>
> "For what, I wonder? I rob nobody."
>
> "To give up our persons to the lust of many, unsanctified by marriage rites!—This we call impurity and wickedness."
>
> "Our priests in Georgia call it by the same names.—It is a sad crime for a young girl with us, to lose her virginity, before she has got a husband; or before her parents have got the market price for it."
>
> "Do your priests teach that doctrine?"
>
> "Certainly—when they have pretty daughters, they sell them like other people—when they have ugly ones, they get them husbands; and tell them what a virtue it is to be chaste."
>
> "Nay, if you are thus taught—but, my dear, there is another article that perplexes me—Did you not feel your delicacy hurt, to be at the will of different men—no affection to return?"
>
> "No affection! Delicacy! I don't understand you."
>
> "You had no feelings of disgust?"
>
> "No—not I."
>
> "Amazing! The idea fills me with horror. I prefer death a thousand times."

"And I prefer a thousand times—to death." She could not finish the sentence for an extravagant fit of laughing. "And you drink no wine either, I observe," says she—"Love and wine, the two best cordials in the cup of life;—how unhappy you are!"

Thus did this wild, untutored, sensible madcap turn and laugh at the most serious arguments I could use. She was, however, one of the best natured creatures in the world, and always disposed to oblige; and I must confess my philosophy not a little indebted to her.[13]

Up to this point, the argument has been deliberately simplified by confining it to the first four novels. Actually, the principles under discussion apply to all of Bage's work: *Hermsprong* is by no means as didactic as it is often thought to be. As has been seen, one of Bage's favorite techniques was the extensive comparison of different points of view in action. Those who protest that the characters in *Hermsprong* are unrealistic should give proper weight to its alternative title—*Man As He Is Not.* To be properly understood, *Man As He Is Not* must be read in conjunction with the novel which immediately preceded it in order of composition—*Man As He Is.* The hero of *Man As He Is* is a wayward young gentleman whose character is quite realistically portrayed. The theme, if one must be derived, seems to be a plea for tolerance and understanding of the weakness of human beings who experience the temptations of fashionable life. Like Fielding, Bage seems to suggest that judgment of human behavior must weigh sincere intentions at least as heavily as performance. The novel as a whole anticipates much of Thackeray in tone and structure. It contrasts violently with *Man As He Is Not,* in which the hero is a "natural man" of impossible perfections, and the principal nobleman is a caricature villain. If *Hermsprong* is interpreted solely as a didactic and satirical work, it must be judged (in spite of many good hits) lamentably unrealistic. However, if its title is kept in mind, and if it is read as part of a larger structure involving (in addition to the social satire) the amused comparison of two very different attitudes and points of view, many of the objections to it disappear.

In one sense Bage was a transition figure between some of the didactic novelists of the eighteenth century, and novelists of ideas in the nineteenth and twentieth centuries. His deism and his liberal, democratic, political ideas colored everything he wrote; but his civilized tolerance and his understanding of the relativity of ideas prevented his falling into most of the awkwardnesses of didacticism. Although he was rarely able to contrast a number of different points of view with the dramatic smoothness and objectivity of a writer like Peacock, the form of his work and his achievement can only be understood in terms of the form and purpose of the novel of ideas. His success should not be underrated. He was not only the best novelist between Fanny Burney and

Jane Austen (a modest enough claim!); he was also a main figure in the development of a form of literature which seems to be of increasing significance in our own age.

Notes

1. Cf. Frederick J. Hoffman, "Aldous Huxley and the Novel of Ideas," in *Forms of Modern Fiction,* ed. William Van O'Connor (University of Minnesota Press, 1948), pp. 189-200; and the discussion of the "anatomy" in Northrop Frye, "The Four Forms of Prose Fiction," *Hudson Review* (Winter, 1950), pp. 582-595.

2. Vaughan Wilkins, ed., *Hermsprong,* by Robert Bage (New York, 1951), p. vii.

3. I use the term "point of view" here for want of a better one. I do not mean by it the formal narrative point of view; I mean, rather, the intellectual perspectives—the philosophical, psychological, or moral positions—which the author presents with understanding and seeming approval. This frequently corresponds with the narrative point of view in Bage, as in other writers; but it need not do so.

4. *The Novels of Swift, Bage, and Cumberland* in *Ballantyne's Novelists' Library,* ed. Sir Walter Scott (London, 1824), IX, 150-151.

5. *Ibid.,* p. 166.

6. In a letter to his wife, Mary Wollstonecraft, quoted in full in C. Kegan Paul, *William Godwin: His Friends and Contemporaries* (Boston, 1876), I, 261-264.

7. *Ballantyne's Novelists' Library,* IX, 371-372.

8. *Ibid.,* p. 468.

9. *Ibid.,* p. 385.

10. *Man As He Is* (London, 1792), III, 195-196.

11. *Ballantyne's Novelists' Library,* IX, xxix-xxx.

12. *Ibid.,* p. 183.

13. *The Fair Syrian* (London, 1787), II, 80-81.

Marilyn Butler (essay date 1975)

SOURCE: Butler, Marilyn. "The Jacobin Novel II: *Caleb Williams* and *Hermsprong*." In *Jane Austen and the War of Ideas,* pp. 57-87. Oxford: Clarendon Press, 1975.

[*In the following excerpt, Butler studies Bage's novels within the tradition of the Jacobin novels of such authors as Thomas Holcroft and William Godwin, noting how Bage's expression of opinions in his works differs from that of his contemporaries and anticipates the expression of ideas in the novels of Jane Austen.*]

2. BAGE'S *HERMSPRONG*

Robert Bage,[1] the paper-maker from Elford, near Derby, is the revolutionary novelist who least resembles the others. He was older than most of them, and moved in a wholly different circle, though in the last few years of his life, after all his novels were written, he twice met Godwin. Bage's contacts in the Derby Philosophical Society included his friend William Hutton, Josiah Wedgwood, and Erasmus Darwin, the two latter also being members of the celebrated Lunar Society of Birmingham. This was a group, and a generation, which shared practical day-to-day interests, a taste for applied science, and a general intellectual approach shaped in the 1760s and 1770s by the French *philosophes* and the Anglo-Scottish empiricists. Bage's writings were evidently sufficiently typical for one member of the Lunar Society to detect in them a kindred spirit. Richard Lovell Edgeworth, enjoying **Hermsprong** in Ireland in 1797, believed that parts of it had been written by one of his own most intimate friends, Erasmus Darwin.[2]

Bage's circle of businessmen and entrepreneurs, inventors and scientists, canal-builders, mechanics, chemists, educators, is the key to an understanding of his intellectual position. It was a world whose textbook was not Godwin's *Political Justice,* still less Paine's *Rights of Man,* but Adam Smith's *Wealth of Nations.* For three decades before the outbreak of the French Revolution, Midlands industrialists had been actively involved in a revolution of their own, and their natural enemy was the only interest powerful enough to stop it—the vested political interest in the capital, that of the landed oligarchy, old corruption. The Lunar members tended for example to be opposed to the American War: not merely for the effect it might have on their immediate business interests, but because Ministerial policy towards the colonists was an interference from the centre with the liberty of the middle-class subject. It was the principle which they detested.

Bage's first novels were written in the aftermath of the American War, and in the end all six of them suggest the period of that Revolution rather than the French.[3] Bage is for individualism much as Adam Smith is for it, and it is for this reason that the fictional format which most appeals to him is that of Smith's compatriot and contemporary, Smollett. The fourth novel, *James Wallace,* indeed comes very near to plagiarizing *Roderick Random*: a hero driven by necessity to become a footman is too memorable a feature to be used more than once. But the fifth, **Man As He Is,** 1792, shows Bage deploying Smollett's loose-knit framework to real advantage, as his hero travels about England and the Continent and purveys a representative, sharply satirical picture of contemporary men and manners. Bage excels at the pointed character-sketch, and in **Man As He Is** the aristocratic brother and sister, Lord Auschamp and Lady Mary Paradyne, are memorable comic creations, as solemn, self-important, and absurd as Jane Austen's Lady Catherine de Burgh. Unlike Holcroft, Bage is content to leave much as he found it the rambling picaresque format, with its haphazard sequence of events and its tolerance of coincidence. He appears innocent of the otherwise universal jacobin obsession with social determinism: his characters are only the pawns of their social environment inasmuch as they choose to be. Essentially free agents, in the aggregate they *are* society, as in the earlier, more naïve eighteenth-century comic manner.

If in social theory and psychology Bage is old-fashioned, he thereby avoids a great many technical difficulties. Moreover, it can at least be said of him that where he adopts stale conventions, he does not do so unthinkingly. The picaresque expresses well enough his individualistic egalitarian philosophy and his admiration for individual energy and effort. And where other conventions of eighteenth-century fiction-writing do not fall in with his themes, he has a neat way (which suggests far greater intellectual flexibility than Holcroft's) of standing them on their head.

The relationship in **Man As He Is** between Sir George Paradyne and Cornelia Colerain must for example have struck the contemporary reader as a most amusing democratic pastiche of Fanny Burney's snobbish central situation in *Cecilia.* And when Lady Mary Paradyne makes the same assumption as Fanny Burney's Mrs. Delvile, that the girl is socially unworthy to become her daughter-in-law, Sir George's rebuke is one that Mortimer Delville would have done well to utter (although it could never have come from Fanny Burney's deferential pen):

> 'The lady on whom you have made such liberal observation, rejects that honour. If she would accept it, I know not of your ladyship's acquaintance, in a comparison of merit, one who would not sink before her. If she would stoop to raise me to herself, I might still be happy; but she rejects me because—I am not worthy of her.'[4]

The plot of **Hermsprong,** 1796, plays havoc with cliché in similar terms. A totally unknown young man, strangely named and of supposed German origin, appears in a Cornish village, saves the life of Lord Grondale's daughter, and is supposed by that peer to be a fortune-hunter bent on marrying above him. Hermsprong does indeed love Caroline Campinet, but not her weaknesses;[5] she still thinks it right to play the part of a dutiful daughter, and it is Hermsprong who refuses to be married while she remains the slave of custom and prejudice.

In the plot of *Hermsprong,* the expectations roused by current literature are continually deployed, only to be over-set. For example, the love-story begins in the standard romantic manner, with Hermsprong seizing the reins of the bolting horse as it drags Caroline's carriage towards the cliff. As a result of this episode, Caroline feels sentimentally bound to Hermsprong, although he drily points out that 'It was an impulse, and it was irresistible.'[6] At other points in the novel he behaves, or appears about to behave, according to the best manner of a hero. In a French garden he encounters Mr. Fillygrove, who is at the moment suffering from a hangover; but Mr. Fillygrove has eloped from Falmouth with Harriet Sumelin, Hermsprong is Mr. Sumelin's friend, and by a conventional sequence of events Mr. Fillygrove has soon challenged Hermsprong to a duel. The unorthodox outcome is in Bage's idiosyncratic vein. Hermsprong retaliates by picking up Fillygrove, and 'giving the young man a hearty shake' . . . 'Mr. Fillygrove was rather inclined to be sick.'[7] In a similar episode later in the novel Hermsprong encounters his rival for Caroline's hand, Sir Philip Chestrum, and, instead of duelling with him, he picks him up and deposits him on the far side of a fence.

The unexpected turns of event have the effect of throwing the protagonist's motives into relief. The reader is bound to ask himself what has made Hermsprong behave differently from other heroes, thus diverting the plot from its usual course. From here it is a short step to engaging the reader as a moral arbiter between the hero who refuses to act as heroes normally do, and the heroine who persists, despite the hero's disapproval, in acting merely like a heroine. The ironic disturbance of conventional expectations promotes an alert and critical attitude in the reader, an effect which is ably supported by further stylistic devices.

What we are to criticize in the principal action is very obvious. Lord Grondale is an archetypal Bage villain, a tyrant in each of his roles, as politician, landlord, and father. As usual, too, in Bage's portrayal of the upper classes, he is corrupt in his morals. He lives with 'a person of merit', Mrs. Stone, and has the impudence to justify himself by the precedent of those unorthodox father-figures, the Hebrew patriarchs.[8] In his garden he has a Temple of Venus, its walls adorned with suggestive pictures, and there he assaults his daughter's friend Maria Fluart:

> However capital these might be, they were such as ladies are not accustomed to admire in the presence of gentlemen. There was, however, a superb sofa, on which a lady might sit down with all possible propriety. Miss Fluart did sit down; but the prospect from thence rather increased than diminished a little matter of confusion which she felt on the view of the company she seemed to have got into.
>
> She was rising to leave the pavilion, when his lordship, in the most gallant manner possible, claimed a fine, due, he said, by the custom of the manor, from every lady who honoured that sofa by sitting upon it. His lordship meant simply a kiss, which I believe he would have taken respectfully enough, had Miss Fluart been passive; but, I know not why, the lady seemed to feel an alarm, for which probably she had no reason; and was intent only upon running away, whilst his lordship was intent only upon seizing his forfeit. A fine muslin apron was ill treated upon this occasion; a handkerchief was ruffled, and some beautiful hair had strayed from its confinement, and wantoned upon its owner's polished neck. She got away, however, from this palace of painting, and its dangerous sofa.
>
> 'Upon my word, my dear Miss Fluart,' said his lordship, getting down after her as fas as he was able, 'you are quite a prude today. I thought you superior to the nonsense of your sex,—the making such a rout about a kiss.'
>
> 'A kiss! Lord bless me,' said Miss Fluart, 'I thought, from the company your lordship had brought me into, and the mode of your attack, you had wanted to undress me.'[9]

Lord Grondale's chief aide—and jointly with him the satiric target of the main plot—is a servile pluralist, the Reverend Mr. Blick. This harsh portrait of a clergyman of the Established Church, in whom religion and every other moral principle are sacrificed to the worldly interest of his patron, is darker in tone than Bage's characteristic satire of earlier years, probably because the circumstances of the times made it so. Bage's friend William Hutton had been a sufferer, along with Joseph Priestley, of the Birmingham Riots in 1791, in which the mob had zealously burnt Dissenters' property in the name of King and Church. It is not merely the oligarchic tendencies of the upper classes and their sycophants that Bage attacks; but, with a more special aptness in this novel, their crimes against religious toleration and free speech. Dr. Blick's actions recall real-life acts of repression which at the time of writing were fresh in the memory—the prosecution of men for their opinions in the Treason Trials of 1794, and the notorious Two Acts of 1795. Blick the so-called divine takes the most energetic part in the prosecution of Hermsprong, and, as perhaps his most generalized and representative act of sycophancy, preaches a sermon on the necessity of submission to the temporal power.

Equally, however, the themes of the novel are developed in the subplot, which concerns the family of Mr. Sumelin at Falmouth. The heroine's friend Miss Fluart is Mr. Sumelin's ward, a fact which often takes Caroline there; luckily for her since, by one of Bage's unashamed coincidences, Hermsprong is Mr. Sumelin's associate in business. The Sumelin *ménage* is the mirror-image of Lord Grondale's household: Mr. Sumelin, dry, intelligent, not at all severe, is the very reverse of a domestic tyrant, while his silly wife and their daughter Harriet are also the reverse of the rational

Caroline Campinet. The lesson of the Falmouth family is that the freedom Mr. Sumelin allows is of little use unless women have minds, and are prepared to use them; for Mrs. Sumelin and Harriet voluntarily submit to the tyranny of fashion and appearances. Even if the action's periodic removal to Falmouth is not well accounted for in terms of plot, the thematic link goes a long way to justify it. Besides, few readers would be willing to forgo conversations which delightfully, and significantly, anticipate *Pride and Prejudice*:

> . . . Mrs. Sumelin, in the course of rapid declamation, so far forgot things as to defend her dear Harriet from head to foot, imprudence and all.
>
> 'Then,' my guardian asked as soon as he could be heard, 'why do you eternally scold her for faults, if she has committed none?'
>
> 'You catch one up so, Mr. Sumelin; to be sure, I did not mean to say quite that; but for your part, you take no pains to instruct your children, nor ever did. I don't believe you have ever said one word to Harriet about this business.'
>
> 'What need? when I have a dear industrious wife, who takes the department of lecturing into her own hands, and performs it so ably.'
>
> 'You are enough to provoke a stone wall. I have not patience with you.'
>
> "I don't expect it, my dear. Only have the goodness not to torment yourself. You were in the humour just now to think Harriet's fault a small one.—With all my heart. The law does not call it an offence at all. It gives young women leave to choose their own husbands after twenty-one; or before, provided they do not marry in England. Harriet, you see, did nothing illegal. She was going out of England, that she might not sin against the law. But the law also allows fathers to dispose of their acquired property as they please. To this inconvenience Harriet must submit. She loves Mr. Fillygrove, I do not. To him, therefore, I shall give nothing . . ."[10]

It is largely in conversation at Falmouth, between Hermsprong, Caroline, and Maria Fluart, that the principal themes of the novel are developed. The most important of these is liberty, especially, in the terms of this novel, the liberty of women. Caroline has the first essential quality, which Mrs. Sumelin and Harriet lack—an educated understanding. But according to Hermsprong the problem for English women is that despite their relative liberty of action they employ too little liberty of mind. Without this, they become slaves to fashion, convention, or their menfolk. To some extent the problem is one of education; but it is even more one of will.[11]

Caroline, too rational to be a slave to fashion or social ambition, nevertheless voluntarily submits to the tyranny of her father. Her combination of just perception and timid orthodoxy reveals itself when she is courted by Sir Philip Chestrum. He has inherited a fortune from his tradesman-father, and a long pedigree from his aris-

tocratic mother, but Caroline rejects him on account of his want of education and intellect. To Lord Grondale, needless to say, he is an eligible suitor, and the peer enters into an unholy alliance with Lady Chestrum. In relation to the match, Caroline adopts the approved stance of the eighteenth-century heroine. She stands on her right to refuse the man she does not love; but she will not assert her right to the man, Hermsprong, whom she does love.[12] Bage criticizes his heroine's passivity by causing the lively Miss Fluart to put up an entertaining resistance on Caroline's behalf both to Sir Philip and to Lord Grondale. The former soon learns to fear the play of her irony—'Miss Fluart talked one thing always, and meant another.'[13] Lord Grondale, at first enchanted with her vivacity, eventually comes to hate her, as she thwarts his plans for Caroline's marriage and dismisses both it and his own suit with more than customary frankness:

> Your Lordship requires Miss Campinet to return, in order to receive the addresses of Sir Philip Chestrum. I would recommend to your Lordship to receive those addresses yourself; for, if they are offered to Caroline in person, they must inspire her with invincible disgust . . . Indeed, my Lord, there should be a little affection, if it be no more than sufficient to prevent a nausea, which possibly might affect an elegant young woman upon the pawings of a bear or monkey. You know, my Lord, that is what I am waiting for: and when it comes, I am ready. But indeed, and indeed, I must wait till it does come; and so ought all sober minded young women, like.
>
> Your Lordship's most obedient servant,
>
> Maria Fluart[14]

What Maria Fluart does that her friend the conventional heroine does not do is to speak her mind with freedom. The reader comes to look for and to value a style in conversation which reveals liberty of mind. Hermsprong and Maria Fluart have the manner to perfection, so bracing that it hits their opponents like a bucketful of cold water. The Rev. Mr. Woodcock displays it in his finest hour, when he turns upon his superior, Dr. Blick.[15] Mr. Sumelin has it, together with other desirable intellectual qualities—decisiveness, as when he tells his wife to end her reproaches to Harriet, and discrimination, as when he corrects his wife's slipshod phrasing:

> One morning, at breakfast, Mr. Sumelin had the misfortune to scald his fingers, simply for the common cause of such accidents, doing one thing, and thinking of another. Mrs. Sumelin, as is usual in these small domestic cases, began to scold.
>
> 'If I had broke the cup, madam,' Mr. Sumelin answered, 'it would have been a crime inexpiable but by a new set. This is, I suppose, a regular tax upon husbands; I submit to it; but I really cannot submit to the not being allowed to scald my own fingers.'
>
> 'It was so thoughtless, Mr. Sumelin,' said his lady.
>
> 'Was it not rather too much thought?' asked Miss Fluart.

'It's all one,' Mrs. Sumelin answered.

'To the tea-cup,' said the husband, 'or to things which want understanding.'[16]

The dialogue of admirable characters habitually suggests this kind of precision and here, if not in boldness, Caroline ranks among the angels. Her scene with Sir Philip Chestrum, in which she quietly discourages him, and in his complacency he fancies the opposite, has more than a touch of Jane Austen about it. Of course it anticipates the proposal scene of John Thorpe, just as it anticipates Sir Philip Baddely's courtship in Maria Edgeworth's *Belinda*: foolish young men who propose and are unexpectedly refused are a favourite stock-in-trade of comedy in the period, perhaps on account of the conceited Mr. Smith in Fanny Burney's *Evelina*. But even more interesting, and more fundamental to the art of Bage's successors, is the carefully controlled use in this scene of the heroine's intelligent tone. Nothing need be said by the author about Sir Philip Chestrum's inept proposal. The flavour of the heroine's restricted remarks is sufficient to put the reader into an active frame of mind in which his own discrimination does the rest.

As a technician Bage is not consistently in the front rank. He adopts a structure in **Hermsprong,** involving a narrator called Gregory Glen, which is irremediably clumsy and after a while seems to get forgotten. Although **Hermsprong** is actually more tightly constructed than his earlier novels, the action still wanders about, and contains too many inset stories. Even in terms of his own clever concept, the heroine who behaves in accordance with convention, and is yet in the wrong, Bage is to some extent at fault. The reader cannot help feeling conned when he discovers that Hermsprong, Caroline's rational choice, the man of no name, is really (in the worst manner of conventional plotting) the long-lost Sir Charles Campinet. At least Holcroft had the intellectual courage to leave Frank Henley to the last a gardener's son. Besides, Caroline's submissiveness is censured only so far. We cannot help suspecting that Bage partly relies on our sympathy for her gentleness and obedience, and the suspicion is confirmed when he makes Lord Grondale fall ill, so that Caroline's weak-willed conformism merges indistinguishably into her general benevolence.

The plot thus fails to maintain its originality and irony to the end, and the lack of consistency and deficiency in intellectual daring are such serious faults that **Hermsprong** falls short of great satirical comedy. What does not disappoint is the formal innovation, the pointed and dramatic use made of intelligent dialogue. Here, at any rate, is the logical connection with the central inspiration of Godwin. For Bage, too, is writing about individualism, and about liberty, and, in an entirely differ-

ent genre from Godwin's sombre tragedy, he too has made his characters enact what they stand for. It is perfectly true that Hermsprong himself is a concoction out of place in a realistic novel, suggesting Voltaire's Huron out of Ferguson or Smith. What matters more is that in speech he really does do battle with dictatorial assurance on the one hand, the empty forms of polite address on the other; and that Miss Fluart's lively freedoms support him. This, too, is a drama of consciousness, though it belongs to the comic mode. And in achieving such a drama, Bage, who is in many ways so old-fashioned, moves towards a novel that speaks for his own time rather than for that of his predecessors.

Here, in fact, is that assault via burlesque on the values of Fanny Burney's world which is sometimes read into Jane Austen.[17] *Pride and Prejudice* especially has been thought of as a disenchanted reappraisal of those plots in which humble heroines aspire to acceptance by the high, mighty, and not self-evidently deserving. But Bage—one of several predecessors of Jane Austen in connecting the words 'pride' and 'prejudice' together[18]—more interestingly anticipates her in challenging the automatic reverence for rank which was an unwritten assumption behind so many stock eighteenth-century fictional situations. The difference between them is that Bage's entire novel sets out to do what is done only by certain scenes and characters in *Pride and Prejudice*—to deflate the swollen pride of the representatives of the State and the Church. Lady Mary Paradyne and Lord Grondale time and again lay claim to pompous dignities, only to have them simply dismissed by their free-minded opponents:

> 'Should you, Miss Fluart, if I should offer to lay my rank, my title, my person, and fortune at your feet—should you think it worth a serious consideration?'

> 'Why, my lord, these are very serious things, no doubt; one should like to tread upon some of them.'[19]

To trample upon peers of the realm *ex officio* was never Jane Austen's intention. But recent enterprise by a bibliographical scholar has shown that she possessed a copy of **Hermsprong.**[20] If she acquired it in the year of publication, 1796, that was also the year in which she received her subscription copy of Fanny Burney's *Camilla* (published July), and began work on the early version of *Pride and Prejudice* (October).[21] Here were seeds for the fertile soil of that great technical intelligence. But it must also be apparent that in **Hermsprong** there was a wholesale and consistent assault upon the idea of inherited authority which Jane Austen showed no sign of repeating.

One device which Bage handed on to his heirs was his form: he mimicked the stale conventions of eighteenth-century fiction in such a manner that he criticized its underlying assumptions, while at the same time availing himself of the popular novelist's power to create an attractive autonomous world. His second contribution was his emphasis on dialogue as an index of value. Here Bage was no doubt influenced by the French philosophic tale, especially Voltaire's and Marmontel's. But he helped to naturalize the convention of a debate on issues of substance, to make it amenable to the full-length romantic plot, and thus to inaugurate one of the most interesting sub-species of the coming generation, the intellectual comedy of Maria Edgeworth, Jane Austen, and Thomas Love Peacock.

Bage was read by three at least of his most important immediate successors: by Jane Austen, who has left no comment on **Hermsprong,** by Maria Edgeworth, who presumably shared her father's approval of it, and by Scott, who wrote a generous appreciation of Bage's work as a whole for the British Novelists' Library. Maria Edgeworth and Jane Austen use conventional plot-motifs much as Bage does. Dialogue which re-enacts a clash of values (though not open debate on national issues) is another corner-stone of their comedy. Of the two, Maria Edgeworth is closer to Bage not only because her novels sometimes also deal frankly with real-life controversial issues, but because she agrees with him in valuing independence above other personal attributes. Even she, however, probably did not write as she did because Bage wrote first. He was not one of the novelists she reread; those were Fanny Burney and Elizabeth Inchbald. It may well be that both Maria Edgeworth and Jane Austen, even if they grasped what he had to teach them, would have felt shy of confessing a debt in this quarter. Bage's politics might not have shocked Maria Edgeworth, or not at first, and not much, but she would have found it hard to take his prurience. The scenes between Lord Grondale and Miss Fluart must have struck a well-bred woman in the period as excessively free, and even a twentieth-century reader is startled to notice how much pleasure the author seems to take himself in Lord Grondale's 'manual operations'.

The point is perhaps merely that from Bage's insights certain formal developments logically followed. In one sense or another he shared his contemporaries' awareness and fear of the power of organized society, which is often most effectively exerted in the moulding of opinion. His humanism takes the form of respect for the mental attributes of people at their best—vitality, independence, humour, and—that old keystone of sentimental optimism—spontaneous sympathy. He is a genuine creator, if a flawed and eccentric one, because the form he develops, his verbal comedy, is a true correlative for what he has to say; his fresh, wry dialogue dramatizes the human characteristic he finds central, which is consciousness itself. Or, at least, the externalized equivalent of it: for it is not the whole consciousness Bage really tries to represent, but that aspect of it which has to do with discriminations about the outside world and

about our moral obligations to it. By restricting himself to a stylized comedy, Bage avoids the falsification inherent in other jacobins' would-be naturalistic portrayals of the rational consciousness, and produces a statement of his ideals which is valid after its kind. If it happens that he also anticipates at least one writer of a very different intellectual persuasion—Jane Austen—it is a sign of the common inheritance of jacobin and conservative, and a sign of the times.

Notes

1. Bage's life (1728-1801) is summarized in William Hutton's *Memoir* in *The Monthly Magazine,* xii (1 Jan. 1802), 479, and in Scott's *Lives of the Novelists.* For his circle, see Eric Robinson, 'The Derby Philosophical Society', in A. E. Musson and E. Robinson, *Science and Technology in the Industrial Revolution,* Manchester, 1969, pp. 190-9, and Robert E. Schofield, *The Lunar Society of Birmingham,* 1963.

2. Unpublished letter of R. L. Edgeworth to Maria Edgeworth, Belfast, 2 Mar. 1797: 'I am reading *Hermsprong* & am much pleased with the original good sense which it contains—part of it is Dr. Darwins.' National Library of Ireland, MS. 10166-7.

3. For Bage's earlier novels, see above, p. 42.

4. *Man As He Is,* 1792, iv. 188. For a parallel with *Pride and Prejudice,* see below, pp. 200-1.

5. *Hermsprong, or Man As He Is Not,* ed. V. Wilkins, London, 1951, ch. lxxvi, p. 233. Subsequent references are to this edition.

6. Ibid., ch. lx, p. 33.

7. Ibid., ch. xvi, p. 61.

8. Ibid., ch. xxv, p. 83.

9. *Hermsprong, or Man As He Is Not,* ch. xxxv, pp. 110-11.

10. Ibid., ch. xv. p. 52.

11. *Hermsprong, or Man As He Is Not,* ch. xliii, pp. 135-7.

12. Ibid., ch. lviii, pp. 183-6.

13. Ibid., ch. lx, p. 191.

14. Ibid., ch. xlix, p. 158.

15. Ibid., ch. xiii, p. 47.

16. Ibid., ch. xlii, p. 129.

17. See below, pp. 198-201.

18. e.g., ch. xxxii, p. 101. Cf. *TLS,* 29 Dec. 1961, p. 929, and 26 Jan. 1962, p. 57.

19. *Hermsprong,* ch. xxxv, p. 111.

20. D. J. Gilson, 'Jane Austen's Books', *The Book Collector,* Spring 1974, p. 31. The copy in question has 'Jane Austen', most probably her own signature, on the front free endpaper of each volume. I am grateful to Mr. Gilson for drawing my attention to his discovery.

21. '*First Impressions* (original of *Pride and Prejudice*), begun October 1796, ended August 1797'. Memorandum by Cassandra Austen, quoted by R. W. Chapman, introductory note to *Sense and Sensibility,* Oxford, 1923, p. xiii.

Gary Kelly (essay date 1976)

SOURCE: Kelly, Gary. "Robert Bage." In *The English Jacobin Novel, 1780-1805,* pp. 20-63. Oxford: The Clarendon Press, 1976.

[*In the following essay, Kelly closely examines Bage's oeuvre, demonstrating that while Bage's narrative skills develop over the course of his writing career and the particular topics he treats in his works vary from novel to novel, the author's overall themes and viewpoint remain constant.*]

I. 'POLITICAL AND PHILOSOPHICAL OPINIONS'

In what remains the best single essay on Robert Bage, Walter Scott rightly emphasizes the novelist's interest in both character and 'political and philosophical opinions'.[1] More recently J. M. S. Tompkins has included Bage in her chapter on 'new life in the novel' precisely because of his seriousness about social and political issues;[2] and Harrison R. Steeves has described Bage's chief merit as 'an unobscured outlook upon contemporary social and political conventions, illusions, and inequities'.[3]

In spite of this unanimity regarding Bage's seriousness as a novelist, no one has yet indicated the precise nature and depth of the political and social interest in his work, or shown how his view of society actually directs his choice of characters, themes, and plots. For the *Ballantyne's Novelist's Library* Scott chose the least provocative of Bage's novels,[4] and G. Barnett Smith suggested that the 'philosophy' of all of them could safely be considered apart from their value as entertainment.[5] But it was Bage's aim to make serious views an essential part of the novel and its entertainment, and his novels were interesting to the other English Jacobin novelists precisely because their political and philosophical themes could not be considered apart from their characters and plots. If Bage's works lack the 'unity of design' which Holcroft and Godwin considered the distinguish-

ing feature of the novel, they still have a kind of unity of their own, a thematic unity, and before attempting to define this unity it is necessary to consider the historical and intellectual milieu which gave Bage his themes.

Little is known about Bage himself, apart from the excellent memoir by Catherine Hutton, daughter of Bage's great friend William Hutton, which Scott inserted in his Preface. Bage was the son of a paper-maker at Darley, near Derby, and his mother died soon after his birth. He was educated at a 'common school' in Derby and gave early evidence of considerable intellectual ability. He learned his father's trade and at twenty-three married a young woman very much like one of the heroines in his novels, possessed of 'beauty, good sense, good temper, and money'.[6]

The great friends of Bage's youth were William Hutton, historian of Derby, and John Whitehurst, a Derby watch-maker and author of miscellaneous technical works. Hutton was also a publisher and bought almost the whole of the paper production of the mill which Bage owned at Tamworth, and it was to Hutton that Bage frequently complained about the Scylla and Charybdis of his existence, the rapacious excisemen on the one hand, and the continual demands of his workmen for higher pay on the other.[7] Like manufacturers ever since, Bage found himself squeezed between government and labour. He seems to have been able to face both with a certain degree of humour.

In religious matters Bage was a materialist.[8] There is ample evidence in his novels that he sympathized with the Dissenters, although Scott was probably incorrect in assuming that he had had a Quaker upbringing.[9] As William Hutton put it, Bage was 'barely a Christian, yet one of the best'.[10] To everyone, including his servants and domestic animals, but excluding perhaps those excisemen, he showed the greatest benevolence.[11]

Although far from the world of literary London, Bage was at the centre of the literary-scientific world of Birmingham and Derby. He did, however, feel himself deprived of a library suitable for more serious literary tasks. 'He believes he should not have written novels, but for want of books to assist him in any other literary undertaking.'[12] And yet Godwin, who had met the cream of London's intellectual and literary society, paid high tribute to the qualities of Bage's mind and conversation: 'When we met him, I had taken no breakfast; and though we had set off from Burton that morning at six, and I spent the whole morning in riding and walking, I felt no inconvenience on waiting for food till our dinner time at two, I was so much interested with Mr. Bage's conversation.'[13] In fact, it is possible to argue that Bage was in touch with a wider spectrum of eighteenth-century thought than Godwin himself. 'Trade, which is thought to corrupt the mind, made no such impression upon his', wrote William Hutton.[14] As the owner of a paper-mill and member of the Derby Philosophical Society Bage was the friend of scientists and entrepreneurs who were creating a revolution in industry that was to equal in importance the revolution in late eighteenth-century politics. An interest in theoretical science was combined with practical application of new knowledge to manufacturing techniques, and the initiative in scientific study was moving away from the established institutions—the Royal Society and its allies the Universities of Oxford and Cambridge—to the centres of provincial manufacture and *their* allies, the Dissenting Academies. 'The important role of the Dissenting Academies in introducing more liberal, scientific and utilitarian studies into English education is well known, and Warrington provided one of the most illustrious examples.'[15]

Science, religious Dissent, and political reform met in the person of one of Warrington's most celebrated members, Joseph Priestley. Priestley also belonged to the best of the new philosophical societies, the Lunar Society of Birmingham.[16] But there were others at Norwich, Northampton, Exeter, Bristol, Bath, Plymouth, Derby, Manchester, Newcastle, and many other places.[17] The Derby Philosophical Society of which Bage was a member did not have quite the diversity of the Lunar Society, but it was an interesting group nevertheless, and included Erasmus Darwin and his son Robert, Josiah Wedgwood and his inventor cousin Ralph, William Strutt, eldest son of Jedediah Strutt and inheritor of much of his father's mechanical genius, William Duesbury the great Derby china manufacturer, three mayors of Derby, and Sir Brooke Boothby,[18] formerly considered a 'pretty gentleman du premier ordre',[19] but subsequently a member of the Lichfield circle, intimate of Rousseau, and critic of Burke during the 1790s.

The Derby Society met to discuss scientific matters and perform experiments, and they possessed a fine library which contained *The Wealth of Nations,* Howard on Prisons, and Paley's *Moral and Political Principles,* in addition to books on travel, politics, economics, and science.[20] The members clearly did not restrict themselves to discussing scientific matters. But in the 1780s, when the society began, it was still possible for men of goodwill to agree to disagree. When some members of the Society sent a message of sympathy to Priestley after the Birmingham Riots, a split resulted when other members felt that the Society was overstepping its role by engaging in controversial politics.[21] The Derby Philosophical Society was not the only group to be so divided in the 1790s.

Nevertheless, through his association with these men Bage had contact with the most liberal thought of the late eighteenth century, as well as with the intellectual life of France and London. Occasionally the rather eccentric scientific interests of these friends appear in Bage's novels, especially in *James Wallace,* written about the time the Society came into existence and published in 1788. When Bage describes the attempts of Paracelsus Holman's father to use electricity to increase the fertility of his land,[22] he was perhaps mocking the experiments of an associate of the Society (though not actually a member), Abraham Bennet, F. R. S., who published *New Experiments on Electricity* at Derby only a year after the appearance of *James Wallace.*

The scientific interests of the Society's members do not play much part in Bage's novels, however. Much more important was the Society's role in bringing together men of many interests, some of whom were Dissenters and many of whom could be expected to have a stake in the movement for political and social reform. In one letter written very early in the Society's life the founder, Erasmus Darwin, referred to it as a kind of Freemasonry.[23] But the Freemasons, along with debating clubs, benefit societies, and probably the scientific societies as well, were regarded by the forces of conservative reaction in the 1790s as hotbeds of Jacobinism, or at least as potential centres for political dissent. In *Proofs of a Conspiracy* (1797) John Robison, Professor of Natural Philosophy at the University of Edinburgh, had claimed to show that there was an international conspiracy, 'carried on in the secret meetings of Free Masons, Illuminati, and Reading Societies', to subvert liberty and monarchy, and had cited Priestley as an open advocate of 'the detestable doctrines of Illuminatism'.[24]

The Birmingham rioters had already carried this view into practical effect in July 1791, and carefully destroyed Priestley's library and scientific apparatus, while shouting 'No Philosophers—Church and King forever'.[25] A co-sufferer in those riots was Bage's friend, William Hutton, who discovered in the midst of his flight from the mob that the mere mention of Bage's name was sufficient to procure him instant credit.[26] When Hutton, along with others, tried to recover damages from the Government, Bage was one of his witnesses in court,[27] facing the same George Hardinge who was later to take such a violent dislike to Mrs. Inchbald's friends Holcroft and Godwin, and to her Jacobin satire *Nature and Art.* But Bage himself, although a man of retired habits, found the political temperature too hot. It is not surprising that critics have found a more bitter tone in the novel Bage wrote after these sad events, *Hermsprong; or, Man As He Is Not* (1796). Godwin too depicted the Riots, as late as 1799, in his second major novel, *St. Leon.*

Living far from the English Jacobin circles of London, Bage was nevertheless in the forefront of most liberal ideas and activities in the late eighteenth century, and managed to write novels which pleased the critics, influenced the most celebrated of English Jacobin writers, and eventually won for himself the scorn of *The Anti-Jacobin Review and Magazine.*[28]

2. BAGE AND THE TRADITION OF THE NOVEL

Bage was connected with the vanguard of innovation in science, industry, religion, and politics, and yet the most immediately striking fact about his fiction is its continuity with the great eighteenth-century tradition of the novel.

There is, first of all, the seriousness without solemnity which is found in Fielding and Smollett, but which had been lacking in their imitators during the heyday of the 'English Popular Novel'. In fact, so unusual was this serious moral purpose that J. M. S. Tompkins has included Bage in her chapter on 'new life in the novel'. Scott, who was a conservative, included Bage in *Ballantyne's Novelist's Library* not because of his Jacobinical views, but because he both 'instructed' and amused.[29] In short, Bage fulfilled the traditional role of the author according to neo-classical standards of criticism—he could both teach and delight.

Bage's early reviewers were also unanimous in praising his acceptance of the moral function of literature, for it was a barren period for the English novel, and reviewers had little to rejoice over. *The Monthly Review* praised Bage's first novel, *Mount Henneth* (1781)[30] in terms which might have been used as a motto for the English Jacobin novelists of the 1790s: 'Its sentiments are liberal and manly, the tendency of it is perfectly moral; for its whole design is to infuse into the heart, by the most engaging examples, the principles of honour and truth, social love, and general benevolence.'[31] And later the same periodical was to describe Bage's third novel, *The Fair Syrian* (1787), as 'a performance in which instruction and entertainment are blended in a manner that is rarely to be found; and which, in the present state of novel writing, we cannot too much commend'.[32]

The important point, however, is that Bage blended instruction and entertainment, in a way seldom found since the days of Fielding and Smollett, whereas other 'serious' novelists, including other English Jacobin novelists, tended to alternate the two. Bage's 'engaging examples' also managed to blend comedy with satire, for he delighted in attacking every form of social and political abuse and, as his son Charles emphasized, Bage could easily become 'indignant at the wantonness of pride and power'.[33] Yet his view of the proper objects of satire was serious and responsible; in a letter to his friend William Hutton, who had just published a 'Dissertation on Juries', Bage wrote: 'I received thy pamphlet; and am not certain whether I have not read it with more pleasure than any of thy former works. It is lively and the reasoning just. Only remember it is some-times against the institution itself of Juries and County courts that you have directed your satire—which I think ought to be confined to the Abuse of them.'[34]

But if Bage was serious, he was not grave or severe, as the other English Jacobin novelists often were. His comic satire did not have the animus of the early Augustans or the French Enlightenment satirists, but was more in line with the 'general' satire acceptable to late eighteenth-century readers and critics, and found for example in Cowper and Goldsmith. Only in his last novel, ***Hermsprong*** (1796), did Bage's satire acquire the harshness found in Holcroft's *Hugh Trevor* (1794-7) and Mrs. Inchbald's *Nature and Art* (1796), a harshness derived from Swift and La Rochefoucauld, La Bruyère and Voltaire. But in spite of his evident admiration for the French opponents of *l'infâme,* there was something peculiarly English about Bage, especially in his early works. It was from these that Scott, who was a great student of eighteenth-century literature, chose the selection for the *Ballantyne's Novelist's Library,* emphasizing Bage's 'rich and truly English vein of humour'.[35] Holcroft too, with his interest in the idea of ruling passions, was in the line of humour which began to take over from the line of wit sometime around the middle of the century,[36] and, like Bage, he aimed at first to reform rather than censure. A recent critic has gone so far as to describe Bage as 'an eighteenth-century Shaw' and has remarked that 'Bage's social satire at its best shows the bland spirit of Chaucer, not the flame of Swift'.[37] Bage's comedy is also softened by borrowings from Richardson and Rousseau, Prévost and Mackenzie (although he could also make fun of sensibility), and his novels are, like Mrs. Inchbald's *Nature and Art,* Holcroft's *Hugh Trevor* and *Bryan Perdue,* and Godwin's *Fleetwood,* a mixture of satire and sentiment. The result, occasionally, was a farrago, but it was highly original. As J. M. S. Tompkins puts it, Bage partook of 'that attitude of benignant irony, based on an equal sense of man's frailty and his worth, which was, indeed, natural to the age, though Fielding gave it its most perfect expression'.[38]

In fact, Bage's humour is almost too disarming; it conceals the real radicalism of his underlying views, a radicalism which grows as his fiction develops in maturity. Even in the 1790s he escaped the censure heaped on other novelists with similar views simply because his fiction possessed the saving grace of humour. The Fieldingesque denial of seriousness, achieved at times even by exaggerated mock-seriousness, leaves his social and political criticism in an advantageously ambiguous light. He could be read and enjoyed by everyone, whereas conservative readers and reviewers gave only grudging praise to the achievements of Godwin and Holcroft, or condemned them outright for their pernicious views. It is only when the contemporary allusions and themes in Bage's novels are examined in detail, and the humour, of necessity, left out of the analysis, that his radicalism becomes apparent.

Even the techniques employed in Bage's novels seem to suggest a fundamental lack of seriousness. In terms of structure, plot, and characterization Bage belonged to the tradition of Smollett rather than of Fielding. His characters, for example, are mostly Theophrastan 'Characters', and in his last novel he jokingly referred to the fact.[39] His plots, too, are Smollettian, being diffuse, digressive, and cumulative in incident and moral effect, gathering events and characters and conversations around certain ideas, rather than working logically to a conclusion like the plots of Holcroft and Godwin. Occasionally a reviewer even complained that Bage's story was *too* close to his model, and *The Critical Review* said of **James Wallace**: 'The adventures of Wallace, as a footman, are so nearly copied from the Roderick Random of our incomparable Smollett, as to displease by a too close imitation. . . .'[40] In the rambling structure of his novels Bage was untypical of the English Jacobin novelists who believed in philosophical necessity and who therefore sought to avoid coincidence and show the *necessary* links in action and the development of character. Holcroft, for example, also drew on Smollett for his second major novel, *Hugh Trevor,* but tried to introduce the same high degree of logic to his plot which he had essayed in *Anna St. Ives.*

Even Bage's borrowings from the novel of sensibility are in a light-hearted vein, and pertain more to Rousseauistic pathos than to Richardsonian domestic tragedy. If Bage's novels abound in depraved aristocrats, fashionable ladies, young rakes, and the occasional bawd, they are also full of virtuous and loyal servants, chaste young women, and incredibly noble lovers. Bage never wrote a fully Richardsonian novel such as Holcroft's *Anna St. Ives.* He was not an 'enthusiast' either in his politics or his literary work. He defies labels such as Richardsonian or Smollettian, and combines influences in a way thoroughly original, if somewhat synthetic. And so once again Bage leaves the impression of lack of seriousness, of indifference to maintaining the purity of his models. In fact he is the most thoroughly 'popular' of all the English Jacobin novelists.

Yet Walter Scott, and the reviewers of the 1790s, considered Bage to be a Jacobin. In 1800 *The Anti-Jacobin Review and Magazine* classed **Man As He Is** and **Hermsprong** with vicious novels such as *Desmond, Nature and Art,* and 'the trash of Mrs. Robinson'.[41] Even though four of his six novels were published before 1789, Bage shared most of the assumptions and values of other English Jacobin novelists, whose important novels were almost entirely a response to the crisis of the 1790s. Like them, Bage was deeply affected by the French Revolution debate in England, and his novels only seem to have more continuity because little attention is usu-

ally paid to the plays which Holcroft and Mrs. Inchbald produced during the 1780s. Their work as a whole shows the same fairly continuous development from liberalism to radicalism which can be traced through the novels of Bage.

In fact the French Revolution itself created little that was new; it accelerated changes which were already taking place, and gave new stimulus to a debate which had been going on ever since the English Civil War and the Settlement which followed the Glorious Revolution.[42] Even in the decade before 1789 the issues of constitutional and social reform, brought to a head by the crisis of the American Revolution, had begun to be discussed with a new earnestness.[43] That this intensification of controversy should affect the novel is not surprising; it was after all a popular form of entertainment and depended more than is now realized on a certain level of topicality. Bage merely extended the range of this kind of reference in the novel.

A similar development has been traced by Dorothy George in graphic satire from the time of Hogarth to that of Gillray: 'The new look was a product of changing techniques and of a more realistic approach to politics.'[44] The 'Classic Age of English Caricature' which she describes is explicable in terms of political rather than artistic history: 'Not only do prints multiply in times of crisis, but their forcefulness varies with the intensity of convictions and passions.'[45] It was a period when, in certain quarters at least, 'intensity of convictions and passions'—enthusiasm—was once more regarded with approval.[46]

In his novels Bage satirizes 'enthusiasm' along with all sorts of other excesses; but it is entirely wrong to see him therefore as a secret conservative,[47] sympathetic to that Establishment which had been fending off Dissenters' and other enthusiasts' demands for reform ever since the Revolution Settlement. Though not a Dissenter himself,[48] Bage knew many, and his own intellectual milieu was amongst those who found that liberal studies produce liberal views. From a circle of men whose sympathies and financial interests were hurt by a war with the American colonies, Bage sent forth novels which admirably expressed their views on Old Corruption and its immoral wars. When events and themes changed, Bage's novels changed too, but they remained a link between the earlier period of crisis and the period of the French Revolution, because the same fundamental issues were at stake. It is in 'intensity and passion' rather than in chronological precedence that Bage differs from the other English Jacobin novelists.

3. 'Unity of Design': The Themes of Bage's Fiction

Aristocrats versus 'The Middling Sort'

It used to be a commonplace, before the rise of social history, that the eighteenth century was an age of aristocrats, and its novelists certainly delighted in creating hundreds of new peers, almost all villainous. Bage's aristocrats are no exception: they are rapacious, boorish, lustful, arrogant, and impecunious. Except for the gruff but kindly Lord Konkeith, who is moreover a Scot, all of the nobles from Sir Richard Stanley in **Mount Henneth** to Lord Grondale in **Hermsprong** are unfeeling tyrants, whose desire to recoup the losses of a life of gaming and dissipation sends them, and their sons, in search of title-hungry merchants and squires with eligible daughters. In **Barham Downs** (1784) Lord Winterbottom, the best of Bage's early villains, tries to avoid the necessity of retrenchment by forcing himself on the daughter of Justice Whitfield, a kindly man who is blinded by a coat of arms and the desire to be called grandfather by a peer.

Scott, naturally enough, disagreed with Bage's picture of the higher ranks of society, but for rather peculiar reasons of his own: 'Men of rank, in the present day, are too indifferent, and too indolent, to indulge any of the stormy passions, and irregular, but vehement desires, which create the petty tyrant, and perhaps formerly animated the feudal oppressor.'[49] He was probably reacting against literary conventions himself in this remark, and thinking of the exaggerated ennui of the 'silver fork' novels of the early nineteenth century, but as far as novel readers were concerned it was always the convention and not reality which mattered. Such readers wanted to applaud the characters whom Bage depicted as the natural enemies of his depraved aristocrats, the merchants and wealthy farmers, or at least their less work-soiled and more handsome sons. Such characters, with their suspicion of the vices of the city and the town, contempt for fashion, and respect for the middle-class domestic virtues, were the front line of what can only be described as the class-war.[50] When Lord Winterbottom is called out by young Henry Osmond, a former merchant, though a genteel one, he merely retorts, 'You cannot call yourself a gentleman, when you reflect upon your past-gone occupation.'[51] Significantly, Winterbottom is also a member of the Government, and thus associated with Lord North's administration, which had been attacked by the independent members and country interest in Parliament for its wasteful expenditure and disastrous policy of war with France. In fact Winterbottom's name may even be a sly reference to North.

If so, Bage's linking of a stock novel character with real and pressing political issues was not unique. During the heyday of 'Wilkes and Liberty' Charles Johnstone had dressed contemporary events in a very thin disguise of fiction in *Chrysal, or The Adventures of a Guinea* (1760-5) and *The Reverie; or, A Flight to the Paradise of Fools* (1762). Nor was Bage the only au-

thor in the 1780s to associate the frivolity of the nobility with the decline of empire. In 1783 Cowper addressed the country's aristocratic rulers:

> There is a public mischief in your mirth;
> It plagues your country. Folly such as your's,
> Grac'd with a sword, and worthier of a fan,
> Has made, what enemies could ne'er have done,
> Our arch of empire, stedfast but for you,
> A mutilated structure, soon to fall.[52]

Bage's friends were merchants and industrialists, and they were being hurt by a war waged, so it seemed, solely by the aristocratic oligarchy who held the reins of power by means of extensive political corruption. It is but natural, then, for Lord Winterbottom and Henry Osmond to be enemies. But Bage also satirized the *nouveaux arrivés* who, once wealth had procured the coronet, sought to shed all trace of the origin of that wealth. In **Hermsprong** Sir Philip Chestrum seeks to impress Miss Campinet with his partly ancient lineage:

> 'My family, Miss Campinet, is very great and noble by my mother's side. She was a Raioule, a great name in English history. I have some thoughts of changing my name to it, by act of parliament; for Chestrum is but an odd sort of name. Beside, my father was in trade once, and his title a new one; so people looking more at his side than my mother's, I don't get so much respect on account of my family as is my due. Should not you like Raioule better than Chestrum, Miss Campinet?'
>
> (ii. 141)

The fact that Sir Philip is deformed physically to match his mental and moral smallness is perhaps an indication of a more Swiftean element in Bage's satire in this last of his novels.

In an earlier novel such as **The Fair Syrian** (1787) his satire on the vanity of high birth retains a more humane warmth. The comic French aristocrat St. Claur protests, when his tyrannical mother finds a rich *bourgeoise* for him, that

> Madame Prévigny was nothing more than the widow of a *Fermier-General*; of no blood; no alliance; nothing to support her in the *grand monde,* but a million or two of livres—yet did this mother of mine, the Marchioness de St. Claur, Prince of Grex, with an *et cetera* half as long as a Spanish title, condescend to court her acquaintance, and to propose the head of the house of St. Claur as a husband for *Mademoiselle,* born and educated at the foot of the Pyrenees, and newly arrived at Paris.[53]

The object of attack in both these examples is the same, and the technique is similar: Bage merely lets the characters talk, and as snobs usually do, they condemn themselves. The character of St. Claur, however, is a reminder that Bage's aristocrats, although they usually have English names, are in fact borrowing a French attitude in their contempt for the lower orders. Bage must have known that, in the north of England especially, the high-born were as actively engaged and interested in commerce and industry as his own self-made friends. The truth is that Bage's villainous lords are drawn mostly from satire and novels rather than from real life.

It is also true that Bage probably wished to satirize the tendency of the English nobility to ape the fashions and attitudes of their European cousins. He was also expressing a real social animus which, however, remained latent until some crisis—the American and French Revolutions—heightened social tensions. As to the real state of 'the middling sort' even Scott agreed with Bage that the golden mean in society offered most opportunity for happiness and virtue:

> Those . . . who weigh equally, will be disposed to think that the state of society most favourable to virtue, will be found amongst those who neither want nor abound, who are neither sufficiently raised above the necessity of labour and industry, to be satiated by the ready gratification of every wild wish as it arises, or so much depressed below the general scale of society, as to be exasperated by struggles against indigence, or seduced by the violence of temptations which that indigence renders it difficult to resist.[54]

Bage's view was a moral and egalitarian one, that nobility was dependent on virtue, not birth. In *Barham Downs* (1784) the Quaker apothecary replies to a demand for the respect due to rank: 'Give me leave to inform thee in my turn, that I am Isaac Arnold, by birth a man, by religion a Quaker, taught to despise all titles that are not the marks of virtue; and of consequence—thine. I rank above thee' (i. 330-1). The idea is hardly original, but it is certainly radical; and Bage held it consistently before 1789.

It is significant that Arnold makes the riposte while defending Kitty Ross from the aristocrat's lust, for sex is the battlefield on which aristocratic *ton* and middle-class morality fight for supremacy. The outcome is always a foregone conclusion. Earlier in *Barham Downs* Sir Ambrose Archer[55] puts the case for middle-class sense when he tells Whitfield that the latter's daughter is not impressed by Lord Winterbottom's titles and appurtenances 'because she thinks well of certain other things, which your great folks who delight in wealth and grandeur seldom think of at all. She thinks well of piety, benevolence, humility, social affection, and the peaceable virtues of domestic life' (i. 155). Sir Ambrose is himself a reformed profligate, and knows what he is talking about.

Bage's novels characteristically proceed by such short pithy speeches as the above. Although not a dramatist like Holcroft and Mrs. Inchbald, Bage could match them for crisp and witty conversation in his novels, and he develops the larger themes of his novels, not by plot, as the other English Jacobin novelists tried to do, but by character and short comments, conversations, or encounters. Bage's novels accumulate points by means of short scenes, dialogues, or satiric Characters, in all of which he reveals his debt to the periodical essay and the seventeenth-century Theophrastan 'Character'. Bage condenses his larger themes into smaller anecdotes, and at times even sets them apart with the heading 'Story'. The tale of Sir Howell Henneth in *Mount Henneth* (1781) is such a vignette, illustrating the themes discussed above, and showing why the ideals cherished by Annabella Whitfield in *Barham Downs* could never be fulfilled in marriage to a vicious noble. Henneth inherits a large fortune, and the rest follows naturally. 'Twelve years he spent in all the pride and pomp of equipage; gave the *ton* to the *beau monde,* and became the fashion of the fair. Half a dozen trips to paris, two to Italy, a score or two of *volant amours,* and a couple of duels, raised him to the summit of reputation.'[56] Gaming leads to a rapid fall, and a rigid economy advocated by the faithful family steward (one of Bage's favourite types) eventually turns Sir Howell into a misanthrope, miser, and hermit—in short, a negation of the neo-Classical ideal of man.

Throughout Bage's fiction the aristocrats follow the *ton* to financial ruin, while 'the middling sorts' pursue love, morality, benevolence, and sobriety; and are rewarded with love, usually a fortune, and occasionally a title. With the poor Bage is not concerned, except as objects of charity for his heroes and heroines, and there are only two references in his novels to the effects of the Poor Law.[57] Both lords and paupers exist in Bage's novels only as foils to middle-class virtues and attitudes. His novels are not only for, they are almost exclusively about the well-to-do 'middling sort'. Although Bage loads his argument by stacking all the advantages on one side, he is not really writing tracts for the class war, because 'the middling sort' had not yet become the middle classes. Bage's novels describe a process of social change which was only just beginning in earnest, but which had been shaping up for some time;[58] and Bage's own view of social conflict is a cross between that of Fielding, with his distinction between nobility, gentry, and commonalty,[59] and that of nineteenth-century supporters of gradual reform, who sought to detach the politically unprivileged 'middle classes' from the artisan and working men's reform movement.[60] Bage's novels display the confidence of the middle-classes, but not in terms of class consciousness, a phrase which was not even used earlier than an English translation of *Kapital* in 1887.[61] Bage in fact phrases his argument in familiar eighteenth-century moral-philosophical terms rather than social or economic ones, and his characters belong to the world of Fielding and Smollett, rather than that of Disraeli, Kingsley, and Mrs. Gaskell; and Bage's moral-philosophical terms are those of Gibbon and Hume, Swift and Voltaire.

'FASHION, LEADER OF A CHATT'RING TRAIN'

The evidence of this moral-philosophical inheritance is seen in the issues over which his middle-class heroes and upper-class villains disagree, and to a large extent the plots of Bage's novels, such as they are, involve the middle-class protagonists in temptation by the corruptions of the aristocratic world. Sensible heroines, like Annabella Whitfield in **Barham Downs** and Julia Foston in **Mount Henneth,** detest the city and its courts, crowds, fops, masquerades, gamesters, and titled debauchees. Lady Bembridge, on the other hand, once the simple Emilia Amington, has married a title and become a leader of the *ton*. She advises her brother Sir John to forget his dislike and moral disapproval of the frivolous and fashionable lord her husband:

> you would have him harangue the house upon the dignity and integrity of past times; and oppose the court; and make protests: Waste the midnight lamp in projects for his country's good; banish luxury, taste, and fashion; build churches, or endow an hospital; and restore the reign of miracles and mince-pyes. Dear Brother, banish these whims; come amongst us, and enjoy your five senses. Do as other people do. Above all, lend my lord this *6000l.*
>
> **(The Fair Syrian,** i. 146-7)

The opposition of the stoic and the epicurean outlook here was to be developed in other Jacobin novels, notably Holcroft's *Anna St. Ives*; but in Bage's novel it is clearly a comment, similar to the lines of Cowper quoted earlier, on the supposed connection between aristocratic frivolity and the loss of an American empire.

Fashion becomes politically significant because it is the means by which the aristocracy defend their exclusiveness. The more expensive the fashion, the more effective it is likely to be in shutting out the *canaille* (even the use of French is part of the process). Sir Antony Havelley the fop in **James Wallace,** for example, prefers a good tailor to liberty and good laws (p. 435). Again and again Bage emphasizes one of the favourite ideas of Augustan England, that luxury breeds decadence, and marks the approaching end of a civilisation.[62] The relation of luxury to politics becomes obvious, for with inexorable logic, political corruption becomes the necessary means of supporting the extravagant projects dictated by fashion.

Moreover, fashion corrupts the whole of society, not just those who indulge in it, and the novels are studded with vignettes which portray humbler versions of Sir Howell Henneth, ruined by fashion and their wives'

vanity. The most interesting example, for the light it throws on other Bagean themes, is also in **Mount Henneth** (ii. 63).[63] Hugh Griffiths is a prosperous shoemaker who is ruined by his family's desire to ape a higher level of society: their ambition, by an inexorable chain of cause and effect, produces the need for improvements in the house and furnishings, better apparel and equipage—all leading to less shoemaking, poorer quality work, bankruptcy, and arrest for debt. What is interesting is the form Sir James Foston's benevolence takes when he decides to intervene: he allows only enough to restore Griffiths to his original humble status. It is a *prudent* kindness. One recalls Bage's assertion that he was compelled to take up his pen in order to pay for his daughters' new gowns, and the droll Scot Dr. Gordon probably speaks for Bage when he denies that *all* such domestic disasters as that suffered by the Griffiths family are due to the rage for fashion: 'No, I am not so unreasonable; nine in ten only' (**Mount Henneth,** ii. 76-7).

THE USE OF RICHES

Since fashion diverts money from virtuous to selfish uses it is related to another theme familiar in the moral literature of the earlier half of the eighteenth century, the idea of the use of riches. The example of Sir James Foston's prudential benevolence is not followed in the later novels. Bage was susceptible enough to the influence of the novel of sentiment to make most of his heroes prodigal in this respect. James Wallace spends his wedding-day, not in enjoying the society of his bride, but in clearing the sponging-houses of Liverpool of debtors (p. 506).

However, to a man in Bage's position, closer to the life of the land than the London Jacobins, another aspect of the use of riches would be of wider relevance. As Cowper wrote:

> Improvement too, the idol of the age,
> Is fed with many a victim.
>
> [*The Task,* iii, lines 764-5]

There are several 'improving' lords of the manor in Bage's novels, and the activities of Squire Garford in **Man As He Is** may have suggested those of Sir Arthur St. Ives in Holcroft's *Anna St. Ives*. Squire Garford is soon forced to live abroad because of these extravagant projects at home, as one of his workmen relates:

> 'Squire Garford married before he came of age, a very pretty young lady from Londonwards. Neither house nor ground was like what it is now; for the ground would have done you good to look at, it was in such condition; but the house was old. Now the ground's old and the house new. Then you see a mort of obelisks they call 'em, and temples up and down; and six hundred acres of prime land as crow e'er flew over, was turned into pleasure ground.'[64]

In the same novel, in which fashion is more than an occasional theme, there is another character who may have been taken up by Holcroft in his portrayal of the difficulties of Sir Arthur St. Ives, Mr. Haubert, a man with architectural projects, like Gray's Lord Holland, but who is ruined and eventually becomes a debtor to his steward.

Bage makes many of his points by means of parallel or contrasting characters—a technique which received its fullest flourish from Mrs. Inchbald in *Nature and Art* (1796)—and against the examples of poor stewardship he sets a sufficient number of counter-examples. Particular acts of benevolence are so numerous in the novels as to have made the Poor Law superfluous had they been carried out in reality. In his emphasis on good stewardship Bage was not only remembering Pope's Man of Ross and attacking aristocratic wastefulness, he was also promoting a tenet of considerable importance to liberal, non-Calvinistic Dissenters, with their stress on works as well as faith. Certainly the Dissenters whom Bage knew personally were of this persuasion.

The positive contrast to the destructive 'improver' is the benevolent landlord, who realizes that concern for his tenants' welfare is both humane and profitable. In *Barham Downs,* for example, the reformed Sir George Osmond restrains his harsh steward Yates from prosecuting several tenants who are in difficulties due to the American war (ii. 188); and in *Man As He Is* the eventual reform of the temporarily wayward Sir George Paradyne is foreshadowed by his indulgence in allowing his (always honest and deserving) tenants to recover from their difficulties (iii. 10). In *Hermsprong* the hero comes to the aid of Mr. Wrigley, who is being persecuted by his former patron Lord Grondale, embodiment of every private and social vice (vol. iii, Ch. xii). Finally, there is the example of the Marquis de St. Claur, who decides to try to become that rarity, a French landlord who is as kind to his tenants as an English one would be (*The Fair Syrian,* ii. 322-3).

Such characters represent Bage's version of that ideal of eighteenth-century liberals, the independent country gentleman, and it would be wrong to see them as evidence that Bage was really a conservative in his view of society.[65] He concentrated on individual virtue, as did the other English Jacobins, and, in any case, there were very few in England in the 1790s who advocated the complete redistribution of wealth and land. The same ideal of benevolent landlordism, based on Biblical traditions of the stewardship of riches, is also found in the novels of Holcroft and Mrs. Inchbald, and even Godwin, who originally felt that charity could not be justified philosophically, came to see the importance of benevolence in the light of his revised attitudes to sympathy and the 'domestic affectations'. And, like the other Jacobin novelists too, Bage showed the opposite side of the question by depicting servants giving the lead in honesty and kindness to their masters. In *Mount Henneth* the steward Smith opens Sir Richard Stanley's eyes to his tyranny in trying to force his daughter to marry money (ii. 233-4). In *The Fair Syrian* Wood points out to Sir John his folly in putting too much credit in the 'World's' view of the distance between himself and the lowlier-born Miss Warren (i. 226-7). And in *Barham Downs* the loyal old steward Timothy Thistle acts as a counter to the iniquitous Yates (ii. 187-8). Bage's ideas of the relations between classes may be based on reverence for order and example, but his basic interest is still in the *moral* equality of men.

However, in the novels before *Man As He Is* much of the material which has to do with the opposing themes of fashion and the use of riches is used only in the digressions and 'stories'; the main plots usually concern some sort of lover's test, and resistance to the temptations of fashion and devotion to benevolence are only two aspects of the whole sequence of adventures. But in the two novels published in the 1790s these two themes actually become a shaping force. *Man As He Is* is still basically a 'lover's test' plot, but it is also a humorous study of the moral education of a young man of fortune. Unlike the perfect hero of Bage's previous novel, James Wallace, whom Judith Lamounde described as 'the preceptor, who taught me the proper use of fortune' (p. 453), Sir George Paradyne is literally 'man as he is', and he struggles from falsehood to *faux pas,* from folly to *folie,* through four volumes, in an effort to merit the hand of the idealized heroine. In many ways this is Bage's best novel,[66] because it is less schematic, more crowded with ideas, diversions, and minor characters than *Hermsprong.* As Mrs. Barbauld put it, '*Man as He Is* has more of a story, and more variety of character.'[67] The plot is as rambling as that of any of Bage's earlier novels, but there is more of a congruence of plot and subject. Sir George's life is in fact, as in narration, a series of digressions and temptations, until Miss Colerain saves him at the end. Many of the digressions in the other novels have an appropriate moral parallel with the main story, but only in *Man As He Is* does the variety of incident and character have a point in itself. In this novel Bage's usual anarchy of plot is both appropriate for the 'adventures' described, and more consistently related to the old central theme, which is the conflict of fashionable corruption—'worldliness' as a negative moral outlook—and the proper aim of life, to use one's possessions, both personal and material, for the benefit of others. The only difference between this view, posited in *Man As He Is* with humour and vivacity, and Godwin's position in *Political Justice,* posited with the utmost philosophical rigour, is that Godwin attempts to make benevolence a matter of justice and reason rather than of human sympathy.

WOMEN

But sympathy became increasingly important in Godwin's life and philosophy, largely because of the importance of women, and the virtuous feelings associated with them, the 'domestic affections'. Bage had already anticipated Godwin, simply by relying on popular novel conventions and an idealized view of the importance of women, expressed in Cowper's lines 'Addressed to Miss—':

> And dwells there in a female heart,
>   By bounteous heav'n design'd
> The choicest raptures to impart,
>   To feel the most refin'd.

(lines 1-4)

Bage's plots are wholly conventional in that they lead eventually to a marriage as the reward of virtue. For middle-class readers the conjugal rites sealed the moral and material progress of hero and heroine, and reconciled the conflict of love with whatever value had been set up in opposition to it in the rest of the novel. However, one of the ways in which Bage's novels were original was in the portrayal of that essential element in these love-plots, the women. Bage's son Charles asserted that his father 'seems, almost always, to have been fonder of the company of ladies than of men'.[68] In several novels Bage directly addresses his 'fair readers', and is not above a few winks and nods over the conventions expected in a product of the Minerva Press.[69] Nevertheless, he took women seriously, and seems, like the other English Jacobins, to have believed strongly in the equality of women. The characters of women, however unrealistically presented, are the main turning-points of his plots.

However Bage was also like the other English Jacobin novelists in that his heroines are not usually impressive or even successful creations. The fact that the same woman will bring out the worst in one man and the best in another has nothing to do with her individual character. Love is a moral litmus paper in Bage's novels, and women are merely part of the test apparatus. However much he preferred the company of women, and consciously wrote for them, he seems to have been incapable of making any of his female characters, apart from the secondary ones, as interesting and vivacious as an Elizabeth Inchbald or a Mary Wollstonecraft.

Bage's love plots are conventional and briefly dealt with. There is full-blown romantic love between heroes and heroines, obstructed by fashionable follies or parental pride and tyranny. The themes tend to radiate out from these simple plot lines, rather than being bound up with them. On the other hand there is the full-blown lust and avarice which the rakes and aristocrats feel towards the same objects which attract the James Wallaces and Henry Osmonds. Initially the sensual lords have the upper hand, because they enjoy the temporary alliance of parental pride; and the pursuit of lust and money allows Bage to indulge in a few Richardsonian elements, with abductions, waiting coaches, and secluded mansions. But eventually the conspiracy of arranged marriage, that cardinal iniquity of women's romantic fiction ever since *Clarissa,* is overthrown, not by rebellion, but by stoic endurance and virtuous candour, the traditional recourse recommended to women.

However, as is often the case, it is Bage's variations which give new life to the old conventions. The most important of his revisions of the schemes of the popular novel has to do with the 'ruined' woman.[70] Bage includes scenes of seduction or near seduction which have that undertone of prurience which Fielding exposed in *Shamela.* At the same time Bage shows an awareness of sexual realities that is far more frank and sophisticated than anything to be found in any of the other Jacobin novelists, and Scott confessed to having cleaned up the three novels which he chose for the *Novelist's Library.*[71]

The most complete example of the 'ruined' woman is in the story of Kitty Ross in **Barham Downs.** She is seduced as a young innocent by the young and equally indiscreet Corrane. After various narrow escapes the couple finally succumb to common frailty: 'Kitty unable to resist the flood of tumultuous sensations, gave herself up to be plundered without resistance; his honour's penitence and virtue were lost in the conflict; and the scene was—Ruin' (i. 73). Ruin of course only for Kitty. Yet she recovers from the slip, with the aid of the kindly Quaker apothecary Arnold. She earns her right to reclaim the title of virtuous woman (she conveniently miscarries while on her way to continue her liaison), and although Corrane later returns to claim her as his mistress by some sort of natural right, she escapes at the last moment from a fate worse than death, maintains her life of virtue, inherits Arnold's fortune, and marries her lawyer Mr. Wyman.

Other young ladies, with no disinterested patron and less determination, fare worse. As Sir George Osmond observes on the fate of Molly Patterson, who was seduced by his steward Yates, 'The custom of society, punishes woman too much for this offence, and man too little' (**Barham Downs,** ii. 189). In the middle of the story of Honoria Warren's escape from the perilous state of slavery in the Levant there is a nice contrast, both to the prevailing social attitude and to the suppressed eroticism of Honoria's situation, in the story of a Georgian slave girl who looks back on her previous eleven masters with a certain amount of affection (**The Fair Syrian,** ii. 68-70); but then she at least need not exhibit the delicacy expected of a European woman.

So while Bage criticizes the literary and social convention of the ruined woman, he still avails himself of the tension caused by the possibility that a woman might be ruined. The outstanding example is the story of Camitha Melton in *Mount Henneth.* An American maiden of fiery independence she had been captured in a seabattle and sent to Mrs. P———'s fashionable brothel. Bage had a fairly liberal view of prostitution as a necessary social evil, and one of the novel's 'good' characters, Henry Cheslyn, tells the old bawd, 'You are a useful woman, in your way, Mrs. P———, I own; populous cities, for ought [sic] I know, might be worse without you; but certainly you should only beat up for volunteers; and not be allowed to *press* into the service' (i. 97). Like Honoria Warren, Miss Melton escapes with her virtue intact, but not before Bage has derived a useful amount of titillation from her plight. Were it not for the saving grace of his humour such hypocrisy might be seen as the kind of thing which gave the Minerva Press a bad name. It is fitting therefore that the most lively of Bage's heroines in peril, Miss Fluart, appeared in his most Jacobin novel, and one which also appeared in the lists of the Minerva Press, *Hermsprong; or, Man As He Is Not.*

SENSIBILITY AND BENEVOLENCE

Bage exploits conventional sensibility in his novels in the same way he exploits the convention of female 'ruin'. Judith Lamounde tells her correspondent Miss Edwards that one day, whilst reading a novel, James Wallace burst in upon her with the exclamation 'O madame! . . . whilst you are weeping the fictitious distresses of a Catharine, did you but know what real calamities are around you!' (p. 427.) Judith suffers at first from an excess of sensibility and it is none other than her footman, James Wallace, who, with his naïvely practical view of the world's ills, eventually teaches her 'the proper use of fortune' (p. 453). So that eventually a charming degree of sensibility is reconciled with a healthy recognition of the real world's ills and enjoyments.

At the end of the novel Judith Lamounde marries her former footman, and another aspect of the sentimental romance or stage comedy, the conflict of love and duty, is developed and reconciled. Some of the examples already cited in this chapter will indicate that Bage felt that duty and love had to be merited before they were received. In opposing love and duty Bage does not accept the normal plot conventions entirely at face value however; although as usual he retains enough of the convention, like that of the 'ruined' woman, to keep his stories moving. This opposition of two values, which he accepts when convenient, but rejects in theory and occasionally uses as the butt of humour, is similar to Bage's use of another feature of eighteenth-century fiction, the opposition of prudence and benevolence, sense and sensibility.

One of Bage's many inset 'stories' will illustrate this point. In *Mount Henneth* Bage uses another of his favourite devices, contrasting characters, in the 'Story' of two Athenian maids whose father is killed in a battle which also deprives the state of some territory on which the family wealth depends. Both ladies are of marriageable age, but the elder sister feels that there is now nothing left for their inheritance but sorrow. 'I give up my portion,' says the younger and trips away to find a husband (ii. 226). She marries, and lives happily, while her sister pines away for young Alcandor, who has suddenly lost interest in the impoverished maid. She dies, while the younger sister lives to enjoy the family prosperity that results from the recovery of their land.

The story has a point in itself, but it also marks the difference of outlook between Laura Stanley, who tells it, and Julia Foston. In many ways they are lineal descendants of Anna Howe and Clarissa. In *The Fair Syrian* there is a similar contrast between the resilient Amelia Clare and the hypersensitive Honoria Warren, and in *Barham Downs* between Annabella Whitfield and her sister Peggy. The contrast between the outspoken Maria Fluart and the retiring Caroline Campinet in *Hermsprong* is even more schematic, and the line of development can also be traced through Holcroft's heroine and her correspondent in *Anna St. Ives.* Bage criticizes oversensibility, then, by the economical means of contrasting characters, a device obviously developed from *Clarissa.* Yet he also makes most of his leading ladies into just the type of saintly symbol which he mocks through their witty and satirical friends. It is only the secondary characters which Bage tempers with Jacobinical rebelliousness, and he nowhere portrays a major female character similar to Mrs. Inchbald's Miss Milner, unless it is in the Miss Fluart of *Hermsprong,* who was created, perhaps significantly, after Mrs. Inchbald published the vicissitudes of her independent heroine.

It remains true that in his treatment of sensibility, as in his treatment of the 'ruined' woman, Bage manages to eat his cake and have it. The same ambiguity is found in his examples of a subject close allied to sensibility, namely benevolence.

Villains and villainesses always have an eye for the main chance, while the heroes are characterized by the sort of imprudent benevolence displayed by James Wallace on his wedding-day. Aristocrats, of course, have no conception of benevolence; Lord Grondale and Dr. Blick agree in condemning Hermsprong's kindness to the village struck by a severe storm:

> 'I suppose he has exerted himself to-day, in order to eclipse the lord of the parish.'
>
> 'I dare say your lordship is right. I saw at once his charity did not flow from Christian benevolence.'
>
> 'For my part, I have no opinion of these charitable ebullitions.'

'Your lordship is perfectly happy in your terms. Yes, ebullitions,—bubbles.'

'Indiscriminate giving is not my taste: I chuse to consider my objects.'

[i. 227]

Although Sir James Foston also liked to consider his objects, his motives were still disinterested. Bage clearly liked to keep the vices all on one side: that Lord Grondale should also be the most thorough-going of the parental tyrants, and a man who has received his peerage for the delivery of his Cornish boroughs into the Government interest, are not incidental traits of his character. The opposing values of passion and prudence, love and duty, benevolence and self-interest arrange themselves along the same lines as those taken up by good or bad characters. And a liberal purse, if directed to good ends, is a sign of a liberal heart. A character's attitude to benevolence is therefore tied up with wider issues and an over-all moral pattern in Bage's novels. And so, in spite of the fact that his novels appear to be rambling structures, full of delightful irrelevancies, Bage still manages to give a unified impression by linking all his moral themes to one central issue, the nature and limitations of freedom and restraint.

DOMESTIC AND SOCIAL TYRANNY

The conflict of freedom and restraint is dealt with most fully in Bage's handling of the conventional plot device of parents' obstruction of the romantic designs and views of the younger generation. Clearly, Bage could not deal with such a subject without having to consider the influence of Richardson. In his very first novel Bage depicts the struggle of poor Julia Foston against the attempts by her father and brother to force her into a marriage with the gross and canting hypocrite, Abraham Pymnel. Julia, of course, is torn between duty and revulsion, and the parallel to *Clarissa* is obvious.

Bage carried this situation right into his last novel, in showing how Lord Grondale tries to force his daughter into a similarly unsuitable match, but his approach is too much tempered with humour for it to develop into a Richardsonian study of the struggle for psychological domination. Bage simply does not allow matters, or the sense of evil, to go so far. But his choice of this by now standard romance plot, with its arranged marriages, threatened or real abductions, and other attempts to treat women as chattels, is more than just acceptance of a popular and commercially successful Richardsonian formula. Every novel has its young lady under parents' house-arrest, but the characters also sit down regularly to the type of round-table discussion typical of Bage's novels,[72] and debate the problems of filial duty and parental oppression. But this rather hackneyed issue is in itself given new impetus and wider relevance by Bage, because he treats parental oppression of romantic lovers as a domestic variety of the same tyranny that led to persecution of individuals such as Wilkes at home, and the American colonies abroad.[73]

He does this by having his characters discuss the matter in the most general terms, thereby leaving them in their particular situation, while at the same time allowing the reader to make the wider application. In this way Bage avoids the didacticism of the discussions in *Anna St. Ives* and *Hugh Trevor.* In his first novel, **Mount Henneth,** Bage already exhibits this method. James Foston tells the story of Miss Winter to Lady Stanley in order to make the latter realize that 'the effect of persecution, whether for love, or faith, is generally contrary to the design' (ii. 268). The observation conjures up a weight of historical reflection to illuminate a mere problem of love, and Sir Ambrose Archer in **Barham Downs** tries to bring Justice Whitfield to his senses by a similar kind of argument. He tells Lord Winterbottom, after Annabella has disappeared from her home-made prison, 'I mean to oppose oppression, by equity' (i. 189). Justice Whitfield's proprietorial attitude, however, is similar to that of Captain Suthall towards Miss Melton in **Mount Henneth,** when he tries to force his other, more high-spirited daughter to reveal where Annabella has fled:

'Suppose I had lost a horse, and the thief had trusted you with the place where it was concealed; you would not tell me because it would be a breach of trust?'

'My sister is not a horse, Papa; nor has she been stolen.'

'But is not she my property, Miss? Answer me that.'

'She is your *daughter,* Sir.'

[i. 252]

Where all these remarks tend is finally revealed in **Man As He Is,** when one character tries to dissuade another from indulging in parental autocracy, by the reminder that 'too peremptory a tone lost us America' (i. 40).

It is significant that the parallel between domestic and public tyranny is made explicit in the first of Bage's novels of the 1790s. In **Man As He Is** Lady Mary Paradyne tries to enforce some sort of filial obedience in her son, and fails simply because he does not respect her views or feel that she is right. Lady Mary also tries to impose her will on her daughter, and succeeds, with disastrous consequences. She arranges for her tender and obedient daughter Emilia to marry Mr. Birimport, a repatriated nabob who defends Warren Hastings's actions in India (ii. 141-2), and who is himself of marked tyrannical tendencies. The association of ideas and ideals here is obvious: reason can be the only legitimate persuader, and children should have the right to invoke it against the irrational prejudices of their parents.

In **Hermsprong** the conflict of love and duty is made even more schematic. Lord Grondale is a complete monster, like Mr. Birimport associated with political corruption and tyrannical attitudes to domestic and public affairs. Caroline Campinet's intention to obey him at all costs is opposed by Miss Fluart, who controls Lord Grondale by teasing him, as Bage perhaps hoped to control oppression by his humour and satire. Miss Fluart remonstrates with Caroline over her excessive dutifulness, and the latter replies:

> 'In pity to me, my dear, . . . you should restrain your lively genius. Lord Grondale is my father; he may have his failings, but is it fit for a daughter to see them? In short, my dear Maria, he is my father; I say every thing in that.'
>
> Miss Fluart, with composed gravity, answered, 'Yes, my dear—that—that sanctifies him.'
>
> 'How can you, Maria, so pervert my meaning? I refer to the duty I owe; a duty which forbids my giving him offence.'
>
> 'Very true, child,' Miss Fluart replied, with continued gravity. 'Yes, about this high transcendent duty—yes, it is all true. Pray, my dear, did you ever hear, or see in the dictionary, the word reciprocity? I assure you, the politicians make great rout about it.'
>
> [ii. 11-12]

Miss Fluart is making a general point as well as a particular one, and it is the same one made in the last of Bage's novels published before the French Revolution, *James Wallace.* Paracelsus Holman tells the hero: 'There are many bad men in the world, James Wallace; many of them are fathers. Now, according to you, they are entitled to reverence and respect from their children: But imitation follows reverence; so your pietyship is only propagating immorality by your patriarchal maxims' (p. 505). Bage's argument is the same one he used against aristocratic pride: authority will receive its due if it is worthy, and seen to be worthy. For those who reverence titles and power must be sure that homage will not be abused, whether at home or in public life.

Behind this argument is the liberal Whig view of the social contract, and the parallel between the family and the state went back, in English political writing, at least as far as Hobbes and the writers of the Commonwealth period.[74] The idea of contract was especially important to the eighteenth-century Commonwealthmen,[75] and Bage's thoroughgoing application of this principle in his fiction suggests that his intellectual roots were in some ways very close to Godwin's. It would not be stretching a point to see behind Paracelsus Holman's rejection of 'patriarchal maxims' the attack by Locke, Tyrrell, and Algernon Sydney on Filmer's paternalistic monarchism, and behind ideas such as Miss Fluart's 'reciprocity' support for the Commonwealthman's ideal of mixed and therefore stable government in the state.[76] This is not to say that Bage is offering the old plot convention of parental tyranny as a political allegory; but it

is significant that his two novels written and published when Commonwealth political literature was being rifled for its contemporary relevance should both contain overt discussion of the parallels between private and public moralities.

RELIGION

But Bage also owed a large debt to the French Enlightenment. Through the pages of his novels breathes the same spirit that animated the *Philosophical Dictionary* and *D'Alembert's Dream,* and this is nowhere more apparent than in his treatment of religion. His condemnation of established religion is universal. Delane, the proud priest in **Barham Downs,** for example, had been a hack journalist in his younger days; and the culminating example of the churchman is, not surprisingly, in **Hermsprong.** Dr. Blick plays the sycophant to Lord Grondale the debauchee and superannuated politician, and he preaches a sermon on the Birmingham Riots which is an accurate representation of the way Dissent and sedition were associated by supporters of Church and King. The sermon, moreover, is an obvious reference to that preached by Bishop Horsley 'Before The Lords Spiritual And Temporal' on 30 January 1793, the anniversary of the 'martyrdom' of Charles I. Horsley's text had been Romans 13: 1: 'Let every soul be subject unto the higher powers', and it contributed greatly to the apprehension felt by all Dissenters and their friends when conservative reaction made itself manifest in the aftermath of the Birmingham Riots.

Against Blick's intolerant sermon is set Hermsprong's tolerant scepticism, an attitude which in 1796 would undoubtedly have been seen to have a political application as well. Once again events had turned one of Bage's favourite themes into a piece of provocative radicalism, for views similar to Hermsprong's had been expressed even in the earliest of Bage's novels (**Mount Henneth,** i. 174). It was established religion of any kind which Bage opposed. The Church of Scotland pastor in **James Wallace,** for example, is inevitably a man 'of great bigotry, and sma' humanity' (p. 461), and Bage also criticized the excessive religious prejudices of Roman Catholics and Jews (**Barham Downs,** ii. 351; **The Fair Syrian,** i. 171), and even on occasion mocked the enthusiasm of Dissenters. There is Arnold the virtuous Quaker apothecary, but there is also Paracelsus Holman's zany father, a Dissenter who is critical of Bage's friend Priestley (**James Wallace,** p. 398). While Mr. Holman devotes himself to ridiculous scientific projects his orthodox wife devotes herself to fashion (p. 381). There is, Bage implies, little to choose between them.

His views on established religion, like those of the English Jacobin Commonwealthmen, can no doubt be traced back to writers such as Milton. But on the subject of religion in general Bage was obviously influenced by the French *philosophes*. Quakers such as Isaac Arnold had been admired ever since Voltaire's *Philosophical Letters*,[77] and Bage must have agreed with the emphasis placed by writers such as Montesquieu on virtuous living rather than the mere outward forms of religion. In the *Persian Letters* Montesquieu had argued that all religions were good if they made men better, and Bage's friend William Hutton had taken a similar line in his pamphlet on the Birmingham Riots: 'Every species of religion tends to improve the man, otherwise it is not religion. Should a Jew cheat me, I have no right to charge it to his religion, but to his *want* of religion: he must have fallen short of its principles.'[78] Perhaps the influence of the *Persian Letters* may also be traced in the particular way in which Bage expresses his views on the subject of religion: in **Mount Henneth** it is an old Indian priest who declares that 'we are all, the universe I mean, brethren of the same faith' (i. 199), and in **The Fair Syrian** Abu Taleb is praised for being a Muslim by action rather than precept (ii. 36). These parallels with eastern religion were a commonplace of Enlightenment thought by the time Bage came to write his novels, but they may suggest at least one line of his intellectual inheritance.

There is more than just a general moral argument behind Bage's views on religion, however. Ever since the Revocation of the Edict of Nantes in 1685 religious intolerance had been institutionalized in France, and an attack on the Revocation was an attack on the established powers of the land. The case had been the same in Britain; the pressure for the removal of religious tests was linked with pressure for a wider political reform, since it came to be felt that the former could not be achieved without the latter. The subject was revived after the September Massacres of 1792, which were compared with the St. Bartholemew Massacres even by English Jacobin writers, such as Mrs. Inchbald.[79] Now the plea for tolerance became a desperate attempt to lower the temperature of controversy, lest the terrible events of September 1792 be repeated in Britain. But Bishop Horsley's sermon marked the point of no return; increasingly pleas for religious and civic toleration were seen as a veil for sedition.

Bage had not changed his ground in any way, but by the 1790s real life Dr. Blicks began to preach that legal emancipation for Dissenters was a threat to liberty and property, and Bage inevitably became associated with those who held more extreme views. It was no coincidence that when Holcroft chose the customary extract for inclusion in his review of **Man As He Is** for *The Monthly Review*, it should be the lively discussion on religious toleration.[80] Bage's example, and his characterization of Churchmen and Dissenters, was followed by Holcroft in *Hugh Trevor* and Mrs. Inchbald in *Nature and Art*, and the association of political and religious

oppression was eventually treated by Godwin in a truly grand manner in *St. Leon* (1799). Bage, perhaps unintentionally, set a pattern for the rest of the English Jacobin novelists to follow. The liberal of 1780 was transformed by events far from his little bailiwick of Tamworth into a model for the English Jacobins, and an object of detestation to *The Anti-Jacobin Review and Magazine*.

POLITICS

A similar process seems to have taken place in the development of the political themes and references in Bage's novels. At least one historian has felt that the English reaction to the American Revolution, which was just approaching its conclusion in defeat for Britain when Bage first appeared in print, marks the real watershed in eighteenth-century politics.[81] The defeat at Yorktown made the fall of Lord North's ministry inevitable, and the advent of Fox to power also brought the constitutional issue of the king's influence to a head. At the same time, the threat of invasion from France had produced the Volunteer Movement in Ireland, which in turn led to greater vociferousness in Irish demands for an independent parliament. The growth of extraparliamentary associations for reform, such as the Petitioning Movement, was partly caused by disgust with the inability of opposition in the House of Commons to prevent what the country interest considered to be wasteful expenditure, or to end an unpopular war which clearly could not be won. All of these issues find their way into Bage's novels of the 1780s.

It has already been noted that Lord Winterbottom in **Barham Downs** is associated with the ministry of the day. This novel, Bage's second, abounds with political incidents and allusions, and this is only natural, for it was published in 1784, during that period which Dorothy Marshall has described as the forcing-house of late eighteenth-century English politics. Winterbottom is a complete ministerial man: 'And Opposition, poor devils, says the Justice. Are silenced and put to flight, replies my Lord. And how should it be otherwise? For wisdom and fine parts, his Majesty's cabinet, although I have the honour to be of it, is absolutely superior to anything the universe has yet beheld' (i. 80). As a member of the Government he naturally looks askance at demands for economy made by advocates of reform, such as Edmund Burke:

> Well but my Lord, says the Justice, is not it pity the King's Friends should not attend a little bit more than they do to œconomy?
>
> National œconomy, my dear Sir, is a very childish term. How can it have escaped the penetration of a man of your sagacity, that the more government spend, the greater circulation is produced; and the greater the circulation, the wealthier and happier, the body of the people.

> [i. 82-3]

Justice Whitaker is appropriately concerned with public expenditure: he is a member of the country interest who abandoned Toryism only when the malt tax was raised (i. 47). We are reminded not only of Bage's running battle with the excisemen, but of the general tendency of the country and mercantile interests, with which of course Bage must have been to some extent associated, to see national politics in terms of shillings and pence.

In the character of Delane there is another object of Opposition abuse since the days of Grub Street, the Government hack, who also appears in Holcroft's *Hugh Trevor.* Lawyer Wyman tells Harry Osmond in Bage's novel: 'The bulk of authors now are become political; and seem to have adapted the precept of Doctor Swift, "Suit your words to your music well." The sweetest of music to an author, is undoubtedly the jingle of guineas; the exchequer furnishes the greatest number of concertos, and requires nothing more but to "suit your words to your music well"' (ii. 34).

Barham Downs also contains references to other leading issues of the 1780s. There is a glance at the Volunteer Movement in Ireland, which, under the sympathetic Lord Lieutenant the Earl of Buckinghamshire, had developed from an organization of Irish Protestants to resist an invasion from Catholic France, into an unofficial militia backing the restless Irish parliament's demands for greater independence and free trade (ii. 340).

References to Irish problems are also plentiful in *The Fair Syrian,* which is partly set in Ireland, and more space is devoted to showing the plight of the unhappy islanders in the face of rapacious landlords and rack-renters such as Lord Cronnot, whose views are similar to those of the autocratic Corrane in *Barham Downs* (i. 320). In *The Fair Syrian* Honoria Warren writes to her friend Miss Clare that she cannot fear death: 'Born and educated in a country where pestilence and famine destroy a large portion of mankind, and where the hand of tyranny plays wantonly with the lives and felicities of those who remain, I have been made familiar with death' (i. 89). In the same novel the Marquis de St. Claur describes the lively debates in an Irish coffee-house: 'Three topics of dispute were distinguishable. Whether the Irish ought to insist upon the English parliament renouncing all right of legislature over them, or be content with renouncing it themselves? Whether the scheme of the Fencibles was or was not insidious? And whether it was possible to entertain a doubt of Miss Warren's guilt?' (i. 124). This amounts to a potted version of the main controversies in Ireland since the achievement of independence for the Irish parliament in January 1783; and only one of the issues mentioned belongs to the fiction of Bage's novel. In November 1783 the Convention of Volunteers met in Dublin, a meeting which was attended by Richard Lovell Edgeworth, who was a member, along with others of Bage's friends, of the Lunar Society of Birmingham.[82] No doubt Edgeworth's reactions to this period of turmoil found their way back to Bage in some form or another. Bage may also have received information from another source, a Mr. Archdale, who was a fellow member of the Derby Philosophical Society, and whom Erasmus Darwin described as one 'who is going to make speeches in the Irish parlament [sic]'.[83]

Irish demands for independence had been accelerated by events in America. As Sir George Osmond tells the comic Irish Captain O'Donnell—who incidentally is forced into French and hence anti-British service because under the Test Act Catholics could not hold the King's commission—'your country is going to recover her lost rights; America restores them to her' (*Barham Downs,* ii. 290). In fact the American war and the example of American independence figure more in these early novels than does the Irish question. In *Mount Henneth* John Cheslyn's fable of Carthage and her colonies is an obvious allegory for the revolt of the American colonies (i. 58). There are even American characters in the book, in the persons of Mr. Melton and his daughter Camitha. *The Fair Syrian* begins in America, where St. Claur is captured by John Amington after some comic skirmishes in the American countryside. As he often does, Bage sets his views aside in a section which is only superficially integrated with the plot. St. Claur describes his encounter with the prosperous American farmer whose wife he had tried in vain to seduce, and who elaborates on some of the paradoxes of the war:

> 'Thou knowest the Americans are struggling for liberty. Thy King, and the King of Spain, who dote upon it so, that they keep it all to themselves, and tell their people it is not for common wear, help us forward in the obtaining it with all their might; and the King of England, who lives but to extend and secure this blessing to all his subjects, is labouring as lustily to deprive us of it. . . .
>
> '. . . Let them give their own people that liberty they endeavour to procure us, and they will be as high in my esteem, almost as William Penn.'
>
> [i. 28-9][84]

Such political sermons are frequently set aside in this way; but just as the minor moral themes in Bage's novels are related to the wider issue of freedom and restraint, so the particular political issues which are discussed are also related to the moral themes. The prime example is in *Barham Downs.* Annabella Whitaker expresses her distaste for London life by a fable of the search of Fashion for its mother, Folly. The search leads from a Masquerade ball through the offices of the secretaries of state, the Guildhall, and the House of Commons, where the whole story turns into a denunciation of the American war. The conclusion is as liberal as it could be: folly produces fashion which can be supported only by the fortunes to be acquired through political corruption and the fat pickings available in wartime. It is a conclusion that can be drawn from all of Bage's novels. He casts his satire in a genial mode it is true—he does not lash folly, he laughs at it; but behind the romance and the comedy is a consistent and liberal view of the ills of the time. If Bage says little about the remedy for these ills, apart from the unexceptionable advocacy of high standards of personal virtue, he at least manages to cover the widest range of abuses and corruptions, which clearly must be removed before men can live happily together, free from *l'infâme,* and therefore free to express the best of human nature.

4. The Development of Bage's Fiction

It is obvious that there is a great deal of contemporary politics in all of Bage's novels, not just in those written in the 1790s; and yet the first modern critic of the English Jacobin novel, Allene Gregory, has felt that **Man As He Is** and **Hermsprong** are different in kind from his earlier work: 'The sharp conflicts of ideas arising from the political crisis have at last crystallized Bage's very liberal sentiments into a genuine radicalism.'[85] *The Anti-Jacobin Review and Magazine* made a similar judgment as early as 1800;[86] such a view, however, needs some qualification.

Contemporary criticism is often a better guide to the important aspects of controversial works than that written by the historian far removed from the passions of the time; and in 1792 *The English Review* greeted the first of Bage's post-Revolutionary novels, **Man As He Is,** with the remark that, 'In this age of disquisitions, religious and political, it was not to be expected that the author of **Man as he is** would omit an opportunity of declaring his opinion.'[87] It was indeed an age of disquisitions and Bage was merely responding to the controversies of the day as he had responded to the Irish controversy, the American controversy, and all the other public issues of the 1780s. In fact the examples already chosen to illustrate the various aspects of Bage's fiction have been taken from all of his novels, and demonstrate the essential continuity of his moral and social satire. If there is any change in Bage's last two novels it is due as much to the change in the times and the normal development of Bage's talents as to any sudden change in his outlook on life.

Man As He Is, for example, was obviously conceived in the context of pre-Revolutionary problems. Bage retains his familiar easy-going air, in a Smollettian fable about the progress of a wealthy young baronet, Sir George Paradyne, towards moral independence and a virtuous bride. There are a large number of serious dialogues and round-table discussions, it is true, but these were also to be found in Bage's earlier novels. Even the political background of the novel is pre-Revolutionary. Bage still attacks Old Corruption, and shows Lord Auschamp trying to buy the pen of Lindsay for the service of the Ministry (i. 49), as Lord Winterbottom had successfully bought Delane's in **Barham Downs,** and as Lord Idford was to buy Hugh Trevor's in Holcroft's novel of 1794. When Lord Auschamp learns that Sir George is going abroad with Lindsay as his tutor, he expresses the hope that the baronet will return with an enlarged affection for his native land. When Lindsay concurs in this hope Auschamp asks him in what he conceives the superiority of England to consist:

> 'In good laws, my Lord; by which personal liberty is as well secured, and private property as well guarded, as is consistent with civil society.'
>
> 'These blessings, says Lord Auschamp, we owe to the indulgent family upon the throne; to which I suppose you will think it just to inculcate a peculiar loyalty.'
>
> 'I hope my Lord, I have the proper sentiments of a subject to this illustrious family; to which all loyalty will be due so long as it continues the faithful guardian and executor of our laws. As to the civil blessings we enjoy, I humbly conceive we owe them to our own good sense and manly exertions; nor do I know that liberty like ours ever flowed, with design at least, from any throne on earth'.
>
> [i. 29-30]

Behind Lindsay's views is of course the idea of social contract so dear to Commonwealthmen and Jacobins, and given classic expression in that sermon by Richard Price which had set Burke to writing his *Reflections,* and in which Price had described as one of the 'rights' established by the Glorious Revolution, 'the right to chuse our own governors; to cashier them for misconduct; and to frame a government for ourselves'.[88] Even the title of Price's sermon has an obvious connection with the conversation of Lindsay and Lord Auschamp. And yet views of this kind can be found in Bage's novels before 1789, and were no different from the claims which Fox and the Whigs had been advancing for years. It was the French Revolution and the reaction to it in Britain which radically changed the context of such views, and made them provocative or profoundly true, depending on which side of the growing controversy one took.

There are a few references to the Revolution in the novel, but Lord Auschamp is drawn on essentially the same lines as Lord Winterbottom, only his objects of fear and contempt have changed. He now fears 'democratic anarchy' rather than the boorish manners of the *canaille,* and observes that young men tend too much to 'maxims of liberty' (i. 43). He and Lady Mary are forced to recall, when contemplating some new attempt to coerce Sir George, that 'too peremptory a tone lost us America'. The novel really belongs in the context of the debate on the American rather than the French Revolution, and in fact the novel is set partly in pre-Revolutionary France. There is a whole chapter devoted to Sir George's encounter in the Tuileries Gardens with the Marquis de Lafayette and the Marquis de Lally Tollendal, and the conversation which results (iii. 110 ff.) is a comparison of French oppression with English liberty that no doubt drew on the reading of Montesquieu and other French writers which Bage had exhibited in his earlier novels.

No doubt Bage inserted some references to more recent events, but on the whole **Man As He Is** represents only a superior example of the fiction Bage had developed in the 1780s, and only on the last page of the novel does he deliver a Jacobinical parting shot as he sends his happily married couples off

> to see if the nation of Francks, so merry when governed by folly, are not grown grave, since wisdom has had a share in the administration. This, I find, is partly the case; but when an English senator had said in a book . . . 'That man has no rights,'—the whole French people fell into a violent fit of laughter, which continues to this day. Some rights, at least, they said, might be allowed to man; the rights of suffering, and of paying taxes; these no courts would dispute.—But if, said they, men have no rights, they have wills at least; and Kings, Lords, and Priests, shall know it.
>
> [iv. 272][89]

When **Man As He Is** came out, in September 1792, Bage could still afford this kind of optimism and humour. Revolutionary enthusiasm in England was reaching a peak with the declaration of the French republic and the checking of the armies of the 'leagued despots' at Valmy. And not too far from Bage's Tamworth five or six thousand members of the Sheffield Constitutional Society celebrated Valmy in a great public demonstration.[90] The September Massacres were a disturbing portent, but could be attributed to reaction against foreign intervention and royalist treachery.[91] War with France and the conservative reaction in Britain still lay in the future. But events had already occurred which were to place such things as Bage's fictionalized conversation on toleration in an entirely new context by the time Holcroft came to quote it in his review of **Man As He Is.**

By the time **Hermsprong** was published in 1796 the Directory ruled France, and Pitt's policy of repression had already sent several men to Botany Bay and driven others, such as Joseph Priestley, into exile. In Ireland Richard Lovell Edgeworth found himself associated with Irish rebels by the undiscriminating prejudice of loyalists.[92] The suspension of Habeas Corpus, the Treason Trials of 1793 and 1794, and the 'Two Acts' of 1795 had stifled English Jacobinism. The experience of Wordsworth and Coleridge with 'Spy Nosy' was soon

to show that Bage was not wide of the mark when he depicted Lord Grondale trying to get rid of the troublesome hero by having him taken up as a French spy (**Hermsprong,** iii. 24-5).

Bage's new novel, like Mrs. Inchbald's *Nature and Art* published in the same year, was an open and vehement attack on this organized repression. There are signs too that Bage was now taking his avocation much more seriously: *The Monthly Review* detected influences from the French philosophical as well as the English Jacobin novel, in the character of Hermsprong: 'This noble character has much originality: but its features may be traced back partly to the native openness and resources of the ingenuous *Huron* of Voltaire, and partly to the systematic sincerity and philosophic courage of *Frank Henley* in Holcroft's *Anna St. Ives.*'[93] *Nature and Art* also had its naïvely wise hero, in the character of young Henry, whose simple common sense and lack of 'civilized' preconceptions enable him to expose, as Hermsprong does, the vanities and illusions of society.

None of the Jacobin novels of the middle 1790s strives for naturalism. *Hugh Trevor, Nature and Art,* and **Hermsprong** are all designed to unfold the errors of 'things as they are' in a kind of satirical procession of vices. Bage's hero, for example, gets embroiled with the law when Lord Grondale tries to have him arrested for treason because he has read *The Rights of Man* (iii. 125), a crime of unquestionably contemporary relevance. Bage makes a distinction drawn at some point by all the English Jacobins after the Treason Trials of 1794, when he describes the plotting of Grondale and his cohorts: 'It was not of justice they talked; it was of law' (iii. 174). The remark also suggests that Bage was familiar with the most philosophical expression of English Jacobinism, Godwin's *Political Justice.*

Hermsprong is also like most of the other English Jacobin novels in that it contains surprisingly little direct reference to the French Revolution. This is partly because such reference was not only dangerous after 1793, it was increasingly embarrassing; but it was also in part because Bage and the other English Jacobin novelists expressed their views in ways acceptable to readers of the 'English popular novel' and these ways included general moral types as well as a high proportion of moral argument, but not, as yet, the attempt to depict the actual 'condition of England'. In any case the English Jacobins saw particular political and social abuses only as outward signs of the deeper moral issues.

Even so, there is a high degree of allusion and indirect reference to particular issues and personalities in the various English Jacobin novels, although this element has not unfortunately been brought out in recent annotated editions of these works. The contrast between the fat pluralist and the poor curate, for example, was a commonplace, and Bage contrasts the toadying Dr. Blick with good parson Brown and the worthy curate Mr. Woodcock. Hermsprong takes the opportunity to discuss with the narrator of the novel the state of the clergy, and emphasizes that the actions of men like Blick are abuses in the clerical office, not the rule (i. 108). This point reminds one immediately of Bage's views on his friend William Hutton's pamphlet on juries. But Blick is also clearly meant to be a caricature of Bishop Horsley—both preach sermons on the Birmingham Riots which are identical for arguments in defence of the *status quo* and intemperance against Dissenters and other advocates of reform. Other English Jacobin novelists too were quick to take up the subject of Horsley's sermon, but Bage had merely developed the contrast between religious Dissent and the established church, present in his earlier novels, into the wider context of the French Revolution debate of the 1790s. It was events themselves and not any change in Bage's outlook, which had created this new context. It was one of Bage's friends, Joseph Priestley, after all, who had been one of the chief victims of the Riots which provided the subject for Dr. Blick's sermon.

Bage's treatment of politics in *Hermsprong* is even more continuous with that found in his earlier novels. Lord Grondale is a politician of the old school—in his youth a leader of the *ton,* he caught politics like a disease. With several Cornish boroughs in his pocket he was soon bought up by the Government; he abandons political independence as Lord Idford had done in *Hugh Trevor,* and like Sir Barnard Bray in the same novel his price is a coronet. It also comes as no surprise to discover that Lord Grondale is an oppressor of the poor like Lord Bendham, another placeman portrayed in Mrs. Inchbald's *Nature and Art.* When the wife of one of his tenants refuses to submit to his foul designs, Grondale persecutes the miserable family, as Tyrrel persecuted his tenants in Godwin's *Things As They Are.* Clearly the English Jacobin novelists all had the same picture of what Holcroft was later to call 'official or pestilential rogues'.[94]

Bage also brings his treatment of the plight of women into line with the latest English Jacobin thought of the 'nineties. He depicts Grondale as the sort of domestic tyrant by now familiar in his novels, but Grondale's attempt to force his dutiful daughter into a marriage with the jumped-up and physically deformed Sir Philip Chestrum allows Bage to insert references to Mary Wollstonecraft (ii. 168) and a conversation in which Miss Fluart argues strenuously for equality of choice in marriage (iii. 94). Finally Hermsprong himself sums up this particular argument of the novel with a plea for complete equality of the sexes (iii. 230). He is a fictional hero of whom Mary Wollstonecraft would have approved—a complete Jacobin hero in fact—but his views had always been present in some form or another in

Bage's novels, and in *Hermsprong* he was merely bringing his 'popular novel' material up to date.

The moral argument of Bage's novels had not, in fact, changed at all. Hermsprong makes a distinction to be found at the base of all of Bage's fiction when he declares, after having saved the life of Lord Grondale's daughter, 'As to rank,—I have been taught only to distinguish men by virtue' (i. 62). What has changed is what might be called the author's moral expectations for the future of mankind. It is true enough that *Hermsprong* has its happy ending and that virtue triumphs over villainy; but the revolutionary parting shot of *Man As He Is* is transformed into Hermsprong's vision of Pantisocracy on the banks of the 'Potowmac'. It is a vision almost identical to the description of the communal life at the end of Bage's first novel, *Mount Henneth.*

Perhaps it is too convenient to see Bage's fiction travelling full circle, but the moral of his last novel—'Give me, heaven! any life, but the life of grandeur!' (ii. 223)—belies the radical views and serious satire to be found in *Man As He Is,* and in most of *Hermsprong* itself. It is a withdrawal from commitment to contemporary issues which is also found in *Nature and Art* (1796) and, even more significantly, in the increasing Romanticism of Godwin's *St. Leon* (1799). By 1796 it was obvious that English Jacobinism had been defeated, and Bage was only following in fiction the path which friends such as Priestley had already followed in fact. The regions of the 'Potowmac' was where Priestley and many others had already gone.

Bage's last two novels seem to be more radical than their predecessors only because the crisis of the 1790s made men speak out more plainly than before. By 1800 Bage's novels, in spite of their most un-Jacobinical humour, could be classed by *The Anti-Jacobin Review and Magazine* along with 'the trash of Mrs. Robinson' and Mrs. Inchbald's *Nature and Art.* On the whole, however, Bage escaped from the opprobrium heaped on the other English Jacobin novelists, partly due to his humour, but partly no doubt because he was harmlessly removed from the centre of political passions in London. And yet Bage's views, as expressed in his novels ever since 1781, were very little different from those of the most outspoken London radicals. *Hermsprong* in particular had a sharper edge to its satire, and although *Man As He Is* had its influence on Holcroft, it was really *Hermsprong,* the least 'typical' of Bage's novels, which made Godwin, in the summer of 1797, so anxious to meet this obscure Midlands paper-manufacturer.[95] *Man As He Is,* with its Smollettian vigour, appealed to Holcroft; *Hermsprong,* with its greater severity and closeness to the French philosophical novel, appealed to Godwin; but neither novel was essentially different from the kind of fiction which Bage had been producing since

1781. As the public issues changed, so too did Bage's incorporation of those issues into his novels. As the more philosophical of the English Jacobins might have put it, following the argument of *Political Justice,* circumstances made character, both in life and in fiction.

It is somewhat of a paradox, then, that Bage was so uninterested in that issue of fundamental importance to the other English Jacobin novelists, the causal relation between circumstances and character. Except to a very small degree in **Hermsprong,** he was only interested to show how a character, already formed, managed the issues that were always at stake in the conflict between coercion and free will, social requirements and the necessities of individual choice and independence. It was, basically, an interest in the eighteenth-century debate on ethics, but it was also, in its way, as much a 'Protestant' or Dissenting interest as anything to be found in the more serious novels of William Godwin. Moreover, Bage's humour and his ability to draw eccentric characters have obscured the fact that he has his own kind of seriousness, and that his novels have their own kind of unity. The view of G. B. Smith has been the dominant one:

> As novels they may not interest strongly by their plot, but there is a distinct originality about them. They were chiefly intended to inculcate certain political and philosophical opinions. . . . Considered altogether apart from their moral and social bearings, the novels of Bage display an unquestionable power in drawing and developing character, while their style is always entertaining and frequently incisive.[96]

By now it should be clear that their 'moral and social bearings' cannot be separated from their ability to entertain. It is true that in theme, structure, and characterization Bage's fiction is often highly conventional; he relied, after all, on the great tradition of the eighteenth-century English novel, as did all of the English Jacobin novelists—it is one sign of their high seriousness. But for Bage the conventions took on new life when invested with his systematic moral purpose; and so the unity of his novels is not that of a syllogism which demonstrates the causal relationship between circumstances and moral character, as in the novels of Holcroft and Godwin, but that of a certain moral 'atmosphere'. He works not in a straight line, but by parallels and digressions which all, eventually, contribute to the 'political and philosophical' view of man which he wished to 'inculcate'.

And in a way Bage's characters are the plots. Ideas and incidents, debates and controversies, adhere to individuals rather than to any concatenation of events which works out a meaning in itself. It is in this way that Bage can make ideas and politics both serious and amusing. The machinery of character and plot is united with the social and moral criticism in a way that is to be found in all of Bage's novels. He came from a part of the country where eccentric and extraordinary individuals were creating a revolution in industry and society; it is not surprising that the characters in his novels should reflect his own circumstances.

The themes of Bage's novels are all the same, the interest in political issues remains the same. Only the particular issues, and the technical skill, change and develop. In turning to the popular novel at the advanced age of fifty-two, Bage tried to correct a situation which one of his own characters described in **James Wallace:**

> My uncle remembers well . . . when no young people of a decent appearance were regarded, unless they could speak upon the publications in vogue—novels then were not—and even make moral sentiments in a tolerable manner.
>
> But then it must be owned, there was sometimes a horrible clash of opinion in very good company, especially when religion or politics were the subject; the two grand sources of disputation. By degrees it became the fashion never to introduce those spoilers of peace; and hence we are said to have now a most gentleman-like religion, never offensive by exuberance of zeal, and a most accomodating public spirit, perfectly acquiescent in every measure of every minister. In short, the good English people, with some exceptions, choose rather to be ignorant and polite, than learned and contentious.

[p. 492]

Robert Bage, the paper-maker from Elford, was one of the exceptions, and there were soon to be many more. He made it seem right that novels should be concerned with the social and political problems of the day. It was a suggestion which other English Jacobin writers were not to miss.

Notes

1. *Ballantyne's Novelist's Library,* ed. Walter Scott (Edinburgh, 1824), vol. ix, pp. xxv-vi.

2. *The Popular Novel in England 1770-1800,* p. 193.

3. *Before Jane Austen* (London, 1966), p. 274.

4. *Mount Henneth* (1781), *Barham Downs* (1784), and *James Wallace* (1788).

5. *Dictionary of National Biography,* s.v. Robert Bage.

6. *Ballantyne's Novelist's Library,* vol. ix, p. xvii. The Memoir comprises pp. xvii-xxv of the Preface.

7. Letters from Bage to Hutton, 1782-1801, in the Local Studies Library, Birmingham Public Library.

8. Kegan Paul, i. 263.

9. *Ballantyne's Novelist's Library,* vol. ix, p. xxvi. Cf. John H. Sutherland, 'Bage's Supposed Quaker Upbringing', *Notes and Queries,* cxcviii (Jan. 1953), 32-3.

10. *Monthly Magazine,* xii (Jan. 1802), 479. William Hutton's Memoir of Bage.

11. *Ballantyne's Novelist's Library,* vol. ix, p. xxiv.

12. Letter from William Godwin to Mary Wollstonecraft, 15 June 1797, in Kegan Paul, i. 263.

13. Kegan Paul, i. 263.

14. *Monthly Magazine,* xii. 478.

15. A. E. Musson and Eric Robinson, *Science and Technology in the Industrial Revolution* (Manchester, 1969), pp. 31, 36-7, 90.

16. Described in full in Robert Schofield, *The Lunar Society of Birmingham* (Oxford, 1963).

17. Musson and Robinson, p. 89.

18. Musson and Robinson, p. 193.

19. *D. N. B.,* s.v. Sir Brooke Boothby.

20. Musson and Robinson, pp. 196, 194.

21. Musson and Robinson, p. 197.

22. *James Wallace,* in *Ballantyne's Novelist's Library,* ix. 390.

23. Musson and Robinson, p. 191.

24. Op. cit. (Edinburgh, 1797), pp. 481-2.

25. Schofield, *The Lunar Society of Birmingham,* p. 360.

26. *Monthly Magazine,* xii. 479.

27. Note to a copy of letters from Bage to Hutton regarding the Riots and the trials, evidently by Hutton's daughter Catherine. Hutton Beale Collection 29A-B, in the Local Studies Library, Birmingham Public Library.

28. Op. cit. v (Feb. 1800), 152, in a review of *St. Leon.*

29. Op. cit., p. xxxiii.

30. Cf. *Notes and Queries,* ccx (Jan. 1965), 27, where H. R. Steeves argues for a publication date of 1782.

31. Op. cit., 1st Ser., lxvi (Feb. 1782), 130.

32. Ibid. lxxvi (Apr. 1787), 329.

33. *Ballantyne's Novelist's Library,* ix. xxv.

34. Letter from Bage to Hutton, dated 29 Apr. 1789, in the Local Studies Library, the Birmingham Public Library. The text is slightly different in the version in Scott's memoir (p. xxi).

35. *Ballantyne's Novelist's Library,* ix. xxvi.

36. James Kinsley and James T. Boulton, edd., *English Satiric Poetry Dryden to Byron* (London, 1966), pp. 17-18.

37. Steeves, *Before Jane Austen,* pp. 272, 289.

38. *The Popular Novel in England,* p. 40.

39. [Robert Bage,] *Hermsprong; or, Man As He Is Not* (London, 1796), i. 43.

40. Op. cit., 1st Ser., lxvii (Jan. 1789), 76.

41. Op. cit. v (Feb. 1800), 152.

42. Cone, *The English Jacobins,* Ch. iii.

43. See Ian R. Christie, *Wilkes, Wyvill and Reform* (London and New York, 1962), Chapters iii-vi.

44. M. D. George, *English Political Caricature* (Oxford, 1959), i. 171.

45. George, i. 176.

46. Susie Tucker, *Protean Shape* (London, 1967), p. 233.

47. P. S. Denenfeld, 'Social Criticism in the Novels of Robert Bage', unpublished Ph.D. dissertation, Northwestern University, 1957, p. 276.

48. John H. Sutherland, 'Bage's Supposed Quaker Upbringing', *Notes and Queries,* cxcviii (Jan. 1953), 32-3.

49. *Ballantyne's Novelist's Library,* ix. xxviii.

50. Cf. Frank Henley, the hero of *Anna St. Ives,* whose father is the steward of Sir Arthur St. Ives, father of the heroine.

51. [Robert Bage,] *Barham Downs* (London, 1784), i. 199.

52. William Cowper, *The Task,* i, lines 769-74, in *Poetical Works,* ed. H. S. Milford, 4th edn., with corrections and additions by Norma Russell (London, 1967).

53. [Robert Bage,] *The Fair Syrian* (Dublin, 1787), ii. 46.

54. *Ballantyne's Novelist's Library,* ix. xxviii.

55. In popular novels, and English Jacobin ones, the line of demarcation between classes seems to lie between baronet and baron. Cf. Sir Vavasour Firebrace's views on the special virtues of baronets in Disraeli's *Sybil* (1845), Book ii, Ch. ii.

56. [Robert Bage,] *Mount Henneth,* 2nd edn. (London, 1788), i. 90.

57. *James Wallace* (1788), p. 485; *Hermsprong* (1796), i. 6.

58. See E. N. Williams, "'Our Merchants are Princes'": The English Middle Classes in the Eighteenth Century', *History Today,* xii (Aug. 1962), 548-57.

59. Asa Briggs, 'Middle-class Consciousness in English Politics, 1780-1846', *Past and Present,* ix (Apr. 1956), 66.

60. Briggs, p. 70.

61. Ibid., p. 67.

62. Cf. James W. Johnson, *The Formation of English Neo-Classical Thought* (Princeton, New Jersey, 1967), pp. 48-9.

63. The account is placed under the title '*Story of* HUGH GRIFFITHS'.

64. [Robert Bage,] *Man As He Is* (London, 1792), i. 70.

65. Philip Stanley Denenfeld, 'Social Criticism in the Novels of Robert Bage', unpublished Ph.D. dissertation, Northwestern University, 1957, p. 276. Perhaps Bage did have the writings of Bolingbroke in mind, but the ideal of the independent country gentleman was a general one, a rallying banner for opponents of Walpole and his system rather than a monopoly of the Tories.

66. J. M. S. Tompkins considers it Bage's best work. See *The Popular Novel in England,* p. 196.

67. *The British Novelists,* vol. xlviii (London, 1820), p. ii.

68. *Ballantyne's Novelist's Library,* ix. xxv.

69. Perhaps it is ironical that Bage's most Jacobinical novels, *Man As He Is* and *Hermsprong,* actually received the Minerva Press imprint. The previous novel, *James Wallace,* bore the imprint of William Lane. See E. A. Osborne, 'A Preliminary Survey for a Bibliography of the Novels of Robert Bage', *Book Handbook,* no. 1 (1947), 30-6.

70. There was, of course, the great example of Rousseau's Julie, but Bage's treatment is humorous rather than sentimental.

71. *Ballantyne's Novelist's Library,* ix. xxx. Crouch asserts however, 'There are no important expurgations in any one of the novels.' W. C. A. Crouch, 'The Novels of Robert Bage', unpublished Ph.D. dissertation, Princeton University, 1937, p. 272.

72. J. H. Sutherland, 'Robert Bage: Novelist of Ideas', *Philological Quarterly,* xxxvi (1957), 214.

73. Bage may also have had in mind the condition of India under Warren Hastings, an issue also dealt with by Mrs. Inchbald in her play *Such Things Are* (1787).

74. See especially Hobbes's *Leviathan,* ed. C. B. Macpherson (Harmondsworth, 1968), pp. 253 ff. (Pt. ii, Ch. 20).

75. Caroline Robbins, *The Eighteenth-Century Commonwealthman,* p. 8.

76. Z. S. Fink, *The Classical Republicans,* 2nd edn. (Evanston, Illinois, 1962), p. 27 n.

77. G. R. Havens, *The Age of Ideas* (New York, 1955), p. 396.

78. [William Hutton,] *The Life of William Hutton, written by himself* (London, 1816), p. 165.

79. In *The Massacre,* which she suppressed at the desire of Holcroft and Godwin.

80. Op. cit., 2nd Ser., x (Mar. 1793), 298.

81. Dorothy Marshall, *Eighteenth Century England* (London, 1962), p. 448.

82. Musson and Robinson, p. 163.

83. Ibid., p. 193.

84. The American farmer is obviously a Quaker.

85. Allene Gregory, *The French Revolution and the English Novel* (New York, 1915), p. 168.

86. Op. cit. v (Feb. 1800), 152.

87. *The English Review,* xx (Dec. 1792), 438.

88. Richard Price, *A Discourse on the Love of Our Country, delivered on November 4, 1789, at the Meeting House in the Old Jewry, to the Society for Commemorating the Revolution in Great Britain* (London, 1789), p. 34.

89. The 'English senator' referred to is Burke.

90. Gwyn A. Williams, *Artisans and Sans-Culottes* (London, 1968), p. 58.

91. Williams, p. 38.

92. Desmond Clarke, *The Ingenious Mr. Edgeworth* (London, 1965), pp. 156, 159-60.

93. Op. cit., 2nd Ser., xxi (Sept. 1796), 21.

94. *Bryan Perdue* (1805), i. 15.

95. The meeting is described in Godwin's letter to Mary Wollstonecraft, Kegan Paul, i. 262-3.

96. *D. N. B.,* s.v. Robert Bage.

Works Cited

I. MANUSCRIPT SOURCES

Hutton-Beale Collection, number 29A-C, Birmingham Public Library, Local Studies Library. Copies of extracts of letters from Bage to William Hutton, and of a letter from Mr. Chavasse, surgeon of Walsall, to William Hutton.

Letters from Robert Bage to William Hutton, 1782-1801. Birmingham Public Library, Local Studies Library, catalogue number 486802. For the most part these are short messages written on invoices for shipments of paper sent from Bage to Hutton.

II. BOOKS

1. GENERAL

(a) Historical

Association for Preserving Liberty and Property against Republicans and Levellers, *Association Papers* (2 parts, London, 1793).

Briggs, Asa, *The Age of Improvement* (corr. edn., London, 1960).

————, 'Middle-class Consciousness in English Politics, 1780-1846', *Past and Present,* ix (Apr. 1956), 65-74.

Brinton, Crane, *The Political Ideas of the English Romanticists* (1926, repr. Ann Arbor, Michigan, 1966).

Brown, Ford K., *Fathers of the Victorians* (Cambridge, 1961).

Brown, Philip A., *The French Revolution in English History* (1918, repr. London, 1965).

Burke, Edmund, *The Works* (6 vols., London, 1882-4).

Christie, Ian R., *Wilkes, Wyvill and Reform* (London and New York, 1962).

Cléry, Jean-Baptiste, *A Journal of the Occurrences . . . During the Confinement of Louis XVI,* trans. R. C. Dallas (London, 1798).

Cobban, Alfred, ed., *The Debate on the French Revolution 1789-1800* (2nd edn., London, 1960).

Coleridge, Samuel Taylor, *The Watchman,* ed. Lewis Patton (London and Princeton, New Jersey, 1970).

————, *Lectures 1795 on Politics and Religion,* ed. Lewis Patton and Peter Mann (London and Princeton, New Jersey, 1971).

Cone, Carl, *The English Jacobins* (New York, 1968).

Creasey, John, 'Some Dissenting Attitudes Towards the French Revolution', *Transactions of the Unitarian Historical Society,* xiii, no. 4 (Oct. 1966), 155-67.

Eaton, Daniel Isaac, ed., *Politics for the People* (4th edn., London, 1794).

Fink, Zera S., *The Classical Republicans* (2nd edn., Evanston, Illinois, 1962).

George, M. Dorothy, *Catalogue of Political and Personal Satires Preserved in the Department of Prints and Drawings in the British Museum,* vol. vii (London, 1942).

Havens, George R., *The Age of Ideas* (New York, 1955).

Marshall, Dorothy, *Eighteenth Century England* (London, 1962).

Martin, Kingsley, *French Liberal Thought in the Eighteenth Century* (3rd rev. edn., New York, 1963).

Place, Francis, *The Autobiography of Francis Place (1771-1854),* ed. Mary Thale (Cambridge, 1972).

Price, Richard, *A Discourse on the Love of Our Country* (London, 1789).

Robbins, Caroline, *The Eighteenth-Century Commonwealthman* (1959, repr. New York, 1968).

Robison, John, *Proofs of a Conspiracy Against All the Religions and Governments of Europe* (Edinburgh, 1797).

Rudé, George, *Wilkes and Liberty* (Oxford, 1962).

Starobinski, Jean, *L'invention de la liberté 1700-1789* (Geneva, 1964).

Thompson, Edward, *The Making of the English Working Class* (rev. edn., Harmondsworth, 1968).

[Towers, Joseph,] *Remarks on the Conduct, Principles, and Publications, of the Association . . .* (London, 1793).

Veitch, G. S., *The Genesis of Parliamentary Reform* (1913, repr. London, 1965).

Williams, E. N., '"Our Merchants are Princes": The English Middle Classes in the Eighteenth Century', *History Today,* xii (1962), 548-57.

Williams, Gwyn A., *Artisans and Sans-Culottes, Popular movements in France and Britain during the French Revolution* (London, 1968).

Williams, Raymond, *Culture and Society 1780-1950* (Harmondsworth, 1961).

(b) Literary

Baker, Ernest A., *The History of the English Novel* (London, 1934), vol. v.

Birkhead, Edith, *The Tale of Terror, A Study of the Gothic Romance* (1921, repr. New York, 1963).

————, 'Sentiment and Sensibility in the Eighteenth Century English Novel', *Essays and Studies,* xi (1925), 92-116.

Boulton, James T., *The Language of Politics in the Age of Wilkes and Burke* (London and Toronto, 1963).

Crane, R. S., 'Suggestions toward a Genealogy of the "Man of Feeling"', *ELH A Journal of English Literary History,* i (1934), 205-30.

Foster, James R., *History of the Pre-romantic Novel in England* (London and New York, 1949).

Fussell, Paul, *The Rhetorical World of Augustan Humanism* (Oxford, 1965).

Giddings, Robert, *The Tradition of Smollett* (London, 1967).

Gregory, Allene, *The French Revolution and the English Novel* (New York, 1915).

Howe, Irving, *Politics and the Novel* (London, 1961).

Johnson, James W., *The Formation of English Neo-Classical Thought* (Princeton, New Jersey, 1967).

Lejeune, Philippe, 'Le Pacte autobiographique', *Poétique,* no. xiv (1973), 137-62.

Lloyd, Charles, *Edmund Oliver* (2 vols., Bristol, 1798).

Lucas, Charles, *The Infernal Quixote* (4 vols., London, 1800).

McClelland, E. M., 'The Novel in Relation to the Dissemination of Liberal Ideas, 1790-1820', unpub. Ph.D. diss., London University, 1952.

Nangle, B. C., *The Monthly Review First Series 1749-1789, Index of Contributors and Articles* (Oxford, 1934).

———, *The Monthly Review Second Series 1790-1815, Index of Contributors and Articles* (Oxford, 1955).

Nicoll, Allardyce, *A History of English Drama, 1660-1900,* vol. iii, *Late Eighteenth Century Drama 1750-1800* (London, 1952).

Proper, C. B. A., *Social Elements in English Prose Fiction Between 1700 and 1832* (Amsterdam, 1929).

Pye, Henry James, [Essay on the Imitative Arts,] *The Artist,* vol. i, no. xviii (11 July 1807), 1-12.

Rodway, A. E., *The Romantic Conflict* (London, 1963).

Steeves, H. R., *Before Jane Austen* (London, 1966).

Tompkins, J. M. S., *The Popular Novel in England 1770-1800* (1932, repr. Lincoln, Nebraska, 1961).

Walker, George, *The Vagabond* (3rd edn., 2 vols., London, 1799).

Williams, Ioan, ed., *Novel and Romance 1700-1800, A Documentary Record* (London, 1970).

Withycombe, E. G., *The Oxford Dictionary of English Christian Names* (2nd edn. corr., Oxford, 1963).

2. ROBERT BAGE

(a) Sources

[Bage, Robert,] *Mount Henneth* (1782, 2nd edn., 2 vols., London, 1788).

[———,] *Barham Downs* (2 vols., London, 1784).

[———,] *The Fair Syrian* (2 vols., Dublin, 1787).

———, *James Wallace* (1788), in *Ballantyne's Novelist's Library,* ed. Walter Scott, vol. ix (Edinburgh, 1824).

[———,] *Man As He Is* (4 vols., London, 1792).

[———,] *Hermsprong: or, Man As He Is Not* (3 vols., London, 1796).

Barbauld, Anna L., Preface to *The British Novelists,* vol. xlviii (London, 1820).

Cowper, William, *The Poetical Works,* ed. H. S. Milford, with corrections and additions by Norma Russell (London, 1967).

Disraeli, Benjamin, *Sybil, or The Two Nations,* Bradenham Edn., vol. ix (London, 1927).

Hobbes, Thomas, *Leviathan,* ed. C. B. Macpherson (Harmondsworth, 1968).

(b) Secondary Sources

Boulton, James T., and Kinsley, James, eds., *English Satiric Poetry Dryden to Byron* (London, 1966).

Clarke, Desmond, *The Ingenious Mr. Edgeworth* (London, 1965).

The Critical Review, lxvii (Jan. 1789), 76-7. Review of *James Wallace.*

Crouch, William, 'The Novels of Robert Bage', unpub. Ph.D. diss., Princeton University, 1937.

Denenfeld, Philip S., 'Social Criticism in the Novels of Robert Bage', unpub. Ph.D. diss., Northwestern University, 1957.

The English Review, xx (Dec. 1792), 437-43. Review of *Man As He Is.*

Faulkner, Peter, 'Robert Bage', *Notes and Queries,* ccxii (Apr. 1967), 144.

George, M. Dorothy, *English Political Caricature* (2 vols., Oxford, 1959).

Hartley, K. H., 'Un Roman philosophique anglais: Hermsprong de Robert Bage', *Revue de littérature comparée,* xxxviii (1964), 558-63.

Hutton, William, *The History of Derby . . . to 1791* (London, 1791).

———, *The Life of William Hutton, . . . written by himself* (London, 1816).

———, 'Memoirs of Mr. Bage', *Monthly Magazine,* xii (Jan. 1802), 478-80.

The Monthly Review, 1st Ser., lxvi (Feb. 1782), 129. Review of *Mount Henneth,* by Samuel Badcock.

————, 1st Ser., lxxvi (Apr. 1787), 325-9. Review of *The Fair Syrian,* by Andrew Becket.

————, 2nd Ser., x (Mar. 1793), 297-302. Review of *Man As He Is* by Thomas Holcroft.

————, 2nd Ser., xxi (Sept. 1796), 21-4. Review of *Hermsprong,* by William Taylor.

Musson, A. E., and Robinson, Eric, *Science and Technology in the Industrial Revolution* (Manchester, 1969).

Osborne, E. A., 'A Preliminary Survey for a Bibliography of the Novels of Robert Bage', *Book Handbook,* i (1947), 30-6.

Schofield, Robert, *The Lunar Society of Birmingham* (Oxford, 1963).

Scott, Walter, 'Prefatory Memoir to Robert Bage', in *Ballantyne's Novelist's Library,* vol. ix (Edinburgh, 1824), pp. xvi-xxxiv.

Smith, G. Barnett, 'Robert Bage', *Dictionary of National Biography.*

Steeves, H. R., 'The Date of Bage's "Mount Henneth"', *Notes and Queries,* ccx (Jan. 1965), 27.

Sutherland, John H., 'Bage's Supposed Quaker Upbringing', *Notes and Queries,* cxcviii (Jan. 1953), 32-3.

————, 'Robert Bage: Novelist of Ideas', *Philological Quarterly,* xxxvi (1957), 211-20.

Sutton, C. W., 'Sir Brooke Boothby', *Dictionary of National Biography.*

Peter Faulkner (essay date 1985)

SOURCE: Faulkner, Peter. Introduction to *Hermsprong; or, Man as He Is Not,* by Robert Bage, edited by Peter Faulkner, pp. vii-xix. Oxford and New York: Oxford University Press, 1985.

[*In the following essay, an introduction to an edition of* Hermsprong; or, Man as He Is Not, *Faulkner outlines the historical and literary significance of the novel, providing context for and explication of the ideas Bage expresses in the work.*]

Robert Bage's **Hermsprong** is one of the liveliest and most entertaining political novels in English, although its publishing history has restricted knowledge of it to a small readership. First published in 1796, it had several early editions;[1] but after the Chiswick Press edition of 1828, it was not to reappear until 1951, and then only in a small edition. The Folio Society edition of 1960 was also not large. It is much to be hoped that the present edition will make possible its acceptance as one of the most interesting—and by far the most amusing—of the contributions to the great political debate in England that followed the French Revolution of 1789.

It was as a political work that **Hermsprong** was certainly regarded at the time. The reviewer who praised it most highly, William Taylor in the *Monthly Review,* related it to other works expressing the 'new philosophy', such as Voltaire's *L'Ingénu* and Thomas Holcroft's *Anna St. Ives* of 1792.[2] When the tide of opinion had turned against radical ideas in the early nineteenth century, the comments reveal the change. Writing in 1810, Mrs Barbauld informed her readers in a preface to the novel: '**Hermsprong** is democratical in its tendency. It was published at a time when sentiments of that nature were prevalent with a large class of people, and was much read.'[3] Sir Walter Scott, who included three of Bage's novels in his *Ballantyne's Novelist's Library* in 1824, felt in necessary to point out Bage's 'speculative errors' as well as his culpable laxity in treating female sexual irregularities (a point which will be discussed later). But he argued that the quality of the characterization and style greatly exceeded the danger from such errors—though considering it necessary to remind the reader that 'a good jest is no argument'.[4] When the preface came out as part of *The Lives of the Novelists* in the following year, Scott was criticized by the *Quarterly Review* for reprinting 'a very inferior novelist' of dangerous subversive views: '[Bage] systematically made his novels the vehicle of all the anti-social, anti-moral and anti-religious theories that were then but too much in vogue among the half-educated classes in this country.'[5] This emphasizes the extent to which Bage's novels belonged to a particular social and political situation that can be explored through an account of his life; it also makes particularly impressive the irony and comic detachment with which Bage treated political issues in the novel itself.

Robert Bage was born in 1728 in the hamlet of Darley on the outskirts of Derby. He learnt his father's trade, that of paper-maker, married Elizabeth Woolley of Mickleover at the age of twenty-three, and was able to buy a small mill in the Staffordshire village of Elford, on the River Tame between Lichfield and Tamworth, probably in 1753. Here he lived quietly and industriously for some fifty years. William Godwin described the Bages's house as being 'floored, every room below stairs, with brick, and like that of a common farmer in all respects. There was, however, the river at the bottom of the garden, skirted with a quickset hedge, and a broad green walk.'[6] Most of our information about Bage comes through William Hutton, a Birmingham bookseller and writer, who was a business associate and, indeed, after 1761, Bage's sole customer, taking and selling all the paper Bage produced at Elford. Hutton later recorded that he paid Bage an annual average of £500 and in forty-five years 'he never gave me one cause of complaint'.[7] Hutton in fact seems to have done very well from their arrangement, becoming a leading citizen of the rapidly expanding Birmingham of the time, whose history he enthusiastically wrote. Bage's other local friends included Erasmus Darwin, who settled at Lichfield in 1756 and was prominent as doctor, scientist, poet, and man of radical ideas.[8]

Bage's social position was thus that of a working paper-miller in the Midlands at a time when industrial development was largely seen as progressive and desirable. Josiah Wedgwood's pottery at Etruria was becoming very well known; Matthew Boulton was joined by James Watt at his Soho Manufactory in 1774, and the business expanded rapidly. On an intellectual plane, the Lunar Society[9] met locally from 1766 onwards for the discussion of scientific topics, and over the years its members included, in addition to Darwin, Wedgwood, Boulton and Watt, the writers R. L. Edgworth and Thomas Day, and the scientists James Keir, John Whitehurst and Joseph Priestley—who was also well known as a Unitarian minister and theological controversialist. Whether Bage knew all these distinguished people personally is impossible to determine, but his enthusiasm for their outlook is expressed in the novel *Man as He Is* (1792), where he refers to Priestley, Keir and Darwin, and to Birmingham as 'a place scarcely more distinguished for useful and ornamental manufacture, than for gentlemen who excel in natural philosophy, in mechanics, in chemistry'.[10] Thus it is clear that Bage was in touch with contemporary ideas, and his novels themselves give plentiful evidence of his wide reading. His familiarity with the ruling class in the countryside would have been much less, but it is interesting to note that the landowner to whom he sold his mill in 1766, while retaining the tenancy, was the Earl of Donegall.[11] Donegall bought Fisherwick Hall in Staffordshire in 1758, and between 1766 and 1774 lavishly reorganized his estate with the help of 'Capability' Brown, the noted landscape-planner, building a large Palladian mansion and planting 100,000 trees. He achieved an English barony in 1790 and an Irish marquisate in 1791, and must have been known to Bage as a striking example of the conspicuous consumer deplored by Augustan moralists, and later by Jane Austen.

Bage seems to have kept mainly to his mill, though there is evidence of an unsuccessful involvement in 'an iron manufactory' from about 1765 to 1780, resulting in a heavy financial loss. It was his need to distract himself from this loss that Bage gave to Godwin as the unusual motive for his having started to write novels when in his fifties.[12] *Mount Henneth* appeared in 1782, to be followed by *Barham Downs* in 1784, *The Fair Syrian* in 1787 and *James Wallace* in 1788. These four epistolary novels were quite well received in the reviews, coming at a time when, as J. M. S. Tompkins succinctly puts it, 'the chief facts about the novel' were 'its popu-

larity as a form of literature, and its inferiority as a form of art'.[13] The novels suggest Bage's familiarity with his great predecessors, Fielding, Richardson, Smollett and Sterne, but have definite characteristics of their own, notably a preoccupation with social and political ideas for which the epistolary form is unhelpful. Nevertheless, they are often amusing as well as doctrinaire in their dramatization of an underlying contrast between upper-class values, associated with a self-indulgent and irresponsible aristocracy, and the realistic and humane behaviour of the middle classes. In *Mount Henneth* the hero is a self-made merchant who establishes a happy community at Henneth Castle, a mercantile version of the conventionally rural myth of communal felicity. In *Barham Downs,* though on a smaller scale, a similar ideal is enacted: 'Beauty without pride. Generosity without ostentation. Dignity without ceremony. And Honour without folly.'[14] *The Fair Syrian,* as its title implies, has more exotic elements, including the Turkish harem, but again it works by contrasts. French pre-Revolutionary society is condemned for its extravagance and sophistication, which are contrasted with American simplicity and integrity. The hero, Sir John Amington, is a model country gentleman who discovers, while serving in the British Army in America, the injustice of the cause for which he is fighting. He rejoices in the success of the American colonists, represented by a sturdy Quaker farmer who eloquently asserts American egalitarianism: 'Every man feels himself a *Man*.'[15] *James Wallace* again ends with the establishment of a community of the good, but the last words of the novel are given to the unrepentant aristocrat Sir Everard Moreton, whose praise of his Parisian companions and denunciation of the rest makes clear the novel's class basis:

> Debauchers and sharpers! good Captain Fanbrook! Tolerably illustrious too, some of them, for birth and family. In the grace of God I believe they are not equal to the upright commercials of Liverpool; nor do they get up matrimony so sweetly: But for the manufactures of wit, mirth and good-humour—I doubt the abilities of your artists must fall short; and curse me if I don't prefer these looms to those for the weaving of saints . . .[16]

Bage, by contrast, is the representative voice of the 'upright commercials' of late eighteenth-century England.

One further aspect of these early novels should be noted: the remarkable liberality in the treatment of sexual morality. In *Mount Henneth* Mr Foston arrives at the wrecked house of a Persian merchant in India too late to save the merchant's daughter Caralia from being raped by soldiers. Later, Foston wishes to court the girl, but she holds back on the grounds that she has read in novels that the loss of a woman's 'honour' is irretrievable. Addressing her father, Foston rejects her attitude: 'It is to be found in books, Sir; and I hope, for the honour of the human intellect, little of it will be found anywhere else.'[17] Later, a female character reflects on the prevailing 'double standard' of morality: 'But in this good town, no one now, I perceive, affixes the idea of criminality to male incontinence. All the guilt, and all the burder of repentance, fall upon the poor woman. Such are the determinations of men.'[18] In *Barham Downs,* the sixteen-year-old Kitty Ross is seduced by a rakish aristocrat; later the shrewd lawyer William Wyman does not hesitate to marry her. In *The Fair Syrian* Honoria Warren is sold into a harem and although she miraculously preserves her virginity, she becomes friendly with the Georgian Amina, who argues that it is better to submit to the inevitable. When Honoria speaks of her fear in the harem, saying, 'The idea fills me with horror. I prefer death a thousand times,' Amina replies, 'And I prefer a thousand times—to death.'[19] Lady Bembridge, whose husband is a rake and a gambler: is allowed to seek an absolute separation from him, thus questioning the conventional assumption about her husband's rights *James Wallace* criticizes the rakish Sir Everard ('A wife, Lamounde, for affairs of state; but for affairs not of state, a maid—a maid'[20]), but is otherwise less concerned with sexual morality. Nevertheless, it can be seen how prominent Bage's liberal ideas are in this area.

If such ideas seem commonplace today, they were certainly not so at the time, as the outraged response of the normally humane Scott suggests. He deplores Bage's 'dangerous tendency to slacken the rein of discipline upon a point where, perhaps, of all others, Society must be benefitted by their curbing restraint'.[21] Fielding and Smollett may have allowed their heroes to be 'rakes and debauchees', but Bage has gone much further; he has 'extended that licence to females' and he 'seems at times even to sport with the ties of marriage'.[22] Scott's attitude to Kitty Ross shows vividly how seriously—and, from a modern point of view, how wrong-headedly—he took the issue of virginity. He concedes that it is possible to imagine a girl being seduced 'under circumstances so peculiar as to excite great compassion', so that it might be reasonable for her eventually to be admitted into society as 'a humble penitent'. But her 'fall' would never have to be forgotten:

> Her disgrace must not be considered as a trivial stain, which may be communicated by a husband as an exceeding good jest to his friend and correspondent; there must be, not penitence and reformation alone, but humiliation and abasement, in the recollection of her errors. This the laws of society demand even from the unfortunate; and to compromise further would open a door to the most unbounded licentiousness.[23]

Since Scott is so fair-minded in his overall treatment of Bage's novels, this passage stands out vividly to appal the modern reader. The measure of our distance from Scott's righteous indignation and unconscious male chauvinism must be our pleasure in Bage's humane and generous treatment of sexual morality, and his evident sympathy with the woman's point of view.

Bage's last two novels, *Man as He Is* (1792) and *Hermsprong; or, Man as He Is Not* (1796), belong to the decade following the French Revolution of 1789. As the titles suggest, the fictional methods are different—in the earlier novel, an attempt at realism, in the later, a more stylized approach—but both reflect the increasing political tensions of the period. The French Revolution was initially broadly welcomed in England, but as time passed and the extent of its claims became clearer, the Establishment, led by Pitt's Ministry, became more and more hostile, while the supporters of the Revolution were represented as becoming more and more extreme; public opinion became polarized.[24] The opposition is most vividly seen in literature by the sweeping reactionary rhetoric of Edmund Burke's *Reflections on the Revolution in France* (1790), answered by many radicals but most powerfully by Thomas Paine in *The Rights of Man* (1791 and 1792) and, more obliquely and intellectually, by William Godwin in *An Enquiry Concerning Political Justice* (1793).

The political history of the period, which can be only briefly summarized here, shows the same increasing polarization. A number of organizations had come into existence seeking reform of various kinds, such as the County Associations of the 1770s and the Society for the Abolition of the Slave Trade in 1787. These groups were followed by others with more directly political aims: the Society for Constitutional Information (1780), the Society of Friends of the People (1792) and the London Corresponding Society (1792). In May 1792 a Royal Proclamation was issued against seditious publications, and *The Rights of Man* was declared a seditious libel in December of that year. Meanwhile, in November 1792, was founded the Association for the Protection of Property against Republicans and Levellers. The declaration of war with France in February 1793 made it easy to represent radical opinions as disloyalty, and the course of the Revolution, with the execution of the King and of Marie Antoinette followed by the Reign of Terror of 1794, alienated many English people who, like Wordsworth and Coleridge, had initially welcomed the Revolution. To go on putting forward radical criticisms of society demanded courage and conviction, but it was nevertheless done both in pamphlets and literary works such as Godwin's novel *Things as They are; or Caleb Williams* (1794) and Thomas Holcroft's *Anna St. Ives* (1792) and *Hugh Trevor* (1794-7). Bage's later works must be seen in this context, which has recently been thoroughly and thoughtfully discussed by Gary Kelly in *The English Jacobin Novel 1780-1805*; but we can also see the continuity of his work and its provincial basis.

The closeness of these concerns to Bage is strikingly demonstrated by the fact that it was in Birmingham in

July 1791 that one of the most alarming and protracted riots of the decade took place. The radicals of the area held a dinner to celebrate 'the ideas of 1789'. News of the dinner was circulated beforehand, and a mob of anti-radicals gathered. The magistrates failed to disperse the mob, which destroyed the Old and New Meeting Houses of the Unitarians (whose minister was Joseph Priestley), as well as the houses and property of many leading radicals.[25] Even Bage's friend William Hutton, a prosperous man but by no means a radical, suffered. He fled with his wife and children to Tamworth, where he was given hospitality on the strength of his friendship with Bage. On 25 July 1791 Bage wrote Hutton a sympathetic and concerned letter about the situation:

> In this country, it is better to be a churchman, with just as much common sense as heaven has been pleased to give on average to Esquimaux, than a dissenter with the understanding of a Priestley or a Locke. I hope, Dear Will, experience will teach thee this great truth and convey thee to peace and orthodoxy, pudding and stupidity. Since the riots, in every company I have had the misfortune to go into, my ears have been insulted with the bigotry of 50 years back—with, damn the presbyterians—with church and king huzza—and with true passive obedience and non-resistance—and may my house be burnt too, if I am not become sick of my species, and as desirous of keeping out of its way, as was ever true hermit.[26]

This is the situation referred to in Dr Blick's sermon in Chapter XXIX of **Hermsprong,** and it helps to make clear the reasons for the more emphatic political note in the later novels. **Man as He Is** appeared in 1792, and is the story of Sir George Paradyne, a young man of good family, seeking a way of life. The choice is between the pursuit of pleasure, as proclaimed by George's rakish friend John Lake Fielding and embodied in Lady Ann Brixworth, a fashionable beauty, and the more responsible attitude encouraged by his tutor Mr Lindsay and represented by the heroine, Cornelia Colerain. As Sir George is shown as a young man with normal appetites (rather like Tom Jones), he takes some time to learn to abjure fashion for sense. Interestingly, Birmingham plays a part in the scheme of ideas, as a contrast to both London and Paris. At one point, Sir George comes to Birmingham, which is praised in the terms quoted earlier for its manufacturers and scientists.[27] Like other travellers of the time, Sir George goes to visit a local factory, where in the exhibition room are displayed views of Southampton; these are found to be the work of the gifted and industrious Cornelia, now living in the neighbourhood, who seems to have become something like the only female member of the Lunar Society referred to earlier. The proprietor of the factory tells Sir George that she has dined with him twice: 'When I have been favoured with the company of Dr. Priestley; with that of Mr. Keir, the well-known translator and

elucidator of Macquer's Chemistry; or the celebrated author of the botanic garden.'[28] (Erasmus Darwin published his scientific poem *The Botanic Garden* in 1789 and 1791.)

Thus the values of the 'upright commerciants of Liverpool' upheld in **James Wallace** are here further supported, and Bage sees no contradiction in making his landed-gentleman hero eventually commit himself to these values rather than those of the decadent aristocracy. His position is thus not extreme. Nevertheless, Bage does mount a direct attack on the leading conservative spokesman of the time, Edmund Burke. While travelling in Italy, Sir George meets a Miss Zaporo, a rigid Roman Catholic who believes that any extension of civil liberty would be disastrous: 'We should have seen no more of that generous loyalty to rank.'[29] The 'I' narrator then breaks into the novel to draw attention to the closeness of these 'enlarged and liberal sentiments' to those of Burke's *Reflections*. The narrator ironically gives praise to Burke's eloquence, referring particularly to the famous passage in which Burke compares Marie Antoinette to a star and laments the passing of chivalric ideals at her execution: 'I thought ten thousand swords must have leaped from their scabbards, to avenge even a look that threatened her with insult!' The narrator then claims to have discussed the passage with a friend:

> I was quoting this with a generous enthusiasm to an old friend who lives a very retired life, and troubles himself but little about the politics of this world. The muscles of his face contracted into a sort of grin—'Ten thousand pens,' said he, 'must start from their inkstands, to punish the man who dares attempt to restore the empire of prejudice and passion. The age of chivalry, heaven be praised, is gone. The age of truth and reason has commenced, and will advance to maturity in spite of cants or bishops.'[30]

Although the narrator wryly dissociates himself from the views of his 'old friend'—'I did not invite my friend to dinner'[31]—the reader is led to see the extravagance and inappropriateness of Burke's ideas in the modern world where law rather than knight-errantry is the method for creating social justice. Although Bage retains his lightness of touch in many parts of **Man as He Is,** the novel situates its social and political discriminations directly in the controversies of the decade.

This is equally true of **Hermsprong,** published in 1796, by which time the war with France and the developments there had combined with internal events in England to make the position of radicals even less comfortable. Spies and informers were widely employed by the Ministry. In Scotland the judges, led by Lord Braxfield, were particularly hostile, and in August 1793 the leading Scottish radical Thomas Muir was sentenced to fourteen years' transportation. Braxfield told the jury that no proof was required for the assumption 'the British Constitution is the best that ever was since the creation of the world, and it is not possible to make it better'.[32] In September T. F. Palmer, a Unitarian minister in Dundee, was convicted for belonging to the Dundee Friends of Liberty and encouraging the reading of Paine, and sentenced to seven years' transportation.[33] In November and December a National Convention was held in Edinburgh, with delegates from many parts of Britain. Maurice Margarot and Joseph Gerrald were sent by the London Corresponding Society. Together with the Scottish secretary of the Convention, W. Skirving, they were arrested and tried. Eventually all three were sentenced to fourteen years' transportation.[34]

In England juries were less inclined to follow the Ministry's policy, but in May 1794 leaders of both the Society for Constitutional Information and the London Corresponding Society were arrested, and a Committee of Secrecy appointed to examine them. Meanwhile, Habeas Corpus was suspended. However, when the radicals were brought for trial in October on a charge of treason, first Thomas Hardy, then Horne Tooke, and then (in December) John Thelwell were acquitted, and the rest, including the writer Thomas Holcroft, were freed.[35] But there was no change in Pitt's policy, which aimed to discredit the radicals by identifying them with the republicanism of Paine and the extremism of the French Jacobins. In 1795 the high price of corn and dissatisfaction with the progress of the war seemed to favour the radicals, but the Ministry raised strong hostility towards them in connection with an incident when the King's coach was attacked on the way to the State Opening of Parliament in October.[36] As a direct result, Pitt introduced in November further repressive measures, known as the Two Acts.[37] By the first, the Treasonable Practices Act, it became a treasonable offence to incite hatred of the Constitution; and by the second, the Seditious Meetings Act, no meetings of more than fifty people could be held without a magistrate's permission. Despite widespread opposition outside Parliament, the Two Acts received the Royal Assent in December, and—with the suspension of Habeas Corpus—were successful in greatly reducing radical activity.

For Bage the period was discouraging, as his surviving letters to Hutton show. When a book by Priestley was published in January 1793, Bage welcomed it, but noted: 'at present—Nothing from him will be attended to. No man's ear is open to anything but Church & King—and Damn the French—and Damn the Presbyterians. I abstain from all society, because respect for my moral principles is scarce sufficient to preserve me from insult on account of my political.'[38]

As a working paper-miller, Bage was also well aware of the economic problems resulting from the war with France. His letters to Hutton reflect his difficulties over increasing taxation, the rising costs of raw materials,

and the need of the workers for higher pay to offset increased prices. In September 1794 he writes: 'This very morning, my men with mighty clamour demand an increase of wages. I am under necessity of complying, for they are low, but thou, much more than I, have the advantage of it.'[39] By Christmas, he is writing with more characteristic sprightliness, but the situation remains the same:

> Eat my breakfast quietly, you monkey? So I do, when my house don't smoak, or my wife scold, or the newspapers tickle me into irritation, or my men clamour for another increase of wages—for I have granted one of about £20 per Annum. But I must get my bread by eating as little of it as possible, for my Lord Pitt will want all I can screw of Overplus.[40]

Despite these problems (which are perhaps reflected in Hermsprong's argument with the miners at the end of the novel), Bage was able to produce his most succinct and entertaining novel, *Hermsprong; or, Man as He Is Not,* published by the Minerva Press in early 1796 and favourably received by its few reviewers.[41]

The novel must speak for itself, but three aspects may perhaps be emphasized here. First, the method. William Taylor, the early reviewer who referred to 'Voltaire's Huron' as a source for the novel,[42] was clearly right to do so, as was Walter Scott in suggesting the relationship of Bage's 'quaint, facetious, ironical style'[43] to French didactic writers like Diderot and Voltaire. Voltaire's fables were early translated and widely known in England. Translations of *L'Ingénu* (with various titles) appeared in 1768, 1771 and 1786. Voltaire's hero is a young Frenchman, brought up in America as an 'Indian', who comes to France eager to learn about the country. His radical frankness and honesty lead him into numerous troubles, including a period in the Bastille, from which he is released only when the woman he loves sacrifices her virtue to a powerful aristocrat. The fable—cautiously set in 1689—is a witty exposure of repressive aspects of the *ancien régime,* making use of a central figure with characteristics recognizably those of the Noble Savage. Bage's novel clearly takes over some of this material, including its hero's background, but places it in an English context and provides a more romantic ending. The influence of Voltaire can be felt in the witty style as well as the overall plan, and also in the oriental anecdotes which Mr Sumelin discusses with his unimaginative wife in Chapter XLII. In following the master of the non-realistic fable, Bage was allowing himself a freedom of approach well suited to his satirical purposes, which rest on the sharp contrast drawn between the State and Church Establishment, represented in caricature by Lord Grondale and Dr Blick, and the various liberal or radical alternatives represented by Hermsprong, Gregory Glen (the narrator whose presence reveals the complementary influence of Laurence Sterne), Mr Sumelin, and Maria Fluart.

The second point for emphasis relates to Miss Fluart, whose liveliness and independence make her a fitting climax to Bage's series of sympathetic heroines. In the earlier novels Bage was consistently liberal in his attitude to women. Here their position is both dramatized and discussed in similar terms. During dinner at the Sumelins' house in Chapter XLIII the discussion deals with the lives and education of women, and Mr Sumelin (and later the narrator) refers explicitly to Mary Wollstonecraft. Her *Vindication of the Rights of Woman* had been published in 1792, so that feminist ideas were part of the controversial atmosphere of the times. Bage shows himself both interested in and concerned for women's emancipation. Like many early novelists, he makes use of a contrasting pair of female heroines, one sweet, the other vivacious. (We may think of Richardson's Clarissa Harlowe and Anna Howe, and later Jane Austen's Jane and Elizabeth Bennet—whose family situation resembles to a considerable extent that of the Sumelin family.) In *Hermsprong,* Caroline Campinet is so consistently sweet and virtuous that the reader's interest focuses much more on Maria Fluart, whose ready wit is as attractive as her determined actions. Her remark to Sir John and Sir Philip in Chapter LX is strikingly to the point: 'Our obligations to men are infinite. Under the name of father, or brother, guardian, or husband, they are always protecting us from liberty.' Her treatment of Lord Grondale combines comedy with morality as she outmanœuvres him in the pavilion in Chapter XXXV, and she proves quite equal to the final crisis in Chapter LXVIII by producing a pistol—a deed of which it is hard to think any other heroine in English literature capable until recent times. Moreover, when the plot involves Hermsprong and Caroline in the conventional ending of marriage, Maria Fluart remains alone, 'not yet willing "to buy herself a master"'.

Thirdly, in the politics of the novel, the relative importance given to America and France should be noticed as evidence of Bage's moderate radicalism. There is no doubt at all of his hostility to the repressive politics of the Ministry, as represented in Hermsprong's trial in Chapter LXXII with its resort to law rather than justice, or to the whole Establishment, as embodied in Lord Grondale. The choice of Cornwall (an area well away from Bage's Midlands) as the setting may, as Stuart Tave has suggested, be accounted for by that county's reputation for over-representation in Parliament and saleable boroughs;[44] Bage must also have known of the troubles at the Poldice mine in 1795 due to rising food prices and low wages, and perhaps of Sir Francis Bassett, whose success in putting down food rioting in Redruth in the following year was rewarded with the title of Baron de Dunstanville of Tehidy.[45] It has been suggested too by Dr Kelly that Dr Blick should be seen as a version of Dr Samuel Horsley, the peroration of whose sermon to the House of Lords in January 1793 on the danger of the revolutionary spirit brought the whole assembly to its feet 'in rapt enthusiasm'[46]—though Horsley's views were those widely promulgated from the pulpits of the Established Church at the time.[47]

Nevertheless, Bage was not a young man whose political attitude was shaped by the French Revolution. His commitment had been made and articulated much earlier, and involved a continuing respect for the values of the American Revolution, as accepted by Sir John Amington in **The Fair Syrian.** In 1796 this enabled Bage to offer a radical perspective that did not have to underwrite every action of the increasingly repressive French government. In the discussion with the Sumelins in Chapter VIII Hermsprong presents a balanced account of recent developments in France; in Chapter XLIII he praises America as the best society ('still at an immense distance from the ultimatum'), a view he repeats and develops in Chapter LXXVII through a detailed criticism of English society; this culminates in his suggestion of taking his friends to establish a community in America. Although the conventional romantic ending of the novel, with its revelation of Hermsprong's parentage, makes this unnecessary, the values contained in the proposal remain valid: American freedom, toleration and adventurousness are endorsed as against the narrow restrictiveness of the English Establishment. The final suggestion of the novel that these values can actually be upheld in England itself, given good will and determination, is evidence of Bage's moderation—and indeed of a subdued optimism particularly courageous in 1796.

Notes

1. It was pirated in Dublin in 1796; the Minerva Press published a revised edition in 1799, and a third in 1809; an unauthorized edition was published in Philadelphia in 1803; Mrs Barbauld included it in *The British Novelists,* 1810, reprinted 1820; Chiswick Press 1828. This edition is photographed from the 1951 Turnstile Press edition.

2. *The Monthly Review,* XXI (September 1796), 21-4.

3. Anne Barbauld, 'Preface, biographical and critical' to *Man as He Is Not, or Hermsprong* in *The British Novelists,* XLVIII (F. & J. Rivington, London, 1810), p. 2.

4. Scott, 'Prefatory Memoir to Bage' in *Ballantyne's Novelist's Library,* vol. IX, *Novels of Swift, Bage and Cumberland* (Hurst, Robinson and Co., London, 1824), pp. xxxiii-iv.

5. *Quarterly Review,* XXXIV (September 1826), 367.

6. C. Kegan Paul, *William Godwin. His Friends and Contemporaries,* 2 vols. (London, 1876), I, pp. 262-3.

7. 'Memoir of Robert Bage' in *Monthly Magazine,* XIII (1802), 479.

8. See D. King-Hele, *Erasmus Darwin 1731-1802* (London, 1963), *passim.*

9. See R. E. Schofield, *The Lunar Society of Birmingham* (Oxford, 1963), especially Parts II and III.

10. *Man as He Is* (London, 1792), II, p. 216.

11. See G. E. Cokayne (ed.), *The Complete Peerage,* IV (London, 1916), p. 392.

12. Kegan Paul, *Godwin,* op. cit., I, p. 263.

13. J. M. S. Tompkins, *The Popular Novel in England 1770-1800* (London, 1932), p. 1.

14. *Barham Downs* (G. Wilkie, London, 1784), II, p. 342.

15. *The Fair Syrian* (J. Walter, London, 1787), I, p. 30.

16. *James Wallace* (1788; *Ballantyne's Novelist's Library,* IX, 1824), p. 508.

17. *Mount Henneth* (T. Lowndes, London, 1782), I, p. 221.

18. Ibid., II, p. 31.

19. *The Fair Syrian,* II, p. 69.

20. *James Wallace,* p. 467.

21. Scott, 'Prefatory Memoir to Bage', op. cit., p. xxix.

22. Ibid.

23. Ibid., p. xxx.

24. See E. P. Thompson, *The Making of the English Working Class* (1963; Harmondsworth, 1968), especially Part I, 'The Liberty Tree', for much of the historical information in this section.

25. See Thompson, op. cit. p. 79; he cites R. B. Rose, 'The Priestley Riots of 1791', *Past and Present* (November 1960), pp. 68-88.

26. Birmingham Public Library, Local Studies Library, MSS 486802, 25 July 1791; for a fuller quotation see P. Faulkner, *Robert Bage* (Boston, 1974), p. 26.

27. See above, p. ix.

28. *Man as He Is,* op. cit., II, pp. 219-20; James Keir (who presided at the dinner preceding the Birmingham Riots in 1791) translated the then well-known scientific work of the French chemist Macquer in 1771.

29. Ibid., IV, 71. Cf. Edmund Burke, *Reflections,* p. 91.

30. *Man as He Is,* IV, p. 73.

31. Ibid., IV, p. 75.

32. See Thompson, op. cit., p. 136.

33. Ibid.

34. Ibid., pp. 138, 140.

35. Ibid., pp. 148-9.

36. Ibid., p. 158.

37. Ibid., p. 161.

38. Birmingham MSS, op. cit., 24 January 1793.

39. Ibid., 27 September 1794.

40. Ibid., 7 December [1794?].

41. *The Analytical Review,* XXIV (1796), 68; *The British Critic,* VII (April 1796), 430; *The Monthly Review,* XXI (September 1796), 21-4.

42. Taylor, *Monthly Review* op. cit., p. 21.

43. Scott, 'Prefatory Memoir', op. cit., p. xxvi.

44. Tave, p. 3.

45. See F. E. Halliday, *A History of Cornwall* (London, 1959; 1975), p. 267.

46. G. Kelly, *The English Jacobin Novel 1780-1805* (Oxford, 1976), p. 105.

47. For other relevant sermon titles see W. T. Laprade, *England and the French Revolution 1789-1797* (1909; New York, 1970), especially pp. 154-7, and notes thereto.

Select Bibliography

BIBLIOGRAPHY

There is no fuller work yet available than E. A. Osborne's early but largely reliable 'A Preliminary Survey for a Bibliography of the Novels of Robert Bage' in *Book Handbook,* edited by R. Horrox (Bracknell, Berkshire, 1951). This may be supplemented by *The New Cambridge Bibliography of English Literature,* II, edited by George Watson (Cambridge, 1971), and Gary Kelly's *The English Jacobin Novel 1780-1805* (Oxford, 1976).

BIOGRAPHY AND CRITICISM

The only full-length study is *Robert Bage* by Peter Faulkner, in Twayne's English Authors series (Boston, 1979); Gary Kelly discusses Bage together with Godwin, Holcroft and Mrs Inchbald in *The English Jacobin Novel* (see above).

The fullest early treatment is in Walter Scott's 'Prefatory Memoir to Bage' in vol. IX of *Ballantyne's Novelist's Library* (London, 1824), which includes biographical information provided by Catherine, the daughter of Bage's friend William Hutton. This is reprinted in Scott's *Lives of the Novelists* and in I. Williams (ed.), *Sir Walter Scott on Novelists and Fiction* (London,

1968). Manuscript letters from Bage to Hutton are in the Local Studies Library of the Birmingham Public Library (MSS 486802). The account of Godwin's visit to Bage in 1797 is in C. Kegan Paul, *William Godwin, His Friends and Contemporaries,* 2 vols. (London, 1876).

Useful earlier scholarly accounts of Bage's novels and ideas are to be found in Edward Dowden, *The French Revolution and English Literature* (London, 1897); Wilbur Cross, *Development of the English Novel* (New York, 1899); Oliver Elton, *Survey of English Literature 1780-1830* (London, 1912); Allene Gregory, *The French Revolution and the English Novel* (London and New York, 1915); George Saintsbury, *The English Novel* (London, 1913), *The Peace of the Augustans* (London, 1916), *The Period of the French Revolution,* vol. IX in the *Cambridge History of English Literature* (Cambridge, 1932); Carl Grabo, 'Robert Bage: A Forgotten Novelist' in *Mid-West Quarterly,* V (1918), 202-26; Hoxie N. Fairchild, *The Noble Savage: A Study in Romantic Naturalism* (New York, 1928); J. M. S. Tompkins, *The Popular Novel in England 1770-1800* (London, 1932); and Dorothy Blakey, *The Minerva Press 1790-1820* (Oxford, 1939).

More recent scholarship and criticism includes J. R. Foster, *History of the Pre-Romantic Novel in England* (New York, 1949); Vaughan Wilkins, Introduction to Turnstile Press edition of *Hermsprong* (London, 1951); J. H. Sutherland, 'Robert Bage: Novelist of Ideas' in *Philological Quarterly,* XXXVI (1957), 214-20; W. L. Renwick, *English Literature 1789-1815,* vol. IX in the *Oxford History of English Literature* (London, 1963); H. R. Steeves, *Before Jane Austen* (London, 1966); and Marilyn Butler, *Jane Austen and the War of Ideas* (Oxford, 1975).

Abbreviations

LD — Longman's Dictionary of English Idioms (1979)

OED — Oxford English Dictionary

Tave — Stuart Tave (ed.), *Hermsprong; or, Man as He Is Not* by Robert Bage (Pennsylvania University Park and London, 1982)

Reflections — Edmund Burke, *Reflections on the Revolution in France* (1790), ed. W. B. Todd (New York, 1959; 1965)

Vindication — Mary Wollstonecraft, *A Vindication of the Rights of Woman* (1792), ed. Miriam Kramnick (Harmondsworth, 1975)

Pam Perkins (essay date winter 1996)

SOURCE: Perkins, Pam. "Playfulness of the Pen: Bage and the Politics of Comedy." *Journal of Narrative Technique* 26, no. 1 (winter 1996): 30-47.

[*In the following essay, Perkins focuses on Bage's use of comedy in* Hermsprong; or, Man as He Is Not.]

. . . your playfulness, I know, is only of the pen, for your heart is good . . .[1]

A beautiful young woman, about to be dashed over a cliff by a runaway horse, is rescued by a handsome stranger. Her tyrannical father, enraged by his daughter's refusal to marry a rich but foolish suitor, imprisons her and attempts to force her to the altar. Persecuted by the heroine's father, a wicked baron, the handsome and mysterious rescuer is finally revealed to be the long-lost rightful heir to the baron's estates. Standard melodrama—except that the heroine has a taste for debating the rights of women. The forced marriage is halted when the heroine's confidante pulls a pistol on the father and would-be bridegroom, and the new lord of the manor is a democrat who disapproves of the entire aristocratic system. Far from being the tired romance that one might expect from the plot outline, Robert Bage's **Hermsprong** (1796) simultaneously employs and mocks conventions of popular melodrama, as the few critics who have written about the book invariably point out. Marilyn Butler, in a brief but very helpful discussion of **Hermsprong,** comments that Bage "mimicked the stale conventions of eighteenth-century fiction in such a manner that he criticized its underlying assumptions, while at the same time availing himself of the popular novelist's power to create an attractive, autonomous world" (86). Similarly, Gary Kelly has observed that one of Bage's characteristic techniques is to "retain enough of [a] convention to keep his story moving" (*English Jacobin Novel* 43) while cheerfully mocking the rest. The novel is not merely a parody, however; **Hermsprong** is usually classified not with the long line of literary burlesques stretching from Charlotte Lennox's *Female Quixote* through E. S. Barrett's *Heroine* and (most famously) Austen's *Northanger Abbey,* but rather among the intensely serious and highly politicized jacobin novels of the 1790s.

While no one would disagree with the contention that Bage's work belongs with that of the jacobin novelists, his use of the comic mode does separate him from his fellow radicals. The jacobin world view was a tragic one, or, at the very least, one that was far more dark than light. Jacobin novelists and their characters tend to seek the absolute conversion of the unregenerate, instead of working toward the literal or figurative marriage of oppositions that usually characterizes comedy. There can be no reconciliation between the principles of Thomas Holcroft's Anna St. Ives and Coke Clifton, for example, or between those of Godwin's Falkland and Caleb Williams. Happy endings ensue only if the good convert the bad. In the more optimistic novels, such as *Anna St. Ives* and the revised version of *Caleb Williams,* characters merely cling stubbornly to their ideals despite all dangers and temptations; in the pessimistic work of writers such as Mary Hays and Mary Wollstonecraft, the clash between principled individuals and a harshly corrupt world usually proves fatal. Such stark oppositions are foreign to Bage's novels. While Bage undoubtedly shares the rather Utopian political ideals of his jacobin contemporaries, he is far less inclined than they are to make the conflict between his enlightened characters and their opponents a literal life-and-death struggle. Not only does he give us happy endings, which are fairly unusual in jacobin fiction (even the relatively cheerful *Anna St. Ives* leads up to its somewhat chastened happy ending with an abduction, an attempted rape, and the near-death of the anti-hero), but also he implies throughout his novel that quiet compromise between opposing world views is both desirable and inevitable. Bage's politics might have been impeccably jacobin, but his choice of the comic mode is jarringly at odds with the literary practices of his fellow radicals.

Initially, it might seem as if in Bage we have that very rare being, a political radical with a sense of humour about his politics. After all, *Hermsprong* is comic in style as well as in mode; it is, quite simply, a very funny book. Yet despite this promising and rather charming combination of deep political engagement and genial comedy, *Hermsprong* is generally agreed to be an unsuccessful novel. Butler, for example, criticizes Bage for his concluding lapse into literary and political conventionality, observing that he fails to maintain either his "irony" or his "intellectual daring" to the end of the novel (84). Mona Scheuermann is more disturbed by Bage's seeming political apostasy than by any failure of plotting, concluding that the novel never really overturns any of the institutions that it attacks. Bage, she argues, begins by making "many basic criticisms of his society," but then retreats and "arrives[s] at his happy ending by ignoring the larger issues he has raised" (225-26). This is a fair criticism, but could it be that the apparent weakness of the conclusion of *Hermsprong* arises not from a failure of nerve or imagination, as these critics imply, but is rather the ironic result of the book's seeming strength—its combination of serious political engagement with a comic insistence upon the necessity of debate and compromise? Similarly, if Bage's play with literary conventions stems from a cheerful iconoclasm, it also, as Kelly points out, implicitly recognizes that for the comedy to work and the plot to keep moving, some elements of literary convention have to be retained. While this point may seem self-evident—the ironic dependence of transgression upon the conventions being transgressed has been explored by critics of genre in some detail[2]—still it is precisely this point upon which Umberto Eco builds his argument that comedy can never be unambiguously radical as a mode. In a brief but highly provocative article, which starts from a critique of Bakhtin's ideas of the carnivalesque, Eco argues that even the most apparently transgressive forms of comedy—such as the carnival—"can exist only as an *authorized* transgression" (6). According to Eco, the most transgressive form of comedy is, rather ironically, one that admits its inability ever to escape either the social or literary conventions by which it is bound.

In *Hermsprong,* one finds precisely the sort of sophisticated awareness of dependence upon the conventions—or "frames"—being mocked that Eco analyzes in his essay. Structurally, the novel balances playful literary iconoclasm with a half-mocking, half-resigned awareness of its inability ever to entirely escape conventionality, a balance that inevitably modifies and undermines the political Utopianism embedded in the plot. Bage continually links his attacks on literary and social conventions throughout the book, and as he does so, he confronts, both openly and implicitly, the possibility that constricting, foolish social structures will be no more easy to do away with entirely than literary ones, some remnants of which he has to continue to cling to in order to write anything at all.

"Remnants" is actually an understatement. *Hermsprong* reads like a cheerful potpourri of almost every familiar type of comic plot imaginable; it opens in a manner reminiscent of Smollett's novels, with a wry first-person account of the conception, birth, and upbringing of the scapegrace narrator, Gregory Glen. Yet Glen has withdrawn from the centre of attention by the fourth chapter, and in chapter ten he announces that he has decided to start referring to himself in the third person and almost completely effaces himself from the novel. Later in the book, Bage again moves away from the main romance plot and dabbles in domestic comedy in his amusing accounts of the homelife of the witty banker Mr. Sumelin and his foolish wife and daughter;[3] these characters are connected to the main plot only by what Butler calls one of Bage's "unashamed coincidences": Mr. Sumelin happens to be both Hermsprong's banker and Miss Fluart's guardian. Finally, at intervals Bage anticipates Peacock's comedy of philosophical debate,[4] stopping the action for animated discussions of topics such as Mary Wollstonecraft's ideas about female liberty and the relative nature of happiness in civilized and "savage" societies. While this mode might seem particularly congenial to Bage's openly didactic purposes, it is ultimately no more than one comic style employed among many.[5]

These sudden shifts from one type of comic plot to another might appear rather clumsy artistically, perhaps even more so than the wooden contrivances used by a number of Bage's contemporaries, yet they are the most basic level at which Bage implies a connection between his literary play and his reformist politics. As the book lurches from one familiar type of plot to another, Bage calls attention to the artificiality of these conventional patterns and invites a critical response from the audience. By refusing to write the picaresque novel that the opening account of Glen's adventures seems to promise, Bage jars his readers into a recognition of the extent to which their expectations have been conditioned by previous experiences with literature. His abrupt switch of direction is not at all improbable on the basic level of plot; after all, it is completely reasonable for Glen to settle near his friends in a beautiful and inexpensive district of the country. Only previous experience with literary wanderers from Don Quixote to Moll Flanders and on down would make us expect that a penniless young adventurer like Glen should keep moving and settle down only on the last page of the novel. More importantly, by making Glen, the hero of the opening chapter, disappear from the novel so suddenly, Bage subtly confronts his readers with the limitations of his own main plot. Glen has a story of his own, quite possibly one just as amusing as Hermsprong's, which he refuses to continue telling or even to complete. His unnamed editor, and his coyness about this mysterious figure, are clear reminders that Glen continues to have a full and active life beyond his self-imposed function as Hermsprong's biographer. By refusing to make his narrator either a central character or a disembodied, omniscient voice, Bage teases his readers, tantalizing them with glimpses of Glen's life—but no more than glimpses. Instead of creating an illusion of comprehensiveness, he reminds us of the arbitrariness and limitations of the story that he is actually telling. Yet by calling attention to the limitations of his story in this manner, Bage is not making a radical critique of the conventions of the picaresque—or of domestic comedy, or of philosophical debates, or of those of any of the other forms that he dabbles in. Suggesting that any particular style of writing has its limitations and that turning to one excludes the particular virtues of other types of comedy is an obvious point, even if it is not one that is often made within the context of the comic works themselves. The more interesting aspect of Bage's play with conventions is his implicit reminder that the use of some conventional elements, however hackneyed and limiting they might be, is necessary to attract and retain an audience. Complete iconoclasm, he implies, might be appealing in theory but is impossible in practice.

Bage makes this point even more clearly through what limited characterization he does provide of the self-consciously self-effacing Gregory Glen. Although reading Glen as a character is difficult in the latter half of the novel, doing so is extremely important. However much one might be tempted to assume that his witty perspective on events provides us with a completely omniscient and objective account of the incidents he relates, there are clear signs of self-deception in his narra-

tive, a fact that fundamentally alters the way in which the reader approaches the text. Glen wants to persuade us of his freedom, a freedom to relate his story independently of any reliance upon the confining laws of fiction. Yet by his very attempts to demonstrate independence from conventions, Glen reveals that he is bound far more tightly by them than he wants to believe. Through Glen's inability to recognize his own contradictions, Bage manages the rather difficult task of amusing his readers by calling their attention to the silliness of several conventions while continuing to draw upon them to increase the appeal of both his novel and his ideas.

One of Glen's characteristic attributes throughout the novel is an amused, rather contemptuous attitude toward the stale and manipulative devices of popular fiction. At several points, Glen openly discusses the way in which novels shape—or rather distort—readers' expectations. For example, when Miss Fluart and Miss Campinet set out on a brief journey, he observes,

> All ladies know—for all ladies read novels—how extremely dangerous the roads of England are for female travellers who happen to be young and handsome . . . lords, knights, and gentle squires [make it] their cruel practice to seize and carry away *vi et armis,* that is, in chaises drawn by flying horses, that distinguished part of the fair sex called heroines, and confine them in very elegant prisons. . . . Surely, I did not consider these things, when I turned my two lovely girls into this wide world of danger, with no other guide but their own discretion.
>
> (122)[6]

He then suggests that he is immune to reliance upon this particular device of conventional plotting by informing us that the two young women arrive without incident. Similarly, near the end of the book, he comments:

> If the careless writer of a novel closes his book without marrying, or putting to death, or somehow disposing not only of his principal personages, but of all who have acted a part in the drama above the degree of a candle snuffer, he creates an unsatisfied want in the minds of his readers, especially his fair ones, and they hardly part friends.
>
> (246)

Once again, Glen implies his own freedom from the bonds of convention, since his means of satisfying this "want" is to inform us that with the exceptions of Hermsprong and Miss Campinet, who predictably get married, almost all of the major characters continue in exactly the same manner as they did throughout the novel.

Yet inevitably, by the very act of mentioning conventions, Glen indicates a certain reliance upon them. He may begrudge us the information that Hermsprong and Miss Campinet get married, and he may not be particularly informative concerning the specific fates of the rest of the characters, but he nonetheless observes the convention that some allusion to those fates must be made. Similarly, he provokes momentary interest in an otherwise very brief and very mundane journey to Falmouth only by the expedient of reminding the reader that heroines' journeys are habitually fraught with danger. Contrary to his claims, Glen does not break the conventional rules of comic narrative; he merely gives the illusion of doing so by employing those conventions openly and self-consciously. Glen himself apparently never notices this unacknowledged dependence upon convention; he appears to be taken in by the illusion of himself as a successful literary iconoclast. He is able to tell the story, he informs us, only because he is reined in by a practical-minded editor. Otherwise, the plot would remain static as he spun out his own ideas (see pp. 15, 58). It is his editor who insists on plot and plausibility, Glen implies; he, being a free-thinker, is interested in neither.

Such "unconventionality" is flawed whichever way one chooses to interpret it. First of all, Glen submits to his editor's observations, despite his show of resistance. Moreover, and far more devastatingly to his position, his supposedly unconventional inability to tell a straightforward story in a straight-forward manner is itself a convention by 1796, derived most obviously from Sterne.[7] Finally, he is far from invariably self-conscious about all conventions. In both of the speeches quoted, and at many other points in the novel, he reveals that his own expectations of women—both as characters and as readers—are shaped by the popular images of them in fiction and conduct guides. Unlike Hermsprong, Miss Fluart, or even Miss Campinet, he remains untouched by Wollstonecraft's ideas and deeply influenced by, presumably, his own novel reading. I do not mean to suggest that one should read Glen as a conscious hypocrite, but rather that conventional literary structures and assumptions are not quite as easy to escape as he rather naïvely assumes them to be. Despite his amusing assumption of the role of iconoclast, he remains trapped by his own comic plot.

Hermsprong is not primarily literary criticism, of course; jacobin that he is, Bage is arguing for the birth of a new social order, not the death of an old form of literature. Yet the book's implicit claim that it is impossible to escape the limitations of convention no matter how self-consciously aware of those conventions one might be, is far from irrelevant to the novel's politics. On the contrary, Glen's entanglement in literary convention both reflects and reinforces the way that characters in the novel express political ideals that they have to modify and compromise both in practice and theory. As they try to escape the social codes binding them, they, much like Glen, discover that these conventions are not very easy to discard entirely, no matter how thoroughly one is aware of their artificiality. Hermsprong himself, the embodiment of freethinking iconoclasm, is fully aware that he is incapable of practicing

all that he preaches. A radical and independent thinker, who has no difficulty in telling Dr. Blick that he does not respect the clergy or in informing Lord Grondale that "he did not mind [his] rank" (22), Hermsprong also quotes Wollstonecraft and reads Paine, certain indications of a freethinker in eighteenth-century terms. Yet he sees nothing wrong in addressing women with elaborate and conventional gallantry, an incongruity that both Miss Campinet and Miss Fluart point out. Miss Campinet, in fact, hints at her own familiarity with Wollstonecraft's ideas when she reproves Hermsprong for his flattery:

> [Miss Campinet said,] ". . . I am sorry you have learned to flatter."
>
> "To flatter! Nay, at most it is only truth a little heightened. In praise of beauty one becomes poetical. Are young ladies pleased to be praised with cold and exact precision?"
>
> "It would be better, perhaps, if they were."
>
> "Possibly so; but since that is not their taste, what can poor young men do?"
>
> "I am sorry our sex should lay yours under the necessity of estimating female merit by a false scale. . . . I could have wished your extravagance in that particular, Mr. Hermsprong, had been less."
>
> (72)[8]

Hermsprong's belief that "the homage men pay to youth and beauty is insidious" (136) is softened and made less outrageous to eighteenth-century tastes by the fact that Hermsprong himself pays this homage. A willing outcast from Lord Grondale's aristocratic but rigidly closed-minded circles because of his views, Hermsprong is not willing to risk exile from society altogether by breaking through the elaborately polite behaviour that he assumes is expected by most ladies. Even knowing that such behaviour is a mere social convention, and a potentially deforming one at that, he is unable—or at the very least unwilling—to free himself from its confines.

It is clear that this inconsistency is not just hypocrisy on Hermsprong's part or carelessness on Bage's. Hermsprong admits his contradictory behaviour and gives two reasons for it. First, despite his egalitarian theory, he is "destined to be an adorer of women" (136) and so cannot help being elaborately flattering when he addresses them. More significantly, he has learned "that in very, very civilized countries, no man [can] hold up the mirror of truth to a lady's face without ill manners" (139). Politeness, Hermsprong implies, and by extension, making oneself liked, is at least in some circumstances more important than shattering conventions and proclaiming universal truths. Just as Glen proclaims his freedom from comic conventions but then retreats and charms his readers by employing them, Hermsprong proclaims his political unconventionality even as he makes himself charming through the elaborate politeness of fashionable social discourse. Recognizing arbitrary rules of behaviour, he tacitly admits, does not necessarily mean that one can or should escape them with impunity.

Bage further suggests the impossibility of escaping social—and by extension any—convention entirely by quietly showing that Hermsprong, the mouthpiece of most of the novel's radical politics, tacitly compromises with those who represent the social status quo and qualifies his political ideas in theory as well as in practice. For example, he repeatedly encourages Miss Campinet to overcome her exaggerated sense of filial duty and disobey her father's tyrannical orders because "there [are no] obligations binding on one party only" (172). Yet he quickly retreats from the full implications of this point when Miss Fluart proposes a test case:

> "Let us try now," said Miss Fluart. "Here am I now, your wife, the most charming creature in the universe; in two years you begin to wonder what made you think so. You find another quite as much to your taste. You play the false. Am I at liberty to return the favour?"
>
> "Yes, my most charming creature in the universe, yes, as far as respects myself. But, in this case, you have contracted an obligation with society also. Society does not think itself so much injured by the lapse of the male. In short, you bear the children. To you I need not point out the important deductions from this single circumstance."
>
> (172-73)

Far from demonstrating a penchant for radical freethinking, Hermsprong here is positioning himself in the long line of eighteenth-century moralists who argued that the transcendent importance of transferring property dictated rigid female propriety.[9]

The fact that the novel's literary iconoclasm does not necessarily reinforce its attack on social custom, even though at first it might seem logical that it do so, is significant. At times, in fact, play with literary convention seems to dampen down political radicalism, or vice versa. For example, Bage may be levelling a political attack on the corrupt aristocracy in his treatment of the wicked Lord Grondale, but as Kelly points out, in literature the figure of both the Bad Baron and the tyrannical father are so commonplace that any political commentary is muted (*English Jacobin Novel* 45). Moreover, as Kelly suggests elsewhere, the novel had become a weapon in the battle for middle-class hegemony by the end of the eighteenth century, so it is scarcely surprising to find attacks on wicked lords in them ("The Limits of Genre" 158-75). In elevating middle-class morality over aristocratic license, Bage was being almost tiresomely conventional in his plotting. Novelists of all

political stripes, from Hannah More and Jane West to Thomas Holcroft and William Godwin, agreed that the private gentleman was more likely to be virtuous and worthy than the aristocrat exposed to the corrupting temptations of public, urban life. Similarly, even though the witty, sexually provocative Miss Fluart is precisely the sort of character who horrified conservative moralists, she is hedged about by so many literary conventions that the shock value of what she says and does in considerably muted.[10] Miss Fluart's ideas are as radical as Hermsprong's, but she does not express them in his polemical manner. Instead, she employs playful debate, as in the passage cited above, or charmingly witty epigrams. "Our obligations to men are infinite," she tells a would-be suitor, "under the name of father, or brother, or guardian, or husband, they are always protecting us from liberty" (191). The statement is quite as radical as any of Wollstonecraft's, but given Miss Fluart's decision to present her ideas as playful epigrams, one laughs at them instead of being roused to an angry sense of injustice. Bage also diffuses some of Miss Fluart's more extreme radicalism through its context. In the case of the epigram just cited, the reader's attention is diverted not just by Miss Fluart's wit and charm, but also by the comic folly of Sir Philip, whose response to it is a dark suspicion that "she don't think women have any obligations to men at all" (191). The dull-witted and conventional-minded Sir Philip both provokes laughter and deflects the reader's own suspicions about the very un-funny implications of Miss Fluart's observation. (Notably, the more intelligent Sir John, to whom the speech is addressed, is reduced to temporary silence by it.) Similarly, Lord Grondale's bewildered or fatuous responses to Miss Fluart's sharp comments increase the emphasis on the conventional comic motif of a foolish old suitor pursuing a rich young woman and decrease the obvious radicalism of the sentiments expressed during the courtship scenes. Finally, the witty confidante of a properly virtuous heroine is a conventional literary figure who goes back at least as far as Shakespeare's Beatrice, and who enters the novel at its birth as a genre in the forms of Anna Howe and Lady G————. As long as the main heroine does and says what she ought and patiently rebukes her witty friend's excesses in a properly ladylike manner, the wit of the secondary heroine is contained and to a certain extent neutralized by this frame. However sharply pointed Miss Fluart's comments on female subordination might be when taken out of context, in the novel itself they are blunted by Miss Campinet's sweetly exemplary sentiments. And, since Caroline gets exactly what she wants by this behavior—her father's penitence and blessing, her friends' admiration, and (somewhat against his will) Hermsprong's devotion—the novel hints that despite Miss Fluart's witty attacks on feminine passivity, being a sweet, traditionally feminine woman is not entirely a handicap. This sop to the conventional-minded might not destroy the radical charm of the secondary heroine, but it does mitigate the force of her message.

Of course, the fact that Miss Fluart's role as a wit is entirely conventional does not make her statements, taken out of context, any less radical. By putting some of the novel's most outrageous statements in the mouth of a character whose conventional role damps them down somewhat, Bage almost manages to carry off a clever literary sleight-of-hand: making the same figure both conventional and unorthodox, according to how one looks at her. This cleverness certainly contributes to the charm of the novel: through it, Bage manages to violate readers' expectations without alienating his audience, because he makes sure that the violation occurs on only one level of the narrative and is counteracted on another. J. M. S. Tompkins suggests that Bage's books were full of "shocks for the conventional" anyway, because of innovations such as "militant Clarissas [who] defend themselves with sarcastic and resolved vigour" (202), but those shocks were certainly not as extreme as they could have been if Beatrice and Anna Howe, as well as Clarissa, did not stand behind young women such as Miss Fluart.

This interaction of social criticism and literary convention might help to account for the relative lack of controversy surrounding Bage's novels in their own day. Radical enough to impress Godwin, who made a point of meeting him, Bage nonetheless won surprisingly favourable reviews, even in the reactionary later 1790s. The conservative *British Critic,* though disapproving of the "pernicious" principles, admired the novel as a whole and singled out the "sprightly and most agreeable Miss Fluart" for particular praise (430). *The Critical Review,* less troubled by Bage's philosophy, went so far as to claim that a reader might well grow "wiser and better by a perusal of this work" (234).[11] The only negative comment on *Hermsprong* published during Bage's lifetime is in a brief note to a review of *St. Leon,* which appeared, predictably enough, in the *Anti-jacobin Review.* Not until Anna Laetitia Barbauld and Sir Walter Scott printed editions of the novel in 1810 and 1824, do we find critics making uneasy apologies for the novel's radical social and sexual politics. Tompkins suggests, plausibly enough, that Bage's surprisingly favourable reception owes more to the flaws of his competitors than to his own merits (194),[12] yet given the importance attached to the moral qualities of novels at the time (an importance that Tompkins herself stresses[13]), it is clear that early reviewers could not have found Bage's radical perspective particularly offensive. Eighteenth-century reviewers were, if anything, even less inclined than Scott to see an amusing plot as an excuse for a corrupt moral.

By using comedy and by framing his social criticism with pleasant mockery of familiar literary devices, Bage glosses over his radical ideas with a patina of innocuous geniality. Unlike the direct, often bitterly angry attacks made by so many of his radical contemporaries, Bage's political criticism amuses more than it enrages. The construction of the novel as a whole mirrors the practice of both Glen and Hermsprong as they question conventions even while charming an audience by fulfilling its expectations and employing them. The problem with this technique is that while Bage's comedy might help to make his political message more palatable for an unconvinced audience, it also risks making that message seem rather frivolous. The point of these observations is certainly not to imply that *Hermsprong* has a reactionary subtext or even that Bage was too nervous or too confused to be consistent in his pro-feminist, pro-democratic, and anti-aristocratic stance. After all, what one remembers after reading the novel is not Hermsprong's inconsistencies and qualifications but his and Miss Fluart's delightfully bold attacks on the stances taken by the more conservative-minded characters. Ultimately, the difference between Bage's work and that of his contemporaries is not that his ideas are more timorous or less radical, but that he treats the "war of ideas" as grist for genial, civilized debate, while the other jacobins see it as a war in good earnest, one with life-and-death issues at stake.

Bage's fairy-tale endings are the point at which the academic nature of the radical debates in his novels becomes most evident. His characters neither change the world nor fall victim to "things as they are"; instead, they form happy communities of the redeemed, living a more politically correct version of the cozy life of country gentry. The facile conventionalism of his endings provokes considerable critical disapproval, particularly in the case of *Hermsprong,* in which the main characters' retreat into domestic bliss is topped off by the revelation of the rather improbable secret of Hermsprong's birth. Butler is representative when she dismisses this conclusion as a collapse into "the worst manner of conventional plotting" (84). Instead of discarding the existing social order entirely—perhaps by having the courage to let Hermsprong remain a nameless wanderer and still marry a baron's daughter, as Butler suggests— Bage makes his democratic-minded hero turn out to be none other than Sir Charles Campinet, Lord Grondale's long-lost nephew and the rightful owner of all of the baron's land. Even with Glen's insistence that Sir Charles is a model landlord, the political orthodoxy involved in making the jacobin Hermsprong turn out to be a member of the landed gentry is discomfiting.

The literary conventionality of the ending is even more marked than the political. The deathbed repentance of Lord Grondale, the revelation of Hermsprong's identity, and the happily-ever-after life at Grondale Hall are part of a fairy-tale ending that undercuts at least some of what is argued in the book about social relations. For example, even as romantic love is being criticized by Miss Fluart's acerbic refusal to marry and "buy herself a master," the concluding image of Miss Campinet being led to the altar "dressed in love and innocence" and "a white polonese" (247-48) affirms precisely what Miss Fluart is so amusingly denying.[14] Glen's self-conscious mockery of conventional fiction does not change the fact that, on the most basic level, that is precisely what he is offering his audience. His claim that he "live[s] but to love and oblige these charming critics [female readers] . . . and give them all the satisfaction I can" (246) is obviously meant to be read ironically, but there is a measure of literal truth in it as well. However much Glen laughs at these readers, his audience, female or otherwise, determines the shape of his story from beginning to end. It is his editor—a reader, speaking for other readers—who initially halts Glen in the middle of his character sketches and starts him on the plot. By the end of the story, Glen no longer needs any such external pressures and is able to decide for himself that it is necessary for him to provide a fittingly happy ending, since readers do not like being left "at liberty to suppose [whatever they] please" (248). Boasts that he is free from any dependence upon convention have been replaced by an ironic admission that he must indeed draw upon them. It is up to us to decide whether this is a simple cop-out, or if, as Glen protests, he indeed has little choice in the matter.

The key to the matter lies perhaps in Glen's rather wistful comment about the artistic sacrifices necessitated if an author and his readers are to "part friends." If the goal is to win friends rather than to make converts, one must entertain as effectively as one harangues. No one has ever doubted Bage's abilities as an entertainer, abilities that have won his books "friends" as diverse as Godwin and Sir Walter Scott. But, as the case of Scott shows, his audience might well enjoy the entertainment while discreetly ignoring the message. "A good jest is no argument," Scott reminds his readers in his preface to Bage's novels, seeming to assume as a corollary that a good argument can't be hidden behind or sweetened with a jest (290). He was attempting, unsuccessfully as it turned out, to repopularize Bage after the political fervour of the 1790s had died away, by instructing readers to enjoy the entertainment offered by the novels while ignoring the politics. The politics interfered and offended—critics scolded Scott for reprinting such morally tendentious material—and the novel sunk from view. Scott's rather guilty pleasure in Bage's comedy and his insistent warnings to readers not to let the charm of the novel seduce them into accepting its ideas, are in themselves a tacit admission that the comedy and the politics of *Hermsprong* are inseparable and that one affects the way the other is read.

The result is a novel in which political didacticism is both tempered and somewhat diluted by the literary play used to convey the message. To use Miss Campinet's description of Miss Fluart's radicalism, it is a playfulness of the pen rather than the heart. The novel certainly charms, but in *Hermsprong* one can see the problems involved in employing a complex structure of the kind that Bage does, one which attempts to convert its readers to a new political vision even while amusing them by self-consciously calling attention to the novel's structuring conventions. The critical unhappiness with the ending is probably an indication that it is, as Eco's ideas imply, impossible for Bage to remain entirely true to his radical intent while busily mocking the conventions of the genre in which he is working. Ultimately, *Hermsprong* is a novel that is both too political simply to amuse and too intent on amusing to be wholeheartedly political. The other jacobins avoid this problem by concentrating exclusively on the failings of society, treating fiction as little more than a convenient tool for disseminating their ideas. As Godwin observes in his preface to *Caleb Williams,* there are large numbers of people who will never open "books of philosophy and science" but who nevertheless ought to be convinced of the "inestimable importance of political principles" (1). The moral comes before the medium; Godwin concludes that if he "shall have taught a valuable lesson, without subtracting from the interest and passion by which a performance of this sort ought to be characterized, he will have reason to congratulate himself on the vehicle he has chosen." Bage never adopts such a casually utilitarian attitude toward fiction, seemingly finding literary conventions just as fascinating a subject for investigation as political principles. While the more single-minded Godwin saw his novel writing as an almost entirely political act—"even the humble novel writer," he announces ironically but rather proudly in the preface to *Caleb Williams,* "might be shown to be constructively a traitor" (2)—Bage implies that his motives for writing are considerably less straightforward. Glen, at the end of *Hermsprong,* imagines indignant and unsatisfied readers asking, "for what END then did you write your book?" (248), as he teasingly skimps on the information about the future fates of Hermsprong and Miss Campinet. It is hard to imagine such a question being posed, even jokingly, about most of the other jacobin novels, in which the end for which the novel is written is hammered home quite relentlessly. Yet Bage seems to want to amuse just as earnestly as he wants to instruct; like Glen, he wants to "part friends" with his readers. Bage is a genuine political radical, and he undoubtedly has a keen sense of humour, but unfortunately he does not find a way to disentangle, on the level of narrative, his political and his comic visions; anticipating Eco, his work shows that one inescapably modifies the other. Far from lacking the intellectual rigour to pursue his political visions to a genuinely radical conclusion, Bage is intellectually honest enough to end his novel on the same note of inconclusive compromise which, because of his divided purpose, has marked both the structure of and the characters in his book. As he closes his novel with an implausibly neat and conventional denouement, Bage might even be suggesting the extremely radical notion that despite the assumptions of his fellow jacobins, the untidy complexities of political ideology cannot be satisfactorily resolved within the necessarily formulaic discourse of fiction.

Notes

1. The epigraph is taken from a letter written by Miss Campinet to Miss Fluart (32).

2. See, in particular, Todorov's "L'origine des genres" and *The Fantastic: A Structural Approach to a Literary Genre* and Culler's *Structuralist Poetics.*

3. Dorothy Blakey sees these scenes as a delightful anticipation of *Pride and Prejudice* (64). However, the motif of the foolish wife and long-suffering husband is a familiar one in eighteenth-century comedy—Cibber, for example, employs it in *The Provok'd Husband*; Goldsmith uses it in *The Vicar of Wakefield*, Sheridan in *The School for Scandal*, and so on.

4. Critics such as J. M. S. Tompkins, Allan Rodway, and Peter Faulkner have drawn parallels between Bage and Peacock. See Tompkins, *The Popular Novel in England 1770-1800*, 194; Rodway, *English Comedy*, 191-93; Faulkner, *Robert Bage*, 154.

5. In any case, the philosophical debate, at least as employed by Peacock, is not necessarily a didactic mode. By letting characters debate among themselves with little or no narrative commentary, the author suggests that a wide range of opinions is available on any given topic, not that one idea is superior to all others.

6. Bage was not alone in mocking this convention; by the beginning of the nineteenth century, making a jocular reference to the danger of heroines' journeys had itself become conventional. Austen, for example, writes in *Northanger Abbey*: "[Catherine's journey] was performed with suitable quietness and uneventful safety. Neither robbers nor tempests befriended them, nor one lucky overturn to introduce them to the hero" (5:43). Similarly, Edgeworth writes in her novella *Angelina*: "[Angelina] had the misfortune—and it is a great misfortune to a young lady of her way of thinking—to meet with no difficulties or adventures, nothing interesting upon her journey. She arrived, with inglorious safety, at Cardiffe" (1:229). The ubiquity

of such references suggests how thoroughly Glen is imbued with the literary tastes of his day.

7. See Wayne C. Booth's *The Rhetoric of Fiction*, 234-40, for a discussion of Sterne imitations in eighteenth-century literature. Booth sees Bage as one of the few successful imitators of Sterne's narrative method, and Faulkner also points out examples of Bage's debt to Sterne in his edition of *Hermsprong*.

8. Admittedly, this is an old complaint, one made by Clarissa as well as by Wollstonecraft, so one can argue that Miss Campinet is showing herself a properly sensible heroine rather than a closet feminist. However, given the novel's ongoing concern with women's rights and Wollstonecraft's ideas, it is perfectly reasonable to hear echoes of Wollstonecraft as well as Richardson in this speech.

9. Samuel Johnson, perhaps not surprisingly, provides one of the most blunt and concise statements of this ideology, which was accepted by thinkers as otherwise different as Rousseau and Hannah More: "*Boswell*. 'To be sure there is a great difference between the offense of infidelity in a man and that of his wife.' *Johnson*. 'The difference is boundless. The man imposes no bastards upon his wife'" (*Life* 1035).

10. Witty women were anathema to conservatives. Popular conduct book writers such as More, Fordyce (117), and Gisborne (263), cautioned women who possess that "dangerous quality" to hide it or at least chasten it.

11. Mary Wollstonecraft also reviewed *Hermsprong* very favourably in the *Analytical Review*, but given Bage's sympathy with her politics, this is not particularly surprising.

12. The two reviews immediately following *Hermsprong* in the *Critical Review* suggest the quality of the reception of the more typical novel of the day: "*Geraldine, a Novel founded on a recent Event*: We are sorry that any person could be so destitute of delicacy as to make the event to which the title alludes the subject of a novel. There must have been an equal want of genius, or the author would not have produced a piece which has so little merit. *Laura, or the Orphan. A Novel. By Mrs. Burton*: A rapid succession of improbabilities."

13. See, in particular, chapter 3 of *The Popular Novel in England*.

14. The delayed revelation that Miss Campinet and Hermsprong are first cousins reinforces the too-neatly coincidental nature of the conclusion and further undermines the radical argument made

throughout. While the fresh perspective offered by Hermsprong might initially seem to represent an attempt to revitalize a moribund class from outside, the endogamous marriage in fact implies how tightly closed that class is. Even change must come from those born within its ranks. One can compare the notoriously troublesome conclusion of *Mansfield Park,* in which actual outsiders, the Crawfords, are firmly rejected and the infusion of "new" blood comes from Fanny, like Hermsprong a cousin of the family that she marries into and revitalizes.

Works Cited

Austen, Jane. *Northanger Abbey.* 1818. *Novels of Jane Austen.* Ed. R. W. Chapman. 6 vols. Oxford: Oxford University Press, 1933.

Bage, Robert. *Hermsprong, or, Man as he is not.* 1796. Ed. Peter Faulkner. Oxford: Oxford University Press, 1985.

Blakey, Dorothy. *The Minerva Press, 1790-1820.* Oxford: The Bibliographical Society, 1939.

Booth, Wayne C. *The Rhetoric of Fiction.* Chicago: Chicago University Press, 1983.

Boswell, James. *The Life of Johnson.* Ed. R. W. Chapman. London: Oxford University Press, 1935.

Butler, Marilyn. *Jane Austen and the War of Ideas.* Oxford: Clarendon Press, 1975.

Culler, Jonathan. *Structuralist Poetics.* Ithaca: Cornell University Press, 1975.

Eco, Umberto. "The Frames of Comic Freedom." *Carnival!* Ed. Thomas A. Sebeok. New York: Mouton, 1984.

Edgeworth, Maria. *Angelina. Tales and Novels.* 10 vols. The Longford Edition, 1893.

Faulkner, Peter. *Robert Bage.* Boston: Twayne, 1979.

Fordyce, James. *Sermons to Young Women.* London, 1767.

Gisborne, Thomas. *An Enquiry into the Duties of the Female Sex.* London, 1797.

Godwin, William. *Caleb Williams.* 1794. Oxford: Oxford University Press, 1982.

Kelly, Gary. *The English Jacobin Novel, 1780-1805.* Oxford: Clarendon Press, 1976.

——. "The Limits of Genre and the Institution of Literature: Romanticism Between Fact and Fiction." *Romantic Revolutions: Criticism and Theory.* Eds. Kenneth R. Johnston et. al. Bloomington: Indiana University Press, 1990. 158-75.

Rev. of *Hermsprong. The British Critic* 7 (1796): 430.

Rev. of *Hermsprong. The Critical Review.* 2nd series. 23 (1798): 234.

Rodway, Allan. *English Comedy.* London: Chatto & Windus, 1975.

Scheuermann, Mona. *Social Protest in the Eighteenth-Century English Novel.* Columbus: University of Ohio Press, 1985.

Scott, Walter. *The Lives of the Novelists.* London. 1824. J. M. Dent, 1928.

Todorov, Tzvetan. *The Fantastic: A Structural Approach to a Literary Genre.* Trans. Richard Howard. Ithaca: Cornell University Press, 1975.

——. "L'origine des genres." *La notion de littérature et autres essais.* Paris: Seuil, 1987. 27-46.

Tompkins, J. M. S. *The Popular Novel in England, 1770-1800.* London: Constable, 1932.

Nancy E. Johnson (essay date autumn 2002)

SOURCE: Johnson, Nancy E. "'Seated on her Bags of Dollars': Representations of America in the English Jacobin Novel." *The Dalhousie Review* 82, no. 3 (autumn 2002): 423-39.

[*In the following essay, Johnson studies the depiction of America as symbolic of the changing "relationship between property and subjectivity and the dilemma it caused for reformers and contractarianism at the end of the eighteenth century" in* Hermsprong; or, Man as He Is Not, *Mary Wollstonecraft's* Maria; or the Wrongs of Woman, *and Charlotte Smith's* The Young Philosopher.]

In the 1790s, the English Jacobin novel engaged in a sustained narrative critique of contractarianism. While it supported the foundational premises of contractarianism—for example, the concept of inalienable rights for the individual—it also exposed the restrictive requirements and specifications that proponents of the social contract were imposing on political agency. In the fiction of Robert Bage, Mary Wollstonecraft, and Charlotte Smith, among others, it becomes evident that liberty is a function of property.[1] To establish political authority, one has to be able to claim the right of property, which begins with self-governance and culminates in proprietorship within society.[2] Financial dependence means disqualification, and it precludes enfranchisement or claims to political authority in any form, thereby excluding large segments of the populations such as women. Consequently, the English Jacobin novel wrestled with this fundamental paradox of property. The right of property was a means of breaking open the franchise, but it also continued to be a divisive force in society. It was necessary to political agency, but its absence was a means of denying subjectivity.

One consistent narrative location for investigations into the role of property is the representation of America. When this newly independent nation appears in the English Jacobin novel, it is almost always a means to exploring the relationship between ownership and subjectivity. America was an especially vital mechanism for this particular inquiry, I suggest, for two main reasons. First, America *was* property: it was abundant in land, a site of new and expansive commerce, and a territory populated by individuals who could lay claim to self-ownership either because of the status of "noble savage" or because of their access to land and commercial enterprise. Second, America bore a significant relationship to France. Not only did they share a common enemy—Great Britain—they were also both engaged in establishing governments based on similar revolutionary sentiments. France was often seen as the exporter of democratic ideals—indeed, one of Robert Bage's characters hears the "tastes of France" in an American speech.[3] It is more likely, however, that France was influenced by the social thought of early America, not to mention that of the British Dissenting movement as well.[4] In either case, a rigorous intellectual exchange between America and France certainly seems to have informed the political philosophy of both nations in the 1790s, and their revolutionary governments shared certain republican goals. For the English Jacobin novel, then, America presented itself as a viable substitute for France when the egregious violence of the French Revolution made it difficult to tout the European nation as a model of liberty. As the decade wore on and revolutionary France turned into Napoleon's empire, America became an increasingly important alternative. Mary Wollstonecraft, when pointing out the errors made by France's revolutionary government in her *Historical and Moral View of the Origin and Progress of the French Revolution* (1794), frequently uses America as an example of "how to do it right," of how forces of resistance may transform themselves into a stable, tolerant authority, rather than a despotic state.[5]

The representations of America that I discuss in this essay are taken from three English Jacobin novels: Robert Bage's *Hermsprong* (1796), Mary Wollstonecraft's *Maria; or the Wrongs of Woman* (1798) and Charlotte Smith's *The Young Philosopher* (1798). Together they exemplify the range of possibilities that America presented to British reformers in the 1790s. In all three instances, I will argue, America in some way signifies the evolving relationship between property and subjectivity and the dilemma it caused for reformers and contractarianism at the end of the eighteenth century. Bage's *Hermsprong* celebrates America in the tradition of po-

litical travelogues, such as Brissot's *Nouveau Voyage Dans Les Etats-Unis* (1791), that set America up as a paradigm of liberty.[6] Likewise, it embraces property through a protagonist who has it all: land, commercial wealth, and self-governance. America is the solution to the dilemma of property because it offers an array of economic opportunities. Wollstonecraft's novel, in contrast, concedes that America is a nation of property, but it is far less optimistic about the benefits. For Wollstonecraft, "adoration of property is the root of all evil," and correspondingly, America is not the answer for her troubled character Henry Darnford.[7] Nonetheless, life without property, especially in the form of self-governance, leaves him vulnerable and victimized; he is trapped in the irresolvable dilemma of property. Finally, Charlotte Smith seems to abandon the struggle altogether when her family of reformers, the Glenmorrises, decides to leave England and embrace exile in America after a series of protracted dealings with the law over family inheritances. Their exile to America, however, is driven in part by the desire to construct a new society in a land that is not yet a nation. It is an act of appropriation that contradicts their efforts to leave the pursuit of property behind them. In the end, none of these novels resolves the paradox of property and subjectivity but their attempts call attention to one of the most significant limitations within contractarianism.

AMERICA: THE LAND OF ECONOMIC OPPORTUNITY

Robert Bage's novel ***Hermsprong; or Man as He Is Not*** is among the most sanguine and confident of the political novels of the 1790s. It is not encumbered by the weight of defeat or the distractions of uncertainty that plague English Jacobin fiction at the end of the decade. It does not bear the often claustrophobic atmosphere of those texts representing "things as they are," in part, because it is presenting "man as he is not," a venture of hope and possibility. Moreover, it is one of the few English Jacobin novels that use a classical comedic structure to expose corruption and advocate reform. The driving force behind this optimism is the protagonist "Hermsprong," who is not only brave, brawny, and debonair but also a great financial success—and an American. He is a celebration of abundance, a cheerful embodiment of property. He is indeed "sprung" from Hermes, the god of commerce, the protector of traders. His triumph over the social forces of evil, which in this novel are the restrictions of outmoded tradition, and his marriage to the lovely Caroline Campinet are the causes of celebration at the close of the text.

In stark contrast to Hermsprong is the narrator and alleged author of the story, Gregory Glen, the illegitimate son of an innocent country maiden who is led astray by a young squire. The chaste Ellen Glen, her son tells us, "defended the citadel of her honour all the preceding summer," but had, alas, "surrendered at the close of it, subdued by a too tender heart, and a flowered cotton gown" (2). In spite of the fact that he was "begot" by a gentleman, Glen regards himself the "son of nobody" (1). He bears his father's Christian name but his mother's family name; thus, he reaps little benefit from, and casts no shame on, a family of status and wealth. In addition, Glen is perceived to be the property of others. As he is shifted from caretaker to caretaker (his great grandmother, his great aunt, the parish's Goody Peat, and, finally, Parson Brown), he is assessed for the financial debt he incurs. When he settles with Parson Brown, Glen observes that Brown "considered me as deodand," a form of chattel that is given over to pious service because it has caused a death (5).[8] In most legal instances, deodand refers to an animal or a vehicle that might have caused a fatal accident. Pollock and Maitland cite "[h]orses, oxen, carts, boats, mill-wheels and cauldrons" as the most common forms of *deodand*.[9] Glen, however, presumably acquires this status because his mother died in childbirth and hence he bears the culpability of her loss. His humanity does not exempt him from being cast as chattel; his entire life as the "son of nobody" prepares the way for this culminating image.

Still, Glen's status as the less-than-human property of others does not protect him from the sway of such human impulses as romantic love, as well as the disappointment that often follows. He is soon besotted with affection for Parson Brown's niece, a young woman well trained in the enchantments of dress and educated on romances and novels. When she throws him over for "a young hero, who measured cloth in a neighbouring town," he is devastated and resolves to commit suicide (6). While Glen's life story thus far is certainly a criticism of specific laws—those governing poverty, illegitimate births, and suicide—it also elucidates an assumption of ownership that becomes strikingly evident after Glen is apparently saved from killing himself. Just as Glen is about to exercise his agency by explaining his intention to Mrs. Garnet, who is nursing him, she lectures Glen on the sinfulness of suicide. According to Mrs. Garnet, he tells us, had he been successful, his damnation would have been assured because the great sin was in "considering my life as my own property, and throwing it away when I was weary of it" (8). His suicide would have been an assertion of the self that is not his to assert and an act of disobedience, akin to that of Adam and Eve; Glen himself confesses that he had "eaten of the tree of knowledge and was ashamed" (7). He has attempted to destroy the self to which others had already laid claim.

Glen's tainted parentage and loss of self sets him up as the antithesis to Hermsprong. On the one hand, Glen seems to have found a kindred spirit in this man who is also an outsider in the village of Grondale and whose odd and seemingly fabricated name obscures *his* parentage. But the singular difference that will distinguish Hermsprong from Glen and render Hermsprong a hero is his access to property, beginning with his ownership of himself. Whereas Hermsprong is able to embrace self-determination and the natural and civil rights that are due him, Glen is not. In a conversation with Glen, Hermsprong boasts, "I see not the difficulty of man's becoming a judge, tolerably just, of the temper of his mind, . . . I have energies, and I feel them; as a man, I have rights, and will support them; and, in acting according to principles I believe to be just, I have not yet learned to fear" (98). Glen's response to Hermsprong's self-assurance is one of both admiration and trepidation. Of Hermsprong's "pretensions," he asks, "[i]s this the stuff of which the pride of our people of rank and fashion is made? That it is pride of some sort, I have no doubt; for I, Gregory Glen, the son of nobody, felt myself raised, exalted by it. I almost began to think myself a man. But it is a word of bad augury. Kings like it not; parsons preach it down; and justices of the peace send out their warrants to apprehend it" (99). The dangers to which Glen refers—the controversy over the publication of Paine's *Rights of Man,* the Treason Trials of 1794, and the network of spies that Pitt set loose on the British populous—were very real and serious impediments to the sort of claims to the "rights of man" that Hermsprong espouses. And it was men like Glen who were most vulnerable. Hermsprong, in contrast, was insulated from these fears, and his ambiguous familial history renders him an "everyman" rather than a "nobody" because of his extraordinary access to property and because of his ties to various nations—including America—that make that access possible.

Hermsprong is a composite of national identities. He is born of an English father and a French mother in America, where he was raised until he comes of age at sixteen. While his father gives him an English title (the revelation of "noble" birth at the end of the narrative), and his mother gives him property in France, Hermsprong's upbringing in America affords him his most powerful sense of self. It is what allows him to forego the strictures of formal patriarchalism and proceed on the strength of his individual talent and merit. It is also what provides him with an alternative model of manhood, one that is stronger than the European version. Hermsprong uses his mythical name and American connections to establish himself as a different kind of "nobleman" who will challenge the forces of traditional rank and title: the "noble savage." Identifying with the Native Americans, among whom he was raised, would seem to marginalize and isolate Hermsprong in the context of English society. But with the romantic persona of the noble savage comes an assumption of innate power and human potential, two ideals that suddenly seemed within reach in the 1790s. Unlike the European, struggling with the allocation of political authority in a system of civil rights, the primitive figure is untroubled by a division between the individual and the community, the personal and the public, the legal subject and the law. Self-determination is a given; it is not bestowed or withheld by the institutions of advanced civilization. Furthermore, the noble savage is closer to that state of nature where, according to contractarians such as Locke and Paine, those endowed and protected by natural rights decide to form a nation while still maintaining certain benefits of natural law.[10]

Significantly, it is not his primitive roots alone that empower Hermsprong. Bolstering his status as a noble savage is his inheritance of "commerce" as a newly respected tradition in its American form. Hermsprong's father, alienated emotionally and financially from his family in England and driven abroad, was a successful fur trader with the Native Americans. He made trade a form of diplomacy and used commerce to bridge the gap between the European world and the "uncivilized" world. He lived among the native inhabitants, learned their language, religion, and philosophy, and in that way "gratif[ied] his ardent desire to know man" and made a good bit of money (166). In the experience of Hermsprong's father, we see one of the most effective manifestations of the transactions of commerce in the midst of a people living in a state of nature.[11] Hermsprong's paternal inheritance, therefore, is the ability to act as a conduit between cultures, and he does so, like his father, through the mechanism of property. Though he claims to be "born a savage," Hermsprong's European parentage affords him distance and allows him to consider himself a philosopher, an observer of the very culture in which he was raised (73). He then functions as something of an ambassador when he explains and interprets American life to those in England. What enables his travel and independence is wealth (gained through the commerce of his father and the land of his mother) and self-ownership, an assumption that lies behind one of the privileges of his American birth, self-determination.

Although Hermsprong's American upbringing (the combined force of the primitive and the commercial) seems to be the primary source of his extraordinary confidence and power, it is the revelation of his true identity at the end of the novel that completes and solidifies his authority. Hermsprong, we learn, is most definitely not akin to "the son of nobody." His real name is Sir Charles Campinet, and he is the rightful heir to Lord Grondale's estate. It turns out that Hermsprong is an offspring of Great Britain, much like America herself. He is a messenger—thereby fulfilling another aspect of his mythical pseudonym—bearing news of the great potential of man and the lessons learned from an alternative civilization. He denies that America is a utopia, and he concedes to an Englishman that "their government

would not do for you," precisely because the wheels of English government are greased with wealth and politicians are addicted to luxury (134). Throughout his ambassadorial discourse, Hermsprong eschews material prosperity and rejects an equation of money with happiness. He depicts America as the land of simplicity and moderation, of "simple plenty, strength, and health" (134). Still, he acknowledges the power of wealth and realizes that it is the source of his independence. He also seems to recognize that it is essential to political authority in England, even in the newly emerging social contract that should incorporate an expansion of the franchise. If Hermsprong is "the new man" endowed with "the rights of man," then the figure of modernity is decidedly a propertied one. As Hermsprong's entire identity unfolds, he becomes the embodiment of all sorts of property: commercial wealth, from his father's trade in America; landed wealth, from his mother in France and Lord Grondale's fortune in England; and lastly, as the undisputed owner of himself, a condition that affords him his "freeborn mind" (73) and sustains him in his efforts to displace the outmoded patriarch. America, rather than the more troublesome revolutionary France, is the site of liberty and this liberty is unequivocally girded by property.

AMERICA: THE LAND OF COMMERCE

In spite of Bage's apparent endorsement of property as the defining factor for enfranchisement in the social contract, he does acknowledge the limitations of this requirement for women. His heroine and counterpart to Hermsprong, Maria Fluart, finds herself restricted rather than freed by wealth. A similar fate awaits Mary Wollstonecraft's protagonist Maria in her unfinished novel *Maria; or the Wrongs of Woman*. Here, too, property plays a central role in the struggle for subjectivity and political agency, but it is far more troublesome than it is in Bage's **Hermsprong.** The manipulation of an inheritance by Maria's uncle, to ensure that it bypasses the clutches of her husband, sets into motion the tragic events that lead to Maria's imprisonment in a madhouse and the loss of her daughter. For Wollstonecraft, property is "an iron hand," a "demon," that preoccupies and dominates society, resulting in gross inequalities and tyrannical laws.[12] Nonetheless, proprietorship of the self—a crucial form of property—remained a cornerstone of contractarianism, creating a dilemma for an English Jacobin author who was at the very heart of the campaign for rights.

In Wollstonecraft's novel, as in Bage's, a representation of America provides an opportunity for a discussion of property and self-determination. America appears when Henry Darnford, Maria's love interest, tells the story of his life. Although he was not born in America, nearly all of his narrative takes place there, and, like Hermsprong, it is where he has come of age. But Darnford is a very different creature than Hermsprong. Whereas Hermsprong is "man as he is not" but would hope to be, Darnford is the more realistic "man as he is" that reflects a dark state of existence. Having been kidnapped by unknown assailants, for mysterious reasons, Darnford is confined to a madhouse. There in the prison, Maria (who has also been forcibly incarcerated) falls in love with him, and they exchange the stories of their lives. They are messengers of a sort (like Hermsprong), and they are exercising agency by communicating their personal narratives; however, they converse inside a prison and within constrictions that are diametrically opposed to Hermsprong's exceptional freedom of movement and expression.

America is not a source of liberation or empowerment for Darnford. He is sent there by the British military, after purchasing a commission in a newly-raised regiment, and fights for Britain against the colonists seeking independence. When he is wounded, he has a political change of heart and decides to buy a piece of land and stay on as a resident. Darnford's description of America, however, is coloured by his disillusionment, a process he undergoes when he grows restless in the countryside, travels the vast terrain in a futile search for aesthetic pleasures, and finally wearies of the false and frenetic disposition of the cities. In fact, his unhappiness with America is what propels him back to London and occasions his present crisis. Darnford casts the young nation as a site of broken promises and lost opportunities, a scene of excessive poverty and wealth, and a place of shallow gestures toward cultivation. His depiction of the *nouveau riche* of America is from the perspective of the British gentry and is delivered in a derisive tone.[13] The wealthy of America, he says, engage in vulgar display for lack of refinement: "the cultivation of the fine arts, or literature, had not introduced into the first circles that polish of manners which renders the rich so essentially superior to the poor in Europe" (45). Perhaps his most biting condemnation of American culture is his image of the American spirit of independence and determination failing to make the transition from the religious prejudice that fueled the revolution to an emancipation of the understanding, a bursting into the light of reason. Instead, the remarkable strength and resolve of the revolutionary colonists turned to commerce, and the figure of the American individual now bears "a head enthusiastically enterprising," and "a cold selfishness of heart" (45).

"Gambling" is how Darnford defines American commerce.[14] With utter contempt, he describes how "[t]he resolution, that led them [colonists], in pursuit of independence, to embark on rivers like seas, to search for unknown shores, and to sleep under the hovering mists of endless forests, whose baleful damps agued their limbs" has now devolved into "commercial speculation." Americans are no better than his own English

parents, people of fortune who were confined to an unhappy marriage and also turned to gambling. "He was fond of the turf," Darnford explains, "she of the card-table."[15] Although Darnford is not a consistent spokesperson for reformers, his disdain for commerce seems to be an aversion to a world view based on chance, which worked against the universal premises that were being espoused by reformers such as Wollstonecraft herself. Speculation is antithetical to reason.[16] It discards the movements of logic, and the sequences of cause and effect. It ignores first principles, rational inquiry, and several of the arguments reformers and *philosophes* of the 1790s were using to promote an expansion of the franchise. Moreover, while gambling is a circulation of wealth, it is a "hyperactive redistribution" that was at odds with efforts to reallocate wealth through a transformation of the body politic.[17] The novel *Wrongs of Woman* itself makes an attempt to show that nothing is the result of pure chance. There are, in the end, reasons why Darnford and Maria are in such dire situations, and it is the job of the enquirer—the novelist and philosopher—to discover and explain those causes.

When Darnford purchases property in the American countryside, builds a house and plants his crops, he establishes himself as a stable proprietor and thus fulfills a contractarian ideal. But obtaining property does not complete, satisfy or seemingly empower Darnford. We do not see it transform him into a spokesperson for the "rights of man" or a citizen endowed with political authority. The ownership of land breeds restlessness, and the option of commerce is abhorrent to Darnford. When he eventually decides to abandon America, Darnford leaves us with a final image of the fledgling nation as "the land of liberty and vulgar aristocracy, seated on her bags of dollars," and he flies back to London. However, only a week after Darnford's return, he is imprisoned. He is "knocked down in a private street, and hurried, in a state of insensibility, into a coach," which brings him to the madhouse where he is now locked up (47). Hence, when Darnford leaves the security of America and returns to England, he is faced with the predicament of a lack of property in the very fundamental form of self-ownership, and this leaves him vulnerable to the law and the outlaw alike. Darnford, like so many women, is in the end caught in the double-bind of property. We are left wondering, in spite of his disparaging depiction of America, whether or not he was better off in the nation of commerce.

America was for Wollstonecraft less a symbol of liberty and more a sign of economic opportunism that corrupted, rather than enhanced, the self. In her representation of America, the fulfillment of subjectivity that is deeply embedded in the American promise is a double-edged sword: necessary for financial independence and political authority, but divisive and oppressive to those without (and there are always those without). America becomes an exquisite example of how the idea that property alone is the basis for freedom is a flawed notion. Still, without property, as we see in the examples of the novel's characters, identity is either imprisoned or denied. Ownership of the self is essential to self-preservation. While Wollstonecraft's novel offers no solution to the dilemma of property and subjectivity, it exposes the difficulties facing contractarians at the end of the eighteenth century.

AMERICA: "LE VRAI BEAU"

When Charlotte Smith confronts the paradox of property in *The Young Philosopher,* she abandons the struggle—and she does so by pointing her protagonists in the direction of America. But this is not before she too examines the forces of wealth and ownership and, like Wollstonecraft, determines them to be if not demonic then certainly destructive. The Glenmorrises, who are the lost and persecuted reformers in the novel, decide that after a series of trials and tribulations the best solution for their difficulties is exile to America. This self-imposed remove, they conclude, is preferable to continuing a losing battle in Britain and condemning themselves to years of abuse and condemnation. In the Glenmorrises' plan, America is represented as a site of childlike innocence and purity, a territory that barely constitutes a nation. The land of commerce is recast in aesthetic terms and transformed into a country of "*le vrai beau,*" defined as "the great simple."[18] Smith addresses the problem of property through this conversion of America—that is, by denying the value of an ostentatious accumulation of wealth and by turning real property (land) back into the form of landscape, owned by no one but appreciated by all. Yet, in spite of her valiant effort to change the parameters of the struggle by walking away from the pursuit of property, Smith's invocation of America as the solution is a romantic gesture, which does not resolve the problem but rather tries to gloss over the social and political realities of a nation.

Smith's novel, published late in the decade of the 1790s, is encumbered by failed efforts at reform within Britain and the dismal reports coming out of France. It is a review of radicalism at the end of a turbulent and, at times, deeply disappointing decade. As in so many English Jacobin novels, at the heart of nearly all of the struggles within *The Young Philosopher* are disputes over rightful inheritances and the dispersal of family wealth. Before the pursuance of property is abandoned, it is a preoccupation of the central characters. George Delmont, the "young philosopher" of the title, is drawn into a series of frustrating financial and legal entanglements because of his brother's avarice. As a result, he becomes acquainted with the dark figures of property: the lawyers, bookies, and loan sharks. Mr. Glenmorris is the character most often treated as property, as "a bale of goods" (II:239). He is kidnapped, held for ransom, and eventually "bought" (his ransom paid) by friends, only to be imprisoned eventually for debt—his person deemed the equivalent of money owed. Meanwhile, Mrs. Glenmorris is on a quest to obtain her daughter's rightful inheritance from her family, the De Verdons. She proceeds in search of justice but learns that the law's *raison d'être* is the protection of property. What employs the lawyers is the myriad of "claims, liens, demands, and rights . . . lying and being in the estates, fortunes, assets and effects, sums of money in government securities, mortgages or bonds, or lands, domains, forests, woods, coppices, parks, warrens, marshes, heaths, orchards, gardens, or paddocks, commons, rights of common, fee farm and copyholds," and the list goes on (3:56-57).[19]

Thus, the action of the novel is driven by characters competing for the rights of ownership. But the pursuance of property, Smith's protagonists find, divides families, isolates individuals, and drags parties into the circular reasoning, confounding discourse, and indefinitely deferring motions of law. Moreover, each pursuit fails. George Delmont's attempts to restore his modest fortune prove to be futile. He never recovers the money he lent his brother and never successfully obtains a large part of his inheritance. Mr. Glenmorris cannot extricate himself from debtor's prison and thereby act with self-governance. It is through the generosity of a cousin that he is finally released. Mrs. Glenmorris's endeavors on behalf of her daughter are not just unsuccessful, they turn out to be dangerous and push her headlong into an emotional and physical breakdown. Striving for property, then, does not seem to be the answer, and property is not the mantle that will be passed on to the succeeding generations in the cases of the Delmonts and the Glenmorrises. By the end of the novel, when the central characters gather together under a cloud of defeat, they must decide how to proceed—and in the instance of Mrs. Glenmorris, it is a matter of the most fundamental form of subjectivity, the preservation of life. When they choose exile to America, they opt to abandon their struggles for property, and, quite significantly, they also try to free subjectivity from the reign of property.

America is the device through which the attempted liberation occurs. And Glenmorris, functioning a bit like Hermsprong, fashions himself America's primary spokesperson. Readers have certainly been set up, thus far, for Delmont's and the Glenmorrises' decision to embrace exile in America. We have been romanced with descriptions of America that render it maybe not the ideal choice but surely the best at hand. Furthermore, the Glenmorrises have already been living in exile in America because of Glenmorris's debt and his political sentiments. Their return to England was only for the purpose of claiming family inheritances, even though it also gave them a chance to reassess their options and reflect on the characters of both nations. The critique of Britain is, expectedly, harsh, though based on history and experience. In contrast, Glenmorris' advocacy of America rests on expectation and vision. His reasons for embracing America are wrapped in future hope and promise, in the unknown, and in the imagination. America's traditional role as a "child" of the mother country renders it only partly formed and therefore a site of possibility and, to some extent, purity. It is a society still waiting to be "raised," to be shaped and molded. In addition, much as Alison Conway observes that, "in radical social theories of the 1790s the child plays a critical role as the image of a citizen as yet unmarked by prejudice or tradition,"[20] America in Smith's novel is thought to provide an opportunity to observe unfettered and untainted humanity. Glenmorris sees in America the "great book of nature [, that] is open" to those who wish to engage in "noble study" and examine "human nature unadulterated by inhuman prejudice" (4:392). America is nature, rather than property.

One consequence of the assumption that America is a primitive, and hence unformed, nation is the further supposition that it does not require national loyalty or even legal citizenship. America is poised to welcome those who are "citizens of the world," those who choose to live where they do, according to their principles, not alliances. America serves Glenmorris's idealistic assertion that "wherever a thinking man enjoys the most uninterrupted domestic felicity, and sees his species the most content, *that* is his country" (4:395). He finds in America a chance to reject outright the restrictions and exclusive identifications of nationalism that have in his experience given governments the opportunity to erect borders of all kinds that inevitably result in dividing and victimizing the populace. As a "child-nation" or as no nation at all, America is not in a position to control political authority, to endow only the propertied with rights and leave the financially dependent without autonomy and without protection. It is not equipped to bestow or withhold self-determination, as is the case in Britain. The "state," in Glenmorris's design, is not America but the family itself, which exercises the subjectivity and personal agency of its individual members by choosing its home regardless of the boundaries and limitations of nationalism. "If I have those I love with me," concludes Glenmorris, "is not every part of the globe equally my country?" (4:390).

The final effort to diminish the importance of property, and to lessen its influence on subjectivity, appears in Glenmorris's use of aesthetic terms to describe the American experience. In defending exile to America in a discussion with the Godwinian Mr. Armitage, Glenmorris explains that he derives pleasure from living in a place "where human life [is] in progressive improvement," and, correspondingly, that he suffers repulsion and disgust from witnessing "abject meanness" used "to obtain the advantages of affluence" (4:201-02). A society in which a rapacious citizenry are relentlessly vying for wealth is ugly, a grotesque "spectacle of court figures in hoops and periwigs," whereas a community in which content visionaries seek only personal integrity and happiness is beautiful, an "exquisitely simple Grecian statue" (4:392). To embrace an aesthetic of simplicity, as Glenmorris does, is to reject the supremacy of property. The accumulation of wealth results only in gaudiness; it weighs one down and distorts one's perceptions like the prejudices and prescriptions of previous generations. It also obscures the self, which may emerge in all its elegant glory, fully intact (like a classical statue), when freed from the concerns of property beyond those of self-ownership. The great pleasure of the aesthetic is in the exercise of personal agency, the creative expression of the self. "To cultivate the earth of another continent," Glenmorris joyously declares, "to carry the arts of civil life, without its misery and its vices, to the wild regions of the globe, had in it a degree of *sublimity*" [my italics] (4:210). In the immense physical expanse of a vast uncultivated American landscape, is the blank sheet of white paper that is Locke's articulation of the *tabula rasa*.[21] It is the infant's mind, on which experience is still to be written, and it is Glenmorris, his family, and other reformers like them who will enjoy inscribing this new society. Therein lies potential and power; therein lies beauty.

Ultimately, America is "*le vrai beau*," the true beauty, and that is because it represents, for Glenmorris, "the great simple" (4:392), the grand abandonment of property. For America to replace France as the New Jerusalem, as the promising new commonwealth for those seeking *liberté,* it has to be transformed from the land of economic opportunity and the land of commerce to an aesthetic form because the pursuit of property has become such a debilitating problem. However, the effort to depict America as a white sheet of paper, a child-nation, or an amorphous territory that serves as a gathering site for citizens of the world, is a gesture to ahistoricize a political entity, thereby working against one of the principles of contractarianism: an acknowledgement of history and process. The contract that binds the governed to the governors is a product of a single moment in a social and political evolution, and it is subject to change, dissolution, and reformation by each succeeding generation. Glenmorris attempts to bypass process and impose a false point of origin. Moreover, to deny America's history and nationhood—to erase its native settlements, even its invasions and re-settlements—is of course an act of appropriation, one that lands the earnest reformers of *The Young Philosopher* right back in the predicament of property that they sought to flee. The expression of self-determination is still manifest through an act of proprietorship.

None of these English Jacobin novels sheds much light on the nuances, developments, or emerging cultures of America. In fact, any reliable information on the newly independent colonies is strikingly missing. Rather, America serves as a terrain upon which the relationship between property and subjectivity is explored and exposed. The confusion that Smith's novel generates conveys turmoil within the ranks of contractarianism at the turn of the century. The optimism of Bage's Hermsprong turns out to be quite justified; he is the figure—the propertied man—who does well by the social contract. And Wollstonecraft's novel is rightfully grim as it illuminates the difficulties that property poses for some members of the commonwealth; they will be excluded from political agency. In one text, America provides opportunities; in the other, America holds false promise. In Smith's novel, the slate is wiped clean and America is relegated to the imagination—but even there ownership creeps back in, and no one, we discover, is ultimately free from Wollstonecraft's "iron hand" of property.

Notes

1. For an extended discussion of liberty as a function of property in early contractarian thought, see C. B. Macpherson, *The Political Theory of Possessive Individualism* (London: Oxford UP, 1962).

2. In *Two Treatises on Government,* Locke establishes ownership of the self as the most fundamental form of proprietorship and an essential precursor to political authority. "Though the Earth, and all inferior Creatures be common to all Man, yet every Man has a *Property* in his own *Person.* This no Body has any Right to but himself." See Locke, *Two Treatises of Government,* ed. Peter Laslett (Cambridge: Cambridge UP, 1960) 287. Nearly a century later in his influential *Rights of Man,* Paine describes citizenship as a "proprietorship in society." See Thomas Paine, *Rights of Man,* 2nd ed. (London: J. S. Jordan, 1791) 53.

3. Robert Bage, *Hermsprong; or Man As He Is Not* (London, 1796; Oxford: Oxford UP, 1985) 73.

4. Seamus Deane, *The French Revolution and Enlightenment in England, 1789-1832* (Cambridge: Harvard UP, 1988) 162-63. Roy Porter, *The Creation of the Modern World* (New York: Norton, 2000) 6-12.

5. Mary Wollstonecraft, *Historical and Moral View of the Origin and Progress of the French Revolution,* in *The Works of Mary Wollstonecraft,* ed. Janet Todd and Marilyn Butler, 7 vols. (New York: New York UP, 1989) 6:1-235.

6. Jean-Pierre Brissot, *Nouveau Voyage Dans Les Etat-Unies de L'Amerique Septentrionale, fait en 1788, part J. P. Brissot (Warville) Citoyen Fran-*cois—*Travels in the United States of North America* (Paris, 1791).

7. Wollstonecraft, *Letters Written in Sweden, Norway and Denmark,* in *Works,* ed. Todd and Butler, 6:325.

8. *Oxford English Dictionary,* s.v. "deodand." See also, Sir William Blackstone, *Commentaries on the Laws of England,* 2 vols. (Philadelphia: J. B. Lippincott & Co., 1870) 1:224-25.

9. Sir Frederick Pollock and Frederic William Maitland, *The History of English Law,* 2nd ed., 2 vols. (Cambridge: Cambridge UP, 1898) 1:473.

10. Locke, *Two Treatises of Government* 330-32; Paine, *Rights of Man* 53-57.

11. The idea of property transactions in a state of nature is also discussed by Locke in his *Two Treatises of Government.* See 301-02.

12. Mary Wollstonecraft, *A Vindication of the Rights of Men,* in *The Works of Mary Wollstonecraft,* ed. Janet Todd and Marilyn Butler, 7 vols. (New York: New York UP, 1989) 5:14, 24.

13. Nancy Armstrong and Leonard Tennenhouse discuss the phenomenon of a "second-tier" English aristocracy in America, in *The Imaginary Puritan* (Berkeley: U of California P, 1992) 43-44.

14. Wollstonecraft's association of speculation with America is derived, at least in part, from personal experience. Her brother Charles and her lover Gilbert Imlay both became involved in speculative schemes in America that often failed. See Janet Todd, *Mary Wollstonecraft: A Revolutionary Life* (New York: Columbia UP, 2000) 197, 232, 260, 290.

15. Mary Wollstonecraft, *Maria; or the Wrongs of Women* (London: J. Johnson, 1798; New York: Norton, 1975) 44.

16. Thomas Kavanaugh, *Enlightenment and the Shadows of Chance* (Baltimore: Johns Hopkins UP, 1993) 4-5.

17. *Enlightenment and the Shadows of Chance* 29-30.

18. Charlotte Smith, *The Young Philosopher: A Novel,* 4 vols. (London: T. Cadell, Jun. and W. Davies, 1798) 4:392.

19. Smith was executor to her father-in-law's estate and was embroiled in a lengthy legal battle as a result; thus, she experienced first hand the law's preoccupation with property and its propensity to complicate and delay rather than solve and expedite matters. See Loraine Fletcher, *Charlotte Smith: A Critical Biography* (New York: St. Martin's Press, 1998) 337.

20. Alison Conway, "Nationalism, Revolution, and the Female Body: Charlotte Smith's *Desmond*," *Women's Studies* 24 (June 1995): 404.

21. See Book II, Chapter 1, Section 2 of John Locke, *An Essay Concerning Human Understanding* (London: J. M. Dent & Sons, 1976) 33.

FURTHER READING

Bibliography

Moran, Michael G. "Robert Bage (1728-1801): A Bibliography." *Bulletin of Bibliography* 38, no. 4 (October-December 1981): 173-78.

Presents a concise bibliography of Bage's writings, along with secondary criticism.

Criticism

Faulkner, Peter. "*Man As He Is*: The Establishment Challenged." In *Robert Bage*, pp. 102-21. Boston: Twayne Publishers, 1979.

Offers a scholarly analysis of *Man As He Is*, maintaining that although the novel follows certain literary and social conventions of the time in its structure and characterization, Bage's views expressed in the novel are a radical departure from those expressed by the majority of his contemporaries.

London, April. "The Discourse of Manliness: Samuel Jackson Pratt and Robert Bage." In *Women and Property in the Eighteenth-Century English Novel*, pp. 141-53. Cambridge: Cambridge University Press, 1999.

Places Bage firmly within the tradition of liberal-minded, class-conscious satire.

Steeves, Harrison R. "An Eighteenth-Century Shaw: Robert Bage." In *Before Jane Austen: The Shaping of the English Novel in the Eighteenth Century*, pp. 272-91. New York: Holt, Rinehart and Winston, 1965.

Traces the development of Bage's views as expressed in his novels and likens this progression to that evidenced in the novels and plays of Bernard Shaw.

Additional coverage of Bage's life and career is contained in the following sources published by Thomson Gale: *Dictionary of Literary Biography*, **Vol. 39; and** *Literature Resource Center.*

Benjamin Constant
1767-1830

(Full name Henri Benjamin Constant de Rebecque) Swiss-born French novelist, essayist, diarist, journalist, autobiographer, speech writer, and translator.

The following entry presents criticism on Constant's works from 1972 to 2002. For further information on Constant's life and career, see *NCLC*, Volume 6.

INTRODUCTION

Renowned during his lifetime as a statesman and political writer, Constant is remembered today for his novel, *Adolphe* (1816). Commonly thought to be based on Constant's romance with the French writer Germaine de Staël, the novel recounts the affair of an egocentric young man and a married woman who dies when she realizes the insincerity of her lover's feelings. Critics particularly praise Constant's keen analysis of the title character, who is caught in the conflict between passion and reason. Hailed as strikingly modern in its theme and analytical nature, *Adolphe* is admired equally for its spare prose style. Constant's precise, unadorned language is considered extraordinarily evocative, and many critics have lauded the author's skill in capturing and relating elusive thoughts and concepts with remarkable clarity.

BIOGRAPHICAL INFORMATION

Constant was born in Lausanne, Switzerland. His mother died two weeks after his birth, and his father placed the boy first in the care of relatives, then with a governess, and finally with a succession of eccentric and difficult tutors. At thirteen Constant was taken to England to enroll at Oxford University, but was turned away because of his age. He subsequently studied at the University of Erlangen in Germany and at Edinburgh University in Scotland. In 1787 Constant initiated the first of a series of notable love affairs when he became involved with Isabelle de Charrière, a woman of letters twenty-seven years his senior. In spite of his marriage in 1789, Constant maintained his relationship with Charrière until approximately 1795, when he became enamored of the noted intellectual and author Staël. Although both were married, Constant and Staël had a daughter together and were involved in a romantic relationship until 1811.

It was during his liaison with Staël that Constant became active in French politics. A supporter of Barras throughout the period of the Directory, Constant was elected to the tribunate, but, opposing the Bonaparte regime, lost his post in 1802 and a year later followed Staël into exile. During the next several years Constant alternated between Switzerland and Weimar, Germany, where he came in contact with the primary forces behind the German Romantic movement: August Wilhelm von Schlegel, Friedrich von Schlegel, Johann Wolfgang von Goethe, and Friedrich von Schiller, whose play *Wallenstein* Constant translated into French. Constant was productive during this period, working on his *De la religion considérée dans sa source, ses formes, et ses développements* (1824-31), a historical consideration of religion that was to be a lifelong project. In addition, Constant composed political essays advancing his strong liberal theories, notably *De l'esprit de conquête et de l'usurpation, dans leurs rapports avec la civilisation européenne* (1814; *Prophecy from the Past. Benjamin Constant on Conquest and Usurpation*), an indictment of Napoleon's regime. Constant subsequently came under criticism by reconciling with the Empire of the Hundred Days, but conditions had stabilized by 1819 so that he was able to win election to the Chamber of Deputies. Until the time of his death Constant served with distinction in various government positions in addition to writing numerous political pamphlets and contributing political articles to newspapers.

MAJOR WORKS

Of his literary endeavors, Constant reportedly took the most pride in his *De la religion considérée dans sa source, ses formes, et ses développements*. Although it was received well in its time, later critics have often overlooked the work. Constant's political works are seldom addressed by English-language critics; somewhat more critical attention has been granted to Constant's autobiographical writings, however, perhaps because they help to illuminate *Adolphe*. The *Journal intime de Benjamin Constant et lettres à sa famille et à ses amis* (1895), which incorporates his diary and selected letters, is generally valued by critics for the revelations it provides into Constant's mind and personality. *Le cahier rouge de Benjamin Constant* (1907; *The Red Note-Book*) is considered a charming, picaresque account of Constant's youthful travels. Of the autobiographical writings, critics most often comment on the novel fragment

Cécile (1951), which was not discovered until the mid-twentieth century. As with *Adolphe,* this unfinished fiction is regarded as a thinly-veiled account of Constant's own life and experience, in this case his relationship with Charlotte von Hardenberg, his second wife.

CRITICAL RECEPTION

While many commentators have studied the biographical elements present in Constant's works, notably *Adolphe* and *Cécile,* a number of critical assessments focus on arguing against such a strictly biographical interpretation. These critics opine that approaching Constant's works as historical documents diminishes the author's artistic achievement. Scholars further examine the theoretical underpinnings of Constant's essays, letters, journals, and autobiography, as well as the various historical, national, theoretical, linguistic, and literary influences upon his narrative style. Most recently, critics discuss Constant's thoughts on liberalism, his refutation of the writings of Jean-Jacques Rousseau, and the relationship between Constant's conception of liberty, or "personal sovereignty," and the democratic ideals espoused by such writers as Alexís de Tocqueville. *Adolphe* has been widely praised for its penetrating character analysis, austere style, and expression of modern sensibility, and is regarded by many scholars as a literary masterpiece.

PRINCIPAL WORKS

Des effets de la terreur (essay) 1797

Des reactions politiques (essay) 1797

Wallstein [translator; from the play *Wallenstein* by Friedrich von Schiller] (play) 1809

De l'esprit de conquête et de l'usurpation, dans leurs rapports avec la civilisation européenne [*Prophecy from the Past. Benjamin Constant on Conquest and Usurpation*] (essay) 1814

Réflexions sur les constitutions, la distribution, et les garanties dans une monarchi constitutionelle (essay) 1814

"De la responsabilité des ministres" ["On the Responsibility of Ministers"] (essay) 1815; published in the journal *Pamphleteer*

Adolphe: Anecdote trouvée dans les papiers d'un inconnu et publiée par M. B. de Constant [*Adolphe: An Anecdote Found among the Papers of an Unknown Person and Published by Benjamin de Constant*] (novel) 1816

Mémoires sur les Cent-Jours en forme de letters. 2 vols. (letters) 1820-22

De la religion considérée dans sa source, ses formes, et ses développements (essay) 1824-31

Mélanges de literature et de politique (essay) 1829

"Réflexions sur la tragédié" (essay) 1829; published in the journal *Revue de Paris*

Lettres de Benjamin Constant à Madame de Récamier, 1807-1830 (letters) 1882

Journal intime de Benjamin Constant et lettres à sa famille et à ses amis (journal and letters) 1895

*Le cahier rouge de Benjamin Constant [*The Red Note-Book*] (autobiography) 1907

Cécile (unfinished novel) 1951

Journaux intimes (journals) 1952

Benjamin Constant: Oeuvres [edited by Alfred Roulin and Charles Roth] (novel, unfinished novel, autobiography, journals, essays, and speeches) 1967

De la liberté chez les modernes. Ecrits politiques [edited by Marcel Gauchet] (essays) 1980

Correspondance générale I (1774-1792) [edited by C. P. Courtney and Dennis Wood] (letters) 1992

*This work was translated by Norman Cameron and published in *Adolphe and The Red Note-Book,* 1948.

CRITICISM

E. Cappadocia (essay date 1972)

SOURCE: Cappadocia, E. "Benjamin Constant and Restoration Liberalism." In *The Triumph of Culture: 18th Century Perspectives,* edited by Paul Fritz and David Williams, pp. 245-59. Toronto, Ontario, Canada: A. M. Hakkert Ltd., 1972.

[*In the following essay, Cappadocia delineates the events and actions that have determined Constant's somewhat mixed reputation as a promoter of Restoration-era liberalism.*]

In a preface to a collection of his essays published in 1829, Benjamin Constant wrote: "j'ai défendu quarante ans le même principe, liberté en tout, en religion, en philosophie, en littérature, en industrie, en politique. . . ."[1] The matter of consistency has remained paramount in any discussion of his political life. In fact, although he was the theoretician of Restoration liberalism and played a key role in the liberal opposition, especially in the first crucial decade of that era, Constant has seldom been accorded the recognition due to him. A cursory glance at Restoration liberalism and at his behaviour during that decade may indicate some of the reasons for this neglect.

The political career of Constant falls into two phases; the first (1795-1802) culminated in his expulsion from the Tribunate by Napoleon. In those years, like all those who feared a return of either the Bourbons or the Jacobins, Constant sought some form of constitutional government, but Napoleon had only contempt for "idéalogues" who wished to raise an English form of constitutional opposition. So Constant as a faithful acolyte of Madame de Staël followed her into exile to continue their opposition. During the period, 1802-1813, he published no political tracts, but the tumultuous events of 1814-1815 that culminated in the second return of the Bourbons, evoked from him his major political works on which his reputation as a political theorist is based. Until the end of his career in December 1830, his pamphlets and his parliamentary activities were responses to day-to-day issues and they elaborated his essentially middle-class, Natural Rights liberalism, the credo that feared the despotism of both the absolute monarch and of the masses. Restoration liberalism[2] was conditioned philosophically by the Revolution and practically by the behaviour, in 1814-15, of Constant and of many of those who were to be leading opposition Liberals.

In 1813 Constant first appeared on the scene in the baggage train of Bernadotte, former Marshal of the Empire and heir designate, on whose hopes of replacing Napoleon he had attached his ambition. Bernadotte never reached Paris, as Constant had already noted in the *Journaux intimes* "son propre terrain est mourant. Ma cabane bâtie le-dessus serait du sable sur du sable."[3] But on 31 December 1813, Constant published his first political tract since his exile, the famous anti-Napoleon philippic, *De l'Esprit de conquête et de l'usurpation dans leurs rapports avec la civilisation européenne.* In it, he expressed a liberal optimistic view of man and a belief in human perfectibility. He did not see Liberty and Pacifism as natural predispositions of man, but rather as the fruit of civilisation and progress that are always threatened by despotism and the spirit of conquest. War was now an anachronism and the important new forces in the world, trade and commerce, tend to peace and liberty. He made direct attacks on Napoleon, the usurper, and argued that legitimacy could be conferred on a ruler only by free elections or by heredity. Unlike legitimate rulers "un usurpateur siège avec effroi sur un trône illégitime, comme sur une pyramide solitaire. Aucun assentiment ne l'appuie."[4]

Although by June 1814 the *Esprit* had gone through four editions, Constant played no part in what was to be seen as the beginning of Restoration liberalism, the fruitless effort by the Imperial Senate to impose terms on the returning Bourbons in April 1814. Contractual monarchy was one of the precepts of Liberals who throughout the Restoration argued that a contract, implied if not explicit, had taken place between the nation and the returning Bourbons. The pre-eminence of Talleyrand as vice-President of the Senate and as a friend of the Russian Tsar was at first cause for despair, but: "La liberté n'est pas perdue. Tâchons de nous faire une place commode dans un système paisible. Essayer vaut la peine."[5] He soon consoled himself: "Tâchons d'être désiré,"[6] and once in Paris he felt that, "il y a de la ressource pour la liberté."[7] . . . "Servons la bonne cause et servons-nous."[8]

In the summer of 1814 all those who during the Restoration were to be spokesmen of liberalism gave the Bourbons their good will.[9] Lafayette, who had never compromised with Napoleon and who was to become the flag of the Liberals, informed Jefferson that he and his friends were striving to make the Bourbon throne as rational and as liberal as possible.[10] Constant even claimed that the French restoration of 1814 combined the advantages of the English restoration of 1660 and of the Revolution of 1688.

Constant continued to elaborate liberal principles and to hope in vain for a place in the new political world: "Les éloges sans résultat me font plus de peine que de plaisir."[11] The praises he was receiving came for a major pamphlet,[12] published in May 1814, on political theory. To the traditional three powers dear to liberal writers since Montesquieu, he added a fourth, the neutral power of the Crown. He stressed the inviolability of the Crown and the responsibility of ministers as the two fundamental principles of a constitutional system.

At a time when the government began to consider the limitations to the freedom of the press, Constant wrote the first of his many pamphlets on that subject. In it he presented the classical liberal argument that only through a free press can the authorities know public opinion, and that "ce que la nation voulait en 1789, c'est à dire une liberté raisonnable, elle le veut encore aujourd'hui."[13] After six months of emotional chaos over Madame Récamier's failure to return his love, Constant re-entered the political world with another pamphlet on the responsibility of ministers.[14] But by that time, February 1815, future Liberals were in despair over the follies of the *émigrés*. Constant wrote to Lafayette: "L'avenir est bien incertain. Il n'y a de sûr qu'une chose, c'est que les purs ne veulent pas de nous. Ils se perdront et nous perdront."[15]

The return of Napoleon from the island of Elba in March 1815 was to be an important factor in determining the fate of Restoration liberalism. Lafayette and Constant at first cast aside recent doubts and rallied to the Bourbons who now made frantic last-minute efforts to identify the Crown with constitutionalism. The Chamber of Representatives characterized the Bourbon Charter of June 1814 as the development of the principles of 1789. Constant wrote on 11 March a bitter anti-Napoleon article which he feared might endanger his life: "Vogue la galère. S'il faut périr, périssons bien."[16] And although he was being approached by Bonapartists, "ils m'amadouent,"[17] on the 18th he wrote the famous diatribe against Napoleon which appeared in the *Journal des débats* the following day. The unequivocal attacks on "the Corsican," on whose side he saw only slavery, anarchy, and war, was accompanied by a spirited defence of the Bourbons, the ensurers of constitutional liberty, safety, and peace, and included the well-known sentence: "Je n'irais pas, misérable transfuge, me traîner, d'un pouvoir à l'autre, couvrir l'infamie par le sophisme et balbutier des mots profanés pour racheter une vie honteuse."[18] Yet by 14 April he rallied to Napoleon, became a member of the Council of State and, as most future Restoration Liberals, convinced himself that Napoleon could become a constitutional monarch.

Napoleon entered Paris on 22 March, two days after Louis XVIII had left it. Since his landing he had voiced the language of constitutional monarchy and of liberalism. He proclaimed freedom of the press and on the 25th the Council of State declared: "La souveraineté réside dans le peuple, il est la source légitime du pouvoir."[19] After an absence of six days, Constant returned on the 27th and by the 31st he was noting in his *Journaux*: "Les intentions sont libérales: la pratique sera despotique. N'importe."[20] On 9 April, Lafayette wrote to Constant that the Emperor's whole career made him inimical to guarantees of liberty, but though Napoleon and liberty were irreconcilable, in comparison with the *émigrés* the emperor's government represented the lesser of the two evils.[21] Meanwhile Constant on 14 April met Napoleon who persuaded him, his opponent since 1800, and his recent detractor, to draw up a constitution. On 7 June, Napoleon told the newly elected Chamber that he was beginning his "monarchie constitutionnelle."

In May 1815, Constant was to see not only the acceptance of his constitution, *L'Acte Additionnel aux Constitutions de L'Empire,* also known as "la Benjamine," but also, and perhaps even more important, a significant book on political theory which he had completed on 13 April.[22] The *Benjamine* was more liberal than the Bourbon Charter, but the plebiscite on it attracted fewer voters than Napoleon's earlier efforts to ascertain popular will. The experiment in Bonapartist constitutionalism never took place because Waterloo rescued the anti-Bourbon Liberals from the dismaying illusion of totalitarian liberalism.

Throughout the Restoration, Liberals had to explain their conduct during the Hundred Days. Constant's defence[23] centred on his claim that his first duty was the defence of liberal principle and that political organisation was merely a means to guarantee specific ends: liberty, order and the happiness of the people. Moreover on 20 March, he had raised his eyes and saw that, though the king had disappeared, France was still there. The fact that France was at war was an additional rea-

son for supporting Napoleon. He had also been convinced that the way was then clear to surround Napoleon with constitutional barriers. Moreover, in his major study on political principles which he finished in April 1815, Constant argued that the English people became free when James II fled from England and his flight was declared to be an abdication. He concluded this important work with the justification:

> Alors, après avoir, pendant 20 ans, réclamé les droits de l'espèce humaine, la sûreté des individus, la liberté de la pensée, la garantie des propriétés, l'abolition de tout arbitraire, j'oserai me féliciter de m'être réuni, avant la victoire, aux institutions qui consacrent tous ces droits. J'avais accompli l'ouvrage de ma vie.[24]

In April 1814, Liberalism had consisted of the futile efforts to impose terms on Louis XVIII; the following year it had centred on surrounding Napoleon with constitutional limitations, and after his defeat it meant the engineering of his second abdication. Constant played no important part after Waterloo neither with regard to the succession nor to the Chamber of Representatives' futile debate on the fundamentals of a liberal constitution—the distillation of the principles of 1789 as understood in 1815.[25]

By the time of the second return of the Bourbons, Constant's reappearance in the political arena had been less than successful. Although he had had a glimpse at fleeting glory in the resplendent uniform of Councillor of State, and he was to wait until the Revolution of 1830 to be again amongst those with political power, he had made more meaningful contributions to liberalism by his writings. But the frantic desire for recognition, the restless ambition for honours and office, the passionate need for acceptance drove him to foolish opportunism. On 31 May, 1814, he confided to his *Journaux*:

> Folies d'imagination. Je me crois dédaigné de tout le monde et personne n'y pense. C'est moi qui ne prends pas ma place, et je crois qu'on me la refuse.[26]

One need not share Henri Guillemin's[27] sardonic view of Constant to recognize that ambition and opportunism went side-by-side with a brilliant intellect and facile pen.

The return of the Bourbons meant that for over two years the Liberals played no part in French politics. They had to depend on Liberalism by princely grace and rejoiced when Louis XVIII followed a policy of reconciliation between the old and the new France. In September 1816, he dissolved the reactionary "Chambre introuvable" elected the previous year, even though this action outraged the Ultras, his more reactionary supporters who followed the leadership of his brother, the future Charles X. Until the murder of the heir to the throne, the Duc de Berri, in February 1820, Louis XVIII encouraged the moderation of the Centre group in the Chamber of Deputies. By 1818 this group split into the Right Centre under the Duc de Richelieu, who did not want the policy of moderation to antagonise the Right, and into Left Centre under Elie Decazes who was willing to rely on the Liberals.

This royal moderation was supported by liberal-minded people who hailed the "coup" of September 1816, and who greeted with enthusiasm the election law of the following year. It was under that law with its restricted franchise (about 90,000 voters in a nation of over thirty million people), that the Liberals were to make their reappearance in the Chamber of Deputies in the partial renewal of that body in the elections of 1817, 1818, and 1819.

Constant, Lafayette and other "Independent"[28] candidates for the partial renewal of 1817 were suspected as the men of the Hundred Days and were considered "anti-dynastic." Constant sought to allay fears aroused by their candidacy in a pamphlet in which he saw the choice presented for the electorate as one among the partisans of the *ancien régime* (the Ultras), those who accepted the new regime but who insisted that, for a while yet, exceptional laws must be maintained (the Centrists), and those who were loyal to the Charter but who wanted to see the constitutional monarchy go forward only with the assistance of "constitutional liberty" (the Independents).[29] Although Lafayette and Constant were not elected, the Independents did make substantial gains.

The Liberals gave only grudging and uncertain support to Decazes and the Left Centre, the only group that could help them realize their hopes for liberal reforms. One of these reforms, the press laws of 1818, led to the appearance of more newspapers, one of the most important of which was to be the Liberal journal *Minerve,* brilliantly edited by Constant. In it he carried out the constitutional education of France.[30] His main theme was stated repeatedly: the purpose of the State is to guarantee personal liberty, that is to free the individual from all restraints that limit his growth. By liberty he meant the guarantee of individual rights for the masses of the common people. Moreover, he argued that this liberty could be established only by wise combination of monarchical power and the rights of the people. He feared the "revolutionary" policy of the Ultras, who, he felt, wanted to undermine the system of government by the Charter:

> C'est parce que je crains les bouleversements, c'est parce que je hais les révolutions, c'est parce que je veux la stabilité de la monarchie constitutionnelle, que je crois qu'il est urgent de repousser les projets qui favorisent tout ce que je crains de voir reparaître, et qui mettent en péril tout ce que je voudrais qui fût conservé.[31]

In the midst of the turmoils of 1821 Constant was to declare in the Chamber that, "la stabilité est bonne en toutes choses," and that to conserve that which exists in order to profit from it, is better than to look for hazardous new things.[32] Revolution was justified only when the rights of the individual could not be attained within the framework of the existing form of government, whatever its nature might be. He spoke of the aristocratic basis of English liberty and praised the English aristocracy which, unlike the French, had never been the enemy of the people. The realization of the liberty of the individual was the paramount issue in the writings of Constant, whose erudite lectures on constitutionalism, the biting sarcasm that characterized the *Minerve*'s attacks on the Ultras and on the government, were to make that journal popular both in France and abroad.

An event equal in significance for Restoration liberalism as the appearance of the *Minerve* was the posthumous publication in 1818 of Madame de Staël's study of the Revolution. This book[33] represented one of the first systematic defences of the Revolution and set the pattern for the interpretation of those momentous years that was to be followed by the Liberals, whose leaders, such as Lafayette and Constant, had been her personal friends and admirers. In the second half of the *Considérations* written in 1816, which was directed towards the existing political situation in France, Madame de Staël was aware of the dangers which liberalism would encounter in France if it identified itself with Bonapartism. She admonished "les amis de la liberté" to separate their cause from that of the Bonapartists and cautioned them not to confound "les principes de la Révolution" with those of Napoleon.[34]

Constant gave the *Considérations* a surprisingly lukewarm reception, and he failed to make any references to her views on Bonapartism and on the danger of identifying it with liberalism. He and writers in other Liberal journals[35] wanted to de-emphasize the inherent contradiction between Liberalism and Bonapartism, because they realized that Bonapartism was popular among the masses.

The Bonapartist issue remained a divisive force between the Liberals and the ministry, and it emerged over the issue whether or not the regicides and those who, because of their activities during the Hundred Days, had been banished temporarily by the law of 1816, should be allowed to return. When a parliamentary committee recommended that the petitions on behalf of the banished be disregarded, and the decision as to who should return to France be left to the king, only twenty votes, all Liberals, were cast against them.

The Liberal press gave little direct attention to Napoleon himself, but Napoleonic military anniversaries were recalled and the songs of Pierre-Jean de Béranger, the famous and popular songster of the Liberal and Bonapartist opposition, were given prominence. The *Indépendant* was disturbed because the memories of Napoleon's triumphs served to worry even certain Liberals about "le destin de la liberté."[36] The identification of Liberalism with Bonapartism was to become more marked after the death of Napoleon in 1821. The Liberals, who no longer had to fear his return, now expected to recruit more followers. Even Lafayette, who had never been a Bonapartist, was relieved by the death because he foresaw that "many Bonapartists" would now attach themselves to the "patriotic" party, as he then called the Liberals.[37]

In the election campaigns of 1818 and 1819, and throughout the stormy events following the assassination of the Duc de Berri the following year, the Liberals stressed the theme that they were the preservers of the *status-quo* because they, unlike the Ultras, wanted no radical change but wished to preserve the gains of the Revolution. They emphasized the need to follow the "strict application" of the Charter. Constant presented his colleagues in 1817 as the true conservatives, the representatives of the peaceful element of the nation whose "true strength" could be found in the middle-class, the defenders of stability in all things.[38]

The Liberal gains in 1818 when, among others, Lafayette was elected, dismayed the Duc de Richelieu who resigned as president of the council of ministers. He had been shocked by the "alliance monstreuse"[39] between the Liberals and the Bonapartists. Decazes, the man responsible for the liberal measures of the previous two years, became more important in the new ministry nominally headed by General Dessoles. But the Liberals, for whom the year 1819 was "une époque d'espérance," gave the new ministry little support, because they were expecting greater gains in the elections of 1819. The Bonapartist undercurrent and the important Liberal success that did materialize convinced Decazes and Louis XVIII, the architect and supporter of the moderate Centrist position, that the time had come to modify their policy. They had presupposed acquiescence, if not positive support, from those who saw themselves as the defenders of the new France. But before Decazes could give a new orientation to his policy, the Duc de Berri was murdered by a young fanatic, on 13 February 1820. This event was fraught with disastrous consequences for French Restoration Liberalism. Although Decazes introduced bills to revise the election law of 1817, to suspend individual liberty and to re-establish press censorship, Louis XVIII bowed to pressure from the Ultras, led by his brother, and dismissed him. The return of the Duc de Richelieu to head the ministry ended the era of Left-Centre moderation.

The new government's measures to reverse the Left-Centre policies evoked from the Liberals a spirited defence of the *status-quo*. They took refuge in the Charter which now became the palladium of Liberalism. To the *Indépendant* the Revolution of 1789 and the Charter were now synonomous. By 1822 the Liberals spoke of the Charter as superior to the king himself and insisted that only a constitutional convention representing the "nation" could revise it.

The Liberals and Constant gave a classic defence of individual liberty and of freedom of the press when bills to curb both were debated in the Chamber of Deputies. In his lecture on individual liberty Constant insisted that all arbitrary governments want to rule by exceptional measures and any law to limit individual freedom attacks not only liberty, justice, and morals, but also the credit system in finance, industry, and the prosperity of France. He accused the government of wanting the powers enjoyed by Napoleon, of wishing to return to absolutism and of overthrowing the Charter. In the measures proposed, he saw the return of 1788 and with it the doom of liberalism.[40]

The Liberals fought tenaciously and eloquently, if to no avail, against changes in the election law of 1817, which had made their success possible. Parliamentary speeches became effective appeals to agitate public opinion, especially students, in the streets. Since the proposed system of the double vote and indirect elections gave the richest electors more power, the Liberals centred their attacks on the aristocracy. They identified the mass of the people with the middle-class and saw the changes as an attack on the Charter. When an Ultra spoke of the Liberals as the men responsible for the march of the women on Versailles on 5 and 6 October 1789, for the September 1792 massacres, for the murder of Louis XVI, and for the return of Napoleon on 20 March 1815, Constant re-interpreted the French Revolution. To him the Liberals were the constitutionalists of 1789 who had defended the throne in 1792, had been the victims of the Terror and the enemies of Napoleon. In 1814 they had warned the king's government of its perilous situation, and who, if listened to, could have saved the Bourbons in March 1815. He now wanted "les Bourbons, rien que les Bourbons avec la Charte, toute la Charte sous les Bourbons."[41] The events of the Revolution and of the 1814 and 1815 restorations were constantly re-examined by speakers on both sides of the Chamber of Deputies. In 1820 Constant began to publish the defence of his actions during the Hundred Days.[42]

In 1820 the Liberals sought comfort from events abroad, the revolution in Naples and, even more important, that in Spain. These revolutions, undertaken in the name of liberalism, were hailed by the Liberals who contrasted the twilight of liberalism at home with the dawn of a new era abroad. Since they feared the intervention of Austria, Prussia, and Russia, the Liberals advocated a policy of open diplomacy and non-intervention. When the Congress of Verona (1822) led to the French invasion of Spain to crush the rebellion, the Liberals saw the invasion as a "hypocriso-politico-religious" war on liberalism.[43] The easy victory in Spain brought prestige to the Ultras and despondency to the Liberals. Their decline, already visible in the partial renewals of 1821 and 1822, was to be confirmed in the crushing defeat they suffered in the general elections of the following year. As Lafayette admitted to Jefferson, the mass of the people in Italy and Spain had been indifferent to liberalism. Only the "less ignorant part" had been alert, the rest were still under the influence of "prejudice and superstition."[44]

Although Constant had been a vigorous debater in the Chamber, and was to be the cause of demonstrations on the part of his supporters and opponents both in Paris and in his constituency of the Sarthe, unlike Lafayette and many other Liberals, he took no part in the military conspiracies of 1820 and 1822. He was essentially a political theorist anxious to lecture France on constitutionalism. In 1818-1819 he published four volumes[45] of his writings to serve as a course on constitutional politics. In 1821 in the Chamber he returned to the theme of the responsibility of ministers, on which he had published a pamphlet six years before. He again based himself on the English practice and insisted that the ministry should lead the defence of, and always uphold, a measure it presented to the Chamber of Deputies. He did not, however, believe that a defeat in that body should lead to the resignation of the government. Constant could not face the logic of responsible parliamentary government, such as was to develop in England after the Reform Bill of 1832, whereby the ministry has to resign when it no longer commands a majority in the House of Commons. To accept such a practice in France in 1821 would have meant an Ultra ministry. To him, a ministry should resign only if it sees no immediate prospects of obtaining a majority.[46]

Constant remained the voice of middle-class liberalism.[47] Unlike such Liberals as the pamphleteer Paul-Louis Courier or the songwriter Béranger, he feared the "mob" and could not appeal to the mass of the "people." Throughout the stormy and angry debates of 1820-1822, unlike many of his colleagues, he believed that it was still possible to convince the Right-Centre and even the Right, if not the extreme Ultras, that their path would lead to the perdition of the monarchy. To him the Charter had consecrated the Revolution, i.e. the political and civil gains of the middle-class. Therefore he wanted some accommodation to maintain the Charter and avoid another revolution. The only "people" he would trust were the educated and the property owners.

Constant, though defeated in 1822, was re-elected in 1824 and for the next six years played an important part in the opposition to the policies of Charles X. Until the crisis of 1829-1830, he devoted most of his energies to gambling and to his study of religion, his major non-political interest. In August 1827 he made a triumphal trip to Alsace and, with Lafayette, became a symbol of opposition to Charles X. During the July Revolution of 1830, which to Constant and to the Liberals became their version of 1688 in England, he wrote the important declaration in favour of the future King Louis-Philippe. By that time Constant and Lafayette were symbols. Power was in the hands of younger men such as Guizot and Thiers. A month later, Constant was named president of a section of the Council of State and the king gave him the large sum of 200,000 francs to pay his debts.

It is important to note that Constant's last speech in the Chamber was in favour of printers and booksellers, but his motion for more liberal measures were defeated. In September he had written to the Duchesse de Broglie:

> Nous avons tous les éléments de la liberté il y a prodige dans les biens. Mais il y a moyen de gâter ce prodige.[48]

When he died in December 1830, his funeral was the occasion of popular demonstration. He finally achieved the popularity for which he had so often yearned.

Louis-Philippe's generosity (or was it repayment?) raises again the question of opportunism in Constant. Was his behaviour during the Hundred Days merely a personal demarche, a clumsy interplay of personal ambition and principles or a benediction of Bonapartism by liberalism? At first it was the one and then became the other. But personal vicissitudes, obvious contradictions, turncoat accusations cannot vitiate the importance of Constant's writings. They are relevant not only to the issues of his day, but to the understanding of Restoration Liberalism and of the Nineteenth-Century Natural Rights school of continental Liberalism.

Notes

1. B. Constant, *Oeuvres*, A. Roulin, ed., Paris, 1957, p. 801.

2. E. Cappadocia, "The Nature of French Liberalism During the Restoration," *Historical Papers, The Canadian Historical Association*, 1961, J. Heisler and P. Dumas eds., pp. 132-141.

3. 11 November, 1813. "Journaux intimes," *Oeuvres*, p. 685.

4. *Ibid.*, p. 1061.

5. 7 April, 1814, *ibid.*, p. 695.

6. 11 April, *ibid.*, p. 695.

7. 15 April, *ibid.*, p. 695.

8. 16 April, *ibid.*, p. 695.

9. E. Cappadocia, "The Liberals and the Crisis of the First Restoration in France," *Historical Papers, The Canadian Historical Association,* 1966, J. Heisler and F. Ouellet eds., pp. 141-154.

10. Lafayette to Jefferson, 14 August, 1814, in *Général Lafayette, Mémoires, correspondance et manuscrits du général Lafayette publiés par sa famille* V, 6 vols., Paris, 1837-48, pp. 486-489.

11. 28 May, 1814. "Journaux intimes," *Oeuvres,* p. 699.

12. *Réflexions sur les constitutions, la distribution et les garanties dans une monarchie constitionnelle,* Paris, 1814.

13. *De La Liberté des brochures, des pamphlets et des journaux considérée sous le rapport de l'intérêt du gouvernement,* Paris, 1814, *Oeuvres,* p. 1243.

14. *De La Responsabilité des ministres,* Paris, 1815.

15. 20 February, 1815, "Journaux intimes," *op. cit.,* p. 739.

16. *Ibid.,* p. 742.

17. 12 March, 1815, p. 742.

18. *Journal des débats,* 19 March, 1815.

19. *Moniteur,* 25 March, 1815.

20. 31 March, 1815. "Journaux intimes," *op. cit.,* p. 744.

21. Lafayette V, p. 416.

22. *Principes de politique applicables à tous les gouvernements réprésentatifs et particulièrement à la constitution actuelle de la France, Oeuvres,* pp. 1065-1215. Constant did not believe that one should talk in the abstract about "sovereignty of the people," although he accepts it as a principle, because such talk does not enhance the liberty of the individual. To him Natural Rights come first. Law is the expression of "la volonté de tous" which becomes "la volonté générale" if one accepts the power of a few when sanctioned by all. He devotes key chapters on the inviolability of property, on press and religious freedom and above all on individual liberty.

23. *Mémoires sur les Cent-Jours,* Paris, 1829.

24. *Principes, op. cit.,* p. 1215.

25. L. Duguit et H. Monnier, *Déclaration des droits des Français et des principes fondamentaux de leurs institutions votés par la chambre des représentants le 5 juillet 1815,* pp. 198-199. This document is important not so much for the stress on liberty and equality, on the demand for the abolition of the nobility, of privilege, but rather for its last article (XIII) which unequivocally declared that no prince could rule until he had taken the oath to observe the present declaration. The restatement of the principles of 1789 were combined with the belief in the contract theory of government—a recurrent theme of Liberals who finally achieved their goal in the Revolution of 1830.

26. "Journaux intimes," *op. cit.,* p. 699.

27. H. Guillemin, *Mme de Staël, Benjamin Constant et Napoléon,* Paris, 1959.

28. In 1817 and 1818 the Liberals called themselves Independents to disassociate themselves from the Centrist followers of the Richelieu-Decazes ministry. To their enemies they were known also as Jacobins, Radicals, Revolutionaries, and the Left.

29. *Journal général de France,* 19 September, 1817.

30. For the aims of the *Minerve,* see I, February, 1818, III, August, 1818, p. 159; IV, November, 1818, p. 100; IX, February, 1820, p. 107.

31. *Ibid.* VIII, December, 1819, p. 295.

32. *Discours de Benjamin Constant à la chambre des députés,* 2 vols., Paris, 1827-28. I, p. 416.

33. Staël-Holstein, Anne-Louise-Germaine Necker, Madame la baronne de, *Considérations sur les principaux événements de la Révolution française, ouvrage posthume de madame la baronne de Staël,* Duc de Broglie and Baron de Staël, eds., 3 vols., Paris, 1818.

34. *Ibid.* III, p. 169.

35. E. Cappadocia, "The Liberals and Madame de Staël in 1818," in R. Herr and H. Parker, eds., *Ideas in History, Essays Presented to Louis Gottschalk by his former students,* Durham, 1965.

36. *Indépendant,* 23 June, 1819.

37. Lafayette VI, p. 128.

38. *Minerve* III, August, 1818, pp. 433-446.

39. Cited in E. Daudet, *Louis XVIII et le duc Decazes 1815-1820, d'après des documents inédits,* Paris, 1899, p. 281.

40. *Archives parlementaires,* 2nd series, XXVI, 1820, p. 354.

41. *Ibid.* XXVIII, pp. 57-61.

42. *Mémoires sur les Cent-Jours.*

43. A. P. XXXVIII, 1823, p. 380.

44. Lafayette to Jefferson, 20 December, 1823, *Massachusetts Historical Society* (Louis Gottschalk photostats).

45. *Collection complète des ouvrages publiés sur le gouvernement représentatif et la constitution actu-elle de la France, formant une espèce de cours de politique constitutionnelle,* 4 vols., Paris, 1818-1819.

46. *A. P.* XXXI, 1821, pp. 672-673.

47. Baron Pasquier, who became minister for foreign affairs in 1820, declared that at that time the youth in the schools, the army, big businessmen, big in-dustrialists, rich capitalists, capable, esteemed, highly considered men were nearly all "partisans des ideés plus ou moins libérales." Pasquier, *Mé-moires du chancelier Pasquier,* 5 vols., Paris, 1892-95, IV, p. 356.

48. Comtesse Jean de Pange, "Quelques lettres in-édites de Benjamin Constant à Auguste et Alber-tine de Staël entre 1815 et 1830," pp. 119-125, in *Benjamin Constant, actes du congrès de Lausanne,* October, 1967, P. Cordey et J. L. Seylaz eds., Geneva, 1968, p. 125.

Ian W. Alexander (essay date 1973)

SOURCE: Alexander, Ian W. "The Conflict of Motives." In *Benjamin Constant*: Adolphe, pp. 22-44. London: Edward Arnold, 1973.

[*In the following excerpt, Alexander examines the nar-rative and thematic significance of Constant's portrayal of Ellénore as emotionally tyrannical in* Adolphe.]

ELLÉNORE

The character of Ellénore is a great deal more complex than may at first appear or than is often recognized. One is tempted to view her in somewhat simplified terms by the undoubted fact that in the novel she is seen reflected in the eyes and mind of Adolphe. But the appreciation of 'character'—one's own as much as that of another—is inevitably mediated through an 'image', the degree of 'reality' or 'truth' of which depends on the perceptiveness and penetration of the eyes and mind that form it. When the eyes and mind are those of an Adolphe, one may be assured that the image—in this case the 'character' of Ellénore—will have all the subtlety, complication and even ambiguity associated with a real, live person, fictive though the latter may be.

The story of Ellénore is not simply the story of a woman destroyed by an unrequited passion, but of a woman tortured and in part led astray by conflicting urges in her nature. She is, above all, a creature of refined and powerful sensibilities and of high personal ideals, re-markable by the 'pureté de ses motifs', the 'dés-intéressement de sa conduite' and 'la noblesse et

l'élévation de ses sentiments' (pp. 33-4). Of these she had already given proof when we first meet her by her loyalty to, and her sacrifices on behalf of, her lover the Comte de P., which had in some degree regularized her *liaison* with him in the eyes of society and reconciled in her own mind the consciousness of her irregular situ-ation and her moral and religious scruples. Yet not wholly so. Thrown by 'la fatalité de sa situation' or her inexperience—Adolphe himself can only speculate—into a 'carrière qui répugnait également à son éduca-tion, à ses habitudes et à la fierté qui faisait une partie très remarquable de son caractère', she was 'en lutte constante avec sa destinée' (pp. 33-4); and this opposi-tion shows itself in excessive moral and religious scruples—scruples carried to the point of puritan-ism—in strict observance of social conventions, in ex-aggerated maternal anxiety, in quick reactions to wounded pride, in bursts of temperament and in alter-nating bouts of taciturnity and impetuous speech:

> Il y avait dans sa manière quelque chose de fougueux et d'inattendu qui la rendait plus piquante qu'elle n'aurait dû l'être naturellement. La bizarrerie de sa po-sition suppléait en elle à la nouveauté des idées. On l'examinait avec intérêt et curiosité comme un bel or-age.

(pp. 35-6)

Those two facets of her passionate temperament—the capacity for whole-hearted personal commitment and the febrile impetuosity and excess of feeling which brooks no resistance to its demands, particularly when pride and self-esteem are activated in conjunction with passion—come to the fore in her relations with Adol-phe. Once her moral, religious and social scruples have been overcome—and that relatively quickly—and she has surrendered to him, her passion and devotion are entire and all-consuming. For him she is prepared to sacrifice security, children, filial duty, social approval it-self. But her situation has been worsened. As she de-taches herself progressively from the Count and at-taches herself to a man so many years younger than herself, the hard-won and precarious recognition of so-ciety is lost and she knows as never before the shame and hurt pride of a lost reputation: 'Ainsi la malheu-reuse Ellénore se voyait tombée pour jamais dans l'état dont, toute sa vie, elle avait voulu sortir. Tout con-tribuait à blesser son âme et à blesser sa fierté' (p. 72). She suffers, however, a still deeper hurt to her self-esteem by Adolphe's failure to respond to her passion-ate and self-sacrificing devotion: 'elle s'était relevée à ses propres yeux par un amour pur de tout calcul, de tout intérêt; elle savait que j'étais bien sûr qu'elle ne m'aimait que pour moi-même' (p. 60). The very disin-terestedness of her passion, proved by the sacrifice of all that she had held most dear, had in some sort com-pensated in her own eyes for her loss of reputation, re-storing the sense of her own moral value and personal worth. Adolphe's failure to respond with a love equally disinterested—and the nature of Ellénore is to demand all or nothing—and, perhaps most of all, his failure to recognize the sacrifices she had made on his behalf, are tantamount not only to a rejection of her love but also to a slight upon her personal dignity, which diminishes her in her own eyes and robs her of all that remains to her of belief in her own value and of trust in herself.

Spurned by society, all but rejected by her lover, Ellénore experiences the anguish of 'cette estime refoulée sur elle-même, et qui ne sait où se placer' (p. 7), and which can find expression only in the violent reproaches or sullen silences that characterize her behaviour and contribute to the quarrels and misunderstandings which finally transform the life of the partners into a 'perpétuel orage' (p. 121). For everything is not readily excusable in Ellénore. Understandable no doubt in view of her position and of Adolphe's subterfuges, evasions and 'paroles acérées', Ellénore's own violence, of which there is repeated mention (e.g. pp. 60, 79-80), must take its due share of blame. All the more so as it is so closely connected with her character. It springs undoubtedly from what is most laudable in it, her need to dedicate herself to an object of preference with an all-consuming and all-absorbing passion, but it is all the same a distortion of this quality, which is only partly excusable by the fact that it is brought about by the strains and stresses of her situation.

This tendency to violent assertion, expressing itself in peremptory language, reproaches and accusations, takes the basic form of an all too demanding possessiveness. We already see traces of the latter before Adolphe ever appears on the scene in her attitude to her children, in her 'anxious' concern for, and preoccupation with, their safety. This 'anxiété', as Adolphe observes, is for the most part accounted for by her situation, since they are a living reproach to her, their unmarried mother: 'On eût dit quelquefois qu'une révolte secrète se mêlait à l'attachement plutôt passionné que tendre qu'elle leur montrait, et les lui rendait en quelque sorte importuns . . . on la voyait pâlir de l'idée qu'il faudrait qu'un jour elle leur avouât leur naissance' (p. 35). And, as if to compensate, she redoubles and exaggerates her attention at the slightest risk of their coming to harm: 'Mais le moindre danger, une heure d'absence, la ramenait à eux avec une anxiété où l'on démêlait une espèce de remords, et le désir de leur donner par ses caresses le bonheur qu'elle n'y trouvait pas elle-même.' Full allowance being made for this explanation, there remains however in this 'anxiété' more than a hint of a possessiveness, of an excessive surveillance, which spring from the very character of her attachment, 'plutôt passionné que tendre'.

'Plutôt passionné que tendre'—is Ellénore's attachment to Adolphe any less so? And need one be surprised to see flow from it similar effects? Possessiveness shows

itself almost from the beginning of the relationship, even when the partners are under the sway of 'le charme de l'amour' and Adolphe begins to find in Ellénore 'un lien' and no longer 'un but':

> Son attachement semblait s'être accru du sacrifice qu'elle m'avait fait. Elle ne me laissait jamais la quitter sans essayer de me retenir. Lorsque je sortais, elle me demandait quand je reviendrais. . . . Elle fixait avec une précision inquiète l'instant de mon retour. . . . Il m'était quelquefois incommode d'avoir tous mes pas marqués d'avance et tous mes moments ainsi comptés.
>
> (p. 58)

This possessiveness quickly becomes a veritable tyranny or 'despotism', as Adolphe calls it (p. 65), which allows him no freedom of action. Not only does she seek to control his actions, but she seems to wish to debar him from any possibility of free choice by confronting him with a *fait accompli* which rivets him to her and allows him no means of escape. Thus, disregarding the counsels of prudence of Adolphe, who is quick to realize the damage her action will do to her reputation, she abandons the Count and completes arrangements to live with him. And when she presents him with the fact, she stifles any possible reproaches or objections he may feel impelled to make: 'Elle s'étourdissait de ses paroles, de peur d'entendre les miennes; elle prolongeait son discours avec activité pour retarder le moment où mes objections la replongeraient dans le désespoir' (p. 68). She does not hesitate to assert her claims over him. When, for example, Adolphe shows himself understanding and tolerant of her 'flirtation' with other men in an attempt to arouse his jealousy (and to prove to herself that she still possesses 'des moyens de plaire'), she profits by his indulgence to claim new rights: 'Ellénore se croyait de nouveaux droits; je me sentais chargé de nouvelles chaînes' (p. 121). She is capable even of using her very sacrifices as a weapon to tyrannize, as when she urges him to accompany her to Poland in response to her father's request and declares that, if he will not do so, she will not go alone and suffer the pangs of separation:

> Je n'ai pas la consolation de me dire que, par le sacrifice de toute ma vie, je sois parvenue à vous inspirer le sentiment que je méritais; mais enfin vous l'avez accepté, ce sacrifice. Je souffre déjà suffisamment par l'aridité de vos manières et la sécheresse de nos rapports; je subis ces souffrances que vous m'infligez; je ne veux pas en braver de volontaires.
>
> (p. 91)

Nor will she listen to Adolphe's pleadings. As he says: 'Je voulus réveiller sa générosité, comme si l'amour n'était pas de tous les sentiments le plus égoïste, et, par conséquent, lorsqu'il est blessé, le moins généreux' (p. 92). This particular episode leads later, indeed, to a positive injustice on Ellénore's part when, her father having died suddenly before they can leave for Poland, she reproaches Adolphe as being the cause of her absence from his death-bed: 'Vous m'avez fait manquer, me dit-elle, à un devoir sacré' (p. 93). In general, throughout the course of events she is frequently apt to render Adolphe wholly responsible for all her troubles: 'Ellénore m'accusa de l'avoir trompée, de n'avoir eu pour elle qu'un goût passager, d'avoir aliéné d'elle l'affection du comte; de l'avoir remise, aux yeux du public, dans la situation équivoque dont elle avait cherché toute sa vie à sortir' (p. 65). There are moments when the reader's sympathies move to the side of Adolphe as being the more 'moral' character of the two in the sense that there is in him a genuinely moral conflict. Allowance made for an initial conflict between love and duty, which is speedily solved, once she falls in love her relationship with Adolphe raises no moral issues and what conflict she experiences is psychological, between her passion and her self-esteem, itself in part a reflection of the conflict between herself and society. Nor is it perhaps correct to speak of conflict, for her pride and violent assertiveness are part of her very passion which, by its all-consuming and all-absorbing nature, makes absolute demands and expects an absolute response. The very fact that it is 'disinterested' and 'pur de tout calcul' is what makes it so demanding, overbearing and so seemingly tyrannical. One sees it in Ellénore's desire not only to control Adolphe's actions, but to take command of his very thoughts and moods—that desire which Sartre has placed at the centre of personal relations and defined as the will to 'capter la liberté d'autrui':

> Il y avait dans la voix et dans le ton d'Ellénore je ne sais quoi d'âpre et de violent qui annonçait plutôt une détermination ferme qu'une émotion profonde ou touchante. . . . Elle aurait voulu pénétrer dans le sanctuaire intime de ma pensée pour y briser une opposition sourde qui la révoltait contre moi.

> (pp. 91-2)

One may further note that this tyranny is exercised not only through words but also, as Sartre again has indicated, through 'le regard', which disturbs, freezes or paralyses: Adolphe is particularly sensitive to its power, both generally and in respect of Ellénore: 'la figure humaine me trouble, et mon mouvement naturel est de la fuir pour délibérer en paix' (p. 22); '. . . je démêlais dans ce sourire une sorte de mépris pour moi' p. 42); 'Vos regards m'observent. Vous êtes embarrassée, presque offensée de mon trouble' (p. 54).

If Ellénore's displays of temperament and her despotic will have as their ultimate cause her all-consuming passion, so too do her errors of judgment. 'Ellénore', observes Adolphe, 'n'avait qu'un esprit ordinaire; mais ses idées étaient justes' (p. 33). Her native judgment, indeed, is sound and this explains her powers of in-

sight. The narrative makes clear that, in the depths of her mind, she is aware of the actual state of affairs. Both she and Adolphe may seek to conceal the truth, but they do so because they, and she just as much as he, know the truth. She shows as much by the letter written after one of their quarrels, which Adolphe found and read after her death: 'Par quelle pitié bizarre n'osez-vous rompre un lien qui vous pèse, et déchirez-vous l'être malheureux près de qui votre pitié vous retient?' (p. 144). And on at least one occasion she admits the truth openly to him: 'vous croyez avoir de l'amour, et vous n'avez que de la pitié' (p. 83).

Two things, however, cloud her judgment. On the one hand, the very 'ordinariness' and limited range of her mind, which make it difficult for her to assess the finer points of the situation and to estimate the consequences of her actions. On the other, and most of all, the strength of her passion, which has two effects. First, it obscures her native perspicacity and ability to form 'idées justes' so that, while with one part of her mind she recognizes the truth, with another she deludes herself into believing the contrary. 'Crédulités du cœur, vous êtes inexplicables!' (p. 89), as Adolphe so rightly exclaims. Secondly, and even more disastrous, her all-consuming passion, reinforced by the limited range of her mind, makes her incapable of adjusting the means to the end. If Adolphe has doubts about his true ends, Ellénore has one single and all-absorbing end, namely Adolphe and the retention of his love, but the means she employs to retain his love are precisely those most designed to lose it. As Adolphe remarks:

> Elle avait l'esprit juste, mais peu étendu; la justesse de son esprit était dénaturée par l'emportement de son caractère, et son peu d'étendue l'empêchait d'apercevoir la ligne la plus habile, et de saisir des nuances délicates. Pour la première fois elle avait un but; et comme elle se précipitait vers ce but, elle le manquait.

> (p. 115)

Thus, her ill-conceived and febrile attempt to regain a 'place honorable' in society, to which the above passage refers, brings her only humiliation: 'Tour à tour haute et suppliante, tantôt prévenante, tantôt susceptible, il y avait dans ses actions et dans ses paroles je ne sais quelle fougue destructive de la considération qui ne se compose que du calme.' The same impetuous miscalculation leads her to adopt the 'calcul faux et déplorable' of trying to win Adolphe back by exciting his jealousy (p. 118); and to employ a friend as an intermediary to plead with him, failing to realize that 'le cœur seul peut plaider sa cause' and that 'tout intermédiaire devient un juge', more likely in his or her impartial role to look for attenuating circumstances in the conduct of the partner than to sympathize deeply with the sufferings of the confider (p. 111).

In this same respect Ellénore must take her share of responsibility for the final tragedy. If nothing else, it is her ill-timed and ill-judged letter, symbolic of her despotic hold over him, which, brought to Adolphe in the presence of the Baron as if designed to humiliate him in the latter's eyes, forces him to declare his intention to break off the relationship once and for all: 'Enfin, comme si tout s'était réuni contre elle, tandis que j'hésitais, elle-même, par sa véhémence, acheva de me décider' (p. 126). Whether from miscalculation or the promptings of a passionate temperament and feeling not fully under control, Ellénore throughout the course of the novel launches out impulsively into actions which are a major factor in precipitating the events that culminate in tragedy.

It is indeed only when, certain of her approaching death, Ellénore achieves a state of resignation that the full clarity of her judgment is restored, for then her passion, rid of all extraneous elements and distortions—reduced, as it were, to its pure essence—can express itself serenely and allow her to acknowledge to herself the final, ultimate truth. Not merely that truth previously acknowledged by her from time to time and referred to in the passages already quoted. That truth was wrenched from her under the compulsion of indignation and self-pity. This truth is one which the deeper insight and understanding that pure feeling alone inspires enables her to accept calmly and serenely. That truth was in any case but a half-truth, throwing by implication the full responsibility on Adolphe by accusing him of concealing his lack of love behind a cloak of compassion. This truth is the deeper truth, acknowledging the common misfortune of two beings caught in a web of fate spun by circumstance, situation and character: 'Ne vous reprochez rien, quoi qu'il arrive. Vous avez été bon pour moi. J'ai voulu ce qui n'était pas possible. L'amour était toute ma vie: il ne pouvait être la vôtre' (p. 135).

For, when all is said and done, in spite of her all too human failings, Ellénore remains in the mind of the reader the moral superior of Adolphe. Not by her ultimate display of compassion and forgiveness—for the strength of Adolphe's pity and sympathy is not in doubt—nor by being the seat of a moral conflict—for it is Adolphe who is the seat of the moral conflict—but by the strength of her personality. What stands out is the enduring quality of her love, the depth and intensity of her feelings and the spirit of total self-sacrifice and whole-hearted devotion. Her faults are distortions of her passionate commitment, it alone is her essence. She is the embodiment of that urge to transcend and to sacrifice the self which is for Constant the principle of true love, of morality and of religion:

> Dans la seule faculté du sacrifice est le germe indestructible de la perfectibilité.[1]

> L'idée de sacrifice est inséparable de toute religion. L'on pourrait dire qu'elle est inséparable de toute af-

fection vive et profonde. L'amour se complaît à immoler à l'être qu'il préfère tout ce que d'ailleurs il a de plus cher.[2]

Ellénore wills this sacrifice of self to the point of sacrificing life itself and, by so doing, she redeems what faults she may have in the eyes and mind of the reader. And it is this absolute surrender to the being of another which, however much she may be at odds with society and even with herself, gives her that underlying unity and continuity of feeling and therefore that strength of personality which are denied to Adolphe.

Notes

1. *Mélanges,* p. 398.

2. *De la religion,* Vol. I (1826), p. 170.

Works Cited

For the purposes of quotation and reference the edition of *Adolphe* by J.-H. Bornecque (Garnier, 1968) has been used, and for Constant's Journals the Pléiade edition of the *Œuvres* edited by A. Roulin (1957). The source of quotations from, and references to, other works by Constant is given in footnotes, as in the case of works by other authors. Unless otherwise stated, the place of publication of books in French is Paris.

Abbreviations

Pléiade edition	*Benjamin Constant. OEuvres,* edited by Alfred Roulin and Charles Roth (Paris: Gallimard, Bibliothèque de la Pléiade, 1957).
Mélanges	*Mélanges de littérature et de politique* (Paris: Pichon et Didier, 1829).
De la religion	*De la religion, considérée dans sa source, ses formes et ses développements,* volume 1 (Paris: Bossange père, Bossange frères, Treuttel et Wurtz, Rey et Gravier, Renouard, Ponthieu, 1824); volumes 2 and 3 (Paris: Béchet aîné, 1825, 1827); volumes 4 and 5 (Paris: Pichon et Didier, 1831).

F. W. J. Hemmings (essay date spring-summer 1979)

SOURCE: Hemmings, F. W. J. "Constant's *Adolphe*: Internal and External Chronology." *Nineteenth-Century French Studies* 7, nos. 3 & 4 (spring-summer 1979): 153-64.

[In the following essay, Hemmings argues that Adolphe *is set during a four-year period at the beginning of the nineteenth century, and that the careful manner in which*

Constant provides this chronological information, particularly with respect to Ellénore's biographical details, are indicative of Constant's views of Ellénore as a distinct and integral character within the narrative.]

"Le 15 mai 1796, le général Bonaparte fit son entrée dans Milan . . ."; "Vers le milieu du mois de juillet de l'année 1838, une de ces voitures nouvellement mises en circulation sur les places de Paris et nommées des *milords,* cheminait, rue de l'Université . . ."; "Le 15 septembre 1840, vers six heures du matin, *la Ville-de-Montereau,* près de partir, fumait à gros tourbillons devant le quai Saint-Bernard." The opening words of three of the most celebrated French novels of the nineteenth century (*La Chartreuse de Parme, La Cousine Bette,* and *L'Éducation sentimentale*), fully confirm what has recently been advanced by Maurice Larkin, that in realist writing of this period, "more often than not time was pinpointed with an uncompromising precision."[1] The probability is that the fashion for referring to the calendar (not necessarily, of course, in the first sentence, nor only there) was started by the authors of historical novels; Mérimée used a date in the title of his fictional account of the Massacre of St. Bartholomew,[2] while Hugo did the same in his late novel about the French Revolution, *Quatre-Vingt-Treize,* and only avoided quoting a date in the first sentence of *Notre-Dame de Paris* by the unfair device of requiring his reader to carry out a complicated subtraction sum: "Il y a aujourd'hui trois cent quarante-huit ans six mois et dix-neuf jours que les Parisiens s'éveillèrent au bruit de toutes les cloches sonnant à grande volée dans la triple enceinte de la Cité, de l'Université et de la Ville."

Whether in historical or contemporary novels, the use of precise dating served the obvious purpose of rooting the action in a specific historical setting, and constitutes one of the significant differences between the nineteenth-century novel and its forerunners. The characteristic procedure of the eighteenth-century novelist was either to omit all mention of dates, or else to use the conventional "En 17**" as a means of blurring too exact a historical indicator: the two last numerals are suppressed in all but seven of the 175 letters constituting *Les Liaisons dangereuses,* and where they are included, this is more likely due to carelessness on Laclos's part than to a desire to help the reader situate the events in historical time. In this respect, if in no other, *Adolphe* is bound to strike the reader as belonging to the older tradition: for Constant quotes no dates anywhere in his novel.[3]

This is not to say that *Adolphe* takes no heed of chronology. "It is certainly not set abstractly outside time," remarks Alison Fairlie, adding that the "carefully worked out details . . . fit coherently together; compare the slips in chronology which have been unearthed in, for example, *Madame Bovary.*"[4] Each of the chapters covers a definite period of time, ranging from a year

(chapter VI) to twenty-four hours (chapter VII). Sometimes the passage of time is quite precisely noted: "M. de P*** fut obligé . . . de s'absenter pendant six semaines (p. 58); "Nous vécûmes ainsi quatre mois" (p. 65); "Deux jours s'écoulèrent" (p. 67); "Les six mois que m'avait accordés mon père étaient expirés" (p. 75).[5] More often the references are a little more vague: "Plusieurs jours se passèrent" (p. 40); "cette histoire de quelques semaines" (p. 51); "les jours suivants" (pp. 110 and 130). Still, thanks to these indications, the action of the novel can be calculated to cover approximately four years in all.

This space of time accords, moreover, with the other and more obvious method Constant uses to make the internal chronology clear: the periodic reminders he gives us of his hero's age. The first of these occurs in the opening sentence, in which Adolphe states that he is beginning his narrative at the point when he completed his studies at the age of twenty-two. Early on in chapter VI his father alludes to the fact that Adolphe has passed his twenty-fourth birthday, while in the following chapter the Baron de T*** observes (p. 99) not only that Adolphe is now twenty-six but also that Ellénore "a dix ans de plus que vous." These statements serve, of course, another purpose than that of establishing the internal chronology of the novel. For a contemporary reader it would be immediately obvious that, for most of the period covered in the novel, the hero was legally a minor, unable to marry without parental consent and risking, perhaps, arrest if he defied his father too openly—a point implied, indeed, in the letter his father writes to him at Caden: "Vous avez vingt-quatre ans . . . : je n'exercerai pas contre vous une autorité qui touche à son terme" (p. 84).

If, however, passing from the internal to the external chronology of *Adolphe,* we aks in what decade of what century these four crucial years in the hero's life are to be situated, we appear to come up against a blank wall. In so far as critics have posed the question, they answer it in one of two ways: either they dismiss it as meaningless, pleading that Constant's masterpiece is not a realist novel tethered to a particular historical period but a psychological drama as a-historical as, say, *King Lear*; or else they situate the action somewhere in the early 1790s, arguing that the novel is so indisputably autobiographical that, when Constant says Adolphe is twenty-two, he is thinking of the period when he himself was twenty-two. Thus in the preface to a recent popular edition of the book, Jean Mistler, after asserting that "le récit n'est guère plus localisé dans le temps que dans l'espace," proceeds to refer to the fact that Adolphe is twenty-two when he meets Ellénore and twenty-six when she dies and comments: "Ces indications, rapportées à la vie de Benjamin Constant, placeraient l'action autour de 1792 . . . mais le milieu social où elle se déroule est un milieu d'Ancien Régime." Mistler further quotes the sentence in chapter VII: "Une de ces vicissitudes communes dans les républiques que des factions agitent rappela son père en Pologne," and glosses tentatively: "Cette mention peut s'appliquer aux événements qui se déroulèrent entre 1791 et 1795, date du dernier partage de la Pologne, mais on aurait grand tort d'y attacher plus d'importance que l'auteur lui-même."[6]

To elucidate the external chronology of **Adolphe,** it is obviously necessary to locate references within the text to datable external events, though the particular instance cited by Mistler may not be the most helpful; there were, after all, so many "vicissitudes" in the history of Poland, throughout the entire course of Constant's life, that one would need to take more factors into account than Mistler does, before one could risk a guess as to the particular occurrence the author had in mind when he wrote the words quoted. Clearly what is required is some more precise allusion to a known event in recorded history, which could serve as a base line for the reconstruction of the total external chronology.

We may begin by selecting, from the potted biography of Ellénore offered in chapter II, one particular detail concerning not her but her protector:

> Ce que je sais, ce que tout le monde a su, c'est que la fortune du comte de P*** ayant été presque entièrement détruite et sa liberté menacée, Ellénore lui avait donné de telles preuves de dévouement, avait rejeté avec un tel mépris les offres les plus brillantes, avait partagé ses périls et sa pauvreté avec tant de zèle et même de joie, que la sévérité la plus scrupuleuse ne pouvait s'empêcher de rendre justice à la pureté de ses motifs et au désintéressement de sa conduite
>
> (p. 33)

Let us forget for a moment the parallel that commentators of the novel have not failed to draw between this account and the devotion shown by Anna Lindsay, one of the "models" for Ellénore, to Auguste de Lamoignon during the French Revolution. We know, from the passage immediately preceding, that Ellénore met the Count in France, to which country her mother, escaping from Poland, had taken her. The reference to the near-ruin of the Count and the risk he incurred of imprisonment suggests very strongly that the Count, as a member of the French aristocracy, had to go into hiding when the Jacobins came to power, and that his estates then became forfeit under the decrees of June 3, 1793, nationalizing the property of *émigrés,* and of July 17, 1793, abolishing without compensation whatever manorial rights had not already been extinguished.

It is difficult to imagine that Ellénore could have effectively devoted herself to the Count's interests, and displayed the "activity, courage, and intelligence" that Constant here credits her with, unless she had already

reached years of discretion by 1793. This would imply that she was born no later than 1772. Now it was in this year that the first partition of Poland took place, with a preliminary treaty signed at St. Petersburg in February between Prussia and Russia and a second treaty, allowing Austria to annex East Galicia, in August.[7] It thus seems reasonable, provisionally at least, to suppose that it was to this disaster that Constant intended referring when he wrote that Ellénore's family, "assez illustre en Pologne, avait été ruinée dans les troubles de cette contrée" (p. 32). Her father had been banished, probably very shortly after her birth since she tells Adolphe (p. 90): "Mon père est un inconnu pour moi." She herself had been taken to France by her mother when she was three (p. 89), that is, in 1775. At some indeterminate point between then and the beginnings of her liaison with the Count, her mother had died.

The chronology of Ellénore's early life allows us to fix that of Adolphe. We know that she was ten years older than he (p. 99). If our earlier deductions are accepted, this would imply that he was born in 1782 and that the starting-point of the novel would therefore be 1804. This date is corroborated by an incidental remark made by Ellénore (p. 67): "J'ai rempli pendant dix ans mes devoirs mieux qu'aucune femme." The context makes it clear that she is referring to her quasi-conjugal "duties" to the Count, and we have already seen that her close relationship with him must date from mid-1793 or shortly after. The "ten years" would take us approximately to 1804.

Our examination of the internal chronology of the book has shown that the final episodes, set in or near Warsaw, must be placed some four years later, i.e. in 1808.[8] We learn that, in the terms of the sentence quoted by Mistler, Ellénore's father was recalled to Poland by "une de ces vicissitudes communes dans les républiques que des factions agitent" (p. 89), and that he regains possession of his estates. He sets afoot inquiries to discover the present whereabouts of his only child Ellénore; and having traced her to Caden, writes inviting her to join him. This she declines to do, knowing it would mean parting from Adolphe. After hesitating for some time, he reaches the point of agreeing to accompany her to Poland, when she receives information that her father has died suddenly (p. 93), whereupon the two of them set out together on the journey to Ellénore's native country.

It is clear that the change in his fortunes that allowed her father to emerge from exile cannot have been, as Mistler supposes, anything that took place between 1791 and 1795; it must have been an event occurring shortly before 1808. Now in July 1807 Napoleon, having defeated the combined Russian and Prussian armies at the battle of Friedland the previous month, had a well-publicized meeting with Tsar Alexander at Tilsit and wrested from the Russian ruler his consent to the establishment of a new Polish state, to be called the Duchy of Warsaw. By this act Poland, obliterated from the map of Europe by the Third Partition (1795-6), was reconstituted in a form that was to last at any rate for the next few years, and it seems highly probable that this new turn of events was what Constant had in mind when he wrote of the "vicissitude" that allowed Ellénore's father to return to his homeland.

Thus the external chronology of *Adolphe* can be seen to be consistent and, given a reasonable interpretation of Constant's vaguely worded allusions, to be firmly linked to a series of well-attested historical events: the first partition of Poland in 1772, the sequestration of estates belonging to French *émigré* aristocrats in 1793, and the re-establishment of Poland, under the name of the Duchy of Warsaw, in 1807. It is noteworthy that all these events touch on the life-story of Ellénore, not of Adolphe, and this may have been one reason why Constant gave them so little prominence and refrained from spelling out the points of reference too clearly: for it was Adolphe, not Ellénore, who was to be the central character; the very form he adopted, the first-person confessional novel, required this. In addition, one has to remember the severe constrictions under which any novelist wrote at a period when the French Empire was all-powerful on the continent. Napoleon's efficiently organized censorship might well have taken steps to impede publication of Constant's novel if it had included overly transparent allusions to delicate political issues. He would not have forgotten the trouble Mme de Staël ran into when she brought out her first novel, *Delphine,* the incautiously pro-British tone of which had provoked the First Consul to remark, menacingly: "J'espère que les amis de madame de Staël l'ont avisée de ne pas venir à Paris; je serais obligé de la faire reconduire à la frontière par la gendarmerie."[9] She was to compound the offence in 1807 with her second novel, *Corinne,* in which it was not merely the marked anglophilia evident in the creation of Lord Oswald Nelvil, but also the diatribes in favour of Italian independence, that aroused the indignation of Napoleon, his ministers, courtiers, and the entire literary establishment in France. So long as the Empire lasted—and who could tell how long that would be?—common prudence obliged authors to delete any overt references in their work to contemporary political issues.

Before drawing any general conclusions from the foregoing argument, we need to consider one fundamental objection that could be made to our reconstruction of the historical background to *Adolphe.* If we accept that the reference in chapter II to the proscription of Ellénore's father is to be linked to the events of 1772, account has to be taken of the fact that the First Partition took the form of a simple transfer of sovereignty, to Russia, Austria, and Prussia, of certain frontier provinces of the Polish Commonwealth, namely those parts of White Russia and modern Latvia lying east of the rivers Dvina and Dnieper, East Galicia and Lodomeria, and West Prussia with the exception of Danzig. These transfers of territory took place without any active resistance on the part of the Poles; the big landowners were left in possession of their estates, and none appears to have been ruined (as we are told Ellénore's father was), imprisoned, or driven into exile. They simply became subjects of different monarchs, and reconciled themselves easily to the change; one of them, Mme Potocka-Kossakowska, is reported to have declared to her Austrian friends: "If you leave me my wealth and my religion, what shall I have to regret?"[10]

It is true that in 1767, a few years before the First Partition, when Catherine was having difficulty in persuading the Diet to grant rights and privileges to Polish subjects of the Greek Orthodox confession, her ambassador in Warsaw, Prince Repnin, had four troublemakers, including the governor of Cracow and two Roman Catholic bishops, arrested and sent as prisoners to Russia.[11] But it seems much less likely that Constant was thinking of this earlier incident than of the desperate struggle for survival that the Poles were finally goaded into making in the early 1790s. Between May and July 1792 the invading Russians were met with armed resistance, the leaders of which, when it collapsed, took refuge abroad. In 1793 the city of Danzig defied Frederick of Prussia's troops for ten weeks, before being starved into surrender. But it was the so-called Kościuszko Insurrection that caught the imagination of European liberals, Constant among them. Kościuszko, who had fought under Prince Józef Poniatowski in 1792, had made his way to revolutionary Paris to enlist support for the Polish cause: but although given a cordial welcome, he could not obtain more than moral backing from the French, and accordingly the Poles were left to fight for their freedom on their own. The insurrection started from Cracow on March 24, 1794, and was at first remarkably successful, even though it was largely a matter of peasants armed with scythes opposing trained troops with guns. Warsaw went over to the patriots on April 17, and later that month the Polish regiments drafted into the Russian army in the Ukraine rose in rebellion. However, Kościuszko was defeated in a pitched battle at Rawka in June and lost Cracow. The rising was finally crushed in November 1794, Kościuszko and some of his comrades being deported to St. Petersburg while others, who had sought asylum in Austria, were also imprisoned.

It was the failure of the Kościuszko Insurrection that led directly to the Russo-Prussian convention of October 24, 1795 by which the Third (and final) Partition of Poland was decided on. "Seeking refuge from persecution, the men of the insurrection, who were the active élite of the nation, went into exile in crowds. . . . State property and estates of which the Polish patriots had been deprived passed into the hands of foreign donatories."[12]

The interest Constant took in the Kościuszko Insurrection is evident from the letters he was writing at the time from Brunswick. "Vous savez l'insurrection de Pologne, les vêpres polonaises," he wrote to one correspondent on March 5, 1794: "la prise de Varsovie et de Cracovie par les insurgés qui y ont trouvé 600 canons et qui sont au nombre de 25.000 hommes de troupes réglées et de 80.000 paysans." Three months later he included in a letter to his aunt Mme de Nassau a further bulletin on the success of the Poles in encounters with the Russians; and in July he recorded their defeat: "Les pauvres Polonais sont très mal dans leurs affaires. Le roi de Prusse les a battus, les Russes s'avancent et les insurgés n'ont ni forteresse, ni munitions."[13]

When he came to write *Adolphe,* twelve or more years later, Constant remembered these events and transposed them mentally to the earlier invasion of Poland which, of course, occurring as it did when he was in his infancy, would have been known to him only by report. In the latter part of 1807 he had temporarily shelved work on his novel in favour of a new adaptation of Schiller's *Wallenstein,* when news of Napoleon's creation of the Duchy of Warsaw reached Coppet and became the subject of eager discussion in Mme de Staël's circle. "La société y était assez 'polonisée'," reports Mme Claire Nicolas. "Il y avait là Zacharias Werner [the German dramatist who had worked as a civil servant in Warsaw and Berlin down to 1807] que Mme de Staël admirait beaucoup, et d'anciens émigrés réfugiés en Pologne, comme Elzéar de Sabran."[14] On September 25 Prosper de Barante arrived hot-foot from Poland and was able to give his hostess first-hand information about the steps leading up to the creation of the Duchy of Warsaw. Napoleon's solution of the Polish question fell far short of satisfying the aspirations of the patriots who had faithfully served under his command, supplying contingents to fight in Italy in 1796 and in San Domingo in 1802, and trusting always that he would fulfil the promise he made at Verona, in September 1796, to "force the Russians to re-establish Poland." That Constant shared to the full the interest the Coppet group took in Barante's account, and their indignation at Napoleon's cynical manoeuvring, is evident from the brief entries in his diary, dated September 25 and 26, 1807: "Prosper arrivé. Il nous donnera des détails curieux. Je ne voudrais pas me remettre en indignation ou en terreur. Mais quel monstre!" "Prosper arrivé. Quels détails! Quelle bizarre, ridicule, atroce chose que l'espèce humaine!"[15]

Included in Napoleon's dispositions for the new duchy was the redistribution of the old crown lands among French marshals and other imperial dignitaries. Additionally, some of the confiscated estates were allotted to those Polish leaders who had served him in the past, Józef Poniatowski, the nephew of the last king of Poland, Jan Henryk Dabrowski who, after making contact with Bonaparte in Milan in 1796, had founded the Polish Legion, and Józef Zajaczek, who had formed another Polish unit to fight with the French in 1799. Such men were not, of course, in the same situation as Ellénore's fictitious father, dispossessed and banished in 1772 and recovering his estates on the creation of the Duchy of Warsaw in 1807. In imagining his shadowy life-story, Constant was taking the same liberties with history as, traditionally, novelists have always been allowed to take, ever since they started giving their novels a historical setting.

Nevertheless, the evidence assembled here is perhaps sufficient to establish that *Adolphe* does have a genuine historical dimension; however timeless the story, it does not take place "outside time." But a more important conclusion concerns Ellénore's reality as a fictional creation. When the novel was first published, and for at least a century afterwards, critics tried to argue that Ellénore, as a character, lacked substance and unity, being a mere piecing together of traits Constant had observed in the various women with whom he had had amorous relations in the course of his life. "Ni les circonstances de la vie, ni celles de la personne n'ont aucune identité," wrote Sismondi within months of the publication of the book. "Il en résulte qu'à quelques égards elle se montre dans le cours du roman tout autre qu'il ne l'a annoncée."[16] Sismondi's view, quoted approvingly by Sainte-Beuve, clearly influenced the judgements passed on Ellénore by Emile Faguet ("il me semble qu'elle est composée un peu artificiellement de parties qui ne sont pas tout à fait d'accord"), and by Anatole France, who in any case detested Ellénore on what would, in today's jargon, be called "male chauvinist" grounds: "Un manque d'unité se trahit entre la femme discrète qui figurait au début du livre et la victime bruyante dont le désespoir s'étale sans mesure pour finir dans la mort."[17] These criticisms, and of course those of Gustave Rudler, were in part founded on the numerous parallels that biographical research had succeeded in establishing between Ellénore and her "models," Germaine de Staël, Anna Lindsay, Charlotte de Hardenberg e tutte quante. In the last few years, a salutary attempt has been made, first and foremost by Alison Fairlie in her article on the creation of character in *Adolphe,*[18] to view Ellénore strictly as a product of the creative writer's imagination, with an internal coherence which does not prevent her, under the stress of her difficult relations with Adolphe, from developing and perhaps deteriorating in the course of the action. One cannot, of course, exclude from all consideration the evidence concerning "models" assembled by earlier generations of scholars; but it is important not to give this evidence more than its due weight. Any novelist of the male sex must create his heroines out of the knowledge of women that experience has brought him. As Paul Bénichou puts it: "Mieux eût valu admettre qu'Ellénore est à la fois plusieurs femmes, *quoiqu'elle ne puisse être aucune d'elles.* Ne pas affronter ce paradoxe, c'est, je le crains, se condamner à ne pas comprendre ce qu'est *Adolphe.*"[19]

What it is hoped the present study will have contributed to the debate is a further argument in favour of the thesis that Ellénore was conceived by Constant as an autonomous fictional character with an independent life-history. This life-history, extending beyond the chronological bounds set by the action as related by Adolphe, was no doubt present in Constant's mind in all its details as he wrote the novel; it is one which, if we take the trouble to draw the necessary conclusions from the occasional clues he gives us, can have the same kind of authenticity for us, linked as it is to verifiable historical events; for Ellénore's biography, in its bare outlines, can be plotted along a series of dates just as though she were a real person: born 1772, taken by her mother to France in 1775, became the mistress of the Count de P*** 1793-4, bore him two children (say) 1796-8, seduced by Adolphe 1804, returned to Poland and died 1808.

Notes

1. Larkin, *Man and Society in Nineteenth-Century Realism* (London: Macmillan, 1977), p. 5.

2. The book was first registered in the *Bibliographie de la France* (March 7, 1829) as *Quinze cent soixante douze. Chronique du temps de Charles IX.*

3. The contrast with *Cécile* is striking. Not only is an exact date quoted in the opening sentence ("Ce fut le 11 janvier 1793 que je fis connaissance avec Cécile de Walterbourg, aujourd'hui ma femme"), but each of the seven "époques" into which the novel, as far as it goes, is divided, is provided with its dating. One cannot tell, of course, whether Constant would have retained these dates if he had completed *Cécile* and published it.

4. Fairlie, "The Art of Constant's *Adolphe*. Structure and Style," *French Studies*, XX (1966), 229, 241 n. 4.

5. Page-references are, here and elsewhere, to the edition of *Adolphe* by Jacques-Henri Bornecque, Paris, Garnier, 1955. A complete list of the internal "repères chronologiques" can be found in Paul Delbouille, *Genèse, structure et destin d' "Adolphe"* (Paris: Les Belles Lettres, 1971), p. 213, n. 18.

6. Constant, *Adolphe,* suivi du *Cahier rouge* et de *Poèmes inédits,* ed. Jean Mistler (Paris: Librairie Générale Française, 1972), p. xii-xiii.

7. For detailed accounts of these events and the subsequent history of Poland referred to in this article, see: *The Cambridge History of Poland from Augustus II to Pilsudski (1697-1935)* (Cambridge: University Press, 1941); Georg von Manteuffel-Szoege, *Geschichte des polnischen Volkes während seiner Unfreiheit, 1772-1914* (Berlin: Duncker & Humblot, 1950); Herbert H. Kaplan, *The First Partition of Poland* (New York: Columbia U.P., 1962); and Piotr S. Wandycz, *The Lands of Partitioned Poland, 1795-1918* (Seattle: U. of Washington Press, 1974).

8. This is not the place to enter into a discussion of the vexed question when Constant may be supposed to have completed the writing of *Adolphe.* Andrew Oliver ("*Cécile* et la genèse d'*Adolphe,*" *Revue des Sciences humaines,* fasc. 125 [1967], 5-28) suggests 1809-10, and none of those who have considered the problem seem inclined to put it much earlier; see Bornecque's introduction to the Classiques Garnier edition of *Adolphe*; Anthony R. Pugh, "*Adolphe* et *Cécile,*" *Revue d'Histoire Littéraire de la France,* LXIII (1963), 415-23; Paul Bénichou, *L'Écrivain et ses travaux* (Paris: Corti, 1967), pp. 91-119 ("La Genèse d'*Adolphe*"); and Delbouille, *op. cit.,* chap. I ("La Naissance d'*Adolphe*").

9. See Paul Gautier, *Madame de Staël et Napoléon* (Paris: Plon, 1921), p. 106.

10. Quoted by Henryk Frankel, *Poland, the Struggle for Power, 1772-1939* (London: Lindsay Drummond, 1946), p. 30.

11. Kaplan, *op. cit.,* p. 89.

12. *Cambridge History . . . ,* p. 175. See also Wandycz, *op. cit.,* pp. 15-22.

13. Constant, *Lettres à sa famille,* ed. J.-H. Ménos (Paris: Stock, 1888), pp. 131-2, 262. See Claire Nicolas, "Pourquoi Ellénore est-elle polonaise?", *Revue d'Histoire Littéraire de la France,* LXVI (1966), 86-7.

14. "Mme de Staël et la Pologne," *Kwartalnik Neofilologiczny,* XV (1968), 42.

15. *Œuvres,* ed. Alfred Roulin (Paris: Gallimard, 1964), p. 628.

16. Quoted by Delbouille, op. cit., p. 405.

17. Emile Faguet, *Politiques et moralistes du XIXe siècle, 1re série* (Paris: Société française d'imprimerie et de librairie, n.d.); France, *Le Génie latin* (Paris: Calmann-Lévy, 1917), pp. 334-5.

18. Fairlie, "The Art of Constant's *Adolphe*: creation of character," *Forum for Modern Language Studies,* II (1966), 253-63.

19. Bénichou, *L'Écrivain et ses travaux* (Paris: Corti, 1967), p. 114. My italics.

Guy Howard Dodge (essay date 1980)

SOURCE: Dodge, Guy Howard. "Popular Sovereignty." In *Benjamin Constant's Philosophy of Liberalism: A Study in Politics and Religion,* pp. 52-79. Chapel Hill: The University of North Carolina Press, 1980.

[*In the following essay, Dodge traces Constant's conception of "popular sovereignty" and links this to the principle assumptions of such writers as Alexís de Tocqueville regarding the true nature of democracy.*]

According to Emile Faguet, "from Jurieu to Robespierre, through Burlamaqui and Rousseau, there is a constant tradition of Jacobinism."[1] Constant sought to refute this Jacobin tradition by reprinting with some additions and alterations a chapter **"De la souveraineté du peuple,"** with which he had begun his ***Principes de politique applicables à tous les gouvernements représentatifs,*** published during the Hundred Days, when Napoleonic rule based on that concept was the menace to freedom. This revised version—**"De la souveraineté des peuples et de ses limites"**—was added to the second edition of Constant's ***Réflexions sur les constitutions, la distribution des pouvoirs et les garanties dans une monarchie constitutionnelle,*** published in 1818.[2] In this essay it is clear that Constant perceived, to use the words of Alexander Passerin D'Entrèves, that "positive liberty [ancient liberty] and popular sovereignty go hand in hand" and that "one is the ideological justification of the other."[3]

Constant begins his essay by explaining in 1818 that four years earlier he had no reason to deal with the subject of popular sovereignty, because at that time liberty was not in jeopardy from that direction. In 1815, however, things were quite different, because Bonaparte, as we have already noted, always had justified his despotic power upon the basis of the sovereignty of the people. Therefore, this theory had to be contested once again during the Hundred Days.

Constant stated first that he had not been able to find anywhere a "precise and exact definition" of the principle of popular sovereignty, but in his analysis he specifically criticizes Montesquieu, Rousseau, and Thomas Hobbes on this subject.[4] He does not, interestingly enough, cite the well-known delineation of popular or national sovereignty by the Abbé Sieyès, who wrote: "The nation is prior to everything. It is the source of everything. Its will is always legal. The manner in which a nation exercises its will does not matter; the point is that it does exercise it; any procedure is adequate and its will is always the supreme law."[5]

Constant's own thesis was then outlined—"The abstract recognition of popular sovereignty in no way increases the sum of the liberty of individuals."[6] Not only that, but "unlimited sovereignty" is positively dangerous. If true, then, why have party leaders or even the lovers of liberty been so "reluctant to limit sovereignty"? It is because they have objected to "this or that kind of government" or "this or that class of governors"; in short, to the "harmful possessors of power and not to the power itself." In other words, "instead of destroying it they have thought only of replacing it."[7]

In a footnote, Constant noted that Montesquieu seemed to limit popular sovereignty in certain passages of *The Spirit of the Laws.* For example, the baron said that "justice existed before the laws," which is "to imply that the laws and consequently the general will of which the laws are only the expression, must be subordinated to justice."[8] But what happened to Montesquieu's proposition? Namely this: that "often the depositories of power are parties of the principle that justice existed before the laws in order to subject individuals to retroactive laws or to deprive them of the benefit of existing laws."

Constant continued that Montesquieu in his definition of liberty had misunderstood the limits of social authority. The baron had interpreted liberty as "a right of doing whatever the laws permit," which is a statement of the rule of law whereby one may do whatever the law does not forbid (prohibit).[9] In other words, liberty consists of that sphere within which man is unrestrained by law. But Constant objected that Montesquieu "had confused two things: liberty and its guarantee." "Individual rights, that is liberty; political rights, that is the guarantee." His famous maxim "that individuals have the right to do whatever the laws permit is a principle of guarantee. I mean that no one has the right to prevent another from doing what the laws do not forbid but it does not explain what the laws have or do not have the right to prohibit."[10] But "there is where liberty resides," because "liberty is nothing more than what individuals have the right to do and what society does not have the right to proscribe."

Now to return to the body of the text. Constant submits that popular sovereignty legitimately means "the supremacy of the general will over all particular wills."[11] To cite the notes again, "the axiom of the sovereignty of the people has been considered as a principle of liberty," whereas instead "it is a principle of guarantee" because it is designed "to prevent one individual from seizing the authority, which only belongs to the entire association."

Constant, however, always denied that "society as a whole exercised unlimited sovereignty over its members," because "there is . . . a part of human life which of necessity remains individual and independent and which, as of right, remains outside the jurisdiction of society.[12] Sovereignty exists only in a limited and relative way. The jurisdiction of this sovereignty stops at the point where the independence of individual life starts. If society crosses this border, it becomes as culpable as the despot whose title rests only on the sword of destruction; society cannot exceed its competence without usurpation; the majority cannot do so without becoming a faction. The consent of the majority by no means suffices in all cases to make its acts legitimate; there are some acts which nothing can make legitimate. When any authority commits acts of this sort, it matters little from what source it claims to derive; it matters little whether it is called an individual or nation, it might be the entire nation with the exception of the citizen whom it oppresses, and the act would still not be legitimate."[13]

By thus equating freedom with independence within a certain sphere, Constant was defining, of course, negative freedom. This places him in what John Stuart Mill called "the newer generation of European liberals . . . who thought the central problem of political theory was the limits of what a government may do." Mill had noted that "the earlier generation saw the central problem in making the ruling power emanate from the periodical choice of the ruled [self-government]."[14] It is instructive to compare Constant's definition of freedom with Tocqueville's. His liberal successor wrote: "According to the modern notion of liberty every man . . . is inherently entitled to be uncontrolled by his fellows in all that only concerns himself and to regulate at his own will his own destiny."[15] In all three—Constant, Tocqueville, and Mill—"there is the same negative definition of liberty as freedom from external control and the same delineation of an area of self-regarding actions, which should be properly left to the individual himself."[16]

Constant's treatment of popular sovereignty in his *Principes de politique* and *Réflexions sur les constitutions* should be compared with his analysis of the same subject later on in his *Commentaire sur l'ouvrage de Filangieri (The Science of Legislation)*: "In the portion of human existence which must rest independent of legislation, resides individual rights, which legislation must not touch, rights over which society has no jurisdiction." Constant adds in summary that "the legitimacy of authority depends on its object as much as on its source. When authority extends over objects, which are beyond its sphere, it becomes illegitimate."[17]

Constant thought that because Gaetano Filangieri, an eighteenth-century Italian philosophe, would have the law fix the rights of each individual, who had only such rights as legislation left to him, his system was just as unlimited in nature as Rousseau's, whose "*Social Contract,* so often invoked on behalf of liberty," was instead "the most terrible auxiliary of all kinds of despotism."[18] But once again Constant repeated in a footnote that he was "far from joining the detractors of Rousseau," who "are numerous in our day. A mob of inferiors, who hope to become successful by calling into question all courageous truths, occupy themselves in an attempt to blemish his glory. That is but one reason the more for being wary of blaming him. He was the first to popularize the feeling for our rights. Generous hearts and independent souls were awakened at the sound of his voice."

Constant was convinced, however, that "what Rousseau felt strongly he did not always define clearly; many chapters of the *Social Contract* are worthy of the scholastic writers of the fifteenth century."[19] Constant adds that "the fomenters of despotism can draw an immense advantage from Rousseau's principles." He then cites one, without naming him. It was Louis-Mathieu Molé, who in his *Essais de morale et de politique* (1806) contended that the power of society's representative was not arbitrary because "it was no longer a man but a people."[20] After such reasoning, how, Constant asks, can Rousseau ever be reproached for his "abstractions?"[21]

In 1820, Constant observed that "every time laws are proposed against liberty Jean-Jacques Rousseau is quoted for authority. With much love for liberty, Rousseau has always been cited by those who wish to establish despotism. Rousseau has served as a pretext for despotism because he had the feeling for liberty but not for theory."[22] Constant, however, thought it was wrong to apply Rousseau's concepts, which were developed in a period of history when liberty was not yet established, to a later generation of men that is wiser after thirty years of unfortunate experiences, such as the French Revolution (The Terror and Babeuf) and Bonapartism.

In his critique of Rousseau, in **"De la souveraineté du peuple et de ses limites,"** Constant devotes special attention to Chapter 6 of Book I of the *Social Contract* entitled "The Social Pact." He points out that Rousseau defines the "contract entered into by society and its members" as

> the complete alienation without reserve of each individual and all his rights to the community. To reassure us as to the consequences of such an absolute abandonment with respect to all phases of our existence for the benefit of an abstract being, he tells us that the sovereign, that is to say, the social body, cannot do injury either to its members collectively or to any one of them in particular; and each giving himself completely, the conditions are the same for all and, therefore, it is in no one's interest to make the conditions onerous for others.

Finally, Rousseau contended that "each in giving himself to all, gives himself to no one; and since each acquires over all his associates the same rights that he surrendered to them, he gains the equivalent of everything he loses, with more power to conserve what he has."[23]

In his detailed refutation, Constant argued that Rousseau

> forgets all these preservative attributes, which he confers upon the abstract being called the sovereign and the consequence of its being composed of every individual without exception. But as soon as the sovereign must make use of the power which he possesses, that is to say, as soon as he finds it necessary to proceed to a practical organization of authority, because the sovereign cannot exercise it himself, he delegates it, and all these attributes disappear.[24] Acts done in the name of all, being necessarily in the control of only one person or a few, the result is that in giving one's self to all it is not true that one gives oneself to nobody: on the contrary, one gives one's self to those who act in the name of all. From that follows that in giving one's self completely the conditions are not the same for all, since some profit exclusively from the sacrifice of the rest. It is not true that it is in no one's interest to make the conditions onerous for others. . . . It is not true that all those associated acquire the same rights, which they cede; they do not gain the equivalent of what they lose.

Continuing with his confutation, Constant is very cogent in his analysis.

> As soon as the general will becomes all powerful, the representatives of this general will will become all the more formidable in that they call themselves only docile instruments of this pretended will. . . . What no tyrant would dare do in his own name, they legitimize through the limitless social authority. . . . The most unjust laws, the most oppressive institutions, are obligatory as the expression of the general will, for, as Rousseau says, individuals being entirely dedicated to the benefit of the social body, can have no will other than this general will. In obeying this will, they obey only themselves.

Constant then reminds his readers that "the consequences of this system . . . unfolded themselves to their full extent during . . . the Revolution"; in fact, "the crudest sophistries of the most impetuous apostles of the Terror were merely perfectly appropriate consequences of Rousseau's principles."[25] Constant quickly added, however, that "Rousseau himself was afraid of these consequences." Therefore, he "declared that sovereignty could be neither transferred nor delegated nor represented."[26] To Constant, however, this simply meant that "it could not be exercised"; in fact, "it amounted in practice to destroying the principle he [Rousseau] had just proclaimed."

At this point, Constant makes reference to Hobbes, who "reduced despotism to a system." The great English theorist had argued that sovereignty was unlimited and

that "it is clear that the absolute character which Hobbes attributed to the people's sovereignty is the basis of his entire system." In fact, however, Hobbes developed the concept of ruler rather than popular sovereignty.

Continuing his examination of Rousseau, Constant states that "this word 'absolute' makes liberty . . . impossible under any kind of institution," for "when sovereignty is not limited there is no means of protecting individuals from governments.[27] It is in vain that you claim to submit governments to the general will. It is they who dictate this will and all precautions become illusory. Rousseau said we are sovereign in one respect and subject in another. But in practice these two aspects are confounded. It is easy for authority to oppress the people as subject in order to force it to manifest as sovereign the will which it prescribes to it."[28]

What is the remedy for this? Constant replied that "you can try a division of powers in vain; but, if the sum total of powers is unlimited, the divided powers have only to form a coalition for despotism to be installed without remedy." This point was also made by Bentham when he treated the subject of the separation of powers. To Constant, then, "what is important . . . is . . . not that . . . rights may not be violated by one power without the approval of another, but rather that such a violation be forbidden to all powers."

Constant concludes that "no authority on earth is unlimited, neither that of the people nor that of the men who claim to be their representative nor that of the king nor that of the law."[29] The boundaries to authority "are fixed by justice and by the rights of individuals," such as personal liberty, religious liberty, industrial liberty, inviolability of property, liberty of opinion, and "the guarantee against *tout arbitraire*."[30] Therefore, "not even the will of an entire people can make just what is unjust. The representatives of a nation do not have the right to do what the nation itself has not the right to do. . . . The consent of a people cannot make legitimate what is illegitimate."[31]

Constant was convinced, unlike the Doctrinaires, that the "limitation of power in the abstract is not sufficient." In addition, "we must look for the foundations of political institutions. . . . Limitation of sovereignty is, therefore, . . . possible. . . . It will be safeguarded first by the force of public opinion and second . . . by the distribution and balance of powers."[32]

Having examined Montesquieu's definition of liberty as "the right of doing whatever the laws permit" and Rousseau's that "liberty is obedience to a law which we prescribe to ourselves," Constant concluded that for him freedom was "the triumph of individuality as much over a government which seeks to rule by despotic methods as over the masses who seek to render the minority a slave to the majority."[33] "Despotism has no rights," however. "The majority has the right to compel the minority to respect public order, but everything which does not disturb public order, everything which is only private, such as our opinions, everything which, in manifestation of opinion, does no harm to others either by provoking physical violence or opposing contrary opinions, everything which, in industry, allows a rival industry to carry on freely—this is something individual that cannot legitimately be subjected to the social power."[34]

In 1859, John Stuart Mill, many of whose ideas are very similar to Constant's noted, in *On Liberty,* chapter 1, that the ideas that "the nation did not need to be protected against its own will" and that "there was no fear of its tyrannizing over itself" were "common among the last generation of European Liberalism."[35] He also stated that "those who admit any limit to what a government may do . . . stand out as brilliant exceptions among the political thinkers of the Continent." Although he was not named, Constant was just such an exception. He had, however, his liberal predecessors and successors, who attacked the theory of popular sovereignty and its chief exponent, Rousseau, as well.

During the French Revolution, Jean Joseph Mounier had contended in 1792 that occasionally in history civil liberty had existed under the absolute power of a king, but never under the absolute power of the people. In fact, he concluded that "the government the least favorable to liberty would be a pure democracy, that is to say, supreme power without limits in the hands of the people, which leads to the majority tyrannizing over the minority."[36] This idea, that all democracies are essentially despotic is, of course, as old as Plato and Kant and as new as Vilfredo Pareto, Gaetano Mosca, and Robert Michels. Moreover, in anticipation of Constant, Mounier had observed in 1789 that "people sustain the despotism of the multitude because they share in it, little realizing that popular despotism often ends in the arbitrary power of one man."[37]

In 1793, the Swiss polemicist Jacques Mallet du Pan suggested that "with the exception of Condorcet, all the revolutionaries of France, beginning with Sieyès and ending with Marat, were the disciples of Rousseau," who "alone innoculated the French with the doctrine of popular sovereignty and with its most extreme consequences."[38] According to Mallet, this theory established the "despotism of the majority, that is, the right of the strongest over the minority." Furthermore, "this unlimited power of the majority can only be based on sheer force unless it is grounded in justice and reason." It was Mallet's conclusion, therefore, that because "Locke and Cicero placed justice and reason above the right of the multitude, they are to be preferred to revolutionaries like Sieyès and Louvet." It is no wonder, then, that the

"English, much more advanced than the rest of Europe in public law, have always despised the *Contrat Social.*"

Counterrevolutionary conservatives, such as Burke and Joseph de Maistre, as well as such liberals as Constant and Madame de Staël, participated at the time in the general denunciation of popular sovereignty.[39] The liberal reaction to the French Revolution, however, is our chief concern. Germaine de Staël depicted in 1795 and again in 1816 the disastrous effect of the French Revolution on civil liberty, yet she always distinguished 1789 from 1792 and the Girondins from the Jacobins. She would have agreed with Charles de Rémusat, who declared later, "Liberal ideas are born in revolutions. It is almost always through revolutions that they are founded and that they prevail."[40]

In the middle of the nineteenth century, Prosper de Barante commented on Rousseau and popular sovereignty in terms that are remarkably similar to those of his friend Benjamin Constant. Barante claims that Rousseau saw no difficulty at all in having each person by contract abdicate his individual rights in favor of the community. He adds that popular sovereignty gives tyranny its most powerful arm. The government that exercises this sovereignty is not an abstract being but instead a man or several men, who are always animated by personal interests and moved by passions and subject to mistakes. Therefore, the doctrine of popular sovereignty results in our not taking sufficient precautions against the abuse of power, which is what makes it so dangerous to liberty. Barante then cites the controversy between Jacques Bossuet and Pierre Jurieu in the seventeenth century. The Catholic bishop accused the Huguenot pastor of asserting a right to do wrong, a right against justice, when Jurieu said that "there needs to be in a society a certain authority which does not need to be right to validate its acts and this authority is only in the people."[41] Barante concludes that there is no right in the people to do wrong, because all authority that does not offer guarantees of justice and reason is usurpation and tyranny.[42]

Saint-Marc Girardin attacked Rousseau as well as the "absolute power of the state and the sovereignty of the people" in his *Cours* given at the Sorbonne in 1848. In his presentation, he argues that "to the end of the seventeenth century the idea of the state was confused with royalty and the expression of Louis XIV 'L'état c'est moi' denoted this theory. With the eighteenth century the idea of the state began to be confused with the idea of the people, and the *Contrat Social* of Rousseau is the strongest expression of this new theory of the state."

Saint-Marc Girardin claims that

> in passing from the hands of royalty to the hands of the sovereignty of the people, the theory of the absolute state, far from becoming more modest and mild, be-

came more haughty and imperious. When the absolute power was only the absolute power of the king, the theory had the prince in favor of it but it had the subjects against it, for our enemy is our master. When it was understood that the state represented the people, and that the sovereignty of the state proceeded from the people, the vanity of everybody was flattered, without thinking that in this theory one is hardly a sovereign for a part and a slave for all the rest. Just as the monarchy of Louis XIV was the apogee of the theory of the state identified with the monarchy the Convention and the Committee of Public Safety are the apogee of the sovereignty of the state proceeding from the sovereignty of the people. But there was no more individual liberty under the Convention and the Committee of Public Safety than there was under the monarchy of Louis XIV.

In the words of Jean Jacques Chevallier, "l'état c'est moi" of Louis XIV becomes "l'état c'est nous" of Rousseau.[43]

Returning to Rousseau, Saint-Marc Girardin referred to the great Swiss thinker's argument in Book 3, chapter 1, of the *Social Contract* that "the more the state is enlarged the more freedom is diminished." Rousseau wrote: "Suppose the state has for his own share only 1/10,000th part of the sovereign authority." But "if the people is increased to 100,000 men," then the subject's "share of the suffrage is reduced to 1/100,000th." But Saint-Marc Girardin asks, what is it to be only 1/35,000,000th part of the sovereignty in a state of thirty-five million souls?[44]

Francis Lieber in America examined the same problem of popular sovereignty employing his own peculiar terminology: "That which . . . must be pronounced to be Gallican liberty is . . . the idea of the universal sovereignty of the people." In fact, "liberty is believed in France . . . to consist in the absolute rule of the majority." Rousseau in his *Social Contract* "assigns all power to the majority and teaches what might be called a divine right of the majority." Furthermore, the "*Contrat Social* was the bible of the most advanced Convention men. Robespierre read it daily and the influence of that book can be traced throughout the Revolution. Indeed we may say that two books had a peculiar influence in the French Revolution; Rousseau's *Social Contract* and Plutarch's *Lives*."[45]

John Stuart Mill also confronted the question of popular sovereignty, which he refuted in 1859:

> The notion that the people have no need to limit their power over themselves, might seem axiomatic when popular government was a thing only dreamed about and read as having existed at some distant period of the past. . . . In time, however, a democratic republic came to occupy a large portion of the earth's surface . . . it was now perceived that such phrases as "self-government" and the "power of the people over them-

selves" do not express the true state of the case. The people who exercise the power are not the same people with those over whom it is exercised; and the "self-government" spoken of is not the government of each by himself but of each by all the rest. The will of the most numerous or the most active . . . part of the people; the majority . . . the people consequently may desire to oppress a part of their number; and precautions are as much needed against this as against any other abuse of power. The limitation, therefore, of the power of government over individuals loses none of its import when the holders of power are regularly accountable to the community.[46]

Another English liberal of the nineteenth century, Lord Acton, also treated the theory of popular sovereignty. His method was to contrast what he called the "true and false democratic principles." First, "the true democratic principle that none shall have power over the people is taken to mean that none shall be able to restrain or elude its power." Second, "the true democratic principle that the people shall not be made to do what it does not like is taken to mean that it shall never be required to tolerate what it does not like." Third, "the true democratic principle that every man's will shall be as unfettered as possible is taken to mean that the free will of the collective people shall be fettered in nothing."[47]

In France, Edouard Laboulaye outlined his position in much the same vein as Constant and Mill, but, following his Swiss-French predecessor, he addressed himself to Rousseau, in particular:

> The government of the *Contrat Social,* instead of being the government of each by himself as Rousseau believed, is in theory the government of each by all the others; in fact, it is the reign of a majority; the most often the rule of a turbulent and audacious minority. In this system the state is everything and the citizen, king but man, nothing.[48]

One other French liberal who had his doubts about popular sovereignty and Rousseau was Henri De Ferron, who was writing at the same time as Edouard Laboulaye. He claimed that the sovereignty of the people had two meanings—"the sovereignty of humanity, that is, the ensemble of generations past, present, and future or the sovereignty of the present generation" alone. But "the only absolute sovereignty that can be accepted, is that of all humanity." The proponents of popular sovereignty have always confused "material force" with "moral force," with the result, especially in Rousseau's theory, of despotism, both in "logic" and in "fact."[49]

Two of Constant's contemporaries, however, the Doctrinaires Pierre Paul Royer-Collard and François Guizot, developed the most ingenious refutation of the theory of popular sovereignty. They both thought that this concept personified the revolutionary rather than the liberal spirit. In fact, Royer-Collard goes so far as to maintain that "as soon as there is sovereignty, there is despotism, whether vested in king, people, or parliament." It is no wonder that the conclusion has been drawn that "there is no sovereignty is the underlying principle of Royer-Collard's whole political theory."[50]

In a *Discours* on electoral reform (17 May 1820), Royer-Collard contended that the "difference between the sovereignty of the people and the sovereignty of free governments is that in the first there are only persons and wills; in the other there are only rights and interests."[51] In another address on the electoral law, he maintained that "there is nothing more difficult than to be liberated from the sovereignty of the people" because "it rests in the minds of most of those who combat it." In the last analysis, however, "privilege, absolute power, popular sovereignty, they are under different forms . . . the empire of force on earth." Therefore, to Royer-Collard, "there are two elements in society: the one material, which is the individual, his force and will; the other moral, which is right resulting from legitimate interests." In developing his argument, Royer-Collard puts this question: "Do you want to make society with the material element?" Then, "the majority of individuals, the majority of wills . . . is the sovereign" and "there is popular sovereignty." But, he asks, "Do you want, on the contrary, to make society with the moral element which is rights (law)?" Then, "the sovereign is justice because it is the rule of rights (law). Free constitutions have for their aim the dethronement of force and the reign of justice. Choose then your sovereign. It is force, if your government represents persons; it is justice, if it represents rights and interests."[52]

Royer-Collard thought that as long as the idea of sovereignty is retained, the problem of limiting the power of the state by law becomes insoluble. How those holding power can legitimately impose their wills by force and to what extent they are to be permitted to do so was discussed by him in a famous speech (4 October 1831) on the occasion of the suppression of the heredity of the peerage, which was regarded as inconsistent with the principle of national sovereignty:

> Yes, nations are sovereign in the sense that they are not possessed like territories but belong to themselves and have in themselves by virtue of their own natural right, the means of providing for their own conservation and their own salvation. They are sovereign also in the sense that general consent is the only true basis of governments, which, therefore, exist through nations and for nations. But these incontestable truths are rather maxims of morals than principles of government; they rather express the divine sovereignty of reason and justice than this human and practical sovereignty that makes laws and administers states.

Continuing to elaborate on his thesis, Royer-Collard then asks: "Is it the majority of individuals, the majority of wills . . . that is sovereign?" He replies: "If that

be so . . . the sovereignty of the people is only a sovereignty of force and the most absolute form of power. Before such a sovereign unguided by rule and unlimited in power, without duty and without conscience, there is no constitution, no law. . . . But force is not destined in this manner to exercise a veritable sovereignty on earth. Force constrains, it does not oblige. To oblige is the attribute of quite another sovereignty."

On what conditions and to what extent can the will of those who govern be imposed on those who are ruled? Royer-Collard's answer is clear: "When such will manifests itself in conformity to law; when it has for its object the protection of the legitimate interests, which have their origin in law." Properly understood, "societies are not numerical assemblies of individuals and wills. They have another element than numbers; they have a stronger bond—law, the privileges of humanity, and the legitimate interests which spring from law. Law does not spring from force, but from justice; societies are formed for the purpose of dethroning force and setting up justice in its place." Furthermore, the division of all "society into rights and interests" instead of "individuals and wills, is . . . the reason for and the sanction of representative government."

Royer-Collard thus appealed from "the sovereignty of the people to another sovereignty, the only one which merits the name, a sovereignty superior to people and to kings, immutable and eternal sovereignty like its author . . . the sovereignty of reason, the only true legislator of humanity," which takes the form of natural law, known to man because he is a rational being.[53]

Royer-Collard's ideas appear again in a "diffused state in the writings . . . of François Guizot," who said that he distinguished two kinds of government.[54] "First, there are those who attribute sovereignty as a right belonging exclusively to individuals, whether one, many, or all those composing a society; and these are, in principle, the founders of despotism. . . . The second class of governments is founded on the truth that sovereignty belongs as a right to no individual whatever, since the perfect and continued apprehension, the fixed and inviolable application of justice and reason do not belong to our imperfect nature."

Guizot is particularly concerned with representative government, which he approached as follows:

> The plurality is society; the unity is truth; it is the united force of the laws of justice and reason, which ought to govern society. If society remains in the condition of plurality; if isolated wills do not combine under the guidance of common rules; if they do not all equally recognize justice and reason; if they do not reduce themselves to unity, there is not a society, there is only confusion. And the unity which does not rise from plurality, which has been violently imposed upon it by

one or many, whatever be their number, in virtue of a prerogative which they appropriate as their exclusive possession, is a false and arbitrary unity; it is tyranny. The aim of representative government is to oppose a barrier at once to tyranny and to confusion and to bring plurality to unity.[55]

It is obvious that Royer-Collard, Guizot, and Constant were all seeking a point of equilibrium or a *juste milieu* between the evils of autocratic power, on the one hand, and the abuses of the multitude, on the other. All three wished to show that there is no sovereignty without limit. But the Doctrinaires, like Royer-Collard and Guizot, stressed reason and justice, especially when they were delineating the bounds of supreme power. They tried, then, not so much to determine the object of power and the manner of its exercise as to find the rule it must obey. The legislator thus does not create law but discovers it. But, it might be asked, is it easier to secure obedience to a superior law of justice and reason or to a law of competence? To the Doctrinaires, government has an absolute competence as long as it uses it within the confines of the moral law.

It will be recalled that Constant placed first the question of competence: "There are objects over which the legislator does not have the right to make a law." He also spoke of the limits of sovereignty as being "laid out by justice and the rights of individuals." This recognition of rights involves a juridical limitation. The Doctrinaires, however, had no faith in the a priori natural rights of individuals. As Royer-Collard put it, "No will, whether of man over man, of society over the individual, of the individual over society, can be exercised against justice and reason," a formula which implies the legitimacy of every action of society over the individual conforming to reason. The Doctrinaires were, therefore, "more moral than liberal."[56]

Royer-Collard, earlier than Tocqueville, was not only interested in the theory of popular sovereignty but also in the political and social implications of the destruction of the *ancien régime*.[57] The French Revolution had changed the whole social order from one of hierarchy to one of equality.[58] In fact, to Lord Acton, the abolition of the intermediate powers characterized the Great Revolution even more than the circumscription of government authority.[59] Royer-Collard was one of the first to face the question whether liberty could exist in a society polarized around the individual and the state. In short, he wondered whether liberty could ever be reconciled with a pulverized, atomized society that was no longer sustained by communal values.[60]

Royer-Collard discussed this matter while considering liberty of the press in 1820.

> We have seen the old society perish and with it that crowd of domestic institutions and independent magistrates, powerful bundles of private rights, true republics

in the monarchy. These institutions, these magistracies did not share . . . the sovereignty; but they provided [opposed] everywhere limits to it. Not one survived and none has risen in its [their] place. The revolution has left standing only individuals. . . . From pulverized society has arisen centralization. . . . Where there are only individuals, all the affairs which are not their own are public affairs, the affairs of state. Where there are no independent magistrates, there are only delegates of power. It is thus that we have become a people *d'administrés,* under the hand of irresponsible functionaries, centralized themselves in the power of which they are the ministers. The Charte constituted the government by the division of sovereignty and the multiplicity of powers. But it is not sufficient, that in order that a nation be free, that it be governed by several powers, whatever their nature and origin. The division of sovereignty is without doubt an important fact . . . but the government which results, although divided in its elements, is one in its action; and if it does not meet outside a barrier that it must respect . . . it is absolute; the nation and its rights are its property . . . it is the avowed doctrine of despotism and revolution, since it implies that there are no fundamental laws or national rights.[61]

What had happened, according to Royer-Collard, was simply this: "In the place of a single despotism we have a multiple despotism; parliamentary omnipotence after the omnipotence of one.[62] In the case of the one as in the other, society deprived of institutions, would be without a defense." Therefore, "it was only in founding the liberty of the press as a public right that the Charte has truly founded all liberties. . . . It is true that liberty of the press has the character and energy of a political institution; it is true that this institution is the only one which has restored to society some rights against the powers which rule it." Elaborating on its importance, Royer-Collard stated that "liberty of the press has this double character of a political institution and a social necessity. Publicity is a kind of resistance to the established powers because it denounces their faults and errors and is capable of causing truth and justice to triumph against them. . . . Publicity is an institution; a public liberty; for public liberties are only resistances."[63]

Royer-Collard then observed that "the voice of aristocratic command is no longer heard among us. A little conventional aristocracy, indulgent fiction of the law, but no more true aristocracy. . . . Equality of rights (this is the true name of democracy) it is the universal form of society and it is thus that democracy is everywhere."[64] Furthermore, only two guarantees have been given to rights—representative government and freedom of the press. It can be seen at once that Tocqueville was not the first to note that the inevitable tendency was in the direction of democracy, defined as equality of condition.

The most famous and influential opponent of *un nouvel arbitraire,* that is, popular sovereignty, was, of course, Alexis de Tocqueville. In his judgment, "The last generation in France showed how a people might organize a stupendous tyranny in the community at the very time when they were baffling the authority of the nobility and braving the power of kings."[65] In other words, "in the French Revolution there were two impulses in opposite directions, which must never be confounded; the one was favorable to liberty [constitutionalism], the other to despotism [popular sovereignty]."[66]

Tocqueville was especially concerned with the fact that the "democratic nations are menaced" by a "species of oppression . . . unlike anything that . . . ever before existed in the world and which cannot be described by such old words as 'despotism' and 'tyranny.'" By this he meant in part that "our contemporaries . . . devise a sole, tutelary, and all powerful government but elected by the people. They combine the principle of centralization and that of popular sovereignty; this gives them a respite; they console themselves for being in tutelage by the reflection that they have chosen their own guardians. Every man allows himself to be put in leading strings, because he sees that it is not a person or a class of persons but the people at large who hold the end of the chain."[67] Tocqueville said that he was astonished that "a great many persons at the present day are quite contented with this sort of compromise between administrative despotism and the sovereignty of the people" and "they think that they have done enough for the protection of individual freedom when they have surrendered it to the power of the nation at large. But this does not satisfy me: the nature of him I am to obey signifies less to me than the fact of extorted obedience."[68]

Tocqueville develops this same theme in many different ways. Two more examples are worth citing. First, "When I feel the hand of power lie heavy on my brow, I care but little to know who oppresses me; and I am not the more disposed to pass beneath the yoke, because it is held out to me by the arms of a million men."[69] Second, "Men do not change their characters by uniting with one another. . . . I cannot believe it; the power to do everything, which I would refuse to one of my equals, I will never grant to any number of them." This is because "unlimited power is in itself a bad and dangerous thing. . . . When I see that the right and the means of absolute command are conferred on any power whatever, be it called a people or a king, an aristocracy or a democracy, a monarchy or a republic, I say there is the germ of tyranny. And I seek to live elsewhere under other laws."[70]

Like Constant, but unlike the Doctrinaires, Tocqueville recognized the existence of sovereignty. "I am, therefore, of the opinion," he wrote, "that social power superior to all others must be placed somewhere" and "have asserted that all authority originates in the will of the majority."[71] He qualified his statement about sovereignty: "I hold it to be an impious and detestable maxim that politically speaking, the people have a right to do anything. . . . A general law which bears the name of justice, has been made and sanctioned, not only by a majority of this or that people, but by a majority of mankind. The rights of every people are therefore confined within the limits of what is just. . . ." Therefore, "when I refuse to obey an unjust law, I do not contest the right of a majority to command, but I simply appeal from the sovereignty of the people to the sovereignty of mankind."[72] Tocqueville concluded that the "power of the majority itself is not unlimited" because "above it in the moral world are humanity, justice, and reason and in the political world, vested rights."[73]

The striking similarity between the political ideas of Constant and Tocqueville is very pronounced not only in their treatment of popular sovereignty but also of liberty, which rested in both cases on religion as well as law. Tocqueville conceived of liberty as "the joy of being able to speak, to act, and to breathe without restraint under no sovereign but God and the law."[74] He always said that he wanted "a balanced regulated liberty held in check by religion, custom, and law."[75] He thought that this made him "a liberal of a new kind," and he said that he sought "a liberal but not a revolutionary party."[76]

From Mounier to Tocqueville, then, the liberal political theorists kept trying, especially in France, to find "a medium between sovereignty of all and the absolute power of one man."[77] Constant and Tocqueville both tended, however, to minimize the despotism of the divine right of kings, which looked to the past, in order to concentrate on the new enemy of individual liberty—popular and national sovereignty—which looked to the future. Although both Constant and Tocqueville distinguished between liberty and popular sovereignty, the latter did not try to oppose the two, whereas the former did just that, faced as he was with Jacobinism and the Terror. Instead, Tocqueville thought that, although "liberty is more difficult to found and maintain in democratic societies . . . like our own, than in certain aristocratic societies which had preceded them," still it is not impossible.[78] He realized that aristocratic liberty with privileges for the few had been replaced by democratic liberty with rights for all, just as the inequality of orders and estates had been supplanted by equality of conditions. As we shall see shortly, although Constant was aware of these changes when he evolved his theory of constitutionalism and pluralism, it was left to Tocqueville to formulate a complete theory of liberal democracy in the sense of both a constitutional and a pluralistic regime.

Notes

1. Emile Faguet, *Le Libéralisme*, pp. 331-32.

2. I have referred to the following sources for partial English translation of the essays quoted in this

chapter: John Plamenatz, *Readings from Liberal Writers,* pp. 199-203, and Walter Simon, *French Liberalism, 1789-1848,* pp. 64-69.

3. Alexander Passerin d'Entrèves, *The Notion of the State,* p. 212.

4. Cf. Joseph de Maistre's refutation of Rousseau in his "Etude sur la souveraineté" and Louis Bonald's in his *Essai analytique sur les lois naturelles de l'ordre social ou du pouvoir, du ministre et du sujet dans la société.* Constant, however, does not connect Rousseau with the French Revolution, as these Ultras did.

5. Joseph Sieyès, *What Is the Third Estate?,* pp. 124, 128. Cf. Antoine Boulay de la Meurthe, *Essai sur les causes qui en 1649 amènerent en Angleterre à l'établissement de la République,* pp. 121, 117, whom Constant answered in *Des suites de la contre-révolution en Angleterre*:

> Quand un changement politique est fait dans l'intérêt et avec l'approbation du peuple, il est évident que toutes les mesures nécessaires à son affermissement sont non seulement autorisées, mais commandées par la justice. . . . Nous distinguons tout-à-l'heure dans un gouvernement la chose et la personne; celle-ci n'est pas moins importante que l'autre; car il est constant que de bons gouvernans rendront le peuple plus heureux avec une mauvaise constitution qu'une bonne constitution ne le fera, confie à de mauvais gouvernans; le peuple est bien meilleur juge de ceux-ci que de celle-là . . . en un mot, s'il n'y a ni liberté publique ni liberté particulière, le peuple le voit, le sent très bien; et sa voix est alors la voix de Dieu.

6. See Montesquieu, *The Spirit of the Laws,* Book 11, chap. 2: "In fine, as in democracies the people seem to act almost as they please, this sort of government has been deemed the most free, and the power of the people has been confounded with their liberty." Cf. Chateaubriand, "Essai historique, politique et moral sur les révolutions anciennes et modernes considérées dans leurs rapports avec la révolution française," *Oeuvres complètes* (1870), 4:238: "Le principe de la souveraineté du peuple n'est d'ailleurs d'aucun intérêt pour la liberté." See also Alexis de Tocqueville, *Recollections,* pp. 201-2. This theorist said of Armand Marrast (1801-52), one of the founders of the republican party under the July Monarchy, that "he belonged to the ordinary type of French revolutionaries, who have always understood the liberty of the people to mean despotism exercised in the name of the people." Tocqueville also said, in "Voyages en Sicile et aux Etats Unis," *Oeuvres complètes,* Paris, 1951-V (1): "The people are always right is a republican dogma just as the 'king can do no wrong' is the religion of monarchical states."

7. Cf. Montesquieu's comment in *Spirit of the Laws,* Book 29, chap. 27, p. 309: "For whoever is able to dethrone an absolute prince has a power sufficient to become absolute himself." When sovereignty was shifted from the king to the people lèse-nation was put in the place of lèse-majesté.

8. The relevant passage in ibid. is to be found in Book 1, chap. 1, p. 2:

> Before laws were made there were relations of possible justice. To say that there is nothing just or unjust but what is commanded or forbidden by positive laws, is the same as saying that before the describing of a circle all the radii were not equal. We must therefore acknowledge relations of justice antecedent to the positive law by which they are established.

9. Ibid., Book 11, chap. 3, p. 150.

10. Cf. Jeremy Bentham, *Deontology or the Science of Morality,* 2:59:

> The usual definition of liberty—that is the right to do everything that the law does not forbid—shows with what carelessness words are used in ordinary discourse or composition; for if the laws are bad, what becomes of liberty? and if they are good, where is its value?

11. See the original chapter 1 of "Principes de politique," *Cours de politique,* 1:8:

> En un mot il n'existe au monde que deux pouvoirs l'un illégitime c'est la force, l'autre légitime c'est la volonté générale.

12. Cf. John Stuart Mill, *On Liberty,* chap. 1:

> "The only part of the conduct of any one, for which he is amenable to society, is that which concerns others. In the part which merely concerns himself, his independence, is, of right, absolute. Over himself, over his own body and mind, the individual is sovereign." Lord Acton agreed that liberty lies in the maintenance of an inner realm immune from the encroachment of state power. Cf. Hannah Arendt's comment that "our philosophical tradition is almost unanimous in holding that freedom begins where men have left the realm of political life . . . , and that it is not experienced in association with others but in intercourse with one's self."

> ("What Is Freedom," p. 157)

13. In his article "De la competence du gouvernement" in *Le temps* for 1830, Constant cites some examples of usurping laws, such as the laws of the Convention against the nobles, those of the Constituent Assembly imposing oaths on the clergy, and all censure laws.

14. *On Liberty,* chap. 1.

15. "Etat social et politique de la France depuis 1789 or Political and Social Condition of France," pp. 165-66.

16. Jack Lively, *The Social and Political Thought of Alexis de Tocqueville*, p. 12.

17. *Commentaire sur l'ouvrage de Filangieri*, 1:51-52.

18. In his article "De la souveraineté" in *Le temps* for 1830, Constant wrote: "Rousseau devenait le précepteur de la tyrannie comme Bossuet." Cf. the judgment of a contemporary scholar of ours, Sir Isaiah Berlin, who has called Rousseau "the most sinister and most formidable enemy of liberty in the whole history of modern thought" (BBC broadcast 5 Nov. 1952 in the series *Freedom and Its Betrayal*).

19.   "Que signifient des droits dont on jouit d'autant plus qu'on les aliène plus complètement: Qu'est-ce qu'une liberté en vertu de laquelle on est d'autant plus libre que chacun fait complètement ce qui contrarie sa volonté?"

      ("De la souveraineté du peuple et de ses limites")

20. In the manuscripts of 1810 Constant comments: "L'auteur de certains *Essais de morale et de politique* [Molé] a reproduit en faveur de l'autorité absolu tous les raisonnements de Rousseau sur la souveraineté" (F 93). In a chapter, however, of *Principes de politique* in the manuscripts of 1810, entitled "De Hobbes et du Hobbisme," Constant connects Molé with Hobbes rather than with Rousseau: "Un écrivain de nos jours l'auteur des *Essais de morale et de politique* [Molé] a renouvelé le système de Hobbes avec beaucoup moins de profondeur seulement et moins d'esprit et de logique" (F 103). "A ses [Constant's] yeux, Rousseau avec sa doctrine de la souveraineté, fondait, dans l'ordre intellectuelle, l'alliance monstreuse de la démocratie et de la monarchie absolue" as developed by Antoine-François-Claude Ferrand, in particular, in *Le rétablissement de la monarchie*. See Jean Roussel, *Jean-Jacques Rousseau en France après la Révolution, 1795-1830*, p. 502.

21. Madame de Staël has already referred to Rousseau's mathematical method. See her "Lettres sur les écrits et le caractère de Jean-Jacques Rousseau" (1788), *Oeuvres complètes de Mme la Baronne de Staël*, 1:6: "Rousseau emprunte la méthode des géometres, pour l'appliquer à l'enchainement des idées; il soumet au calcul les problèmes politiques."

22. *Discours de M. Benjamin Constant à la Chambre des Députés*, 1:211. Some modern critics have reached a conclusion similar to Constant's. See Peter Gay's introduction to his translation of Ernst Cassirer's *The Question of Jean Jacques Rous-* seau, p. 27: "Used as a critical yardstick, Rousseau's political thought has been invaluable to democratic movements; used as a political blueprint, it has had a pernicious effect on libertarian ideas and institutions." Gay said that he owed to Franz Neumann the judgment: "Rousseau is the theorist of democratic movements but not of the democratic state." Cf. Judith N. Shklar, *Men and Citizens*, p. 17, who wrote that Rousseau's *Social Contract* "was not meant to be a plan for any future society, but a standard for judging existing institutions. It was a yardstick, not a program."

23. To Isaiah Berlin, *Four Essays on Liberty*, p. 164, "Constant could not see why, even though the sovereign is 'everybody' it should not oppress one of the 'members' of its indivisible self, if it so decided."

24. Constant seems not to have read carefully enough Book 3, chap. 1, "On Government in General" of the *Social Contract*, where Rousseau said that "the executive power cannot belong to the general public in its legislator's or sovereign capacity." Constant is confusing government with sovereignty, something Rousseau never did.

25. See Edwin Mims, *The Majority of the People*, p. 154:

      Rousseau was too close to the sources of Jacobinism to have any misapprehension as to what the real Rousseau thought about liberty.

26.   For Sieyès, as for the French Revolution, the full power of the absolute and unlimited sovereignty of the people was attributed to a representative assembly, which, it was assumed, being the embodiment of the people, was not susceptible of any limitations nor of needing any, for the people could not be supposed to be capable of exercising tyranny over itself. The logical consequence of popular or national sovereignty is to identify contrary to fact the people with the government, and the rulers with the ruled.

      (Alfred Cobban, *A History of Modern France*, 1:162)

27. "Avant moi, il s'est trouvé des hommes célèbres pour s'élever contre la maxime de Rousseau. Beccaria, Condorcet, Franklin, Payne et enfin Sieyès, qui, dans une opinion, émise à la tribune, a déclaré que l'autorité social n'était point illimitée. Mais il ne parait pas que la logique de ces écrivains ait fait impression. L'on parle encore sans cesse d'un pouvoir sans bornes, qui réside dans le peuple ou dans ses chefs, comme une chose hors de doute" (Manuscrits de 1810, F, 93).

28. "Le triomphe de la force tyrannique est de contraindre les esclaves à se proclamer libres; mais en se prêtant à ce simulacre monsonger de liberté,

les esclaves devus complices aussi méprisables que leurs maîtres" (*Discours,* 2:60).

29. Cf. a statement Constant made in *De la religion considerée dans sa source, ses formes et ses dével-oppements,* 1:75-76, which demonstrates the close connection between his religious and political ideas: "Il en est de la raison infaillible du genre humain comme de la souveraineté illimitée du peuple. Les uns ont cru qu'il devait y avoir quelque part une raison infaillible; ils l'ont placée dans l'autorité. Les autres ont cru qu'il devait y avoir quelque part une souveraineté illimitée; ils l'ont placée dans le peuple." To Constant, however, "il n'y a point de raison infaillible; il n'y a point de souveraineté illimitée." Constant especially denounced legislative omnipotence, referring particularly to the Constituent Assembly in France and the Long Parliament in England, a subject to be considered later.

30. "Il y a deux dogmas également dangéreux: l'un de droit divin et l'autre la souveraineté illimitée du peuple; l'un et l'autre ont fait beaucoup de mal. Il n'y a de divin que la divinité. Il n'y a souveraineté que la justice" (*Discours,* 1:211). It is interesting to note that in America John Quincy Adams in "Publicola," pp. 70-71, relied upon the same concept of justice and individual rights to refute Thomas Paine's position in *The Rights of Man,* p. 13, that "whatever a nation chooses to do it has the right to do." Adams wrote: "This principle that a whole nation has a right to do whatever it pleases, cannot in any sense whatever be admitted as true. The eternal and immutable laws of justice and morality are paramount to all human legislation. The violation of those laws is certainly within the power, but it is not among the rights of nations. The power of a nation is the collected power of all the individuals which compose it. . . . If, therefore, a majority . . . are bound by no law human or divine, and have no other rule but their sovereign will and pleasure to direct them, what possible security can any citizen of the nation have for the protection of his unalienable rights. The principles of liberty must still be the sport of arbitrary power, and the hideous form of despotism must lay aside the diadem and the scepter, only to assume the party-colored garments of democracy."

31.   Le peuple peut errer en masse comme chaque citoyen en particulier et quand il fait des lois injustes, sa volonté n'est pas plus légitime que celle du tyran.

                       (*De la religion,* 1:76)

32.   L'on peut affirmer que, lorsque de certains principes sont complètement et clairement démontrés, ils se servent en quelque sorte de ga-

rantie à eux-mêmes. . . . S'il est reconnu que la souveraineté n'est pas sans bornes, c'est-à-dire, qu'il n'existe sur la terre aucune puissance illimitée, nul, dans aucun temps, n'osera reclamer une semblable puissance. . . . L'on n'attribue plus, par exemple, à la société entière, le droit de vie et de mort sans jugement. Aussi, nul gouvernement ne prétend exercer un pareil droit.

In other words, the mere discovery of the truth was optimistically seen as the guarantee of its victory. As for the "distribution and balance of powers," it is interesting to note that Tocqueville believed that mixed government was a chimera (*Democracy in America,* 1:260).

33. Constant, *Mélanges de littérature et de politique,* Preface. Cf. Mill, who argued that "the tyranny of the majority is as menacing as any tyrant of old" (*On Liberty,* chap. 1). Constant quotes Thomas Jefferson (First Inaugural Address, 4 March 1801) in the preface written in 1810 (Manuscrits) to his *Principes de politique*: "Though the will of the majority is in all cases to prevail, that will, to be rightful, must be reasonable. The minority possesses their equal rights, which equal laws must protect and to violate them would be oppression."

34. Cf. *Mélanges,* Preface. See Mill's conception of "the appropriate region of human liberty" (*On Liberty,* chap. 1). First, "liberty of conscience in the most comprehensive sense; liberty of thought and feeling; absolute freedom of opinion and sentiment on all subjects practical or speculative, scientific, moral or theological; liberty of expressing and publishing opinions"; second, "liberty of tastes and pursuits; of framing a plan of our life to suit our own character; of doing as we like, subject to such consequences as may follow: without impediment from other creatures, so long as what we do does not harm them, even though they should think our conduct foolish, perverse or wrong"; third, "the liberty, within the same limits, of combinations among individuals."

35. Mill is referring here to Bentham's idea of an omnipotent legislature rather than to Rousseau.

36. Jean Joseph Mounier, *Recherches sur les causes qui ont empêché les Français de devenir libres et sur les moyens qui leur restent pour acquérir la liberté,* chap. 1, pp. 1-8. Cf. De Lolme, who in the *Constitution de l'Angleterre,* p. 188, stated that the result of popular sovereignty would be the submergence of the individual "in the crowd," which is an interesting anticipation of Tocqueville and Mill.

37. Jean Joseph Mounier, *Considérations sur les gouvernements et principalement sur celui qui convient à la France,* p. 9.

38. Jacques Mallet du Pan, *Considerations on the Nature of the French Revolution and on the Causes which Prolong the Duration*, p. 8; "Du degré d'influence qu'a eu la philosophie française sous la révolution," p. 362; *Correspondance politique pour servir à l'histoire du républicanisme française*, pp. xx-xxi.

39. See Joseph de Maistre, "Etude sur la souveraineté," Book 2, chap. 6, pp. 385-86. Louis de Bonald presents a more detailed condemnation in "Essai analytique sur les lois naturelles de l'ordre social dans la société" (1800), *Oeuvres complètes de M. de Bonald*, 1:1018:

> Après les détails dans lesquels nous venons d'entrer, il en coute à l'homme qui a quelque justesse dans les idées, de discuter l'opinion de la souveraineté du peuple, néant, c'est-à-dire, abstractions sans réalité, système où Dieu n'est pas, où l'homme seul est tout et, même les extrèmes, pouvoir et sujet, faux puis qu'il est impracticable de l'aveu même de ses défenseurs, et où l'on est toujours placé entre une conséquence et un blasphème. En effet, si l'on fait craindre aux apologistes de cette souveraineté que l'ignorance et les passions humaines n'égarent la faculté législative de l'homme ou du peuple ils vous répondent tantôt avec Jurieu. Que le peuple est la seule autorité qui n'avait pas besoin d'avoir raison pour valider ses actes, tantôt que le peuple est juste et bon et qu'il ne saurait faillir, et par de là seul ils reconnaissent une justice et une bonté au dessus de peuple, puis qu'il y conforme ses pensées, et une règle antérieure au peuple, dont il ne peut s'écarter dans ses actions; et ils sont ainsi ramenés à la souveraineté de Dieu . . . auteur nécessaire de tout ordre.

40. Prosper Duvergier de Hauranne, "M. Charles de Rémusat," p. 335.

41. See my *The Political Theory of the Huguenots of the Dispersion*, pp. 67-68.

42. Prosper de Barante, *Questions constitutionnelles*, chap. 1, "De la souveraineté," pp. 1-17. Cf. Jean-Claude Clausel de Coussergues, *Considérations sur l'origine, la rédaction, la promulgation et l'exécution de la Charte*, pp. lxxviii-lxxix. This conservative argued that the king, in granting the Charte to France, repudiated the pernicious doctrine of popular sovereignty:

> La dernière conséquence de cette doctrine est que la justice ne vient pas des lois éternelles établis par Dieu même, mais qu'elle n'est autre chose que la volonté du peuple; de sorte que (comme l'a exprimé formellement Jurieu, disciple de Buchanan, et après Jurieu, Rousseau et les encyclopédistes) le peuple est la seule autorité qui n'ait pas besoin d'avoir raison pour légitimer ses actes; principe monstrueux repoussé par tous les philosophes de l'antiquité, et avec tant de force et d'éloquence, par Ciceron, etc.

43. Jean Jacques Chevallier, *Les grandes oeuvres politiques de Machiavel à nos jours*, p. 153.

44. Saint-Marc Girardin, *Jean-Jacques Rousseau*, 2: chap. 15, "Le Contrat Social. Du pouvoir absolu de l'état et de la souveraineté du peuple," pp. 356-411, 358, 360, 364-65.

45. Francis Lieber, *Civil Liberty and Self Government*, 1:301. Lieber defined Anglican liberty as "the guarantee of those rights which experience has shown to be most exposed to the danger of attack by the strongest power in the state, namely, the executive."

46. Mill, *On Liberty*, chap. 1. Cf. Alexander Hamilton, *The Federalist* No. 84, who asserted that the people did not need to be protected against its own will:

> They [bill of rights] have no application to constitutions professedly founded upon the power of the people, and executed by their immediate representatives and servants. . . . "We, the People of the United States . . . do ordain and establish this Constitution of the United States of America". Here is a better recognition of popular rights, than the volumes of those aphorisms which . . . sound better in a treatise of ethics than in a constitution of government.

See also James Madison, *The Federalist* No. 51, who wrote that "a dependence on the people is, no doubt, the primary control on the government, but experience has taught mankind the necessity of auxiliary precautions."

47. John Emerich Acton, *The History of Freedom and Other Essays*, pp. 93-94.

48. Edouard Laboulaye, *L'état et ses limites*, p. 38. Cf. the conservative thinker, Hippolyte-Adolphe Taine, in *The Ancient Regime*, p. 246:

> In the place of the sovereignty of the king the *Contrat Social* substitutes the sovereignty of the people. The latter, however, is much more absolute than the former and in the democratic convent (layman's monastery) which Rousseau constructs on the Spartan and Roman model, the individual is nothing and the State is everything.

49. Henri De Ferron, *Théorie du Progrès*, 1:247-48.

50. Emile Faguet, *Politiques et moralistes du dix-neuvième siècle*, p. 260.

51. Prosper de Barante, *La vie politique de Royer-Collard, ses discours et ses écrits*, 2:18. For English translations in part see Léon Duguit, "The Law and the State," pp. 1-185. Quotations below are from Duguit.

52. Barante, *Vie politique de Royer-Collard*, 2:32-33.

53. Ibid., 2:459. Cf. ibid., 1:298, where Royer-Collard speaks of "des principes de la Charte qui sont les

principes éternels de la raison et de la justice." Cf. Barante, *Mélanges historiques et littéraires,* 3:20: "Dès qu'une volonté peut prévaloir contre la justice il y a despotisme. . . . Rois, sénats, assemblées, peuples, tous sont coupables d'usurpation, dès qu'ils prétendent supérieure à la justice."

54. See Duguit, "The Law and the State," p. 169. It is interesting to note that José Ortega y Gasset in *La révolte des masses,* p. 23, thought that Royer-Collard and Guizot "ont forgé la doctrine politique le plus estimable de tout le siècle."

55. François Guizot, *History of the Origin of Representative Government in Europe,* 55-64. See also his *Democracy and Its Mission,* p. 39. Cf. his *Du gouvernement de la France depuis la Restauration et du ministère actuel,* p. 201:

> Je ne crois ni au droit divin ni a la souveraineté du peuple, comme on les entend presque toujours. Je ne puis voir là que les usurpations de la force. Je crois à la souveraineté de la raison, de la justice, du droit: c'est là le souverain légitime que cherche le monde et qu'il cherchera toujours; car la raison, la vérité, la justice ne résident nulle part complètes et infaillibles. Nul homme, nulle réunion d'hommes ne les possède et ne peut les posséder sans lacune et sans limite. Les meilleures formes de gouvernement sont celles qui nous placent plus sûrement et nous font plus rapidement avancer sous l'empire de leur loi sainte. C'est la vertu du gouvernment représentatif.

56. M. Berthould, "Deux individualistes," pp. 172-209.

57. See Prosper de Barante, "Réflexions sur les oeuvres politiques de Jean-Jacques Rousseau," p. 301:

> Dès les premiers moments de la Révolution, il sembla qu'un vaste et ardente opinion, plus démocratique que libérale, désirait et espérait, non pas des libertés et des garanties, mais bien plutôt la formation d'une société nouvelle. Elle voulait avant tout la disparition de l'aristocratie nobiliaire; il lui fallait proclamer que le Tiers Etat, c'était la nation.

58. Barante, *Vie politique de Royer-Collard,* 2:17:

> La pairie seul excepté, une société nouvelle est instituée sur la base de l'égalité. La liberté française, toutes nos libertés, même la liberté de conscience, c'est l'égalité.

59. See George H. Sabine, "The Two Democratic Traditions," pp. 451-74, and R. R. Palmer, "Man and Citizen." André de Chénier, during the French Revolution, had asserted:

> Unwise and unhappy is the state where there exist various associations—collective bodies whose members on entering into them acquire a different spirit and different interests from the general spirit and the general interest. Happy is the land where there is no form of association but the state, no collective body but the country, no interest but the general good.

Note the Loi le Chapelier (14-17 June 1791) abolishing trade guilds and all professional societies. "There are no longer any guilds in the state but only private interests of each individual and the general interest. No one may arouse in the citizen any intermediate interest or separate them from the public welfare by corporate sentiment." Rousseau's dislike of "partial associations" within the state was now translated into legislative action.

60. See Prosper de Barante, *Des communes et de l'aristocratie,* pp. 127-28:

> Si les individus d'une nation restent isolés les un; ils seront sans défense contre l'usurpation de leurs droits; mais si par leur consentement implicite ou explicite, il se forme une élite de citoyens éclairés et indépendants en qui se concentrent la force et l'opinion nationale, alors les choses publiques se passent dans le sein de cette nation restreinte et choisie, l'autorité y trouvera résistance contre les abus, protection contre les désordres.

61. Barante, *Vie politique de Royer-Collard,* 2:131.

62. Cf. Herbert Spencer, *Man versus the State,* p. 183: "The function of Liberalism in the past was that of putting a limit to the power of kings. The function of true Liberalism will be that of putting a limit to the powers of Parliament."

63. Barante, *Vie politique de Royer-Collard,* 2:130.

64. Ibid., pp. 137, 133-34. On 22 January 1822, Royer-Collard quoted M. de Serre, who, presenting a law "sur la répression des délits de la presse," said: "La démocratie chez nous . . . est partout pleine de sève et d'énergie; elle est dans l'industrie, dans la propriété, dans les lois. . . . Le torrent coule à pleins bords dans de faibles digues qui le contiennent à peine." Royer-Collard replied: "A mon tours, prenant, comme je le dois, la démocratie dans une acception purement politique, et comme opposée ou seulement comparée à l'aristocratie, je conviens que la démocratie coule à pleins bords dans la France, telle que les siècles et les événements l'ont faite . . . pour moi, je rends grace à la Providence de ce qu'elle a appelé aux bienfaits de la civilisation un plus grand nombre de ses créatures," which is a point to be made by Tocqueville.

65. Tocqueville, *Democracy in America,* 2:314.

66. Ibid., 1:96.

67. Ibid., 2:319.

68. Ibid., pp. 319-20.

69. Ibid., p. 12.

70. Ibid., 1:259-60 and 227. "Nothing is so irresistible as a tyrannical power commanding in the name of the people."

71. Ibid., p. 259.

72. Ibid. Tocqueville also said that the "maxim that everything is permissible for the interests of society" is "an impious adage which seems to have been invented in an age of freedom to shelter all future tyrants" (ibid., p. 305).

73. Ibid., p. 416.

74. Alexis de Tocqueville, *Oeuvres complètes,* 2:pt. 2, 344.

75. Alexis de Tocqueville, *Recollections,* p. 72.

76. Letter to Royer-Collard (25 Sept. 1841) in Léon De Lanzac de Laborie, "L'amitié de Alexis de Tocqueville et Royer-Collard," p. 907.

77. Tocqueville, *Democracy in America,* 1:53.

78. Tocqueville, *Oeuvres complètes,* 9:280, "Correspondance d'Alexis de Tocqueville et d'Arthur de Gobineau."

Bibliography

PRIMARY SOURCES

MANUSCRIPTS

France

Paris

Bibliothèque Nationale.

Constant, Benjamin. Oeuvres Manuscrits de 1810.

Fonds Davray. Nouvelles acquisitions françaises.

Principes de politique applicables à tous les gouvernements.

Fragments d'un ouvrage abandonné sur la possibilité d'une constitution républicaine dans un grand pays.

Fragments d'un essai sur la littérature du XVIII siècle dans ses rapports avec la liberté.

De la perfectibilité de l'espèce humaine.

Fragments d'un essai sur la perfectibilité de l'espèce humaine.

De la justice politique de Godwin.

De Godwin, de ses principes et de son ouvrage sur la justice politique.

Clermont-Créans

Chateau de Créans, Archives d'Estournelles de Constant.

Cours sur la constitution anglaise.

Première lecture à l'Athenée Royal de Paris.

Switzerland

Lausanne

Bibliothèque Cantonale et Universitaire.

Fonds d'Estournelles de Constant.

Nouveau Fonds d'Estournelles de Constant.

Du moment actuel et de la destinée de l'espèce humaine ou histoire abrégée de l'égalité.

PRINTED WORKS BY BENJAMIN CONSTANT

"Trois lettres à un député à la Convention." *Nouvelles politiques nationales et étrangères,* 24, 25, 26 June 1795. Published in Beatrice W. Jasinski, *L'engagement de Benjamin Constant,* pp. 110-25. Paris, 1971.

A Charles His, rédacteur du Républicain français, 24 July 1795. Published in ibid., pp. 134-41.

"De la restitution des droits politiques aux descendants des religionnaires français." *Le moniteur universel,* 26 Aug. 1796.

De la force du gouvernement actuel de la France et de la nécessité de s'y rallier. 1796.

Aux citoyens représentants du peuple composant le conseil Cinq-Cent. 1796.

Des réactions politiques. 1797.

Des effets de la terreur. 1797.

Discours prononcé au cercle constitutionnel pour la plantation de l'arbre de la liberté le 30 fructidor an V. 1797. Published in Carlo Cordie, *Gli scritti politici givanili di Benjamin Constant, 1796-1797.* Como, 1944.

Discours prononcé au cercle constitutionnel le 9 ventôse an VI. 1798.

A ses collègues de l'assemblé électoral du départment de Seine-et-Oise le germinal an VI. 1798.

Des suites de la contre-révolution en Angleterre. 1799. Republished in 1818-19 under the title *Essai sur la contre-révolution d'Angleterre.*

Discours prononcé sur le projet concernant la formation de la loi, Tribunat, séance du 15 nivôse an VII. 1799.

Opinion sur le projet de loi qui met à la disposition du gouvernement les citoyens qui ont atteint leur vingtième année au premier vendémiaire an VIII, Tribunat, séance du 15 ventôse an VIII. 1800.

Opinion sur le projet de loi relatif aux rentes foncières, Tribunat, séance du 27 ventôse an VIII. 1800.

Discours sur les victoires de l'armée d'Italie, Tribunat, séance du 3 messidor an VIII. 1800.

Opinion sur le projet de loi concernant l'établissement de tribunaux criminels spéciaux, séance du 5 pluviôse an IX. 1801.

Opinion sur le projet de loi concernant la réduction des justices de paix, Tribunat, séance du 2 pluviôse an IX. 1801.

Mémoires sur les communications à établir avec l'intérieur de la France, le 18 novembre, 1813. In Bengt Hasselrot, ed., *Benjamin Constant: Lettres à Bernadotte,* pp. 3-6. Geneva, 1952.

Commentaire sur la réponse faite par Buonaparte à la députation du Sénat le 14 novembre, 1813.

De l'esprit de conquête et de l'usurpation dans leurs rapports avec la civilisation européenne. Hanover, 1814. Partial translation by Helen B. Lippmann, *Prophecy from the Past: Benjamin Constant on Conquest and Usurpation.* New York, 1941.

Réflexions sur les constitutions, la distribution des pouvoirs et les garanties dans une monarchie constitutionnelle. 1814.

Des révolutions de 1660 et de 1688 en Angleterre et de celle de 1814 en France. Journal des débats, 21 April 1814.

De la liberté des brochures, des pamphlets et des journaux considérées sous le rapport de l'intérêt du gouvernement. 1814. English translation in *Pamphleteer* 6 (London, 1815): 206-38.

Observations sur le discours prononcé par S. E. le ministre de l'intérieur en faveur du projet de loi sur la liberté de la presse. 1814.

"Observations sur une déclaration du Congrès de Vienne." *Journal de Paris,* 24 April 1815.

"Comparaison de l'ordonnance de réformation de Louis XVIII avec la constitution proposée à la France le 22 avril 1815." *Journal des débats,* 1 May 1815.

De la responsabilité des ministres. 1815. English translation, "On the Responsibility of Ministers," in *Pamphleteer* 5 (London, 1815): 302-29.

Principes de politique applicables à tous les gouvernements représentatifs. 1815.

De la doctrine politique qui peut réunir les partis en France. 1815.

Adolphe. London, 1816.

Considérations sur le projet de loi relatif aux élections, adopté par la Chambre des Députés. 1817.

Questions sur la législation actuelle de la presse en France et sur la doctrine du ministre public relativement à la saisie des écrits et à la responsabilité des auteurs et imprimeurs. 1817.

Des élections prochaines. 1817.

Note sur quelques articles de journaux. 1817.

Entretien d'un électeur avec lui-même. 1817.

Histoire de la session de la Chambre des Députés depuis 1816 jusqu'en 1819.

Annales de la session de 1817 à 1818.

Annales de la session de 1818 à 1819.

Lettre à M. Charles Durand, avocat, en réponse aux questions contenus dans la troisième partie de son ouvrage intitulé Marseilles, Nîmes et ses environs en 1815. 1818.

De l'appel en calomnie de M. le marquis Blosserville contre Wilfrid-Regnault. 1818.

Des élections de 1818. 1818.

Lettre de M. Benjamin Constant à M. Odillon-Barrot sur le procès M. Lainé, serrurier, entraîné au crime de fausse monnais par un agent de la gendarmerie et condamné à mort. 1818.

A MM les électeurs de Paris le 23 octobre 1818.

A MM les électeurs de Paris le 29 octobre 1818.

Collection complète des ouvrages publiés sur le gouvernement représentatif et la constitution actuelle de la France, formant une espèce de politique constitutionnel. 4 vols. Paris, 1818-20. See also the J. P. Pagès edition of the *Cours de politique constitutionnelle* (Brussels, 1837); and the Edouard Laboulaye editions of 1861 and 1872 published in Paris in 2 volumes. Note also Charles Louandre, *Oeuvres politiques de Benjamin Constant* (Paris, 1874); and finally Olivier Pozzo di Borgo, *Benjamin Constant: Ecrits et discours politiques* (Paris, 1964), and his *Benjamin Constant: Choix de textes politiques* (Paris, 1965).

Eloge de Sir Samuel Romilly, prononcé à l'Athenée Royal de Paris le 26 décembre 1818. 1819.

Lettre à MM les habitants de département de la Sarthe. 1819.

De l'état de la France et des bruits qui circulent. 1819.

De la liberté des anciens comparée à celle des modernes. 1819.

Mémoires sur les Cent Jours en formes de lettres. 1820. Published first in *La minerve française* (Paris, 1818-20). See also Olivier Pozzo di Borgo, *Mémoires sur les Cent Jours par Benjamin Constant* (Paris, 1961).

Des motifs qui ont dicté le nouveau projet de loi sur les élections. 1820.

De la dissolution de la Chambre de Députés. 1820. English translation in *Pamphleteer* 18 (London, 1821).

Troisième lettre à MM les habitants du département de la Sarthe (21 March 1820).

Lettre à M. le marquis de Latour-Mauborg, ministre de la guerre sur ce qui s'est passé à Saumur les 7 et 8 octobre 1820.

Pièces relatives à la saisie de lettres et papiers dans le domicile de MM Goyet et Pasquier. 1820.

Du triomphe inévitable et prochain des principes constitutionnels en Prusse d'après un ouvrage imprimé traduit de l'allemand de M. Koreff, conseiller intime de régence par M. avec un avant-propos et des notes de M. Benjamin Constant, député de la Sarthe. 1821.

Lettre à M. le Procureur général de la cour royal de Poitiers. 1822.

Note sur la plainte en défamation adressé à MM les conseillers, membres de la cour de cassation contre M. Mangin. 1822.

Commentaire sur l'ouvrage de Filangieri. 2 vols. 1822.

Appel aux nations chrétiennes en faveur des Grecs. 1825.

"Coup d'oeil sur la tendance générale des esprits dans le XIX siècle, extrait du discours prononcé dans le séance d'ouverture de l'Athenée royal de Paris, le 3 décembre 1825." *Revue encyclopédique,* 1825.

"Christianisme." *Encyclopédie moderne* 7 (1825): 30-52. Also published in Charles-François Dupuis, *Abrégé de l'origine de tous les cultes* (Paris, 1895).

"Religion." *Encyclopédie progressive ou collection des traités sur l'histoire, l'état actuel et les progrès des connaissances humaines.* 1826.

Discours de M. Benjamin Constant à la Chambre des Députés. 2 vols. Paris, 1827-28. For the complete discourses of Benjamin Constant, especially from 1827-30, see *Archives parlementaires 1789-1860: Receuil complète des débats des chambres françaises* (Paris, 1862-).

Mélanges de littérature et de politique. Paris, 1829.

"Souvenirs historiques à l'occasion de l'ouvrage de M. Bignon." *Revue de Paris* 9 (1830): 115-25; 16 (1830): 102-12, 221-33.

De la religion considérée dans sa source, ses formes et ses développements. 5 vols. Paris, 1824-31. Note Pierre Deguise, *Benjamin Constant De la religion Livre I* (Lausanne, 1971); and Patrice Thompson, *Deux chapitres inédits de l'Esprit des religions, 1803-1804* (Geneva, 1970).

Du polythéisme romain considérée dans ses rapports avec la philosophie grecque et la religion chrétienne. 2 vols. Ouvrage posthume, 1833.

Le cahier rouge. Paris, 1907.

Journaux intimes. Edited by Alfred Roulin and Charles Roth. Paris, 1952.

Cécile. Edited by Norman Cameron. London, 1952.

CORRESPONDENCE

Baldensperger, Ferdinand. "Lettres de Constant à Bottiger, 1804-1815." *Revue politique et littéraire* 9 (1908): 481-86.

Berthoud, Dorette. "Belle et Benjamin. Lettres inédites de Benjamin Constant." *Revue de Paris* 7-12 (Oct. 1964): 65-75.

Colet, Louise. *Lettres de Benjamin Constant à Madame Récamier.* Paris, 1864.

Constant de Rebecque, Adrien de. "Lettres de Benjamin Constant à sa famille." *Revue internationale* 14 (1887): 25-53, 200-32, 355-76, 584-605.

Crepet, Eugène. "Benjamin Constant d'après une correspondance de famille complètement inédite." *Revue nationale et étrangère* 27 (1867): 161-89, 415-60.

De Lauris, Georges. "Lettres inédites de Benjamin Constant." *La revue* (1904): 1-18, 151-59.

Dierolf, George. "Lettres de Benjamin Constant à Prosper de Barante, 1805-1830." *Revue de deux mondes* 34 (1906): 241-72, 528-67.

———. "Lettres inédites de Benjamin Constant." *Gaulois du Dimanche,* Jan. 1906.

Gaullieur, Eusèbe H. "Benjamin Constant et Madame de Charrière ou la jeunesse de Benjamin Constant racontée par lui-même. Lettres inédites, communiquées et annotées." *Revue des deux mondes* 15 (1844): 193-264.

———. "Benjamin Constant pendant la Révolution d'après de nouvelles lettres inédites à Madame de Charrière." *Bibliothèque universelle de Genève* 6 (1847): 236-67, 344-75; 7 (1848): 50-84, 271-95.

Glachant, Paul et Victor. "Lettres de Benjamin Constant à Fauriel." *La nouvelle revue,* Jan. 1902, pp. 63-68.

———. "Lettres de Benjamin Constant à Fauriel." *Revue politique et littéraire* 5 (Jan. 1906): 36-41.

———. "Lettres inédites de Benjamin Constant à Rosalie de Constant." *La nouvelle revue* Oct. 1903, pp. 289-95.

Harpaz, Ephraim. *Benjamin Constant et Goyet de la Sarthe correspondance, 1818-1822.* Geneva, 1973.

———. *Benjamin Constant. Lettres à Mme Récamier 1807-1830.* Paris, 1977.

Hasselrot, Bengt. *Lettres à Bernadotte par Benjamin Constant. Sources et origines de l'esprit de conquête et de l'usurpation.* Geneva, 1952.

Isler, Johann and Witmer. *Briefe von Constant, Görres, Goethe . . . und vielen Anderen. Auswahl aus dem Landschaftlichen Nachlasse des Charles de Villers,* pp. 5-59. Hamburg, 1879.

Lenormant, A. *Lettres de Benjamin Constant à Madame Récamier, 1807-1830.* Paris, 1882.

Ley, Francis. *Bernardin de Sainte-Pierre, Madame de Staël, Chateaubriand, Benjamin Constant et Madame de Krudener.* Aubier, 1967.

L'inconnue d'Adolphe. Correspondance de Benjamin Constant à d'Anna Lindsay. Paris, 1930.

Melegari, D. "Benjamin Constant à Saumur." *Nouvelle revue retrospective,* 1901, pp. 1-36.

——. *Journal intime de Benjamin Constant et lettres à sa famille et à ses amis.* Paris, 1895.

——. "Lettres de Benjamin Constant à Madame de Charrière, 1792-1795." *Revue de Paris* 5 (1894): 673-718.

Menos, Jean H. *Lettres de Benjamin Constant à sa famille, 1795-1830.* Paris, 1888.

——. "Lettres inédites à la Comtesse de Nassau." *Revue internationale* 21 (1889): 9-31, 149-76, 302-34.

Mistler, Jean. "Benjamin Constant et Madame Récamier." *Revue des deux mondes* 5 (1950): 81-95.

——. *Lettres à un ami: Cent onze lettres inédites de Benjamin Constant et de Madame de Staël à Claude Hochet.* Neuchâtel, 1949.

Pellegrini, Carlo. "Lettere inédite di Benjamin Constant al Sismondi." *Pegaso* 4 (1932): 641-60.

Roulin, Alfred and Suzanne. *Benjamin et Rosalie Constant: Correspondance, 1786-1830.* Paris, 1955.

Rudler, Gustave. "Une correspondance inédite. Benjamin Constant et Louvet." *Bibliothèque universelle et revue suisse* 67 (1912): 225-47.

——. "Lettres à Philippe Stapfer." *Mélanges de philologie, d'histoire et de littérature offerts à Joseph Vianey,* pp. 321-33. Paris, 1934.

——. "Lettres de Benjamin Constant à M. et Mme De Gérando." *Bibliothèque universelle et revue suisse* 69 (1913): 449-85.

Seznec, J. "Deux lettres de Benjamin Constant sur Adolphe et les Cent Jours." *The French Mind: Studies in Honour of Gustave Rudler,* pp. 208-19. Oxford, 1952.

Thomas, L. "Lettres à Anna Lindsay." *Revue des deux mondes* 60 (Nov.-Dec. 1930): 781-818; and 61 (Jan.-Feb. 1931): 62-97, 373-404.

——. "Lettres inédites de Benjamin Constant." *Revue politique et littéraire* 21-22 (1914): 481-86, 519-24.

"Trois lettres inédites de Benjamin Constant à Madame de Krudener." *Journal de Genève,* March 1908.

Vauthier, Gabriel. "Une lettre inédite de Benjamin Constant le 24 brumaire 1799." *Annales révolutionaires* 13 (1921): 413-18.

JOURNALS WITH ARTICLES BY OR ABOUT BENJAMIN CONSTANT

Note the collections by Ephraim Harpaz: *Benjamin Constant: Receuil d'Articles, 1817-1820. Le Mercure, La Minerve et La Renommée,* 2 vols. (Geneva, 1972); *Benjamin Constant: Receuil d'articles, 1795-1817* (Geneva, 1978); and *Benjamin Constant; Receuil d'articles, 1820-1830* (forthcoming).

"L'ambigu ou variétés littéraires et politiques, 1804-18." *Christian Examiner* 10 (1831); 17 (1834).

Le constitutionnel, journal politique et littéraire, 1815-17, 1827.

Le courrier français, journal du commerce, politique et littéraire, 1819-30.

Edinburgh Review 24 (1814-15); and 26 (1816).

Journal du commerce, de politique et de littérature, 1817-19.

Journal des débats, 1814-30.

Journal de Paris, 1811-27.

Le mercure de France, journal politique, littéraire et dramatique, 1789-1820.

Le mercure de France au XIX siècle XXXI, 1830.

La minerve française 1817-20.

Le moniteur universel ou gazette nationale, 1789-1830.

Nouvelles politiques, nationales et étrangères, 1792-97.

La renommée, 1818-20.

Le Républicain français, 1795.

La sentinelle, 1795.

Le temps, journal des politiques, scientifiques, littéraires et industriels, 1829-30.

ANONYMOUS WORKS ON BENJAMIN CONSTANT

Adresse à tous les amis de la France sur la brochure de Benjamin Constant "Des causes de la contre-révolution en Angleterre." 1799.

A MM les députés des départements. 1829.

A MM les membres de la Chambre des Députés. 1829.

A MM les membres de la Chambre des Députés au sujet de la proposition de M. B. Constant tendant à rendre libres les professions d'imprimeur de libraire. 1830.

Combat des six. 1829.

Consultation pour M. B. Constant. 1822.

Critique raisonné dans laquelle on signale les fautes d'orthographe, de construction, de solécismes, les barbarismes, les néologismes, les imprissions impropres et inconvénients dont est remplie la brochure que vient de publier M. B. Constant sur la "Dissolution de la Chambre" par un auteur de la pureté de langage. 1820.

De la loterie et des maisons de jeu. Lettre à M. B. Constant. 1822.

Lettre à M. B. Constant au sujet de l'attentat de Saumur. 1820.

Lettre à M. B. Constant sur celle qu'il a écrit à M. Ch. Durand, insérée dans le livraison de la Minerve française, auteur de l'écrit intitulé, "L'impartial." 1818.

Lettre à M. B. Constant sur l'obligation d'improviser dans les assemblées législatives.

Lettre à M. B. Constant et Manuel membres de la Chambre des Députés en réponse à quelques passages des discours qu'ils ont prononcé sur la traité des noirs dans la séance du 27 juin 1821. 1821.

Lettre à M. Esmangart, conseiller d'état, préfet du département du Bas Rhin, par un saucissier de Strasbourg en réponse à un article inséré dans le journal ministériel du département au sujet d'un banquet offert à M. B. Constant. 1827.

Lettre d'un républicain du département de la Gironde à un de ses amis à Bordeaux sur le discours prononcé par B. Constant au cercle constitutionnel du Palais Royal de 9 ventôse. 1798.

Le cri d'un ultra ou le vade-mecum de l'électeur honnête homme suivi de "Quelques mots sur les élections de 1818." 1818.

M. B. Constant, est-il français, est-il éligible? 1818.

M. B. Constant de Rebecque Suisse d'origine, est-il ami de la Charte? 1818.

Note historique et biographique sur B. Constant député de France. 1830.

Note sur la note de M. B. Constant de Rebecque. 1817.

Ordre du convoi funèbre de B. Constant, commençant par de mots "Le convoi de B. Constant." 1830.

Quelques mots à M. le vicomte de Chateaubriand et à M. B. Constant par M. le marquis de Paris. 1818.

Sur l'ouvrage de M. B. Constant intitulé "Des élections prochaines." 1817.

Trois têtes dans un bonnet ou MM Constant, Jay et Guizot. 1820.

Vie patriotique de B. Constant dédié à la jeune France. 1830.

RELATED ORIGINAL WORKS IN THE NINETEENTH AND TWENTIETH CENTURIES

Acton, John Emerich. *Essays on Freedom and Power.* Edited by Gertrude Himmelfarb. New York, 1948.

———. *Lectures on Modern History.* London, 1906.

———. *Lectures on the French Revolution.* London, 1910.

———. *The History of Freedom and Other Essays.* London, 1907.

Adams, John. *A Defense of the Constitutions of Government of the United States of America.* London, 1787.

Adams, John Quincy, "Publicola" (1791). In *The Writings of John Quincy Adams,* edited by W. C. Ford. 7 vols. New York, 1913-17.

Barante, Prosper de. *Des communes et de l'aristocratie.* Paris, 1821.

———. *La vie politique de Royer-Collard, ses discours et ses écrits.* 2 vols. Paris, 1861.

———. *Mélanges historiques et littéraires.* 3 vols. Paris, 1835.

———. *Questions constitutionnelles.* Paris, 1849.

———. "Réflexions sur les oeuvres politiques de Jean-Jacques Rousseau" and "De la souveraineté." In *Etudes littéraires et historiques.* 2 vols., 1:275-351, 352-62. Paris, 1859.

———. *Souvenirs du Baron de Barante, 1782-1866.* 8 vols. Paris, 1890-1901.

Bentham, Jeremy. *Deontology or the Science of Morality.* 2 vols. London, 1834.

———. *Works.* 11 vols. London, 1843.

Bonald, Louis G. A., Vicomte de. *Essai analytique sur les lois naturelles de l'ordre social dans la société ou du pouvoir, du ministre et du sujet dans la société.* 1800.

———. *Législation primitive considérée dans les derniers temps par les seules lumières de la raison.* 1802.

———. *Oeuvres complètes de M. de Bonald.* 3 vols. Paris, 1959.

———. *Théorie du pouvoir politique et religieux dans la société civile, démontrée par le raisonnement et par l'histoire.* 1796.

Boulainvilliers, Comte de. *Histoire de l'ancien gouvernement de la France.* Paris, 1727.

Boulay de la Meurthe, Antoine. *Essai sur les causes qui en 1649 amenèrent en Angleterre à l'établissement de la République.* Paris, 1799.

Boyer-Fonfrède, F. B. *Des avantages d'une constitution libérale.* Paris, 1814.

Broglie, Duc Victor de. *Souvenirs, 1785-1870.* 4 vols. Paris, 1886.

Buchez, P. J. B., and Roux, P. C. *Histoire parlementaire de la révolution française.* 40 vols. Paris, 1834-1938.

Chateaubriand, François Auguste René, Vicomte de. *De Bonaparte et des Bourbons et de la nécessité de se rallier à nos princes légitimes pour le bonheur de la France et celui de l'Europe.* 1814.

——. *De la monarchie selon la Charte.* 1816.

——. *Essai historique, politique et moral sur les révolutions anciennes et modernes considérées dans leurs rapports avec la révolution française.* 1797.

——. *Le génie du Christianisme et défense du génie du Christianisme.* 1802.

——. *Mémoires d'outre tombe.* 6 vols. Paris, 1898-1900. See Robert Baldrick, ed., *The Memoirs of Chateaubriand.* New York, 1961.

——. *Oeuvres complètes.* 28 vols. Paris, 1826-31, and 12 vols. Paris, 1870.

Clausel de Coussergues, Jean Claude. *Considérations sur l'origine, la rédaction, la promulgation et l'exécution de la Charte.* Paris, 1830.

——. *De la souveraineté du peuple et du serment demandé aux membres des collèges électoraux.* Paris, 1830.

De Ferron, Henri. *Théorie du Progrès. 2 vols. Paris, 1867.*

Duvergier de Hauranne, Prosper. *Histoire du gouvernement parlementaire en France, 1814-1848.* 10 vols. Paris, 1857-71.

——. "M. Charles de Rémusat." *Revue des deux mondes* 12 (1875): 315-69.

The Federalist, New York, 1971.

Filangieri, Gaetano. *The Science of Legislation.* London, 1816.

Guizot, François. *Democracy and Its Mission.* London, 1848.

——. *Du gouvernement de la France depuis la Restauration et du ministère actuel.* Paris, 1820.

——. *Du gouvernement représentatif et de l'état actuel de la France.* Paris, 1820.

——. *Histoire générale de la civilisation en Europe.* Paris, 1828.

——. *Historical Essays and Lectures.* Edited by Stanley Mellon. Chicago, 1972.

——. *History of the Origin of Representative Government in Europe.* London, 1861.

——. *Mémoires pour servir à l'histoire de mon temps.* 8 vols. Paris, 1858-67.

Hobbes, Thomas. *Leviathan.* London, 1914.

Jefferson, Thomas. "First Inaugural Address" (March 4, 1801). In *A Compilation of the Messages and Papers of the Presidents,* compiled by James D. Richardson, 1:309-12. New York, 1897.

Kant, Immanuel. "On a Supposed Right to Lie from Altruistic Motives." In *Critique of Practical Reason and Other Writings in Moral Philosophy,* pp. 346-50. Edited by L. W. Beck. Chicago, 1949.

Laboulaye, Edouard. "Benjamin Constant." *Revue nationale et étrangère* 5 (1861): 321-57, 489-533; 6 (1861):6-43, 161-210, 481-513; 7 (1861):5-27, 321-64.

——. "Benjamin Constant et les Cent Jours." *Revue nationale et étrangère* 25 (1866): 385-411; 26 (1866-67): 55-77, 161-79, 404-31.

——. "La liberté antique et la liberté moderne." In *L'état et ses limites: Suivis d'essais politiques.* Paris, 1871.

Lieber, Francis. "Anglican and Gallican Liberty" (1849). In *Miscellaneous Writings.* 2 vols., 2:371-88. Philadelphia, 1881.

——. *Civil Liberty and Self-Government.* 2 vols. Boston, 1853.

Madison, James. "Vices of the Political System of the United States" (1787). In *The Writings of James Madison,* edited by Gaillard Hunt. 9 vols. 2:361-69. New York, 1901.

Maistre, Joseph de. *Considérations sur la France.* 1796. English translation by Richard A. Lebrun. London, 1974.

——. *Essai sur le principe générateur des constitutions politiques et des autres institutions humaines (1808-1809).* 1814. See the edition in English by Elisha Greifer (Chicago, 1959).

——. "Etude sur la souveraineté." In *Oeuvres inédites du Comte Joseph de Maistre.* Paris, 1870.

——. *Oeuvres complètes.* 14 vols. Lyons, 1884-86. See Jack Lively, *The Works of Joseph de Maistre.* New York, 1965.

Mallet du Pan, Jacques. *Considérations sur la nature de la révolution française et sur les causes qui en prolongent la durée.* Brussels, 1793. English translation, *Considerations on the Nature of the French Revolution and on the Causes which Prolong the Duration.* Introduction by Paul Beik. New York, 1974.

————. *Correspondance inédite de Mallet du Pan avec la Cour de Vienne (1794-1798)*. 2 vols. Paris, 1884.

————. *Correspondance politique pour servir à l'histoire du républicanisme française*. Hamburg, 1796.

————. "Du degré d'influence qu'a eu la philosophie française sur la révolution," le 20 mars 1799. *Mercure britannique; ou notices historiques et critiques sur les affaires du temps*. 5 vols., 2:342-70. London, 1798-99.

Mill, John Stuart. *On Liberty*. London, 1859.

————. *Considerations on Representative Government*. London, 1861.

Mirabeau, Marquis de. *L'ami des hommes*. Paris, 1756.

Molé, Louis-Mathieu, Comte de. *Essais de morale et de politique*. Paris, 1806.

Montesquieu, Charles de Secondat, Baron de. *The Spirit of the Laws*. Translated by Thomas Nugent. New York, 1949. See also the edition of David W. Carrithers (Berkeley, 1977), and selections by Melvin Richter, *The Political Theory of Montesquieu* (New York, 1977).

Mounier, Jean Joseph. *Considérations sur les gouvernements et principalement sur celui qui convient à la France*. Paris, 1789.

————. *Recherches sur les causes qui ont empêché les Français de devenir libres et sur les moyens qui leur restent pour acquérir la liberté*. Paris, 1792.

Paine, Thomas. *The Age of Reason*. London, 1794.

————. *The Rights of Man*. London, 1791. Everyman edition, London, 1915.

Rousseau, Jean-Jacques. *The First and Second Discourses*. Edited by Roger D. Masters and Judith R. Masters. New York, 1964.

————. *The Government of Poland*. Edited by Willmore Kendall. New York, 1972.

————. *Lettres écrites de la Montagne*. Amsterdam, 1764.

————. *The Miscellaneous Works of Mr. Jean-Jacques Rousseau*. 5 vols. London, 1767.

————. *Oeuvres complètes*. Edited by Bernard Gagnebin and Marcel Raymond. 3 vols. Paris, 1959-64.

————. *On the Social Contract with Geneva Manuscript and Political Economy*. Edited by Roger D. Masters and Judith R. Masters. New York, 1975.

————. *The Social Contract*. Translated by Maurice Cranston. London, 1968.

Saint-Marc Girardin, François A. *Jean Jacques Rousseau: Sa vie et ses ouvrages*. 2 vols. Paris, 1875.

Sieyès, Joseph. *Qu'est-ce que le Tiers Etat?* Paris, 1789. English translation, *What Is the Third Estate?*, edited by S. E. Finer. London, 1963.

Spencer, Herbert. *The Man versus the State*. Edited by Donald G. Macrae. London, 1969.

Staël, Germaine de. *Considérations sur les principaux événements de la révolution française*. 1817. English translation, *Considerations on the Principal Events of the French Revolution*. 2 vols. New York, 1818.

————. *De l'Allemagne*. Paris, 1810.

————. *De l'influence des passions sur le bonheur des individus et des nations*. Paris, 1796.

————. *Des circonstances actuelles qui peuvent terminer la révolution et des principes qui doivent fonder la République en France* (1799). Edited by John Vienot. Paris, 1896. See also Edouard Herriot, *Un ouvrage inédit de Madame de Staël. Les fragments d'écrits politiques de 1799*. Paris, 1904.

————. "Dix années d'exil." In *Mémoires de Mme de Staël*. Paris, 1861.

————. *Lettres de Madame de Staël à Benjamin Constant*. Paris, 1928.

————. *Lettres sur les écrits et le caractère de Jean Jacques Rousseau*. [Paris?] 1788.

————. *Oeuvres complètes de Mme la Baronne de Staël*. 20 vols. Paris, 1820-21.

————. *Portrait d'Atilla*. Paris, 1814.

————. *Réflexions sur la paix intérieure*. Paris, 1795.

Taine, Hippolyte-Adolphe. *The Origins of Contemporary France*. Vol. 1, *The Ancien Regime*. New York, 1885.

Tocqueville, Alexis de. *Democracy in America*. Introduction by Phillip Bradley. 2 vols. New York, 1946.

————. "Etat social et politique de la France depuis 1789 or Political Science and Social Condition of France." *London and Westminster Review*, April 1836.

————. *Oeuvres complètes*. Edited by J. P. Mayer. 13 vols. Paris, 1951—

————. *Oeuvres complètes*. Edited by Gustave de Beaumont. 9 vols. Paris, 1864-66.

————. *Oeuvres et correspondance inédites*. 2 vols. Paris, 1861.

————. *The Old Regime and the French Revolution*. Translated by Stuart Gilbert. New York, 1955.

————. *Recollections*. Edited by J. P. Mayer. London, 1948.

SECONDARY SOURCES

Actes du Congrès Benjamin Constant à Lausanne, Octobre, 1967. Geneva, 1968.

Bastid, Paul. *Benjamin Constant et sa doctrine.* 2 vols. Paris, 1966.

———. *Les institutions politiques de la monarchie parlementaire française.* Paris, 1954.

———. *Sieyès et sa pensée.* Paris, 1939.

———. "Tocqueville et la doctrine constitutionnelle." In *Alexis de Tocqueville: Livre du centenaire, 1859-1959,* pp. 45-56. Paris, 1961.

Berlin, Isaiah. *Four Essays on Liberty.* Oxford, 1969.

———. "Montesquieu." *British Academy Proceedings* 40 (1956): 267-96.

Berthauld, M. "Deux individualistes: Benjamin Constant et Daunou." In *Mémoires de l'Académie des sciences de Caen,* 1863, pp. 172-209.

Cassirer, Ernst. *The Philosophy of the Enlightenment.* Boston, 1951.

———. *The Question of Jean Jacques Rousseau.* Introduction by Peter Gay. New York, 1954.

———. *Rousseau, Kant, Goethe.* Princeton, 1947.

Chevallier, Jean Jacques. *Les grandes oeuvres politiques de Machiavel à nos jours.* Paris, 1849.

———. *Histoire des institutions politiques de la France moderne (1789-1945).* Paris, 1958.

———. "Montesquieu ou le libéralisme aristocratique." *Revue internationale de la philosophie* 9 (1955): 330-45.

Cobban, Alfred. *A History of Modern France.* 2 vols. London, 1957 and 1961.

———. *In Search of Humanity: The Role of the Enlightenment in Modern History.* London, 1960.

De Lanzac de Laborie, Léon. "L'amitié d'Alexis de Tocqueville et de Royer Collard." *Revue des deux mondes* 58 (15 Aug. 1930): 876-911.

———. *Un royaliste libérale en 1789: Jean Joseph Mounier, sa vie politique et ses écrits.* Paris, 1887.

D'Entrèves, Alexander Passerin. "Mallet du Pan." *Occidente* 7 (1951): 371-403.

———. "Mallet du Pan: Swiss Critic of Democracy." *Cambridge Journal* 1 (1947): 99-108.

———. *The Notion of the State.* Oxford, 1967.

Dodge, Guy H. *The Political Theory of the Huguenots of the Dispersion.* New York, 1947 and 1972.

———, ed. *Jean-Jacques Rousseau: Authoritarian, Libertarian?* Lexington, Mass., 1971.

Duguit, Leon. "The Law and the State." *Harvard Law Review* 31 (1917-18): 1-185.

Faguet, Emile. *Le libéralisme.* Paris, 1902.

———. *Politiques et moralistes du dix-neuvième siècle.* Paris, 1888.

Lively, Jack. *The Social and Political Thought of Alexis de Tocqueville.* Oxford, 1962.

Mims, Edwin. "Henri Benjamin Constant de Rebecque (1767-1830)." *Encyclopedia of the Social Sciences,* 4: 241-42. New York, 1931.

———. *The Majority of the People.* New York, 1941.

Ortega y Gasset, José. *Invertebrate Spain.* New York, 1937.

———. *La révolte des masses.* Paris, 1961.

Palmer, R. R. "Man and Citizen: Applications of Individualism in the French Revolution." In *Essays in Political Theory Presented to George H. Sabine,* pp. 130-52. Ithaca, 1948.

Palmenatz, John. "Liberalism." *Dictionary of the History of Ideas,* 3: 36-61. New York, 1973.

———. *Readings from Liberal Writers.* New York, 1965.

Sabine, George H. *A History of Political Theory.* Revised by Thomas T. Thorson. New York, 1973.

———. "The Two Democratic Traditions." *Philosophical Review* 61 (Oct. 1952): 451-74.

Shklar, Judith N. *After Utopia: The Decline of Political Faith.* Princeton, 1957.

———. *Men and Citizens: A Study of Rousseau's Social Theory.* Cambridge, England, 1969.

Simon, Walter. *French Liberalism, 1789-1848.* New York, 1972.

Robert J. Benton (essay date January-March 1982)

SOURCE: Benton, Robert J. "Political Expedience and Lying: Kant vs Benjamin Constant." *Journal of the History of Ideas* 43, no. 1 (January-March 1982): 135-44.

[*In the following essay, Benton illuminates the theoretical underpinnings of Constant's* Des reactions politiques *in order to provide context for Immanuel Kant's essay, "On a Supposed Right to Tell a Lie from Altruistic Motives," which was written in response to* Des reactions politiques.]

The notorious essay "On a Supposed Right to Tell a Lie from Altruistic Motives"[1] is probably the work most often cited to prove that Kant was a moral legalist in the strongest (and worst) sense of the term. And the evidence provided by the essay does indeed seem damning: in it Kant claims that it is wrong to tell a lie even to save a friend from probable murder.

This claim is so clearly abhorrent that many writers have attempted to save Kant from himself by offering interpretations of the essay that are more in keeping with common sense. Paton, for example, in a sensible and scholarly article, has argued that the position Kant takes in this essay does not reflect his more considered views on the possibility of exceptions to practical rules.[2] H. E. M. Hofmeister has argued for the importance of Kant's distinguishing in the essay between truth and truthfulness; he maintains that Kant had in mind a notion of truthfulness defined not by agreement of one's statement with what he believes to be the facts, but rather by one's conviction of the moral character of the statement.[3] Perhaps the most dauntless of Kant's supporters has been W. Schwarz, who maintains that Kant was right in distinguishing between, on the one hand, the harm done by telling the truth to the murderer, and, on the other, the injustice of lying; Schwarz agrees with Kant that one should be held responsible not for the harm but for the injustice of the lie.[4]

Of these three sample interpretations, Paton's seems to me to be the most reasonable. Hofmeister's interpretation, while correctly pointing out a distinction that Kant himself emphasizes, nevertheless interprets the distinction in such a way that being truthful no longer requires even the *intention* of telling the truth (as Schwarz points out); and this cannot be an acceptable interpretation of what Kant meant by truthfulness. Schwarz, on the other hand, remains true to Kant's text, but as a result he is forced to accept as correct Kant's claim that a person is not responsible for the harm caused by a truthful statement. This conclusion is so strongly opposed to common judgments of right and wrong action—a criterion that Kant himself held in high esteem—that though it may represent an accurate account of Kant's meaning, it cannot make Kant's essay more acceptable.

Even Paton's interpretation, however, is less than perfectly satisfying. Paton's basic approach is, on the one hand, to undermine the credibility of the essay (for example, on the grounds of Kant's advanced age and ill health, and by internal evidence of pique supposedly aroused by a feeling of injured national pride), and, on the other hand, to cite other texts in which Kant is less legalistic in order to supply grounds for arguing that the essay on lying is an aberration.

I think Paton is correct in arguing that there is a "better" Kant who does not hold a rigid legalistic view of practical reasoning, but, at the same time, the "worse" Kant must also be acknowledged. The problem of legalism (in this sense) arises with the notion of perfect duties: the concept of a perfect duty is—from the *Ground-work* on (although by no means consistently)—associated with the refusal to admit any exceptions to obeying a duty.[5] But the very concept of a duty that allows *no* exceptions (unless it be a duty on a very abstract level) seems to be intrinsically legalistic. Hence, even though it may be possible to read the essay in a selective way so as to save the "better" Kant, I think we must not do so at the expense of recognizing the real difficulties presented by the essay, difficulties that reflect real problems in Kant's practical philosophy. Thus, we are not justified in dismissing the apparent legalism of the essay as a mere result of advancing age or injured national pride. On the other hand, without recourse to such explanations, it may not be possible to account fully for the essay's rigorism. Nevertheless, I propose a way of reading the essay that may provide a partial explanation and a partial justification for the extreme position that Kant takes there.

My proposed reading of the essay focuses on an aspect that is sometimes noted but has rarely been pursued consistently.[6] The clue to this reading is provided by Kant's assertion that the essay is concerned with lying *not* as an ethical problem but rather as a problem of *Recht*.[7] Moreover, I would like to suggest that the problem of *Recht* arising here is not simply a problem of justice (in either the sense of positive law or in the sense of the principles on which positive law should be based) but rather of *Recht* as it applies to politics. I think politics plays a role in the essay on both the theoretical level of how political principles are justified and the practical level of deciding which political principles are the right ones to act on—and this latter aspect of the problem requires a reference to the historical and political context of the essay. My aim in proposing this interpretation of the essay is to show why Kant would have supported such an extreme position and what might be correct in Kant's basic approach, despite the fact that his conclusions in the example of the murderer remain unacceptable.

As a first step in this analysis, to make our proposed political reading of the essay plausible, I call attention to a striking feature of Kant's argument: He refers, in the example of lying to save one's friend from murder, to a question of *expediency* (*Convenienz,* G427; E363). In the context of the example this seems to be a singularly inappropriate way to describe the well-intentioned liar's action: presumably one would lie to save one's friend from murder because one believed that to be the *right* thing to do in that situation. Even the mention of "altruism" or "love of humanity" (*Menschenliebe*) in the title of the essay does not make this interpretation of the act any more palatable.[8] To understand why Kant thought of the example as relating to expediency and what he meant by that, it is important to recall the historical context within which Kant's essay was written. It was a reply to a pamphlet by Benjamin Constant entitled *On Political Reactions,* published in 1797.[9] Constant's pamphlet was a political work in two senses: its subject matter was a topic of political importance, and it was written essentially as propaganda for the Directory who had gained power in France in 1795 as a result of the Thermidorean reaction against the Jacobins. The Directory presented itself publicly as the heir to the principles of the French Revolution, and it was on this that its claim to legitimate authority rested. However, at the same time, the Directory was formed as a reaction against the more radical tendencies in the Revolution (in particular, universal suffrage and the demand for equality of wealth). Thus, under the Directory, the Jacobins were branded as extremists. Since Constant's pamphlet was written to provide a justification of the policies of the Directory,[10] it reflects their views: it professes a firm commitment to principles, but at the same time its primary aim is to guard against "excess" by fixing strict limits in the application of principles.

Thus, Constant's allusion to Kant (whom he mentions only as a "German Philosopher"[11]) and the use of the example of lying occur in a section of the pamphlet concerned with showing that if principles are applied too strictly, they lead to excess and the destruction of society. Constant's argument is that society would be endangered if people were prohibited from lying even to murderers; on the contrary, a person is justified in lying to save someone from harm. Now, while it is true that lying is justified in some such cases, it is clear that a prohibition on such lying would constitute no real danger to society. Hence, the real significance of the example of the murderer must be its role in a more general argument designed to justify the bending of principles in the name of preserving society. And in this case the preservation of society means the preservation of elements of pre-Revolution society (in particular, the influence of the aristocracy).

Kant was firmly and publicly committed to the principles of the French Revolution: in fact he was one of the few leading intellectual figures in Germany who continued to support the Revolution even through the Terror.[12] Kant had thus developed the reputation of being a Jacobin, and an attack on Kant in a political pamphlet would by itself have been a clear indication of the anti-Jacobin character of the pamphlet. Moreover, the argument that the "excesses" of the Terror were the result of a fanatical attempt to apply abstract philosophical principles directly to real-life situations was already familiar in 1797; for example, Burke had done endless variations on that theme in his *Reflections on the Revolution in France*[13] (and Burke had also already argued at length that the destruction of the power of the aristocracy meant the destruction of society[14]).

Thus Kant would not have viewed Constant's pamphlet simply as an abstract essay on political principles containing a passing attack on himself. Rather, he would have recognized it as propaganda for the reaction against the more democratic principles of the Revolution. More explicitly, he would have recognized that Constant's purpose in undermining the strictness of principles was to support the political claims of the Directory. In this context, then, we can see why Kant would have considered Constant's principle one of expediency: to him Constant's pamphlet would have appeared as an exercise in political opportunism—in the deliberate misuse of political principles to achieve private ends.[15] Thus, a major theme of the essay is an attack on mere expediency in political theory and an attempt to show how truly principled action is both necessary and possible.

Kant replies to the pamphlet in its own terms, that is, he takes up and defends the example of refusing to lie to a potential murderer.[16] He does so without explicitly mentioning the political events of the day, but, as we have seen, Kant must have had the political issues in mind in writing his essay. Moreover, he does not restrict himself solely to the example of the murderer: he also takes up a second, explicitly political, example given by Constant, namely, the principle that "no man can be bound by any laws except those to the formation of which he has contributed."[17] And he does not merely mention the second example in passing; he devotes a substantial portion of the essay to it.

These aspects of the exchange between Constant and Kant indicate that politics is at least as much at stake as civil law (in spite of the fact that the example of the murderer is used as a merely legal example). To see what role the political theme plays in the two works we need to look more closely at Constant's argument. The passage in which Constant refers to the "German Philosopher" is in a chapter entitled "On Principles."[18] Constant argues there that there exist generally recognized principles that must not be abandoned and whose essence is to be "fixed."[19] The problem, then, is how these "fixed" principles can be applied in concrete cases where they might not seem to apply. Constant's solution, in cases where a principle is known to be true but seems inapplicable, is to find a more particular intermediary principle that will allow the application of the general principle.[20]

This argument is reasonable enough, and in fact Kant himself subscribes to it.[21] In the example of obedience only to self-given laws, in the case of a society too large for each member to be a legislator, Constant adduces the intermediary principle of representative government; and Kant quotes Constant approvingly (although, as we shall see, he gives his own interpretation of how the mediating principle is to be derived).

In the case of the "fixed" principle that "truth is a duty," however, Constant does something quite different from merely supplying an intermediary principle. He argues as follows:

> Say that truth is a duty. What is a duty? . . . A duty is that which in one being corresponds to the rights of another. Where there are no rights there are no duties. Truth then is a duty, but only towards those who have a right to the truth. But no man has a right to the truth who harms others.[22]

What Constant has actually supplied here is not a more particular mediating principle for the duty of telling the truth; instead, he has moved to a more general principle concerning the relation of rights to duties as such. And by saying that "where there are no rights there are no duties" he implies that, in effect, rights precede duties.

Now, Constant seems to have had no well thought-out political philosophy to support his claim of the priority of rights over duties, and it is possible that he introduced it casually, merely as support for his argument. But to Kant such a claim would have suggested a very definite political theory—a theory that Kant was quite concerned with combatting—namely, the Hobbesian view.[23] For Hobbes, the subordination of duties to rights is one aspect of a well-articulated political theory and psychology that (from Kant's viewpoint) destroys the very concepts of right and duty by reducing them to mere expediency. Hobbes's understanding of human action relies on a mechanistic psychology and an understanding of "human nature" that can offer no justification for actions except their pleasurable or painful consequences. Thus, for example, the authority for constituting a commonwealth is sheer physical necessity: to avoid the fear of violent death when one remains in the state of nature. Moreover, no obligation can exist for Hobbes except within a constituted state, and it is in this sense that duties are subordinate to rights: duties arise only with the social contract, and the sole grounds for the necessity of the contract itself is to avoid physical compulsion and economic insecurity. For the same reason, there can be no rights or duties that are more basic than the claims of the state (whatever form it may have) except the right to preserve one's own life and property.

Kant's view of the relation between rights and duties, and of the justification of both, is diametrically opposed to this view[24]; for him, the concepts of right and duty cannot be meaningful if we understand human action merely mechanistically. The only alternative, for Kant, is to think of human action as free action; but, on Kant's view, freedom can be known only through the fact of moral obligation under the fundamental law of practical reason (the moral law). The fundamental principle of *Recht,* in turn, is derived from the moral law. Thus, for Kant, duty (as moral obligation) logically precedes all

rights and is a condition of their possibility. Moreover, the fundamental principle of *Recht* (the harmony of the freedom of each with the freedom of all) is logically prior to the state and in fact is the immediate justification for the social contract that must be considered as the merely ideal basis of all states. The obligation to form a state is therefore tied up with an obligation to form a certain kind of state, namely, one that ensures fundamental rights (among others, political equality and freedom).

We can now begin to see how Constant's example of lying is significant on the level of political theory. In the first place, his way of applying the principle of truthfulness reveals that in Kant's terms Constant can have no theoretical justification, other than an arbitrary one, for principles of *Recht.* From Kant's viewpoint, no matter how much Constant may profess his belief in freedom and equality, he can provide no philosophical grounds for those principles if he believes that rights precede duties. But, in addition, the fact that it is lying that is in question takes on added significance in the context of Kant's political theory. Even though Kant did not believe in the social contract as an historical event, he did believe that an original contract must be the ideal presupposition of all states; and in that context a principle asserting that the duty to truthfulness is contingent upon a right to truthfulness contradicts the very idea of political philosophy. As Kant argues, "truthfulness is a duty that must be regarded as the basis of all duties founded on contract"[25] since it "constitutes the supreme condition of justice in utterances"[26] and hence to make a principle of lying "vitiates the source of justice."[27] Viewed politically in terms of a social contract theory, the duty of truthfulness is one of the most fundamental of all duties: it must logically precede even the social contract itself since the obligation to truthfulness is a presupposition of any justifiable contract.

In this context, too, it becomes clear why Kant picked up Constant's phrase "the German philosopher" and then referred to Constant as "the French philosopher." Far from being motivated by injured national pride (as Paton suggests), Kant was using the phrase ironically. For Kant, just as the fundamental universal principles of *Recht* are logically prior to the establishment of any constituted state, so the philosophy of *Recht* (or metaphysic of *Recht,* as he calls it at G429; E364) is intrinsically international. *Recht* cannot vary from state to state but must transcend all states—in fact, it is their presupposition. And the philosopher, when considering questions of *Recht,* must transcend national prejudice and become cosmopolitan.[28] Therefore, when Kant finally enunciates his own derivation of the intermediary principle of representative government, he significantly drops the national denomination and asserts simply "the philosopher will enunciate."[29] Kant's pique is directed against Constant's use of national distinctions, not against an imagined slur on his own nationality.

Kant's insistence upon the universality of the principles of *Recht* (specifically their international character) is tied logically to his belief that the fundamental principles of *Recht* must be a priori and therefore universal and necessary. It is this belief that accounts for his insistence that duty must take precedence over rights, since the alternative would (at least in his view) ultimately reduce all obligation to mere expediency, to pleasure and pain, which can provide only a contingent basis for action. This becomes explicit in his derivation of the second principle mentioned above, namely, the principle of representative government.

Kant's derivation of this principle is significantly different from that of Constant. Constant presents the principle of representation as merely a matter of expediency—it would not be practicable to have everyone make laws, so representatives must be chosen. Of course, Kant, too, acknowledges an inevitable element of mere expediency in politics, but he is also anxious to distinguish different levels of principles of *Recht*—ranging from apodictic, fundamental principles to principles that can be applied in experience and thus must take into account questions of expediency.[30]

Thus Kant (speaking as "the philosopher") enunciates (G429; E364) first an *axiom,* which he defines as "an apodictically certain proposition that follows immediately from the definition of external *Recht* (Harmony of the freedom of each with the freedom of all by a universal law)," The axiom as a priori and apodictic, can admit of no arbitrariness. Likewise necessary, although not apodictic (since it is not immediately derivable from the definition of external *Recht* although it is necessary for the realization of the latter), is Kant's second principle, the *postulate* of "external public law as the united will of all on the principle of *equality.*" With the third step in the progression, the *problem* of how freedom and equality may be guaranteed even in a large society, Kant introduces the representative system—but still as a fundamental principle ("a principle of politics"). It is only with the introduction of politics as the realm of the empirical application of principles such as the principle of representation that elements of expediency enter in: ". . . enactments which, drawn from empirical knowledge (*Erfahrungserkenntnis*) of human beings, have in view only the mechanism of the administration of *Recht*, and how this is to be arranged in accordance with given ends."[31]

Kant's purpose in this rather ponderous derivation is to show the difference between the concrete application of political principles (which must always be adjusted to suit the circumstances) and the formulation of basic

principles of *Recht* that are presupposed by all concrete political principles. Principles of *Recht* are not simply more general than political principles; they are more fundamental because they provide the only possible justification for political principles. Thus "*Recht* must never be accommodated to politics, but always politics to *Recht*" (G429; E365). Kant's criticism, therefore, is that Constant makes political expediency more fundamental in principle than *Recht,* and in doing so undermines the foundations of politics itself.

My purpose in emphasizing the political context of Kant's essay has been to explain why Kant adopted such a rigoristic stance on the question of lying and to see what, if any, justification there might be for that stance. I think we now have the elements of such an explanation, but to draw them together we need to note the following points. In the first place, it must simply be acknowledged that Kant's position on lying is untenable. The principle of truthfulness (even if it is interpreted as a political principle) cannot be made into an absolute principle in the strong sense asserted by Kant, i.e., one allowing no exceptions whatsoever. It would be only in an ideal society that one could assert categorically that lying is never permissible. And certainly, in the example of the murderer, lying is not only necessary but justified (if we grant Kant's condition that there is no other way to save the friend's life).

But, in the second place, the extreme legalistic position that Kant takes in his essay on lying is not even required by his own views. It is true that even in other writings Kant sometimes uses rigorous conceptions of duty, the prime example being his understanding of perfect duties as those that allow of no exceptions.[32] But, at the same time, he frequently makes claims that suggest a very different position, namely, that the application of any principle requires personal judgment, which cannot itself be determined by further rules.[33] Such a position seems to be a methodological one, in which principles are understood as procedures for deciding what actions are right or wrong rather than as rules that immediately dictate their own application.[34]

So it seems that Kant does not need to take such a legalistic position; moreover, elsewhere he takes what seems to be a very different position. But that leaves us with the question of why he adopts the legalistic stance in this particular essay. I think the answer to that question may lie in the fact that although Kant's practical philosophy does not need rigorism in the concrete application of principles, it does need rigorism of fundamental principles. On Kant's view there must be some practical principles or a principle that is apodictic in the strictest sense—otherwise there can be no moral or legal obligation at all but only mechanical compulsion. In the debate with Constant fundamental principles are at stake rather than particular principles like the prohibition on lying; and fundamental principles are at stake here both theoretically and practically.

On the level of the theoretical understanding of principles of action Kant makes this clear, especially with his distinction of degrees of generality of principles. He acknowledges there that some principles are flexible insofar as they are based solely on "practical knowledge of men" (G429; E365), but at the same time he denies that all principles are equally flexible. Constant, on the other hand, treats all principles as alike subject to modification; and thus, form Kant's viewpoint, Constant's pratical philosophy is sheer opportunism and fundamentally opposed to his own.

On the level of the practical application of principles, however, Kant does not make explicit his radical disagreement with Constant. In particular, he never once mentions in the essay the French Revolution or the Directory. One obvious reason for this omission is that Kant did not need to remind contemporary readers of the political events of their own day—the mere mention of the journal title (*France*) and the title of Constant's pamphlet (**"On Political Reactions"**) in the opening sentence of his essay would have been sufficient. It was also, of course, dangerous for Kant to express Jacobin sympathies at that time. Nevertheless, in spite of Kant's silence on his political disagreement with Constant, he cannot have failed to recognize that Constant's pamphlet was written in support of a government that was undermining the principles of the French Revolution, a revolution that Kant had hailed as empirical evidence for his view that humanity was capable of progress, both politically and morally.[35] Thus Constant's views would have appeared to Kant as reactionary in the most literal sense. And so, on the practical level too, the real disagreement between Constant and Kant went much deeper than the particular question of whether or not lying is justifiable.

Thus, if my proposed political reading of the essay is correct, then Kant's lapse into legalism might be at least partially explained by the fact that under the guise of defending a position on lying, he was actually defending the foundations of his moral and political views. The result is a conflation of the specific question of lying with the more general questions of how actions are justifiable and what political principles are right; in this conflation Kant's generally more methodological views rigidified into strict legalism. Such a confusion of issues would of course not have been possible in his essay if it did not reflect a more general problem in Kant's views of how principles are applied in action. Still, the legalism of his essay should be seen as an expression of an implicit problem in Kant's thought, and not simply as a momentary aberration or as the authoritative presentation of his views.

By reading Kant's essay in its historical and political context, therefore, although we cannot resolve all of the essay's internal contradictions, we can at least see how they arise. And I think this reading indicates that the contradictions have their origins in the historical context as well as in the context of Kant's philosophy.

Notes

1. The essay, "Ueber eine vermeintes Recht, aus Menschenliebe zu lügen, *Berlinésche Blätter,*" I (Sept. 6, 1797) appears in Vol. VIII of the Royal Prussian Academy edition of Kant's works, 23 vols. (Berlin, 1902-55), 425-30, and in English translation in *Kant's Critique of Practical Reason and Other Works on the Theory of Ethics,* transl. Thomas Kingsmill Abbott (London, 1963, repr. from the 6th ed. of 1909), 361-65. The essay was also translated by Lewis White Beck and included in *Critique of Practical Reason and Other Writings in Moral Philosophy* (Chicago, 1949; repr. New York, 1977). In citing passages from the essay I quote page numbers from the German text and from Abbott's English translation in the following form: G111; E399.

2. H. J. Paton, "An Alleged Right to Lie, A Problem in Kantian Ethics," *Kant-Studien,* 45 (1953), 190.

3. Heimo E. M. Hofmeister, "The Ethical Problem of the Lie in Kant," *Kant-Studien,* 63 (1972), 353; cf. also "Truth and Truthfulness: A Reply to Dr. Schwarz," *Ethics,* 82 (1972), 262.

4. Wolfgang Schwarz, "Kant's Refutation of Charitable Lies," *Ethics,* 81 (1970), 62; "Truth and Truthfulness: A Rejoinder," *Ethics,* 83 (1972-73), 173-75.

5. *Groundwork of the Metaphysic of Morals,* transl. H. J. Paton (New York, 1964), G53; E89. (Here and throughout, page number citations to German texts of Kant's works are to the Academy edition.)

6. See, for example, Schwarz's article, "Kant's Refutation . . ." cited above, Note 4, 63, par. 3; Paton, *op. cit.,* 194-95. The point has been followed up by Hans Wagner in an article that was called to my attention after the completion of this essay: "Kant gegen 'ein vermeintes Recht, aus Menschenliebe zu lügen,'" *Kant-Studien,* 69 (1978), 90. See also the paper by John E. Atwell (Philosophy Dept., Temple University): "Kant on an Alleged Right to Lie from Benevolence," read before the New Jersey Philosophical Association in Jan. 1981 at Princeton, N. J.

7. G426 n; E362 n 1. I have chosen not to translate Kant's term *Recht,* since (as I argue below) I think that neither "justice," "law," nor "right" is an adequate translation for the meaning Kant intends here.

8. Hofmeister is certainly right that the word *Men-schenliebe* in the title of the essay could point to the distinction between acting from the mere feeling of "tender sympathy" and acting on principle (cf. p. 266 of Hofmeister's article in *Ethics*, 266, cited in note 3 above). But that distinction, as concerning motives, would be appropriate to ethics and not to Recht.

9. Benjamin Constant," Des réactions politiques," first printed 1797, repr. in *Écrits et discours politiques*, ed. O. Pozzo di Borgo (Paris, 1964), 21-85. Translations are my own. Passages from this pamphlet will be cited using only Constant's name and the page number.

10. Constant apparently wrote this pamphlet, as he did several others during that period, in hopes of gaining a position in the government of the Directory. Cf. Harold Nicolson's biography *Benjamin Constant* (London, 1949), Chaps. 8 and 9. Constant was himself a constitutional monarchist, and he supported the Directory (as he later, briefly, supported Napoleon) in the hope that they would restore the monarchy.

11. Constant himself identified Kant as the German Philosopher in question, as is explained in a footnote to Kant's essay (G425 n; E361 n). This identification was, of course, incorrect, and one of the more puzzling things about Kant's essay is why he thought he had previously committed himself to that position when in fact he never had. Failure of memory is not, by itself, a sufficient explanation, since Kant could have qualified or retracted a previous statement if he no longer thought it correct. Kant's confusion here about what he said in print seems to point to a more basic confusion in his thinking about the question.

12. Cf. Part II of the *Strife of the Faculties*, "An Old Question Raised Again: Is the Human Race Constantly Progressing?" Section 6: "Concerning an Event of Our Time which Demonstrates this Moral Tendency of the Human Race," esp. Academy edition, 85 (in Lewis White Beck, ed., *On History* [New York, 1963], 143; transl. Robert E. Anchor). Kant thus developed the reputation of being a Jacobin. For example, in the anti-Jacobin reaction in Bavaria, in 1794, Kant's works were banned and burned (cf. Georges Lefebvre, *The French Revolution*, transl. J. H. Stewart and J. Friguglietti, 1964, II, 33). In that same year Kant was forbidden by the Prussian government to lecture or write on religious subjects—a prohibition with more than theological implications, since it was his criticism of political clericalism that immediately prompted the censorship (cf. Beck's Introduction to the volume *On History*, X).

13. Edmund Burke, *Reflections on the Revolution in France* [1790] (New York, 1955). Burke in fact blamed what were in his view the worst horrors of the Revolution on the Enlightenment. This theme runs throughout the *Reflections*, but see esp. 70-73, 95-101, 126-27, *et passim*.

14. Burke, *op. cit.*, 159-60.

15. An (admittedly ad hominem) argument for the essentially opportunistic nature of Constant's views is provided both by the propagandistic and self-serving character of Constant's pamphlets and by his subsequent career, which even his most charitable biographers admit was guided by opportunistic principles. (Nicolson defends him as "one of the most extraordinary opportunists that has ever lived," Nicolson, *op. cit.*, 229; cf. 145-46).

16. Actually, Constant had introduced the example as pertaining to morals (although he also speaks of the "right" to truth). It is significant that Kant reinterprets the example as a question of *Recht.*

17. Constant, 67-68; Kant G427; E363. This second example (as well as a third one introduced by Constant, namely, the principle of equality) was at the time particularly politically charged; the Directory had proposed a new constitution in which, among other things, universal suffrage was abolished and replaced by a property requirement (cf. Lefebvre, *op. cit.*, II, 160-64). Of course, Kant's own later views on suffrage were scarcely more radical than those of the constitution of the year III—cf. "On the Common Saying: 'This May Be True in Theory but it Does Not Apply in Practice,'" Academy ed., VIII, 273-313, in Hans Reiss, ed., *Kant's Political Writings*, transl. H. B. Nisbet (Cambridge, U. K., 1970), 77-78. See also the *Rechtslehre* of the *Metaphysic of Morals*, Academy ed., VI, 313-15, English transl. John Ladd (New York, 1965), 78-80.

18. Constant, 63-71.

19. Constant, 65.

20. Constant, 64.

21. Kant, G427; E363.

22. Constant, 69.

23. Part II of *Theory and Practice* (cited in note 17 above) is subtitled "Against Hobbes."

24. See *Theory and Practice*, Part II; cf. Appendix I to *Perpetual Peace* (in the volume *On History* cited in note 11 above), esp. G375 ff.; E123 ff.

25. G427; E363.

26. G429; E365.

27. G426; E362.

28. Cf. the "Secret Article of a Perpetual Peace," *Perpetual Peace* (note 24 above), G368-369; E115-16.

29. G429; E364.

30. He describes the progression as going from a "*metaphysic* of Recht" to a "principle of *politics,*" G429; E364.

31. G429; E365. The phrase "in accordance with given ends" is a translation of *zweckmässig*; it is here that the concept of expediency enters in for Kant, since it is a question of the choice of means appropriate to the end in view.

32. Cf. note 4 above; also the *Doctrine of Virtue* of the *Metaphysic of Morals* (English transl. Mary Gregor, (Philadelphia, 1964), G389 f.; E49 f.; G421-37; E84-103.

33. See, for example, the first two paragraphs of "Theory and Practice" (cited in note 17 above); note how close to Constant's views Kant's remarks sound here. Cf. also the *Doctrine of Virtue* (cited in note 32), G433 n; E97 n.

34. Cf. John Silber, "Procedural Formalism in Kant's Ethics," *The Review of Metaphysics XXVIII* (1974), 197.

35. See "An Old Question Raised Again . . . ," (*On History,* esp. Sec. 6.)

Timothy Unwin (essay date 1986)

SOURCE: Unwin, Timothy. "Organization of the Text." In *Constant*: Adolphe, pp. 13-50. London: Grant & Cutler Ltd., 1986.

[*In the following excerpt, Unwin illustrates how* Adolphe *follows the construction of the classical tragedy.*]

6. STRUCTURE

It will perhaps be accepted, on the basis of the remarks of the foregoing pages [of *Constant*: *Adolphe,* by Timothy Unwin], that the composition of **Adolphe,** far from offering a loose and episodic development such as might have been expected from Constant's original subtitle to his work (*Anecdote trouvée dans les papiers d'un inconnu*), shows extremely careful attention to the interrelation of detail. In fact the work is anything but anecdotal in its style, and Constant is merely exploiting a well-worn eighteenth-century convention (the chance discovery of an 'authentic' manuscript) as a means of presentation. We are beginning to discover a quite new conception of the novel. The loose linking together of sequences in a linear progression (of which the picaresque novel had been the extreme form) is now being replaced by an approach to the text as an organic totality in which the inner unity dictates the disposition of its elements. In this respect, if one takes a crude historical view, Constant has his rightful place in literary history between Laclos and Flaubert, who both raised the novel to new peaks of perfection while exploiting the prevailing conventions. Having seen something of this approach in the various stylistic devices used by Constant, we should hope to find it again at the level of overall structure. My use of the term 'structure' is intended to cover two aspects: first, the internal mechanisms which motivate the plot; second, the external proportions and divisions of the tale. Let us take these in turn.

It has often been said that Constant's novel has some of the properties of a Racinian drama, with its almost claustrophobic concentration on a central dilemma (for discussion of this see *15,* p. 34 and pp. 43-46). There are, of course, some essential points of difference: Constant's attention to the disappearance of passion rather than its growth, his choice of a prolonged time-scale, the setting of the drama in varied geographical locations, not to mention the preference of a different genre. Of the unities of time and place Constant once wrote:

> [Elles] circonscrivent nos tragédies dans un espace qui en rend la composition difficile, la marche précipitée, l'action fatigante et invraisemblable. Elles contraignent le poète à négliger souvent, dans les événements et les caractères, la vérité de la gradation.

(*1,* p. 884)

Yet for all that, the parallel with Racine is a valid one, and is perhaps most evident in Constant's attention to unity of the action.

In addition to all the events in the story being subordinate to the central problem, the tragic incompatibility of the lovers is relentlessly exposed until we reach the final climax. What matters is not the detail of individual developments, but the manner in which each new change intensifies the emotional dilemma. Adolphe's accompaniment of Ellénore to Poland, the recovered inheritance, even the heroine's death—the events in themselves are described with bare simplicity; what interests us in them is their contribution to an overall scheme and the manner in which they combine to produce the total effect. The emphasis is always on the unifying force, never on the constituent elements of the narrative. Even that which comes before the encounter with Ellénore, although in some senses standing apart from the narrative proper, contributes closely to our understanding of the tragic predicament. As in Racinian drama, the problem is present before the introduction of specific circumstances which bring the action into play;

and the arrival of Ellénore is the individual element which highlights the complexities of the original matrix.

Unity of action in *Adolphe* is greatly reinforced by the sense of fatality which looms over the story. Most obvious and most immediate among the devices used by Constant is the description of the hero by an outside observer at the outset. Now it is important to stress that, when we see Adolphe through the eyes of the editor, the affair with Ellénore is already in the past and the manuscript already written. It is therefore impossible for the story, when we read it, to have any bearing at all on the fictional present (especially since the editor claims to have delayed ten years before publishing the manuscript). The reader knows and must accept this. Compare such a situation with, for example, that of *Manon Lescaut,* where the Homme de qualité meets Des Grieux for the first time before the latter's departure to America, and then again on his return, at which point the story is recounted. The explanation in *Manon Lescaut* thus finds a natural focal point, which is the journey to America, and it is geared towards a listener who has witnessed some of the earlier events in the story. But the editor in *Adolphe* has not, like his counterpart in *Manon Lescaut,* had any influence on the course of the story; and even his correspondent's claims to have known the participants stand unconfirmed by Adolphe's own account. Nor do we have any real impression that this account is in any way directed towards a specific listener, as is the case in *Manon Lescaut*; indeed, the so-called 'narratee' is, as one critic has pointed out,[1] strangely absent, and only once does Adolphe make an appeal to a second person in his story ('Qui que vous soyez, ne remettez jamais à un autre les intérêts de votre cœur', p. 95). The account is deliberately, almost overbearingly, fixed and static, a characteristic which is reinforced by the presence of the maxims: what took place is not in question, the issue is how and why it took place. As in Racinian tragedy, disaster is known to be inevitable, and the focus shifts to how the human mind may bear with dignity what it is powerless to avoid.

Also in the tragic tradition, Constant is careful to balance inner and outer forces in order to prevent any facile judgement of his hero's guilt or innocence. Adolphe's failures do not in themselves decide the turn of events; the reactions of other people (which he cannot foresee or control) combine with them to produce the tragic outcome. In this respect, Adolphe's avowal of his true sentiments about Ellénore to her friend is something like Phèdre's admission to Œnone of her incestuous passion for Hippolyte, for both confidantes make more active use of the information than had been envisaged by its disclosers. Similarly, the baron de T***'s action in sending Adolphe's letter on to Ellénore shows an outside character taking an unexpected responsibility over feelings which the central character cannot himself fully account for. As Constant suggested in his tribute to Madame de Staël written after her death, it is the artist's duty to suggest the sense of guilt and responsibility, as well as the insidious nature of moral problems, but without pointing the finger of blame in any unequivocal manner:

> Un ouvrage d'imagination ne doit pas avoir un but moral, mais un résultat moral. Il doit ressembler, à cet égard, à la vie humaine qui n'a pas un but, mais qui toujours a un résultat dans lequel la morale trouve nécessairement sa place.
>
> (*1*, p. 834)

The most frequent point of comparison to which attention is drawn between Constant's novel and classical tragedy is the particular use he makes of the presence of society. Society represents, either in the form of specific individuals or in the general form of its attitudes, that sense of constraint which is alternately seen either as wholesome discipline or as cruel oppression. Society was, moreover, held by Constant to be something of a modern equivalent to the gods of the ancients, and in one of the most telling remarks he ever penned on the link between his aesthetic and his social beliefs he tells us:

> L'ordre social, l'action de la société sur l'individu, dans les diverses phases et aux diverses époques, ce réseau d'institutions et de conventions qui nous enveloppe dès notre naissance et ne se rompt qu'à notre mort, sont des ressorts tragiques qu'il ne faut que savoir manier. Ils sont tout à fait équivalents à la fatalité des anciens.
>
> (*1*, p. 918)

The presence of society, together with the differing responses to its demands on the part of the two lovers, is an important motivating element in the story. Society is most obviously a hostile outer force in the case of Ellénore, bent as it is on her destruction: allowing her a precarious respect before her encounter with Adolphe, expressing its outrage when she abandons all for her lover, treating her as an outcast when she sets up with Adolphe in her father's house. The absolute ascendant of society, which commands total obedience or else exacts dire punishment, is clearly expressed by Adolphe at the beginning of his account when he says: 'Cette société d'ailleurs n'a rien à . . . craindre. Elle pèse tellement sur nous, son influence sourde est tellement puissante, qu'elle ne tarde pas à nous façonner d'après le moule universel' (p. 40). Herein lies the difference between Adolphe's and Ellénore's attitude, a difference which leads to their inevitable separation. Adolphe, critical of society though he may be, ultimately respects its values and refrains from goading it into anger. If he despises the hypocrisy and the facility of its judgements, he nevertheless looks to it for satisfaction of his own ego: his eagerness to earn the respect of key social figures such as the baron de T***, his yearning for the pleasure of career satisfaction, his dream of an acceptable emotional partner, these reveal a conservative attitude not to be found in the more single-minded Ellénore. As the novel progresses, the social gap between the lovers becomes symbolically wider. At first we see them together in the society of the comte de P***, but later we find them apart when Adolphe receives an invitation to the house of the baron de T*** and when Ellénore remains in hiding: she has become, in the baron de T***'s words, one of those women 'que l'on ne voit que chez elles' (p. 104). Society provides a measure by which the two central characters' development in opposite directions can be gauged. More than this, it forces the issues by its very presence in their world; and finally it offers, chorus-like, a running commentary on the actions of the characters—from the range of reactions displayed when Ellénore leaves the comte de P***, through the attitude of Adolphe's father who pinpoints the social implications of his son's behaviour, to the interventions of the baron de T***, and then, all passion spent, to the two judgements offered at the end of the narrative by the editor and his correspondent. Society is part of the internal structure of the novel, and a key element in its equilibrium.

Together with that sense of tragic ambiguity and the delicate balance of inner and outer forces, the reader may also be struck by the external proportions of the novel. It has been said that the ten chapters of this story, taken in pairs, might be seen as having something of the nature of the five acts of a tragedy (*24*, pp. 250-54). An alternative scheme which has been suggested is to see the novel as falling naturally into three groups of three chapters, with the tenth and final chapter offering the dénouement (*14*, pp. 303-6). What I should prefer to stress, rather than any external scheme, is the careful interrelation in the novel of climaxes of events and climaxes of emotion. These separate orders are now staggered, now brought together, and the author's use of such a technique has significant consequences for our reading of the text.

The first part of the novel is marked by one major event, which is the seduction of Ellénore in the third chapter. The emotional climax which is the corollary of this event is held over until the beginning of the fourth chapter: it is the well-known one-paragraph celebration of love. The simple technique of delay might not appear in any way unusual (is it not a conventional means of maintaining interest?) until we reflect that it could, perhaps, have been more logically inserted into the narrative in the closing stages of chapter three, where the narrator is already expressing his joy. As it stands, it gives the impression of being slightly isolated. It is known that this paragraph was absent from the 1810 manuscript of **Adolphe** and that it was added for the

first edition of the novel, but does that alone account for the effect of disjunction? I would prefer to argue that such an effect was deliberately sought by the author, who wishes to show his hero's inner life as fragmented in the early stages, or at least as lacking in continuity. For the introspective young Adolphe, the real world of cause and effect is at some distance, and he lives more in the fitful and sporadic domain of the inner life. As he tells us: 'Je ne demandais alors qu'à me livrer à ces impressions primitives et fougueuses que jettent l'âme hors de la sphère commune' (pp. 35-36). The relation between the outer and inner world has not yet been fully established. Ironically, it will come only in the latter stages of the story.

The interplay between facts and feelings becomes much more complicated in the middle stages of the novel (i.e. the rest of chapter four to the end of chapter six). In this section there are three, or perhaps four, main external events. The first is Ellénore's departure from the comte de P*** at the end of chapter four. The second is Adolphe's departure from D*** to return to his father, half-way through chapter five. The third—a double event—is the synthesis of the preceding departures as Adolphe and Ellénore leave together, first for Caden at the end of chapter five, then for Poland at the end of chapter six (the journey to Poland is, in terms of the action of the story, a reiteration and a reinforcement rather than an entirely new occurrence). The symmetry of these departures is itself an eloquent statement of the anxiety and agitation of the lovers, but into this scheme Constant injects three emotional climaxes which maintain the intensity of the drama at an almost unbearable pitch.

The first of these is the bitter dispute which occurs between Adolphe and Ellénore half-way through chapter four, and which prompts the dark diagnosis that 'une première barrière était franchie. Nous avions prononcé tous deux des mots irréparables . . .' (p. 65). The second is Adolphe's act of rebellion against his father and his decision to remain with Ellénore at the end of chapter five, together with Ellénore's clear-sighted response ('Vous n'avez que de la pitié'). The third comes shortly later in chapter six, when Adolphe makes his own attempt to be forthright ('L'amour [. . .] je ne l'ai plus', p. 81). As Alison Fairlie has pointed out (*17*, p. 226), this moment stands in conspicuous equilibrium with Ellénore's own moment of truth (moreover, it is one of the ironies that Adolphe is doing no more than tell her what she had told him). We find something of the symmetry of the external action echoed at the level of inner, emotional high points.

But let us look also to the correlation between external fact and internal change in these middle chapters. Here we will find that in two out of three cases an emotional climax actually precedes the event which will accompany it: the dispute between Adolphe and Ellénore in chapter four is followed by Ellénore's separation from the compte de P***; and Adolphe's revelation to Ellénore in chapter six that he is no longer in love with her is followed by the departure to Poland. In both cases, the ordering of the narrative is an ironic reinforcement of the helplessness of Adolphe's and Ellénore's situation, for their actions are carried out at a time when irreparable damage has already been done. Only once in the middle section of the novel do external and internal events coincide, and this is when Ellénore accuses Adolphe of experiencing no more than pity at the moment when the lovers are departing for Caden. Appropriately, this occurs at the precise midway point of the novel, and Ellénore's insight is given a privileged status amidst the surrounding confusion. It is the first occasion when an event immediately elicits an adjacent emotional response.

In the latter stages of the story (chapters seven to ten) there is an apparent return to the pattern of its early stages, with emotional climaxes following on from external actions. The difference is that the delay no longer appears as a process of disjunction, but rather as the temporal progression of cause and effect. It is as though the memory of Ellénore's insight has jolted the narrator, who now gradually emerges from the confusion and begins to perceive a coherent pattern in his past conduct. There are three points at which we see this. The first is in chapter seven, where the significant first encounter with the baron de T*** prompts a new moment of inner intensity as Adolphe wanders alone at night. The second is in chapter eight where two external events— the intercession of Ellénore's friend, and Ellénore's invitation of local people into her house—have their backlash in the scenes of frenzied conflict between the lovers described in the final paragraph of the chapter. And the third, perhaps most obviously, is the baron de T***'s action to separate the couple (chapter nine) followed by Ellénore's emotional delirium at the beginning of the final chapter as she falls into fatal sickness.

This device of separation and intertwining of the external and internal high points in the novel has considerable advantages in a text of such small proportions. It creates, through its pattern of intermittences and echoes, the impression of density and depth; and with great economy of means, the author is able to scatter the moments of tension more evenly and more widely. But the overall distribution tells us something else. At first, for the inexperienced and introverted young hero, the world of emotions and the world of real events are unsynchronized and separate; in the confused middle stages of his relationship they seem even to be of two different orders altogether. But they are forced together in the middle of the novel with Ellénore's insight, and thereafter an overall pattern of cause and effect begins to emerge. Whilst Adolphe's explicit account of his rela-

tionship with Ellénore stresses its progression towards increasing disorder, the underlying structure of that account shows the gradual emergence of order. This is an irony which reinforces Constant's deliberately ambivalent presentation of his hero.

The careful and controlled structuring of the novel is confirmed again by the move to the epistolary level with which it is concluded. Although an apparent sop to an eighteenth-century convention, Constant's use of the two letters of judgement by way of epilogue is an amplification of what is already present within the narrative: the turning of Adolphe's judgements against him, and the alternative interpretations of events which are to be found in the extracts given from other people's letters (the two trends coming together in the final pages of the story, where Ellénore's letter provides the transition to the external point of view). It is perhaps of interest to note that the 1810 manuscript of **Adolphe** did not contain the concluding letters, and that the *Avis de l'éditeur* correspondingly offered different reasons for the publication of the manuscript (this, we are told, was found together with some diamonds, and it is in the hope of returning them to their rightful owner that the editor is having the story printed).[2] The manifest superiority of the reworked ending comes of its being structurally an integral part of the work. The earlier convention, which often implied that literary merit was the very last reason for publication, is now turned upside down by Constant. He is using it in order to complete the effect of unity for which he strives.[3] But there is a further aspect of the epistolary conclusion which merits a moment's attention, for it also exploits another fascinating undercurrent in the novel.

That undercurrent—which has implications on the whole way in which we look at the structure of the work—is the existence of letters and documents which the reader never gets to see. In his reply to the editor, the correspondent refers to a series of letters which he is sending and which, he says, will give some insight into what later happened to Adolphe. The editor himself replies, after reading these letters, that he could have guessed at the continued misery of Adolphe's existence even had he not received this further information. What we have here is a text or a series of texts, known to the characters and discussed by them, but quite unknowable to the reader. This is an ironic inversion of what so often happens in the epistolary novel, where the reader holds documents unknown to at least some of the characters. Now these letters and documents referred to at the end of the story are far from being the only source of alternative information which is mentioned. What they do is increase our sense of the possible extensions in different directions of Adolphe's account: whether it be in Ellénore's direction, in the series of documents and personal papers which she leaves after her death, or in her correspondence with Adolphe when the latter is at his father's house; or in the comte de P***'s direction, for we know that he writes to Ellénore while she is away in chapter two, and that he writes to her again later offering her half of his recovered fortune; or in the direction of Adolphe's father, for we read but fragments of the correspondence between him and his son, and we know also that he corresponds with the baron de T***. Of the innumerable documents, letters, conversations, reminiscences and interpretations, the final account has been wrested in all its incompleteness. We are aware of the difference and the potential conflict between Adolphe's own version and the other possible versions of the story.

For all its classical structure and elegant proportions there is, then, a deliberate air of asymmetry about **Adolphe.** The directness of its line of action, the careful patterning of its themes and images, the totality of effect created by the organization of the text, are undercut by our awareness that we are in possession of a limited segment of the story, the incompleteness of which is epitomized by the final withholding of extra information about the hero. Beneath the unified surface of the text we discern gaps, additions and alterations, and our attention is drawn to the fact that the process of converting lived experience into written form is by no means the monopoly of the narrating Adolphe. The continued mention within his own account of other written documents underlines that others are doing precisely the same as he, and the only reason that his own story happens to have a privileged status is because it is the only one we possess. We are not therefore left with the impression (as we may be, say, in classical theatre) that we have a perfect and unalterable representation of an action. The work is lacunary in its very conception, posing the problem of how reality can be perceived through words and thus evoking a theme which will be a major concern of modern writers.

Just as we are in the end obliged to judge Constant's style by a standard other than that of formal completeness, so too we must look in his presentation of character for something other than well-proportioned exemplars of human psychology or morality. Although presented in the light of specific themes, Constant's characters are distinguished above all by their personal responses to given situations. Through them, the author's view of the world comes to life in individual ways, and through them the general and the particular are fused.

Notes

1. John T. Booker, 'The implied "narrataire" in *Adolphe*', *The French Review*, 51 (1977-78), 666-73.

2. For the text of the variant in the original *Avis* see *4*, p. 15.

3. For a full discussion of this aspect of the novel see Alison Fairlie, 'Framework as a suggestive art in Constant's *Adolphe* (with remarks on its relation to Chateaubriand's *René*)', *Australian Journal of French Studies,* Special Number, 16, pts. 1-2 (1979), 6-16.

Works Cited

Italicized numbers in parentheses refer to items in the Select Bibliography. References to the text of *Adolphe* are to the Folio edition *(7)*. Quotations from other works by Constant are taken from the Pléiade selection *(1)*; however, the *Journal* entries are, for convenience, identified by their date alone.

This study draws upon many ideas and insights from other works, and it has not been possible to detail its sources exhaustively. However, I should like here first to express my admiration for the writings of Georges Poulet, and second to acknowledge a profound debt to the work by Alison Fairlie. I would urge my own readers either to read or to re-read her trio of articles (listed in the Select Bibliography) which are as central and as relevant now to the study of *Adolphe* as when they were first published twenty years ago.

Select Bibliography

I. EDITIONS

1. Constant, Benjamin, *Œuvres,* texte présenté et annoté par Alfred Roulin, Paris, Gallimard, Bibliothèque de la Pléiade, 1957.

2.———, *Adolphe,* édition historique et critique par Gustave Rudler, Manchester University Press, 1919.

3.———, *Adolphe,* chronologie et introduction par Antoine Adam, Paris, Garnier-Flammarion, 1965.

4.———, *Adolphe,* ed. Jacques-Henry Bornecque, Paris, Garnier, 1968.

5.———, *Adolphe, anecdote trouvée dans les papiers d'un inconnu,* ed. W. Andrew Oliver, London, Macmillan, 1968.

6.———, *Adolphe, suivi du Cahier rouge et de Poèmes inédits,* ed. Jean Mistler, Paris, Livre de Poche, 1972.

7.———, *Adolphe, Le Cahier rouge, Cécile,* ed. Alfred Roulin, Paris, Folio (Gallimard, 1957).

8.———, *Adolphe, anecdote trouvée dans les papiers d'un inconnu,* ed. Paul Delbouille, Paris, Les Belles Lettres, 1977.

II. CRITICAL WORKS

9. Alexander, Ian W., *Benjamin Constant: 'Adolphe',* London, Edward Arnold, 1973.

10. Baguley, David, 'The role of letters in Constant's *Adolphe*', *Forum for Modern Language Studies,* 11 (1975), 29-35.

11. Bowman, Frank Paul, 'Nouvelles lectures d'*Adolphe*', in *Annales Benjamin Constant,* 1, Geneva, Droz, 1980, 27-42.

12. Brady-Papadopoulou, Valentini, 'The killing of the "mother" in Constant's *Adolphe'*, *Neophilologus*, 65 (1981), 6-14.

13. Charles, Michel, 'Adolphe ou l'inconstance', in *Rhétorique de la lecture*, Paris, Seuil, 1977, pp. 215-47.

14. Delbouille, Paul, *Genèse, structure et destin d''Adolphe'*, Paris, Les Belles Lettres, 1971.

15. Fairlie, Alison, 'The art of Constant's *Adolphe*: the stylization of experience', *Modern Language Review*, 62 (1967), 31-47.

16.———, 'The art of Constant's *Adolphe*: creation of character', *Forum for Modern Language Studies*, 2 (1966), 253-63.

17. Fairlie, Alison, 'The art of Constant's *Adolphe*: structure and style', *French Studies*, 20 (1966), 226-42.

(The essays by Alison Fairlie, together with four further studies on *Adolphe*, may be found in the collective volume of her articles on nineteenth-century authors, *Imagination and Language*, Cambridge University Press, 1981).

18. Gonin, Eve, *Le Point de vue d'Ellénore: une réécriture d''Adolphe'*, Paris, José Corti, 1981.

19. Jallat, Jeannine, 'Adolphe, la parole et l'autre', *Littérature*, 2 (1971), 71-88.

20. King, Norman, 'Structure et stratégies d'*Adolphe'*, in *Benjamin Constant, Madame de Staël et le Groupe de Coppet, Actes du deuxième congrès de Lausanne, 1980*, Lausanne, Institut Benjamin Constant, Oxford, The Voltaire Foundation, 1982, pp. 267-85.

21. Le Hir, Yves, 'Lignes de force sur l'imagination de B. Constant dans *Adolphe'*, *Convivium*, 26 (1958), 328-31.

22. Mercken-Spass, Godeliève, *Alienation in Constant's 'Adolphe': an exercise in structural thematics*, Bern, Peter Lang, 1977.

23. Morrison, Ian R., 'Emotional involvement and the failure of analysis in *Adolphe'*, *Neophilologus*, 60 (1976), 334-41.

24. Oliver, Andrew, *Benjamin Constant: écriture et conquête du moi*, Paris, Minard, 1970.

25. Poulet, Georges, *Etudes sur le temps humain*, Edinburgh University Press, 1949.

26.———, *Benjamin Constant par lui-même*, Paris, Seuil, 1968.

27.———, 'Benjamin Constant et le thème de l'abnégation', in *Actes du Congrès Benjamin Constant, Lausanne, octobre 1967*, Geneva, Droz, 1968, pp. 153-59.

28. Schilling, Robert, 'Encadrement du récit et structure d'*Adolphe'*, *Bulletin de la Faculté des Lettres de Mulhouse*, 4 (1971-72), 49-58.

29. Scott, M., 'The Romanticism of *Adolphe'*, *Nottingham French Studies*, V, 2 (1967), 58-66.

30. Thomas, Ruth P., 'The ambiguous narrator of *Adolphe'*, *Romance Notes*, 14 (1972-73), 486-95.

31. Todorov, Tzvetan, 'La Parole selon Constant', in *Poétique de la prose*, Paris, Seuil, 1971, pp. 100-17.

32. Turnell, Martin, *The Novel in France*, New York, Plainview, 1951 (repr. 1972).

33. Verhoeff, Han, *'Adolphe' et Constant: une étude psychocritique*, Paris, Klincksieck, 1976.

III. BIBLIOGRAPHICAL

34. Hofmann, Etienne et al., *Bibliographie analytique des écrits sur Benjamin Constant (1796-1980)*, Lausanne, Institut Benjamin Constant, Oxford, The Voltaire Foundation, 1980.

35. Lowe, David K., *Benjamin Constant: an annotated bibliography of critical editions and studies, 1946-1978*, London, Grant and Cutler, Research Bibliographies and Checklists, No. 26, 1979.

Robert Wilcocks (essay date fall-winter 1988)

SOURCE: Wilcocks, Robert. "The Demystification of Rousseau: Benjamin Constant's Critique of Rhetoric, Abstraction, and Consequence in *Du contrat social*." *Stanford French Review* 12, nos. 2-3 (fall-winter 1988): 231-44.

[*In the following essay, Wilcocks presents Constant's steadfast refutation of the theories and writings of Jean-Jacques Rousseau.*]

In a BBC broadcast in 1952 for the series *Freedom and Its Betrayal*, Sir Isaiah Berlin called Jean-Jacques Rousseau "the most sinister and most formidable enemy of liberty in the whole history of modern thought."[1] In our century, this judgment has been shared by thinkers as diverse as Bertrand Russell who, when writing his *History of Western Philosophy* during World War II, was moved to conclude his opening paragraph on Rousseau thus: "At the present time, Hitler is an outcome of Rousseau; Roosevelt and Churchill, of Locke," and Albert Camus who, with perhaps greater political acumen, saw in the *déification* of the *volonté générale* a precursor of Leninism and Stalinism.[2] Certainly a theoretical basis for the systematic alienation from early infancy of the child from his family by the State—something that even Stalin had not argued—is to be found in the "Discours sur l'économie politique."[3] The scene in the Roland Joffé film *The Killing Fields* of the Khmer Rouge child-indoctrination center is a moving indictment of this *mise-en-pratique* of theories elaborated in Rousseau's political writings. Nonetheless, it was without irony, I am sure, that twenty-one years ago Bernard Gagnebin wrote in his preface to the Pléiade edition of *Du contrat social*:

> De nombreux hommes politiques africains ou asiatiques de langue française se sont mis à lire Rousseau, au moment où leurs pays accédaient à l'indépendance.

D'éminents hommes d'Etat vietnamiens, guinéens, sénégalais, etc., ont affirmé que leurs carrières *avaient été orientées vers la politique par la lecture des oeuvres de Rousseau.*

(Rousseau xxvi; my emphasis)

Conor Cruise O'Brien has argued in a trenchant article entitled "Virtue and Terror" (*The New York Review of Books,* September 26, 1985:28-31) against "putting liberal interpretations on work which is in fact not liberal" (O'Brien 29). He seems to have in mind as his audience—or his targets—those American political science and literature departments that teach Rousseau as if he were a wild and brilliant eccentric (which he was) whose political thought however expressed is susceptible of translation into the framework of liberal representative democracy (which it is not).

It was, of course, as a *liberal* that Benjamin Constant argued so powerfully throughout his adult life against the political writings of Rousseau. In that sense, Conor Cruise O'Brien's article is less a call for a re-assessment of Rousseau than an appeal for a return to an original liberal assessment made in the nineteenth century by those who had first-hand experience of the consequences, direct and indirect, of Rousseau's persuasive rhetorical abstractions. Such an appeal, repetitive in principle (and O'Brien makes no claim to theoretical or historical novelty), may well be salutary in practice if we accept the *obiter dictum* on the need to repeat to the present generation what was once said but is now forgotten or neglected.

Rousseau's influence on the thoughts and actions of the leading figures of the French Revolution is undeniable. While Heine may have been exaggerating when he wrote "Maximilien Robespierre was merely the hand of Jean-Jacques Rousseau, the bloody hand that drew from the womb of time the body whose soul Rousseau had created,"[4] there is no doubt that Saint-Just's *Essai de constitution pour la France* and *Esprit de la Révolution*[5] were rhetorically and theoretically inspired by Rousseau. However, between inspiration and influence on the one hand, and responsibility on the other, there is a divide that one crosses with trepidation and that perhaps not even solid documentation can resolve. Constant himself (strangely enough, given the position he took on the duties of the writer to his readers in his famous dispute with Goethe) was more concerned with the influence of Rousseau's writings than with an assessment of personal responsibility. One is tempted to recall Voltaire's soothing comment to Rousseau on the limits of authorial responsibility: "Avouez que le badinage de Marot n'a pas produit La St Barthelemi, et que la tragédie du Cid ne causa pas les guerres de la Fronde. Les grands crimes n'ont été commis que par de célèbres ignorants" (Rousseau 1380).

Voltaire was not always so sanguine about the likely effects of Rousseau's texts, nor so gentle in his remonstrations. The caustic marginalia in his own copy of *Du contrat social* are savage in their brusque uncovering of Rousseau's antinomies. If Constant was the first liberal theoretician of the nineteenth century to demolish in detail (and in public) the theses of *Du contrat social* many of his arguments were anticipated—at least in outline—in Voltaire's marginalia written some fifty years earlier. This point is brought out by the French political scientist Jacques Julliard in *La faute à Rousseau* published in 1985.[6] Like Conor Cruise O'Brien, though with much greater scholarly depth, Jacques Julliard writes with a sustained polemical verve. He is careful to distinguish Rousseau's speculative intentions—"Le *Contrat social* est un conte, une parabole philosophique" (Julliard 36)—from the intentions of those who used his work as a practical textbook on how to achieve absolutist tyranny. Julliard attempts, *inter alia,* an overview of Rousseau's reception in France from the Revolution onward[7] and naturally includes a detailed assessment of Constant's refutations of Rousseau's sociopolitical utopia. Julliard is critical of the historical limitations of Constant's liberal vision; but he recognizes and pays tribute to Constant's perspicacity in his reading of the past (the writings of Rousseau) and of what was, for him, the very recent past (the excesses of 1793-1794). He concludes "Constant joue 1789 contre 1793, les droits de l'homme contre la logique du citoyen. Et d'énumérer des droits fondamentaux auxquels aucune autorité ne saurait porter atteinte sans détruire sa propre légitimité" (Julliard 111).

Julliard's references to Constant's criticisms of Rousseau are, for the most part, drawn from the ***Principes de politique*** elaborated by Constant at the beginning of the nineteenth century in the immediate aftermath of the Bonapartiste response to the *chienlit* that the Revolution had become.[8] But even in the last year of his life, 1830, Constant continued to repudiate the theses and the seductive (and hence, in his eyes, misleading) rhetoric of Rousseau. In an article in *Le Temps,* **"De la souveraineté,"** written a few months before his death, Constant declared unambiguously "Rousseau devenait le précepteur de la tyrannie comme Bossuet."[9]

Stephen Holmes has pointed out in *Benjamin Constant and the Making of Modern Liberalism*:

> The anti-Rousseauist strain in Constant's thought is undeniable and important. Nevertheless, it has frequently been exaggerated. As a result, the important ways in which Constant had an irreducibly ambivalent attitude toward Rousseau have been neglected.[10]

In an attempt to minimize the dangerous rhetorical consequences of Rousseau's works, and in a subtle demonstration of the ambiguities which, for him, appear to link Constant with Rousseau, Holmes tends to disregard the power of Rousseau's rhetoric and to dismiss as "banal" those interpretations or "misinterpretations" (as he calls them)—presumably a reference to J. L. Talmon—which have seen in *Du contrat social* an outline for, and a defense of, a prototalitarian democratic tyranny (Holmes 86).

It seems to me that Holmes is mistaken in this attempt to lessen Constant's divergences from Rousseau and for three reasons. In the first place, Constant, educated in Germany and Britain (he was a fellow student of Walter Scott at Edinburgh University), familiar with Blackstone's *Commentaries* and a firm supporter all his life of the British system of common-law, constitutional monarchy, and parliamentary democracy, was always and without exception a *political* opponent of the political theories of Rousseau and of the use made of them by Saint-Just and Robespierre.[11] He had experienced and understood the parliamentary practice of the "loyal opposition"—a notion alien to Rousseau, incomprehensible to Robespierre, and anathema to Saint-Just.[12] In the second place, he knew, virtually from first-hand experience, what horrors could be produced by the putting into practice of the abstractions created in Rousseau's political writings. And, thirdly, Holmes seems not to understand the usages of formal rhetorical courtesy employed by Constant in his speeches and in his writings. This is, in my view, a serious error of historico-literary judgment. It is true that one can find, for example, in a footnote to *De l'esprit de conquête* (1814) a long paragraph which begins "Je suis loin de me joindre aux détracteurs de Rousseau; ils sont nombreux dans le moment actuel."[13]

To read this as an indication of a sympathy for Rousseau's political doctrines is to misread the rhetorical code of early nineteenth-century discourse on politics (which was in many respects a *mise-en-question* by demonstration of the rhetorical code of the *jacobins*). As Roland Barthes wrote in a different context "ça ne signifie pas, ça signale!" Constant's signal is double-edged. On the one hand, this opening formula is devised to distinguish him from the conservatives and this message is intended as much for them as for his fellow liberals. On the other hand, it is a parade of ironic and elegant courtesy (so much a feature of Constant's speeches in the *Chambre*), which heralds a sustained critique of the consequences of Rousseau's theories.

Where it would be justified to make a *rapprochement* between Rousseau and Constant is in the area of that hypersensitivity, which marked the emotional relationships in their respective private lives. But, unlike Rousseau, Constant was able to bring to his political writings a kind of reasoned pragmatic empiricism—at once a memory of Locke and a foretaste of J. S. Mill—certainly more English than continental in its style and theoretical basis. There is no evidence in his political writings of the hysteria that seemed to be an essential part of his amatory correspondence. Nor is there any evidence that he felt one ounce of sympathy for Rousseau's political theorizing, although he may well have felt sympathy and indeed empathy for Rousseau's personal predicaments and sensitive nature.

In this extensive footnote to *De l'esprit de conquête,* Constant briefly praises Rousseau: "Il a le premier rendu populaire le sentiment de nos droits" (Constant 1049). He then launches into an attack on Rousseau's inability to think carefully, to write clearly, and to understand the implications of his rhetoric. In a vein similar to Raymond Aron's celebrated attack on Sartre's *Critique de la raison dialectique,* which ends with the suggestion that Hitler would have found it a useful textbook, Constant writes of Rousseau:

> . . . ce qu'il sentait avec force, il n'a pas su le définir avec précision. Plusieurs chapitres du *Contrat social* sont dignes des écrivains scolastiques du quinzième siècle. Que signifient des droits dont on jouit d'autant plus qu'on les aliène complètement?[14] qu'est-ce qu'une liberté en vertu de laquelle on est d'autant plus libre, que chacun fait plus complètement ce qui contrarie sa volonté propre? Les fauteurs du despotisme peuvent tirer un immense avantage des principes de Rousseau.
>
> (Constant 1049)

In a way this footnote gives in a nutshell Constant's major criticisms of Rousseau: lack of clarity of language (and hence of thought); a use of dishonest or self-deceptive rhetoric removed from the observed and observable realities of modern Europe and worthy of the worst excesses of scholasticism; a confused and confusing notion of rights, which are given not to that empirical entity so dear to Constant's liberal heart, "the individual," but to that abstraction "le peuple" and then only to be immediately alienated to that other abstraction "la patrie";[15] and, finally, a style and a set of theories ready-made for tyrants to justify their repression of individual liberties.

On March 10, 1820, in response to a government motion to restrict individual freedom following the assassination on February 13, 1820, of the Duc de Berry by the saddler Louvel (the isolated act of a madman, not the result of a political conspiracy), Benjamin Constant included this observation in his address to the *Chambre*:

> Monsieur le ministre des affaires étrangères . . . a invoqué Rousseau; mais toutes les fois qu'on a voulu proposer des lois contre la liberté, on s'est appuyé de l'autorité de J.-J. Rousseau. Avec beaucoup d'amour pour la liberté, Rousseau a toujours été cité par ceux qui ont voulu établir le despotisme. Rousseau a servi de prétexte au despotisme, parce qu'il avait le sentiment de la liberté, et qu'il n'en avait pas la théorie.[16]

As Kurt Kloocke points out,[17] Constant was fearful of a repressive counter-revolution ("J'entends, Messieurs, par contre-révolution un système qui attaquera graduellement tous les droits, toutes les garanties que la nation voulut en 1789, et qu'elle avait obtenues en 1814" [Constant, *Discours* 203]), which would use as a pretext this isolated assassination. From March 7, 1820, to June 30, 1820, he produced over twenty-five major speeches or interventions in the Chamber in all of which may be read the putting into practice of the criticisms of Rousseau and their theoretical foundation that he had mediated some ten years before and published in 1815. The *Principes de politique* (sometimes called *Cours de politique*) were a sober, sustained, and closely argued treatise in defense of individual freedoms, the necessity of the principle of representation in a democracy (whether republican or monarchical), and of the necessary limitations to sovereignty.

This text, fundamental to French liberal thought during the nineteenth century, and indeed to much of the political organization of the Western democracies of today, was re-edited in 1980 by Marcel Gauchet together with a selection of other political writings by Constant under the title *De la liberté chez les modernes.* An English version of these texts would have the tenor, if not quite the flavor, of J. S. Mill's two essays "Representative Government" and "On Liberty." In fact, some passages of "On Liberty" read as virtual translations of the *Principes.*

Constant discriminates carefully between those passages in *Du contrat social* and elsewhere in Rousseau's, which have led (mainly Anglo-Saxon) readers to see Jean-Jacques as a proto-liberal democrat and the underlying theories that he recognized as being at odds with those often rhetorically powerful pleas for tolerance and, in *Emile,* for sweetness and light—what Conor Cruise O'Brien called the "nice cop" Rousseau as opposed to the "tough cop" Rousseau of the *Contrat* (O'Brien 28). Constant was the first major critic—and the value of his criticism has endured—to go to the heart of the Rousseau-problem. Given the horrors of the Revolution, some of which he knew at firsthand, it is surprising that the tone of the *Principes* is, generally, so restrained.

The final paragraph of the March 10 (1820) speech to the Chamber states the essence of the critique of *Du contrat social,* which informs the *Principes de politique*:

> Il y a deux dogmes également dangereux, l'un le droit divin, l'autre la souveraineté illimitée du peuple. L'un et l'autre ont fait beaucoup de mal. Il n'y a de divin que la divinité, il n'y a de souverain que la justice. Il ne faut pas prendre les avis d'un ami fougueux, mais peu éclairé de la liberté, à une époque où la liberté n'était pas encore établie, et les proposer pour règles à des hommes qui ont acquis des idées plus saines par une expérience de trente ans de malheurs.

(Constant, *Discours* 211)

Constant attacks Rousseau on grounds of theory, on grounds of incoherence in argumentation, on grounds of false or unreliable definitions, and finally, and most importantly, on grounds perhaps misanthropically recognized by Rousseau himself when he wrote in Book II, chapter 7 of the *Contrat* "Il faudroit des Dieux pour donner des loix aux hommes" (Rousseau 381), that is to say, on grounds of practical application. Where Rousseau is absolute and full of imaginative references to Antiquity (witness his life-long fancy-dress love affair with Sparta and Rome and his outright rejection of the principle of representation in Book II, chapter 16), Constant is relativist, practical, and draws his analogies from the lived and understood realities of the British constitution. For him sovereignty is limited and divisible, and government is representative as, indeed, is a parliamentary opposition to it. Rousseau's statement in the letter to Christophe de Beaumont on the refusal to allow foreign religions without the consent of the Sovereign "car si ce n'est pas directement désobéir à Dieu, c'est désobéir aux loix: et qui désobéit aux loix, désobéit à Dieu" (Rousseau 90) may be usefully contrasted with Constant's "les lois ne sont pas la justice, ce sont les formes pour l'administrer" (Constant 1611) as an indication of the radical difference of attitude between the two men as far as jurisprudence is concerned.

I should perhaps mention here—for it is an important matter affecting the training of many of our young undergraduates—that there seems to be a conspiracy of silence in Political Science departments that teach Rousseau on this continent (in Canada as well as in the U.S.A.). Neither the widely used English translation, *The Social Contract,* by Judith R. Masters, edited by Roger D. Masters, which appeared in 1978, nor the more recent Cress translation (with an Introduction and Bibliography by Peter Gay), published in 1983, makes one reference, editorial or bibliographical, to the damaging and coherent critiques of Constant.[18] The footnotes of the Masters edition, while highly informative as to the *background* of Rousseau's text, are strangely silent as to its reception and use.[19] They are replete with the special pleading of the kind mocked by Conor Cruise O'Brien; there is an absence of scholarly confrontation with unpalatable facts first unearthed and investigated by Benjamin Constant.

The vexed question, subject of so many papers on Rousseau,[20] of what exactly he meant by the *volonté générale* is not for Constant an important issue. Now here, one might think, was surely the stumbling block that allowed such apologists for popular butcheries as, at different times, Marat, Danton, Saint-Just, and even Robespierre, to invoke the name of Rousseau. But no! For Constant this was an ancillary issue, secondary in importance (theoretically and practically) to that of the un-limited sovereignty of the people. To this question he addresses the whole of the first chapter of the ***Principes de politique.***

Two lines of attack are mounted. To begin with, Constant argues that the whole idea of popular sovereignty came from a misunderstanding of tyrannical sovereignty, so that the argument was directed by Rousseau and his followers against the *possession* of such sovereign power rather than against such undivided, absolute power itself. In consequence, he says:

> Au lieu de détruire, ils n'ont songé qu'à le déplacer. C'était un fléau, ils l'ont considéré comme une conquête. Ils en ont doté la société entière. Il a passé forcément d'elle à la majorité, de la majorité entre les mains de quelques hommes, souvent dans une seule main: il a fait tout autant de mal qu'auparavant: et les exemples, les objections, les arguments et les faits se sont multipliés contre toutes les institutions politiques. Dans une société fondée sur la souveraineté du peuple, il est certain qu'il n'appartient à aucun individu, à aucune classe, de soumettre le reste à sa volonté particulière; mais il est faux que la société tout entière possède sur ses membres une souveraineté sans bornes.
>
> (Constant 1104-05)

In the second place, and really almost as a consequence of this, an abstraction was created—"le peuple"—in whom this revised, *displaced* abstraction "sovereign power" was invested.

Once this was unleashed all kinds of horrors could, quite logically, follow. Individuals, their liberties alienated not to their fellow-men reciprocally, but to an abstraction, would be deprived of those specifically liberal (and in my view indispensable) liberties of publication, opinion, dissent, and assembly.

Constant sees Rousseau as being aware of this and horrified by its implications, as being powerless to undo in practice what he has elaborated in theory. And so Rousseau, still for Constant (writing with liberal charity!) a lover of freedom, but theoretically confused—a kind of Frankenstein of the New Social Order trying desperately to turn off the voltage before his creation can destroy its maker—attempts to ensure that his theory will not, *cannot,* be enacted. Here is the powerful paragraph in which Constant sums up this section of the ***Principes***:

> Rousseau lui-même a été effrayé de ces conséquences; frappé de terreur à l'aspect de l'immensité du pouvoir social qu'il venait de créer, il n'a su dans quelles mains déposer ce pouvoir monstrueux, et n'a trouvé de préservatif contre le danger inséparable d'une pareille souveraineté, qu'un expédient qui rendit l'exercice impossible. Il a déclaré que la souveraineté ne pouvait être ni aliénée, ni déléguée, ni représentée. C'était déclarer en d'autres termes qu'elle ne pouvait être exercée; c'était anéantir de fait le principe qu'il venait de proclamer.
>
> (Constant 1106)

Constant's point is, or should be, well taken. In fact it required Lenin's invention of the one-party state to resolve this dilemma, although for Julliard this was less a solution than a radically divergent amendment:

> Il est pourtant un point où le système léniniste diffère fondamentalement du modèle rousseauiste: c'est la question de la représentation. Incompatible avec la souveraineté du peuple chez Rousseau, elle est au contraire, sous la forme du Parti, consubstantielle avec la souveraineté de classe chez Lénine.
>
> (Julliard 170)

If Lenin's solution, following Julliard's suggestion, departs from Rousseau, there is a sense in which it may be seen as a historical evolution of what Constant called "tout l'affreux système de Hobbes" (Constant 1108). If unlimited sovereignty is the thesis attacked in the first chapter of ***Principes,*** the two theorists who are the object of Constant's recriminations are Hobbes (whom he saw as more frankly and *spirituellement* aware of his systematic defense of despotism) and Rousseau (whom he sees as misguided: see the whole paragraph beginning "Rousseau a méconnu cette vérité . . ." [Constant 1105-06]).

On the question of the division of powers, or "sovereignty," and of representation, Constant broadly follows the English model of constitutional monarchy, government by ministers and a two-chamber parliament. Although these issues of division and representation clearly distinguish his proposals from those of the *Contrat,* so aware is Constant of the dangers posed by *unlimited* sovereignty that he realizes that even these salutary measures are insufficient to avoid the threat of a new version of despotism if sovereignty is not first to be very carefully defined and delimited:

> Lorsque la souveraineté n'est pas limitée, il n'y a nul moyen de mettre les individus à l'abri des gouvernements . . . Le peuple, dit Rousseau, est souverain sous un rapport, et sujet sous un autre: mais dans la pratique, ces deux rapports se confondent . . . Aucune organisation politique ne peut écarter ce danger. Vous avez beau diviser les pouvoirs: si la somme totale du pouvoir est illimitée, les pouvoirs divisés n'ont qu'à former une coalition, et le despotisme est sans remède. Ce qui nous importe, ce n'est pas que nos droits ne puissent être violés par tel pouvoir, sans l'approbation de tel autre, mais que cette violation soit interdite à tous les pouvoirs.
>
> (Constant 1108)

At the heart of Constant's demonstration is a concern for that negative liberty (freedom *from*), which would guarantee for each citizen certain rights in his quality as an individual human entity and would diminish the capacity of the state to eliminate human individuality in its search for cogs to function (and, in a way, *only* as such) in a despotic social machine. Unlike the *Contrat,*

Constant's treatise has a whole chapter on the liberty of the press. The Rousseau equivalent would be, I suppose, Book IV, chapter 7 of the *Contrat,* which has the ominous title "De la censure." Both writers are in favor of the subject of their respective chapter headings and the choice of title is indicative of the choice of argument. Constant considered liberty of the press and *absence* of censorship to be fundamental to any sane and equitable society. Constant distinguishes between liberty and license (indeed he was in his lifetime known for his litigation against writers of libels), and he shares the respect for the law, which is a feature of Rousseau's chapter. But whereas Rousseau cites Rome and, especially, Sparta as his examples, Constant writes "l'Angleterre est assurément, pour la liberté de la presse, la terre classique" (Constant 1214).

Constant's *Principes de politique* also has a chapter on the inviolability of property. For Constant, property is a *social* not a *natural* right; but he argues, as did Locke, that it extends to the person of the individual. In a sense he goes beyond Locke to argue that thoughts and opinions are intellectual property and, as such, are social rights. This allows him in chapter 17, **"De la liberté religieuse"** (which follows **"De la liberté de la presse"** as Rousseau's "De la religion civile" follows "De la censure"), to hammer Rousseau's grotesque statement (Rousseau 468) requiring the death penalty for whoever behaves as if he did not believe the instituted state religion to which, *in order to remain a citizen,* he has had to declare public allegiance. Constant, writing presciently before Lenin and Stalin, but, it is true, after Robespierre's splendid Halloween trick-or-treat creation of the state religion of the Supreme Being, notes: "Je ne connais aucun système de servitude, qui ait consacré des erreurs plus funestes que l'éternelle métaphysique du *Contrat social*" (Constant 1216).

Constant's reading of this state institutionalization of faith (he quotes Rousseau directly in the text and in an extensive footnote describes with humanity and realism the probable private griefs attendant upon such a decree [Constant 1215-16], understands the difference between Rousseau's oft-stated love of liberty—"Rousseau, qui chérissait toutes les théories de la liberté" (Constant 1215)—and the uses to which his texts had been put—"et qui a fourni des prétextes à toutes les prétentions de la tyrannie" (Constant 1215). As in the footnote to *De l'esprit de conquête* cited earlier in this paper, he notes the disparity between the "sentiments" and the "principes." Nonetheless, he was aware that Saint-Just had not entirely misunderstood the theory nor Robespierre the rhetoric of the passionate *citoyen de Genève.*

But Constant's reading of the past extends beyond the condemnation of Rousseau's absolutist, unempirical, anti-historicist approach and its consequences in the hands of the *jacobins.* It includes also, especially in the

Principes, a re-reading of an earlier French political theorist whom he found more congenial, Montesquieu. His interpretation of Montesquieu, with its sober realization that the central feature of *L'esprit des lois* is a moderation of authority and plurality of state powers, is very close to the excellent presentation by Tzvetan Todorov "Droit naturel et formes de gouvernement dans *L'esprit des lois,*" which appeared in *Esprit* in March 1983.

Even here, Constant's interpretation is culturally complex. Not only does he read Montesquieu as a francophone, but as a francophone who also speaks and reads English and who had read Locke's two treatises on government (in English) and that *vade mecum* for English magistrates of the eighteenth century, William Blackstone's *Commentaries* on English law. Given his polyglot formation and his liberal sympathies, it was almost inevitable that from the moment he started to consider writing about politics, Rousseau would have to be seen as the prime target of his lucid refusal of despotism in whatever form.

In "un romantique libéral, Benjamin Constant," Philippe Raynaud has written:

> Toute l'oeuvre de Constant milite pour la défense de la liberté individuelle, et la définition, dans les *Principes de politique,* d'un domaine "privé", hors de toute compétence sociale, comme la démonstration de l'accord entre les "exigences" de la "liberté des modernes" et les nécessités de la société contemporaine, n'ont pas d'autre signification. Il n'est donc nullement indifférent que Constant ait dû poser la défense des droits de l'individu comme une exigence éthique qui définit un *devoir* et non une revendication arbitraire ou une nécessité sociale.[21]

It was this that made Constant fight against the dangers he saw in Rousseau's rhetorical appeal to totalitarian abstractions and against what he considered to be the profound anachronism of Rousseau's political theories in the Europe of his time.

Notes

1. Quoted (p. 57) in Guy Howard Dodge, *Benjamin Constant's Philosophy of Liberalism* (Chapel Hill: University of North Carolina Press, 1980). Berlin is speaking of the dangers inherent in Rousseau's passionate rhetoric and of the practical elaboration from his theories of "popular democracy" in which the individual is at the mercy of the State. For his appreciation of Constant's thoughts on liberty, i.e., the "negative" liberty of the individual as opposed to the "positive" freedom of the collective, see Sir Isaiah Berlin, *Two Concepts of Liberty* (Oxford: Clarendon, 1958) 47-52.

2. See the section "Les régicides" of *L'homme révolté* (esp. 524-26) in Albert Camus, *Essais,* eds. R. Quilliot and L. Faucon (Pléiade, 1965).

3. This argument, which begins, in fact, with systematic alienation from *birth* (!), will be found in Jean-Jacques Rousseau, *Du contrat social. Ecrits politiques, Oeuvres complètes,* ed. Bernard Gagnebin et al. (Pléiade, 1964) 3:259-62. All future references are indicated in the text by "Rousseau" followed by page numbers.

4. Quoted in Andrew Levine, "Robespierre: Critic of Rousseau," *Canadian Journal of Philosophy* 8.3 (1978) 544.

5. These works are reprinted in *Saint-Just, théoricien de la Révolution,* ed. Charles Vellay (Monaco: L. Jaspard, 1946).

6. Jacques Julliard, *La faute à Rousseau* (Seuil, 1985).

7. One of the best accounts of the nineteenth-century reception of Rousseau, including a detailed discussion of Constant's criticisms, is in Robert Derathé's "Les réfutations du *Contrat social* en France dans la première moitié du dix-neuvième siècle" in Simon Harvey et al., eds., *Reappraisals of Rousseau: Studies in Honour of R. A. Leigh* (Manchester: Manchester University Press, 1980).

8. What will doubtless remain for some time the standard study of this period of Constant's evolution is Etienne Hofmann's *Les 'Principes de politique' de Benjamin Constant: la genèse d'une oeuvre et l'évolution de la pensée de leur auteur (1789-1806),* 2 vols. (Geneva: Droz, 1980).

9. Dodge 57.

10. Stephen Holmes, *Benjamin Constant and the Making of Modern Liberalism* (New Haven: Yale University Press, 1984).

11. The dangerous implications of the Rousseauist "la volonté générale est indivisible" (Vellay 116) are followed faithfully in Saint-Just's *Essai de constitution pour la France.* Saint-Just, however, it should be noted, was one of the few *jacobins* to publish theoretical criticisms of Rousseau; he strongly disagreed with the theory and practice of criminal law proposed by Rousseau (see Vellay 68-69). Almost any of Robespierre's speeches will be found to be deeply indebted to Rousseau, but see in particular the long speech on religion and morals culminating with the decrees on the *Etre suprême* presented to the Convention nationale "au nom du Comité du salut public" on 18 Floréal An II (i.e., May 7, 1794), *Oeuvres de Maximilien Robespierre, Tome X. Discours 27 juillet 1793-27 juillet 1794,* eds. M. Bouloiseau and A. Soboul (PUF, 1967) 460-63.

12. For example, in his report "Sur les factions de l'étranger" presented to the Convention on March 13, 1974, Saint-Just declared: "un patriote est celui qui soutient la République en masse: quiconque la combat en détail est un traître" (Vellay 184).

13. Benjamin Constant, *Oeuvres,* ed. Alfred Roulin (Pléiade, 1957) 1049. All future references are indicated in the text by "Constant" followed by page numbers.

14. Constant is presumably thinking not only of the "newspeak" argumentations on the positive rights of live citizens in the *Contrat,* but also of the kind of strange twist of logic in the "Discours sur l'économie politique" on testamentary rights (or proposed absence thereof) whereby if the State alienates the estate of a deceased citizen "c'est au fond moins altérer son droit en apparence, qui l'étendre en effet" (Rousseau 263 and, for editorial commentary, 1402-03).

15. Why does no current English translation of the *Contrat* give "Fatherland" for this term? Has the Nazi misuse of this term so intimidated translators?

16. Benjamin Constant, *Discours de M. Benjamin Constant à la Chambre des députés,* 2 vols. (Ambroise Dupont, 1827) 1:211. All future references are indicated in the text by "Constant, *Discours*" followed by page numbers.

17. Kurt Kloocke, *Benjamin Constant: une biographie intellectuelle* (Geneva: Droz, 1984) 246 *et seq.*

18. Nor, one should add, is there mention of the long history of serious French criticism of Rousseau from all shades of opinion (conservative, liberal, positivist, socialist). This silence which, one assumes, is not the result of ignorance, is, at least, a disservice to the students for whom these translations are primarily intended. The same lacunae mar the earlier translation by Charles Frankel for The Hafner Library of Classics and this ran through nine printings (from 1947 to 1961).

19. This criticism also applies to the full-scale study by Roger D. Masters, *The Political Philosophy of Rousseau,* where the only hostile critics referred to more than once (and then only in footnotes) are J. L. Talmon and Lester G. Crocker.

20. Of which the most thorough is Ellen Meiksins Wood, "The State and Popular Sovereignty in French Political Thought: A Genealogy of Rousseau's 'General Will,'" *History of Political Thought* 4.2 (1983) 281-315.

21. Philippe Raynaud, "Un romantique libéral, Benjamin Constant," *Esprit* (March 1983) 65.

Derek J. Turton (essay date winter 1991)

SOURCE: Turton, Derek J. "First Love: Benjamin Constant's Recollection of Madame Johannot in *Le Cahier rouge*." *Nineteenth-Century French Studies* 19, no. 2 (winter 1991): 187-202.

[*In the following essay, Turton offers a textual analysis of Constant's "psychological perturbation," as evidenced by his recollection of his love affair with Madame Johannot in* La Cahier rouge.]

Mon père arriva lui-même à Paris et m'emmena à Bruxelles, où il me laissa pour retourner à son régiment. Je restai à Bruxelles depuis le mois d'août jusqu'à la fin de novembre, partageant mon temps entre les maisons d'Anet et d'Aremberg, anciennes connaissances de mon père, et qui, en cette qualité, me firent un très bon accueil, et une coterie de Genevois, plus obscure, mais qui me devint bien plus agréable.

Il y avait dans cette coterie une femme d'environ vingt-six à vingt-huit ans, d'une figure très séduisante et d'un esprit fort distingué. Je me sentais entraîné vers elle, sans me l'avouer bien clairement, lorsque, par quelques mots qui me surprirent d'abord encore plus qu'ils ne me charmèrent, elle me laissa découvrir qu'elle m'aimait. Il y a, dans le moment où j'écris, vingt-cinq ans d'écoulés depuis le moment où je fis cette découverte, et j'éprouve encore un sentiment de reconnaissance en me retraçant le plaisir que j'en ressentis.

Mme Johannot, c'était son nom, s'est placée dans mon souvenir, différemment de toutes les femmes que j'ai connues: ma liaison avec elle a été bien courte et s'est réduite à bien peu de chose. Mais elle ne m'a fait acheter les sensations douces qu'elle m'a données par aucun mélange d'agitation ou de peine: et à quarante-quatre ans je lui sais encore gré du bonheur que je lui ai dû lorsque j'en avais dix-huit.

La pauvre femme a fini bien tristement. Mariée à un homme très méprisable de caractère et de moeurs très corrompues, elle fut d'abord traînée par lui à Paris, où il se mit au service du parti qui dominait, devint, quoique étranger, membre de la Convention, condamna le roi à mort et continua jusqu'à la fin de cette trop célèbre assemblée à y jouer un rôle lâche et équivoque. Elle fut ensuite reléguée dans un village d'Alsace pour faire place à une maîtresse que son mari entretenait dans sa maison. Elle fut enfin rappelée à Paris pour y vivre avec cette maîtresse que son mari voulait l'obliger à servir, et les mauvais traitements dont il l'accabla la poussèrent à s'empoisonner. J'étais alors à Paris moi-même et je demeurais dans son voisinage; mais j'ignorais qu'elle y fût, et elle est morte à quelques pas d'un homme qu'elle avait aimé et qui n'a jamais pu entendre prononcer son nom sans être ému jusqu'au fond de l'âme; elle est morte, dis-je, se croyant oubliée et abandonnée de toute la terre.

Il y avait à peine un mois que je jouissais de son amour, quand mon père vint me prendre pour me ramener en Suisse. Mme Johannot et moi nous nous écrivîmes de tristes et tendres lettres, au moment de mon départ. Elle me donna une adresse sous laquelle elle consentit

à ce que je continuasse à lui écrire: mais elle ne me répondit pas. Je me consolai sans l'oublier, et l'on verra que bientôt d'autres objets prirent sa place. Je la revis deux ans après une seule fois à Paris, quelques années avant ses malheurs. Je me repris de goût pour elle. Je lui fis une seconde visite; elle était partie: lorsqu'on me le dit, j'éprouvai une émotion d'une nature tout à fait extraordinaire par sa tristesse et sa violence. C'était une sorte de pressentiment funeste que sa fin déplorable n'a que trop justifié.

(Benjamin Constant, *Oeuvres,* texte présenté et annoté par Alfred Roulin, Paris: Bibliothèque de la Pléiade, [1957] 1964, 93-95)

The young Constant's liaison with Mme Johannot occupies a special position in his unfinished autobiography: in Rudler's words, "Chose curieuse, nulle part *le Cahier Rouge* n'est plus personnel, et nulle part il n'est plus voisin des *Confessions*;" "Il est évident que ce premier amour a laissé une trace profonde, a fait tache de lumière dans sa mémoire."[1] Despite this reference to the highly intimate and confessional nature of Constant's memory, Rudler does not examine the form of that memory, but passes immediately to a consideration of the psychological and emotional effects of the experience: "*Le Cahier Rouge* présente visiblement, à cet endroit de son récit, une brusque rupture d'équilibre. Le système nerveux de Benjamin avait reçu de cette révélation [de l'amour de Mme Johannot pour lui] un choc trop fort. Ses excentricités, relativement simples jusque-là, se compliquent follement et tournent à l'insanité."[2] Rudler here fails to distinguish the two roles and identities of Constant in the autobiography, the man who lived the events and the man who wrote about them, the protagonist and the narrator; indeed, the former is acknowledged as Benjamin, while the latter is denied an existence, and his functions hidden behind the title *Le Cahier rouge.* Just as the narrator is eliminated, so is any consideration of the "temps de la narration". Rudler's discussion remains on the level of the "temps du narré" and seeks to elucidate the information which is presented concerning Constant's life, rather than examine the manner in which that information is presented by the narrator. In this paper, instead of examining the psychic disturbance caused by this first love and its consequences with respect to the behaviour of the eighteen-year-old Constant (what Rudler terms the search for "pure sensation" and "complications sentimentales")[3] it seems more useful to explore the psychological perturbation which is manifest in Constant the narrator at the moment when he remembers this episode of his youth, a perturbation which reveals itself at the level of the text by means of linguistic, syntactic, and structural features.[4]

In order to illustrate the degree of disturbance that our text exhibits, it is desirable to examine briefly the principal formal characteristics of the preceding pages which, by virtue of their position at the very beginning of the autobiography, serve as exposition and hence create certain expectations in the reader.

Le Cahier rouge appears at first as a narrative summary, a succession of episodes whose discontinuity is marked by mostly imprecise references to years or to the protagonist's age, or to spatial movements centered solely on the hero. The text is linear, consisting of concise, abrupt notes, placed end to end, without any effort to soften the transitions, and always in strict chronological sequence. No attempt is made to dramatize the episodes. This essentially narrative account is dominated by the *passé simple* and therefore rarely leaves the foreground to develop circumstantial details or examine temporal perspectives. In short, a text which is characterized by discontinuity, juxtaposition, contraction of time, absence of commentary, of background, of perspective, emphasis on events rather than on thoughts or feelings.

Constant's early life up to the age of eighteen is presented as a succession of geographical displacements from town to town, from country to country, discontinuous involvements and broken or failed relationships, enforced departures or sudden rescues, parental absence or neglect interrupted by unforeseen interventions, studious concentration followed by passionate spurts of dissipation and gambling—above all, the absence of any sense of continuity in the formative years of Constant's life, the all-pervasive feeling that life is composed of independent episodes, whose consequences are never serious because they are so easily evaded or because paternal intervention prevents a natural conclusion to any event.

The opening pages of *Le Cahier rouge* are concerned essentially with Constant's education, intellectual, social, and emotional, and may be divided into three movements: his private education, entrusted to a succession of tutors, covers the first fourteen years of his life (1767-1782); his public education at the universities of Edinburgh and Erlangen extends from February 1782 to May 1785; and his sentimental education, through his liaison with Mme Johannot, took place during his stay in Brussels from August to November 1785. Linguistically these three phases are distinguished in the following ways. Phase one is dominated by the narrative tenses with *il* as subject; Constant as character in his own life appears rarely as *je*, but frequently as the object pronoun *me*, or less directly in the possessive adjectives. Phase two marks the much more frequent use of the subject pronoun *je* in combination with the *passé simple*: in fact, *je* appears more frequently than *il*, the only other statistically significant pronoun. Phase three marks the sudden irruption of the tenses of *discours* in a hitherto narrative text, thereby shifting the focus of attention from the past of the character-I to the present of the narrator-I. In Phase 1 Constant is under the tutelage of the other, exclusively male, *il*; he presents the other as actor, himself as object. In Phase 2 he achieves a measure of autonomy and assumes his role as protagonist. In Phase 3 he assumes responsibility for the narrative by establishing himself as narrator. This brief episode is then not only of paramount importance in determining the character-I (as Rudler so rightly insists), but also in constituting the narrator-I; it is highly revelatory of both aspects of the self.

It is clear that *histoire,* as Benveniste defines the term, is almost totally absent from the first pages of Constant's text. His ideal of "le récit des événements passés" by means of third-person pronouns and past tenses (especially the past definite) would exclude all reference to the time, place, or person of the narrator, thereby giving the impression that "personne ne parle ici: les événements semblent se raconter eux-mêmes."[5] On the contrary, the person of the narrator is constantly evoked by the recurrent use of the first-person pronoun in combination with the essentially narrative tense, the past definite. The result is Starobinski's mixed entity, discourse-history, in which the first person is treated as a quasi-third person, a *je-il.*[6] As the vehicle of an irreversible past, the aorist emphasizes the part of the protagonist. Yet this hybrid form has great potential for establishing a mood of detachment, or of ironic distance, a picaresque tone which draws attention to "the role of the interpretative consciousness in the drama before us,"[7] the *je narrateur* endowed with superior knowledge and experience. Full attention is focused on the narrator in *discours,* with its autobiographical linguistic forms (*je; ici; maintenant*): "les indicateurs de la *deixis*—démonstratifs, adverbes, adjectifs, qui organisent les relations spatiales et temporelles autour du "sujet" pris comme repère [. . .] Ils ont en commun ce trait de se définir seulement par rapport à l'instance de discours où ils sont produits, c'est-à-dire sous la dépendance du *je* qui s'y énonce."[8] The narrator is presented with immediacy by use of the present tense, while the *passé composé* underlines the continuity of feeling from past to present.

SYMMETRY

In the opening paragraph of our text, factual circumstances are arranged with economy and clarity in an increasingly intricate binary system. Constant's move from Paris to Brussels is expressed by parallel coordinated propositions, concluded by a relative clause indicating the respective situations of father and son. His stay at Brussels is seen in terms of its limits, and his time is divided between two groups of people, his father's acquaintances of long standing and new friends of his own making, in a sequence of balanced oppositions (consisting in each case of an attribute and a coordinated relative clause) which make clear Constant's personal preference. Just as the syntax reveals polarities and oppositions, in like manner Constant's docility to paternal authority is balanced by a further expression of his independence.

The second and third paragraphs, with their needless semantic and syntactical reduplication, reveal that rhythmical balance is just as important as the information conveyed: five sentences of considerable length (average 48 syllables; shortest 33 syllables) and remarkable equilibrium due to the continual recurrence of binary elements and parallel structures. The last sentence of each paragraph is of identical length (55 syllables): each is divided symmetrically into two parts (28 and 27 syllables) by means of an *"et" de mouvement,* ushering in a closing formula of identical import—the permanence of gratitude after a period of twenty-five years (stressed by the repetition of "encore"), and the contrast between present gratitude and past pleasure.

Coming in the wake of such elegant periods, the initial sentence of the fourth paragraph is of the utmost brevity and simplicity (10 syllables) and offers a most poignant summary of a wasted life. The three sentences which relate Mme Johannot's biography form a ternary movement composed of symmetrical passive constructions whose chronological sequence is stressed by temporal and spatial indications ("d'abord"—"ensuite"—"enfin"; "à Paris"—"dans un village d'Alsace"—"à Paris"). The final sentence has a tripartite structure—three clauses juxtaposed and separated by semi-colons, and each containing at least one binary structure. The balance of the sentence is clear from its syllabification (9-10; 7-15-13-9; 4-15).

The final paragraph returns to simple narrative, a desolate prose that results from the juxtaposition of essentially unadorned propositions beginning abruptly with subject pronouns. Subordination is reduced to a minimum. Instead the text is composed of an accumulation of simple clauses, juxtaposed without any attempt to relieve the monotony of the presentation. After the persuasive eloquence and depth of emotion of the preceding paragraphs, the aridity of this narration is shocking—a sense of lifelessness that results from the recollection of death, a lifelessness which culminates in an explosion of grief.

Delbouille maintains that the balancing of sentences in binary, and especially ternary, movements is characteristic of Constant's time.[9] What is remarkable in this text is the sudden appearance of such forms in such concentration. Evidently, for Constant, the material warranted such eloquence.

What distinguishes this episode from previous ones in **Le Cahier rouge** is that the immediate narration of the memory is interrupted by the narrator's commentary on that memory. The real (or feigned) detachment of the previous narrative is abandoned as Constant focuses on the act of memory itself, marvelling at the persistence of emotion over a twenty-five year period, at the readiness with which the recollection of past happiness can inspire feeling across long expanses of time. However, the redundant duplication of information which concludes successive paragraphs (2 & 3), undermines, even as it affirms, the very serenity of gratitude for past pleasures which Constant feels as he distances himself from his adolescence.

The compulsion to repeat almost identical information in varied form hints at subterranean emotion which the text will soon bring to the surface. The scrupulous precision of temporal references serves to hold emotion under control, in the ordered universe of autobiographical fixity. But the narratorial serenity proves to be fragile for the very preoccupation with such details draws the narrator away from the exploration of the initial episode of the protagonist's discovery of love—and hence an optimistic, even idyllic, prospect of unlimited pleasure—and instead, by the affective power of the *passé composé,* the narrator floats free of temporal and autobiographical constraints to recall the death of Mme Johannot, to recount her biography (which he knows only by hearsay) instead of his own.

Constant's double presentation of identical material in the different registers of *histoire* and *discours* gives an illusion of a double reading. It is as if Constant were showing the reader the way in which his text is to be read, for the manner in which the memory is told reflects the reduplication of lived events which are the result of chance: two episodes, separated by a period of two years; both episodes divided into two parts, the first into her declaration and their parting, the second into reunion and abandonment. The superimposition of episodes reveals the desire to repeat, while at the same time it is pervaded by the uncanny sense of "déjà vu." The second episode is split into a forward and a backward vision—renewed contact inspires the prospective vision of desire, while the unexpected departure of Mme Johannot recalls the earlier separation. Positive and negative feelings are juxtaposed: Constant's wish for love is confronted by the awareness of Mme Johannot's indifference. The text stresses the feeling that history is repeating itself—a sense of destiny, but also a sense of death, projected into the future and linked by the narrator to the real death which he has already recounted.

The passage ends on the prospect of death. The intuitive sense of impending death becomes a self-fulfilling prophecy; the subjective, internal feeling is justified or proven to be appropriate by real events, i.e. the "extraordinary" (= disproportionate) emotion of the protagonist is subsequently proven to be appropriate—the twenty-year-old Constant reacted to Mme Johannot's departure as to her death.

The conclusion of the memory reestablishes the persistent oscillation between *histoire* and *discours,* between past and present, just as the text, while projecting a forward move chronologically, refers back to itself in a circular movement which confers a closure upon the memory, isolating it from the autobiographical narrative, and inviting the reader to linger in the circularity of the episode.

CHRONOLOGY

The narrator's recollections of Mme Johannot are presented as a global memory which disrupts the chronological narration of his own life. Constant makes no effort to integrate the information into the account according to the order of knowledge of the protagonist. Objective chronology and protagonist's awareness have been replaced by the psychic time of the narrator who blends memories from different, often unspecified periods.

There is a double deviation from the textual norm. Firstly, the occurrence of events in chronological time does not coincide with the order of their disposition in the text. By means of the interplay of *passé simple* and *passé composé,* the text oscillates between the past of the protagonist and the epic situation of the narrator: Constant's stay in Brussels (August—November, 1785) is recalled at Hardenburg (mid-August—end of October, 1811).[10] Between these two poles several anticipations further disrupt the chronological axis. After the initial evocation of the past (1785), the narrator interposes, in reverse order, his present feelings (1811) and his most recent knowledge (1806 = discovery of her death)[11] before attempting to relate the conclusion of the first stages of their relationship (1785 and 1787). He deals essentially with absence and loss before completing his treatment of presence.

Secondly, Constant breaks the bounds of his autobiographical project, *Ma Vie* [1767 -1787], by exceeding the temporal limit of 1787 in order to include the death of Mme Johannot (which occurred between 1792 and 1797) and his discovery of her death much later in 1806. The text is silent on these important dates.

The dislocation of the chronological sequence of events prevents the reader, and the narrator himself, from embracing the perspective of the protagonist. The wretched biography of Mme Johannot, culminating in a suicide of which Constant was ignorant for at least ten years, serves as a lens with which to view the protagonist's feelings. His emotional reaction at the moment of separation, which the protagonist cannot have known to be final, is nonetheless experienced as a foreboding of death, even more a foreboding of the horrible death which the narrator has previously recounted. The linking of these two instances of loss—separation and death—is not simply a structural device designed for climactic effect: it derives rather from a psychic urge which the narrator was compelled to satisfy.

There are five distinct time-periods involved in this text: 1. Brussels, August—November, 1785; 2. Paris, 1787; 3. Paris, several years later (Mme Johannot's suicide); 4. place unknown, date unknown (Constant's discovery of Mme Johannot's death); 5. epic situation, 1811 (place not given, date inferred from text). Each time-period presupposes a different identity for the hero and the heroine, and offers the narrator the choice of three perspectives—his own, that of the hero, and that of the heroine. Given the large number of possible perspectives, it is not surprising that many are not exploited, but what is of interest is the emphasis given to some and the silence accorded to others. The potential for evasion is equal to that for confession; what is not said determines the sense of what is said.

SPEECH—SILENCE

In the early pages of **Le Cahier rouge** the reader is struck by the repetition of inappropriate behaviour by the young Constant, especially in the presence of women. Desire is presented as a game, a challenge, a duty, a convention, but cannot be acknowledged as real. Constant seems bent on presenting to the world a false self composed of verbal pyrotechnics and histrionic posturings, which belie his genuine emotions. From his superior standpoint as narrator, Constant readily exposes the immaturity and inexperience of himself as youth, indulging in self-mockery in a tone that has been termed "picaresque" by several critics.[12]

By contrast, the magic of Constant's love affair with Mme Johannot is due in large part to a reversal of the usual roles in the declaration of love, and to Constant's silence. Reciprocal desire is marked by the reticence of the one, overcome by the frankness of the other. No longer spurred by desire of intellectual origin, the young Constant is the passive victim of feelings which he cannot admit unequivocally even to himself: "Je me sentais entraîné vers elle, sans me l'avouer bien clairement." The passive construction ("entraîné") evades responsibility for the act or for the feelings of attraction and desire. Desire cannot be fully admitted nor owned. Constant's taciturnity concerning his own feelings is not then the concealing from others of clearly felt emotion—it indicates the concealing from the self of true desires and needs: the true self desires but dare not name the desire, for to own the desire is to expose it to the humiliation of rejection.

But the silence is eloquent for those who can read it. It is Mme Johannot's ability to read Constant's silence which is critical. To his unspoken need for love corresponds her rejection of the ritual need for skirmish which in the young Constant's experience characterizes the struggle of the sexes. Mme Johannot's straightforward gift of love penetrates to the reality of Constant's desire and acts like magic on this misunderstood soul. From Constant's perspective, this intuitive understanding on the part of Mme Johannot implies the idyllic happiness of childhood when the mother divines and satisfies the child's unspoken needs.

It is her declaration which makes possible the lovers' dialogue (though the narrator excludes any treatment of it). An exchange of letters at the moment of separation briefly unites the lovers ("Mme Johannot et moi nous nous écrivîmes de tristes et tendres lettres") but the promise of a continued correspondence is broken. Her unexplained silence destroys the dialogue that she had created. The passive role that Constant had assumed in this liaison is transformed into an active one in the face of loss, but his written voice is powerless before her obstinate silence.

The pattern is repeated two years later (1787). Constant's attempt to offer his love, to resume the lovers' dialogue, is destroyed by Mme Johannot's sudden, unsuspected departure. The desire for dialogue is met with silence. Mme Johannot's initial free gift of love is twice withdrawn without explanation, at precisely the moment when Constant's gift of love is offered.

Constant as narrator has no hesitation in naming the emotion that Mme Johannot feels for him ("elle m'aimait;" "un homme qu'elle avait aimé;" "son amour"), but refuses to call love his own varied feelings of the past and the present ("surprise;" "charme;" "reconnaissance;" "plaisir;" "sensations douces;" "absence d'agitation ou de peine;" "bonheur").

Significantly, the initial mention of love causes the narrator to abandon the historical perspective in favor of the commentative point of view, causing an evident displacement of attention from the feelings at the moment of experience to the feelings inspired by the recollection of that experience. The narrator conceals the protagonist's silence by substituting his own voice. Ironically, the confessional intimacy of *discours,* blocking the exploration of the past precisely at the mention of love, produces a sense of detachment. Clearly, at this stage of the recollection, the feelings of the narrator are more easily confessed than those of the protagonist: the avowal of gratitude is preferable to the (non)avowal of love. Structurally, to the lady's offer of love corresponds the narrator's gratitude for the protagonist's pleasure. A deliberate filtering, and censoring, device has been interposed between the two partners in the experience, with the result that the treatment of the initial contact of the two lovers is achieved by a separation of identities: Mme Johannot and Benjamin Constant protagonist; Mme Johannot and Constant narrator; and ultimately

Constant protagonist and Constant narrator. To this list must be added the split that exists within Constant protagonist: namely, the withholding from the self of awareness of feeling, or simply the rift between feelings and thoughts. Separations are to be found everywhere in this text. Besides the physical partings of 1785 and 1787, and Mme Johannot's death, syntactically the two lovers remain distinct (*je—elle*), and the text continually juxtaposes separate existences, as is especially apparent in the treatment of Mme Johannot's death.

FIDELITY—INFIDELITY

The recollection of Mme Johannot coincides with Constant's assumption of responsibility for his text. The narrator intervenes, in consecutive paragraphs, to characterize this memory as unique; the permanence of feeling over a twenty-five year period is especially remarkable to Constant who draws attention to the disproportion between the event and its repercussions. His attachment to Mme Johannot seems arrested at the moment of contact, and is impervious to growth or destruction by time and changes of circumstance. The initial assurances of gratitude are inadequate to explain the nature of Constant's sensitivity to this one woman; his emotional vulnerability is like an open wound—even at the age of 44, he confesses to being incapable of hearing her name "sans être ému jusqu'au fond de l'âme." Progressive recollections have released in the narrator a depth of emotion that contrasts sharply with the intellectual formulations of the earlier paragraphs. The suppressed violence of the narrative of Mme Johannot's tragic existence gives way to an outburst of personal passion in *discours.* In the subsequent narrative of the protagonist's loss of Mme Johannot, grief is finally confessed and is assumed by the narrator who transposes it from its original cause, her unexpected departure (where it appears as a disproportionate reaction) to its proper place, her death.

Constant and Mme Johannot are parted twice, in 1785 and 1787. The first loss inspires in the protagonist sadness and tenderness, while the second gives rise to "une émotion d'une nature tout à fait extraordinaire par sa tristesse et sa violence." The impact of the first separation is alleviated by several factors. Firstly, it is Constant who leaves, and Mme Johannot who remains behind.[13] Neither he nor she is to blame, since it is Constant's father, as usual, who enforces the separation ("mon père vint me prendre pour me ramener en Suisse"). Secondly, an exchange of emotion in the face of separation supplies consolation ("nous nous écrivîmes de tristes et tendres lettres, au moment de mon départ"—the adjectives are complementary and integrative).

The effect of the second loss is catastrophic. Constant's former passion for Mme Johannot is instantly revived two years later at their first and only meeting, but no expression of his desire is possible in the face of her sudden, unexplained and inexplicable departure ("Je lui fis une seconde visite; elle était partie"). The brutal juxtaposition of terse, narrative sentences emphasizes the unexpectedness of the loss, which has the force of a rejection, a betrayal. Loss unleashes in Constant not only sadness which aims at recovering the lost object, but also violence, murderous rage, which seeks to annihilate that same object ("j'éprouvai une émotion d'une nature tout à fait extraordinaire par sa tristesse et sa violence.") The binary opposition well expresses the ambivalence characteristic of grief. Further, this complex "extraordinary" emotion is felt as a presentiment of death, a fear of death, a wish to cause death, a death that was ultimately realized.[14] It is the narrator's commentary that reveals the true sense of the protagonist's emotion.

Mme Johannot's death is treated twice, in the different modes of *histoire* and *discours*. The seemingly objective account of her wretched life culminates in suicide as a direct result of her husband's brutality. At the mention of death the narrator intervenes, not to express his own, or the protagonist's, reaction to that death, but rather to explain his own ignorance of her presence in Paris. Instead of revealing his own feelings, the narrator states her feelings, which, in the absence of first-hand knowledge, are his own projections—the revelation of his own feelings transposed onto her. The feeling of abandonment is not to be explained by the previous biographical details, but rather by the emotions preoccupying the narrator himself. Loss is an abandonment.

The syntactic repetition, with its emphatic *incise* ("elle est morte;" "elle est morte, dis-je") appears to introduce a conclusive recapitulation, but the implied semantic link is not logically present. Instead, the narrator imagines Mme Johannot's final feelings in a highly charged closing formula of assonant past participles ("se croyant oubliée et abandonnée") and alliteration ("de toute la terre"). Formally, the narrator emphasizes the distinction between the forgetfulness of others and his own affective fidelity, which prevents his ignorance from being considered as neglect. The accusation of others, coupled with the protestation of his own innocence, becomes an act of self-condemnation. He appears to be defending himself against an unspoken charge.

IDENTIFICATION[15]

The cryptic biography of Mme Johannot does not come from the lived experience of the protagonist, but from the *post facto* discovery of the narrator. Logically it has no place in the autobiographical project that Constant has undertaken thus far—the chronological sequence of the events in his life, respecting the state of knowledge of the protagonist. Thematically, however, Mme Johannot's story is so akin to Constant's own experience that

the narrator's need to recount this seemingly irrelevant biography is to be explained not only as the expression of pity and compassion for this woman, but also, by virtue of his own identification with her, as an indirect commentary upon his own life.

The dominant motif of this biography—geographical displacement at the whim of another—which is graphically presented by a symmetrical, ternary series of passive structures, initiated by the violent and disdainful "traînée," is echoed, in anodyne terms, in the resumed narrative of Constant's own life, by Juste de Constant's untimely intrusion into his young son's life ("Il y avait à peine un mois que je jouissais de son amour, quand mon père vint me prendre pour me ramener en Suisse"). This motif is, in fact, merely the physical manifestation of a greater psychological theme—the humiliation of servitude. It seems characteristic that Constant should displace the emphasis by subordinating the cruelty of Mme Johannot's husband to spatial and temporal considerations. Similarly, Constant's anger concerning his own life and his own father is displaced on to Mme Johannot and her husband. As a youth, Constant was subject to the capricious movements of his father; then, as a man, he became slave to Mme de Staël, the "homme-femme" who dominated his life for eleven years. Victim of male and female domination, incapable of exercising his own authority over either party, just as Mme Johannot was subjected within her own household to both her husband and his mistress, Constant must indeed have identified closely with this woman who was the first to love him.

By an ironic twist of fate, Mme Johannot took her own life by the very means that Constant himself had attempted, or feigned, on several occasions in response to rejection by women—suicide by poison. It is therefore highly revelatory of Constant's attitude that he should imagine Mme Johannot's thoughts at the moment of death to be directed to "oubli" and "abandon." Constant's categorical statement of her thoughts should not deceive us, for these thoughts are clearly the projection of Constant's own feelings. It is as if the narrator is confessing that, by turning his own weapon against him, she is responding to his rejection of her. Such is the grandiosity that guilt can confer.

Constant distances himself from Jean Johannot by refusing to name him, emphasizing his function as husband. By means of a symmetrical opposition, Constant seeks to establish the cruelty of the husband and his own sensitivity, referring to Johannot and himself as "un homme," a stylistic equivalence that has an emotional origin. Mme Johannot's entire existence is viewed in terms of the polar opposition of two men, and the overt brutality of the one is balanced by the unspoken empathy of the other. The symmetrical structure of the paragraph, the rhetorical amplification of the concluding period, and the dramatization of function at the expense of individualization, all contribute to an impassioned, yet strangely theatrical, idealization of life. Constant has abandoned narrative, reflection, retrospection; he is delivering a "plaidoyer," a violent denunciation of Johannot's brutality and an emotional defence of his own inaction. Separated from Mme Johannot's death by space and time, doubly impotent to prevent this needless death or to change the past, Constant's only opportunity to "save" this woman is to rescue her from oblivion, to guarantee her immortality by writing this encomium. Without him, without his text, she would indeed be "oubliée et abandonnée de toute la terre." Constant's text presents itself as the redemption of her wasted life.

Constant dramatizes the situation by casting Johannot and himself in oppositional roles of executioner and frustrated saviour. The condemnation of the one is followed by the exculpation of the other in an unrealistic conflict which mirrors an internal split. For this very polarity is to be found within Constant himself, but separated in chronological time and textual space, and presented in reverse order. The empathy ("reconnaissance-plaisir") of the narrator starts the memory while the violence ("pressentiment funeste") of the protagonist concludes it. Once one realizes that the loss of Mme Johannot unleashed in the 20-year-old Constant an extraordinary sense of violence, a new light is cast on the violent and despicable role allotted to Johannot. The condemnation of the husband's violence is simultaneously an identification with that violence.

CONCLUSION

Constant's text is characterized by its essential ambivalence: positive and negative emotions are intertwined at every point. In a well-known formula, Stendhal described *Adolphe* as "a tragic *marivaudage,* in which the difficulty lies, not, as in Marivaux, in making a declaration of love, but in making a declaration of hatred. Once this has been made, the story is at an end."[16] The point is surely that the declaration of "hatred" is not made, or, at least, not openly. *Adolphe* is rather a study of the ways in which negative feelings are transmuted into positive ones, by means of a complex psycholinguistic process which involves self-appeasement as much as a desire to appease the other. Denial of love is only permissible for Adolphe within the context of dependence; indeed, denial is repeatedly balanced by the avowal of love, since Adolphe cannot suffer the consequences of his own denial.

In this memory, Constant professes the pleasure of the narrator, but recounts the pain of the protagonist. In this way the text represents a double silence—the narrative of past pleasure is missing, as is the narrative of present pain. It is as if the pain has disappeared to leave an unalloyed pleasure at the remembrance of the past, whereas in reality it is the inability to assert openly the continuing hurt that blocks the possibility of release from the haunting of the past. The obsessive repetition results from the inability to mourn "over what has happened over the irreversibility of the past."[17] Recurrent parallelisms in this text prolong thoughts beyond the requirements of strict sense. It would seem that Constant is preoccupied as much with rhythm as with meaning, and the pervasive symmetry of phrase, sentence, or paragraph, evidently creates for him a sense of balance akin to emotional satisfaction, a sort of exorcism that assuages the malaise inextricably associated with this memory. In this way textual equilibrium substitutes for psychic peace and provides a linguistic resolution of an unresolved love.

Notes

1. G. Rudler, *La Jeunesse de Benjamin Constant, 1767-1794* (Paris: Librairie Armand Colin, 1909) 124 note 2 and 506.

2. Rudler, *La Jeunesse de Benjamin Constant, 1767-1794* 125.

3. Rudler, *La Jeunesse de Benjamin Constant, 1767-1794* 125. P. L. Léon interprets this first love affair in the same way: "Ce fut la première et peut-être la seule fois que Benjamin se donne tout entier et cet abandon de lui-même, en dehors de toute analyse intellectuelle, lui fit entrevoir un bonheur dont il ne s'était jamais douté. Toute sa sensibilité devait en recevoir une force et une signification nouvelles; ce jour-là, il dut perdre le mépris des sentiments qui lui empoisonnait et lui empoisonna la vie. Mais en même temps cette expérience lui offrit un but pour sa sensibilité qui devait avoir des effets désastreux dans les années suivantes. Revivre ce moment d'abandon, d'oubli devient pour lui une nécessité, une idée absorbante et fixe. Faute d'un objet éveillant spontanément ces émotions sincères, il veut les faire naître coûte que coûte. Il en résulte un tissu d'extravagances, de folies, de chasses à la sensation toute nue, de complications sentimentales et romanesques qui vont remplir les années qui viennent" (*Benjamin Constant,* Paris: Riedler, 1930, 25-26). Simone Balayé a drawn attention to the biographical orientation of Rudler's text: "Rudler, dans sa bible constantienne, a raconté les vingt premières années de la vie de Constant en utilisant le *Cahier rouge*; il ne s'est pas posé de problème autre que l'exactitude biographique, sans des moyens suffisants de contrôle, comme il le dit lui-même" ("Les degrés de l'autobiographie chez Benjamin Constant: une écriture de crise", in *Benjamin Constant, Mme de Staël et le groupe de*

Coppet, Actes du IIe Congrès de Lausanne et du IIIe Colloque de Coppet, 15-19 juillet 1980, Oxford: The Voltaire Foundation; Lausanne: Institut Benjamin Constant, 1982, 361 n.9).

4. Rousseau, in the "Ebauches des *Confessions*", is fully aware of such intricacies of the autobiographical text: "En me livrant à la fois au souvenir de l'impression receue et au sentiment présent, je peindrai doublement l'état de mon âme, savoir au moment où l'événement m'est arrivé et au moment où je l'ai décrit; mon style inégal et naturel . . . fera lui-même partie de mon histoire." (Cited by Huntington Williams, *Rousseau and Romantic Autobiography,* Oxford: Oxford University Press, 1983, 127; and by Jean Starobinski, "The Style of Autobiography," in *Literary Style: A Symposium,* ed. Seymour Chatman, London and New York: Oxford University Press, 1971, 292).

5. E. Benveniste, *Problèmes de linguistique générale* (Paris: Gallimard, 1966) 241.

6. Starobinski, "The Style of Autobiography" 288, 290.

7. D. Goldknopf, *The Life of the Novel* (Chicago and London: The University of Chicago Press, 1972) 31.

8. Benveniste, *Problèmes de linguistique générale,* 241.

9. P. Delbouille, *Genèse, structure et destin d'Adolphe* (Paris: Les Belles Lettres, 1971) 254, n.54.

10. Benjamin Constant, *Oeuvres,* ed. Alfred Roulin (Paris: Pléiade, 1957 [1964]) 1420.

11. It would appear that Constant learned of the death of Mme Johannot in 1806: "De longues années, il [Constant] ne connut plus rien d'elle [Mme Johannot]; rien à elle n'eût été plus facile que de se rappeler à son souvenir qu'elle pouvait croire fidèle. Par une sorte de pudeur, elle s'en abstint. Le hasard, seul, renseigna Benjamin sur sa triste destinée. Au mois de juin 1806, à Auxerre et à Vincelles, dans les plus sombres heures de ses querelles avec Mme de Staël exilée, il rencontra chez celle-ci Mme Roman, une amie de Genève, et par elle il apprit le sort navrant de cette délicieuse 'Marie-Charlotte Johannot Aguiton', la première femme qui l'ait aimé," (M. Levaillant, *Les Amours de Benjamin Constant,* Paris: Hachette, 1958, 21). See the entry in Constant's *Journal abrégé* for June 27, 1806: "Dîné chez Mme Roman. Souvenirs de Mme Johannot Aguiton, la première femme qui m'ait aimé."

12. Georges May refers to Starobinski's comments on Rousseau's use of a picaresque tone, which consists of treating his own past "avec ironie, condescendance, apitoiement, allégresse." May detects a similar tone in *Le Cahier rouge,* when "Benjamin Constant fait choix du ton héroi-comique pour raconter sa tentative de suicide à l'opium après son aventure avec Mme et Mlle Pourrat" (*L'Autobiographie,* Paris: PUF, 1979, 82). W. W. Holdheim goes so far as to state that "the *Cahier rouge* as a whole is very much a picaresque novel. Perhaps there is an even closer parallel with Voltaire's 'philosophical' adventure story, notably *Candide,* which is itself largely picaresque in technique. There is the same sober precision and rapidity of style, the same contraction of time. Above all, the novelistic world shows the same weightlessness which paradoxically enables a hero who is buffeted by the vicissitudes of fortune to move about as if he were not subject to the resistance of matter. This is a world where anything may happen and where nothing seems to be irrevocably serious" (*Benjamin Constant,* London: Bowes and Bowes, 1961, 34).

13. See R. Barthes, *Fragments d'un discours amoureux,* Paris: Seuil, 1977, under the entry *L'Absent*: "ABSENCE. Tout épisode de langage qui met en scène l'absence de l'objet aimé—quelles qu'en soient la cause et la durée—et tend à transformer cette absence en épreuve d'abandon" (19); "L'absence amoureuse va seulement dans un sens, et ne peut se dire qu'à partir de qui reste—et non de qui part: *je,* toujours présent, ne se constitue qu'en face de *toi,* sans cesse absent. Dire l'absence, c'est d'emblée poser que la place du sujet et la place de l'autre ne peuvent permuter; c'est dire: 'Je suis moins aimé que je n'aime'" (19); "Historiquement, le discours de l'absence est tenu par la Femme: la Femme est sédentaire, l'Homme est chasseur, voyageur; la Femme est fidèle (elle attend), l'Homme est coureur (il navigue, il drague) [. . .] Il s'ensuit que dans tout homme qui parle l'absence de l'autre, du *féminin* se déclare: cet homme qui attend et qui en souffre, est miraculeusement féminisé. Un homme n'est pas féminisé parce qu'il est inverti, mais parce qu'il est amoureux" (20).

14. "Pressentiment: sentiment vague, confus, irraisonné, qui fait prévoir, craindre, ou espérer, sans qu'on puisse savoir pourquoi" (H. Bénac, *Dictionnaire des synonymes,* Paris: Librairie Hachette, 1956).

15. In his introduction to the Garnier edition of *Adolphe* (1966), J.-H. Bornecque gives several instances of Constant's identification with his father (x, xi).

16. The statement is to be found in a review of the third edition of *Adolphe,* published in the *New Monthly Magazine,* December 1824.

17. Alice Miller, *For Your Own Good. Hidden Cruelty in Child-Rearing and the Roots of Violence.* Translated by Hildegarde and Hunter Hannum (New York: Farrar, Straus, Giroux, 1983) 270.

Renee Winegarten (essay date February 1995)

SOURCE: Winegarten, Renee. "A Concept of Liberty: Benjamin Constant." *The New Criterion* 13, no. 6 (February 1995): 30-7.

[*In the following essay, Winegarten surveys Constant's innovative and complex interpretation of liberalism.*]

On April 11, 1804, when Benjamin Constant was thirty-six, he confided to his diary: "I have excellent qualities . . . but I am not quite a real being. Inside me there are two people, one the observer of the other." It might have been the voice of the self-analytical Adolphe, the destructive and self-destructive anti-hero of Constant's celebrated autobiographical novel. Part womanizing Valmont and part sensitive Werther (the author of *Adolphe* met the creators of both, Laclos and Goethe), Constant was a skeptic rationalist and a self-tormenting introvert, a man fascinated by suicide and obsessed with death. To a confidante of his youth he seemed "a true chameleon." He was also one of the founding fathers of French political liberalism (a word used here throughout in its European sense). It was he who shaped a diverse mass of liberal notions into a clear and coherent practical political doctrine. Strange that a man with such a strong sense of nothingness (commonly an attribute of those inclined to the political extreme) should strive for so hopeful and positive an aim as the freedom of the individual in a society governed by just laws.

Benjamin Constant (1767-1830) has been called the "most eloquent of all defenders of freedom and privacy." That was the view of Isaiah Berlin in his influential essay "Two Concepts of Liberty." "No one saw the conflict between the two types of liberty better, or expressed it more clearly, than Benjamin Constant," observed Berlin. Constant took his stand on the area of "negative liberty," where an individual should be left in peace to think, speak, and act without interference from authority. The individual must have inner space, with freedom of religion, opinion, and expression guaranteed. This was by no means the case in France in Constant's own troubled times, whether under the *ancien régime* of Louis XVI, Robespierre's revolutionary Committee of Public Safety, the military dictatorship of Napoleon Bonaparte, or the reactionary Bourbon Restoration. Even today, this standpoint of Constant's can

scarcely be taken for granted, or regarded simply as old hat, in view of the insidious spread of fanaticism and the undermining of the role of the individual in theory and practice.

While professing deep admiration for Jean-Jacques Rousseau as a thinker who cherished theories of liberty, Constant denounced him for furnishing weapons and pretexts for all kinds of tyranny, whether of one man or of many. "It is in the name of liberty that we were given prisons, scaffolds, countless varieties of harassment," wrote Constant, ever mindful of the bloodstained French revolutionary Terror of 1793-94. Constant envisaged Rousseau and his disciples as the proponents of what Isaiah Berlin has named "positive liberty," the kind favored by those who believe they know best and who interfere ostensibly for one's own good. Constant's acute penetration of the corrosive nature of tyranny and its consequences would prove to be startlingly prophetic of all kinds of modern authoritarianism and totalitarianism, whether of Left or Right.

After Constant's death in December 1830, and the astonishing scenes at his funeral, attended by crowds of young people—for whom he had become the hero and instructor of parliamentary liberalism, the tireless fighter against injustice—his role and his writings began to fade from view. Other doctrines would be vying for public attention: among them, varieties of utopian socialism, Marxism, nationalism. Toward the end of the nineteenth century, however, his subtle short novel *Adolphe,* first published in London in 1816, and for which he himself professed to care little, found admirers among leading men of letters and soon entered the literary canon. In politics, though, he remained a controversial figure: he was naturally loathed by all those on the Left and the Right who despised and rejected liberal ideas and values; and condemned out of hand by some as a cynic and an opportunist.

Certainly, his was a name that cropped up here and there in various contexts historical, literary, and biographical. Yet although a selection of his works was published in the Pléiade collection in 1957, many of his important political writings were comparatively little known. A possible exception was his powerful pamphlet against Napoleon Bonaparte, *De l'Esprit de conquête et de l'usurpation* (where the word "usurpation" was substituted for "despotism" and "arbitrary rule"). It was not until the late 1970s, and especially since 1980, the 150th anniversary of Constant's death, that he and his work became the subject of numerous studies, not only in France but also in the United States and Great Britain.[1] Some of his political works were now reprinted in scholarly editions. In 1980 there were three editions of *De l'Esprit de conquête* alone. Documents began to turn up and continue to do so.

The immediate cause of this activity in France (and elsewhere) was evidently the disillusion of hitherto fellow-traveling writers and intellectuals with revolutionism in general, with discredited ideology, with Soviet Marxism and the Soviet regime. Some deluded spirits transferred their allegiance to Mao's China, but in the end, especially after the collapse of arbitrary East European regimes, the Communist dream in practice could scarcely fail to be seen for the nightmare it was. In France, the so-called "new philosophers," disillusioned Marxist intellectuals and former activists in the would-be revolutionary events of 1968, floated on the wave of "neo-liberalism." Raymond Aron replaced Sartre (who died in 1980) as the leading intellectual guru. The most dire insult of all, the dread charge of being a "bourgeois liberal," ceased to be heard. There was renewed interest in the origins of French liberalism and therefore in the role of Benjamin Constant in its development.

The object of all this fresh inquiry was not a straightforward being to be easily assimilated. Diverse, disturbed, and disturbing, Constant was inclined to mockery and self-mockery, irony and paradox. Learned in Greek as well as Latin, fluent in German and English, he was not only the author of fiction and drama but also a self-probing diarist and autobiographer, a brilliant literary and political journalist, a scholar, a moralist, a religious and political thinker, polemicist, orator, ardent parliamentarian, and opposition député (from 1819 to 1822, and from 1824 until his death). He belonged to a cosmopolitan age when the word "literature" (in Germaine de Staël's definition) embraced everything except the physical sciences; and it was in the broad field of literature that his early ambitions lay. He would often start a work—for instance, his translation of William Godwin's *Enquiry Concerning Political Justice* or his refutation of Edmund Burke's *Reflections on the Revolution in France*—only to abandon it. Some of his writings, left unpublished in manuscript, together with various pamphlets, articles, and parliamentary speeches, have only recently been made available to modern readers.

The fact that many of Constant's political writings were incomplete, unpublished, or dispersed, goes some way to explain their relative neglect. He often used works he had earlier abandoned to furnish the arguments of later, completed ones, like his ***Principes de politique applicables à tous les gouvernements représentatifs.*** Throughout his life, just like Coleridge, though from a different angle, he was preoccupied with a *magnum opus* on religion. Where Coleridge labored on a defense of Christianity, Constant aimed to promote the lasting value of religious feeling irrespective of the established churches. Although in his youth Constant had tended to irreligion, he experienced periods of pietism, and even amusingly observed that he was too skeptical to be an unbeliever. He once claimed that he had upheld the same principle for forty years: "liberty in everything, in religion, philosophy, literature, industry, politics: and by liberty I mean the triumph of individuality, both over authority which would seek to rule by despotism, and over the masses who demand the right to enslave the minority to the majority." Yet he was really too complicated and self-contradictory to be entirely consistent.

Wits had fun with his name and liked to call him "Constant the inconstant." Besides, he held that in every question there is always some idea that upsets everything; and that a truth is only complete when it contains its contrary. Observations of that sort foxed contemporaries who preferred matters to be cut and dried, and earned him the reputation of a scoffer, a person who was not in earnest, an opportunist. That was the unfavorable opinion of the poet and critic Sainte-Beuve, who cordially disliked Constant—but then, whom did he like among his fellow writers?

Born a Swiss aristocrat in Lausanne, Henri-Benjamin de Constant de Rebecque was the descendant of French Protestants who had fled persecution during the sixteenth-century Wars of Religion. How could he be politically active in France? French citizenship was granted during the French Revolution to *bona fide* descendants of Huguenot victims of religious persecution under the *ancien régime*. In addition, the purchase of landed property in France would entitle Constant to stand for election to the Chambre des Députés. But throughout his life there were always some who queried the authenticity of his French citizenship and commitment, and who created difficulties for him. In their eyes he would always be an outsider, and not only for the decades he spent in political opposition.

Any novelist who ventured to give a fictional character the upbringing and education of Benjamin Constant would be derided for an excessively lurid imagination. It was Constant's private tragedy that his mother died shortly after his birth. The child passed first into the hands of various female relatives, and then from the age of four he was looked after by the young peasant girl his father had seduced and eventually married in secret. Constant's father followed the path of many Vaudois aristocrats who, kept out of office by the ruling Bernese, served in the armies of foreign princes: he was therefore frequently absent. Withdrawn, formidable, demanding, convinced that his son was an infant prodigy, he entrusted the boy to a succession of improbable tutors. One was a sadist; another turned out to be an atheist and a libertine, who moved into a brothel with the boy. (Constant would keep his taste for prostitutes.) Various shady pedagogues followed, among them a one-time lawyer who (it later appeared) had had to leave France in a hurry. His successor was a defrocked monk who ended in suicide. Nothing, however, could quell the boy's curiosity and passion for learning.

Almost fourteen, Constant entered the University of Erlangen, in Bavaria, and through his father's connections he was appointed gentleman of the bedchamber to the Margrave of Anspach-Bayreuth. It was at Erlangen that he is said to have acquired his love of gambling, which would often lead him heavily into debt throughout his life. While studying seriously there, Constant also became involved in numerous scrapes, and he finally blotted his copybook by sardonically mocking the Margravine, his benefactress.

The precocious youth of sixteen was next dispatched to the University of Edinburgh, where, he said, he spent the "most agreeable" year of his life. It was the dazzling age of the Scottish Enlightenment. Constant distinguished himself in the grave debates of the Speculative Society, where political, philosophical, and metaphysical matters were discussed. Some of his Whig fellow students would remain lifelong friends. One close friend observed of Constant that he seemed "to have drawn freedom with his first breath," while commenting on the "endless mazes of his character." However, Constant was obliged to discontinue his studies in Edinburgh, apparently because of his failure to pay his gambling debts.

He was sent to Paris, where he stayed with the well-known journalist J.-B. Suard, friend of the liberal-minded *philosophe* Condorcet. In Paris, Constant continued his career at the gaming table and in the brothel. It was possibly at an intellectual gathering at Suard's that he met the first of the two remarkable women who influenced the course of his life. This was Isabelle van Tuyll, now Mme de Charrière, daughter of a Dutch nobleman and many years older than Constant. (James Boswell thought she had "more genius than any woman I ever saw, and more acquired perfections," and he therefore decided that it would be "madness to marry her.") She was a woman of sharp wit, far too clear-sighted and brilliant for her milieu.

Mme de Charrière (1740-1805) had already published three novels, including *Lettres de Mistriss Henley,* and she was on the point of publishing *Caliste,* her best-known work of fiction. With Constant she would collaborate on a novel entitled *Lettres de d'Arsillé fils* (first published in 1981). Skeptical, embittered, she shared her "scorn for the rest of the human race" with young Constant. It was she who (so he said) inspired him to run off alone to England—a country he chose because he thought it was the place with the most freedom. In this way she hoped to liberate him from dependence on his eccentric father.

However, in 1788 his father obtained a post for him at the court of the Duke of Brunswick. Constant's youthful radicalism, which was reinforced by the French Revolution of 1789, did not make him popular among the stiff Prussian courtiers. It was the period of his revolutionism at one remove. "The human race is born stupid and led by rogues, that is the norm," he had once reminded Mme de Charrière, but if he had to choose between rogues he still preferred the reformers to the royalists. Although he was stunned when he learned of the ghastly summary executions under the Terror, he would never abandon his underlying trust in the fundamental principles of the French Revolution itself.

His private life was in turmoil. In 1789 he had rashly married a lady-in-waiting to the Duchess of Brunswick. This ill-considered match would end in divorce. Oddly, Constant appears to have regarded matrimony as a safe haven that offered a solution to all his inner conflicts. He had already had several love affairs—mostly of the sort that Stendhal would later define as love-in-the-head—where his favorite method of trying to advance his cause was to make a show of taking poison, with threats to kill himself. In Brunswick he encountered the placid Charlotte von Hardenberg, then estranged from her first husband: she became Constant's mistress. Later (in 1808), after many vicissitudes, the long-suffering Charlotte would become Constant's second wife. His account of this strangely disconcerting affair is to be found in his potent autobiographical narrative *Cécile* (first published in 1951).

Meanwhile, in 1794 he had met the extraordinary woman writer and political thinker with whom his name was always to be linked, the one who propelled into the world of French politics his hitherto unfocused ambition to create a name for himself. Germaine de Staël (1766-1817), prodigiously gifted daughter of Jacques Necker, the wealthy self-made Swiss banker and finance minister under Louis XVI, was by then the author of plays, stories, and nonfiction works. She was already called "la trop célèbre" (to be freely translated as "too famous for a woman") by her detractors. As the wife of the Swedish Ambassador, she had presided over an extremely influential literary-political Parisian salon. She had absorbed politics from her adored father, and she knew that her only means of achieving power—at second hand—lay through the talented men she attracted into her circle and whose career she promoted.

Germaine de Staël found the tall, willowy Constant unprepossessing in appearance, but at the same time "extraordinarily amusing." He shone (again like Coleridge) as a brilliant talker who could vie in eloquence with herself. Equal in intellect, they stimulated each other. According to those who heard Constant in conversation, he was "perhaps the greatest wit since Voltaire." Dazzled by her courtly charm and intelligence, Constant pursued her for eighteen months, staging a (possibly fake) suicide in his by now customary manner, until she succumbed.

In May 1795, they left Switzerland together for the Paris of the precarious Directoire. "With all my impetuosity and with a youthful ardour belied by my years [he was then in his late twenties] I devoted myself to revolutionary opinions. I was in thrall to ambition and I saw only two things to be desired: to be the citizen of a republic and the leader of a party," said Constant. Since organized political parties did not yet exist, he presumably meant by "party" an association of freedom-loving individuals who shared the same interests and battled for the same constitutional changes. In Germaine de Staël's salon he met the men of the hour. Through her, he found himself talking with Sieyès, the power-broker and constitution-maker, and Barras, the strong man of the Directoire. Assiduously, Constant attended the debates in the Convention. Political articles of his began to attract notice.

The main drift of his ideas at the time in various pamphlets coincided with those of Germaine de Staël in her political writings. Whereas formerly Montesquieu and Rousseau had believed that a republic was suited only to a small country, the new American Republic showed that it was possible to have a viable republic in a large one. Constant, along with Germaine de Staël, stressed the importance of rallying to the French Republic all those of moderate views, in order to counter the very real threats against it from ultra-royalists on the Right and Jacobins on the Left.

With the coup d'état of 18 Brumaire (November 9, 1799), which ended the Directoire, the advent of Napoleon Bonaparte as First Consul aroused Constant's misgivings. He saw at once that Bonaparte was only concerned with his own power. Through Sieyès, Constant was appointed to the Tribunate, where he distinguished himself by his opposition to measures he believed were instruments of tyranny. On January 5, 1800, he spoke out eloquently in favor of free discussion and independence for the Assembly, "without which there is merely servitude and silence, a silence that the whole of Europe would hear." Bonaparte's elder brother, Joseph, conveyed the First Consul's displeasure to the recalcitrant pair. Nonetheless, Constant protested when special courts were introduced to deal with suspects. Unsurprisingly, Bonaparte was seriously irritated by this libertarian gadfly and his troublesome companion. Constant was among those expelled from the Tribunate in 1802. It was the end of the hopes of a political career that he had harbored since 1795. Years would pass before those hopes were to be renewed in an extraordinary reversal that damaged his reputation forever.

Constant followed Germaine de Staël into exile, either at her home at Coppet close by Lake Geneva, or to the places of internal exile in France to which Napoleon condemned her for her eloquent defiance. When she traveled to Germany in 1804, to prepare for her influen-

tial work *De l'Allemagne,* Constant accompanied her and they conversed with the great men of the day, including Goethe and Schiller. Constant was inspired to write an adaptation of Schiller's drama about Wallenstein, that ambitious enigmatic leader of the Thirty Years War, whose indecision must have struck a chord.

Running errands, Constant was often at Germaine de Staël's beck and call. The more he became dependent on her, the more he veered between affection and resentment. He sought ways of escape without being able to make a wounding irrevocable break. The two engaged in scenes of high emotional drama. He contemplated marriage with a perfectly ordinary girl whom he thought he could control. At times he recognized the folly of this course, noting in his diary: "Germaine said to me yesterday, accurately enough, that as soon as I was bound to Amélie my imagination would move into reverse: instead of seeing as I do now the drawbacks of a woman of wit who is far too famous I should see those of a mediocre woman." This would be the fate of Oswald, who marries mediocrity, in Mme de Staël's epoch-making novel *Corinne.* When Constant was spending long hours in Germaine de Staël's salon, he was yearning for solitude in the country. When he was on his country estate, he missed the brilliant and stimulating discussions in her circle of the leading thinkers of the day. Later, when Constant was at home with his devoted wife Charlotte, he was often bored. He privately owned that Germaine de Staël was the only person who really understood him. And long after the pair had gone their separate ways, "How I miss Mme de Staël!" he confided to his diary when his work was not progressing well.

Constant's novel *Adolphe* chronicles the idiosyncratic character of the young eponymous anti-hero. In accordance with the disreputable manners of the day, Adolphe decides, à la Valmont, to become the lover of Ellénore, a lady who has been living with a nobleman, by whom she has had two children. Ellénore falls deeply in love with Adolphe, and gives up her secure if equivocal position to be with him. By subtle gradations, the more enmeshed Adolphe becomes in all the sacrifices she makes for him, the more he yearns for freedom to pursue his neglected ambition and occupy the place that is his due in society. When Ellénore discovers that Adolphe intends to break with her, she falls ill and dies. Adolphe is free, but in destroying Ellénore he has destroyed himself. He remains incapable of action.

According to the moralizing preface to the second edition, it is an oppressive society that has defeated Adolphe, and it would have made no difference had he really been in love with Ellénore. Their irregular relationship was doomed. To delineate Adolphe, with his weaknesses and egoism, Constant relied on ruthlessly probing his own failings, the way even his generous instincts worked against his own freedom. He could draw on his liaisons with numerous women, among them not only Mme de Staël but also the Irish courtesan Anna Lindsay, and even his former mistress (now his wife) Charlotte. How to reconcile personal freedom with obligation and responsibility? To that query this ever intriguing novel gives a dusty answer.

A reminder from Germaine de Staël: on April 17, 1813, she could still write to stir Constant, "And what are you actually doing with your rare genius?" She herself had been working tirelessly for the downfall of Napoleon, and she had traveled across Europe to win support for the indecisive General Bernadotte, Crown Prince of Sweden, in whom she saw a liberal replacement for the Emperor as ruler of France. Seized once again by "the crazy restlessness of ambition," Constant too gambled on this unlikely candidate. It was in support of Bernadotte that he wrote *De l'Esprit de conquête,* his potent criticism of Napoleon's authoritarian regime, an analysis that stays valid for all ages.

Constant's originality lay in demonstrating that Napoleon's dictatorship, resting as it did upon bloody wars of conquest and the suppression of dissent, was not in accord with a modern society, which needed peace and freedom for the pursuit of commerce. The idea that the form of government should be in harmony with the spirit of the age, and that the modern world spelled commerce, was not new. It was the application that Constant made of it that struck many of his contemporaries as novel. The modern individual citizen wanted freedom to live quietly in quest of private ends, Constant maintained, and that freedom had to be guaranteed by any government that could be regarded as modern.

For Constant, the Napoleonic empire was rooted in hypocrisy, spying, and lies. Wars of aggression were fought not in the name of world conquest but of honor, national independence, and the defense of hearth and home. With telling irony Constant observed: "you might say that they call their hearths all the places that they have set alight." The system of hypocrisy, spying, and lies permeated the whole of society. Constant perceived that such an authoritarian regime, in its quest for uniformity, mutilated the inner life: "it pursues [man] into the intimate sanctuary of his thought and, forcing him to lie to his conscience, it robs him of the last remaining consolation of the oppressed." Moreover, the individual is left at the mercy of the master's subordinates. According to Constant, under arbitrary rule it is not enough for you to stand aside when others are struck down, for you yourself have contributed to shape degraded public opinion: "Innocent people have disappeared, you have judged them guilty. So you have opened the path along which you tread in your turn." These impassioned warnings remain as forceful as when they were written.

His bitter scorn is directed to writers, many of them suborned by Napoleon. How fond they were of the words "necessity," "public safety," and *"raison d'état"*! Would these specious words ever fall into disuse? inquired Constant. "The mania of writers is to show themselves to be statesmen . . . The author, peaceably seated at his desk . . . believes for the moment that he is clothed in power, because he preaches the abuse of it. . . . He loudly repeats the big words of public safety, supreme law. . . . Poor fool! He is speaking to men who . . . will practice his theory on himself." Constant's analysis of the "vanity that has warped the judgment of so many writers" has unfortunately remained true for a large number of major and minor literary figures on Right and Left in the twentieth century.

The news that the defeated and exiled Napoleon had escaped from Elba in March 1815, and was marching on Paris, stunned the world. One day Constant was defending constitutional monarchy under Louis XVIII, newly enthroned by the Allies, while qualifying the deposed Emperor as Attila and Genghis Khan; and the next he was closeted with Napoleon's brother, Joseph. Then Napoleon himself received Constant, who admitted in his diary that the Emperor was an "astonishing man." After the second audience, however, Constant noted: "It is not precisely freedom that he wants." Nonetheless, Benjamin Constant was entrusted with the task of making amendments to the constitution of the Empire, the new version being familiarly known as "la benjamine." He was appointed to the Council of State and, as a courtier, he wore the splendid gold-embroidered uniform of his rank.

Why did he do it? Was it, as Sainte-Beuve would harshly declare, that Constant really believed in nothing? Constant gambled on the Napoleon of the Hundred Days as he had gambled on Bernadotte, and on both occasions he had chosen losers. It is hard to imagine that, with all his experience and understanding of Napoleon's tyranny, he could believe even for a moment in the supposed transformation of Machiavellian lion into liberal lamb. The skeptical Constant could scarcely have dreamed that Napoleon's forced conversion to liberalism would endure once the emperor was restored to full power.

After Napoleon's defeat at Waterloo and his abdication in June 1815, Constant went into voluntary exile in Brussels and London. When he returned in 1816 to the Paris of the second restoration of Louis XVIII, the rest of his life was devoted—in exemplary fashion—to pursuing liberal ends, both as writer and député. If, as he proclaimed, his political principles were applicable to all representative regimes, they could be applied to constitutional monarchy. Like most French liberals from Montesquieu to Mme de Staël, he took for his model an idealized view of constitutional arrangements in England, adding modifications of his own. Royal power must be neutral, and ministers responsible to the elected representatives rather than to the monarch. What he wanted was religious toleration, and he advocated the separation of Church and State to that end. Recognizing the vital importance of the freedom of the press, he battled hard for it. He defended individuals who had been unjustly condemned; opposed the slave trade; fought for political rights for the blacks of Martinique and Guadeloupe; and urged the independence of Greece, among other noble causes.

It was not an easy ride, especially under reactionary ministers, notably those of the blinkered authoritarian Charles X. Constant did have contact with the liberal-minded Louis-Philippe, duc d'Orléans. When, after the Revolution of July 1830, Louis-Philippe ascended the throne, the "Citizen King" offered Constant a post (which he declined) and helped him to settle his gambling debts. By then Constant was a very sick man with only a few months to live. It did not take long, though, for him to feel doubts about the liberal credentials of the new regime, and so he remained in opposition to the last.

Like many eighteenth- and nineteenth-century liberals—and despite his sense of nothingness, his conviction that truth is many-sided, and at times his cynicism—Constant overvalued the role of reason and enlightenment in human affairs. The notion that fanaticism and war were incompatible with the modern world was to be shattered by the pursuit of irrationalism, by ever more savage wars and nationalistic barbarism. For him, too, a certain amount of property was an essential requisite for elector and elected alike: only the property-owner possessed the education and experience for true judgment. In his day the masses were illiterate, and he could not forget the frightening role of the wild, unpredictable crowds in the Revolution of 1789. With talent and through education, however, he believed the number of property owners would necessarily increase.

At the same time he was far from indifferent to the fate of the poor and hungry. He defended poor working people against injustice and oppression, objecting to the increasing concentration of land in the hands of the few, a development which, he said, was driving the proletariat to despair and rebellion. All the same, he did not appear to realize that the laboring classes had interests of their own and that they would soon be clamoring to defend these interests for themselves.

Few in his day understood so well as Constant the corrupting effects of arbitrary rule and false ideology not only upon society at large but upon the individual spirit. Notwithstanding his scarcely exemplary lifestyle as libertine and perennial gambler, there was a moral spark in his writings, whose eloquence and irony still have power to move. If the revival of interest in liberal thought persists—not least as a challenge to various surviving forms of "socialism"—it seems likely that the reputation of Benjamin Constant will grow with it. It is worth exploring the writer who proclaimed that "uniformity is death," and who stigmatized those who "offer up in sacrifice to the abstract being real human beings of flesh and blood."

Note

1. Among the more recent see *Benjamin Constant and the Post-Revolutionary Mind,* by Biancamaria Fontana (Yale University Press, 1991), and *Benjamin Constant: A Biography,* by Dennis Wood (Routledge, 1993).

Roy Dineen (essay date November 1996)

SOURCE: Dineen, Roy. "Love and Absurdity in Constant's *Adolphe.*" *Journal of the Australasian Universities Language and Literature Association,* no. 86 (November 1996): 1-16.

[*In the following essay, Dineen studies Constant's commentary on the absurd and pessimistic aspects of the human condition as represented by Adolphe's experiences with love.*]

'Charme de l'amour, qui pourrait vous peindre!' (p. 60)[1] This rhetorical exclamation begins the fourth chapter of Benjamin Constant's novel, *Adolphe.* For one who admits that his life up to this point has had no experience nor understanding of love whatsoever, the eponymous hero, now believing himself to be truly in love, proceeds nonetheless to deliver a quite superb description of this most profound of human emotions:

> Cette persuasion que nous avons trouvé l'être que la nature avait destiné pour nous, ce jour subit répandu sur la vie, et qui nous semble en expliquer le mystère, cette valeur inconnue attachée aux moindres circonstances, ces heures rapides, dont tous les détails échappent au souvenir par leur douceur même, et qui ne laissent dans notre âme qu'une longue trace de bonheur, cette gaieté folâtre qui se mêle quelquefois sans cause à un attendrissement habituel, tant de plaisir dans la présence, et dans l'absence tant d'espoir, ce détachement de tous les soins vulgaires, cette supériorité sur tout ce qui nous entoure, cette certitude que désormais le monde ne peut nous atteindre où nous vivons, cette intelligence mutuelle qui devine chaque pensée et qui répond à chaque émotion, charme de l'amour, qui vous éprouva ne saurait vous décrire!
>
> (p. 60)[2]

The lyricism of this evocation of his feelings for his beloved Ellénore is to be of the greatest irony. The very quality of total communication which entrances him at present will prove his undoing, for he will not be able to hide from her his true feelings when later he falls out of love. Adolphe knows very little about the emotions, and certainly the true effects of love are as yet a complete mystery to him. He has had a brilliant university career, his intellectual abilities and achievements are of the highest order, but he is a simpleton when it is a question of the emotional aspects of life. As for love, or even affection, he has never experienced these, and may be considered to be little more than an emotional cripple. At the conclusion of the affair, however, he will have learnt a great deal about love, will have experienced its transient glories, and will have confirmed his initial suspicion that the human condition is shaded above all by pessimism and absurdity.

In a text of some ten short chapters, Adolphe tells the story of a three-year *éducation sentimentale,* seeing his actions with the painful illumination provided by hindsight. Before meeting Ellénore, the older woman whom he is to destroy along with himself as a functional human being, he has grown up into a young man almost totally alienated from the world around him. He knows nothing about life and the initial responsibility for this is undoubtedly his father's. This career soldier is victim of a paralysing timidity, one of the most crippling of social disabilities: he is quite incapable of expressing his emotions, loving his son dearly, but unable to demonstrate the reality of this love. Adolphe, motherless from birth, cannot understand, and thinks himself unloved. Inheriting this timidity from his father, the adolescent discovers the difficulties inherent in relationships with others exacerbated as a result. It is to be noted that the word timidity is in itself a quite unsatisfactory term to describe the paralysing lack of self-confidence and the lack of a sense of reality to which it refers. He speaks with sensitivity of this handicap in one of the novel's many subtle insights into human frailty:

> Je ne savais pas alors ce que c'était que la timidité, cette souffrance intérieure [. . .] qui refoule sur notre cœur les impressions les plus profondes, qui glace nos paroles, qui dénature dans notre bouche tout ce que nous essayons de dire, et ne nous permet de nous exprimer que par des mots vagues ou une ironie plus ou moins amère, comme si nous voulions nous venger sur nos sentiments mêmes de la douleur que nous éprouvons à ne pouvoir les faire connaître.
>
> (p. 36)

This constraint experienced in his first relationship with another human being corrupts all subsequent relationships. Adolphe, taciturn and extraordinarily introspective, flees all contact with the Other. Hindsight shows him the problem to have been in part one of emotional deprivation. He has had no experience whatsoever of human warmth and will be consequently all the more vulnerable to the first onslaught of love:

> Je portais au fond de mon cœur un besoin de sensibilité dont je ne m'apercevais pas, mais qui, ne trouvant point à se satisfaire, me détachait successivement de tous les objets qui tour à tour attiraient ma curiosité.
>
> (p. 37)

The father has also inculcated in his adolescent offspring the view of his own generation regarding the female sex. The youth learns that, as a calculating seducer, he should not permit the emotion love to enter into his relationships with women:

> J'avais [. . .] adopté sur les femmes un système assez immoral. Mon père [. . .] considérait le mariage seul sous un rapport sérieux. [. . .] toutes les femmes, aussi longtemps qu'il ne s'agissait pas de les épouser, lui paraissaient pouvoir, sans inconvénient, être prises, puis être quittées; et je l'avais vu sourire avec une sorte d'approbation à cette parodie d'un mot connu: *Cela leur fait si peu de mal, et à nous tant de plaisir!*
>
> (p. 42)

Unable to give expression to his love for his son, the father overcompensates. Indulgent of his son's misdemeanours, he removes all difficulties which arise from the youth's misconduct. As a result, Adolphe, on the threshold of adulthood, has no concept of responsibility for things done to others, and consequently no concept of cause and effect. There is irony in the fact that the father will unfortunately not only be unable to deal with the problems inherent in his son's first real crisis, the affair with Ellénore, but will intensify them by interfering, misunderstanding their complexities and thus worsening an already impossible situation. This state of affairs might be considered quite serious enough, but Adolphe is also a product of the beginning of the Romantic age and shares its obsession with time and the impermanence of all things. Death is viewed by the young man as an absurdity, the ultimate negation which he suspects he may perhaps temporarily escape through a love affair with Ellénore, but to which he will inexorably return.[3] He becomes convinced that with death as the inevitable outcome of all existence, nothing is worth any real effort: 'Je trouvais qu'aucun but ne valait la peine d'aucun effort.' (p. 38)

This is his state at the conclusion of the expository first chapter, at which point in his young life his understanding of himself and of society reveals a worrying degree of cynicism:

> Je ne veux point ici me justifier [. . .]; je veux simplement dire [. . .], qu'il faut du temps pour s'accoutumer à l'espèce humaine, telle que l'intérêt, l'affectation, la vanité, la peur nous l'ont faite.
>
> (p. 40)

His cynicism extends to self-analysis and at the beginning of the second chapter he can make a disturbing assessment of his present situation, seeing himself as

'Distrait, inattentif, ennuyé [. . .]'. (p. 41) This functional alienation is not a pleasant state to be in for he is not a true rebel, wishing instead to be part of the human race. Consequently, his seduction of a woman ten years his senior may be seen as more of an unconscious attempt to belong to reality than the dispassionate, coldly planned, egoistic seduction he, in his inexperience, believes it to be. The attempt is, however, doomed to failure, and life will give him at the end the ultimate negative: the human condition is an absurd labyrinth from which there is no escape.

But he is as yet unaware of this bitter truth, and begins a lengthy and painful learning experience. He catches glimpses of what love and feeling may be all about, imperfect glimpses as yet, but he suspects love to be better than the quiescent emptiness of the first chapter. Characteristically, Adolphe does not initiate the new development. Observing the quite extraordinary joy of an acquaintance who has succeeded in love, he allows himself to drift into an imitation of the acquaintance's behaviour in order to see if in this way the void which is his existence may be filled. The text now refers increasingly to the rôle of fate, of chance, *le hasard*. It is this element which provides the counterpoint to his awareness of death as a nullifying factor in all existence. Death is the one and only certainty in this universe, but it is also the ultimately futile and absurd end to which all things proceed: on the way to this end, however, all is controlled by the purest uncertainty, chance. Adolphe is convinced he has no control, no volition, no power over his life, and that he is the plaything of forces greater than himself. At the precise moment when he fortuitously becomes aware of love, chance also dictates that Ellénore should appear: 'Offerte à mes regards dans un moment où mon cœur avait besoin d'amour, [. . .] Ellénore me parut une conquête digne de moi.' (p. 45) As the affair progresses, with a great deal less facility than he in his ignorance had foreseen, he is struck by the series of random events, such as the absences of Ellénore's de facto husband, which smooth the progress of the seduction. Adolphe's conviction that chance rules this world and that we are lost, without control or power in the labyrinth that is the human condition, is reinforced.

He approaches Ellénore with his father's hazardous illusions about the nature of women, and is amazed to note that the results of his initial courtship of her are not as foreseen. The indeterminate process of falling in love has in fact begun, and he notes this with a subtle use of what might be termed the imperfect tense of hindsight:[4]

> Je pensais faire, en observateur froid et impartial, le tour de son caractère et de son esprit; mais chaque mot qu'elle disait me semblait revêtu d'une grâce inexplicable. Le dessein de lui plaire, mettant dans ma vie un nouvel intérêt, animait mon existence d'une manière inusitée. J'attribuais à son charme cet effet presque magique.

> (p. 46)

Having put the supposedly calculated seduction into operation, he is the first victim of his own snare. Life now has an interest, a purpose for existence has been found, and the paralysing awareness of impermanence disappears from his perception; chance for once has done things properly![5] Convinced that chance rules the world, and also that words descriptive of the emotions are obscure in meaning and consequently to be distrusted, he discovers that words are in fact not only untrustworthy but positively dangerous: they create love. Paralysed by timidity, he cannot speak to Ellénore face to face. But, in a letter to her, he is so successful at feigning love that his pretence takes on a magical reality of its own:

> Les combats que j'avais livrés longtemps à mon propre caractère, l'impatience que j'éprouvais de n'avoir pu le surmonter, mon incertitude sur le succès de ma tentative, jetèrent dans ma lettre une agitation qui ressemblait fort à l'amour. Echauffé d'ailleurs que j'étais par mon propre style, je ressentis, en finissant d'écrire, un peu de la passion que j'avais cherché à exprimer avec toute la force possible.

> (p. 48)

Still unable to attach any real importance to actions, he is astonished at the anguish he feels when, as a result of this letter, Ellénore, who is very aware of the extreme vulnerability of her position, refuses to see him again. Exasperated by his lack of success, 'Il me tardait d'avoir parlé, car il me semblait que je n'avais qu'à parler pour réussir' (pp. 46-47), he continues his pursuit, until Ellénore, worn down by his melodramatic persistence, and by a natural pleasure at having attracted a younger man, agrees that he should continue to see her and talk of love. Familiarity breeds contempt and Adolphe concludes the chapter in a state far removed from that of its beginning. The emptiness which characterized the beginning of the chapter has been transformed into the tortures of unrequited love. He is now in a state of emotional torment, an unpleasant state responsibility for which he quite unfairly lays at Ellénore's door, but one which from the stress and tension it brings, at least offers some proof of existence, of reality, of life. The conviction that love is in fact life is coming upon him: '«Vous voyez [. . .] que vous disposez de toute mon existence; que vous aije fait pour que vous trouviez du plaisir à la tourmenter?»' (p. 52).

By the beginning of the third chapter he sincerely believes himself to be in love. It may very well be merely a sincerity of the moment, but it is certainly not the cynical hypocrisy of the calculating seducer he had at first prided himself on being: 'Je passai la nuit sans dormir. Il n'était plus question dans mon âme ni de calculs ni de projets; je me sentais, de la meilleure foi du monde, véritablement amoureux' (p. 52). In love, he now gives voice to another intuition which he has had about the complex nature of this emotion. This insight, that love of this intensity will last forever ('Cet amour [. . .] est indestructible' p. 53), will be seen later as yet another delusion. It is a counterbalance to the attitude learned from his father that women may be emotionally abused without suffering any permanent harm, and it will prove equally damaging. In this cautionary tale on the dangers of ignorance of the true nature of love, Adolphe is painfully prophetic, although not yet realising the significance of his words, as he speaks to her of the therapeutic nature of love:

> «Vous connaissez ma situation, ce caractère qu'on dit bizarre et sauvage, ce cœur étranger à tous les intérêts du monde, solitaire au milieu des hommes, et qui souffre pourtant de l'isolement auquel il est condamné. Votre amitié me soutenait: sans cette amitié je ne puis vivre. [. . .] qu'aije fait pour perdre cette unique consolation d'une existence si triste et si sombre? Je suis horriblement malheureux; je n'ai plus le courage de supporter un si long malheur; je n'espère rien, je ne demande rien, je ne veux que vous voir: mais je dois vous voir s'il faut que je vive [. . .], arraché par votre présence à la souffrance et au désespoir».

> (pp. 53-54)

He could hardly be more specific. This is no cynical Don Juan; this is in every syllable the pure and ungarnished truth, even if he is not yet fully aware of the import of his words, including that of the word *étranger*, prophetic of the ending of the story. Love does rescue him from alienation, but his understanding is still imperfect and he is unaware that the cure, and love itself, are only temporary, controlled as they are by the immutable law of the universe that all things must end. Incapable of assimilating this fact, Adolphe is for the moment carried away by his certainty, expounding magnificently on love, indeed mentioning, but in essence ignoring, its inherent transience:

> [. . .] cette histoire de quelques semaines nous semblait être celle d'une vie entière. L'amour supplée aux longs souvenirs, par une sorte de magie. Toutes les autres affections ont besoin du passé: l'amour crée, comme par enchantement, un passé dont il nous entoure. Il nous donne, pour ainsi dire, la conscience d'avoir vécu, durant des années, avec un être qui naguère nous était presque étranger. L'amour n'est qu'un point lumineux, et néanmoins il semble s'emparer du temps. Il y a peu de jours qu'il n'existait pas, bientôt il n'existera plus; mais, tant qu'il existe, il répand sa clarté sur l'époque qui l'a précédé, comme sur celle qui doit le suivre.

> (p. 56)

His conception of love is still imbued with that inexplicably magical quality he had remarked upon earlier. For love has the inestimable ability to create a past, that sense of having always been together, of having at last met the *âme sœur* destined for us by heaven.[6] From childhood, immeasurably spoiled by his indulgent but inarticulate father, he has had nothing on which to anchor the past. Never having been called upon to suffer the consequences of his misdeeds, he has been unable to develop any sense of cause and effect. Were he possessed of this faculty, it may be surmised that he would have been infinitely more circumspect in his taking up with Ellénore in the first place. Nothing has ever been real to him. The immediate resolution by his father of any difficulties resulting from his transgressions has led to a feeling of intemporality in which the transgressions and therefore the past itself appear unreal, a state of mind where the present is fleeting and the future is that most vague and uncertain of things but which, paradoxically, is carrying us to a certain destruction. Now presented almost miraculously with a sense of the past, of time, he understands that love has done everything for him, and may perhaps be able to overcome the threat posed by the future. Specifically, love has destroyed that alienation which has always beset him. The equation that love equals life is proposed, one in which unfortunately he will not totally believe until too late, at Ellénore's death. All this constitutes a superlative description of love from a man who appears to distrust words since they can never do anything beyond designate areas of emotional response, and are never capable of providing a truly satisfactory description of an emotion.[7] This is a man who knows apparently nothing about love, who has indicated an obsessive distrust of the actual meaning of words, but who is, however, beginning to discern the true nature of the emotion, having managed to comprehend that love creates time, creates that past which he has never had. Through love, the world is suddenly made real and purposeful to him.

His new understanding is by no means exclusive to the Romantic period but is certainly fundamental to it. It is intriguing to wonder whether Adolphe should have met other stars of Romanticism: his comprehension of love parallels that expounded for example in George Sand's *Indiana*. Sand's protagonists are usually in no doubt whatsoever about their total comprehension of this mysterious emotion, and, just as important, are convinced that love justifies anything. The definition of love in *Indiana* is more dramatic, feverish and in the final analysis less convincing than the simplicity basic to Constant's ***Adolphe***. Raymon de Ramière can for example wax most eloquent to Indiana, his intended conquest:

> [. . .] si le ciel [. . .] vous eût donnée à moi [. . .]. Je vous aurais portée dans mes bras pour empêcher vos pieds de se blesser; je les aurais réchauffés de mon haleine. [. . .] Tu es la femme que j'avais rêvée, la pureté que j'adorais; la chimère qui m'avait toujours fui, l'étoile brillante qui luisait devant moi pour me dire: «Marche encore dans cette vie de misère, et le ciel t'enverra un de ses anges pour t'accompagner.» De tout

temps, tu m'étais destinée [. . .]. Les hommes [. . .] m'ont arraché la compagne que Dieu m'eût choisie [. . .]. Ne me reconnais-tu pas? ne te semble-t-il pas qu'il y a vingt ans que nous ne nous sommes vus? [. . .]. Et maintenant, rien ne peut nous désunir . . .[8]

The evocation of love in *Indiana* conveys many of the aspects of this emotion as presented in ***Adolphe,*** but with none of the convincing desperation of Constant's text. Indiana, like Adolphe, is convinced that love legitimizes everything, and indeed Ellénore, who has abandoned much, including her children, for an untried and unreliable male ten years her junior, was able to take such an irrevocable step for that very reason:

> «Laissez-moir me livrer à présent, me dit-elle, aux devoirs de ma religion; j'ai bien des fautes à expier: mon amour pour vous fut peut-être une faute; je ne le croirais pourtant pas, si cet amour avait pu vous rendre heureux.»

(p. 114)

Despite Raymon's and Adolphe's conviction that love is for ever, in the latter's case certainly, this proves to be desperately inaccurate. The next development in his understanding comes with his realization that love is indeed all those things he has thus far assimilated, but is, in addition, quintessentially temporary. This is that obsession with time so perfectly evoked by Rousseau who in the previous century had already spoken of the Romantic despair when faced with the absurdity of existence:

> Aussi n'a-t-on guère ici-bas que du plaisir qui passe; pour le bonheur qui dure je doute qu'il soit connu. A peine est-il dans nos plus vives jouissances un instant où le cœur puisse véritablement nous dire: *Je voudrais que cet instant durât toujours*; et comment peut-on appeler bonheur un état fugitif qui nous laisse encore le cœur inquiet et vide, qui nous fait regretter quelque chose avant, ou désirer encore quelque chose après?[9]

With Ellénore conquered, Adolphe reverts almost immediately to purposelessness, overcome once again by the inevitability of future annihilation, and by the consequent profound awareness of the *à quoi bon?* Nothing lasts. There is no purpose to anything. The Ecclesiast was right; vanity of vanities, all is vanity. He knows this, has always known it, but had been able, temporarily, to forget it in the exhilarating moments of his courtship and conquest of Ellénore. It was, however, never all that far removed from his consciousness:

> Malheur à l'homme qui, dans les premiers moments d'une liaison d'amour, ne croit pas que cette liaison doit être éternelle! Malheur à qui, dans les bras de sa maîtresse qu'il vient d'obtenir, conserve une funeste prescience, et prévoit qu'il pourra s'en détacher!

(p. 59)

Within a very short space of time he is desperate for escape from her suffocating possessiveness. The novel from this point on resounds with the claustrophobic im-

agery of asphyxiation and imprisonment. Ellénore is transformed from his beloved to his gaoler in rather less than one page of text: 'Ellénore était sans doute un vif plaisir dans mon existence, mais elle n'était plus un but: elle était devenue un lien'. (p. 61) It is only because he is as yet unaware of his true dependency on her that Adolphe is able to make such statements and to believe them, at least with one portion of his mind. Believing that love is forever, at the same time he also believes to an equal degree in his father's delusion according to which trifling with a woman's feelings is of no real consequence. His earlier conviction that chance rules the world, allied to the paralysing effect of the awareness of temporality, helps also to convince him that any decisive action on his part is unnecessary. Sooner or later, chance will resolve everything:

> D'ailleurs, l'idée confuse que, par la seule nature des choses, cette liaison ne pouvait durer [. . .] servait néanmoins à me calmer dans mes accès de fatigue ou d'impatience. Les liens d'Ellénore avec le comte de P***, la disproportion de nos âges, la différence de nos situations, mon départ que déjà diverses circonstances avaient retardé, mais dont l'époque était prochaine, toutes ces considérations m'engageaient à donner et à recevoir encore le plus de bonheur qu'il était possible: je me croyais sûr des années, je ne disputais pas les jours.

(p. 62)

It is only a careful reading of the first chapter which makes this apparently abrupt change in his disposition towards Ellénore credible. Time, with his father's help, has always resolved all problems, and there is irony in the fact that this present difficulty can be solved neither by time nor by his father. When the latter endeavours, from his own generation's viewpoint, to assist his son to escape the woman's clutches, all he manages to do is to complicate the situation, forcing his son and Ellénore even further into a claustrophobic prison of emotional tension.

The remaining six chapters of the novel relate the limitless agony that Adolphe and Ellénore inflict on each other as the affair progressively deteriorates over a period of three years. The progress of the dissolution of the affair is analysed in the most careful detail, each irrevocable step commented upon in a manner which may strike more than one echo in the heart of the reader. It is a penetrating analysis of the human heart and its frailties:

> Je me plaignis de ma vie contrainte, de ma jeunesse consumée dans l'inaction, du despotisme qu'elle exerçait sur toutes mes démarches. En parlant ainsi, je vis son visage couvert tout à coup de pleurs: je m'arrêtai, je revins sur mes pas, je désavouai, j'expliquai. Nous nous embrassâmes: mais un premier coup était porté, une première barrière était franchie. Nous avions prononcé tous deux des mots irréparables; nous pouvi-

ons nous taire, mais non les oublier. Il y a des choses qu'on est longtemps sans se dire, mais quand une fois elles sont dites, on ne cesse jamais de les répéter.

(p. 65)

From this point, the affair is on an increasingly precipitous slope. Because, as Adolphe is now so quick to understand, whatever love is, and it must be said that he still has a very good idea, he is himself no longer in love. He feels, almost certainly erroneously, that had he been still in love, it is conceivable that he might perhaps have overcome all the pressures, both external and internal, which beset the couple. A Romantic, and therefore by now convinced that any absence of emotion is in itself something reprehensible, he desperately attempts to force himself back into love with Ellénore. This he cannot do, for the mind may not control the heart. Ellénore is herself aware that what he does feel for her is little more than a form of pity. By the sixth chapter a crisis is reached during which he is at such a pitch of emotional intensity that he cannot stop himself making the ultimate confession to her, with predictable results. He conducts this exchange exactly as he set about the seduction two years before, full of misplaced confidence in his own abilities and with, apparently, the same initial degree of determined calculation:

> Je retournai chez Ellénore, me croyant inébranlable dans le dessein de la forcer à ne pas rejeter les offres du comte de P*** et pour lui déclarer, s'il le fallait, que je n'avais plus d'amour pour elle.

(p. 80)

A confrontation easy to plan, much harder to execute: still a Romantic and therefore willing to consider himself to some degree a victim of society, Adolphe provides first a reasoned and indeed how seemingly noble an argument about life and its unfortunate but necessary hardships, followed by another brief but effective evocation of his now more complete understanding of love, at least in its immediate effects:

> «Chère amie, [. . .] on lutte quelque temps contre sa destinée, mais on finit toujours par céder. Les lois de la société sont plus fortes que les volontés des hommes; les sentiments les plus impérieux se brisent contre la fatalité des circonstances. En vain l'on s'obstine à ne consulter que son cœur; on est condamné tôt ou tard à écouter la raison. Je ne puis vous retenir plus longtemps dans une position également indigne de vous et de moi [. . .].» A mesure que je parlais, sans regarder Ellénore, je sentais mes idées devenir plus vagues et ma résolution faiblir. Je voulus ressaisir mes forces, et je continuai d'une voix précipitée: «Je serai toujours votre ami; j'aurai toujours pour vous l'affection la plus profonde. Les deux années de notre liaison ne s'effaceront pas de ma mémoire; elles seront à jamais l'époque la plus belle de ma vie. Mais l'amour, ce transport des sens, cette ivresse involontaire, cet oubli de tous les intérêts, de tous les devoirs, Ellénore, je ne le puis plus.»

(pp. 80-81)

The eternity promised for love is now transferred to a feeling which he admits to being now no more intense than affection. Love may legitimize all behaviours, but Adolphe is no longer possessed of this emotion, confessing it in a final outburst, brutal in its stressful monosyllabic haste, opposed carefully to the controlled beginning of the exchange.

The labyrinth, the inescapable symbol of the human condition, is reasserting its dominance.[10] Adolphe has had a temporary sense of purpose and now understands a great deal more of love than before, but he does not yet understand everything. He has finished his life before really beginning it. The first words of the novel are negative, intimating in paradoxical fashion a conclusion: 'Je venais de finir à vingt-deux ans mes études [. . .]'. (p. 35) This is an of course innocuous and perfectly normal beginning, but nonetheless it conveys an impression of disquiet, of pessimism, of a mismanaged beginning to life; he has finished at the age of twenty-two! Life, love, affection are in vain, empty, and nothing lasts. This effectively negative use of the past tense is unconsciously prophetic, for the affair with Ellénore does not prove in the end to be Adolphe's salvation, but rather the reverse. The novel is related in the *passé simple,* a tense in itself suggesting an element of finality and reinforcing the dominant image of something fated, from which there never was any real escape. It is indeed a portrayal of the human condition in its most stark form, the maze, the labyrinth, the Piranesi *Carceri* with the bolted trapdoor in the ceiling of the vault. The sense of inevitability is further highlighted by the frequent use of the imperfect tense of hindsight, of truths about the nature of love which ought to have been understood, but which were not so comprehended until too late. The text is singularly lacking in the future tense although Ellénore twice indulges in prophecy concerning Adolphe's negative future. In this way she closely parallels the two occasions when he himself uses the future for unconscious prophecy: once when commencing the affair, and then again when desperately trying to conclude it. In the first instance, if she continues to refuse to see him, he threatens self-destruction in an exact evocation of what his future will in fact prove to be on her death. A supposed philanderer, he considers this is an empty threat which will do its work upon her. It is not; it is the precise description of his ultimate future:

> [J]e pars à l'instant, j'abandonne mon pays, ma famille et mon père, je romps tous mes liens, j'abjure tous mes devoirs, et je vais, n'importe où, finir au plus tôt une vie que vous vous plaisez à empoisonner. [. . .]

(p. 51)

Then, later in the affair, he makes that commitment to her of future affection, a bitter contrast to the frenzied love of so short a time before:

Je serai toujours votre ami; j'aurai toujours pour vous l'affection la plus profonde. Les deux années de notre liaison ne s'effaceront pas de ma mémoire; elles seront à jamais l'époque la plus belle de ma vie. [. . .]

(p. 81)

The point is reinforced by Ellénore's earlier prediction of her own fate:

Elle m'écouta longtemps en silence; elle était pâle comme la mort. «De manière ou d'autre, me dit-elle enfin, vous partirez bientôt; ne devançons pas ce moment [. . .]. Gagnons des jours, gagnons des heures: des jours, des heures, c'est tout ce qu'il me faut. Je ne sais quel pressentiment me dit, Adolphe, que je mourrai dans vos bras.»

(p. 63)

She offers here a variation on Adolphe's own concept of time as something which will sooner or later solve everything with chance continuing to rule all aspects of existence. He is quite sure of the years and will not dispute the immediate future. She, however, is interested only in the immediate present. And at the end of the affair in the concluding lines of the novel, in a letter never sent but which he comes upon after her death, she speaks directly to him of what her life with him has been. Addressing him from beyond the grave, she delineates the only future which could ever be his, and which is nothing but that ending, that past he unconsciously evoked in the opening line of the novel, the beginning which is in reality a conclusion:

Vous êtes bon; vos actions sont nobles et dévouées: mais quelles actions effaceraient vos paroles? Ces paroles acérées retentissent autour de moi: je les entends la nuit; elles me suivent, elles me dévorent, elles flétrissent tout ce que vous faites. Faut-il donc que je meure, Adolphe? Eh bien, vous serez content; elle mourra, cette pauvre créature [. . .] que vous frappez à coups redoublés. Elle mourra, cette importune Ellénore que vous ne pouvez supporter autour de vous, que vous regardez comme un obstacle, pour qui vous ne trouvez pas sur la terre une place qui ne vous fatigue; elle mourra: vous marcherez seul au milieu de cette foule à laquelle vous êtes impatient de vous mêler! Vous les connaîtrez, ces hommes que vous remerciez aujourd'hui d'être indifférents; et peut-être un jour, froissé par ces cœurs arides, vous regretterez ce cœur dont vous disposiez, qui vivait de votre affection, qui eût bravé mille périls pour votre défense, et que vous ne daignez plus récompenser d'un regard.

(p. 118)

This moving conclusion to the novel by Ellénore is proved to be absolutely correct. Adolphe fulfils both his own prophecies and Ellénore's to the letter. Confirmation of this is provided in a short introduction to the novel given by its supposed editor who met the person whom he later discovered to be Adolphe some years after Ellénore's death. The editor relates how he was once delayed for several days by a flooded river in Italy. In a village in itself of no importance whatsoever and therefore constituting yet another proof of the rôle of chance in human affairs, he fortuitously meets a traveller, an *étranger* whose pessimistic inertia and aimlessness are precisely those of Adolphe, who, having tried once to escape alienation and in so doing destroyed the woman who loved him, will never again face the pain, anguish and indeed responsibility involved. The human condition, the labyrinth, is capricious in its operation but inescapable. Love works its balm only temporarily, cannot be ordered by the mind and is purely of the intractable heart:

Je parcourais l'Italie, il y a bien des années. Je fus arrêté dans une auberge de Cerenza, petit village de la Calabre, par un débordement du Neto; il y avait dans la même auberge un étranger qui se trouvait forcé d'y séjourner pour la même cause. Il était fort silencieux et paraissait triste. Il ne témoignait aucune impatience. Je me plaignais quelquefois à lui, comme au seul homme à qui je puisse parler, dans ce lieu, du retard que notre marche éprouvait. «Il m'est égal,[11] me répondit-il, d'être ici ou ailleurs.»

(p. 33)

This is the state to which Adolphe has been reduced, a state of definitive apathy. He has learned, too late, that Ellénore was necessary to him.[12] The scales lifted at last from his eyes and in full knowledge of what love is, he uses a series of absolutes to record in terms of the most lancing despair, the bitter reality of the human condition:

Je demeurai longtemps immobile, près d'Ellénore sans vie. [. . .] ce fut alors que j'éprouvai la douleur déchirante et toute l'horreur de l'adieu sans retour. Tant de mouvement, cette activité de la vie vulgaire, tant de soins et d'agitations qui ne la regardaient plus, dissipèrent cette illusion que je prolongeais, cette illusion par laquelle je croyais encore exister avec Ellénore. Je sentis le dernier lien se rompre, et l'affreuse réalité se placer à jamais entre elle et moi. Combien elle me pesait, cette liberté que j'avais tant regrettée! [. . .]. J'étais libre, en effet, je n'étais plus aimé: j'étais étranger pour tout le monde.

(pp. 116-117)

Thus are fulfilled the prophecies. There is now little difference between the respective states of Adolphe and Ellénore. Both have escaped the human condition in the only way possible. Truth, real truth, has now removed all illusions about our unenviable situation, and Adolphe for one has been afforded an almost Sartrian glimpse of the void that is in fact our much vaunted freedom. He is indeed a *salaud,* having since Ellénore's death done nothing with the freedom for which he had striven so hard. Aware of the absurdity consequent upon impermanence even before meeting Ellénore, he was at the time of her passing in no way moved to mock the consolation afforded by religious belief, giving instead expression to a quite existential *angoisse:*

Ma surprise n'est pas que l'homme ait besoin d'une religion; ce qui m'étonne, c'est qu'il se croie jamais assez fort, assez à l'abri du malheur pour oser en rejeter
une: il devrait, ce me semble, être porté, dans sa fai-
blesse, à les invoquer toutes; dans la nuit épaisse qui
nous entoure, est-il une lueur que nous puissions re-
pousser? Au milieu du torrent qui nous entraîne, est-il
une branche à laquelle nous osions refuser de nous re-
tenir?

(p. 115)

We are born alone, we live alone and we die alone,
étrangers in each of these stages, as is carefully delineated in three aspects of the text corresponding each
with the three periods of our lives, the past, the present
and the future. Each of these times is 'dead' for Adolphe, each gives him a negative answer indicative of futility to the question 'why?', 'what is the point of it
all?'. He is paralysed by the vanity of all human effort:

Ah! renonçons à ces efforts inutiles; jouissons de voir
ce temps s'écouler, mes jours se précipiter les uns sur
les autres; demeurons immobile, spectateur indifférent
d'une existence à demi passée; qu'on s'en empare,
qu'on la déchire: on n'en prolongera pas la durée!
Vaut-il la peine de la disputer?

(p. 93)

The past has never existed except when the equation
'love equals life' created a temporary one for him. The
present also is intangible and fleeting, and he is the
stranger, alone in the midst of crowds, in the void which
prefigures the *néant,* the ultimate negation from which
we came, in which we stay and to which on death we
are to return. And the future is in itself a threat, the one
thing paradoxically certain in this life ruled by chance.
He began life with a negative use of the past tense and
ends it, to all intents and purposes, with Ellénore's
prophecy from beyond the grave of an empty future,
the exact parallel of the negative past with which he began his story; the story begins and ends with a negation. And what he has understood of love is that it is indeed as wonderful as he suspected it to be, but only
temporarily! His two misconceptions on the nature of
love, his father's view according to which women suffer no lasting emotional harm on being abandoned, and
his own conviction that love is eternal, are both replaced by the truth; and this truth is that love is very
much part of the human condition, part of that labyrinth
from which we escape only for a brief moment in an illusory rapture because it cannot last, having no more
reality than any of the Utopias to which we strive. We
are in that recurrent symbol of the human condition, the
labyrinth of time and existence, in an empty vicious
circle where past, present and future merge into the
same meaningless and inescapable horror. Tantalizing in
its transient magnificence, the pinnacle of emotional experience, love is to be understood as a full part of creation and therefore subject to the corrosive effects of

time. Chance rules, and we may as well take the next
left turn in the maze, or the right, or go straight ahead
or turn back; it is all so inconsequential. *Il m'est égal
d'être ici ou ailleurs* must be one of the most despair-
ing of human utterances, indicative of total dismissal of
everything positive in this existence. Whichever way
we choose, we can do nothing except return to the spot
whence we began: the past is the future, Chapter 1 is
Chapter 10, the past tenses are the future tense. We
circle in the labyrinth with no control over our lives
and any escape is in essence a mirage. We are fated to
disaster, to a negative answer to our aspirations.

Love, as portrayed in this novel, is Utopian. But Adolphe is finally led to understand it to lack that one quality essential to Utopia, timelessness.[13] Time in the labyrinth of human existence sooner rather than later
reestablishes itself, the Utopia disappears, and the paralysing obsession with impermanence and the rôle of
chance in human affairs returns. In this cautionary tale
concerning the very real dangers presented by human
emotions, love justifying everything was perceived as a
possible escape from the human condition; yet there is
no way out, death is the ultimate absurdity, the ultimate
negation, the one thing really to be understood. Life,
the novel, everything, is an inescapable tragedy; it is
the *Il n'y avait pas d'issue* of Camus[14], and, indeed,
Adolphe ends his story with that understanding of life
which characterizes Meursault at the commencement of
his. Both are irremediably *étrangers* with no way out of
the labyrinth. Constant's preface to the second edition
of the novel in 1816 is clear on this point, considering
the account of the affair between Adolphe and Ellénore
to be the very essence of ineluctable tragedy:

[. . .] qu'aurait dû faire Adolphe, pour éprouver et
causer moins de peine? Sa position et celle d'Ellénore
étaient sans ressource [. . .]. Je l'ai montré tourmenté,
parce qu'il n'aimait que faiblement Ellénore; mais il
n'eût pas été moins tourmenté, s'il l'eût aimée davan-
tage. Il souffrait par elle, faute de sentiment: avec un
sentiment plus passionné, il eût souffert pour elle. La
société, désapprobatrice et dédaigneuse, aurait versé
tous ses venins sur l'affection que son aveu n'eût pas
sanctionnée. C'est ne pas commencer de telles liaisons
qu'il faut pour le bonheur de la vie: quand on est entré
dans cette route, on n'a plus que le choix des maux.

(p. 29)

Notes

1. Page references are taken from the 1978 Gallimard Folio edition of *Adolphe* which includes *Le
   Cahier rouge* and *Cécile*. The novel, *Adolphe,* was
   first published in 1816 but Constant had begun
   work on it as early as 1806.

2. Although much has been written on Constant's
   novel, three articles by Alison Fairlie must be considered of especial significance: 'The Art of Con-

stant's *Adolphe*', *Modern Language Review*, 62 (1967), pp. 32-47, 'Creation of Character', *Forum for Modern Language Studies*, II, 3 (1966), pp. 253-263, and 'Structure and Style', *French Studies*, XX (1966), pp. 226-242.

3. Georges Poulet analyses Adolphe's paralysing view of death in his *Etudes sur le Temps humain*, (University of Edinburgh Press, 1949), pp. 239-262.

4. See Fairlie, 'The Art of Constant's *Adolphe*', p. 38.

5. Fairlie deals at length with the importance of the goal, the obstacle as a galvanizing force in the psychological make-up of Adolphe in 'The Art of Constant's *Adolphe*', p. 38ff.

6. «Et si je vous avais rencontrée plus tôt, vous auriez pu être à moi! J'aurais serré dans mes bras la seule créature que la nature ait formée pour mon cœur, pour ce cœur qui a tant souffert parce qu'il vous cherchait et qu'il ne vous a trouvée que trop tard! [. . .]». (p. 57)

7. Adolphe refers on several occasions to this aspect. It is also an important component of Fairlie's 'The Art of Constant's *Adolphe*'. The theme begins early in the novel in one of the frequent maxims on the nature of the human condition: «Les sentiments de l'homme sont confus et mélangés; ils se composent d'une multitude d'impressions variées qui échappent à l'observation; et la parole, toujours trop grossière et trop générale, peut bien servir à les désigner, mais ne sert jamais à les définir.» (p. 42)

8. George Sand, *Indiana* (Folio, 1989), pp. 94-96.

9. Jean-Jacques Rousseau, *Les Rêveries du Promeneur solitaire* (Folio, 1984), *Cinquième promenade*, p. 101.

10. Chapter 7, for example, is thematically and structurally the circling around by Adolphe in the labyrinth of his emotional involvement with Ellénore, seeking an impossible escape from her, the "Minotaur" at its centre.

11. The phrase is also used by that other *étranger*, Camus's Meursault and is indicative of his similarly unusual attitude to existence.

12. One is almost inevitably reminded of Lamartine's poignant statement of loss composed in 1818: 'Un seul être vous manque, et tout est dépeuplé!', *L'Isolement*, line 28. Both Constant and Lamartine are attempting to come to terms with a painful aspect of the human condition, and both use the same word, *l'isolement*, to describe their state of mind.

13. The importance of this absolutely indispensable attribute of any Utopia is underlined by Rousseau in his evocation of a very personal *vrai bonheur* in, for example, the *Deuxième*, the *Cinquième*, the *Neuvième* and the *Dixième Promenades* of the *Rêveries*.

14. Albert Camus, *L'Etranger* (Folio, 1989), p. 30.

Elena Russo (essay date 1996)

SOURCE: Russo, Elena. "Knowing the Authentic Subject: *Adolphe*." In *Skeptical Selves: Empiricism and Modernity in the French Novel*, pp. 67-111. Stanford, Calif.: Stanford University Press, 1996.

[*In the following essay, Russo analyzes Constant's assertion that the strength of social and historical precedents and circumstances determine individual behavior and perception.*]

In the small provincial Court of D***, in spite of the rule of an enlightened prince who apparently "governed with mildness" and "favored freedom of thought," society is in the grip of a covert despotism that foreshadows the stifling atmosphere of Stendhal's Cour de Parme. There, it is easy for Adolphe to win for himself the privileged but somewhat cumbersome reputation of a "libertine" seeking the destruction of prejudice, "acquiring a strong reputation for satire and maliciousness" as well as immorality. Embarking upon the career of freethinker and seducer allows Adolphe to escape the narrow constraints of the court while at the same time endowing him with an identity and a direction. "In my father's home I had adopted a somewhat immoral attitude towards women": the typical libertine, given primarily to intellectual activity, displays a desire for power and control that he satisfies thanks to his superior knowledge of human nature. "I thought I was a cool impartial observer exploring her mind and character," writes Adolphe referring to Ellénore; his ambition to seduce her leads him to invent "clever plans and subtle schemes": "Anyone who could have read my heart when I was away from her would have taken me for a cold and heartless seducer."[1]

Constant's hero inherits a tradition whose paradigmatic figure is to be found in *Les Liaisons dangereuses*. On a first impression, Adolphe and Laclos's Valmont share certain qualities and actions: both are engaged in a dangerous liaison, as Constant suggests in the preface to the second edition. There, he warns the reader against "the danger of those irregular liaisons" and concludes that "it is the never having commenced such liaisons which is necessary for the happiness of life: when we have once entered on that career, we have no longer but the choice of evils" (29). ***Adolphe*** is in many ways a reading of Laclos's novel, but a critical one, focused on the seducer's use of language. Adolphe and Valmont's methods are similar in many respects: both make ample use of their verbal and stylistic skills and both end up caught in the web they wove for their victims. In his game of deceit the seducer is carried away by the power of his own words and led to believe his own fictions. "And indeed, warmed up as I was by my own rhetoric, by the time I had finished writing I really felt some of the passion I had been at such pains to express," writes Adolphe (50). In a similar way, by the time of his death, Valmont has almost merged with the image of himself he carefully constructed in his letters to Mme de Tourvel, in which he portrayed himself as a passionate lover.

It is in the mechanics of seduction, however, that the two stories meet most closely. In both cases the mediation of a third person is instrumental in setting events in motion as well as in bringing about their closure. Mme de Merteuil, dictating to Valmont the cruel verse letter of breakup with the Présidente, is mirrored by the Baron of T***, an accomplice of Adolphe's father. In addition to inspiring and receiving the letter in which Adolphe announces his decision to put an end to the liaison, the Baron is also responsible for diverting the letter to Ellénore, thus causing her death: "She had read in my own hand my promises to leave her, promises dictated only by the desire to stay with her a little longer. . . . But he had the cruelty to calculate that Ellénore would take that all for an irrevocable decree" (114). In both episodes the seducer loses control of his strategy and of his language, as his final and most crucial moves are activated by a malevolent and cruel spectator (Merteuil for Valmont; in the case of Adolphe, the mediators vary, though they all are embodiments of a father figure). The intruder gradually interferes between the two main actors and eventually takes over. When Valmont writes the fateful letter to Tourvel, he is so unaware of its consequences that he is in fact planning a future reconciliation with her. Similarly, in announcing his separation from his mistress, Adolphe convinces himself that he is only trying to postpone his decision and win more time for reflection.

As a commentary on the text of *Les Liaisons,* Constant's novel emphasizes the weakness and the shallowness of the seducer: Adolphe's shortcomings—his words that continually misfire, his wavering between opposite directions, and his infinite irresolution—are rooted in the hollow point of Valmont's strategy. Adolphe's failure echoes, and amplifies, the weakness of his model. The end of the *Liaisons,* with Valmont falling prey to the Marquise's plan, and its variant in *Adolphe* show that seduction is a deceptive game of power, in which those who seem to be leading are in fact enslaved in turn. Valmont sacrifices his passion for Tourvel to his desire to have Merteuil acknowledge his superiority: he needs her to authenticate his identity as a libertine.

Adolphe acts out his role in front of a public he has interiorized but which nevertheless will never give him the recognition he needs. Following the seventeenth-century moralist tradition, Adolphe calls this invasion of the self by the others "vanity" or "amour propre": the alienating desire to "live in others an imaginary life"[2] which induces the individual to sacrifice his own self in the hope of achieving public recognition. Love is in *Adolphe* just one of the side effects of amour propre: "I would have enjoyed it even more fully had I not given certain hostages to my own amour-propre. This amour-propre stood as a third party between Ellénore and me" (56). Amour propre has, in the case of Adolphe, a precise genealogy, which the text traces back in time:

> In my father's home I had adopted a somewhat immoral attitude towards women. My father was a strict observer of outward appearances, but he quite often indulged in loose talk about love affairs. He looked upon them, if not as legitimate amusements, at any rate excusable ones. . . . So long as marriage was not contemplated, there was no harm in taking any woman and then dropping her. I had seen him smile, almost with approval at the parody of the well-known saying: it does them so little harm and gives us so much pleasure!
>
> (44-45)

At the origin of Adolphe's moral predicament we find his father's teachings and example. Adolphe's story is nothing but an interpretation of the paternal words,[3] as he acts them out while at the same time subverting their content. Ellénore's death contradicts the father's words: it is not true that women can be taken and discarded without consequence, and far from eliciting "pleasure," Adolphe's experience affords him nothing but guilt.

The father's words have left, however, an even deeper mark on his son. Adolphe's discourse, like his, is based on irony, sarcasm, and a playful use of language: "When I was tired of my own silence," he writes, "I ventured on a few pleasantries, and once my wit began to move, it carried me beyond all bounds" (41). Irony in the text turns out to be destructive, carrying the speaker "beyond all bounds," making him lose control over his words. The father's language is devious, relying on parody and quotation and referring to a set of rules that belong to a past society. It is from his father that Adolphe has inherited his inability to speak his mind openly—a weakness which condemns him to equivocal words, to a devious discourse that perverts his intentions, "miserable ambiguities, tortuous language which I deplored to find so obscure but dreaded making any clearer" (77). Irony follows its own laws, regardless of the speaker's intentions. With the Baron of T***, Adolphe utters, almost without control, malevolent words about his liaison: "My fixed intention was to speak well of [Ellénore] at all times, but without realizing it I was referring to her in freer and more detached terms, sometimes showing by general aphorisms that I accepted the necessity of a separation, sometimes letting jokes come to my rescue and laughing about women and how hard it was breaking with them" (108).

Adolphe is among the first novels in which the protagonist has not only lost hold of the outside world but where he has also been divested of the capacity to know and express himself. In contrast to the case with Laclos's characters, language is no longer a rhetorical tool used to shape the self and to act upon others: it has ceased to be a neutral instrument at the service of the self. While Valmont grounds his expression entirely in his drive to seduce, Adolphe has no unified project; there is no set of actions that would express the content of his self.

Like Valmont, Marivaux's Marianne is contained within the boundaries of an ambition that leads her to the projection of an aristocratic identity entirely of her own devising; even Prévost's narrator in *Histoire d'une Grecque moderne* is nothing more nor less than a man in love with a woman he does not understand. For them, the relationship to others and to language does not represent a problem as such: the self is not separable from its language because it is, after all, just an effect of that language. But such is not the case of Adolphe. Adolphe's failure in self-expression bears witness not only to the triumph of the private sphere over the public one but also to the severing of the ties between character and its rhetorical and public expression that many eighteenth-century novels displayed. As the self is "emancipated" from linguistic expression, its integrity and unity gradually come under scrutiny: the individual self is barely more than the converging point of a multitude, and there is no solid substratum beneath the show of appearances. Adolphe is inhabited by otherness: the legacy of his father's devious shyness, the rules of a society he finds frivolous and superficial. "General maxims" and fragmented stereotypes are the medium through which he is compelled to give vent to his innermost intentions. Precisely because there is a keener sense of individuality, otherness is perceived as an invasion of the self and as a threat of dissolution: perhaps following Rousseau, Constant shows in this novel that language has become the instrument of that alienation. *Adolphe* is still indebted to eighteenth-century language and style, but the relationship between language and the individual has radically changed. Language is no longer a mere instrument at the service of the individual, rather, it has a character of its own, which interferes with the individual's will to express himself. This new relationship between language and the individual in the novel parallels the transformations undergone by the philosophy of language in the early nineteenth century. The new vision of language that emerges after Kant departs from the basic tenets of empiricism: language is no longer a universal and ahistorical medium conditioned only by the universal structure of the experience. It is now seen as an a priori, as the precondition to our experience; its structure shapes experience and thought.

Through the figure of Adolphe, Constant demonstrates a sharp awareness of the historical determinacies that shape a person; the seventeenth-century universalistic critique of amour propre has been replaced by a historicization of the notion of the self's invasion by others. In other words, amour propre is no longer the permanent aspect of a generic and atemporal human nature, but rather the product of precise social and historical circumstances.[4] What is more, history in this novel means violence: Adolphe is represented as a product of his times, he shoulders the weight of a tradition that thwarts his own self and keeps him from developing his individuality. Such a tradition manifests itself in a language burdened by irony: "This kind of talk amused an elderly official whose soul had dried out," writes Adolphe (108), referring to the elderly Baron of T***, recipient and appreciator of his ironical observations about women. Irony and laughter are the signs of decrepitude and corruption; through them Adolphe has been infected, since his early years, with the sickness of old age. Constant describes it in the preface as "a doctrine of unfeeling vanity, a fatal tradition, which bequeaths to the folly of the generation which arises the corruption of the generation which has grown old—an irony become trivial, but which seduces the mind by satirical style, as if any style could change the basis of things" (28).

This "deadly tradition" of irony and playful use of a language endowed with an irresistible seduction, which appears in his father's discourse—"the pleasantries that seem to them to contain the secret of life"—has for Constant a precise origin. The reference to "satirical style," puns and witticisms, targets the tradition of eighteenth-century salon conversation: the laughter not only of the libertine and the *petit-maître* of the old regime, but also of a class that made ample use of satire and epigram, whose brilliant and seductive language, Constant thought, was bent on the destruction of moral values. He has in mind the laughter of Voltaire and with it that of Enlightenment culture—a negative and destructive irony, undermining the foundations of morality and of religion; affirmation of atheism and of a general refusal to believe. In this laughter Constant—born in Lausanne to an ancient Huguenot family, and reared in a relatively tolerant bourgeois Protestantism—does not hear any liberating accent: "Strange philosophy, deriding its own principles, amusing itself by leaving nothing untouched by ridicule, by degrading, defiling everything."[5]

With Mme de Staël and her circle, Constant considered certain aspects of Enlightenment thought potentially destructive, in particular the morality of enlightened self-interest advocated by materialist thinkers such as Helvétius. Because the Enlightenment's initial motivation and inner drive seemed to them lost in the process of its negative activity, they saw atheism as leading toward the destruction of moral and ultimately civic values.[6] The philosophes' atheism, Constant thought, was responsible for the excesses of the Revolution (a revolution whose basic egalitarian principles he had nonetheless always endorsed) and for the reestablishment of despotism. The destruction of values left a void that had to be filled with total submission to substitute forms of power as oppressive, Constant thought, as the former ones: "Ephemeral men," he wrote of the philosophes, ". . . writing only to spur the next generation—which certainly took advantage of their lesson—to selfishness and degradation."[7]

Adolphe embodies the end of a society, and the paternal sin he must expiate is the sin of the absence of all belief. His life is the expression of lack and deprivation, and the narration explores all the possible manifestations of such a want: "weakness," the absence of "conviction" and "truth." Adolphe begins his career with a feeling of emptiness expressed in the opening of his memoirs: "I felt that no object was worth striving for." Such a declaration would have applied equally to the young Constant himself at the time of his friendship with Mme de Charrière.[8] Irony and laughter are interpreted in a resolutely ideological way: they destroy every value, Constant writes repeatedly, thus joining the chorus of the postrevolutionary rhetoric of "degeneration" which pervaded much of nineteenth-century writing, liberal and reactionary alike: "One laughs at one's own foolishness and enslavement, at one's corruption, without being any less enslaved, foolish and corrupt. This indiscriminate and unbounded persiflage, a kind of vertigo which takes hold of an adulterated race, is itself the symptom of an incurable degeneration."[9] The laughter of persiflage knows no "boundary" because its negative purport has no limits: it is a "vertigo" that carries away with it not only "dullness," "slavery," and "corruption" but also every transcendent value. Irony—at first the response to a sense of impotence on the part of those who foresee no escape from their situation as "slaves"—ends up losing, in its excess, all motivation. Irony is the language of impotence. An "indiscriminate" laughter, it shakes the very foundations of reference and renders meaning impossible. That same satirical criticism, coupled with a sense of void and meaninglessness in his life, leads Adolphe, at the court of D***, "beyond any proper bound," exposing everybody's weaknesses and thus alienating the whole community. Such, according to Constant, is the legacy of eighteenth-century thought. In evoking the state of mind of an unbelieving people submitted to tyranny (his target here is France under the Empire), Constant emphatically condemns the degradation of the people's language: "De-plorable state of a nation that has reached that stage! The dishonored word flies from mouth to mouth, cumbersome noise that brings no conviction, and which does not leave to truth and justice a single undefiled utterance."[10]

In a projected preface, set aside probably because of its somewhat dogmatic overtones, Constant presents Adolphe as a manifestation of "one of the most important moral sicknesses of our century" (a sickness destined to reach the stardom of stereotype in the celebrated *mal du siècle*): "This sickness of the soul is much more common than we think, and many young people show symptoms of it. The senescence of civilization has caught them. They sought enlightenment in the experience of their fathers, but they only inherited their satiety."[11] "Satiety" involves the loss of all motivation: nothing seems worth any effort to the young man who has been contaminated by the decrepitude of civilization. Adolphe's identity is shaped by absence and want; what he does or says is always defined by reference to what he has not done or said: "Such is the *strength* of a *true* feeling that *false* interpretations and artificial conventions fall silent when it speaks. But I was an ordinary *weak* man, both grateful and enslaved, not driven by any motive power from my heart" (72). Strength/weakness, truth/falsity: Adolphe's position is nearly always the negation of an alternative position that he is unable to take; he is always elsewhere, and never where he was meant to be. In that respect, his narrative has, like Prévost's, the quality of an unsolvable moral problem. The characters' predicament is so tightly knit that none of their actions bears any weight, and only a catastrophe would allow them to escape—hence the plot's obsessive and repetitive structure. "This story was written with the sole purpose," writes Constant in the preface to his third edition, "of proving . . . that it was possible to infuse a kind of interest into a novel with characters numbering only two and a situation remaining the same throughout" (30).

"I can at least solemnly claim that I have always been guided by truthful and natural feelings. How comes it that with such feelings I have for so long brought about nothing but my own misfortune and that of others?" asks Adolphe (105). If the text does not allow anybody—neither the reader nor the textual commentators (the publisher and the correspondent)—to answer that question, the reason is that throughout the narration, the reference to and the use of key words like "nature" and "truth" are rendered infinitely problematic. The novel's hermeneutical mood is based not on the knowledge of the outside world, as was the case for Prévost, but on the evaluation of the instruments that make interpretation possible. With Prévost, the delirium of the self puts the world into question. What is in doubt here is the unity and integrity of the self as well as the use it makes of language.

(2)

At the origin of the self's coming to consciousness there is amour propre or imitation. Adolphe's behavior is nothing but the interpretation of a previous discourse, be it his father's ironical speech or, more generally, society's set of rules. Even the central event of his life, his involvement with Ellénore, has its origin outside his own self:

> For some time a young man with whom I was fairly intimate had been paying attention to one of the less vapid women in our circle, and he had chosen me as a disinterested party in whom to confide his aspirations. . . . The sight of such happiness made me regret not having tried such an experience myself, for until then I had had no affair with a woman which could possibly have flattered my amour-propre, and a new future seemed to unfold before my eyes and a fresh need stir into life in my heart.
>
> (44)[12]

Adolphe's story interprets and develops someone else's story, which has left only a slight trace in the text. His passion originates in this "new desire" born out of the imitation of his confidant: "Some people would never have been in love if they had never heard of love," writes La Rochefoucauld.[13] To the awareness of the social and theatrical character of the individual's "private" conscience that is the legacy of seventeenth-century moralist tradition and that Constant still shares is added an entirely new interpretation: there is no absolute original moment in experience, but every new experience is mediated by a previous discourse that frames the approach to the object.

Such a structure is mirrored at the narrative level in our reading of Adolphe's memoirs. Although written in the first person, the text is not the creation of a unified point of view or of a voice rising above the other voices in the novel; it is rather the product of interaction with voices opposed to it. This aspect emerges in its full light when we examine the role of the narrative frame, but even in Adolphe's narrative alone, such interdependence is obvious. Here lies the cause of what many critics have labeled the "complexity" of the text and its characters. What we find, however, is not so much psychological complexity (a notion always conveniently invoked in order to brush aside the intricacies of reading) as complete reversal of the configuration of the characters' interactions. In the conflict that opposes Adolphe to Ellénore and to society, the structure of the conflict must incessantly be redefined. The text proceeds by reversals, and the characters change identity by shifting their positions with respect to each other. Ellénore, for instance, is alternatively a "pleasure" and a "burden," and society, shunned by Adolphe at the beginning of his story, becomes subsequently the object of his longing. Every situation evolves, at some point or other, into its exact opposite. Adolphe in particular embodies unexpected reversal: "I went out as I finished this speech. But who can explain what instability made the sentiment that was dictating it perish before I had even finished saying the words?" (93). Such "instability" is the effect of a sudden change of desire, but a change so instantaneous that its motivation is hardly knowable. Adolphe constantly seems to be elsewhere: as soon as he has uttered some words, their referent, his intention, is askew with his utterance. One would say that the content of his conscience escapes all principles of continuity: he thus appears to be deprived of a stable identity.

When, for instance, upon Ellénore's entreaties, Adolphe writes to his father in order to obtain permission to extend his stay in his mistress' town, his letter expresses both Ellénore's and his own desires:

> I fell at her feet, threw my arms around her, swore I loved her, and then went off to write to my father. And indeed I wrote under the impulse that Ellénore's grief had inspired. I alleged a thousand reasons for this delay; I stressed the advisability of going on with some courses of study at D*** that I had not been able to take at Gottingen. When I posted the letter I desperately wanted to get the consent I was asking for.
>
> (66)

Adolphe's plea is emblematic in another way as well: the structure of this desire is triadic, involving Adolphe, Ellénore and the father. To be more specific: Adolphe can manifest his desire for Ellénore only in relation to an antagonist, embodied in this case by the father. The antagonist allows Adolphe to establish himself as a subject. He mediates between Adolphe and the object of his desire, and, as we shall see, the protagonist's relationship to the outside world, whether to a person or to a particular value, is never directly expressed but needs the intervention of an opponent.

Adolphe's passion for Ellénore is shaped and defined by his exaltation of the obstacle which seems to acquire an importance far superior to that of the avowed focus of his desire. "Inflamed by this obstacle, my imagination took possession of my whole life" (50): this line synthesizes Adolphe's whole story. Regardless of the variations of circumstances and the metamorphosis of his desire, his imagination follows the same structure. The mediation of a third element is what allows Adolphe to function as an acting character: without the antagonist there would be no action, but only stagnation and eventually death. His language bears also the traces of that pattern, since the moments rhetorically most intense are those celebrating separation and distance. A sense of constraint is what allows desire and seduction to find their expression: without them there can be no meaning, since Adolphe's discourse is rooted in the negation of an antagonistic discourse that burdens him with its implicit threat.[14] This is true from a narrative and formal standpoint, as well as from a psychological one. As soon as the obstacle disappears, the structure of desire is subverted: since desire is constituted as the negation of a contrary position, once the latter has vanished, the negative drive turns against desire itself:

> My father's reply came with all speed. As I opened the letter I trembled at the thought of the grief a refusal would inflict upon Ellénore. Lever felt that I would be as grief stricken as she was; but as I read the consent he agreed to give, all the disadvantages of an extension to my stay suddenly leapt to my mind. "Six more months of embarrassment and constraint!" I exclaimed to myself.
>
> (67)

The positive answer from the father brings about an unexpected and sudden reversal in Adolphe's intentions, creating a sort of revolution. With his assent the father has deprived his son of the opposition that was vital for maintaining the balance of his decision, and left him alone to face the object.[15] The change that occurs is not merely an alteration in the content of consciousness, but its utter negation. The self appears fragmented into discontinuous moments.

In fact, the missing link that would reestablish some logic between these contradictory moments is not to be found in Adolphe alone but in the dialectical relationship that Adolphe entertains with the antagonist—in the present case, the father's projected and imaginary authority. Yet, we should not identify the obstacle with any conventional authority figure such as the father and his representatives. The opponent has no thematic unity and no content but merely a formal role. If such were the case, Adolphe would have been endowed with a greater coherence and ideological consistency than he actually has; we shall see later that while Adolphe himself is empty, the totality of his relationship to others is ideologically significant to Constant.

The opponent is a *function* and, as such, constantly changes its content and value. Ellénore herself turns from an object of desire into an obstacle as threatening as the father himself: "Ellénore was a great joy in my life, of course, but she was no longer an objective, she had become a tie" (64). She is now the one who keeps Adolphe in chains, away from a society that he imagines projected in the distance, and that looks all the more desirable as it appears out of reach: "All careers are open to you: literature, the army, administration, and you can aspire to the most brilliant of marriages, you are born to succeed in any direction," the Baron of T*** tells Adolphe, "but you must bear in mind that between you and all kinds of success there is an insuperable obstacle, and this obstacle is Ellénore" (92). The brilliant future that the Baron of T*** paints with seductive colors appears eminently desirable to Adolphe only because Ellénore is an obstacle to their realization.

Ironically, Ellénore herself echoes the Baron's words in her "posthumous" letter: "She will die, this wearisome Ellénore whom you regard as an obstacle" (122). She has indeed become the embodiment of absence and deprivation, the negative focus of Adolphe's aspirations, but also that which gives those aspirations a direction and a purpose: she makes his desire for the world possible: "As misers conjure up in the treasures they have amassed all the goods those treasures could buy, so I saw in Ellénore the deprivation of all the successes I might have expected" (94).

Adolphe's formal promise to the Baron to abandon Ellénore, however, is enough to turn the situation around and resurrect his desire for her, rekindled by the obstacle his own words have raised: "I had implored Heaven for some insurmountable obstacle to come between Ellénore and me. This obstacle had now arisen and I looked upon Ellénore as a being I was about to lose. . . . All my impatience had gone, and in its place there was an unacknowledged desire to postpone the fateful moment" (112). By invoking a supernatural obstacle, such as only "Heaven" could send, Adolphe expresses his nostalgia for a transcendent interdiction: only such an interdiction would be able to engender in him a desire eternal and absolute for an object eternally unavailable. But Adolphe's drama is that all his obstacles are transient and human. For the time being, contemplating Ellénore as "an object on the point of being lost" forever, Adolphe can dwell on that liminal zone between presence and absence: a unique moment when everything is still possible, when all roads are open to action. This possibility is an ideal Adolphe would like to protract indefinitely, in his desire "to postpone the fateful moment."

(3)

The novel's political significance lies precisely in the logic of desire that emerges from the individual's confrontation with an obstacle. A number of commentators have noted ***Adolphe***'s thematic relation to the main body of Constant's writings on liberal democracy. But the novel's political significance is not where most critics have sought it, in the explicit representation of society. The small German court of D***, Caden, and the Polish aristocratic community are all schematizations of a generic notion of society; they function in the novel as a necessary background to Adolphe's adventure, but they do not themselves carry any ideological content.[16]

The novel's political reflection operates on a deeper, structural level in the representation of the individual: in its relationship to the other and in its need to find a point of reference—even a negative one—to its action. In that sense, Adolphe's psychological representation is political throughout. Hume had already found a parallel between internal order and political order, in a metaphor reminiscent of the ancient microcosm/macrocosm mirroring: "I cannot compare the soul more properly to anything than a republic or commonwealth in which several members are united by the reciprocal ties of government and subordination."[17] Conscience is like a well-ordered republic where all the members sit together observing common rules.

What is then the inner order that rules Adolphe's conscience? To what type of government can we compare it? The sudden reversals in his intentions, the dynamic of antagonism that forms a precondition to the expression of his will, and the fragmentation and discontinuity of his thoughts are the image not of a well-organized republic but of a state in revolution. His actions are based on the negation and the reversal of a contrary position which provides him with both a foil and a necessary point of reference; without such a reference, he would not act at all. Adolphe needs to set himself against values he questions: he cannot do without the very power he wants to repudiate. Adolphe exists only as far as he is being related to some other—left to himself he is barely alive:

> How my heart now cried for that dependence which I had often hated! Only recently all my actions had one single object. . . . There was nobody to watch over my movements now, they interested nobody; there was none to dispute my comings and goings, no voice to call me back as I was going out. I was free, truly, for I was no longer loved. I was stranger to the whole world.
>
> (120-21)

With the death of Ellénore, his own private tyrant, Adolphe is left alone in the world, without the necessary context that provided a motivation to his actions. With that death, the conflict that allowed him to express his identity through the language of revolt disappears, and with it he loses the structure of dependence that functioned as a background to his claim for liberty. Freedom exists in relation to its opposite—a two-faced medal carrying on the other side the inscription of subjection. In Constant's novel, in order to experience "freedom," the person needs to live under someone else's gaze: "I felt resentment that a benevolent eye should watch over all my movements. . . . There was nobody to watch over my movements now, they interested nobody" (121). With Ellénore's death, Adolphe is thrown back into the same state of shapeless anonymity that threatened him at the beginning of his story, when he spoke of "all [those] people who stare at me with an indifferent eye, who, knowing nothing of what is going on in my mind, look on with dull curiosity and callous astonishment" (59). Left to himself, Adolphe is close to death, he is the ghostlike character that the publisher has known, "always alone" and spending "whole days sitting motionless, with his head in his hands" (33).

Freedom is presented in the novel as a disturbing value. Echoing one another, all the characters evoke it as a burden, as a state of lack and deprivation, rather than as a positive value: "I was going to live on without her in the desert of this world, in which I had so often wanted to be an independent traveler" (117); "how irksome this liberty now was, that I had missed so grievously!" (121). "You will walk alone in the midst of this crowd you are so anxious to join," Ellénore had written in her last message, and the correspondent tells us that Adolphe "made no use of the freedom regained at the cost of so much grief and so many tears," offering us a glimpse of Adolphe's after-life. The freedom Adolphe has regained from his subjection to Ellénore turns out to be absolutely empty: he has made no use of it.

It would be impossible to read these words without thinking of the concern at the core of Constant's reflection, as well as at the center of political thought of his time—namely, the crisis of the concept of freedom in the aftermath of the revolutionary Terror.[18] The "freedom regained" during the Revolution, with its "cost" of violence, raises important questions concerning the "use" that has been made of it, not only because that freedom was immediately alienated to new tyrants (the violent outbursts of the Revolution were, according to Constant, greatly responsible for the weakness and the servility of those who accepted the Empire and made Napoleon possible), but most of all because—once the accepted forms of authority have fallen under a newly conquered freedom of thought—the winner is left to face a void:

> Man, having triumphed in the combats he has launched, looks at a world emptied of its tutelary powers, and stands still, astonished at his victory. The agitation of the struggle, the challenge of a danger that he loved to defy, the desire to reclaim the rights that had been disputed to him, no longer sustain him. His imagination—until then bent on the pursuit of a success that was denied him, now idle and deserted—turns back against itself.[19]

In this moral description of political life we can single out the same structure of behavior that motivated Adolphe's actions. With an almost Nietzschean accent, Constant evokes the work of creative imagination as an energy constantly overcoming itself, striving to find something beyond its own achievements. Imagination burns all its energies for the idea of an obstacle to overcome, and the "agitation of the struggle," the "challenge of danger," keeps it alive in the hope of reconquering its "disputed rights." The work of imagination lies entirely in its effort to transcend itself; once the struggle is over and the goal has been reached—when the idols have been overthrown—the imagination loses its grip on reality and "turns against itself."[20] Here the romantic move would have been to turn the work of art into a possible outlet for the striving of the imagination, as the only hope for its salvation. But Constant has no bent for mythical vision: his intent is not to lose reference to the reality of active life. When the transcendent object has been lost, the imagination, in Constant's view, finds a whole host of replacement objects: new idols and new forms of subjection surface, which are all the more extreme as the new power has no binding legitimacy.

The new power is deemed "weak" not because of any nostalgia on Constant's part for a "legitimate" monarchy based on divine right but because the very notion of legitimacy has been put into question, especially since the new power does not have any democratic assent. Constant witnessed the political passivity of citizens during the Empire, and he considers the establishment of tyranny to be the result of such indifference. But tyranny is also weak. The "usurper" Napoleon, abandoning his conquests at his first defeat, is for Constant an example of such weakness: "the usurper stands in fear on an illegitimate throne as he would stand on top of a solitary pyramid. No consent is there to sustain him."[21] Constant has also in mind the government of the Directoire, unable to protect its citizens from chaos and paralyzed by opposite and violent forces. Adolphe is representative of all those who have been unable to accept and make use of the newly acquired freedom: those who, bent on their individual interests, do not participate in public life. His weakness is thus extended to the entire society, for the sources of authority are represented as equally weak, though subtly pervasive.

Adolphe's troubles do not lie in his being openly oppressed, but rather in the fact that the forms of authority he must confront are ambivalent and elusive: his father is "very indulgent towards some errors [Adolphe had] committed"; the Prince at the Court of D*** "governed with mildness . . . and left all opinions to express themselves in perfect freedom"—though that does not prevent his society from being secretly repressive. "I will not exercise against you an authority that soon I will have to give up, and that I never used with you," writes the father, but this tolerance is paradoxically the cause of Adolphe's anxiety: "I would have preferred reproaches and threats: I would have taken pride in standing up to him and felt it was necessary to muster my strength. . . . But there were no perils; I was being left perfectly free, and this freedom only made me the less patient in bearing a burden apparently of my own choosing" (82-83). In an ironical reversal, oppression is invoked as a necessity, a way to "muster strength." By the reaction it provokes, oppression induces meaning to appear, whereas "freedom," empty and obscure, is merely the coexistence of weak and ambivalent forms of discourse in the pluralism of a world where nobody can reach truth or has the strength to affirm it. Constant's diagnosis of the weakness of a postrevolutionary world, where all reference to a stable authority has been lost, prefigures Nietzsche's analysis of man's drive toward religion and authority: "Belief is always most de-

sired, most pressingly needed, where there is a lack of will . . . that is to say, the less a person knows how to command, the more urgent is his desire for that which commands, and commands sternly,—a God, prince, caste, physician, father, confessor, dogma or party conscience."[22] Adolphe is the product of a postrevolutionary world where freedom is no longer a goal, but where its triumph is only apparent. Liberated from external forms of oppression, the individual has internalized an inescapable need for authority. New forms of the old oppression emerge from within the individual, all the more dangerous because they cannot be recognized under their disguise and cannot be projected onto an outside enemy.

If *Adolphe* is a novel that still appeals to us, this is due, I think, to the fact that in its pages we can witness the emergence of an essentially modern conflict: there is no truth about the nature of the object itself but only difficult negotiations between different interpretations; meaning has become "political." There is no code of interpretation, because any reference to an ultimate meaning has been lost. Constant's position in respect to meaning is essentially ambivalent. On the one hand, the inability to fix interpretation is represented as "weakness," emptiness, and apathy; it gives rise to a desire, and even a nostalgia, for a discourse whose "force" would triumph over others, a discourse that would succeed in fixing the meaning of fundamental values such as "feeling," "nature," "truth." On the other, such weakness can be seen in a positive light when placed in the context of Constant's political choices. His recognition of the absence of transcendent values is at the root of his choice of liberalism; it is the only condition for the coexistence of a variety of "weak" discourses—weak in the sense of being nonuniversal but only relative to the subject's point of view. The novel stages the conflict between these two views, but it does not succeed in taking a position—or, rather, it does not seek a single, unequivocal position. If on the one hand the text incessantly makes reference to the validity of a notion of nature that, though absent, is still a regulative ideal, on the other, the whole story of Adolphe demonstrates the impossibility of reaching a definitive certainty and a conclusion as to the meaning of "nature."

In that respect, the analysis of Adolphe's moral fall and "corruption" is also a search for his lost "nature." The narrator may well declare "I have never acted out of calculation, but have always been guided by genuine and natural feelings": "nature"'s referent is determined by the vagaries of circumstance and self-interest. "Nature" in *Adolphe* may sometimes imply Rousseauistic values of "sentiment" and a desire to distance oneself from society's corruption—values embodied mostly by women. "Weak beings, having no real life but in the heart, no deep interest but in the affections, without activity to occupy them, without career to command them, confiding by nature," as the author writes in the preface (27), women are the representatives of a "morality of sentiments" that stands opposed to the "morality of self-interest" ruling society. Following this view, the liaison with Ellénore—a woman who, as a concubine, has only "natural" ties to the Count of P*** and who lives on the fringes of respectable society—should be able to reconcile Adolphe with nature. On the contrary, during his melancholic wandering on the isolated lands of the Polish countryside, Adolphe muses about the "slow and shameful degradation" that Ellénore has imposed on him: "I was forced to thrust aside the most delectable visions and *natural* aspirations as if they were guilty thoughts" (95). In a striking reversal, "nature" designates here all the values that Adolphe had previously opposed to nature, namely, the social order—ambition, career, acceptable marriage, and integration into the father's moral horizon—and that, in the past, he had rejected. At that point, it becomes impossible to draw the line between what belongs to nature's "truth" and what belongs to social "corruption": irony "denatures" and falsehood "depraves," but is there a state prior to corruption? Is there an individual untouched by history, language, and the insidious socialization of amour propre?

(4)

We cannot attempt to answer these questions without taking into account the elaborate value-laden language that pervades the novel and structures the prefaces and the afterwords. Few first-person novels come accompanied by so heavy an editorial apparatus: two prefaces signed by Constant, the publisher's notice at the opening of the text, and at its closure an exchange of letters between the publisher and his anonymous correspondent. We must acknowledge that fictional memoirs as a genre seem to require a particularly elaborate narrative frame in order to establish their historical credibility—as if the use of the first person were in need of legitimization more than any other form. Moreover, besides the necessities of a traditional *captatio benevolentiae,* prefaces have a normative and descriptive function:[23] the editorial frame initiates a dialogue with the text that will provide the basis for a moral and evaluative attitude on the reader's part.

In *Adolphe,* however, such a judiciary structure is undermined by a deep irony. Far from enabling the reader to shape his judgment, the value-laden language seems to have no unity and no direction. Each voice ascribes to the text a specific motivation, each justifies its existence according to different rules. In the first preface, the author points our attention to Ellénore—"I speak not of the positive ills which result from intimacies formed and broken. . . . I speak of those sufferings of the heart, of that wretched amazement of a mind deceived" (27)—but in the second, the focus shifts to Adolphe:

"What I wanted to describe was the pain inflicted upon even the hardest hearted by the suffering they cause to others, and the illusion which makes them more fickle and corrupt than they really are" (30). The author comments, interprets, declares what he "meant to say" and "what he wanted to describe" in the text; the publisher, in the final exchange of letters with the correspondent that we find in the appendix to Adolphe's narrative, repeats the same gesture: "Yes, I will certainly publish the manuscript you return. . . . I shall publish it as a true story of the misery of the human heart" (124-25). The language of the prefaces is judiciary in its tone: here we witness a trial whose verdict—whether Adolphe is guilty—depends on the question, Who is Adolphe? "Ellénore's tragedy *proves* that even the most intense emotion cannot struggle against the accepted order of things," writes the correspondent (123). But the publisher expresses a different point of view when he shifts the burden of responsibility from society to the individual, and to Adolphe in particular: "If it has any instructive lesson, that lesson is for men, for it *proves* that intellect, which they are so proud of, can neither find happiness nor bestow it" (125).

In spite of their different views, the publisher and his correspondent agree on one point: the text "proves" something of the order of a moral exemplum. But what? The inadequacies of the heart or, rather, those of the mind? Who carries the blame for Adolphe's and Ellénore's tragedy—the protagonist's moral "character" or society ("the order of things")? Significantly, the dialogue between the publisher and the correspondent dramatizes the fundamental duality of the conception of the individual in this novel: on the one hand, the notion of an autonomous self, endowed with an essential nature—a character—who is such as he is regardless of society's influence; on the other the idea that the individual character is only a function within a larger structure, and that his qualities are determined by the dynamics of the whole. To the correspondent, things are clear, the blame lies with society: "Society is too powerful, it takes too many forms, mixes too much bitterness with any love it has not sanctioned" (123). Such a position echoes Adolphe's self-justification, his declaring to the reader that "[society] presses down so heavily upon us and its imperceptible influence is so strong" (42), and to Ellénore that "the laws of society are stronger than the will of men. The most compelling emotions dash themselves to pieces against the fatality of circumstances" (84). Constant also used a similar language when he condemned in the preface "the rigour of public judgement, the malevolence of that implacable society" (27).

At the opposite pole, what is questioned is not society but Adolphe's moral character. "Circumstances are quite unimportant, character is everything," writes the publisher (125); Adolphe's shortcomings are assumed to transcend his person and to be representative of the "misery of the human heart." But how does one describe that misery—in the words of Adolphe "this character of mine which people call difficult and strange" (55)? In fact, not only are Adolphe's character and its evaluation contradictory, but nobody can agree on the meaning of the words used to evaluate it. Here is an example. "I hate that weakness which is always blaming others for its own impotence and which cannot see that the trouble is not in its surroundings but in itself" (125), writes the publisher; "Why do you show yourself so angry and weak? Why do you deny me the paltry satisfaction of believing you to be at any rate generous?" echoes Ellénore in her posthumous letter (121); and Adolphe adds his voice to Ellénore's judgment: "I was an ordinary weak man, both grateful and enslaved" (72); "to give up to her was not an act of generosity but a dangerous weakness" (83). But in spite of the repetitions and echoes rebounding from speaker to speaker, nothing is less certain than the value we can attribute to each term in the polarization generosity/weakness. To Adolphe, his initial "generous" devotion to Ellénore has by the end turned into a "weakness" dangerous to both him- and herself, a weakness that he should overcome. Yet the author subverts this polarization in the preface: "If [men] wish to overcome that which they habitually call weakness, it is necessary that they descend into that miserable heart, that they crush there whatever is generous" (28). What if the impulse that Adolphe calls "weakness" (his devotion to Ellénore's sufferings) was in fact generosity, a quality that, the author suggests, men are usually induced to repress? Who can determine the content of terms invested with a value judgment? When Adolphe happens to confess his predicament to a benevolent auditor, a woman friend whom Ellénore has entrusted with the task of mediating between herself and Adolphe, the friend's personal evaluation of the events adds a further uncertainty to the vocabulary used: "The woman I was speaking to was touched by my story, seeing generosity in what I called weakness, misfortune in what I called hardness of heart" (99).

The fact is that terms of value such as "generosity," "weakness," "unhappiness" are not descriptive but prescriptive. That is to say, they do not describe an existent object but rely on a conventional and accepted view of reality: they are a set of instructions for interpreting an event. In Locke's terminology, still current in Constant's time, those terms are "mixed modes," "made by a voluntary collection of ideas, put together in the mind, independent from any original patterns in nature." Locke states that "for the most part, in the framing of these ideas, the mind searches not its patterns in nature, nor refers the ideas it makes to the real existence of things, but puts together as may best serve its own purposes, without tying itself to a precise imitation of anything that really exists."[24] As such, they cannot, like "names of substances," be wholly traced to a sensory

experience. Mixed modes are tied specifically to a prescription or a law: the examples Locke gives are from the language of justice. The "ideas" connected to them are culturally determined by a specific convention and are not, therefore, universal, as the fact that they are often not adequately translatable into another language clearly indicates. How is it possible then to establish their meaning and to test their applicability to an object? They differ from words of substances which, being "the imitation" (the nominal essences) of something that "really exists" (the real essences), can be analyzed into their components—the simple signs that refer to sensory experience and that are in principle the same for all men. But value words and juridical words (for instance, "incest" or "adultery") have only a nominal essence that cannot be measured against the standard of reality; they signify something only insofar as men agree on their content; their use is tied to culture-specific situations involving a specific behavior. That is to say that their meaning depends on the use a community makes of them.

Is there such a community in Constant's novel? If there is, how does it hold together? More important, can it ever reach an agreement regarding the meaning of value-laden terms and their applicability to actual behavior? In other words, is there a consensus that would cement the group and establish a uniformity of interpretation for human action—in this case, Adolphe's action?

In fact, the same fragmentation and internal discontinuity that affected Adolphe's identity is at work on a larger scale in the society represented in the novel. The text is a stage where different actors deliver their speeches without ever engaging in dialogue. There is no metalanguage in the text, no critical discourse or commentary that would exert some authority over the other voices. And in spite of its elaborate structure and its heavily judgmental tone, the editorial frame is in fact as much the expression of a subjective viewpoint as Adolphe's speech itself. Its main role is to distance the reader from Adolphe's narration and to reduce its direct impact. This is what in the end distinguishes this novel from a typical *Bildungsroman,* describing the coming of age of a young man discovering the intricacies of life and the heart, in which the narrator—now grown older and wiser—can muse upon his youthful errors for the enlightenment of future generations of readers. Without the editorial frame, the narrator's frequent forays into sententious and aphoristic language—characteristic of someone judging his past from the standpoint of the knowledge extracted from it—would seem to be one of the markers of that genre. In a *Bildungsroman* the older narrator can rely on his knowledge of the nature of his past errors; the temporal and cognitive distance that divides the two halves of the protagonist's self—the one who lived the events narrated and the one who now reshapes them in his narrative—provides the basis for that fundamental irony which is the main quality of a first-person novel of formation. The self is precisely a product of that ironic distancing, which provides it with the richness and density of temporal stratification.

There is in *Adolphe* a tragic irony (the narrator writes from the standpoint of his knowledge of Ellénore's death) that seems to suggest a moral development in the narrator. But the comforting notion of autobiography as the progressive coming to consciousness of an autonomous self is radically undermined by the impact of the editorial frame. There, the distance between the self as protagonist and the self as a narrator (distance which is the foundation of autobiography and of the structure of the *Bildungsroman*) is narrowed. "After spurning the woman who loved him he was no less restless, upset, and unhappy; he made no use of the liberty regained at the cost of so much grief and so many tears" (124). These words from the correspondent are confirmed and reinforced by the publisher's reply: "We change our circumstances, but we transfer with us into each new situation the torment we had hoped to leave behind" (125). Adolphe is always the "same": every apparent "change" is reduced to nothing more than the "transfer" to a different context of the same structure of behavior. Variety is only a disguise for the repetition of the identical: "If you want proofs of all this, Sir, read these letters which will acquaint you with Adolphe's later life. You will see him in many varied circumstances, but always the victim of that mingled selfishness and emotionalism," suggests the correspondent (124). To what purpose should we read further? Those new letters would only present us with a story all too similar to the one we have just read, even granting its occurring under "different circumstances."[25]

The narrative thus appears as a vicious circle, the obsessive repetition of the same dilemma; instead of a coming of age, we have Adolphe's neurotic reenacting of an identical pattern of events, due to a "character" with whom one "cannot break." And because, viewed in this light, Adolphe as a narrator is not in any real sense distinct from Adolphe as a protagonist, the narrative voice is deprived of any authority over the meaning and the interpretation of the events it narrates: there is no distinction between *discours* and *histoire*. Let us read the publisher further: "I hate the vanity of a mind which thinks it excuses what it explains, I hate the conceit which is concerned only with itself while narrating the evil it has done, which tries to arouse pity by self-description and which, soaring indestructible among the ruins, analyses itself while it should be repenting" (125). In this sweeping condemnation of the activity of writing—narration, explanation, analysis, self-description (strange, when we consider that it is precisely the publisher who decides to give a sympathetic public to Adolphe's secret story!)—the publisher tries to analyze the

origin and motivation of Adolphe's writing. If the latter took up the pen, it was out of "vanity" and self-infatuation, in order to manipulate the reader's sympathy and compassion, to present a flattering image of himself: in a word, to seduce. It is clear whence came the publisher's words if we remember how Adolphe himself analyzed the motivations of his drive to seduce: "Of course there was a great deal of vanity in it, but it was not merely vanity, and perhaps there was less of it than I believed myself" (44). But the publisher's words are a moralistic and schematic reduction of Adolphe's subtle, ambiguous, and deeply ironic psychology. What is at stake in this example of internal reading is the fact that—according to the publisher—the older Adolphe succumbs, as a narrator, to the same logic he followed as a young protagonist: vanity and a desire to seduce. Once more, the distance between the two is ironically reduced.

A network of echoes, inverted repetitions, and mirroring statements establishes between the different utterances a complex system of internal reference that deprives each individual voice of any conclusiveness. The publisher's discourse is also, in its turn, anticipated by and assimilated into Adolphe's own utterance, and thus exposed to a hidden but sharp irony. Adolphe has experienced the horror of being exposed to public attention and commentary:

> It was a large gathering, and I was looked at with great interest. I could hear my father's name and those of Ellénore and Count P*** whispered all around me. People stopped talking as I approached and began again as I passed on. It was clear to me *that my story was being related, and no doubt each was telling it in its own way.* My position was intolerable, and a cold sweat broke out on my forehead. I blushed and went white again and again.
>
> (109)

Like Constant himself, who claims in *Amélie et Germaine* to abhor the "perpetual parlance of the salons," Adolphe cannot stand to be talked about in the third person. This torture is the reversal of amour propre, offering to him a distorted image of himself. Turned into the object of common gossip, torn between multiple and contradictory identities that are all categorically attributed to him, Adolphe is keenly aware of the corrosive effect of public words:[26] "It was said that I was an immoral and unreliable person" (43); "it was said that my conduct was that of a seducer, of an ungrateful person" (72). Communal discourse clothes itself with objectivity, but it cannot hide its fundamentally arbitrary and subjective character: "My story was being related, and no doubt each told it in its own way." The voice of the correspondent—claiming that he "knew most of the characters in this story," that he "often saw the strange and unhappy Adolphe," and confessing to have played some role in the events by trying to "warn Ellénore, that charming woman worthy of a happier fate and a more faithful heart against that tyrannical person who dominated her" (123)—discreetly betrays him as a member of that same "small audience" which, like the parody of a classical chorus, accompanies the protagonist's action. The editorial frame turns out to be an essentially ironic structure: the last words belong not to the protagonist but to a few outsiders, representatives of that fragmented and dissonant public voice that has only been able to produce conflicting versions of the events, each of them telling the story "in its own way."

Constant's novel depicts a community where there is no consensus and where moral concepts have no unified meaning. There is no convergence and consequently no possible truth, especially not in public language. But the need for truth subsists nonetheless in the text, both at the thematic level and as a textual practice. Let us see how the two are articulated.

(5)

In the realm of promises, the seducer is constantly held liable by other people for the content of his own utterance, and Adolphe is no exception. He must confront either his father or Ellénore on charges of his breach of promise. Truth in the text, however, appears under two different forms, each of them related to a specific conception of language. The first one is the most explicitly stated: there are things "out there" whose qualities are what they are regardless of our apprehension of them. A proposition is true when it corresponds to a state of fact: roughly speaking, we can say that truth is the correspondence between discourse and events. In this case, man does not constitute truth; he just finds or discovers it. This is the theory of language underlying statements like this one: "I had not said what was in my mind. My letter showed no signs of sincerity. The arguments I invented were feeble because they were not the genuine ones" (77). The letter that Adolphe writes to Ellénore is not "sincere" because it does not correspond to his secret thoughts.

But Adolphe's lie does not succeed in suppressing entirely the feeling that he has tried to mask with his false words. On the contrary, the repressed referent will sooner or later violently resurface: "The truth emerged at every turn, and in order to make my meaning clear I resorted to the harshest and the most pitiless expressions" (106). If truth can resurface from the depth of consciousness, then consciousness has an objective reality; mental and affective states have their own peculiar qualities even before they find verbal expression. In a similar perspective, Prévost's narrator can scrupulously ask whether his language corresponds to his inner feelings as faithfully as possible ("Who will trust my sincerity in the narration of my pleasure and my suffering? Will a pen guided by love not alter the nature

of everything my eyes and my senses have witnessed?" [59]). A true language, therefore, is a language adequate to the intrinsic "nature" of things; the world of signs has to adapt to the world of things. It is in reference to this type of truth that Adolphe has to answer for his actions and his words; to that conception of truth he is liable and held responsible.

There is, however, in the text another conception of language which, although not explicitly stated, nonetheless governs the protagonist's action and can be inferred from the modes of human interchange exemplified in the text. According to it, the realm of mental states belongs to the world of signs, and its reality is not distinct from its representation. In that sense, language is not a simple reproduction, but it carries all the weight of action: it is performative. Words are true only insofar as *they are interpreted as such* by the speaker and by the addressee. "While I was saying all this I was not contemplating anything beyond that object, and I was sincere in my promises" (71). In the act of promising, words are not preceded by, but they must be followed by, the appropriate action.[27] In *Adolphe,* every discourse seems to be performative; words have the power to affect the reality they claim only to reproduce:

> I managed to control myself, and kept even the tiniest signs of dissatisfaction locked in my heart, calling upon all the resources of my mind to create an artificial gaiety to conceal my profound melancholy. This effort had an unhoped-for effect upon me. We are such unstable creatures that the feelings we pretend to have we really do have in the end. I found myself half forgetting the resentments I was concealing.
>
> (83)

The work of simulation produces a discourse that does not originate in an authentic feeling. But the signs of Adolphe's fictive happiness, which initially only "conceal" his melancholy, end up becoming true. The mask has merged with his true face. Turning his personal experience into a general statement about human nature, the narrator affirms that fictional feelings can eventually become true, provided they are interpreted as such: "we are such unstable creatures." Constant does not believe in an essential human nature: habit leads men and women from mask to reality; the mask is the manifestation of our social persona and a sign of society's formative power over the self, of our vulnerability to the other's gaze. It may even be seen, at times, as a positive socializing tool.[28]

Todorov has observed that in *Adolphe* "the relationship between words and things is not static but dynamic."[29] Objects do not stay the same after they have been named, because words are not merely transparent labels attached to them but are events carrying with them a burden of consequences. Nietzsche generalized this principle by saying that a thing is the sum of its effects, and Peirce gave it a more precise formulation when he wrote, following a pragmatic conception of language, that the meaning of a sentence is the sum of its effects.[30] In Constant's novel, everybody is particularly aware of the fact that words constitute an event: moreover, the action value of a discourse is shown to be more important than the actual content of its words: "I was no longer considering the meaning my words must convey but the effect they could not fail to produce" (77).

According to our standard view of language, words "convey" a meaning and "produce" an effect, the latter being described as the consequence of meaning. These two poles correspond to the distinction between the participants in the verbal exchange: the speaker, the active producer of the discourse, controls the meaning; the addressee, a passive recipient, experiences the effect of the words' meaning. Such a hierarchy, however, cannot explain the vicissitudes of discourse in this novel: it cannot account for the deviations of Adolphe's initial message as it is received by his different interlocutors or for the endless variations of interpretations his words are exposed to, all facts that give us the impression that Adolphe's words constantly misfire. What is more, we have also seen that the meaning of certain words indicating value, such as "truth," "generosity," "weakness," and "freedom," is by no means fixed and stable but varies according to the word's context and to the speaker who defines it. The meaning of such words is constantly redefined within an ever-changing structure of communication.

How can we define the "effect" of signs in the text? How is interpretation articulated, and can there be more than one interpretation of the same event? Is anybody able to control it? More specifically, does the producer of discourse—in most cases Adolphe—exert any control over the effect his words will have on his many interlocutors? Let us take as an example the letter that is the immediate cause of Ellénore's death. Its content is certainly ambiguous. Adolphe addresses it to the Baron of T***, a friend and an ally of his father, as a follow-up to one of their conversations. There he promises to abandon Ellénore and the life of an exile that she has forced upon him in order to regain his proper place in society and to engage, as his father wished, in an "honorable career." But all these pledges, Adolphe tells the reader, are not entirely sincere; rather they are intended to produce an effect contrary to the meaning they convey: "she had read in my own hand my promises to leave her, promises dictated only by my desire to stay with her a little longer and which the strength of that desire had made me reiterate and enlarge upon in countless ways" (114). Adolphe is supposed to have written the letter with the secret purpose of reassuring his father and thus winning some more time to delay his final decision about Ellénore. But the Baron, who can read through Adolphe's rhetoric, understands both intentions:

"M. de T***'s dispassionate eye had easily read between the lines of these repeated protestations the irresolution I was disguising and the shifts of my own uncertainty" (114).

Adolphe's message is certainly an open sign, exposed to different interpretations among which it would be difficult to single out the "true" one. The very emphasis of Adolphe's style is a sign of the "weakness" of his intentions, which renders his message duplicitous and allows him and others to take advantage of the indeterminacy of his language. Adolphe's letter has potentially two contradictory effects: on the one hand to free him from Ellénore (with the disadvantage of binding him to his father), on the other to bind him to Ellénore but free him from his father. By sending it to Ellénore, the Baron is the one who chooses between them: "He had the cruelty to calculate that Ellénore would take all that for an irrevocable decree" (114). Through the Baron's reading, Ellénore's death becomes the meaning of Adolphe's letter; a meaning that might in the end be more adequate to Adolphe's secret intention than his avowed desire to tie his life to hers. To read the whole episode as a simple mishap in communication would be in fact reductive. The deviation of the letter has a deeper narrative justification when seen in the novel's broader context: it is the ultimate, perverse effect of the father's principles on women, the result of Adolphe's ambivalent attitude toward his father's authority. Establishing the meaning of Adolphe's words seems thus to involve a collective effort, since its originary source does not in any way exert an exclusive control over it: Adolphe has no privileged access to his own intentions; indeed, he does not even seem to have any determinate intentions.

The question of truth in this novel is defined in a way that is radically different than in Prévost's novel. There nature existed regardless of interpretation: it had the face and the body of an undecipherable woman, and the narrator's helpless desire turned it into a tangible reality. Prévost's narrator strove with his language to define the object as closely and as faithfully as possible, in a constant search for the correspondence between object and sign—even if it was only to discover that his description was also an interpretation. Here, however, language does not try to be merely descriptive, for in the realm of mental states there is nothing stable to describe. Value-charged language does not conform to the object but it creates its object: by naming a moral entity invested with human interest, the sign produces its referent and prescribes an action. Contrary to the empiricist theory of meaning (a complex word's meaning must conform to the qualities of the collection of individual objects the word denotes, except in Locke's mixed modes), a word, any word, is a *regulative principle* whose function is to direct our perception and our use of both the external world and the world of mental objects. A word does not conform to the nature of the object, but our approach to the object will conform to the use we make of that word. Words in *Adolphe* have the power to create and alter situations not because they betray their object but because their meaning lies in their effect, in the activity they set in motion. This is all the more evident in Adolphe's language of seduction, which constantly engages in promises and oaths—that is to say, in speech acts. The prescription will function only insofar as it will be accepted as such by a community, and as far as the speakers will conform to it.

Those questions were central to Constant's thought, particularly to his conception of society. In the novel the conflict revolves around the value given to Adolphe's actions by his interlocutors, by the publisher's exchange with the correspondent, and by the author, all paradigmatic figures of the reader. Such an evaluation involves finding the appropriate words to define the character's actions, hence the necessity to interpret his actions by reference to general rules of behavior that are prescribed by the words we want to use: does Adolphe's action correspond to what we intend by the terms "generosity," "weakness," "sincerity," and so on? The text's ironical structure introduces discordant notes between the different voices involved in that process. What is at stake is not only what value to attribute to Adolphe's actions but most of all the use made in the text of the tools available for interpretation: the interpretive activity is in fact doubled by a constant reflection on its own instruments.

At first glance, the community in the novel appears quite homogeneous. Even its outsiders, like Ellénore, share its values and its "prejudices" ("She had many prejudices, but they were all directly opposed to her own interests" [46]). The society in power, embodied in Adolphe's father and in the baron, is bourgeois in its appreciation of work and career, but it is aristocratic in its valorization of family "renown" and political influence. The distribution of allegiances is, however, more complex. The "morality of self-interest" clashes with Ellénore's "morality of sentiment"; the old regime libertinage of Adolphe's father is opposed to the sentimental, bourgeois, and proto-romantic aesthetic that Adolphe wants at times to follow. The hero's weakness, therefore, originates in the different tendencies that inhabit him simultaneously: as a true product of his "degenerate" times, Adolphe is open to a variety of conflicting influences. There is no strength in such plurality: in the novel, only those who act single mindedly in agreement with their own interests have the strength and the power to make their own meaning triumph over others. Naming something is an act involving a conflict that only the "strongest" can win, no matter what his or her values are.

We touch here on the central problem of the novel's representation of the use of language: only those who have the strength and the power to affirm their interpre-

tation can impose it successfully over other alternative meanings; only they can be said to have a self. If Adolphe has no privileged access to his intentions but lets others take control, this is because, Constant suggests, where there is no direction and no project, there is no self. In that case, the power belongs to the old baron, who has the backing of a covert but all-pervading set of rules that dominates the society Adolphe belongs to. In a world where truth is a value to be negotiated, only the discourse that succeeds in imposing itself with the greatest strength prevails. The narrator cannot impose his own interpretation because he does not have that strength: "Such is the strength of a true feeling," he remarks, "that false interpretations and artificial conventions fall silent when it speaks. But I was an ordinary weak man, both grateful and enslaved, not driven by any motive power from the heart" (72). But Constant is by no means a proto-Nietzschean proponent of meaning as will to power. Constant has lost the Enlightenment ambition of finding a firm and objective foundation for morality but not the desire of attaining it, somehow, sometime. Nietzsche, on the other hand, is not interested in establishing the universal validity of moral judgments, nor in finding any foundation for them.[31] Nietzsche might indeed have judged Constant as he did Carlyle: one who is "continually agitated by the desire of a strong faith *and* the feeling of incapacity for it (in this a typical Romantic!)."[32]

The strength that is so often referred to in the novel originates in *belief,* and ultimately in the passionate endorsement of that belief. In the projected preface, Adolphe's moral weakness and lack of conviction are ascribed to the whole postrevolutionary generation: "Fidelity in love is a strength, like religious belief, like the enthusiasm for freedom. But we no longer have any strength." Adolphe's inability to love is interpreted in moral and political terms: his shaky love for Ellénore is the emblem of a whole generation's uncertain relationship to liberty; Adolphe stands for those who, having lost passion, are torn between the conflicting needs of a weakened sense of justice and a concern for their self-interest. "Although being exclusively interested in myself, I was only unsteadily interested in myself," Adolphe writes (39): absorption in the self is a way to lose oneself, and the hero's indifference and weakness prefigure his future disappearance into insignificance. If on the one hand the fragile balance of self-interest is ultimately dangerous and destructive for the whole community,[33] on the other, impassioned and fanatical individuals end up being self-destructive as well, as Ellénore's own drama proves. Indifference and impassioned belief can both tear a society apart, but objectivity and noncommitment are not a viable option either: one of the most frequently repeated lessons of the novel is that neutrality is impossible. We are always, in some way or other, deeply involved and compromised, we are always in context. Stepping out of the conflict and endorsing indifference can lead to the useless and ultimately unhelpful impartiality of Ellénore's friend, who is unable to reconcile and mediate between the two parties at war:

> The very explanations which infuriated the passionate Ellénore carried conviction in the mind of her impartial friend. How fair we all are when we are not involved ourselves! Whoever you may be, never discuss with another the interests of your own heart. . . . Any intermediary becomes a judge who analyses, comes to a compromise, realizes that indifference can exist, indeed allows it to be possible, recognizes it as inevitable, hence excuses it.
>
> (99-100)

"We are unable to love, to believe, to will. Everybody doubts the truth of what he says, mocks the fervor of what he affirms and foresees the end of what he feels," Constant writes in the projected preface to his novel.[34] Will and belief rely upon the "force" originating in the reference to a form of spiritual transcendence; God is absent and there is in the novel a clear nostalgia for a reference to him. Describing the scene of Ellénore's death, Adolphe observes:

> I heard these people mechanically repeating the words of the prayers for the dying, as though they themselves were not some day to die too. And yet I was far from scorning such practices, for is there a single one of them which man in his ignorance can dare call useless? . . . What surprises me is not that man needs a religion, but rather that he should ever think himself strong enough or sufficiently secure from trouble to dare reject any one of them. I think he ought, in his weakness, to call upon them all. In the dense night that surrounds us is there any gleam of light we can afford to reject? In the torrent bearing us all away is there a single branch we dare refuse to cling to?
>
> (119)

Adolphe's sense of moral weakness, his estrangement from the scene together with his longing to belong to it, are paradigmatic of a whole generation. Constant was well acquainted with such estrangement, loss, and desire to belong, since he spent most of his energy and time trying to define them and recapture them historically in what he considered his major work, *De la Religion.*

(6)

The notion of an autonomous self may well have been put into question in the novel, but this does not mitigate Constant's preoccupation with the representation of individuality. In fact, we might say that a keener awareness of the question of individuality is precisely what is involved in the undermining of such a notion. Is it surprising that once individuality has been posited as an ideal, its validity should be questioned? When, in narrative practice, the individual dissolves under the combined influence of amour propre and of historical and linguistic determinacies, then individuality becomes a regulative ideal, a principle to safeguard and protect. We might go as far as to say that Constant's writing revolves almost obsessively around the question of how to preserve the integrity and the privacy of the self from contamination by language and expression—or, at any rate, from contact with degraded forms of language.[35]

This apparent paradox gradually unravels when we see how the self is repeatedly characterized by mobility, whereas language is allegedly made of "general" and "stable" signs. The experience of the self is composed of a succession of individual moments that are irreducible to language, the realm of generality. The conflict between the individuality of experience and the so-called generality of language is common to most autobiographical enterprises, and in contemporary autobiography, whether fictive or not, it can go so far as to affect the form of the narration itself.[36] In *Adolphe,* we witness the dawning of such awareness, which is a current theme in contemporary autobiography and first-person narrative; in Constant's writing this reflection is kept under control on the thematic level, without really affecting the form of the novel itself.

The tension between particularity and generality (the story of an exceptional event or a parable representative of the "human heart") which affects every classical form of narrative[37] is crucial in first-person narrative. There, in the absence of a third person, the narrator's "I" and the reader's "you" are reconciled and united in the generality of the first person plural. The latter mediates between the two poles of discourse with its reassuring thesaurus of common rules, maxims, and instructions for reading and interpreting. First-person narrative that maintains the mask of "history" always belongs, to some extent, to the genre of the "exemplum." In *Adolphe* critics have often noticed that, in full contrast with the image of a secretive and almost aphasic narrator who has given up all communication ("He was very silent and looked sad. . . . He went for walks in the evening, always alone, and often spent whole days sitting motionless" [33]), the manuscript addresses a wide audience, inviting humankind to witness Adolphe's personal story. The story becomes, indeed, the starting point for generalizations, advice, and didactic remarks intended, very often, to legitimize and justify the protagonist's actions.[38]

And yet, the narrator's aversion to maxims and generalizations is repeatedly underlined in the text, which dwells at length on the "corruption" of that form of expression: "[I developed] an insurmountable aversion," Adolphe remarks, "for all commonplace aphorisms and dogmatic formulae. . . . In any case some warning instinct made me mistrust general axioms" (41). In spite of his avowed mistrust of discourses of indefinite or uncertain reference, "general" language (a notion that is often, but not invariably, coextensive with the maxim and the aphorism in the text) allows Adolphe to express a hidden and forbidden meaning: "By a strange inconsistency, while I was most indignantly repudiating the slightest insinuation against Ellénore, my general conversation was helping to do her harm. I was constantly inveighing against [women's] fickleness, their tyranny, their exacting exhibitions of grief. I made a display of the harshest principles" (74). "General" discourse, not always endorsed by its speaker, loaded with ideology, the repository of a commonplace morality that seems all the more unquestionable as it is shared by general parlance, has in the text a strategic value. It allows Adolphe to give vent to a desire that has been repressed because of its destructive content. Its apparent neutrality mediates between Adolphe's experience and the audience he has to confront, an audience whose repressive function he has internalized by dint of amour propre: "My fixed intention was to speak well of her at all times, but without realizing it I was referring to her in freer and more detached terms, sometimes showing by general remarks that I accepted the necessity of a separation, sometimes letting jokes come to my rescue and laughing about women and how hard it was to break with them" (108). The general maxim is in that case a discourse referring to an indefinite object (some man, every man, women in general, etc.) and prescribing some action. In Adolphe's speech, however, its reference becomes specific, targeting only one person, Ellénore.[39] There is clearly a tension between the two instances of Adolphe's speech: his avowed respect for his mistress on the one hand, and on the other his indirect rejection of her, mediated by a safe and acceptable discourse that is not his own, but that speaks through him.

But is there actually an individual language of feelings? Constant's private journals witness his skepticism on that score. The influence of amour propre is too strong and too pervading to allow any of us to ever stop performing: "At the beginning I made myself a rule to write down everything I felt. I have observed that rule to the best of my ability, but the habit of speaking to the gallery is so strong that I have not always and completely observed it. . . . One dons a character like one wears a suit, to entertain guests."[40] While on the one hand "public," "general," "aphoristic," and degraded language is a fiction serving as a foil for the defense of a personal and "innocent" form of expression, on the other, advocating the ideal of such an alternative, private, and more authentic language might indicate not so much a positive belief on Constant's part as a desire and a longing for it. Indeed Adolphe's reliance on the audience and the total, albeit painful, socialization of his conscience betray a very "unromantic" mistrust in the integrity of the self.

And yet, with an ambivalence that is characteristic of Constant's writing, such an ideal occupies a central place in a text that universalizes the conclusions drawn from Adolphe's case: "general" language is fundamentally incompatible with the content of consciousness: "Man's emotions are so confused and tangled, they are made up of a *multitude* of various impressions unrecognizable by observation, and language, always too rudimentary and *too general,* can *designate* them but never really *define* them" (44). Feelings are "confused and tangled," and a "multitude" of "various impressions" condemns consciousness to perpetual anarchy. These words appear frequently in the text: according to the correspondent, Adolphe is "the victim of this mixture of selfishness and emotionalism which worked together in him for his own undoing and that of others" (124); it was a "peculiar mixture of melancholy and vivacity" that seduced Ellénore (48); "I felt a mixture of pleasure and regret" writes Adolphe (65), and again: "I cannot describe the mixture of gratitude, emotion, terror and love that showed itself on Ellénore's face" (75).[41] Every mental state is composed of a variety of contradictory elements. Even though inner life may appear as an indivisible continuum, when submitted to the rules of descriptive language and analyzed into its components, it appears as a variegated combination of distinct elements irreducible to unity. There is no stable hierarchy: consciousness is characterized by dynamism, by the mobility of its elements in constant rearrangement.

This representation of personal identity was familiar enough in Constant's time. Its roots can be found in Hume, whom Constant probably knew quite well, since from 1783 to 1785 he was enrolled at the University of Edinburgh where he became well acquainted with the major works of the Scottish Enlightenment.[42] As persons we are a sort of text, Hume demonstrates; our identity is fictional because the continuity we seem to experience between our distinct sensory impressions is only illusory. The self is no longer a Cartesian substratum, a stable and originary substance, nor is there any reflexive consciousness: there is no such thing as a "self" separate from its perceptions. The self is like a theater where different perceptions succeed each other on the scene: we know the play, but we know nothing about the theater where the play takes place (in fact, there is no theater building at all). The "mobility" by which the person is described in *Adolphe* is very similar to the Humean conception of a multiform self. According to Hume's well-known definition, a person is "nothing but a bundle or collection of different perceptions, which succeed each other with an inconceivable rapidity and are in a perpetual flux and movement. . . . The mind is a kind of theatre, where several perceptions successively make their appearance; pass, repass, glide away, and mingle in an infinite variety of postures and situations."[43]

For Hume, although the self may well be a collection of fugitive moments, it is still able to enjoy a sense of identity, however imaginary. All these impressions, in spite of their mobility, are in fact related to each other by discursive laws:

> 'Tis therefore on some of these three relations of resemblance, contiguity and causation that identity depends; and as the very essence of these relations consists in their producing an easy transition of ideas, it follows that our notions of personal identity proceed entirely from the smooth and uninterrupted progress of thought along a train of connected ideas, according to the principles above explained.
>
> (260)

The law of identity obeys the same rhetorical principles that regulate a coherent discourse: a person is also a well-constructed text in which each idea is motivated by the previous one, in a regular progression. Analyzed in its atomistic components, conscience is fragmented—it is a bundle of perceptions and impressions—but its own activity produces an effect of continuity.[44] For Hume it is important that there be an "easy transition of ideas" in the flow of conscience; a "change produced gradually and insensibly" is the main outcome of the three principles regulating the connection of ideas. But with Constant, even the Humean notion of continuity is put into question: if there were a law regulating the flow of thoughts in *Adolphe,* it would be discontinuity and fragmentation, abrupt and seemingly unjustified change. And while for Hume no overall unifying principle such as essence or substratum keeps consciousness together, the *experience* of the self is nevertheless one of unity—no matter how illusory that unity may be. The three principles allow us to perceive, to imagine, and therefore to live mental life as unified. For Constant, even the experience of consciousness, with its infinite variety and its unbound potential for sudden reversal, lacks that unity. Language is of no use either, since it cannot function as a unifying principle.

(7)

However strange such a sweeping condemnation may sound, when contrasted with mental life, language appears "too rudimentary" and "too general." We have seen with Locke that every linguistic sign is, of course, general, because it does not refer to a particular individual but to a class, which is a logical construct. Only the primitive mind was entirely nominalistic and thus able to approach the world as a collection of particular objects. There is in Constant the explicit nostalgia for a lost edenic language that would allow us to name each object, to get closer to reality and touch more solid ground—a language that would enable us to escape the constrictions of our subjective representations and, at the same time (regardless of the contradiction implicit here), provide us with a more faithful description of in-

ner life. It is ultimately a language that would enable us to really know our inner experience.

This is not a romantic theme, because Constant is still indebted to the empiricist's critique of generality conceived as abstraction and vagueness—a generality to which they oppose a careful analysis of the semantic components of general terms (the atomistic decomposition of "complex signs"). But Constant's condemnation of such an obvious and widely accepted aspect of language as generality *per se* is not as unjustified as it may appear at first sight. There is in fact a long tradition behind it. We have already mentioned Rousseau's nominalism: general words and concepts have no model in nature but are products of the mind; not only man in the state of nature ignores them, but they are also useless for the imagination: "Every general idea is purely intellectual; when the imagination gets involved, it immediately becomes particular."[45] Locke himself is not always entirely clear on the question. He acknowledges that only the use of categories and the classification of objects according to their properties make thought possible: "It is impossible that every particular Thing should have a distinct peculiar Name. . . . If it were possible, it would be useless; because it would not serve the main chief of Language."[46] Locke gives several reasons for the need to use general terms: the limits of our memory, which make it impossible for a general to remember the name of "every soldier in the army," or for anybody to know the name of "each sheep in the flock or crow that flies over his head;" the necessity to communicate words that would mean the same "idea" and would thus refer to an experience in the mind of the other which is similar to mine but which is not the same experience;[47] and finally the fact that a simple name (functioning like a deictic or an index) would not give us any information about the object, but would be nothing more than a blind label attached to it.[48] A language composed only of particular names would not only be unable to refer, it also would not allow anyone to have any thought at all: for thought involves conceiving relations and identities between objects. Borges's prodigious character Funes the Memorious is living proof of that:

> He was almost incapable of ideas of a general, Platonic sort. Not only was it difficult for him to comprehend that the generic symbol *dog* embraces so many unlike individuals of diverse size and form; it bothered him that the dog at three fourteen (seen from the side) should have the same name as the dog at three fifteen (seen from the front). . . . I suspect, however, that he was not very capable of thought. To think is to forget differences, generalize, make abstractions. In the teeming world of Funes, there were only details, almost immediate in their presence.[49]

But the very fact that Locke cares to give all these reasons proves that even if he thought the idea impractical, he saw it at least worthy of attention and deserving serious rebuttal. In fact, Locke and most of his followers could not shake off the idea that generality represented, in some way or other, a fall from grace, and the loss of an originary state of harmony and unity with the world. Locke goes so far as to state it explicitly: "One has reason to suspect such [general and abstract] Ideas are marks of our Imperfection; at least, this is enough to shew, that the most abstract and general Ideas, are not those that the Mind is first and most easily acquainted with, nor such as its earliest Knowledge is conversant about."[50]

As for Constant, "language can only designate [man's emotions] but never really define them": when it comes to the description of mental life, words can designate or indicate, but they cannot signify or have a general meaning. The content of consciousness belongs to the realm of the particular and cannot be subsumed under any classification: it can only be, at best, indicated or named. A name is an index, pointing not to a class, but to an individual object in a spatio-temporal context. This idea is central to Constant's thought in many ways. It recurs in different contexts, and Constant is well aware of its aesthetic and political implications:

> All our intimate personal sentiments seem to make sport of the efforts of language: speech [*parole*] is recalcitrant because it generalizes and expresses, and it can designate and differentiate rather than define.[51]

> I would like to find out how we could ever define with precision that deep part of our moral sensations which, by their very nature, defy all the efforts of language.[52]

In spite of the different contexts in which these and other similar remarks appear and the time that separates them, Constant's language is remarkably stable in its terms. To "define" is to determine the number of characters that are predicated from the object and that belong to the class under which the object can be subsumed. To "designate" involves no description and no categorization, since the name functions as a tag appended to the object, directly pointing to it, without the mediation of properties.

In this novel, such an opposition between the generality of language and the individuality of the self is expressed in terms of a conflict between the individual Adolphe and the interpretive position embodied by society. The latter is fundamentally repressive, not because of the content of the rules it seeks to apply but rather because of the way it uses language:

> [I developed] an insurmountable aversion for all commonplace aphorisms and dogmatic formulae. So when I heard mediocrity personified pontificate complacently about established and incontrovertible *principles* of morality, behaviour, and religion (which are usually put in the same class) I felt moved to contradict them, not that I would necessarily have held opposite views my-

self, but because such ponderous, unshakeable convictions exasperated me. Some warning instinct made me mistrust general axioms uttered without any reservation, so innocent of any shade of distinction. Fools keep their moral code in a compact and indivisible whole so that it may interfere as little as possible with their actions and leave them freedom in all matters of detail.

(41)

The language of society is precisely this "rudimentary" and "general" expression unable to grasp the "shades of distinction" among individual experiences. Generality involves not only abstraction, but also the immutability of a conventional form: "maxim," "formula," "axiom," "conviction." The power it exerts over the individual lies in the totalizing assurance of its opinions and in its pseudo-scientific language, which Constant ironically emphasizes. On the one hand, there is the dynamism, nuance, and multitude of the elements of consciousness; on the other "ponderous, unshakeable convictions," a "compact and indivisible whole."

To Constant, any attempt at universalizing moral principles is bound to fail and is open to the manipulations of power. "Society presses down so heavily upon us and its imperceptible influence is so powerful," Adolphe remarks, "that it soon moulds us into the *universal pattern*. And then we are no longer surprised . . . and we feel quite at home in our new form" (42). The "universal mould," evoking a degraded image of the act of creation, giving "shape" to indistinct matter, seems to point, beyond the present context, toward a universal damnation of form: what is in question here is every "form," be it the aesthetic form, or the very form that the mind gives to reality through language and conceptualization.[53] Constant's search exceeds the boundaries of the aesthetic realm: it is not limited to the romantic criticism of the expressive shortcomings of language but questions the very function of signs. Is it possible to reconcile the individual with language? In other terms, is there an aesthetic of individuality?

In this novel, public judgments categorically impose on the individual an irrevocable identity: regarding the protagonist, "It was said that I was an immoral and unreliable person, two epithets happily chosen. . . . It was said that my conduct was that of a seducer, of an ungrateful person"; and about Ellénore: "no distinction was made between her and all the other women of her class. . . . For leaving her children she was regarded as an unnatural mother" (72). Public opinion classifies individuals by turning them into types: the degenerate mother, the seducer, the immoral man, and so on. Similarly, in classical comedy, there were, according to Constant, no individuals or "characters" but only theatrical "passions." In his adaptation of *Wallenstein* by Schiller, Constant expresses the same rejection of categorization together with the same need for complexity in the representation of a character: "The French in their tragedies . . . only represent one event or one passion; the Germans, in theirs, represent a whole life and a complete character. . . . Characters are infinite, while theatrical passions are limited in number." German theater is superior to French theater because it represents more complete characters: "The Germans do not set aside in their characters anything of what constitutes their individuality; they show them with their weaknesses, their incongruities and the ebb and flow of that mobility that characterizes human nature and that forms real human beings." However, such a choice involves new aesthetic problems: "Individual characters, always complex and mixed, prevent the unity of expression"—problems Constant is fully aware of, since he paid for them personally with the failure of his French adaptation of Schiller's play. But his last words are more radically pessimistic: "There are no words to share in common what is always and only individual."[54]

Such an analysis, however, goes far beyond the realm of epistemology: Constant shifts epistemological problems and concerns to the moral domain and in so doing he carries on the Enlightenment project of a linguistic and conceptual reform. By dint of the analysis of language (the atomistic decomposition of complex signs), Locke and the empiricists had hoped to perform the critique of scholastic concepts; in the following century, the analysis of signs would also involve a critique of moral concepts and principles. Such had been the specific project of the Ideologues, Constant's own contemporaries, and Condillac had already prefigured that move when he showed not only that thinking is entirely dependent upon the acquisition of linguistic signs but also that our mental and moral development themselves have a semiotic nature.

The self is irreducible to the generality of language because the elements that compose the self are all particularized and *sui generis*: "feelings" are incompatible with the meaning of words (the "nominal essence") because their properties (their "real essence") are volatile and infinitely nuanced. Constant's concerns are not primarily epistemological, since what matters to him are the moral and political implications of the *uses* of language—but without such an epistemological tradition behind him, the claims he makes would be unthinkable. Constant's critique of language benefits from a whole tradition of eighteenth-century linguistic skepticism. The need for a new language that would represent the dynamics of the evolution of consciousness, together with the desire to overcome the limitations of accepted literary rules, borrows here the voice of a pre-Kantian view of language that sees signs as stable forms (generality, classification, categorization) within which

we classify experience a posteriori, rather than as part of a dynamic process that transcends experience and makes it possible.

Constant shares the typical nominalistic belief: "The only means we have at our disposal to render what we feel is language, and language is an invention of the mind. This is why language is only able to express what pertains to its domain. But we cannot find any words that would translate the sensations of the body and of the soul."[55] Language appears as an "invention" of the mind; it is deprived of the necessity of natural objects. Its conventional character relegates it to the expression of "what pertains to its domain," denying it any grasp on the world of experience—quite a paradoxical outcome for a philosophy of language that was based precisely on sensation! Emotions can be experienced from within, but they cannot be captured in language; the realm of the experience thus becomes individual and *private*: public discourse, degraded by opportunistic politics, cannot and should not penetrate it. Here we touch at the core of Constant's ambivalent thoughts on the relationship between the individual and language. On the one hand, the experience of the self transcends language; the latter, being unable to capture the experience, betrays us and leaves us isolated among others and separated from ourselves, unable to see and know our inner life. But on the other, as Constant shows in *Adolphe* and throughout his whole work, we are indeed captured by our language and by our linguistically coded social roles, and are therefore removed from any intimacy with our own experiences.

In this respect, Constant's mistrust of language also has its roots in his actual experience of successive forms of government that exercised tyranny in the name of rallying words—such as "liberty," "majority," "legitimacy"—which he felt had been emptied of their meaning in order to fit different situations. He could have said, with Tocqueville, that in political life abstract terms are like "a box with a false bottom; you may put in it what ideas you please, and take them out again without being observed."[56] There is in Constant's work a desire to flee a medium of expression that has been corrupted by political interests: "I have started to prefer painting to any other mode of literary composition because painting does not need language, and language has been so tortured lately, that it damages everything it expresses," he wrote in a letter.[57] Constant's liberal thought is the source of his desire to preserve the unique and private aspect of the person, a principle he has been deeply concerned with throughout his political career. By being aware of the incompatibility of language and authentic consciousness, Constant suggests, the private self can attempt to achieve and preserve some integrity and elude the intrusion of the public gaze. The reductive generality of despotic law should not—as it does in *Adolphe*—penetrate the individual realm and invade it.

"Variety is life, uniformity is death," Constant writes in *De l'esprit de conquête et de l'usurpation,* echo-ing Montesquieu's advocacy of individual differentiation, against the forced uniformity that despotic rule imposes on its subjects.[58]

As a dialectical thinker, though, Constant is aware that there is another side to protecting the individual consciousness from the intrusion of linguistic categories, which Adolphe fully exemplifies—namely, the flight from direct involvement and from responsibilities. If Adolphe reacts so strongly against the generality of language and the reductiveness of moral rules, such reaction is a defensive one, mainly due to his need to escape the condemnation implicit in such rules and to evade his own guilt. The claim to uniqueness has clearly in his case an apologetic value. Torn between a desire to abandon the community and his dependence on it (because of his amour propre), Adolphe demonstrates that the incompatibility between language and authentic consciousness might also become antisocial: one needs a common language and shared values in order to negotiate an interaction between the individuals' needs and representations.

In spite of the threats of dissolution hovering over the individual in society, Constant's regulative ideal of what constitutes a person is very much indebted to the Enlightenment atomistic notion of a society composed of a collection of individuals rather than to the holistic romantic view of a unified society imbued with a common collective spirit, where the individual is absorbed into the totality. In a significant passage of *De l'esprit de conquête,* Constant, with a polemical tone tinged with irony, explicitly merges, in the same language, the epistemological and the political sides of the question:

> We [referring to himself and to Degérando] do not believe, like the scholastics did, *in the reality of universals* in themselves. We do not think that there are in a State any real interests other than local ones: local interests brought together when they are the same, or balanced against each other when they are different. . . . Individual connections strengthen the general bond, instead of weakening it.[59]

Reacting against the revolutionary rhetoric of a state ruled by the absolute and "general will" of a single "people" in accordance with abstract principles of universality (which, like many other liberals, he traced back to Rousseau's *Social Contract*), Constant advocates a type of federalism and decentralization that would preserve local and regional interests in the state as a form of protection against the danger of totalitarianism. Constant's own brand of political "nominalism" makes him envision a community made up of a collection of particularized and distinct members, whose convergence under common federal laws should not in any way erase their intrinsic differences and their individu-ality. Constant's political nominalism is a reaction against the revolutionary rhetoric which placed abstractions of an idealized collectivity above individuals.[60] In spite of the impending skepticism looming in the background of his thought, Constant's social outlook is far more optimistic than his theories on language and the outlook of his novel would have allowed us to think. We are a far cry from the world of *Adolphe,* from the struggle and the fragmentation of the individual and his community.

Notes

1. Constant, *Adolphe,* trans. Tancock, 44, 50. I have frequently modified Tancock's translation and supplied my own emphases.

2. "We are not content with the life we have in us, in our own being: we want to live in others an imaginary life, and this is why we try to put ourselves on display [*nous nous efforçons de paraître*]" (Pascal, *Pensées,* ed. Brunschvicg, no. 147).

3. For an analysis of the father's symbolic role in the text see Reichler, "Adolphe ou le texte enfoui": "The son is therefore forced, by the language he speaks, the money he spends and the love he profanates, to reenact and to expiate the father's fault and the contradiction carried by his speech" (34).

4. In his *Réflexions sur la tragédie,* Constant stresses the molding action of society on the individual, the formative power of circumstances on the individual character: "It is evident that this action of society is the most important thing in human life. Everything stems from there; everything comes to an end there; to this unacknowledged, unknown predetermination we have to submit, if we do not want to be broken. . . . Passion and character are mere accessories; society's action is what counts mostly" (*Oeuvres,* 910). Constant seems no longer to believe in the Enlightenment atomistic view of a society composed of autonomous individuals; however, he also seems to deplore the emergence of a holistic view, whereby society predetermines the space, the possibilities, and the forms of individual action. In this tension, in this awareness of irreconcilable contradictions, lies the power of Constant's thought.

5. Constant, *Journaux intimes,* 21 November 1804, in *Oeuvres,* 378.

6. See Mortier, "Constant et les Lumières." Constant's reading of eighteenth-century authors was "directly influenced by the political evolution of revolutionary France seen through the eyes of a moderate." Like Tocqueville, he saw in the phenomenon of atheism the abolition of moral and spiritual values, as well as a milieu favorable to the development of an attitude of servile submis-

sion to any political power. Napoleon's opportunistic politics of interest seemed to him the direct product of the "morality of self-interest" of Diderot, Helvétius, and d'Holbach. Constant shared that vision with those liberal thinkers who, while rejecting the dogmatism of catholic religion, according to Bénichou still "believed in the necessity of a constitutive revision of eighteenth-century philosophy." See *Le Temps des prophètes,* 45. This is not to say, however, that Constant rejected the basic tenets of the progressive Enlightenment: the critique of inherited privilege, the necessity of making political participation accessible to the greatest number. Constant's attitude toward the Enlightenment is complex, and it evolves throughout his career. See Holmes, *Benjamin Constant and the Making of Modern Liberalism.*

7. Constant, *Journaux intimes,* in *Oeuvres,* 378.

8. As Starobinski pointed out, a tendency to indifference and a form of nihilism characterized Constant's youth. See "Benjamin Constant et l'éloquence," in Hoffman, ed., *Benjamin Constant, Mme de Stael et le groupe de Coppet.* There are a number of important contributions to the study of Constant's political and aesthetic thought in the same collection, most notably Kloocke, "Benjamin Constant et les débuts de la pensée nihiliste en Europe"; Mueller-Vollmer, "Politique et esthétique: l'idéalisme concret de Benjamin Constant, Guillaume de Humboldt et Mme de Stael."

9. Constant, *De la Religion,* quoted in Starobinski, "Benjamin Constant et l'éloquence," 325.

10. Ibid.

11. *Adolphe,* ed. Delbouille, 246-47.

12. In the Tancock translation, *amour-propre* is translated as "self-esteem."

13. La Rochefoucauld, *Oeuvres complètes,* 421.

14. This dynamics between desire and obstacle is close to the structure Girard describes in his *Deceit, Desire and the Novel.* Girard stresses the fact that the mediator, the hidden figure behind romantic desire, has a metaphysical significance, being the degraded expression of transcendental authority. In Constant's novel, authority has vanished and the empty place of God is filled only with the desire to restore belief, a desire tempered yet by the awareness that, historically speaking, the time for belief is over. Both "mediator" and "opponent" manifest therefore the individual's need to define itself in relation to a source of authority which constitutes its point of reference.

15. Adolphe's behavior fits well with the Freudian notion of the oedipal triangle: the child desires the mother not only for his own satisfaction but also because she is a forbidden object—between her and the child, the father intrudes as a rival and as a figure of authority which invests the object he possesses with boundless value. These two qualities, the object's use and its unavailability, are two essential components of desire; once one of them disappears, desire can no longer subsist.

16. See, for instance, Fairlie, "L'individu et l'ordre social dans *Adolphe.*" Instead of looking for a mimetic representation of social conflicts in the novel, Fontana, in her admirable book *Benjamin Constant and the Post-Revolutionary Mind,* rightly points out that *Adolphe* "appears on first reading very remote from any political theme, and even from any recognizable socio-historical background. . . . However, it was through this novel that Constant succeeded in giving full expression to his understanding of the complexity of the modern condition; it was his literary imagination which best enabled him to explore the difficulties in the exercise of that personal liberty which post-revolutionary society promised to its members" (120).

17. Hume, *A Treatise of Human Nature,* 261.

18. See Holmes, *Benjamin Constant*: "Constant's political thought can be understood as an original response to a crisis in the concept and experience of freedom. Reflecting on the Revolution, Constant always stressed that arbitrary imprisonment and judicial butchery had been justified in the name of liberty. Although he stubbornly refused to attenuate his commitment to liberty and democracy, he was forced, as his eighteenth-century predecessors were not, to incorporate into his thinking some reaction to bloody tyranny publicly justified by an appeal to freedom and popular sovereignty" (24).

19. Constant, *De la Religion,* 1: 46, quoted in Poulet, *Etudes sur le temps humain,* 1: 271.

20. Nietzsche will also dwell on the sense of emptiness experienced after victory, but he will come to conclusions opposite to those of Constant: "The value of a thing sometimes lies not in what one attains with it, but in what one pays for it—in what it *costs* us" (*Twilight of the Idols,* 92).

21. Constant, *De l'esprit de conquête et de l'usurpation,* in *Oeuvres,* 1095. This book is in many respects not typical of Constant's positions. Put together hastily from previously existing notes in 1814, after the defeat of Napoleon, it had a "disconcertingly Legitimist flavor" (see Holmes, *Benjamin Constant,* 16), which clashes both with his earlier and his mature defense of democratic participation in government. Constant, contrary to

Mme de Staël, was never an advocate of the hereditary right to the throne.

22. Nietzsche, *The Gay Science,* 347.

23. See Avni, "Dico vobis: préface, pacte, pari."

24. Locke, *An Essay Concerning Human Understanding,* 430, 431.

25. In his *Rhétorique de la lecture* Michel Charles criticizes the editor for his seemingly arbitrary choice among Adolphe's letters and memoirs in the fictional "box" containing Adolphe's papers. The editor may well have censored much of the publishable material, but his censure, however, suggests that more would only mean more of the same.

26. The horror of being talked about, the anxiety of gossip, is very well described by Barthes: "Gossip reduces the other to *he/she* and this reduction is unbearable to me. For me the other is neither *he* nor *she*; the other has only a name of his own, and her own name. The third-person pronoun is a wicked pronoun: it is the pronoun of the non-person, it absents, it annuls" (*A Lover's Discourse,* 185).

27. In *How To Do Things with Words,* Austin draws a distinction between "constative" statements that can be described as either true or false, and performative statements that can only be happy or unhappy. This basic distinction holds, even though Austin shows later on that it is not as clear-cut as we might have thought at first (see lecture 5).

28. This belief in the homeopathic function of masks and in man's ability to fully endorse, in the long run, the attitude he has been mimicking for a long time was a principle Constant applied to public life as well. Holmes writes that "Constant, at times, attributed a creative function to masks, lies and public feigning. . . . One of Constant's main arguments in favor of representative government ran as follows: periodic popular elections will force wealthy elites to *pretend* that they are concerned with the well-being of average and poor citizens. By dint of habit, this pretense will eventually become a genuine concern. Men are not psychologically robust enough to be consistent fakers. In social life, appearance has a tendency to become reality" (*Benjamin Constant,* 26). For a provocative analysis of the dialectic of sincerity and mask, see Felman, "A la recherche de la sincérité perdue."

29. Todorov, "La Parole selon Constant," 760.

30. "Consider what effects that might conceivably have practical bearing you conceive the object of your conception to have. Then your conception of those effects is the WHOLE of your conception of the object" (Peirce, *Collected Papers,* 5.422).

31. "There are no moral facts whatever. . . . Morality is merely sign-language, merely symptomatology: one must know already what it is about to derive profit from it" (Nietzsche, "The Improver of Mankind," *Twilight of the Idols,* 55).

32. Nietzsche, "Expeditions of an Untimely Man," *Twilight of the Idols,* 74.

33. See Constant's "Of Ancient and Modern Liberty": "The danger of modern liberty is that, absorbed in the enjoyment of our private independence and in the pursuit of our particular interests, we will renounce too easily our right to share in political power" (Constant, "Of Ancient and Modern Liberty," quoted in Holmes, *Benjamin Constant,* 19). The weakness and indifference of individuals is, according to Constant, the source of oppressive and totalitarian governments.

34. *Adolphe,* ed. Delbouille, 247.

35. For an analysis of the tension between particularity and generality in *Adolphe* see Scott, "The Romanticism of *Adolphe.*"

36. Leiris's *L'Age d'homme,* which is composed of fragments, is one of the numerous examples of experiments with form in the autobiographical genre. For a discussion of these aspects of the genre see Lejeune, *Le Pacte autobiographique* and *Je est un autre.* Such a "mobility" of the self affects the process of narration, introducing a fundamental cleavage between the past self—the object of narration (*énoncé*)—and the present self who, here and now, in the process of narration, gradually discovers and unravels his past self. Since the self is a relational entity, his identity shifting according to his position within a structure of interaction, he cannot but be affected and transformed by the narrative act. Constant is well aware of the fact that the object is inseparable from the point of view when he writes in his journal, "the object that escapes us is by necessity entirely different from the object that pursues us." Lejeune speaks of "cleaved subject," and of a "fundamental split that turns the speaking subject into a vanishing being" (*Le Pacte autobiographique,* 38). The elusiveness of the referent of first-person narrative confirms the difficulty of giving a content to the self.

37. See Genette, "Vraisemblance et motivation," in *Figures II,* and Todorov, "La Lecture comme construction," in *Les Genres du discours.*

38. The narrative role and the use of the maxim and aphorism are signs of Constant's indebtedness to

the seventeenth-century moralist tradition, which informs both his style and his conception of the self. For a discussion of the role of the maxim in the novel see Fairlie, "The Art of Constant's *Adolphe*": "Few authors have at the same time so challenged the criteria of abstract judgement, and yet exercised judgement so relentlessly, have more mistrusted general terms, yet been more irresistibly drawn to the maxim, the epigram, the precise formula" (37). For a good stylistic analysis of the aphoristic form see also Colette Coman, "Le Paradoxe de la maxime dans *Adolphe.*"

39. When discourse strikes a blow, it resorts to generality: "And so we took turns at attacking each other with indirect remarks, only to retreat afterwards into general protestations and vague self-justifications, finally relapsing into silence" (87). Or again: "Soon she began expressing in devious ways certain general observations which were really nothing less than personal attacks [*idées générales . . . attaques particulières*]" (100).

40. Constant, *Journaux intimes,* 18 December 1804, in *Oeuvres,* 394.

41. While in the English translation *mélange*—which connotes both "variety" and "combination"—appears under a variety of synonyms, I have replaced it by one word.

42. See also Marivaux, *Le Spectateur Français,* 17e feuille, 12 May 1723, in *Journaux et oeuvres diverses de Marivaux,* 207: "I am seventy-four at the moment I am writing this: I have been living for a long time. A long time? alas! I am certainly mistaken, because to be precise, I only live in this present instant, which is now passing. Another replaces it, which is already gone, where I lived, it is true, but where I no longer am, and it is as if I had never been there. Could not I say, then, that my life has no duration, but only beginnings? Young and old, we would all have the same age." Consciousness of the present is the only certainty, as time and consciousness are dissolved into their atomistic elements, a succession of instants that do not form any synthesis, since the present moment is replaced by the next, which erases the memory of the previous one. Marivaux's paradoxical consequences ("young and old, we would all have the same age") seem to anticipate Borges's own paradoxical conclusions in "A New Refutation of Time," in *Other Inquisitions 1937-1952.*

43. Hume, *A Treatise of Human Nature,* 253.

44. Hume's conception of a person is definitely nominalistic: nothing can unify or turn the atomistic elements that compose the self into a single entity. Continuity itself is not an objective fact; rather it is to be attributed solely to the works of imagination which give our thoughts an imaginary unity. In our mind we get the impression that a thought is motivated by one immediately preceding it (contiguity or metonymy) and resembles the first (resemblance or metaphor) thanks to the work of memory which, "raising the images of past perceptions," lets us imagine a resemblance between contiguous thoughts. Among these three rules, only the first, causation, is of a logical nature; the other two are rhetorical. But then again, causation itself is a notion that Hume has seriously put into question elsewhere and which he attributes to the sole effects of the imagination: the link of causation is nothing but the succession of two events contiguous to each other, a succession continuously and regularly repeated: "Even the union of cause and effect, when strictly examined, resolves itself into a customary association of ideas" (*Treatise,* 73).

45. Rousseau, *Second discours,* in *Oeuvres complètes,* 3: 150.

46. Locke, *Essay,* 410.

47. "Men would in vain heap up Names of particular Things, that would not serve them to communicate their Thoughts. . . . The Names of them could not be significant or intelligible to another, who was not acquainted with all those very particular Things, which had fallen under my Notice" (Locke, *Essay,* 409).

48. Ibid., 410.

49. Borges, "Funes the Memorious," in *Labyrinths,* 65-66.

50. Locke, *Essay,* 595.

51. Constant, *De la religion,* quoted in Fairlie, "The Art of Constant's *Adolphe,*" p. 35.

52. Constant, *Principes de politique,* quoted in Fairlie, "The Art of Constant's *Adolphe,*" p. 35. See also Voltaire, in a fragment on language: "There is no language complete enough as to be able to express all our ideas and all our sensations; their nuances are too imperceptible and too numerous. Nobody can communicate with precision the intensity of the feeling that affects him. We are compelled, for instance, to designate under the general name of *love* and *hate* a thousand different forms of love and hate; this also goes for our pleasures and our pains. All languages are as imperfect as we are" (quoted in the 1860 Hachette edition of the *Dictionnaire Philosophique* 3: 98).

53. We hear in *Adolphe* an echo of Rousseau's condemnation, in *Emile,* of society's molding action, of its denaturing and transmuting the individual

from its original shape: "Our entire wisdom is nothing but servile prejudices; all our customs are subjugation, confinement and restraint. Civil man is born, lives, and dies in slavery: at his birth he is sewn into swaddles; at his death he is nailed into a coffin; as long as he keeps a human face, he is chained by our institutions" (*Emile*, in *Oeuvres complètes*, 4: 253).

54. Constant, *Mélanges de littérature et de politique,* in *Oeuvres,* 867.

55. Letter to Prosper de Barante, September 18, 1808, in "Lettres de B. Constant à Prosper de Barante," 266.

56. Tocqueville, *De la démocratie en Amérique,* 2: 89.

57. Letter to his cousin Rosalie, June 4, 1811, *Correspondence de Benjamin et Rosalie de Constant,* 143.

58. Constant, *De l'esprit de conquête,* in *Oeuvres,* 984. In Montesquieu's *Persian Letters,* letter 63, Rica writes to Usbek: "With us everyone's character is uniformly the same, because they are forced. People do not seem what they are, but what they are obliged to be. Because of that enslavement of heart and mind, nothing is heard but the voice of fear, which has only one language, instead of nature, which expresses itself so diversely and appears in so many different forms" (129-30).

59. Constant, *De l'esprit de conquête,* in *Oeuvres,* 1059.

60. See Largeault, *Enquête sur le nominalisme*: "Nominalism seems to be linked to a choice of civilization: it is strictly connected to a political and social philosophy which states that individual preferences must count" (34).

Works Cited

Apel, Karl-Otto. *C. S. Peirce, From Pragmatism to Pragmaticism.* Trans. John Michael Krois. Amherst: University of Massachusetts Press, 1981.

Arnauld, Antoine, and Pierre Nicole. *La Logique ou l'art de penser.* Ed. Pierre Clair and François Girbal. Paris: Vrin, 1981.

Auerbach, Erich. *Scenes from the Drama of European Literature.* Minneapolis: University of Minnesota Press, 1984.

Austin, John. *How To Do Things with Words.* 2d ed. Ed. Marina Sbisà and J. O. Urmson. Cambridge, Mass.: Harvard University Press, 1981.

Avni, Ora. "Dico vobis: préface, pacte, pari." *Romanic Review* 85, no. 2 (1984): 119-30.

———. *The Resistance of Reference.* Baltimore: Johns Hopkins University Press, 1991.

———. "Silence, vérité et lecture dans l'oeuvre de Louis-René des Forêts." *Modern Language Notes* 102 (Sept. 1987): 877-97.

Barthes, Roland. *Leçon inaugurale au Collège de France.* Paris: Publications du Collège de France, 1977.

———. *A Lover's Discourse.* Trans. Richard Howard. New York: Hill and Wang, 1978.

Bataille, Georges. *L'Erotisme.* Paris: Minuit, 1957.

Beckett, Samuel. *Texts for Nothing.* In *No's Knife Collected Shorter Prose. 1945-1966.* London: Calder and Boyars, 1967.

Bénichou, Paul. *Le Temps des prophètes.* Paris: Gallimard, 1977.

Benveniste, Emile. *Problèmes de linguistique générale.* Paris: Gallimard, 1966.

Blanchot, Maurice. *La Parole vaine.* Afterword to *Le Bavard* by Louis-René des Forêts. Paris: Gallimard, 1946.

———. *La Part du feu.* Paris: Gallimard, 1949.

Borges, Jorge Louis. *Labyrinths.* Trans. James E. Irby. New York: New Directions, 1964.

———. *Other Inquisitions 1937-1952.* Trans. Ruth L. C. Simms. New York: Simon and Schuster, 1964.

Butor, Michel. *La Modification.* Paris: Minuit, 1957.

Calvino, Italo. *Six Memos for the Next Millennium.* Cambridge, Mass.: Harvard University Press, 1988.

Cassirer, Ernst. *The Philosophy of the Enlightenment.* Princeton, N.J.: Princeton University Press, 1951.

Chardin, Chevalier de. *Voyages en Perse.* 5 vols. Ed. L. Langlès. Paris, 1811 [orig. ed. 1687].

Charles, Michel. *Rhétorique de la lecture.* Paris: Seuil, 1977.

Coman, Colette. "Le Paradoxe de la maxime dans *Adolphe.*" *Romanic Review* 73 (1982): 196-208.

Condillac, Etienne Bonnot de. *Essai sur l'origine des connaissances humaines.* 1746. Paris: Galilée, 1973.

Conroy, Peter V. "Image claire, image trouble dans l'*Histoire d'une Grecque moderne* de Prévost." *Studies on Voltaire and the Eighteenth Century* 217 (1983): 187-97.

Constant, Benjamin. *Adolphe.* Trans. Leonard Tancock. Harmondsworth, Eng.: Penguin Books, 1964.

———. *Adolphe.* Ed. Paul Delbouille. Paris: Société d'Edition "Les Belles Lettres," 1977.

————. *Correspondence de Benjamin et Rosalie de Constant.* Ed. Alfred and Suzanne Roulin. Paris: Gallimard, 1955.

————. *De l'esprit de conquête et de l'usurpation.* In *Oeuvres,* 951-1062.

————. *Journaux intimes.* In *Oeuvres,* 225-789.

————. "Lettres de B. Constant à Prosper de Barante." *Revue des deux mondes* 34 (1906): 240-72.

————. *Mélanges de littérature et de politique.* In *Oeuvres,* 801-97.

————. *Oeuvres.* Ed. Alfred Roulin. Paris: Gallimard, 1957.

Dante. *The Banquet.* Trans. Christopher Ryan. Saratoga, Calif.: Anma Libri, 1989.

De Brosses, Charles. *Traité de la formation méchanique des langues.* 2 vols. Paris: Terrelonge, 1801.

De Man, Paul. *Allegories of Reading.* New Haven, Conn.: Yale University Press, 1979.

De Mauro, Tullio. *Introduzione alla Semantica.* Bari: Laterza, 1965.

Demoris, René. *Le Roman à la première personne: Du Classicisme aux Lumières.* Paris: Armand Colin, 1975.

Deprun, J. "Thèmes malebranchistes dans l'oeuvre de Prévost." In *L'Abbé Prévost: Acts du colloque en Aix-en-Provence, Dec. 1963.* Aix-en-Provence: Publications des annales de la Faculté des Lettres, 1965.

Derrida, Jacques. *Margins of Philosophy.* Trans. Alan Bass. Chicago: University of Chicago Press, 1982.

————. *Of Grammatology.* Trans. Gayatri C. Spivak. Baltimore: Johns Hopkins University Press, 1974.

Descartes, René. *Méditations métaphysiques.* Ed. Charles Adam and Paul Tannery. Paris: Garnier-Flammarion, 1976.

Des Forêts, Louis-René. *Le Bavard.* Paris: Gallimard, 1973.

————. *La Chambre des enfants.* Paris: Gallimard, 1983.

————. *Voies et détours de la fiction.* Paris: Fata Morgana, 1985.

Diderot, Denis. *La Religieuse.* Paris: Garnier-Flammarion, 1968.

————. *Lettre sur les aveugles.* In *Oeuvres philosophiques.* Ed. Paul Vernière. Paris: Garnier, 1964.

————. *Sur les femmes.* In *Oeuvres complètes,* vol. 10. Ed. Roger Lewinter. Paris: Le Club Français du Livre, 1971.

Dostoievski, Fiodor. *Notes from Underground.* Trans. Michael Katz. New York: W. W. Norton, 1989.

Douthwaite, Julia V. *Exotic Women. Literary Heroines and Cultural Strategies in Ancien Régime France.* Philadelphia: University of Pennsylvania Press, 1992.

Dufrenoy, Marie-Louise. *L'Orient Romanesque.* Montreal: Beauchemin, 1946.

Eco, Umberto. *The Role of the Reader.* Bloomington: Indiana University Press, 1979.

————. *Semiotics and the Philosophy of Language.* Bloomington: Indiana University Press, 1984.

————. *The Limits of Interpretation.* Bloomington: Indiana University Press, 1991.

Fairlie, Allison. "The Art of Constant's *Adolphe*: The Stylization of Experience." *Modern Language Review* 62 (1967): 31-47.

————. "L'individu et l'ordre social dans *Adolphe.*" *Europe* (March 1968): 30-37.

Felman, Shoshana. "A la recherche de la sincérité perdue." *Europe* (March 1968): 93-107.

Fénelon, François de Salignac de la Mothe de. *De l'education des filles.* In *Oeuvres.* Ed. Jacques Le Brun. Paris: Gallimard, 1965.

Fontana, Biancamaria. *Benjamin Constant and the Post-Revolutionary Mind.* New Haven, Conn.: Yale University Press, 1991.

Formigari, Lia. *Maupertuis, Turgot, Maine de Biran: Origine e funzione del linguaggio.* Bari: Laterza, 1971.

Foucault, Michel. "Débat sur le Roman." *Tel Quel* 17 (1964): 12-54.

————. *The Order of Things.* New York: Pantheon Books, 1970.

————. "The Subject and Power." *Critical Inquiry* 8 (1982): 777-95.

Genette, Gérard. *Figures II.* Paris: Seuil, 1969.

Gilroy, James P. "Prévost's Théophé: A Liberated Heroine in Search of Herself." *French Review* 60 (1987): 311-18.

Girard, René. *Deceit, Desire and the Novel.* Trans. Yvonne Freccero. Baltimore: Johns Hopkins University Press, 1965.

Gossman, Lionel. "Literature and Society in the Early Enlightenment: The Case of Marivaux," *Modern Language Notes* 82 (1967): 306-33.

————. "Male and Female in Two Short Novels by Prévost." *Modern Language Review* 77 (1982): 29-37.

Harari, Josué. *Scenarios of the Imaginary: Theorizing the French Enlightenment.* Ithaca, N.Y.: Cornell University Press, 1987.

Hoffmann, Etienne, ed. *Benjamin Constant, Mme de Stael et le groupe de Coppet*. Actes du deuxième congrès de Lausanne, 15-16 July 1980. Lausanne: Institut Benjamin Constant, 1982.

Holmes, Stephen. *Benjamin Constant and the Making of Modern Liberalism*. New Haven, Conn.: Yale University Press, 1984.

Hume, David. *A Treatise of Human Nature*. Ed. P. Nidditch. Oxford: Oxford University Press, 1978.

Jones, Shirley. "Virtue, Freedom and Happiness in the *Histoire d'une Grecque moderne*." *Nottingham French Studies* 29, no. 2 (1990): 22-30.

L'Abbé Prévost. Actes du colloque d'Aix-en-Provence, December 1963. Aix-en-Provence: Publications des annales de la Faculté des Lettres, 1965.

Largeault, Jean. *Enquête sur le nominalisme*. Paris-Louvain: Editions Nauwelaerts, 1971.

La Rochefoucauld, François, duc de. *Maximes*. In *Oeuvres complètes*. Ed. L. Martin-Chauffier and Jean Marchand. Paris: Gallimard, 1964.

Lautréamont, Isidore Ducasse. *Maldoror*. Trans. Alexis Lykiard. London: Allison and Busby, 1970.

Leiris, Michel. *Manhood*. Trans. Richard Howard. New York: Grossman Publishers, 1963.

Lejeune, Philippe. *Le Pacte autobiographique*. Paris: Seuil, 1978.

———. *Je est un autre*. Paris: Seuil, 1980.

Locke, John. *An Essay Concerning Human Understanding*. Ed. Peter Nidditch. Oxford: Oxford University Press, 1975.

Malebranche, Nicolas. *La Recherche de la vérité*. Paris: Gallimard, 1979.

Mallarmé, Stéphane. *Mallarmé: Selected Prose Poems, Essays and Letters*. Trans. Bradford Cook. Baltimore: Johns Hopkins University Press, 1956.

Marivaux, Pierre Carlet de Chamblain de. *La Vie de Marianne*. Paris: Garnier, 1957.

———. *Le Spectateur Français*. In *Journaux et oeuvres diverses de Marivaux*. Ed. Frédéric Deloffre and Michel Gilot. Paris: Garnier, 1988.

Maupertuis, Pierre Louis Moreau de. *Réflexions philosophiques sur l'origine des langues, et la signification des mots*. In R. Grimsley, ed. *Maupertuis, Turpot, Maine du Biran: Sur l'origine du langage*. Geneva: Droz, 1971.

Mauss, Marcel. "Essai sur le don." In his *Sociologie et anthropologie*. Paris: Presses Universitaires de France, 1950.

Mauzi, Robert. "Foreword" to *Histoire d'une Grecque moderne*, by the Abbé Prévost. Paris: Union Générale d'Edition, 1965.

May, Georges. *Le Dilemme du roman au XVIIIe siècle*. New Haven, Conn.: Yale University Press, 1965.

Miller, Nancy K. "*L'Histoire d'une Grecque Moderne*: No-Win Hermeneutics." *Forum Houston* 16, no. 2 (1978): 2-10.

Montaigne, Michel de. *The Essays of Michel de Montaigne*. Trans. M. A. Screech. London: Allen Lane, 1987.

Montesquieu, Charles-Louis de Secondat. *Persian Letters*. Trans. C. J. Betts. Harmondsworth, Eng.: Penguin Books, 1973.

———. *De l'esprit des lois*. Paris: Garnier, 1973.

Mortier, Roland. "Constant et les Lumières." *Europe* 467 (March 1968): 5-18.

Nietzsche, Friedrich. *The Gay Science*. Trans. Walter Kaufmann. New York: Vintage, 1974.

———. *The Genealogy of Morals*. Ed. and trans. Walter Kaufmann. New York: Random House, 1989.

———. *Twilight of the Idols*. Trans. R. J. Hollingdale. Harmondsworth: Penguin Books, 1968.

Pascal, Blaise. *Pensées*. Ed. Léon Brunschvicg. Paris: Garnier-Flammarion, 1976.

Pateman, Carol. *The Sexual Contract*. Cambridge, Eng.: Polity, 1988.

Pavel, Thomas. *Fictional Worlds*. Cambridge, Mass.: Harvard University Press, 1986.

Peirce, Charles Sanders. *Collected Papers*. Ed. Charles Hartshorne and Paul Weiss. 8 vols. Cambridge, Mass.: Harvard University Press, 1931-58.

———. *The New Elements of Mathematics*. Ed. Caroline Eisele. 4 vols. The Hague: Mouton, 1976.

Pirandello, Luigi. *Uno, Nessuno e Centomila*. Milan: Bemporad, 1926.

Poulet, Georges. *Etudes sur le temps humain, 1*. Paris: Plon, 1952.

Poullain de la Barre, François. *De l'egalité des deux sexes*. Paris: Fayard, 1984.

Prévost, Antoine-François d'Exiles, abbé. *Histoire du Chevalier des Grieux et de Manon Lescaut*. Ed. Frédéric Deloffre and Raymond Picard. Paris: Garnier, 1965.

———. *Histoire d'une Grecque moderne*. Ed. Alan Singerman. Paris: Garnier-Flammarion, 1990.

———. *Mémoires et aventures d'un homme de qualité*. In *Oeuvres de Prévost*, vol. 1.

———. *Oeuvres de Prévost.* Ed. Jean Sgard. 8 vols. Grenoble: Presses Universitaires, 1977-86.

———. *The Story of a Fair Greek of Yesteryear.* Trans. J. F. Jones, Jr. Potomac, Maryland: Scripta Humanistica, 1984.

Pruner, F. "Psychologie de la Grecque moderne." *Actes du colloque d'Aix-en-Provence,* December 1963. Aix-en-Provence: Publications des annales de la Faculté des Lettres, 1965.

Queneau, Raymond. *Bâtons, chiffres et lettres.* Paris: Gallimard, 1965.

Quine, W. V. O. *The Ways of Paradox.* Cambridge, Mass.: Harvard University Press, 1976.

Reichler, Claude. "Adolphe ou le texte enfoui." *Critique* 33.357 (1977): 131-45.

Ricaut, Sir Paul. *Histoire de l'etat présent de l'Empire ottoman.* London, 1671.

Richelieu, Armand-Jean du Plessis, cardinal de (attributed to). *Political Testament.* Trans. Henri Bertram Hill. Madison: University of Wisconsin Press, 1961.

Rorty, Amélie Oskenberg. *The Identity of Persons.* Berkeley: University of California Press, 1976.

Rorty, Richard. *Consequences of Pragmatism.* Minneapolis: University of Minnesota Press, 1982.

Rousseau, Jean-Jacques. *Essai sur l'origine des langues.* Ed. Charles Porset. Paris: Nizet, 1970.

———. *Oeuvres complètes.* Prepared under the supervision of Bernard Gagnebin and Marcel Raymond. 4 vols. Paris: Gallimard, 1959-69.

Rousset, Jean. *Narcisse romancier.* Paris: Corti, 1973.

Russell, Bertrand. *Mysticism and Logic.* New York: Longmans, Green and Co., 1921.

Sartre, Jean-Paul. *Situations IX.* Paris: Gallimard, 1972.

———. *What is Literature?* Trans. Bernard Frechtman. New York: Philosophical Library, 1949.

Scott, Malcolm. "The Romanticism of *Adolphe.*" *Nottingham French Studies* 6, no. 2 (1967): 58-66.

Sermain, Jean-Paul. "*L'Histoire d'une Grecque moderne* de Prévost: Une rhétorique de l'exemple." *Dix-Huitième Siècle* 16 (1984): 357-67.

Sextus Empiricus. *Against the Logicians.* Trans. R. G. Bury. Cambridge, Mass.: Harvard University Press, 1935.

Sgard, Jean. *Prévost Romancier.* Paris: Corti, 1968.

Singerman, Alan J. Introduction. In Antoine-François d'Exiles, abbé Prévost, *Histoire d'une Grecque Moderne.* Paris: Garnier-Flammarion, 1990.

Smith, Adam. *Considerations Concerning the First Formation of Languages.* Tübingen: Gunter Narr, 1970.

Smith, John. "Community and Reality." In Richard Bernstein, ed., *Perspectives on Peirce.* New Haven, Conn.: Yale University Press, 1965.

Sontag, Susan. *Styles of Radical Will.* New York: Farrar, Straus and Giroux, 1976.

Starobinski, Jean. "Benjamin Constant et l'éloquence." In Etienne Hoffmann, ed., *Benjamin Constant, Mme de Stael et le groupe de Coppet.* Actes du deuxième congrès de Lausanne, 15-16 July 1980. Lausanne, Institut Benjamin Constant, 1982.

Sterne, Laurence. *The Life and Opinions of Tristram Shandy, Gentleman.* Indianapolis: The Odyssey Press, 1940.

Tocqueville, Alexis de. *De la démocratie en Amérique.* 2 vols. Paris: Garnier-Flammarion, 1981.

Todorov, Tzvetan. "La Parole selon Constant." *Critique* 26, nos. 255-56 (1968): 751-71.

———. *Les Genres du discours.* Paris: Seuil, 1972.

Voltaire. *Dictionnaire Philosophique.* 3 vols. Paris: Hachette, 1860.

Patrick Coleman (essay date 1998)

SOURCE: Coleman, Patrick. "The Authority of Pain in *Adolphe.*" In *Reparative Realism: Mourning and Modernity in the French Novel, 1730-1830,* pp. 79-101. Geneva, Switzerland: Librairie Droz S. A., 1998.

[*In the following essay, Coleman maintains that a careful examination of the narrative structure in* Adolphe *provides evidence of Constant's preoccupation with theorizing the significance of pain and with conveying his ideas on pain within a realistic, albeit fictional, context.*]

Central to *Adolphe* is what Alison Fairlie has called "the logic and illogic of pain."[1] Haunted by the thought of hurting a woman who depends on him, Adolphe cannot bring himself to leave his mistress Ellénore. His scruples, which also spring from his own weakness of character, only make matters worse. Ellénore sees through to Adolphe's lack of love, but she cannot help relying on his protests of devotion. Finally, she falls sick and dies. Her death fills Adolphe with a guilt even more paralyzing than his earlier anxiety about being the cause of sorrow. Yet, it also confirms the source of that anxiety: Adolphe's belief that the harmful results of action confound ordinary expectations about the proportionality of cause and effect.

Constant's novel does not, however, present the problem of pain solely in terms of the hero's personal relationships. At each level of *Adolphe,* whether it be the hero's conduct, the shaping of the narrative, or the author's decision to publish, we find a tension between an anxious preoccupation with the effects of action and a countervailing skepticism about the urge to control those effects. For Constant, this is not only a moral, but a literary and political, problem. Can one provide a containing context for the analysis of *douleur* when the theme itself seems to resist any attempt to define its boundaries or to put it in a larger perspective? In *Adolphe,* pain seems to be endowed with its own authority, but in Constant's novel that authority does not provide a foundation on which to construct a system of positive values. On the contrary, the emphasis on pain seems to cut short any attempt to differentiate levels of action or meaning. I want to suggest that Constant's fascination with *douleur,* in which scruple seems to collapse into paralysis, is the starting-point for an active exploration of the conditions needed to build a richer and more stable symbolic world. *Adolphe* invites misunderstanding, however, because it is not cast in the lyrical mode of feeling favored by other Romantic writers; it favors the abstract language of reflection and analysis characteristic of the preceding century. Precisely because the idea of pain is so overwhelming, Constant needs that language to control the fiction through which he imagines a way beyond the obsession with control.

Constant began *Adolphe* in October 1806, driven by his rekindled passion for Charlotte Hardenburg to compose "un roman qui sera notre histoire."[2] He had met Charlotte in Brunswick in 1793, lost sight of her during the tumultuous years of the Revolution and his liaison with Germaine de Staël, and found her again in Paris in 1806, when the relationship with Staël had become a burden. From the available evidence it seems most likely that *Adolphe* was first conceived as a story with a happy ending: like Aeneas, the hero would, after many perils and temptations, find safe harbor at last.[3] Soon, however, the novel took another direction. Torn between Charlotte and Germaine, Constant found himself unable to extricate himself from a tangle of conflicting demands. He could not bring himself to end his long relationship with Mme. de Staël. As he wrote, the novel gradually gave way to an "episode" concerning "Ellénore," a second woman who prevents the hero from pursuing his goal.[4] As if the work of composition were destined to mirror the plot itself, Constant gave up on the original conception of the novel entirely, and the episode became an autonomous entity culminating in Ellénore's death. In Constant's journal, the last clear reference to *Adolphe*'s composition shows the author worried that this death is "amenée trop brusquement" (31 Dec. 1806). How long the story of Charlotte, which Constant took up again later in *Cécile,* remained in some way part of the novel, we do not know,[5] but whatever extension of the novel Constant envisaged very soon came to be located within and not beyond Ellénore's story.

Interest in the novel's genesis was originally sparked by scholars seeking the real-life models for the book's heroine, for in addition to Charlotte and Germaine, Anna Lindsay, another lover of Constant's from the beginning of the decade, provided some of the details of Ellénore's character. Over the years, the urge to identify Ellénore with a particular person has given way to an appreciation of the ways in which ordinary reality was transformed by the author's imagination into an autonomous work of art. But this shift in emphasis has never been complete. Because Constant does not discuss his book in aesthetic terms, and because the first-person from of the literary work resembles that of the journals, critics such as Francis Jeanson or Henri Guillemin could feel confident judging the book in terms of the motives they detected behind it.[6]

Constant's decision to adopt a more circumscribed form of narrative does, however, indicate an effort to distinguish the work from the context of its creation. Not only does the author call attention to the contingent, almost anonymous status of the book in the subtitle he finally adopted ("anecdote trouvée dans les papiers d'un inconnu"), but the frame-structure he added later seems designed to prevent the narrative from being read as the unmediated expression of its author. But the move from novel to episode lends itself to conflicting interpretations. For Paul Bénichou, it represents the moment when the book ceased to be a compensatory fantasy and gained independent reality as art.[7] Constant's concern about Ellénore's illness arriving "too abruptly" would mark the beginning of an effort to recreate, within the world of the text, some of the fullness of space and time lost when the "novel" became the "episode." On the other hand, the way Constant formulates that concern may suggest some uneasiness about imaginative creation itself. He could be admitting that his writing is an aggressive act situated on the same plane of reality as his arguments with Madame de Staël. If this were true, then deferring the heroine's illness, far from indicating the author's aesthetic and moral scruples, would only prove that Constant was no more able to confront his own impulses in art than he was in life.

Anxiety about the interpenetration of art and life is no doubt often a factor in literary creation when there is no tradition to authorize the act of writing. Like other French novelists before him, Constant wrote a preface to legitimize his work in a genre that was often criticized precisely for blending empirical and imaginative reality in ways that undermined the hierarchy of cultural categories. In the past, prefaces such as the ones Rousseau wrote for his novel could argue that the very fact of the book's coming into being in a sense justifies the author's having written it: the work has a reality of its own as undeniable as the reality it represents. In *Julie,* as we have seen, the complications of the prefatory dialogue derive from the author's desire, in the face of his own scruples, to articulate his sense of achievement. This is not the case with *Adolphe.* Having revised his text in such a way as to defer Ellénore's illness, Constant then deferred publication of his novel. Yet, when he did publish the book, it was at a moment when, far from being pushed into the background, his motives for writing could once again be questioned.

Ten years separate the first composition of *Adolphe* from its appearance in 1816. Like the author's other semi-autobiographical works, *Cécile* and *Le Cahier rouge,* it might well have remained uncompleted and unpublished during the author's lifetime had there not occurred the series of wrenching personal and political events that followed Constant's return to Paris after the Allies occupied it in 1814. Constant had opposed Napoleon's dictatorship from the start and published violent attacks against him during the last years of the Empire, but when the "usurper" escaped from Elba Constant surprised everyone by accepting his invitation to work on a new and ostensibly more liberal constitution. Overtaken by the events of the following year, he realized that his conduct was a poor recommendation in the eyes of the public. The lucid analysis of Adolphe's indecisiveness and abrupt changes of course Constant published in 1816 can therefore be seen as a kind of confession. This confession was personal as well as political. Constant's decision to remain in Paris during the Hundred Days was motivated in part by a sudden passion for Juliette de Récamier, and the suffering brought on by her unresponsiveness made him aware more strongly than before of the pain he might have caused others. As Pierre Deguise has suggested, Constant's desire to express his remorse probably contributed to his decision to publish *Adolphe.*[8] But the fact that Constant also wanted to position himself for a political comeback has led some observers to view Adolphe's confession more as an attempt to justify the author than as a true expression of regret or a disinterested clinical portrait.

Constant made a pointed effort, however, to anticipate his reader's objections. Adolphe's first-person narrative is followed by an exchange of letters between the "publisher" of the manuscript and an anonymous acquaintance of the unhappy couple. In a sentence that is often taken as the "the final summing-up of the book,"[9] the publisher, who judges Adolphe very harshly, bases his opinion on a principle formulated in the most general terms. "La grande question dans la vie, c'est la douleur que l'on cause, et la métaphysique la plus ingénieuse ne justifie pas l'homme qui a déchiré le cœur qui l'aimait" (209). At first sight, nothing could be more definitive than this declaration. But Constant's use of a simple co-ordinating conjunction leaves the logic of the sentence ambiguous. Ordinarily, one would read the first clause as a rhetorical preparation for the second, designed to underscore the gravity of what some readers might take to be only a sad fact of life. But the publisher's peremptory tone suggests that he is proposing an absolute standard of conduct, applied here to a particular case. One might ask how it could make sense to say that "la douleur que l'on cause" is *the* question in life. Since it is precisely Adolphe's obsession with the possibility of causing pain that brings about the story's unhappy ending, putting pain first is not always a sure moral principle. On the contrary, it may be a way of indulging in the metaphysics the publisher condemns. The logic and illogic of pain that informs Adolphe's behavior also contaminates the terms by which that behavior is judged.

Similar problems of judgment arise concerning the novel itself as a creative act. *Adolphe* is framed not only by the reflections of a fictional publisher but by a preface in which the author, speaking in his own name, discusses "le caractère et le résultat moral de cet ouvrage" (99). The immediate reason for inserting this preface was to deny there was any (harmful) reference to real people (especially Germaine de Staël) in this "autobiographical" novel. But Constant also defends his presentation of a story that offers the characters no way out. Such a story may dispirit readers looking for moral solutions, but placing the characters (and, implicitly, the reader) in a position that is "sans ressource" (103) is warranted by the gravity of the problem the author wants to expose. People do not realize how much suffering is caused by "la simple habitude d'emprunter le langage de l'amour et de se donner ou de faire naître en d'autres des émotions de cœur passagères" (101). Constant feels justified in publishing a narrative limited to an unflinching depiction of that pain.

On the surface, Constant's preface echoes the reasons earlier novelists gave in reply to the charge that the genre was an immoral or, at the very least, demoralizing one. But Constant is not concerned merely to preserve the moral integrity of his book; he wants it to serve a political purpose as well. The latter should not, however, be equated with the promotion of his own personal career. After all, Constant could have done so more surely with a less disturbing kind of story. In a draft version of the preface, Constant suggests a link between Adolphe's conduct in love and an issue of concern to all citizens: the strength of will that underpins political freedom. "Tout se tient dans la nature. La fidélité en amour est une force comme la croyance religieuse, comme l'enthousiasme de la liberté. Or nous n'avons plus aucune force. Nous ne savons plus aimer, ni croire, ni vouloir" (247).[10] If this energy is so crucial a value, then the author's determination to follow his fictional premise to its logical conclusion without mitigating its harshness is not only aesthetically excusable but politically laudable.

In the end, Constant did not include this passage in the published text. Perhaps he felt it protested too much on his own behalf. But there were philosophical grounds, too, for dropping so categorical a statement. The idea that freedom requires strength of purpose in the citizen is only one aspect of Constant's doctrine. The publisher's insistence on "la douleur que l'on cause" should remind us of a central tenet of Constant's liberalism. This is that the state's mission is above all to protect the citizens from harm, the harm they do each other but especially the damage caused by the state itself.[11] Far from advocating a politics of virtue driven by a Rousseauian general will, Constant was concerned to safeguard the citizen's freedom to develop his own idea of the good life, even if that idea led him away from active participation in public affairs.[12] Not that the two points of view are necessarily contradictory. The first focuses on the activity of the citizen while the second seeks to limit the power of the state. But there is an unresolved tension between the two ideas. It is not immediately clear how a neutral, pluralistic view of politics is to be reconciled with the claim that human life is all of a piece. Perhaps, as Charles Larmore suggests, that claim is simply one we have some reason to wish were valid. Although we know in our more lucid moments that this is only a wish, this may be enough for positive notions of love and liberty not to give way entirely to a purely negative ideal such as the avoidance of pain in all human action.[13] We have already seen how problematic such a reduction can be at the thematic level of *Adolphe.* The tension makes itself felt even more acutely at the level of authorial initiative. In 1816, Constant is both a citizen among others and a public figure who has played a major role in government and hopes to do so again. The publication of *Adolphe* constitutes an intervention on the stage of political opinion: it is less the work of a professional novelist than of a *publiciste* claiming a voice in the direction of public affairs. The authority of Constant's literary work is thus uncertain. In one sense it represents an assertion from above or outside the public it addresses; in another it presents itself as a contribution from within the internal dynamic of cultural life.

Constant's decision to surround Adolphe's first-person story with an elaborate frame structure suggests a further uncertainty about the availability, in the community of readers, of a context of understanding within which this tension can be absorbed. In the preface, he points to a pervasive weakness of will among his contemporaries, hidden behind a mask of vanity. Does *Adolphe* provide a remedy by assisting in its own interpretation? One would think that a novel that elaborated so complicated a hierarchy of narrative levels, and in which analysis and reflection feature as prominently as the

story itself, must furnish the tools to do so. But this is by no means clear. As Marian Hobson has remarked, Adolphe's reflections are expressed in the same mode of sober, generalizing statement we find in the framing remarks of the publisher, his correspondent, and the author himself.[14] The tone adopted by each of these speakers is also remarkably similar, so that although the emphasis may vary, each level of commentary seems merely to mirror the elements it frames. The most insidious manifestation of the logic and illogic of pain is, finally, the way it blurs crucial discursive and ethical distinctions. Personal allusions in a novel are imagined to have the same kind of moral consequences as an unhappy ending. More important, despite the multiplication of narrative levels, the book's instrumental value for the author and its broader cultural significance find themselves being weighed on the same scale.

So much, at least, can be inferred from the reception of *Adolphe* over the years. Like other "autobiographical" fictions, Constant's novel has often been taken as a direct reflection of the author's life. Indeed, the tendency to assimilate the novel to the motives that prompted Constant to write and publish it has persisted, to a degree—and with a vehemence—unusual in modern criticism. In the late 1940s, Jeanson and Guillemin's influential essays denounced the novel as an exercise in bad faith, as an "umbrella" designed to ward off the brimstone its author's conduct deserved. And it is not rare to find other such critiques, expressed with a harshness seldom applied to a comparably "self-centered" work such as *René.*[15] Maurice Blanchot and Georges Poulet defended Constant by showing how his self-examination attains a rare degree of subtlety and rigor,[16] but only in the 1960s did Alison Fairlie develop a sustained argument for an "aesthetic" view of the novel as a carefully-constructed and self-contained pattern of themes and linguistic relations independent of the man. Yet, perhaps inevitably, these analyses erred in the opposite direction by minimizing the extent to which *Adolphe* is intended to persuade as well as to portray. The difficulty of mediating between these aspects of the novel persists in more recent criticism, except for a curious reversal of positions. Now it is the formalist critics who express some skepticism about the possibility of distinguishing the work's artistic from its practical intentions. According to Michel Charles, for example, *Adolphe* blurs important boundaries by encouraging the reader to take "des mots pour des maux, et inversement."[17] Conversely, a more positive assessment has emerged among those who discuss the novel as a political statement. A brief review of these discussions is necessary if we are to avoid perpetuating the dualistic dynamic of earlier interpretations.

Constant's reputation as a political thinker and activist has risen remarkably in recent years, both in France, where the influence of Marxism has declined, and in

America, where the rise of neo-conservatism has driven liberals to rethink the premises of their thought. As might be expected, these shifts in opinion have been reflected in discussions of the Revolution, but just as remarkable has been the revival of interest in the Restoration, when, having successfully managed his re-entry into political life, Constant played a prominent role in the liberal opposition to Charles X. This aspect of his career has traditionally been slighted, especially in France, where the Restoration has usually been regarded as a period of reaction during which progressive historical forces could find no institutional expression without being hopelessly compromised. It is significant, in this regard, that Guillemin and Jeanson, two of *Adolphe*'s harshest critics, wrote their essays in the years following the Second World War, when the traditional view of the Restoration combined with the revulsion and guilt over French collaboration during the Occupation era to make a considered assessment of Constant's activity particularly difficult. In sharp contrast, scholars have now come to believe that the Restoration left greater room for maneuver in public life than did many earlier periods and that the prestige of the Revolution and the Empire had cast the succeeding years in undeserved shadow.[18] No longer is Constant's later career dismissed as an opportunistic compromise. Whatever its failings, it is now seen as representing a constructive attempt to increase the margin of freedom in a country slowly adjusting to constitutional rule. In this context, Constant's use of *Adolphe* to help start a new career acquires retrospective justification.

American liberals, on the other hand, accused by conservative "communitarian" thinkers of a sterile individualism, have looked to European romanticism as a movement which recognized legitimate aspirations to both individual independence and to group identity. Especially important for liberals are Romanticism's early years, when the Groupe de Coppet sought to bring together English principles of government, the German emphasis on national community, and the insights of French psychological analysis. Thus for Stephen Holmes, the author of a major reinterpretation of Constant's work, *Adolphe* is rooted in a sophisticated approach to political psychology.[19] As an example, Holmes points to a passage in the 1806 *Principes de politique* describing the revolutionary crowd. In contrast with the conventional image of popular fervor, Constant underscores the lack of real "enthusiasm" displayed for political leaders. Even as the crowd applauds them, it looks forward to "le moment où ils doivent tomber et vous apercevrez dans son exaltation factice un mélange bizarre d'analyse et de moquerie."[20] Constant's novel does not emerge from an apolitical preoccupation with the solitary individual. Although he argued passionately for what Isaiah Berlin has called "negative liberty"— the freedom not to have one's private life invaded in the name of the supreme value of political participa-

tion—Constant was concerned to foster a sense of commitment to the wider community. *Adolphe,* Holmes suggests, is not a symptom but a critique of liberal weakness. It offers "a commentary on the human emptiness of negative freedom."[21]

Holmes does not, however, consider possible ambiguities in the novel's presentation. On the contrary, ignoring the problem of the frame, he compares *Adolphe* favorably with *Werther* in this regard. "Goethe reserved for himself all limiting commentary on Werther's tempestuous passions. Constant, by contrast, granted an illusion-shattering clarity to Adolphe. That is why Adolphe was not allowed the self-dramatizing gesture of suicide and why there could never arise a cult of his protagonist for Constant to repudiate, as there did for Goethe."[22] But what has distressed some readers about *Adolphe* is not the seduction of extravagant gestures but an "arid" tendency to self-analysis that exaggerates the possible risks of commitment and thus provides another kind of cover for narcissism.[23] Giving Adolphe an "illusion-shattering clarity," one might reply, is an effective strategy only if the limiting commentary is embedded in a story that (like *Werther*) preserves the immediacy and vitality of experience. It misses the mark if reflection narrows the range and intensity of experience itself. Adolphe's lucidity becomes part of the problem, since it keeps him from acting to any positive effect. The question, therefore, is whether we can distinguish between the character's false lucidity and that the genuine lucidity of the author. Since the novel is written in the first person, the difference must manifest itself somehow in what Adolphe says as narrator of his own story.

This problem is squarely faced in Marian Hobson's analysis of *Adolphe*'s narrative structure. Constant claims in the preface to the second edition of *Adolphe* that the book is not centered on the character's intentions or actions, good or bad, but on a tragic situation whose terms are those of general, not individual, experience. Thus, there is an objective point of view incorporated in the story. Hobson points out, however, that "the tragic dilemma, when narrated in the first person, takes on an 'intentional' aspect." In other words, the story may appear "as the deliberate construction of a situation which will exempt that person from responsibility."[24] How can this contradiction be resolved? Hobson begins from her conviction that the novel's frame structure does not in fact compensate for the drift from tragic fate to personal responsibility. The fact that in analytic and stylistic quality these passages mirror Adolphe's own self-analysis robs the framing discourses of their power over the story. Indeed, their effect is all the weaker because they are not grounded, as Adolphe's story is, in a dramatically specified experience. But this does not mean the novel is incoherent. On the contrary, Hobson credits Constant with valuable insight into the limits of moral analysis. *Adolphe,* she writes, is a self-reflexive novel in which "the criteria for the analyzing and ordering of experience are built into the novel itself which orders that experience."[25] The absence of any sharp demarcation between Adolphe's discourse and that of the frame does not signal the collapse of necessary distinctions; it is designed to convey the insight that no language can master experience. Adolphe's tragedy may take on an "intentional" cast, but the source of the apparent intention is not in his—or any one's—consciousness. "The only sure criterion for events is . . . where they lead to." Hobson thus respects Constant's morality of effects while asserting that the novel does possess a symbolic coherence. On this view, *Adolphe* is self-reflexive in a special sense. It anticipates its own effects only to show more dramatically that the interconnection of theme and structure leaves an unresolved remainder beyond the totalizing reach of the text. The moral thrust of the novel lies in showing that affirming an all-encompassing moral discourse only undermines the moral authority of effects. The inward turn of *Adolphe* is a way of being faithful to the external world by deconstructing the subject.

Still, it is one thing to appreciate the unmasterability of experience. It is quite another not to want to control "la douleur que l'on cause," not just in one's practice but on the psychological level as well by developing some kind of imaginative framework to make sense of the problem. Like Holmes, Hobson does not consider the objection that the peculiar form of the novel may betray its theme. Here, Han Verhoeff's psychoanalytic approach can help us forge a link between the problem of intention and the prospect of pain. In *Adolphe,* he claims, we see "the *production,* the new and active reproduction of Constant's deep trauma."[26] He discusses in detail the similarities between Adolphe and his creator: the loss of the mother, the hostile dependence on other parental figures (including Ellénore, a substitute mother as well as a lover). Adolphe's aggressive behavior springs not only from a desire for independence, but also from a deep identification with Ellénore's vulnerable social position. Verhoeff finds the aggressive element in Adolphe's character to be present in the author as well, and, what is rare among defenders of the novel, recognizes that the presentation of Ellénore is conditioned by that aggression. Indeed, the value of *Adolphe* lies, very simply, in the way it faces the facts of the hero's (and the author's) situation. If the novel offers no resolution of its conflicts, it is because "reality, Adolphe's reality, demanded it be so."[27] From a psychoanalytic point of view, recognition of this reality is no mean achievement, given the obstacles presented by Constant's difficult childhood and the strength of his defenses.

But how does Constant reach this insight? Or, more precisely, in what sense can the novel be said to distance itself from the impulses it portrays? Whereas Holmes identified lucidity as the key factor and Hobson located the distancing agency in the novel's reflexive structure, Verhoeff speaks of the novel as a "sublimation" of the author's melancholy.[28] It is curious that while Verhoeff interprets Adolphe's actions according to a broadly Kleinian model of object-relations (emphasizing the role of good and bad maternal figures in defining a containing context for aggressive impulses), he should shift to the Freudian notion of sublimation to define the dynamics of literary creation. This shift allows him to fall back on an overly idealistic view of the work of art. The concept of sublimation fails to take account of a possible ambivalence in the author's relation to the text and defines the reader's relation to that text in terms of unexamined cultural premises: since the novel exists and possesses shapeliness of form and style, one can assume the author's inner chaos was overcome. A Kleinian analysis, on the other hand, would speak of reparation rather than sublimation in order to retain the connection with the conflictual world of object-relations evoked in the analysis of the character.[29] Retaining such a connection is, indeed, vital in view of *Adolphe*'s insistence on "la douleur que l'on cause" at every level of the work.

The key issue here is Ellénore's death. Verhoeff suggests that "Ellénore's death is the culmination of Adolphe's aggressivity and also of his identification with her."[30] This seems to suggest that Éllénore is a figure in Adolphe's fantasy and that by ending the novel with her death the author is being true to that fantasy. But responsibility for the shape of the story surely lies with the author, not the hero. Like more naive readers, Verhoeff conflates author and character, only for a different and critically more interesting reason. For it follows from his analysis that the successful coming to terms with reality that is the achievement of *Adolphe* depends on Constant's decision to kill of Ellénore. If Verhoeff hesitates to draw this conclusion, it is no doubt because it casts doubt on the novel's aesthetic autonomy. And yet this possibility must be faced.

Constant does in fact say, in the preface to the second edition, that he wanted to create a situation "sans ressource" (103). Once a man such as Adolphe, by nature sensitive but imbued with the thoughtless frivolity and self-centeredness of his age, begins an illicit relationship with a vulnerable woman such as Ellénore, there is no way to avoid catastrophe. "C'est de ne pas commencer de telles liaisons qu'il faut pour le bonheur de la vie: quand on est entré dans cette route, on n'a plus que le choix des maux" (103). This is Constant's reply to those who ask what Adolphe could or should have done to avoid the novel's unhappy ending, and it is an appropriate defense. Still, it is disturbing that Constant should have excluded any reparative gestures in the telling of that story.[31] Many readers would probably feel less uncomfortable if Constant had described Ellénore's suffering and death with greater pathos, or if her fate, like that of Staël's Corinne, were accompanied by the prospect of eventual redemption. But not only does Adolphe recount Ellénore's last days in almost clinical fashion, the characters in the frame story decline the opportunity to supply what is lacking in Adolphe's story. The publisher's correspondent, who claims to have known Ellénore, does say she was "digne d'un sort plus doux et d'un cœur plus fidèle" (207), but he supplies no details that would counterbalance Adolphe's judgment of her mediocre intelligence, emotional instability, or erratic behavior. Nor does the publisher, in his determination to berate Adolphe, praise the virtues of his mistress. On the contrary, he suggests that her effect even on women readers will be nullified by these readers' assumption that they are superior to her. No doubt the publisher, as the voice of social morality, could not champion too strongly the interests of a kept woman who is hardly a model of social rectitude. Nonetheless, his attitude turns out to be less generous than that of the supposedly callous Adolphe. It does nothing to redeem Ellénore's memory, although it may lead the reader to question the publisher's own moral authority. This is indeed to create a "situation sans ressource." But if we return in greater detail to the circumstances that shaped the novel, we shall find that it is precisely the refusal to surround Ellénore's death with comforting thoughts that allows Constant to include reparative elements in his book.

Constant's shift from novel to episode is understandable enough in personal terms, given the emotional paralysis of 1806. But one may ask why, even in later years, Constant did not expand the novel's scope. By 1816, the circumstances that originally led Constant to limit himself to the "episode" no longer obtained. Had he wished to do so, he could have recast the Ellénore story in such a way as to set it in a different and broader context, one in which her death—and the hero's conduct—could appear in a less scandalous light. But the revisions Constant did make neither mitigate the impact of Ellénore's death nor soften the hard edges of the work. I emphasize the possibility of expanding the text's perspective because Constant did precisely this in the political text he was composing while preparing *Adolphe* for the press. Although the *Mémoires sur les Cent-Jours* has often been linked with *Adolphe* as part of Constant's campaign to re-establish his reputation after the Restoration, the close relationship—and instructive differences—between the two texts have been overlooked.

Like *Adolphe,* the *Mémoires* emerged from a moment of crisis in which opportunity for action was combined with inexplicable paralysis and guilty betrayal. But what began as a brief **"Mémoire apologétique"** addressed to the King became an extended work of political discussion.[32] To *Adolphe* Constant added two short letters. The *Mémoires* also were cast in letter form: as open letters they were eventually serialized in the liberal journal *La Minerve* beginning in 1819. These letters take a wide-ranging look at the political scene of the preceding years. Constant explains his conduct in terms of the complex interplay of forces at work during the Hundred Days and the Restoration of 1814 that preceded them. By the time the *Mémoires* were published, Constant could also integrate into his story the struggles over the meaning of Louis XVIII's Charter in the second Restoration's Chamber of Deputies. By situating his actions in the context of a detailed historical analysis, Constant is able to give his conduct a greater degree of plausibility, and at the very least to argue that his actions were no more distorted by the circumstances or motives of the moment than those of anyone else.[33] Looking back on his career in the introduction he wrote for a second edition of the *Mémoires* in 1829, Constant could even echo the verdict of Adolphe's publisher in a remark on Napoleon's apparent conversion to constitutional rule in 1815. "Lorsqu'on a fait à l'espèce humaine un certain degré de mal, on n'a plus ni la faculté ni le droit de lui faire du bien."[34] That Constant clearly does not feel included in such a judgment shows he was satisfied that his own failings had not precluded him from repairing whatever damage he had done. Of course, it is easy to make such a judgment retrospectively, after being given a second chance. But Constant's conclusion reflects an attitude present in the *Mémoires* from the beginning, a basic confidence that, unlike Napoleon, he had always been working within a framework of persuasion and compromise, knowing the relativity of human affairs. The text's form supports the author's contention that whatever mistakes he may have made do not destroy the overall "fit" between his choices and the context in which they were made.

The contrast with *Adolphe* is striking. The reason for the difference is that although the novel was given its frame structure in 1816, its origin lay in Constant's situation in 1806: not only the personal entanglement with Mme. de Staël, but, just as important, the state of Constant's political thought at the time. The composition of *Adolphe* interrupted work on Constant's major political treatise, the *Principes de politique.*[35] This work would remain unpublished as such during Constant's lifetime, but he drew on it extensively for shorter, more directly polemical books published during the transitional years of 1813-1815. In fact, the novel's evolution provides a vital link between the early political philosophy and the parliamentary activism of the Restoration as reflected in the *Mémoires.* For the notion of authorial initiative and control in the novel's logic of pain may be linked with the problem of a controlling judgment in Constant's political philosophy. Since *Adolphe* is not explicitly a political novel, it dramatizes the issue in terms of personal relationships, in particular through its analysis of men's power over women. In his preface to the second edition of **Adolphe,** Constant warns men against taking advantage of women, who are characterized by "la noble et dangereuse faculté de vivre dans un autre et pour un autre" (101). Yet, because Adolphe is only too conscious of Ellénore's dependence, the admonition seems to miss the mark. Indeed, Adolphe's obsession with the dangers of controlling responsibility only exacerbates the situation. It certainly does not diminish the centrality of male agency, despite the value judgment attached to it. In fact, Adolphe's scruples merely reverse the cynical adage quoted by his father to justify men's casual treatment of women in sexual affairs: "*Cela leur fait si peu de mal, et à nous tant de plaisir!*" (118). In neither case is the woman's subjectivity (including the possibility of her own pleasure) granted any reality of its own.

Constant never did reconsider the problem of sex roles, but he was aware that his political liberalism would not offer an adequate response to modern civil society if it focused too much on the dangers of state power and defined the citizen in purely negative terms as an individual whose private space should not be violated. Constant also sought to develop a concept of self-realization that would involve more than a mechanical calculation of utility even though it would not appeal to any coercive metaphysical ideal.[36] What *Adolphe* illustrates is the difficulty of getting beyond utilitarian calculations of pleasure and pain when moral pain remains a purely abstract idea. We are told that Adolphe's outlook on life is indelibly marked by his witnessing, while still very young, the death of an older woman who had been his only confidante. This early experience impressed upon him with paralyzing clarity the futility of human endeavor. But what is opposed here is not brute reality and the purposes men invent for themselves. Adolphe is obsessed by "l'*idée* de la mort" (112, my emphasis). Despite his disenchanted tone, he has not accepted death as a fact. This is apparent in his behavior, which, far from manifesting a mature appreciation of the boundaries of human action, displays constant anxiety about the lack of any real boundaries at all. Adolphe notes that he was never made to feel the consequences of his actions, and in his preoccupation about the effect of his words on Ellénore we see how difficult it is for him to distinguish any degrees of pain. Ellénore he describes as a "lien" (140), an obstacle to his freedom, but she herself, by her unstable character and her precarious social status, does not appear to him in clear outline. The situation changes only when she falls ill. This is the turning-point of the story, and if the author worried about arriving at it too abruptly, it was because it was hard to see how this death could be at once the sad result of Adolphe's insensitivity and the solution to the author's problem with the issue of psychological and political control. For only when pain and death are felt to be facts separate from immobilizing or omnipotent fantasy will it be possible to effect a real change in the way authority is conceived.

Constant's literary strategy will therefore be just the opposite of what we find in Chateaubriand's *René,* which served as an anti-model for **Adolphe.** René, too, is characterized by the boundlessness of his desires, and Chateaubriand's explicit intention is to make him accept the limitations of "les voies communes."[37] But these common paths remain, in the end, as vaguely defined as René's desires were, and it is significant that Chateaubriand, instead of seeking to clarify these limits, immediately incorporates René's story into another vast, idealizing synthesis—the *Génie du Christianisme*—whose capacity to integrate that story has always appeared problematic. Rather than extend Adolphe's story in this way, Constant opens it up within the confines of the "episode" so that the hero's struggle with limits goes hand in hand with the author's coming to terms with the boundaries of his text. As in *René,* the dénouement of the story is precipitated by a letter the hero receives after the death of the woman closest to him. But whereas the announcement of Amélie's death remains external to the narrative, merely providing the occasion for René's telling his story, Ellénore's letter to Adolphe is crucial to the inner coherence of Constant's text.

During her final illness, Ellénore asks Adolphe to destroy a letter he would find among her papers after her death. The letter bitterly expressed all her resentment against him, but as Ellénore began to find inner peace under the influence of religion she changed her mind about attacking Adolphe in this way. Adolphe comes across the letter without at first knowing what it is. He reads a few words and then cannot help going on out of a need to know what Ellénore had said (204). In his narrative, the older Adolphe quotes excerpts from the letter, which form the concluding paragraphs of his story. Thus Ellénore is given the last word, for Adolphe does not reply to her anguished cry: "l'idée de ma douleur vous poursuit, et le spectacle de cette douleur ne peut vous arrêter!" (204).

Ellénore's words prepare the way for the publisher's judgment. As Michel Charles has pointed out, they serve as a bridge between narration and commentary in the novel,[38] so that by including them in the hero's own story, Adolphe seems at last to recognize the authority of a perspective other than his own. But there is one troubling fact: Adolphe quotes only parts of Ellénore's letter. It may appear, therefore, that he exercises a final control over what is said about him, allowing into his story only the kind of criticism he is prepared to accept.[39] Adolphe claims he lacks the strength to transcribe the whole letter, and of course it is not clear that he intended his manuscript to be published. But if his story is only a kind of journal entry designed for private use, why quote the letter at all, since he has it before him? If, on the other hand, his text is supposed to be a full confession—to a reader whom he knows has no other access to the events of the story—Adolphe's enfeebled state does not excuse his omission.

Before equating this evidence of compositional arrangement with the narrator's bad faith, we should look at the effect of quoting Ellénore's letter rather than reproducing it. By isolating these two passages from their (absent) context, Constant gives special resonance to the sentences themselves as independent entities, especially to the verbs of action that feature so prominently in them. The first passage ends with a three-part sentence emphasizing Ellénore's dependence on Adolphe's power to produce a decisive event. "Vous ne me la donnerez pas," she writes, referring to the strength she would need to leave Adolphe, "vous me ferez languir dans les larmes, vous me ferez mourir à vos pieds" (205). The second passage ends with the anaphoric repetition of the phrase "elle mourra," as Ellénore speaks of herself in the third person.

> Eh bien, vous serez content; elle mourra, cette pauvre créature que vous avez protégée, mais que vous frappez à coups redoublés. Elle mourra, cette importune Ellénore que vous ne pouvez supporter autour de vous, que vous regardez comme un obstacle, pour qui vous ne trouvez pas sur la terre une place qui ne vous fatigue; elle mourra: vous marcherez seul au milieu de cette foule à laquelle vous êtes impatient de vous mêler!

Both passages focus on Ellénore's death, not as part of a long chain of circumstances and attitudes (detailed, perhaps, in the rest of the letter), but as a single, decisive event. Ellénore's reference to herself in the third person is also significant (again, one assumes she does not do so throughout her letter). It is Ellénore's way of paraphrasing Adolphe's unspoken wish, but the impersonality of the formulation detaches it from the speech of any character. Understandably so, since at the moment we read this passage Ellénore has already died and Adolphe has ceased to desire her death (assuming that he could have consciously formulated such a wish before her actual demise).

Isolating the image of Ellénore's death in this way, far from suggesting an effort on the narrator's part to control the text, indicates for the first time the possibility of separating reality from fantasy, the integrity of the event from the endless regress of analysis that prevented Adolphe from coming to terms with the world. The omission of the rest of Ellénore's letter does not contradict this interpretation. Adolphe's pursuit of Ellénore and his subsequent inability to break off while there is still time derived precisely from an excessive identification with her. It is his own lack of clear boundaries that aggravated the pain of their relationship. The omission of part of her letter ironically marks the appearance of an initial boundary. The legitimacy of this omission, we

note, is implicitly endorsed by the censorious publisher himself. Although supplied by his correspondent with further documents concerning Adolphe and Ellénore, he withholds them from his text. Just as important as this isolation of Ellénore's words, however, is the way they open up the text from within the deliberately restricted boundaries of the "episode." The use of the future tense projects her speech beyond Adolphe's own story. Constant offers us Ellénore's death as a *prospect* that comes into focus for Adolphe only after the event. Adolphe begins the work of mourning Ellénore at least to this extent: as narrator he makes the words "elle mourra" his own. This perspective is incorporated in the text as a potential space. In this sense, Ellénore's death is not brought on "too abruptly" and it becomes possible for the author to distinguish between completing the book and closing it off by an act of arbitrary will.

Creating this space involves a reconsideration of the problem of *douleur*. If we reread the long, almost clinical description of Ellénore's final moments, what is perhaps most remarkable is that the word "douleur," which blurs the boundaries between physical and mental experience, is replaced by the expression "souffrance physique." The passage gains its special resonance from its insistence on the specific quality of her pain:

> Je vis, spectacle humiliant et déplorable, ce caractère énergique et fier recevoir de la *souffrance physique* mille impressions confuses et incohérentes, comme si, dans ces instants terribles, l'âme, froissée par le corps, se métamorphosait en tout sens pour se plier avec moins de peine à la dégradation des organes.
>
> (200, my emphasis)

The same perspective is underscored later: "on eût dit qu'elle luttait contre une *puissance physique* invisible . . ." (203).

Ellénore's death is thus hardly a Romantic one. As in the case of Emma Bovary, the author's refusal to indulge in compensatory rhetoric gives it the special dignity of sober precision. In Adolphe's comment, "ce fut alors que j'éprouvai la douleur déchirante et toute l'horreur de l'adieu sans retour" (203), we do find the word *douleur,* but in a context that balances the idea of boundlessness with the hero's first genuine experience of separation. Although he has not overcome the paralysis that underlay his conduct from the beginning, Adolphe can be said to experience Ellénore's death as a fact and not as a fantasy. He thus arrives at the point where it is possible for him to feel genuine guilt instead of being overwhelmed by his own split-off and projected impulses. If some uneasiness remains, it is because Adolphe's story ends here without that possibility being dramatized. But Constant's concern, finally, is not to develop the character (and in the light of Ellénore's fate, how could he show us Adolphe redeemed?). The differentiation that counts is that between author and book. The careful selection of terms tells us that Ellénore's death is now bound to the imaginative world of the text and no longer to the author's daydream—or nightmare. The literary work becomes an independent, impersonal entity which can no longer be viewed as an extension of the self.

The separation of fact and fantasy in the handling of Ellénore's death is only one of the ways this symbolic differentiation is achieved. In his final revisions of the novel, Constant added a passage that complements the difficult opening to the future at the end of the book by reinterpreting the past.[40] This is the paragraph inserted at the beginning of chapter four, at the point where Adolphe and Ellénore are enjoying their brief period of happiness. Like the selection from Ellénore's last letter, it is tenuously linked to its context and is characterized by rhetorical repetition. The narrator interrupts his story to dwell on the difficulty of portraying the magic spell of love.

> Charme de l'amour, qui pourrait vous peindre! Cette persuasion que nous avons trouvé l'être que la nature nous avait destiné, ce jour subit répandu sur la vie . . . ces heures rapides . . . cette gaieté folâtre . . .

The narrator rings nine variations on the theme, only to exclaim: "charme de l'amour, qui vous éprouva ne saurait vous peindre!" (139).

In his essay on time in *Adolphe,* Wolfgang Holdheim draws attention to the incongruity in Constant's use of the past historic ("éprouva") in a passage meant to celebrate the power of love to lift us out of ordinary time. He points out that at the end of the previous chapter Adolphe also used this tense to describe his feelings after Ellénore has given herself to him for the first time. After proclaiming: "Malheur à l'homme qui, dans les premiers moments d'une liaison d'amour, ne croit pas que cette liaison doit être éternelle!" (137), he betrays his own state of mind in those first moments by the form he chooses to express them. "J'aimai, je respectai mille fois plus Ellénore après qu'elle se fut donnée." According to Holdheim, this feature of the narrative "represents the onslaught of forgotten mutability . . . the clarion call of inexorable time."[41] Because character and narrator are so closely identified, however, what in another book would simply be an impersonal generalization takes on existential overtones. It would seem that not only the younger but also the older Adolphe, who is supposed to have learned something from his experience and to have undertaken the narrative to make up for his mistakes, is still unable to lift his feelings for Ellénore above the realm of disenchanted calculation. For Holdheim, these passages have "the grammatical and tonal effect of an icy shower."

True enough, but if we extend our perspective beyond the character and the narrator to the author's struggle with the composition of his book, Holdheim's argument can be turned against itself. As in the passage relating Ellénore's death, the real problem is not the mutability but the indeterminacy of experience, and it is only when some preliminary shape can be given to that experience that it becomes meaningful to speak of change. The rhetorical flourishes that at first sound like conventional Romantic efforts to transcend time are in fact designed to highlight by contrast the specific experience of time marked by the past historic. Contrary to what has often been said, this experience is not necessarily negative. On the contrary, to be able to say "j'aimai" or "j'éprouvai" is, in the world of *Adolphe,* a difficult achievement. The *passé simple* protects the feelings named in this way from the endless reconsideration and reinterpretation that characterizes Adolphe's behavior. Elsewhere in the novel, Constant speaks of wounding words between the lovers that, once uttered, cannot be taken back. By the same token, however, Adolphe's avowals of love, once cast in such definite form, cannot be reabsorbed into the flux of his self-reflection. The feeling for Ellénore is given a definition it would not otherwise have.

It is true that the simple past is standard when narrating past events in French, and so normally carries no exceptional meaning. But Constant is not by nature a novelist, nor indeed is he at ease with any sustained narrative. As can be seen from the long gestation of his major works, he had great difficulty in giving his ideas an overall form—most famously, he hesitated for many years between a narrative and a systematic presentation of his work on religion—and in letting go of the work once he had done so. That he completed and published *Adolphe* is thus remarkable. The defensive structure of pre-emptive judgments he erected around the novel suggests how uneasy he felt about using a tragic love story for what would inevitably be seen as personal gain. But although it has some basis in fact, that reproach is really justified only from the perspective of an impoverished and polarized culture, whose narrow definition of "fact"—and complementary exaltation of transcendent moral norms—is precisely what Constant is struggling to repair through his art. The use of the *passé simple* in this passage is incongruous only if we assume that *Adolphe* should conform to the more congenial model of Romantic irony represented by, say, Friedrich Schlegel's *Lucinde,* published just a few years earlier (1799), and strive to transcend experience through reflection. *Adolphe* should be acknowledged instead for its effort to find a way to give experience greater symbolic resonance while acknowledging and remaining within the bounds of the ordinary world. There is, perhaps, something paradoxical about such a use of the fictional imagination, and it may be that in some ways *Adolphe* works against its own intentions, but such is the underlying logic of its composition.

Notes

1. Alison Fairlie, "*Adolphe*: the stylization of experience," in her *Imagination and Language. Collected essays on Constant, Baudelaire, Nerval, and Flaubert* (Cambridge: Cambridge UP, 1981), 11.

2. Benjamin Constant, *Journaux intimes,* in *Œuvres,* ed. Alfred Roulin (Paris: Gallimard, Bibliothèque de la Pléiade, 1957), 30 October 1806. References to this edition of the journals will be by date.

3. Claude Reichler, "*Adolphe* et le texte enfoui," *Critique* 33 (1977), 131-45, discusses Constant's references to Virgil at key moments in his work.

4. *Journaux intimes,* 12 November 1806.

5. The scholarly debate on the issue is reviewed by Paul Delbouille in his *Genèse, structure et destin d'"Adolphe"* (Paris: Les Belles lettres, 1971) and in his critical edition of *Adolphe* (Paris: Les Belles lettres, 1977), both of which contain extensive bibliographies. References to *Adolphe* will be to the Delbouille edition. Page numbers will be included parenthetically in the text.

6. Henri Guillemin, "Adolphe ou le parapluie de Benjamin," in *Éclaircissements* (Paris: Gallimard, 1961), 87-147; Francis Jeanson, "Benjamin Constant ou l'indifférence en liberté," in *Lignes de départ* (Paris: Seuil, 1963), 7-36 (originally published in 1948).

7. Paul Bénichou, "La Genèse d'*Adolphe,*" in *L'Écrivain et ses travaux* (Paris: Corti, 1967), 116.

8. Pierre Deguise, *Benjamin Constant méconnu: le livre "De la Religion"* (Geneva: Droz, 1966), 198.

9. Fairlie, 11.

10. A similar statement appears in Constant's unpublished political treatise of 1806, now published as *Les "Principes de politique" de Benjamin Constant,* ed. Étienne Hofmann (Geneva: Droz, 1980) 2: 147: "toutes les facultés de l'homme se tiennent."

11. *"Principes de politique"* 2: 369: "L'autorité n'a qu'une seule chose à faire, c'est que les hommes ne se nuisent pas. S'ils ne se nuisent pas, ils se servent."

12. Constant, "De la liberté des anciens comparée à celle des modernes" (1819), in Benjamin Constant, *De la liberté chez les modernes,* ed. Marcel Gauchet (Paris: Livre de poche, 1980), 491-515. An English translation is available in Benjamin Constant, *Political Writings,* trans. and ed. Biancamaria Fontana (Cambridge: Cambridge UP, 1988), 309-28.

13. Charles Larmore, personal communication. For an excellent general discussion of these issues, see Larmore's book, *Modernité et morale* (Paris: Presses universitaires de France, 1993).

14. See Marian Hobson, "Theme and Structure in *Adolphe,*" *Modern Language Review* 66 (1971): 306-14.

15. A recent example is Ghislain de Diesbach's *Madame de Staël* (Paris: Perrin, 1983).

16. Maurice Blanchot, "*Adolphe,* ou le malheur des sentiments vrais," in *La Part du feu* (Paris: Gallimard, 1949); Georges Poulet, *Benjamin Constant par lui-même* (Paris: Seuil, 1968).

17. Michel Charles, "Adolphe ou l'inconstance," in *Rhétorique de la lecture* (Paris: Seuil, 1977), 246.

18. See Tzvetan Todorov, "La liberté et les lettres sous la Restauration," *Commentaire* 11 (1988): 497-504; F. W. J. Hemmings, *Culture and Society in France 1789-1848* (Leicester: Leicester UP, 1987); Paul Bénichou, *Le Temps des prophètes. Doctrines de l'âge romantique* (Paris: Gallimard, 1977); and the historical works of Pierre Rosenvallon.

19. Stephen Holmes, *Benjamin Constant and the Making of Modern Liberalism* (New Haven: Yale UP, 1984). Cheryl Welch's *Liberty and Utility: the French Idéologues and the Transformation of Liberalism* (New York: Columbia UP, 1984) offers important historical background. See also Nancy L. Rosenblum, *Another Liberalism* (Cambridge, MA: Harvard UP, 1987). For a liberalism less centered on traditions of thought in the United States, see Charles Taylor, *Sources of the Self* (Cambridge, MA: Harvard UP, 1989), whose work has been extended by other Canadian scholars such as Will Kymlicka and James Tully.

20. *"Principes de politique,"* 2: 434.

21. Holmes, 13.

22. Holmes, 166-67.

23. See Philippe Garcin's well-argued "*Adolphe* ou les embarras de l'innocence," in *Partis-pris* (Paris: Payot, 1977), 131.

24. Hobson, 306.

25. Hobson, 314.

26. Han Verhoeff, *"Adolphe" et Constant. Une étude psychanalytique* (Paris: Klincksieck, 1976), 119.

27. Verhoeff, 74.

28. Verhoeff, 120.

29. See Melanie Klein, "Love, Guilt, and Reparation," (1937) in *Love, Guilt and Reparation and other works 1921-1945* (New York: Dell, 1975).

30. Verhoeff, 74.

31. In the 1806 manuscript, Constant distinguishes between what is "natural" and what is "artificial" by arguing that "il existe dans la nature [des choses] une force réparatrice. Tout ce qui est naturel porte son remède avec soi." *Les "Principes de politique" de Benjamin Constant* 2: 51 (cf. also 2: 316).

32. The initial text is reprinted as an appendix to O. Pozzo di Borgo's edition of Constant's *Mémoires sur les Cent-Jours* (Paris: Pauvert, 1961). Further details on the genesis of the *Mémoires* can be found in Norman King, "Après les Cent-Jours: trois lettres de Benjamin Constant écrites en 1815," *Cahiers staëliens* n.s. no. 25 (1978), 25-44.

33. This is also the assessment of Biancamaria Fontana in Benjamin Constant, *Political Writings,* 12.

34. *Mémoires sur les Cent-Jours,* 6.

35. See the *Journaux intimes* for 5 and 15 October 1806, where Constant expresses satisfaction with his treatise but says it needs a different organization to pull it together.

36. Many commentators would emphasize here the importance of Constant's remarks on self-sacrifice, which Constant suggests is the basis of human perfectibility. See "De la perfectibilité de l'esprit humain," written in 1805, in *De la liberté chez les modernes,* 586. Without denying the importance of this idea, whose connection with the rest of Constant's political thought would require an extended discussion, I believe it is of limited relevance to *Adolphe*.

37. Chateaubriand, *Atala/René/Les Natchez,* ed. Jean-Claude Berchet (Paris: Livre de poche, 1989), 343. See the analysis by Eric Gans, "*René* and the Romantic Model of Self-Centralization," *Studies in Romanticism* 22 (1983): 421-35.

38. Charles, 228; also Ian W. Alexander, *Benjamin Constant: "Adolphe"* (London: Edward Arnold, 1973), 17.

39. Charles, 221.

40. According to Delbouille (*Adolphe,* 228), the change was certainly made after 1810 and probably shortly before publication of the novel.

41. Wolfgang W. Holdheim, "The Culmination of Love in Benjamin Constant's *Adolphe,*" in *The Hermeneutic Mode* (Ithaca: Cornell UP, 1984), 62. The essay originally appeared in German in *Interpretation und Vergleich: Festschrift für Walter Papst,* ed. E. Leube and L. Shrader (Berlin: Erich Schmidt Verlag, 1972), 108-28.

Mark R. Blackwell (essay date spring 1999)

SOURCE: Blackwell, Mark R. "Constant, Napoleon, and the Mechanics of Political Action in *Wallstein.*" *Studies in Romanticism* 38, no. 1 (spring 1999): 63-88.

[*In the following essay, Blackwell studies the influence of Thermidorian scientific principles and their relation to Napoleon's policies on* Wallstein, *Constant's translation of Friedrich von Schiller's* Wallenstein.]

> Quoi! vous avez une nation entière pour levier, la raison pour point d'appui, et vous n'avez pas encore bouleversé le monde!
>
> ["What! You have an entire nation for a lever, reason for a fulcrum, and you have not yet overturned the world!"]
>
> —Georges Danton, *le Moniteur,* session of March 10, 1793[1]

> For the course in mechanics (then called "*Mechanique*"), the following materials were supplied: . . . a machine for studying central forces; an inclined plane; a machine for studying vibrating cords; a reflexion apparatus; an Archimedean screw; a Bullinger globe (*sic,* still mentioned in 1807 under *Glassware*) [probably the terrestrial globe of Louis Boulengier, 1518, according to Margaret Bradley's notes]; levers; tribometers for measuring friction; and a lever balance for demonstrating pulleys. . . . For *Géographie* and *Astronomie,* various globes were taken, and a small model of the Copernican system was made by Fortin.
>
> —list of materials requisitioned in 1794-95 for the *Ecole centrale des travaux publics,* from Margaret Bradley, "The Facilities for Practical Instruction in Science during the Early Years of the *Ecole Polytechnique*"[2]

> There were no honorary members [in the National Institute of Sciences and Arts established in 1795], though concessions to political expediency occurred. A prominent example was the election of General Napoleon Bonaparte in 1797, after the Italian Campaign, to the "Mechanics" section of the First Class.
>
> —Martin S. Straum, "Science and Government in the French Revolution"[3]

> A *Throne* the Δος που στω ["Give me a fulcrum (and I will move the world)"] of Archimedes—Poet Bonaparte—Layer out of a World-garden—
>
> —Samuel Taylor Coleridge, unpublished memorandum, 1802[4]

According to Bronislaw Baczko, the word "reaction" and its French derivatives, "réacteur" and "réactionnaire," first entered the political vocabulary at the end of the Thermidorian period and were used to describe a counteraction, a movement in response to another movement.[5] Baczko further notes that two other words, "revolution" and "progress," were earlier borrowed from scientific discourse to describe politico-historical events.[6] Baczko's association of the Thermidorian raid on the contemporary scientific vocabulary with such previous events would seem to suggest that the language of mechanical physics was always fertile ground for newly emerging political concepts and that the Thermidorian appropriation of "reaction" is of anecdotal interest rather than of a narrow historical specificity.

But manifold references to science, the manipulation of a scientific vocabulary, and the reorganization of scientific institutions in Thermidorian or, perhaps more properly and broadly, post-Jacobin France demonstrate that science was a central and privileged site of cultural and political contest in the period. In the wake of a Jacobin régime which was broadly anti-science and which dismantled much of science's institutional structure, many post-Jacobin intellectuals both reinvested in science and invoked scientific models and lexicons for political purposes. These post-Jacobin thinkers wanted to distinguish themselves from their dangerously unbalanced Jacobin predecessors, and they did so both by rebuilding a scientific establishment and by borrowing from science a suitably neutral and un-inflammatory political language.[7] These two projects were not necessarily complementary. On one hand, science was invoked because its destruction represented everything capricious, unstable, unpredictable about the Terror. On the other hand, science itself became a political player whose terms, concepts, and status as the repository of stable, universally agreeable ends could be manipulated for political gain.

The epigraphic references above are intended to hint at Napoleon's involvement in both the reconstruction and the manipulation of science after Thermidor. Napoleon in turn embodied the Thermidorian dream of political stability grounded in scientific principles and the nightmare of a science perverted by personal political motivations. This Thermidorian sensibility, and its changing relation to Napoleon, finds fullest expression in the early work of Benjamin Constant. Constant's early political writings deploy a rhetoric of balance 1) because it provides a model of dynamic stasis (action and reaction, for example) particularly suitable to Constant's argument for moderation, and 2) because its aura of scientific rigor creates an illusion of dispassionate objectivity that validitates Constant's political principles and his defense of the Convention. Constant's rhetoric manifests his Thermidorian turn-of-mind and reveals a broad reliance on the notion of "balance" as a cognitive paradigm shaping his political philosophy, swaying his shifting political allegiances, and influencing at least one of his artistic endeavors—the 1807 translation of Schiller's *Wallenstein*. This essay will explore what might be called the phenomenology of balance in Constant's work, with an eye towards ultimately presenting a "balanced" reading of Constant's *Wallstein*.

Thermidorian Science

The demarcation of a liminal political space poised between past and future is the quintessential Thermidorian fantasy. Such a fantasy involves the generation of a positive program from a politics "defined primarily in negative terms: neither Terror nor monarchy" (Baczko 408). According to Bronislaw Baczko, the Constitution of Year III documents the Thermidorian imagination, which "conceived of the political space at best in terms of a balance of powers and the exercise of sovereignty" but "was never able to conceive of or imagine that space as necessarily divided by opposing political tendencies, hence inevitably contradictory and in conflict" (Baczko 410).

Interestingly, these Thermidorian political fancies accompanied the very real rebirth of an organized science dismantled by revolutionary extremists (the Constitution of the Year III, in fact, made provision for the establishment of a National Institute of Sciences and Arts). Though the scientific rigor of the *encyclopédistes* and others may have had much to do with softening faith in the king and the pope and with providing intellectual kindling for the revolutionary conflagration, the hierarchical structure and elitism of an institution like the Royal Academy of Sciences of Paris could only stoke the waxing anger and resentment of practicing artisans excluded by its theoretical bent and sans-culottes for whom science and aristocratic privilege were inextricably linked:

> In the Revolutionary context, the Academy's position seemed anachronistic and arrogant. The National Assembly in 1790 and 1791 liberated the marketplace by dissolving guilds, industrial monopolies, and professional corporations. Yet privilege persisted in the world of ideas. The most implacable opponents of academic privilege came to power or to prominence because of the circumstances of revolution.[8]

Hence such outbursts as Claude-Antoine Rudel's to the National Convention in December of 1792: "Does it matter to the Republic that a number of citizens busy themselves with lofty speculations?" Or Durand-Maillane's the same month:

> Perhaps we are so corrupted only because we are too learned. . . . To be happy, the French people need only those sciences necessary for the attainment of virtue. . . . It is quite strange that, under the pretext of science and enlightenment, we propose that the nation create, at its own expense, a particular and permanent station for one class of citizens; and what citizens? The men most capable of dominating public opinion by directing it, because there is a superstition about those we call savants, as there was for kings and priests . . .[9]

Or that of a Jacobin deputy to the Convention in 1793:

> Free nations have no need of a caste of speculative savants. Pure science . . . in the end proves a poison which infects, weakens, and destroys a republic.
>
> (Straum 105)

Orders to execute scientists like Bailly, Lavoisier, and Condorcet (who actually took his own life while incarcerated), the imprisonment of numerous others (many of whom were not released until 9 Thermidor), and the abolishment of the Academy of Sciences followed quickly.[10]

The heavy emphasis on "class" or "caste" and the finely drawn distinctions between "pure science" and the health and virtue of the republic demonstrate that the attacks on science excerpted above were likely motivated less by deep-seated qualms about speculative science and the pursuit of esoteric knowledge than by the social and political circumstances that made members of science academies the beneficiaries and supporters of vast patronage systems.[11] As Roger Hahn contends in his work on the Paris Academy of Sciences, "when partisan politics made its way into the academic sanctum, it was by way of disagreements over the organizational structure of the institution and its relation to the two centers of governmental authority rather than by its occupational concerns" (Hahn 166-67).

Therefore, despite a general anti-science climate which culminated in the abolition of France's scientific institutions, "partly as survivals of the old regime, partly, too, in a fit of vulgar, sentimental petulance against the hauteur of abstract science, the impersonal tyranny of mathematics, the superiority of the scientist over the artisan," not all scientists suffered during the Jacobin ascendancy.[12] Many later encyclopedists, who worked on copycat editions or extensions like that of Panckoucke, were protected by their associations with Jacobin extremists and lived to help organize the *Ecole polytechnique* (men like Monge, Fourcroy, Guyton de Morveau, and Chaussier).[13] In fact, the most esoteric of the volumes in Panckoucke's *Encyclopédie,* those on physics and chemistry, appeared during the Terror, no doubt made more palatable for Jacobin authorities by the Jacobinism of their authors, Monge and Fourcroy. But though some scientists, even theoretically abstruse ones like Monge and Fourcroy, participated in Jacobin politics and seem not to have been affected by anything like a wave of anti-science sentiment in Jacobin France, their interest in pure scientific speculation had to be subordinated to the practical needs of the Republic. Panckoucke's anxiety about the fate of his *Encyclopédie* during the Revolution—an anxiety not merely about the difficulties of printing and marketing a big book during a time of social and political upheaval, but also about its reception among Revolutionary extremists—testifies to a Jacobin attitude toward science and "enlightenment" different from that after Thermidor, as does the fate of most scientists and science academies during the Terror. Indeed, "pure science" and encyclopedism were still popularly linked to pre-Revolutionary privilege as late as 9 Thermidor.[14]

While science at the height of the Revolution is, at best, acceptable only insofar as it contributes to the health of the Republic and the spread of an independently conceived Republican virtue, popular post-Terror rhetoric represents science as a neutral, objective, non-combative space, as a disinterested "purposefulness without purpose" that serves, incidentally, political and national ends.[15] Certainly, the Thermidorian discourse of scientific objectivity is mystifying rhetoric in the service of a program of political moderation, but it manifests a different vision of the relationship between science and society (a distinctly modern one, perhaps) than that of Robespierre's France. The vision culminated in something of a "return" to scientific bureaucracy and encyclopedism proper: the Thermidorian establishment of what Roger Hahn describes as that "elitist and encyclopedic French temple of knowledge," the National Institute of Sciences and Arts in 1795. The change of the *Ecole centrale des travaux publique*'s name to the *Ecole polytechnique* the same year offers another example of this renewed focus on encyclopedism and science. "Polytechnique" is, after all, something of a synonym for "encyclopédique"; the school was to be a scholastic embodiment of the book's comprehensiveness.[16] Charles Gillispie describes the post-Jacobin transformation as follows:

> Upon the *tabula rasa* left by the Jacobins, the Directory erected a new set of scientific institutions: the first *École normale,* the *École polytechnique,* new medical facilities . . . the *Conservatoire des arts et métiers.* . . . Other schools were revived, the *École des mines,* the *École des ponts et chausées,* the *Collège de France.* Finally at the summit was created the *Institut de France.*
>
> (Gillispie, *Edge* 176)

Even if the Jacobin attitude toward science was more conflicted than its characterization in this paper might suggest—and it was, for at least a few of the initiatives pursued by Thermidorians had their tentative beginnings at the end of the Terror—the Thermidorian Convention did not hesitate to depict its Terrorist predecessors as "vandals" whose suppression of science academies and brutish neglect of "enlightenment" epitomized their irrational, chaotic, and destructive extremism.[17] The scientific initiative of the Thermidorians was a means of distancing and differentiating the new Convention from the old, a sort of lever with which the "Conventionnels" could pry the old associations of Jacobinism, Terror, and anarchy from the new government and its rational, encyclopedic ambitions. The strategy worked, in a sense, for the scientist of the National Institute achieved "an unprecedented position of primacy in French culture," becoming almost "the cultural hero of the post-Themidorian Republic" and the symbol of "a reordered system of social values in the Directorate" (Hahn 301).

Only "in a sense," however, because Napoleon himself "patronized science and its devotees on a scale heretofore unknown" in order to consolidate power, usurp cultural hero status, and finally reorganize the scientific establishment to serve his own very interested military and ideological ends. Scientists like Monge and Berthollet were enlisted to propagandize the Egyptian campaign as a scientific and cultural venture, but Bonaparte returned as the hero.[18] Coleridge's "Poet Bonaparte" could just as easily have been dubbed "Scientist Bonaparte." Science was Napoleon's fulcrum.

Constant Thermidorian

Perhaps a summary of Constant's early political trajectory will provide a map useful for charting some of the connections I will make between *Wallstein,* Constant's political thought, and the mechanics of balance.[19] Constant's support for the revolution of 1789 and his tepid sympathy for the Jacobins in the early 90s gave way to Thermidorian moderation and remorse. Biancamaria Fontana, translator of Constant's political writings and something of an apologist for the apparent unevenness of Constant's political maneuvers, notes that this recantation came with Constant's realization that Jacobin republicanism and absolute monarchy—and, in fact, the political philosophies of Hobbes and Rousseau—were two sides of the same coin (Fontana 21). An unlimited authority vested in the sovereignty of the people (for example, the supreme, boundless, and "monstrous force" granted by Rousseau to the general will over any particular will) is for Constant a despotism as frightening as the absolute monarchy supported by Hobbes. For Constant, the only legitimate sovereignty is popular and issues from the general will, but political authority of whatever form must be limited by certain inalienable individual rights—among them, individual freedom, freedom of opinion, religious freedom, the enjoyment of property, and a guarantee against all arbitrary power. These rights are not "natural" (a notion with which Constant was uncomfortable, according to Fontana), but rather represent the products of a complex and irreversible historical process (Fontana 22-23).

In Constant's opinion, revolutionary theorists and governments were confounded by their inability to comprehend the "balance" of history. They suffered either from historical anachronism, a failure to understand that the movements of history (with a capital "H") had finally discarded political models like monarchical absolutism (which infected revolutionary thought in the form of popular absolutism) and ancient republicanism (with what Fontana calls "its ideal of the full subjection and dedication of the individual to the community"), or from historical anticipation, a headlong attempt to impose a new system of government on a public not yet ready for it (Fontana 25). In Fontana's words,

> The purpose of a revolution was that of re-establishing a balance which had been upset by the development of civil society on the one hand and by the persistence of old-fashioned and inadequate institutions on the other. However, when a revolution went beyond this limit, when it established institutions which were too advanced for the ruling ideas of a society, or destroyed those which corresponded to them, it would inevitably produce reactions.

(Fontana 31)

The complex attitude toward science after Thermidor—the felt imperative to make simple and reductive distinctions between the violent Jacobin and rational Thermidorian stages of the Revolution by citing a pre-Revolutionary, encyclopedic tradition of objective inquiry, and the concomitant need to do so without raising the specter of royalism—provides the backdrop for Benjamin Constant's political writings of 1796-97. For example, Constant begins his *De la force du gouvernement actuel de la France et de la nécessité de s'y rallier [Of the Force of the Present Government of France and of the Necessity of Rallying behind It]* (1796) with the following synopsis of the contemporary political scene:

> Le moment actuel est l'un des plus importants de la Révolution. L'ordre et la liberté sont d'un côté, l'anarchie et le despotisme, de l'autre. Peu d'instants sont encore données pour se prononcer; il faut se hâter de déposer les souvenirs et les haines, ou demain ces haines seront remplacées par d'inutiles regrets, ces souvenirs par d'amers remords.

> [The present moment is one of the most important of the Revolution. Order and liberty are to one side, anarchy and despotism to the other. Little time remains to decide; we must hasten to lay aside memories and hatreds, or tomorrow these hatreds will be replaced by useless regrets, these memories by bitter remorse.][20]

What is striking about this passage is the rhetorical effectiveness of Constant's use of balanced pairs—order/anarchy, liberty/despotism, memories/hatreds, regrets/remorse—which create the illusion of measured, even-handed presentation while reducing complicated political issues to a more accessible binary logic. The second sentence, for example, distills the political complexity of Thermidorian France into a simple choice between two alternatives.[21] Constant's disingenuous grouping of terms, order and liberty on the one hand and anarchy and despotism on the other, so weights the binary option it pretends to establish that it offers the French people no real choice at all. Yet the convenient obviousness of choice framed by Constant's manipulation of terms conceals the difficult balance he hopes to strike, a balance that can only be achieved by transcending the factionalism of more traditional political taxonomies pitting monarchists against radical revolutionaries.

Hence the difference between Constant's first binaries, where the scale clearly tips in favor of liberty and order, and the confusing chiasmus of remembrance: hate::

regret (springing from hate): remorse (product of remembrance), which more faithfully depicts the difficulty of fashioning a present politics from an abandoned Bourbon past and a forsaken Jacobin future. Constant hopes to cull the best—order and liberty—from both absolutist and popular forms of government, to establish an equilibrium between traditional stability and visionary freedom by jettisoning (in fact, *deposing*) both the royalist memories that induce bitter remorse about what was and the petty Jacobin jealousy and spite that result in regrets about what might have been. Too-forward and too-backward looking political programs must be blended in order to forge a politics appropriate to "le moment actuel," to the steady present which must neither rush rashly ahead nor linger bitterly behind.

The illusory evenhandedness and deceptive obviousness of Constant's balanced syntactic structure, described above, is a rhetorical strategy designed to represent contingent political decisions as neutral and objective facts—to suggest that Jacobins and Bourbon sympathizers are tinged by political bias but Convention moderates, attached to transcendent principles like liberty and order, are not. It comes as no surprise that Constant pleads his own objectivity six paragraphs later—"N'étant attachee à aucun parti par aucun intérêt, inconnu même à la plupart des individus, nul motif personnel n'a pu diriger mes jugements" ["Not being attached to any party by any interest, unknown, even, to the majority of individuals, no personal motive could have guided my judgments"] (*De la force* 30)—or that "la réhabilitation des principes" (130) called for in *Des réactions politiques* (1797) involves establishing "des calculs politiques, rapprochés des sciences exactes par leur précision" ["political calculations, approximating the exact sciences in their precision"] (152). Constant portrays the present government as the natural result of revolutionary geometry, as a sort of vector product of oppositional Jacobin and monarchist forces whose equilibrated steadiness and rightness are guaranteed by the neutrality and objectivity of scientific method.

Constant consistently manipulates this lexicon of balance. "Moment" signifies an important interval, a point in time, a resting place between regrets about failed expectations and remorse over lost traditions. It is the fulcrum between headlong anarchy and reactionary despotism, between visions of the future and remembrances of the past. The moment is "actual"—tangible and present—and as such is dependent upon neither unsubstantiated theory nor antiquated, anachronistic fact. To be a proper moment, a proper present, it must be between, bringing what *has* been into contact with what *will* be. Anarchy and despotism cannot, according to Constant, actualize that balanced, momentary contact, but liberty and order can.[22]

Constant's call for an attention to the present moment is of course a call for unity, for a rallying around a central point—hence the title of his tract. The "moment actuel" is intimately connected with the "gouvernement actuel" and its particular "force." That force seems a peculiarly static and passive one; implicit in Constant's argument is that the government derives its strength not from anything it does or can do, but from the fact that it *is* the present government, the government of the moment (*De la force* 38-39). Hence his assertion,

> Il faut que ces hommes se rapprochent du Gouvernement, et non le Gouvernement de ces hommes. Lorsqu'ils entrent dans son sens, ils y portent l'honnêteté et la modération, mais lorsqu'ils font entrer dans le leur, ils lui donnent de la vacillation et de la faiblesse.

> (*De la force* 29)

> [These men must bring themselves closer to the government, and not the government to these men. When they move in the government's direction, they bring honesty and moderation with them, but when they make it go in theirs, they give it unsteadiness and weakness.]

Note Constant's valuation of moderation over impulsive "revolutionary" action, of unity through an "encyclopedic" centralized government over dispersal through the diffuse political desires of individuals, of stasis over vacillation.[23] Constant subordinates the revol(v/t)ing constelled hubbub of the French citizenry to the fixed hub of a stable, moderate, inertial government. In other words, he solves the problems of constructing a coherent national identity and of ensuring proper popular representation by turning the question of governmental responsibility on its head: French citizens should not ask what France can do for them, but rather what they can do for their country.

For this very reason, Constant wants to see the Revolution end and ardently desires the steadying of the Republic ("voir se terminer la Révolution" and "[désire] ardemment aussi l'affermissement de la République") (*De la force* 30). The vicissitudes of personal desire, the tempestuous ebbings and flowings and turnings of revolutionary fervor must be replaced by something more solid and inert; the *res publica*—the public thing, the thing of the people—must succeed the *res volutans* or *res volens* or *res volitans*—the twisting or frighteningly volitional or unsteadily fluttering thing (to indulge some fanciful etymologies). Of course, the *revolution* and the *res publica* differ little in theory, for the "willingness" of the revolution, becomes willfulness at its dangerous extreme during the Terror, and the sense of commonality in the public good central to a republic manifests a shared interest in consent which promises a blend of liberty and order. Perhaps that explains Constant's use of the resonant "se terminer," which suggests that the revolution must finish itself, bring itself to a close, fix itself, as if the static "affermissement" of the republic were just a frozen stage, a moment of inertia, a *tableau vivant* of revolutionary action: "dans toutes les nations, la masse veut essentiellement et presque exclusivement le repos" ["in all nations, the multitude (or mass) wants essentially and almost exclusively rest"] (*De la force* 69).[24] The republican mass[es] must, and will, according to Constant's version of Newton, dampen destructive revolutionary energies.

BONAPARTE MÉCANICIEN

Constant's desire for the end of the Revolution and the "affermissement" of the Republic can perhaps be read as an uncanny and prophetic invocation of Napoleon, described by François Furet as the man "chosen by the Revolution . . . to embody the new nation" and as "the ultimate incarnation of that crisis of political representation that was the essence of the Revolution."[25] William Hazlitt's portrait of Napoleon's triumphant return from Egypt in 1799 harmonizes with Furet's assessment:

> It was not like the return of a citizen to his country, or of a general at the head of a victorious army, but seemed to imply something more than this. . . . "We are numerous, we are brave," the people seemed every where to say, "and yet we are conquered. We want a leader to direct us—we now behold him, and our glory will once more shine forth."[26]

The "something more than this" to which Hazlitt alludes intimates Napoleon's ability to represent the unrepresentable, to fulfill a popular national need that would otherwise remain unfulfilled.

The sense of national helplessness and dependency adumbrated in this passage also evokes another of the senses of "affermissement," which can mean "support," "prop," or "stay" as well as "consolidation" or "establishment." Napoleon is the French Atlas incarnate, as Hazlitt's transcription of a supposed dialogue between Sieyès and Napoleon before the coup makes clear:

> "You hear them, General," said he; "they talk while they should be acting. Bodies of men are wholly unfit to direct armies, for they know not the value of time or occasion. You have nothing to do here; go, General, consult your genius and the situation of the country; the hopes of the Republic rest on you alone."

> (Hazlitt, *Napoleon* 61)

Bonaparte, Sieyès implies, must use his genius, his comprehension of the object's situation, and his calculation of the proper moment or occasion to save a Republic delicately balanced on his shoulders. "Value" even seems to suggest a quantitative measure, as if Napoleon could successfully solve an equation to determine the moment or torque necessary to turn the country around. Perhaps that explains why "he went frequently to the Institute [the National Institute of Sciences and Arts], but seldom to the theatres" (Hazlitt,

Napoleon 62). Studying mechanics, or pretending to, is more important than theatrical diversions in a time of national disequilibrium.

Bonaparte seems less a fulfillment of Constant's prophecy than a good reader of Constant's political writings and of the political climate of post-Thermidorian France. He impersonates a scientist, a man of cool judgment, objectivity, and disinterestedness, a leader whose stony dispassion signifies not the paralytic impotency of inactivity, but the profound potential of inertial repose (*De la force* 71). Hence Napoleon's enigmatic silence and placidity in the face of a national crisis and the sublime force of that pose in Hazlitt's eyes:

> Napoleon looked steadfastly at him, without replying a word. . . . He related to them, without any comment or without any expression of countenance which could betray his own opinion. . . . But Napoleon, who had already taken his measures, replied that he had nothing in view . . . and put an end to the interview. . . . The citizens of Paris also complained of Napoleon's keeping so close; they went to the theatres and reviews in the hope of seeing him, but he was not there. Nobody could account for this shyness. "It is now," they said, "a fortnight since his arrival" (an age to the levity and short-sightedness of these people) "and as yet he has done nothing . . ." But the decisive hour approached.

> (*Napoleon* 64)

A political scientist worthy the name, Napoleon "takes his measures" and bides his time, untroubled by sly, insinuating colleagues and unmoved by the importunate expectations of a confused citizenry. This Bonaparte is not stirred, but stirs; he is not a cog in the machine, but a man "combin[ing] a deep sense of internal power, with imaginations capable of bodying forth lofty undertakings."[27]

This vision of a kind of self-engenderment ("bodying forth") as the supreme sign of the commanding genius' self-possession is not uniquely Coleridgean. Here's Hazlitt's tribute to Burke:

> With respect to most other speakers, a specimen is generally enough, or more than enough. When you are acquainted with their manner, and see what proficiency they have made in the mechanical exercise of their profession, with what facility they can borrow a simile, or round a period, how dexterously they can argue, and object, and rejoin, you are satisfied; there is no other difference in their speeches than what arises from the difference of the subjects. But this was not the case with Burke. He brought his subjects along with him; he drew his materials from himself.[28]

Interestingly, Hazlitt contrasts the aesthetic power of a self-sufficient orator who commands, arranges, and "bodies forth" his materials with the "mechanical exercise" of a second-rate speaker. The distinction seems to be between Burke's control of his words, the seamless harmony of rhetoric and meaning in his speech, and the slapdash clunkiness of a less masterful orator whose rhetorical flourishes seem like props that are somehow independent of the speaker's government. Burke may be an excellent mechanic, one whose words perform work on others, but he is not mechanical, not a sprocket whose profession "exercises" him rather than vice versa. His oratory does not awkwardly articulate a series of borrowed formulae, but transforms a latent, inertial potential into a commanding presence. Like the sublimely detached Bonaparte, this version of Burke has internalized one of Constant's fundamental precepts of good government: "Impassible, mais fort, le gouvernement doit tout faire par sa propre force, n'appelar à son secours aucune force étrangère . . ." ["Impassive, but strong, the government must do all by means of its own power, calling to its aid no foreign force"] (*Des réactions* 102).

Another way of characterizing Hazlitt's reading of Burke is to view it as a distinction between good and bad scientist, between charlatan and Institute member. These are the very terms in which Coleridge expresses his disillusionment with Bonaparte in the *Morning Post* of January 10, 1800. Coleridge contends that Bonaparte's decree of 13th Nivose "becomes to the eye of a just observer no more than a handsome patch in the motley coat of a Charlatan—one trick more in the low Harlequinade of Usurpation." Coleridge continues:

> Bonaparte, who so ambitiously prefixed the title of Member of the National Institute to Commander in Chief—Philosopher in Egypt—Mahometan in Syria, has now commenced preacher of the great mystery of Transubstantiation. . . . The whole faculties of man must be exerted in order to noble energies; and he who is not in earnest, self-mutilated, self-paralysed, lives in but half his being.[29]

Irrepressible "energies" identify the usurper, a hyperactive child who, in his selfish desire to possess everything, fails to tame or "noble" his myriad drives into the staid serenity and coherent selfhood of a Washington or a Kemble. Napoleon proceeds ad hoc, piecemeal, in any fashion that serves his narrow ends. His patchwork costume signifies his halting policy-making, his need to stitch the frayed fragments of selfish ambition into a motley coat that hides the naked ugliness of the usurper. Bonaparte has become mechanical, in Hazlitt's sense of the word; the stitched together patches recall the articulated rhetorical devices of the bad orator. Rather than calmly and scientifically following the steps of a guiding methodology to arrive at objective truth, Napoleon participates in an elaborate charade. Indeed, Coleridge's critique of Bonaparte reads like the exposure of a quack applicant to a science academy. Here, Coleridge is the journalist-mechanic and Bonaparte the charlatan-pretender to science, more like Mesmer than Monge.[30]

Hazlitt reaches a like conclusion at the end of the "Eighteenth of Brumaire" chapter of his *Life of Napoleon*. Bonaparte's initial failing comes before the Council of Five Hundred, where he miscalculates the force necessary to sway a roomful of agitated Council members and is himself moved—literally rushed out of the chamber by a flood of would-be assassins and armed guards (72). Hazlitt's bemused description of the incident's dénouement generates a bathos especially appropriate to Napoleon the Harlequin: "Meanwhile, Buonaparte had some difficulty, on coming out of the Council of Five Hundred, in recovering from his embarrassment. Little accustomed to scenes of popular violence, he had been a good deal staggered" (72). The spell of Napoleon's sublime inertia has been broken by a burlesque failure. His is an aesthetic shortcoming, an inability to play properly the role of the commanding genius (or the scientist), and it sets up the subsequent unravelling of Napoleon's character effected by a lying and "womanish" proclamation that attempts to rewrite a scene of comic ineptitude as a moment of sublime majesty. Even an apologist for Bonaparte like Hazlitt first detects in this scene a loose thread that reveals the truth of Bonaparte's motley.[31]

WALLSTEIN

Constant first describes his plan to translate Schiller's *Wallenstein* as a diversionary tactic designed to distract him from the distressing personal circumstances of a romantic balancing act. His journal entries from September 1807 document the mental anguish caused by the awkward love triangle involving himself, Charlotte de Marenholtz, and Mme de Staël. The "Nuit convulsive" of 1 September becomes the "Journée douleureuse" of the second, and Constant still remains uncertain what to do about Mme de Staël: "Je n'ai pas la force de persister à lui dire que je veux rompre, et pourtant je ne puis lui dire que je reviens à elle. Elle s'agite et je souffre" ["I do not have the strength to persist in telling her that I want to break it off, and yet I cannot tell her that I will come back to her. She is uneasy and I suffer"].[32] Having complained of a "tête toute brisée," a "head entirely broken" or "exhausted," on the third, Constant makes something of a breakthrough the next day: "Je vais me mettre à travailler pour tuer le temps d'ici à 15 octobre. Fait le plan d'une tragedie de *Wallstein*" ["I am going to put myself to work in order to kill time between now and October 15. Make the outline for a tragedy of *Wallstein*"] (*Journaux* 348).

Constant's use of the process of translation as a means of maintaining emotional equilibrium seems pertinent to the idiosyncratic reading of the play offerred here. Nonetheless, it would be unfair to put too much emphasis on Constant's glib and detached announcement of the project. *Wallstein* may begin as self-prescribed therapy, but it soon becomes "cette tragédie qui fera peut-être ma réputation dans un genre tout nouveau" ["this tragedy which will perhaps establish my reputation in a completely new genre"], with scenes which are "ce qu'il y a de plus touchant en vers français" ["the most touching in French verse"] (*Journaux* 351, 356). The pride evident in the self-congratulatory journal entries that chart the progress of the play suggests that Constant takes more than a pedestrian interest in the work; he intends it to represent his artistry, not merely translate Schiller's.

As Lesley Sharpe notes, the course the French Revolution had taken by the late 1790s convinced Schiller of "the inability of individuals to exert any lasting control over the movement of events," showed him that "even the most apparently powerful" historical figures are "subject to circumstances and to the tide of events."[33] Applying the "extreme pessimism of Schiller's view of history" to a consideration of *Wallenstein,* Sharpe argues that Wallenstein's reluctance to act proceeds from the contradiction between his conviction that he may "act without consequences, without regard for the laws which govern events," on one hand, and his "keen awareness of the incalculability of the effects of action and [his] unwillingness to unleash a chain of events over which he has no control," on the other.[34] Wallenstein compromises by respecting the laws which govern events while nonetheless believing that only he can "stand outside history until the perfect moment for action arrives and he can stride on to the 'Welttheater' and take control" (Sharpe 90). One context for Wallenstein's "perfect moment" is "Der prägnante Moment," the pregnant moment so central to German aesthetic theory late in the eighteenth century.[35] Ilse Graham argues convincingly that Goethe's and Schiller's shared interest in "the climactic moment when permanence becomes pellucid with transcience and stable structures are seen inexorably to dissolve" finds expression in "the dialectic of movement and stasis" which characterizes the Wallenstein trilogy (281). Graham even describes the pregnant moment as an "Archimedean point" and a "still pivot," though without pursuing the mechanical connotations of the metaphor (280, 283).

I would argue that one aspect of Constant's artistry as a translator of Schiller consists in his pursuit of that scientific metaphor, and that this artistry is as much political as dramaturgical. Constant's investment in the play proceeds in part from the fact that it lends itself to manipulation as a form of political commentary upon Napoleonic France. Indeed, Constant's heavy use of the word "appui," or fulcrum, which appears much more frequently in his condensed translation than in Schiller's original, can be used as a lever to open up a reading of *Wallstein* informed by the imbrication of science, politics, and balance discussed above.

The word "appui" was used in two basic senses in the late eighteenth and early nineteenth centuries. Com-

monly, the term meant "support," "prop," or "stay," along with any of the attendant metaphorical takes on these substantives. The second, more technical meaning referred to the fulcrum or turning point of a lever. Though the more specific term is "point d'appui," "appui" *tout simple* was the word of choice two hundred years ago, as in, for example, most references to mechanics in Diderot's *Encyclopédie*. The *Encyclopédie,* in fact, demonstrates the pervasive mechanical connotations of the word in comparative examples intended to illustrate the different usages of "appui," "soutien," and "support":

> l'appui fortifie, le soutien porte, le support aide; l'appui est à côté, le soutien dessous, l'aide à l'un des bouts; . . . ce qui est violemmennt poussé a besoin d'appui. Au figuré, l'appui a plus de rapport à la force et à l'autorité; le soutien, au crédit et à l'habileté; le support, à l'affection et à l'amitié.
>
> ("Appui," *Encyclopédie* 1: 559)
>
> [the *appui* strengthens, the *soutien* bears, the *support* helps; the *appui* is beside, the *soutien* below, the *support* at one end; . . . that which is violently pushed needs an *appui*. Figuratively, the *appui* has a greater connection with force and authority, the *soutien* with trust and skill; the *support* with affection and friendship.]
>
> (my emphases)

"Appui" connotes a particular kind of human dependency, not on the sustenance of affection and friendship (interesting with regard to the relationship between Wallstein and Gallas in Constant's play), but on another's ability to give one force and authority, to fort-ify, to provide the strength and stability necessary to resist movement. An "appui" in this sense resembles a Derridean supplement or, to cite Constant's contemporaries, the sort of mechanical prosthesis that Hazlitt explicitly and Coleridge implicitly criticize.

As noted above, Constant lets slip ideal, aestheticized notions of governmental self-dependence: "Impassible, mais fort, le gouvernement doit tout faire par sa propre force n'appeler à son secours aucune force étrangère . . ." (*Des réactions* 102). Fundamentally, though, he is a pragmatist who understands that this highly prized inertia can only come as the product of a careful calculation of very complex systems of reciprocity and motion. His attack on the First Estate's ignorance of the power of ideas furnishes an example:

> Les rois, les grands, et ceux qui les défendent semblent ignorer la puissance des idées. Accoutumés à ce que des forces visibles dominent d'invisibles opinions, ils ne sentent pas que c'est à ces opinions que cette force est due. L'habitude les rend indifférents sur le miracle de l'autorité. Ils voient le mouvement, mais comme ils méconnaissent le ressort, la société ne leur paraît qu'un grossier mécanisme. Ils prennent le pouvoir pour une cause, tandis que ce n'est qu'un effet, et ils veulent se servir de l'effet contre la cause.
>
> (*De la force* 77)

[Kings, nobles and those who defend them seem not to be aware of the power of ideas. Accustomed to visible forces dominating invisible opinions, they do not sense that it is to those opinions that that force is due. Habit renders them indifferent to the miracle of authority. They see the movement, but as they do not recognize the spring, society appears to them but a rude mechanism. They take power for a cause, whereas it is only an effect, and they wish to make use of the effect against the cause.]

In effect, Constant's eerily Foucauldian analysis accuses royalists and aristocrats of forgetting their "appuis." The problem is not that they are mechanistic materialists, but that they are mediocre mechanics who can only comprehend "un grossier mécanisme." For Constant, the real danger to political stability lies in the potential failure of political actors to remember that their authority is not self-engendered, but contingent upon their ability to parse, measure and balance scrupulously the web of forces entangling them.

Constant's acute awareness of the mechanics of political action helps explain the ubiquity of the word "appui" in *Wallstein.* There does not seem to be anything of its like consistently used in Schiller's trilogy (or in Coleridge's more faithful English translation, for that matter).[36] But the word is everywhere in *Wallstein,* usually to describe one character's dependence on another, and there is often something provisional and hesitant about its use, as if the "appui" were a pivotal term in a mathematical proof, as if systems of thought, courses of action, or lives were mapped out based on the assumption that these supporters will, when necessary, support.

"Appui" initially appears within the opening twenty lines of *Wallstein.* The first two times Constant employs the word, it refers to Wallstein himself, first as a supporter of the Protestant cause, then as a chief upon whom his men can rely.[37] The play thus immediately suggests that Wallstein is at the center of the action and that the army, the political and religious order of Europe, and the play itself turn around him. Of course, one gets the same impression of Schiller's Wallenstein during the only scene in which anything like the word "appui" is used.[38] Constant's version differs from Schiller's, however, in the subtle slippages of power that occur in connection with the term. When, for example, the emperor's emissary, Géraldin, calls Gallas (Constant's Octavio) "notre appui secret" ["our secret support"] (74) in the second scene, the balance shifts as one realizes that the nexus of political force and influence is considerably more complicated than a simple first-order reading of Wallstein as the axis of power might suggest.

Géraldin goes on to intimate that Wallstein is as poor a mechanic as Constant's First Estate, for he does not understand "quels sont les satellites / Sur qui s'est appuyé son pouvoir sans limites" ["what are the satellites / Upon which is supported his limitless power"] (I.ii.75-76). Géraldin's comment refers to Gallas and the other soldiers from whom Wallstein draws his power, but it also alludes disparagingly to Wallstein's superstitious dependence upon astrology. In his science as in his politics, Wallstein relies upon what Gallas calls eight lines later "un art merveilleux" to keep together "Les élémens confus que son génie assemble" ["The confused elements which his genius gathers together"] (I.ii.76). That marvellous art might advert to Wallstein's quack interpretations of the movements of stars and planets or anticipate the trickery involved in his attempt to collect compromising signatures from his subordinates while their wills are weak (I.vi.94). Both acts involve a sort of false writing far removed from the objective "truth" of science, in that Wallstein's subjective desires inscribe upon the heavens, and his comrades, what he wants to read.[39]

Wallstein most gravely misinterprets his friend, Gallas, whom he calls "un appui que m'ont donné les cieux" ["a stay given me by the heavens"] (II.i.96). Gallas is not simply a support, but a fulcrum whom Wallstein needs in order to get leverage on other generals:

TERSKY

Ils suivront l'exemple de Gallas. . . .
[They will follow the example of Gallas. . . .]

WALLSTEIN

Je puis compter sur eux?
[I can count on them?]

TERSKY

Si vous comptez sur lui.
[If you [can] count on him.]

WALLSTEIN

Gallas, en tous les tems, fut mon plus ferme appui.
[Gallas, in all seasons, was always my strongest prop.]

(I.vi.86-87)

Wallstein's destiny turns not with the stars, but around Gallas, and he mistakes how much he can depend on his friend—literally, how much weight he can rest on him. Read this way, *Wallstein* becomes a play about a general who miscalculates the balance of forces necessary to make a successful political move because he's a poor study at mechanics.

The pivotal scene between Gallas and Wallstein, a monologue spoken by Wallstein in Act II, Scene vii, simmers with dramatic irony for careful followers of "appui":

Approche, vieil appui de ton chef outragé:
J'ai reçu tes sermens, j'en accepte l'hommage,
Et je vais dès ce jour achever mon ouvrage.
. . . Je n'exige de toi qu'un service facile.
Il est de mes guerriers dont l'esprit indocile
A mon juste courroux peut craindre de s'unir.
Pour un jour seulement il les faut contenir.
Tu le peux. Avec eux balance, temporise.
. . . Wallstein n'a plus besoin de secours empruntés,
Et dédaigne l'appui des rois qu'il a domptés.

(111)

[Approach, old stay of your insulted chief:
I have received your promises, I welcome their ser-
  vice,
And beginning today I am going to complete my work.
. . . I demand of you but an easy duty.
It concerns my soldiers whose indocile spirit
May fear to join itself with my just anger.
For one day only it is necessary to restrain them.
You can do it. With them, hesitate, delay.
. . . Wallstein no longer needs borrowed help,
And scorns the support of kings whom he has sub-
  dued.]

Wallstein recruits his "old supporter" to counterpoise the willful indocility of those soldiers who may refuse to join the rebellion. Though he professes not to need "borrowed assistance" and to scorn the "support of kings he has subdued," Wallstein still relies upon Gallas' ability to sway the troops, or rather, to keep them from swaying. Wallstein calls on Gallas to hold the soldiers in check, to delay and contain them, without realizing that Gallas himself threatens the very balance Wallstein expects him to maintain. Gallas becomes the play's fulcrum without speaking a word during the entire scene. In a sense, his early prognostication has come true: "En cet état funeste / Wallstein contre lui-même est l'appui qui nous reste" ["In that deadly state / Wallstein against himself is the one *appui* remaining for us"] (I.ii.78).

Wallstein realizes exactly what he has lost as soon as he learns of Gallas' treachery: "D'un appui, dans l'ingrat, ils ont cru me priver" ["They think to have deprived me of a prop in the ingrate"] (III.iv.137). His old friend was not simply his strongest supporter, but the fulcrum with which he expected to move the army, and by extension, the European world. Wallstein's enlightenment signals a dramatic turn of events which occurs, appropriately enough, at the play's midpoint—the third act. The balance has shifted, and the remainder of Constant's work consists of Wallstein's doomed efforts to right this newly wrought disequilibrium. Thécla's impassioned apostrophe to her dead mother discloses the apparent hopelessness of the situation and ends the third act with a resonant and fitting word: "Que ton bras nous protège et nous serve d'appui" ["May your arm protect us and serve as our stay"] (III.v.140).

Wallstein responds to his changed circumstances with defiant self-assurance: "Le destin des héros qui m'ont donné leur foi / Ne dépend désormais que du ciel et de moi" ["The destiny of the heroes who have placed in me their faith / Henceforth depends only upon heaven and me"] (IV.v.147). But his manifest disdain for temporal assistance merely displays a petulant and ultimately deadly self-delusion that blinds him to his continuing dependence on others, like Buttler and Isolan. Wallstein proudly refuses Alfred's request to become "votre appui" (IV.vi.150) and continues to blame "Impitoyable sort! quelle est donc ta justice? / Pourquoi ton bras sur nous vient-il s'appesantir" ["pitiless fate! What then is your justice? / Why does your arm come to weigh down upon us?"] (IV.vi.154)? His stubborn belief that fate's heavy arm tips the scales to his disadvantage renders him unable to perform the practical, mechanical work necessary to succeed politically. Wallstein's abdication of such responsibilities leaves his faithful few to pursue their desperate solutions ad hoc: Alfred mistakenly seeks Buttler's promise "de lui servir d'appui" ["to serve as his support"] (IV.vii.157), while Tersky, a sort of crypto-Robespierrist, believes that "La rigueur est l'appui de tout nouvel empire" ["Severity is the prop of every new empire"] (V.i.160).

Wallstein's awareness of political realities has developed by the time he delivers his last soliloquy near the end of Act v. Bitterly complaining that "L'amitié m'a trahi" ["Friendship has betrayed me"] and noting sadly that he is "Seul, et sans un ami . . . me servant d'appui" ["Alone, and without a friend . . . serving as my support"], Wallstein takes as the lesson of his experience that one should "Ne voir dans les mortels qu'un instrument" ["See in mortals only an instrument"] (V.x. 181). The danger of a mechanics of political action lies in its potential abuse by men like Wallstein and Napoleon, who can use their mechanical expertise to effect the brutal instrumentalization of society's human agents. Wallstein's insight accurately reflects the truth of science in Bonaparte's France, where Napoleon's generous patronage of science and scientists has evolved into a massive reorganization of the country's scientific infrastructure to suit the emperor's military needs—Napoleonic France's equivalent of a military-industrial complex.[40] The hope for progressive "Enlightenment" conveyed in Thermidorian citations of scientific discourse has been betrayed by Bonaparte's usurpation of science in the service of both an anachronistic militarism and his purely selfish imperial ambitions.[41]

Discussing the usurper's need to display constantly the power upon which his rule depends, Constant quotes Napoleon: "'One must give the French something new every three months,' a man who is an expert in the matter used to say, and he acted on his word" (*Spirit* 89). Constant's concern about Bonaparte's penchant for creating extravagant effects recalls his treatment of the differences between the contemporary German stage and French theatrical decorum in an 1804 journal entry:

> Les Français ne pensent qu'à faire effet. . . . En conséquence, si on leur permet de tout essayer pour arriver à ce but, ils se jettent infailliblement dans l'extravagance et le mauvais goût. Les règles sont une barrière contre la vanité entreprenante, et cette barrière a été posée par la vanité des spectateurs, qui ne veut pas qu'on hasarde trop, parce qu'on a l'air de trop compter sur ses forces.
>
> (*Journaux* 72)
>
> [The French think only about creating an effect. . . . Consequently, if one permits them to attempt anything in order to achieve this goal, they inevitably throw themselves into extravagance and bad taste. The rules (of theatrical decorum) are a barrier against daring vanity, and this barrier has been erected by the vanity of the spectators, who don't want anyone to risk too much, because doing so suggests that one counts too much on one's own (on their) powers.][42]

This early version of Constant's rationale for transforming the *Wallstein* trilogy into a single play in rhymed couplets organized by the unities represents more than a clash between national aesthetics. In the context of Napoleon's own "vanité entreprenante," it suggests that the translator's task of tempering Schiller's German romantic "individualism" in order to make *Wallenstein* suitable for the French stage performs a kind of political work on Bonaparte.[43] Constant's effort to curb extravagance and bad taste on the French boards adumbrates an analogous desire to check Napoleon's imperial enterprise, which puts undue strain on the nation and its "forces." As my equivocal translation above suggests, Napoleon's enterprising ambition taxes his own forces as well, for it threatens to burst the seams of his disguise as the embodiment of France and thus, as in Constant's analysis of the relation between playwright and audience, to pose the vanity of Bonaparte against that of the spectating nation whose will he is supposed to incarnate. Constant hopes to use *Wallstein* as a lever, not to move the world, but to equilibrate a France unbalanced since Bonaparte's rapid rise to power. *Wallstein* counters the bad faith of the theatrical emperor, for whom science is just another spectacular effect, with the dramaturgical mechanics of a liberal playwright.

Notes

1. Quoted in the entry "Appui," *Le Grand Robert de la Langue Française,* 2nd ed. (Paris, 1986) 1: 487; my English translation.

2. See *Annals of Science* 33 (1976): 429.

3. See *Science, Technology, and Culture in Historical Perspective, Studies in History* 1 (1976) 120.

4. Quoted by David Erdman in his introduction to Coleridge's *Essays on His Times,* ed. David Erdman (Princeton: Princeton UP, 1978) 1.cv.

5. Bronislaw Baczko, "Thermidorians," *A Critical Dictionary of the French Revolution,* ed. François Furet and Mona Ozouf, trans. Arthur Goldhammer (Cambridge: Belknap/Harvard UP, 1989) 407.

6. The adjective "revolutionary," however, was also coined during the French Revolution. See Janis Langins, "Words and Institutions during the French Revolution: The Case of 'Revolutionary' Scientific and Technical Education," *The Social History of Language,* ed. Peter Burke and Roy Porter, Cambridge Studies in Oral and Literature Culture 12 (Cambridge: Cambridge UP, 1987) 136-60.

7. For an analysis of the importance of political language during the Revolution, see Jacques Guilhamou, *La langue politique et la Révolution française: de l'événement à la raison linguistique* (Paris: Meridiens Klincksieck, 1989). Particularly interesting is Guilhamou's account of "l'abus des mots" in the early 1790s and of subsequent Jacobin efforts, particularly those of François-Urbain Domergue, to elaborate a more stable and analytical political language, a "langue bien faite." My argument here is that a rhetoric of balance, strongly resonant with a contemporary scientific lexicon, offers Thermidorians like Constant just such a political language.

8. Straum 110. For example, Marat. For an interesting discussion of the exclusion of "charlatans" like Marat and Mesmer by the scientific establishment, see Charles Coulston Gillispie, *Science and Polity in France at the End of the Old Regime* (Princeton: Princeton UP, 1980).

9. Both quotations are gleaned from Joseph Fayet, *La Révolution Française et la Science 1789-1795* (Paris: Marcel Rivière, 1960) 198; my English translations.

10. See Nicole Dhombres, *Les savants en Révolution: 1789-1799* (Paris: Cité des sciences et de l'industrie, 1987).

11. Among the most interesting takes on Jacobin hostility to science are Gillispie, "The *Encyclopédie* and the Jacobin Philosophy of Science," *Critical Problems in the History of Science: Proceedings of the* Institute for the History of Science *at the University of Wisconsin, September 1-11, 1957,* ed. Marshall Clagett (Madison: U of Wisconsin P, 1959) 255-89 and "Science in the French Revolution," *Behavioral Science* 4.1 (1959): 67-73; Roger Hahn, *The Anatomy of a Scientific Institution: The Paris Academy of Sciences, 1666-1803* (Berkeley: U of California P, 1971); Fayet and Straum. For the contrary view that a strong association cannot be found between political affiliation and anti-

science sentiment in Revolutionary France, see Henry Moss, "Scientists and Sans-culottes: The Spread of Scientific Literacy in the Revolutionary Year II," *Fundamenta Scientiae* 4.2 (1983): 101-15; and L. Pearce Williams, "The Politics of Science in the French Revolution," *Critical Problems* 291-308; also see the comments by Henry Guerlac and Henry Bertram Hill on Williams' and Gillispie's papers, collected in *Critical Problems.*

12. Gillispie, *The Edge of Objectivity: An Essay in the History of Scientific Ideas* (Princeton: Princeton UP, 1960) 175.

13. See Robert Darnton, *The Business of Enlightenment: A Publishing History of the* Encyclopédie *1775-1800* (Cambridge: Belknap/Harvard UP, 1979).

14. This despite the fact that hostility to the pure sciences and geometry was abundant in Diderot's *Encyclopédie,* especially with regard to their dubious value in the pursuit of more practical knowledge. See, for example, the critique of the application of geometric and mechanical principles to the study of human anatomy in the entry, "Méchanicien."

15. A late example is Napoleon's response to his 1797 election to the National Institute of Sciences and Arts: "True victories, the ones which have no regret, are those made over ignorance. The most honorable occupation and the most useful to nations is to contribute to the extension of human ideas. The true power of the French Republic must henceforth consist in not allowing there to be new ideas which do not belong to it" (Straum 120).

16. On the name change and its significance, see Langins 147-48. Although the post-Jacobin legacy of the encyclopedists is difficult to assess, it seems less likely that "encyclopédies," whether Diderot's or his successors', were viewed as the site of "popular utilitarianism" and "half-democratic sentimentality," as Gillispie suggests, and more likely that they offered France after the Terror an idealized vision of social progress, political stability, and comprehensive unity to be achieved through the neutral objectivity of scientific endeavor. See Gillispie, "Science" 68-69, Hahn 304, and, on the diffusion and reception of encyclopedias (and an account of the relations between encyclopedism and Jacobinism that differs from mine), Darnton's excellent *The Business of Enlightenment.*

17. Straum 120-21. Rousseauian natural philosophy, for example, enjoyed a ground swell of support from Jacobins, as the Convention converted the *Jardin du Roi* into the *Museum d'histoire naturelle* and established twelve chairs in the biological sciences. Gillispie argues that there was nothing paradoxical about popular enthusiasm for the natural sciences in the context of a broader anti-science sensibility, "for the Revolution, which suppressed organized physics, provides institutional testimony to the deep instinct of romanticism to seek shelter in the humane metaphors of biology, which proposed organism rather than mechanism as the model of order." The short-lived official sanction for a less alienating, more subjective science ended with the fall of Robespierre and the revivification of an encyclopedist scientific tradition. See Gillispie, "Science" 68 and *Edge* 176.

18. Hahn 311. Also see Bradley, "Scientific Education versus Military Training: The Influence of Napoleon Bonaparte on the *Ecole Polytechnique,*" *Annals of Science* 32 (1975): 415-49; and Williams, "Science, Education, and Napoleon I," *Isis* 47.4 (1956): 369-82.

19. The broad view of Constant's political philosophy offered here is drawn predominantly from Biancamaria Fontana's *Benjamin Constant and the Post-Revolutionary Mind* (New Haven: Yale UP, 1991). Constant's own (and very early—before the embarrassing vicissitudes of his relationship with Napoleon) response to charges that he is an "inconséquent, versatile, insidieux" political chameleon, a refutation replete with the rhetoric of stability and equilibrium, is as follows:

> I imagine proffered here the charge of machiavellianism. You want, someone will say, to do all according to circumstances, after having pretended for so long not to count them. You abandon your principles as soon as they no longer serve your ends. You slander your adversaries when they reason using the very bases that you have forced them to admit. It is you who are inconsistent, changeable, insidious, you who oppose the most rigorous abstractions to the interests that you wish to offend, and who make countless exceptions in favor of your own interests.
>
> I am far from meriting this reproach. While rebuffing those for whom abstract reasoning is an evolution, and metaphysics a stratagem, no one has guarded himself more than I against the partisans of a contrary excess, against those eternal panegyrists of modification who, always searching out the middle, do everything by halves, and, not believing that the social order can be founded on fixed bases, take wavering for balance, and fluctuation for equilibrium.
>
> (*Des reactions politiques* 129-30; my English translation)

For evidence that Constant's "inconstancy" was something of a popular issue during his lifetime, see the political cartoon of uncertain date in Georges Poulet, *Benjamin Constant par lui-même* (Paris: Editions du seuil, 1968) 17.

20. *De la force du gouvernement actuel de la France et de la nécessité de s'y rallier (1796); Des reactions politiques; Des effets de la Terreur (1797)* (Paris: Flammarion, 1988) 29. All further references to this and to the other pamphlets included in this volume will be cited in the body of the text by page number. English translations of Constant's work are mine throughout, except where otherwise noted.

21. Perhaps I should clarify my use of Thermidorian. I use the word here as a temporal qualifier signifying the chaotic period between 9 Thermidor, Year II (the fall of Robespierre), and 4 Brumaire, Year IV (the end of the Convention). Elsewhere, Thermidorian also refers to the moderate or "liberal" political sensibility that I associate with this period.

22. The "moment" that Constant invokes here, a point of contact between Bourbon monarchy and Jacobin republic, a sort of limit at the abject edge where one ceases to be and the other begins, perhaps enjoys a resonance borrowed from the language of mathematics, in which "moment" signifies the infinitely small quantity of difference employed in differential calculus. See Diderot's (et al.) *Encyclopédie ou Dictionnaire raisonné des sciences, des arts et des métiers* (Samuel Faulche: Neufchastel [sic], 1765) 10: 633.

23. On the waning popularity of the word "revolutionary" as the '90s wore on, likely because it connoted abrupt change, ad hoc political and educational policy (the "revolutionary courses" of the Jacobin period were almost literally brought to the people), and the anarchy at the Revolution's height, see Langins 146-47.

24. In physics, a moment of inertia is the quantitative measure of a body's resistance to rotation or revolution about an axis. I mean the phrase to evoke both this technical, "revolutionary" sense and a more straightforward reading as "brief time of inertial passivity."

25. "Napoleon Bonaparte," *Critical Dictionary* 273, 281. See also Lucien Jaume, *Le discours jacobin et la démocratie* (Paris: Fayard, 1989) 174. Jaume writes, "Napoleon, or the people become king, as Guizot put it, represented the reconciliation, for a time, between the sovereignty of the multitude and the power of a preeminent individual" (my English translation).

26. "The Eighteenth of Brumaire," *Life of Napoleon, Complete Works of William Hazlitt* ed. P. P. Howe (London: J. M. Dent, 1930) 14: 55.

27. Coleridge on the commanding genius of Washington in "General Washington I: Obituary," *Essays* I: 131.

28. "Character of Mr. Burke, 1807," *Political Essays 1819* (Oxford: Woodstock Books, 1990) 361.

29. "Bonaparte's Harlequinade," *Essays* 1: 91. Compare the patchwork rags and self-mutilation of Constant's personification of Usurpation: "Usurpation alone, bare and stripped of all those things, wanders around haphazardly, sword in hand, seeking on all sides to cover its shame, its rags, which it tears and bloodies in snatching." Constant, *The Spirit of Conquest and Usurpation and their Relation to European Civilization, Political Writings*, trans. and ed. Biancamaria Fontana (Cambridge: Cambridge UP, 1988) 94. Future references will be cited in the body of the paper by page number.

30. On Southey's and Coleridge's early enthusiasm for Bonaparte as a "man of Science," see Simon Bainbridge, *Napoleon and English Romanticism* (Cambridge: Cambridge UP, 1995) 22, 24.

31. On Hazlitt's "ambiguous" representation of Napoleon, see Bainbridge 199-201.

32. Constant, *Journaux intimes,* ed. Alfred Roulin and Charles Roth (Paris: Gallimard, 1952) 348. Future references will be cited in the text. For a reading of *Wallstein* that makes more of these biographical events, see Jean-Pierre Perchellet, "*Wallstein* ou le jeu de miroirs," *Annales Benjamin Constant* 14 (1993): 29-49.

33. Lesley Sharpe, *Schiller and the Historical Character* (Oxford: Oxford UP, 1982) 73.

34. Sharpe 105, 90. For a different account of *Wallenstein*'s "recognition of the incommensurability between agent and act," of the "frustration of heroes whose vision simultaneously qualifies them for and disqualifies them from active leadership in the world," see Julie A. Carlson, "Coleridge's German Revolution: Schiller's *Wallenstein*," *In the Theatre of Romanticism: Coleridge, Nationalism, Women* (Cambridge: Cambridge UP, 1994) 77, 78.

35. Ilse Graham, "The pregnant moment: Wallenstein's debt to Laocoon," *Schiller's Drama: Talent and Integrity* (New York: Harper, 1974) 245-83.

36. The words "Mittelpunkt" (center or midpoint), "Halt" (support, stability, foothold, or stop), "Kraft" (force), and "Säule" (column, pillar, or pile) all appear in one important section of *Die Piccolomini* in which Max praises Wallenstein to Questenberg (Act II, lines 409-33). The absence of mechanical language elsewhere—and more specifically, of "appui"—suggests 1) that Max's mechanical metaphors signify a kind of political naiveté, 2) that the language of mechanics is discredited as a political vocabulary, given the machinations of Wallenstein for which it cannot

account (a variation on #1), or 3) that the scientific idiom in Schiller does not "count" as it does in Constant. See Schiller, *Wallenstein,* ed. Max Winkler (New York: Macmillan, 1901) 63 for the scene in question. For a straightforward, line-by-line translation, see *Wallenstein,* trans. Charles E. Passage (New York: Ungar, 1958).

37. Constant, *Wallstein,* ed. Jean-René Derré (Paris: Société d'édition, 1965) I.i, pages 72, 74. Further references will be cited in the body of the paper by act, scene, and page number (Derré's edition does not provide line numbers).

38. See n. 32 above. It seems worth noting that Constant reads the first play in Schiller's trilogy, *Wallstein's Camp,* as an elaborate sketch of Wallstein as the static point around which all else revolves— the (apparent) orchestrator of moves and turns who nevertheless remains unmoved:

> *The Camp* is a sort of prologue without any action. We see there the habits of soldiers, in the tents where they live: some sing, others drink, others come home enriched from the plunder of the peasants. They recount their exploits; they talk about their commander, of the freedom he allows them, of the rewards he showers on them. The scenes follow one another, without anything tying one to the next: but this incoherence is natural, it's a tableau mouvant, where there is no past, no future. However, the genius of Wallstein presides over this apparent disorder. Everyone's head is full of him: everyone sings his praise, worries over the rumors spread about the dissatisfaction of the court, swears not to abandon the General who protects them. We see all the symptoms of an insurrection [against Austria] ready to erupt, if the signal is given by Wallstein. We discern at the same time the secret motives which, in each individual, modify his devotion; the fears, the suspicions, the selfish designs, which come to thwart the universal impulse.

I'm suggesting that Constant's first uses of the word "appui" work to the same end, setting up Wallstein as fulcrum and then slowly revealing the complex interdependencies of the social machine that generates his power. See Constant, "Quelques Réflexions sur la Tragédie de Wallstein et sur le Théâtre Allemand," *Wallstein* 50; my English translation.

39. Certainly, though, both the signature collection and the superstition lose some of the centrality they enjoy in Schiller.

40. See Bradley, "Scientific Education versus Military Training," and Williams, "Science, Education, and Napoleon I."

41. Consider the contrast between the promise of repose and the anachronism of war in *The Spirit of Conquest and Usurpation*: "The sole aim of modern nations is repose, and with repose comfort, and, as source of comfort, industry. War becomes every day a more ineffective means of attaining this aim" (54).

42. The final sentence here is peculiarly resistant to strict translation. The antecedent of "ses forces" appears to be "on," but it seems to me possible to see "ses forces" as referring to the spectators as well. Constant's "veut" must take "la vanité" as its subject, but if it does, vanity becomes a personification, an embodiment of the spectators themselves in a particular state of being vain; it is, after all, "la vanité des spectateurs." "Ses forces" can thus refer to the powers of a personified vanity and thus to the powers of the spectators in a state of vanity. My point is not to claim that we *must* read the passage this way, but merely that we *can,* that Constant himself has left unclear whether the antecedent of "ses forces" is theater performers or theatergoers. That conflation of performers and spectators is in fact consistent with his confusing suggestion that spectators motivated *by* vanity have erected a barrier *against* the vanity of too-enterprising performers, a claim that at once establishes and effaces the boundary between audience member and actor.

43. Constant's epigraphic citation of *Wallstein* in his *The Spirit of Conquest and Usurpation* (at the opening of a chapter entitled "Differences between Usurpation and Monarchy") clearly suggests that Constant felt a connection between the play and the political circumstances of Napoleonic France. Though *The Spirit* was first published in 1814, Constant assembled the treatise from notes compiled while working in 1806 on a political tract he later abandoned, *Principes de politique.* Thus the anti-Napoleonic thinking suffusing *The Spirit* dates from roughly the same time that Constant decided to translate Schiller (1807). See Fontana 12-13. For a reading of Coleridge's *Wallenstein* translation as a sort of "Character of Bonaparte," see Carlson 89.

Tzvetan Todorov (essay date 1999)

SOURCE: Todorov, Tzvetan. "Liberal Democracy." In *A Passion for Democracy—Benjamin Constant,* translated by Alice Seberry, pp. 33-46. New York: Algora Publishing, 1999.

[*In the following essay, Todorov illustrates how Constant's liberal philosophy embodies a combination and revision of the political philosophies of Jean-Jacques Rousseau and Charles-Louis de Secondat Montesquieu.*]

AUTONOMY AND MODERATION

Constant's political thought can be presented as a synthesis and a transformation of the two major currents of 18th century French political philosophy, that of Montesquieu and that of Rousseau. The very first sentence of his great treatise ***Principes de politique*** refers to both *L'Esprit des lois* and to the *Contrat social*. Both these famous predecessors reflect upon the nature of the best political regime; but they do not see it in the same way.

For Montesquieu, it is not the number of people who hold power that matters (monarchy, aristocracy, democracy), but the way in which power is wielded. In his eyes, power is legitimate when it is not unlimited. One can limit it either by laws or by another power. Montesquieu thus wants the government to be subject to existing laws, and for the executive, legislature, and judiciary powers not to be concentrated in the same hands, so that one can counterbalance the other. If these precepts are followed, the result is a "moderate" or, as we would say today, liberal, regime. It does not matter much whether it is a monarchy or a republic; the moderate regime is, in itself, good. In the contrary case, the regime is despotic, and despotism must be fought always and everywhere.

Rousseau reasons in very different terms. For him autonomy is essential, i.e. whether an action is the result of its subject's will, in other words, whether one lives under laws that one has given oneself. Descartes required that reason not be subject to any external authority; Rousseau transposes this requirement to the political field and he declares: only that government is legitimate that has us live according to the law that we ourselves wanted. It is not how power is exercised that makes it good, but the way in which it is instituted. Monarchy is founded by tradition; but tradition can be only the result of a past injustice and it is always the effect of force, not of what is right. Only the republic is legitimate, in that here it is the sovereign people that decides the law according to which it will live.

Constant initially accepts Rousseau's postulate without hesitation: power must be the expression of the people's will; the good political regime is democratic. "In a word, there are only two powers in the world. One is illegitimate; that is force. The other is legitimate, and that is the general will" (***Principes,*** 1806, I, 2, 22). But he is not satisfied with that and adds a constraint that takes Montesquieu as its starting point. It is not enough that power should be legitimate in its origins; it also must be exercised legitimately—in other words, it must not be unlimited. "When this authority extends over objects outside its sphere, it becomes illegitimate" (II, 2, 50). In other words, Constant adds together Rousseau's and Montesquieu's requirements for the best political regime. It must be both instituted *and* exercised in a

certain manner, the general will having to be applied with moderation. The best regime is neither democracy nor liberalism, it is liberal democracy.

A synthesis of Montesquieu's and Rousseau's stipulations, Constant's thought is at the same time a criticism addressed to both. Rousseau, giddy with the discovery that political autonomy is possible, forgot or did not foresee a probable complication, to wit, that the autonomy of the community enters into conflict with the autonomy of the individual. The regime resulting from the French Revolution was quite democratic in that it derived from the sovereignty of the people; however, it was also a regime that could become despotic, as demonstrated by the Terror. This historical fact revealed a weakness in Rousseau's reasoning. It is not sufficient to require that the people be sovereign, still it must be specified that this sovereignty extends only up to a certain limit and not beyond. Indeed, the people, as legitimate sovereign, can exert a terror worse than that of the illegitimate monarch. "The people that is all-powerful is as dangerous as, or more dangerous than, a tyrant" (I, 6, 38). Thus it is necessary to build a wall that stops the general will at the edge of the individual's private territory and ensures the latter's protection.

> Democracy is authority deposited in the hands of all, but only that sum of authority necessary for the security of the group [. . .] The people can give up this authority in favor of just one man or a small number, but their power is limited, like that of the people who gave them this mantle.
>
> (I, 7, 41)

Sovereignty is total only within certain bounds. Even if there is just one individual in dissension with all the others, these latter should not be able to impose their will upon him in his private life.

On the other side of this boundary begins the private space, where the individual alone is master. In disagreement with Rousseau, here Constant discovers an insurmountable heterogeneity within the social body. The individual cannot be reduced to his society; the principles that one and the other proclaim do not form a continuum. Constant cannot accept what Rousseau calls "the total alienation to the whole communityof each associate with all his rights" (*Le Contrat social* I, 6, 360). That the source of power is legitimate by no means prevents abuse. The reason for Rousseau's error is, according to Constant, in the abstraction of his system—he forgot that, in practice, the general will will be deposited in the hands of just a few individuals, and that this fact makes possible all forms of abuse. "In giving oneself up entirely, one does not enter into a condition that is equal for all, since some benefit exclusively from the sacrifice of the others" (***Principes,*** 1806, I, 4, 34).

However, Montesquieu's solution, which requires that power be limited by laws and by other powers, is not enough for Constant either. Power may be distributed between distinct entities (the legislature, the executive and the judiciary) in vain. If their sum deprives me of a private territory, then I cannot approve such a regime:

> What matters to me is not that my personal rights cannot be violated by one power, without the approval of another; but that this violation should be prohibited to all the powers. It is not enough that the executive agents need to appeal for authorization by the legislator, it is essential that the legislator be able to authorize actions only within a given sphere.
>
> (II, 3, 54)

Montesquieu says all the power should not be given into *the same hands,* Constant retorts: *all* the power should not be given away. Montesquieu takes care to make sure that power will stop power. Constant asks: "How can we limit power other than by power?" (II, 4, 55), and he answers: by establishing a territory on which no societal power, legitimate or illegitimate, divided or unified, has any right—the territory of the individual.

At the same time Constant, who observed the Revolution from close at hand, knows that the law can be as tyrannical as governments. Nothing prevents those who have seized power from drafting laws that authorize them to terrorize the population. Iniquitous laws are not hypothetical, they really exist. Therefore, a standard is needed that makes it possible to judge the laws. Constant recovers here the spirit of modern natural rights, which was present but veiled in Montesquieu's thought. Which characteristics make a law contrary to people's rights? Constant enumerates three of them: retroactivity; the prescription of actions contrary to morals, such as the refusal of compassion, or denunciations; and finally, collective responsibility, under which one could be punished for actions that one did not oneself commit. If laws do not transgress these principles, it is better to obey them, even when one may not agree with them. Order is preferable to disorder. But if they do contravene these principles, civic disobedience is not only licit, it is required. "Nothing excuses the man who lends his support to the law that he believes to be iniquitous" (XVIII, 6, 484). Constant would have no difficulty understanding the concept of a crime against humanity, an act that might be allowable under the laws in force but that transgresses the principles of rights and morals, the underpinnings of any law.

If obedience to positive laws and the separation of power are not enough, by what means can we ensure that freedom will be maintained? Above all, by establishing a fundamental law or constitution that states and specifies the possible extent of all the laws and all the powers; after that, by vigilance at every moment to ensure that the constitutional principles are not abrogated in practice. Certainly, this is why the writing of constitutions, and reflecting upon them, is one of Constant's

passions—as testified by some of his works such as *La Constitution républicaine, Réflexions sur les constitutions et les garanties, Cours de politique constitutionnelle,* and *l'Acte additionnel* (a supplement to the Constitution) intended for Napoleon during the Hundred Days. This is also why, every time circumstances allow it, he participates in the country's political life.

Constant invents neither the democratic (or republican) principle of the sovereignty of the people nor the liberal principle of the limitation of power. Nonetheless it is he who articulates them, who holds them up against the real-life experience of the Revolution, the Empire, and the Restoration, who thus gives flesh to abstractions. It is he who reveals their consequences and sometimes their dangers. Constant is one of the first, and one of the most brilliant, authors who chose, among all the options that arose at the time, the one that appears to us today to be obvious (even if we are far from fulfilling it in all its perfection)—Revolution without Terror, popular sovereignty with respect for personal freedoms. In this, he is the first French theorist of liberal democracy.

THE PRINCIPLE OF FREEDOM

And what is personal freedom? Constant's ideas on the subject were fixed since 1806; he would only revisit them and reformulate them over the rest of his life. Perhaps the simplest definition is the following. "Freedom is nothing more than that which individuals have the right to do and that which society does not have the right to prevent" (*Principes,* 1806, I, 3, 28). Any human being's existence is divided into two domains, one public, the other private; one in which society exerts control, the other governed by the individual himself. *Freedom* is the name given to the border separating these two domains, to the barrier beyond which any intervention of society is illegitimate, where the individual decides everything by himself.

This is the point to which Constant returns most often, this is what he himself considers the leitmotiv of his political philosophy—the territory of the individual is not subject to societal sovereignty, whatever form that may take. When he tallies up the results of his battles, at the end of his life, in the foreword of his *Mélanges de littérature et de politique,* he repeats, "I defended the same principle for forty years, freedom in everything: religion, philosophy, literature, industry, politics" (519). Only "industrial" freedom (that is, that of productive labor) was added along the way. At this time, indeed, Constant thinks that competition must be permitted and the entrepreneurial spirit should not be regulated. The activity of production deserves these considerations, for it inherently belongs to the individual, as opposed to goods passed along through heritage. "The real estate asset is the value of the thing; the industrial one, the value of the man" (521).

In the *Principes* of 1806, the enumeration is a little different. Four subdivisions are found: 1. Freedom of action; 2. Freedom of conviction (or religious freedom); 3. Freedom of expression; and 4. Physical guarantee (one must be treated in accordance with the laws) (II, 6, 58). No limitation must apply to anything that is internal—no civil religion as in Rousseau. Such is also the conclusion of the work on religion. "Men, that is, those in power, the material force, must not interfere with religion" (*Religion,* V, XV, 4, 206). In this respect, Constant's vast study follows a construction parallel to that of his political treatises. The "Montesquieu" aspect is still visible here (for some time Constant wanted to call his great work *L'Esprit des religions*). In politics, as we have seen, it is not the opposition between one and many, monarchy and republic, that matters (Constant would defend the latter in 1800, the former in 1815), but that between limited and unlimited power. In the same way, in religion, the difference between polytheism and monotheism counts less, actually, than that between "sacerdotal" and "nonsacerdotal" religion, that is, containing or not containing a clergy, and thus also participating or not participating in political power. The first is, indeed, potentially "despotic," in that it can lead to a concentration of all the power in the same hands; the second, by contrast, is intrinsically "moderate."

Freedom of the press is also complete, except for that which harms the integrity of the person (slander, incitement to violence) or of the community (appealing to the population or to a foreign enemy to overthrow the ruling power). These exceptions do not justify the institution of censorship since, as infringements of the general law, they will be punished by that general law.

This segregation of freedom into various types is further refined, in other contexts, into additional segments. One can distinguish the pact between the government and the governed, which provides the guarantees of personal freedom, and the exercise of this freedom, or enjoyment. Absence of the former, notes Constant, would destroy the latter. From another perspective, one might also speak of a "moral freedom, which consists of making us independent of the passions that degrade us" (*Liberté politique,* 258). The latter is no longer identified with the protected territory of societal supervision, but with an internal purification; nevertheless, it benefits from personal freedom.

However, the most telling distinction is still to come. That is the distinction between the freedom of the individuals thus described and a very different form of social action, which consists of participating in the political life of one's country, which signifies another meaning of the word "freedom." To indicate this new contrast, Constant sometimes speaks of civil freedom and political freedom, or even of negative freedom and positive freedom, or again, as in his talk at the Atheneum in 1819, of the liberty of the Moderns and that of the Ancients.

Constant starts with a simple historical observation. Not every people recognized the same ideal of personal liberty; it has existed, actually, only since the 16th and especially the 18th century (*Liberté politique,* 257). The ancient Greeks, in particular, had no place for it; they were not concerned with preserving a space where the individual would decide everything by himself, because for them, "the individual was entirely sacrificed to the ensemble" (*Principes,* 1806, XVI, 1, 419). On the other hand, they cultivated a very different form of freedom, "active participation in collective power" (*Conquête,* II, 7, 164). "The aim of the Ancients was to share social power among all the citizens of a fatherland. That is what they called freedom (*liberté*). The aim of the Moderns is the security of private pleasures; and they call freedom the guarantees granted to these pleasures by social institutions" (*Liberté,* 502). For the Ancients, the individual is entirely subject to society; for the Moderns, it is society that must be put to the service of the individuals. The freedom of the Ancients is thus connected to the general will of Rousseau; that of the Moderns, to social moderation according to Montesquieu.

Where does this distinction between the Ancients and the Moderns originate? The quarrel by the same name was, itself, already old at that time, but the meaning of the distinction had changed. In Rousseau, one finds the intellectual articulation but not the terms: the Ancients, for him, are *citizens,* i.e. parts of a whole, "fractional unities"; the Moderns become, in the best case, *men,* that is, each one an individual, "an absolute entirety" (*cf. Emile,* I, 249). But Constant's immediate source (and Mme. de Staël's—both share the same political ideas) is Condorcet. He already defends a concept similar to liberty: the majority, even if it is legitimate, should not be able to encroach on the territory of the individual; now, only the Moderns discovered this principle. "The Ancients did not have any concept of this kind of liberty," writes Condorcet (*Oeuvres,* VII, 202). It is in this distinction and in this debate that the modern idea of the individual is born.

Note

References given within parentheses refer to publications listed [in the List of Works Cited.] The last number designates the page of the quoted text; the number immediately prior designates the internal subdivision of the cited text (the part, section, or chapter number).

Works Cited

CONSTANT'S WORKS

REFERENCES AND ABBREVIATIONS

In the absence of any standard edition of Constant's writings, one is obliged to consult very diverse publications, some of them long unobtainable. Unless otherwise specified, the place of publication is Paris. When necessary, I indicate the abbreviation used in this book for each work.

I. COLLECTIONS

Ecrits et discours politiques, J. J. Pauvert, 1964, 2 vol. (contains a useful selection of Benjamin Constant's speeches of 1800-1801 and 1824-1830).

Force = De la force du gouvernement actuel de la France, etc., Flammarion-Champs, 1988.

Modernes = De la liberté chez les Modernes, LGF-Livre de Poche-Pluriel, 1980 (republished in 1997 by Gallimard-Folio under the title *Ecrits politiques*).

OC = Œuvres complètes, Tübingen, M. Niemeyer, 1993 s.

Œuvres = Œuvres, Gallimard-Pléiade, 1979. (*Adolphe, Cécile* and *Ma Vie* are also available in a volume in the "Folio" collection.)

Portraits = Portraits. Mémoires. Souvenirs, Champion, 1992.

Recueil = Recueil d'articles 1795-1817, Geneva, Droz, 1978 (six other collections of articles were published, all under the direction of E. Harpaz, all at Droz, between 1972 and 1992).

II. INDIVIDUAL PUBLICATIONS

A. Works

Conquête = De l'esprit de conquête et de l'usurpation, Garnier-Flammarion, 1986.

Constitution républicaine = Fragments d'un ouvrage abandonné sur la possibilité d'une constitution républicaine dans un grand pays, Aubier, 1991.

Filangieri = G. Filangieri, Œuvres, Vol. III, 1840, commentary by Benjamin Constant.

Polythéisme = Du polythéisme romain, 2 vols., 1833.

Principes 1806 = Principes de politique applicables à tous les gouvernements, Genève, Droz, 1980; republished in 1997 by Hachette-Pluriel.

Religion = De la religion considérée dans sa source, ses formes et ses développements, Vol. I, 1824; Vol. II, 1825; Vol. III, 1827, Vols. IV and V, 1831.

B. Correspondence

"Lettres à Prosper de Barante," *Revue des Deux Mondes,* July 15 and August 1, 1906.

"Letters to Isabelle de Charrière," in: I. de Charrière, *Œuvres complètes.* Amsterdam, G. A. Van Oorschot and Geneva, Slatkine, in particular Vol. III, 1981 and Vol. IV, 1982.

Benjamin and Rosalie de Constant, *Correspondance.* Gallimard, 1955.

Journal intime de Benjamin Constant et lettres à sa famille et à ses amis, 1895.

Lettres de Benjamin Constant à sa famille, 1775-1830, Stock, 1931 (these two publications are quite flawed; however, they contain the letters to his aunt, the countess of Nassau, which are of interest).

Benjamin Constant and Mme. Récamier, *Lettres 1807-1830,* Champion, 1992 (also contains his letters to Annette de Gérando).

Benjamin Constant and Mme. de Staël, *Lettres à un ami (Claude Hochet),* Neuchâtel, à la Baconnière, 1949.

III. SPECIFIC TEXTS

Adolphe, in: *Œuvres.*

Amélie et Germaine, in: *Œuvres.*

Article = article in the *Journal des débats,* March 19, 1815, in: *Recueil.*

Cécile, in: *Œuvres.*

Cent-Jours = Mémoires sur les Cent-Jours: OC, Vol. XIV, 1993.

Dunoyer = De M. Dunoyer et de quelques-uns de ses ouvrages, in: *Modernes.*

Education = De la juridiction du gouvernement sur l'éducation, in: *Modernes.*

Godwin = De Godwin et de son ouvrage sur la justice politique, in: *Modernes.*

Guerre de Trente Ans, in: *Œuvres*

Histoire abrégée de l'égalité, in: *OC,* Vol. III, 1995.

Idées religieuses = Du développement progressif des idées religieuses, in: *Modernes*

Journal, in: *Œuvres.*

Julie = Lettre sur Julie, in: *Portraits.*

Liberté = De la liberté des Anciens comparée à celle des Modernes, in: *Modernes.*

Liberté politique = La Liberté politique, essentielle à la liberté civile, in: *Recueil.*

Littérature du XVIII siècle = Esquisse d'un essai sur la littérature du XVIII siècle, in: *OC,* Vol. III, vol. I, 1995.

Ma Vie, in: *Œuvres* (under the title *Le Cahier rouge*).

Mémoires de Juliette, in: *Portraits.*

Madame de Staël = De madame de Staël et de ses ouvrages, in: *Portraits.*

Passions religieuses = Des passions religieuses et de leurs rapports avec la morale, in: *P. Déguise, Benjamin Constant inconnu,* Geneva, Droz, 1966.

Pensées détachées, in: *Modernes.*

Perfectibility I = De la perfectibilité de l'espèce humaine, in: *Modernes.*

Perfectibility II = Fragment d'un essai sur la perfectibilité de l'espèce humaine, in: *Modernes.*

Préface abandonnée d'Adolphe in: *OC,* Vol. III, t. 1, 1995.

Préface aux Mélanges, in: *Modernes.*

Principes = Principes de politique, in: *Modernes.*

Souvenirs historiques, in: *Portraits.*

Sur la censure des journaux, in: *Œuvres.*

Tragédie = Réflexions sur la tragédie, in: *Œuvres*

J. Wilde, in: *OC, serie Correspondance générale,* Vol. I, 1993.

IV. A SELECTION OF CONSTANT'S WORKS IN ENGLISH TRANSLATION

Adolphe. New York: B. Blackwell, 1989.

Adolphe and *The Red Notebook* (= *Ma Vie*) With an introduction by Harold Nicolson. New York: New American Library, 1959; and Indianapolis: Bobbs-Merrill, 1959.

Cecile. Edited and annotated by Alfred Roulin; translated by Norman Cameron. Norfolk, CT: James Laughlin, 1953.

Political Writings. New York: Cambridge University Press, 1988.

Prophecy from the Past: Benjamin Constant on conquest and usurpation, edited and translated by Helen Byrne Lippmann. New York: Reynal & Hitchcock, c. 1941.

V. OTHER AUTHORS CITED

Condorcet, "Mémoires sur l'instruction publique," *Œuvres complètes,* Vol. VII, 1849.

I. Kant, "Sur un prétendu droit de mentir par droit de mentir par humanité," *Œuvres complètes,* Gallimard-Pléiade, Vol. III, 1986. In English see: "On a supposed right to lie because of philanthropic concerns" in *Grounding for the metaphysics of morals,* translated by James W. Ellington, Indianapolis: Hackett Pub. Co., c. 1993.

J. J. Rousseau, *Œuvres complètes,* Gallimard-Pléiade, Vol. II, 1964 (*La Nouvelle Héloïse*), Vol. III, 1964 (*Discours sur l'origine de l'inégalité, Le Contrat Social*), Vol. IV, 1969 (*Emile*).

Stendhal, *Courrier anglais,* Vol. V, Le Divan, 1936.

Selective Bibliography

REFERENCE WORKS:

C. Courtney, *A Bibliography of Editions of the Writings of Benjamin Constant to 1833.* London: The Modern Humanities Research Association, 1981.

E. Hofmann (*under the direction of*), *Bibliographie analytique des écrits sur Benjamin Constant, 1796-1980.* Lausanne: Institut Benjamin-Constant, and Oxford: The Voltaire Foundation, 1980.

A more succinct bibliography may be found in the above-mentioned edition of *L'Esprit de conquête,* p. 301-319, by Ephraïm Harpaz.

D. Verrey, *Chronologie de la vie et de l'oeuvre de Benjamin Constant,* Vol. I, 1767-1805. Geneva: Slatkine, 1992.

Annales Benjamin Constant, a magazine dedicated to studies of Constant (published in Lausanne since 1980).

The notes and forewords accompanying recent republications of Constant's works are also helpful in determining how to approach his thought.

TWO GENERAL STUDIES HAVE THE MERIT OF TAKING INTO ACCOUNT THE VARIOUS FACETS OF HIS WORK:

G. Poulet, *Benjamin Constant par lui-même.* Le Seuil, 1968.

B. Fontana, *Benjamin Constant and the Post-Revolutionary Mind,* New Haven and London: Yale University Press, 1991.

TWO RECENT BIOGRAPHIES ARE CONVENIENTLY COMPLEMENTARY, ONE FOCUSING ON HIS DOCTRINES, THE OTHER ON HIS LIFE:

K. Klooke, *Benjamin Constant, Une biographie intellectuelle,* Geneva: Droz, 1984.

D. Wood, *Benjamin Constant, A Biography,* London & New York: Routledge, 1993.

ON THE FIRST YEARS OF HIS LIFE, THE BEST REFERENCE WORK IS:

G. Rudler, *La Jeunesse de Benjamin Constant.* A. Colin, 1908.

ON THE BEGINNINGS OF HIS POLITICAL LIFE AND LOVE LIFE, AN EXCELLENT CLARIFICATION:

B. W. Jasinski, *L'Engagement de Benjamin Constant.* Minard, 1971.

ON THE ROLE OF THE MOTHER IN CONSTANT'S WORK:

H. Verhoeff, *"Adolphe" et Constant: une étude psychocritique.* Klincksieck, 1976.

ON POLITICAL THOUGHT, SEE IN PARTICULAR:

S. Holmes, *Benjamin Constant and the Making of Modern Liberalism*. New Haven: Yale University Press, 1984. The studies by M. Gauchet, Ph. Reynaud, and P. Manent contributed to awakening interest in France for Constant's political thought.

ON THE HISTORY OF POLITICAL AND SOCIAL THOUGHT AT THE TIME OF CONSTANT, THE STANDARD WORK IS:

P. Bénichou, *Le Temps des prophètes*. Gallimard, 1977.

ON CONSTANT'S WRITINGS DEVOTED TO RELIGION, TWO WORKS ALSO COMPLEMENTARY, ONE MORE HISTORICAL, THE OTHER MORE SYSTEMATIC:

P. Déguise, *Benjamin Constant méconnu*. Genève: Droz, 1966.

H. Gouhier, *Benjamin Constant*. Desclée de Brouwer (Les écrivains devant Dieu), 1967.

ON THE *JOURNAL INTIME* AND ITS PLACE AMONG OTHER DIARIES OF THE TIME:

A. Girard, *Le Journal intime*. PUF, 1963.

ON *ADOLPHE*, SEE THE VOLUMINOUS STUDY:

P. Delbouille, *Genèse, structure et destin d' "Adolphe."* Les Belles Lettres, 1971.

Patrick Coleman (essay date 2001)

SOURCE: Coleman, Patrick. Introduction to *Adolphe*, by Benjamin Constant, edited by Patrick Coleman and translated by Margaret Mauldon, pp. vii-xxvii. Oxford: Oxford University Press, 2001.

[*In the following essay, Coleman discusses the biographical and historical circumstances surrounding Constant's composition of* Adolphe, *and surveys critical response to the novel.*]

Adolphe is a novel for a disenchanted age. When Benjamin Constant published the book in 1816 France had just emerged from a quarter-century of revolution and war. It had seen the reformist Enlightenment turn into Robespierre's dictatorship of virtue, religious tolerance proclaimed and then replaced by campaigns to 'de-Christianize' the country by force. It had seen Napoleon overthrow the republic he was supposed to save, forge a new alliance with the Church, and cover himself in military glory only to end in despotism and defeat. For Constant, disenchantment was a good thing, to the extent that it fostered scepticism about utopian schemes. In a pluralistic and imperfect world, attempts to impose uniformity of belief or unrealistic norms of conduct could only end in oppression and unhappiness. On the other hand, when disenchantment becomes so pervasive that it undermines all conviction, it saps the moral energy on which a free and flourishing society depends. *Adolphe* does not deny the necessity of disenchantment in public policy, but it was written to diagnose its dispiriting psychological effects. Two centuries on, Constant's portrait of a man so focused on the ultimate emptiness of existence, so mistrustful of his own feelings, that he finds himself unable to sustain any personal or public commitment, has lost none of its point.

Although the novel was published only after Napoleon's fall, it was largely written in 1806, at the height of the emperor's power. For Constant this was a period of enforced idleness and emotional impatience. His relationship with his lover and partner, the writer Germaine de Staël (1766-1817), had for some time become a burden to him. Despite the similarity of their intellectual outlook they had always been temperamentally at odds. She was brilliant and generous, but also needy and controlling. He craved autonomy but was too weak to strike out on his own; he felt responsible for her, yet resented her demands. In the early years of their affair, when the lovers were swept up in the excitement of political life, this emotional unbalance did not matter so much. They had met in 1794, not in France but in Switzerland. Constant and Staël both came from Swiss Protestant families. She was the daughter of Jacques Necker, a Genevan banker who had been de facto finance minister in France just before the Revolution. In 1786, she had married the Swedish ambassador to France (a match of family interests rather than of love), and her early stories and essays had begun to earn her a considerable reputation as a writer, but as the Revolutionary government became more extreme in 1792 she had decided to retire to her family's Swiss estate at Coppet. Constant was descended from French Protestants forced by religious persecution to leave the country after the Reformation. Until 1798 his native city, as part of the Pays de Vaud, was subject to the canton of Berne, and the only public careers open to the local gentry were military service as an officer in a foreign army (Constant's father served in Holland), or civil service at a foreign court. Constant himself spent the years 1788 to 1793 in the service of the Duke of Brunswick. He had married a Brunswick lady, Wilhelmina von Cramm, but the match was not a happy one (the couple were officially divorced in 1795), nor did Constant enjoy government service in a small, convention-bound German principality. His closest confidante at this time was Isabelle de Charrière (1740-1805), a Dutch-born writer whose novels, including *Caliste* (1787)—a distant influence on *Adolphe*—have recently come to be recognized for their sensitive portraits of women's lives in constricting provincial settings. Charrière expressed dissatisfaction with her own marriage to a worthy but boring Swiss country gentleman in her conversations with Constant, and her disenchanted view of life is echoed by the 'older woman' mentioned in the first chapter of *Adolphe.* Constant himself found comfort in Charrière's friendship, which was something more than intellectual and maternal, although it did not lead to an actual affair.

Constant was therefore ready to be swept up by Staël's energy and enthusiasm; he soon fell in love. Staël, emerging from an unsatisfactory love affair of her own, did not immediately return the feeling, although she found in Constant the intellectual companion she needed. After the fall of Robespierre he followed her back to Paris, where together they were determined to play a role in public affairs. They collaborated on political pamphlets in support of the more moderate republicans. A brilliant conversationalist, Madame de Staël hosted an influential salon, where she helped shape elite public opinion on political and cultural issues. Her own more systematic reflections on *Literature Considered in its Relationships with Social Institutions,* published in 1800, would become a classic of what would later be called the sociology of literature. Meanwhile, Constant sought a more official kind of position. A recent law had given descendants of French Protestant families like his own the right to claim French nationality, and Constant took advantage of this opportunity. Success came in 1799, when, after Napoleon's *coup d'état,* he was appointed to the Tribunate, an advisory political body. But in January 1802 his public opposition to Napoleon's increasingly dictatorial policies led to his dismissal. Later in the same year Madame de Staël also incurred Napoleon's wrath for her persistent expression of liberal views in her novel *Delphine,* and simply for daring, as a woman, to speak out in public on political matters. She was told to leave Paris. This humiliation reinforced Constant's sense of obligation to her, and even though their relationship had lost its former intimacy, he followed Staël (whose husband died en route to Switzerland) in her exile.

As fate would have it—and the indecisive Constant often put himself in the hands of fate in moments of stress, usually in the form of gambling, sometimes incurring large debts—during a visit to Paris in late 1804 he found Charlotte von Hardenburg (1769-1845), whom he had known in Germany a decade earlier when they were each unhappily married. They had thought of marrying each other after their divorces were pronounced, but the plan had come to nothing: Charlotte's father was opposed, misunderstandings had ensued, and after Constant's resignation from the Duke of Brunswick's service and return to Switzerland they had lost touch. Charlotte now had a second husband, a former French émigré, but they were not a united couple, and in 1806 Constant began an affair with her which surprised him by the intensity of its joy. He would marry Charlotte, he decided, as soon as she could get a divorce from M. Du Tertre and he could find a way to leave Staël. So

great was his happiness at finding a new sense of direction—Constant was almost forty, and acutely conscious of time's passing—that he decided to turn the story of his relationship with Charlotte into a novel. Writing it down was probably a way to explore the new sense of continuity he felt existed between the past he remembered and the future he imagined. Not coincidentally, Staël was already engaged in writing a novel of her own, which dealt in a different way, and on a different scale, with the relationship between past, present, and future. In 1805 she had travelled extensively in Italy, much of which was ruled by Napoleon and other foreign powers, and on her return she wrote *Corinne* (1807), the story of a brilliant woman poet who bridges both cultural divides (she is half-English, half-Italian) and historical eras: she evokes in her work the glorious republican past of Rome, Venice, and Florence in order to spur the Italians to recover the energy they have lost through centuries of oppression. In contrast to Constant's story, however, Staël's ends unhappily. Corinne falls in love with a Scottish lord named Oswald, but the latter is too weak and too much influenced by the patriarchal prejudices of British society to commit himself fully to such an unconventional woman. Ironically enough, from the perspective of gender conventions, it is not the prospect of personal happiness that gives Staël's novel its energy and direction, but the ambition to present a portrait of European culture comprehensive enough to rival the oppressive vision Napoleon was imposing on the continent. In its own way Constant's *Adolphe* also stakes a claim to broader cultural significance, but it did so only after a longer and more tortuous period of gestation, and in spite of the fact that the time and space of the story are much narrower. The backdrop to *Adolphe* is not the imaginative vastness of the Roman and British empires but the claustrophobic atmosphere of small German and Polish cities. Indeed, *Adolphe*'s German setting, and Constant's familiarity with German literature and thought, also invite us to define the novel's literary character in relation to works in that tradition, to Friedrich Schlegel's *Lucinde,* for example, or to Goethe's *Elective Affinities,* each written in a style very different from Constant's but presenting views about men and women that are worth comparing to *Adolphe*'s, and, whose characters, like Adolphe, speculate about past and future from within the confines of paralysed present moments.

The decision to compose a novel, that is, a narrative of characters living in time and whose actions form a meaningful plot, represented a new departure for Constant the writer as well as for Constant the man. To some extent, it is true, the ground had been well prepared by developments in his political writing. The pamphlets of the 1790s, his only publications up to this point, were distinguished by a keen analytical sense, but they had been occasional works, designed to address the crises of the moment. In the more comprehensive *Principles of Politics* that preoccupied him in the first decade of the new century Constant, stepping back from circumstances he could no longer influence in any case, focused on the larger question of the relationship between politics and the progress of human institutions. Instead of taking sides in the conflict between French monarchists and republicans, he asked what constitutional guarantees were necessary to preserve individual freedom under any form of government. A crucial step in this process was to define the similarities and differences between freedom as conceived by the ancients (briefly stated, the freedom to participate in government as an active citizen), and the freedom most needed by modern people (the freedom of individuals from government interference in their private pursuits). By the summer of 1806 Constant had completed a long manuscript treatise on the subject, distinguished by a broad historical conception of the evolution of civil society. He was buoyed up by his accomplishment, but also frustrated. Not only was there no prospect of putting his own ideas into practice under Napoleon's regime, the very act of publishing his book would be foolhardy. Under these circumstances he found it difficult to give his manuscript a definitive form.

A deeper hesitation about the shape of the work hindered his researches on the nature and history of religion, a project on which Constant worked almost all his adult life. Should he proceed chronologically, focusing on the evolution of religious ideas, or should he focus on a typology of the forms of religious organization which tended to reappear at various times in different cultures? He changed his mind several times, so difficult was it for him to find an organizing principle that would enable him to integrate into the disenchanted theory of religious institutions his increasingly respectful, if still tentative, appreciation of 'that impulse toward the unknown, the infinite' whose integrity seems to be at odds with any institutional embodiment. Finally, the narrative continuity of the novel stood in most obvious contrast to the diary in which Constant recorded the ups and downs of his moods. Here too there was a perpetual conflict between good intentions and the patterns of behaviour in which those intentions were obscured and distorted. Constant even devised a coded series of numbers so that he could record his most frequently recurring impulses more economically, as one might record the cycles of the weather. His yearnings for freedom and his guilty swings back to concern for, and dependence on, Madame de Staël, had come to seem like impersonal, isolated facts, devoid of meaning or shape. Interestingly, at one point in 1803, with the short-lived prospect of marriage to a Genevan lady, the journal turned into a more continuous narrative, to which Constant gave the title 'Amélie and Germaine'. But both marriage and *récit* were abandoned. It is in contrast with all these forms of writing that Constant turns with obvious enthusiasm to creating something with both a practical and an imaginative direction.

And yet, within a short time the focus of the novel changed. Although the evidence from Constant's journal and correspondence is fragmentary and the process must be reconstructed, it seems that he became increasingly preoccupied with what was originally only an 'episode' in the larger narrative. This episode involved the hero's relationship with another woman. In *Adolphe* as we have it this attachment is so strong that the idea of breaking it paralyses the hero with guilt. That such was the case at the earliest stage of composition we can only surmise, but what is clear and significant is that the episode not only stood in the way of the hero's reaching his goal, it also blocked the author's progress on the narrative, so much so that in the end the episode took over the work and displaced the original story. That story was to have culminated in the happy fulfilment of a destiny. Its spirit could be symbolized by a quotation from Virgil that Constant used in a later text: the happy cry of 'Italy, Italy' when Aeneas and his crew first sight their goal (*Aeneid,* iii, 523). The episode (the subtitle of the final *Adolphe* is 'an anecdote') ends with the death of the other woman, the fictional Ellénore, and with a devastated Adolphe alienated from all human relationships and aimlessly wandering the earth, more like Cain than Aeneas.

Ellénore's death seems, in fact, to have imposed itself on Constant as the work's necessary climactic event. Indeed, even as the novel's original goal came to be deferred indefinitely, Constant found on rereading his work that Ellénore's fatal illness 'is brought about too abruptly' (*Journals,* 31 December 1806). It was as if he had been driven to get to the new conclusion without delay. He then revised the text, expanding it once again from within, but this time to make the conclusion emerge more plausibly from the temporality of the episode. Interpretation of *Adolphe* thus centres on the meaning of Ellénore's death, which appears as an event in both the life of the hero and in the story the author tells his readers. The close connection between the two levels of composition, all the more apparent because of Constant's decision not to incorporate the Ellénore episode in a more comprehensive literary structure, has provoked a number of questions about the relation of literature to life. Is Ellénore's death a wish-fulfilment fantasy, masked by the novel's sorrowful tone—a criticism recently revived by some feminist readers—or is it, as other critics of a more psychoanalytic bent have argued, an imaginative device through which Constant tries to overcome a destructive and paralysing pattern of behaviour? If we acknowledge the legitimacy of the book's therapeutic function—and of course Constant argues that he is not the only one who needs such therapy—another question arises. Does the book's practical purpose support or compromise its integrity as a work of art? In thinking about these questions, we need to recognize that it is Constant's own disenchanted perspective, reflected in the starkness of the episode's story and style, that encourages us to wonder about the uses of imagination in his book. In this respect *Adolphe* stands in contrast to the more expansively 'Romantic' works of the same period, including Staël's own *Corinne*. But we should beware of using *Adolphe*'s disenchanted lucidity to support a reductively instrumental approach to human motivation that Constant himself seeks to condemn. Still, by limiting the narrative of *Adolphe* to a single episode, deliberately isolated from a more thickly layered context of circumstantial detail, Constant takes a considerable risk. While he probably did so to avoid the kind of embellishment that might dull the edge of the pain he portrays, the story is so soberly told that any evidence of artistic shaping stands out the more starkly, and by that very fact may strike the reader as problematic when contrasted with the rawness of the experience it conveys.

Some early readers, aware of Constant's predicament, were tempted to see in Ellénore a fictionalized portrait of Madame de Staël, and in the preface to the novel's second edition (written while Staël was still alive) Constant is at pains to dispel this impression. The reality is in fact much more complicated. Adolphe's indecisive attempts to break off his affair with Ellénore do reflect something of Constant's own relationship with Staël, but the latter's emotional resilience, as well as her high rank, gave her resources unavailable to the fictional Ellénore. The latter's social vulnerability owes something to Anna Lindsay (1764-1820), an Irishwoman with whom Constant had an intense affair in 1800-1. For eleven years she had been the companion of a Frenchman with whom she had two children, only to be reduced to the status of mistress when her lover returned to his wife. Like Ellénore, therefore, Anna's position in good society was a marginal one, although she too was more resilient than the fictional character. Ellénore's final agony is based on that of Julie Talma (1756-1805), not one of Constant's lovers but perhaps his closest and most understanding friend. The wife of France's leading actor of the period, Julie was a woman of great intelligence and insight, and Constant's **'Letter on Julie'** shows how much he valued her support. He had faithfully sat by her side during her final illness and was keenly affected by her death. One may speculate that this experience of loss touched Constant all the more because his own mother had died shortly after he was born. The absence of any adequate maternal figure in his own childhood, coupled with the defences he had built up to deal with the brusqueness of his father, had prevented him from coming to terms with his own unresolved need for an attachment that could help him deal with this early and fundamental loss.

Finally, although the Ellénore character emerged in contrast with that of Charlotte von Hardenburg, Adolphe's gratitude for Ellénore's gift of herself also draws on Constant's experience with Charlotte as they resumed their relationship in 1806. The writing of *Adolphe,* now made possible by the prospect of marriage to Charlotte, may in fact be seen as a way not only of imagining a break with the past, but of forestalling the recurrence of old patterns of behaviour that would spoil his new relationship with a woman to whom he owed a second chance at happiness. This aspect of the biographical context has not been sufficiently appreciated, perhaps because Constant returned to the story of his relationship with Charlotte in *Cécile,* an unfinished novel written after their marriage and the definitive break with Madame de Staël (most probably in 1810), but not published until 1951. This interweaving, in the depiction of the fictional Ellénore, of a future haunted by the past and a past blocking the future makes the novel, even at this early stage of composition, much more than a wish-fulfilment fantasy about getting rid of an obstacle. Far from being a convenience, Ellénore's death represents a disconcertingly obstructive prospect that must be faced if the principles guiding Constant's behaviour—including neurotic forms of pity and self-sacrifice—are themselves to be more than disguised conveniences, narcissistic defences dressed up as moral norms.

Constant completed a first version of *Adolphe* within a few weeks and read it aloud to a few friends, but in 1807 he set it aside for some time. Whatever the therapeutic value of the writing, it produced no immediately apparent results. Constant still hesitated to break decisively with Madame de Staël. He found temporary comfort in the Lausanne meetings of a group of Pietists (Protestants of mystical bent), who encouraged him to abandon his will entirely to God's. While Constant's turn to religion was sincere, his yearning for selflessness had about it something of the passivity of his attraction to the gambling table, and so was bound to fall short of its aim. In 1808 he and Charlotte were finally married, but Madame de Staël was kept in the dark about this until a year later, when, tired of his evasions, Charlotte herself broke the news. At some point in 1809 Constant revised the novel, and a recently discovered 'chronology' in his hand supports the hypothesis that he modified the time-scheme of the story to remove the 'abruptness' of the final crisis. Finally, in 1811 Constant made a decisive break both with Staël and with his habit of shuttling back and forth between Paris and Switzerland. With Charlotte he moved to Germany, settling near her family in Göttingen, a university town whose library allowed him to pursue in scholarly tranquillity his long-delayed work on religion.

Not that he had abandoned literature altogether. In 1809 he published a translation-adaptation of Schiller's dramatic trilogy *Wallenstein,* with whose fate-obsessed, indecisive hero he felt some affinity (interestingly, Constant's English contemporary, Samuel Taylor Coleridge, another writer prone to procrastination, was also drawn to translate these plays). In the period 1810-12 Constant also composed two short, quasi-autobiographical works. *Ma Vie* (*My Life,* formerly known as the **'Red Notebook'** and first published in 1907) looks back on his youth, and especially on his English escapades of 1787, in a light-hearted, humorous way. *Cécile* is a more serious work, but except for its last part is not as sombre as *Adolphe.* The story of the hero's relationship with Cécile-Charlotte is structured as a series of 'epochs', as if it were a history book governed by a firm overall pattern, but the narrative breaks off after relating a particularly heart-rending episode. Cécile, despondent at her lover's failure to extricate himself from his relationship with Madame de Malbée (Staël), falls violently ill and comes close to death. Dennis Wood plausibly speculates that the real Charlotte may have attempted suicide, but in the absence of documentary evidence this cannot be confirmed. What can be said is that Constant abandoned *Cécile* at this point, as if, despite his intention to express his gratitude to Charlotte, the pain and guilt associated with this incident could not be integrated into a story ending in serenity.

In 1813, after Napoleon's disastrous Russian campaign, it became apparent that the emperor's power was weakening. Constant began to dream of re-entering politics and of helping to design the limited, constitutional monarchy he believed was now the only reasonable option for France. At the beginning of 1814 he won wide acclaim for his brilliant essay *On the Spirit of Conquest and Usurpation,* in which he used an anti-Napoleon polemic to present some of the constructive ideas he had developed in the manuscript *Principles of Politics* (a book with this title, also drawing on the earlier treatise, would appear in 1815). Leaving his wife in Germany, Constant returned to Paris, determined to make his mark in the restored Bourbon monarchy of Louis XVIII. Two unexpected developments upset his plans. He became obsessively infatuated with Juliette Récamier (1777-1849), one of the great beauties of the day, who would later become the devoted companion of Chateaubriand. She remained indifferent, however, to Constant's passion, and her coldness drove him to distraction, as it had done others before him. Then, when Napoleon escaped from captivity on Elba in 1815 and marched triumphantly back to Paris, Constant persuaded himself that the emperor, chastened by experience, was prepared to transform himself into a democratic ruler. He switched allegiances and drafted a constitution for the very man he had assailed for usurping all constitutional authority. But Napoleon's 'Hundred Days' of glory ended at Waterloo, and Constant, avoiding an anticipated order of exile and awakening from his obsession with Juliette, left Paris to join Charlotte in Brus-

sels. They went on to London, where he was well received in liberal circles, and it was there that he finally published *Adolphe* in 1816 (in French; an English translation followed shortly afterwards). A Paris edition appeared the same year.

Why did Constant publish the novel? The first reason was simply financial. His situation was precarious, and he was able to sell the rights for a good price. The second reason was to show the world that he was not as erratic and irresponsible as his recent behaviour made him appear. While another work, the *Memoirs on the Hundred Days* (published serially in 1819-20) would offer a reasoned defence of his political manoeuvring, *Adolphe* would attest to the essential sincerity and good intentions of the author as a person. In the year before publication Constant had again read his novel aloud to groups of friends in Paris and London. These readings would end with both audience and author in tears, although Constant would sometimes apparently react against the pathos of the moment by bursting into hysterical laughter. Publishing the novel allowed him to achieve some distance from the story while also accepting that readers would draw their own conclusions from it in his absence. Indeed, it was not long before publication that he composed the **'Letter to the Editor'** and the **'Reply',** which add other voices to that of Adolphe and invite debate about the lessons to be learned from his fate. Not long after the novel appeared Constant also stopped writing his personal journal, which ends on the eve of his final return to France in September 1816.

From that point on, although he went on to publish essays paying warm tribute to Madame de Staël (who died in 1817) and other friends, and although personal feeling emerges in several passages of his work on religion (especially on the mysteries of suffering and death), he does not seem to have needed to explore his emotions in autobiographical writing. Constant threw himself instead into politics, devoting himself to liberal causes, including the abolition of the slave trade and the struggles for Greek independence and freedom of the press. He was several times elected to the Chamber of Deputies where, despite growing infirmity, he spoke out eloquently against the increasingly authoritarian government of Charles X, who succeeded Louis XVIII in 1824. The long-delayed multi-volume work on religion finally began to appear that same year (as did the third and definitive edition of *Adolphe*), but it was not a success. Its mass of erudite and often dusty detail put readers off, and its tentative attitude toward faith pleased neither Christians nor secular rationalists. Constant welcomed the July Revolution of 1830 which placed Louis-Philippe on the throne, accepting a gift from the new king to pay off more gambling debts, but reiterating his commitment to further reform. He died in December 1830, having won the reputation of a tireless champion of liberty, and was given a national funeral.

As is often the case, Constant's reputation declined in the first few decades after his death, although Balzac was inspired to 'reply' to *Adolphe* in his novel *The Muse of the Department* (1843), and George Eliot would cite Constant approvingly, as we shall see below, in her political novel *Felix Holt* (1866). In the ideologically polarized France of the late nineteenth and early twentieth century, however, Constant's moderately progressive liberalism appealed neither to the right nor the left. When interest in *Adolphe* revived in the 1880s, it was focused on its merits as an essay in self-analysis, and much of the discussion concentrated on the biographical sources of the fiction. In the last few decades, however, as a more pluralistic view of politics has replaced narrow certainties, and then as the triumph of a postmodern, relativistic view of cultural difference has made all certainties suspect, it has become possible to appreciate the broader historical and philosophical considerations that inform Constant's narrative.

In some draft fragments of his preface to the novel's second edition Constant sketches the background against which the story is to be understood. 'Everything in nature is connected', he writes. 'Inconstancy or exhaustion in love; in religion, incredulity in a thousand drab or frightening forms; servility in politics are symptoms that go together.' And again, 'Fidelity in love is a strength . . . We have no more strength. We no longer know how to love, or to believe, or to will.' These words suggest that much more is at stake in the portrayal of Adolphe's indecisiveness in love than the novel's plot first suggests. The story focuses primarily on the destructive consequences of Adolphe's inability either to commit himself to the vulnerable Ellénore or to end their affair, but Constant defines his theme in such a way as to encourage reflection on its broader social implications. Earlier French love stories had often portrayed conflicts between love and duty. Generally speaking, in such stories (from Lafayette's *Princesse de Cleves* to Rousseau's *Julie, or the New Heloise*) love was attractive but illicit or uncertain; duty was difficult but ordered and clear. In *Adolphe* this situation is given a new twist. The hero is torn between an illicit relationship to which he feels duty-bound and the dream of a career in which he would find personal fulfilment.

The irony is that while Adolphe's integration into society is not blocked by problems of social standing, education, ideology, or lack of opportunity, he lacks the inner resources needed to establish a meaningful connection with the world around him. In this respect, his situation differs markedly from that of most heroes in earlier French fiction, who aspire to better their lot or who struggle against social convention. It does, however, resemble that of Oswald in Staël's *Corinne,* for although Oswald's reluctance to marry Corinne stems in part from his duty—as a gentleman serving his country as a military officer and member of the House of Lords—to have a wife who meets British standards of female behaviour, it also reflects a deeper lack of energy and initiative. For both Oswald and Adolphe the source of the problem is the same, although the problem itself takes opposite forms. Oswald is paralysed by the image of his father, whose influence over his son, even from beyond the grave, is so great that he cannot undertake any action, however legitimate, of which his father might not approve. Adolphe's father is remote but indulgent, so that the son has never had to confront the consequences of his actions. Lacking any boundaries, and at the same time deprived of a containing context of love, Adolphe finds himself emotionally adrift. While explanations for the respective sons' condition may be found in the biographies of Staël and Constant, one might also see in this change of narrative pattern signs of a broader crisis of paternity in late eighteenth- and early nineteenth-century France. The smooth transmission of values has broken down in the wake of political revolution (culminating in the execution of the ultimate father-figure, the king) and of the crisis in religious belief. Cultural historians and literary critics are now also looking at tensions within families, where the geographical separations necessitated by the search for work in a modernizing economy, along with established habits of sending children away to wet-nurses and later to residential schools, coexisted uneasily with new ideals of 'bourgeois' intimacy within a narrower, if not nuclear, family circle (over this period, for example, we can trace increasingly frequent use of the familiar *tu,* as opposed to the formal *vous,* in letters between children and parents). And if one of the slogans of the Revolution called for careers to be open to talent rather than status, the very meaning of a 'worthy' or 'manly' career had lost its clarity in a world where the prestige associated with war and libertine sexual conquest had vanished without the down-to-earth pursuits of business or practical politics offering any compensating glory.

Fragility of connection is also the dominant note in the novel's treatment of religion. While in eighteenth-century French literature references to God were as often ironic as they were pious, there was at least a clearly defined God to be exalted or mocked. In Chapter 7 of Constant's novel Adolphe is drawn into an extended metaphysical meditation on his place in the universe. His thoughts take on a tone that is undoubtedly religious, and yet they avoid any reference to the divinity. Constant's discretion can be explained by the tentativeness of his own religious beliefs. He had abandoned the sceptical views he had inherited from the Enlightenment, but he was not prepared to embrace any organized religion. As Pierre Deguise has aptly remarked,

Constant's religion consisted more of hope than of faith. He certainly did not want the message of *Adolphe* to be confused with that of *René* (1802), the best-selling story written by his conservative literary and political rival, the royalist Chateaubriand. That novel's hero was to some extent a model for Adolphe, in that he too found himself unable to connect with anything or anyone. René's alienation, however, derived primarily from his aristocratic sense of unrecognized superiority and his conviction that no career was really worth his while, and Chateaubriand answers his hero's inchoate rebellion with an answer which Constant derided as tritely conventional: the story ends with a priest urging René to overcome his sinful self-absorption and return to the 'common paths' marked out by religious and social tradition. Chateaubriand's mature views were much less schematic than this, but even as he moved toward an acceptance of modernity he maintained his belief in the saving prestige of tradition, and in Catholicism as the most imaginatively compelling form of religion. Constant, who had been raised a Protestant, rejected this approach as reactionary obscurantism. He wanted to move beyond disenchantment, but without falling back into illusion. He had come to believe that religious feeling was a basic element of human nature, and that philosophers were wrong to discount it. As Adolphe says toward the end of the novel: 'My surprise is not that man should need a religion; what astonishes me is that he should ever believe himself sufficiently strong, sufficiently protected against misfortune to dare to reject a single one.' Religious institutions and dogmas were another matter. Indeed, in his treatise *On Religion* Constant portrayed a recurring conflict between the dynamism of religious feeling, which fosters an ethic of self-sacrifice crucial to humanity's moral progress, and the ecclesiastical institutions that channel the expression of that feeling: the believer's search for spiritual support is too often used to make him dependent on priestly authority.

It was probably Constant's awareness that his own statements could be exploited in this way that led him to drop the fragments quoted above from the final text of his preface. *Adolphe,* after all, is a novel, not a tract. Nor is the energy of personal conviction liable to be distorted only by religious institutions. Political freedom depends on the citizen's willingness to look beyond his immediate interests, but it is not the government's role to dictate the direction of that gaze, or to demand the sacrifice of the citizen's individuality. Within a general framework of laws protecting them from each other and from interference by the state, citizens, Constant believed, should be free to pursue their own ideal of the good life. This philosophy informs his view of art as well: while the force of the scene or story it presents may have a moral result, giving art a direct moral goal constricts the range of communication and response from which art derives its broader psychological value.

Emotional commitments, the central issue in *Adolphe,* are another, more complicated matter. They should not be enforced by religious or secular law (both Constant and his second wife had earlier been married and divorced in Germany, but in France divorce, legalized by the Revolution in 1792, was forbidden again in 1816), but so crucial is responsibility in love to society's moral health that Constant is more willing to underscore in his prefaces the lesson his male readers should draw from the story. 'Flirtatious women', he writes, 'cause sufficient harm' to men, but women are the ones more vulnerable to suffering, because men 'are less likely than are women to develop the noble and dangerous faculty of living through another and for another.' Today's reader may well concur, but will likely balk at the way Constant develops the point. Women are 'weak creatures, whose only real life is in the heart . . . who have no activity to direct them, no career to direct them, who are . . . credulous out of an excusable vanity . . . and who are always prone to confuse the need for support with the need for love!' There is no suggestion here that, rather than encourage men to assume the role of 'protector', it is women's need for protection that itself needs be reduced. Constant seems to be contradicting the liberal principle that what individuals need protection from is paternalistic authority itself. A quasi-religious feeling of respect for women as models of self-sacrifice takes on problematic social embodiment in unequal gender roles. Readers today, dissatisfied as they may be with the moral side-effects of free-market ideology, might detect similar ambiguities in calls for a return to 'virtue', 'community', or 'family values'. Moving beyond disenchantment without succumbing to the lure of dubious idealizations is no easy task.

Fortunately, *Adolphe* itself is much more subtle than the statements Constant makes about it. Indeed, one of its principal themes is the tendency of generalizing judgements to ignore, even to erase, the complexities and contradictions of personal experience. Near the beginning of the novel Adolphe gives the point a polemical edge. At various points in the narrative we are shown how third-party judgements about both Ellénore's and Adolphe's conduct, whether malicious or well-meaning, not only prove to be inadequate but in fact aggravate the painful dilemmas they are supposed to resolve. At the same time, we are not to view Adolphe's first-person perspective as so unique and authentic that it must be held to speak for itself. On the contrary, his difficulties arise in large measure because he is alienated from himself, observing himself from the outside as if he were another person—and so he is as prone as anyone else to mis-describing his own behaviour. The older Adolphe who tells the story has been made wiser by suffering, but because his narrative stands at some remove from the events it relates, and because he wants to relate his experience to some general 'truths' about human nature at which he has arrived, his own judgements are still questionable. They may be distorted by another kind of detachment from experience, and also by the fact that he is still judging his own case. A further ambiguity may be found in the exchange of letters, after the end of Adolphe's story, between the 'editor' and an anonymous correspondent. These texts provide a necessary balance to the narrator's perspective, yet they do not place it in a neatly delimited frame. These characters belong to Constant's fictional world, which offers no examples of unprejudiced judgement, and one notes that the letters employ the same vocabulary and analytical devices we find used in Adolphe's own self-analysis. The correspondents also begin from contradictory premisses: for one, society is ultimately to blame; for the other, character. Their statements, too, invite assessment rather than assent.

Take, for example, the moral principle advanced by the 'editor' in his 'Reply' to his correspondent at the end of the book. 'The great question in life is the suffering we cause, and the most ingenious metaphysics do not justify the man who has broken the heart that loved him.' At first sight the statement carries an undeniable force. But is it always true that the suffering one causes should be the supreme question? We are reminded of the physician's Hippocratic oath, with its injunction 'Never do harm'; yet doctors do order painful treatments to cure a worse ill. One might well argue that it is precisely because Adolphe was so obsessed by the prospect of the harm he might do Ellénore by breaking off his relationship with her that he ultimately caused her more pain. And yet, contemplating Ellenore's suffering, readers will surely feel that summing up the story as an instance of 'having to be cruel to be kind' would be a crudely inadequate response. The implications of the 'editor's' statement do not stop there, as George Eliot understood when she used it as the epigraph to Chapter 50 of *Felix Holt*. Dressed-up by an 'ingenious metaphysics', the cruel-to-be-kind principle has been used by political and religious leaders to justify questionable actions undertaken for the people's own ultimate good. The events of the last two centuries have taught us to be wary of such arguments. On the other hand, the refusal to intervene for fear of possibly causing harm may sometimes be a way of rationalizing our indifference or our refusal of risk. In Constant's story, Adolphe's own father (himself, it is worth recalling, the director of a government department in an enlightened German principality) was scrupulous in not interfering with his son's freedom, but the result is hardly reassuring.

Thinking about paternal authority leads us to another point. If, as suggested before, there is something paternalistic in the way Constant speaks about women's need for protection, then it is equally presumptuous for a man to assume, even when he wants to shoulder the blame, that in the life of a couple all the agency is on his side. To see Ellénore merely as a passive victim to be pitied is to rob her of her status as a character in her own right, and to turn her into a symbol. A closer look at her character shows an element of pride and wilfulness in her self-abasement; her devotion is as destructive as it is noble, and if we reread the 'editor's' Reply more carefully in this light, we see that his statement is more nuanced than it first appears. When considered attentively, the first part of the sentence invites us to a philosophical debate in which the fashionable slogan, 'the personal is the political', is shown to generate more questions than answers. Still, in pursuing these questions we should beware lest an 'ingenious metaphysics' of our own absorb us to the point of obscuring the emotional scandal of broken human connection, to which that sentence returns at its end.

The whole of **Adolphe** repays a close reading of this kind, which moves from a first, overall assessment of each incident or statement to a separate, many-sided consideration of its various parts, and back again to the whole. We are accustomed, when reading a novel, to distinguish between what is shown and what is told, and we are well advised to follow D. H. Lawrence's injunction to trust the tale more than the teller. **Adolphe,** however, belongs to a distinctive French tradition of concentrated first-person narratives or *récits* that includes such works as Gide's *The Immoralist* and Camus's *The Stranger,* as well as such contemporary examples of fictional self-disclosure as the novels of Annie Ernaux. In these works, in which a limited number of incidents are related and analysed at length, the telling, to a considerable degree, is part of the showing. Or, perhaps more precisely, we should say that the 'saying' is the showing, since so much of the narrative's dynamism lies in the relationship between the various parts (words and abstract ideas) of sentences carefully arranged to stimulate fresh reflection as much as to formulate a judgement on the action or to propel the reader on through the story. Among other examples, one may cite Adolphe's judgement on his younger self: 'although I was interested solely in myself, I was only faintly interested in myself', where one wonders whether the two 'myselfs' refer to the same thing (indeed, in the French text they are designated by *moi* and *moi-même*, a distinction difficult to reproduce in English). Another example might be Adolphe's description of the letters he writes to Ellénore to reassure her: 'without ever saying enough to satisfy, I always said enough to deceive her.' Or again, when the couple is trying inauthentically to recreate a sense of intimacy: 'we spoke constantly of love; but we spoke of love because we were afraid to speak of other things.'

In their terse suggestiveness, the novel's more general statements recall the 'maxims' devised by seventeenth-century *moralistes* such as La Rochefoucauld to provoke drawing-room debate: 'Fools make of their morality a compact and indivisible mass, so that it interferes as little as possible with their actions and leaves them free in all the details.' 'We had both spoken irreparable words; we could keep silent, but we could not forget them. There are things which for a long period are left unsaid, but once they are said, one never ceases to repeat them.' Other statements invite us to weigh not only their general truth, but the truthfulness of Adolphe's own narrative, even when it is at its most apparently self-critical. 'We are such changeable creatures that we eventually come to experience the feelings that we counterfeit.' Does this apply to the older Adolphe telling the story as much as to the younger one who first pretended to be in love with Ellénore? Is Constant unmasking the inauthenticity of human life—and by extension of the narrative we are reading—or expressing a paradoxical form of hope within and beyond disenchantment? In its intellectual and emotional complexity *Adolphe* remains, as Alison Fairlie, one its most sensitive commentators, once called it, 'the most quietly disruptive of all French novels'.

Select Bibliography

EDITIONS OF CONSTANT

Œuvres complètes, ed. Paul Delbouille *et al.* (Tübingen, 1993-). This will be the standard critical edition of all Constant's works. *Adolphe* appears in vol. III.

Adolphe, ed. Paul Delbouille (Paris, 1977). A fine critical edition, with extensive introduction, notes, and bibliography.

Adolphe, ed. C. P. Courtney (Bristol, 1990). An edition of the French text by a leading British scholar.

Adolphe, ed. Gilles Ernst (Paris, 1995). A handy pocket edition of the French text, with helpful linguistic notes.

Political Writings, trans. and ed. Biancamaria Fontana (Cambridge, 1988).

BIOGRAPHY

Dennis Wood, *Benjamin Constant: A Biography* (London, 1993). Up-to-date, scholarly, and very readable biography.

Harold Nicolson, *Benjamin Constant* (London, 1949). Needs to be corrected by subsequent findings, but offers many shrewd remarks on Constant's life and times.

CRITICAL WORKS

Only works in English are listed here. For full bibliographies of studies in French and other languages, see *Bibliographie analytique des écrits de Benjamin Constant (1796-1980)*, ed. Étienne Hofmann (Lausanne-Oxford, 1980); François Vallotton, *Bibliographie analytique des écrits sur Benjamin Constant (1980-1995)* (Paris, 1997); and the yearly *Annales Benjamin Constant*.

Patrick Coleman, *Reparative Realism: Mourning and Modernity in the French Novel 1730-1830* (Geneva, 1998).

John Cruickshank, *Benjamin Constant* (New York, 1974).

Alison Fairlie, *Imagination and Language: Collected Essays on Constant, Baudelaire, Nerval, and Flaubert* (Cambridge, 1981). Fundamental.

Biancamaria Fontana, *Benjamin Constant and the Post-Revolutionary Mind* (New Haven, Conn., 1991).

F. W. J. Hemmings, *Culture and Society in France 1789-1848* (Leicester, 1987).

Marian Hobson, 'Theme and Structure in *Adolphe*', *Modern Language Review,* 66 (1971): 306-14.

Wolfgang W. Holdheim, *The Hermeneutic Mode* (Ithaca, NY, 1984). Excellent chapter on the style of *Adolphe*.

Stephen Holmes, *Benjamin Constant and the Making of Modern Liberalism* (New Haven, Conn., 1984). A major reinterpretation and rehabilitation of Constant as political thinker.

Lynn Hunt, *The Family Romance of the French Revolution* (Berkeley, 1992).

Charles E. Larmore, *The Romantic Legacy* (New York, 1996).

Allan H. Pasco, *Sick Heroes: French Society and Culture in the Romantic Age, 1750-1850* (Exeter, 1997).

Naomi Segal, *Narcissus and Echo: Women in the French Récit* (Manchester, 1988).

Margaret Waller, *The Male Malady: Fictions of Impotence in the French Romantic Novel* (New Brunswick, NJ, 1993).

Dennis Wood, *Constant: Adolphe* (Cambridge, 1987).

Timothy Unwin, *Constant, Adolphe* (London, 1986).

———(ed.), *The Cambridge Companion to the French Novel from 1800 to the Present* (Cambridge, 1997).

FURTHER READING IN OXFORD WORLD'S CLASSICS

J. W. von Goethe, *Elective Affinities,* trans. and ed. David Constantine.

Choderlos de Laclos, *Les Liaisons dangereuses,* trans. and ed. Douglas Parmée, with an introduction by David Coward.

Madame de Staël, *Corinne, or Italy,* trans. and ed. Sylvia Raphael, with an introduction by John Claiborne Isbell.

Patrick Coleman (essay date fall 2002)

SOURCE: Coleman, Patrick. "Constant and the *Froissement* of Form." *Historical Reflections* 28, no. 3 (fall 2002): 385-96.

[*In the following essay, Coleman illuminates Constant's discussion of the relationship between literary form and emotional expression in his works.*]

Benjamin Constant is well known for his disenchanted lucidity about the forms—political, literary and religious—that embody, safeguard or stifle the free expression of human sentiments. If, as Constant asserted, the common denominator of his whole career was a commitment to "liberty in everything,"[1] and if "all man's faculties hang together,"[2] then an interdisciplinary study of his work should include a comparative analysis of the forms generated by those faculties, and of the interaction between form and freedom of feeling or will. Of course, such an enterprise runs the risk of abstraction and unwarranted generalization. Wary of imposing a reductive totalizing philosophical scheme on the diversity of human institutions, uncomfortable also with the tendency of all universalizing language to distort the elusive particularity of human emotions, Constant tended to present his ideas on religion, politics and art in provisional ways, through responses to specific external occasions. Even the long-meditated treatise on religion, which was not published until late in his life, bears the marks of Restoration polemics. All forms for Constant were derivative constructs, to be discussed and evaluated in such a way as to respect the primacy of the sentiments through which humanity expresses its freedom and capacity for progress.

And yet, if the dynamic of human agency is to be defined at all clearly then we must attend, in a more comprehensive way, to Constant's ideas about form. A common objection to Constant's analysis of religion, for example, is that while doctrines and institutions are extensively discussed, the contours of the *sentiment religieux* itself remain disappointingly vague. In literary criticism, there has been long and often acrimonious debate about the relation between form and feeling in Constant's novel *Adolphe,* both within the world of the text and in the author's relation to his work. While the novel offers a multiplicity of framing devices (prefaces, editor's note, an exchange of letters commenting on the

story), the very prominence of these forms has encouraged suspicions about the nature and authenticity of the hero's feelings. Similar suspicions about the motives behind Constant's sometimes erratic political career have prompted in the past similar questions about his motives, and even now sympathetic critics have asked whether the freedom of the "moderns" can in fact energize the institutions devised to protect it. Comparing his writings on different subjects may not lead to resolution of these difficulties, but it may help us understand the nature of the interplay between form and feeling in Constant's thinking.

The distinction between feeling and form is not, of course, absolute. For example, religious feeling as Constant comprehends it stands on a different level from, say, fear or gratitude; as a "disposition" or "tendency" that reflexively enjoys other emotions and can compel us to believe, it possesses some degree of organization and stability.[3] Still, we can begin by considering form separately, and by distinguishing three kinds or aspects of form in Constant's work.

First, there is form as the embodiment or objectification of feeling. As such, form is a necessary, indeed inevitable, component of any human action or communication.[4] In his remarks on language in *Adolphe,* Constant shows how feeling may be betrayed or distorted by the hackneyed words that must be used to express it, but he also shows, in Adolphe's relationship to Ellénore, that not putting feelings into words can be even more hurtful to others and paralyzing to the self. The question raised is whether such personal relationships may be mediated through a larger social or cultural context of communication in which the expression of feeling can be stabilized, its worst consequences blocked or minimized, and its positive potential enhanced.

This brings us to a second idea of form as containing context, a notion developed at greatest length in Constant's political philosophy. Condemning as outmoded and ultimately oppressive the ancient Greek notion of politics as participation—as the collective embodiment of freedom—Constant argued that political institutions should instead provide a regulatory framework. Within that framework, citizens could pursue their own vision of the good life without damaging others and without being required to cast that vision in terms of an ideal imposed upon them, or even being compelled to articulate any systematic vision at all. The danger, of course, is that if they are not animated by a clear sense of purpose or unifying collective agency, political forms may collapse into mechanical routines. In an unpublished text, Constant declared that "enthusiasm for liberty" cannot exist independently of such "forces" as faithful love and religious belief,[5] but what the relationship might be between these forces and the forms of politics is not clear. Political institutions could also be captured by interests all the more difficult to identify and oppose in that they hide behind the impersonality of the forms.

This alienation of form from free feeling appears most starkly in religion. The uncertainty of communication with an elusive divinity means that any form devised to institutionalize the expression of religious feeling—as embodiment or as framework—will tend to become oppressive, especially when controlled by a priesthood. It is notable in this regard that Constant, in his account of the establishment of collective religious forms (that is, all those that go beyond the level of low-level fetishism, which he views as individualistic), does not ascribe any initiative to the members of the community. The people only respond, either to the actions of leaders set apart from them (for Constant even the prophets of ancient Israel were not popular figures but were to be classified as priests[6]) or to such impersonal forces as climate and "given" cultural factors. It is true that for reasons of prudence Constant's analysis of religious forms focuses on the past rather than the present,[7] and so the issue of agency in religion now does not arise except in negative comments about Lamennais and other Catholic apologists. But one wonders whether there is not some connection here between Constant's reluctance to envisage community agency in religion—owing in large part to the heritage of the Enlightenment and the ecclesiology of militant Restoration Catholicism—and the absence of any consideration of collective moral agency within the civil society protected by politics.[8] A comparison with Tocqueville's *De la démocratie en Amérique* might be illuminating in this regard.

The only exception to Constant's denial of agency in religion "from below" is the polytheism of ancient Greece. There, Constant identifies a dynamic linked to a third kind of form. This is form as refinement, of which Constant distinguishes several different kinds. When discussing an existing form, then refinement may be considered embellishment or adornment, if the form is solidly established; it is idealization, or what Constant calls *épuration*, if the form is not entirely fixed. The Gods as the Greeks inherited them from their primitive past and contacts with other peoples were still rather crude, and the conduct attributed to them less than admirable; but in Homer, and then in Athenian tragedy, we can see a characteristic Greek effort of idealization, through which the most vulgar and immoral aspects of polytheism were discarded. According to Constant, this process was made possible by the absence in Greece of a powerful priesthood, for while educated priestly castes may not share the more vulgar beliefs of the people, they are careful not to abandon cruder religious forms that serve their interests by keeping the people under their control. There is no real *épuration* from above or outside; the intellectual work of priests is, rather, syncretistic and as such *stationnaire*

rather than progressive.[9] In the absence of such a controlling agency, the forms of the Greek gods were not fully determined, and so they could be redefined and reinterpreted.

Yet, it does not follow from this that in Greece the people at large worked on their own religious forms. Constant does claim that Homeric epic reflects the dynamic of Greek culture, but it is unclear in what way Homer's agency (or that of the Athenian tragedians) mirrors that of the community from which the author springs. To the extent that literature constitutes the main evidence he has for Greek religion in the period, it is not surprising that Constant is not able to pursue the question, which is obviously linked to the problem of the artist's agency within any society. Does an author (who must be the product of a society already refined to some degree) merely "adorn" through his style already-existing cultural attitudes, or does he contribute to refining those attitudes? In some sense, of course, he does both, and in his literary criticism Constant will investigate the question further. In *De la religion,* however, it seems that the unanalyzed but assumed complexity of the artist's agency in the *Iliad* or the *Oresteia* allows Constant not to probe into that of the Greek people as a differentiated community. The German Romantic view of the ancient Greeks as a people of artists, giving idealized form to all aspects of their existence, may also have left its mark here. By way of contrast, Constant does not consider the scriptures of Eastern religions, or even the Hebrew Bible, either as works of art or as reflections of community agency. Had he done so, his characterization of the dynamic of religion in each case, and certainly for ancient Israel, would have had to be modified. As it is, these writings are considered almost exclusively as the instrumental creations of the priestly caste.

It is true that Constant does distinguish a more authentic cultural agency within Hebrew religion in the work of Moses, who is distinguished by the purity of his monotheistic theology and moral teaching. But Moses is very different from Homer. First, his refinement is exclusively moral. It does not involve an aesthetic redeeming of appearances. Rather, it centers on a code of law, one in which *sentiment* plays little part. Not coincidentally, I think, Moses is viewed as being ahead of his time, rather than the embodiment of his age. No doubt Constant's attitude reflects a common Enlightenment view of ancient Israel as a primitive culture. Constant, it is true, does not see in Moses one of those legislators who use religion only as a means to govern,[10] that is, who do not believe the doctrines they preach. Yet, Moses' focus on moral legislation, and the need to accommodate the pure language of law to the "grossness" of the popular mind,[11] puts him at much more of a distance from his community than does the artistry of Homer or Sophocles. It is useful in this regard to compare Constant's Moses with the isolated hero of Vigny's famous poem "Moïse." For Vigny, refinement of sensibility principally distinguishes the spiritual leader, like the artist, from other people. What decisively isolates Constant's Moses is that he must channel refinement in the form of a law code which, however admirable in its way, must necessarily involve an alienating effect.

Some of Constant's vagueness in his discussion of Jesus may indeed be traced to this half-articulated intuition about the nature of the religious leader's mission as mediator of the divine. In line with his eighteenth-century predecessors, Constant wants to present Jesus essentially as a man who introduced a more refined and universal morality. At the same time, he realizes that to do so goes against his own fundamental conviction that religious feeling is not a matter of conformity to laws, divine or human, and that its refinement is only possible through a deeper awareness of "all that is good" in the world. Such a revelation, if we may call it that, can no more derive "from above" in the conventional sense of divine self-manifestation than it can be the work of a leader or legislator. In a way Constant never makes clear, it seems to come *to* humankind but from *within* humanity as part of that "good." This approach clearly owes much to the idea of the incarnate Christ, but this is a doctrine as uncongenial to Constant as the alternative doctrine of pantheism.[12]

The problem is an important one since a number of passages in Constant's work suggest that a refined morality is the key to resolving the tension between feeling and form in both politics and religion. A morality no longer seen as compulsion or command, but as a framework of behavior almost coincident with a *sentiment* freed from the immediate impulses of pleasure and pain—a "practical idealism," as one critic has called it[13]—would seem to be the goal toward which Constant's thinking tends. The "almost" would not represent the alienation of form from feeling but the space for further progress, driven by that dynamic of free self-sacrifice from below to which Constant, like Staël, attributes so much importance. What drives the progress of civilization is the human capacity to forego immediate satisfaction, even at the cost of some pain, for the sake of one's own future good or for that of another. The notion of self-sacrifice, however, must not be misunderstood. It is not a self-alienation subordinating the self to an external agency or institution.[14] Rather, the *douleur* associated with self-sacrifice is sorrow more than pain (the French word can mean both): a sorrow that comes from the realization of the absence or inadequacy of fulfillment within currently-existing forms of life. What is "sacrificed" is not feeling but the illusion of solidity, revealed as such by experience in time. I have argued elsewhere, for example, that the purpose of **Adolphe** is not to transcend raw experience through reflection, to enshrine in acceptable form the wayward re-

ality of feeling, but rather to arrive at the disenchanted reality of feeling by deconstructing the falsely idealizing forms of reflection that bar access to human reality.[15]

The negativity of *douleur* makes room for growth in sympathy with others and for the imagination of new ways of life. Yet, it is not oriented to an abstract ideal but to the rehabilitation of experience, including physical experience—the French *sentiment* encompassing both sensuous and moral feelings. One is tempted to link this recovery with revelation as the experience of "all that is good," since in this formulation of the process it is possible to maintain that a revelation comes to the self from outside, but in a sense still from within. However, modeling, let alone effecting, this rehabilitation, which is a key element in any authentic refinement of feeling, is beyond the capacity of a disincarnated religion. A moral code, however enlightened, will not serve either. It remains to be seen whether art, as the embodiment in language of the tension between form and feeling, can illustrate a possible resolution.

Constant's literary criticism is only now beginning to attract scholarly attention.[16] This is probably because of its fragmentary and somewhat diffident character. In discussing his translation of Schiller's *Wallenstein*, Constant does speak of his struggle to convey the atmosphere of the German work while following the "rules" of the French theatre, but his discussion does not engage a broader view of literary form. Instead, the rules are seen merely as reflections of the audience's prejudices. In another essay Constant envisions a new kind of tragedy focused precisely on the power of social prejudice, but his analysis concentrates on theme rather than form. There is no echo here of the philosophical history of genres developed by the German Romantics. Instead, the process of artistic refinement centers on the progress of style and taste. In his unfinished essay on literature in its relation to freedom, Constant writes of "that suppleness of wit, that finesse in shades of meaning, that quickness of allusion, that propriety of language that conduce to the perfection of art."[17] As in his discussion of Homeric religion, he uses the word *épuration*, long associated with the idea of taste, to encapsulate this process of refinement. But does refinement in this sense necessarily go together with freedom of expression? Against La Harpe and other defenders of authoritarian rule, who argued that the golden ages of Latin and French literature coincided with periods of absolutism, Constant maintains that Virgil and Horace, Corneille and Massillon were animated by the memory or the anticipation of political freedom, without which they would not have achieved greatness.

Yet, Constant's analysis neither explains how this process of refinement operates, nor how it manifests itself in the formal elaboration of the work. Indeed, as Beatrice Fink has remarked, when analyzing a work of art Constant speaks more of the author's character than of the work's form.[18] However, we need not conclude from this that Constant's criticism tells us nothing about form and refinement. If, following Buffon, we take style, broadly defined, as the expression of personality, then perhaps art criticism for Constant is really a way of talking about personality, that is to say, about the form of the human individual.[19] To focus on the person is not necessarily to descend from the level of form to that of unstructured feeling—a reproach often and wrongly leveled at Staël's aesthetics, be it said in passing. It may be to arrive at the site where the relation between feeling and form most commands our attention. It is worth reflecting on the fact that one of Constant's most moving essays, the **"Letter about Julie,"** appears in the *Mélanges de littérature et de politique,* even though Julie Talma was neither an author nor a politician.[20]

In the eighteenth century form and feeling at the level of the person met in the notion of *character,* the object of the literary genre of the "portrait," and a notion given renewed currency by Constant's English contemporary, William Hazlitt. Constant's outlook in his personal essays is similar in that he wishes to frame the analysis of the ways a personality defines itself without appealing directly to moral categories. As with art, one could say that while for Constant the self-definition of personality should have a moral result or outcome, it should not be directed by a predetermined moral purpose. The essay **"On Mme. de Staël and her works"** illustrates this point by placing the author's character on the same level as her works, and the preface to the "second edition" of *Adolphe,* significantly subtitled **"Essay on the nature and moral effect of the work,"** makes a similar argument. Unfortunately, despite his spirited defense of authors and books against simplistic moralism, Constant sheds little light on the process of refinement from within or below. On the contrary, he does not hesitate to appeal to a more traditional notion of delicacy associated with *mondanité.* When Constant wants to condemn those who see in *Adolphe* a vulgar *roman à clef* rather than an autonomous work of art, he associates them with "those men who, not being accepted in society, observe it with uncouth curiosity and wounded vanity from the outside, and attempt to discover or to create scandal in a sphere which is above them."[21] Here, the notion of art as disinterested, as moving beyond personal experience toward a broader and more socially useful meaning, is linked to an idea of good manners. However powerful a civilizing force it may have been in its original seventeenth-century context, the appeal to manners hardly responds adequately to the circumstances of nineteenth-century civil society, unless the idea of "manners" is redefined and expanded. Nor is the ethic of free self-sacrifice productively developed in the same text by an association with gender roles, as when Constant writes of women as possessing more than men

the "noble and dangerous faculty of living through another and for another."[22]

If the key to art, however, is style, then perhaps we should look to Constant's style, rather than to his thematic statements, for clues as to how the refinement of cultural forms is re-imagined in terms linked to the idea of the individual person.[23] I will conclude this paper by exploring a feature of Constant's vocabulary which I believe provides one such clue.

In rereading Constant I have been struck with his use of the word *froisser,* a word which can mean, depending on the context, to bruise, crumple, wrinkle or vex. The most vivid example occurs in *Adolphe* in the description of Ellénore's suffering:

> I saw—what a humiliating and pitiable sight!—that energetic, proud personality experience countless confused and discordant impressions of physical suffering, as if, in those terrible moments, the soul, bruised [*froissée*] by the body, underwent every possible metamorphosis so as to conform the more easily to the deterioration of the organs.[24]

The word appears again in the **"Preface to the second edition,"** as Constant describes men whose good instincts are checked by the influence of "une doctrine de fatuité" inherited from the frivolous eighteenth century. Surprised by the movement of their own hearts,

> if they want to overcome what out of habit they call weakness, they must go deep into that wretched heart and bruise [*froissent*] what is generous in it, break what is faithful, and kill what is good.[25]

The first of these contexts may be categorized as religious in a broad sense, the second as moral. But the word also occurs twice in Constant's first formulation of his most original political concept, that of the "neutral or preservative power [*pouvoir neutre ou préservateur*]" necessary to the proper functioning of any constitutional government. Constant is arguing that the administrative branch of government should not be directly dependent on the branch entrusted with the executive power. If they are fused, "the interests of those administered will be hurt [*froissés*], because the administrators will want to please a superior authority."[26] A few pages later, he sums up his discussion of the neutral power in this way:

> The preservative power has no connection with individuals; it in no way trammels individual progress; it sanctions no opinion, but in preserving the different branches of government from their reciprocal frictions [*froissements*], it contributes to the happiness and the perfectioning of the governed, as the architect who by turns strengthens or corrects the various parts of a building contributes to the happiness of those who inhabit it, without restricting their independence, but by ensuring their safety.[27]

In the first of these four instances, *froisser* seems to involve damage to feeling inflicted in the first case by the suffering of the body; in the second, by the calculations of egoism. The body may be identified with the outward earthly form of the soul, while egoism is the psychological analogue of a frozen, and, to use a term favored by Constant, *stationnaire* social structure. On the other hand, in the third and fourth instances, what is *froissé* is itself a form: the structure of interests of the people and political institutions. In the latter case "froissement" might in fact be translated (as I have done above) as "friction," as between the parts of a machine, with the *pouvoir préservateur* acting not as a stationary form, but as a judiciously-applied lubricant. The image of the house and its architect develops this reversal of perspective. The house is a protective and enabling form, provided of course it is modified over time by an architect concerned less with the permanence of his monument than with the responsiveness of his art.

This evolving house offers an interesting contrast to the image of the ruin, which is so important to other Romantic writers, including Chateaubriand and Staël. In the ruin we see the visible embodiment of religious or political forms (a medieval church, the Roman forum) worn away by time. But the ruin also has positive value, in that its incompleteness invites imaginative recreation, which can be the first step toward the development of new forms. What we have in Constant's image of the building is a form beyond form, a form which, rooted in free, personal activity, looks more like a manifestation of *sentiment*. That the neutral power stands in contrast to "form" even as it emerges as the linchpin of constitutional order is made clear in another, remarkable passage of the **Fragments.** "Why not combine the preservative power," Constant asks, "with the judicial power? Because it is impossible to pass from the exercise of a discretionary authority to the exercise of an authority bound by formal constraints."[28]

Let us return now to the use of the term *froisser* in **Adolphe.** It is not quite correct to say that what we see there is the destructive activity of form on feeling. In speaking of Ellénore's suffering, Constant might just as easily have spoken of her tender soul as being *meurtri* ("bruised") or *écrasé* ("crushed") by her body.[29] We have learned, however, from Alison Fairlie and other close readers of Constant's style to appreciate the subtlety of his word choices. It seems clear that the echo with *froisser* in the sense of a transgression of standards of delicacy (a sense present in the quotation from the preface) is deliberate here. Not only is Ellénore's suffering the result of Adolphe's lack of moral delicacy, but the stark physicality in the way he describes her death is yet another offence against contemporary notions of literary tact. But to say this is to say that the contrast here is not simply innocent feeling and a hostile form. Rather, Ellénore's soul is also a

kind of concrete form, whose beautiful surface has been "froissé" in the sense of crumpled (*chiffonné*). What distinguishes *froisser* from its alternatives is the connotation of a constructed appearance (clothing, hair) being wrinkled, or the smooth surface of social *égards* roughened. The distance between the passages from **Adolphe** and those from the **Fragments** may not be that great. If generosity and interest may both be *froissé,* then the difference between them may not be as fundamental as Constant makes them out to be in his more polemical statements. But rather than reducing generosity to the level of interest, it is the latter that is incorporated into a vision of moral and political delicacy (just as the concreteness of Ellénore's death scene does not reduce her to a mere body, but integrates her physical suffering into the story of her moral ordeal). As Constant writes in another context: "man in his march to civilization endeavors to bring down to himself that which is too elevated, and to raise that which is too base."[30] Although it is only glimpsed *en creux,* in negative examples, a new relationship between form and feeling begins to emerge here in the art of Constant's prose.

Notes

1. "Preface" to *Mélanges de littérature et de politique* in Benjamin Constant, *Œuvres,* ed. Alfred Roulin (Paris, 1957), p. 802. Unless otherwise indicated, all translations from the French are my own.

2. *Les "Principes de politique" de Benjamin Constant,* ed. Etienne Hofmann (Geneva, 1980), 2:147.

3. *De la religion considérée dans sa source, ses formes, et ses développements* (Paris, 1824-31), livre I, chapitre 1; I:18, 32. Further reference to this work will be to book and chapter, then to the volume and page of this edition.

4. I say "human" because for Constant God's activity in the world is embodied only as "a constant and intimate appeal at the center of all that is good." See *De la religion* XII, 12; IV:509. He is hostile to the notion of an incarnate God (*De la religion* V, 6; II:445, note b).

5. See the drafts for a preface to the second edition of *Adolphe* in Benjamin Constant, *Œuvres complètes* (Tübingen, 1995-) III.1:197. Future references to the critical edition in progress will be abbreviated as *OC.* It should be noted that "enthusiasm" here does not carry the overtones of fanaticism it does in earlier writers such as Shaftesbury or Voltaire. The word designates an energy of will and feeling that stands in opposition not to enlightenment, but to cynicism and passivity.

6. *De la religion* IV, 10; II:205. Pierre Deguise underscores the point in the notes to his edition of *De la religion* in Benjamin Constant, *OC* XVIII.2:

163. [At the time of writing only one part of volume 18, devoted to *De la religion,* has been published.]

7. Constant does analyze Indian and other non-Western religions as they existed in his time, but in his scheme of religious evolution they belong to the past. For the distorting effect of Constant's decision not to discuss contemporary Christianity directly, see Patrice Thompson, "Benjamin Constant: L'allégorie du polythéisme," *Annales Benjamin Constant* 12 (1991): 7-18.

8. Significantly, Constant nowhere invokes the idea of the priesthood of all believers.

9. *De la religion* VI, 3; III:33 ("The priests always added, and never cut back.")

10. *De la religion,* IV, 11; II:230.

11. *De la religion,* IV, 11; II:215.

12. It would be worth investigating why Constant should express such hostility to pantheism, which, in rather traditional anti-Spinozist fashion, he pairs with atheism. See *De la religion* VI, 3; III:28-29.

13. See Kurt Mueller-Vollmer, "Politique et esthétique: l'idéalisme concret de Benjamin Constant, Guillaume de Humboldt et Madame de Staël," *Benjamin Constant, Madame de Staël et le groupe de Coppet,* ed. Etienne Hofmann (Oxford, Lausanne, 1982), pp. 453-73.

14. Constant differs from Staël in placing less stress on a Kantian conception of duty.

15. Patrick Coleman, *Reparative Realism: Mourning and Modernity in the French Novel 1730-1830* (Geneva: 1998), pp. 79-101.

16. See Béatrice Fink, "Benjamin Constant devant le sens du littéraire," *Les Lumières en Hongrie, en Europe centrale et en Europe orientale. Actes du 6e Colloque de Matrafüred 20-25 octobre 1984* (Budapest-Paris, 1987), pp. 245-254; Martine de Rougemont, "Benjamin Constant critique littéraire," *Annales Benjamin Constant* 12 (1991): 99-107; and the introductions to the essays published in *OC* III.

17. Constant, *OC* III.1:500.

18. Fink, p. 249.

19. As distinguished from *personnalité,* which in the writings of Constant and others of his time designates the asertiveness of the selfish ego.

20. The essay was begun in late 1806 and finished in early 1807, and was originally supposed to preface a memorial volume of letters Julie Talma had written to her friends. The volume was never published, but Constant attached considerable importance to this text. For a critical edition, see *OC* III.1: 207-223.

21. Benjamin Constant, *Adolphe,* trans. Margaret Mauldon, ed. Patrick Coleman (Oxford, 2001), p. 81. For the French text, se *OC* III.1:99. References to *Adolphe* will be first, to the translation, then to the *OC* text.

22. *Adolphe,* 82; III.1:100.

23. See, however, the discussion of another image in Markus Winkler, "Benjamin Constant et la métaphore de la poussière," *Annales Benjamin Constant* 4 (1984): 53-73.

24. *Adolphe,* 72; III.1:174.

25. *Adolphe,* 83; III.1:101. In the Preface to the third edition, Constant replaced "bruise what is generous in it" with "destroying everything in you that is generous" (*Adolphe,* 4; III.1:104). Littré's dictionary (s.v."froisser") cites a sermon of Bossuet in which the two words are used together to describe Jesus' suffering as a "victim which must be destroyed [*détruite*] and bruised [*froissée*] of body."

26. Benjamin Constant, *Fragments d'un ouvrage abandonné sur la possibilité d'une constitution républicaine dans un grand pays,* ed. Henri Grange (Paris, 1991), p. 410. The passage is recycled in chapter XII of the *Principes de politique of 1815* (Constant, *Œuvres,* p. 1155).

27. *Fragments,* p. 417. This image disappears when Constant later reformulates the idea of a neutral power in the context of constitutional monarchy. He would not want the king to assume the role of architect. Perhaps that role should devolve to a *publiciste* such as himself.

28. *Fragments,* p. 381n.

29. While Margaret Mauldon employs "bruise," Leonard Tancock uses "crushed" in his translation. See Benjamin Constant, *Adolphe* (Harmondsworth, 1964), p. 117.

30. *De la religion* III, 2; II:6. The context is that of primitive fetishism.

James Mitchell Lee (essay date 2002)

SOURCE: Lee, James Mitchell. "*Doux commerce,* Social Organization, and Modern Liberty in the Thought of Benjamin Constant." *Annales Benjamin Constant* 26 (2002): 117-49.

[*In the following essay, Lee characterizes Constant's political liberalism as "liberal humanism," based upon the author's emphasis that committed adherents to political liberty should possess moral integrity.*]

The history of political thought has consistently regarded Benjamin Constant as one of the first historical spokesmen for modern liberalism. This representation of Constant identifies individual liberty as his chief concern, while political liberty is seen as playing a secondary, defensive role in his thought[1]. In this view, Constant becomes extolled and excoriated as a celebrant of negative freedom, of laissez-faire capitalism, of an amoral world blind to forms of tyranny occurring within frameworks of legal rights. This reading of Constant has recently been renewed by historians and political theorists exploring the possibilities of modern republicanism[2]. These scholars adopt the picture of Constant as the preeminent theorist of modern liberalism, and consequently charge him with having helped dismantle republicanism. Specifically in the terrain of French history, they highlight the Revolution as a republican moment during which moderate republicans integrated Enlightenment commercial discourse with civic values and restraints on capitalism's "depleting moral legacy"[3]. This modernized republicanism was meant to solve the "wealth and virtue problem", and emancipate itself from classical, Rousseauean, or Jacobin associations[4]. Soon after the Revolution, so the story goes, Benjamin Constant slew republicanism with the dagger of modern liberalism, heralding an era of individual liberty, bourgeois enjoyments, and legal rights. We need to ask, however, whether this portrait of Constant is correct. Was he a modern liberal in these terms? What happened to Constant's own Revolutionary-era allegiance to republicanism? And how does the liberalism—republicanism distinction help us explain the history of French political thought between 1789 and 1830?

Agreement on modern liberalism's characteristics notwithstanding, the traditional view misunderstands Constant because it ignores how his vision of modern liberty incorporated both individual liberty and political liberty and how it arose from his own youthful modern republicanism. Constant undoubtedly prized individual liberty. He justified it on the basis of developments in socio-economic organization, thus sharing the economic interpretation of the civilizing process to which commercially-minded republicans subscribed. Moreover, Constant's full vision of modern liberty also stressed political liberty, assigning it a vital humanistic role. He stood arm-in-arm with moderate republicans who called for political liberty in the form of representative government. But, Constant went far beyond his well-known view that political liberty existed merely to guarantee individual liberty. He thought that, by promoting humankind's "perfectibilité", political liberty could save civilization from the egoism and materialism encouraged by modern commercial attitudes.

Between the 1790s and the 1820s an important transformation in French political thought occurred, as erstwhile republicans like Constant, P. L. Rœderer, or J.-B.

Say digested the implications of the economic vision of civilization and accommodated themselves to non-republican forms of government. We can plot this change by looking closely at the development of Constant's concept of modern liberty. In the first section of this article, we shall investigate the longer-term ideological context of French and Scottish political economy, to see how questions of individual and political liberty became imbedded in an economic *Weltanschauung*. In the second section, we shall explore the political implications of that worldview by examining how Constant first coined the concept of modern liberty to refute the absolutist theory of civilized monarchy, which was likewise predicated on commercial discourse and individual liberty. Here, the fundamental tension between the economic and civic perspectives came to the fore, as moderate republicans put their faith in utility and industry rather than the republic or political liberty. In the final section, we shall illuminate Constant's mature understanding of civilization and political liberty by comparing it with that of his liberal allies among the *industrialistes,* Say and Charles Dunoyer.

Historically speaking, a distinction between modern liberalism and modern republicanism becomes difficult to sustain in this context. The key players all predicated modernity's benefits on the rise of commercial societies, and shortly after 1800, abandoned their insistence on a republican form of government. The new-born liberalism of the French Restoration too closely resembled its modern republican father, who perished from neglect rather than patricide. By the 1820s, a dispute among liberals arose over their patrimony. The *industrialistes* transported their republican commitments into the economic categories of *industrie,* utility, and *intérêt bien entendu.* Constant saw their utilitarianism as forsaking humanity's higher ends. Faced with the triumph of an economic view of humankind, he responded with an appeal to political liberty.

DOUX COMMERCE AND MODERN LIBERTY

Constant rooted his concept of modern liberty in political economy and the history of social organization[5]. In the opening pages of **"De la liberté des anciens"**, Constant contended that modern socio-economic needs and desires necessitated a different sort of liberty than the ancients had possessed[6]. Ancient liberty consisted of political liberty, or the direct participation in public sovereignty. It entailed the public deliberation of laws, of questions of war and peace, of foreign alliances, of state finances, and the overseeing of the magistrates. While the ancients derived great satisfaction from political life, they did not require private, individual enjoyments. In defining modern liberty, Constant maintained political liberty in the form of representative government and added individual liberty in areas of religion, profession, property, industry, and the press.

Moderns called for individual liberty, he perceived, to satisfy the private wants that had arisen in the course of history. Individuals asked to be free above all from arbitrary authority[7]. But, Constant saw modern commercial societies threatened by attempts to revive ancient liberty and antiquated political systems, as in Mably, Rousseau, the Jacobins, the Ultras, and Napoleon[8]. Their lack of limitations on authority linked them together in Constant's eyes. Despite his criticisms of radical republicanism, Constant felt political liberty remained crucial for modernity because it both guaranteed individual liberty and was "le plus puissant, le plus énergique moyen de perfectionnement que le Ciel nous ait donné". Both individual and political liberty, in Constant's view, thus comprised modern liberty[9].

In Constant's exposition, the requirement for different kinds of liberty stemmed from alterations in "l'organisation sociale" which had occurred in the transition from ancient warrior and feudal societies to modern commercial ones. Ancient republics were small, Constant argued, and as a result "l'esprit de ces républiques était belliqueux". Repeated mutual threats prevented them from adopting pacific ways. Their security, independence, and "existence entière" could only be "achet[ées] [. . .] au prix de la guerre"[10]. The ancients satisfied their economic needs by conquering, enslaving, and demanding tribute from other nations. The desire for participation in sovereignty issued from their martial situation. But, Constant emphasized, "Leur organisation sociale les conduisait à désirer une liberté toute différente de celle que ce système [le commerce] nous assure"[11]. In the modern world, according to Constant, trade had successfully replaced warfare. It not only enriched modern societies, it also made them "douces", thus promoting peace and cooperation between states: "Le commerce n'est qu'un hommage rendu à la force du possesseur par l'aspirant à la possession. C'est une tentative pour obtenir de gré à gré ce qu'on n'espère plus conquérir par la violence". In addition to softening manners and civilizing social relations, trade placed wealth in private hands and thereby enabled individuals to assert themselves politically against despotism. Commerce "affranchit les individus", while public credit "rend l'autorité dépendante"[12]. Thus Constant bound the economic interpretation of the civilizing process together with the history of liberty.

In grounding modern liberty in the transformation of socio-economic relations, and specifically highlighting the rise of commerce, Constant was a classic *doux commerce* theorist, to apply Albert O. Hirschman's apt concept[13]. He stood in a tradition of political economic thought, whose exponents can be found throughout the European Enlightenments. Identifying commerce as a civilizing agent, this discourse credited a wide range of social and political benefits to commerce's account, progress in the arts and sciences, the refinement of man-

ners, orderly government, justice, and individual independence. Originally the argument had been used in the sixteenth century to legitimate the pursuit of empire: commerce was a gentler means than war to acquire new possessions. By at least 1700, thinkers like Daniel Defoe were pointing out how commerce itself provided a set of social institutions operating independently of politics and indeed profoundly affecting political calculations[14]. Trade came to be seen as restraining "Machiavellianism", fostering mannerly behavior, and encouraging the growth of individual independence.

In an enduring dialogue with the language of civic republicanism, *doux commerce* offered an alternative to its austere terms. Whereas republicanism defined personality in the *civic* terms of virtue and political liberty, a *civil* model challenged it, as trade, interests, and manners started to be perceived as part of a self-directing social system. These traditional corruptors of virtue could accordingly achieve mannerly behavior without the severe moralism of the civic conception[15]. Following J. Pocock's lead, the historiography has tended to associate republicanism with political liberty and to bind individual liberty to the new commercial discourse. Q. Skinner and others have contested this view, insisting on a long tradition in which both forms of liberty existed side-by-side[16]. Nevertheless, in the intellectual history of the Enlightenment and French Revolution, the "wealth and virtue problem" always raised questions about the relationship of individual and political liberty.

In France, the Revolution brought civic and commercial discourses to the political forefront, as the Jacobins harnessed Mably and Rousseau to their aims and as commercial republicans like Condorcet, Sieyès, Rœderer, and Say combined the promises of *doux commerce* with republican notions of equality, virtue, and moral education[17]. From even before 1789 until long into the Restoration, political economy and the history of civilization were among the cardinal points of political debate. The perspectives ranged from those of absolutists like Bonald and de Maistre, to those of left and right liberals like Constant, Say, the *industrialistes,* or Guizot, as well as eventually to those of the Saint-Simonians and Fourier. Dunoyer esteemed Constant's discussion of ancient and modern liberty as a major contribution to the history of civilization[18].

But, the commercial and the civic in commercial republicanism proved difficult to reconcile. In 1803, J.-B. Say drove a wedge between politics and economics in order to privilege economics as the science that would supply modern solutions to problems of poverty, morality, and liberty. He thus dropped his insistence for a republican form of government, turning his hope instead to utility and enlightened self-interest. In 1806 Constant aimed to find "les principes de politiques applicables à tous les gouvernements" by looking at the political requirements of modern commercial societies[19]. Constant was provoked by Louis-Mathieu Molé's *Essais de morale et de politique,* which had anonymously appeared at the end of 1805[20]. Molé had embraced the idea of a civilized absolutist monarchy, one which granted individual liberty within an absolutist regime that accorded no political liberty. Constant discerned in Molé's book nothing but an apology for despotism. The universally valid principles that Constant offered in contrast drew upon an extended discussion of economic issues and voluminous citations to Say, Adam Smith, J.-C.-L. Sismondi, and Charles Ganilh. Drawn from French and Scottish political economy, the *doux commerce* tradition gave Constant's work, indeed his entire mature political thought, its theoretical foundation[21]. As we shall see below, Molé's text derived its essential argument from the same view of modern commercial societies. Constant recognized that modern commercial societies inherently possessed a strong de-politicizing tendency bound to the satisfaction of material happiness and pleasures. That is why modern liberty needed to remain political.

From the "esprit de conquête" to modernity in Charles Ganilh

Although well-read in French and Scottish political economy himself, Constant gained his most direct contact with *doux commerce* arguments through his liberal confederate, Charles Ganilh. In the 1806 **Principes,** Constant often referenced Ganilh's *Essai politique sur le revenu public,* also published that year[22]. First coming to Paris as an elector in 1789, Ganilh enjoyed a political career parallel to Constant's, as a member of the Tribunat from 1799 until 1802 and in the liberal opposition during the Restoration[23]. Ganilh's numerous volumes on political economy were reputed for their obsessive statistical precision[24]. The *Essai politique* relied heavily on Scottish thinking, with abundant mention of William Robertson, David Hume, and Adam Smith. Concentrating on the history of public finance, Ganilh modeled his work on Robertson's *History of the Reign of Emperor Charles V,* but followed Hume's example by beginning with antiquity rather than the Middle Ages. While Ganilh also cited factual material from French sources, he drew his conceptual structure from the Scots.

In the *Essai politique sur le revenu public,* Ganilh asserted that the economic organization, and specifically systems of public revenue, determined the social and political character of an age. Public revenue in antiquity, he stated, was founded on the "esprit de conquête"[25]. Ancient city-states were organized around plundering, exacting tribute, and capturing slaves. Although a new form of social organization, feudalism, according to Ganilh, was likewise based on a martial spirit, and serfdom functioned similarly to slavery[26]. Modern com-

mercial societies, by contrast, took their particular shape because commerce remained outside the "empire de force". Consequently, government revenue became dependent upon taxation and thus the people's prosperity. Since their interests now coincided with those of private citizens, princes no longer benefited from capriciously appropriating private wealth. Commerce and especially public credit offered moderns a source of strength with which to resist arbitrary power and made individual liberty possible[27]. After the overview sketched in the introduction, Ganilh simplified the antiquity—feudalism—modernity sequence into an antiquity—modernity one[28]. Turning on the war—commerce opposition, his historical conceptualization placed him squarely in the *doux commerce* tradition.

Centering his case on fundamental differences in socioeconomic institutions, Ganilh exploited two arguments which Constant later used to define modern liberty. First, he explicitly linked social organization to the means of generating subsistence. Discussing antiquity, he wrote,

> Cet esprit général de guerre permanente, de conquête et de domination, imprimait à tous les citoyens un ardent amour pour la patrie, développait tous les sentiments énergiques, et conduisait à cet héroïsme gigantesque qui [. . .] fait de l'état social un état militaire, de la patrie un camp, et de tous les citoyens une armée.[29]

By contrast, he continued on the next page, "le système social des peuples modernes se compose d'autres éléments, est réglé par d'autres principes et marche à un but différent. Les peuples modernes reconnaissent leur indépendance mutuelle"[30]. Modern independence was a direct product of the commercial system.

Second, Ganilh noted the inappropriateness of ancient liberty to modern life. He adopted Rousseau's definition of the social contract—"l'aliénation totale de chaque associé avec tous ses droits à toute la communauté"—as a description of ancient political association. For moderns, by contrast, "le pacte social [. . .] c'est une simple confédération à frais communs pour défendre, assurer, étendre, et perfectionner la jouissance des facultés individuelles"[31]. This language of individual development became a centerpiece of Constant's plea for modern liberty. As Constant would do in the 1806 **Principes** and in **"De la liberté des anciens"**, Ganilh declared ancient politics incompatible with modern social organization, casting Rousseau and, by implication, the Jacobins as obsolete.

In *Essay politique,* Ganilh also brandished the ancient conquest—modern commerce opposition to delegitimate martial values. He thus supplied Constant with the motivating argument for the **Esprit de conquête et de l'usurpation** as well as **"De la liberté des anciens"**. In a passage which reveals the extent of Constant's debt, Ganilh proclaimed,

Ne serait-il pas plus sage et plus utile de laisser aux anciens leur système militaire, et de nous pénétrer des avantages du système civil et commercial qui lie tous les peuples, civilise tous les hommes, et les unit par le sentiment de leur utilité mutuelle et réciproque? Loin de nous l'éclat des vertus guerrières, de la puissance des armes, de la grandeur des conquêtes! Elles ne peuvent s'allier avec les vertus sociales et pacifiques du système commercial; elles ne conviennent pas à nos mœurs, à notre esprit, à nos besoins[32].

Using the conditional mode, Ganilh called for the abandonment of the spirit of conquest in modern commercial societies. Writing in 1806, he must have had Napoleon's martial appetite in mind.

Constant commended Ganilh for his brave words. In a chapter of **Usurpation** entitled "Causes qui rendent le despotisme particulièrement impossible à notre époque de la civilisation", Constant noted how trade, the circulation of money, and public credit made despotism undesirable and even restrained abusive power. He ended the segment with a laudatory footnote to Ganilh:

> J'aime à rendre justice au courage et aux lumières d'un de mes collègues, qui a imprimé, il y a quelques années, sous la tyrannie, la vérité que je développe ici, mais en l'appuyant de preuves d'un genre différent de celles que j'allègue, et qui ne pouvaient se publier alors. «Dans l'état actuel de la civilisation, et dans le système commercial sous lequel nous vivons, tout pouvoir public doit être limité, et un pouvoir absolu ne peut subsister».[33]

Thus Constant appreciated Ganilh's characterization of the civilizing process. Both Constant and Ganilh bound their analysis of social organization directly to the commerce—conquest opposition, collapsing antiquity and feudalism into the "esprit de conquête", a social system entirely at odds with modern commerce. Modernity's spirit of commerce had transformed society to make absolute power over individuals especially onerous and catastrophic in the long run.

With such arguments, both Ganilh and Constant were drawing upon the *doux commerce* tradition. In this tradition, trade promoted individual independence, regular government, and a civil, not civic, understanding of personality and society. This emphasis on the social and economic as the spheres of human satisfaction created the possibility that a civilized absolutist monarchy might provide security and individual freedom without any concessions to political liberty. In the Scottish Enlightenment, the play of the monarchy versus republic and commerce versus war oppositions bore directly on theories of individual and political liberty. In post-Revolutionary French debates, the interaction of the commercial and civic languages structured how Constant and Ganilh thought about a range of political problems, including the nature of modern liberty. To understand how this was so, we must first fill in a few more details in the eighteenth-century French and Scottish *doux commerce* background.

COMMERCE & THE CIVILIZING PROCESS IN MONTESQUIEU & THE SCOTTISH ENLIGHTENMENT

With his oft-cited statement, "partout où il y a des mœurs douces, il y a du commerce; et [. . .] partout où il y a du commerce, il y a des mœurs douces", Montesquieu provided the *doux commerce* tradition with its epigraph[34]. Commerce, according to Montesquieu, tended to civilize both individuals in their manners and nations in their policy. It brought the fortunate situation where, "pendant que leurs passions leur inspirent la pensée d'être méchants, ils ont pourtant intérêt de ne pas l'être"[35]. It promoted peace by making nations "réciproquement dépendantes", thus replacing the feudal violence[36]. By making princes increasingly dependent on the tax revenue of their commercial subjects, it moderated the arbitrary rule of "machiavélisme". Since "il n'y a plus que la bonté du gouvernement qui donne de la prospérité", princes learned to govern wisely[37]. In a discussion of ancient commerce, Montesquieu enunciated a basic point on which virtually every other eighteenth-century author agreed: commerce generated wealth, wealth precipitated luxury and leisure, and luxury spurred the cultivation of the arts[38]. Yet, Montesquieu did not historically confine the "commerce, leisure, cultivation" sequence to modernity[39].

The celebrated Scottish historian, William Robertson, who guided Constant's studies in Edinburgh and upon whose work Ganilh drew, echoed Montesquieu when he commented that commerce "softens and polishes the manners of men. It unites them, by one of the strongest of all ties, the desire of supplying their mutual wants. It disposes them to peace, by establishing in every state an order of citizens bound by their interest to be the public guardians of tranquillity"[40]. But, in also asserting that commerce had moved society away from the "spirit of domination" to something more refined and modern, Robertson historicized Montesquieu's static argument. In ascribing the transformation from feudalism to modern society to commerce, Robertson turned commerce into an agent of progressive civilization[41]. Constant and Ganilh therefore drew their historical reading of *doux commerce* more from Scottish sources than from Montesquieu. For members of the Scottish Enlightenment, history was an essential tool in elucidating commercial societies' benefits and problems. Writing historically about the rise of commerce led these thinkers to predict a sanguine future for the arts, refinement, justice, and liberty[42]. The distinction between ancient and modern performed the important task of legitimizing the political configuration of regular justice, the stability of property, and individual liberty.

David Hume attributed the advance of civilization to commercial opulence, coupling antiquity with conquest and political liberty: "the ancient republics were almost in perpetual war, a natural effect of their martial spirit, their love of liberty, their mutual emulation"[43]. The ancients may have valued the civic qualities of "poverty and rusticity, virtue and public spirit", but, through their warlike disposition and reliance on slavery, these attributes spawned "barbarous manners". While praising their civic virtue, Hume contended that the lack of thriving "trade, manufactures, [and] industry" made ancient nations "inferior to the modern, both for the happiness and encrease of mankind"[44]. Similarly, in medieval Europe feudal lords constantly went to war, producing social disorder worse than despotism[45]. Modern societies, Hume argued, had attained superiority in wealth, pacific relations, regular government, and individual independence as a result of their commerce and manufactures.

Along the same lines, Adam Smith's economic arguments in the *Wealth of Nations*—the division of labor, capital accumulation, and the monopoly problem—showed how commercial society would fulfill the *doux commerce* promises. The historical Book III of the *Wealth of Nations,* drew rhetorical force from the linguistic oppositions of the *doux commerce* tradition, with feudal, barbaric, rude, savage, warlike, anarchic, poor, and retrograde societies set against commercial, civilized, peaceful, orderly, rich, and forward-looking ones[46]. Smith's famous four-stage view of history examined how economic organization enhanced the development of orderly government and justice[47]. Smith and Hume both combined an historical analysis of the rise of commerce with a natural one, so that the recovery of commerce at the end of the Middle Ages amounted to a return to "natural" sequences of investment[48]. In their eyes, societies thus naturally gravitated toward the social, economic, and political refinements offered by *doux commerce,* and the history of Europe exhibited that this potential could be fulfilled.

According to Hume, Smith, and Smith's student, John Millar, commerce also encouraged individual independence for increasing numbers in society. "Nourished" by luxury, Hume opined, commerce and industry allowed peasants to "become rich and independent; while the tradesmen and merchants acquired a share of the property, and drew authority and consideration to that middling rank of men, who are the best and firmest basis of public liberty". Although he never expected trade to drive away inequality, he believed it would raise the economic position of artisans and the working poor. Superior economic means also advanced fortunate political ends. The enlarged middling ranks could be counted upon to "covet equal laws which may secure their property, and preserve them from monarchical as well as

aristocratical tyranny"[49]. In short, for Hume, commerce and industry were responsible for cultivating individual independence and thereby checking abuses of authority.

Smith concurred and turned his attention specifically to how commerce destroyed the dependence and injustice typical of feudalism. In addition to furthering "order and good government" and the "liberty and security of individuals", Smith thought, commerce undermined the "servile dependence" on superiors and impeded feudal lords from interrupting the "regular execution of justice"[50]. Commercial societies were thus most able to enjoy the "system of natural liberty", which included justice, protection of property, enforcement of contracts, and liberty and security for the individual under the law[51]. Independence carried with it distinct moral benefits: "Nothing tends so much to corrupt mankind as dependencey, while independencey still encreases the honesty of the people. The establishment of commerce and manufactures, which brings about this independencey, is the best police for preventing crimes". The material advantages of commercial societies meant that the "common people have better wages than in any other", which successively led to "probity of manners" and industriousness[52]. John Millar elaborated on his teacher's views by observing that rising wages facilitated the acquisition of property for middle and eventually lower ranks in society, hence creating a material basis for both individual and political "independence" and contributing to the overall "spirit of liberty"[53]. Thus, Smith and Millar, like Hume, held that, inequality notwithstanding, this affluence and independence was vastly preferable to the feudal and ancient alternatives.

Over the last twenty-five years, the historiography of the Scottish Enlightenment has explored these themes in the context of the civic humanist tradition[54]. While the vastness of this literature prohibits summary, several of its main points bear directly on Constant's conception of modern liberty and the fate of French Revolutionary republicanism, which we shall examine shortly. Smith and Hume, and, with more reservations, Millar, held that the expansion of commercial prosperity and individual liberty could occur in a monarchy as easily as under a "free government" upholding political liberty[55]. As long as the rule of law prevailed, such a "civilized monarchy" could accommodate the "system of natural liberty". Attacking the civic humanist arguments in vogue in Britain at the time, Hume resorted to the ancient—modern polarity to disparage unreasonable claims for political liberty by its "zealous partizans". Hume did rank modern republics with civilized monarchies, mostly because they possessed the "justice, lenity, and stability" necessary for flourishing trade[56]. He feared, however, that "the passionate admirers of the ancients" might sacrifice the gains of modern commercial societies, returning them to a state of war, disorder, and slavery[57]. Similarly, Smith's ideal of the "system of natural liberty" did not require political liberty, although he, too, probably preferred modern republics[58]. With more evident allegiances to the Commonwealth tradition, Millar accorded political liberty a more important role in his notion of independence, noting its requirement for guaranteeing individual liberty[59]. All three nonetheless struggled with the possibility that monarchy might satisfy the needs of commercial societies, justice, security of possession, and individual liberty, while the political liberty cherished by republicanism might even endanger those benefits[60]. Yet, as their measured praise for the ancients' public spirit and their skepticism about commerce's "depleting moral legacy" revealed, it remained for them a dilemma.

As a consequence of the *doux commerce* discourse, *homo œconomicus* seemed to supplant *zōon politikon.* This result did not mean that political liberty became unimportant, just that it did not foster happiness as it had come to be valued in modern commercial societies. The eighteenth-century configuration of commerce, civilization, rule of law, and individual liberty was rooted in a civil understanding of human relations and personality. The civic humanist view of man could consequently recede into the background[61]. Ganilh and Constant adopted the terms of the *doux commerce* tradition, using it to contest despotism, unlimited authority, and the spirit of conquest. The French Revolution brought the civic—civil opposition into sharp focus. Although starting as an attempt to reform the monarchy, the Revolution polarized monarchic and republican alternatives. Moderate republicans employed civic virtue, equality, and political liberty to oppose absolutism and aristocratic privilege, while they applied social and economic language to embrace individual freedom, wealth, and the advance of civilization. But, this resolution to the wealth and virtue problem scarcely survived the Revolution, as thinkers responded differently to the prospect that modern enjoyments no longer necessitated political liberty.

SOCIAL ORGANIZATION AND THE ECONOMIZATION OF LIBERTY IN FRENCH REPUBLICANISM

In France, during the Revolution and the first several decades of the nineteenth century, political economy stood square in the middle of the debates about individual and political liberty, governmental form, and the means to happiness in modern civilization. With his links to commercially-minded republicans like Condorcet, Rœderer, Sieyès, Cabanis, and Say, Constant did not fortuitously turn to political economy in 1806 when he engaged Molé's absolutism. With his statement that there existed political principles "applicables sous tous les gouvernements, n'attaquant les bases d'aucune organisation sociale, compatibles avec la royauté comme avec la république", Constant organized the work around socio-economic concept of "l'organisation sociale"[62]. It shifted his long-standing concern for arbitrary authority onto a terrain that let the discursive fields of the *doux commerce* discourse undercut his opponents. By lumping together absolutists like Molé and classical republicans like Rousseau, Mably, or the Jacobins, he could furthermore surmount the monarchy—republic opposition characteristic of the Revolution[63]. It also made obsolete his ***Fragments sur une constitution républicaine,*** which had insisted that a republic alone could protect liberty[64]. Modern liberty was justified because it fit modern commercial society and did not depend on any particular political form. But, it cannot be overlooked that Constant arrived at this standpoint through a refutation of both radical republicanism and "civilized" absolutism, and that he never surrendered his view that political liberty manifestly comprised part of modern liberty.

Constant grasped onto the term "l'organisation sociale" because his adversary, Molé had resorted to the idea himself to describe the social hierarchy of an ideal civilized absolutism. In Molé's model, all social classes bound themselves by a chain that stretched from the king to the lowest members. Assimilating Montesquieu to Bossuet and Hobbes, he contended that the intermediary rank of the aristocracy thus hindered the king from growing into a despot. The social sequence joined the monarch to society, causing him to become "la société elle-même". The king reciprocally prevented any class from abusing its position[65]. Liberty, in Molé's view, consisted of security and "bonheur" and occurred naturally in a monarchy. Because, for Molé, monarchies themselves were natural, he could claim without contradiction that liberty "dépend de l'organisation de la société, et non de la forme du gouvernement". Republican governments and the republican conception of freedom, he posited, corrupted the natural order and stemmed from a people's desire to rid itself of despotism, which had resulted from the breakdown of the proper hierarchical and monarchical social organization. The struggle against tyranny produced the unnatural habit of valuing liberty in itself. Republicans mistakenly came to cherish "la passion de la liberté" above "le désir du bien-être". They, therefore, "restèrent dans cette erreur que la liberté devoit être l'objet des institutions, et non le résultat de l'organisation sociale"[66]. He did not distinguish between different kinds of liberty, but nevertheless spurned republican political liberty in favor of an individual liberty which a civilized monarchy could provide.

In his discussion, Molé related the growth of "naturels" and "artistiquement faits" governments to the civilizing process. Following the *doux commerce* tradition, he declared that the progress of civilization had made humanity "moins guerrière" wanting simply "repos" and "jouir mollement du fruit de ses travaux". Through "industrie", humankind had attained the point of civilization where it could benefit from its leisure. Civilization had rendered despotism in a monarchy impossible: "Il y auroit trop de lumières à éteindre, d'industrie à étouffer, d'opinions, d'habitudes, de préjugés même à faire oublier"[67]. The republican passion for liberty nevertheless threatened to corrupt monarchy, and the Revolution loomed large as a silently present example of corruption and fervor for liberty. Molé asserted, "l'âge de la vigueur et des passions étoit passé". In order for human beings to enjoy the diversity of their tastes, the stability in monarchy "est donc aujourd'hui la condition la plus nécessaire aux institutions humaines". In fact, civilization seemed to Molé to have reached a happy situation where peoples "se reposent ou ils se corrompent"[68]. Monarchies allowed the former, while republics encouraged the latter. For Molé, monarchies were natural, modern, and civilized.

Constant's assertion that moderns required a form of liberty suitable to a social organization of stability, repose, and commercial prosperity rested upon the same conceptual foundation. Constant, of course, drew the opposite conclusion: as civilized as it might be, absolutism would guarantee neither the liberty nor the security appropriate to modernity, for it would permit unlimited authority[69]. Constant and Molé thus gave different answers to the questions posed to them by the ideological context of French and Scottish political economy and the political setting of the Empire.

In using the term "l'organisation sociale", Molé was himself participating in a decade-old discussion in which the concept signaled attention to the socio-economic sphere of human association. During the Revolution, commercially-minded republicans, including Condorcet, Sieyès, Rœderer, Cabanis, and Say, implemented terms like "l'organisation sociale", "l'art social", and "l'état social", in forwarding their political goals. From as early as his return from Edingburgh in 1785, Constant had personal ties to members of the Auteuil and Condorcet salons, most of whom were well-versed in French and Scottish political economy[70]. Invested in republican notions of equality, virtue, and moral education, these men and women faced the ideological task of integrating commercial ideas with republican ones. They rejected the classical republican view, lately invigorated by Rousseau and Mably, that set wealth against virtue. In their view, free trade, security of property, and individual liberty justified a republican constitution, and if properly channeled, would promote equality and virtues like industriousness and frugality[71]. These commercial republicans, too, confronted the possibility that a non-despotic, civilized monarchy would guarantee security, "bonheur", and individual liberty better than a republic could. After 1800 many forsook their demand for a republican government, as some condoned the Empire outright while others quietly waited and accepted the constitutional monarchy in

1815. Since they believed that political economy, not politics, provided prosperity, they came to accept that an overemphasis on political liberty demanded too high a price. During the Revolution, however, they still worked hard to deny the modernity of monarchy and to prove the compatibility of a republican constitution with modern commercial institutions.

For Sieyès, the discovery of the principles of political economy or "l'art social" was the privilege of modernity, and they conferred legitimacy on its political institutions. In his famous pamphlet, *Qu'est-ce que le Tiers état,* Sieyès explicitly linked the political rights of the Third Estate to modern social organization, and built his notion of representation on the division of labor. The thrust of this text was, of course, to show that the Third Estate deserved a voice because it performed the preponderance of work. The Revolution needed to destroy noble privilege, he argued, and "il faut prouver encore que l'ordre noble n'entre point dans l'organisation sociale"[72]. Not engaging in labor or commercial activity, the nobility stood outside the social organization of the nation and therefore failed to earn the right to political participation. He developed this position while refuting the Physiocrats in 1775. Labor, not land, produced prosperity: "le travail général est donc le fondement de la société, et l'ordre social n'est que le meilleur ordre possible des travaux"[73]. Citing Smith, he asserted sometime later that the division of labor was "le véritable principe des progrès de l'état social"[74]. This leading principle, for Sieyès, dictated that the representative system uniquely sustained political unity in a nation united by commercial sociability[75].

Pierre Louis Rœderer, a member of the Institut with close relations to Mme de Staël and Constant in the second half of the 1790s, turned to the idea of social organization to distinguish between modern political economy and the anti-commercialism of classical republicanism[76]. He made it clear that social organization was primarily an economic or social category, not a political one: "L'organisation sociale ne consiste pas seulement dans l'organisation du gouvernement". Rather, it emanated from the human disposition to self-preservation through property, labor, agricultural production, and capital investment[77]. The study of social organization meant analysis of "une autre division des personnes" than found in Rousseau or Mably. It subordinated the *polis* to the social units of families, villages, and cities. In this way, civil society based itself on natural impulses to which a political constitution should conform[78].

From this perspective, Rœderer attacked the modern "niveleurs"—Rousseau, Mably, and "plusieurs membres de la Convention"—whom he compared to citizens of ancient republics[79]. Edmund Burke had introduced the term "levelers" to denounce the Revolution *tout court,* but Rœderer cleverly employed it here to separate radical from moderate republicanism[80]. While praising the radicals' celebration of equality and virtue, Rœderer rejected their equation of wealth, commerce, manufactures, and the division of labor with corruption and the destruction of public "bonheur". Instead, a correct calculation of interests, frugal morals, and moderate wealth would not only satisfy society's material needs better but would stay in perfect accord with the civic ethic and would also promote industriousness[81]. The expansion of trade and manufactures furthermore increased the range of "jouissances" and the "sociabilité" which unified society. Stressing his disagreement with the levelers, Rœderer claimed that equality and liberty remained paramount but it should be "l'égalité dans l'abondance et non dans la disette" and "la liberté qui féconde, non celle qui stérilise"[82]. Rœderer fused the commercial language of prosperity with republican notions of moderation, while mistrusting the appropriateness of classical republicanism to modernity.

In 1799, Rœderer's fellow member at the Institut and an associate of Constant, P.-J.-G. Cabanis also used the term social organization and the ancient—modern opposition to discuss the relationship between socioeconomic and political forms[83]. While some human needs endured perennially, he contended, others arose with the advance of civilization, thus altering notions of "bonheur" and "repos". The best "système social" addressed both the fixed needs and "tous les besoins plus mobiles que de nouvelles circonstances politiques, et sur-tout les progrès de la civilisation peuvent amener". The course of civilization, he argued, had also shown that the progress of ideas had "adouci" arbitrary power. Modern perceptions of commerce, property, and industry had created the "force de la classe moyenne" and encouraged the growth of talents and "les solides vertus"[84]. These historical developments made a representative system with a separation of powers the best political organization for a modern republic. Cabanis's model called for a strong executive to obviate the administrative weaknesses of disorder-prone democracies, while the legislature prevented executive abuse of authority[85]. Cabanis in this manner followed Sieyès in justifying representative institutions on the political economy of modernity. Constant also defended representative government from the same basis. He nevertheless dissented from their approval of 18 brumaire because he judged it a betrayal of the republican faith in popular elections[86].

The term "l'organisation sociale" thus functioned as a tool in a larger dialogue about the appropriate kind of political system for modern commercial societies. Molé rejected the republican position, and Constant repudiated Molé's monarchism in turn. All agreeing on the primacy of the economic, the social, and the private, rather than the political, in satisfying modern needs and desires, Constant, Sieyès, Rœderer, Cabanis, and Molé

were working out the implications of the Enlightenment discourses on commerce, liberty, the civilizing process, and civic humanism. As the Scots had claimed earlier, individual liberty did not require political liberty, and the institutions of security of property and orderly government, which caused trade and manufactures to flourish, might do more for the happiness of humankind than the ancient values of political liberty and civic virtue. The ancient and modern idiom allowed these thinkers to privilege commerce, individual liberty, and gentle manners, by historicizing classical republicanism. With the intellectual categories so established, moderate republicans braved a challenge when they tried to refute absolutism, aristocratic privilege, and Physiocratic economics by combining commercial and republican ideologies.

MODERNITY AND THE FATE OF POLITICAL LIBERTY

Constant's effort in 1806 to discover "les principes politiques applicables à tous les gouvernements" was an important step in his intellectual maturation because it struck right at the heart of these questions. Did this move, as M. Gauchet has suggested, amount to the invention of modern liberalism? Did Constant abandon his previous republican views for liberal ones? In recent debates about modern republicanism and liberalism, these have become central issues both for Constant studies and the history of political thought[87]. Historically speaking, Constant's shift—no longer insisting upon a republic—mirrored the direction taken by many moderate republicans in the early nineteenth century. Their defection suggests that the economization of civilization and liberty had altered the ideological landscape so thoroughly that republican manners, but not republican politics, were all that remained of republicanism[88]. In response to this context, Constant adopted a liberal humanism which called for sustaining political liberty to promote human perfectibility and to stem the moral erosion of modern commercial societies at the hands of egoism, atomism, and mere material happiness.

Along with many others in the *Idéologue* circles of the Institut and the *Décade philosophique* journal, Say and Destutt de Tracy joined Constant in dropping their demands for a republican government. Setting aside political liberty, Say and Destutt de Tracy expected the proper understanding of economic principles to satisfy material needs and even generate virtues like frugality. Say's connections to commercial republican circles predated the Revolution and he partially owed his ideas on political economy, especially those of utility and industry, to Rœderer[89]. On the first page of the 1803 edition of the *Traité d'économie politique*, Say stated that prosperity could be achieved in a well-administered state, regardless of its political form[90]. As he had emphasized in his 1800 utopian essay, *Olbie*, citizens needed education in political economy to gain the capacity to determine their true self-interests[91]. Correctly identified, interests would harmonize and, along with individual liberty and industriousness, promote utility and wealth. From his revolutionary-era writings and through the numerous editions of his *Traité*, Say underlined the republican values of frugality, equality, and virtue[92]. In the science of political economy, Say thus sought to build in moral restraints to rein in the raw self-interested behavior which commercial societies encouraged.

Destutt de Tracy shared this belief in the harmony of self-interests, distilling it from the study of sensations and ideas in the hallmark fashion of the *Idéologues*[93]. While he preferred a representative system, he nevertheless considered happiness a pure matter of individual liberty, and thus effectively dismissed concern for political liberty:

> le gouvernement sous lequel on est le plus libre, quelle que soit sa forme, est celui qui gouverne le mieux; car c'est celui où le plus grand nombre est le plus heureux; et quand on est aussi heureux qu'on peut l'être, les volontés sont accomplies autant qu'il est possible. Si le prince qui exerce le pouvoir le plus despotique, administrait parfaitement, on serait sous son empire au comble du bonheur, qui est une seule et même chose avec la liberté. Ce n'est donc pas la forme du gouvernement qui en elle-même est une chose importante.[94]

Striking in its apology for despotism, Destutt's statement showed how far from political liberty the commercial ideology could drift. Say never went so far and suffered the *Traité*'s confiscation after rebuffing Napoléon's demands for changes to it. Nonetheless, in the combination of *intérêt bien entendu*, individual liberty, and utility, Say and Destutt de Tracy believed they had found the formula to achieve the greatest happiness without much regard for political liberty.

As we have seen, Constant shared the view of modern commercial societies which spawned these conclusions and it formed the conceptual foundation of his modern liberalism. But, in the last decade of his life, if not well before, he grew weary of utilitarianism and its French expression in the industrial doctrine of Say, Dunoyer, and Charles Comte[95]. Constant insisted that civilization needed moral and political restraints if it hoped to survive its own destructive tendencies[96]. Political liberty served this important role. The scholarship has often noted how Constant meant to protect individual liberty through political liberty exercised in representative government and vigorous public opinion. When, in the second half of **"De la liberté"**, he analyzed modern liberty and how modernity required it, Constant also questioned the privatized, acquisitive world which justified individual liberty. And, in answering his query, Constant assigned to political liberty a much higher, even sacred value:

> Est-il donc si vrai que le bonheur, de quelque genre qu'il puisse être, soit le but unique de l'espèce humaine? En ce cas, notre carrière serait bien étroite et notre destination bien peu relevée [. . .] ce n'est pas au bonheur seul, c'est au perfectionnement que notre destin nous appelle. La liberté politique est le plus puissant, le plus énergique moyen de perfectionnement que le Ciel nous ait donné. La liberté politique soumettant à tous les citoyens, sans exception, l'examen et l'étude de leurs intérêts les plus sacrés, agrandit leur esprit, anoblit leurs pensées, établit une sort d'égalité intellectuelle qui fait la gloire et la puissance d'un peuple.[97]

In a striking departure from the egocentric connotation of "intérêts" offered by his liberal contemporaries, Constant appealed to interests whose value derived from their civic and religious character. He intended them to pull citizens out of a base concern for their private happiness. Furthermore, Constant ascribed to political institutions the duty of educating and elevating citizens to their highest moral position[98]. Although he did not specify how representative institutions could achieve these goals, he intended to encourage interests that were civic in spirit and religious in their devotion.

By contrasting Constant's argument against those of his liberal compatriots, we may best see the full import of his humanist perspective. In 1826, Constant criticized Dunoyer's conception of civilization for its excessive focus on material well-being and its utilitarian implications[99]. In 1814 Dunoyer, with his colleague, C. Comte, had pronounced themselves disciples of Say's economics and Constant's politics. During the first years of the Restoration, Constant was closely allied with the *industrialistes* in the left-liberal opposition[100]. In 1826, Constant reviewed Dunoyer partly in order to defend himself against Dunoyer's accusation that he believed in the decline of civilizations. He easily dispelled Dunoyer's error[101]. Dunoyer had, however, rightly pinpointed Constant's worry that "l'Europe marche à grands pas vers un état pareil à celui de la Chine, que [Constant] représente à la fois comme très civilisée et très asservie"[102]. Constant, in fact, wanted nothing more than to find a way to sustain both civilization and liberty, and to keep the former from destroying the latter.

Their disagreement revolved around whether industrial civilization could manage itself politically without external controls. Dismissing the understanding of liberty as a matter of rights and duties, Dunoyer explained it as the development of physical and moral faculties to permit the satisfaction of needs. He wrote, "la vraie mesure de la liberté c'est la civilisation"[103]. The industrial doctrine therefore pertained itself foremost to "du travail et des échanges", which would best further the advance of material well-being, and thereby morality and liberty. Government became likewise "une compagnie commerciale", charged with little more than enforcement of the law[104]. Because he saw in this argument a fatal tendency to put the utility of material well-being before right, Constant portrayed Dunoyer as a Benthamite. Constant deemed it vital to "contrebalancer" such a definition of civilization with "les sentiments nobles et désintéressés [. . .] afin de préserver la civilisation elle-même des dangers qui résultent pour elle de sa propre tendance"[105]. Civilization, Constant continued, was part of "la destinée de l'espèce humaine" insofar as "l'homme a été créé pour s'instruire, pour s'éclairer, et par là même, pour s'adoucir et s'améliorer". These ends were not material and had nothing to do with self-interest, even in its enlightened form. Utility and material happiness, for all their merit, remained base motives, insufficient to human dignity[106].

Constant situated his life-long work, *De la religion,* at the crossroads of these questions about liberty and civilization. He beseeched his fellow "amis de la liberté" not to replace ennobling morality with "intérêt bien entendu", which would lead to atomization. With eloquence worthy of Rousseau, Constant implored:

> Contemplez l'homme dominé par ses sens, assiégé par ses besoins, amolli par la civilisation, et d'autant plus esclave de ses jouissances, que cette civilisation les lui rend plus faciles. Voyez combien de prise il offre à la corruption. Songez à cette flexibilité du langage qui l'entoure d'excuses, et met la pudeur de l'égoïsme à couvert. N'anéantissez donc pas en lui le seul mobile désintéressé qui lutte contre tant de causes d'avilissement. Tous les systèmes se réduisent à deux. L'un nous assigne l'intérêt pour guide, et le bien-être pour but. L'autre nous propose pour but le perfectionnement, et pour guide le sentiment intime, l'abnégation de nous-mêmes et la faculté du sacrifice.[107]

The opulence of civilization aided "corruption". The very "jouissances" that comprised modern satisfactions, that justified individual liberty, that rendered ancient sacrifices intolerable, had enslaved moderns to their desires. Human beings could select between "intérêt" leading to mere "bien-être" and the nobler sentiments of "sacrifice" and self-abnegation which strove toward perfectibility.

When placed next to his concluding plea for political liberty in **"De la liberté"**, Constant's stress on perfectibility, self-abnegation, and sacrifice demonstrated an important aspect of his conception of liberal civilization. Individual liberty and the amenities of civilization, what Kant had called "schimmerndes Elend", inadequately fulfilled man's *telos*[108]. When following only their self-interest, Constant asserted, civilized human beings put themselves merely "au sommet de cette hiérarchie matérielle" as "le plus sagace des animaux", rather than striving to escape the bonds of that hierarchy altogether[109]. In order to achieve perfectibility, Constant advocated abiding by religious sentiment and ex-

ercising political liberty. Both called for sacrifice to succor true freedom. Sacrifice entailed willingly striving to transcend self-interest. Constant ended the preface to **De la religion** with a further entreaty to the friends of liberty: "La liberté se nourrit de sacrifices. Rendez la puissance du sacrifice à la race énervée qui l'a perdue. La liberté veut toujours des citoyens, quelquefois des héros. N'éteignez pas les convictions qui servent de base aux vertus des citoyens, et qui créent les héros, en leur donnant la force d'être des martyrs"[110]. In short, a liberty based on self-interest was not deserving of the name, and it was this kind of liberty that Constant saw in the utilitarianism of Say and Dunoyer.

The vision of liberty and civilization forwarded in **De la religion** and in **"De la liberté"** amounted to a liberal humanism, mordantly critical of self-interest as the basis for freedom. Constant ascribed to political liberty the moral aim of perfectibility, a loftier end than the mere guarantee of individual liberty. Political liberty and individual liberty thus reinforced each other. The sacrifices demanded by political liberty could only become moral acts if they were voluntary, which in turn necessitated individual liberty. Ancient liberty seemed inferior to Constant for this additional reason: its exercise had been an obligation, not a choice. All of this suggests that his **"De la liberté"** lecture was less an unconditional call for individual liberty than an appeal to the bourgeois youths of the Athénée royal to take the commitments of political liberty seriously. Any discussion of Constant's thought must account for this moral dimension of political liberty.

With recognition of the moral character of Constant's liberalism, it becomes difficult to affirm differences between modern republicanism and modern liberalism at the start of the nineteenth century. Say, Rœderer, and Constant were all once committed to moderate republicanism. They all shared the economic interpretation of the civilizing process, which they imagined compatible with republican values of equality, frugality, and liberty. Shortly after 1800, they all surrendered their insistence on a republican form of government. But, when faced with the possibility that material prosperity and happiness could be satisfied in the civilized monarchy suggested by Molé, in Napoleon's empire, or in the representative monarchy of the Restoration, they reacted differently. Only Constant sustained a humanist commitment to political liberty, albeit in the pale form of representative government. By the 1820s, the terms of the debate had changed, even if republicanism's old nemesis, self-interest, remained ever in need of restriction. In this altered context, Constant recoiled from the economized view of humanity of his fellow liberals in the utilitarian camp. This vision of modern liberty thus revealed the limits of the *doux commerce* discourse. For all his *douceur, homo oeconomicus* knew no ethical restraints to his self-interest. Even when the promises of commerce were attained, modern societies still required the sacrifices encouraged by political liberty and religious sentiment—not only to safeguard themselves against despotism, but also to achieve the perfectibility which Constant felt to be human destiny.

Notes

1. Sir Isaiah Berlin, "Two Concepts of Liberty", in *Four Essays on Liberty,* New York, Oxford University Press, 1969, p. 118-172. In variance to Berlin's negative and positive liberty categories, the present article employs individual and political liberty in accord with Constant's usage: individual liberty means the right to act without intrusion from the state or other individuals; whereas political liberty refers to participation in sovereignty. The distinction between these two sides of modern liberty should not be conflated with his modern—ancient liberty distinction. See Benjamin Constant, "De la liberté des anciens comparée avec celle des modernes", in *Ecrits politiques,* Marcel Gauchet (ed.), Paris, Gallimard, 1997, especially p. 613-619.

2. For recent portrayals of Constant as the apotheosis of bourgeois, laissez-faire liberalism in contrast to the republican or "neo-roman" tradition, see Quentin Skinner, *Liberty before Liberalism,* Cambridge, Cambridge University Press, 1998, p. 60, 117; Philip Pettit, *Republicanism: a Theory of Freedom and Government,* Oxford, Oxford University Press, 1997, p. 17-18, 50; Richard Whatmore, *Republicanism and the French Revolution: An Intellectual History of Jean-Baptiste Say's Political Economy,* Oxford, Oxford University Press, 2000, p. xiii, 5, 190, 199; Alain Boyer, "De l'actualité des Anciens Républicains", in Stéphane Chauvier (ed.), *Libéralisme et républicanisme,* Caen, Presses Universitaires de Caen, 2000, p. 37-38.

3. R. Whatmore, *Republicanism, op. cit.,* p. 17-31; Michael Sonenscher, "The Nation's Debt and the Birth of the Modern Republic", *History of Political Thought,* vol. 18, 1997, p. 64-103, 267-325. On the idea of capitalism's "depleting moral legacy" and its expression in the eighteenth century, see Fred Hirsch, *Social Limits to Growth,* Cambridge, Harvard University Press, 1976, p. 117-122, 137-151.

4. John Pocock, Q. Skinner, Istvan Hont, Laurence Dickey, Donald Winch, and many others have enriched our understanding of the "wealth and virtue problem" in Anglo-American contexts. It has recently become a part of French debates in the work of I. Hont, M. Sonenscher, Jean-Fabien Spitz, R. Whatmore, S. Chauvier, and A. Boyer. See throughout for citations to their work. Other significant collections pertaining to the history of

republicanism are François Furet and Mona Ozouf (eds.), *Le siècle de l'avènement républicain,* Paris, Gallimard, 1993; Biancamaria Fontana (ed.), *The Invention of the Modern Republic,* Cambridge, Cambridge University Press, 1994; and David Wootton (ed.), *Republicanism, Liberty, and Commercial Society, 1649-1776,* Stanford, Stanford University Press, 1994.

5. Exceptions to a general neglect of the political economy in Constant's work are Biancamaria Fontana, "The Shaping of Modern Liberty: Commerce and Civilization in the Writings of Benjamin Constant", *Annales Benjamin Constant,* vol. 5, 1985, p. 3-15; and Pasquale Pasquino, *Sieyès et l'invention de la constitution en France,* Paris, Odile Jacob, 1998, p. 31-48.

6. To stress their historicity, Constant's texts and ideas, including that of modern liberty, are discussed in the past tense.

7. B. Constant, "De la liberté", *art. cit.,* p. 593-600. Most of the important aspects of the ancient—modern liberty comparison, including its foundation in political economy, first appeared in 1806 in B. Constant, *Principes de politique applicables à tous les gouvernements,* in *Les 'Principes de politique' de Benjamin Constant,* Etienne Hofmann (ed.), Geneva, Droz, 1980, especially bk. XVI, vol. II, p. 419-455.

8. Constant's criticisms of these figures appeared throughout his work, singly and often in combination. See B. Constant, "De la liberté", *art. cit.,* p. 591-593; *De l'esprit de conquête et de l'usurpation,* in *Ecrits politiques, op. cit.,* p. 127-134, 160-163; and *Principes de politique* (1806), *op. cit.,* vol. II, p. 21-45, 432, 437-444.

9. B. Constant, "De la liberté", *art. cit.,* p. 612, 617. Constant employed ancient and modern liberty as temporal categories and individual and political liberty as conceptual ones. The scholarship has consistently downplayed the vital and positive role which he gave to political liberty in modernity. Refreshing acknowledgements of this aspect of Constant's thought are beginning to appear: see Giovanni Paoletti, "Relire Constant: la question des anciens", *Annales Benjamin Constant,* vol. 23-24, 2000, p. 119-133; and J.-F. Spitz, *La liberté politique: essai de généalogie conceptuelle,* Paris, PUF, 1995, coll. "Léviathan", p. 481-483.

10. B. Constant, "De la liberté", *art. cit.,* p. 593, 596, *De l'esprit de conquête et de l'usurpation, op. cit.,* p. 127-134, especially 129, *Principes de politique* (1806), *op. cit.,* vol. II, p. 420-428, especially 422; cf. vol. II, p. 419, where he used "l'organisation politique" instead. Did Constant

briefly consider describing the ancients as having political organization in contrast to the moderns' social organization? In several texts, he did use the term "l'organisation politique" to refer to the form of government, but only in this rare instance did he apply it to the whole of society.

11. B. Constant, "De la liberté", *art. cit.,* p. 593-596, quote p. 593.

12. *Ibid.,* p. 597, 613-614. Passages adapted from *Principes de politique* (1806), *op. cit.,* vol. II, p. 425-426, and similarly used in *De l'esprit de conquête et de l'usurpation, op. cit.,* p. 130, 264-266.

13. Albert O. Hirschman, *The Passions and the Interests: Political Arguments for Capitalism before Its Triumph,* Princeton, Princeton University Press, 1977. Alternatively, see J. Pocock's work, especially, "Virtue, Rights, and Manners", in *Virtue, Commerce, and History,* Cambridge, Cambridge University Press, 1985, p. 37-50. The *doux commerce* tradition in France has been well discussed in Catherine Larrère, *L'Invention de l'économie au XVIIIᵉ siècle: du droit naturel à la physiocratie,* Paris, PUF, 1992, coll. "Léviathan".

14. L. Dickey, "Power, Commerce and Natural Law in Daniel Defoe's Political Writings 1698-1707", in John Robertson (ed.), *A Union for Empire: Political Thought and the British Union of 1707,* Cambridge, Cambridge University Press, 1995, p. 63-96; A. Hirschman, *Passions and Interests, op. cit., passim.*

15. J. Pocock, "Virtue, Rights, and Manners", *art. cit.,* p. 37-50; J. Pocock, "Cambridge Paradigms and Scotch Philosophers: a Study of the Relations Between the Civic Humanist and the Civil Jurisprudential Interpretation of Eighteenth-Century Social Thought", in I. Hont and M. Ignatieff (eds.), *Wealth and Virtue: The Shaping of Political Economy in the Scottish Enlightenment,* Cambridge, Cambridge University Press, 1983, p. 235-252. On civic republicanism more generally, see J. Pocock, *The Machiavellian Moment,* Princeton, Princeton University Press, 1975; J.-F. Spitz, *La liberté politique, op. cit.* Many essays in the now classic, I. Hont and M. Ignatieff (eds.), *Wealth and Virtue, op. cit.,* bear directly on these questions.

16. Most recently, Q. Skinner, *Liberty before Liberalism, op cit.*; Steve Pincus, "Neither Machiavellian Moment nor Possessive Individualism: Commercial Society and the Defenders of the English Commonwealth", *American Historical Review,* vol. 103, 3, 1998, p. 705-736.

17. R. Whatmore, *Republicanism, op. cit., passim*; I. Hont, "The Permanent Crisis of a Divided Mankind: 'Contemporary Crisis of the Nation State in Historical Perspective", *Political Studies,* vol. 42, 1994, p. 166-231; M. Sonenscher, "Nation's Debt", *art. cit., passim.* D. Winch has remarked that after 1776 the republic—monarchy opposition attained heightened significance. In France, it became the key political question at least by 1792 (D. Winch, *Adam Smith's Politics: an Essay in Historiographic Revision,* Cambridge, Cambridge University Press, 1978, p. 40-45).

18. Charles Dunoyer, "Notice historique sur l'industrialisme", in *Œuvres,* Anatole Dunoyer (ed.), Paris, Guillaumin, 1879, vol. 3, p. 175-180.

19. Jean-Baptiste Say, *Traité d'économie politique, ou, Simple exposition de la manière dont se forment, se distribuent, et se consomment les richesses,* Paris, Crapelet, 1803, vol. I, p. i-vi. B. Constant, *Principes de politique* (1806), *op. cit.,* vol. II, p. 20-23, quotation taken from Constant's subtitle.

20. E. Hofmann, *Les 'Principes de politique' de Constant, op. cit.,* vol. I, p. 232-234; [Louis-Mathieu Molé], *Essais de morale et de politique,* Paris, Nicolle, 1806. On Molé's life, see Jacques-Alain de Sédouy, *Le comte Molé: ou la séduction du pouvoir,* Paris, Perrin, 1994; and [Prosper de Barante], "Molé", in *Biographie Universelle,* Paris, Desplaces, 1854, vol. 28, p. 536-540.

21. From the manuscript version of the *Principes de politique,* Constant drew sentences, passages, and almost entire chapters for his subsequent political texts, including the 1819 ancient and modern liberty lecture. Although itself partially assembled from earlier writings, the 1806 *Principes de politique* marked the maturity of his ideas, especially because of its inclusion of political economy. On the work's composition, see E. Hofmann, *Les 'Principes de politique' de Constant, op. cit.,* vol. I, especially p. 232-237.

22. Charles Ganilh, *Essai politique sur le revenu public,* 2 vols., Paris, Giguet et Michaud, 1806.

23. Around 1800-1802, while on the Tribunat, Ganilh and Constant worked together on several legal projects (Dominique Verrey, *Chronologie de la vie et de l'œuvre de Benjamin Constant, 1767-1805,* Geneva, Slatkine, 1992, vol. 1, p. 367).

24. Michel Bruguière, "Le tribun Ganilh et la liquidation de la dette publique par le Consulat", *Revue de l'Institut Napoléon,* vol. 111, April, 1969, p. 83-88; Philippe Steiner, "Quels principes pour l'économie politique? Charles Ganilh, Germain Garnier, Jean-Baptiste Say et la critique de la physiocratie", *Economies et Sociétés,* vol. 29, 1-2, 1995, p. 209-230.

25. C. Ganilh, *Essai politique . . . , op. cit.,* vol. I, p. 121, 139, 140.

26. *Ibid.,* vol. I, p. 38-40, 45-49, 88-90.

27. *Ibid.,* vol. I, p. 151-162, quote 154.

28. Condorcet's *Equisse* and *Mémoires sur l'instruction publique* conveyed a similar message, resorting to the same opposition, as did the works of the moderate republicans discussed below. As G. Paoletti has shown, Condorcet also significantly influenced Constant's use of the ancient—modern duality (G. Paoletti, "Relire Constant", *art. cit.,* p. 119-133).

29. C. Ganilh, *Essai politique, op. cit.,* vol. I, p. 226.

30. *Ibid.,* vol. I, p. 227-228.

31. *Ibid.,* vol. I, p. 233-234, citing Jean-Jacques Rousseau, *Du contrat social,* in J.-J. Rousseau, *Œuvres complètes,* Bernard Gagnebin and Marcel Raymond (eds.), 4 vols., Paris, Gallimard, 1959-1966, "Bibliothèque de la Pléiade", bk. I, ch. 6; vol. III, p. 360.

32. C. Ganilh, *Essai politique, op. cit.,* vol. I, p. 235-236.

33. B. Constant, *De l'esprit de conquête et de l'usurpation, op. cit.,* p. 264-267, quote p. 266-267, quoting C. Ganilh, *Essai politique, op. cit.,* vol. I, p. 419. Also cited in B. Constant, *Principes de politique* (1806), *op. cit.,* vol. II, p. 449.

34. Charles Louis Secondat de Montesquieu, *De l'esprit des lois,* Victor Goldschmidt (ed.), Paris, Garnier-Flammarion, 1979, bk. XX, ch. 1; vol. 2, p. 9. A. Hirschman, *Passions and Interests, op. cit.,* p. 60, 70-80.

35. C. Montesquieu, *Esprit des lois, op. cit.,* bk. XXI, ch. 20; vol. 2, p. 65.

36. *Ibid.,* bk. XX, ch. 2; vol. 2, p. 10.

37. *Ibid.,* bk. XXI, ch. 20; vol. 2, p. 64.

38. *Ibid.,* bk. XXI, ch. 6; vol. 2, p. 30. J. Pocock refers to this as the "commerce, leisure, cultivation" sequence ("Virtue, Rights, Manners", *art. cit.,* p. 49).

39. Although Montesquieu wrote that "qu'on ne s'étonne donc point si nos mœurs sont moins féroces qu'elles ne l'étaient autrefois", his illustrations of the benefits and drawbacks of commerce were as frequently ancient as modern, just as were his examples of commercial republics, e.g. Tyre, Carthage, Florence, Venice, or Holland (C. Montesquieu, *Esprit des lois, op. cit.,* bk. XX, chs. 1, 4-5; vol. 2, p. 9, 11-13). See Duncan Forbes, "Scientific Whiggism: Adam Smith and John Millar", *Cambridge Journal,* vol. 7, 1954, p. 646; D. Forbes, "Sceptical Whiggism, Commerce, and Liberty", in Andrew S. Skinner and Thomas Wilson (eds.), *Essays on Adam Smith,* Oxford, Clarendon Press, 1975, p. 185-186. In his minimal discussion of historical development, Montesquieu differed notably from other French *philosophes,* such as Voltaire, Turgot, and Condorcet, all of whom were historically-minded about commerce.

40. William Robertson, *The Progress of Society in Europe,* Felix Gilbert (ed.), Chicago, University of Chicago Press, 1972, p. 67. This text was published separately and as the introduction to his 1769 masterpiece, *History of the Reign of Emperor Charles V,* which received its French translation in 1771 by J.-B. Suard (Daniel Gordon, *Citizens without Sovereignty: Equality and Sociability in French Thought, 1670-1789,* Princeton, Princeton University Press, 1994, p. 150-160). Constant resided with Suard in Paris in the mid-1780s after two years' attendance at the University of Edinburgh. While Constant's studies in Edinburgh have left little evidence of contact with the lions of the Scottish Enlightenment, Scotland should be taken seriously as an ideological context for Constant, due to his thorough reading of Hume, Smith, and Ferguson and his ties to French circles in which the Scots were discussed. See Fontana, "Shaping of Modern Liberty", *art. cit.;* and cf. C. P. Courtney, "An Eighteenth-Century Education: Benjamin Constant at Erlangen and Edinburgh (1782-1785)", in Marian Hobson, J. T. A. Leigh, and Robert Wokler (eds.), *Rousseau and the Eighteenth Century,* Oxford, Voltaire Foundation, 1992, p. 295-324.

41. D. Gordon, *Citizens, op. cit.,* p. 156. For recent discussion of Robertson, see J. Pocock, *Barbarism and Religion: Narratives of Civil Government,* Cambridge, Cambridge University Press, 1999, vol. 2, p. 258-305.

42. History also allowed them to contest aspects of the civic republican tradition by relegating it to an outmoded past. See J. Pocock, "Modes of Political and Historical Time in Early Eighteenth-Century England", in *Virtue, Commerce, and History, op. cit.,* p. 98.

43. David Hume, "Of the Populousness of Ancient Nations", in *Essays, Moral, Political, and Literary,* Eugene Miller (ed.), Indianapolis, Liberty Classics, 1985, p. 404. Liberty here was "political", meaning participation in sovereignty not individual independence. Constant knew Hume's *Essays* and his *History of England.*

44. D. Hume, "Populousness of Ancient Nations", *art. cit.,* p. 383, 384, 401-405, 416. See J. Robertson, "The Scottish Enlightenment at the Limits of the Civic Tradition", in I. Hont and M. Ignatieff (eds.), *Wealth and Virtue, op. cit.,* p. 165.

45. D. Hume, "Of Refinement in the Arts", in *Essays, op. cit.,* p. 276-277.

46. A. Smith, *An Inquiry into the Nature and Causes of the Wealth of Nations,* R. H. Campbell, A. S. Skinner, and W. B. Todd (eds.), *The Glasgow Edition of the Works and Correspondence of Adam Smith,* Oxford, Clarendon Press, 1976, III.i-iv. *passim.* Following convention, the *Wealth of Nations* are cited by book, chapter, section, and paragraph number, rather than by page number. The *Lectures on Jurisprudence* are labeled (A) and (B) for the 1762-63 and 1766 versions, with page numbers referring to manuscript pagination as reproduced in the Glasgow edition. On Smith and *doux commerce,* see A. Hirschman, *Passions and Interests, op. cit.,* p. 100-112; L. Dickey, *"Doux Commerce* and the 'Mediocrity of Money' in the Ideological Context of the Wealth and Virtue Problem", in A. Smith, *An Inquiry into the Nature and Causes of the Wealth of Nations,* L. Dickey (ed.), Indianapolis, Hackett, 1993, p. 243-259. On the terminological pairings in Smith, see L. Dickey, "'The Nature of Things' and the Monetarization of History in Smith's discussion of Feudalism", in *ibid.,* p. 220-222.

47. A. Smith, *Lectures on Jurisprudence (A),* R. L. Meek, D. D. Raphael, and P. G. Stein (eds.), *The Glasgow Edition, op. cit.,* 1978, p. 27-32. On the Four-Stages theory, see Ronald L. Meek, "Smith, Turgot and the 'Four Stages' Theory", in *Smith, Marx, & After,* London, Chapman & Hall, 1977, p. 18-32.

48. L. Dickey, "'The Nature of Things'", *art. cit.,* p. 220-225.

49. D. Hume, "Refinement in the Arts", *art. cit.,* p. 277-278. Hume maintained, "Every person, if possible, ought to enjoy the fruits of his labour, in a full possession of all the necessaries, and many of the conveniences of life. No one can doubt, but such an equality is most suitable to human nature, and diminishes much less from the *happiness* of the rich than it adds to that of the poor" (D. Hume, "Of Commerce", *art. cit.,* p. 265). See I. Hont, "Rich Country—Poor Country Debate", in I. Hont and M. Ignatieff (eds.), *Wealth and Virtue, op. cit.,* p. 273.

50. A. Smith, *Wealth of Nations, op. cit.,* III.iii.12, III.iv.4, 15. D. Forbes, "Sceptical Whiggism", *art. cit.,* p. 185-187. Taxation exemplified the progress of liberty, Smith believed, because it showed that one was subject to a regular government and possessor of property in contrast to being "the property of a master" (A. Smith, *Wealth of Nations, op. cit.,* V.ii.g.11).

51. *Ibid.,* IV.x.50-52, V.i.b.2; cf. III.iii.12, 19; III.iii.4; *Lectures (B), op. cit.,* p. 210. See D. Forbes, "Sceptical Whiggism", *art. cit.,* p. 186-7, and D. Winch, *Adam Smith's Politics,* p. 40, 70-71.

52. A. Smith, *Lectures (B), op. cit.,* p. 205; cf. A. Smith, *Wealth of Nations, op. cit.,* III.iv.12-16. Smith's attack on mercantilism noted the injustice of keeping wages low. A "liberal reward for labor" was a sign of increasing prosperity, not corruption (I. Hont and M. Ignatieff, "Needs and Justice", in *Wealth and Virtue, op. cit.,* p. 2-5).

53. J. Millar, *An Historical View of the English Government,* London, Mawman, 1818, vol. IV, p. 114-119; vol. II, p. 383-384. A long-standing civic humanist view regarded the possession of property as necessary for political participation. Millar's notion of "independence" thus combined both individual and political liberty. See M. Ignatieff, "John Millar and Individualism", in I. Hont and M. Ignatieff (eds.), *Wealth and Virtue, op. cit.,* p. 321; John Pocock, "The Mobility of Property and the Rise of Eighteenth-Century Sociology", in *Virtue, Commerce, and History, op. cit.,* p. 103-123, especially, p. 103-109; and A. Hirschman, *Passions and Interests, op. cit.,* p. 87-93.

54. Above all, see I. Hont and M. Ignatieff (eds.), *Wealth and Virtue, op. cit.*

55. "Civilized monarchy" is thus distinct from a "mixed government" monarchies which possessed some political liberty. Smith used the term "despotism" to refer to arbitrary rule, independent of government form (D. Forbes, "Sceptical Whiggism", *art. cit.,* p. 186, 189-190). See D. Hume, "Of Civil Liberty", in *Essays, op. cit.,* p. 94; D. Hume, "Of the Rise and Progress of the Arts and Sciences", in *Essays, op. cit.,* p. 126-127.

56. D. Hume, "Populousness of Ancient Nations", *art. cit.,* p. 383, 416. Modern republics, for Hume, were milder than ancient ones partly because they were all "well-tempered Aristocracies" tamed by social dependencies. On Hume's preference for modern republics also see "Idea of a Perfect Commonwealth", in D. Hume, *Essays, op. cit.,* p. 512-529; J. Robertson, "Scottish Enlightenment", *art. cit.,* p. 165.

57. D. Hume, "Populousness of Ancient Nations", *art cit.,* p. 383, 419. This attack on the "admirers of the ancients" was directed at those like Andrew Fletcher who in the context of the Union debate advocated a civic conception for Scotland (J. Robertson, "Scottish Enlightenment", *op. cit.,* p. 137-178).

58. D. Winch, *Adam Smith's Politics, op. cit.,* p. 40-45.

59. M. Ignatieff, "Millar and Individualism", *art. cit.,* p. 321.

60. J. Robertson, "Scottish Enlightenment", *art. cit.*, p. 137-138, 161-162; D. Forbes, "Sceptical Whiggism", *art. cit.*, p. 198-199.

61. J. Pocock, "Virtue, Rights, Manners", *art. cit.*, p. 37-50.

62. B. Constant, *Principes de politique* (1806), *op. cit.*, vol. II, p. 21.

63. M. Gauchet concludes that Constant's 1806 search for principles independent of political form marked the moment at which Constant became a liberal. But, if the core of those principles, summarized in the term modern liberty, rested on the commercial discourse outlined here, this notion of liberalism fails to distinguish liberalism from modern republicanism or civilized monarchism (M. Gauchet, "Constant", in F. Furet and M. Ozouf (eds.), *Dictionnaire critique de la Révolution française,* Paris, Flammarion, 1988, p. 951). Steven Holmes finds it "enigmatic" that Constant's accepted the "illiberal" notion of hereditary monarchy in *De l'esprit de conquête et de l'usurpation* and in the 1806 *Principes de politique.* Holmes's perplexity results from his focus on categories derived from government form, which is exactly what Constant tried to avoid (S. Holmes, *Benjamin Constant and the Making of Modern Liberalism,* New Haven, Yale University Press, 1984, p. 208, 211).

64. Although their exact relationship remains difficult to decipher, the *Fragments* preceded the *Principes de politique.* Constant may have briefly imagined publishing them together. But, built around political economy and the progress of civilization, the broader perspective of the *Principes de politique* rendered the institutional focus of the *Fragments* less philosophically satisfying. See E. Hofmann's helpful list of passages found in both works (B. Constant, *Principes de politique* (1806), *op. cit.,* vol. II, p. 661-662). B. Constant, *Fragments d'un ouvrage abandonné sur la possibilité d'une constitution républicaine dans un grand pays,* Henri Grange (ed.), Paris, Aubier, 1991. On the institutional focus of Constant's political writings before 1806, see H. Grange "Introduction", in *ibid.*; and K. Steven Vincent, "Benjamin Constant, The French Revolution, and the Origins of French Romantic Liberalism", *French Historical Studies,* vol. 23, 4, 2000, p. 607-637.

65. [L. Molé], *Essais de morale et politique, op. cit.,* p. 142, 146-153. Molé's use of the term "l'organisation sociale" may have derived from Rœderer or Cabanis, but connections between them are difficult to establish. For discussion of Rœderer and Cabanis, see below.

66. *Ibid.,* p. 194-197.

67. *Ibid.,* p. 144, 200-201.

68. *Ibid.,* p. 202, 205, 210.

69. B. Constant, *Principes de politique* (1806), *op. cit.,* vol. II, p. 19-45.

70. Constant witnessed the first half of the Revolution from Braunschweig. His entry into French political affairs in 1795-1796 was nurtured by above all by Mme de Staël and Jacques Necker, and Constant moved in the same circles as Sieyès, Rœderer, Say, and Sophie Grouchy-Condorcet.

71. R. Whatmore, *Republicanism, op. cit., passim*; M. Sonenscher, "Nation's Debt", *art. cit.,* p. 64-103, 267-325. After 1789, or perhaps 1792, the term "republic" was ripe with uncertainty concerning its precise form. Could a constitutional monarchy upholding political liberty be "republican"? Was a republic of any kind possible in a large country like France? B. Constant's *Fragments sur une constitution républicaine* addressed these questions.

72. Emmanuel-Joseph Sieyès, *Qu'est-ce que le Tiers état,* Roberto Zapperi (ed.), Geneva, Droz, 1970, p. 124. Like the Scots, whose work he knew intimately, Sieyès thought commerce and industriousness had destroyed feudal hierarchies and fostered individual independence (E. Sieyès, "Notes et fragments inédits", in *Ecrits politiques,* R. Zapperi (ed.), Paris, Editions des archives contemporaines, 1985, p. 79).

73. E. Sieyès, "Lettres aux économistes sur leur système de politique et de morale", in *Ecrits politiques, op. cit.,* p. 32. For Sieyès's opposition to Physiocracy, see R. Whatmore, *Republicanism, op. cit.,* p. 68-70.

74. E. Sieyès, "Notes et fragments inédits", *art. cit.,* p. 62, cf. 87-89.

75. On representation as a consequence of the division of labor, see I. Hont, "Permanent Crisis", *art. cit.* 192-205; M. Sonenscher, "Nation's Debt", *art. cit.,* p. 296-322; P. Pasquino, *Sieyès, op. cit.,* p. 37-44; Keith M. Baker, *Inventing the French Revolution,* Cambridge, Cambridge University Press, 1990, p. 224-251.

76. Rœderer, an *idéologue,* leading member of the Institut, and publisher of journals devoted to political economy, severed many friendships by rallying to Bonaparte and becoming a leading minister in the Empire. See Martin S. Staum, *Minerva's Message: Stabilizing the French Revolution,* Montreal, Buffalo, McGill-Queen's University Press, 1996; and, specifically for the connection to Mme de Staël and Constant, Anne-Louise-Germaine de Staël, *Des circonstances actuelles qui peuvent terminer la Révolution et des principes qui doivent*

fonder la République en France, Lucia Omacini (ed.), Geneva, Droz, 1979, p. 300, n. 9.

77. P. Rœderer, *Cours d'organisation sociale fait au lycée en 1793,* in *Œuvres,* A. M. Roederer (éd.), Paris, Firmin Didot frères, 1853, vol. VIII, p. 130. See R. Whatmore, *Republicanism, op. cit.,* p. 98-100.

78. P. Rœderer, *Cours d'organisation sociale, op. cit.,* p. 134-136.

79. *Ibid.,* p. 134, 144-150.

80. Edmund Burke, *Reflections on the Revolution in France,* J. Pocock (ed.), Indianapolis, Hackett, 1987, p. 43. Already in 1790, Constant proposed to refute Burke's assault on "les Levelers français" (B. Constant, Lettre à Isabelle de Charrière, 10 December, in *Correspondance générale,* C. P. Courtney (ed.), Tübingen, Niemeyer, vol. 1, 1994, p. 271). This reference to these seventeenth-century English radicals was just one of the Revolution's many rhetorical categories which drew their origin from Burke's *Reflections.* See J. Pocock, "Edmund Burke and the Redefinition of Enthusiasm: the Context as Counter-Revolution", in F. Furet and M. Ozouf (eds.), *The Transformation of Political Culture 1789-1848,* Oxford, Pergamon Press, 1989, vol. 3, p. 19-43.

81. P. Rœderer, *Cours d'organisation sociale, op. cit.,* p. 146-153.

82. *Ibid.,* p. 151, 155-156.

83. Pierre-Jean-Georges Cabanis, *Quelques considérations sur l'organisation sociale en général et particulièrement sur la nouvelle constitution,* Paris, Imprimerie nationale, An VIII (1799). His essay, written to fulfill an assignment from the *Conseil des Cinq-Cents,* justified the form of representative government implemented after 18 brumaire.

84. *Ibid.,* p. 13, 36-37.

85. *Ibid.,* p. 21-23, 30. Displaying the uneasiness about direct democracy felt by many moderates in 1799, Cabanis, however, echoed the long-held view of republics as turbulent and prone to falling into tyranny.

86. Constant disputed Cabanis's and Rœderer's Sieyès-inspired view that, while sovereignty lay with the nation, it was delegated to the representatives. Cabanis's assurances about surveillance of the government did not convince Constant that arbitrary power would be adequately impeded (B. Constant, *Fragments, op. cit.,* p. 304-310; cf. Cabanis, *L'organisation sociale, op. cit.,* p. 36).

87. M. Gauchet, "Constant", *art. cit.,* p. 951; R. Whatmore, *Republicanism, op. cit.,* p. xi-xiii. See note 63 above.

88. With a fresh reading of Say's work, R. Whatmore has recently stressed the republicanism in Say's utilitarianism, accentuating its egalitarianism and attempts to restrain self-interest with moral virtues like frugality. R. Whatmore misses however the heart of Constant's complaint to Say: did *intérêt bien entendu* remain at all moral or political, or did it become just scientific and administrative? As such, could it control egoism's darker side? See *ibid.,* p. 205-214. For the older view, which regards *utilité* and *intérêt bien entendu* as more morally problematic, see Michael James, "Pierre-Louis Roederer, Jean-Baptiste Say, and the Concept of *Industrie*", *History of Political Economy,* vol. 9, 3, 1977, p. 455-475; Thomas E. Kaiser, "Politics and Political Economy in the Thought of the Idéologues", *History of Political Economy,* vol. 12, 2, 1980, p. 141-160; Cheryl B. Welch, *Liberty and Utility,* New York, Columbia University Press, 1984.

89. R. Whatmore, *Republicanism,* p. 119, 144; M. James "Concept of *Industrie*", *art. cit.,* p. 455-456; Evelyn L. Forget, *The Social Economics of Jean-Baptiste Say: Markets and Virtue,* London, Routledge, 1999, p. 63-79.

90. J.-B. Say, *Traité, op. cit.,* vol. I, p. i-vi. The *Traité* earned Say the moniker, "the French Smith". The literature has subsequently wrestled over the extent of Say's divergence from Smith. For recent discussions, see R. Whatmore, *Republicanism, op. cit.,* p. 3-12; and E. Forget, *Say, op. cit.,* p. 106-118.

91. J.-B. Say, "Olbie, ou Essai sur les moyens d'améliorer les mœurs d'une nation", in *Œuvres diverses,* Paris, Guillaumin, 1848, p. 582-583, 587-588. Say wrote "le premier livre de morale fut-il, pour les Olbiens, un bon traité d'Economie politique" (*ibid.,* p. 594). In "Olbie", Say referred to "vrais intérêts" which instruction might "éclairer". In the *Traité,* he employed the same construction as well as "intérêt bien entendu". Say echoed Smith in according instruction a vital role in mitigating the negative effects of the division of labor (*Traité, op. cit.,* vol. II, p. 428-440).

92. E. Forget, *Say, op. cit.,* p. 110-111, 115-118; R. Whatmore, *Republicanism, op. cit.,* p. 127-129. Say's notion of "industrie", which formed the basis of the industrial doctrine, was predicated on hard-work as a moral quality, just as it had been for the Scots. While highlighting Say's enduring commitment to republican "manners", R. Whatmore concedes that Say was "no longer an orthodox republican" after 1803 (*ibid.,* p. 152). In becoming "manners", virtues scarcely retained anything of their civic nature. See, J. Pocock, "Virtue, Rights, Manners", *art. cit.,* p. 47-50.

93. On Destutt de Tracy, see especially C. Welch, *Liberty and Utility, op. cit.*

94. A. L. C. Destutt de Tracy, *Commentaire sur l'Esprit des Lois de Montesquieu* (1806), *Œuvres de Montesquieu*, A. Destutt de Tracy and Villemain (ed.), vol. 8, Paris, H. Féret, 1827, p. 151-152. T. Kaiser, "Political economy and the *Idéologues*", *art. cit.*, p. 145-147.

95. While in the 1820s he confronted the French utilitarians with the moral argument, Constant had already in 1806 criticized Bentham's doctrine for permissiveness toward the encroachments of arbitrary authority (B. Constant, *Principes de politique* (1806), *op. cit.*, vol. II, p. 58-79).

96. Jean Starobinski observes that Constant perceived better than his nineteenth-century counterparts that "Quelque chose, dans la civilisation, travaille contre la civilisation" (J. Starobinski, "Le mot civilisation", in *Le Remède dans le mal: Critique et légitimation de l'artifice à l'âge des Lumières*, Paris, Gallimard, 1989, p. 41). Also see his most recent contribution to this theme, J. Starobinski, "Benjamin Constant: la pensée du progrès et l'analyse des réactions", *Annales Benjamin Constant*, vol. 23-24, 2000, p. 39-62. Similarly, see George Armstrong Kelly, *The Humane Comedy: Constant, Tocqueville and French Liberalism*, Cambridge, Cambridge University Press, 1992.

97. B. Constant, "De la liberté", *art. cit.*, p. 617. G. Paoletti appropriately highlights these criticisms of modernity (G. Paoletti, "Relire Constant", *art. cit.*, p. 123-125).

98. B. Constant, "De la liberté", *art. cit.*, p. 618.

99. B. Constant, "De M. Dunoyer et quelques-uns de ses ouvrages", in *Ecrits politiques, op. cit.*, p. 654-678, which reviewed C. Dunoyer, *L'industrie et la morale considérées dans leurs rapports avec la liberté*, Paris, Sautelet, 1825.

100. They had in mind Say's *Traité* and Constant's *De l'esprit de conquête et de l'usurpation*, and particularly his discussion of ancient and modern civilization. See C. Comte and C. Dunoyer, *Le Censeur*, vol. VII, Paris, 1815; and C. Dunoyer, "Notice Historique", *art. cit.*, p. 175-180. On Constant's ties to the *industrialistes*, see Ephraïm Harpaz, *L'école libérale sous la Restauration*, Geneva, Droz, 1968; and Shirley Gruner, "Political Historiography in Restoration France", *History and Theory*, vol. 8, 4, 1969, p. 347-365.

101. B. Constant, "De M. Dunoyer", *art. cit.*, p. 657-658; C. Dunoyer, *L'industrie, op. cit.*, p. 94-95, citing B. Constant, *De la religion considérée dans sa source, ses formes et ses développements*, Paris, Bossange Père, 1824-1831, vol. I, p. 236. In his defense, B. Constant referenced *ibid.*, vol. I, p. xl-xli, n. 1.

102. C. Dunoyer, *L'industrie, op. cit.*, p. 5-6; alluding to B. Constant, *De la religion, op. cit.*, vol. I, p. 236.

103. C. Dunoyer, *L'industrie, op. cit.*, p. 40, 28-40.

104. *Ibid.*, p. 16, 358, cf. p. i-v, 321-397.

105. B. Constant, "De M. Dunoyer", *art. cit.*, p. 659, 665-668. Given Dunoyer's close relationship to Say, one wonders if Constant was reminding the *industrialistes* of their mentor's earlier words with this near quote of Say's "Olbie". Say had written, "l'amour du gain [. . .] étouffe une foule de sentiments nobles et désintéressés qui doivent entrer dans l'âme humaine perfectionnée" (J.-B. Say, "Olbie", *art. cit.*, p. 596).

106. B. Constant, "De M. Dunoyer", *art. cit.*, p. 659, 662, 664-668. Say contrasted his utilitarianism to Constant's views expressed in *De la religion* and linked Constant to the German-informed ideas of Victor Cousin and Mme de Staël (J.-B. Say, "Lettre à Etienne Dumont, à Genève, de Paris, le 10 mai 1829", in *Mélanges et correspondance d'économie politique; l'ouvrage posthume de J. B. Say*, Charles Comte (ed.), Paris, Chamerot, 1833, p. 366-367). Say wrote this letter while preparing his "Essai sur le principe de l'utilité", in which he parried Mme de Staël's criticisms of utilitarianism's aridness (in J.-B. Say, *Mélanges, op. cit.*, p. 406-455, especially p. 436-441).

107. B. Constant, *De la religion, op. cit.*, vol. I, p. xxxvii-xxxviii. We may surmise that the "amis de la liberté" were his associates among the *industrialistes*, such as Dunoyer and Say, whose reactions to *De la religion* seemed to confirm their growing disagreement. The "seul mobile désintéressé" here was "le sentiment religieux".

108. Immanuel Kant, "Idee zu einer allgemeinen Geschichte in weltbürgerlicher Absicht", in *Was is Aufklärung? Ausgewählte kleine Schriften*, Horst D. Brandt (ed.), Hamburg, F. Meiner, 1999, p. 14.

109. B. Constant, *De la religion, op. cit.*, vol. I, p. xxxix.

110. *Ibid.*, vol. I, p. xliv. Compare Constant's use of the term "sacrifice" here with his statement in "De la liberté" that moderns were no longer willing to sacrifice their individual liberty as the ancients had done (B. Constant, "De la liberté", *art. cit.*, p. 602). Constant was suggesting that modern liberty only attained meaning when the sacrifices of duty occurred in the context of individual freedom.

FURTHER READING

Bibliography

Lowe, David K. *Benjamin Constant: An Annotated Bibliography of Critical Editions and Studies.* London: Grant & Cutler Ltd., 1979, 141 p.

Offers a comprehensive bibliography of Constant's works, along with secondary criticism.

Biography

Wood, Dennis. *Benjamin Constant: A Biography.* London: Routledge, 1993, 308 p.

Comprehensive biography of Constant.

Criticism

Call, Michael J. "*Adolphe*: Obstruction and the Lost Order." In *Back to the Garden: Chateaubriand, Senancour and Constant,* pp. 95-124. Saratoga, Calif.: Anma Libri, 1988.

Asserts that in *Adolphe* Constant expresses frustration and regret over his own personal weaknesses and failures as well as over the political events in France at the time the novel was written.

Cruickshank, John. "Literary Theory." In *Benjamin Constant,* pp. 107-20. New York: Twayne Publishers, 1974.

Outlines the social and political views and literary influences—German, French, and Classical Greek—that inform Constant's literary theories.

Fontana, Biancamaria. *Benjamin Constant and the Post-Revolutionary Mind.* New Haven, Conn.: Yale University Press, 1991, 165 p.

Book-length study of Constant's political thought and career as an activist.

Holmes, Stephen. *Benjamin Constant and the Making of Modern Liberalism.* New Haven, Conn.: Yale University Press, 1984, 340 p.

In-depth study of Constant's political and social thought.

Kelly, George Armstrong. *The Humane Comedy: Constant, Tocqueville and French Liberalism.* Cambridge: Cambridge University Press, 1992, 262 p.

Compares and contrasts the thought of Constant and Alexís de Tocqueville in relation to French Enlightenment thought.

Mossman, Carol A. "Production, Reproduction, and Narrative Form: *Adolphe.*" In *Politics and Narratives of Birth: Gynocolonization from Rousseau to Zola,* pp. 72-138. Cambridge: Cambridge University Press, 1993.

Takes the position that "birth is central to *Adolphe,*" focusing on the notion of matricide through childbirth.

Additional coverage of Constant's life and career is contained in the following sources published by Thomson Gale: *Dictionary of Literary Biography,* **Vol. 119;** *European Writers,* **Vol. 4;** *Guide to French Literature, 1789 to the Present*; *Literature Resource Center*; **and** *Nineteenth-Century Literature Criticism,* **Vol. 6.**

Susanna Haswell Rowson
1762-1824

English-born American novelist, playwright, poet, essayist, and textbook writer.

The following entry presents criticism on Rowson's works from 1976 to 2003. For further information on Rowson's life and career, see *NCLC*, Volumes 5 and 69.

INTRODUCTION

Susanna Haswell Rowson was one of the first women to write professionally in the United States. Her novel, *Charlotte: A Tale of Truth* (1791; subsequently published as *Charlotte Temple: A Tale of Truth*), achieved unprecedented popularity, exceeding 160 editions during the three years following its first publication in the United States in 1794. The breadth and duration of this novel's circulation permanently influenced the reading habits of the American public. With her blend of sensationalism and didacticism, Rowson helped popularize the novel in colonial America, where novel-reading had long been considered immoral.

BIOGRAPHICAL INFORMATION

Susanna Haswell was born in 1762 in Portsmouth, England, to William Haswell, a British naval lieutenant, and Susanna Margrove, who died shortly after her daughter's birth. At the age of five, the young Susanna moved to America to live with her father and stepmother. As political tensions increased in the colonies, William Haswell remained loyal to the crown; consequently, his property was eventually confiscated, and in 1778 the family was sent back to England. There, Susanna was employed for some time as a governess and in 1786 her first novel, *Victoria*, was published. She married William Rowson that same year. Rowson wrote poetry and several other novels over the next few years, including the semi-autobiographical *Rebecca, or, The Fille de Chambre* (1792). In 1792, Rowson, her husband, and her sister-in-law joined a theater company, and in the following year they immigrated to America. In addition to acting, Rowson continued to write to help support her family. Of her plays, only one—*Slaves in Algiers; or, A Struggle for Freedom* (1794)—remains extant, and this is only in fragments. In 1797 Rowson opened a school for young girls in Boston. While teach-

ing, Rowson also wrote three more novels, and a number of textbooks that were used in her school as well as in others. In addition, she contributed regularly to journals, and served as the editor of the *Boston Weekly Magazine*. Rowson continued to write novels, plays, educational texts, poetry, and songs until her death in 1824.

MAJOR WORKS

Concern for the education of women pervades Rowson's work. In *Mentoria; or, The Young Lady's Friend* (1791), she states that her purpose in writing is to show women that "happiness can never be met within the temple of dissipation and folly." Rowson's early novels, including *Victoria, The Inquisitor; or, Invisible Rambler* (1788), *Charlotte,* and *Trials of the Human Heart* (1795), each portray, ostensibly, a good woman who is seduced, then realizes her error and repents her weakness. Rowson's works feature many characteristics of the sentimental genre, emphasizing such themes as filial obedience and Christian morality, and make use of the "seduction plot," which had been popularized earlier in England by novelists such as Samuel Richardson. Although Rowson appropriates the sensationalism of the seduction plot in *Charlotte,* her style is realistic, and in the subtitle and the preface of the novel, she emphasizes that the novel is based on the actual seduction and abandonment of a young girl, Charlotte, at the hands of American army Lieutenant Montraville. Rowson's later heroines are more independent and resilient. *Sarah; or, The Exemplary Wife* (1813) and *Charlotte's Daughter; or, The Three Orphans* (1828; also published as *Lucy Temple*), depict resourceful women who overcome adversity and maintain their personal integrity. In *Slaves in Algiers* and *Reuben and Rachel; or, Tales of Old Times* (1798), Rowson explores the struggle against political tyranny and the fight for women's rights.

CRITICAL RECEPTION

Rowson's novels were generally dismissed by her contemporaries as highly stylized, mawkish imitations of the works of Richardson. Although *Charlotte* enjoyed tremendous popular success, critics dismissed the novel as lacking literary and artistic merit. Later critics have praised Rowson's realistic rendering of character and situation and her skillful handling of plot. Modern criticism of Rowson's works generally concerns her treatment of women and women's issues. While some critics argue that the author's use of sentimental-novel conventions reinforces a stereotype of the weak, dependent woman, others have declared that Rowson's works reveal a strongly feminist sensibility. The latter group maintains that her genteel, sentimentalized novels were more than mere entertainment; they served as expressions of Rowson's contempt for those who freely victimize women, and of her belief in education and full equality for women. Some commentators, studying the characterization of Charlotte Temple, have regarded Charlotte as an embodiment of matriarchal authority, and attribute *Charlotte*'s popularity to the readers' identification with the title character's maternity. Critic Paul Barton has interpreted the character as a mouthpiece that allows Rowson to take on the role of spiritual advisor in a daring, covert subversion of the Puritanical ban against women in positions of church authority. Rowson is now regarded by many scholars as a pioneer in prose fiction in American literature, although critics such as Jane Tompkins have argued that prejudicial attitudes against women writers have prevented Rowson's works from being recognized as equal, or even greater, in importance to American literary development to such male authors as Charles Brockden Brown. Despite the absence of critical approval for Rowson's works by her contemporaries and by succeeding generations of literary scholars, the popularity of her works precipitated an important change of attitude which prompted the public's acceptance of the novel as a legitimate literary form. In addition, because she championed women's education, both in her novels and in her personal life, Rowson has been noted as an important early advocate of feminism in America.

PRINCIPAL WORKS

Victoria (novel) 1786

The Inquisitor; or Invisible Rambler (novel) 1788

Poems on Various Subjects (poetry) 1788

A Trip to Parnassus; or, The Judgement of Apollo on Dramatic Authors and Performers (poetry) 1788

Mary; or, The Test of Honour, A Novel. By a Young Lady (novel) 1789

Charlotte: A Tale of Truth (novel) 1791; also published as *Charlotte Temple: A Tale of Truth,* 1797

Mentoria; or, The Young Lady's Friend (novel) 1791

Rebecca; or, The Fille de Chambre (novel) 1792

Slaves in Algiers; or, A Struggle for Freedom (play) 1794

Trials of the Human Heart (novel) 1795

Reuben and Rachel; or, Tales of Old Times (novel) 1798

Miscellaneous Poems (poetry) 1804

An Abridgement of Universal Geography, Together with Sketches of History (textbook) 1806

A Present for Young Ladies (poetry and essays) 1811

Sarah; or, The Exemplary Wife (novel) 1813

Youth's First Step in Geography (textbook) 1818

Biblical Dialogues between a Father and His Family (essays) 1822

Exercises in History, Chronology, and Biography, in Question and Answer (textbook) 1822

Charlotte's Daughter; or, The Three Orphans. A Sequel to Charlotte Temple (novel) 1828; also published as *Lucy Temple,* 1842

CRITICISM

Dorothy Weil (essay date 1976)

SOURCE: Weil, Dorothy. "Inferior to None." In *In Defense of Women: Susanna Rowson (1762-1824),* pp. 31-64. University Park: The Pennsylvania State University Press, 1976.

[*In the following essay, Weil discusses how Rowson dispels commonly-held prejudices about women and encourages equal treatment for women in her works.*]

> The union of masculine virtues, feminine softness, and christian meekness, form the most illustrious assemblage. . . . The name of christian unites in it all that is lovely and amiable in nature. . . .
>
> (*A Present for Young Ladies,* 1811)

Under the banner of Christianity and with a battalion of literary forms at her command, Mrs. Rowson met the major issues concerning women, and claimed freedom for her sex. She did not deal with specific political rights; Mrs. Rowson died when Elizabeth Cady Stanton was nine years old—twenty-four years before the Women's Rights Convention held by Mrs. Stanton and Susan B. Anthony at Seneca Falls, New York, in 1848. But at a time when the prevailing ideal for women in both Britain and America was that of "a gentle but capable mistress in a sheltered home,"[1] Mrs. Rowson attacked the myths and stereotypes that surrounded women and taught her reader that she could be the equal of the male in most of the important spheres of life, and that she should see herself as a person capable of great achievement. Mrs. Rowson's attempt to work through the problems that such a belief entails, and her recommendations for social change, are her major themes.

A glance at the situation of women in the period in which Mrs. Rowson worked places her feminist ideas in perspective. Many English women novelists had complained of the narrowness of their world and the masculine attempt to confine them to the domestic scene.[2] In America, as well as England, women were much discussed: their fundamental nature, their proper social rôle, and their rights.

The literature that dealt explicitly with women was pretty much the same in England and America during Mrs. Rowson's writing years. In her study *Women in Eighteenth-Century America,* Mary Benson divides the writers into those who denied women equality with men and saw them as objects to please the male (the Rousseau-Chesterfield point of view); those who might grant women equality with men, but still based their worth on their influence upon husbands and children (Hannah More and Mrs. Chapone); and, in a category by herself, Mary Wollstonecraft, who argued that women were responsible to themselves and that virtue was worth attaining for a woman's *own* self-respect. Writers on the subject crossed these divisions, of course; some argued that women were inferior, but granted them a "higher" destiny than that of pleasing the male. Some even argued that women were morally superior to men, but this approach still led to defining their worth according to their uplifting effect on men. These elementary areas of discussion had been established by European writers, and the various writers were available to American readers.

Mary Wollstonecraft, while not at first attacked in America, lost favor due to fear of radicalism and her connection with the ideas and thinkers of the French Revolution (Benson, p. 86). On the other hand, the works of Hannah More were very popular; and More, notes William Wasserstrom, "urged women to respect themselves and women's work, avoid encroaching upon masculine interests or entering the 'theatre of masculine activities.'"[3]

Education for women was generally approved of in America; the distinguishing feature of the genuine advocate for women is often a matter of tone. The clergy favored female education, but as Mary Benson points out, their concern had the effect of forestalling the influence of Mary Wollstonecraft and other advanced thinkers (Benson, p. 145). Further, some of the most enthusiastic supporters of feminine intellectual development phrase their ideas in patronizing language. James Neal, an educator himself, wrote in defense of scientific, rigorous education for women, yet apparently regarded it as a form of beautification. In his *Essay on the Education and Genius of the Female Sex* (1795), in which he praises the Ladies' Academy of Philadelphia, and even approves Mary Wollstonecraft, he advises the pupils to "adorn and beautify your minds."[4] Neal uses the words "ornament" and "ornamental" over and over until his original premises appear in doubt. The commencement address delivered by a pupil at the academy

(such pieces were generally written by teachers) also belies to some degree Neal's enthusiasm for the female mind. The young lady attempts to refute certain myths about feminine temperament, then goes on to say in support of separate roles and education for men and women.

> To undergo the fatigues and toils of war, to tread the thorny path of politics, and to move in the more active scenes of life, belongs to men.
>
> "Nothing," says Milton, "is lovelier in a woman, than to study household good."
>
>   (Neal, p. 18)

For all the talk, women were the "second sex." Whether the ideas of women were "high or low," says Mary Benson, the vision of the woman's proper rôle was that of "a gentle but capable mistress in a sheltered home." In the periodicals, for example,

> Women . . . save for some unconvincing fiction, were not idealized figures on pedestals, but more ordinary creatures whose moderate education gave them a taste for the milder forms of literature but did not lead them to deep reasoning or serious study. They formed a part, and a most important one, of the community in their relation to men's pleasures and in their specialized duties as mistresses of families. Their character was a subject of interest and study rather in social than in intellectual aspects although interest in the latter was increasing. Despite these signs of change women remained, for most of the men who wrote popular essays and sketches, objects to be smiled at, scolded, loved, perhaps praised, but rarely to be treated as men's equals.
>
>   (Benson, p. 222)

Frank L. Mott, in his *History of American Magazines,* examines the periodicals' interest in the rôle and education of women. Notes of counsel and advice were ubiquitous; several periodicals, among them the *American Magazine* and *Massachusetts Magazine,* were designed for, and explicitly appealed to feminine readers.[5] Mott points out one instance of a discussion of the equality of the sexes, but most of the excerpts he provides from the periodicals of the day involve the education of women. These consist of suggestions for curricula and warnings that women must not drink too deeply of learning. Noah Webster and Benjamin Rush agree on teaching females English, Arithmetic, and Geography, and in forbidding them novels (p. 64).

The "learned woman" faces much opposition, and the magazines increase the prejudice against her. Mott quotes Webster's *American Magazine* (1788) as advising women to "be mild, social and sentimental" and to avoid the "profound researches of study" (p. 64). The *Ladies Magazine* (1792) says of women writers that "We admire them more as authors than esteem them as women" (Mott, p. 66), while the *American Moral and Sentimental Magazine* (1797) paints a completely traditional view of "Domestic Felicity" (Mott, p. 65).

Charles Brockden Brown and Judith Sargent Murray, who according to Mary Benson in *Women in Eighteenth-Century America* represented "radical thought" (p. 177), brought out portions of their works in periodicals. Parts I and II of Brown's *Alcuin,* a dialogue between a pedantic male teacher and a somewhat cynical bluestocking who discuss the issues of sexual equality, was published as a book and serialized (in altered form) in the *Weekly Magazine* in 1798. The final two parts, however, in which the narrator, Alcuin, describes a utopia in which the only difference between the sexes is the biological function, were not published until 1815, after Brown's death.[6] Judith Sargent Murray's *The Gleaner* (1798), a collection of miscellaneous writings begun in 1792 in the *Massachusetts Magazine,* defends independent lives for women.[7]

Brown and Murray aside, the magazines continue to express doubts about the strength of the female mind. The *Portico* (1816) refuses intellectual equality to women, for their minds "were never designed to soar into the higher regions of literature and science" (Mott, p. 143). The notion of women as beings of superior sensibility and capacity for civilization lives on in the *Literary Magazine* in 1805, and the idea that the highest female rôle is that of a companion to and an influence upon the male survives in 1816 in *Portico* (Mott, pp. 141, 143). Physical education joins music and dancing as possible threats to female domesticity; the *American Journal of Education* (1826) finds it "unfeminine" (Mott, p. 143).

Studies of early American fiction and drama also reveal few examples of liberal treatment of the female. Mrs. Benson discovers a mild note of feminism in Sally Wood's *Dorval* (1801)[8] while arguing that the novel is basically adverse to the ideas of Mary Wollstonecraft; she grants a few unusual female portraits to Charles Brockden Brown (pp. 194, 198), but finds almost none in early American drama. The heroines' lives, according to Benson, culminate in marriage, and there is little variety in the type of female presented.

In her study *The Stereotype of the Single Woman in American Novels,* Dorothy Yost Deegan finds in the early fiction mainly disgust for any feminine type but the happily married woman:

> In fact, it was in this early period that this concept of spinsterhood was translated and took deep root in American fiction. Only one novelist, Charles Brockden Brown, influenced by the radical theories of Godwin, dared to present the unmarried woman as somewhat admirable. But he too adopts the Richardsonian suicide motif, and in some of his minor characters, makes the gossiping spinster the villain.

There can be little doubt or question as to the social attitude toward single women in this early period of American fiction. Herbert Ross Brown in his recent study on the sentimental novel, observes that the "new woman" who entertained ambition outside the home was regarded as the moral horror of the time. He summarizes tersely the prevailing opinion: if happiness beyond the bonds of wedlock was criminal in a man, it was the unpardonable sin for a woman.[9]

The actual situation of the woman in the late eighteenth and early nineteenth centuries was akin to limbo. The single woman might be an outcast socially, but she was better off economically and legally than her married sister. The married woman, though accepted socially, was economically and legally a slave. If a woman married— and marriage was practically forced upon the female— she suddenly found the oppressive law of "coverture" descend upon her and herself deprived of control of her property, her earnings, her ability to engage in contracts, collect debts, or enter a business. Husband and wife had been declared by Blackstone to be a legal unit, and that unit was the husband. American law followed the British in this regard, so that until the mid-nineteenth century, when married women's property laws were passed, these restrictions of coverture (as well as others equally demeaning to the wife) prevailed here. The husband chose the place to live, and the wife had to follow. He had the right to inflict punishment upon his wife as long as he used a small stick. Torts and crimes committed in the presence of the husband were presumed to be his responsibility.[10]

At the time that Mrs. Rowson wrote, divorce was almost impossible to obtain in England. No secular court divorce was instituted in England until 1857 with the Divorce and Matrimonial Causes Act. During the late eighteenth and early nineteenth centuries, the only relief from a bad marriage was a "legislative" divorce; that is, dissolution of a marriage required an act of Parliament concerning the specific case. This process was expensive, time-consuming, and was available only to the privileged. In America after the Revolution, legislative divorce existed alongside newly emerging judicial divorce (with strict, explicit grounds) as the various states instituted new laws on the subject. The difficulty of obtaining a divorce was viewed as a protection for the female, and it may have operated as such in a society that provided so few options. Still, the difficulty of the process, reinforced by social disapproval of divorce, made it virtually impossible for a woman to break the "bonds" of matrimony.

In other areas women were equally disadvantaged. Although, as Mary Benson notes, some women had participated in the Revolution (through economic boycotts, for example), they were left out of the Constitution. Several important women had exerted political influence with their husbands and brothers—Mercy Warren,

Hannah Winthrop, and Abigail Adams are cases in point—but politics was still considered beyond the feminine sphere (Benson, p. 258). Women were not, of course, permitted to vote, to serve on juries, or to hold public office. An item in the *Monthly Magazine and American Review* illustrates the feeling of one writer about females in politics. It describes a case of a young woman who denies herself an interest in the political arena in favor of "tranquillizing" her husband. Literature is open to her, judges the writer, but not the "agitation" of politics.[11] The opinion of Thomas Jefferson was that "the tender breasts of ladies were not formed for political convulsion" (Benson, p. 246). John Adams's answer to Abigail when she suggested that the Constitution guarantee rights to women as well as to men was even less liberal.[12]

In her study *Economic Feminism in American Literature Prior to 1848*,[13] Augusta Violette confirms the fact that no really radical or profound moves were accomplished in behalf of women until the convention at Seneca Falls, New York, in 1848, although there were pro-feminist forces (the Quakers, for instance) from the beginning, and the anti-slavery movement somewhat later, working in that direction. The Fanny Wright societies[14] and writers such as Thomas Paine and John Neal, says Violette, contributed to the eventual changes.

Thelma Smith, in her article "Feminism in Philadelphia, 1790-1850,"[15] concurs in seeing little movement toward emancipation during Mrs. Rowson's period. While the leisure attained by many Philadelphia women, the interest in European ideas, and the Quaker influence encouraged change, such forces as the rise of romanticism in literature and the lack of educational opportunities kept feminism at a low ebb (p. 245).

This is the atmosphere into which Mrs. Rowson, with her emancipated ways, arrived in 1793. Mrs. Rowson was thoroughly aware of the controversies concerning women and had already begun to chip away at what she considered misconceptions about the nature of the female. She emphatically rejected the advice to be "mild, social and sentimental," and although she described the contemporary woman's rôle as inevitably one of influence upon the male, she insisted that women are capable of high intellectual development and success in "any profession whatever."

One aspect of woman's basic nature upon which Mrs. Rowson never wavered was her sex's equality with the male. She states her view clearly in **"Sketches of Female Biography,"** a series of vignettes of famous women in history who excelled in various ways. These sketches are part of *A Present For Young Ladies* (1811), the collection of pieces in prose and poetry written by Mrs. Rowson and recited by her students at the annual exhibitions of her academy. In this work,

Mrs. Rowson declares, "It would be absurd to imagine that talents or virtue were confined to sex or station" (p. 88). She believes, then, in both intellectual and moral equality of the sexes, and she supports this view in all phases of her literary work.

The matter of sex and temperament is somewhat more complex for Mrs. Rowson. She has been included among writers who perpetuated the myth of the delicate, sensitive, passive woman, and the lustful, brutal, active male; she does tend at times to present this view. She often uses phrases like "the delicacy natural to our sex." On the other hand, Mrs. Rowson devotes a good deal of energy to refuting feminine stereotypes. As noted, she resolves such problems by resorting to a religious standard. A Christian, she argues, should combine the softer female virtues and the harder masculine ones. She cannot quite bring herself to drop the male-female dichotomy, so she retains it and still asserts a non-sex-linked personality for women. The Christian female person will conform to the pattern outlined in the following passage:

> A woman who to the graces and gentleness of her own sex, adds the knowledge and fortitude of the other, exhibits the most perfect combination of human excellence; and since innumerable instances may be produced of female courage, fortitude, talent, and virtue of every description, why should not we start forward with generous ardour in the pursuit of what is praiseworthy, and substitute for the evanescent graces of beauty the durable attractions of a cultivated mind.

("Female Biography," *A Present*, pp. 84-85)

Mrs. Rowson manages to come to at least compromise terms even with the notion of sex-associated emotional patterns. As early as her second novel, ***The Test of Honour*** (1789), Mrs. Rowson was dealing unequivocally with the idea that women were morally special. The story attempts to show that women may possess virtue and character equal to that of men. Mary, the protagonist, is fifteen when her parents die; she is moderately well-off financially and is left with two sets of guardians. Mary has spirit and integrity, and she leaves Mrs. Fentum, one of her guardians, when she discovers that the lady intends to marry her to her son, Harry Fentum. The main action of the novel turns upon Mary's refusal of a paragon of a suitor, Frederick Stephens, because he does not have his father's blessing to propose to her. Mr. Stephens wishes Frederick to marry a wealthy young girl. He cannot believe that Mary, because she is a female, could want Frederick for other than mercenary reasons and he sees her behavior as a stratagem to catch a husband. Mr. Stephens's dislike of women is general. He expostulates to his son, "I tell you Fred you know no more of women than an ideot. Why, I'll be d—d if there ever was a generous disinterested woman in the world; they are all as artful as serpents; they study every look, word, and action, and are ever laying plans to compass some favorite end" (I, 134). But Mary's actions prove her to be above art.

On receiving a letter from an uncle in Jamaica, Mary leaves the country to avoid Frederick. Frederick follows and is captured by Algerians. After several years, during which she meets many trials with courage and sense, Mary returns to England. She is approached by Mr. Stephens, who despairs of Fred's ever being returned to his home. The broken old man apologizes for having parted the lovers and brought on Fred's captivity. He is sickened by the venality of his son's acquaintances, who have tried to ingratiate themselves with him. To expiate his own guilt, and because Mary was loved by his son, he offers to adopt Mary and make her his heir. Mary refuses the offer, of course. She extends Mr. Stephens her affection only, so that the old misogynist is forced to admit that "there might be true generosity, even in a woman" (II, 160).

In a story within the story, Frederick's tale of his adventures in Algiers, a woman, Semira, saves her father and sister by marrying the chief of the Algerians, Hali, and swearing that she will embrace the Mohammedan religion. Semira fulfills her promises, but then produces a dagger, and is about to kill herself when the infidel, moved by her filial love as well as her religious and moral integrity, releases her from her vows and arranges for passage for the entire English group back to England (chapter XX, **"Female Fortitude and Filial Duty Rewarded,"** II, 196). Twice Frederick is returned to his father through the efforts of a woman. Two unbelievers, Hali and Mr. Stephens, are converted to a new and respectful view of women.

Mrs. Rowson's heroines tend to combine the "graces and gentleness" of their own sex and the "knowledge and fortitude of the other" rather than to possess a rare, specifically feminine, religious and moral sensibility. Weak, passive vessels like Charlotte and Victoria may be in good standing "in futurity," but cause themselves and others great distress in the present. The heroines Mrs. Rowson presents as models to copy possess an active moral sense, and they face up to the tribulations involved in their choices as well as any man. Rebecca, who must support herself financially, faces poverty and ignominy when she refuses on two occasions to assist her employers in immoral intrigues. In several instances the power of Christian women to influence others is given special focus. Meriel's example is an inspiration to Rooksby and Clara to repent; but Meriel has had to struggle, as a man would, to attain a Christian frame of mind.

In *Slaves in Algiers* (1794), which is ostensibly organized around a patriotic theme—the enslavement of Americans by the Barbary Pirates—the courage and fortitude of women takes precedence. The plot is very similar to that of Frederick's narrative of his captivity in *The Test of Honour.* A group of Americans enslaved by the Dey of Algiers escape, partly through the efforts of two women. Olivia promises to marry the Dey in exchange for her fellow prisoners' lives. Olivia has resolved, of course, to kill herself after the ceremony, but is saved when a slave revolt intervenes. The slaves have been incited by Fetnah, a courageous young woman who has been given to the Dey by her father in exchange for pecuniary advancement.

Fetnah explicitly rejects the concept that women are inferior to men. She has learned to appreciate liberty in spite of being the daughter of Ben Hassan, a Jew and keeper of slaves. She says, "Woman was never form'd to be the slave of man. Nature made us equal with them, and gave us the power to render ourselves superior" (II.1.9). Fetnah also rejects the notion that the character of a woman should express itself differently from that of a man. When she, Frederick, Henry, and others who encourage the revolt are hiding in a cave and Frederick tells her to retreat to the back of the grotto while he goes off to rescue Olivia, she refuses. She intends to accompany Frederick on his mission. Fetnah asserts,

> A woman!—Why, so I am; but in the cause of love or friendship, a woman can face danger with as much spirit, and as little fear, as the bravest man amongst you.—Do you lead the way, I'll follow to the end.
>
> (III.1.47)

In response, Sebastian, a servant, who has witnessed Fetnah's performance, exults,

> Bravo! Excellent! Bravissimo!—Why, 'tis a little body; but ecod, she's a devil of a spirit.—It's a fine thing to meet with a woman that has a little fire in her composition. I never much lik'd your milk and water ladies; to be sure, they are easily manag'd—but your spirit'd ladies; require taming; they make a man look about him—dear, sweet angry creatures, here's to their health.
>
> (III.1.47)

Fetnah is Mrs. Rowson's version of a Shakespearean comic heroine, the girl who shows her spirited, active side. In helping the plot along, Fetnah must dress in men's clothing, thus underlining her relationship to Rosalind, Viola, et al.

In the epilogue to the play, Mrs. Rowson not only assumes equality with men, but incites her female audience to claim precedence:

> Well, Ladies tell me—how d'ye like my play?
> "The creature has some sense," methinks you say.
> "She says that we should have supreme dominion.
> "And in good truth, we're all of her opinion.
> "Women were born for universal sway,
> "Men to adore, be silent, and obey."

In character and virtue, Mrs. Rowson asserted, women could rival men, and their morality should be judged by similar standards. As to intellect, men may appear superior to women, but Mrs. Rowson viewed this situation as a function of society, not nature. She made conventional apologies for the artistic quality of her own intellectual efforts in several prefaces, but usually accompanied these expressions with a plea for better education for the female. In the preface to *Mentoria,* Mrs. Rowson writes,

> a-well-a-day for me, I must also be judged by some sage male critic, who, "with spectacle on nose, and pouch by's side," with lengthened visage and contemptuous smile, sits down to review the literary productions of a woman. He turns over a few pages, and then
>
> > Catching the Author at some that or therefore,
> > At once condemns her without why or wherefore.
>
> Then alas! What may not be my fate? whose education, as a female, was necessarily circumscribed, whose little knowledge has been simply gleaned from pure nature, and who, on a subject of such importance, write as I feel with enthusiasm.
>
> > (p. iii)

In the preface to *Slaves in Algiers,* Mrs. Rowson writes of the disadvantages of "a confined education" and heads off the male critics by adding that she does not expect to be found equal to masculine playwrights who have "from their sex or situation in life" had the advantage of a classical education (p. ii).

The works themselves exhibit men and women of about equal mental ability. The heroines of the fiction are great readers and writers. The examples of the original poetry written by Victoria. Meriel, Rebecca, Charlotte, and Sarah do not impress the reader with the quality of the intellects that produced them; still these efforts are introduced to create minds for the protagonists as well as to provide an elegant artistic effect. Several women in the fiction are attracted to literature and learning; Rebecca, Sarah, and Lucy are well enough educated to teach. Several women writers and artists appear in *The Inquisitor.*

In the nonfiction, Mrs. Rowson makes a strong claim for the intellectual ability of women. **"Female Biography"** (*A Present*) is replete with examples of women who developed their minds to a high level. Among many others, Mrs. Rowson cites Hypatia, a fourth-century Egyptian who was educated by her father and succeeded him as head of his school after he died (pp. 85-86), Lucretia Cornaro, a Venetian who attained a doctor's degree in the seventeenth century and excelled in mathematics (p. 86), and Mrs. Macaulay, the English historian, whose work was "inferior to none" (p. 88).

These stories are echoed in the pages of the *Boston Weekly Magazine.* The types of women celebrated in the biographical department of the paper parallel those

in **"Female Biography"** and the texts, and thus suggest the hand of Mrs. Rowson. The issue of 17 November 1804 (vol. 3) includes a sketch of the life of Donna Maria Agnesi, a prodigy and professor of mathematics and philosophy in Bologna. The writer refutes the idea that great talents appear only in men. On 29 December 1804, four columns are devoted to a Miss Linwood, an artist in needlework whose copies in tapestry of famous paintings had been praised by Sir Joshua Reynolds as well as the president of the Royal Academy. Volume 3, 26 January 1805, brings a sketch of the religious insight of Catherine Paar, wife of Henry VIII. There are praises for Mrs. Johnson, the "Stella" of Swift (13 April 1805, vol. 3), and for Mrs. Chapone, the famed writer on women (25 May 1805). The biographical subject for 28 September 1805 (vol. 3) is Ann Eliza Bleecker, the American writer known as a poet and author of the 1797 novel *The History of Maria Kittle.*

In her poetry, Mrs. Rowson underlines her belief in the natural intellectual equality of the sexes. Her poem **"The Birth of Genius,"** a long and ambitious dramatic piece that appears in *Miscellaneous Poems* (1804), personifies "Genius" as a male, but the young fellow is told by Apollo,

> A few words beside! And, my son ever mind them,
> Love talent and merit, wherever you find them.
> To no sex, to no station, no climate confin'd,
> They ever will reign uncontroll'd in the mind.
>
> > (p. 25)

Queen Elizabeth, a favorite figure with Mrs. Rowson, as she was with Anne Bradstreet, appears in a manuscript poem **"Commemorative of the Genius of Shakespeare."** Mrs. Rowson celebrates the Elizabethan age as the greatest for literature and art. She writes of the Queen,

> Elizabeth, who in retirement bred,
> Had drank of Wisdom at the fountain head,
> Whose high taught mind, discriminating eye,
> Knew native worth and genius to discry;
> Who called the tuneful Nine around her throne,
> And made the muse of Shakespeare, all her own.
> Drew all his talents forth her reign to adorn,
> Then gave his works to ages yet unborn.[16]

If men and women are born with an equal capacity for moral and intellectual growth, are there any intrinsic differences besides gender? As has been stated, Mrs. Rowson tended to answer this question ambiguously. In her analysis of Catherine II in *An Abridgment of Universal Geography,* she ascribes the queen's penchant for murder (Mrs. Rowson says she ordered the death of the emperor John) to Catherine's "masculine understanding, ambitious, haughty, and revengeful" (p. 287).

In poems like **"To Anna,"** which appears in both *Victoria* and *Mentoria,* women are called "Weak womankind" and "the helpless fair." The "tyrant" man is compared to a hawk and woman to a small bird liable to be devoured:

> Be circumspect, be cautious then,
> Beware of all, but *most* of *men.*
> For they will study to betray,
> And make our helpless sex, their prey,
> From virtue's bright, refulgent, throne,
> With baleful hand, will drag you down.
> Dishonor first, then leave to mourn
> Those blessings, which can ne'er return.
> As the young bird, who from the nest,
> Its mother's fost'ring wings and breast.
> Timidly ventures through the air,
> Far from the tender parents' care,
> If chance some hawk beholds it fly,
> He views it with an eager eye,
> Pursues, & clench'd within his power
> It falls poor bird to rise no more.[17]

This picture of the sexes is echoed in other passages in Mrs. Rowson's work. In *The Test of Honour,* she speaks of woman's character as being soft and tractable, for "nature formed them friendly, affectionate, noble, and unsuspicious" (p. 61). Her poem **"Maria, A Fiction"** in *Miscellaneous Poems,* a dramatic piece about a seduction, reflects the same point of view; the woman is passive, while the man is "the cruel spoiler." In a more playful vein, in the song **"He is Not Worth the Trouble,"** Mrs. Rowson writes,

> Ye Maidens then beware of men,
>   They're all alike believe me,
> They all proceed on Damon's plan
>   And flatter to deceive ye.
> Then let not love your senses blind,
>   And be not made their bubble,
> For should you meet one to your mind,
>   And marry! ten to one you'll find,
>   He is not worth the trouble.[18]

Such warnings in Mrs. Rowson's work tend to suggest that she conceived women—if treated properly—as naturally gentle, tractable, and affectionate, and men—if unchecked by religion and morality—as exploitative, destructive, and irresponsible. Mrs. Rowson often quotes Milton's line about women as "nature's last, best gift"; yet in the fallen world she writes of, she must grant the sexes an equal propensity for vice and virtue. In general, she does. In *The Inquisitor* she presents us with "Lassonia":

> It is such women as Lassonia, who cast an odium on the whole sex; and such women are not only objects of contempt, but detestation. I am not of [the] opinion that women would never degenerate into vice, were they not at first seduced by man; certain I am . . . that there are many women, who are abandoned to all manner of wickedness, entirely through the depravity of their inclinations.—Oh! how my soul rises with indignation, to

see the fairest works of the Creator's hand so far forget their native dignity, as to glory in actions which debase them beneath the lowest reptile that crawls upon the earth!

(III, 232)

In the novels, both sexes can both be exploitative and destructive. Victoria is not a victim simply of "male scheming." A haughty, ambitious female, Lady Maskwell, who has married an aged earl for money, captures Victoria's Harry. This same woman nearly allows her mother and sisters to starve in order to devote herself to her social schemes. There is no implication that Lady Maskwell's nature is a result of a "masculine understanding." Mademoiselle La Rue in *Charlotte,* even more the villain than Montraville, is a prime mover in Charlotte's seduction—she is a go-between for Montraville and urges fifteen-year-old Charlotte to see the young man against her school's and her parents' wishes. Mrs. Bellamy in *Sarah,* more persuasively than the male, urges Sarah to lower her moral standards for financial security. The analogy of the hawk and the small bird is not meant to be confined only to sexual nature, either. Here too, the woman can be as predatory as the male. Lady Ossiter of *The Fille de Chambre* matches her husband's affairs with her own, and Clara of *Trials of the Human Heart* seduces poor Rooksby, the heroine's young man, in his own home.

Mrs. Rowson often attributes a specifically feminine twist to the vicious behavior she satirizes. In *The Inquisitor,* she presents an episode about a young girl whose literary aspirations are squelched by an older woman. The woman, Mrs. Greenham, encourages Ellen, the aspiring writer, to recite some of her poems in public so that she will be ridiculed. First hearing of Mrs. Greenham's encouragement, the narrator muses, "It is rather surprising . . . that one woman should be so liberal in the praises of another" (II, 143). When Ellen's humiliation proves his cynicism accurate, the Inquisitor declares,

> Friendship is a word universally used, but little understood; there are a number of people who stile themselves friends, who never knew that it was to have an anxious thought for the person for whom they pretend this violent friendship, in the female world in particular. I make no doubt but there are numbers of women who, should they be informed whilst at cards, of the greatest misfortune having befallen one of their most intimate friends, would cry, Poor thing, I am vastly sorry—I had a great regard for her—and then inquire what is trumps? or how gows [sic] the game?

(II, 148)

When out of patience with some supposedly female foible, Mrs. Rowson will give the advantage to men. In *Sarah,* Ann, with whom Sarah exchanges letters, writes to Elenor, "It is a humiliating circumstance to confess, that beauty, wit and talents, are by no means possessions to secure a friend in our own sex. Why is this? Why do women suffer that degrading quality envy, to predominate in their bosoms? Men naturally esteem those who are most worthy esteem . . ." (p. 35).

For the most part, Mrs. Rowson works from the theory that human temperament, guided properly, can be the same in both sexes. The virtuous male, like the virtuous female, would aspire to a similar goal, a combination of the "knowledge and fortitude" of his own sex and the "gentleness" of the other. As a Christian he would make the best of the two sides of his nature.

The narrator designated in the title of *The Inquisitor* is a male, the typical man of feeling. He is interested in others, helpful, and compassionate. Like Mackenzie's man of feeling, his compassion extends to prostitutes and persons of other races, as well as to animals and old soldiers. The heroes of the fiction are men of action, but they all possess understanding and some degree of sensitivity. Columbus appears in *Reuben and Rachel* as both a man of feeling and an intrepid adventurer. The masculine types who dominate Mrs. Rowson's poetry are such men as Washington and Adams.[19] These figures are praised for their deeds as well as their intellects. In her 1799 tribute to John Adams, in *Miscellaneous Poems,* Mrs. Rowson puts Adams above the mythical Alcides, for he "took rigid honour for his guide," and "Firm to her cause, / Enforc'd the laws, / That made his country free" (p. 39). Washington is praised as a soldier but is certainly not cast in the *Miles Gloriosus* mold. In her **"Eulogy,"** also in *Miscellaneous Poems,* Mrs. Rowson has "wisdom" say,

> "Yet martial ardour go with wisdom hand in hand.
> There was a man who has this wonder done;
> A man! my much lamented darling son!
> Columbia's guardian genius—Washington!"

> (p. 48)

In her **"Commemorative"** on Shakespeare, the poet is praised for his moral influence as well as for his artistic style. The best types of each sex use the full range of their potentialities. In spite of her slips in splitting temperamental characteristics into feminine and masculine, Mrs. Rowson finds the sexes capable of the same emotional responses.

To underline her view, Mrs. Rowson questions the stereotypes of female temperament. In the fictional works, she frequently pauses to question whether men or women are the worse gossips or the more capable of true friendship, and so on. In *Reuben and Rachel,* she comments,

> Curiosity, when once awakened, is hard to be repelled, at least in women, say the opposite sex. Whether we are more troubled with the impulse than our fathers, brothers, or husbands, I will not now dispute; it is a certainty Dinah stopped to listen to a conversation which had powerfully excited her's.

> (II, 281)

Of course, the novels provide one long argument that the female is not the weaker sex. Mrs. Rowson's heroines confront physical as well as moral dangers. Mary survives being marooned on a desert island (a female may share Robinson Crusoe's adventures), Rebecca endures near starvation on the voyage to America, and helps to bury a dead Revolutionary soldier, Meriel is shipwrecked, and Sarah courageously faces a storm at sea. In *Reuben and Rachel,* Rachel Dudley (aunt of the modern day Reuben and Rachel), and her Indian sister-in-law, Oberea, accompany their men into war (I, 161). Even demure little Lucy Temple, Charlotte's mother, shows her grit; she helps support her father by taking on needlework and painting (*Charlotte,* p. 34). Isabelle, granddaughter of Christopher Columbus, closes the gap between conformity to standards of feminine delicacy (which Mrs. Rowson could not quite relinquish) and the qualities needed to endure and survive in real life. In *Reuben and Rachel,* she says to Columbia, her daughter, when they face life alone,

> I have a trifle, my child . . . and we must summon all our fortitude to brave even hardship and danger without shrinking. We are women it is true, and ought not to forget the delicacy of our sex; but real delicacy consists in purity of thought, and chastity of words and actions; not in shuddering at an accidental blast of wind, or increasing the unavoidable evils of life by affected weakness and timidity. How many of our sex are obliged by hard and daily labour, to procure for themselves and children the bare means of existence!

> (I, 113)

In **"Female Biography"** (*A Present*), Mrs. Rowson questions the idea that women are weak by nature:

> They [women] are generally called the weaker sex, and perhaps through constitution, habit, and education in some degre [sic] they are so; but there have been numberless instances of women who have proved themselves adequate to every trial, that proves their attachment to their husbands, children, parents or country.

> (p. 90)

She follows this statement with examples from history of female fortitude: there is Chelonis, daughter of a king of Sparta, who accompanies her husband "into perpetual exile" (p. 91), and Eponina, a Roman woman who lives in a subterranean vault for nine years to help her husband evade his enemies, and when he is finally caught, demands to be executed with him (pp. 92-93). In *Exercises in History* and *Biblical Dialogues,* Mrs. Rowson tells the stories of many other such women.

Mrs. Rowson also attacks the myth that women cannot keep secrets. She cites in **"Female Biography"** (*A Present*) the story of Tymicha of Lacedemonia, who is threatened with torture by an enemy who, in attempting to pry state secrets from her, relies upon woman's propensity to talk. Tymicha bites off her tongue and spits in the tyrant's face. Leona, an Athenian woman who follows suit, was honored, Mrs. Rowson tells us, by a monument erected to her that bore the inscription "a lioness without a tongue" (p. 97). Surely, there could be no greater conscientiousness in secret-keeping than these women showed!

With all these virtues and talents, the female might be expected to claim almost any social rôle, but Mrs. Rowson does not suggest such a sweeping program. The prevailing social ideal envisioned woman as a good influence upon the male, with marriage as the principal means of influence. Susanna Rowson defers to this trend, even while she recognizes that marriage will not be the lot of every woman and will provide none with an eternally comfortable haven. She does not preclude the participation of women in any other kind of activity.

Mrs. Rowson sees the rôles of men and women as complementary. She advances in **"Outline of Universal History"** (*A Present*) the importance of history in teaching the sexes "as in a faithful mirror their respective duties" (p. 53). In all the pedagogical works, Mrs. Rowson stresses the importance of women as an influence upon men and children. In the **"Concluding Address For 1808"** (*A Present*) she speaks of "reforming" the opposite sex as the job of the woman (p. 148). Her rationale for the education of women is often based on the uplifting effect educated women will have on their families; as she states in **"Female Biography,"** such women become "friends and rational companions to our fathers and brothers" (p. 122). Still, she stresses the value of the works of individual women, and offers some alternatives to marriage.

In the fiction, the destiny of most of the protagonists is marriage. Only a few escape husbands for useful single lives. Of course, Mrs. Rowson's novels, aside from *Victoria* and *Charlotte,* are comic in the sense that there are alternatives for the protagonists, and the final reversal of fortune moves from bad to good; and marriage is the traditional resolution of the comic plot. *The Inquisitor* contains a little paean to married love as exhibited in the royal marriage, in which Mrs. Rowson envisions Hymen "triumphant o'er the British nation" (III, 176). The assertive epilogue to *Slaves in Algiers* continues in a similar vein:

> True, Ladies—bounteous nature made us fair,
> To strew sweet roses round the bed of care.
> A parent's heart of sorrow to beguile,
> *Cheer an afflicted husband by a smile.*
> To bind the truant, that's inclined to roam,
> Good humour makes *a paradise at home.*
> To raise the fall'n—to pity and forgive,
> This is our noblest, best prerogative.

> By these, pursuing nature's gentle plan,
> We hold in silken chains—the lordly tyrant man.

(italics mine)

The poem **"Rights of Woman"** in *Miscellaneous Poems* also stresses the domestic scene. Addressed at the outset to a masculine audience, it proclaims:

> Poor woman has her rights as well as you [men];
> And if she's wise, she will assert them too.
> If you have patience, and your wrath forbear,
> In a few words I'll tell you what they are.

(p. 98)

The "rights" are to be competent in the household (p. 99), to make a "paradise at home," and to share the woes of "father, brothers, friends, oppress'd with care" (p. 100). The widow, the orphan, and the sick are to share the good woman's ministrations, but the influence upon the male is paramount.

Mrs. Rowson's enthusiasm for the domestic rôle is laid on a little thick in this poem; she ends with a paean to "Domestic duty—oh how blest we are!" (p. 103). But many of the individual pieces in *Miscellaneous Poems* were written years before the 1804 publication. **"Rights of Woman"** is probably a very early effort, for under full sail Mrs. Rowson tempers her enthusiasm for domesticity with emphasis upon intellectual attainment. In this poem, knowledge makes only a brief appearance as the poet concludes, now addressing her own sex,

> Then ever let it be our pride, ye fair,
> To merit their [the good and brave man's]
>   protection, love, and care;
> With useful knowledge be our heads well stor'd,
> While in our hearts we every virtue hoard.
> These rights we may assert, and tho' thought common
> These, and these only are the RIGHTS OF WOMAN.

(p. 104)

Mrs. Rowson's poem **"To Anna"** and many of her other works contain advice on how to maintain a good marriage, but there is little joy held out for the woman. She tells a young woman about to marry,

> If e'er your heart feels joy sincere,
> Twill be to dry affliction's tear
> To visit the distress'd and poor,
> And chase pale famine from their door.

(7379-a, Rowson Collection)

The joys of matrimony are also seen from the man's point of view in her poem **"Women As They Are"** in *Miscellaneous Poems*:

> The happiest lot that can to man be given,
> To smooth the rugged path, and sweeten life,
> Is an affectionate and faithful wife.

(p. 115)

For the woman, marriage is one more possible briar in that "thorny path of life" Mrs. Rowson offers to her audience. It may be fulfilling: one feminine type frequently encountered in the works is the generous, philanthropic, happily married woman. She is embodied in Victoria's best friend, Arabella Hartley Selton, in *Victoria,* and in Mrs. Beauchamp in *Charlotte.* Both these women are more compassionate toward the disgraced heroine than is society at large. Rebecca in *Slaves in Algiers,* Mrs. Rooksby in *Trials of the Human Heart,* and Lady Mary Worthy in *The Fille* conform to this pattern. They are not only happily married but extend the blessings of their enviable state to people outside their homes. At best, marriage can be a fine institution, good not only for the participants but for the rest of society.

At worst, marriage is legalized prostitution. This idea is stated in *Charlotte,* where marriage forced upon women as their only alternative is quietly attacked. Mrs. Rowson's language in this passage conveys her disgust with such a system:

> Mr. Temple was the youngest son of a nobleman whose fortune was by no means adequate to the antiquity, grandeur, and I may add, pride of the family. He saw his elder brother made completely wretched by marrying a disagreeable woman, whose fortune helped to prop the sinking dignity of the house, and he beheld his sisters legally prostituted to old, decrepid men, whose titles gave them consequence in the eyes of the world, and whose affluence rendered them splendidly miserable.
>
> (p. 26)

Mrs. Rowson continues this argument against society's insistence upon marriage in *Charlotte, Trials of the Human Heart,* and *Sarah.* The virtue of a woman who does not marry or retain masculine protection is open to assault and gossip. In *Charlotte,* the father of Montraville enunciates the difference in the situations of the sexes:

> "My daughters," said he, "have been educated like gentlewomen; and should I die before they are settled, they must have some provision made to place them above the snares and temptations which vice ever holds out to the elegant, accomplished female, when oppressed by the frowns of poverty and the sting of dependence: my boys, with only moderate incomes, when placed in the church, at the bar, or in the field, may exert their talents, make themselves friends, and raise their fortunes on the basis of merit."
>
> (p. 52)

In *Trials of the Human Heart,* the unmarried Meriel is frequently accused of illicit relationships. If she attempts to establish a friendship with a man, the gossips assume she is having an affair. She is fair game for the machinations of married employers and the suspicions

of their wives. Near the conclusion of the novel, when Meriel is living with her father, she is safe. Mr. Kingly states that he is free to visit her without censure—"For under the shelter of paternal protection, who shall dare to arraign her conduct?" (IV, 158). Without this protection, Meriel, who has no practical training, sinks according to the elder Montraville's prescription, to the lowest level of the job market and is almost forced into prostitution.

Sarah provides a strong case against marriage as the only respectable rôle for a woman. Sarah marries because her mother is dead and her father has abandoned her. She and her husband are completely incompatible; but when Sarah tries to escape and live apart from her husband, she is defeated. Her reputation suffers; an earl who is infatuated with Sarah makes a false judgment about her availability. She faces poverty. Sarah puts it thus to her beloved, Frederick:

> "My separation from him was enforced by necessity: but had I known the misery of a state of separation, how forlorn, how desolate, how totally unprotected a married woman is, when separated from her husband; how every one thinks he may insult her with impunity, and no one will take the trouble to defend her, but rather unite in aspersing and depressing her, even to the very earth—I would have never thrown myself into so deplorable a situation. I will make no overtures towards a reunion; but should he solicit me to pardon his unkind neglect, and again share his fate, I shall certainly do it. . . . I am convinced I shall never again appear respectable in the eyes of the world, until I am again under my husband's protection."
>
> (p. 182)

The subtitle of *Sarah, The Exemplary Wife,* contains an ironic twist. Sarah has no legal recourse against her husband; she has few skills; there is little she can do but passively endure the marriage. In doing so, she is the "exemplary" wife, that is, worthy of imitation, but she is also exemplary to serve as a warning. Mrs. Rowson sounds both notes in her preface.

In making Sarah's confidante, Anne, a single woman—and a likeable one—surely Mrs. Rowson comments upon the possibilities for happiness in and out of the married state. Anne is well off by contrast to Sarah, and Mrs. Rowson develops her to some degree as a character in order to bring out this point. Anne is not only sympathetic, concerned, and fond of Sarah, but has a witty, analytical attitude toward life—including her own single state—which is far from the stereotype of the dried-up, vicious spinster. In *Sarah,* Anne jokes to Elenor as she extols the virtue of patience:

> . . . in the married state, I believe a double portion is absolutely necessary. I cannot speak from experience, as I have never entered the holy pale, and being now on the wrong side of thirty-five, in all probability never

shall, unless some spruce young squire of twenty-one (I would not marry one older) very rich and gallant, should fancy me the *Ninon* of the age and fall in love with me. But this is not very likely; it does not happen very often that men become seriously attached to women considerable older than themselves, though often that they are deeply enamoured of their fortunes. Now and then indeed, a woman appears, who, like the celebrated madam Maintenon, maintains her sovereignty over the young, the wealthy, the noble, the learned; and is beloved and courted to the very verge of her grand climacteric; but never was such a phenomenon known as such a woman being an old maid—

(p. 234)

Anne is typical of Mrs. Rowson's treatment of the single woman. While she presents a few portraits in the early fiction that conform to the pattern outlined by Dorothy Deegan, Mrs. Rowson is usually kind to the unmarried. A "superannuated" female appears in *Victoria,* and Miss Abigail Prune in *The Fille de Chambre* is an example of the grotesque old maid; but these portraits are outweighed by Mentoria, the epitome of feminine wisdom, a widow who does not remarry; Meriel's friend Celia, a nun; Fetnah in *Slaves in Algiers,* and Aunt Rachel, who guides and helps the two young protagonists of *Reuben and Rachel.*

In her school-oriented works, Mrs. Rowson did not forget the unmarried. She makes a distinction that many people fail to recognize as they advocate the home or the job market as the place for women: not all situations are alike. In her **"Concluding Address, 1810"** (*A Present for Young Ladies*), Mrs. Rowson writes that most women must be domestic, but that the wealthy and single have time to learn and should therefore develop themselves to the fullest (p. 151). In **"Female Biography"** (*A Present*), she provides an interesting example of a woman who—though not unmarried—proved that marriage was not the only honorable estate. Catherine of Cline, an actress, managed to live separately from her husband and still maintain "a spotless reputation." Furthermore, she was buried in Westminster Abbey (pp. 89-90).

What social rôles outside of marriage are available to women? Mentoria takes on the traditional governess role. Fetnah will remain in Algiers to devote herself to the care of her father, and to instruct the dey in morality (Fetnah's escape from marriage may be due simply to Mrs. Rowson's reluctance to unite her Christian hero with a girl of Jewish ancestry). Lucy Blakeney is the only really successful career girl in the fiction. When Lucy's enamored is discovered to be her very own half-brother, son of the notorious Montraville who seduced her mother, Lucy turns to her natural altruism and uses her inherited wealth to open a school for girls.

The incest theme in *Charlotte's Daughter* and the belated punishment of Montraville (he grows faint with guilt when he first beholds Lucy, and eventually dies)

has been used by Leslie Fiedler as a prime example of the dire treatment in American literature of the trespassing male. In *Love and Death in the American Novel,* Fiedler places Montraville among dejected hulks ruined by excess sexuality.[20] Helen Papashvily would agree and see the near incest and the guilt suffered by Montraville as part of the "witches broth" cooked up by the early American women writers.[21] In the context of Mrs. Rowson's time, however, this kind of situation was one of the few acceptable ways to excuse a heroine from matrimony. An insurmountable problem would be needed to justify a single life for a heroine. What more irrefragable obstacle to marriage than the threat of incest?

Other women in Mrs. Rowson's fiction besides Lucy aspire to careers, but they do not attain them because the attitudes of society toward women prevent success. Mrs. Greenham's ill treatment of Ellen in *The Inquisitor* is due to these attitudes. Mrs. Greenham confesses, "I should like to see her heartily laughed at—I am sure women have no business with pens in their hands, they had better mend their cloaths, and look after their family" (II, 143-144).

Meriel, in *Trials of the Human Heart,* is discouraged from pursuing a writing career. She is told by a Mr. Friendly, the attorney of her benefactor, that she is not only too obscure socially to win praise, but also of the wrong gender:

> "burn your pens and paper, and believe me, a woman makes as awkward a figure engaged in literary pursuits, as a counsellor would do seated at a tambour frame or busied in assorting colours for embroidery."

(II, 68)

Meriel takes Mr. Friendly's advice. However, one of the interesting aspects of Meriel's struggle is that she does not write to enrich family life or help a man's career; she simply likes to write. She tells Celia, her confidante,

> "I would like to obtain a living by the exertion of my natural talents, than by following the straight-forward path of the plodding world of business. . . ."

(II, 58)

Careers for women are defended by Mrs. Rowson. An "old gentlemen" stands up for Ellen in *The Inquisitor*:

> And pray, why not, Madam, said an old gentleman, who had listened attentively to this loquacious harangue, why may not a woman, if she has leisure and genius, take up her pen to gratify both herself and friends. I am not ashamed to acknowledge that I have perused the productions of some of our female pens, with the highest satisfaction; and am happy when I find any woman has so large a fund of amusement in her own mind. I never heard a woman, who was fond of

her pen, complain of the tediousness of time; nor, did I ever know such a woman extravagantly fond of dress, public amusements, or expensive gaiety; yet, I have seen many women of genius prove themselves excellent mothers, wives, and daughters.

(II, 144)

The Inquisitor himself defends a professional actress whose character has been questioned. He contends,

> I have frequently been engaged in disputes concerning women of this profession—it puts me beyond all patience to hear people advance an opinion so very contracted and illiberal, as that of supposing no woman can be virtuous who is on the stage—I know many at this time who are ornaments not only to their profession, but to the sex in general: even the lady I have just mentioned, is generous, humane and prudent, pride is her only fault—Charming woman! I have often said, when I was enchanted with her performance of some amiable character—conquer but that one foible, and our admiration will rise into veneration.—I am confident a woman may, if she is so inclined; be as virtuous as Lucrece behind the scenes of a theatre.

(I, 71)

Two social rôles are consistently downgraded in Mrs. Rowson's work, the woman of fashion and the household drudge. Neither of these rôles permits expression of the total woman. The fashionable female—that is, one who devotes her life to being ornamental and to her own pleasure—may be noble or poor, she may work or not. Her identifying characteristic is her selfish pursuit of personal aggrandizement. This type is represented by Lady Maskwell in *Victoria*; she takes on West Indian hue in *The Test of Honour* where she appears as the indolent Jamaican wife of Mary's scheming cousin. La Rue plays the role in *Charlotte.* Lady Ossiter in *The Fille de Chambre* is one of the best-drawn portraits of the heartless society woman. She and Rebecca appear in a scene not unlike Proust's between Swann and Madame de Guermantes in ironic intention. Lady Ossiter's absorption in her mourning clothes is played off against Rebecca's genuine sorrow over the death of Lady Ossiter's mother. Knapp quotes the scene in full in his 1828 *Memoir,* so impressed was he with the writing.[22]

These women see their function in society as ornamental only. They are castigated in Mrs. Rowson's **"Women As They Are"** in *Miscellaneous Poems*:

> The girl, who from her birth is thought a beauty,
> Scarce ever hears of virtue, sense or duty;
> Mamma, delighted with each limb and feature,
> Declares, she is a fascinating creature;
> Forbids all study, work, or wise reflection;
> 'Twill spoil her eyes, or injure her complexion.
> "Hold up your head, my dear; turn out your toes;
> Bless me, what's that? a pimple on your nose;
> It smarts, dear, don't it? how can you endure it?
> Here's some *Pomade divine,* to heal and cure it."
> . . . . .

> Thus, ere one proper wish her heart can move,
> She's taught to think of lovers, and of love;
> She's told she is a beauty, does not doubt it;
> What need of sense? beauties can wed without it.
> And then her eyes, her teeth, her lips, her hair,
> And shape, are all that can be worth her care;
> She thinks a kneeling world should bow before her,
> And men were but created to adore her.

(pp. 105-108)

The purely domestic woman is portrayed as equally incomplete. She appears in the fiction as Mrs. Penure (née Prune) in *The Fille de Chambre* and in *Reuben and Rachel* as Tabitha who hates all forms of literature and is interested only in "pickles and preserves" (II, 220). This female too is ridiculed in **"Women As They Are"** in *Miscellaneous Poems*:

> "Dear," cries mamma, whose only merit lies
> In making puddings, good preserves, and pies;
> Who rises with Aurora, blythe and cheery,
> Feeds pigs and poultry, overlooks her dairy,
> Brews her own beer, makes her own household linen,
> And scolds her girls, to make them mind their spinning—
> "Dear, surely Tom was blind; what could he see,
> To think of marrying such a thing as she?
> She was a beauty; what is beauty? pshaw!
> I never knew a *beauty* worth a straw.
> She's so eat up with pride, conceit, and folly,
> I vow she knows no more than little Molly,
> Whether a pig were better roast or boil'd;
> I warrant many a dinner will be spoil'd.
> But I'll take care, whoever weds my daughter
> Shall find a different lesson, I have taught her.
> My Bett's fifteen next May; I'd lay a crown,
> She'd cook a dinner with the best in town;
> To roast, or boil, make pudding, pye or jelly,
> There's not her equal far or near, I tell ye.
> Then at her needle, making, mending, darning,
> What is there else that's worth a woman's larnings?
> With my good will, a girl should never look
> In any but a pray'r or cook'ry book:
> Reading 'bout kings, and states, and foreign nations,
> Will only fill their heads with proclamations."
> If of these documents a girl's observant,
> What is she fit for, but an upper servant?

(pp. 108-109)

Mrs. Rowson's rejection of a narrow or reduced rôle for women is underlined by the comments in her texts. In *An Abridgment of Universal Geography,* Mrs. Rowson disapproves of the Thibetans' treatment of women because "They consider women as very inferior to men; that they were created only to people the world, and to look after household affairs" (p. 110).

Ideally, the woman who has a family would combine the practice of the household arts with the attainment of knowledge. Intellectual or cultural activities must be curtailed only if they are incompatible with one's financial and social situation, if they interfere with domestic and family duties, or if they are carried to "extremes." If the motive of the learned woman is simply to show off, Mrs. Rowson disapproves, for she believes that knowledge should be useful. In **"Concluding Address, 1810"** (*A Present for Young Ladies*), she states that "pedantry and presumption in a woman is more disgusting than an entire want of literary information" (p. 152). But in the same passage, she had defended the maligned bluestocking:

> Many are the prejudices entertained, and the witticisms thrown out against what are called learned women; but surely a woman will not be less acceptable in the world, or worse qualified for performing her part in it, for having devoted a large portion of her early years to the cultivation of her understanding.
>
> (p. 151)

Some areas of endeavor appear to be outside the woman's province. In **"The Rights of Woman"** in *Miscellaneous Poems,* Mrs. Rowson may be haunted by Dr. Johnson's simile describing the performing female, for she declares,

> But know you not that woman's sphere
> Is the domestic walk? To interfere
> With politics, divinity, or law,
> As much deserved ridicule would draw
> On woman, as the learned, grave divine,
> Cooking the soup on which he means to dine;
> Or formal judge, the winders at his knee,
> Preparing silk to work embroidery.
>
> (p. 103)

But this sentiment does not represent Mrs. Rowson's final judgment on this issue. In her later work, **"Female Biography"** (*A Present*), she notes,

> Though few of our sex are called to sway the regal sceptre; yet among those who have filled the important station of queen, many might be mentioned as examples of their political abilities; amongst whom may be reckoned preeminent, Elizabeth queen of England.
>
> (p. 98)

The many stories of other female monarchs bring home Mrs. Rowson's point. Besides that of Elizabeth, the careers of Anne of Austria, Catherine the Great of Russia, and Catherine the Second are sketched in **"Female Biography."** Elizabeth appears in nearly all of the historical surveys. In *Exercises in History,* Mrs. Rowson praises Margaret of Denmark, a fourteenth-century ruler, for her "great qualities for government and policy" (p. 138), Queen Christina of Sweden for her support of learning (p. 143), and Queen Anne of England for having achieved one of the "most illustrious" reigns in the history of Britain (p. 99). In *Abridgment of Universal Geography,* Mrs. Rowson points to Catherine II of Russia: Catherine was "successful in her military pursuits,

and her reign has been the admiration of all Europe"; she is also praised for abolishing torture to elicit confession of crime and for encouraging commerce (p. 287). Mrs. Rowson underlines the implications of her historical examples by noting in **"Female Biography"** that "The exercise of brilliant talents in *any profession whatever,* does not prevent the practice of virtue" (*A Present,* pp. 88-89, italics mine).

As to the rights of women, education is certainly first. This point needs little further development, except to note that while Mrs. Rowson admits that all women need not "study with the closeness of application which is essentially requisite in the education of a boy" (**"Concluding Address, 1808,"** *A Present,* p. 153), she makes no concession to the male pundits who advised women to avoid the "profound researches of study." In **"Female Biography"** she emphasizes the encouragement she has offered women to go beyond dabbling in intellectual pursuits; she argues, "when literature, or the study of the fine arts, can be engaged in, without neglect of our feminine duties, why may not we attain the goal of perfection as well as the other sex?" (*A Present,* p. 85). The forcefulness of Mrs. Rowson's statements on this subject can be illustrated best by comparing her language to that of others who supposedly advocated female intellectual attainment. The commencement speaker at the Philadelphia Ladies' Academy (1794) assures the girls that "A sprig from the top of Parnassus would certainly be allowed a pleasing and fragrant decoration for a lady."[23]

Mrs. Rowson says little about specific legal rights, although in the novels she shows her single heroines exercising their property rights, and her married heroines deprived of redress to law. In *Sarah,* the heroine endures even the ignominy of physical abuse (as does Meriel in *Trials*) rather than seek legal help. She writes to Anne of her husband,

> "D—n," said he, in an under voice, and being on the opposite side to my female companion, he actually struck my arm with his open hand. The blow was not heavy, but it was a blow; and I felt that it had broken the last small link that remained between us. Dishonored—insulted—struck! Anne, Anne! I am a woman; the law will not redress my grievances, and if it would, could I appeal publicly? No; I can suffer in silence, but I could not bear to appear openly as the accuser of the man I had once sworn to honor.
>
> (p. 94)

Charlotte's Daughter also touches upon the legal rights of women. Mary Lumly is an example of the sorrows that overwhelm a female foolish enough to surrender not only her body but her property to a man. Her guardian, the Reverend Matthews, tries to convince Mary to cool her ardor for her fiancé long enough to allow him to negotiate a sensible property settlement for her. But

Mary gives her all; she says, "When I make him master of my person, I shall also give him possession of my property, and I trust he is of too generous a disposition ever to abuse my confidence" (p. 83). Mary is, of course, seduced, abandoned, and robbed.

The rights of woman begin, Mrs. Rowson believed, with changes in the attitudes of society. She calls for abandonment of the stereotypes that confine the woman's world educationally and professionally, in the way men view women, and in the treatment of women by the social mores.

All that has been said to this point shows Mrs. Rowson's disapproval of the limited world of the average female. Ellen's and Meriel's stories of blighted ambition make this point. One after another, the women in the fiction find that there is practically no work obtainable except teaching as a governess or assisting in a hat shop. Meriel works as a milliner's assistant and attempts prostitution. Rebecca is mistreated by the children she is assigned to teach; as a governess, she is only a step from being a maid. Sarah is also treated badly in her attempt at teaching. Such conditions are criticized in other important feminist works. In *A Vindication of the Rights of Woman* (1792), Mary Wollstonecraft complains of the menial and demeaning work open to the female. The rôle of governess amounts to "degradation," for the woman does not receive the respect given a male tutor; the job of milliner's assistant "could sink them [women forced to earn a living] almost to the level of those poor abandoned creatures, who live by prostitution. For are not milliners and mantua-makers reckoned the next class?"[24]

The rights of women also include treatment from men as the equals they are and the abandonment of the image of women as children or "sex objects." One small episode in *Reuben and Rachel* makes this point. Dinah, wife of Jacob Holmes, presumes to offer her opinion that Reuben is an honest young man, and she is chided by her father for judging "on her own" (II, 282). Of course, her opinion is correct.

Sarah states the woman's right to adult status most clearly. She tells Anne in *Sarah,*

> "You have never been married, Anne; so cannot inform me whether it is so or not, but if every married man is so captious, and petulant, so angry at their wives' only expressing a difference in opinions in the mildest words: I wonder how any woman can be so passionately attached to them. But, perhaps, that passionate attachment prevents their seeing any fault in them, and they, supposing all the man, thus idolized, says, does, or thinks is right, never take the trouble of contradicting him; assent implicitly to his opinions, however absurd, and will not exert their own mental powers to think or decide for themselves."
>
> (pp. 43-44)

The same heroine writes to Frederick, describing her friendship with Reverend Hayley:

> Of my own sex, I have seldom met with any who are formed for more than the companion of an hour. Your sex, in general, accustom themselves to consider women in so inferior a light, that they oftener treat us like children and playthings, than intelligent beings. I must be candid enough to confess, it is too frequently our own fault, that we are not held in higher estimation. How gratifying, then, was it to my self love, to be considered by a man of sense and erudition as an equal, and to be conversed with as a rational companion.
>
> (p. 258)

To Anne, Sarah emphasizes her point; when trying to escape her husband, she says, "but to be treated either like a child, an idiot, or a slave, is what I cannot, will not submit to" (p. 114). The friendship between Sarah and Mr. Hayley is unique in Mrs. Rowson's fiction. Other characters dream of such a relationship, but societal pressures intervene.

Women, claims Mrs. Rowson, have the right to be judged on a par with men. The sexual double standard is implicitly criticized throughout her works. In *Victoria,* she attempts to formulate her disgust with this phase of society's mores. Her heroine says to her best friend, Arabella Hartley,

> How cruel is it, that if one of us poor weak mortals only once step aside from the path of rectitude, we are never suffered to return. Penitence may make us acceptable in the sight of Heaven, but the world will never pardon us; while man may plunge into every idle vice, and yet be received in all companies, and too often caressed by the brave and worthy. Can you tell me why this is, Bell? Are crimes less so when committed by men than women? Are not they allowed to be wiser than we? Ought not they then to be better?"
>
> (I, 131-132)

Mrs. Rowson's unflagging championship of the "fallen" woman is an important part of her plea for change in society's attitudes toward women. She never forgot the figure of the "fallen woman," and her compassion for the plight of such women is illustrated forcefully by the appearance of this motif even in her early critical piece *A Trip to Parnassus* (1788). Apollo, bestowing plaudits upon various playwrights and actors, praises Harriet Lee for her compassion:

> "You my kindest protection shall share;
> "For the woman who stoops, a fall'n sister to raise,
> "Shall find her own temples encircl'd with bays."
>
> (p. 6)

The type of the fallen woman appears in *The Inquisitor* (1788). The narrator writes to the prostitute Annie, whom he finds begging for a drink near a tavern, "Now let the icy sons of philosophy say what they please. I could no more have left this poor girl . . . than I could travel barefoot over the burning deserts of Arabia" (II, 160). With the help of the narrator, Annie's reformation is brought about (III, 178).

Mary's best friend Emily (little Emily?) in *The Test of Honour* (1789) is seduced by Harry Fentum, who marries and then abandons her. Mary later finds the girl wandering about and takes her in. Harry repents, and Mary hopes to see the couple and the child reunited. But the good news of Harry's return is too much for poor Emily, and she expires. In *Trials of the Human Heart,* as has been noted, the protagonist herself nearly indulges in prostitution to support her starving mother.

The besmirched protagonists, Charlotte and Victoria, must die—but more by society's and the reader's decree than Mrs. Rowson's. Through the many secondary characters, Mrs. Rowson argues for compassion for the erring female, and in some cases presents us with examples of full recovery from the supposedly fatal effects of seduction. True Christianity demands forgiveness of the fallen; mankind is fallen. In both *Victoria* and *Charlotte,* there is a sympathetic woman to defend the transgressor. Arabella Hartley (now Lady Selton) writes to a friend of the difference between her own and her husband's attitudes toward Victoria. Lord Selton, who is in general a very decent man, sees only Victoria's disobedience to her mother. Bell sees and writes of the unfairness to Victoria:

> How well does it teach us to be careful how we confer favours on the unworthy of the other:—Strange beings! who at the moment we are giving them the highest proofs of affection, despise us for those very errors themselves have urged us to commit.
>
> (I, 189)

Mrs. Beauchamp in *Charlotte* argues that Charlotte might "in spite of her former errors, become a useful and respectable member of society" (p. 82).

Two women in *Charlotte's Daughter* who encounter Mary Lumly at an inn where her seducer has left her exhibit the proper attitude toward the fallen woman:

> These truly virtuous, respectable women did not think that the commission of one fault was sufficient to banish a human being from society, or excuse in others the want of humanity or kindness.
>
> (p. 136)

Chastity is very important in Mrs. Rowson's system of values; in one passage she calls chastity the cornerstone of virtue; but if, as Margaret Wyman contends in her article "The Rise of the Fallen Woman," Mrs. Rowson conceived of "a Providence upholding the absolute value of feminine chastity,"[25] she surely emphasizes the spiritual meaning of chastity. Mrs. Rowson's belief in

the ability of the individual female to recover from sexual mistakes shows that bodily purity is not her prime concern. Only when the mind becomes corrupt is "purity" lost. Charlotte bears the surname "Temple," which represents in Christian symbolism the body as a reflection of the soul rather than an entity valuable in itself. To emphasize sexual chastity would be indeed to reduce the female to an object, and Mrs. Rowson's purpose is to avoid such reduction.

Women are entitled to be judged as whole personalities rather than by one virtue alone, argues Mrs. Rowson. She teaches women that they are equal to men in virtue, intellect, emotional range and fortitude, and that the ideal they should strive for is not feminine as defined by society, but androgynous, combining the best of the "masculine" and "feminine" traits. She points out the unfairness of narrowing the female's sphere of activity to the domestic, emphasizes her right to education and decent employment, and calls for the abandonment of stereotypes along with the treatment of women as children and objects.

The exact boundaries of Mrs. Rowson's feminism are impossible to establish. Other writers examined one phase or another of the problems of women, and some of the recommendations Rowson made appear in a variety of sources. Further, as more early British and American women writers are rediscovered, we find feminist concepts and phrases appearing in earlier and less publicized texts. Even a lurid romance like *The Happy-Unfortunate* (1732) by Elizabeth Boyd[26] protests masculine preemption of the arts. Mary Wollstonecraft, as noted, considers several of the same issues as Mrs. Rowson, but the latter had already published seven books dedicated to female emancipation before *A Vindication of the Rights of Woman* appeared.

Notes

1. Benson, *Women in Eighteenth-Century America,* p. 99.

2. Tompkins, *The Popular Novel in England, passim,* and see page 163 for the term "legal prostitution" in reference to marriage as used by Mrs. Griffith, later discussed in the present chapter. Also see MacCarthy, *Female Pen,* vol. 1, pp. 260-261, for attitudes and expressions in Sarah Fielding's *David Simple* (1744) that—as will become clear—parallel similar elements in some of Susanna Rowson's works. Fielding's heroine has free-wheeling views on love and marriage, refuses to be an unpaid "upper servant."

3. William Wasserstrom, *Heiress of All the Ages: Sex and Sentiment in the Genteel Tradition* (Minneapolis: University of Minnesota Press, 1959), p. 5.

4. Neal, *Essay*, p. 2.

5. Frank L. Mott, *A History of American Magazines: 1741-1850* (New York: D. Appleton & Company, 1930), p. 65.

6. A modern edition that includes all parts of Brown's dialogue is *Alcuin: A Dialogue,* ed. Lee R. Edwards (New York: Grossman Publishers, 1971).

7. Mary Benson summarizes the ideas of Mrs. Murray as expressed in the latter's collection, *The Gleaner,* published in Boston, 1798. Mrs. Murray approved of "the revolution of thought in recent years which made it possible for them [women] to devote time to studies other than the needle. . . . [She] drew a glowing picture of this new and more enlightened era in female history, which was to manifest itself in the intellectual development of women free from romantic ideas of marriage and ready to act as enlightened and thoughtful mothers. She believed that women might become as independent as Mary Wollstonecraft had wished, if they were taught to earn their own living and to regard matrimony only as a probable contingency. Education for economic independence would enable women to make choices in marriage with much greater freedom" (Benson, *Women in Eighteenth-Century America,* pp. 176-177). Mrs. Rowson agrees with all these ideas.

8. Sally Sayward Barrell Keating Wood, *Dorval; or the Speculator* (Portsmouth, N.H.: Nutting & Whitelock, 1801). Published anonymously.

9. Dorothy Yost Deegan, *The Stereotype of the Single Woman in American Novels: A Social Study with Implications for the Education of Women* (New York: King's Crown Press, Columbia University, 1951), pp. 131-132.

10. A 1960 case in which a wife filed suit for damages against a defendant who had incapacitated her husband by injuring him in an auto accident, and thus deprived her of his services, impelled a modern judge to describe the earlier legal position of women with a perceptiveness difficult to paraphrase:

> Such being the mother's "rights" with respect to her children it follows, with the relentless logic of the common law, that her rights respecting her property and her person are no more generous. She was his chattel. What was hers was his. The wife says Bracton, "has nothing which is not her husband's." They were one, and, as one opinion put it, he was that one. All of her personal property, money, goods and chattels of every description, became his upon marriage. Since she was "under the power of her husband," it followed that she had "no will of her own" and having no will of her own could not enter into a contract. Of course, he was entitled to her services in the home as he would be to those of any servant in his employ. Should he lose them through the acts of another that other must respond in damages. But should the husband be injured, and she thus lose his protection and solace, might she equally with him, maintain a like suit for her loss? In light of what has been said the question is nonsensical. To have a lawsuit we must have to start with, someone capable of suing another. She, however, could not bring any action in her own name, for she was a legal nonentity. But this was not all. What if she were so injured by another as to be incapable of performing her wifely duties? Has the husband suffered a legally recognizable loss, so that he might cause that other to respond in damages? The answer is clear from the common law, as is the theory upon which it was based. He had. It was an actionable trespass for one to interfere with the services of another's servant. This menial in the house, this chattel, responding to the term "wife," also rendered services. It would follow, and it did follow, that the husband had a right of action for injury to her, grounded upon the theory that she was his servant. But could she sue for the loss of services of the master? Clearly not.
>
> J. Smith in Montgomery v. Stephen, 359 Mich. 33, 101 N.W. 2d 227 (1960).

11. *Monthly Magazine and American Review* 3 (September 1800), no. 3.

12. Katherine Anthony, *First Lady of the Revolution: The Life of Mercy Otis Warren* (Garden City, N.Y.: Doubleday & Company, 1958), p. 95. John Adams is quoted as replying to Abigail's request that the husband not be allowed to continue absolute master of his wife:

> I begin to think the Ministry as deep as they are wicked. After stirring up Tories . . . bigots, Canadians, Indians. . . . At last they have stimulated the [women] to demand new privileges and threaten to rebel.

13. *Economic Feminism in American Literature Prior to 1848,* University of Maine Studies, 2d ser., no. 2 (Orono: University of Maine Press, 1925).

14. Fanny Wright (1795-1852), general reformer and utopian, wrote and worked late in Mrs. Rowson's career. She lectured at societies in her name, and helped get the Married Women's Property Law enacted (ibid., p. 54; *Rossi, Feminist Papers,* pp. 86 ff.).

15. *Pennsylvania Magazine of History and Biography* 68, no. 3 (July 1944), pp. 243-268.

16. Rowson Collection, 7379a, n.d.

17. "To Anna: An Address to a Young Lady Leaving School" (n.d. 7379a. Rowson Collection). This

poem, slightly altered, appears in the preface to *Mentoria* and in *Victoria* ("To Sophie," pp. 87 ff.).

18. "He is Not Worth the Trouble," J. Hewitt, composer (Boston: J. Hewitt, [ca. 1813]); see bibliography for discussion of dating.

19. Adams is praised in "Ode, on the Birth Day of John Adams, Esquire" (1799), in *Miscellaneous Poems* (pp. 32-39), as well as in the "Eulogy to George Washington, Esquire" (pp. 44-54). Washington appears in many selections.

20. *Love and Death in the American Novel,* new rev. ed. (New York: Dell Publishing Co., 1969), pp. 74-75.

21. *All The Happy Endings: A Study of the Domestic Novel in America* (New York: Harper & Brothers Publishers, 1956), p. xvii.

22. Samuel L. Knapp, "A Memoir of the Author," in *Charlotte's Daughter* (Boston: Richardson & Lord, 1828).

23. Neal, *Essay,* p. 20.

24. *A Vindication of the Rights of Woman, with Strictures on Political and Moral Subjects,* ed. Charles W. Hagelman, Jr. (New York: W. W. Norton & Company, Norton Library, 1967), p. 222.

25. Margaret Wyman, "The Rise of the Fallen Woman," *American Quarterly* 3 (1951), p. 161. Wyman sees Mrs. Rowson's support for the erring female, and her pique at the "unfeeling world which rejects such women." On this same subject, Wendy Martin (using only *Charlotte* as a basis for judgment) takes the more familiar view that Mrs. Rowson's treatment of the seduced is punitive and illiberal ("Seduced and Abandoned in the New World, 1970: The Fallen Women in American Fiction," in *American Sisterhood,* pp. 257-273).

26. Elizabeth Boyd, *The Happy-Unfortunate or the Female-Page,* ed. William Graves. Garland Series, Foundations of the Novel (New York: Garland Publishing, 1972).

Bibliography

WORKS BY SUSANNA ROWSON

The following bibliography is an attempt to provide an up-to-date and usable list of Rowson's works, and to suggest the extent of her production. It includes at least one edition of all the works that appear in current bibliographies, but does not attempt to track down all the editions of any work. The multifarious editions of *Charlotte Temple* and *Charlotte's Daughter* require separate treatment, and the sheet music could also be the subject of a separate bibliographical study. R. W. G. Vail lists

158 editions of *Charlotte Temple* in his fully researched bibliography; Lyle Wright adds ten to Vail's total. Several other Rowson works went through multiple editions. The following pages list the first editions of Rowson's works, those mentioned in this study, and in several instances, the second or third editions of works that received a small number of reprintings. R. W. G. Vail's entry number is given in many cases, and where there is nothing to add to the information, I have relied on Vail. Locations are listed only in cases where a book was not previously located, or is extremely rare. The following bibliographical sources are mentioned:

Allibone, S. Austin. *A Critical Dictionary of English Literature and British and American Authors Living and Deceased. From the Earliest Accounts to the Latter Half of the Nineteenth Century.* 2 vols., 2 suppls. Philadelphia: J. B. Lippincott Company, 1899.

Dunlap, William. *History of the American Theatre and Anecdotes of the Principal Actors.* 2d ed. 3 vols. in 1. Burt Franklin Research and Source Works Series, no. 36. New York: Burt Franklin, 1963.

Durang, Charles. "The Philadelphia Stage: 1749-1821," *Philadelphia Dispatch,* 15 October 1854.

Evans, Charles. *American Bibliography; a Chronological Dictionary of all Books, Pamphlets, and Periodical Publications Printed in the United States from the Genesis of Printing in 1630 Down to and Including the Year 1820.* Chicago: Printed for the Author, Blakey Press, 1903-1959. Subtitle and publisher vary.

Odell, George C. D. *Annals of the New York Stage, 1798-1821,* vol. 2. New York: Columbia University Press, 1927.

Quinn, Arthur Hobson. *A History of the American Drama From the Beginning to the Civil War.* New York: Harper & Brothers, 1923.

Sabin, Joseph. *A Dictionary of Books Relating to America, from its discovery to The Present Time,* Vol. 18. New York: Sabin, 1889.

Seilhamer, George O. *History of the American Theatre: New Foundations.* 3 vols. Philadelphia: Globe Printing House, 1888-1891.

Sonneck, Oscar George, and William Treat Upton. *A Bibliography of Early Secular Music: Eighteenth Century.* Rev. and enlarged, preface by Irving Lowens. New York: Da Capo Press, 1964.

Vail, R. W. G. "Susanna Haswell Rowson, The Author of Charlotte Temple: A Bibliographical Study," *Proceedings of the American Antiquarian Society* 42 (1932), pp. 47-160.

Wolfe, Richard J. *Secular Music in America: 1801-1825. A Bibliography.* Introduction by Carleton Sprague

Smith. New York: New York Public Library, Astor, Lenox and Tilden Foundations, 1964.

Wright, Lyle. *American Fiction 1774-1850, A Contribution Towards a Bibliography.* New rev. ed. San Marino, Calif.: Huntington Library, 1960.

FICTION

Charlotte: A Tale of Truth. 2 vols. London: William Lane, Minerva, MDLCXCI. Unique copy of the first edition is in the Clifton Waller Barrett Library at the University of Virginia. Prefatory remarks by "Minerva," presumably a mask assumed by the publisher William Lane, to "Ladies and Gentlemen" readers, assure them that the press's products will be respectable, informative, and entertaining.

————, in *Three Early American Novels.* Ed. William S. Kable. Columbus, Ohio: Charles E. Merrill Publishing Co., 1970.

Charlotte's Daughter: or, The Three Orphans. A Sequel to Charlotte Temple. To Which is prefixed, A Memoir of the Author. Boston: Richardson & Lord, 1828.

The Lamentable History of the Beautiful and Accomplished Charlotte Temple, With An Account of Her Elopement With Lieutenant Montroville [sic], *and Her Misfortunes and Painful Sufferings, Are Herein Pathetically Depicted.* Philadelphia: Barclay & Co., 1865.

Charlotte Temple: A Tale of Truth. Ed. Francis W. Halsey. New York: Funk & Wagnalls Co., 1905.

————. Ed. Clara M. and Rudolph Kirk. Twayne's United States Classics Series. New York: Twayne Publishers, 1964.

The Fille de Chambre, A Novel, in Three Volumes, by the Author of The Inquisitor, & c. & c. London: Printed for William Lane, at the Minerva, MDCCXCII. Vail (201) lists this first edition as *Rebecca, or the Fille de Chambre*; there was no copy known when Vail prepared his study. Volume 2 of this novel, located at Indiana University Library (vols. 1 and 3 missing), is entitled as above.

————, A Novel. By Mrs. Rowson of the New Theatre, Philadelphia; Author of *Charlotte,* the *Inquisitor, Victoria,* & c. [1st American ed.] Philadelphia: H.& P. Rice, and J. Rice & Co., 1794.

————. *Rebecca, or the Fille de Chambre.* A Novel. By Mrs. Rowson, Author of Charlotte, The Inquisitor, Victoria, & c. The Second American Edition, Corrected and Revised by the Author. Boston: R. P. & C. Williams, 1814.

The Inquisitor; or, Invisible Rambler. In three volumes. By Mrs. Rowson, author of Victoria. London: G. G. J. and J. Robinson, X.DCC.LXXXVIII. (Vail 191).

————. In three volumes. By Mrs. Rowson, author of Victoria. The first American edition. Philadelphia: William Gibbons, 1793 (Vail 192).

————. In three volumes. By Mrs. Rowson, Author of Victoria. Second American Edition. Philadelphia: Mathew Carey, 1794.

Mentoria; or The Young Lady's Friend: in Two Volumes. By Mrs. Rowson, *Author of Victoria,* & c. & c. London: printed for William Lane, at the Minerva, [1791]. The title page of the first edition does not include a printed date. The date appears to be well established by the evidence Vail cites (195): advertisements and reviews dated 1791. Locations in addition to the New York Public Library, are the Barrett Library, University of Virginia, and the Indiana University Library.

————. By Mrs. Rowson, author of Victoria, & c. & c. Dublin: Printed by Thomas Morton Bates for P. Wogan, A. Grueber, J. Halpern, J. Moore, R. M'Allister, J. Rice, W. Jones, and R. White, 1791 (Vail 196).

————. In two volumes. By Mrs. Rowson, of the New-Theatre, Philadelphia: Author of *The Inquisitor, Fille de Chambre, Victoria, Charlotte,* & c. & c. Philadelphia: Robert Campbell, M.DCC.XCIV.

Reuben and Rachel; or, Tales of Old Times. A Novel. By Mrs. Rowson, Author of Charlotte, Trials of the Heart, Fille de Chambre, & c. & c. Boston: Manning & Loring, 1798.

————. A novel in two volumes. By Mrs. Rowson, author of Charlotte, Mentoria, Fille de chambre, & c. & c. London: Printed at the Minerva-Press, for William Lane, 1799 (Vail 206).

Sarah, or The Exemplary Wife. By Susanna Rowson, Author of Charlotte Temple, Reuben and Rachel, Fille de Chambre, & c. & c. Boston: Charles Williams, 1813. Rev. from the serial version, *Sincerity,* in *Boston Weekly Magazine,* 4 June 1803-30 June 1804.

The Test of Honour, A Novel. By a Young Lady. In Two Volumes. London: John Abraham, 1789. The running title of this work is *Mary, or the Test of Honour,* and is so listed by Vail (194), who got the title from Knapp. Below the title is a seven-line passage of poetry:

> Take Honour for thy guide, and on just Heaven
> Place thy reliance, there's a secret charm
> In virtuous actions, that o'er awes the wicked,
> And, maugre all the malice of the world,
> Honour thy shield, Religion thy support,
> And happiness await thee in the end.

The full imprint reads "Printed by and for JOHN ABRAHAM, at his Circulating-Library, St. Swithin's Lane, Lombard-Street, 1789." A copy—as far as I know, unique—is located at Houghton Library, Harvard University.

Trials of the Human Heart, A Novel. in four volumes. By Mrs. Rowson, of the New Theatre, Philadelphia, Author of Charlotte, Fille de Chambre, Inquisitor, & c. & c. Philadelphia: Wrigley & Berriman, M.DCC.XCV.

Victoria. A Novel. In Two Volumes. The Characters taken from real Life, and Calculated to Improve the Morals of the Female Sex, By impressing them with a just Sense of The Merits of Filial Piety. By Susannah Haswell. London: J. P. Cooke, 1786. Copies at the New York Historical Society and Indiana University Library.

PEDAGOGICAL WORKS

An Abridgment of Universal Geography, Together with Sketches of History. Designed for the Use of Schools and Academies in the United States. By Susanna Rowson. Boston: John West [1805]. Vail (159) notes that the date is not on the title page, and agrees with Nason on 1805, which coincides with the printer's location in Cambridge Street, the address given in the imprint.

Biblical Dialogues Between A Father and His Family: Comprising Sacred History, From the Creation to the Death of our Saviour Christ. The Lives of the Apostles, and the Promulgation of the Gospel; with a Sketch of the History of the Church Down to the Reformation. The Whole Carried on in Conjunction with Profane History. In Two Volumes. By Susanna Rowson. Boston: Richardson and Lord, 1822.

Exercises in History, Chronology, and Biography, in Question and Answer. For the Use of Schools. Comprising, Ancient History, Greece, Rome, & c. Modern History, England, France, Spain, Portugal, & c. The Discovery of America, Rise, Progress and Final Independence of the United States. By Susanna Rowson, Author of Biblical Dialogues, & c. & c. Boston: Richardson and Lord, 1822.

A Present for Young Ladies; Containing Poems, Dialogues, Addresses, & c. & c. & c. As Recited by the Pupils of Mrs. Rowson's Academy, at the Annual Exhibitions. By Susanna Rowson. Boston: John West & Co., 1811.

A Spelling Dictionary, divided into Short Lessons, For the Easier Committing to Memory By Children and Young Persons; and Calculated to Assist Youth in Comprehending What they Read. Selected From Johnson's Dictionary, For the Use of Her Pupils, By Susanna Rowson. Boston: John West, 1807.

————. 2d ed. Portland: Isaac Adams, 1815.

Youth's First Step in Geography, Being a Series of Exercises Making the Tour of the Habitable Globe. For The use of Schools. By Susannah [!] Rowson, Preceptress. Boston: Wells and Lilly, 1818.

PERIODICALS

The Boston Weekly Magazine; Devoted to Morality, Literature, Biography, History, the Fine Arts, Agriculture, & c. & c. 3 vols. Boston: Gilbert and Dean. 1802-1805. The title pages bear the following verse:

> To soar aloft on Fancy's Wing,
> And bathe in Heliconia's Spring;
> Cull Every Flower With Careful Hand,
> And Strew them O'er our Native Land.

New England Galaxy. Boston: 1817-1839[?] Subtitle varies. Mrs. Rowson's contributions are found in early issues under the initials "S. R."

POETRY

Poems on Various Subjects. By Mrs. Rowson, author of the Inquisitor, & c. London: G. G. J. and J. Robinson, M.DCC.LXXXVIII. No copy known (Vail 199). Vail takes this title from Allibone and the imprint from the first edition of *The Inquisitor.*

Miscellaneous Poems. Susanna Rowson, preceptress. Boston: Gilbert and Dean, 1804.

A Trip to Parnassus; or, the Judgment of Apollo on Dramatic Authors and Performers. A Poem. London: John Abraham, 1788. The title page of *A Trip* includes a one-line quotation: "Laugh where we must, be candid where we can.—Pope." The full imprint reads, "Printed by and for John Abraham, No. 3, St. Swithin's Lane, Lombard-Street; and sold by all other Booksellers, in Town and Country. 1788. (Price Two-Shillings.)" There is a copy of this rare work at Houghton Library. Harvard University.

DRAMA

The American Tar, or the Press Gang Defeated. A "ballet founded on a recent fact at Liverpool . . . the music entirely new and composed by R. Taylor." Directed by William Francis and performed at the New Theatre, Philadelphia, June 17, 1796 (Sonneck-Upton, p. 22). Vail (160) quotes Seilhamer to the effect that the piece was probably an adaptation from a work by Jacob Morton, and was probably never published. Seilhamer (vol. 3, p. 213) lists the characters as Will Steady, Tom Capstan, Captain Trunion, Midshipmen, Dick Hauser [Mr. Rowson], Susan [Charlotte Rowson] and Jane.

Americans in England, or, Lessons for Daughters. A comedy. Boston: 1796. No copy known (Vail 161). Vail notes disagreement over the possibility of this work having been printed. It was performed at the Federal Street Theater, 19 April 1797, and said to have been produced later under the title "The Columbian Daughter, or Americans in England," a fact which suggests that the play was printed. Seilhamer provides a list of characters, which may denote the flavor of the play. The English characters are Courtland, Folio, Snap, Waiter, Captain Ormsby, Jack Acorn, Thomas, Bailiff's Man, Rhymer, Mrs. Ormsby, Arabella, Betty, and Melissa; the Americans are named Ezekiel Plainly, Horace Winship, and Jemima Winship. Mrs. Ormsby and

Jemima Winship were played by Mrs. Rowson, Betty by her sister-in-law, Charlotte Rowson, and Snap by Mr. Rowson (vol. 3, p. 340).

The Female Patriot; or, Nature's Rights. [Altered from Philip Massinger's "Bondman."] Philadelphia: 1794. Vail (184) takes the title from Durang, Knapp, Sabin, and Evans. No copy is known and there is disagreement as to whether the play was printed. Vail cites evidence from Dunlap (an early edition) and Durang that this farce was performed 19 June 1795. Seilhamer's list of characters suggests that Mrs. Rowson stayed pretty close to Massinger: Timoleon, Archidamus, Leothenes, Hernando, Diphilus, Jailor, Graculo, Pymbrio, Pysander, Cleora, Olympio, Statilla, Xanthia. Statilla was played by Mrs. Rowson (p. 181).

Hearts of Oak. [Boston? 1810-1811]. Probably not published (Vail 190). Vail quotes John Bernard (*Retrospections of America 1797-1811* [New York: Harper and Brothers, 1887]), who ascribes this play to Mrs. Rowson, and notes that the play was probably adapted from John Till Allingham's *Hearts of Oak* (Drury Lane, 1803). Allingham's play is a sentimental comedy, with patriotic overtones expressed in the prologue and epilogue. The central action is mainly domestic and involves the departure of one Dorland from his wife Eliza because he had concluded, on seeing her embrace her brother, that she had a lover. There is a money-grubbing land dealer, Ten-Per-Cent, a humorous Irishman, Brian O'Bradleigh, and an orphan heroine (John Till Allingham, *Hearts of Oak. A Comedy. Five Acts. Drury Lane*, London: Alexandra & Fredricksburg, Cotton & Stewart, [1804]).

Slaves in Algiers; or, a Struggle for Freedom: A Play Interspersed with songs, In three acts. [Music composed by Alexander Reinagle]. Philadelphia: Wrigley and Berriman, M,DCC,XCIV, 1794. Vail (208) says this was first performed at the New Theatre, Chestnut Street, Philadelphia, 30 June 1794, and notes Mrs. Rowson's early use of national themes. Seilhamer declares, "The style was wretched, the dramatic quality tawdry, and the sentiment strained and stilted" (vol. 3, p. 156). He claims the play owes its popularity to William Cobbett's attack. Evans assumes a reprinting of *Slaves*, Boston, 1796, from an advertisement (Evans 31130).

The Standard of Liberty: a Poetical Address. Baltimore: 1795. No copy known (Vail 211). Vail takes the title from Knapp and Evans via Sabin, and notes that it probably was printed by George Keatinge, who advertised works by New Theatre playwrights. Published in the *Baltimore Telegraphe*, 31 October 1795, as "The standard of liberty. A poetic tale." Appears in *Miscellaneous Poems*, pp. 94-97.

The Volunteers. A musical entertainment as performed at the New Theatre. Composed by Alex Reinagle. The words by Mrs. Rowson. Philadelphia: Printed for the author and sold at the music shops [1795]. Vail (249) notes that Durang, Seilhamer, and Sonneck agree that the work was performed first at the New Theatre, Philadelphia, 21 January 1795. Doubt exists as to whether there was a separately printed libretto. Evans describes the piece as a farce based upon the Whiskey Rebellion. The available score contains fourteen songs with music, all but one with lyrics by Mrs. Rowson. Copies of the score are located at the Library of Congress and The Historical Society of Pennsylvania.

SONGS

"America, Commerce and Freedom." Comp. A. Reinagle. Philadelphia: Carr's Musical Repository [1794] (Vail 216). Date assumed by Sonneck, from ad. The piece was part of "The Sailor's Landlady," produced at the New Theatre, Philadelphia, 19 March 1794. Seilhamer describes this "ballet pantomine" as having been quite popular, and the third of such works by William Francis; the same name appears as the director of *The American Tar* (pp. 151-152).

———. Comp. A. Reinagle. Baltimore: Carr's Musical Repository, [1794-1796].

———. "New Song." Sung by Mr. Darley. [Philadelphia]: M. Carey, [1794] (Evans 27648).

"Captn Truxton or Huzza! for the Constellation," Sung Mr. Tyler at the Theatre with the greatest applause. New York: Printed and Sold at J. HEWITT'S Musical Repository, [ca. 1799] (Evans 36246). "Captain Truxton," "Huzza for the Constellation," and "Truxton's Victory," while all commemorate the same occasion, and are dated the same year, have different words.

"Charity." [An ode. Music by John Bray] (Vail 220). Part of an elaborate religious performance for the anniversary of the Boston Fatherless and Widow's Society. Performed at Boylston Hall, Boston, 11 October 1820.

"Child of Mortality." Duett and Chorus. Written by Mrs. Rowson. Composed by John Bray. Portsmouth, N.H.: T. H. Miller [ca. 1824] (Vail 222); (Wolfe 1276).

"The Columbian Sailor." Written by Mrs. Rowson, Composed by J. Bray. Philadelphia: G. E. Blake, [1816?]. Vail (223) dates this song [1816-1820?]; Wolfe (1284) gives it as [1816?]. It was number 6 of Blake's Musical Miscellany.

"Come Strike the Silver String. A Sacred Song." Written by Mrs. Rowson. Composed by Oliver Shaw. Providence: Oliver Shaw [1817-1823]. Wolfe (7935) narrows Vail's "1818-1825" to "1817-1823." Reissued in Shaw: *Sacred Songs, Duetts, Anthems, & c.* Providence [1823].

"A Dirge" [to George Washington]. Words by Mrs. Rowson, of Medford. In *Sacred Dirges, Hymns, and Anthems, Commemorative of the Death of General George Washington, The Guardian of His Country, and*

The Friend of Man. An Original Composition. By a Citizen of Massachusetts [Oliver Holden]. Boston: I. Thomas and E. and E. T. Andrews, [1800] (Evans 37635-37638).

"Drink to Me Only With Thine Eyes" (Vail 226). Three four-line stanzas. "This first verse also is from the original song" [by Ben Jonson], the last two verses by Mrs. Rowson. Published in *Miscellaneous Poems*, p. 198.

"He is Not Worth the Trouble." Written by Mrs. Rowson. Composed by J. Hewitt. Boston: J. Hewitt, [18—?]. Vail's entry for this song lists the place and publisher as "New-York: Firth & Hall No. 1 Franklin Sq.," and dates the song [1832?] on the evidence that the publisher appeared at the given address between 1832 and 1847. The copy I have bears the above information, and is dated "ca. 1813."

"How Cold and Piercing Blows the Wind." A Favorite Ballad, Sung with great applause by Mrs. Graupner at the Philharmonic Concert, Boston. The Words by Mrs. Rowson. Music by J. Hewitt. New York: J. Hewitt's Musical Repository and Library, [1809]. Wolfe (3721) gives the date as [1809]; evidence from an advertisement of 12 September 1809 in the *New York Evening Post* features it among "new songs just published." Wolfe's entry has Mrs. Rowson listed as Mrs. Rawson. My copy has her name correct.

"Huzza for the Constellation." Sung by Mr. Fox at the Theatre. Printed and sold at B. Carr's Musical Repository, Philadelphia, & Carr's, Baltimore, & P. Hewitt's, N. York [1799] (Evans 36247).

"Hymn to the Deity." (Vail 228). Twelve four-line stanzas. Published in *Miscellaneous Poems*, pp. 53-58.

"Hymn." [For Washington?] *Hymns and Odes Composed on the death of General Washington.* Portsmouth: 1800.

"I'd Rather Be Excus'd." Composed by Mr. Hook. Boston: J. Hewitt, [1814-1815]. (Wolfe 4086).

Reissued from same plates; Boston: E. W. Jackson [1821-1824] (Wolfe 4086A).

Reissued from same plates; Music Saloon 325 Broadway [n.d.], ca. 1825 (Wolfe 4086B).

In The *Songster's New Pocket Companion*, Boston: 1817 (Wolfe 4087).

"Independent and Free," From the AMERICAN TAR or the PRESS GANG DEFEATED. Sung by Mr. Rowson at the New Theatre Philadelphia. The Words by Mrs. Rowson, the Music by R. Taylor. Printed for the Author . . . & Sold at Carr's Repository's [1796] (Evans 47929), (Sonneck, p. 207). Location, Historical Society of Pennsylvania.

"The Independent Farmer." A song. Three twelve-line stanzas. Published in *Miscellaneous Poems*, pp. 191-193 (Vail 231).

"I Never will be Married." The words by Mrs. Rowson. The music by Mr. Hook. London: Polyhymnian Company. [1790-1820] (Vail 229).

"In Vain is the Verdure of Spring." A new song composed by Mr. Carr. The words by Mrs. Rowson [Philadelphia:] Printed and sold by G. Willig, [1797-1798?]. Vail (230) notes that the Willig music store appears in the Philadelphia directories between 1797 and 1854, and the fact that Nason dates this song prior to 1799. Wolfe (10186) says "[1799-1802]," and lists "Mrs. I. Rowson" as lyricist.

"Kiss the Brim and Bid it Pass." A new song. Written by Mrs. Rowson. The music composed by P. A. Von Hagen. Boston: P. A. Von Hagen's Piano Forte Warehouse [1802]. Vail (232) and Wolfe agree on date, Vail by means of ads, Wolfe (3292) from copyright granted Von Hagen, 21 August 1802.

"The Little Sailor Boy." A Ballad Sung at the Theatres & other Public Places in Philadelphia, Baltimore, New York & c. by Messrs Darley, Williamson, Miss Broadhurst, M. Hodgkinson. Written by Mrs. Rowson. Composed by B. Carr. Printed and sold at the Authors Musical Repository, Philadelphia, J. Carrs, Baltimore & J. Hewitts New York [1798] (Vail 233; Evans 34489). See Vail and Sonneck-Upton for the many editions of this song, and see Wolfe for problems in dating.

"Ma Jolie Petite Fille." A New Song. Set to Music by Mr. R. Taylor—the words by Mrs. Rowson/Of Medford, near Boston. In *The Philadelphia Repository and Weekly Register* 1, no. 26 (9 May 1801), fol. p. 205.

"National Song for the 4th of July the Birthday of American Independence." Words by Mrs. Rowson of Boston, Massachusetts, the music composed by Dr. Arnold. Boston: G. Graupner [181—]. Vail (235) gives the date [1818]; Wolfe (269) says [1815].

"Ode. To the Memory of John Warren." Published in *An Oration Occasioned by the Death of John Warren . . . Delivered . . . by Josiah Bartlett . . .* Boston: C. Stebbins, 1815 (Vail 236).

"Original Ode." Boston Fatherless and Widow's Society Order of Performance at Park St. Church, 16 October 1825. Annual Meeting. Boston, 1825.

"Orphan Nosegay Girl." The words by Mrs. Rowson. Boston: G. Graupner. Vail (237) dates [1818-1825]; Wolfe (7466), [1803-1806]. Vail notes that Graupner appears in the Boston directory between 1805 and 1825.

A second state of the preceeding. In Shaw, "A Selection of Progressive Airs and Songs." Dedham, 1810 (Wolfe 7467A).

"Parody on the Marseilles Hymn, adapted for the sons of Columbia." Three eleven-line stanzas. Published in *Miscellaneous Poems*, pp. 186-188 (Vail 238).

"Peace and Holy Love, a Sacred Song"; Sung by Master Ayling, at the Handel & Haydn Society: Written by Mrs. Rowson, the Music Composed by John Bray. Boston: S. Wood [1820] (Vail 238); (Wolfe 1323).

Reissued on the same plates, imprint altered to: "Boston: Published by E. W. Jackson [1822-1826] (Wolfe 1323A). My copy has S. Wood scratched out and E. W. Jackson apparently written in.

"Soft As Yon Silver Ray That Sleeps." A song, With an accompaniment for the piano forte. The words by Mrs. Rowson. The music composed by J. Bray. Boston: G. Graupner. Vail (240) gives the date of this song as [1814-1825]; Wolfe (1346) says [1820-1825]. Wolfe lists seven issues of this song, the lyrics for which, as he and Vail both note, are from Anne Radcliffe's *The Mysteries of Udolpho*. Only the one version is ascribed to Mrs. Rowson.

"A Soldier is the Noblest Name." [First published in *The Highland Reel*. A comic opera, in three acts. As performed with universal applause, at the Theatre—Federal—Street. By John O'Keeffe. Boston: Printed [by Joseph Bumstead] for Wm. P. and L. Blake, 1797 (Vail 241). Produced at the New Theatre, Chestnut St., Philadelphia, 5 April 1794; music by Alexander Reinagle.

"Song." [First line:] "Fragile sweets, how frail ye are." Three eight-line stanzas. Published in *Miscellaneous Poems*, pp. 184-185 (Vail 242).

"Song." [First line:] "The rose just bursting into bloom." Two eight-line stanzas. Published in *Miscellaneous Poems*, pp. 204-205 (Vail 243).

"Song." [First line:] "Welcome is the morning light." Three eight-line stanzas. Published in *Miscellaneous Poems*, pp. 206-207 (Vail 244).

"Song." [First line:] "When far from freedom's happy court." Two ten-line stanzas. Published in *Miscellaneous Poems*, pp. 194-195 (Vail 245).

"Song." [First line:] "When hoarse winds roar, and lightnings gleam." Two eight-line stanzas. Published in *Miscellaneous Poems*, pp. 199-200 (Vail 246).

"Song. Written for the celebration of the Birthday of George Washington, Esq." and sung on that occasion, in Boston, February 11th, 1798. Air—Anacreon in Heaven. Three eight-line stanzas. Title from *Miscellaneous Poems*, pp. 178-179 (Vail 247).

"Truxton's Victory." A Naval Patriotic song. Sung by Mr. Hodgkinson. Written by Mrs. Rowson, of Boston. [Boston: Printed by Thomas & Andrews, 1799?]. Imprint in ink (Vail 248); (Evans 36248); (Sonneck-Upton, p. 438). Sonneck notes that "Truxton's Victory" was advertised in March 1799 as "published, at P. A. von Hagen, jun. and Co's, No. 55, Marlboro' Street . . ." Boston.

"When the Cloud Has Pass'd Away." Air, in *A Sacred Concert*, in Two Parts/To Be Performed on Sunday Evening Dec. 9, 1821. by the "Neponset Sacred Music Society" at their Hall Near Milton Bridge. Order of Performance. Words by Mrs. Rowson, Music by John Bray. Vail locates at The American Antiquarian Society; my copy from Barrett Library, University of Virginia.

"Where Can Peace of Mind Be Found." A Duett. Written by Mrs. Rowson. The Music Composed by John Bray. Boston: G. Graupner [1821]. Wolfe (1356) notes that the copyright was granted Graupner in 1821.

"Will Not Dare Not Tell." A New Song Written by Mrs. Rowson. The Music Composed by P. A. von Hagen. Boston: P. A. von Hagen's Piano Forte Warehouse, [1802] (Vail 251; Wolfe 3296). Wolfe notes copyright granted von Hagen September 1802; both he and Vail cite advertisements that support date.

"Will You Rise My Belov'd." Words by Mrs. Rowson—Adapted to the Music of "Will You Come to the Bower." Boston: G. Graupner. Vail (252) gives the date as [1818-1825]; Wolfe (6061) as [1811?].

WORKS REFERRED TO

Adams, Oscar Fay. "Susanna Haswell Rowson." *Christian Register,* 17 March 1913, pp. 296-299; 3 April 1913, p. 321.

Angoff, Charles. *A Literary History of the American People.* 2 vols. in 1. New ed. New York: Tudor Publishing Co., 1935.

Anthony, Katherine. *First Lady of the Revolution: The Life of Mercy Otis Warren.* Garden City, N.Y.: Doubleday & Company, 1958.

Baker, Ernest A. *The History of the English Novel: The Novel of Sentiment and the Gothic Romance.* Vol. 5. London: H. F.& G. Witherby, 1934.

Benson, Mary Sumner. *Women in Eighteenth-Century America: A Study of Opinion and Social Usage.* New York: Columbia University Press, 1935.

Bernard, John. *Retrospections of America: 1797-1811.* Ed. Laurence Hutton and Brander Matthews. New York: Harper & Brothers, 1887.

Blakey, Dorothy. *The Minerva Press 1790-1820.* London: Oxford University Press, 1939.

Boyd, Elizabeth. *The Happy-Unfortunate, or the Female-Page.* Ed. William Graves. Garland Series, Foundations of the Novel. New York: Garland Publishing, 1972.

Bradsher, Earl L. *Mathew Carey. Editor, Author and Publisher. A Study in American Literary Development.* New York: Columbia University Press, 1912.

Bradstreet, Anne. *The Works of Anne Bradstreet.* Ed. Jeannine Hensley, Adrienne Rich. Cambridge, Mass.: Harvard University Press, 1967.

Brown, Charles Brockden. *Alcuin: A Dialogue,* 1935; reprint ed. with afterwords by Lee R: Edwards. New York: Grossman Publishers, 1971.

Brown, Herbert Ross. *The Sentimental Novel in America, 1789-1860.* Durham, N.C.: Duke University Press, 1940.

Brown, William Hill. *The Power of Sympathy, or, the Triumph of Nature. Founded in Truth,* in *The Power of Sympathy and The Coquette.* Ed. William S. Osborne. Masterworks of Literature Series. New Haven, Conn.: College and University Press, 1970.

Buckingham, Joseph Tinker, *Personal Memoirs and Recollections of Editorial Life . . .* Vol. 1. Boston: Ticknor, Reed, & Fields, 1852.

Burney, Frances. *Evelina, or the History of a Young Ladies Entrance into the World.* Ed. Edward A. Bloom. London: Oxford University Press, 1968.

The Cambridge History of American Literature. Colonial and Revolutionary Literature; Early National Literature. Vol. 1. Ed. William Peterfield Trent, John Erskine, Stuart P. Sherman, Carl Van Doren. New York: G. P. Putnam's Sons, 1917.

Charvat, William. *The Profession of Authorship in America, 1800-1870.* Ed. Matthew J. Bruccoli. Foreword by Howard Mumford Jones. Columbus: Ohio State University Press, 1968.

————. *Literary Publishing in America, 1790-1850.* Philadelphia: University of Pennsylvania Press, 1959.

Cobbett, William [Peter Porcupine, pseud.]. *A Kick For a Bite; or, Review upon Review; with a Critical Essay, on the Works of Mrs. S. Rowson, in a Letter to the Editor, or Editors, of The American Monthly Review.* Philadelphia: Thomas Bradford, 1795.

Cowie, Alexander. *The Rise of the American Novel.* New York: American Book Co., 1948.

Dall, [Caroline Wells Healey]. *The Romance of the Association; or, One Last Glimpse of Charlotte Temple and Eliza Wharton. A Curiosity of Literature and Life.* Cambridge: Press of John Wilson and Son, 1875.

Davis, Elizabeth Gould. *The First Sex.* New York: G. P. Putnam's Sons, 1970.

de Beauvoir, Simone. *The Second Sex.* Ed. and trans. H. M. Parshley, 1953; reprint ed., New York: Bantam Books, 1961.

Deegan, Dorothy Yost. *The Stereotype of the Single Woman in American Novels: A Social Study with Implications for the Education of Women.* New York: King's Crown Press, Columbia University, 1951.

Eastman, Arthur M., et al., eds. *The Norton Reader: An Anthology of Expository Prose.* 3d ed. New York: W. W. Norton & Company, 1973.

Fiedler, Leslie A. *Love and Death in the American Novel.* New rev. ed. New York: Dell Publishing Co., 1969.

Field, Vena Bernadette. *Constantia: A Study of the Life and Works of Judith Sargent Murray 1751-1820.* University of Maine Studies, 2d ser., no. 17. Orono: University of Maine Press, 1931.

[Foster, Hannah]. *The Boarding School; or, Lessons of a Preceptress to her Pupils: consisting of Information, Instruction, and Advice, Calculated to Improve the Manners, and form the Character of* YOUNG LADIES. *to which is added, A Collection of* LETTERS, *Written by the* PUPILS, *to their Instructor, their Friends, and each other.* By a Lady of Massachusetts; Author of The Coquette. Boston: I. Thomas and E. J. Andrews, 1798.

————. *The Coquette, or, The History of Eliza Wharton. A Novel Founded on Fact,* in *The Power of Sympathy and The Coquette.* Ed. William S. Osborne. Masterworks of Literature Series. New Haven, Conn.: College and University Press, 1970.

Friedan, Betty. *The Feminine Mystique.* New York: Dell Publishing Co., 1963.

Goulianos, Joan, ed. *By a Woman Writt: Literature From Six Centuries By and About Women.* Baltimore: Penguin Books, 1973.

Hahn, Emily. *Once Upon a Pedestal.* New York: Thomas Y. Crowell, 1974.

Hale, Nancy. *New England Discovery: A Personal View.* New York: Coward, McCann, 1963.

Hall, Ernest Jackson. "The Satirical Element in The American Novel." Ph.D. diss., University of Pennsylvania, 1922.

Halsey, Francis W. "Historical and Biographical Introduction," *Charlotte Temple: a Tale of Truth.* New York: Funk and Wagnalls Company, 1905.

Hart, James D. *The Popular Book. A History of America's Literary Taste,* 1950. Reprint ed., Berkeley: University of California Press, 1963.

Heilbrun, Carolyn G. *Toward a Recognition of Androgyny.* New York: Alfred A. Knopf, 1973.

Heilman, Robert Bechtold. *America in English Fiction, 1760-1800: The Influences of the American Revolution.* Baton Rouge: Louisiana State University Press, 1937.

Jones, Mary Gwladys. *Hannah More.* Cambridge: Cambridge University Press, 1952.

Kable, William S. "Introduction," *Three Early American Novels.* Columbus, Ohio: Charles E. Merrill Publishing Co., 1970.

Kettler, Robert Ronald. "The Eighteenth-Century American Novel: The Beginning of a Fictional Tradition." Ph.D. diss., Purdue University, 1968.

Knapp, Samuel L. "A Memoir of the Author," in *Charlotte's Daughter: or, The Three Orphans. A Sequel to Charlotte Temple*. Boston: Richardson & Lord, 1828.

Literary History of the United States: History. Ed. Robert E. Spiller, Willard Thorp, Thomas H. Johnson, Henry Seidel Canby, Richard M. Ludwig. 3d ed., rev. New York: Macmillan, 1964.

Loshe, Lillie Deming. *The Early American Novel.* New York: Columbia University Press, 1907.

MacCarthy, B. G. *The Female Pen.* 2 vols. New York: William Salloch, 1948.

Mackenzie, Henry. *The Man of Feeling.* Ed. Brian Vickers. London: Oxford University Press, 1967.

Manvill, P. P. *Lucinda; or, the Mountain Mourner. Being Recent Facts, in a series of Letters, from Mrs. Manvill, in the State of New York, to her sister in Pennsylvania.* 2d ed., rev. Ballston Spa, N.Y.: William Child, 1810.

Martin, Terence. "The Emergence of the Novel in America. A Study in the Cultural History of an Art Form." Ph.D. diss., Ohio State University, 1954.

————. *The Instructed Vision; Scottish Common Sense Philosophy and the Origins of American Fiction.* Indiana University Humanities Series no. 48. Bloomington: Indiana University Press, 1961.

Martin, Wendy. "Seduced and Abandoned in the New World, 1970: The Fallen Women in American Fiction." *The American Sisterhood: Writings of the Feminist Movement from Colonial Times to the Present.* Ed. Wendy Martin. New York: Harper & Row, Publishers, 1972.

Martineau, Harriet. *Society in America.* New York: Saunders and Otley, 1837.

Mates, Julian. *The American Musical Stage Before 1800.* New Brunswick, N.J.: Rutgers University Press, 1962.

Mead, Margaret. *Sex and Temperament in Three Primitive Societies.* New York: Mentor Books, 1950.

Melville, Herman. *Redburn, His First Voyage. Being the Sailor-boy Confessions and Reminiscences of the Son-of-a-Gentleman, in the Merchant Service.* Ed., Harrison Hayford, Hershel Parker, G. Thomas Tanselle. Vol. 4 of Northwestern-Newberry Edition. General ed. Harrison Hayford. Evanston, Ill.: Northwestern University Press, 1960.

Millett, Kate. *Sexual Politics.* Garden City, N.Y.: Doubleday & Company, 1970.

Montagu, Ashley. *The Natural Superiority of Women.* New York: Macmillan, 1953.

More, Hannah. *Works: Strictures on the Modern System of Female Education-Sacred Dramas.* Vol. 6. New York: Harper & Brothers, Publishers, 1855.

Morgan, Robin, ed. *Sisterhood is Powerful: An Anthology of Writings from the Women's Liberation Movement.* New York: Vintage Books, 1970.

Mott, Frank Luther. *Golden Multitudes: The Story of Best Sellers in the United States.* New York: Macmillan, 1947.

————. *A History of American Magazines, 1741-1850.* Vol. 1. New York: D. Appleton & Company, 1930.

Murray, Judith Sargent. "On the Equality of the Sexes." *The Feminist Papers: From Adams to de Beauvoir.* Ed. Alice S. Rossi. New York: Columbia University Press, 1973.

Nason, Elias. *A Memoir of Mrs. Susanna Rowson, with Elegant and Illustrative Extracts From her Writings in Prose and Poetry.* Albany, N.Y.: Joel Munsell, 1870.

Neal, James. *An Essay on the Education and Genius of the Female Sex. To Which is Added, An Account, of the Commencement of the Young Ladies' Academy of Philadelphia, Held the 18th of December, 1794. Under the Direction of Mr. John Poor, A. M. Principal.* Philadelphia: Jacob Johnson & Co., 1795.

Orians, G. Harrison. *A Short History of American Literature. Analyzed By Decades.* New York: F. S. Crofts & Co., 1940.

Papashvily, Helen Waite. *All the Happy Endings: A Study of the Domestic Novel in America, the Women Who Wrote It, the Women Who Read It, in the Nineteenth Century.* New York: Harper & Brothers Publishers, 1956.

Parker, Gail, ed. *The Oven Birds: American Women on Womanhood, 1820-1920.* Garden City, N.Y.: Doubleday & Company, Anchor Books, 1972.

Pattee, Fred Lewis. *The First Century of American Literature, 1770-1870.* New York: D. Appleton-Century Company, 1935.

Petter, Henri. *The Early American Novel.* Columbus: Ohio State University Press, 1971.

Plumb, Harriet Pixley. *Charlotte Temple, A Historical Drama,* Three Acts With Prologue. Chicago and London: Publishers Printing Co., T. Fisher Unwin [1899].

Quinn, Arthur Hobson. *American Fiction: An Historical and Critical Survey.* New York: Appleton-Century-Crofts, 1936.

Richardson, Charles F. *American Literature 1607-1885.* Vol. 2. New York: G. P. Putnam's Sons, 1889.

Richardson, Samuel. *Clarissa, or the History of a Young Lady.* Ed. George Sherburn. Boston: Houghton Mifflin Co., 1962.

————. *Pamela, or Virtue Rewarded.* Ed. William M. Sale, Jr. New York: W. W. Norton and Co., 1958.

Rossi, Alice S., ed. *The Feminist Papers: From Adams to de Beauvoir.* New York: Columbia University Press, 1973.

Rourke, Constance. *The Roots of American Culture, and Other Essays.* New York: Harcourt, Brace and Co., 1942.

[Sansay, Leonora]. *Laura.* By a Lady of Philadelphia. Philadelphia: Bradford & Inskeep, 1809.

Sargent, Mary E. "Susanna Rowson." *Medford Historical Register,* 7 April 1904, pp. 24-40.

Scott, Anne Firor. *Women in American Life. Selected Readings.* New York: Houghton Mifflin Co., 1970.

Sedgwick, Catherine Maria. *The Poor Rich Man, and The Rich Poor Man.* New York: Harper & Brothers, 1836.

Sewall, Samuel. "Talitha Cumi," Sewall *Letter Book, Coll. Mass. Hist. Soc.,* ser. 6, vols. 1-2, 1886-1888.

Smith, Thelma M. "Feminism in Philadelphia, 1790-1850." *Pennsylvania Magazine of History and Biography* 68, no. 3 (July 1944), pp. 243-268.

Sonneck, Oscar George. *Early Opera in America.* New York, London, and Boston: G. Shirmer, 1915.

Southworth, E. D. E. N. *Self-Raised, or From the Depths.* New York: Grosset & Dunlap, 1864.

[Swanwick, John]. *A Rub from Snub; or a cursory analytical Epistle: addressed to Peter Porcupine, Author of the* BONE TO GNAW, KICK FOR A BITE, *& c. & c. containing* GLAD TIDINGS *for the* DEMOCRATS, *and a Word of* COMFORT *to Mrs. S. Rowson. Wherein the Said Porcupine's Moral, Political, Critical and Literary character is Fully Illustrated.* Philadelphia: Printed for the Purchasers, 1795.

Tompkins, J. M. S. *The Popular Novel in England, 1770-1800.* London: Constable & Co., 1932.

Twain, Mark. "The Literary Offenses of Fenimore Cooper." *The Portable Mark Twain.* Ed. Bernard de Voto. New York: Viking Press, 1946.

Violette, Augusta Genevieve. *Economic Feminism in American Literature Prior to 1848.* University of Maine Studies, 2d ser., no. 2. Orono: University of Maine Press, 1925.

Wasserstrom, William. *Heiress of All the Ages: Sex and Sentiment in the Genteel Tradition.* Minneapolis: University of Minnesota Press, 1959.

Watt, Ian. *The Rise of the Novel: Studies in Defoe, Richardson and Fielding,* 1957; reprint ed., Berkeley: University of California Press, 1967.

Whittier, John Greenleaf. *Whittier on Writers and Writing: The Uncollected Critical Writings of John Green- leaf Whittier.* Ed., Edwin Harrison Cady and Harry Hayden Clark. Syracuse, N.Y.: Syracuse University Press, 1950.

Wollstonecraft, Mary. *A Vindication of the Rights of Woman, with Strictures on Political and Moral Subjects.* Ed. Charles W. Hagelman, Jr. New York: W. W. Norton & Company, 1967.

[Wood, Sally Sayward Barrell Keating]. *Dorval; or the Speculator. A Novel. Founded on Recent Facts.* By a Lady. Author of "Julia." Portsmouth, N.H.: Nutting & Whitelock, 1801.

———. *Julia and the Illuminated Baron. A Novel. Founded on Recent Facts. . . .* By a Lady of Massachusetts. Portsmouth, N.H.: United States Oracle Press, 1800.

Woolf, Virginia. *A Room of One's Own.* New York: Harcourt, Brace & World, 1957.

Wyman, Margaret. "The Rise of the Fallen Woman." *American Quarterly* 3 (1951), pp. 161-177.

Patricia L. Parker (essay date 1986)

SOURCE: Parker, Patricia L. "Literature of the Stage." In *Susanna Rowson,* pp. 61-82. Boston: Twayne Publishers, 1986.

[*In the following essay, Parker studies Rowson's poetry treating the dramatic arts, as well as the author's own plays and song lyrics.*]

A TRIP TO PARNASSUS

Rowson's first publication suggests her early involvement with the theater. In 1788 she published ***A Trip to Parnassus; or, the Judgment of Apollo on Dramatic Authors and Performers,*** a thirty-page, lighthearted work inscribed to Thomas Harris, manager of the theater at Covent Garden.[1] The poem describes in couplets of anapestic quatrameter the approach to Apollo's throne of some thirty-four actors and writers. With merciless abruptness Apollo either welcomes them with bay leaves and laurels or casts them aside as undeserving of praise.

The poem reflects an intimate acquaintance with the performers and writers of Covent Garden, one of London's three patent theaters, and it reflects Rowson's considerable interest in theater art. Almost all of the actors who come before Apollo for judgment were part of the Covent Garden company, and the writers were those whose works constituted part of the company repertoire. Except Sheridan, few of the dramatists are recognizable today, for with the notable exception of Sheridan and Goldsmith, late eighteenth-century theater engaged the attention of only second- or third-rate writers. Few distinguished plays were written during Rowson's theatrical career. Most of the best acting appeared in the comedy and other light genres, and those are the forms that attracted Rowson. She liked especially the sentimental comedies of Elizabeth Inchbald, John O'Keefe, and the George Colmans, senior and junior.

The dramatists appear first in **Parnassus**. The first playwright she brought for Apollonian judgment was Edward Topham, a dramatist known for his sartorial taste. But Rowson disliked vanity, and so she dismissed him quickly:

> The first that advanc'd, without order or rule,
> Was that Tip-Top* of taste, whose first borne was a
> Fool.
> Apollo, displeas'd, push'd the upstart away.
>
> (3)

"The Fool" was Topham's second, not first, play, a farce in two acts performed at Covent Garden and printed in 1786.[2]

As corollary to her disapproval of vanity, Rowson held morality up as a standard for the writing of drama, a position shared by most eighteenth-century playwrights, who stressed the rewards of virtue. Thus she praised George Colman, the second dramatist introduced to Apollo, for his "honour and virtue":

> . . . a man in [Apollo's] service grown grey,
> Who, pourtraying the heart of a Freeport, has shown
> The honour and virtue which glow in his own:
> The Deity smiled, and the Muses drew near
> To welcome a brother they ever held dear.
>
> (3)

Colman at age fifty-six continued to act as proprietor of Covent Garden despite the effects of a paralytic stroke suffered three years earlier. A writer and adapter of some thirty dramatic pieces, he had spent his inheritance on the purchase of Covent Garden Theatre in 1767.[3]

Rowson repeated her belief in drama as purveyor of virtue in a novel she published the following year, **Mary; or, the Test of Honour.** The title character, an avid theatergoer, calls for moral drama:

> Why are there such scenes represented on the stage as we should blush to see practiced in private life? Why cannot all their comedies be written in the same chaste style which some are? It appears to me highly improper to represent before an audience, the greatest part of which are composed of the youthful of both sexes, scenes of immoral tendency, which may not only be a means of leading them into numerous errors, but may corrupt and vitiate their minds in such a manner as to be an irreparable injury to the rising generation.
>
> (43)

Rowson held to her standards of moral taste, regardless of popular opinion. Hannah Cowley, for example, had written many plays that met with audience acclaim at both Drury Lane and Covent Garden, but Rowson did not approve of her works and did not fail to say so:

> Next Cowley approach'd, but Apollo looked down,
> While his features divine were deform'd by a frown;
> 'Hold, woman (he cried) approach not too near,
> 'I dictate no line that can wound the chaste ear;
> 'When your sex take the pen, it is shocking to find,
> 'From their writing loose thoughts have a place in
>   their mind.'
>
> (4)

A similar objection to Cowley was expressed in the *Gentleman's Magazine*.[4]

As for acting, Rowson's standard was naturalness, an ideal she sought in her own stage performances as well as in her literary productions. The semblance of natural behavior on stage was in the eighteenth century by no means a given, especially in performance of tragedy. The "roaring styles" of tragic representation had been replaced in the eighteenth century by an "indolently-dignified, monotonous declamation" which failed to distinguish one tragic character from another except by costume. Rowson would have agreed with this contemporary description of James Quin, who epitomized this style of acting:

> With very little variation of cadency, and in a deep, full tone, accompanied by a sawing kind of action, which had more of the senate than of the stage in it, he rolled out his heroics with an air of dignified indifference that seemed to disdain the plaudits that were bestowed upon him. Unable to express emotions, whether violent or tender, he was forced or languid in action and ponderous and sluggish in movement.[5]

Rowson and others who shared her preference for natural acting may have been influenced by David Garrick, who had sought to change this declamatory style of tragic performance. Garrick had endeavored to make tragic characters more real by introducing variety in their representation. He had tried to replace the conventional rhetorical techniques with individuality in characters that even the dullest audience could recognize as distinctive. As stage manager of Drury Lane for thirty years, he had tried to teach others his techniques, but his principles were slow to spread. Though Rowson had never seen Garrick, who had retired two years before her return to England, she adhered to at least some of his principles. "Make Nature your copy," she advised.

Another famous actor who had introduced realism into his characters was Charles Macklin. Rowson so enthusiastically approved of his techniques that she gave him an especially long section in her poem. "To dame Nature you've paid due regard," Rowson's Apollo said,

"And trod in the steps of my favourite bard." Apollo's "favourite bard" was of course Shakespeare, for Macklin had made his career with his portrayal of Shylock. Instead of playing the Jew as a comic buffoon, which had long been the tradition, Macklin made him an obstinate, passionate man—much like Macklin himself. This new interpretation had been enthusiastically received ever since Macklin had first played the role at Drury Lane in 1741. Macklin was still performing his Shylock even as he approached the age of eighty, and Rowson had seen and delighted in his creation:

> Could Shakespeare himself from the silent tomb rise,
> He'd view your performance with joyful surprise;
> And charm'd with your excellence, freely wou'd own,
> That Macklin in Shylock can ne'er be out-done.
>
> (10)

Perhaps her insistence upon a natural acting style influenced her preference for comic over tragic drama, for comic art, never having lapsed into stiff and colorless declamation, produced better acting. Rowson's preference for comedy may account for her association with Covent Garden, where more comedies than serious plays were being produced.

But Rowson was not so naive as to believe an actor could act "naturally" without concerted effort. "There is genius and judgment in acting required." She advised one aspiring young actress to perform with genuine feeling:

> . . . beauty alone will not do on the stage.
> You must have animation, must feel what you speak.
> Call a tear to your eye, or a blush to your cheek.
> It is wrong, on the stage, when performing a part,
> Like a school girl, to con o'er your lesson by heart.
> The merely repeating a speech will not do;
> You must feel it yourself, and make others feel too.
> A public performer must study to please,
> And for public applause, must give up their own ease.
> A task that's more difficult scarce can be known
> Than an actress to please the caprice of the town.
>
> (18)

Rowson may have learned the necessity of feeling a part intently from Sarah Siddons, who, it was said, never spoke a line on stage that she did not feel. Rowson found much to admire in the great Siddons, who combined beauty, talent, hard work, and an emotional commitment to her profession with a virtuous personal life.[6] As such personal role models seemed important to the young and ambitious Rowson, she later searched through history to find models for other young women.

In addition to presenting Rowson's theories of dramatic art, *A Trip to Parnassus* expressed her view of one contemporary issue, the opening of the Royalty Theatre. In this controversy Rowson sided conservatively with the established theaters and thus showed herself as the rather proper, conservative woman she would remain all

her life. The Royalty Theatre had been built in 1785 in Wellclose Square by John Palmer (1742-98), an actor whose career seemed dogged by misfortune.[7] Against the advice of theatrical friends, he opened on June 20, 1787. The managers of the three patent theaters so successfully fought his efforts to obtain the necessary licenses that the Royalty closed after the first performance. A pamphlet war ensued. On July 3 Palmer reopened for the performance of "pantomime and irregular pieces," anything not defined as a "play." Despite her interest in pantomime and light entertainment for the masses, Rowson frowned upon this arrangement, which attracted crowds and thereby reduced audiences at the large patent theaters. Others found nothing wrong with it, however, and several actors, among them one Mary Wells, left Covent Garden for a few weeks to take advantage of Palmer's extravagant salaries. To applauding Royalty audiences Mary Wells mimicked great actresses such as Siddons, but for her troubles she earned Rowson's condemnation. "She had never much claim to my favour," said Apollo.

> And her folly has made me abjure her for ever.
> Then angry commanded her hence to be hurl'd,
> And declar'd she had praises enough in the World.[8]
>
> (13)

Rowson described John Palmer himself as a "poor Pantomimical hero," whose youthful fame would wither with age (17). She was, unfortunately for Palmer, correct.

Despite the seriousness of much of *A Trip to Parnassus,* Rowson's tone throughout the poem was light. In the end she brought forward her narrator to direct the last laugh at herself. (Recall that in *The Inquisitor* she used the narrator as a main character throughout the book.) From the throng of dramatists and performers pressing to appear before Apollo, Rowson herself steps up to the god. That she who had as yet neither produced a play nor appeared on a London stage should dare to join the company of accomplished playwrights and actors suggests her courage and willingness to assert herself. But she knew her limits, felt a decorous modesty, and would go only so far. Rowson's Apollo rejects her narrator, though she is spared the actual sentence:

> He seem'd much offended, and gave me a look,
> To see it, the Muses themselves must have shook.
> Thick clouds gather'd round him, the hollow winds
>   howl'd,
> The blue lightnings flash'd, and the hoarse thunder
>   roll'd'
> I fell prostrate before him, and fain wou'd have spoke,
> But my fears were so great, that I trembling awoke.
>
> (26)

And thus the poem ends.

A Trip to Parnassus shows Rowson's early interest in and skill with rhyme. The poem uses full, near, and internal rhymes, and the lines contain simple sound patterns of assonance, consonance, and alliteration. But she attempted nothing more complicated, as her more natural mode was prose, not poetry, and though she published **Poems on Various Subjects**[9] in London the same year, she did not again attempt poetry for many years.

Perhaps because it was her first publication, Rowson published **A Trip to Parnassus** anonymously. She dedicated the book to Thomas Harris, manager of the Covent Garden theater, whose company provided the subject matter. She sold the manuscript to John Abraham, a relatively small publisher in St. Swithin's Lane, Lombard Street, London, who printed the book as a quarto and sold it for two shillings.

A Trip to Parnassus received a mildly favorable review in the *Monthly Review*:

> The plan of the "Session of the Poets," by Sir John Suckling, hath been adopted by many of the sons of Apollo, with various success, from Rochester and Mulgrave, down to the author of the "Children of Thespis," and the fair writer of this *poetical* dream: who is not the least successful of Suckling's imitators; and is a much better versifier than was Sir John—though Congreve styled him *natural* and easy.—In appreciating the respective merits of our present race of dramatic authors, and actors, she is careful to throw out no reflection on private characters; but, as public performers, whether in the closet or *on the boards,* she considers them as proper objects of critical investigation. . . .[10]

But the *Critical Review* of the same month judged her first effort more harshly. Calling her a fly without a sting, the reviewer disagreed with her evaluations of dramatists and actors but admitted that she was more inclined to praise than blame and would not "sacrifice each well-meaning candidate for fame, to raise a pile to some favourite idol of fashion or prejudice." Of her verse, the reviewer said, it had neither "gross defects" nor "striking beauties."[11]

AMERICAN PUBLICATIONS

SLAVES IN ALGIERS

As a member of Thomas Wignell's Philadelphia acting company, Rowson contributed her several skills. In addition to acting she wrote lyrics and plays. Her first American play, **Slaves in Algiers,** was hastily conceived and executed, taking no more than two months from conception to first performance. Thanks to one irate critic, however, the play received publicity for months.

Slaves in Algiers capitalized on current interest in attacks on American ships by Barbary pirates. Rowson had known in England of the piracy of the Barbary states, Algiers, Morocco, Tripoli, and Tunis. From her father she had long ago learned that the worst among them were the Algerians, and that their practice of capturing goods, ships, and men had gone on since English ships had first sailed the seas. Italian, Spanish, and German ships also suffered these attacks, not only in the Mediterranean but far into the Atlantic. By paying ransom, these nations had encouraged the piracy, and now the Barbary governments sought to extract the same blackmail from the United States. In America Rowson learned of the new nation's concern with the problem, for America had been losing ships and captives to Algerian pirates in the Mediterranean for about ten years. When the United States refused to pay tribute to the Dey of Algiers, American ships, like the English and Europeans before them, suffered degrading abuse. By the time Rowson arrived in Philadelphia, well over a hundred American sailors were enslaved in Algiers and more were being brought in weekly.

Rowson's play was not the only literary work to capitalize on the resentment Americans were feeling.[12] In 1787 Royall Tyler published *The Algerine Captive,* and in 1794 the bookseller Mathew Carey wrote *A Short Account of Algiers.* Rowson may have read Carey's forty-six page account, which contained a general description of Algeria, a chapter on customs and religion, another on the origin of the present government, and a discussion entitled "The State of America as to Algiers." Carey mentioned no names of particular places in Algiers, but he did refer to the many gardens and to the use of rows of fig trees for walls. Rowson set her scenes in palace gardens and hid her characters behind fig trees, but she too seemed only slightly acquainted or little concerned with specific facts about the nation. She did know that olives and figs grew there and that Jews lived among the Moors without discrimination. Rowson's interest, however, lay not in Algeria itself but in the subject of tyranny in general and of tyranny of men over women in particular. She used this popular topic to make her first feminist statement on stage.

The plot involves a beautiful young woman, Olivia, who has been captured by Algerian pirates and sold to Muley Moloc, the Dey of Algiers. The character of Olivia derived from the character of Semira the Greek in Rowson's earlier novel, **Mary; or, the Test of Honour,** and it seems significant that Rowson transformed her into an American for her American audience. Olivia's father, Constant, and her fiancé, Henry, have separately had themselves captured in attempts to free Olivia. To this story is added the subplot of Fetnah, the outspoken and courageous daughter of the Jew, Ben Hassan. Fetnah has been taught to love liberty and independence by Rebecca, an American woman prisoner to Ben Hassan. Fetnah falls in love with another Christian slave, Frederic, and longs to escape to democratic America with her Christian lover. All of these prisoners contrive an escape under the plan of Zoriana, the daughter of the Dey and a secret convert to Christianity. When

Olivia learns that Zoriana has fallen in love with her own fiancé Henry, Olivia decides not to try to escape with the others but to stay behind and sacrifice herself to the Dey's wrath. The escape fails, so Olivia, secretly planning suicide, offers herself in marriage to the Dey if he will permit her father and fiancé to go free. Suddenly a slave revolt leaves Muley Moloc helplessly surrounded, so he agrees to free all Algerian captives and provide for their passage home. Olivia is united with Henry, and in a standard recognition scene Rebecca finds her long-lost husband and daughter—none other than Constant and Olivia.

As this plot summary shows, the play was contrived, the characters stereotyped, and the language stilted, and yet it enjoyed a surprising popularity. It became a part of the repertoire of the Philadelphia company and was performed in Baltimore as well as in Philadelphia. Unlike most plays written during this period, *Slaves* was sufficiently well received to merit publication, and Rowson had it printed the same year it was first produced.[13]

How can the play's popularity be accounted for? Rowson's name alone could not have caused the play to succeed, even though she had a slight reputation as actress at the New Theater, and she had begun to create a reading public through republication of her earlier novels. A more likely factor would have been the topic of the play and its American chauvinism. Although Rowson created this play as a revision of a brief subplot from her earlier novel *Mary; or, The Test of Honour,* she altered it to appeal to an American audience. She changed the heroine from Semira, a captive Greek, to Olivia, a young American woman, and she made all the main characters American—patriotic Americans at that. Whereas in *A Test of Honour* England served as Rowson's symbol of liberty and democracy, in *Slaves* she transferred that symbol to America. She dedicated the printed version to "the citizens of the United-States of North-America." An additional appeal, at least for some audiences, was that the American chauvinism in the play served the larger purpose of celebrating the concept of freedom for all people. The plot involving prisoners for ransom permitted Rowson to contrast an oppressive with a free society:

> Who barters countrymen, honour, faith, to save
> His life, tho' free in person, is a slave.
> While he, enchan'd, imprison'd tho he be,
> Who lifts his arm for liberty, is free.[14]

Rowson's slave characters suffer the same longings for freedom as an imprisoned American feels. The author's comments about liberty would have been well received by democrats in the pit, at a time when feelings about the French Revolution still ran high.

Significantly, this political rhetoric did not occur in Rowson's novels and stories, nor was it found in novels by other authors before 1800, though it was found frequently in poetry and drama. The reading public in the United States at that time, thought to consist largely of young, unmarried women, was considerably smaller than the numbers who regularly attended the theater. That theater audience was comparatively unrestrained. They interrupted a musical number with demands to hear "Yankee Doodle," and threw gin bottles and orange peels if they did not get it. They loved to hear repeated praise for American patriotism and virtue.[15] Rowson had worked in the Chestnut Street Theater for only one year when she wrote *Slaves in Algiers,* but she was obviously sensitive to the nationalistic rhetoric and the demands of her theater audience.

Rowson carried her rhetoric about America and liberty a step further. If all men love and need freedom, then the same is true for women, and Rowson joined the love of political liberty with the love of sexual liberty. She put into the character of Fetnah her most outspoken comments on the position of women. Fetnah has been taught by another English woman captive and has herself come to believe in women's inequality:

> Woman was never formed to be the abject slave of man. Nature made us equal with them, and gave us the power to render ourselves superior.
>
> (1.1.9)

> . . . A woman can face danger with as much spirit, and as little fear as the bravest man amongst you.
>
> (3.1.47)

Fetnah objects particularly to her own sexual enslavement to a man she does not love, for, she claims, women as well as men love freedom:

> Woman when by nature drest
> In charms devoid of art
> Can warm the stoic's icy breast,
> Can triumph o'er each heart.
> Can bid the soul to virtue rise,
> To glory prompt the brave,
> But sinks oppress'd and drooping dies,
> When once she's made a slave.
>
> (1.1.10)

When asked if she does not love her master, Fetnah's reply indicates Rowson's rejection of sexual dominance or forced "love":

> No—he is old and ugly,—then he wears such tremendous whiskers, and when he makes love, he looks so grave and stately, that I declare, if it was not for his huge scymitar, I shou'd burst out a laughing in his face.
>
> (1.1.6)

Fetnah's enforced subservience makes the sexual relationship, emphasized with phallic symbolism, repugnant to her. She plainly states her objection to slavery:

I think I see him now . . . a long pipe in his mouth. Oh! how charmingly the tobacco must perfume his whiskers—here, Mustapha, says he, 'Go bid the slave Selima come to me'—well it does not signify,—I wonder how any woman of spirit can gulp it down.

(2.2.39)

Rowson did not here reject male sexuality but tyranny based on sex, the use of women as sexual commodities. Fetnah longs for both physical freedom from her position as slave and the freedom of a genuine sexual love. She wishes to go to America, where she dreams a woman does just as she pleases.

For 1794 this protest of sexual domination seemed audacious. Admittedly some discussion of women's rights had taken place; Mary Wollstonecraft's *Vindication of the Rights of Women* had been published in Philadelphia in 1792, and the subject of education for women occasionally served as the topic for a debate. But no one seriously considered any change in the status of women. Why did Rowson choose this play to make her most forthright assertions about the equality of women? Was she, in this hastily written drama, carried along by her own rhetoric about liberty, so that equal rights for women seemed a logical extension of her own argument? That would imply that Rowson was not entirely in control, and such a conclusion seems inconsistent with the Susanna Rowson who so carefully determined her life. A more likely theory is that Rowson constructed her political rhetoric as a vehicle for her feminist assertions.

In fact, a careful reading of the play indicates that she was not as patriotic as she might at first glance have seemed. Fetnah's line about America as a place where a woman does just as she pleases seems incredibly naive. The line assumes perspective when we recall that Fetnah is here dreaming of a country she knows only secondhand. She has never set foot outside Algiers. The American women who do know America speak only of the freedom offered to men: "Columbia's sons be free," and "A boy born in Columbia claims liberty as his birthright." The characters seem unconscious of the irony, but Rowson was not.

Because of her position in a theater company, Rowson was able to have her play performed a number of times. It was first presented on June 30, 1794 and then repeated as a popular stock piece when the company performed in Baltimore and New York.[16] By November, 1795, Rowson had shortened the play for use as an afterpiece.[17] Cutting the play would have intensified the comic elements, which Rowson had made effective by writing parts for particular actors. She wrote the role of the drunken Spaniard Sebastian, for example, for the experienced low comedian Billy Bates, who specialized in pantomime. Sebastian drew applause with a boisterous rhythmic drinking song that lent itself to pantomime. (The music to the play has not been preserved.) Rowson created the other roles for other company members: Ben Hassan was played by the ballet master, William Francis, and the young Moreton played Frederic. The role of Rebecca's son was acted by the son of the Warrells, one of the families in the company. The role of Fetnah, the opinionated and daring slave, was played by Mrs. Marshall, one of Wignell's most talented actresses; and Rebecca and Constant, who in the end discover themselves wife and husband, were played by Mr. and Mrs. Whitlock. Eliza Whitlock, a large, heavy woman, suited the maternal role. Rowson herself played Olivia, Rebecca's daughter. Though Rowson at thirty-two was beginning to grow heavy, she relished the part and spoke with feeling the final lines of the play:

May Freedom spread her benign influence thro' every nation, till the bright Eagle, united with the dove and olive branch, wave high, the acknowledged standard of the world.

(3.7.72)

With **Slaves in Algiers,** Rowson entered the mainstream of popular American culture. Americans were demanding new plays; theater managers had to meet those demands. As an actress Rowson found herself in a position to satisfy both the needs of her theater manager and the needs of her audience. She knew what her audience wanted, and she knew the limitations of her company. Though English, she had no trouble adapting herself to the new nationalistic rhetoric, for she believed in democratic ideals as firmly as if she had been a third-generation patriot. She felt no disloyalty in celebrating American freedom, and she was not the only English playwright to do so. In fact, American audiences liked these English actors and actresses who constituted the majority of the theater companies, and they seemed to prefer plays by English, rather than American, playwrights.[18] Other English actors and actresses who wrote plays during this decade were J. Robinson, a comedian in the Old American Company who wrote and published *The Yorker's Strategy; or, Banana's Wedding* (1792), a popular farce; James Fennell, in Rowson's own Philadelphia company, who wrote *The Advertisement; or, a New Way to Get Married* (1798); John Beete, an actor in Charleston; and John B. Williamson, for whom Rowson was later to work.[19]

Though Rowson knew of other Englishmen writing plays for the American stage, she knew of few other women.[20] The one other woman who did write a play during this time could not have lent Rowson much encouragement. Three months before **Slaves in Algiers** appeared, Anne Kemble Hatton produced *Tammany; or, The Indian Chief,* in New York. Hatton was one of the numerous Kemble offspring, a sister of Sarah Siddons, and she had arrived in New York about the same time as Rowson had arrived in Philadelphia. Seizing upon a local issue, Hatton produced the play under the auspices of the Tammany Society at the John Street Theater. The play received praise from the Republicans and the Irish who supported the Tammany Society, but its opening night aroused enough antagonism to interrupt the performance. Federalist critics objected to its "popular notions of liberty,"[21] but at least the music merited publication. Thus Rowson had precedent for writing, as a woman, a topical play on a nationalistic note, but that did not spare her from criticism.

Although theater reviews as we know them today were almost nonexistent in the 1790s, Rowson's published play elicited one reaction—not so much a review as a political debate. On March 6, 1795, William Cobbett, the pamphleteer, published *A Kick for a Bite,* commenting on a number of subjects and signed "Peter Porcupine," Cobbett's first use of this pseudonym. He addressed the article to Samuel Harrison Smith, publisher of the *American Literary Review,* and included this castigation of Smith:

> . . . what excuse have you for having omitted to take notice of the voluminous productions of the celebrated Mrs. Rowson? Sins of omission were ever expiable when a lady is in the case; the fair do generally in the long run, pardon sins of commission, but those of omission they never do. Indeed, Sir, it was giving them but a pitiful idea of your gallantry, to slip by without casting a single glance at our American Sappho.[22]

Cobbett then offered his "Review on the roma-drama-poetic works of Mrs. Susanna Rowson of the New Theatre, Philadelphia." Since space did not permit him to analyze all of her performances, he wrote that he must content himself with extracts from **Slaves in Algiers,** which "may be looked upon as a criterion of her style and manner."

William Cobbett, an Englishman, had spent a few years in France before emigrating to Philadelphia at the same time Rowson arrived. During his fourteen months in Delaware as a teacher of French, he had cultivated an animosity toward things American. He had returned to Philadelphia the same month that the New Theater opened and had seen Rowson in several productions there. He had read her books and had seen her "poetical address," **"The Standard of Liberty,"** performed in Baltimore.

Rowson epitomized all that Cobbett abhorred in women; her role as actress made her life public and her writings sought to pass her ideas on to others. When she went so far as to announce from the Philadelphia stage the superiority of women over men, Cobbett's ire would not be contained. Though he protested against her figures of speech and her grammar, his real objection was clearly her feminism. He attacked Rowson's vanity for claiming women's equality with men. As for the couplet from the epilogue, "Women were born for universal sway / Men to adore, be silent, and obey," he asserted, "Sentiments like these could not be otherwise than well received in a country, where the authority of the wife is so universally acknowledged." He anticipated, he said, a House of Representatives constituted entirely of women. To discredit Rowson personally, he intimated the adulterous behavior of people in the theater.

Cobbett's second main objective was to the patriotic language of the play. Cobbett was an arch-Federalist, and this attack on Rowson's democratic principles anticipated his attacks on the Republican Mathew Carey and others. Cobbett claimed to disbelieve in what he called Rowson's sudden conversion to republicanism. Her use of the word *liberty* particularly rankled:

> Is not the sound of Liberty, glorious Liberty! heard to ring from one end of the continent to the other? . . . What else is heard in the senate, the pulpit, the jail, the parlour, the kitchen, and the cradle?[23]

Rowson thus became one of the first of an impressive list of Cobbett's pamphlet targets, which included Benjamin Rush, Thomas Paine, Benjamin Franklin, Albert Gallatin, Edmund Randolph, and James Monroe. Abigail Adams described Cobbett as "low and vulgar as a fishwife,"[24] and Nathaniel Hawthorne spoke of "the ferocity of the true bloodhound of literature—such as Swift, Churchill, or Cobbett—which fastens upon the throat of the victim, and would fain drink his life-blood."[25] But Rowson, like so many of Cobbett's later targets, had a reputation and a popular following, so it did not take long for a defender to appear.

John Swanwick (1740-1798), congressman from Pennsylvania, published his first defense of Rowson and attack on Cobbett in a pamphlet entitled *A Rub from Snub: A Cursory Epistle: Addressed to Peter Porcupine Containing Glad Tidings for the Democrats and A Word of Comfort to Mrs. Rowson.* As a politician with literary interests, Swanwick had written a number of pamphlets and was well acquainted with Rowson and her works. He sized up Cobbett accurately. "This 'review,' as you term it, appears to be merely an expletive, in order to swell your pamphlet to a more respectable bulk. . . ." Swanwick then returned Cobbett's fire with vindictiveness. He called Cobbett "Mr. Hedge-Hog" and defined him as an ass with prickly skin. He denied Cobbett's qualifications as critic and faulted him for waiting for months after the play's first production. Despite Swanwick's good intentions toward Rowson, his counter to Cobbett's attack on Rowson's feminism suggests even Swanwick did not take the statements in her play seriously. He described some of Rowson's comments as only fun:

> merely a sally of humor, intended to create a smile, and not to enforce a conviction of women's superiority. In all polite circles (with which I presume you [William

Cobbett] have little intercourse) the superiority is always ascribed to women, when in fact they may possess an inferiority.[26]

But Swanwick by no means shared Cobbett's view of woman as drudge. He believed that the distinctions between the sexes were based on "customs and manners," and that a male education would qualify a woman for "all the duties of a man."

Swanwick also defended Rowson's praise of "charity, friendship, and philanthropy" as attributes of the American character. He confessed that he did not know Rowson personally and hoped she would not find his vindication officious or presumptuous but would take it "as a candid eulogium to the intrinsic merit of works which we cannot sufficiently applaud." He then recommended that Rowson ignore Cobbett, not condescend to reply to him, and should she "indulge her audience with another epilogue at her next benefit I would particularly advise her not to mention . . . [Cobbett's] name."

As for Cobbett, Swanwick warned him against future attacks on Rowson in terms of suggesting Swanwick had heard of Rowson's temper:

> Should you provoke the vengeance of Rowson, you would stand no more chance than insects beneath a discharge of thunderbolts. Whippets that seize the heels of horses often get their brains kicked out.[27]

Indeed Rowson had a fierce temper when provoked, but just now she contained her anger. She knew that such publicity as both Cobbett and Swanwick provided could only benefit sales of her novels and plays as well as box office sales at the New Theater. She knew too that to condescend to become a pamphleteer would invite more criticism, perhaps from those more respected than William Cobbett. And so, at least publicly, she withheld her temper.

In keeping with her public image of a dignified and morally upright actress, she restrained her reply, limiting it to a single defense in the preface of her upcoming novel, *Trials of the Human Heart*:

> It is with reluctance I find myself obliged to remark that the literary world is infested with a kind of loathsome reptile, of the class of non-descripts, for it cannot be ranked, with propriety among either authors or critics, not possessing the qualifications necessary to form either, and being in itself remarkable for nothing but its noxious qualities: its only aim is to prevent the success of any work of genius; and swelling with envy, should the smallest part of public favour, be conferred on another, spits out its malignant poison, in scurrility and detraction. One of these noisome reptiles, has lately crawled over the volumes, which I have had the temerity to submit to the public eye. I say *crawled* because I am certain it has never penetrated beyond the title of any.[28]

Rowson called all of Cobbett's allegations "false and scurrilous," and to demonstrate how her loyalties had grown "equally attached" to both Great Britain and the United States, she used the metaphor of a family:

> The unhappy dissentions affected me in the same manner as a person may be imagined to feel, who having a tender lover, and an affectionate brother who are equally dear to her heart . . . sees them engaged in a quarrel with, and fighting against each other, when let whichsoever party conquer, she cannot be supposed insensible to the fate of the vanquished.

(xviii-xix)

Rowson remained silent about Cobbett's attacks on her feminism. To proclaim female superiority in the context of a play was one thing, but to defend that proclamation in the clear light of a preface was another. The dramatic work had served its purpose. She had stated her position and had gained publicity by being attacked and defended.

Cobbett, however, loved the fray, and he entered the arena again in May with a reply to Swanwick entitled "A Bone to Gnaw for the Democrats. Part II."[29] He prefaced this essay by saying that readers would not get from him "an answer to citizen Scrub" because "I hate controversy more, if possible, than I do sans-culottism." Though most of the pamphlet ridiculed Swanwick, Cobbett's only reference to Rowson was the protest that his motive had been to "deliver her unfortunate play, *The Slaves in Algiers,* from obscurity."

The following year Swanwick published two other pamphlets condemning Cobbett, *British Honour and Humanity; or the Wonders of American Patience* and *A Roaster; or a Check to the Progress of Political Blasphemy intended as a brief reply to Peter Porcupine.*[30] The latter contained no reference to Rowson, and the first one briefly alluded to Cobbett's "furious attack" on *Slaves in Algiers.*

OTHER PLAYS.

So ended Rowson's only venture into politics. She did not like the strident voice of pamphlet politics and in the future avoided such controversy. She refused, however, to let Cobbett prevent her from writing plays about political events. Her next play dealt with the so-called Whisky Rebellion, an outbreak in southwestern Pennsylvania which occurred in the fall of 1794, as farmers resisted the federal excise tax. The play was entitled *The Volunteers.* In defiance of Cobbett's objection to her use of the word *liberty,* Rowson wrote lyrics that exuberantly celebrated liberty. The volunteers, that is, the militia called by Washington to enforce the law, sing of love, of the joys of simple frontier life, and of their American freedom.[31]

For this play, or "musical entertainment" as it was described, Rowson collaborated with Wignell's comanager of the New Theater, Alexander Reinagle.[32] Rowson had warmed to Reinagle as soon as they met and discovered they both came from Portsmouth, England. Six years older that she, Reinagle had come to the United States in 1786, while Rowson was entering the world of the English theater. Reinagle had lived first in New York, teaching pianoforte, harpsichord, and violin. He had moved to Philadelphia in 1786 and since then had been sponsoring "city concerts" and giving music lessons. His connections with leading Philadelphia families had greatly promoted the theater since 1791, when he became the theater comanager. Reinagle had found his theater responsibilities gratifying, for he and Wignell shared a belief in the importance of music on the public stage. Together they were offering the Philadelphia public more musical productions than any other theater, and Reinagle was writing music for all productions as well as directing the twenty-five member orchestra. Rowson responded enthusiastically to Reinagle's love of music and found him a demanding but dignified man with whom to work. He welcomed her eagerness to write musical numbers, and very shortly after the company opened they began to collaborate. By mid-March they had produced the popular **"America, Commerce, and Freedom,"** for the ballet pantomime *The Sailor's Landlady.* Then they wrote a new song for an old work, **"A Soldier is the Noblest Name,"** for the O'Keefe opera *The Highland Reel.* By mid-April when Rowson approached Reinagle with her proposed *Slaves in Algiers,* they were experienced collaborators. Although today these numbers are the only extant songs by Rowson and Reinagle, the pair undoubtedly wrote others. Reinagle constantly searched for more musical material, and he found in Rowson a company member who could write lyrics as readily as she could sing them.

The score remains the only extant part of *The Volunteers,* and it is located in the Library of Congress. It consists of thirteen songs by Rowson and Reinagle and one borrowed from a London song published three years earlier. The Rowson/Reinagle numbers are of a sort that would easily become popular with theater audiences, light, simple melodies in major keys. This duet opens the ballad-opera:

THOMAS:

> Here beneath our lowly Cott
> Tranquil peace and pleasure dwell
> If contented with out lot
> Smiling Joy can grace excel.

JEMIMA:

> Natures wants are all supply'd
> Food and raiment, house and fire,
> Let others swell the courts of pride
> This is all that we require.

THOMAS:

> When day just glimmers in the east
> Blythesome we leave our humble bed
> Chearful at night partake the feast
> By bounteous nature kindly spread.

JEMIMA:

> We'll chearful our endeavours blend,
> Yes ev'ry future moment spend

BOTH:

> To make your time pass cheerily
> To make your time pass cheerily.

Other songs include delicate love lyrics, humorous numbers, and a lively soldier's song.

Another play of Rowson's, *The Female Patriot; or, Nature's Rights,* was performed by the company some time in 1794.[33] No known copy exists, and indeed the play, like most at the time, may never have been printed. The title suggests that Rowson continued her feminist theme in this play, which she based on Philip Massinger's *The Bondman,* keeping many of Massinger's characters. Massinger's popular Jacobean comedy, like *Slaves in Algiers,* concerns a slave revolt and a female hero. *The Female Patriot* apparently included no music. For her benefit night on June 17, 1796, Rowson wrote another play, *The American Tar, or the Press Gang Defeated.*[34] As with *Slaves in Algiers* and *The Volunteers,* this "ballet," as it was subtitled, was based on a current event, a "recent fact at Liverpool." For the music Rowson collaborated with Raynor Taylor, another emigrant musician, previously music director at Sadler's Wells Theatre in London, and a friend and teacher of Alexander Reinagle.[35] As this production called for little actual acting, Rowson wrote parts for both her husband and her husband's sister, Charlotte—a treat for them, since William Rowson seldom performed on the Philadelphia stage, and Charlotte, young and not greatly talented, usually performed only minor roles. William sang "Independent and Free," a number that became quite popular. *The American Tar* was probably an adaptation from a work by Jacob Morton and was probably never published; no known copy exists today. Rowson sold or gave the rights to this play to the actor and manager-partner of the Old American Company, John Hodgkinson, who produced and performed in the play at the opening of the Park Street Theater on January 29, 1798.[36]

When Rowson moved to Boston she continued her dramatic writing in addition to her writing of fiction. Her comedy, *Americans in England; or Lessons for Daughters,* was first performed on April 19, 1797.[37] Only the list of characters remains to tantalize the dramatic historian today. The English characters' names imply their English eccentricities: Courtland, Frolic, Snap, Waiter,

Jack, and Arabella Acorn; while the American characters convey sturdy American qualities: Ezekiel Plainly, Horace Winship, Jemima Winship. Rowson herself played the roles of Mrs. Ormsby and Jemima Winship, the heroine, and she again wrote roles for her husband and sister-in-law. The title and list of characters suggest that the play praised the United States through a strong-minded woman, a daughter of Columbia, played by the author. The Boston audience received the play enthusiastically, delaying Rowson's delivery of the epilogue with their applause and following her exit with three "distinct plaudits," according to an anonymous review in the *Massachusetts Mercury* of April 21, 1797.[38] Despite this reception Rowson made no money from the production, so she gave the rights to John Hodgkinson, who renamed it *The Columbia Daughter: or, Americans in England* and used it for his benefit at the New York Mt. Vernon Gardens Theater on September 10, 1800.

Song Lyrics

Rowson's Philadelphia musical contacts provided her with a ready introduction into the musical circles of Boston, and within a short time after her arrival there she had met the musicians of the day, again English and European immigrants: Samuel Arnold, Oliver Holden, James Hewitt, Peter Van Hagen, and Gottlieb Graupner. Of these, Hewitt, Arnold, and Graupner came from the theater; Peter Van Hagen taught music both at his own music school and later for Rowson's Boston Academy while operating a music store with his son. Rowson soon began writing lyrics for the songs of these composers and for others. She wrote a variety of songs, love songs, sea chanties, and patriotic numbers.

When Benjamin Carr, whom she had met in Philadelphia, came to Boston in 1797 or 1798, he composed the music for Rowson's **"In Vain is the Verdure of Spring,"** a love song published in Philadelphia in 1798. This song typifies her pastoral love songs:

> Restrain'd from the sight of my dear
> No object with pleasure I see
> Tho' thousands around me appear
> The world's but a desert to me.
> In vain is the verdure of spring
> The trees look so blooming and gay
> The Birds as they whistle and sing
> The Birds as they whistle and sing
> Delight not when William's away. . . .[39]

This song achieved some popularity and was reprinted in several collections.

Many of Rowson's love songs, however, are of a different sort and do not convey the sweet innocence of **"Willy of the Dale"** or **"In Vain is the Verdure of Spring."** Often they reflect an impertinence: **"I Never Will Be Married, I'd Rather Be Excus'd."** Typical of these is **"He is Not Worth the Trouble"**:

> Ye Maidens then beware of men,
>   They're all alike believe me,
> They all proceed on Damon's plan
>   And flatter to deceive ye.
> Then let not love your senses blind,
> For should you meet one to your mind,
>   And marry! ten to one you'll find,
>   He is not worth the trouble.[40]

Carr also wrote the music for Rowson's **"The Little Sailor Boy,"** which he took back with him to Philadelphia to have Rowson's ex-colleagues in the Chestnut Street Theater company sing in Philadelphia, Baltimore, and New York. Benjamin Carr printed and sold it as sheet music as did his father, Joseph Carr, in Baltimore, and their fellow musician and music publisher, James Hewitt, in New York. This song falls somewhere between Rowson's love songs and her sea chanties, being a love song about a boy away at sea. The lyrics might have been prompted either by her half brother William or by her husband's natural son, whom she raised. The poignancy of the lyrics and the simple tune made the song popular in east coast cities and towns. Even in this maritime love song Rowson inserted a word about tyranny:

> Oh may he never be compell'd
> To cringe to pow'r or mix with Slaves;
> May love and Peace his steps attend,
> Each future hour be wing'd with Joy,
> Like that when I again shall meet
> My much lov'd little Sailor Boy.[41]

Love songs, however, were not Rowson's favorite genre. She excelled at sea chanties, with rollicking, quick-moving rhythms and boisterous lyrics, atypical of women's poetry. **"America, Commerce, and Freedom"** was one of the most popular of this genre, written originally for the ballet pantomime, *The Sailor's Landlady* in 1794. The third stanza reflects the sailor's language and attitudes Rowson had picked up from her family and family friends:

> Our prizes sold, the chink we share,
>   And gladly we receive it;
> And when we meet a brother tar,
>   That wants, we freely give it;
> No freeborn sailor yet had store,
>   But cheerfully would lend it;
> And when 'tis gone—to sea for more:
>   We earn it but to spend it.
> Then drink round, my boys, 'tis the first of our joys,
>   To relieve the distress'd, clothe, and feed 'em;
> 'Tis a duty we share with the brave and the fair,
>   In this land of Commerce and Freedom.[42]

Each verse contains a reference to drinking, both by sailors and by their "bonnie lasses," and this song remained popular for years in the New England area.

Notes

1. *A Trip to Parnassus* (London, 1788); hereafter page references cited in parentheses in the text.

2. See W. P. Courtney, "Edward Topham," *DNB* [*Dictionary of National Biography*] (1909). The asterisk referred to Rowson's footnote identifying Topham by name.

3. *DNB* (1909), s.v. "George Colman."

4. Tompkins, *The Popular Novel in England,* 125.

5. Quoted in Karl Mantzius, *History of Theatrical Art in Ancient and Modern Times,* trans. Louise von Cossel (1909: reprint, Gloucester: Peter Smith, 1979), 5:368.

6. See Roger Manvell's *Sarah Siddons: Portrait of an Actress* (New York: Putnam, 1971).

7. *The Thespian Dictionary, or Dramatic Biography of the Eighteenth Century* (London: J. Cundee, 1805), n.p.

8. *The World* was a newspaper run by Edward Topham, the playwright and journalist with whom Wells had been living for several years.

9. *Poems on Various Subjects* (London, 1788). No known copy exists.

10. *Monthly Review* (March, 1788), 241.

11. *Critical Review* (March, 1788), 225.

12. Another dramatist's work on the same topic as Rowson's *Slaves in Algiers* shows that interest in the subject remained high for several years after her play. *Slaves in Barbary* by Caleb Bingham dealt with a slave auction in Tunis, with the dialogue a debate between a slaver and the more humanitarian Bashaw of Tunis. This play was never performed but was published in *The Columbian Orator* in 1797. For a discussion of the play, see Walter J. Meserve, *An Emerging Entertainment: The Drama of the American People to 1828* (Bloomington, 1977), 156.

13. Charles Evans, *American Bibliography* (Chicago: Blakely Press, 1925) lists a second printing in 1796 but no known copies exist. Mathew Carey intended to include the play in a 1796 collection of American drama, but it is not known whether that intention ever materialized. See Roger Stoddard, "Some Corrigenda and addenda to Hill's American Plays Printed 1714-1830," *Papers of the Bibliographical Society of America* 65 (1971):278-95.

14. *Slaves in Algiers* (Philadelphia, 1794) 1.1.2; hereafter references to act, scene, and line cited in the text.

15. The most popular play of the period was John Daly Burke's *Bunker Hill; or the Death of General Warren,* which first appeared at the Boston Haymarket on February 17, 1797. Despite its flat characters, pompous blank verse, disjointed plot, and propagandistic speeches, the play enjoyed tremendous success, in part because audiences loved its spectacle. The production required construction of an actual hill which eighteen or twenty British could roll down when fired upon. It ended with a "Grand Procession in honor of General Warren," with "American music only" played between acts. See Meserve, *Emerging Entertainment,* 119-23.

16. George O. Seilhamer, *History of the American Theatre from 1774-1797* (New York: Harper, 1896), 3:182.

17. The *Baltimore Telegraph* of November 26, 1795, advertised it on the same program as *A Bold Stroke for a Husband* by Hannah Cowley.

18. Wignell's company was composed entirely of new English immigrants with the exception of one couple, Mr. and Mrs. Morris, and himself. Meserve (*Emerging Entertainment,* 127-28) concludes that theater Meserve (*Emerging Entertainment,* 127-28) concludes that theater managers, themselves usually British, discriminated against American playwrights.

19. Meserve (*Emerging Entertainment,* 127-62) discusses plays and playwrights of this period.

20. Judith Sargent Murray wrote anonymous plays but refused to sign her name or even acknowledge them as her own.

21. "Calm Observer," *Daily Advertiser,* March 7, 1794, quoted in Meserve, *Emerging Entertainment,* 140.

22. William Cobbett, *A Kick for a Bite; or a Review Upon a Review; with a Critical Essay on the Works of Mrs. Rowson: in a letter to the editors of the American Monthly Review* (Philadelphia: Thomas Bradford, 1795), 78.

23. Ibid., 90.

24. Page Smith, *John Adams* (Garden City: Doubleday, 1956), 956.

25. *The Complete Works of Nathaniel Hawthorne* (Boston: Houghton Mifflin, 1883), 7:255-56.

26. John Swanwick, *A Rub from Snub* (Philadelphia: Printed for the Purchaser, 1795), 76.

27. Ibid., 79, 77.

28. *Trials of the Human Heart* (Philadelphia, 1795), xiii-xiv; hereafter page numbers cited in parentheses in the text.

29. Part I had appeared on January 8, 1795, as an answer to a brochure published in England by James

Thomson Callendar, an attack on church and state which got Callendar arrested. Cobbett's "Bone to Gnaw" had relied chiefly on personal abuse of Callendar, which attack elicited a review by Smith in his *American Monthly Review,* which in turn was attacked by Cobbett in "A Kick for a Bite."

30. Evans's *American Bibliography* attributes these anonymous pamphlets to Swanwick.

31. The script of the play has been lost, but the lyrics and score are in the Library of Congress.

32. For biography, see Ernst C. Krohn, "Alexander Reinagle," *DNB* (1935); Charles Durang, *History of the Philadelphia Stage between the Years 1749 and 1855* (Philadelphia, 1868), 1:35; and Julian Mates, *The American Musical Stage Before 1800* (New Brunswick, 1962), 35.

33. See Vail, *Bibliographical Study,* for evidence that the play was also performed on June 19, 1795 for the Rowsons' benefit night.

34. Benefit nights were held annually to supplement actors' salaries; the actor honored for the evening could advertise and sell tickets in any way she or he chose and kept all proceeds from the evening's performance. Rowson apparently wrote her own production for each of her benefit nights, including roles for her husband in all of them.

35. The dancing for *The American Tar* was choreographed by William Francis.

36. Joseph Ireland, *Records of the New York Stage* (New York, 1866), 1:174.

37. See Vail, *Bibliographical Study,* 161.

38. Anon., "Theatrical," *Massachusetts Mercury,* April 21, 1797, n.p.

39. "In Vain is the Verdure of Spring," [Philadelphia]: G. Willey, [1797-98?].

40. "He is Not Worth the Trouble," written by Mrs. Rowson. Composed by J. Jewitt (Boston: J. Hewitt, n.d.).

41. *A Ballad Sung at the Theatres and Other Public Places in Philadelphia, Baltimore, New York etc. by Messrs. Daly, Williamson, Miss Broadhurst, M. Hodgkinson. Written by Mrs. Rowson. Composed by B. Carr* (Philadelphia); Printed and sold at the Authors Music Repository (Baltimore: J. Carr, and New York: J. Hewitt, [1798]).

42. "America, Commerce, and Freedom" (Philadelphia: Carr's Musical Repository, [1794]).

Selected Bibliography

PRIMARY SOURCES

1. NOVELS

Charlotte: A Tale of Truth. London: William Lane, 1791.

Charlotte's Daughter; or, The Three Orphans. A Sequel to Charlotte Temple. To Which is Prefixed, A Memoir of the Author. Boston: Richardson & Lord, 1828.

The Fille de Chambre. London: William Lane, 1792.

The Inquisitor; or Invisible Rambler. London: G. G. J. & J. Robinson, 1788.

Mentoria; or the Young Lady's Friend. London: William Lane, [1791].

Reuben and Rachel; or, The Tales of Old Times. Boston: Manning & Loring, 1798.

Sarah, or The Exemplary Wife. Boston: Charles Williams, 1813.

Trials of the Human Heart. Philadelphia: Wrigley & Berriman, 1795.

Victoria, A Novel. In Two Volumes. The Characters Taken from Real Life, and Calculated to Improve the Morals of the Female Sex, By Impressing Them with a Just Sense of the Merits of Filial Piety. London: J. P. Cooke, 1786.

2. DRAMATIC WORKS

The American Tar, or the Press Gang Defeated. [Performed in Philadelphia June 17, 1796. Probably never published.]

Americans in England; or, Lessons for Daughters. A Comedy. Boston: n.p., 1796. [No copy known.]

The Female Patriot; or, Nature's Rights. Philadelphia: n.p., 1794. [No copy known.]

Hearts of Oak. [Boston: n.p., 1810-11. Probably not published.]

Slaves in Algiers; or, a Struggle for Freedom: A Play Interspersed with Songs. Philadelphia: Wrigley & Berriman, 1794.

The Standard of Liberty: a Poetical Address. Baltimore: n.p., 1795. [No copy known.]

A Trip to Parnassus; or, the Judgment of Apollo on Dramatic Authors and Performers. A Poem. London: John Abraham, 1788.

The Volunteers. Philadelphia: Printed for the Author, [1795].

3. EDUCATIONAL WRITINGS

An Abridgment of Universal Geography, Together with Sketches of History. Designed for the Use of Schools and Academies in the United States. Boston: John West, [1805].

Biblical Dialogues Between a Father and His Family: Comprising Sacred History, From the Creation to the Death of our Saviour Christ. The Lives of the Apostles, and the Promulgation of the Gospel; with a Sketch of the History of the Church down to the Reformation. The Whole Carried on in Conjunction with Profane History. Boston: Richardson & Lord, 1822.

Exercises in History, Chronology, and Biography, in Question and Answer. For the Use of Schools. Comprising Ancient History, Greece, Rome, & c. Modern History, England, France, Spain, Portugal, & c. The Discovery of America, Rise, Progress and Final Independence of the United States. Boston: Richardson & Lord, 1822.

A Present for Young Ladies; Containing Poems, Dialogues, Addresses, & c. As Recited by the Pupils of Mrs. Rowson's Academy, at the Annual Exhibitions. Boston: John West, 1811.

A Spelling Dictionary, Divided into Short Lessons, for the Easier Committing to Memory by Children and Young Persons; and Calculated to Assist Youth in Comprehending What They Read. Boston: John West, 1807.

Youth's First Steps in Geography. Being a Series of Exercises Making the Tour of the Habitable Globe. For the Use of Schools. Boston: Wells & Lilly, 1818.

4. POETICAL WORKS

Miscellaneous Poems. Boston: Gilbert & Dean, 1804.

Poems on Various Subjects. London: G. G. J. & J. Robinson, 1788. [No copy known.]

SECONDARY SOURCES

1. BIBLIOGRAPHIES

Parker, Patricia L. *Early American Fiction: A Reference Guide.* Boston: G. K. Hall, 1984. [Annotated bibliography of critical works.]

Vail, Robert W. G. *Susanna Haswell Rowson, The Author of Charlotte Temple. A Bibliographical Study.* Worcester: American Antiquarian Society, 1933. [Lists editions of Rowson's works.]

2. BOOKS AND PARTS OF BOOKS

Meserve, Walter J. *An Emerging Entertainment: The Drama of the American People to 1828.* Bloomington: Indiana University Press, 1977.

Tompkins, Joyce M. S. *The Popular Novel in England 1770-1800.* London: Constable, 1933.

Blythe Forcey (essay date June 1991)

SOURCE: Forcey, Blythe. "*Charlotte Temple* and the End of Epistolary." *American Literature* 63, no. 2 (June 1991): 225-41.

[*In the following essay, Forcey examines the reasons for Rowson's contemporaries' preference for her narrative, rather than epistolary, approach in* Charlotte Temple, *and asserts that this reception led to the subsequent popularity of the American domestic novel.*]

One of the few universally acknowledged truths of modern literary studies is that the roots of the British and, by extension, American novel can be traced to the epistolary form. What has not been adequately explained, however, is why the effective lifespan of this form was nearly as brief as those of its typically benighted heroines. I propose that the epistolary novel could not survive as a dominant form because, in the fast-changing, polyglot world of late eighteenth-century Anglo-America, it fell victim to the same forces of seduction and betrayal that its heroines were unable to avoid. *Charlotte Temple,* with a traditional Richardsonian plot and an authoritative, unifying narrative voice, exposes the forces that combined to render the epistolary novel obsolete.

I

In 1794, when *Charlotte Temple* emerged as America's first publishing sensation, the new nation was changing and growing at an unprecedented rate.[1] New York City, for example, more than doubled its population in the forty years between 1749 and 1789.[2] Even though over seventy-five percent of the white population was of English, Scotch, or Irish origin, and most were Protestant, the community did not feel homogeneous or stable. This majority was highly mobile and various, a significant portion of it was made up of recent immigrants, and it was constantly blended with other groups. The remaining white twenty-five percent was a dynamic blend of mostly German, French, Dutch, and Spanish. Also present, and even more volatile, was a large minority of Black slaves, indentured servants, and Native Americans. New people were arriving in the cities each day from Europe and the surrounding rural communities. Some of these new people stayed for a while, some moved on. Most of the people who did stay in the cities had only known a rural way of life, and a majority of them had been born in Europe.

Of this diverse and disoriented population, the actual readers were usually young and at least as likely to be female as male. As one commentator points out, "because of the high mortality rate during the Revolutionary War and the population explosion in its aftermath, by the first decades of the nineteenth century, a full two-thirds of the white population of America was under the age of twenty-four. Furthermore, because of the increasing attention to childhood education in the later part of the eighteenth century, young people, especially women, tended to be more literate than old people."[3]

However, even those early American readers who were anything but innocent young girls could have found much to identify with in *Charlotte Temple.* The revolution just over, a new government laboring to gain support and control, and all foundations seemingly left behind, fears of chaos, rootlessness, and abandonment dominated.[4] Most potential readers, even those seemingly least likely to identify with Charlotte Temple—battle-scarred old soldiers, jaded prostitutes, sophisticated society matrons, successful merchants, or ambitious young entrepreneurs—would still have been affected by the pervasive sense of "homelessness." The general mood was one of distrust, alienation, and isolation, which was exaggerated by a nostalgic idealization of a supposedly stable, communal, and cooperative colonial or European past.[5]

Thus, the anonymity and volatility of the New World created many new freedoms and, along with them, many new problems. No longer could all Americans know their neighbors; class boundaries were blurred; channels of authority shifted; and, as a result, the force of community could not be relied upon to provide effective social control. Without a recognizable common community, correspondence between individuals could not be assumed; coming from many different places, people did not necessarily speak in the same idiom; misreading of even the simplest exchanges became very possible, and an individual could not anticipate the rules on which a social encounter would be based.[6] Neither the ways nor the words of the Old World appeared to work in their original form. For most early Americans, the passage from Old World to New had brought on many unexpected and frightening changes to which they were struggling to adapt. *Charlotte Temple* could be read by the American reader as a parable of this very struggle, as it is a tale of a crossing that tears Charlotte Temple from her "mother country" and brings her to a New World where homelessness and foreignness define the conditions of her life.

II

With its warm, motherly narrator, *Charlotte Temple* tells a terrifying cautionary tale in a way that comfortably allows readers to approach and acknowledge their feelings of homelessness and rootlessness without ever feeling lost or abandoned. It conforms, externally, to "the commonest of all plots of the eighteenth-century Gothic novel," which, according to Marilyn Butler, "involves a frail protagonist in terrible danger." The result "is a nightmare, and perhaps the reason for its potent appeal is that it enables the reader to live vicariously through nightmare. . . . Facing up to one's fears is emotionally satisfying. Besides, there is something comforting, again almost magical, in anticipating the worst. It is a common intuition that the known evil never comes."[7] Early American readers were able, as they read this novel, to live through a nightmare of dislocation, alienation, and abandonment that mapped their worst fears. But, guided by the careful and caring narrative of Mrs. Rowson, they emerged safe and unscathed, with all troubling ambiguities and terrors temporarily put to rest.

The motherly character of Rowson's narrative voice is evident from her first addresses to the reader. In her preface, she states that it is "for the perusal of the young and thoughtless of the fair sex, [that] this Tale of Truth is designed."[8] She expresses her desire to be "of use . . . to the many daughters of Misfortune who, deprived of natural friends, or spoilt by mistaken education, are thrown on an unfeeling world without the least power to defend themselves from the snares not only of the other sex, but from the more dangerous arts of the profligate of their own" (p. 5). Thus she offers, quite explicitly, to stand in for those "natural friends" that the reader might have lost and to protect them from the horrors of the world.

Lacking the support of such narrative guidance, the epistolary novel could not make the successful crossing to the New World. As Richardson once said, the epistolary novel was addressed to an imaginary "country reader," a person who shared a common (albeit idealized) culture with the writer: a stable rural culture governed by a fixed and well-understood set of common rules.[9] In her excellent study of epistolarity, Janet Gurkin Altman states that "the epistolary form is unique in making the reader (narratee) almost as important an agent in the narrative as the writer (narrator). . . . The letter is by definition . . . the result of a union of writer and reader."[10] She goes on to say that "for the external reader, reading an epistolary novel is very much like reading over the shoulder of another character whose own readings—and misreadings—must enter into our experience of the work."[11] This implies that for readers to "narrate" an epistolary novel properly, they must have a reasonably thorough understanding of the sorts of characters over whose shoulders they are figuratively peering.

The epistolary novel thus assumes not only correspondence between the writers within the novel but also a correspondence between the writer of the novel and its readers. Readers of an epistolary novel must function as their own narrators. The author's narrative role is more like that of an editor. Authors exercise narrative control in the composition and presentation of the letters but then assume that readers will read the letters correctly and, unaided, will understand the underlying purpose or message. Writers of epistolary novels trust that they know their readers and that their readers know them; for the form to work properly, they must correspond.

As the eighteenth century drew to a close, writers for the Anglo-American market could no longer sustain this assumption. Knowing that they were writing in a time of rapid transition and for many possible audiences (rural/urban, British/American, naive/worldly, male/female, moral/amoral), they could no longer trust readers to interpret on their own. Even Samuel Richardson must have realized this when faced with the varied readings of *Pamela* and *Clarissa.* The existence of *Shamela* (1741), Fielding's satirical "re-reading" of *Pamela,* and of the many other spoofs and re-writings of epistolary novels that proliferated at the time, highlights the facility with which a "narrator-less" novel could be reinterpreted according to the predilections of the current reader.[12] Though these problems were already beginning to lead to the decline of the epistolary form in Britain, they became immediately significant in the volatile and polyglot market of early America.

The openness of epistolary novels to reinterpretation could be even more problematic with novels written by women, about women, and for women. As Ruth Perry suggests, the lack of boundaries in an epistolary novel can be equated with the lack of boundaries that traditionally surround a woman's person and allow her to be molded to fit others' needs rather than her own. In an epistolary novel, the audience is allowed direct access to a woman's consciousness: "Reading the letters written and intended for other eyes is the most reprehensible invasion of privacy and consciousness in epistolary fiction. There are overtones of sexual invasion . . . in the intercepting or 'violating' of another's words."[13] Without the protective boundaries established by a controlling narrative presence, the epistolary novel leaves the female protagonist exposed, vulnerable, and even invisible.

If Rowson had not intervened, Charlotte's simple, quiet voice could easily have been misread or ignored. Most readers would have found the persuasive, self-justifying speeches of her seducers at least as compelling. Charlotte would have been unfairly represented and her story misconstrued. Rowson's narrative intervention thus addresses the inherent contradiction of a tale of seduction and betrayal told through letters alone. Letters, so open to misreading and abuse themselves, cannot possibly suffice to tell a story of a young girl subject to the same sort of misinterpretation and misrepresentation; Rowson, seeking to protect those "daughters of misfortune" most likely to benefit from Charlotte's experience, must intervene to ensure that her message is effectively delivered.

Linda S. Kauffman, in her study of amorous epistolary discourse, has also shown how the critical and literary response to epistolary novels (and collections of letters) by women illustrates this very point. Without a "guardian" narrator, readers can interpret letters in any way that fits comfortably with their preconceived notions.[14] According to Kauffman, modern readers have continued to re-interpret epistolary novels and collections of letters quite freely and easily. Without the guidance of a controlling narrator, it appears that readers can, often irrefutably, choose to "narrate" the text in a way that fits with their preconceived expectations.

Thus, Rowson, thinking explicitly about a young woman who had been seduced, abused, misrepresented, and abandoned, understandably rejected the epistolary form. Instead, she entered the novel herself and introduced the narrator as a character in her own right. A warm, motherly presence, this narrator acts as an editor, moralizer, translator, and guide for her young readers. Rowson eschewed the role of mere passive compiler of letters and, in the process, ensured that Charlotte Temple's voice was not misconstrued or erased.

III

Rowson guides the reader through the tale much as an ideal mother would guide her child through difficult passages of life. Her narrative voice is unselfish, affectionate, gently admonitory, helpful, teacherly, and attentive. From the opening passages of the text, she creates a homey atmosphere that is never saccharine or idealized. She does not hide unpleasant realities or try to soften their impact on the reader. Warm, comfortable, and nurturing, yet intelligent, honest, and pragmatic, she provides an implicit example of the proper way to mother as she exhibits the disastrous effects of improper mothering on young Charlotte.

In the preface she addresses her two primary audiences as she expresses her altruistic and didactic intent: "If the following tale should save one hapless fair one from the errors which ruined poor Charlotte, or rescue from impending misery the heart of one anxious parent, I shall feel a much higher gratification in reflecting on this trifling performance, than could possibly result from the applause which might attend the most elegant finished piece of literature whose tendency might deprave the heart or mislead the understanding" (p. 6). She speaks, thus, to young girls and their parents, and has placed herself in the position of a "parental supplement" of sorts. This novel will help young girls who have not got enough help from their parents, will help parents who do not know how to help their daughters, and will help anyone else who needs guidance and support in an uncertain world.

Even with the primary didactic intent, however, "teacherly" narrative digressions do not dominate the novel. The story moves at a lively pace, and the authorial incursions seem to appear only at moments where proper interpretation of a scene might be in question. Usually, narrative intrusions are brief and to the point, and they often explicitly address the reader most likely to have misread the passage or scene. However, at several points, Rowson intervenes more extensively. Significantly, these more forceful interventions usually occur when a potentially damaging letter has been delivered. Rowson replaces the text of the letter with an interpretive passage that neutralizes its potentially negative effect.

The first such intervention occurs when Charlotte receives her initial letter from Montraville, the man who is to be her seducer. Rowson does not include the text of the letter but, rather, informs us that "any reader who has the least knowledge of the world, will easily imagine the letter was made up of encomiums on [Charlotte's] beauty, and vows of everlasting love and constancy" (p. 28). Rowson thus re-aligns the reader's potential identification with Charlotte through a distancing ironic stance—reducing a passionate letter (the mainstay of the epistolary tradition) to an almost ironic cliché. Rowson goes on to point out, however, that Charlotte, who does not have the least knowledge of the world, would respond to such a letter with "a heart open to every gentle, generous sentiment, [which felt] itself warmed by gratitude for a man who professed to feel so much for her" (p. 28). And in case a young reader, perhaps just as innocent as Charlotte, had missed the irony behind these statements, she goes on to warn her explicitly that "in affairs of love, a young heart is never in more danger than when attempted by a handsome young soldier . . . ah! well-a-day for the poor girl who gazes on him: she is in imminent danger; but if she listens to him with pleasure, 'tis all over with her, and from that moment she has neither eyes nor ears for any other object" (p. 28).

Next, realizing that in spite of her admonitions, she might have worried mothers by referring at all to the potential attractions of a handsome soldier, Rowson shifts narrative attention: "Now, my dear sober matron, (if a sober matron should deign to turn over these pages, before she trusts them to the eye of a darling daughter,) let me intreat you not to put on a grave face and throw down the book in a passion and declare 'tis enough to turn the heads of half the girls in England; I do solemnly protest, my dear madam, I mean no more by what I have here advanced than to ridicule those romantic girls, who foolishly imagine a red coat and silver epaulet constitute a fine gentleman" (p. 28). As Alexander Cowie points out, such reassurance may well have been needed for many readers. Although the value of didactic novels was not disputed, "there were those who felt that the moral lessons might be learned at too great peril. Tender readers might be singed if they witnessed at too close range the blaze of passion which consumed the frail characters of a novel. The serpent of evil, if studied too intently, might claim a new victim in the observer. To be wholly innocuous a novel must recommend virtue without even describing vice."[15] Rowson effectively uses her narrative voice to avoid this dilemma. Not only does she erase the text of the letter, along with its possible misinterpretations and temptations, she also replaces it with specific moral lessons for each of the readers it might have negatively affected.

After addressing the innocent young maiden and the sober matron, she becomes even more emotional as she imagines the feelings of the fathers of young girls like Charlotte: "Gracious heaven! when I think on the miseries that must rend the heart of a doating parent, when he sees the darling of his age at first seduced from his protection, and afterwards abandoned, by the very wretch whose promises of love decoyed her from the paternal roof . . . when fancy paints to me the good old man stooping to raise the weeping penitent, while every tear from her eye is numbered by drops from his bleeding heart, my bosom glows with honest indignation, and I wish for power to extirpate these monsters of seduction from the earth" (pp. 28-29).

Finally, the nearly two pages of narrative incursion that follow the delivery of the letter are concluded with another strong plea to "my dear girls—for to such only am I writing—listen not to the voice of love, unless sanctioned by paternal approbation: be assured, it is now past the days of romance: no woman can be run away with contrary to her own inclination: then kneel down each morning, and request kind heaven to keep you free from temptation, or, should it please to suffer you to be tried, pray for fortitude to resist the impulse of inclination when it runs counter to the precepts of religion and virtue" (p. 29).

I have quoted extensively from this first narrative intervention, for it is, in form, tone, and audiences addressed, typical of those that follow (though it is much longer than most). A difficult moment has been reached in the text—one that, in epistolary novels of seduction and betrayal, could only have been handled by including the letter. In *Charlotte Temple,* the text of the actual letter is omitted, along with the potential romantic excitement and danger it might provide, and is replaced, strategically, with the narrator's clear-cut moral guidelines. This reveals one of the most serious problems of the epistolary form. As all characters, even the villains, are allowed to "speak for themselves" through the inclusion of their letters, they each have an opportunity to attract the sympathy and identification of the reader. Wayne Booth has shown that in any novel, "a prolonged intimate view of a character works against our capacity for judgment."[16] Further, he has pointed out that this effect is intensified by the unmediated intimate contact provided in the epistolary form. For, "unlike our reaction to villains presented only from the outside, [in *Clarissa*] our feeling is a combination of natural detestation and natural fellow feeling; bad as [Lovelace] is, he is made of the same stuff we are."[17] Rowson uses her narrative role to counteract this effect. She fills the space that the potentially seductive letter would occupy with thoughtful and persuasive addresses to all who could be affected (in various ways) by such a letter, thus ensuring that each of these potential readers will respond to it appropriately.

Charlotte, essentially virtuous even though naive, *does* know that she should not read this letter: "my mother has often told me, I should never read a letter given me by a young man, without first giving it to her" (p. 31). Rowson, by omitting the letter and replacing it with sensible motherly admonitions, has thus performed the duty of a good mother. We must assume that if Charlotte had given her mother the letter before she read it, the mother, like Rowson, would have destroyed it and replaced it with a moral lecture. Disaster probably would have been averted. Charlotte does not give her mother the letter, however. After Mlle. La Rue, her persuasive and self-interested French teacher, convinces her to overcome her many moral scruples, Charlotte eventually opens it and reads it. Thus, explicitly, begins her fall.

Although none of the "evil letters" written by Montraville is included in the text, "virtuous letters" occasionally are. For example, just as Charlotte is about to elope with Montraville, she is nearly prevented by a loving letter from her mother asking her to come home to celebrate her sixteenth birthday. This letter, the entire text of which is included, has a powerful effect on the extremely torn and confused Charlotte. As she puts it, "I am snatched by a miracle from destruction! This letter has saved me: it has opened my eyes to the folly I was so near committing. I will not go. . . . How shall I rejoice . . . when in the arms of my affectionate parents . . . I look back on the dangers I have escaped" (p. 46).

Nevertheless, the "miracle" of the letter cannot be sustained in the face of the immediate persuasion of Mlle. La Rue and Montraville. They have the advantage of direct address. Rowson again does not include the actual text of the final seduction, for, as she puts it, "it would be useless to reprint the conversation that here ensued; suffice it to say, that Montraville used every argument that had formerly been successful, Charlotte's resolution began to waver, and he drew her almost imperceptibly towards the chaise" (p. 47). Drawn into the chaise, Charlotte "shrieked" as it drove off, "and fainted into the arms of her betrayer" (p. 48). This physical collapse effectively illustrates the total collapse of Charlotte's will to resist. Montraville's persuasion has proven stronger than the force of a letter from Charlotte's mother.

Rowson, trying to help young girls who might find themselves in situations like Charlotte's, has thus shrewdly chosen to enter the narrative with direct addresses to the reader. In a world where a lover's strongest assaults often occur outside of letters and can prove even more powerful than a letter from a virtuous and caring mother, a novelist who genuinely wishes to combat such forces must allow her own persuasive voice to enter the narrative in order to compete successfully with the written and spoken appeals of a verbally sophisticated would-be seducer.

Although Rowson uses her narrative voice most often to warn her readers about the specific risks of seduction and betrayal, she also, at times, offers more general passages about ways to achieve happiness in life. In one such passage of almost two pages, addressed to "ye giddy flutterers in the fantastic round of dissipation," she proposes that the way to happiness is "worshipping content": "Content, my dear friends, will blunt even the arrows of adversity. . . . She will pass with you through life, smoothing the rough paths . . . and, chearing you with smiles of her heaven-born-sister, Hope, lead you triumphant to blissful eternity" (pp. 34-35). The rhetoric is nearly biblical, and the intent appears stronger than mere didacticism; it can be better described as evangelical. Thus, Rowson also uses her narrative prerogative to guide her readers to a happier life by teaching them the lessons she has learned from her own experience of the world.

And aware, apparently, that such a lengthy digression might seem intrusive, Rowson follows it with an explicit justification of her motherly narrative intent: "I confess I have rambled strangely from my story: but what of that? If I have been so lucky as to find the road to happiness, why should I . . . omit so good an opportunity of pointing out the way to others. The very basis of true peace of mind is a benevolent wish to see all the world as happy as one's self. . . . For my own part, I can safely declare, there is not a human being in the universe, whose prosperity I should not rejoice in, and to whose happiness I would not contribute to the utmost limit of my power" (p. 35).

Rowson's narrative role is thus three-fold. First, she acts to protect Charlotte from misrepresentation and erasure. She enters the narrative to tell Charlotte's story, since if this were an epistolary novel without an active narrator Charlotte's experience would have been seriously distorted or even obscured. Second, she intervenes to protect and guide the reader at difficult, confusing, or dangerous moments of the tale. At such moments, her narration ensures that each potential reader understands the text properly and does not entertain any damaging misconceptions. And, third, she includes passages of explicit advice and guidance. Such passages are intended to inform, improve, and enrich the lives of her readers in ways that extend far beyond the lessons to be learned from Charlotte's tragic tale.

IV

Taken together, Rowson's narrative incursions provide an authoritative unifying voice which gives structure and guidance to the reader. An epistolary novel can have no such unifying voice; inherently multi-vocal, its linguistic duplicity resists the explicit direction and control possible in the narrated form. As in real life, the characters who speak most persuasively, frequently, and emphatically are at least as likely to be heard as characters who speak most truthfully, virtuously, and morally.

Intriguingly, multi-vocality in the novel becomes an explicit metaphor for duplicity. Charlotte's fate is effected largely—and not coincidentally—by a French teacher. Indeed, all three of the novel's villains are French, at least in name: La Rue, Montraville, and Belcour. Partly, this might hark back to the fact that Rousseau, with such epistolary novels as *La Nouvelle Héloise* (1761), was considered the great novelistic "seducer" of the eighteenth century. It also confirms the general British impression of the profligate French. But, more specifically, it reflects the conservative, xenophobic mood of 1790s Britain and the general fear of rebellious "contamination" by French Revolutionaries. Butler has shown that much of late-eighteenth-century British literature was influenced by Francophobia.[18] This anti-French strain in English and American literature rested not only on a horror of the French Revolution but also on the idea that the French, through their vaunted verbal arts, could seduce even the sane into hysterical behavior. Were **Charlotte Temple** to be "translated" into an epistolary novel, the immediate effect would be entire dominance of the multilingual "foreign" voices of the villains at the expense of Charlotte's voice. Rowson, with her domestic and very British voice of reason, retains control of the narrative, guards, supports, and amplifies Charlotte's voice, and ensures that this erasure does not occur.

Such intervention is badly needed as, in the hands of her worldly seducers, Charlotte cannot communicate her will. Although this incapacity is illustrated graphically through her inability to ensure the delivery of her letters, it also occurs on an interpersonal level. Raised in idyllic patriarchal seclusion and trained to be trusting, obedient, and virtuous, the painfully naive Charlotte cannot speak or understand the language of the new world she has entered. Her language has no effect on La Rue, Montraville, Belcour, or, eventually, herself. The simple, open, pastoral idiom provided by her parents cannot withstand the force of worldly persuasion. And, because she is unable to adapt to the requirements of her new situation by learning to speak, or even reliably understand, the idiom of her captors, she becomes effectively mute.

La Rue, Montraville, and Belcour, on the other hand, are multilingual—they know Charlotte's morally pure language even though they do not adhere to the principles that underlie it. With self-serving and hypocritical appeals for help and compassion, they transparently play on her exaggerated sensibility whenever she feels qualms or tries to escape. Charlotte cannot resist or even question such pleas. As she is entirely honorable, cynicism is impossible for her. Without imagination or initiative, she accepts their histrionic banalities as if they were the genuine outpourings of the heart, for that is the only language she knows how to speak or understand.

This underscores the necessity of a narrator to "translate" such utterances. If this were an epistolary novel, naive readers might, along with Charlotte, unwittingly be seduced by the deceptive blandishments of the verbally sophisticated foreign villains. Readers as innocent as Charlotte would be just as unable to distinguish between heartfelt truths and the self-serving lies of a seducer. Rowson teaches not only the conventional message that young ladies should avoid dangerous seducers but also, most significantly, how to recognize them.

This added guidance would have been especially significant to early Americans. In the bustling, multicultural, multilingual new world, survival depended on the ability to learn to be one's own best guide. Rowson emphasizes that readers must learn to distinguish between honesty and dishonesty by themselves. Charlotte's fate is explicitly tied to her inability to learn to make such distinctions. Her credulous attachment to her betrayers persists in spite of overwhelming evidence that they might not have her best interests at heart.

For the perfidy of the villains goes beyond their insincere words. Their irreverence for honest spoken language extends to an equally dangerous irreverence for the written word aptly illustrated by the name of the arch-villain, Belcour. Belcour means "elegant/fashionable/handsome seducer" and could not better describe the man who is to emerge as the most thoroughly malevolent character in the tale. However, *cour* is a word rich in meanings, including courtier, rogue, pursuer, philanderer, and, also, significantly, runner, messenger, or letter carrier.

Indeed, Charlotte's letters are constantly being destroyed. Although she writes many letters to her parents, begging them to rescue her, her seducers confiscate all but one before they can be delivered. When she "throws herself entirely on the protection of Montraville" (p. 43), Charlotte loses her ability to direct her writings; her identity is entirely obscured behind his. Not only does her maladapted language render her dumb, it also effectively renders her illiterate. Without the power of voice or pen, Charlotte has no control over her situation or the narrative. Thus, without the intercession of the narrator, she would have been almost entirely effaced. If this tale were presented in epistolary form, it would be told by Charlotte's self-justifying and persuasive seducers. Rowson, by actively narrating the novel, retains and protects Charlotte's voice and tells a story that could not have been properly or fairly told through the letters delivered during its course.

Letter writing becomes futile the moment Charlotte boards the ship that will take her to America. While they are still in the harbor, waiting for favorable winds in order to depart, Charlotte decides to write her parents to explain her decision "in the most affecting, artless manner, entreating their pardon and blessing, and describing the dreadful situation of her mind" (p. 55). Charlotte becomes reconciled to the voyage after she "had committed the letter to the care of Montraville to be sent to the post office" (p. 55). She cannot conceive of his action, which is "to walk on the deck, tear it in pieces, and commit the fragments to the care of Neptune, who might or might not, as it suited his convenience, convey them on shore" (p. 55).

Charlotte, an entire believer in the sanctity of letter writing, never imagines that her letters have not been delivered. Even as she becomes more worldly about certain things, the possibility that her letters are not being sent does not cross her mind. In the world she has been educated to believe in, the destruction or misdirection of letters would be unthinkable. Letters were treated as nearly sacred objects. They were the primary method of communication between respectable middle-class women. As Ruth Perry points out, "letters were an important line of communication with the outside world in this time when women lived rather cloistered lives. Women generally stayed at home writing letters which were at once a way of being involved with the world and of keeping it at a respectable arm's length. Correspondence became the medium for weaving the social fabric of family and friendships in letters of invitation, acceptance, news, condolence, and congratulations."[19]

Thus, Belcour and Montraville reveal the instability of the established social order as they violate the sanctity of the letter. Their disregard of traditional conventions destroys the mutual trust that allows the epistolary novel to be read as it should, a properly naive young maiden to remain virtuous, or early Americans to rely on the traditions and customs of their past. In a world where miscommunication, seduction, and even revolution are possible, the epistolary novel is no longer viable. Further, its openness to misinterpretation and abuse makes it an especially inappropriate form for the traditional Richardsonian tale of the seduction and betrayal of a virtuous young girl.

V

A solution to this problem is suggested when Charlotte finally manages to deliver successfully one letter with the help of another woman. Mrs. Beauchamp, her country neighbor, mails the letter that, after over a year, finally reaches Charlotte's parents. Although Mrs. Beauchamp, like the villains, has a French name, she is an American, and she is honorable. This suggests that the answer lies not in xenophobic and naive retreat but in enlightened multilingualism. Mrs. Beauchamp is both worldly *and* honorable. She immediately understands how Charlotte has been duped and, in spite of Charlotte's now dubious social status, responds with a genuine desire to help. Very significantly, this also suggests that women must work together and help each other, that they cannot throw themselves entirely on the protection of men if they wish to maintain any reliable networks of communication. Women (and men) who wished to survive and thrive in the "foreign" and multilingual environment of the New World thus needed to create new and imaginative ways to communicate effectively with each other and the world. The narrated novel could be used to serve this purpose.

After *Charlotte Temple,* the American audience continued to favor the narrated novel. In fact, the epistolary novel never acquired much of a foothold in the New World. Rowson's authoritatively maternal narrative style can thus be seen to mark the beginning of a trend which was to become a powerful force in American literature. The extraordinary success of the "domestic" novels of the nineteenth century—a time when the United States was continuing to change and expand at a phenomenal rate—can be linked to the continuing need for reliable guidance and to the effectiveness of the solution Rowson proposed. Thus, as Rowson's most popular novel marked the end of epistolarity, it also heralded the emergence of the American domestic novel, a form uniquely suited to address the needs of a young nation.

Notes

1. *Charlotte Temple* was first published in England as *Charlotte: A Tale of Truth* (1791). Though some copies of the English edition were immediately distributed in America, it was not widely available or widely known there until it was published in Philadelphia by Mathew Carey in 1794.

2. John Tebbel, *A History of Book Publishing in the United States,* (New York: Bowker, 1972), I, 83.

3. Cathy N. Davidson, *Revolution and the Word: The Rise of the Novel in America* (New York: Oxford Univ. Press, 1986), p. 112.

4. Everett Emerson, "The Cultural Context of the American Revolution," in *American Literature, 1764-1789: The Revolutionary Years,* ed. Everett Emerson (Madison: Univ. of Wisconsin Press, 1977), p. 4.

5. Gary B. Nash, *Red, White, and Black: The Peoples of Early America* (Englewood Cliffs, N. J.: Prentice-Hall, 1982), p. 212.

6. Alexander Cowie, *The Rise of the American Novel* (New York: American Book Co., 1948), p. 1. Cowie tells us, in fact, that "speech varied so

sharply in different parts of the country that at the time of the First Continental Congress members had difficulty in understanding each other."

7. *Romantics, Rebels, and Reactionaries: English Literature and Its Background, 1760-1830.* (New York: Oxford Univ. Press, 1981), p. 29.

8. Susanna Rowson, *Charlotte Temple,* ed. Cathy N. Davidson (1791; New York: Oxford Univ. Press, 1986), p. 5. All further references to this work will be included parenthetically in the text.

9. As quoted by William M. Sale in his introduction to *Pamela* (1740; New York: Norton, 1958), p. v.

10. *Epistolarity: Approaches to a Form* (Columbus: Ohio State Univ. Press, 1982), p. 88.

11. Altman, p. 111.

12. Martin C. Battestin in his introduction to Henry Fielding, *Joseph Andrews and Shamela* (1742 and 1741; Boston: Houghton Mifflin, 1961), p. vii.

13. *Women, Letters, and the Novel* (New York: AMS Press, 1980), p. 130.

14. *Discourses of Desire: Gender, Genre, and Epistolary Fictions* (Ithaca: Cornell Univ. Press, 1986), p. 314.

15. Cowie, p. 17.

16. *The Rhetoric of Fiction,* 2nd ed. (Chicago: Univ. of Chicago Press, 1983), p. 322.

17. *Rhetoric,* p. 323.

18. Butler, pp. 53-56.

19. Perry, p. 69.

Dennis Barone (essay date December 1991)

SOURCE: Barone, Dennis. "'My Vile Arts': Male and Female Discourse in *Charlotte Temple.*" *Studies in the Humanities* 18, no. 2 (December 1991): 135-45.

[*In the following essay, Barone maintains that "[i]n* Charlotte Temple *not only are the ravages of class antagonism apparent, but bound together are issues of class, gender, language, and power relations."*]

The early American novel has frequently been condemned. This condemnation has led scholars to biased and partial interpretations. For example, Leslie Fiedler asserted that in early American fiction the sentimental form "proved almost everywhere a *blight,* a universal influence which was also a universal calamity" (58). Fiedler added that the Richardsonian tradition lost its "vigor" "after its capture by women" (69) and that the sentimental novel in America became "an *anti-literature*" (77). Despite Davidson's recent ethnography of the early American novel and studies such as Terry Eagleton's *The Rape of Clarissa* in which Eagleton notes that scholars' critiques of the novel have "ritually re-enacted" the rape of Clarissa (101), one can find blanket condemnations in work more recent than Fielder's. For example, John Seelye in the recent *Columbia History of the United States* has written that "American writing during the Federal Period and for some time after is often dreary stuff" (168). More specifically, *Charlotte Temple,* according to Seelye, "shares many of the unfortunate characteristics of early American fiction, and like modern writers who seek wide readership, she [Rowson] did not perplex her audience with complex characterization or puzzle it with difficult philosophical issues" (170). If not distressing, it is embarrassing that one of our most noted literary scholars when speaking of a rich and complex novel concerned with difficult questions regarding communication and ethics must repeat, though in different words, Hawthorne's comment regarding scribbling women.

One of the omissions that results from a Fiedler-like vitriolic condemnation is the issue of class. Indeed, Fiedler contended that "in America . . . the class-war meanings of the sentimental novel are lost" (72). These meanings are everywhere in the early American novel. Harrington in William Hill Brown's *The Power of Sympathy,* for example, tells Worthy that he will not marry Harriot even though he loves her because

> Harriot has no father—no mother—neither is there aunt, cousin, or kindred of any degree who claim any kind of relationship to her. She is companion to Mrs. Francis and, as I understand, totally dependent on that lady. Now, Mr. Worthy, I must take the liberty to acquaint you that I am not so much of a republican as formally to wed any person of this class.
>
> (33-34)

In *Charlotte Temple* not only are the ravages of class antagonism apparent, but bound together are issues of class, gender, language, and power relations.

In the first paragraph of the second chapter of *Charlotte Temple,* the most popular novel in Federal Era America, Susanna Rowson introduces the travesty of class relations. The reader discovers that "Mr. Temple was the youngest son of a nobleman whose fortune" had been all but lost. Because of the family's weakened financial condition, Temple's "elder brother" had been "made completely wretched by marrying a disagreeable [though wealthy] woman . . ." and "his sisters legally prostituted to old decrepid [though wealthy] men . . ." (11-12).[1] In *Charlotte Temple* women may marry beneath their social station (Julia Franklin and Montraville), but men must marry at least their social equals. Both Montraville's and Temple's fathers lecture their sons on proper marriages. Though the rules for men and women differ, the results are the same. The system does not work. Like a Shakespearean tragedy, the end of this novel brings death or melancholy to all the characters therein.

Due to his benevolent disposition, Mr. Temple assists the distressed Eldridge family. Temple's benevolence is not tempered by reason, and this irrational kindheartedness introduces Rowson's critique of a Hutchesonian moral philosophy. According to Hutchesonian moral philosophy, Temple's good deeds should assure unending domestic bliss, but instead tragedy follows his good deeds. As a young man Temple became attracted to Eldridge's daughter, Lucy, a young lady who had already just escaped ruin. For Lucy Eldridge's brother brought home a friend, Lewis, from school who liked Lucy's appearance, but Lewis was such a villain that without any hesitation he informed Lucy's brother that he could not possibly consider marrying Lucy for she was beneath him. Then Lewis betrays the entire Eldridge family: he kills his schoolmate in a duel and lands his friend's father in debtors' prison while the grief stricken mother passes quickly from this life. Lucy's father recounts all this woe to Temple who has come to the aid of the poor father and daughter. While telling Temple his sad tale, Eldridge becomes distraught with emotion and says, "But pardon me. The horrors of that night unman me. I cannot proceed," and then for some minutes he is silent (16). Clearly, in this passage class and gender and the untenableness of their construction are evident. Lucy cannot marry a possible suitor because he is above her in social rank. Mr. Eldridge becomes "unmanned" by emotion and then silent.

Lucy who is "artless" and does "fine needlework," who is, in other words, the ideal woman, becomes a threat to the Temple family. Temple's father tells his son that to marry for love and not for money is foolish. Rather than approving of Lucy, he encourages his son to consider Miss Weatherby, a very wealthy woman but one who, as Rowson describes her in verse, was "Born just to be admir'd and die"; "in whose breast no virtues glow" (23). Temple disobeys his father and marries Lucy while his father marries the much wealthier as well as much younger Miss Weatherby.

Similarly, Montraville's father lectures Montraville on proper marriage. Unlike Temple who ignored the stern warning of his father, Montraville heeds his father's warning. Yet, neither Montraville nor Temple attains domestic bliss: Temple's daughter, Montraville's lover, dies. This death destroys the happiness of two couples: Temple and Lucy; Montraville and Julia. Montraville's father points out in the course of his lecture that his daughters have been well educated and that before he dies he must see to it that they are well married, too.

"Should I die before they are settled," he says, "they must have some provision made, to place them above the snares and temptations which vice ever holds out to the elegant, accomplished female" (40). The implication here seems to be that the elite female can be a wife or courtesan (whereas all other women can be wives or whores). Montraville's father warns Montraville: "mark me, boy, if . . . you rush into a precipitate union with a girl of little or no fortune . . . I will leave you to enjoy the blessed fruits of your rashness . . . therefore imprint this conversation on your memory, and let it influence your future conduct" (40-41). Impressed indeed was Montraville for within a few hours time he had decided that "it was impossible he should ever marry Charlotte Temple" (41).

On the other hand, Julia Franklin, "who possessed an independent fortune," "resolved to be happy with the man of her heart, though his rank and fortune were by no means so exalted as she had a right to expect" (82). Julia's attraction to Montraville grows because he seems to her to keep somewhat distant. She attributes this distance to the difference in their social rank and attempts to bridge it. In truth, it is guilt that keeps Montraville from Julia Franklin. For while they are in New York socializing, Charlotte, alone in the country, is about to give birth to Montraville's illegitimate child. Julia Franklin never asks Montraville what causes his unease because "that innate modesty, which nature has implanted in the female breast, prevented her enquiring" (88). Soon they do marry. Julia Franklin knows nothing of her husband's prior attachment to Charlotte Temple. Then on the day of Charlotte's funeral, she dies after giving birth to a daughter, Montraville discovers how his friend Belcour had attempted to take advantage of the distressed and abandoned Charlotte. Montraville prostrates himself on Charlotte's grave, saying, "Hold, hold, one moment. . . . Close not the grave of the injured Charlotte Temple till I have taken vengeance on her murderer." Montraville asks Mr. Temple—just arrived from England—to kill him (Temple refuses to do so). Montraville flies "like lightning" to Belcour's lodgings; kills Belcour; receives a wound; others carry him "in a state of insensibility to his distracted wife." Though "a dangerous illness and obstinate delirium ensued," "He recovered; but to the end of his life was subject to severe fits of melancholy" for he could not forget how he had wronged Charlotte Temple (118). In the troublesome relationship of Julia Franklin and Montraville we see once again the interrelationship of class and gender conflicts and the role of language in the perpetuation of those conflicts. Julia follows the convention regarding women and speech. Because she follows the rules, she does not find out the real reason for Montraville's initial reticence. By the time she understands that Montraville's mistreatment of Charlotte was the reason behind his distance at the start of their relationship, the knowledge does not bring Julia happiness. Instead, she is sad because she will live the rest of her life with a melancholy husband. As Julia follows the rules for women, Montraville follows the rules for men. He refuses to marry his social inferior, Charlotte, but accepts the hand of a wealthier woman. This social system and the language used to perpetuate it are not examples of "divine goodness," they bring happiness to no one.

William Smith, Provost of the College of Philadelphia and one of the period's leading Anglican intellectuals, admits in his "Lectures on Rhetoric" that rhetoric "may be abused in the Hands of Men." Smith uses a gendered comparison of proper speech and proper dress versus improper speech and wayward dress. Evil men, he says, "have often made Rhetoric the Engine of Ambition, and rifled her of her amiable and engaging Charms to dress out the Harlot Form of Vice." Yet, according to Smith, "in the Possession of a good Man, the Power of eloquence is a Blessing indeed!" (129)[2] Either there are no good men in *Charlotte Temple* or Susanna Rowson does not ascribe to Smith's view. Throughout the novel Rowson describes characters as either "artful" or "artless." The division is not simply that good men equal artful speakers and good women equal artless speakers. Members of both sexes may be at times artful or artless, but whichever mode of discourse they choose, the results are similarly unhappy. Artful speakers take advantage of others; the artless, others take advantage of. To be bad or to be abused are the only possibilities here. The faculty of speech in *Charlotte Temple* is much less noble than in Smith's lectures.

Charlotte's mother, who was nearly ruined by Lewis as a young woman, "was unaffectedly artless" (1). Lucy's "artlessness," combined with strict obedience to her parents' wishes, saved her from Lewis' evil scheme.[3] But Charlotte, Lucy's daughter, is not so fortunate. Away at boarding school, Charlotte succumbs to a barrage of artificers. La Rue, "the artful woman," uses hypocritical emotional appeals to persuade Charlotte that there can be no wrong in a clandestine meeting with Montraville. Because they are always together as a group in their early meetings, Charlotte also has to contend with the persuasive skill of Montraville and Belcour. Belcour knew that La Rue's agreement to go away with him "added to the rhetoric of Montraville, would persuade Charlotte to go with them" (38). Simply put, power to persuade is an evil, but not to have that power is to be oppressed.

Montraville uses emotional appeals to persuade Charlotte. According to Rowson "emotions of the soul influence the body" (48). Thus, Charlotte knew that "when Montraville at parting would earnestly intreat one more interview, that treacherous heart betrayed her" (42). Nowhere is Montraville's calculating behavior more apparent then in the machination he uses to win Julia Frank-

lin's heart. One night a fire breaks out that destroys the Franklin house. During the confusion, Julia's father entrusts a box of family valuables to Montraville and then disappears into the crowd. Among the items in the box is a locket with a picture inside. Later, at a public assembly Montraville sees Julia Franklin, and he believes that the picture in the locket is of her. (Actually, it is a picture of Julia's deceased mother.) Introduced, they form an immediate attraction. Montraville is to return the box at breakfast the next morning. Rowson wrote: "He arose, dressed himself, and taking the picture out, I will reserve this from the rest,' said he,'and by presenting it to her when she thinks it is lost, enhance the value of the obligation'" (70). This stratagem succeeds.

Montraville's stratagems succeed with Charlotte, too. In a letter to her parents Charlotte states that Montraville's "art has made" her "miserable" (80). Though Charlotte is cognizant of Montraville's art, she is powerless to do anything about it. Indeed, she is further humiliated, for Belcour is next to "triumph over the virtue of the artless cottager" (98). Nowhere is the power of art over the artless more poetically expressed than in La Rue's remorseful statement at the novel's end: "Such was the fair bud of innocence that my vile arts blasted ere it was half blown" (119). Either artful and evil, or artless and naive, the end one meets is tragic: wretchedness, insanity, death.

Another opposition in the novel is benevolence and self-interest. Again, Rowson called the efficacy of both into question. In the spirit of the moral philosophy of the day, Rowson wrote that "the very basis of true peace of mind is a benevolent wish to see all the world as happy as one's self" (35). Belcour, on the other hand, "paid little regard to the moral duties. . . . Self, darling self, was the idol he worshiped, and to that he would have sacrificed the interest and happiness of all mankind"(37). While it is true that Belcour's wickedness is avenged, what is Crayton's crime? Crayton, Rowson writes, "was beloved for his humanity and benevolence by all who knew him, but," Rowson adds, "he was easy and unsuspicious himself, and became a dupe to the artifice of others" (58). Once again, we have a cultural stalemate. On the one hand, one can be selfish and smart, or on the other, one can be benevolent and naive. Crayton becomes the wretched husband of "designing, artful, and selfish" La Rue.

Temple, too, suffers from the same fault as Crayton. According to Rowson, as a young man Temple's feelings were "warm and impetuous; unacquainted with the world, his heart had not been rendered callous by being convinced of its fraud and hypocrisy" (21-22). It was this naive impetuosity that led Temple to extreme benevolence such as mortgaging his entire inheritance in order to assist the distressed Eldridge family.

According to traditional beliefs, by helping others, one's own lot in life increases. For example, Benjamin Franklin, who gave two of his three "great puffy rolls" to a woman and her child when he first arrived in Philadelphia, supposedly rose to social prominence because he helped others. There is one example of this sort of natural connection between self-interest and the common good in *Charlotte Temple.* However, it is an example that perhaps reveals the great gulf and disparity between the classes in early America. A servant of Mrs. Crayton takes pity on Charlotte and decides to help her. "The benevolent man" brings Charlotte to his "poor little hovel" (109). Mrs. Beauchamp, Crayton's daughter by his first marriage and Charlotte's only friend, "amply rewarded him for his benevolence" (113). Here good deeds and self-interest seem linked in the traditional manner. Yet, upon Mrs. Beauchamp's entrance into "honest John's" hovel, Rowson notes that she "had never before beheld such a scene of poverty . . ." (112). Mrs. Beauchamp nearly faints amidst the squalor. In other words, Mrs. Beauchamp, like her father and like Charlotte's father, may be an agent of benevolence, but she acts in complete ignorance and naivete. Not only does this scene reveal class disparity, but it may also indicate that the wealthy had little knowledge of the lower sort.

Ironically, the only person whom Charlotte convinces of her plight is the poor servant, honest but powerless John.[4] Again, Rowson interweaves issues of class, gender, language, and power. The only person Charlotte—from a fairly well off family—persuades to help her is a laborer. Yet, even here she does not persuade John because of what she says, but because of how she looks. Penniless, abandoned, and pregnant, Charlotte, thrown out of her countryside cottage, seeks the aid of La Rue, now living in splendor as Mrs. Crayton. Cold and miserable, Charlotte reaches the Craytons' door. "When the door was opened, Charlotte, in a voice rendered scarcely articulate, through cold and the extreme agitation of her mind, demanded whether Mrs. Crayton was at home." John, the servant, at first unmoved by Charlotte's barely articulate speech, pities her because of how distressed she appears. As Rowson writes, "there was something in her countenance that rather interested him in her favour" (107). Charlotte's appearance, then, and not her voice, finally convinces someone of something. Yet, even this is ineffectual. Mrs. Crayton refuses to aid Charlotte and John then takes Charlotte, the granddaughter of an English Earl, to the servant hovel where after giving birth she dies.

Earlier in the novel Charlotte almost won over Belcour. At this instance. Belcour, though touched by Charlotte's appeal, is not moved to act. Indeed, after Charlotte's appeal, Belcour only redoubles his efforts to increase Charlotte's misery. As Rowson writes,

> Something like humanity was awakened in Belcour's breast by this pathetic speech: he arose and walked towards the window; but the selfish passion which had taken possession of his heart, soon stifled these finer emotions; and he thought if Charlotte was once convinced she had no longer any dependence on Montraville, she would more readily throw herself on his protection.
>
> (96)

Belcour soon tires of Charlotte, however: "confined as she now was to a bed of sickness, she was no longer an object of desire: it is true for several days he went constantly to see her, but her pale, emaciated appearance disgusted him" (98).

Charlotte's next visitor is the wife of the farmer from whom Montraville had rented the cottage. After marrying Julia, Montraville leaves money with Belcour to discharge the rent and Charlotte's other basic needs, but villainous Belcour keeps his friend's money. And so, rent unpaid, the farmer's wife visits Charlotte only to turn her out. Charlotte

> was thunder-struck; she hardly knew what answer to make, yet it was absolutely necessary that she should say something; and judging of the gentleness of every female disposition by her own, she thought the best way to interest the woman in her favour would be to tell her candidly to what a situation she was reduced, and how little probability there was of her ever paying any body.
>
> (102)

Despite the fact that an earlier chapter bears the title "Natural Sense Of Propriety Inherent In The Female Bosom," Rowson continues, "Alas poor Charlotte, how confined was her knowledge of human nature, or she would have been convinced that the only way to insure the friendship and assistance of your surrounding acquaintance is to convince them you do not require it" (102). The farmer's wife, in the most insulting language possible, tells Charlotte to get out. Charlotte's eloquence fails and in that failure, Rowson calls into question the notion of an innate moral sense. Jefferson may have said "State a moral case to a ploughman and a professor. The former will decide it as well, and often better than the latter, because he has not been led astray by artificial rules" (425), but in Rowson's novel it seems that neither a farmer nor a professor can correctly decide a moral case because nothing can be adequately communicated. Once again. "Charlotte bowed her head in silence; but the anguish of her heart was too great to permit her to articulate a single word" (104).

There are many, many more examples of Charlotte's inability to articulate her needs or to persuade others to do her wishes. Charlotte is unable to finish her last sentence (115). At one point earlier in the novel when addressing Montraville she stops and starts a single sentence twice and then fails to finish her hesitant thought. Had she finished it, it is apparent that the thought would have been a question, not a statement or a command. Montraville replies to Charlotte's unfinished question with classical allusion and poetic parallelism: "Judge not so meanly of me. . . . The moment we reach our destination, Hymen shall sanctify our love; and when I shall forget your goodness, may heaven forget me" (44).

In addition to speech, written communication also repeatedly fails. Letters written are not sent, letters sent are not received, letters received are not read or if read, the news they bring comes too late. The only letter in the whole novel that is both timely and efficacious is the one Montraville sends to Charlotte at the start of the novel. Yet even in this instance Montraville has to slip five guineas to La Rue in order to be sure that Charlotte will read the letter. Montraville knows that he can count on Mademoiselle La Rue to convince cautious Charlotte to read his letter.

In *Charlotte Temple* language for women is a no win situation. La Rue doesn't do what she should, but instead she speaks and by her speech she brands herself a wayward woman. Charlotte blushes and silently retires. Charlotte does what she should, but to no avail. By following convention, others—La Rue, Montraville, Belcour—are able to take advantage of Charlotte. The novel is dystopian rather than utopian. It reveals untenable hierarchies and the linguistic and philosophical structures that uphold them. For example, Rowson directly addresses her audience nine times. Emotional appeals to a mother's and a daughter's sense of duty predominate in these direct addresses. The penultimate direct address, however, is to men and their rationality. Whereas other appeals are to the emotions, this one addresses men's rational faculties. Rowson writes, "but let me entreat these wise, penetrating gentlemen to reflect that when Charlotte left England, it was in such haste that there was no time to purchase any thing more than what was wanted for immediate use of the voyage" (106). Rowson speculates in this direct address that her male readers may wonder why Charlotte could not sell some possession of hers in order to alleviate her impoverished state. In other words, men are able to ask or are allowed to ask more probing questions than women.

As Charlotte lay dying in her father's arms, Rowson, the author, seems to say that eventually all communication comes to naught: "to describe the agony of his sufferings is past the power of any one, who, though they may readily conceive, cannot delineate the dreadful scene" (115). When Montraville asks Temple to kill him, to revenge the crime he committed against Temple's daughter, Temple refuses. Let "thine own reflections be thy punishment," Temple says. "I wrest not the power from the hand of omnipotence" (117). Though Montraville took advantage of Charlotte, Temple will not take advantage of Montraville. Hence, an ordered society seems restored. Speech fails everywhere in *Charlotte Temple*; there is no reason to believe that it will succeed here. The cycle of sin, unswayed by silence or speech, will continue. In the posthumous *Charlotte's Daughter,* Lucy, named after Charlotte's mother, nearly marries the son of Montraville and Julia—nearly marries her step-brother.

There could be no complement of motive and result in the republic because the members of one sex, class, and race attempted to control language. Although the members of that sex, class, and race could speak in poetic parallelism, they were not, as William Smith suggested, patrons of honour, protectors of the injured, defenders of justice (129). In *Charlotte Temple,* rhetoric had become divorced from virtue. Those who spoke well were not necessarily good and those who were good did not necessarily speak at all. To speak was to exercise a corrupt power; to remain silent was to remain oppressed.

Notes

1. All quotations are from Davidson's edition of *Charlotte Temple*. Another recent edition is that edited and introduced by Ann Douglas. This volume also includes Rowson's sequel to *Charlotte Temple, Lucy Temple.* The former was first published in London in 1791; it was republished in Philadelphia twice in 1794 (D. Humphreys for Mathew Carey) and many times thereafter. Susan Greenfield examines the failure of Charlotte's language. However, unlike the present essay, Greenfield does not consider the variety of discourses, male and female, in *Charlotte Temple.* Furthermore, she ignores the important class issue in the novel, and she says nothing of the (feminized) sons who disobey their fathers. I see *Charlotte Temple,* like other novels of the 1790s, not so much about the failure of woman's language as it is about the failure of all language.

2. See Parker's "Motivated Rhetorics" for a relevant discussion of the relationship between gender and social order and logic and rhetoric.

3. For information on parental authority in late eighteenth-century America see Fliegleman, *Prodigals and Pilgrims.*

4. O'Barr and Atkins have suggested that Robin Lakoff's notion of "women's language" should be qualified. "Woman's language," they believe, "is in large part a language of powerlessness" and "that the features of 'women's language' are not restricted to women;" therefore, they suggest "renaming the concept 'powerless' language due to its close association with persons having low social power" (94).

Works Cited

Brown, William Hill. *The Power of Sympathy.* Ed. William S. Osborne. Schenectady: New College and UP, 1970.

Davidson, Cathy N. *Revolution and the Word: The Rise of the Novel in America.* New York: Oxford UP, 1986.

Eagleton, Terry. *The Rape of Clarissa.* Minneapolis: U of Minnesota P, 1982.

Fiedler, Leslie A. *Love and Death in the American Novel.* New York: Dell, 1969.

Fliegleman, Jay. *Prodigals and Pilgrims: The American Revolution Against Patriarchal Authority, 1750-1800.* Cambridge: Cambridge UP, 1982.

Greenfield, Susan. "*Charlotte Temple* and *Charlotte's Daughter: The Reproduction of Woman's Word.*" *Women's Studies* 18 (1990): 269-86.

Jefferson, Thomas. Letter to Peter Carr, 10 August 1787, *The Portable Thomas Jefferson.* Ed. Merrill D. Peterson. New York: Penguin, 1979.

O'Barr, William M., and Bowman K. Atkins. "'Women's Language' or 'Powerless Language'?" *Women and Language in Literature and Society.* Ed. Sally McConnell-Genet, Ruth Barker, and Nelly Freeman, New York: Prager P. 1980: 93-110.

Parker, Patricia. "Motivated Rhetorics: Gender, Order, Rule." *Literary Fat Ladies: Rhetoric, Gender, Property.* London: Methuen, 1987: 97-125.

Rowson, Susanna. *Charlotte Temple.* Ed. Cathy N. Davidson. New York: Oxford UP, 1986.

———. *Charlotte Temple and Lucy Temple.* Ed. Ann Douglas. New York: Penguin, 1991.

Seelye, John. "Charles Brockden Brown and Early American Fiction." *Columbia Literary History of the United States.* Ed. Emory Elliott, et al. New York: Columbia UP, 1988: 168-86.

Smith, William. "The Substance of a Course of Lectures on Rhetoric." Ed. Dennis Barone. *Proceedings of the American Philosophical Society* 134 (1990): 111-60.

Julia Stern (essay date winter 1993)

SOURCE: Stern, Julia. "Working through the Frame: *Charlotte Temple* and the Poetics of Maternal Melancholia." *Arizona Quarterly* 49, no. 4 (winter 1993): 1-32.

[*In the following essay, Stern suggests that the lasting appeal of* Charlotte Temple *can be attributed to readers' identification with the novel's embodiment of the maternal and with matriarchal authority.*]

No critic of the early American novel has explained in any convincing way the enduring popularity of Susanna Rowson's **Charlotte Temple** (1791), a seemingly conventional eighteenth-century tale of seduction and abandonment that unfolds against the backdrop of transatlantic emigration and the coming of the American revolution. From its first American printing in 1794 well into the twentieth century, readers have wept, grieved, and purchased copies of Rowson's novel at astonishing rates.[1] Scholars as various as Herbert Ross Brown, writing on the American sentimental novel of the 1940s, and Jay Fliegelman and Cathy N. Davidson, whose recent studies of the early American period and its fiction have transformed our understanding of the genre, all classify **Charlotte Temple** as the first American bestseller, and all three remark upon **Charlotte**'s deep and enduring appeal.[2] Despite this sustained attention to Rowson's story, the source of **Charlotte**'s capacity to provoke affective response in an audience whose constitution has changed significantly over two hundred years remains curiously elusive.[3] By focusing exclusively on the inner story of Charlotte's woe, scholars have failed to recognize that the powers of readerly sympathy the novel conjures emanate from a different, and an unlikely, place: the framing discourse of Rowson's narrator, a symbolic mother figure who seizes hold of and dominates the novel world with remarkable authority.

What compels us to lose ourselves in the seemingly primitive fable that is **Charlotte Temple** lies not in the framed narrative of virtue imperiled, but in the figure working through the frame: the maternal voice that presides over and attempts to control the losses exacted within her narrative. Without its complex narratology, **Charlotte Temple** would remain a simple story of seduction and abandonment, indistinguishable from the work of other eighteenth-century sentimental writers. At best, it might retain some historical significance as the inaugural women's narrative of this American tradition. What sets **Charlotte Temple** apart from the conventions that would seem to define it is its unique mode of *performing loss*: its distinctive narrative *form* makes **Charlotte Temple** an extraordinary artifact, possessed of a specifically *gendered* mode of cultural power.

In order to reconstruct the cultural force that underwrites **Charlotte Temple**'s capacity to compel, we must consider not only the framed tale of seduction, but also the significance of the frame, not simply the narrative matter of **Charlotte,** but also its manner, expressed in disruptions and discontents. As we unpack the complexity of **Charlotte**'s concentric narratives and explore the ways in which the outer story permeates the inner, we will come to a better understanding of Rowson's contribution to a subtle and important cultural conversation concerning gender and loss that was taking place in the post-Revolutionary context of the early American novel.[4]

The key to much that remains unexplained about both *Charlotte Temple* and late eighteenth-century American fiction in general is contained within the dynamics of narrative form. Reading for the poetics of this form clarifies both how and why it is that *Charlotte Temple* occupies a central place in the cultural and representational history of an affect, the feminization of loss that pervades late eighteenth- and nineteenth-century American sentimental fiction.

At the heart of *Charlotte*'s performance of such loss lies a feminine representation, the novel's narrator, whose symbolic maternal voice permeates the framed fictional world. This unnamed and overly present narrator functions as the novel's absent emblem of matriarchal power, and it is she who does *Charlotte Temple*'s most important cultural work.[5] The symbolic mother stands in analogous relation to the "patriarchal authority" that Fliegelman identifies as central to classic early American novels of the family in distress.[6] Literally absent from the fiction, fated to remain a disembodied figure, Rowson's narrator never achieves representational status as a dramatic character. Her force is metaphorical. In fact, the narrator's maternal authority needs no augmentation by visual representation, and actually is enhanced by its non-corporeal status in the novel's figurative regime.[7] For though she cannot be seen, her symbolic power is felt through the all-pervasive presence of her voice, which resonates throughout the novel, in both framed tale and framing discourse.

In imagining this figure, Rowson rings a change on conventional Anglo-American novelistic representation of women in the late eighteenth century; she creates a maternal voice notable for its extraordinary *rationality,* a pragmatic worldliness that stands in stark contrast to the tableau of female hysteria it frames. Speaking within the highly artificial context of a novelistic discourse, the narrator is fully aware that young female readers of fiction need to be grounded in the hard realities of the world in which they live. Her goal is to pre-empt what later would come to be termed as "Bovaryism":

> Oh my dear girls—for to such only am I writing—listen not to the voice of love, unless sanctioned by paternal approbation: be assured, *it is now past the days of romance: no woman can be run away with contrary to her own inclination.*[8]

In the social code of the eighteenth century, a zealous enthusiasm for sensational novels was thought to debase the faculties of reason;[9] ever mindful of her culture's stereotype of female sensibility, in which all women bear a latent propensity for hysterical dissolution, Rowson's narrator will not dignify such identifications for her community of readers.

But the narrator's rationality, the highly logical mode in which she casts her arguments and which is crucial to rendering a persuasive case against seduction, repre-

sents only one level of her affective experience in *Charlotte Temple.* The narrator is equally capable of *acting out* her enthusiasms and passions, in a dramatic performative mode which, though never hysterical (it remains Charlotte's fate to dissolve into madness), is nevertheless fully felt and graphically expressed through subtle modulations of vocal tone. For at the moment in which she registers her soundest judgments, with a striking confidence, she also inadvertently gives voice to a melancholic grief. Perhaps even more interesting than the narrator's insistence that young female readers not be gulled by fantasies of romantic rescue is her emphasis on proper and improper ways in which to listen to the voice of love. Though the narrator would seem to be promulgating paternal approbation as the value of choice (with the incestuous implication of a daughter-father-lover triad), she actually sets herself up as an alternative (maternal) object of affective desire for her readership.

Throughout the course of the novel, the commitment the narrator offers to her audience is total: she is willing to lavish an unstinting flow of love, support, and advice upon the "young ladies" she identifies as her readers. But this outpouring of generosity and concern is marked by an almost disturbing emotional extravagance. The narrator's insistence upon her readers' approving response suggests that her investment goes beyond that of the civic-minded woman who wishes to educate young girls in the meaning of true virtue: the affect betrays the nature of her need. For what she attempts to redress through her relationship with the reader is nothing less than a sense of loss that is both unidentified and, at the same time, so overwhelming that it blights every other idea in *Charlotte Temple.*

By asserting that the affective significance of *Charlotte Temple* inheres in the practices of Rowson's narrator, a figure who has at best been known for her intrusive preachiness, I am suggesting that we shift the ground of early American novel criticism to a psychoanalytic and cultural analysis of form. Scholars writing as recently as Susan K. Harris, who take the female narrator's frequent moralistic interruptions at face value, continue to identify the novel as a didactic fable warning against the dangers of seduction and advocating greater social tolerance for wayward girls.[10] By resting comfortably at the level of moral prescription, such critics accept that *Charlotte Temple* is a novel about ethics. But this line of inquiry stops short of questioning whether or not the narrator's didacticism may itself be symptomatic of an entirely other set of concerns, pertaining not to action but to affect. The didactic reading reduces to monologue the significantly more complicated and pluralized maneuvers of a narrative voice for whom female chastity is not, in fact, the final word.

To unravel the multiple voices that together constitute the text that is *Charlotte Temple* is to discover a feminist anatomy-*manqué* of eighteenth-centural patriarchal culture. Punctuating the central tale of the virgin seduced and abandoned is a less visible but perhaps even more powerful story: the tale of a narrator so haunted by the threat of loss that she has generated the tightly controlled narrative universe to which we have alluded, a fictive world that encodes its own readership and modes of response in order to perform a pre-emptive and potentially reparative ritual of maternal mourning.[11]

This powerful wish for control and restitution is acted out not only at the level of narratorial interruption, but also through an obsessive retelling of Charlotte's story in the epistolary discourse,[12] the melodramatic spectacle, and the oral tradition deployed *within* the novel's mimetic world. Rowson's narrative economy functions according to a law of ultra-legibility: the more often the story can be retold, the better. Repetition insures that the affective core of the novel—its horror over loss—will be communicated without obstruction. If, as Freud argues in "Mourning and Melancholia," mourning is a process of recuperating the ego's investment of libido in the lost object through a ritual of commemoration and farewell,[13] the generic multiplicity at work within *Charlotte Temple* would seem to attest to the mournful nature of the narrator's psychological enterprise.[14]

And yet, the narrator's framing discourse does not, ultimately, contain the grief unleashed by Charlotte's story. The moralistic interruptions, highly rational exhortations deployed to appeal to the mind as well as merely to the feelings of the reader, take us back to the scene of loss and replay it without allowing us to move on. The narrator's grief is unrequited by the end of the tale, her working-through incomplete, verging on the very sort of impasse that, according to Freud, is the mark of melancholia.[15] The frame does not close. Written during a period of renewed Anglo-American discussion about the place of women in post-revolutionary culture,[16] the multi-national genealogy of *Charlotte Temple,* with its discourse of maternal loss and a mourning that remains unresolved, speaks to the unfinished business of post-revolutionary American society. The ongoing appeal of *Charlotte Temple* inheres in its staging of maternal grief as a kind of cultural work in progress.[17]

II

In taking for my title the phrase "working through the frame," I have two intentions. The first is to communicate something quite literal: the narrator of *Charlotte Temple* attempts to do her "work," which I shall identify as maternal mourning, by creating a unique framed structure for her storytelling, one whose narrative boundaries she constantly disrupts. My second use of the term working-through refers to the process of therapeutic healing outlined by Freud, Laplanche and Pontalis define the term as the:

Process by means of which analysis implants an interpretation and overcomes the resistances to which it has given rise. Working-through is to be taken as a sort of psychical work which allows the subject to accept certain repressed elements and to free himself from the grip of mechanisms of repetition. It is a constant factor in treatment, but it operates more especially during certain phases where progress seems to have come to a halt and where a resistance persists despite its having been interpreted.[18]

In his essay on the subject, "Remembering, Repeating, and Working-Through" (1914), Freud coins the term working-through to describe the outcome of the continual process of remembering, repeating, and coming to understanding that is psychoanalysis.

Working-through is also the dynamic that marks the operation of mourning: over time, and with much pain, the survivor reviews the "archive of the dead,"[19] conjuring memories of lost love, images that can be multiple and contradictory. The task of mourning involves the attempt to reweave the rent in life's fabric that death has exacted; it is the effort to resolve, by working-through, the multiple images into a single portrait with which the survivor can live.

The relevance of Freud's theory to my reading of narratorial working-through in *Charlotte* lies in the centrality of storytelling and representation to both processes. In psychoanalysis, the patient continually revises the tale of her life. Repeating elements in the narrative, she places different emphases upon them.[20] The patient constantly amends her interpretation to suit the working hypothesis she has created with the collaboration of the analyst, a hypothesis that is, itself, always undergoing revision.

In *Charlotte Temple,* the narrator's storytelling follows two dialectically opposed trajectories that, taken together, constitute an attempt at "doing and undoing" or working-through. Within the framed tale, the narrator relates the seduction and abandonment of Charlotte Temple, a fifteen-year-old girl whose emotional development remains at the level of a young child.[21] Charlotte is unable to tolerate parental, and particularly maternal, separation, and, in keeping with this characterological disorder, she projects the identity of mother onto any available female object. Charlotte's inability to separate from her mother and her propensity to misjudge all potential maternal objects as figures of benevolence both mark her infantilization and prevent her from functioning as an adult female in a brutally patriarchal world.

To the mind of the narrator, such a scenario as Charlotte's, featuring as it does the prospect of both abandonment and death, is guaranteed to inspire agony in any reader of feeling. Overcome by the compulsion to assuage readerly anguish *in advance of its experience,* the narrator of **Charlotte,** who is linked with maternity by her empathy, her mode of address, and her connection with all of the mother figures in the novel, violates the boundaries of her mimetic world with a series of increasingly maddening interruptions and digressions.

So obsessed is this narrator with controlling the potential distance between authorial intention and reader response that she inaugurates her pre-emptive, intratextual interpretive practices in the authorial preface, where she declares,

> conscious that I wrote with a mind *anxious* for the happiness of that sex whose morals and conduct have so powerful an influence on mankind in general; and convinced that I have not wrote one line that conveys a wrong idea to the head or a corrupt wish to the heart, I shall *rest satisfied* in the purity of my own intentions, and if I merit not applause, I feel that I dread not censure.
>
> (my emphasis)

Although she claims to be fully content with the righteousness of her endeavor, what is really at stake for the narrator is the persistence of her anxiety: the assertion that she has banished concern at this very early moment is betrayed by the fact that she cannot and will not "rest satisfied" in the belief that readers will keep faith with the program. Refusing to entertain the possibility that she may have to cut her readerly losses (the very willingness to "let go" that is required, psychologically, before one can complete the work of mourning), the narrator is determined to avoid abandonment by any one segment of her audience. Hence, she imagines a panoply of potential readers: "sober matron" (25), "dear girls" (26), "dear young readers" (56), "dear madam" (67-68), "young volatile reader" (108), and "penetrating gentleman, dear sir" (116-17), are all addressed in turn. The narrator's determination to control the response to her story is the mark of a chronic unease that fuels the repetitive barrage of didactic interjections that punctuate the entire narrative of **Charlotte Temple.**

Undergirding such obsessive, presumptuously intrusive behavior is the narrator's longing, the wish to bridge the distance between a female readership (symbolic daughters) and a maternal voice determined to undo loss. But the term "bridge" may be too mild a description of the dynamic Rowson's narrator would seem to require: "fusion" would be a more accurate description of her true desire. This narratorial longing for fusion with the reader manifests itself most pointedly in a remarkable digression very early in the novel. (Such incursions into Charlotte's story function as formal cues that we are entering the psychological heart of Rowson's matter. The following example is paradigmatic.) The narrator proclaims:

I confess I have rambled strangely from my story: but what of that? if I have been so lucky as to find the road to happiness, why should I be such a niggard as to omit so good an opportunity of pointing out the way to others. The very basis of true peace of mind is a benevolent wish to see all the world as happy as one's self. . . . For my own part, I can safely declare, there is not a human being in the universe, whose prosperity I should not rejoice in, and to whose happiness I would not contribute to the utmost limit of my power: and may my offenses be no more remembered in the day of general retribution, than as from my soul I forgive every offence or injury received from a fellow creature. Merciful heaven! who would exchange the rapture of such a reflexion for all the gaudy tinsel which the world calls pleasure!

(33-34)

The narrator seeks to surround her reader with a blanket of comfort made of words; her language of care attempts to approximate what, in a different context, feminist theorist Kaja Silverman has coined "the maternal envelope." In her work on the female voice in psychoanalysis and cinema, Silverman uses this vocal and spatial metaphor to describe "the sonorous plenitude of the mother's voice" as experienced by the infant, a voice whose powerful cadences conjure an almost "theological" authority (*The Acoustic Mirror* 72, 49).

In relation to such an omnipotent female voice, the reader/auditor would occupy the subject position of the infant who perceives this parent as all-powerful, godlike. Rowson's narrator herself longs to embody such maternal power in this passage, and she personifies it in the figure of the goddess "Content," who functions as her deified double:

> her name is *Content*; she holds in her hand the cup of true felicity, and when once you have formed an intimate acquaintance with these her attendants . . . then, whatever may be your situation in life, the meek eyed Virgin will immediately take up her abode with you.
>
> (32-33)

In this fantasy, omnipotence, standing in for the narrator, takes up residence with the reader. At the end of a long list of potential roles Content could play in the lives of audience members occupying disparate ranks on the great chain of being (Content is a democrat), the narrator concludes:

> She will pass with you through life, smoothing the rough paths and tread to earth those thorns which every one must meet with as they journey onward to the appointed goal. She will *soften the pains of sickness, continue with you even in the cold gloomy hour of death,* and chearing you with the smiles of her heaven-born sister, Hope, lead you triumphant to a blissful eternity.
>
> (33)

In her medical ministrations, and in her capacity to surround the sufferer with a blanket of care that bridges distance in the passage between life and eternity (a kind of midwifery for the dying), Content stands in for the narrator as the maternal envelope; what the goddess achieves in a digressive moment in the mimesis, the narrator echoes at the level of voice.

Even within the narratorial fantasy, such blissful moments of fusion exert a powerful violence. For not every reader is in tune with the narratorial project of counter-abandonment, which involves a kind of cannibalism of the audience. In effect, the narrator kidnaps the reader from the unbearableness of her own fictional creation. Holding the reader hostage, the narrator subjects her[22] to a powerful and repetitive emotional barrage whose surface message concerns female education and sexual self-control. The subtext, however, has little to do with proper behavior; instead it involves the horrors of filial separation and loss. The narrator attempts to ward off the pain of Charlotte's experience by creating a counter-experience at the level of the frame, one that would obviate such sorrow. Thus, the moralizing functions as a defense, and the didacticism operates as a smokescreen for the narrator's real project: the working-through of unresolved maternal mourning.

In her obsessive exhortation of the reader to fuse with her perspective, in her insistence that the reader swerve away from making filial choices that would break a mother's heart, the narrator attempts to engage the reader by resorting to the theatrical gestures and imprecations associated with melodrama. Despite the power of her performance, one that reveals the truth of her desire for merging, she is unable to bridge any potential distance between herself and her auditors; such a distance makes the narrator so profoundly uneasy that it motivates her obsessive attempt at working-through loss *in advance* of its experience. But these efforts to seize control repeat rather than exact revenge upon the reality of grief, and the narrator only succeeds in reinscribing the gap between herself and the readerly other. Mourning becomes melancholia.

The chapter entitled "Maternal Sorrow" (XIV), which renders its melodramatic tableau of losses in a language of excess virtually unmatched by any other moment in the novel, constitutes a microcosm of the novel's larger psychology of female grief: most significant is the way in which the subject positions of daughter and mother—power relations whose hierarchical fixity has been clear up until this point—become fluid, interchangeable. And, it is here that Rowson's portrait of maternal loss becomes almost luridly visceral. The narrator exclaims: "A mother's anguish, when disappointed in her tenderest hopes, none but a mother *can conceive*" (55, my emphasis).

As the narrator catalogues a virtual compendium of maternal devotions erased from the minds of the ungrateful daughters who have broken their mothers' hearts,

one senses a double vision at work: we are made to see through both maternal and filial eyes simultaneously. The general exhortation on the subject of potential daughterly ingratitude would seem to have been provoked by Charlotte's disloyalty to Mrs. Temple within the framed narrative: thus, the roster of highlights in the history of motherly care would seem to be a flashback, related from the perspective of a mother just like Mrs. Temple.

Yet at the level of feeling, the narrator communicates an additional sense of longing and loss, an emotion that is not quite congruent with memory per se. Instead, the tender representation of mother-child communion reads as a kind of projected wish fulfillment, an imaginative enactment of devotions not experienced, but perhaps only longed for, and originating from the perspective of a daughter deprived of such care. As we watch the narrator conjure and rehearse the scenes of maternal attention as nostalgia for a state of connection that is now lost, something oddly filial also emerges at the level of represented affect. The maternal tableau unfolded in this episode renders such loss a reflexive female experience,[23] and the polymorphous female subject positions that the passage inscribes—positions that are simultaneously occupied by narrator *and* reader—may account for the uncanny appeal *Charlotte Temple* has had for woman readers across two centuries.

Maternal connection becomes the space of female salvation in the world of *Charlotte Temple* precisely because, as Rowson will reveal throughout her story, late eighteenth-century patriarchy takes a fatal toll on disorderly female bodies.[24] And yet, in keeping with a persistent female homosociality operating within the narrative unconscious of *Charlotte Temple,* the most virulent misogynists in this novel are women; one could go so far as to argue that male identity is itself an afterthought in Rowson's fictional universe. The most villainous seducer of young womanhood in *Charlotte Temple* is herself female, as is the heartless landlady who evicts the pregnant and penniless Charlotte from her only refuge. The Law of the Name-of-the-Father,[25] in other words, is in the hands of "phallic" women acting as men. It is only the sound of the speaking mother, the maternally constructed narrative overvoice who interrupts the story in the ways that have been mentioned, that interrogates the psychological efficacy of that law, and it is this female narrator who posits a more nurturing counter-text of her own, one that seeks to obviate maternal loss by an act of pre-emptive mourning. If novels are structured by a certain degree of wish fulfillment, we must take seriously Susanna Rowson's political desire to make men extraneous and to heed the maternal voice. *Charlotte Temple* embodies such forms of desire.

III

Though it is the creation of a female author, **Charlotte Temple** does not escape inflection by the late eighteenth-century Anglo-American climate in which it was written, and in this milieu, women are figured as property. But the novel does provide two different attitudes toward female chattel. The scene in which Montraville, Charlotte's disaffected paramour, recovers the jewel box of his soon-to-be beloved Julia Franklin constitutes a wonderful microcosm of the sexual politics of the novel. In seducing the virtuous Charlotte, or rather, once the girl's teacher La Rue has seduced her into eloping from school and he has relieved her of her virginity, Montraville can be said to have "stolen" Charlotte's "jewels." Consumed by a sexual passion that cannot be controlled, Montraville essentially "spends" Charlotte's "treasure" until it is used up; parental injunction has forbidden him from even considering marriage to a woman of no fortune such as Charlotte Temple. Montraville has taken possession of that which, for the eighteenth-century female, constitutes her wealth, integrity, and honor: he has appropriated what does not belong to him, and he has squandered it. Charlotte herself employs the jewel metaphor to describe her transformation into shame: "I was conscious of having forfeited the only gem that could render me respectable in the eyes of the world" (84).

In contrast, Montraville restores to the wealthy and well-born Julia Franklin a box of jewels that an old man apparently rescued from Julia's burning domicile and turned over to the young and handsome soldier. In the face of a literal fire that rages out of control, patriarchy, in the form of the old man, comes in to save the treasure that represents Julia's purity and hands it off to the figure most fit to assure its future security, Montraville. Montraville *makes an investment* in Julia's jewels; he is their preserver.

In the elaborate scene of exchange that follows Montraville's temporary receipt of this prize, the theme of the absent mother recurs. Julia remarks that a treasured miniature is missing from the jewel box. Having thought the likeness was a portrait of his new object of desire, Montraville had planned to maintain furtive possession of the image; the impulse to steal what is not his and to cashier it away parallels, symbolically, his treatment of Charlotte. But Julia indicates that the portrait is a likeness of *her mother,* the loss of whom, Montraville quickly realizes from her black armband, Julia is *mourning.* Touched by her filial sorrow, he immediately returns the image to the grieving daughter. Montraville is willing to (figuratively) rip Charlotte from her live, though distant, maternal connection, because her lowly place on the ladder of class and rank renders her of little value, but the maternal-filial bonds of the daughter of privilege must be respected. Moreover, the fact of a dead mother opens up affective space in the life of that young heiress, who must now seek a proper surrogate: Montraville has perfect entré. As Belcour, the depraved libertine who professes false friendship to Montraville cynically advises, the latter should "seize the gifts of fortune while they are within [his] reach" (88).

The real tragedy of seduction, argues the narrator, is that it puts young girls in the structural position of orphans. The "fallen woman"

> has no redress, no friendly, soothing companion to pour into her wounded mind the balm of consolation, no benevolent hand to lead her back to the path of rectitude; she has *disgraced her friends,* forfeited the good opinion of the world, and undone herself; she feels herself a *poor solitary being in the midst of surrounding multitudes*; shame bows her to earth, remorse tears her distracted mind, and guilt, poverty, and disease close the dreadful scene: she sinks *unnoticed* to oblivion.
>
> (69, my emphasis)

It is the poor "friendless" woman's tragic destiny to find that her sexual identity has become merely a form of private property, subject only to (black) market conditions, and unregulated by the law. This sad fact forms a striking contrast to the reality of Montraville's sanctified affection for Julia, which belongs to the public sphere. Belcour will break Charlotte's heart when he sadistically informs the pregnant girl that Montraville "addresses her [Julia Franklin] publicly" (106).

Who is Montraville to play such a crucial role in Charlotte's affective life, particularly if, as we have seen, Charlotte is an emotional infant? How can adult sexual yearning emanate from a mere child? Charlotte's attachment, though technically a sexual one, is actually a tie that evokes the pre-oedipal relation to a maternal object. Montraville simply constitutes the last link in a chain of surrogate parents to whom Charlotte has clung throughout the tale. These surrogates include the headmistress of her school, Madame Du Pont, whose name suggests her symbolic function of providing a bridge between home and world, and Mademoiselle La Rue, whose evocative appellation conjures associations to the street, to sexuality and revolutionary danger (the red—"rouge"—one), and to regret (as in "I rue the day . . ."). Charlotte's education at the hands of Mme. Du Pont has been woefully incomplete, in part because the size of her school prevents this able mistress from exercising personal control over every aspect of its functioning (23). The "bridge" has failed to do its duty.

Fatally, given the principle of repetition compulsion at work in both the frame and the framed tales, Charlotte has gone to Mme. Du Pont's to take up the interrupted education of her mother Lucy, another female unable to endure parental separation. When faced with the trauma of her mother's and brother's deaths and her father's imprisonment for debt, Lucy fantasizes a tableau of merging into the grave with her remaining parent:

> "Oh, my father!" cried Miss Eldridge, tenderly taking his hand, "be not anxious on that account, for daily are my prayers offered to heaven that *our lives may terminate at the same instant, and one grave receive us both*; for why should I live when deprived of my only friend."
>
> (9, my emphasis)

The narrator represents all conflict, misfortune, and evil experienced by members of the Eldridge-Temple clan as the tearing, ripping, and violent separation of bodies caught up in a familial embrace. The family is figured maternally, while anyone divided from it is cast in the structural role of orphaned babe. Mr. Eldridge describes the experience of being arrested for debt in rending metaphors: "an officer entered, and *tore me from the embraces of my family.*" He depicts the episode as a castration: "The horrors of that night *unman me.*" He concludes: "what a mere infant I am!" (11, my emphasis).

It is only the "maternal" manipulation of Charlotte's emotions by the surrogate mother figure, La Rue, that goads Charlotte into behavior of which her real mother would never approve; ironically, La Rue taunts the girl with the charge of being infantile: "have you a mind to be in leading strings all your life time" (28), she asks sadistically. In a counter-scene that rings of the uncanny, Mrs. Temple plans to bring Charlotte home from school in order to celebrate her daughter's *birthday,* the only festival in the Anglo-American cultural tradition, prior to the advent of Mother's Day at the turn of the nineteenth century, that commemorates the mother-child bond. Charlotte never attends the celebration, for it is against the background of this ruined birthday idyll that she elopes from school with La Rue into the arms of Montraville. With this setting for seduction, the maternal bond is violated at its symbolic heart. And it is no accident that this episode sets off an extended round of narratorial moralizing par excellence (32): in her role as maternal representative for all of the betrayed mothers in her reading audience, the narrator takes the body-blow of Charlotte's infidelity.

It is also no accident that Charlotte literally must be *unconscious* to enact the elopment (she has "fainted," 48). More accurately, since Charlotte, an emotional infant, is not an agent in her own life, she cannot be said to have enacted anything: in the getaway scene, she is rendered passive at the crucial moment, because to assent to such a brutal divorce from her family would be unthinkable. Even prior to sailing, Charlotte doesn't want to separate from her parents: she writes to them that "her only hope for future comfort consisted in the (perhaps delusive) idea she indulged, of being once more folded in their protecting arms, and hearing the words of peace and pardon from their lips" (57).

Mrs. Temple fantasizes caring for Charlotte when she initially believes that her daughter is ill: unregulated female sexuality is registered, unconsciously, as disease. This mother will fancy her daughter afflicted before she will contemplate the idea that she may have eloped. The imaginary rescue scenario is expressed by an image of fusional mirroring. Mrs. Temple exclaims:

> "Then she is very ill, else why did she not come [home to the birthday celebration]? But I will go to her: the chaise is still at the door: let me go instantly to the dear girl. If I was ill, she would fly to attend me, to alleviate my sufferings, and chear me with her love."
>
> (54)

This blurring of identity within the maternal fantasy is characteristic of the fusional female parent, one version of which feminist theorist E. Ann Kaplan has termed the "overindulgent mother." This excessively involved figure uncannily constitutes the flip side of the phallic maternal coin represented by a character like La Rue. Kaplan explains that:

> the two kinds of mother so criticized by establishment patriarchal discourses . . . i.e., the over-indulgent mother and the phallic mother—both represent strategies whereby the mother-as-constructed-in-patriarchy attempts to get something for herself in a situation where that is not supposed to happen . . . fusional mothers, the one identifying with the child to the extent of vicariously mothering herself, the second getting gratification through exercising control over the child, can be found in many . . . melodramas. The indulgent mother takes something for herself by satisfying needs for love, nurturance and merging through the child; while the phallic mother satisfies needs for power that her ideal function prohibits. . . . Like the master-slave psychic phenomenon analyzed by Hegel and then Franz Fanon, in which those who are (or were) slaves identify with the master position once freed, mothers take out their subjection to their husbands [as La Rue takes out her subjection under patriarchy] on their children. They identify with the Law of the Father when interacting with the child, who is now given over to the "slave" position.[26]

This linking of the fusional mother with the phallic mother helps us to make theoretical sense of an otherwise baffling moment at the climax of the novel. At this point, the pregnant and consumptive Charlotte, on the very verge of death, journeys on foot to New York City in a raging snowstorm. Her mission is to supplicate and obtain relief from the now well-married and socially powerful La Rue, whom she still believes, in her infantile blindness, to be a loyal mother-figure. In this, the most melodramatic scene of the novel, Charlotte's plea to La Rue is charged with the pain of filial imprecation.

Upon being rebuffed by her former mentor, Charlotte begins to speak in psychologically resonant non sequiturs: "but *I will not leave you*; they shall not *tear me from you*," she cries to the brutal woman who refuses to be moved (119, my emphasis). In this bizarrely dissociative moment, Charlotte's fantasy of La Rue as good mother utterly overtakes the reality of the situation, which is, in fact, a scene of abject repudiation.

Such rejection in the framed tale provokes in the narrator, at the level of the frame, the equal and opposite fantasy of possessing a maternal power so strong that it could circumvent and even annul the sorrow of a mother like Mrs. Temple; this is the wish that the narrator attempts to work-through by means of her intrusive story-telling. Though the framed tale of Charlotte's undoing would seem to focus upon the child, the frame knows better: this is a mother's story. The narrator's very first exclamation says it all:

> While the tear of compassion still trembled in my eye for the fate of the unhappy Charlotte, *I may have children of my own*, said I, to whom this recital may be of use, and if to your own children, said Benevolence, why not to the many daughters of Misfortune who, deprived of *natural friends*, or spoilt by mistaken education, are thrown on an unfeeling world without the least power to defend themselves from the snares not only of the other sex, but from the *more dangerous arts of the profligate of their own.*
>
> (xlix-1, my emphasis)

The first narratorial interruption, addressed to "my dear sober matron" (25), to "my dear girls" (26), is filled with maternal fury and proto-feminism: "it is now past the days of romance; no woman can be run away with" (26). As we have noted earlier, the argument here calls for female rationality; in making this case for women's ability to use reason, *pace* Wollstonecraft, the narrator deploys in advance, works-through, an ironic critique of Charlotte's eventual fate.[27]

Maternal identity proliferates throughout the novel world. When Mrs. Temple learns that Charlotte has eloped, her first plea to God is to "make her not a mother" (55). The narrator, symbolically fused with Mrs. Temple in her maternal affect, continues where Lucy Temple leaves off:

> A mother's anguish, when disappointed in her tenderest hopes, none but a mother can conceive. Yet, my dear young readers, I would have you read this scene with attention, and reflect that you may yourselves one day be mothers. Oh my friends, as you value your eternal happiness, wound not, by thoughtless ingratitude, the peace of the mother who bore you: remember the tenderness, the care, the unremitting anxiety with which she has attended to all your wants and wishes from earliest infancy to the present day; behold the mild ray of affectionate applause that beams from her eye on the performance of your duty: listen to her reproofs with silent attention; they proceed from a heart anxious for your future felicity: you must love her; nature, all-powerful nature, has planted the seeds of filial affection in your bosoms.
>
> (55-56)

In an earlier glimpse of this passage, we focused upon the way in which the sacramental vision of a maternal care no longer valued spoke to the longing of the daughter who had not known such attention; like infants whose sensory experience functions according to primary process, and who hallucinate visual representations of an object world that has disappeared, the fictive orphaned daughter conjures images of the absent mother of her desire. But the narrator's complete identification with the imaginary mother of this passage is also striking. In what must be described as nothing less than a rhapsodic lamentation for the forgotten parent whose devoted solicitude has been erased from filial memory, she attempts to restore the mother to readerly presence by making a visual fetish out of her nurture.

One need not be a good mother in order to understand the powerful force of maternity. When La Rue determines to trick Col. Crayton into an immediate (mercenary) marriage, she expedites her plan by passing herself off as an old school chum of the late Mrs. Crayton, who like La Rue was also French, and who died after giving birth to her daughter Emily, now Mrs. Beauchamp (61). By invoking the maternal connection, La Rue enters the marriage market with deliberation and by stealth; the alleged tie to the dead mother is strong enough to negate the force of La Rue's degraded status as a seduced and abandoned woman.

In the fictive world of **Charlotte Temple,** those who lose their mothers gain a special kind of empathly, for who but a motherless daughter like Mrs. Beauchamp can fully appreciate the toll maternal deprivation might exact upon the mind and heart of the innocent female? It is no accident that Mrs. Beauchamp plays a crucial role in the novel's most significant acting out of an expressly maternal psychodynamic. And, tellingly, there is at this moment no breaking of the frame with a narratorial interruption. Upon disembarking, Mrs. Beauchamp responds to seeing the forlorn figure of Charlotte by saying "what a pity" (66). Charlotte catches Mrs. Beauchamp's words and, for the first time in the novel, she interrogates herself about the way in which she has jeopardized her future. In the next chapter, which follows this scene immediately, and which is appropriately titled "Reflections" (67), Charlotte again subjects herself to a brief but soul-searching process of self examination. The motif of mirroring functions at the level of form and at the level of content: the two facing pages echo each other. Charlotte will repeat her own ruminations: "Charlotte caught the word pity. 'And am I already fallen so low,' said she" (66). "'And am I indeed fallen so low,' said Charlotte, 'as to be only pitied'" (67). Mrs. Beauchamp precipitates Charlotte into the awareness of her own (mournful) separateness; she becomes the maternal mirror reflecting Charlotte's abjection, rather than the enabling reflection of Charlotte's emerging, independent subjectivity, an autonomy which is never to be.[28] Up until this mirror scene, Charlotte, metaphorically an infant, has had no real understanding of the abysmal separation she has inaugurated by eloping.

The sorrow witnessed by Mrs. Beauchamp at the harbor prefigures another blow Charlotte is soon to suffer, when Montraville rejects her. In order to make full sense of the mourning Charlotte undergoes for the loss of Montraville, it is necessary to remember that he is a maternal object in man's clothing. In the face of Montraville's neglect, Charlotte's affect is "plaintive" and "mourn[ful]" (68); she plays a kind of *fort-da* game to cope with his absence:

> she would sit at a window which looked toward a field he used to cross, counting the minutes and straining her eyes to catch the first glimpse of his person, till blinded with tears of disappointment, she would lean her head on her hands, and give free vent to her sorrows: then catching at some new hope, she would again renew her watchful position, till the shades of evening enveloped every object in a dusky cloud. . . .
>
> (68)

Unlike Freud's grandson, who attempted to master maternal separation by creating a game in which a spool on a string was made to appear and disappear, Charlotte knows no such working-through, for the object of her longing is inconstant. Once she has willfully and violently separated from her biological parent in an act of supreme infidelity, Charlotte is psychically destined to be failed by all of the surrogate mothers she has conjured. The compulsion to repeat her own flight *from* independence can lead only to the ultimate state of merging: death.[29]

In her sympathy for Charlotte, Mrs. Beauchamp becomes a surrogate for the narrator (77). The thought that finally enables Mrs. Beauchamp to reach out to Charlotte is the notion that the latter is someone's *child*: "who knows but she has left some kind, affectionate parents . . ." (78). The dying Charlotte only wishes to see her mother (82). She writes to Mrs. Temple: "Even [when I eloped] *I loved you most*" (84, my emphasis). She continues: "It seemed like a separation of body and soul" (84). Charlotte, as a mother-to-be, has begun to understand the privilege that is maternal grief (85).

And it is a mother's sorrow that motivates the narrator's final sustained intrusion into the novelistic world: in an uncanny outburst that anticipates violent readerly resistance, the narrator encodes the reader's empathy, to the point that fusion is required. In the penultimate moments of her storytelling, she attempts to seize absolute control of her reader as if, by a law of narrative physics, the anguish provoked by the drama itself requires an equal and opposite narratorial reaction that will quell all pain. Thus, the narrator goes on for two pages, assaulting the reader, challenging her disbelief. Employing reverse psychology to ensure closure, the narrator dares the audience member to quit reading, and thus, makes the prospect of finishing the novel a matter of pride:

> "Bless my heart," cries my young volatile reader, "I shall never have patience to get through these volumes, there are so many ahs! and ohs! so much fainting, tears, and distress, I am sick to death of the subject." My dear, chearful, innocent girl, for innocent I will suppose you to be, or you would acutely feel the woes of Charlotte, did conscience say, thus it might have been with me, had Providence not interposed to snatch me from destruction: therefore my lively, innocent girl, I must request your patience; I am writing a tale of truth, *I mean to write it to the heart*; but if perchance the heart is rendered impenetrable by unbounded prosperity, or a continuance in vice, I expect not my tale to please, nay, *I even expect it will be thrown by with disgust.*
>
> (108)

It is here, at the moment of figurative hemorrhage, that narrative working-through attempts its heroic task of "undoing" loss: by attempting to incorporate the reader, to fuse the vision of the audience with her own view of Charlotte's story, Rowson's narrator would erase the distance that marks separation and that she finds psychically intolerable.

But the narrative unconscious of **Charlotte Temple** will not allow separation to be bridged: even literal mothers and daughters who co-exist in the same physical space cannot experience union. In the final pages of the novel, Charlotte disassociates from her newborn child and doesn't recognize the baby as her own, nor does she begin to fathom the fact that she is a mother. Charlotte's only comprehension of the mother-child dyad involves seeing herself as exclusive inhabitant of the infantile role. Thus, the narrator explains, "she was not conscious of being a mother, nor took the least notice of her child except to ask *whose it was, and why it was not carried to its parents*" (122, my emphasis). In perhaps her most revealing speech, Charlotte exclaims:

> "Why will you keep that child here: I am sure you would not if you knew how hard it was for a mother to be parted from her infant: it is like tearing the cords of life asunder. Oh could you see the horrid sight I now behold—there—there stands my dear mother, her poor bosom bleeding at every vein, her gentle, affectionate heart torn in a thousand pieces, and all for the loss of a ruined, ungrateful child. Save me—save me—from her frown. *I* dare not—indeed I dare not speak to her."
>
> (122)

The fantasy of maternal separation is figured as an apocalypse worked out upon the mother's body: the cords of life are ripped; the bosom, locus of maternal nurture, is awash in blood, while life bleeds out at every other vessel; the heart itself is shredded by the force of filial disobedience. In a total inversion of the mother's power to bestow life, the child becomes the vehicle for the cataclysmic destruction of the woman who bore her.

Charlotte's vision of violence directed against a maternal figure would seem to be the tragic side effect of a daughterly will to be separate, and not a calculated assault conceived in rage. Yet this graphic representation of brutal destruction of the maternal body is so excessive, so ferocious, that it gives pause, requires further commentary. What might this image of maternal mutilation have to tell us about the connection between female mourning and melancholia, between women's grief and women's rage?

The tableau of apocalyptic violence against maternity that Charlotte Temple conjures in the course of her psychotic postpartum ravings can be seen as both a masochistic and sadistic fantasy. Separated perhaps too early from the loving blanket of maternal care, betrayed by a false surrogate mother-figure, and seduced and forsaken by a brutally indifferent male object, Charlotte Temple is undone by the grief of these successive abandonments. The image of maternal dismemberment she summons expresses her rage over being forsaken: onto the safe, because externalized, ground of another female body she projects fury against a series of inadequate mother figures that now includes herself.

It is no coincidence that the framed story comes most vividly to life in these moments: Charlotte, who, until her traumatic journey through the blinding snow on the eve of delivery, has impressed the modern reader more as helpless victim than as compelling heroine, suddenly bursts into a flame of interest in the heat of her own rage and madness *as a mother-to-be*.[30] Through two crucial tableaux—Charlotte's wrenchingly unsuccessful imprecations to La Rue and soon after, in her postpartum psychotic nightmare—Rowson reveals the way in which pathological grief may itself be only an intermediate step *en route* to affective bedrock, another form of defense against an even more painful and culturally prohibited emotion: woman's fury.

Moving from framed to framing tale, shifting from the level of the visual spectacle of suffering to that of the narrator's expressive attempt to master the dynamic of loss, Charlotte's masochistic fantasy can be reread as a veiled and inverted acting out of female rage. For if beneath the narrator's rational and beneficent insight about women's conditions in patriarchal culture lies an all-consuming and unresolvable sorrow over female object loss, which patriarchy exacts as the price of cultural adulthood for women, that sorrow is an emotion in which women may indulge. Thus Rowson's narrative strategy conforms with eighteenth-century norms of female decorum.

And yet, as we have seen, the mourning process inaugurated by the narrative frame is incomplete, unsuccessful, pathological, disturbed. Working-through has broken down, become fixed at the level of obsession; melancholia expresses an internalized rage against women's place in patriarchy. Only once does Rowson's narrator give direct voice to what we might call her maternal fury: tellingly, this outburst erupts in the same passage in which she angrily insists that women know that it is now past the days of romance and that they cannot be swept away by delusions of love. Immediately prior to that statement, the narrator writes: "my bosom glows with honest indignation, and I wish for the power to *extirpate* those monsters of seduction from the earth" (26, my emphasis).

In this fantasy of revenge against male villainy, retribution is inflected by maternity: the site of motherly nurture is the specific bodily location of burning rage; and even the desire to exterminate seducers is expressed in a metaphor of twisted organic reproduction, in which the narrator figures herself as all-powerful gardener, brutally ripping the noxious weeds, symbolizing predatory libertines, out of her walled garden. The motif of revenge through organic blight reaches its apotheosis in La Rue's final fate: in a move that literalizes the earlier, figurative wish to plague those figures guilty of seducing and destroying innocence, Rowson will strike La Rue with smallpox, inscribing upon her body a living emblem of the disease that festers within.

The signature of the narrator's projected rage is punishment at the level of the framed tale: working-through becomes acting out when the narrator afflicts Montraville, inadequate parental surrogate, with her own inconsolable grief. Suffused with fury upon learning that Belcour has betrayed him in his reports about Charlotte's fidelity, Montraville kills his former friend and dissolves into an incurable melancholia. The narrator writes:

> but to the end of his life [Montraville] was subject to severe fits of melancholy, and while he remained at New York, frequently retired to the church-yard, where he would weep over the grave, and regret the untimely fate of the lovely Charlotte Temple.
>
> (130)

In the imagined world of *Charlotte Temple,* such is the penalty a maternal surrogate must pay for failing to perform a nurturing object relation: a life sentence, in which the malefactor is fated to dwell until he dies with the very affect that proves so undoing to a mother, the grief that will not heal.

The wish expressed in **Charlotte Temple** is ultimately conservative, or more precisely, regressive: Rowson's message to young women would seem to be "if at all possible, do not separate." Yet the reality principle at work in **Charlotte** is much more hard-headed: since separation is the likely fate of most young women, and since patriarchal culture is brutally hostile to females, it is crucial to be educated, rational, pragmatic, and aware. Not for nothing does Rowson cast La Rue and the landlady as central antagonists who represent the foreign worlds of sexual and economic politics. Looking for maternal nurture in all the wrong places, while a natural impulse, can also become a fatal compulsion to repeat.

In her act of framing the tale, Rowson's narrator attempts to contain her grief, to make it into a picture.[31] Despite her herculean efforts of control, the image will neither resolve into a final stasis nor move beyond its own all-encompassing sorrow, a grief that hints at a deeper rage. The result is a novel written as a ritual of commemoration that cannot say farewell.[32] But perhaps, being unwilling or unable to let go is just the point. Registering the limitations of fictive wish fulfillment as a space for reparative working-through, the complex narratology of **Charlotte Temple** also attests to what we might term the *psychic realism* of the sentimental form. When it comes to the representation of female losses, a narrator's inconsolable grief may be all that stands between an author's rage and her audience. The history of reader response to **Charlotte Temple** would suggest that female devotees of the novel, far from being overwhelmed by the grief it exhibits or repulsed by the rage that it cannot quite contain, are deeply attuned to and identified with both.

Notes

I am grateful to the following colleagues and friends without whose help this essay could not have been written: Ann Douglas, who generously shared with me the manuscript version of her introduction to the Penguin edition of *Charlotte Temple and Lucy Temple,* prior to publication; and Robert A. Ferguson, who tirelessly commented on multiple drafts of this essay and whose generosity and encouragement have been vital to my work. Thanks as well go to Helen Deutsch, Susan Mizruchi, and my anonymous readers for their insightful suggestions, which enabled me to clarify and enrich my argument in important ways.

1. *Charlotte Temple* defies easy efforts of classification on national grounds; it is most accurate to consider the novel in terms of an Anglo-American literary tradition. I use the term Anglo American to emphasize the interconnectedness of the transatlantic British colonial and post-colonial world in the period of 1760-1799, as well as to describe the dual national identity of Rowson. Rowson emigrated from England to America to join her father, an officer in the British Navy stationed in Boston, when she was five years old. She returned to England in 1778, after living under house arrest during the Revolution. *Charlotte* was written and published in England in 1791, where it achieved almost no recognition or readership. It was only with the American publication of the novel in 1794, a year after Rowson returned to the new republic—where she was to live the rest of her life—that the book took hold of the popular imagination and became a bestseller. As the tale itself concerns the dangers of emigration, of leaving both mother and mother country, the fact of its Anglo-American genealogy and of its rejection by the English reading audience adds an interesting element to the maternal drama the novel stages in both its plot and its narrative form. For recent studies of Rowson's life, see Dorothy Weil, *In Defense of Woman: Susanna Rowson,* and Patricia Parker, *Susanna Rowson.*

2. See Herbert Ross Brown, *The Sentimental Novel in America, 1789-1860.* Between the publication of Brown's work and the late 1970s, scholarly treatment of the early American novel remained confined to brief chapters in volumes surveying the larger colonial and early national American literary landscape. The ground-breaking work of Jay Fliegelman and Cathy N. Davidson in the early and mid-1980s created its own critical revolution, and put the early American novel back on the scholarly map as an artifact worthy of study. See Fliegelman, *Prodigals and Pilgrims: The American Revolution Against Patriarchal Authority, 1750-1800,* and Davidson, Introduction, *Charlotte Temple,* xi-xxxiii; *Revolution and the Word: The Rise of the Novel in America* 110-51; and "The Life and Times of *Charlotte Temple*: The Biography of a Book," in *Reading in America: Literature and Social History* 157-80.

3. For the history and sociology of reader response to *Charlotte,* see Davidson's "The Life and Times of *Charlotte Temple*: The Biography of a Book," in *Reading in America.*

4. The phrase "gendering of melancholia" is Juliana Schiesari's, as is the notion that affects can have "a cultural status," or, in the case of the sentimental, melodramatic, and Gothic American novel, a cultural and representational history. See Schiesari, *The Gendering of Melancholia: Feminism, Psychoanalysis, and the Symbolics of Loss in Renaissance Literature* ix.

5. This important phrase was coined by Jane Tompkins in her discussion of the antebellum American novel. See Jane P. Tompkins, *Sensational Designs: The Cultural Work of American Fiction 1790-1860*

xv, 38, 200. The ongoing cultural power of *Charlotte Temple* may be attributed, in part, to its compelling representation of a fully rational speaking mother, the narrator of *Charlotte*'s frame.

6. See Fliegelman's *Prodigals and Pilgrims* for an extended treatment of this theme. See also Jane P. Tompkins, *Sensational Designs,* and Shirley Samuels, "The Family, the State, and the Novel in the Early Republic," for further elaboration of Fhegelman's notion that the family stands symbolically for the state in early American fiction.

7. I am proposing here that we expand the ways in which we think about the novelistic mimesis of sensory detail: though an unillustrated literary text must employ the mediation of the graphic mode—print—in order to convey the experience of an imagined visual tableau, or make use of the transformation of the written word into the sound image that plays in the reader's mind as an auditory experience, it is possible, in fact, to talk of fictional narrative that is organized in terms of visual and acoustic tracks. See Roland Barthes, *Image, Music, Text*; W. J. T. Mitchell, *Iconology: Image, Text, Ideology*; and Garret Stewart, *Reading Voices: Literature and the Phonotext*. It is my claim that the early American novel in general, and *Charlotte Temple* in particular, has a generic polymorphousness that features mimetic realism, epistolarity, and most importantly, a melodramatic theatricality based upon the centrality of descriptive visual tableaux. With the exception of Ann Douglas, who writes about *Charlotte Temple*'s connections to melodrama in her introduction to the Penguin edition of *Charlotte,* critics have failed to acknowledge the complex generic multiplicity at work in what has been misread as a simple novel (vii-xliii). While Charlotte's *story* may in fact be primitive, Rowson's narratology is anything but, and the building blocks of her tale derive from a rich and diffuse compendium of literary and theatrical sources. Rowson's personal experience as a stage actress and a playwright in the 1780s and 1790s, the heyday of melodrama in the Anglo-American theater, goes far toward explaining the case with which she employed melodramatic motifs and techniques in her novelistic fiction.

8. Susanna Rowson, *Charlotte Temple*, 1791, in *Charlotte Temple and Lucy Temple,* ed. and introd. Ann Douglas 26, my emphasis. All future references will be to this edition of the novel and will be noted parenthetically.

9. The sexual downfall of the heroine of Hannah Foster's 1797 novel, *The Coquette,* another tale of seduction, abandonment, and death based on the real life of Elizabeth Whitman, a woman poet from Connecticut, is also linked to excessive reading practices. In both the novel and the contemporary reports about Whitman herself, detractors attempting to trace the etiology of her ruin repeatedly point to the woman's overindulgence in certain (depraved) forms of reading: an imagination overworked and overheated by sensational novels has no defense against the seductive strains of the libertine.

10. See Harris, *Nineteenth-Century American Women's Novels: Interpretive Strategies* 39-50.

11. In her introduction to the 1986 Oxford University Press edition of *Charlotte Temple,* Davidson asserts that the novel's foregrounding of separation anxiety during a period of widespread political upheaval goes far toward explaining the great psychological appeal of the novel. She writes, "*Charlotte Temple* addressed the insecurities rampant in the early republic" (xii). My reading of the novel attempts to explore the psychological and cultural ramifications of Davidson's insight in specifically feminist (maternal) terms by focusing upon the way that separation anxiety relates to mourning and operates at the level of novelistic form, particularly through narrative voice.

12. See Blythe Forccy, "*Charlotte Temple* and the End of Epistolarity" 241, for a different reading of the role of epistolarity in *Charlotte Temple*. Forcey argues that in Rowson's tale, epistolarity reaches the end of its historical efficacy as a viable narrative form. While I find much in Forcey's reading that is compelling, it is my sense, nevertheless, that epistolarity operates as one of several co-operative generic discourses, all of which achieve full semiosis within *Charlotte Temple*'s framed narrative.

13. See Sigmund Freud, "Mourning and Melancholia" 237-58.

14. *Charlotte*'s narrative functions textually through its embedded epistolarity; Rowson includes the texts of multiple letters. The novel operates aurally in its employment of dialogue, in its use of narratorial interruption, and in its depiction of an oral tradition about Charlotte (the living legend) that springs up at the end of the novel and is passed from character to character by word of mouth. Finally, much of the power of *Charlotte* is produced by the brilliant set-pieces that punctuate the novel. Scenic tableaux proliferate: we see Charlotte swooning into the carriage at her elopment; we follow the pregnant and consumptive Charlotte, dressed in rags, as she makes her way through a blinding snowstorm to New York City; and we witness Montraville in the act of virtually throwing himself upon Charlotte's open gave.

Though it lies beyond the scope of my argument here, it is nevertheless important to note the relationship between generic multiplicity and Rowson's narrative strategy. The repetitive redeployment of the story of loss through multiple embedded genres within the novel form marks a crucial way in which this narrative moves between mourning and melancholia.

15. In "Mourning and Melancholia," Freud argues that melancholia is a pathological disturbance of the mourning process in which the ego, unable to decathect from the lost object, introjects that object (incorporates the object cathexis) into the ego. The superego, enraged over the abandonment suffered in the external world, then turns its fury against the encrypted lost object, which by virtue of the process of introjection, has now become part of the survivor's self. Melancholia is the process of internal self-devouring, the replaying of loss and punishment that occurs in the inner world of the mourner who cannot cut his or her losses and let go in order to begin the work of grief that ultimately enables the survivor to resume living.

16. See Linda K. Kerber, *Women of the Republic: Intellect and Ideology in Revolutionary America,* for a discussion of the post-Revolutionary conditions that initially opened up and soon afterward shut down American optimism over expanded opportunities for women in the late eighteenth century. Many factors contributed to cultural anxiety in the period. Among the most important were: discontent over the ratification of the Constitution among Republicans; Federalist dread of faction; xenophobia in the face of the sudden emigration of Continental refugees in flight from European revolution; Federalist fear of French Jacobin influences infecting the new republic; a series of yellow fever epidemics in the Northeast; and concern over the possibility of an economic depression.

17. Kaja Silverman's theories about gender, the oedipal phase, and melancholia are pertinent here. In *The Acoustic Mirror: The Female Voice in Psychoanalysis and Cinema,* Silverman argues that for females, the oedipal phase, in which the girl child must relinquish her homosexual object cathexis to the mother in order to embrace a heterosexual identification, involves a melancholic form of loss. Since the girl must give up her connection to that which she also *is,* the loss constitutes a *loss of self,* and thus, never can be fully mourned. Instead, the loss is taken inside the self, incorporated as a central feature of female identity. For Silverman, to be a heterosexual female is to be, by definition, melancholic. See *The Acoustic Mirror* 155-59. While this hypothesis demands historicization, it nevertheless constitutes a compelling theoretical backdrop to my speculations about why the melancholic substrate of *Charlotte* has appealed to readers across different historical eras. This is not to suggest that female melancholia *is* a trans-historical phenomenon; rather, I am attempting to locate a particular social construction of female melancholia within the formation of the female subject in the post-Revolutionary period.

18. See J. Laplanche and J.-B. Pontalis, *The Language of Psychoanalysis* 488.

19. The phrase is Mitchell Breitwieser's. My understanding of Freud's "Mourning and Melancholia" has been enriched by Breitwieser's discussion of grief in *American Puritanism and the Defense of Mourning: Religion, Grief, and Ethnology in Mary White Rowlandson's Captivity Narrative.*

20. Another species of repetition goes on at the symptomatic level, in the lived life of the patient. It is this sort of repetition about which Freud writes in his "Working-Through" essay. I shall argue that narrative repetition *is itself symptomatic* and can function as a kind of "represented" principle of working-through within the novelistic universe. Rowson accomplishes this by employing melodrama, epistolarity, and visual tableaux within the frame of *Charlotte.* The compulsion to repeat takes narrative form as different genres and modes work in concert to tell what is essentially the same story of loss.

21. Ann Douglas was the first critic to note Charlotte's arrested psychic development. In her introduction to the Penguin edition of the novel, Douglas writes, "But, at bottom, Charlotte is looking for a parent, not a lover; she is a child in years and even more so in mind. Her enormous pathos in the later portions of the story comes from our sense of her as a helpless child, a trapped and defenseless animal, looking frantically to see where it can reattach and be safe. . . . Without love— without, to be more precise, symbiosis—the child must die." See Douglas' introduction to *Charlotte Temple and Lucy Temple* xxviii. My reading takes off from Douglas' formulations, which she generously shared with me in manuscript form prior to the publication of her introduction in the 1991 Penguin edition of *Charlotte.*

22. Tellingly, there is only one representation of a male reader encoded within the text of *Charlotte:* he rears his disgruntled head toward the end of the novel, when the narrator conjures him up to object to the lack of realism at work in the episode of Charlotte's impoverished flight to New York City. It is no accident that this male reader takes exception to Charlotte's ignorance of money and economics; he angrily charges the narrator

with concocting an unbelievable scenario when she has Charlotte elope from England without first availing herself of material resources, even keepsakes that could be pawned for cash. The narrator responds to this imaginary protest with irritation, explaining that Charlotte was *unthinking* in her flight; I would add that Charlotte, symbolically no more developed than an infant, personifies unthinkingness. Here, Rowson's narrator practices her ethics of exclusion by conjuring the male reader only to discredit him: by revealing that his fixation on petty detail has caused him to miss the heart of Charlotte's matter, Rowson's narrator dispatches the masculine principle from her audience. Controlling the gender identities as well as the responses of her readers constitutes another way in which the narrator seeks to recreate a maternal relation through her storytelling.

23. Susanna Rowson's own biography constitutes a haunting background for the maternal object relations I am attempting to trace: her mother, Susanna Musgrave Haswell, died of puerperal fever shortly after her daughter's birth; when the child Rowson joined her father in America five years later, he had married a woman whom she did not like. During the Revolutionary War, the Haswell family were interned as loyalists, which so demoralized both Haswell and his second wife that they were incapable of earning a living for the family: thus, it devolved upon the adolescent Rowson to care for and support the woman who had taken her mother's place. In her own marriage, years later, Rowson was ultimately the sole financial provider, as a writer of novels, plays, and patriotic songs and as the successful headmistress of a girls' school that flourished for over twenty years; having no biological children of her own, Rowson nevertheless supported her husband William's illegitimate son with her earnings and, toward the end of her life, took in two surrogate teenage daughters, one the child of a relative, and the other the orphaned daughter of a theatrical colleague. For recent biographies of Rowson, see Dorothy Weil, *In Defense of Woman: Susanna Rowson* and Patricia Parker, *Susanna Rowson*.

I would assert that the aura of wish fulfillment that envelops the maternal-filial object relations in *Charlotte* constitutes Rowson's imaginative attempt to work through her significant psychic losses via the figure of the narrator. The multiple subject positions I have attempted to unveil in this passage speak to the complexity of her own identifications in such a mother-daughter hierarchy; one could argue that, in some crucial way, Susanna Musgrave Haswell Rowson was never allowed to be *either* the young daughter of a mother, *or* the mother of a young daughter, and that the

maternal grief that so suffuses *Charlotte Temple* is a projection of sorrow for herself.

24. Charlotte will die after giving birth to her baby daughter; the cause of death is unspecified, but we know that she has been wasting away during her pregnancy, both from hunger and want and from the despair caused by Montraville's neglect. The unmarried, "uncovertured" woman, whose education is incomplete and whose middle-class origins make the prospect of undertaking manual labor unlikely, cannot fend for herself. Charlotte's evil teacher, La Rue, will ultimately die of the pox, contracted, so it would seem, through sexual contact. These two diametrically opposed female constructions of a male-dominated culture, patriarchy's purest and most depraved products, respectively, are ultimately destroyed by the system that has both created them and that has, ultimately, used them up.

25. See Ellie Ragland-Sullivan, *Jacques Lacan and the Philosophy of Psychoanalysis* 34, for a definition of Lacan's term as a metaphor for the reality principle. Ragland-Sullivan's work on Lacan, and specifically on Lacan's theoretical position in the context of Freudian and post-Freudian psychoanalytic theory (both object relations theory and ego and self psychology), has helped me to clarify my thinking about issues of identity and object relations in *Charlotte Temple*.

26. See E. Ann Kaplan, *Motherhood and Representation: The Mother in Popular Culture and Melodrama* 47-48, my interpolation.

27. See Ruth H. Bloch, "American Feminine Ideals in Transition: The Rise of the Moral Mother, 1785-1815" 117-18, for a discussion of Wollstonecraft's influence on the movement for female education in post-revolutionary America.

28. For object-relations psychoanalyst D. W. Winnicott, the mother is the mirror for the baby. Winnicott writes: "What does the baby see when he or she looks at the mother's face? I am suggesting that, ordinarily, what the baby sees is him or herself. In other words the mother is looking at the baby and *what she looks like is related to what she sees there*" (*Playing and Reality* 112).

29. See Madelon Sprengnether, *The Spectral Mother: Freud, Feminism, and Psychoanalysis* 5 and 219, for discussion of the fusional desire for the mother that is the death instinct. See also Douglas, who writes in her introduction to the novel: "The power of [Charlotte's] story comes from a kind of death wish; for what is the death wish but the drive to escape separation, individuation, and maturation?" (xxx).

30. Eighteenth-century readers, theatergoers, novelists, and playwrights had no such ambivalence about female victimization, embodied as virtue distress; the proliferation of such plots and the enthusiastic responses of audiences to post-revolutionary melodrama would seem to attest to the fact that the sight of the suffering female body produced salutary *frissons* rather than enlightened outrage on the part of the audience. See Peter Brooks, *The Melodramatic Imagination: Balzac, Henry James, Melodrama, and the Mode of Excess,* particularly 1-23 and 24-35.

31. I borrow here from the eloquent language of Mitchell R. Breitwieser, who expands upon this concept in his *American Puritanism and the Defense of Mourning.*

32. The kind of failure to contain grief I have attempted to identify as existing between the framed and the framing narratives of *Charlotte Temple*— its affective leakage—extends beyond the fictive world into literary history. Davidson and Douglas have both written about the fact that late into the nineteenth century, devoted readers of *Charlotte* made pilgrimages to a gravestone in Trinity Churchyard, New York City, to tend the burial site of a woman they believed to be the actual Charlotte Temple. Historians have maintained that no such real-life Charlotte lies buried in Trinity Churchyard (the marker is a monument covering no actual grave) and that the hagiography and reliquary surrounding *this* Charlotte attest only to the power of the novel to arouse the grief and sympathy of a loving audience decades beyond its initial publication. In this regard, the narrator's desire to incarnate filial sympathy is utterly successful, for we can read these pilgrimages as part of the mourning process, a working-through *beyond* the frame, at the level of real life, of a grief that was, originally, only imaginative.

Works Cited

Barthes, Roland. *Image, Music, Text.* Trans. Stephen Heath. New York: Hill and Wang, 1977.

Bloch, Ruth H. "American Feminine Ideals in Transition: The Rise of the Moral Mother, 1785-1815," *Feminist Studies* 4 (June 1978): 100-26.

Breitwieser, Mitchell R. *American Puritanism and the Defense of Mourning: Religion, Grief, and Ethnology in Mary White Rowlandson's Captivity Narrative.* Madison: University of Wisconsin Press, 1990.

Brooks, Peter. *The Melodramatic Imagination: Balzac, Henry James, Melodrama, and the Mode of Excess,* 1976. New York: Columbia University Press, 1985.

Brown, Herbert Ross. *The Sentimental Novel in America, 1789-1860.* Durham: Duke University Press, 1940.

Butler, Judith. *Gender Trouble: Feminism and the Subversion of Identity.* New York: Routledge, 1990.

Davidson, Cathy N. Introduction. Susanna Rowson, 1791. *Charlotte Temple.* New York: Oxford University Press, 1986.

———. "The Life and Times of *Charlotte Temple*: The Biography of a Book." In *Reading in America: Literature and Social History.* Ed. Cathy N. Davidson. Baltimore: The Johns Hopkins University Press, 1989.

———. *Revolution and The Word: The Rise of the Novel in America.* New York: Oxford University Press, 1986.

Douglas, Ann. Introduction. Susanna Rowson. *Charlotte Temple and Lucy Temple.* 1794 and 1828. New York: Penguin Books, 1991.

Fliegelman, Jay. *Prodigals and Pilgrims: The American Revolution Against Patriarchal Authority, 1750-1800.* New York: Cambridge University Press, 1982.

Forcey, Blythe. "*Charlotte Temple* and the End of Epistolarity." *American Literature* 63.2 (June 1991): 225-41.

Freud, Sigmund. *The Standard Edition of the Complete Psychological Works of Sigmund Freud.* 24 vols. Trans. James Strachey et al., ed. James Strachey. London: Hogarth, 1974; rpt. 1986.

———. "Mourning and Melancholia." 1917. *S. E.* 14:237-58.

———. "Remembering, Repeating, and Working-Through (Further Recommendations on the Technique of Psycho-Analysis, II)." *S. E.* 12:147.

Fuss, Diana. *Essentially Speaking: Feminism, Nature, and Difference.* New York: Routledge, 1989.

Gallop, Jane. *The Daughter's Seduction: Feminism and Psychoanalysis.* Ithaca: Cornell University Press, 1982.

———. *Reading Lacan.* Ithaca: Cornell University Press, 1985.

Gledhill, Christine, ed. *Home is Where the Heart Is: Studies in Melodrama and the Woman's Film.* London: British Film Institute, 1987.

Harris, Susan K. *Nineteenth-Century American Women's Novels: Interpretive Strategies.* New York: Oxford University Press, 1990.

Hirsch, Marianne. *The Mother/Daughter Plot: Narrative, Psychoanalysis, Feminism.* Bloomington: Indiana University Press, 1989.

Kaplan, E. Ann. *Motherhood and Representation: The Mother in Popular Culture and Melodrama.* New York: Routledge, 1992.

Kerber, Linda K. *Women of the Republic: Intellect and Ideology in Revolutionary America.* Chapel Hill: University of North Carolina Press, 1980.

Kristeva, Julia. *Black Sun: Depression and Melancholia.* Trans. Leon S. Roudiez. New York: Columbia University Press, 1989.

Laplanche, J., and J.-B. Pontalis. *The Language of Psychoanalysis.* Trans. Donald Nicholson-Smith. New York: Norton, 1973.

Mitchell, W. J. T. *Iconology: Image, Text, Ideology.* Chicago: University of Chicago Press, 1986.

Parker, Patricia L. *Susanna Rowson.* Boston: Twayne, 1986.

Ragland-Sullivan, Ellie. *Jacques Lacan and the Philosophy of Psychoanalysis.* London: Basil Blackwell, 1986.

————. "The Sexual Masquerade: A Lacanian Theory of Sexual Difference." In *Lacan and the Subject of Language.* Ed. Ellie Ragland-Sullivan and Mark Bracher. New York: Routledge, 1991.

Riley, Denise. *"Am I That Name.": Feminism and the Category of "Women" in History.* Minneapolis: University of Minnesota Press, 1988.

Rose, Jacqueline. *Sexuality in the Field of Vision.* London: Verso, 1986.

Rowson, Susanna. *Charlotte: A Tale of Truth.* 2 vols. London: William Lane, Minerva 1791. Rpt. Philadelphia: Matthew Carey, 1794.

Samuels, Shirley. "The Family, The State, and the Novel in the Early Republic." *American Quarterly* (1986): 381-92.

Schiesari, Juliana. *The Gendering of Melancholia: Feminism, Psychoanalysis, and the Symbolies of Loss in Renaissance Literature.* Ithaca: Cornell University Press, 1992.

Silverman, Kaja. *The Acoustic Mirror: The Female Voice in Psychoanalysis and Cinema.* Bloomington: Indiana University Press, 1988.

Slotkin, Richard. *Regeneration Through Violence: The Myth of the American Frontier, 1600-1860.* Middletown: Wesleyan University Press, 1973.

Sprengnether, Madelon. *The Spectral Mother: Freud, Fentinism, and Psychoanalysis.* Ithaca: Cornell University Press, 1990.

Stewart, Garrett. *Reading Voices: Literature and the Phonotext.* Berkeley: University of California Press, 1990.

Tompkins, Jane P. *Sensational Designs: The Cultural Work of American Fiction 1790-1860.* New York: Oxford University Press, 1985.

Weil, Dorothy. *In Defense of Women: Susanna Rowson (1762-1824).* University Park: Pennsylvania State University Press, 1976.

Winnicott, D. W. *Playing and Reality.* 1971. London: Routledge, 1990.

Zwinger, Lynda. *Daughters, Fathers, and the Novel: The Sentimental Romance of Heterosexuality.* Madison: University of Wisconsin Press, 1991.

Jane Tompkins (essay date 1993)

SOURCE: Tompkins, Jane. "Susanna Rowson, Father of the American Novel." In *The (Other) American Traditions: Nineteenth-Century Women Writers,* edited by Joyce W. Warren, pp. 29-38. New Brunswick, N.J.: Rutgers University Press, 1993.

[*In the following essay, Tompkins explains her argument that Susanna Rowson, rather than Charles Brockden Brown, should be credited with establishing the novel as a popular American literary form, and discusses the traditions and values that have led to Rowson's exclusion from the canon of influential American authors.*]

The point I have to make in this essay is so simple and obvious that I have trouble believing it myself. It is that by any normal, reasonable standard, the title "father of the American novel" or, alternately, "first American man of letters," should have gone not to Charles Brockden Brown, who has always held it (Brown is referred to variously as "father of the American novel,"[1] "the first of our novelists,"[2] "our first professional author,"[3] "the first of our writers to make a profession of literature,"[4] "the first professional man of letters in America,"[5] "the first American to make authorship his sole career,"[6] "the first American writer to devote himself wholly to a literary career"[7]) but to a person named Susanna Rowson, who wrote at the same time Brown did, whose literary production far exceeded his, whose influence on American culture was incomparably greater, and whose name was misspelled in the MLA program the year I gave the paper from which this essay derives.

If you have never heard of Rowson, do not feel bad. She is not someone you were supposed to have studied for your Ph.D. orals; nor have people who write for *Critical Inquiry* and *Representations* been dropping her name lately. She wasn't the father of the American novel; I am going to talk about why.

One reason is that the terminology of literary history is made for describing men, not women. One has never heard the phrase "mother of the American novel" (or the British novel or the Russian novel). Novels do not have mothers; nor do literary traditions of any sort, at least none that I know of. There is no mother of the Renaissance pastoral, or of the German theater, or of the Portuguese epic. We speak of masterpieces and masterworks and "Masters of Modern Drama." And whether or not sex is specified overtly, the general terms we use to refer to people in the field of literature always designate men, not women. Words like "author," "artist," "creator," "poet," and "genius" automatically evoke a male image, even though women are commonly known to have been authors, artists, creators, poets, and, albeit rarely, geniuses (women do not as a rule get, that accolade). It follows then that if, when we say "author," we mean a man, literary genealogies will be patrilineal. Especially so in a country that has a political father (George Washington) and a spiritual father (the male Christian god), but no political or spiritual mothers. Such a country *must* have a father, not a mother, for its literature as well. I say this in order to assert that the sex of our literary progenitor was scripted from the start. No matter what the facts were.

Now let us look at the facts. If, taking into account the number, variety, and influence of their words, you compare the careers of Susanna Rowson and Charles Brockden Brown, there is no escaping the conclusion that Rowson is the more important and substantial figure by a considerable margin. Although she is known chiefly as the author of *Charlotte Temple,* one of the all-time bestsellers in our literature and by far the most popular novel of its period, Susanna Rowson published seven other novels, two sets of fictional sketches, seven theatrical works, two collections of poetry, six pedagogical works, many occasional pieces and song lyrics, and contributed to two periodicals. Her writing career spanned the thirty-six years between 1786 and 1822. Of the works she produced besides *Charlotte Temple,* several were very popular in her own day: the sequel to *Charlotte Temple, Charlotte's Daughter,* was published in over thirty editions; *The Fille de Chambre,* another of her novels, sold extremely well, as did *Reuben and Rachel*; *Trials of the Human Heart,* a four-volume novel, had a large number of socially prominent subscribers; *Slaves in Algiers* was popular as a theatrical stock piece; and the song **"America, Commerce, and Freedom"** was still recognized as popular in the 1820s.

On the other hand, with the exception of a few essays published in 1789, Charles Brockden Brown's literary production is confined to a three-year period, 1798 to 1801, during which he published a dialogue on the rights of women, and six novels. From then on he devoted himself to editing a magazine and wrote four political pamphlets. Whether or not we count the nonliterary productions of these authors, the contrast in their output is remarkable. Its nature can be gauged by some comments Evert and George Duyckinck make in their account of Brown in the *Cyclopedia of American Literature.*[8] The Duyckincks convey, with obvious relish, the image of a man, passionate, intense, introverted, and plagued by ill health (Brown died of consumption). As part of this picture they mention several unpublished

or uncompleted works he had embarked on at various times in his life: sketches for three epic poems on the model of Virgil and Homer, a geography (geography, they say, was Brown's great love), and a history of Rome under the Antonines. Brown had also written two acts of a tragedy, according to *The Cambridge History of American Literature,* but, told that the play wouldn't act, he burned the manuscript and kept the ashes in a snuffbox.[9] When you turn to the entry for Susanna Rowson in the Duyckincks' encyclopedia, you find that she actually published translations of Virgil and Horace and wrote two geography textbooks, one history textbook, and seven works for the theater, all of which were performed and one of which became part of the period's standard repertory.[10] The contrast here between the doer and the dreamer, money in the bank and ashes in the snuffbox, the published and the unpublished, the read and the unread only adds to the overall contrast between a woman who worked hard at writing over a period of more than three decades, stuck to her work through thick and thin, and exerted an extraordinary influence over the public imagination through one bestseller and several other very popular works, and a man who, in a burst of creativity, wrote six novels in a very short period, grew discouraged, and then turned his mind to other tasks. The question then is, if Rowson outproduces Brown, and outsells him, and has a much greater impact on American society, why don't we have a mother of the American novel instead of a father?

There are several ways of answering this question, one of which I touched on earlier, having to do with sexual attitudes. I will return to that in a moment, but first let me take up some more conservative suggestions for why Rowson didn't get the job. The first two reasons are technical. One is that although Rowson did write a great deal of imaginative literature, she did not devote herself solely to a literary career, and that is why the title went to Charles Brockden Brown. (Rowson began work as a governess to support herself and her parents, married, went on the stage with her husband, whose business had failed, and eventually founded a school for young ladies. She wrote throughout her adult life as a way of supplementing her income.) This would be a powerful argument were it not for the fact that Charles Brockden Brown started out studying for the law, edited a magazine, wrote his novels, went back to editing, and then from 1801 to 1806 became an active partner with his brothers in the mercantile firm of James Brown and Company; when the firm dissolved, he "continued until his death to conduct a small retail business alone, selling pots and pans by day and editorializing by night."[11] In view of these facts, it would be quite easy to argue, if one wanted to (although I do not), that Rowson had never actually engaged in business but had followed exclusively professional callings—teaching, acting, and writing—and that therefore hers was the better claim.

The second technical difficulty is that Rowson was not born in the United States. But this objection is, precisely, technical. Rowson is considered an American author by all of the literary historians who write about her; her Americanness, as far as I know, has never been in dispute. It becomes an issue only if you want to deny her importance on other grounds.

There are other grounds. Someone will say, why not cut through all this patriarchal-attitudes-and-cultural-influence stuff and admit what everybody knows: that *Charlotte Temple* is a sentimental tear-jerker, that Brown's first four novels are fascinating works of fiction, the beginning of an important tradition in American writing (in the nineteenth-century, Poe and Hawthorne, in the twentieth, Faulkner), and that all this talk about numbers of works written and length of career is just substituting quantity for quality. Brown was a truly interesting writer and Rowson was not and that is why he is the father of the American novel.

Why not admit all this? Because it isn't true. *Charlotte Temple* was interesting to tens, perhaps hundreds, of thousands of people for an extraordinarily long period of time. Between 1794 and 1860 it went through 160 *known* editions. It exercised such power over the minds of its readers that in 1905, more than a hundred years after its publication, people were still visiting the heroine's supposed tomb in Trinity churchyard in New York. On the other hand, if you count three French translations, Charles Brockden Brown's most successful novel, *Wieland,* went through thirteen editions before 1860. Yet the number of articles and reviews written on Brown in this period is greater than the number written on Rowson by a factor of almost thirteen to one. To say that *Charlotte Temple* is not interesting and that *Wieland* is is simply not to *count* the interest shown by a certain sector of the population. It is to define "interest" as that which attracts only a small group of literati. Moreover, to say that the value or quality of a work has nothing to do with considerations such as commercial success or the lack of it, or the size and character of its readership, is simply to ignore the data of literary history.

Facts about popularity, number of editions, and the inverse ratio of critical interest in a book to the book's popular success are not extrinsic to questions of literary merit, they are constitutive of it. They determine the way a text is identified, labeled, and transmitted to future generations; they determine whether an author will be seen as a literary ancestor or not. In the next few paragraphs I want to sketch in what I see as the determinants of the critical, as opposed to popular, success, in the cases of Susanna Rowson and Charles Brockden Brown. I want to suggest that the answer to the question why, given her superior productivity and influence, Rowson did not become the first professional author in America, is that given the class structure, given the gender system, given the economic hierarchy, given the relationship of literature to all of these, and given a complex set of interrelated cultural attitudes, for the author of *Charlotte Temple* to have become an important literary figure was not simply an impossibility, it was literally unimaginable. "Why wasn't Susanna Rowson the mother of the American novel?" is a stupid question. Not because *Charlotte Temple* is a trashy book, but because, given the nature of American culture since the late eighteenth century, it could never have been seen as anything else by the people whose opinions counted.

These are the people who write literary histories, and in their portraits of Brown and Rowson you can see the entrenched habits of thought and standards of evaluation that produced the story of early American fiction we have now. The portrait of Brown that emerges from these histories reflects what we might call the "ashes-in-the-snuffbox" view of him that makes Brown out to be a sort of brilliant romantic failure. "Few have failed of 'greatness' by so narrow a margin," says the *Literary History of the United States,*[12] summing up a chorus of similar pronouncements made before and since. Although as editor first of *The Literary Magazine and American Register* and then of *The American Register, or General Repository of History, Politics, and Science,* he wrote quite a bit of literary criticism, lengthy historical surveys, and reports on recently published books at home and abroad, these solid accomplishments tend to be glossed over by the people who created the role of first professional man-of-letters. They like their Brown pale and distraught, the victim of "tortured nerves" and author of unfinished or unpublished works. They admire him for his passionate though brief dedication to imaginative literature at a time when no one else (allegedly) was writing fiction, and they like to picture him struggling to reach a disapproving, puritanical public. But Brown's commercial failure only adds luster to his reputation. The Duyckincks say, "We are not aware that the author ever derived any pecuniary advantage" from the novels, and William Peterfield Trent observes that despite their legendary status "new editions were not called for."[13] While it is true that in Brown's lifetime there were no new editions, by the time Trent wrote there had been almost a score.[14] His ignoring this is evidence of the general rule that commercial failure *is* success where literary distinction is concerned, for the subtext of such remarks is that only the discriminating few were able to appreciate Brown's peculiar genius. The fact that this genius was also failed, in the opinion of the critics, only enhances his attractiveness as a literary forebear. Here is a representative statement of the "flawed genius" position: "His novels are all structurally weak. The best of them, it must be admitted, are among the most seriously flawed."[15] But "overriding the major flaws are strong virtues which clearly reveal the undeniable genius of the author."[16] What is notable about these pronouncements is how clearly they show that Brown's "genius" exists not so much in spite of as because of its flaws. Accompanying this irresistible cliché is always an intimation that the present critic alone understands the special character of Brown's art. "Brown has been underestimated: he had powers that approached genius. . . . He had a creative imagination. . . . He had, more than this, the power to project his reader into the inner life of his characters; . . . he had poetic vision."[17] Literary portraits of Brown reflect an image of the artist as a tragic, sensitive, misunderstood "failure" so predictably and so often that one cannot help wondering why literary critics and their audiences needed this image so badly. Whatever other functions it serves, however, it clearly separates the sheep from the goats where taste and sensibility are concerned. Those who appreciate Brown appreciate passion, intellect, and genius; they look beyond the superficial faults that mislead others; they see the tortured nerves, the inner life, the poetic vision. And they are few and far between. The way this kind of portrait creates a special group of highly perceptive readers, a chosen few who alone understand genius, provides a clue as to why the author of *Charlotte Temple* could never have been taken seriously by the literary establishment.

If Charles Brockden Brown won critical success through commercial and artistic failure, Susanna Rowson, whose popular fame as a novelist was unequaled until Stowe wrote *Uncle Tom's Cabin,* won critical failure through popular success. Yet even to speak of her as a critical failure is to exaggerate her importance, because it implies that she had been at some point a *candidate* for critical success. It is quite clear that this was never the case. Although *Charlotte Temple* had gone through most of its 160 editions before the Duyckincks wrote, they were so little impressed with Rowson's fame that they didn't even bother to write an original entry for her in their *Cyclopedia* but reprinted an obituary from the *Boston Gazette* which they had found in the appendix to something called Moore's Historical Collections for 1824. In 1824, the year of Rowson's death, and over thirty years before the Duycknicks wrote, it appears that *Charlotte Temple*'s enormous sales garnered it small respect; the author of the obituary refers to it dismissively as "a popular little romance."[18] The ensuing description is worth attending to, because it expresses what became the general attitude toward this novel among literary people from that time forward.

> Of the latter [*Charlotte Temple*] twenty-five thousand copies were sold in a few years. It is a tale of seduction, the story of a young girl brought over to America by a British officer and deserted, and being written in a melodramatic style has drawn tears from the public freely as any similar production on the stage. It is still a popular classic at the cheap book-stall and with travelling chapmen.[19]

This description, which seems neutral enough, combines all the ways in which *Charlotte Temple* has been devalued in American criticism. The apparently factual account, delivered offhand and deadpan, places the novel automatically beyond the pale of literature and writes it off without even trying. First of all, the novel's cheapness and general availability set it at a discount. Because it cost practically nothing, it is worth practically nothing, the equation of monetary value with literary value being unstated but assumed. Second, it is read by the wrong class of people—those who buy at cheap bookstalls and from traveling chapmen; hence, it is associated with readers who are at the bottom of the socioeconomic ladder, low social status and lack of literary taste being tacitly equated. (The tacit nature of these assumptions testifies to their strength; it is because they don't have to be argued that they can remain undeclared.) Third, its contents aren't nice. It is "a tale of seduction," and the moral degradation of the heroine lines up with the cheapness of the price and the socially undesirable character of the readers to reinforce an image of debased value, of something that has been cheapened by being made too accessible, too common. More than a hint of prostitution hangs about descriptions of this book—its easy availability becomes conflated with the heroine's easy virtue, the social status of its readers with the social status of unwed mothers, the low price with low behavior, so that the subject matter of the book and the object itself seem to merge and the book becomes a female thing that is passed from hand to hand for the purpose of illicit arousal.[20] Thus, the negative aesthetic judgment that arrives at the end is inevitable: inevitable and integrally related to the attitudes toward sex, social class, and economic status that subtend the preceding description. The terms of the judgment—tears and melodrama—are identifiable as an inferior, feminine form of response to literature, one that is implicitly contrasted to a superior male rationality and implicitly linked to the poorly controlled instincts of a proletarian readership. There is even a tiny hint of politically subversive behavior in the reference to the unruly feelings the novel provokes "freely as any similar production on the stage." The novel, in a word, is vulgar: loved by the *vulgus,* the crowd, and therefore bad.

The female-male, vulgar-genteel opposition established by the contrast between Rowson and Brown, as literary history has constituted them, perfectly illustrates Pierre Bourdieu's notion that art works function to define and maintain hierarchical social distinctions within a culture. Indeed, the oxymoronic term "popular classic" that the *Boston Gazette* uses to describe *Charlotte Temple* flags the work as something valued by the lower classes and therefore automatically excluded from consideration as a real classic. One might almost say that in order for Brown to be seen as the founder of our novelistic tradition, there had to be a Rowson to define his exclusiveness and distinction by contrast to her commonness, in both senses of the term. In fact William Peterfield Trent, in concluding his discussion of Rowson and the other "amiable ladies" who were her contemporaries, says, "Thus early did the American novel acquire the permanent background of neutral domestic fiction against which the notable figures stand out in contrast."[21] The "father of the American novel"—tragic, conflicted, failed, unappreciated except by a few—depends for his profile and his status upon his opposite number, the popular female novelist loved by the unwashed millions, whose vulgarity and debasement ratify and enable his preeminence.

The places assigned to discussions of Brown and Rowson in the literary histories tend to support this claim. These authors are assigned to separate spheres not only in the literary hierarchy but also in the volumes that "record" it; so complete is their segregation that although they were published at exactly the same time and shared at least one common element—seduction—they are never mentioned in the same paragraph, much less the same breath. This separation, which now we take for granted, goes with ways of thinking about gender, social class, and political and economic structures, all of which are inseparable from the way we think about literature. There is nothing natural or inevitable about any of these ways of thinking, but they are so ingrained and so intertwined that statements that challenge their authority—such as that Susanna Rowson should by rights be known as America's first professional author—seem not only counterintuitive, but absurd.

What is the upshot of all this? It is that, as members of the academy, we have for too long been the purveyors of a literary tradition to whose social and ideological bases we no longer subscribe. It means that when we teach early American fiction, it is time we stopped behaving as if Charles Brockden Brown were the only pebble on the beach. As Cathy Davidson demonstrates, the late eighteenth century produced an extremely varied and interesting array of novelists, many of them women, whose works performed a crucial role in shaping American culture.[22] The present genealogy of American novelists, which begins with Brown and proceeds to Cooper, Irving, Hawthorne, Melville, Twain, James, and on down the line, must be revised, because it rests on a set of values that are not worth giving our lives for.

Notes

This essay is based on a talk originally delivered at the Modern Language Association in December 1985.

1. Harry R. Warfel, *Charles Brockden Brown: American Gothic Novelist* (Gainesville: University of Florida Press, 1949), ix.

2. Evert A. Duyckinck and George L. Duyckinck, eds., *Cyclopedia of American Literature: Embracing Personal and Critical Notices of Authors and Selections from Their Writings from the Earliest Period to the Present Day* (New York: Charles Scribner, 1855), 1:586.

3. F. O. Matthiessen, *American Renaissance: Art and Expression in the Age of Emerson and Whitman* (London: Oxford University Press, 1941), 202.

4. Robert E. Spiller, Willard Thorp, Thomas H. Johnson, Henry Seidel Canby, eds., *Literary History of the United States* (New York: Macmillan, 1948), 1:181.

5. Fred Lewis Pattee, ed., *Century Readings for a Course in American Literature,* 3rd ed. (New York: Century, 1926), 168.

6. William Peterfield Trent, John Erskine, Stuart P. Sherman, Carl Van Doren, eds., *The Cambridge History of American Literature* (New York: G. P. Putnam's Sons, 1917), 1:287.

7. Darrel Abel, ed., *American Literature* (Great Neck, N.Y.: Barron's Educational Series, 1963), 1:294.

8. Duyckinck, *Cyclopedia,* 586-591.

9. Trent, et al. *Cambridge History,* 292.

10. Duyckinck, *Cyclopedia,* 502-504.

11. David Lee Clark, *Charles Brockden Brown: Pioneer Voice of America* (Durham, N.C.: Duke University Press, 1952), 216.

12. Spiller et al., *Literary History,* 181.

13. Duyckinck, *Cyclopedia,* 590; Trent, *Cambridge History,* 292.

14. Sydney J. Krause and Jane Nieset, "A Census of the Works of Charles Brockden Brown," *The Serif. Kent State University Library Quarterly* 3 (December 1966): 27-55.

15. Donald A. Ringe, *Charles Brockden Brown,* Twayne's United States Author Series, ed. Sylvia E. Bowman, no. 98 (New York: Twayne, 1966), 138.

16. Ibid., 140.

17. Charles Brockden Brown, *Wieland,* ed. Fred Lewis Pattee (New York, 1926), Introduction, xiv; quoted in Clark, *Charles Brockden Brown,* 316.

18. Duyckinck, *Cyclopedia,* 502.

19. Ibid.

20. See Susanna Haswell Rowson, *Charlotte Temple: A Tale of Truth,* ed. Francis W. Halsey (New York: Funk & Wagnalls, 1905), Introduction, xxxv-xxxvi.

21. Trent et al., *Cambridge History,* 285.

22. Cathy N. Davidson, ed., *Reading in America: Literature and Social History* (Baltimore: The Johns Hopkins University Press, 1989). Since this essay was written, Cathy Davidson's *Revolution and the Word* (New York: Oxford University Press, 1986) has reconstituted American literary history of the Revolutionary and post-Revolutionary period, giving Susanna Rowson and her contemporaries their proper place in the record.

Keith Fudge (essay date spring 1996)

SOURCE: Fudge, Keith. "Sisterhood Born from Seduction: Susanna Rowson's *Charlotte Temple,* and Stephen Crane's *Maggie Johnson.*" *Journal of American Culture* 19, no. 1 (spring 1996): 43-50.

[*In the following essay, Fudge compares and contrasts* Charlotte Temple *and Stephen Crane's* Maggie: A Girl of the Streets, *and declares that both novels can be viewed as "seduction narrative[s]."*]

After the American publication of Susanna Rowson's **Charlotte Temple,** in 1794, readers became so captivated by the ill-fated heroine that the book became the young nation's first best-selling novel. This tragic story of Charlotte's seduction, betrayal, and eventual demise would remain popular well into the nineteenth century, with the text eventually going through more than 200 editions. Almost a century after the publication of Rowson's text, another variation on the theme of seduction and betrayal was made available to the reading public. Stephen Crane's first novel, *Maggie: A Girl of the Streets,* appeared on the shelves of Brentano's Book Shop in New York City in 1893. Although this cheaply printed and poorly published first edition of *Maggie* did not sell (it was printed at Crane's own expense under the name of Johnston Smith), it would later be reissued and reevaluated after Crane's popularity was established. After its second publication in 1896, the novel took on a greater importance when it was praised by one of the most important literary figures of the times, William Dean Howells.

The ensuing criticism regarding *Maggie* primarily dealt with how environmental or economic determinism affected the lives of the book's characters. In recapping the plot, the heroine, young Maggie Johnson, is forced into a life of prostitution, roaming the bowery streets of New York in order to survive. At the novel's end, overcome by the shame she has brought upon herself as the result of being seduced and abandoned, she is found dead, the result of suicide by drowning.

Maggie: A Girl of the Streets is often referred to as Naturalism's first novel, and by depicting the harsh, realistic conditions of bowery life, it is indeed that; however, it is much more. *Maggie* is a novel that clearly defines the consequences of seduction and betrayal as well as Rowson's **Charlotte Temple,** and through the birth and death of Crane's "girl of the streets," to the heroine of each text there has been bestowed an inherent kinship resulting in a "sisterhood through seduction."

An initial comparison of the two betrayed victims yields several common traits shared by the two women: both are depicted as beautiful; both are seduced and betrayed; and both die (spiritually as well as physically) at the end of their respective stories. What I would like to do in the scope of this study is to delve deeper into the "kinship" of the two heroines, exposing more than these "obvious" similarities. It is important to pay close attention to those influential characters who surround each heroine and to attempt to evaluate each player's role in the fate of that particular heroine. But before this examination can be conducted, it is essential to look at two important elements which tie the two "sisters" together: a brief history of the seduction narrative, and a closer look at the archetype of the fallen woman.

In *Love and Death in the American Novel* (1966), Leslie Fiedler states, "The novel proper could not be launched until some author imagined a prose narrative in which the Seducer and the Pure Maiden were brought face to face in a ritual combat destined to end in marriage or death" (62). Fiedler pays tribute to Samuel Richardson as the father of the seduction narrative, citing the importance of *Clarissa* as the influential text regarding the theme of seduction and betrayal. Fiedler then addresses the "American Clarissa," **Charlotte Temple,** and asserts that this tale of seduction is wholly inferior to its English predecessor. And despite the novel's success, Fiedler clearly admits to his confusion regarding **Temple**'s popularity:

> To be sure, the popularity of **Charlotte** poses a real problem. Why a book which barely climbs above the lower limits of literacy, and which handles, without psychological acuteness or dramatic power, a handful of stereotyped characters in a situation already hopelessly banal by 1790, should have had more than two hundred editions and have survived among certain readers for a hundred and fifty years is a question that cannot be ignored. It is tempting to say that popular taste given the choice between a better and worse book will inevitably choose the worse; but this is an anti-sentimental simplification no more helpful than its sentimental opposite number. Only certain bad books succeed, apparently not by the simple virtue of their badness, but because of the theme they have chosen to handle badly.
>
> (94)

Here, Fiedler is obviously making a distinction between "high and low" literature and is representing an elitist ideology regarding the lack of "art" in lieu of a novel which enjoys a commercial success, an attitude that is still widely prevalent today. In fact, he goes even further in his judgment that Rowson's text is not literature at all, but is "published in the guise of literature" (94). What must be kept in mind regarding Fiedler's comments on *Charlotte Temple* is the time in which his book was written. In the 1960s the importance and popularity of Susanna Rowson's book had faded, and at that time it had become virtually ignored by critics and scholars. However, during the 1970s, with the rise of feminist theory, critics such as Wendy Martin addressed the plight of those who had been victimized by the "arts of seduction."

In "Seduced and Abandoned in the New World: The Fallen Woman in American Fiction," Wendy Martin opens with direct reference to the importance of Susanna Rowson's most famous novel. Martin's article reinforces that these "fallen heroines" are not only the result of a reenactment of Eve's fall from grace, thus becoming an integral part of the concept of Christianity, but also a type of "bourgeois economic commodity" where a woman's virtue (or lack of it) is determinate of her value in the eyes of her community (258-9). Martin cites Ian Watt's *The Rise of the Novel* (1959) as the basis for her "economic twist," when she reiterates:

> The moral values of the novel reinforce bourgeois economic reality in which women are totally dependent on marriage for economic survival. In this economic system, virtue is a commodity to be sold to the highest bidder, and virginity relinquished before marriage inevitably means that a woman is less marketable and is therefore less likely to survive economically.
>
> (259)

Martin then goes on to state that according to this hypothesis, "Charlotte Temple would have died of starvation had she not first died in childbirth" (259).

With the character of Charlotte Temple, there is indeed the strong possibility that retaining her virtue could possibly lead to a "more marketable" future; however, in the case of Maggie Johnson, there is little hope that she could ever improve her "destiny." This theory regarding Maggie is also a strong part of Martin's argument when she refers to fallen women as "passive, dependent creatures" (259). Martin points out that this myth or archetype is perpetuated by a type of "conditioning process" that the writer has imposed upon the reader:

> Because many of the most important American novels from *Charlotte Temple* to *A Farewell to Arms* define women as essentially passive, dependent creatures who are doomed to tragic lives if they deviate from convention, an analysis of the numerous ways in which some of these novels perpetuate the archetype of the fallen woman, thereby conditioning women to accept their inferior status, reveals the extent to which a myth can in-

fluence behavior long after widespread belief in the formal religious or economic mythology that gave rise to it has ceased to exist.

> (259-60)

Martin encourages the reader to be aware of this type of condition concerning the tragic circumstances of many of these ill-fated heroines. "A thorough understanding of this conditioning process as it occurs in the American novel—a conditioning process that in turn represents an aspect of the larger cultural conditioning—is necessary in order to sensitize readers to the often subtle but pervasive negative influence of destructive archetypes" (260). Although Martin never does mention the fate of Maggie Johnson in her article, it is clear that nearly a century after Rowson's book, Crane's heroine reinforces Martin's hypothesis regarding the perpetuation of these archetypes.

One of the most recent treatments of the seduction narrative is Cathy N. Davidson's *Revolution and the Word: The Rise of the Novel in America* (1986). Davidson traces the history of the seduction narrative in American print culture, paying particular attention to *Charlotte Temple* and Hannah W. Foster's *The Coquette*. Her interest in these two works is evident as she furnishes introductions for each work in recent editions. But Davidson, like Martin, does not mention Crane's *Maggie* as a seduction narrative directly influenced by its eighteenth century predecessors. The reason for this omission is the early cataloging of Crane's book as a startling portrayal of realism depicting the cruelty of bowery life. Even today, *Maggie* is rarely considered or viewed as a seduction narrative.

Although the novels of *Charlotte Temple* and *Maggie: A Girl of the Streets* are similar in theme, they also are quite different in regard to the context in which they were written. Whereas Susanna Rowson "issued a warning to young women and their parents," Crane saw his work rather as a case study of the fallen woman around the turn of the century and made no moral proclamation regarding the virtue or vice of his characters. He simply reported the facts. Rowson's romanticized approach and didactic style delivered the plight of the fallen woman in much different terms by implying the horrible consequences of being "unclean."

Another difference in the author's treatment of the two heroines is that Charlotte speaks throughout her novel, always protesting, or lamenting the consequences of her actions. Maggie is virtually void of voice, never able to either defend or justify the course of her actions. Perhaps Crane's impressionistic style led to the absence of Maggie's voice, or possibly he stifled Maggie because of his own regard for women. What must be considered in Crane's case is the concept of Victorian domesticity, where a man wanted "a lady in the parlor and a whore in the bedroom." Relationships with mistresses were a common practice at the turn of the century, and the concept was even accepted by wives during that time. In his youth, Crane had difficulty relating to "nice girls," even though he sought out several relationships. Keeping these thoughts in mind, it is imperative to remember that one of the texts is written by a female, and one by a male,[1] and in turn, it is then necessary to examine how each author addresses their "seduced sister."

Crane's research for depicting life in the bowery was literally exhausting. On more than one occasion, he fell ill due to exposure from the harsh winter weather after standing in soup kitchen lines. Although he endured these abysmal conditions, we must also remember that, to understand the life of the type of fallen woman he was to write about, he must have had to spend time in just the sort of places that he depicts in his book. What we know of Crane's supposed appetites, the reader could assume that perhaps all of Crane's research was not as harsh and painful as one might be led to believe.

As Crane researched the lifestyle of his Maggie, in fairness, we must also ask, how did Susanna Rowson so completely understand the nature of her heroine, Charlotte? Was the creation of Rowson's heroine simply influenced by Richardson's *Clarissa,* or was she an actual person? Perhaps the character of Charlotte was drafted from Rowson's own life experience, a life in a society where Rowson and other women were viewed as "merely her husband's property"? Although there are probably no absolute answers for the above questions regarding Rowson's work, that does not imply that the questions themselves should be dismissed—on the contrary, they should be considered. In turning toward the texts themselves, the reader must be aware of how the interpretation of these two novels affect each other. Is Crane's text simply an effort to report the conditions of the bowery, or does it address the consequences of being seduced and betrayed? Given Crane's obsession with virtue and vice and the influence of the realism of Howells, Garland, and others, I believe *Maggie* does both, and it is these thoughts and questions that move the reader to take a closer look at Charlotte, Maggie, and their supporting casts.

One of the most startling contrasts between the two heroines is that of their childhood environments and the relationships with their respective families. The reader of the two novels can easily distinguish the difference, but then is faced to ponder the fact that the outcome of each girl's life is virtually a parallel of the other's. How much of a role does proper (clean, Godfearing, moral) environment play? Also an interesting contrast is found in the "education" of each girl. While Charlotte's family has made sacrifices to send her to boarding school, Maggie's parents do nothing to see that she is exposed to any type of schooling. Her education is in the curriculum of the street, and to some degree, at least through Crane's eyes, it makes her the wiser of the two girls.

In relation to family, Charlotte came from a loving and comfortable atmosphere. Although we know nothing of Charlotte's early childhood as we do Maggie's, we do know that Charlotte was an only child, or as Rowson writes, Charlotte "was the only pledge of their [her parent's] mutual love" (26). By contrast Maggie was the middle child, sandwiched between a younger, neglected brother, and an older brother who seemingly preferred fighting to anything else. Whereas the Temple family enjoyed a modest income and lived comfortably, the Johnson family endured the depths of poverty.

The relationship between Maggie's parents is opposite that of Charlotte's. Maggie's mother and father constantly engaged in behavior more conducive to life in a combat zone rather than an environment typical of where children could grow and prosper in order to become productive members of society. For example, alcohol played a large role in the dysfunctional relationship between Maggie's family members. Maggie's mother constantly drank from "a yellow-brown bottle" (signifying alcohol) (14), and the ensuing comments from her husband confirm her alcoholism: "You've been drinkin', Mary. You'd better let up on the bot' ol' woman, or you'll git done" (13). The entire blame for this environment, however, cannot be thrust upon Maggie's mother, for after an argument between the spouses at the text's beginning, the father also contributes to the dysfunction within the family. "In the quarrel between husband and wife, the woman was victor. The man seized his hat and rushed from the room, apparently determined upon a vengeful drunk" (14).

With this knowledge, it is reasonable to assume that Charlotte and Maggie would lead different lives. While Charlotte actively pursued the life that a young lady should, Maggie, on the other hand, chose the only course available to her in order to insure her survival—a silent vigilance which she hoped would present the opportunity for a better quality of life. As the heroines are, in fact, extremely different in terms of environment and filial relations, the irony lies in the fact that both girls suffer the same fate, death as the result of seduction and betrayal. This fact is also another reason that Rowson's novel was commercially successful. Readers were interested to learn that the fate of one seduced and betrayed was not exclusive to members of the poverty-riddled lower class, but could indeed happen to anyone. Rowson caught her readers off guard here and it worked to her advantage. However, in the case of Maggie, even though a tragic ending is predetermined, readers are still horrified at the cold, harsh, and impersonal outcome of the novel. But for Rowson and Crane the treatment of their girls seems to have been successful in one aspect or another—Rowson's commercially, Crane's critically. It is evident that the fall of an educated girl from a decent family interested the reading public far more than the story of the tragic fate of a fair, yet pathetic street urchin. Also, what is interesting here is the stark contrast in world views. Any recognition of the concepts of determinism was alien to Rowson's work, while Crane's text is defined by it.

Another trait continuously emphasized throughout both texts is each heroine's beauty. In *Charlotte Temple,* Montraville, the seducer, is immediately captivated by the young Charlotte's appearance when she was a girl of thirteen. Two years later, as she grows into a young woman, Montraville proclaims to his companion, Belcour, that her beauty stole his heart. "She is the sweetest girl in the world . . . she had on a blue bonnet, and with a pair of lovely eyes the same colour, has contrived to make me feel devilish odd about the heart" (10). From the above passage, the perception of Charlotte's beauty is established when she is a young girl, and from this implication we are led to believe she has and will always be so. For Maggie Johnson, beauty was not nearly as eminent.

Our first vision of Maggie is hardly impressive: "A small ragged girl dragged a red, bawling infant along the crowded ways" (11). The following scenes then imply that Maggie was probably undernourished and abused as a small child, as were her two brothers (the infant previously mentioned dies with no explanation regarding the cause of death—probably abuse). Maggie's behavior also exemplifies one who is "gun-shy" from being beaten or severely abused: "Maggie, with side glances of fear of interruption, ate like a small pursued tigress" (14). Indeed Maggie's childhood was quite different than Charlotte's, but, despite all obstacles, she grew to be an attractive young girl. Crane's description of Maggie's impending womanhood is one of the most frequently quoted passages in the book. "The girl, Maggie, blossomed in a mud puddle. She grew to be a most rare and wonderful production of a tenement district, a pretty girl (24).

The reader is here caught off guard by Crane who takes a "weed" and turns it into a "blossom" (later to be deflowered). Charlotte's "blooming" was evident from story's beginning, but Maggie's beauty arises despite all the circumstances which should stifle it. Interestingly enough, both heroines "wither" like dying flowers near their death. Charlotte endures delirious fits of sickness in childbirth, and Maggie has begun to lead such a hardened life that she is mistaken for her alcoholic mother on the final night of her life. It is natural that each woman had an unusually alluring amount of beauty. It was commonplace to equate beauty with virtue in the eyes of society, and the fact that both women lost their attractiveness is also given as a consequence

of becoming a fallen woman. Naturally each heroine would be beautiful in her pure state for these attributes make them a greater, or more valuable conquest (commodity, property) in the eyes of their would-be seducer.

In the seduction of Charlotte, Rowson uses a strategy common among seducers in the narratives of that time. In this practice, the seducer calls attention to the fact that, if the girl does not give in to his desires, he will invariably perish by the result of someone else's hand (in the case of Montraville—war), or to more dramatically convey his act of despair, that he should even perish by his own. Montraville uses his ploy effectively in convincing Charlotte that the two should never be separated. In Chapter XI, "Conflict of Love and Duty," Montraville succeeds in driving a wedge between Charlotte and her parents by making her choose between her love for him or the honor of filial duty. He is most convincing to the young and naive Charlotte as he delivers his finest "arts" in convincing her to stray. After Charlotte proclaims her loyalty to her parents' wishes, Montraville eloquently convinces her that his life is more or less over:

> Well, Charlotte, since that is the case, I find I have deceived myself with fallacious hopes. I had flattered my fond heart, that I was dearer to Charlotte than anything in the world beside. I thought that you would for my sake have braved the dangers of the ocean, that you would, by your affection and smiles, have softened the hardships of war, and, had it been my fate to fall, that your tenderness would chear [sic] the hour of death and smooth my passage to another world. But farewel [sic], Charlotte! I see you never loved me. I shall now welcome the friendly ball that deprives me of the sense of my misery.
>
> (42-3)

After receiving this artful oration, Charlotte weakens and agrees to elope with Montraville.

The initial seduction proposition to Maggie from Pete was more crude and direct. Pete, whom Maggie considered to be "a very elegant bartender," gave the appearance of a dandy. Impressed with his wardrobe and his presence, Maggie listened attentively to his tales of barroom brawling conquests when he spoke to Maggie's brother, Jimmie. This impressionistic view of Pete does indeed portray a character with power and control:

> His mannerisms stamped him as a man who had a correct sense of his personal superiority. There was valor and contempt for circumstances in the glance of his eye. He waved his hands like a man of the world, who dismisses religion and philosophy, and says "Rats!" He had certainly seen everything and with each curl of his lip, he declared that it amounted to nothing . . .
>
> (25)

In essence, Maggie was seduced before Pete ever spoke to her. After observing him, she knew that there was something between them. "Maggie perceived that here was the ideal man. Her dim thoughts were often searching for far away lands where, as God says, the little hills sing together in the morning. Under the trees of her dream-gardens there had always walked a lover" (26). In Maggie's world, the "dream-gardens" were anywhere that would free her from the hellish existence shared with her family, or her "sweatshop" job at the cuff and collar factory. Maggie felt she had indeed found her saviour. When Pete left the Johnson house that evening, she observed him as he walked with Jimmie. Deeper and deeper she became immersed in Pete's world. If anyone could save her from the life of the bowery, it was surely Pete. Maggie thought to herself, "Here was a formidable man who disdained the strength of a world full of fists. Here was one who had contempt for brass-clothed power; one whose knuckles could defiantly ring against the granite of law. He was a knight" (28).

Pete's approach to Maggie was anything but chivalrous and knightlike for his language and manner were vulgar to say the least. "Say, Mag, I'm stuck on your shape. It's outa sight" (26). Upon his return a few nights later, he stayed long enough to ask Maggie for a date in this gentlemanly fashion, "Say, Mag, put on yer bes' duds Friday night an' I'll take yehs t' d' show. See?" (29). Maggie needed no encouragement to accept. Despite the ravings of her alcohol-crazed mother, she eventually left home to live under the protection of Pete. However, like Charlotte, Maggie did not immediately give in to vice. After her first date with Pete, she refused his request for a good night kiss. This refusal in all probability made Pete more determined to conquer Maggie, just as Charlotte's opposition to Montraville's plans made him more adamant in possessing her.

The consequences of each seducer's conquest are well known; however, there is something different in their methods of betrayal. With Montraville, it is arguable that he never meant to truly betray Charlotte. His problem arose from the circumstance that he simply fell in love with another woman. But in this already tragic situation, the reader's ire begins to turn away from Montraville and toward his friend, Belcour. Although Montraville knew he had wronged Charlotte by falling for another woman, the situation was further complicated by Belcour as he lied to Montraville regarding Charlotte's own fidelity. Belcour's selfish motives (for he wanted Charlotte for his own) assured that no reconciliation could ever take place. He was willing to do anything even if it included betraying his best friend. It never occurred to him that she wanted nothing to do with him.

Montraville never suspected his friend of wrong-doing until he learned the truth after Charlotte's death. Upon finding out, Montraville killed Belcour, but he himself was wounded in the fight. Physically he recovered, but he would spend the rest of his days in regret. As Rowson writes, "He recovered; but to the end of his life was subject to severe fits of melancholy, and while he remained at New-York frequently retired to the churchyard, where he would weep over the grave, and regret the untimely fate of the lovely Charlotte Temple" (118).

The motive and fate of Maggie's seducer are quite different. Pete, unlike Montraville, set out only to rob a girl of her virtue, and then Maggie simply served Pete's purpose until one of his former "flames" returned to town. Pete's treatment of Maggie is harshly cruel as he literally "dumps" her in the middle of "a night on the town." While Maggie and Pete are in a saloon, Pete spies Nell, the object of his previous affection. Deserting Maggie to greet his former lover and her date, a man whom Crane describes as "a mere boy," Pete then calls Maggie to the table to join them. The conversation is dominated by Pete and Nell, leaving Maggie and the "boy" to suffer an existence as resentful outsiders. And it is obvious from the dialog between Pete and Nell that she is a "professional" woman:

> "I thought you were gone for good," began Pete, at once.
>
> "When did yeh git back? How did dat Buff'lo bus'ness turn out?"
>
> The woman shrugged her shoulders. "Well, he didn't have as many stamps as he tried to make out, so I shook him, that's all."
>
> (58)

Nell is a professional in her trade, and she leaves nothing to chance when sizing up her next "client." "The woman [Nell] was familiar with all his affairs, asked him about mutual friends, and knew the amount of his salary" (58). Nell openly tries to lure Pete away for the evening, casting aside any consideration of the other two partners. She begins to badger Pete to leave with her after a short time in the saloon.

> "Say," whispered she, leaning forward, "let's go over to Billie's and have a heluva time."
>
> "Well, it's dis way! See?." said Pete. "I got dis lady frien' here."
>
> "Oh, t' hell with her," argued the woman Pete appeared disturbed.
>
> "All right," said she, nodding her head at him. "All right for you! We'll see the next you ask me to go anywheres with you."
>
> (59)

Here, Nell attempts a ploy used by the seducer in a majority of seduction narratives. Naturally, she does not imply that "death" will keep her from seeing Pete again, but something far worse: alienation by choice. Feeling pressured by Nell, it is Pete who is now seduced. He leaves Maggie and Freddie, the mere boy, in the saloon on the pretense of having a private conversation with Nell. Pete steps outside the saloon with Nell, never intending to return to Maggie later that evening, or for that matter, ever again.

By Pete's actions, Maggie is immediately transformed into the status of a whore. Realizing that they have both been deserted, Freddie then sets his sights on Maggie, much in the same way that Belcour took aim at Charlotte. And like Charlotte, Maggie refused to have any relations with her lecherous counterpart. Sadly enough, however, Maggie would soon find it necessary to accommodate men such as Freddie—for like Charlotte, she could not return home. Whereas Charlotte would not return out of shame, Maggie could not bear returning to the hellish environment where her drunken mother would continue to abuse her. Maggie made a decision based on her fallen status; for a short time, she would function mechanically, in order to survive. Later, she would choose the other option given a fallen woman.

Later, the reader finds Pete drunk and in the company of Nell and several other prostitutes. A pathetic scene ensues in which the seducer finally passes out and the girls relieve him of his money. On the way out the door, Nell stoops over him and says, "What a damn fool" (74). This different twist added by Crane, that of the aggressor being used and abused, affords the female reader an added sense of satisfaction.

The death scenes of the two heroines are depicted differently. Charlotte's death in childbirth, in the company of those who tried to save her, is more personal than Maggie's fate of suicide. One aspect that the two deaths do have in common is the forgiving parent. Charlotte's father forgives her and then takes his granddaughter to raise. When informed of Maggie's death, while being consoled by a neighbor, Mary Johnson hysterically screams "Oh, yes, I'll fergive her! I'll fergive her!" (77). But there is no hope for renewal in the next generation.

Another quotation from the scene clearly depicts the influence of early seduction narratives on Crane's text. Looking further at the text, on more than one occasion the neighbor who consoles Mary Johnson mentions "what a ter'ble affliction is dis" (75). Two lines later, the woman clarifies this statement: "Me poor Mary, how I feel fer yehs! Ah, what a ter'ble affliction is a disobed'ent chil'" (75). How ironic that Maggie be viewed as an affliction when clearly it was an abusive mother, afflicted with alcoholism, that drove her from home. Also, the term *afflicted* coincides with instances of "demonic possession," or unnatural behavior. The term was used frequently through the eighteenth century in both witchcraft and seduction narratives, and the

implication of disobedient children is a standard warning issued in seduction narratives as the cause that precludes the death and dishonor in the case of the "fallen woman."

In studying the fate of the heroines and their seducers, the reader of these two texts should also recognize that the seducer was not alone at fault and that another character had equal influence over each heroine's fate. In her article, "The Alternate Fallen Woman in *Maggie: A Girl of the Streets*," Laura Hapke discusses the influence of Nell on the fate of Maggie. Hapke describes the differences between Nell and Maggie as prostitutes and points out that there was little chance that Maggie could survive in this cold and unemotional atmosphere. Perhaps the obvious implication of the article is that if Nell had not lured Pete away from Maggie, perhaps she would have never turned to the streets and eventually would not have to consider the final option of suicide to come to terms with her guilt. Nell, as well as Charlotte's teacher, Mademoiselle LaRue, are interchangeable as "alternate fallen women." Like Nell, LaRue is a business woman who can manipulate any situation to her own advantage. The only difference between the two is in the depiction of each at story's end. LaRue has fallen into the path of vice and its ensuing illness and makes a feeble attempt at redemption by confessing her evils to Charlotte's parents. With Nell, we see her "fleecing" Pete's pockets and strutting off to conquer another victim. We are only left to imagine that she will suffer the same misfortunes (poverty, disease, and eventual death) as does LaRue.

Charlotte Temple and Maggie Johnson are indeed sisters. Each suffers the consequences of being seduced and abandoned and in each case that outcome is death.

Although the texts vary in style from eighteenth century sentimentalism to late nineteenth century naturalism, their themes, characters, and messages are incredibly similar. Crane's novel is hardly ever treated as a seduction narrative, where as Rowson's is exclusively regarded as such. Obviously, how critics and scholars view these works often depends on their own fields of interests. But what is important to realize is that hardly ever does a work fit into a single category simply because it was placed there by those who feel that canonical validity is threatened if one crosses the boundaries set by eminent scholars decades ago. For *Maggie,* Stephen Crane was influenced by the theme of seduction and betrayal, and the concepts of virtue and vice. Perhaps, he never read **Charlotte Temple,** but he realized the significance and popularity of its heroine's plight for its theme was a popular one. Crane was only twenty-one years old when he began writing *Maggie,* an impressionable age in the budding career of a writer. Charlotte's type of character impressed him, and Maggie Johnson was born from that impression.

Notes

1. In his creation of Maggie Johnson, Crane elaborated on his fascination regarding the concepts of virtue and vice—a subject, later an obsession, from which he would never be free (to insure himself that he would continue to endure this tug-of-war, Crane would eventually marry the madam of a Jacksonville, Florida, "nightclub"). Born the son of a Methodist minister, Crane wavered on religious principles, at times seeming to deny the existence of a superior being altogether, yet he would never be free from the strict dogma his father imposed upon him (Crane's own religious convictions are best found in his poetry). His rebellious nature led to his subsequent Bohemian days in New York where he found comfort with those who endured the day to day suffering of the artist's lifestyle.

In *The Double Life of Stephen Crane,* Christopher Benfey argues that Crane approached life and art quite unlike other writers. Benfey asserts that the majority of writers first experience certain episodes or aspects of life and then write about them. In the case of Crane, Benfey believes just the opposite to be true, that Crane wrote the story, and then set out to live the adventure. By recounting Crane's work and by following his actions, Benfey's allegation is partially accurate; however, for *Maggie,* Crane did his homework first.

Works Cited

Benfey, Christopher. *The Double Life of Stephen Crane.* New York: Alfred A. Knopf, 1992.

Crane, Stephen. *Maggie: A Girl of the Streets.* 1893. Charlottesville: U of Virginia P, 1969. Vol 1 of *The Works of Stephen Crane.* Ed. Fredson Bowers. 10 vols. 1969-76.

Davidson, Cathy N. *Revolution and the Word: The Rise of the Novel in America.* New York: Oxford UP, 1986.

Dooley, Patrick K. *Stephen Crane: An Annotated Bibliography of Secondary Scholarship.* New York: G. K. Hall & Co., 1992.

Fiedler, Leslie A. *Love and Death in the American Novel.* New York: Stein and Day, 1966.

Hapke, Laura. "The Alternate Fallen Woman in *Maggie: A Girl of the Streets.*" *The Markham Review.* 12.3 (1983): 41-43.

Hardwick, Elizabeth. *Seduction and Betrayal: Women and Literature.* New York: Random House, 1970.

Lewis, Jan. "The Republican Wife: Virtue and Seduction in the Early Republic," *The William and Mary Quarterly.* 44. 4 (1987): 689-722.

Martin, Wendy. "Seduced and Abandoned in the New World: The Fallen Woman in American Fiction," *Woman in Sexist Society.* New York: Basic Books, 1971.

Rowson, Susanna Haswell. *Charlotte Temple.* Ed. Cathy N. Davidson. New York: Oxford P, 1986.

Kay Ferguson Ryals (essay date 1998)

SOURCE: Ryals, Kay Ferguson. "America, Romance, and the Fate of the Wandering Woman: The Case of *Charlotte Temple.*" In *Women, America, and Movement: Narratives of Relocation,* edited by Susan L. Roberson, pp. 81-105. Columbia: University of Missouri Press, 1998.

[*In the following essay, Ryals studies* Charlotte Temple *as a "quest romance" written in response to the social and political circumstances that existed in the United States during the time in which it was written. Ryals asserts that Rowson presents her protagonist in such a manner, and within such a narrative, as to convey her own personal social and political beliefs and to encourage her readers to question the conditions—in particular, society's enforcement of women's dependency—that lead to her heroine's inability to realize her goal.*]

A strong case could be made that Susanna Rowson's **Charlotte Temple,** published in Philadelphia in 1794, was the first great American novel. Leslie Fiedler has called it "the first book by an American to move American readers," and indeed its popularity with the reading public was such that it remained the top seller of any American novel until the publication of *Uncle Tom's Cabin* over half-a-century later.[1] Such success might strike the modern reader as surprising, for Rowson's tale of virtue-under-threat seems entirely conventional, the stuff of sentimental melodrama. The novel recounts the migration of its eponymous heroine from England to America during the Revolutionary War, a migration that begins with the false promises of a seducer and ends tragically with Charlotte's death as an abandoned "fallen" woman. Still, the very popularity of the novel in the early years of the Republic suggests that the story of Charlotte's misadventure provided a model in terms of which readers, many of whom were women, could imagine the promises and perils of their own novel political and cultural adventure.

In this essay, I will examine the connections between **Charlotte Temple** and the political and cultural circumstances of its publication during the United States' own "post-colonial" moment. I will argue, first, that **Charlotte Temple** is best understood not as a sentimental novel, but rather as a kind of quest romance in which a female character attempts to occupy the position of the wandering, "errant" hero; second, that Charlotte's failure as a romance hero is linked to a certain gendered "inadequacy," and that the novel thus invites readers to consider the social and institutional constraints that contributed to that inadequacy; and, finally, that Rowson's subsequent career as an early feminist and educational reformer constituted a response to the conditions fictionalized in *Charlotte Temple,* conditions that—in reducing women to a state of dependency—threaten to corrupt both women's sexual virtue and the Republic's political virtue. The concepts of "virtue" and "corruption" are key here, for they are central not only to the didactic sexual language of women's fiction, but also to the political vocabulary of the founding era. Indeed, Rowson's novel can be read as a feminist intervention in the post-revolutionary debate about the extent to which the American polity should continue to be imagined in terms of the ideology of classical civic republicanism; the relationship between virtue, commerce, and corruption is the decisive point of contention in this debate. It is against the backdrop of such ideological struggle that we can begin to see what is at stake in Fiedler's observation that *Charlotte Temple* is, in effect, the novel in which many early American *readers* are able for the first time to recognize themselves as *American* readers. What sets *Charlotte Temple* apart from the more overtly politically minded novels of the period— and what makes it relevant to ongoing discussions about the role of "otherness" in the history of the American experience—is the fact that Rowson's project for imagining America is one in which the protagonist's dual status as a woman and a wanderer is absolutely crucial.

THE ERROR OF HER WAYS

Charlotte Temple opens with a question posed by Montraville, the heroine's seducer, to his even more treacherous friend Belcour: "Are you for a walk?" The men's ensuing amble takes them on a side trip through the village of Chichester as they make their way to Portsmouth, which is at once their immediate destination and their point of departure on a military expedition bound for the rebellious American colonies. Significantly, this detour through Chichester—which results in Montraville's meeting of and ultimately in his seduction of Charlotte—both begins and prefigures the men's journey to America, a journey which, replete with ocean crossing and battles set at a moment of national founding, is in many ways an archetypal romance journey. But the walk through Chichester is also a *diversion* from the men's journey, a moment of wandering or "errancy" that postpones their more serious military mission. Montraville and Belcour head towards Chichester "knowing they [have] sufficient time to reach the place of destination before dark, yet allow them a walk." Hence within the framework of the men's own itinerary, this casual stroll is both a *part* of their journey and a departure *from* it, a wandering away from their goal that nevertheless moves them toward their destination.

The genre of romance is characterized by precisely such a structural tension between the quester's progress towards his destination and moments of errancy that swerve away from that destination. Indeed, the ubiquity of such tension in romance narratives has led Patricia Parker to describe romance as "a form which both projects and postpones or wanders from a projected ending." Moreover, Parker has shown how, throughout the long tradition of Western romance, the term "error" itself has functioned as "a romance pun," for its own meaning has wandered to include not only geographical, mental, and moral deviation, but also the semantic wandering or slippage that emerges from the rhetorical and figurative dimension of language as such.[2]

But the traditional romance paradigm of progress-via-errancy is also marked by a persistent pattern of gendering. Describing romance as a genre that "necessitates the projection of an Other," Parker maintains that romance is typically structured around "the narrative topos of overcoming a female enchantress or obstacle en route to completion and ending."[3] In many a classic romance, an enclosed, feminine space of temptation—be it Circe's island, Dido's cave, or Acrasia's Bower of Bliss—serves as the male hero's testing ground, and the conquest of that feminine space constitutes his "education." In *Charlotte Temple,* Montraville's diversionary walk, made in order to "take a survey of the Chichester ladies as they returned from their devotions" (3), also functions in accordance with this gendered logic, for his detour into the cloistered feminine space of Chichester and thence into a distracting liaison with Charlotte is but a *temporary* deviation, a moment of moral errancy that he overcomes in the New World. There, as a determined male quester, Montraville achieves military honor, economic prosperity, and sanctioned marriage— with, of course, someone other than the pregnant and abandoned Charlotte. While Montraville's sexual wandering is represented as causing him some emotional anguish, his errancy does not ultimately interfere with either his military promotion or his social advancement; indeed, his affair with Charlotte even generates a certain moral profit by teaching him the "value" of Julia Franklin's chaste love.

In its traditional form, then, the romance plot unfolds according to a *speculative* pattern that is explicitly gendered: the male hero's errancy can be understood as a *strategic* loss—one that will be retroactively transformed into an "investment"—because the generic conventions of romance preordain that the hero's swerving away from his goal in an encounter with a female "otherness" will eventually be recouped in a moment of triumphal return. Yet if, as Northrop Frye maintains, romance is in some sense "the structural core of all fiction," this is perhaps because the story of language has itself so often been told *as* a romance—one that exhibits this same gendered, speculative logic. Thus Margaret Homans has observed that "the dominant myth of Western languages has their operation structured as a quest romance, based on the boy's postoedipal renunciation of the mother and his quest for substituted objects of desire." In the "myth" of language put forward by Jacques Lacan, for example, signification entails—at least for men—an economy of sacrifice and gain that makes it a speculative venture with a logic akin to that of romance. For Lacan, the loss of a pre-oedipal state of imaginary wholeness is the "sacrifice" that is necessary for the subject's accession to the symbolic order of language; the signifier of this "self-sacrifice" is the phallus, "that pound of flesh which is mortgaged in [the male subject's] relationship to the signifier."[4] This "mortgage" is a sound investment, yielding precisely the ability to signify and to symbolize that makes possible successful action within those complex modern institutions in which all power is, to some extent, discursive power.

As feminist critics like Homans have noted, the Lacanian account of language, with its emphasis on the phallic quality of signification, represents the relationship of women to language as problematic, given woman's biological "lack": to already lack the penis, to be "literally" castrated, is to be identified with the literal. As Homans observes, this identification means that those social structures and institutions through which power is exercised are grounded in a form of symbolization from which women are by "nature" excluded: "The symbolic order, both the legal system and language, depends on the identification of the woman with the literal, and then on the denial that the literal has any connection with masculine figurations."[5] Thus while the male Lacanian subject, like the romance hero, supposedly "has what it takes" to navigate the treacherous and deceptive shoals of the signifying chain, the alignment of women with the literal condemns them to a position of passivity and powerlessness outside the symbolic order.

Bearing in mind the gendering of romance, both in its strictly generic sense and in its broader alignment with Western narratives of language and identity, we can return to Rowson's novel. Immediately, however, we must address a difficulty: for obviously, although **Charlotte Temple** accords with the narrative logic of romance when we take Montraville as the questing hero, the book is named not after its male adventurer but after its "fallen" heroine. Yet, there are a number of ways in which the novel invites us to read its plot in terms of the generic conventions of romance, but of a romance filtered through the lens of a gender reversal in which a female character occupies—or attempts to occupy—the subject position of the quester. For example, Charlotte's journey to America begins on her birthday, an occasion that would, in the narrative of the traditional romance quester, mark a rite of passage signifying the hero's

transition into independent adulthood. Thus it is not surprising that, at the start of Charlotte's "maiden voyage," Montraville promises the girl love, marriage, and motherhood—the New-World-as-family—so that her wandering appears to her to offer a route to personal fulfillment and the assumption of her proper social role. Moreover, throughout the novel Charlotte invokes the language of the romance quest to describe her own circumstances, as when she responds to Mrs. Beauchamp's query about whether she would return to her parents should they agree to take her back: "Would I! . . . would not the poor sailor, tost on a tempestuous ocean, threatened every moment with death, gladly return to the shore he had left to trust to its deceitful calmness? Oh, my dear Madam, I would return, though to do it I were obliged to walk barefoot over a burning desert [*sic*]" (82).

Yet the romance pattern of testing and return invoked by this last image is precisely what Charlotte will be denied, and this denial is evidence that—given the pattern of gendering so crucial to romance—Rowson's attempt to narrate a quest romance from a uniquely female perspective is bound to be extremely problematic. In fact, the shift from a male to a female protagonist within a fairly conventional romance plot structure and the jarring disruptions that result from that shift are central to Rowson's project in **Charlotte Temple.** The imagery of the novel often calls attention to the consequences of this gender reversal. Hence while Charlotte is persistently depicted in accordance with the traditions of the romance quester, the cumulative effect of such imagery is ironic, for it makes clear that she is unable to become either an epic Columbus or a bourgeois Robinson Crusoe, whose shipwreck proved to be but the perfect opportunity for his heroic self-assertion and "progress." On the contrary, Charlotte finds that having "trusted [her] happiness on a tempestuous ocean," she is "wrecked and lost forever" (115) when her chastity is forfeited during passage from the Old World to the New.

Such imagery becomes even more poignant and ironic when we note that Charlotte is in part seduced away from her home shore by rhetoric in which Montraville portrays *himself* as the adventurous hero in danger of shipwreck. He urges her, for example, to "reflect, that when I leave my native land, perhaps a few short weeks may terminate my existence; the perils of the ocean—the dangers of war—" (37); Montraville's plea, which the overwrought Charlotte breaks off, is able to elicit Charlotte's sympathy precisely because it alludes to that realm of "generic" threats that confronts the romance hero. Similarly, when Montraville's father warns him against "a precipitate union with a girl of little or no fortune"—a warning that will cause Montraville to desert Charlotte—his advice employs imagery of peril that ultimately proves relevant not so much to Montraville as to Charlotte: "Your happiness will always be dear to me," Montraville's father tells him, "and I wish to warn you of a rock on which the peace of many an honest fellow has been wrecked" (40). That rock, of course, is Charlotte herself. From Montraville's perspective, the female wanderer is but, to recall Parker's formulation, an "enchantress or obstacle" to be overcome; the ambitious young man's entanglement with this girl of modest means poses a threat to his own quest for social advancement through prudent marriage.

Clearly, then, errancy has very different and far more dangerous connotations for Charlotte, the female quester, than it does for the male hero. Although Montraville successfully recoups his wayward dalliance with Charlotte, Charlotte's "error"—as Rowson insistently calls it—takes her away from the "path of rectitude" (35) to which she, unlike the errant male of romance, cannot return. This essential difference is especially evident in Charlotte's illegitimate pregnancy. Although Montraville's own moral errancy is in effect invisible, it nevertheless inscribes itself quite visibly on Charlotte's body in the form of her swollen womb. Yet Rowson is at pains to make clear what actually prevents Charlotte's "return," what makes her—in contrast to her seducer—unable to recoup her errancy: the culprit is society's sexual double standard, a form of institutionalized hypocrisy that insists on regarding the physical sign of a woman's temporary moral errancy as evidence of an irredeemable fallenness. A poignant scene near the end of the novel makes this double standard painfully clear: very pregnant and deathly ill, the forsaken Charlotte wanders in the cold in search of refuge, only to hear a soldier exclaim, "[M]ay God bless [Montraville], for a better officer never lived, he is so good to us all" (117). For Montraville, the male quester, a speculative gap exists between body and character that allows a space for self-fashioning and thus for the projection of a virtuous public reputation. By contrast, Charlotte's pregnant body represents a literalizing of symbolic moral errancy in which signifier and signified are collapsed; the moral character of this *female* quester is allowed no redemptive wandering from the site of her body, which is presumed to serve as an "inerrant," strictly determined material signifier of an errant inner state.

Unlike her male lover, then, Charlotte is already marked as fallen when she enters the "new Eden," and consequently she is forbidden access to whatever social and economic opportunity America might have offered to women immigrants. Charlotte's movement is, as we shall see, always circumscribed by the institutions of patriarchy, and yet—paradoxically—the way that patriarchy constrains and limits her mobility causes her wandering to be one from which there is no way home. Because she does *not* "have what it takes" to succeed as an autonomous agent within this patriarchal world, because she lacks the underwriting by phallic authority

that could ensure the recuperation of error, adventure leads Charlotte not to triumphal return, but to an absolute and literal errancy. For this "dear wanderer" (97), this "poor forsaken wanderer" (116), errancy leads not to advancement-by-trial and accession to a privileged position in the symbolic order, but rather to madness, regression, and that ultimate form of errancy without return—death.

THE STING OF DEPENDENCE

As chronicles of a hero's adventures, traditional romances tend to be episodic, recounting a series of seemingly random incidents and encounters that, despite their initially threatening nature, end up benefiting the hero. Northrop Frye sees the hero's conspicuously fortuitous relationship to chance as central to the romance genre: "The success of the hero," he writes, "derives from a current of energy which is partly from him and partly outside him. . . . The most basic term for this current of energy is luck." I would add that the "luck" that comes from "without" the hero is constituted by the generic conventions that govern romance as a literary form, conventions that function in a sense as the institutional supports that guarantee in advance the hero's success; those favorable gods who pull the strings behind the scenes in classical romances can perhaps be seen as personifications of these generic guarantees. Of course, luck is also important to romance at the more mundane level of character and story, but the luck that comes from "within" the hero—his uncanny ability to master whatever contingencies fortune throws his way—is of a specific kind. For the hero's success in overcoming obstacles depends in large part upon his epistemological sophistication—that is, his ability first to interpret or "read" correctly the circumstances in which he finds himself and then to act so as to turn those circumstances to his advantage. Above all, he must be able to distinguish truth from dissembling, and this requires in turn that he be able both to understand and to employ for his own ends the gap between signifiers and signifieds that marks the rhetorical errancy of language and of other symbolic systems. Just as, in the stories about language told by critics like Lacan and Jacques Derrida, symbolization is an effect of errancy, deriving from a space of difference and deferral that sunders any univocal and "necessary" relationship between signifier and signified, so too the romance hero's "luck"—his ability to manage his own physical and moral errancy—is an effect of his ability to manage the space of epistemological errancy that intervenes between surface appearance and actual reality.[6]

In *Charlotte Temple,* Montraville's career seems to follow this pattern of "luck," of chance turned to advantage. For example, Montraville's introduction to Julia Franklin, his wife-to-be, is occasioned by an "accident" (71). When a fire breaks out next to the Franklins' house, a stranger who is helping to save the house places in Montraville's hands for safekeeping a box containing "jewels to a large amount, about two hundred pounds in money, and a miniature picture set for a bracelet" (72); this picture is of Julia's deceased mother, whose painted likeness to her daughter conveniently leads Montraville to the box's owner. Julia's box is an emblem for her financial fortune and her intact sexual "virtue," both of which are delivered to Montraville through a stroke of good fortune so improbable as to seem almost destined from "outside him" (to use Frye's terminology). Yet Montraville's luck is also "partly from him," for he plans and profits from this initial boon. Even before he has met Julia—and even as he continues to admit his responsibility towards Charlotte—Montraville schemes to increase Julia's "debt" to him for recovering her treasure; thus when he returns the box to Julia, he slyly removes the picture of her mother so that "by presenting it to her when she thinks it is lost," he will "enhance the value of the obligation" that Julia feels towards him (72). His strategy is, of course, successful, and the wily speculator embarks upon his own romance with Julia.

Montraville's relationship with Charlotte is also driven by a combination of luck from without and acuity from within. After he gets an initial glance at Charlotte and spends "three whole days in thinking on her and in endeavouring to form some plan for seeing her," Montraville determines once again "to set off for Chichester, and trust *to chance* either to favour or frustrate his designs" (4, my emphasis). Yet the language here is rather misleading, for "chance" is only imagined as helping or hindering a plan that has already been devised by Montraville. Thus when he does "chance" upon Charlotte on this trip, Montraville is prepared with "a letter he [has] *purposely* written" to her (5, my emphasis), a letter that effects her seduction. To ensure that happenstance has no further part in his meetings with Charlotte, he bribes her teacher, Mademoiselle La Rue, to continue to bring Charlotte "into the field" (5). Indeed, in a passage describing Montraville's interception of a letter written by Charlotte that would have summoned her parents to her aid and averted her departure for America, the novel mocks the very notion that chance has any role in determining Charlotte's future: "Montraville knew too well the consequences that must unavoidably ensue, should this letter reach Mr. Temple: he therefore wisely resolved to walk on the deck, tear it in pieces, and commit the fragments to the care of Neptune, who might or might not, as suited his convenience, convey them to shore" (58). Obviously, the future course of Charlotte's errant letter, and thus of Charlotte herself, is not actually subject to the realm of chance such that it "might or might not" reach its destination, depending on the heroine's "luck"; instead, the letter's "fate" is controlled from without by the scheming Montraville who, like the figure of Neptune, stands for the constraining exter-

nal "reality" that in the end determines the female quester's destiny. This irony suggests that for Charlotte the possibility of a properly "speculative" subjectivity—one that can profit from errancy—is foreclosed from the outset, not by any essential deficiency of Charlotte's but rather by the institutional forces that Montraville-as-Neptune represents and that ensure that the female quester is never "lucky." Thus while chance in the traditional romance plot allows the male hero a certain space of indeterminacy in which to prove his mettle and plot his course, the female quester quite literally never *has a chance*; what appears to happen by accident to Charlotte is in fact the result of the ruthless machinations of the "plotting" men who surround her.

In subjecting romance conventions such as that of the errant letter to a heavy dose of dramatic irony, Rowson's novel invites readers to consider ways that women's "accidental" failures are often a consequence of invisible but pervasive institutional constraints, just as the "accidents" of a conventional romance plot are not really fortuitous at all but are in fact the determined effects of generic norms and authorial decisions, and just as—within the story—the "accidents" that befall Charlotte are really the designs of men. Indeed, to lay bare the gendering at work in romance is also, by analogy, to critique those patriarchal social and political institutions in the young Republic that, rather like the generic supports guaranteeing the male romance hero's success, ensure that only male citizens "have what it takes" to act as autonomous agents. Because such institutions—university, counting house, legislative assembly—at once impart to and demand of their initiates considerable discursive power and symbolic acuity, they share with the literary institution of romance a valorization of speculative subjectivity; whether as rhetorician, merchant adventurer, or revolutionary founding father, the successful male quester displays an epistemological sophistication that enables him to manage errancy in all its forms, and so to reap *symbolic* profit (signification, money, political power) from the threat of *literal* loss (castration, shipwreck, execution). Charlotte's attempt to play the role of quester demonstrates that women's exclusion from the symbolic order and its speculative errancy dooms the female romance plot to failure.

Moreover, set as it is during the United States' founding moment, ***Charlotte Temple*** is engaged in an analysis of the politics of gender. The story of Charlotte's fall demonstrates that if the adventuress cannot make her way in the world, it is largely because the kind of flexible subjectivity that makes possible effective agency in a world of contingency is itself an effect of epistemological power, a power that has been denied to all women insofar as they have been systematically excluded from the institutions that cultivate it. Lacking this power, women also lack the ability to act as autonomous subjects, and this in turn places them in a precarious condition of which Charlotte's own is exemplary. In contrast to men, whose success lies largely in their own hands, women face an enforced dependence on those with power, and this dependence makes their "virtue" vulnerable to attack and thus to corruption. As Montraville's father expounds the matter, Montraville's "success in life depends entirely on [himself]," for young men "may exert their talents, make themselves friends, and raise their fortunes on the basis of merit" (39). Montraville's sisters, however, must "have some [economic] provision made, to place them above the snares and temptations which vice ever holds out to the elegant, accomplished female, when oppressed by the frowns of poverty and the sting of dependance [*sic*]" (39).

Rowson's analysis of the institutional constraints that render women vulnerable to manipulation employs a vocabulary that would have had a powerful political resonance in the 1790s, for the notions of dependency, corruption, and virtue—so central to Rowson's novel—are also central to the vocabulary of civic republicanism, an ideology that historians have come to regard as a dominant conceptual force of the founding era. J. G. A. Pocock, in particular, has traced the genealogy of civic republicanism from eighteenth-century Britain and America back to its decisive articulation in the writings of Machiavelli. This mode of thought maintains that man is by nature a political being who can fulfill his *telos* only when he "acts as a citizen, that is as a conscious and autonomous participant in . . . the polis or republic." Arrayed against the ever-present threat of the polis's decay or "corruption"—symbolized by the female figure of Fortune—is the citizens' capacity for masculine *virtù*, that "active ruling quality . . . practiced in republics by citizens equal with one another and devoted to the public good." Republican virtue is presumed to be strictly incompatible with any kind of economic or social dependency on the part of the citizen, for only personal independence would enable the citizen, as Drew McCoy explains, "to pursue spontaneously the common or public good, rather than the narrow interest of the men . . . on whom he depended for his support." But republican virtue also entails a crucial cognitive dimension, which Pocock calls "the epistemology of the particular"; in order to enact the public good, the citizen must first be able to discern what constitutes the good under particular circumstances and act accordingly. Rather like the romance quester, then, the citizen must be—as Quentin Skinner puts it, glossing Machiavelli—"a man of 'flexible disposition': he must be capable of varying his conduct . . . 'as fortune and circumstances dictate.'"[7]

Given the emphasis on epistemological power that we have seen in both romance and republicanism, then, it is hardly surprising that the heroine's "dependence" in **Charlotte Temple** is not simply economic, but also epis-

temological. The most obvious sign of this is her initial rhetorical ineptness, her inability to understand or to deploy words effectively. At the novel's beginning, it is clear that Charlotte's sheltered experience has left her with a naive, literalist understanding of language, making her an easy prey for the "sophistical arguments" (102) and skillful duplicity of Belcour and Montraville. The "eloquent harangue[s]" of Montraville's accomplice, La Rue, typically leave Charlotte "so confused, that she [knows] not what to say" (47), and La Rue's "advice and machinations" (51) are largely responsible for Charlotte's surrender to Montraville. Yet, in presenting Charlotte's epistemological dependence, Rowson is at pains to make clear its origins in the social and political realities of the day. Thus, as we have seen, once Charlotte begins to see through Montraville's promises of marriage, she does attempt both to shake off passivity and to employ language to effect her escape, only to be thwarted by Montraville. By calling attention to the way that Charlotte's epistemological dependence itself *depends upon* the constraining power of patriarchal institutions (as figured in the "machinations" and thefts by Montraville, Belcour, and their accomplices), the novel subverts republican assumptions about the *inherent* incapacity of women even as it acknowledges the *de facto* state of dependence in which women like Charlotte find themselves. Rowson's appropriation of such republican motifs as virtue and corruption is thus trenchantly critical. That the female quester's missives are never even "posted" is emblematic of her exclusion from the institutional networks through which symbolic power circulates, an exclusion that leaves her dependent.

One institution that quite clearly abets the relegation of Charlotte to silence and dependency is the legal system. Charlotte's sense both of her own lowly status before the law and of the tenuous nature of her legal claims on Montraville is evident in her failed attempts to hold the seducer to his promise of marriage, most notably in a plea that begins eloquently but that breaks off in mid-sentence: "But should you, forgetful of your promises, and repenting the engagement you here voluntarily enter into, forsake and leave me on a foreign shore—" (44). The absence of a main clause that marks Charlotte's retreat into silence here is indicative of the harsh truth that the fallen woman has no access to legal redress. But while Charlotte's seduction renders her particularly dependent upon the very men who seek her undoing, married women in the founding era were subject to a similar dependence. According to the common law policy of coverture, which continued after the revolution to regulate most marital contracts in the United States, the legal identity of the wife, the *feme covert,* was "covered," or "hidden," by that of her husband, who took legal possession of her property and whose rights and will were presumed to represent hers. The "protective interpretation" of coverture argued that the law was "protective rather than restrictive in nature" because, in jurist William Blackstone's words, "[e]ven the disabilities, which the wife lies under, are for the most part intended for her protection and benefit."[8]

Yet this "protective" system placed even married women in a position of vulnerability not unlike that of the fallen Charlotte. Indeed, to be "under the protection" of a man was at this time also a euphemistic expression for being a mistress, as when Belcour calculates that if Charlotte were rendered completely destitute, "she would more readily throw herself on his protection" (105); for him, this clearly means only that she would submit to sexual servitude. This link between the female body and "protection" as a form of economic exchange is presented as being so tenacious that it infects almost every male-female relationship in the novel. The distinction between marriage and prostitution thus emerges as a tenuous one, and the fundamental difference between them proves to lie in the degree of female dependency each entails, not in the fact of dependency. Rowson suggests as much in describing the genteel marriages of Mr. Temple's sisters—alliances made to "old, decrepit men" for the sake of wealth, security, and social status—as "legal prostitution" (6). Such unsettling similarities between wife and mistress suggest the degree to which women's multiple dependencies continually threaten female virtue and, by extension, the integrity and virtue of the Republic itself.

Throughout **Charlotte Temple,** then, the speculative systems of exchange governing language and money are shown to be related, and women's "inadequacy" in negotiating such systems is shown to lead to a corrupting dependency. The defining event of the novel—Montraville's seduction or "corruption" of Charlotte—is itself presented as a consequence of these two forms of symbolic power working together, for when, on their first meeting, Montraville places that "letter he [has] purposely written, into Charlotte's hand," he simultaneously "[slips] . . . five guineas into that of Mademoiselle [La Rue]" (5). Similarly, the letters that Charlotte writes to Montraville after he has been tricked into believing that Charlotte has become Belcour's mistress are intercepted by Belcour, who prevails upon Montraville's servant to steal them by means of "the powerful persuasion of a bribe" (92); as this phrase suggests, rhetorical "persuasion" and economic exchange work together in a powerful alliance to ensure that the dependent woman remains in a position of dependency. It is not surprising, then, that as Charlotte is driven to the conclusion of her plot—the plot of the thwarted female quester—she is rendered both penniless and increasingly silent. When the indignant farmer's wife throws her out of the house for which she can no longer pay rent, Charlotte "bow[s] her head in silence," for "the anguish of her heart was too great to permit her to articulate a single word" (114). In desperation, she wanders to the home of La Rue, now Mrs. Crayton, to seek shelter, where her appeal is made with "a voice rendered scarcely articulate" (118). When the hardened Mrs. Crayton refuses to respond to her last desperate missive, Charlotte is finally pushed into madness: after giving birth, "she lay for some hours in a kind of stupor; and if at any time she spoke, it was with a quickness and incoherence that plainly evinced the total deprivation of her reason" (120).

Denied every avenue of rational appeal, Charlotte is thus forced back upon a different kind of language, for in response to her powerlessness she succumbs to hysteria, the language of the so-called "wandering womb." This dangerous, literalizing language of the body is reflected in the text's increasingly melodramatic style. As the novel winds down, more and more episodes dissolve from narrative progress into static display, as Charlotte's emotional states are signified not only by reports of tears, shrieking, convulsions, delirium, and fainting, but also by the narrative retardation effected by these sentimental tableaux, a retardation that ultimately precludes the narrative closure of Charlotte's romance plot. Hence the very form of Rowson's novel becomes a kind of allegory of its theme, for these scenes of emotive display function as "feminine" obstacles that the forward thrust of the plot seems ever less able to overcome. In a sense, then, this devolution to the conventions of female *sentiment* registers the failure of a female *romance* fully to constitute itself as such.

Of course, the language of emotional display at work in **Charlotte Temple** is in one sense merely typical of the sentimental novel. As John Mullan has argued, this "language of feeling," or of "sensibility," arises from the typically eighteenth-century hope—shared by Shaftesbury, Hutcheson, Hume, and Adam Smith—of overcoming the centrifugal forces of modernity by creating a community founded upon bonds of sympathy. Mullan argues that this hope for community fails because the celebration of sensibility—with its valorization of the female body as a locus of sympathy—is marked by an inherent ambiguity, as a result of which the emotional intensity that is supposed to be the basis of sympathy and thus of community always threatens to "become excessive and self-destructive." Sentimental novels thus describe "a sociability whose fate is isolation."[9] Yet I have argued that the generic shift to sentimental melodrama near the conclusion of Rowson's text should be interpreted as a self-conscious sign of the novel's failure fully to become a female quest romance, and that this failure in turn points towards the social and political strictures that foreclose the possibility of female agency and citizenship in a civic republican polity. Thus, if **Charlotte Temple** does exemplify the paradox noted by Mullan—i.e., that sentiment leads away from the goal of community and towards individual isolation—it also offers an alternative analysis of that paradox. For Rowson's novel represents the isolation wrought by the dangerous literalness of sentiment's hysterical language as not simply a threat to an already existing community, but as itself a consequence of a *prior* failure of community: the exclusion of women from those social institutions that, by providing epistemological power, make possible autonomous agency and thus a truly "virtuous" community.

AMERICA, COMMERCE, AND THE VIRTUOUS ADVENTURESS

There is a certain irony in the fact that Susanna Rowson is best known for her account of an unfortunate American immigrant whose trip across the ocean proves disastrous: Rowson herself was an extraordinarily successful immigrant, and in her post-*Charlotte Temple* literary career, she not only showed a decided penchant for composing popular sea chanteys, but also created numerous female characters who *do* wander abroad and successfully survive "real" shipwrecks with "virtue" intact. She created so many such heroines that one commentator has characterized her as primarily "a vivid portrayer of the virtuous woman adventuress."[10] In a sense, then, *Charlotte Temple* is merely the pre-text for the rest of Rowson's corpus; that is, the novel delineates a problem that the balance of Rowson's literary career sets out to resolve. By looking to one of Rowson's best-known chanteys we can begin both to see how Rowson conceives of the virtuous adventuress as a response to the aporias of female romance dramatized in *Charlotte Temple* and to understand more fully how that novel might be read as a commentary on the civic republican political context from which it emerged.

Rowson's song **"America, Commerce, and Freedom"** was written in 1794, the year of *Charlotte Temple*'s American publication. The song, which celebrates sea life, trade, and the hardy sailors who "earn [money] but to spend it," maintained its popularity throughout the decade. The first stanza and refrain are particularly relevant:

> How blessed the life a sailor leads
> From clime to clime still ranging
> For as the calm the storm succeeds
> The scene delights by changing.
> Tho' tempests howl along the main
> Some object will remind us,
> and cheer, with hope to meet again,
> the friends we left behind us.

> For under snug sail, we laugh at the gale;
> and tho' landsmen look pale, never heed 'em;
> But toss off the glass, to a favourite lass,
> To America, commerce, and freedom.[11]

Like the classic romance, these lines feature a sailor-quester seeking to "profit" from a world highly changeable and subject to storm and tempest, and like the romance hero, the sailor endures a dangerous adventure that finally ends in his return home. Yet what is significant about this song for the problematic put forward in *Charlotte Temple* is its reversal of the conventional opposition between domestic security and seafaring danger: here it is the "landsmen"—those who should be snugly secure on shore—who nevertheless "look pale" and are fearful of the storm, while the sailors, out in the midst of the turbulence, "laugh at the gale" from "under snug sail." According to this inverted image of vulnerability and safety, those dependent upon shelter are exposed to danger while those whose experiences have equipped them to adapt to and indeed to control the contingency of the storm are the more secure. A similar irony is evident in the phrase "still ranging," for the one constant of the "blessed life" the sailor leads is its "ranging" from "clime to clime"—its mobility and openness to variety and chance. Rowson's song thus implies that in a world in which contingency can be neither prevented nor evaded, it is far better to be prepared to maneuver in a gale than to seek the illusory safety of a harbor removed from fortune's tempests.

But the inversion of shelter and storm also recalls that irony—so central to *Charlotte Temple*—that results from the fact that attempts to preserve a woman's "virtue" by sheltering her and making her passively dependent upon a man's "protection" instead render her virtue highly vulnerable to the machinations of eloquent "adventures." The circumscription of female mobility in *Charlotte Temple* results not in safety, but in a wandering without return. It is just here, however, that we can begin to see how Rowson's chantey points towards a solution, equally paradoxical, to the dilemma of female dependency. In the song, the sailors acquire the autonomy or "virtue" that enables them to combat the storms of fortune precisely from their continual exposure to varied circumstances and conditions, an exposure that is part and parcel of their pursuit of commerce. Hence commerce, broadly understood as a heightened mobility and *interdependence* of both people and things, emerges as an aid to the cultivation of virtue and *independence*.[12]

From a civic republican point of view, however, such talk must seem less a paradox than sheer nonsense, for republican purists understood commerce to lead to myriad dependencies and thus to the corruption of civic life. Only property in the form of land was seen to grant the personal independence and impartial zeal for the public good that the citizen needed if he was to avoid corruption; as Pocock explains, for eighteenth-century republicans "the function of property remained the assurance of virtue. It was hard to see how [the citizen] could become involved in exchange relationships . . . without becoming involved in dependence and corruption. The ideals of virtue and commerce could not therefore be reconciled." But Rowson has here moved beyond the republican paradigm, as is obvious from the way that her song links the term "commerce" in a trinity with "freedom" and "America." Indeed, the song's later stanzas suggest that civic life and sociability are themselves dependent upon the sailors' "speculative" adventure abroad, for their return gives rise to song, dance, and communal celebration, even as it brings the material goods on which the community depends. The material exchanges of commercial life and the social exchanges of civic life are seen to be intimately connected, not diametrically opposed. Rowson's project must thus be assigned a place within that late eighteenth-century countercurrent to civic republicanism that eventually issued forth in liberalism, "an ideology and a perception of history which," as Pocock puts it, "depicted political society and social personality as founded upon commerce: upon the exchange of forms of mobile property and upon modes of consciousness suited to a world of moving objects."[13]

It was above all in the social philosophy of the Scottish Enlightenment that a historic transition from a paradigm of civic republicanism to one of commerce was explicitly theorized. Whereas republicanism had advocated a political society in which autonomous citizens relied on their virtue to ensure that they acted strictly for the public good rather than out of base self-interest or vassalage, thinkers like David Hume and Adam Smith began to argue that the refinement of manners brought about by the rise of commercial society itself entails the pursuit of "virtue" by other means. They maintained that propriety—acting in a manner appropriate to one's circumstances—also demands what Smith calls the "virtue of self-command," the sacrificing of self-interest for the sake of "civil" society. However, such decorum is possible only if society's members— like the romance quester and the republican citizen— are able accurately to "read" the particular social context in which we are to act. In the final edition of his influential *The Theory of Moral Sentiments* (which appeared in 1790, a year before the English publication of *Charlotte Temple*), Smith gave definitive form to his argument that "mannered" cognition requires first that we abstract from our self-interest in order to see our actions through the eyes of an ideal "Impartial Spectator," and second that we discipline our own feelings (or "sympathy") so as to accord with the Spectator's judgments. In effect, Smith's theory builds on the cognitive element already latent in Machiavellian *virtù* in order to transform virtue from an essentially political capacity for self-rule into an essentially epistemological capacity for a speculative self-distancing that allows us to make impartial judgments about complex social situations. Pocock neatly summarizes this drift in commercial ideology by saying that "[v]irtue was redefined . . . with the aid of a concept of 'manners'" and that commercial man lost his "antique virtue" but gained in its stead an "infinite enrichment of his personality."[14]

Indeed, what makes Smith's project especially relevant to Rowson's is the decisive role that Smith attributes to "commerce," in the broad sense, in creating a mannered personality. He maintains that the sophisticated appreciation of one's surroundings necessary for mannered behavior is achieved not through isolation from social intercourse, but rather through immersion in it. Polite conversation offers one important form of "exchange" by providing an education in variety that helps to refine perception. Yet Smith holds that the highest virtues of character are forged from a more worldly and adventuresome kind of commerce: the "man of real constancy and firmness," writes Smith, "has been thoroughly bred in the great school of self-command, in the bustle and business of the world, exposed, perhaps, to the violence and injustice of faction, and to the hardships and hazards of war." In a paradox already familiar to us from "America, Commerce, and Freedom," it is precisely the exposure to tumult and contingency that teaches firmness and a mastery of fortune, for it provides what Smith calls "constant practice" in the exercise of mannered cognition.[15]

If, however, the logic that links "commerce" to the republican shibboleths of "America" and "freedom" in Rowson's song seems to emerge from that broad movement toward a liberal conception of society of which Smith's work is an exemplar, then the story of Charlotte Temple's failure in the "great school of self-command" nevertheless subjects Smith's commercial logic to a decidedly feminist twist. Indeed, a cursory reading of **Charlotte Temple** might lead us to conclude that the novel—as opposed to **"America, Commerce, and Freedom"**—shares republicanism's suspicion of commerce, since it is Charlotte's exposure to the hazards of romance that leads to disaster; immersion in "commerce" proves not the making of the heroine, but her undoing. And yet, unlike Smith's "man of real constancy," Charlotte has not been "thoroughly bred" in the bustle of worldly ways. On the contrary, her confinement to a sheltered domestic space and her restricted education have left her lacking in just those epistemological skills that might have enabled her to read the intentions of the men around her and thus to steer a "virtuous" course once she found herself afloat and exposed. Charlotte's predicament is, to borrow the language of Rowson's chantey, that of a "landsman" suddenly set adrift in a gale, with predictably unhappy results.

A scene early in the novel perfectly captures the way that confinement and isolation make women vulnerable to conquest. When Montraville goes in search of Charlotte at the secluded boarding school, he finds that "the wall which surrounded it was high" and fears that "perhaps the Argus's who guarded the Hesperian fruit within, were more watchful than those famed of old" (4). The hyperbole in this allusion only calls ironic attention to the ease with which Montraville, who leans on a "broken gate" as he surveys the erstwhile barrier, will attack Charlotte's integrity. A similar irony is evident in the account of the Temples' preparations for Charlotte's birthday. Anticipating their daughter's return from school, Charlotte's parents have planned a party in a doubly protected area—the "little alcove at the bottom of the garden" that they will "deck . . . out in a fanciful manner" (31) and in which Charlotte will entertain her visitors. That this secluded, enclosed space goes unused because of Charlotte's elopement is itself evidence of the inadequacy of a purely defensive approach to the preservation of female virtue. The rural house where Montraville "keeps" Charlotte, and which becomes her prison in America, is yet another image of female confinement, but in this instance the incarcerating function of the supposedly protective domestic space is more clearly evident. When Charlotte is eventually forced out of this isolated house, she is unable to fend for herself because she "knew so little of the ways of the world": "Alas poor Charlotte," the narrator laments, "how confined was her knowledge of human nature" (112).

In a sense, then, the problem that *Charlotte Temple* reveals is the vulnerability of the passive, naive woman who does not know how to "read" the world around her, a world whose institutions do not work to protect women. Conversely, this very revelation suggests that if female confinement and passivity are simply an invitation to attack, a more reasonable strategy for preserving female virtue would seem to lie in providing women with adequate preparation for an active engagement with the world; the wandering woman must, in sum, be empowered to face the contingencies of experience. The notion that a structured introduction to the ways of the world rather than seclusion from the world offers the best defense against the lures of vice had, in fact, been put forward by John Locke's influential educational writings, in which he suggested that "[t]he only Fence against the World, is thorough Knowledge of it; into which a young Gentleman should be enter'd by degrees, as he can bear it; and the earlier the better, so he be in safe and skillful hands to guide him."[16] For Locke, however, such knowledge "enter'd by degrees" remained the exclusive provenance of men, and this fact points to the innovative nature of Rowson's project. Unlike the liberal texts of British philosophy, Rowson's literary texts of the 1790s point toward the quite novel conclusion that women, too, must be taught to participate in the bustle and business of civic life.

At the same time, this suggestion that women should be prepared to lead active lives constitutes an important element of the novel's sustained critique of republican commonplaces. Indeed, Charlotte's fall serves to demonstrate an inherent shortcoming of republicanism's patriarchal logic: the social and economic dependency of all women, including sexually virtuous women, places them in a position of extreme vulnerability that almost inevitably invites attempts at seduction. In republican terms, the political "corruption" of women-as-dependents leads all too easily to their sexual corruption. But because republican thought did tend to allot women a significant role in the early education of male citizens, such endemic moral decay in the domestic heart of the body politic must—from a republican perspective—eventually exert a corrosive and corrupting influence on the life of the republic itself; *sexual* corruption, in short, has *political* consequences.[17] I would argue, then, that Rowson's program incorporates elements of both republican and liberal theory while rejecting the traditional sexual politics of each: For Rowson, the virtuous republic must not only rethink its rejection of commerce, but it must allow women to explore those mutual interdependencies that, as a school for epistemological virtue, laid a foundation for the kind of independence and autonomy on women's part that alone could equip them to maintain their sexual virtue.

EDUCATING CHARLOTTE

If Rowson's dramatization of the failures of republican community at once provides a worst-case scenario regarding women's status in America and gestures broadly towards the necessity of a more "liberal" and inclusive conception of women's roles, it also begins to articulate a practical strategy through which that conception might be realized. The author's preface to *Charlotte Temple* explicitly notes that the novel is intended as a cautionary tale for "the many daughters of misfortune" who are in danger of repeating Charlotte's tragedy because they are either "deprived of natural friends, or spoilt by a mistaken education" (xlix). These twin impediments—a failure of friendship and a failure of education—in turn suggest a twofold remedy to the threat of corruption posed to, and by, the isolated and dependent woman, a remedy that Rowson sought both to represent in her novel and to effect in her career as an educator.

On the one hand, the novel argues for the vital importance of friendship and community between women in light of the disadvantages that they faced in a nation built around a legal framework of patriarchal custom and an ideological framework of civic republicanism. Indeed, what Charlotte laments most often throughout her ordeal is not that she has left her parents, not even that Montraville has abandoned her, but that she has no female companionship: "Alas!" she sighs, "how can I be happy, deserted and forsaken as I am, without a friend of my own sex to whom I can unburthen my full heart" (104). The narrator characteristically intrudes into the tale to insist that "many an unfortunate female, who has once strayed into the thorny paths of vice, would gladly return to virtue, was any generous friend to endeavour to raise and re-assure her" (70), and the doctor's prescription for the distracted Charlotte is "the soothing balm of friendly consolation" (123). Such a consoling friend is figured within the novel by Mrs. Beauchamp, who is moved to help her "wandering sister" because she is "a witness to the solitary life Charlotte led" (77), and who claims to empathize with Charlotte because they "are both strangers in this country" (80). Both the respectable, married Mrs. Beauchamp and the single, stigmatized Charlotte are isolated within the domestic sphere, and thus they are "strangers" to the institutions that make self-determination possible. The book's portrayal of the women's friendship at once serves as a model for and calls into being what might be termed a "community of strangers" composed of like-minded readers who are alive to Charlotte's isolation and recognize it as representative of their own. Like Mrs. Beauchamp, the members of this community would be able, in spite of Charlotte's sexual vagrancy, to read correctly "the goodness of her heart" (66)—that is, to reinterpret female "virtue" as a symbolic rather than a literal, physical quality. By recognizing the possibility of a disjunction between apparent signifiers of female vice and the reality of inner virtue—and by thus opening up to women the kind of "flexible disposition" and creative agency that republican men already enjoyed—such a community would allow even the "fallen" woman to "become an useful and respectable member of society" (125); Mrs. Beauchamp holds out just this hope for Charlotte until it becomes clear that she is going to die. With its emphasis on an interdependent community of women, *Charlotte Temple* suggests as a solution to the problem of women's isolation, dependence, and corruption, a kind of female commerce between "natural friends."

On the other hand, Rowson's novel also works to redress the second great impediment women face, for by employing Charlotte's career as a negative exemplum, it seeks to correct the kind of "mistaken education" that Charlotte herself has received. By illustrating the dangers that sexual "errancy" posed for women in a society with a sexual double standard, the novel provides moral instruction, but by providing descriptions of worldly affairs it also serves in part as a substitute for the formal education provided for men at academic institutions. In this didactic role, *Charlotte Temple* is typical of the early American novel, which, as Cathy Davidson has observed, "regularly provided a kind of education that could even parallel—admittedly, in a minor key—that which was provided by the men's colleges." But *Charlotte Temple* does not represent the only "parallel" to male education extended by Rowson, for in her own eventual capacity as a founder of girls' schools and author of textbooks for girls, Rowson continued to push for the twin goals of female education and female community. Her commitment to education was evidenced above all in the establishment of her Young Ladies' Academies in the Boston area (established in 1797) and

in her creation of textbooks dedicated specifically to "the arduous (though inexpressibly delightful) task of cultivating the minds and expanding the ideas of the female part of the rising generation." These textbooks were written, she claimed, because "it is observable that the generality of books intended for children are written for boys," and her project thus reflected the increasing interest in women's education that occurred at the end of the eighteenth century. At the same time, the founding of women's schools with a distinctive curriculum was an important impetus for the creation of a sense of female community and solidarity, a process that Nancy Cott has called the "construction of a sex-group identity." Cott argues that this development constituted a key step in the evolution towards the broader feminism of the nineteenth century, for this later movement was "predicated on the appearance of women as a discrete class and on the concomitant group-consciousness of sisterhood."[18]

In the early Republic, then, girls' academies such as Rowson's were essential in providing both the education and the friendship needed to constitute the community of strangers that Rowson suggests is vital to the preservation of female "virtue" in a republican polity. Even though Rowson's education agenda was, by modern standards, largely conservative, her vision of "commerce" seems to demand that women's horizons be expanded beyond the narrow path that leads from girls' academy to republican homestead. For example, Rowson routinely complains of the limits placed on her own education. In the preface to *Mentoria,* she includes a preemptive apology for her stylistic shortcomings, citing the constraints imposed on her education by the conventions of the day that had denied her the kind of broad familiarity with the world so vital to a serious writer: "Then alas!" she complains, sounding more than a little like Charlotte Temple, "What may not be my fate? whose education, as a female, was necessarily *circumscribed,* whose little knowledge has been simply gleaned from pure nature?" Similarly, in the preface to her play *Slaves in Algiers,* Rowson asserts that if her work is not found to be equal to that of male dramatists, it is because she has suffered the disadvantages of a *"confined* education" rather than benefiting from the classical education granted the typical male writer due to his "sex or situation in life."[19]

The imagery of spatial constriction in these passages links the limits placed on female education with the notion that women's civic role should not exceed the bounds of the domestic, private sphere. Hence it is hardly a coincidence—especially given the fact that Charlotte's "fall" is figured by the ocean voyage during which it takes place—that an abiding concern with geography was central to Rowson's own attempts to redress the female's "circumscribed" education. In her textbook *An Abridgment of Universal Geography,*

Rowson explains that geography was a subject that "I had myself ever found . . . an interesting and amusing study."[20] In fact, two of the six books that Rowson wrote for her female students were geography texts. These included descriptions not only of various countries' physical terrains but also of their cultural characteristics, which Rowson often evaluated according to the prescribed treatment of women.

Yet perhaps an even more telling sign of the concerns underlying Rowson's innovative approach to the female curriculum was her supplementation of these protofeminist geography lessons with instruction in the principles of nautical navigation—a subject on which her students were often required to deliver orations. This concern that women be able to reckon or "plot" their physical coordinates under even the extreme conditions of oceanic voyage is simply a logical extension of Rowson's more general commitment to the epistemological empowerment of women. Indeed, we can see Rowson's broader project, both literary and pedagogical, as aimed at enabling all female "questers" to engage in what Fredric Jameson has termed "cognitive mapping." Such mapping permits "a situational representation on the part of the individual subject to that vaster and properly unrepresentable totality which is the ensemble of society's structures as a whole." Jameson maintains that this "situational representation" is effected through the construction of a kind of mental grid that allows the subject to "map and remap [her position] along the moments of mobile, alternative trajectories," and that thus entails "the practical reconquest of a sense of place." It is a tempting anachronism in this context to imagine Rowson's educational program—with its ethos of female mobility—in dialogue with two instances of quest imagery in nineteenth-century American letters: first as a prescient rejoinder to Melville's nautical tales, which exploit sailing as the most masculine of professions and the ship as a metaphor for the patriarchal state; and second as a model for Margaret Fuller's "radical" vision of what full equality of rights could someday mean for women: "But if you ask me what offices [women] may fill, I reply—any. I do not care what case you put; *let them be sea-captains, if you will*"![21] If, for Fuller, navigation was at the extreme margin of female possibility, for Rowson it was the central metaphor, and Rowson's personal quest, whether as fiction writer, social critic, or educational reformer, was to enable American women better to map their own experience and to plot their own destinies.

Notes

1. Leslie A. Fiedler, *Love and Death in the American Novel* (Cleveland: Meridian, 1962), 68.

2. Susanna Rowson, *Charlotte Temple,* in *Charlotte Temple and Lucy Temple,* ed. Ann Douglas (1791; reprint, New York: Penguin, 1991), 3, 3. Subsequent citations will appear parenthetically in the text. Patricia Parker, *Irresistible Romance: Studies in the Poetics of a Mode* (Princeton: Princeton University Press, 1979), 13, 20.

3. Parker, *Irresistible Romance,* 4; Patricia Parker, *Literary Fat Ladies: Rhetoric, Gender, Property* (London: Methuen, 1987), 11.

4. Northrop Frye, *The Secular Scripture: A Study of the Structure of Romance* (Cambridge: Harvard University Press, 1976), 15; Margaret Homans, *Bearing the Word: Language and Female Experience in Nineteenth-Century Women's Writing* (Chicago: University of Chicago Press, 1986), 40; Jacques Lacan, "Desire and the Interpretation of Desire in *Hamlet,*" in *Literature and Psychoanalysis: The Question of Reading: Otherwise,* ed. Shoshana Felman (Baltimore: Johns Hopkins University Press, 1982), 28.

5. Homans, *Bearing the Word,* 10.

6. Frye, *Secular Scripture,* 67; for Derrida's account of linguistic "presence" as an effect of difference and deferral within the signifying chain, see Jacques Derrida, *Margins of Philosophy,* trans. Alan Bass (Chicago: University of Chicago Press, 1982), 1-27.

7. J. G. A. Pocock, *Politics, Language, and Time: Essays on Political Thought and History* (New York: Atheneum, 1971), 85; J. G. A. Pocock, *Virtue, Commerce, and History: Essays on Political Thought and History, Chiefly in the Eighteenth Century* (Cambridge: Cambridge University Press, 1985), 41; Drew McCoy, *The Elusive Republic: Political Economy in Jeffersonian America* (Chapel Hill: University of North Carolina Press, 1980), 68; J. G. A. Pocock, *The Machiavellian Moment: Florentine Political Thought and the Atlantic Republican Tradition* (Princeton: Princeton University Press, 1975), 117; Quentin Skinner, *The Foundations of Modern Political Thought,* vol. 1, *The Renaissance* (Cambridge: Cambridge University Press, 1978), 138.

8. Linda Kerber, *Women of the Republic: Intellect and Ideology in Revolutionary America* (New York: W. W. Norton, 1980), 139; quoted in Kerber, *Women of the Republic,* 140; for an account of how "law in the new Republic did not protect the seduced (or raped) woman," see Cathy N. Davidson, *Revolution and the Word: The Rise of the Novel in America* (New York: Oxford University Press, 1986), 107.

9. John Mullan, *Sentiment and Sociability: The Language of Feeling in the Eighteenth Century* (Oxford: Clarendon Press, 1988), 201, 235.

10. Arthur Hobson Quinn, *American Fiction: An Historical and Critical Survey* (New York: Appleton-

Century-Crofts, 1936), 17; for critical biographies of Rowson, see Dorothy Weil, *In Defense of Women: Susanna Rowson (1762-1824)* (University Park: Pennsylvania State University Press, 1976); and Patricia L. Parker, *Susanna Rowson* (Boston: Twayne, 1986).

11. Susanna Rowson, "America, Commerce, and Freedom," composed by A. Reinagle (Philadelphia: Carr's Musical Repository, 1794).

12. For the central text on the evolution of the term *commerce,* see Albert O. Hirschman, *The Passions and the Interests: Political Arguments for Capitalism before Its Triumph* (Princeton: Princeton University Press, 1977).

13. Pocock, *Virtue, Commerce, and History,* 48, 109.

14. Ibid., 48, 48, 49.

15. Adam Smith, *The Theory of Moral Sentiments* (1790; reprint, Oxford: Oxford University Press, 1976), 146, 147.

16. John Locke, *Some Thoughts Concerning Education,* in *The Educational Writings of John Locke,* ed. James Axtell (Cambridge: Cambridge University Press, 1968), 195.

17. For a discussion of the ideology of the term *Republican Motherhood,* according to which women were seen as important to the Republic due to their role as mothers to the future male citizens, see Kerber, *Women of the Republic.*

18. Davidson, *Revolution and the Word,* 73; Susanna Rowson, *Reuben and Rachel; or Tales of Old Times* (Boston: Manning & Loring, 1798), iii, iii; Nancy F. Cott, *The Bonds of Womanhood* (New Haven: Yale University Press, 1977), 190, 194.

19. Susanna Rowson, *Mentoria; or The Young Girl's Friend* (Philadelphia: Robert Campbell, 1794), iii, my emphasis; Susanna Rowson, *Slaves in Algiers; or a Struggle for Freedom: A Play Interspersed with Songs* (Philadelphia: Wrigley and Berriman, 1794), my emphasis.

20. Susanna Rowson, *An Abridgment of Universal Geography, Together with Sketches of History. Designed for the Use of Schools and Academies in the United States* (Boston: John West, 1805), iii.

21. Fredric Jameson, *Postmodernism, or The Cultural Logic of Late Capitalism* (Durham: Duke University Press, 1991), 51; Margaret Fuller, *Woman in the Nineteenth Century* (1855; reprint, New York: W. W. Norton, 1971), 174, my emphasis.

Paul Barton (essay date spring 2000)

SOURCE: Barton, Paul. "Narrative Intrusion in *Charlotte Temple.*" *Women & Language* 23, no. 1 (spring 2000): 26-32.

[*In the following essay, Barton disputes the common critical interpretation of Charlotte as an expression of Rowson's desire to provide a maternal figure to guide her readers and argues instead that in* Charlotte Temple *Rowson adopts the role of spiritual advisor, opposing the Puritans' exclusion of women from such roles.*]

In the late eighteenth century, American women were expected to conform to the nascent yet already rigid social protocol assigned them by their English-born forebears who had settled the North American continent the preceding century. Women in America, in so many words, were expected at that time to behave and perform their duties no differently than their female relations in England or anywhere in Europe. Casualties of a patriarchal society, women were largely divested of any sense of economic, political, or cultural power.

The female identity was overshadowed and oftentimes even eclipsed by that of her male counterpart. Paul Broca, among others, would seek to demonstrate the intellectual inferiority of women. Theologians, long before, had already argued that women were quite probably born without souls. If women were to be recognized, if they were to have any chance of proving such conclusions wrong, then women would need to find a voice that would afford them the power to redefine their identity in their own terms. Such a voice was to be found in the sentimental novel. It was here that a woman could articulate what she could express nowhere else. The sentimental novel would become a vehicle for female expression; it would grant women the voice they needed to both defend and demonstrate their credibility as a gender deserving of equality in a male-dominated world.

Considering the broad appeal the Puritan ministry maintained in eighteenth-century colonial America, it should come as no surprise that the minister, speaking from his pulpit, possessed not only tremendous spiritual influence over the public, but political and social influence as well. A minister undoubtedly wielded the power to effect changes even at the cultural level. Susanna Rowson recognized this power and knew that if she could find a means to tap it, she would have at her disposal a mouthpiece forbidden to her gender with which she could touch the minds and souls of women throughout colonial America.

It will be the purpose of this article to demonstrate that Rowson—contrary to Julia Sterne's argument that Rowson's novel was inspired by a wish to install herself as an "emblem" of "matriarchal power"—by writing *Charlotte Temple,* intended to employ the sentimental novel as a means to appropriate the voice and attendant powers of a Puritan minister and thereby reach out to her "congregation" of female readers. If we are to truly understand Rowson's identity and motives as a writer, such a distinction is vital. Acceptance of Rowson as an author prompted by only a maternal inclination to dispel the social naiveté of young women serves only to diminish, if not deny, that part of her identity which Rowson deemed to be of most urgent importance: her spiritual mission to tend to and guide the souls of her readers. Yet before presenting this argument, a brief explanation of both the late eighteenth-century American social and religious ethos and the background of the sentimental novel are needful in ways of clarifying and better understanding the context and form in which *Charlotte Temple* was written.

Mikhail Bakhtin, in his essay "Epic and Novel," comments on the peculiar history of the novel: "It is by its nature, not canonic. It is plasticity itself. It is a genre that is ever questing, ever examining itself, and subjecting its established forms to review" (37). With its inception in 1740 marked by the publication of Samuel Richardson's *Pamela,* the sentimental novel embarked upon a turbulent and oftentimes uncertain journey towards acceptance and eventual admission to the literary canon. From the very beginning, the sentimental novel met with extraordinary adversity in America.

Recognized by its "fanciful" prose style, the sentimental novel was almost immediately relegated to the scandalous species of books branded as romances, which, due to their sordid themes and seamy characters, were the frequent target of conservative and Puritan invectives. Romances, novels, and their kin were inveighed against by the majority of American readers because such writing was believed to be a corrupting and misleading influence quite capable of envenoming the minds of America's youth with depraved and misguided intentions.

Susanna Rowson's *Charlotte Temple* (1794), with its innovative plot structure and unconventional narrative technique, was one of only a handful of eighteenth-century American sentimental novels to rebuff the baleful eye of American conservatism and meet with mass public approval. In the past fifteen years critics have been much concerned with this novel's tremendous acclaim and in large part attribute its success to the author's enigmatic use of narrative intrusion—enigmatic, of course, being used in reference to Rowson's motivation for disrupting the structure of her novel with a series of personal interpolations.

Whereas Julia Sterne, among others, believes the narrator of *Charlotte Temple* to be an "emblem of matriarchal power . . . [whose] symbolic power is felt through the all-pervasive presence of her voice . . . "(3), I believe Rowson's narrative presence to be symptomatic of a well-developed sense of Christian duty. Rowson was a dedicated reader of scripture and a staunch exponent of the Puritan faith, but because she was a woman she was denied the opportunity to assume any liturgical or clerical responsibilities, much less those of an ordained minister. Quakerism, in radical contrast with the Puritan Church's oppressively close-minded response to women, encouraged its female membership to assume an active role in religious celebrations, and even awarded to some women the venerable position of preacher. Elizabeth Ashbridge, a late eighteenth-century writer and critic of Puritanism, received considerable attention when she published a diary recounting her dilemma in choosing between Puritanism and Quakerism. Her eventual decision, and explanation thereof, to convert to the more egalitarian congregation of the Quakers stirred up considerable controversy within the Puritan ranks. Ashbridge's conversion in many ways stimulated Puritan women to question the credibility and value of their diminutive role in the church. Furthermore, it prompted many women to reassess their sense of contentment in a church where they were accorded no voice, rights, or responsibilities. Rowson was one such woman, not at all satisfied with her muted station in the church.

Considering her strong religious background, it is surprising that critics have done so little in ways of tying in Rowson's unmistakably homiletic narrative intrusions to the strong Puritan sentiment prevalent in the 1790s. Wendy Martin is in fact the only critic to make notable mention of the homiletic rhetoric in *Charlotte Temple*: "The guilt and anguish which Charlotte Temple experiences as a fallen woman are not unlike the emotions evoked by Jonathan Edwards's 'Sinners in the Hands of an Angry God'" (4).

In the pages to follow I will seek to disprove Sterne's asseveration that Rowson through her powerful narrative presence and frequent intrusions, sought to provide her novel with a "maternal voice notable for its extraordinary rationality . . . that stands in stark contrast to the tableau of female hysteria it frames" (3). By refuting Rowson's putative "maternal" narrative intentions, I will have ample latitude to discuss Rowson's adoption of the preacher's role in *Charlotte Temple,* which I believe was her primary motive for utilizing an intrusive narrative approach.

It is not my intention to deny the presence of maternal tendencies on the part of *Charlotte Temple*'s narrator, for indeed, such tendencies do in fact exist. However, it is my aim to illuminate the presence of various ministerial propensities which abound within the narrator's frequent intrusions. The author of *Charlotte Temple* should be appreciated for her nurturing role as a maternal figure but should be admired for her courage and cunning in adopting the role of a minister, a commanding and influential position reserved for men alone.

Rowson's narrative is twofold in the sense that, first, it successfully preserves Charlotte's voice from misrepresentation or even possible obliteration, and, second, its carefully arranged sequence of homiletic interruptions meld together to form a representation of a Puritan minister's sermon. It was through this device that Rowson designed to voice her moral and spiritual advice to her readers. Rowson not only hoped to entertain her readers, but also wished to provide them with moral guidance and "intended to inform, improve, and enrich the lives of her readers in ways that extend far beyond the lessons to be learned from Charlotte's tragic tale" (Forcey 236).

Rowson with *Charlotte Temple,* which was immensely more popular than even many contemporary sentimental novelists' most successful works—Foster's *The Coquette* (1797), Mackenzie's *Man of Feeling* (1771), and Brown's *Power of Sympathy* (1789), eluded the reproof of American conservatism by shaping her novel within the Puritan mould: replete with Christian rhetoric, moral lessons, and homiletic perspective.[1] In *Charlotte Temple,* a book, according to its preface, intended to provide "the young and thoughtless of the fair sex [with the knowledge] . . . to defend themselves from the snares not only of the other sex, but from the more dangerous arts of the profligate of their own" (5), Rowson effectively implemented didacticism as a defensive stratagem, and thus escaped the censure of her morally sensitive readership.

Rowson had an innate desire to instill within her readers the knowledge and means essential to finding the path of virtue and right Christian living. Dorothy Weil, in her book *Defense of Women,* asserts that this desire to teach was "the organizing principle of Mrs. Rowson's work. . . . Each of Mrs. Rowson's fictional works aims at and is organized by a moral (or two). . . . The textbooks carry on the teachings of the fiction and offer moral reflection as well as instruction in specific subject areas" (14). Rowson, in the penultimate paragraph of her preface to *Charlotte Temple,* defends the moral tendencies of her novel—"I have not wrote a line that conveys a wrong idea to the head or a corrupt wish to the heart, I shall rest satisfied in the purity of my own intentions, and if I merit not applause, I feel that I dread not censure"[2] (6)—and thus averred, on her own, part both a moral rectitude and genuine endeavor to improve her readers' sense of virtue.

Julia Sterne in her essay "*Charlotte Temple* and the Poetics of Maternal Melancholia," astutely observes that, "At the heart of Charlotte's performance . . . lies a feminine representation, the novel's narrator. . . . This unnamed and overly present narrator functions as the novel's absent emblem" (2). Unlike her contemporaries, Rowson did not believe the epistolary form to be an effective means of communicating the precepts of virtue to her readers.[3] By adopting a narrative approach, Rowson could introduce herself as a functional character capable of elucidating the story she was relating and thereby gain a greater degree of authority and control over her work. It is likely that Rowson was compelled to assert such authority and control over her novels to counter the prevailing social attitude towards female sensibility, "in which all women bear a latent propensity for hysterical dissolution" (Sterne 3).

In the case of *Charlotte Temple* it has also been argued that Rowson deviated from the epistolary form so as to ensure that the diminutive voice of Charlotte would not be smothered by the overpowering rhetoric of her adversaries. Without the aid of the author's timely and insightful narrative intrusions Charlotte's message would undoubtedly have been lost. Rowson took every precaution within her means to ensure that her heroine's pleas for sympathy would be heard.

By taking advantage of the tremendous authority afforded by narrative intrusions, Rowson effectively steered Charlotte away from the muted fate shared by most heroines of epistolary novels. As Blythe Forcey remarks in "*Charlotte Temple* and the End of Epistolarity": "Without the protective boundaries established by a controlling narrative pressure, the epistolary novel leaves the female protagonist exposed, vulnerable, and even invisible" (230). By maintaining a strong narrative presence throughout the novel, Rowson not only succeeded in preventing Charlotte's quiet voice from being ignored or misinterpreted, but also succeeded in creating a narrative voice capable of guiding her readers to "sensible" conclusions.

The simple structure of *Charlotte Temple,* two volumes comprised of thirty-five chapters ranging from one to four pages in length, allowed Rowson to interpolate her personal addresses to her audience with relative ease. With only a single exception (Rowson opens and uses more than half of chapter twenty-eight to personally address her readers), Rowson situates her narrative intrusions, of which there are ten, in the latter half of the chapters in which they occur. While these authorial intrusions comprise only a small portion of the text, they are a vital and indispensable part of the novel and the crucial message it seeks to impart.

In the course of the first narrative interruption, in which "romantic girls" are urged to be watchful of their "honour," especially when in the company of a "handsome young soldier," the narrator exhorts female readers to resist the oftentimes deceptive language of love "unless sanctioned by paternal approbation" (29). The narrator further comments on the dangers of illicit love and charges those women weak in resolve to "kneel down each morning, and request kind heaven to keep [them] . . . free from temptation, or, should it please [them] to suffer to be tried, pray for fortitude to resist the impulse of inclination when it runs counter to the precepts of religion and virtue" (29). In this passage the narrator suggests that young women, once beyond the auspices of parental supervision, are exposed to the appetites of dishonorable men. This notion of the female's honor as imperiled by a roving seducer (once removed from the aegis of paternal protection) is substantiated by the title of the novel and the subsequent development of an insular "temple" theme in the initial twelve of the novel's thirty-five chapters.

The "temple" theme to which I have referred is introduced in the first chapter in the form of a description of the "mansion which contained the lovely Charlotte Temple" (10). Within the safe confines of the mansion/temple Charlotte is almost secure from the vice and depravity which abound outside. It is certainly no coincidence that the sanctuary which Charlotte inhabits is situated "in the midst of an extensive pleasure ground" (10). Montraville, Charlotte's eventual seducer, looks "earnestly at the house" from beyond and provides a metaphoric description of the amply fortified mansion: "The wall which surrounded it was high, and perhaps the Argus's who guarded the Hesperian fruit within, were more watchful than those famed of old" (10). While these lines specifically refer to Argus, the hundred-eyed sentinel whom Hera charged to guard Zeus's infamous mistress Io, there is also a subtle allusion to the edenic myth.

The "Hesperian fruit" was, not unlike the fruit of the tree of knowledge, forbidden from human consumption. This "fruit" can be interpreted as a symbol representative of Charlotte's "honour." In a narrative intrusion which follows soon after Charlotte's betrayal in chapter eighteen, a connection is formed between Charlotte's "parting with her honour" and "the fruit of her own folly" (66-67). On one other occasion preceding the above-cited intrusion the symbol of "fruit" is used to imply a notion of retribution for engagement in forbidden activity. This allusion occurs in a retrospective passage in which Montraville's father warns him against impetuous marriages: "if . . . you rush into a precipitate union [and] . . . take the poor creature from a comfortable home and kind friends . . . I will leave you to enjoy the blessed fruits of your rashness" (40).

It is not difficult to trace the plot structure and characters of *Charlotte Temple* back to the edenic myth recounted in Genesis. Indeed both stories begin within the secure boundaries of a garden, both involve a plot motivated by deception and seduction, and in each story the guilty characters are expelled from a realm of hap-

piness and prosperity and are left to fend for themselves. The sense of guilt and anguish which Charlotte suffers after having eaten of the forbidden fruit and thereby forfeiting her "honour"—"the only gem that could render [her] . . . respectable in the eye of the world" (80)—is clearly a manifestation of Rowson's Puritan upbringing.

While Rowson does in fact attempt to promote both sympathy and forgiveness through her narrative intrusions, the plot structure is clearly molded in a Puritan cast. True to the Puritan belief system, Charlotte, once she has transgressed, must make expiation for her sin and thereby endure a harrowing journey into the realms of loneliness, unremitting despair, and eventually death. Mona Scheuermann explains that "there is no outlet for the remission of sin for the Puritan such as exists for the Catholic or the Anglican." Because there is no possibility for the remission of Charlotte's sin, she is fated to a bleak future, and thus "sin and its aftermath take on [an] almost morbid fascination" (116).

However, it is important to note that Rowson deviated from the rigid precepts of Puritan tradition in two fundamental ways: first, she refuted the Calvinist belief in mankind's depraved and unpardonable condition and embraced the redeeming powers of forgiveness and sympathy, and, second, Rowson confronted the prevailing Puritan belief that the female's role was an inferior one. Weil suggests that Rowson as a novelist attempted to "establish a basis upon which women might share religious life free from the many anti-female traditions of the church, which ranged from the use of Scripture . . . [to] prohibiting them from preaching" (76). In *Charlotte Temple,* Rowson, by means of narrative intrusion, succeeds in both endeavors.

The third narrative interruption, which occurs in chapter eight, provides us with a clear illustration of Rowson's intentions:

> Look, my dear friends, at yonder lovely Virgin, arrayed in a white robe devoid of ornament; behold the meekness of her countenance, the modesty of her gait; her handmaids are Humility, Filial Piety, Conjugal Affection, Industry, and Benevolence; her name is Content; she holds in her hand the cup of true felicity, and when once you have formed an intimate acquaintance with these her attendants, nay you must admit them as your bosom friends and chief counsellors . . . Is your state mediocrity?
>
> (34-35)

Rowson poses a poignant question near the middle of this narrative interruption; a question that she is not content to leave unanswered. Rowson, rather than risk misinterpretation or leading her audience astray, supplies her readers with a panegyric explaining how spiritual content fulfills our every need, and in so doing guides us ever closer to God's light and a future of "blissful eternity":

She will heighten every blessing you enjoy by informing you how grateful you should be to that bountiful
Providence who might have placed you in the most abject situation; and, by teaching you to weigh your blessings against your deserts, show you how much more
you receive than you have a right to expect. . . . Content, my dear friends . . . will soften the pains of sickness, continue with you even in the cold gloomy hours
of death, and, cheering you with smiles of her heaven-
born sister, Hope, lead you triumphant to a blissful
eternity. . . . For my own part, I can safely declare
there is no human being in the universe whose propriety I should not rejoice in, and to whose happiness I
would not contribute to the utmost limit of my power:
and may my offenses be no more remembered in the
day of general retribution, than as from my soul I forgive every offense of injury received from a fellow
creature.

(35-36)

In this lengthy narrative intrusion we see the narrator
assume the pulpit, and from that position make an elegant homiletic address to her "congregation" of "giddy
flutterers," as Rowson often and affectionately referred
to her readers. Both the language and pious method of
address employed by the narrator follow unmistakable
homiletic conventions. Illustrative metaphor and the
personification of Christian virtues were devices frequently used by eighteenth century Puritan ministers in
their sermons. Near the end of this homiletic intrusion
the narrator inserts a brief pronouncement extolling the
benevolent powers of forgiveness.[4]

In *Charlotte Temple* we encounter a narrator who promotes the virtues of sympathy and pardon at, what
seems, every possible turn. Throughout the novel the
reader frequently meets with the narrator's urgings to
reject Puritanism's stern disavowal of forgiveness and
rather "charitably . . . overlook the errors" of others
(68): "when we consider this, we surely may pity the
faults of others . . . how shall we erring mortals dare
to look up to thy mercy in the great day of retribution,
if we now uncharitably refuse to overlook the errors, or
alleviate miseries, of our fellow-creatures" (68); "the
heart that is truly virtuous is ever inclined to pity and
forgive the errors of its fellow-creatures" (75); "the tear
of compassion shall fall for the fate of Charlotte. . . .
For Charlotte, the soul melts with sympathy" (99). Even
the characters of Mr. and Mrs. Temple, the novel's para-
gons of Christian virtue, promote forgiveness: "'And
shall we not forgive her?' said Mr. Temple. 'Forgive
her!' exclaimed the mother. 'Oh yes, whatever be our
errors, is she not our child?'" (56).

While forgiveness is indeed a controversial yet central
theme in *Charlotte Temple,* Rowson places significantly
more emphasis on the aforementioned controversy surrounding the females' inferior role in the Puritan
Church. I am careful here to specify the "Puritan"
church because, and as Weil indicates in her book, some

denominations, including "the Quakers[,] allowed
women to speak in church" (79). Rowson, through her
writing, hoped to vitiate the prevailing Puritan beliefs
about the female's subordinate functions in the church
and thereby procure for women increased respectability
and, specifically, the right to speak in church.

By employing narrative intrusions in *Charlotte Temple,*
Rowson provided herself the opportunity not only to
speak publicly (to her readers) but to speak from a vantage point denied her by the church, namely the pulpit.
By assuming a ministerial role, Rowson was undoubtedly aware that she might incur harsh censure from her
church—her "encouragement of women in public speaking . . . may [have] . . . been seen as an assault on
[Puritan] restrictions, for the fear of church participation was linked to the suspicion in women engaging in
any form of public vocal expression . . ." (Weil 79).
Due to this growing sense of dissatisfaction with her
church, Rowson, unlike her female contemporaries, was
not content to maintain a traditional participation in her
novels; "Instead, she entered the novel herself . . . as
an editor, moralizer, translator, and guide for her young
readers" (Forcey 230).

In *Charlotte Temple* Rowson ignored the conventional
parameters of the sentimental novel. Rather than simply
providing her book with a standard didactic plot structure, in which the characters and their actions disclose
to the reader various moral lessons, Rowson opted to
clarify and elaborate upon important narrative sequences
to ensure that her readers would draw the appropriate
conclusions. Because the traditional epistolary format
of the genre prohibited authorial insertions, Rowson
consequently dispensed with it altogether and wrote
Charlotte Temple in narrative form. By doing so Rowson effectively provided herself with an authoritative
unifying narrative structure in which she could intervene and address her readers directly, and, as Forcey
asserts, "expose the forces that combined to render the
epistolary novel obsolete" (225).

The preachy and oftentimes effusive spiritualizing rhetoric employed by Rowson in the course of her narrative
intrusions is undeniably homiletic. The homily or homiletic genre, as defined by Holman and Harmon, is "a
form of oral [or written] religious instruction given by a
minister to a church congregation . . . [and] usually
gives practical moral counsel rather than discussion of
doctrine" (231). Sterne, who refers to Rowson's "maddening interruptions and digressions" as maternal bonds
that connect the author "with all of the mother figures
in the novel" (7), fails to recognize Rowson's passionate desire to minister to her readers not only in the
guise of a mother figure but as a preacher.

In two significant narrative intrusions in which Rowson
does seem to adopt a maternal function—an address in
chapter six to "my dear sober matron," and a disquisi-

tion in chapter fourteen on "a mother's anguish, when disappointed in her tenderest hopes"—the reader will observe that in both cases Rowson concludes, in respective order, with spiritual advice: "Kneel down each morning, and request kind heaven to keep you from temptation" (29); "remember, the mother whom you so dearly love and venerate will feel the same [sorrows], when you are forgetful of the respect due to your maker and yourself, forsake the paths of virtue for those of vice and folly" (54).

However, in a lengthier narrative interruption, which occurs in the second volume, the reader observes the homiletic form in full swing. In chapter eighteen Rowson exhorts her readers not to follow Charlotte's example, else they be led down the same harrowing path: "the poor girl by thoughtless passion led astray, who, in parting with her honour, had forfeited the esteem of the very man to whom she sacrificed every thing dear and valuable in life . . ." (67). Yet Rowson, true to the bleak homiletic style employed by Jonathan Edwards, Michael Wigglesworth, and other early Puritan ministers in their sermons, paints the aftermath of sin with exceedingly grim strokes of despair and anguish:

> she has no redress, no friendly soothing companion to pour into her wounded mind the balm of consolation . . . she has disgraced her friends, forfeited the good opinion of the world, and undone herself; she feels herself a poor solitary being in the surrounding midst of multitudes; shame bows her to the earth, remorse tears her distracted mind, and guilt, poverty, and disease close the dreadful scene: she sinks unnoticed to oblivion.
>
> (67)

In "Sinners in the Hands of an Angry God," Edwards's account of the terrible suffering brought upon the sinner by his transgression is similar to that of Rowson. It is important to note that Rowson was familiar with and did draw upon the sermons of celebrated ministers in writing her own; the diction, tone, and syntactical structure of her homiletic intrusions evenly match those of earlier sermons. The only departure she takes from her model ministers is that of audience; whereas ministers typically directed their sermons at a congregation comprised of both men and women, Rowson is interested in addressing issues that specifically confront a female audience:

> My dear Madam, contract not your brow into a frown of disapprobation. I mean not to extenuate the faults of those unhappy women who fall victims to guilt and folly; but surely when we reflect how many errors we are ourselves subject to, how many secret faults lie hid in the recesses of our hearts, which we should blush to have brought into open day (and yet those faults require the lenity and pity of a benevolent judge, or awful would be our prospect of futurity) I say, my dear Madam, when we consider this, we surely may pity the faults of others. Believe me, many an unfortunate female, who has once strayed into the thorny paths of vice, would gladly return to virtue, was any generous friend to endeavor to raise and re-assure her; but alas! it cannot be, you say; the world would deride and scoff. Then let me tell you, Madam, 'tis a very unfeeling world, and does not deserve half the blessings which a bountiful Providence showers upon it.
>
> (68)

In the course of this narrative departure Rowson alludes to one of the Biblical themes most frequently addressed by Puritan ministers in their sermons: the fall of mankind. Earlier I made reference to the presence of a possible edenic subtext in **Charlotte Temple** in which Charlotte, by yielding her fruit/honor to a seducer, endures an agonizing fall from God's grace not unlike "the fall" of Adam and Eve recounted in Genesis. Charlotte, by "parting with her honour has forfeited . . . everything dear and valuable in life" and realizes only too late "the fruit of her own folly" (66-67). While Montraville is partially responsible for Charlotte's downfall (for he is the one who partakes of her "honour"), his character should not be confused with the seducer/serpent of the edenic myth.

Rowson is careful to dissuade the reader from interpreting Montraville as such: "Montraville was a different character: generous in his position, liberal in his opinions, and good natured almost to a fault" (38). His one fault, which he shares with Eve, is his failure to consider the consequences of his actions: "eager and impetuous in the pursuit of a favorite object [Charlotte's honor/fruit], he staid not to reflect on the consequences which might follow the attainment of his wishes . . ." (38). I compare Montraville to Eve, rather than to Adam, for the simple reason that it is Eve who prompts Adam to partake of the fruit—"And when the woman saw that the tree was good for food, and that it was pleasant to the eyes . . . [she] gave also to her husband with her, and he did eat" (Gen. 3:6)—as, in turn it is Montraville who persuades Charlotte to relinquish her honor.

In this elaborate edenic metaphor, Belcour, a soldier and alleged friend of Montraville, and La Rue, Charlotte's governess, are immediately recognized as the serpents—"more subtil than any beast of the field" (Gen. 3:1)—who seduced Montraville and Charlotte into tasting the forbidden fruit of Charlotte's honor. Belcour is a malefic character—"dissipated, thoughtless, and capricious . . . he minded not the miseries he inflicted on others, provided his own wishes, however extravagant, were gratified. Self, darling self, was the idol he worshipped" (Rowson 37)—whose sinister personality mirrors that of Milton's Satan: "To do ought good never will be our task, / But never to do ill our sole delight" (*Paradise Lost,* Book I: 159-160).

La Rue, who in the final pages admits to her part as the serpent—"I am the viper that stung your peace" (119), is the embodiment of malice, which according to Milton was, aside from pride, Satan's chief sin: "To waste his whole creation, or possess / All as our own, and drive as we were driven, / The puny habitants, or if not drive, / Seduce them to our party . . . This would surpass / Common revenge . . . when his darling Sons / Hurl'd headlong to partake with us, shall curse / This frail Original, and fated bliss . . ." (II: 365-68, 370-71, 373-75). La Rue is a fallen woman who "has lost sight of the basis on which reputation, honour, [and] everything that should be dear to the female heart" (32). Jealous of Charlotte, who still possesses her reputation and honor, La Rue seeks to destroy in Charlotte the respectability that she herself has lost: "she grows hardened in guilt, and will spare no pains to bring down innocence and beauty to the shocking level with herself" (32).

In chapter seven La Rue inveigles Charlotte through her dexterous and deceptive use of language. La Rue is persuasive, and Charlotte is quickly enticed into reading a forbidden letter: "have you a mind to be in leading strings all your life time? Prithee open the letter, read it, and judge it for yourself. . . . Have you no curiosity to see the inside now? for my part I could no more let a letter addressed to me lie unopened so long, than I could work miracles . . ." (31). La Rue's fork-tongued rhetoric is little different than the serpent's in *Paradise Lost*: "do not believe / those rigid threats of Death; ye shall not Die: / How should ye? by the Fruit? it gives you Life / To Knowledge: By the Threat'ner? look on mee, / Me who have touch'd and tasted, yet both live / And life more perfect have attained than Fate / Meant mee . . ." (IX: 684-90). In both stories the seducer/serpent is successful in enticing its artless victim into the realm of the forbidden.

The consequences suffered by Charlotte due to her transgression mirror the pain endured by Adam and Eve: Charlotte, expelled from the garden of "familial bliss" becomes "a poor solitary being, without society, here wearing out her heavy hours in deep regret and anguish of heart . . . Charlotte is fallen . . ." (65). In chapters thirty-two and thirty-three Rowson further extends the parallel of Charlotte's suffering to the edenic myth by subjecting her heroine to the gripping pains of childbirth, which Eve was condemned to suffer by God's decree: "Unto the woman he said, I will greatly multiply thy sorrow and thy conception; in sorrow thou shalt bring forth children . . ." (Gen. 3:16).

Rowson's strong Puritan background, her invocation of an edenic theme, and a conspicuously ministerial voice, which she adopts in addressing her reader, are factors that both validate and substantiate interpretation of Rowson's narrative intrusions in **Charlotte Temple** as homiletic exhortations. As Weil observes: "Susanna

Rowson's religion is the controlling system from which the author's main concerns take their shape and support" (65). While indeed there are definite maternal tendencies played out by the narrator in **Charlotte Temple,** these tendencies do not, as Sterne alleges, serve to define the narrator as "the novel's absent emblem of matriarchal power" (2). The desire to assume the pulpit as a woman in the Puritan Church was a far greater compulsion for Rowson than the call of motherhood.

Certainly Rowson believed the maternal role to be an important one, but one that afforded her little authority within the household, and none beyond. She recognized that the role of minister was one through which she could achieve far greater authority and influence and thereby touch the spiritual lives of hundreds, if not thousands, of women. To identify Rowson's motivations for writing **Charlotte Temple** as purely maternal, as Sterne and other critics have regrettably done, not only misrepresents, but diminishes the scope of Rowson's vision to become a guiding light to her gender. Rowson was clearly an advocate of Republican Motherhood, and in turn sought to extend her range of utility beyond the cramped quarters of the house and hearth to the expansive spheres of political, social, and spiritual influence. For this reason both she and her work must be reassessed from a broader cultural vantage point that looks beyond the narrow maternal purview.

Notes

1. The strong tide of anti-novelistic sentiment was further exacerbated by critics who, roused by public opinion, took to their pens unleashing a barrage of essays and pamphlets decrying the novel's turpitude. "Novel Reading, A Cause of Female Depravity," published in England in 1797, among other scathing attacks on the genre, imperiled the novel's survival into the nineteenth century. However, novel writers, aware of their dire circumstances, immediately devised a means to ensure the viability of their trade. And thus the notion of didacticism was introduced as an integral and "ennobling" purpose of the novel. Hannah Webster Foster, William Hill Brown, Susanna Rowson, and many other novel-writers relied heavily upon didacticism to merit their works the approval of the American public.

2. As it turned out, Rowson was premature in her declaration that she need not "dread" censure of critics. Soon following the 1794 publication of *Charlotte Temple* in America, Rowson was charged by Puritan critics on the count of "false sentiment." Rowson had not considered the possibility that critics would, in their scrutiny of *Charlotte Temple,* presume to inveigh against the "credibility" of her solicitude for her audiences' morality. Yet despite the critics' abusive and wholly unmer-

ited treatment of Rowson's character, *Charlotte Temple* met with tremendous success: "It is conjectured that her novel . . . has been read by more than a million and a half readers since its first edition in England in 1791 and in 1794 in America" (Martin 1).

3. As Mona Scheuermann points out in her essay "The American Novel of Seduction": "American sentimental novels, especially those dealing with seduction, seem . . . to render a favorite English theme: Virtuous Woman Fallen" (106). Having for its focus such a morally charged issue, the sentimental novel of course suffered a predisposition towards the sensational. Not only this, the authors of such novels, as Wendy Martin observes in her "Profile of Susanna Rowson," were prone to follow step for step in the "Richardsonian sentimental vein" and narrate "episodes of infidelity, penury, seduction, abduction, rape, and suicide" (2). While Rowson yielded to many of these same generic tendencies, she did, in the production of *Charlotte Temple,* succeed in departing from the established epistolary form by incorporating herself into the narrative structure as a disembodied yet highly functional character.

4. The notion of forgiveness is a recurring theme in *Charlotte Temple* and became for Rowson a critical issue in her later works, in which she "appears to question the notion of human depravity" (Weil 70). In a later novel, *Reuben and Rachel* (1798), Rowson extends her argumentation for forgiveness: "Revenge is a principle inherent in human nature, and it is only the sublime and heavenly doctrine of Christianity that teaches us to repel the impulse, and return good for evil" (142). Even one-quarter century later, with the 1822 publication of *Biblical Dialogues,* Rowson remained adamant in her advocacy of forgiveness: "We are none of us without fault, we are all prone to evil from our very childhood . . ." (36).

References

Bakhtin, Mikhail. "Epic and Novel." *The Dialogic Imagination: Four Essays.* Trans. Caryl Emerson and Michael Holquist. Austin: University of Texas UP, 1981. 37-39.

Dauber, Kenneth. "American Culture as Genre." *Criticism* 22 (1980): 101-115.

Edwards, Jonathan. *A Jonathan Edwards Reader.* Ed. John Smith, et al. New Haven: Yale UP, 1995.

Forcey, Blythe. "*Charlotte Temple* and the End of Epistolarity." *American Literature* 63 (1991): 225-241.

Ginsberg, Elaine. "The Female Initiation Theme in American Fiction." *Studies in American Fiction* 3 (1975): 27-37.

Hart, James. *The Popular Book.* Westport, CT: Greenwood, 1976.

Holman, Hugh C., and William Harmon, eds. *A Handbook to Literature.* 6th ed. New York: Macmillan, 1992.

King James Version. Nashville: Thomas Nelson Publishers, 1984.

Martin, Wendy. "Profile: Susanna Rowson, Early American Novelist." *Women's Studies* 2 (1974): 1-8.

Milton, John. *Complete Poems and Major Prose.* Ed. Merritt Hughes. New York: Macmillan, 1957.

Rowson, Susanna. *Charlotte Temple.* Ed. Cathy Davidson. New York: Oxford UP, 1986. Originally published in 1791.

———. *Biblical Dialogues Between a Father and His Family.* Boston: Richardson and Lord, 1822.

———. *Reuben and Rachel.* Boston: Manning and Loring, 1798.

Scheuermann, Mona. "The American Novel of Seduction: An Exploration of the Omission of the Sex Act in *The Scarlet Letter.*" *Nathaniel Hawthorne Journal* 8 (1978): 105-118.

Sterne, Julia. "Working Through the Frame: *Charlotte Temple* and the Poetics of Maternal Melancholia." *Arizona Quarterly* 49.4 (1993): 1-32.

Weil, Dorothy. *In Defense of Women: Susanna Rowson, 1762-1824.* University Park: Pennsylvania State UP, 1976.

Joseph C. Schöpp (essay date 2000)

SOURCE: Schöpp, Joseph C. "Liberty's Sons and Daughters: Susanna Haswell Rowson's and Royall Tyler's Algerine Captives." In *Early America Re-Explored: New Readings in Colonial, Early National, and Antebellum Culture,* edited by Klaus H. Schmidt and Fritz Fleischmann, pp. 291-307. New York: Peter Lang, 2000.

[*In the following essay, Schöpp compares and contrasts* Slaves in Algiers *and Royall Tyler's novel* The Algerine Captive *to explore the effects of the authors' gender on their conception and treatment of captivity in their works.*]

In the eighteenth century the orient was clearly on the upswing in the occident. Travelers from either side of the Atlantic explored oriental countries, scholars developed interest in oriental languages and literatures, and writers filled a still largely vacant space with all kinds of exotic fantasies. The literary market abounded with oriental tales. Composers and playwrights produced and theaters performed operas and plays with Turkish, Egyptian or Algerian subjects; essayists discoursed on such remote subjects as the domestic life of the Arabs.[1] Maidens, captured by corsairs, put up for sale at slave markets or abducted into a sultan's seraglio were common subjects and undoubtedly accounted for the success of such questionable aesthetic products. Susanna Haswell Rowson, who in 1791 had published her best-selling novel **Charlotte Temple,** tried to repeat her success as a novelist with an oriental play, **Slaves in Algiers; Or, A Struggle for Freedom,** which premiered in Philadelphia's Chestnut Street Theatre on June 30, 1794. Three years later Royall Tyler, author of the once highly acclaimed play *The Contrast* (1787), tried his hand at an oriental novel, *The Algerine Captive; Or, The Life and Adventures of Doctor Updike Underhill, Six Years a Prisoner Among the Algerines* (1797). Yet neither Rowson nor Tyler, now working in a different genre, could repeat their former success. As early as 1810 the Boston *Monthly Anthology* lamented that Tyler's "little work [was] very undeservedly hastening to oblivion" (Tanselle 148), and twelve years later James Fenimore Cooper, in one of his early critical essays, referred to "Tyler's forgotten, and we fear, lost narrative of the Algerine Captive" and advised any "future collector of our national tales . . . to snatch [it] from oblivion, and to give [it] that place among the memorials of other days, which is due to the early and authentic historians of a country" (97-98). Rowson's initially successful play also disappeared from the stage when the theater troupe which she had founded with her husband disbanded at the end of the 1797 season (Kritzer, *Plays* 11). Although neither Tyler's novel nor Rowson's play can be counted among the undisputed masterpieces of their time, they deserve to be more fully explored than has hitherto been the case as historic markers and "memorials of other days."[2] As the works of two highly acclaimed authors representing different genders who also worked in different genres, they are here singled out to confront the question of how this difference in both genre and gender also offers differing views on the question of captivity and how each of them, in its own distinct way, participates and intervenes in the political debates of the time.

Since the early days of the Puritans, captivity narratives had been seriously engaged in such debates. As stories which told of remarkably providential events, they not only provided a popular and successful formula for the Puritan artist but, what is at least as important, also developed into a uniquely American genre in which central issues of cultural significance could be negotiated. The captivity formula reduced, as it were, "a complex of religious beliefs, philosophical concepts, and historical experiences to a single, compelling, symbolic ritual-drama" of separation, transformation and return. The captive, alienated from his or her happy state, was "plunged into a trial and ordeal" which would ulti-

mately lead to his or her "figurative rebirth" (Slotkin 101). In the Revolutionary era the captivity narrative, "by transforming the captivity experience into a potent metaphor for the Revolution" (Sieminski 52), was instrumentalized for largely propagandistic purposes. Not only in the Declaration of Independence but in various other political and literary documents of the time, the American Revolutionary was cast as a captive who, after long and "patient sufferance," was ready to "throw off" the shackles of "absolute tyranny." In the postrevolutionary period, when the United States had to face new threats and saw its newly gained freedom once more imperiled from outside, the captivity narrative again came to serve as a potent formula and provided a framework for the discussion of the pressing political issues of the time. The American wilderness, once the site of Indian trial and ordeal, was now replaced by an African wilderness in which brutal Barbary pirates and despotic oriental potentates were at work and severely threatened their captives' cultural values. For over a decade (1785-1797), during the almost "forgotten American-Algerian War" (Barnby), Barbary corsairs captured American ships and led their captains and crews into captivity. When Rowson's and Tyler's works appeared, the conflict had reached its climax. "At one time in the early 1790s there were 1200 Christian slaves in Algiers, exposed to cruelty and plagues" (Tanselle 142) and exposed to a culture utterly alien to their own. Under the conditions of oriental despotism, the American values of life, liberty and the pursuit of happiness were suddenly in great danger. Where tyrants ruled over their male subjects and patriarchal despots degraded women into sexual objects, the American sons and daughters of Liberty were indeed plunged into severe trials. The question of how to face such threats had vexed the new American government since the mid-1780s when the Barbary conflict developed and the new nation still lacked the naval power to counter it successfully. To liberate the enslaved sons and daughters was one of the most urgent patriotic duties of the time.

The alien scenario of an Algerine captivity also functioned as an ideal simulation space in which unresolved domestic problems with which postrevolutionary America saw itself confronted could be negotiated and proleptically resolved in a fictional context. Since man is estranged from that with which he is most familiar, as the Russian Formalists argue, a reader would respond to such dislocated and defamiliarized negotiations with an increased awareness. Tyler's protagonist obviously knows about the cognitive value of such dislocations when he remarks, "If a man is desirous to know how he loves his country, let him go far from home; if to know how he loves his countrymen, let him be with them in misery in a strange land" (Tyler II.174).[3] Thus North Africa may be seen as an ideal site for the trials and ordeals which the early republic was to undergo in the struggle for its true identity. How and to what purpose Rowson and Tyler made use of their Algerine space needs to be further explored.

* * *

On the textual surface Rowson's **Slaves in Algiers** at first sight presents itself as a rather conventional formula-play hastily stitched together. Stock figures who hardly ever develop into full-blooded characters dominate the scene. The oriental despot ruling with arbitrary power, the innocent young maiden as the object of his sexual desire, the valiant young man who hopes to rescue the damsel in distress, the greedy Jew, the quixotically comic Spaniard, are only the more strikingly conspicuous of the stereotypical dramatis personae. Disguises and deceptions, cross-dressings and cover-ups, sexual advances, slave mutinies, or elopement schemes planned in nocturnal grotto and garden scenes, enhance the conventional character of the play. A closer second look, however, reveals that Rowson does not just slavishly reproduce the melodramatic formula of a well-made sentimental play but at times makes attempts to use the conventions productively by parodying and thereby subverting them. When the Spaniard Sebastian, a typical comic relief figure, ridicules the stock "milk-and-water ladies" of the Anglo-American sentimental novel, whom he would like to have replaced by a more Mediterranean type of "woman that has a little fire in her composition" (Rowson 80), or when Frederic, the young modern American, in a chivalric fashion dreams of "some distressed damsel who wanted a knight-errant to deliver her from captivity" (Rowson 72), Rowson clearly parodies some of the sentimental conventions of her time. More important than these occasional moments of self-parody, however, are the attempts which Rowson makes to recode and reconfigure the basic constellations of a typical sentimental play. As an educator who a few years after the premiere of the play would open her "Young Ladies' Academy" in Boston, she sees the stage as an efficacious educational space in which new configurations would help articulate and transmit new political ideas. With Judith Sargent Murray, her contemporary, Rowson regards the stage as "a very powerful engine in forming the opinions and manners of a people" (qtd. in Schofield 268).

The most significant recoding of the stage takes place when Rowson redefines the traditionally male-dominated oriental space. Muley Moloc, the Dey of Algiers, who in a conventional context would have reigned supreme, remains absent most of the time in Rowson's play. Hidden behind the scene, he makes his appearance only at the very end of the final act. He is thus clearly removed from center stage and replaced by a new configuration of women who begin to exercise power. From the very first scene, Rowson's play foreshadows this male disempowerment when Fetnah, sold to the Dey as his sexual slave by her father Ben Hassan, rebels against her condition and articulates a deeply felt desire for liberty. This desire, atypical of an oriental woman at that time, was awakened in her by Rebecca, a true American daughter of Liberty, now held captive by the Dey, who, in this opening scene, is only symbolically represented by Fetnah's rather irreverent description. Twisting "his whiskers" and knitting "his great beetle brows," he exercises his power preferably with his scimitar, the most prominent attribute of his masculinity. When he lays "his hand upon the scimitar" and when Fetnah sees "[it] half drawn" (Rowson 60), the phallic connotations are all too obvious and expose his power as pure animal lust. Governed by his unruly passions, he is described as a slave of "lawless love," of pure "licentiousness" (Rowson 87; 63) which invests a ruler with arbitrary power—both political and sexual—over his subjects. The Dey's patriarchal potency is, on a somewhat smaller scale, reproduced by the behavior of the other two oriental male figures, Mustapha, "the horrid-looking creature" and "great, ugly thing" (Rowson 59), and Ben Hassan, Fetnah's father, a Jewish apostate and "a most extortionate old rogue" (Rowson 64), who in his greed does not even refrain from selling his daughter to the Dey. By depicting, on the one side, the traditionally male-encoded oriental space as one of vicious sexual degradation and political arbitrariness, the play, on the other side, upgrades and highlights the American counter-space as one in which the virtues of love and liberty are seen as dominant.

Thus slavery and liberty, the two key concepts of the American Revolution, are brought into play. In true eighteenth-century fashion, however, liberty is not conceived as limited to America; its claim is universal, as the "Prologue" makes unmistakably clear. Wherever Columbia's sons and daughters breathe, "there must be liberty" (Rowson 58). Thus it is only logical that even in Algiers, where the Americans lie captured, liberty must retain its validity. While Columbia's sons, verbally declaiming their liberty creed, play a rather peripheral role in Rowson's play, it is the daughters who move to center stage and become liberty's real agents. They publicly assume power—if only in a world of fiction—which was still largely denied to them in reality. The play thus simulates a situation and negotiates an issue which at the time was seen to be of crucial political importance.

The central figure in the play is Rebecca who, with her son Augustus, was captured by the Algerines and during her captivity learns about the fate of her daughter Olivia and her husband, aptly called Constant, who are also held captive in Algiers and show great moral constancy.[4] After a series of complications typical of a sentimental plot, Rowson reunites the family, once separated by the Barbary pirates, in a melodramatically effective finale. What is more important, however, than the scheming devices on the plot level are the political issues negotiated in the play. Rebecca clearly assumes the role of the republican wife and mother, whose main task, as a "custodian of civic morality," it is "to educate future generations of sensible republicans" (Kerber 10-11). Unlike "matrimony, among savages, having no object but propagation and slavery" (Lewis 708), republican motherhood elevates and ennobles the degraded woman by de-emphasizing her biological function of reproduction and highlighting her productive role. By instilling such "social virtues" (Rowson 57) as liberty, piety, patriotism or affection in her children, she fulfills this eminently productive political task. Rebecca's influence, however, does not remain restricted to the biological family; it includes, as Fetnah and Zoriana, the two Moriscan women in the play, make unmistakably clear, the entire community of women. Thanks to her civilizing influence, Zoriana, who loves "a Christian slave," has already become "a Christian in [her] heart," while Fetnah still dreams of "some dear, sweet, Christian man [who] would fall in love with [her], break open the garden gates, and carry [her] off." Her desire articulates itself in a passage abounding with sexual connotations:

> And take me to that charming place where there are no bolts and bars, no mutes and guards, no bowstrings and scimitars. Oh, it must be a dear, delightful country, where women do just what they please!
>
> (Rowson 73)

Such a dream of a free space, "where women do just what they please," sounds still in part naive and may be explained as an inverted version of the male fantasies of sexual licentiousness and arbitrary power. Fetnah entirely disregards the function of the republican wife and mother who, as a guardian of civic morality, also has to act in a morally responsible way. Her dream of a paradise of mutual affection between man and woman, however, in which bolts, bars and scimitars, the intimidating symbols of phallic power, have lost their threat is far from naive. It has, at least in part, already been realized in America. The republican wife is no longer the powerless object of a man's sexual desires but his equal partner in love. Since it was a central tenet of the American Revolution, as Jay Fliegelman has pointed out, that "in an ideal world all relationships would be contractual" (123), that is, based on the idea of equal partnership, the partners in love could serve as an ideal republican model. In her **"Concluding Address. For 1808,"** Rowson has one of the young ladies of her Academy declaim:

> It is humiliating to our sex to reflect, that in those countries where the admiration of beautiful women is carried to the highest excess they are slaves, and their moral and intellectual degradation increases in direct proportion to the adoration which is paid to mere external charms; to such a length is this degradation carried,

and of so little consequence are they deemed in the scale of intelligent beings, that the voluptuous prophet of Arabia excluded them from light, liberty, and knowledge, and from all the joys of paradise.

> (qtd. in Weil 97)

Thus Rebecca and the other American captives regard it as their highest duty to abolish all forms of degradations and to carve out a space for "concordant minds" (Lewis 710) which would include both men and women as equal partners and in which light, liberty, knowledge and all the joys of paradise would be equally shared.

It was Rowson's deliberate strategy to replace the "unfeeling world" (Rowson 62) of a hierarchically structured patriarchy by a world of affection in which women as its custodians could play a central role. Rowson's reconfigurations in *Slaves in Algiers* may therefore be seen as an attempt to create a social order based on "affectionate unions" (Fliegelman 123) rather than on patriarchal gradations, an order which was gradually emerging in America in the latter half of the eighteenth century and in which "man [was] Lord, woman *Lordess*," as Abigail Adams once put it (qtd. in Norton 250). Through these reconfigurations Rowson was also able to invert the traditional hierarchy between oriental master and slave and thereby could question, if not subvert, the entire social order. The male oriental despot who ruled with absolute power over his harem is here exposed as the voluptuous slave of his passions, while the female captives, free at heart, may be seen as Liberty's true daughters. In three further respects Rowson subverts, as Doreen Alvarez Saar has convincingly shown, "the bounds of the traditional sentimental plot." She, firstly, depicts her female captives no longer as objects who passively wait for the knight-errant to rescue them from their distress but as agents who are able to work out their own liberation. She, secondly, conceives her two Moriscans, Fetnah and Zoriana, as atypical in the sense that they rebel against the patriarchal system of their fathers and thus question it from within. And she, thirdly, violates the sentimentalist conventions when she has her play end with the reunion of the family rather than the traditional marriage vow (Saar 240-41). What Henry and Olivia, the two lovers, profess in their concluding statements is not their love for one another but the patriotic love of their "native land, where liberty has established her court—where the warlike Eagle extends his glittering pinions in the sunshine of prosperity" (Rowson 93).

Not surprisingly, Rowson came under heavy attack with her subversive tactics. Her epilogue, recited by herself, inverts the traditional patriarchal order, suggesting that "Women were born for universal sway; / Men to adore, be silent, and obey" (Rowson 94) to make her audience aware of the absurdity of a non-egalitarian partnership. This infuriated such conservative critics as William

Cobbett who commented rather sarcastically that "sentiments like these could not be otherwise than well received in a country, where the authority of the wife is so unequivocally acknowledged" (qtd. in Saar 242). The very fact, however, that numerous other critics came to Rowson's support indicates that a major change was under way in postrevolutionary America, that a newly (en)gendered American order was dawning and that Rowson's play was, as Judith Sargent Murray had put it, "a very powerful engine in forming" this *novus ordo*.

* * *

At first sight, Royall Tyler's novel *The Algerine Captive* seems to situate itself on the diametrically opposite end of the literary spectrum. Updike Underhill, the authorial narrator, emphatically rejects certain conventions to which Rowson, at least in part, still subscribes. For him the melodramatic moments enacted publicly in Rowson's play are, if at all, only to be admitted in a private closet. If performed "on the stage," he can watch such scenes as the following only with the greatest amusement:

> I saw the lady descend the rope-ladder: heard the old man and his servants pursue; saw the lady carried off breathless in the arms of her knight; arrive safe in Spain, was present at the lady's baptism into the catholic church, and at her marriage with her noble deliverer. I was myself almost stifled with the caresses of the noble family.
>
> (Tyler II.16-17)

As a male captive sold at an auction who had to work as a slave in a quarry and, when found "not so active as the rest," was struck with the whip (Tyler II.23), Updike prefers a more 'realistic' mode of representation. He exchanges, as Alexander Cowie puts it, the "sugary sentiment" for a more "intellectual diet" which is reflected in a "crisp, classic prose" (66; 68). Since he cannot count himself among "the rich and the noble" men of rank, he does not have the means to put up for ransom. The Italian duke, the Spanish don or the French marquis are as much absent in Tyler's narrative as are the contrived cross-dressings and deceptions which are part and parcel of the sentimental plot. The "sober character of the historian," Underhill declares, "compels me to assure my readers, that, whatever may have happened in the sixteenth century, I never saw during my captivity a man of any rank, family, or fortune, among the menial slaves" (Tyler II.17). The rich are replaced by "the wretched" who "are all of one family, and ever regard each other as brethren" (Tyler II.14).

The closed, emotionally charged dramatic space of Rowson's play gives way in Tyler's novel, due to its "sober character," to a less emotional, more open spatial organization. The two different genres with which both authors work may, at least in part, account for the two different spatial models. Whereas Rowson contracts her dramatic space to intensify "the caresses of the noble family," Tyler in his novel works with a counterstrategy of spatial expansion; he strings a series of events together and thereby gradually widens his space. The changes in the novel's setting from New England southward to Virginia, then seaward to England and the coast of West Africa, from there to the Barbary Shore, later eastward to Mecca and Medina and, to complete the circle, westward to his native New England where it all began, symbolize this continuous spatial widening. Unlike Rowson, with her sentimental strategy of reuniting a family, a strategy that asked for a closed space in which the familial bonds and affections would become more plausible, Tyler's two-part narrative is marked by the protagonist's desire to break down such narrow boundaries, "to see the world, to acquire practical knowledge" (Tyler I.145). He therefore expands his space, and at the same time the generic spectrum of the novel widens considerably. Critics have almost unanimously called *The Algerine Captive* a highly "eclectic, incongruous, and sprawling" book (Cook 7), a kind of grab bag which draws on various genres and therefore fails "to achieve a unity of tone that would hold both volumes together" (Tanselle 175).

While Updike Underhill in the first part travels along the Atlantic seaboard like a picaro, experiencing and relating a series of remarkable adventures with the intent to satirize some of the cultural deficiencies of his country, the narrative tone suddenly changes toward the end of the first part when the protagonist, still the naive picaro, boards the *Sympathy,* a ship "bound to the coast of Africa" (Tyler I.163), and becomes unknowingly involved in the African slave trade. When Updike at this point witnesses the cruel separation of families, the rending of "all the tender endearing ties of natural and social affection" (I.166), the picaresque mode proves utterly inefficacious and begins to give way to the sentimental. His increasing sympathy with the slaves calls for such a tonal shift. When he himself is captured by Barbary pirates and sold into slavery at an auction in Algiers, Updike again changes the narrative mode because he is not the sentimentalist who would only lament his fate. He now resorts to the captivity genre, which allows him to analyze at length the cultural and religious differences between Algiers and America and his inner conflict caused by these differences. Like whites in Indian captivity, the Algerine captive in his deepest dejection and greatest despair begins to recognize the benefits of his native American culture which the picaro was unable to see because he used it primarily as a satirical target:

> Let those of our fellow citizens [he exclaims] who set at nought the rich blessings of our federal union, go like me to a land of slavery, and they will then learn how to appreciate the value of our free government.
>
> (Tyler II.27)

A further shift occurs when Updike, now enjoying certain privileges as a respected physician in the city of Algiers, is able to gain a more balanced view and recognize both the differences and similarities characterizing the two cultures. Now it is the travel narrative that offers itself as the ideal mode of representation. In long descriptive chapters which critics have often regarded as the weakest, least inventive sections of the book,[5] Updike relates the history, geography, government, religion and other habits and customs of the Algerines before he again resumes "the thread of [his] more appropriate narrative" which now presents itself as a typical oriental adventure story with the familiar stock figures, delaying complications and remarkable coincidences which will ultimately lead to a happy ending. An artful "wily Israelite" (Tyler II.188), reminiscent of Rowson's Ben Hassan, the Jewish apostate and extortionate old rogue, extorts Updike's ransom and plays various villainous tricks on him before a Portuguese frigate, in deus-ex-machina fashion, finally delivers Updike from his captivity and restores him to his native New England.

William C. Spengemann explains these generic inconsistencies, which account for the incongruous and sprawling character of the novel, with Tyler's changing intentions while he wrote the book (123). Tyler, however, from the very first chapter of the book, intends to draw his protagonist as a very consistent character whose main trait is his love of liberty and his desire to see and explore the world. This desire is reflected on the level of both plot and genre in a continuous transgression of boundaries. Updike is too much the nonconformist to conform to the given social norms and the generic rules. With his ancestor Captain John Underhill, who "had early imbibed an ardent love of liberty" (Tyler I.2) and had come to Massachusetts Bay, the descendant shares the love of freedom, which he seeks in other countries. Like the Captain, who only a few years after his arrival had been banished from the Bay Colony as an antinomian and whom Jeremy Belknap, "that elegant, accurate and interesting historian" (Tyler I.1-2), had described as "a striking instance of that species of false religion" that had "its seat in the imagination" (qtd. in Cook 22), Updike is also a highly imaginative antinomian who constantly violates the rules. He not only rebels against the cultural narrowness of his native New England but, with his imaginative talents, also satirizes its deficiencies. Employed and then dismissed as a country schoolmaster, he sees his dismissal as a fortunate moment of deliverance which affords him a similar joy as his later "emancipation from real slavery in Algiers" (Tyler I.52-53). Disappointed by the cultural poverty of New England, he seeks treasures in "the southern states spoken of as the high road to fortune" (Tyler I.127). On his way to the South, Updike stops in Philadelphia to visit Benjamin Franklin, author of "The Way to Wealth," who had risen "from small beginnings, by the sole exertion of native genius and indefatigable industry," and could therefore function as a model on Updike's way upward (Tyler I.129).[6] The South, however, where he had hoped to free himself of his Yankee provincialism and live the life of a cosmopolitan amongst elegantly clad cavaliers, also proves a failure. Disgusted with the hypocrisy and dissipation of the slave-holding planters as well as their "poverty of spirit" in a country where "books were not the prime article of commerce" (Tyler I.142-43), Updike turns eastward aboard the *Freedom*. In London, where he meets Tom Paine, once like Franklin a champion of America's political liberty, he is utterly disillusioned by Paine's anti-egalitarian ideas and the fact that his tongue now flowed most freely only "when he was most intoxicated with 'ale or viler liquors'" (Tyler I.160). Updike now seems farther from his ideal of freedom than before:

> Men of unbounded affluence, in plain attire, living within the rules of the most rigid economy; crowds of no substance strutting in embroidery and lace; people whose little smoky fire of coals was rendered cheerless by excise, and their daily draught of beer embittered by taxes; . . . who are entangled by innumerable penal laws, to the breach of which banishment and the gallows are almost universally annexed.
>
> (Tyler I.147-48)

Paradoxically, Updike's search for freedom proves more and more a self-entanglement. As "surgeon on board the ship Sympathy," he not only becomes a witness of the cruelties of the slave trade but also an "active part of this inhuman transaction." His Yankee "conscience" and "humanity" begin to awaken, however, and he not only blushes when he thinks of his country but execrates himself "for even the involuntary part [he] bore in this execrable traffic." His later Algerine captivity he conceives as an act of expiation "for the inhumanity [he] was necessitated to exercise towards these [HIS] BRETHREN OF THE HUMAN RACE." In his deepest degradation he becomes aware that he is part of "the great family of the universe" which is "of one flesh and blood" (Tyler I.162-70). His entire life, he vows, will be dedicated to the abolition of slavery:

> Grant me [he prays toward the end of the first part] once more to taste the freedom of my native country, and every moment of my life shall be dedicated to preaching against this detestable commerce. I will fly to our fellow citizens in the southern states; I will on my knees conjure them, in the name of humanity, to abolish a traffic which causes it to bleed in every pore. If they are deaf to the pleadings of nature, I will conjure them for the sake of consistency to cease to de-

prive their fellow creatures of freedom, which their writers, their orators, representatives, senators, and even their constitutions of government, have declared to be the unalienable birth-right of man.

(Tyler I.189)

When Updike therefore in the second part speaks with increasing fervor "of the privileges of [his] native land" (Tyler II.184), he shows that his own captivity has taught him the lesson of the "inalienable birth-right of man," an American right which the Dey's despotic government can never guarantee. At the same time, however, he, who suffered the fate of a slave, cannot and will not forget that there still is that 'peculiar institution' of slavery in the Southern states. Larry Dennis, who criticizes Tyler for the blatantly nationalistic and "chauvinistic coda" of the novel (79), not only fails to contextualize the book as a memorial of the days of postrevolutionary nationalism but also disregards the skeptical undertones which clearly resonate in the coda. When Updike, on the final page of the book, ardently wishes that his fellow citizens may profit from his captivity and when he urges them to keep the union among themselves because "BY UNITING WE STAND, BY DIVIDING WE FALL" (Tyler II.228), slavery remains present as a threat from within which may, if the fellow citizens refuse to learn the lesson of Updike's captivity, eventually destroy the political union.[7] That slavery is here mentioned only indirectly may be explained by Tyler's primary concern, which was the discovery of true republican liberty rather than the abolition of slavery. The one, however, cannot be thought of without the other. Updike's travelings may therefore be seen as stages in a process of self-realization and self-education during which he begins to realize that liberty is not given but has to be fought for daily—even in a self-proclaimed land of the free. *The Algerine Captive* can therefore rightly be called a political *Bildungsroman* in which the gradual discovery and unfolding of a general conviction takes precedence over individual characterizations.

* * *

The two Algerine captivities which capitalized on the American-Algerian war of 1785-1797 were, as I have shown, eminently political in the sense that they engaged and intervened in the debates of the time. Both Tyler and Rowson, who lacked any firsthand knowledge of the oriental world, construed the orient as an imaginary space, an "ORIENT de l'esprit," a "ménagerie mentale" (Valéry 1041; 1044) based on fantasy rather than fact and relying heavily on the literary products *en vogue* at the time. As interventions in a political conflict, both works construed, as might be expected, a rather schematic space in which the lines between good and evil, right and wrong, light and darkness were clearly drawn. By investing the orient with primarily

negative qualities, both works helped justify the American strategies of political containment or, as Edward Said argues, of "dominating, restructuring, and having authority over the Orient" (3). What the United States navy at the Barbary coast failed to achieve, works of fiction, as it were, could bring about. For both Tyler and Rowson Algiers functioned, first of all, as a totalitarian system which would capture free American citizens, sell them into slavery and deprive them of their "inalienable birth-right" of liberty. Yet both also made use of the orient as an alien space in which issues of American national importance such as the role of the republican woman or the contradictions of slavery on the one hand and the nation's universal claim for liberty on the other could be negotiated and, due to the displacement strategy, brought to a recipient's awareness. For her distinct feminist purpose, Susanna Rowson designed the orient as an emotionally charged sentimental space in which she could "spotlight communities of women" (Kritzer, "Playing" 153) enslaved by tyrannical potentates, who would rebel against male arbitrary power, work out both their political and sexual liberation and be in the end reborn as true republican women. Tyler's male-dominated 'gentry novel,'[8] in which women remain, as it were, hidden behind their oriental veils, construed a more permeable, less schematic space in which he could compare two political systems and discover both their differences as well as their similarities. Algiers was to make one aware of slavery as one of the central problems of the time, a problem which threatened the state of the American union and was felt as a painful thorn in the flesh of the body politic. Though very different in form, both captivities share a common political purpose. They both plunge their protagonists into a series of trials and ordeals which will ultimately lead to their political rebirth. While Rowson's women are reborn into a sisterhood of republican women, Tyler's primary concern is with the rebirth of man into a brotherhood beyond slavery, the great family "of one flesh and one blood" (Tyler I.169). Both see their works and their protagonists as "powerful engines" transmitting their gendered messages which would dominate the debates for decades to come.

Notes

1. "Domestic Life of the Arabs," published in the *General Magazine and Review* (July 1798): 34-36, was only one among numerous articles of a similar kind which appeared in magazines of the time.

2. Rowson's play only in the last two decades received some critical attention. Among the more noteworthy discussions are those of Dorothy Weil (1976), Patricia L. Parker (1986), Doreen Alvarez Saar (1991) and Amelia Howe Kritzer (1996). Tyler's novel has fared somewhat better with the critics. Among the earlier discussions are those of Alexander Cowie (1951) and Teut Riese (1958).

Since its republication by Jack B. Moore (1967) and Don L. Cook (1970) critics have been more attentive to it. Cf. G. Thomas Tanselle (1967), Larry R. Dennis (1974), Cathy N. and Arnold E. Davidson (1976), William C. Spengemann (1977), Cathy N. Davidson (1986) and John Engell (1989).

3. Temporal and spatial dislocations were common strategies in literary works of the early republic to raise a reader's consciousness. The 14th-century Swiss struggle for independence, for instance, was a favorite subject, since it offered striking parallels to America's own struggle for political sovereignty. Titles such as *Altorf* (1818), a play by Frances Wright, or "The Waldstetten: A Swiss Tale," anonymously published in *The Atlantic Souvenir* (1826), document the American interest in the Swiss struggle for independence.

4. In Mozart's oriental opera *Die Entführung aus dem Serail,* Konstanze, the female protagonist, captured by the Turks and held captive in the seraglio by Selim Bassa, shows a similar 'constancy.'

5. Teut Riese and Cathy Davidson take an exceptional view here and underline the enlightening function of the long descriptive passages (chs. XV-XXVII). Riese argues that only in the second half of the book with its deep moral sense of values (*sittliches Wertebewußtsein*) "—und nicht in den neuenglischen Anfangskapiteln, wie A. Cowie meint—erreicht Tyler die Höhe seines künstlerischen Vermögens [—rather than in the New England chapters, as A. Cowie argues—is Tyler at his best artistically]" (Riese 148). Cathy Davidson sees the function of the descriptive Algiers chapters as "the mirror version that especially shows up American distortions" (*Revolution* 209). With a similar intention, Montesquieu, with his *Lettres Persanes* (1721), or Voltaire, with his 'histoire orientale' *Zadig* (1747), had depicted the orient to hold up a mirror to the occident.

6. Benjamin Franklin was also the author of a satirical letter to the editor of the *Federal Gazette* (1790), signed under the pseudonym Historicus, in which one Sidi Mehemet Ibrahim, member of the Divan of Algiers, argues against the abolition of piracy and slavery as advocated by the *Erika,* a clear resonance of *Amerika* and its abolitionists. Like Tyler Franklin polemicizes against American slavery by displacing the problem to Algiers.

7. Lincoln's speech delivered at the Republican State Convention in Springfield, Illinois, on June 16, 1858, in which he referred to the house divided against itself which cannot stand, made use of the same biblical source. Such parallel use may be seen as coincidental; the fact, however, that both Tyler and Lincoln see the union endangered by slavery is more than just a coincidence.

8. For an excellent discussion of the two dominant narrative modes of the time, the sentimental and the gentry novel, see Winfried Fluck, *Das kulturelle Imaginäre* (1997), to which this paper owes valuable insights.

Works Cited

Barnby, H. G. *The Prisoners of Algiers: An Account of the Forgotten American-Algerian War 1785-1797*. London: Oxford UP, 1966.

Cook, Don L., ed. *The Algerine Captive*. By Royall Tyler. New Haven: College and UP, 1970.

Cooper, James Fenimore. *Early Critical Essays (1820-1822)*. Ed. James F. Beard. Gainesville: Scholars' Facsimiles and Reprints, 1955.

Cowie, Alexander. *The Rise of the American Novel*. New York: American Book Co., 1951.

Davidson, Cathy N. *Revolution and the Word: The Rise of the Novel in America*. New York: Oxford UP, 1986.

———, and Arnold E. Davidson. "Royall Tyler's *The Algerine Captive*: A Study in Contrasts." *Ariel* 7.3 (1976): 53-67.

Dennis, Larry R. "Legitimizing the Novel: Royall Tyler's *The Algerine Captive*." *Early American Literature* 9 (1974): 71-80.

Engell, John. "Narrative Irony and National Character in Royall Tyler's *The Algerine Captive*." *Studies in American Fiction* 17 (1989): 19-32.

Fliegelman, Jay. *Prodigals and Pilgrims: The American Revolution Against Patriarchal Authority, 1750-1800*. Cambridge: Cambridge UP, 1982.

Fluck, Winfried. *Das kulturelle Imaginäre: Eine Funktionsgeschichte des amerikanischen Romans 1790-1900*. Frankfurt: Suhrkamp, 1997.

Kerber, Linda. *Women of the Republic: Intellect and Ideology in Revolutionary America*. New York: Norton, 1986.

Kritzer, Amelia Howe. "Playing with Republican Motherhood: Self-Representation in Plays by Susanna Haswell Rowson and Judith Sargent Murray." *Early American Literature* 31 (1996): 150-66.

———, ed. *Plays by Early American Women, 1775-1850*. Ann Arbor: U of Michigan P, 1995.

Lewis, Jan. "The Republican Wife: Virtue and Seduction in the Early Republic." *William and Mary Quarterly* 44 (1987): 689-721.

Norton, Mary Beth. *Liberty's Daughters: The Revolutionary Experience of American Women, 1750-1800*. Boston: Little, 1980.

Parker, Patricia L. *Susanna Rowson*. Boston: Twayne, 1986.

Riese, Teut. *Das englische Erbe in der amerikanischen Literatur*. Bochum-Langendreer: H. Pöppinghaus, 1958.

Rowson, Susanna Haswell. *Slaves in Algiers; Or, A Struggle for Freedom*. 1794. Kritzer, ed., *Plays* 55-95.

Saar, Doreen Alvarez. "Susanna Rowson: Feminist and Democrat." *Curtain Calls: British and American Women and the Theater, 1660-1820*. Ed. Mary Anne Schofield and Cecilia Macheski. Athens: Ohio UP, 1991. 231-46.

Said, Edward. *Orientalism: Western Conceptions of the Orient*. Harmonds-worth: Penguin, 1991.

Schofield, Mary Anne. "'Quitting the Loom and Distaff': Eighteenth-Century American Women Dramatists." *Curtain Calls: British and American Women and the Theater, 1660-1820*. Ed. Mary Anne Schofield and Cecilia Macheski. Athens: Ohio UP, 1991. 260-73.

Sieminski, Captain Greg. "The Puritan Captivity Narrative and the Politics of the American Revolution." *American Quarterly* 42 (1990): 35-56.

Slotkin, Richard. *Regeneration Through Violence: The Mythology of the American Frontier, 1600-1860*. Middletown: Wesleyan UP, 1973.

Spengemann, William C. *The Adventurous Muse: The Poetics of American Fiction, 1789-1900*. New Haven: Yale UP, 1977.

Tanselle, G. Thomas. *Royall Tyler*. Cambridge: Harvard UP, 1967.

Tyler, Royall. *The Algerine Captive; Or, The Life and Adventures of Doctor Updike Underhill, Six Years a Prisoner Among the Algerines*. 1797. Ed. Jack B. Moore. Gainesville: Scholars' Facsimiles and Reprints, 1967.

Valéry, Paul. "Orientem Versus." *Oeuvres II*. Ed. Jean Hytier. Paris: Gallimard, 1960. 1040-45.

Weil, Dorothy. *In Defense of Women: Susanna Rowson (1762-1824)*. University Park: Penn State UP, 1976.

Patricia L. Parker (essay date 2000)

SOURCE: Parker, Patricia L. "Susanna Haswell Rowson: America's First Best-Selling Author." In *Ordinary Women, Extraordinary Lives: Women in American History*, edited by Kriste Lindenmeyer, pp. 25-38. Wilmington, Del.: Scholarly Resources Inc., 2000.

[*In the following essay, Parker surveys Rowson's life and works.*]

Susanna Haswell Rowson (1762-1824), author of America's first best-seller, lived through the tumultuous time of the American Revolution. Afterwards, when the war-weary public longed for entertainment, she helped introduce the popular theatrical arts to the New Republic. Then as America became interested in women's education, she opened Boston's first schools for girls and young women. Throughout her lifetime, Rowson continued to write popular novels for and about women. Thus, her life paralleled the rise of the arts in the New Republic and the growing concern for women's rights and education.

At the age of five, Susanna Haswell had her first sea adventure when she traveled from England with her father, William Haswell, a lieutenant in the British navy. Susanna had been born in Plymouth, England (probably in February 1762). Her mother, Susanna Musgrave Haswell, had died shortly after Susanna's birth, so as a young child she lived with relatives. But in October 1766 she said good-bye to the family she had known and to the bustling port town of Plymouth. She, her father, and a nursemaid boarded a ship bound for the colony of Massachusetts Bay. Having grown up in a family of naval men, the child Susanna relished the idea of her first sea voyage, but anticipation and delight soon turned to fear as the ship encountered a storm. Twenty-five years later, the memory remained vivid enough for Susanna Rowson to recount it in her novel *Rebecca; or, The Fille de Chambre*:

> A fair wind presently took them out of the channel, and they flattered themselves with a prosperous voyage; but these flattering appearances were soon reversed, for the wind suddenly changed, rising almost to a hurricane, so that it was impossible to pursue their intended course or return to port, and they continued tossing about in the Atlantic till the latter end of December, and then had not half made their passage, though their provision was so exhausted that they were obliged to live on a very small allowance of bread; water and salt and meat they had, and a few pease, but of these they were extremely careful.[1]

Ten long weeks later, the crew sighted and flagged down a ship to plead for food. But they received no answer and the crew and passengers again faced death by starvation. Ten days later another ship passed. This time a sympathetic captain and his sailors fed their own dinners to the hungry passengers and equipped them with provisions for the remaining journey to Boston. *Rebecca* movingly describes the kindness of the sailors and their captain, who refused recompense.

Susanna's first sea experience had not yet ended, however. As their vessel entered Boston Harbor, it was hit by wind, sleet, and snow that froze the ropes and obscured the lighthouse at the harbor entrance. Her father dared not let his daughter descend the icy rope ladder to the waiting boat, nor did he trust himself to carry her, "lest a false step or slip might destroy them both."[2] An old sailor suggested tying the child around the waist and lowering her down the ship's side. Like a bundle of straw, Susanna Haswell arrived for the first time in America. Small wonder that shipwrecks and dangerous sea adventures figure in six of her later novels. Harrowing voyages had been the experience of many colonists who settled in America, and such scenes in Rowson's novels appealed to many who had suffered similarly.

Compared to the traumas of her arrival, the young Susanna enjoyed a peaceful childhood. Her father remarried, to American Rachel Woodward, acquired a little property, and settled on the Nantasket Peninsula, south of Boston. The nature of his work remains unclear, but he may have served as a customs officer. Susanna's two half-brothers, Robert and William Jr., were soon added to the family. Susanna learned to read and enjoyed the benefits of her father's small library, which included Homer, Spenser, Dryden, and Shakespeare. Though boys might attend a local grammar school and then a preparatory school, girls in colonial New England usually learned to read and do sums from parents at home or from a local dame school. A neighbor, the controversial patriot James Otis, called her his little pupil and often engaged Susanna in conversation. This rural idyll was broken, however, by the onset of the American Revolution.

The Haswells' war experience was typical of many families labeled "Tory" by their neighbors despite attempts to maintain neutrality. Lieutenant Haswell's employment with the Royal Navy placed him under suspicion by his American neighbors, who accused him of communicating with British ships nearing Boston Harbor. In the fall of 1775 the family was forcibly removed from its home and placed under house arrest in Hingham, on the south shore of Boston Harbor, about twelve miles by land from the city. Cut off from his employment and salary, Lieutenant Haswell was promised public assistance for food and firewood, but both sympathy and relief were in short supply during these tense times. Two years later the family was forced to move further inland, to Abingdon, where both Lieutenant Haswell and his wife grew ill. They relied upon young Susanna to find and chop firewood and cook their meager meals. By spring 1778 the Massachusetts legislature had negotiated a prisoner exchange and sent the Haswells to Nova Scotia, where they were allowed to board a boat for England. Susanna Haswell's American childhood had ended, leaving her with memories both bitter and sweet that would find their way into her later novels.

At the age of sixteen, Susanna Haswell and her family joined hundreds of American war refugees in London, waiting for the war to end so that they might either return to their homes and property or gain recompense for it from the British government. Her father, at age forty-four, felt physically and psychologically defeated. His third son, John Montresor, was born while the family lived in London. As years passed and Lieutenant Haswell continued to try to claim retirement pay and compensation, he relied upon his daughter for financial support. But as a young woman in eighteenth-century England, Susanna Haswell had few wage-earning avenues open to her. Women could be seamstresses, hatmakers, ladies' maids, or governesses. All placed women in vulnerable positions, and none earned enough to support a family of six. In her later novels Susanna's fictional heroines face similar situations, forced to seek employment to support themselves and sometimes their aging parents. Despite the apparent hopelessness of their condition, these characters regard work as a valuable, indeed ennobling, middle-class virtue. They enter the working world with pride and enthusiasm. With equal pride and determination they meet its disappointments.

No evidence exists, but it may be supposed that Susanna Haswell became a governess. Her skills qualified her for teaching. She could conduct herself with propriety, converse with charm and intelligence, sing, and sew plain and fancy needlework. She loved books and was as well read as any self-educated woman blessed with a father's moderately good library. Most important, she had a genuine interest in education, especially of girls. In the 1814 preface to *Rebecca; or, The Fille de Chambre,* the author described as autobiographical the scene in which young Rebecca becomes the maligned governess. If Susanna Haswell did take up a position as governess, she did not keep it for long, because her immediate interests rested elsewhere.

In 1786, Susanna Haswell did what many women of the coming decades did to earn money: she wrote a novel. Four years earlier, Fanny Burney had earned £250 for her novel, *Celia,* though more common were the 5- and 10-guinea amounts most booksellers offered authors, especially women. Haswell may have been acquainted with the few women writers in England at the time: Ann Radcliffe (1764-1823), Elizabeth Inchbald (1753-1821), Maria Edgeworth (1767-1849), and Hannah Moore (1745-1833), to name the best known. From the successful writer Samuel Richardson they learned to draw upon the world of the middle class and its values and virtues. Between 1770 and 1800 these women's novels dealt with the world of the home, the farthest reaches being the French convent or a debtors' prison. Haswell's first novel was *Victoria, a Novel. In Two Volumes. The Characters Taken from Real Life, and Calculated to Improve the MORALS OF THE FEMALE SEX, by Impressing Them with a Just Sense of THE MERITS OF FILIAL PIETY* (1786). The plot follows the adventures of young Victoria Baldwin, daughter of a deceased naval officer. Following a standard female-tragedy plot in which seduction is followed by pregnancy and abandonment, the book includes at least five subplots and several brief stories within stories, all of which reinforce the theme of filial piety. Haswell's first publication thus followed recently established conventions of the new genre of fiction. Susanna Haswell had begun what would become a long writing career.

But having been ill treated by the bookseller who bought her manuscript, Haswell found another career more immediately appealing. She was drawn by the lure of the stage. Eighteenth-century London offered a rich variety of popular entertainments, such as the acrobatic exhibitions at Sadler's Wells and Astley's Amphitheater and the pleasure gardens of Vauxhall and Ranelagh. Young Haswell wrote songs for the vocalists at Vauxhall and Ranelagh, discovering in herself a quick talent for light lyrics. More appealing, however, were the theaters, especially Drury Lane and Covent Garden, where American refugees most frequently attended productions. For a shilling or two, Haswell could enjoy a performance that lasted from three-and-one-half to five-and-one-half hours, beginning with music, followed by a five-act play, entr'acte entertainment, and finally an afterpiece of farce or pantomime. Haswell grew intimately acquainted with these theaters and their performers, so intimately that in 1786 she married a minor singer, actor, and trumpeter, William Rowson. The heroine of Haswell's autobiographical novel *Sarah; or, The Exemplary Wife* (1813) describes her decision to marry without love:

> I found I must accede to his proposals, or be thrown on the world, censured by my relations, robbed of my good name, and being poor, open to the pursuits and insults of the profligate. One thing which encouraged me to hope that I might be tolerably happy in this union was—though my heart felt no strong emotions in his favor, it was totally free from all partiality towards any other. He always appeared good-humored and obliging; and though his mind was not cultivated, I thought time might improve him in that particular.[3]

Though great marital unhappiness lay ahead of her, life with William Rowson at first offered new excitement in a career as public performer. Evidence exists that Susanna Rowson performed with a company of London actors at Brighton in the summer of 1786, and it is likely that she, William, and his sister Elizabeth performed with provincial companies when they could not find opportunities in competitive London. "Strolling players," as they were called, affiliated themselves with towns such as Bath, Norwich, York, Liverpool, Manchester, Bristol, or Newcastle, all under royal patent. Wages ran about thirteen shilling sixpence a week, which compared favorably with those of a laborer, who might earn an average of eight or nine shillings a week, but which seemed paltry in contrast to the hundreds of pounds earned by the favorites of the great London stages.

Neither Susanna nor William evidenced great talent, though of the two, Susanna performed more frequently and in more-significant roles. She supplemented her

rather average ability for acting, singing, and pantomime with a conscientious effort to learn her parts and regularly attend rehearsals, behavior that distinguished her from the other performers. Provincial actors were notorious for their inability to act and their disinclination to work, although the demands of learning and performing up to twenty roles at a time might have taxed even the most conscientious. Susanna Rowson refused to stoop to the behavior of most actors, who laughed or swore at the audience and ad-libbed to draw attention to themselves. She made known her standards as well as her evaluation of the most popular performers of the day in her second publication, a thirty-page, lighthearted poem entitled **"A Trip to Parnassus"** (1788). In couplets of anapestic quatrameters, Rowson describes the approach to Apollo's throne of some thirty-four actors and writers. Without mercy, Apollo either welcomes them with bay leaves and laurels or casts them aside as undeserving of praise. The book shows clearly Rowson's standards of honesty, conventionally moral living, and clean language and behavior on stage. She preferred a natural approach to acting rather than the overly rhetorical and heavy-handed lack of realism that marked most performances at the time.

Four more novels followed: *A Test of Honour* (1789); *Mentoria, or the Young Ladies' Friend* (1791); *Charlotte, a Tale of Truth* (1791); and *Rebecca; or, The Fille de Chambre* (1792). None earned her much money, and the reviews did not encourage her. She continued to act, performing at least once in London in a minor role in 1792. The following year, Susanna, William, and Charlotte, another of William's sisters, journeyed to Edinburgh, where they joined the Theatre Royal company, but the company, beset by competition and financial problems, performed little. The future looked bleak.

In 1793, the Rowsons met Thomas Wignell, who had come to England from the United States to recruit actors for his new Philadelphia theater. The war between England and its colonies had closed American theaters, but by 1793 many had reopened, and Wignell sensed a growing market as a population long deprived of luxuries clamored for entertainment. He hastily enlisted the Rowsons and about fifty others; all boarded a ship scheduled to arrive in Philadelphia that fall. This time, Susanna Rowson's journey was uneventful, but she and the others arrived to find the entire city of Philadelphia shut down with a yellow fever epidemic. Rerouted to New Jersey, the company eventually debuted in Annapolis, Maryland, and finally moved on to Philadelphia in January 1794.

Susanna Rowson took to her new job with the energy that characterized her entire career. She learned and performed thirty-five different roles in the first four-and-one-half-month season. She found American audi-

ences more responsive and enthusiastic than British audiences; Americans threw eggs or rotted fruit when they
disliked a performer, and they often interrupted a dull
song with demands for "Yankee Doodle." Managers
constantly needed new material to provide variety for
audiences, who attended several performances a week.
Rowson contributed both plays and songs. Music was
an inherent part of these stage productions, and Rowson
skillfully and quickly wrote lyrics. With her genuine affection for America and its people, she set patriotic
themes to rhythmic, catchy lines. Her **"America, Commerce, and Freedom"** became a popular song for a
ballet pantomime.

Rowson also wrote plays. In her first year with the New
Theater, as it was called, Rowson wrote two plays based
on current political issues, *Slaves in Algiers* and *The
Volunteers.* In *Slaves in Algiers* she capitalized on public anger toward Algerian pirates capturing American
ships. Though she set the play in Algeria, she had less
interest in Algeria than in the subject of tyranny. And
Americans, still feeling boastful about their success
over Britain's tyranny, responded with enthusiasm. The
key word to popularity with such audiences was "liberty," and Rowson stressed it.

> Who barters countrymen, honour, faith, to save
> His life, tho' free in person, is a slave.
> While he, enchan'd, imprison'd tho he be,
> Who lifts his arm for liberty, is free.[4]

With memories still vivid of Americans' fight for liberty, and with feelings about the French Revolution still
running high, such lines generated positive reaction.
But audiences also responded to Rowson's bold feminism, which she effected by turning the topic of Algerian tyranny to the subject of the tyranny of women.
"Woman was never formed to be the abject slave of
man. Nature made us equal with them, and gave us the
power to render ourselves superior. . . . A woman can
face danger with as much spirit, and as little fear as the
bravest man amongst you."[5] The character of Fetnah the
slave asserts that women, as well as men, love freedom.
Fetnah has been a part of the Dey's harem, but once informed of the principles of liberty, she rejects forced
"love." She makes fun of the Dey, saying, "He looks so
grave and stately, that I declare, if it was not for his
huge scymitar, I shou'd burst out a laughing in his
face."[6] The phallic symbolism makes clear the forced
nature of the sexuality, and the play plainly speaks
against tyranny based on sex.

Although Rowson was not the only woman to speak up
for women, most people were unaware of intellectuals
such as Mary Wollstonecraft, whose *Vindication of the
Rights of Women* had been published in Philadelphia
shortly before Rowson's play appeared, or of Abigail
Adams's 1776 private request to her husband to "re-

member the ladies" when forming the new American
government. Although *Slaves in Algiers* continued to
attract audiences, at least one critic expressed strong
objections to it. William Cobbett, an Englishman who
had spent some years in France before emigrating to the
United States the same year that Rowson arrived, became known as a vitriolic political pamphleteer. His targets included Benjamin Rush, Thomas Paine, Benjamin
Franklin, Albert Gallatin, Edmund Randolph, James
Monroe, and Susanna Rowson. Cobbett objected to
Rowson's overuse of the word "liberty," as well as her
grammar and figures of speech. But clearly his real objection lay with her feminism, particularly the couplet
from the epilogue:

> Women were born for universal sway,
> Men to adore, be silent, and obey.

He anticipated, he said, a House of Representatives
constituted entirely of women. To discredit Rowson, he
intimated that people in the theater behaved adulter-
ously.

Rowson had a defender, however little she may have
approved of his defense. John Swanwick, congressman
from Pennsylvania, although personally unacquainted
with Rowson, wrote a retaliatory pamphlet denying
Cobbett's qualification as a critic and insisting that the
distinctions between the sexes were primarily based on
custom and that a male education would qualify a
woman for any of the duties of a man. But Rowson
could not have been happy with Swanwick's assertion
that Rowson's play was merely "a sally of humor, intended to create a smile, and not to enforce a conviction
of women's superiority."[7] Rowson saved her reply for
the preface to her next novel, *Trials of the Human
Heart* (1794), where she called Cobbett a "loathsome
reptile" and his allegations "false and scurrilous." She
obviously strenuously objected to his assertion that her
patriotism was less than genuine. She felt "equally attached" to both Great Britain and the United States. She
declined to reply to Cobbett's objections to feminism,
perhaps feeling that her drama had achieved its purpose.

Little remains of the other plays Rowson wrote for the
Philadelphia company. *The Volunteers,* performed in
1794, dealt with the Whiskey Rebellion in southwestern
Pennsylvania, when farmers resisted the federal excise
tax. In defiance of Cobbett's objection to her overuse of
the word, the thirteen extant songs for this play exuberantly celebrate "liberty." Also in the same year, the
Philadelphia company performed Rowson's *The Female Patriot; or, Nature's Rights,* whose title certainly
suggests continuation of the feminist theme begun in
Slaves in Algiers. Unfortunately, the play has been lost.
Two years later the company performed Rowson's *The
American Tar; or the Press Gang Defeated,* also now

lost. But the list of characters indicated that Rowson wrote parts for her husband and sister-in-law.

Although Rowson gained a small reputation as actress and playwright in Philadelphia, she enjoyed greater prestige as a novelist. Republication of three of her English novels might not have generated much income, but it did provide Rowson with a growing audience. *Rebecca; or, The Fille de Chambre,* apparently without appeal for English audiences, struck a responsive chord in American readers. Perhaps citizens of a youthful country liked the story of a heroine's coming of age, an initiation novel in which the heroine achieves maturity and knowledge of the world. At a time when cartoons and literature depicted the young United States as a woman cast off by a cruel and abusive parent, this story of a young woman abandoned by both her real mother and her female patron aroused nationalistic interest. And possibly the Massachusetts interlude and references to hardships suffered during the American Revolution added further interest for American readers.

But Rowson's greatest success proved to be *Charlotte.* One hundred sixty-one editions have been documented, and the book has remained in print since its 1794 publication. One reason for the novel's success was Rowson's choice of publisher. Mathew Carey had been a publisher and bookseller on Market Street in Philadelphia for six years and had developed effective distribution techniques. Long distances between towns and poor or nonexistent roads had effectively restricted readership of newspapers, magazines, and books. By 1794 communications networks had improved, thereby expanding audiences for all such publications. And among the growing American middle class, women were becoming increasingly literate and even finding a few hours a week of leisure, despite the chores required for family survival or home industry.

Part of *Charlotte*'s appeal is its simple plot. Charlotte, a fifteen-year-old girl in a Chichester boarding school, is persuaded by her dissolute French teacher, Mademoiselle LaRue, to run away to America with a dashing young army officer, Lieutenant Montraville, who claims to love her. Once in New York, Montraville ignores his promise to marry Charlotte and soon falls in love with the beautiful and wealthy Julia Franklin. But his guilt over Charlotte prevents his proposing marriage to Julia. Montraville's false friend, Belcour, who would like to have Charlotte as his own mistress, treacherously convinces Montraville that Charlotte is unfaithful and persuades Charlotte that Montraville has left her for another woman. Pregnant and abandoned, Charlotte is turned out of her lodging and struggles through a snowstorm to seek assistance from her former friend and French teacher, LaRue. But LaRue has found a new lover and refuses to jeopardize her home and social position by helping Charlotte. Finally taken in by some poor servants, Charlotte gives birth to a daughter and goes insane. Her father arrives from England just in time to forgive her before she dies, and he brings home to his hearbroken wife, not their lost daughter, but their orphaned grandchild, Lucy. The novel ends with Belcour's death in a duel, LaRue's dying penniless and alone, and Montraville "to the end of his life subject to fits of melancholy."

The plot thus follows the conventions of the eighteenth-century sentimental novel. It also follows convention by purporting to be "a tale of truth," as fiction still faced opposition among many who thought all literature should be educational and edifying. Those opposing fiction protested that novels were often tales of seduction and incest, hardly "suitable subjects" for young unmarried women, who were assumed to constitute the primary reading audience. Newspapers, magazines, and often the prefaces to novels carried arguments denouncing this claim. Defenders argued that stories of seduced maidens served as moral lessons, severe warnings of the perils posed by the male sex. Others countered that novel reading detracted from hours better spent at spinning, sewing, cooking, or even praying.

In the preface to *Charlotte,* Rowson attested that the story had been told to her by a woman acquainted with a real-life Charlotte and that she as author had merely "thrown over the whole a slight veil of fiction." In none of her previous works had Rowson insisted upon the truth of her fiction, and when she did, many believed her. Fans of the novel soon concluded that the heroine was one Charlotte Stanley, daughter of the eleventh earl of Derby, and Montraville was in real life John Montresor, Rowson's cousin. Rowson herself never commented upon the veracity of such claims. But evidence does support the conclusion that the character of Montraville derived from the life of Montresor. Within the first year of publication, Mathew Carey issued a second edition. Readers liked it and sometimes bought tickets to the New Theater just to see "Mrs. Rowson." But her success as an actress would never rival her achievement as author of *Charlotte Temple,* as the novel was renamed in 1797.

By 1796 Rowson realized that the New Theater was in financial trouble. Though Wignell continued to meet payrolls, he was beset by a competing theater in the same city, yellow fever outbreaks that closed the theaters, and expenses incurred by the production of operas rather than ordinary plays. Rowson wrote to her half-brother Robert Haswell, who lived in Boston, for advice about the theater prospects there, and soon the Rowsons joined seven other actors in a defection from Philadelphia to a Boston company. Rowson's books had already earned her a reputation in Boston. Her work with immigrant musicians, who often moved from city to city giving lessons, holding concerts, writing music for theatrical productions, and opening music stores, meant that she had friends and connections awaiting her. In Boston she found the right combination of opportunities, people, and shared interests to hold her there for the remaining twenty-seven years of her life. She worked with Williamson's Federal Street Theater Company for only a year, performing and writing songs and at least one more play, before resigning from the theater forever in 1797 and turning to a new career—women's education.

Having experienced the atrocities of war during the American Revolution, Rowson spent her mature years enjoying the benefits of that war and suffering the social upheaval it caused. One effect was a change in the position of women. During the war, women had, of necessity, breached decorum and taken over family businesses or farms for absent or dead husbands. Many women discovered new capabilities and interests but, unable to inherit property or businesses, felt shackled by restrictive laws that gave them virtually no rights. After the war, women's diaries, letters, poems, essays, and plays such as Rowson's asked for "freedom," "liberty," even "equal rights." Such requests generated discussions of women's inferiority, equality, or superiority, which led to debates about women's educability. Into this discourse entered Susanna Rowson. But Rowson did more than talk: she acted.

Boston in 1797 had no schools for girls. Many girls still learned to read and write at dame schools. The Boston Act of 1789 stipulated that girls and boys be taught the same subjects, but girls were required to attend school for fewer hours per day and fewer months per year than boys. Yet the public desire for education for females had been shown just two years earlier, when the American Philosophical Society sponsored a contest on the topic of American educational improvements. Every submission had included a proposal for universal free education, that is, education open to all white men and women. Bostonians were ready for a woman's academy, and in November 1797 Rowson launched "Mrs. Rowson's Young Ladies' Academy." The school opened with three pupils; in a year it enrolled one hundred.

Despite the controversy over women's education, public opinion still held that intellectual accomplishments were inappropriate and perhaps unattainable for women. Many feared that a woman educated as a man was educated would abandon her proper sphere; a female pedant would never be a careful housekeeper. Few defied such assumptions outright. Even the most radical, such as the outspoken character of Mrs. Carter in Charles Brockden Brown's novel *Alcuin* (1797), never assumed that women should give up making puddings and nursing babies. But Rowson felt strongly about women's need to learn practical subjects, and her first curriculum consisted of reading, writing, arithmetic, geography,

and needlework. Girls' schools founded later in other cities might include "accomplishments" such as painting on velvet and singing in Italian, but Rowson sought a more serious education for her girls. Still, her love of music and her desire to attract daughters of the best families led her to add lighter and more enjoyable subjects to her curriculum. In 1799 she bought a pianoforte, an instrument still exotic enough to merit newspaper notice, and called upon her theatrical colleague, Mr. R. Laumont, to teach music. She added dancing lessons and sometimes joined her students in the classes, where they found her "a light and pretty dancer." Rowson moved her academy several times, first to Medford, then to Newton, then back to Boston, each time improving and enlarging her facilities.

Rowson's love of performance led her to hold "exhibitions," public demonstrations of her students' talents. Students displayed their maps and needlework and read aloud their own poems, dialogues, or essays or they read works written by Susanna Rowson. These exhibitions were open to parents and the public and indeed became so popular that Rowson profited by charging fifty cents admission. The *Boston Weekly Magazine* reviewed the events. By 1811 the most popular part of the program had become the "female biographies," in which each student recounted a memorized account of a woman from ancient or modern history. Each woman's life exemplified her equality with, if not superiority to, men. The students looked forward to these annual presentations. Although women speaking in public often met with disapproval, Rowson offered no apologies and continued her student exhibitions throughout the history of the academy. She collected some of these demonstration pieces and published them as *A Present for Young Ladies*. The book characterizes the school as an institution where girls and young women learned self-respect, the importance of education, and confidence in the abilities of women.

Throughout her lifetime, Susanna and William remained married, even though William seldom held steady employment and the academy pupils often laughed privately at his obvious drunkenness. William's debts and the mortgage he took on the Hollis Street property caused Susanna Rowson grief and worry during her last years, as she was unable to pay the mortgage. The couple never had children, but some evidence exists that Susanna raised William's illegitimate son. Although childless herself, she informally adopted at least one girl and cared for her pupils as her own. She was fondly remembered by her pupils, whose letters describe her as a strict but caring headmistress.

No matter how great the other demands on her, Rowson always found time to continue her writing. In addition to novels and poetry, Rowson published textbooks. *An Abridgement of Universal Geography* (1805) included her own moral judgments of peoples, religions, and cultures, for no student, teacher, or critic at the time would have valued objectivity in the study of history or geography. She expressed disapproval of slavery, both in the United States and elsewhere; tyranny, whether religious (as in the Catholic Church), political, or otherwise; laziness, induced by warm climates; and immoral behavior, especially among political leaders. She included a section of "Geographical Exercises" reflective of her own fascination with navigation, with graduated exercises designed to teach girls rudimentary principles such as how to find the latitude and the longitude of a place and how, given the latitude and longitude of a place, to find it. Clearly, Rowson expected her students to learn more than mending and simple arithmetic. Even her youngest pupils, the audience for her *Youth's First Steps in Geography* (1818), were expected to learn maps of their state, country, and the world, as well as elementary navigation principles.

Rowson's *Spelling Dictionary* (1807) shows a pedagogical approach remarkably ahead of her time. She wanted to help students associate ideas and to think, not merely memorize. She sought to keep each lesson short and to help students see the rationality for learning, not simply feel forced to learn. Her *Exercises in History, Chronology, and Biography* (1822) included biographies of women, which shows that Rowson read history to find role models for her students. Her last text, *Biblical Dialogues* (1822), written when she had become ill and increasingly interested in religion, placed complex Bible stories within a narrative framework designed to appeal to young readers.

Though Rowson's later fiction never achieved the popularity of *Charlotte Temple,* she continued to entertain her reading audience with *Reuben and Rachel; or, Tales of Old Times* (1798) and a serialized novel, *Sincerity* (1803-1804). A sequel to *Charlotte Temple* appeared posthumously as *Charlotte's Daughter; or, The Three Orphans* (1828). But nothing touched the hearts of the American reading public like *Charlotte Temple.* Nineteenth-century editions added illustrations, including portraits of Charlotte and scenes from the novel. Some illustrations even depicted scenes that were not in the novel, such as a young woman leaning against a tombstone. Readers known as the "Charlotte cult" believed in the literal truth of the novel, as newspapers printed portraits of Charlotte and popular lore identified her house in New York on the corner of Pell and Doyers Streets. Charlotte's gravesite in Trinity Churchyard became the object of pilgrimages for the romantic. Nineteenth-century dramatic versions, such as one published by Charlotte Pixley Plumb in 1899, freely omitted much of the plot, added and deleted characters, and changed both action and dialogue. The novel remained in print for well over a hundred years. Today it is still available in paperback and continues to hold the interest of students in college literature courses.

Rowson died March 2, 1824, after a two-year illness. She was interred in the Gottlieb Graupner family vault in St. Matthew's Church, South Boston. When the church was demolished in 1866, her remains were transferred to Mt. Hope Cemetery in Dorchester, Massachusetts, and a granite monument was erected later in Forest Hills Cemetery, Roxbury, by her descendants, Mary and Haswell C. Clarke and Ellen Murdock Osgood. After his wife's death, William Rowson again mortgaged the Hollis Street house and land, remarried, and lived until 1843.

Susanna Rowson was a prolific writer, producing over her lifetime ten novels, six theatrical works, six textbooks, two collections of poems, and countless songs. As she lived during a crucial period during the nation's history, her writings reflect the taste and interest of the people of the new American Republic, who struggled to decide how to live with their acquired independence. Her life also demonstrates the way in which people who earned their livelihoods in the arts during this early federal period crossed boundaries freely from one field to another, considering themselves artists and entertainers, not merely playwrights or actors, novelists or lyricists. And Rowson's career change from entertainer to headmistress epitomizes the popular emphasis on women's education that characterized American debate at the turn of the century. Rowson thus seems a transition figure, a bridge between women of the colonial period and women of the nineteenth century. Though she never achieved wealth or great fame in her lifetime, she continues to hold reader interest today.

Notes

1. Susanna Haswell Rowson, *Rebecca; or, The Fille de Chambre* (Philadelphia: H. and T. Rice, 1794), 161.

2. Ibid., 116.

3. Susanna Haswell Rowson, *Sarah; or, The Exemplary Wife* (Boston: Charles Williams, 1813), 4.

4. Susanna Haswell Rowson, *Slaves in Algiers; or, A Struggle for Freedom* (Philadelphia: Wrigley and Berriman, 1794), 1.

5. Ibid., 9, 47.

6. Ibid., 39.

7. Susanna Haswell Rowson, *A Rub from Snub* (Philadelphia: Wrigley and Berriman, 1795), 76.

Suggested Readings

Letters from Rowson's family and students are found in the Barrett Collection at the University of Virginia,

Charlottesville, Virginia. A complete bibliography of Rowson's writings was published in 1933 by R. W. G. Vail and the American Antiquarian Society in Worcester, Massachusetts. Vail documents 161 editions of *Charlotte Temple*. Most recently the novel has been edited by Cathy Davidson and published by Oxford University Press (1986). Of all Rowson's writings, only *Charlotte Temple* and *Charlotte's Daughter* are in print today. The only book-length biography, with an accompanying bibliography, is Patricia Parker's *Susanna Rowson,* published in Boston by Twayne (1986). There is another book-length study, Dorothy Weil's *In Defense of Women,* published by Pennsylvania State University Press (1976). Earlier biographies include Francis W. Halsey's Historical and Biographical Introduction to *Charlotte Temple: A Tale of Truth,* by Susanna Rowson (New York: Funk and Wagnalls, 1904), and Samuel Lorenzo Knapp's "A Memoir of the Author" in *Charlotte's Daughter; or, The Three Orphans. A Sequel to Charlotte Temple,* by Susanna Rowson (Boston: Richardson and Lord, 1828). Critical articles include Cathy Davidson's chapter, *"Charlotte Temple,"* in *Reading in America: Literature and Social History,* ed. Cathy Davidson (Baltimore: Johns Hopkins University Press, 1989); Blythe Forcey's "*Charlotte Temple* and the End of Epistolarity," in *American Literature* 63 (1991): 225-41; and Klaus Hansen's "The Sentimental Novel and Its Feminist Critique" in *Early American Literature* 26 (1991): 39-54.

Marion Rust (essay date January 2003)

SOURCE: Rust, Marion. "What's Wrong with *Charlotte Temple?" The William and Mary Quarterly* 60, no. 1 (January 2003): 99-118.

[*In the following essay, Rust considers Rowson's treatment of the themes of women's sexual responsibility and personal agency within eighteenth-century American society in* Charlotte Temple.]

Charlotte Temple, the eponymous heroine of Susanna Rowson's late eighteenth-century best-selling novel, is fond of "lying softly down," and her timing is terrible. She faints into a chaise in Chichester; she crawls into the bed where her seducer, the dashing Lieutenant Montraville, already sleeps; and she takes an afternoon nap that allows his even less scrupulous "brother officer" in the British army, Belcour, to position himself beside her in time for her beloved to discover them together.[1] Given Charlotte's propensity for putting her feet up, it is no wonder that critics have taken the book bearing her name as an exemplar of the novel of seduction, a genre wherein the reader "is asked to deplore the very acts which provide his enjoyment." Some see the novel as evidence of "the appalling popularity of the seduc-

tion motif" in early American sentimental fiction, while others take a gentler view of how the genre "blended the histrionic and pedagogic modes." But whether they favor pleasure or instruction as the primary narrative impetus behind Charlotte's loss of virginity out of wedlock, most scholars take the centrality of the sex act—and with it, of Charlotte's presumed lust—for granted. A story of "the fatal consequence of . . . illicit sexuality," the novel is said to depict a woman "betrayed by her own naive passions" and thereby to provide an "example of virtue fallen through seduction and sexuality."[2]

A closer look calls this emphasis on Charlotte's passion, and its ill-effects on her virtue, into question.[3] The novel rarely mentions sex: there is no indication of how the "kindness and attention" that Montraville shows a seasick Charlotte during their voyage from Portsmouth, England, to New York leads, five chapters later, to the first allusion to her "visible situation" (pp. 62, 81). And while Charlotte's pregnancy attracts other euphemisms, such as "present condition," it receives little actual discussion beyond Charlotte's brief description of "an innocent witness of my guilt" in a letter to her mother and a posthumous reference to a "poor girl . . . big with child" (pp. 99, 85, 129). This reticence cannot be attributed merely to a desire to spare the reader's feelings, since Rowson had no qualms about sensationalizing sexuality in other work. At the same time that the novel was taking off in America, Rowson was in Philadelphia writing stage comedies and patriotic drinking songs in which lust, albeit parodied, racially marked lust, played a central role. Her play *Slaves in Algiers,* first performed in 1794 in Philadelphia and Baltimore, makes much of the Algerian Dey's "huge scimitar" and includes a scene in which the cross-dressed heroine makes a "mighty pretty boy" in the eyes of her unknowing lover. The sailors drinking to their lasses in **"America, Commerce and Freedom,"** Rowson's popular song of the same year, show "eager haste" to join the young women running across the beach to meet them over the "full flowing bowl." Even in the novel at hand, desire is given its due as long as it occurs within the sanctified bonds of marriage.[4] Mrs. Temple, Charlotte's mother, is the very picture of marital satisfaction, in continual possession of "the delightful sensation that dilated her heart . . . and heightened the vermillion on her cheeks" (p. 34) in the presence of her husband. The woman who speaks to Charlotte when no one else will and ministers to her in the hours before her family arrives (in opposition to Charlotte's female undoer, the malicious and cunning boarding school teacher Mademoiselle La Rue, this angel of mercy's name is "Mrs. Beauchamp") is similarly blessed, as "the most delightful sensations pervaded her heart" at the "encomiums bestowed upon her by a beloved husband" (p. 79). Clearly, Rowson is capable of alluding to heteroerotic attraction—it is just not what she is after in Charlotte's case.[5]

Charlotte is "disappointed" in the only "pleasure" she does expect, that of the liberal provisions promised by Mademoiselle La Rue at the party to which she is lured early on, where she meets Montraville. Here, Charlotte experiences a rare instance of clear determination: she "heartily wished herself at home again in her own chamber" (p. 24). The narrator then acknowledges Charlotte's "gratitude" at Montraville's praises of her and, it must be admitted, a certain amount of satisfaction in his "agreeable person and martial appearance" (pp. 24, 25). But her subsequent "blushes" are from shame, not pleasure, and her strongest sensation almost immediately becomes that of not knowing what to do. After Montraville gives her a letter, she turns to her teacher, asking, "What shall I do with it?" (p. 28). With every moment of indecision, La Rue steps in to direct Charlotte's path—"Read it, to be sure" (p. 31)—and it is thus and not through any overwhelming desire of her own that Charlotte is impregnated. She meets her lover to tell him she will see him no more, is persuaded by fits and starts to approach his carriage, and ends up literally fainting into it, whereby we are to assume that the fatal deed is done.[6] The less Charlotte credits her own instincts, the more her behavior is described as a form of collapse, in which her future direction is determined by nothing more deliberate than her center of gravity.

To seduce is to "induce (a woman) to surrender her chastity."[7] And yes, the reader anticipates Charlotte's defloration from her "blushes" and "sighs" and witnesses its effects in her subsequent condition. The word "passion" is even used a couple of times. But the sex itself exists only through its after-effects, and Charlotte's behavior in this regard is never explained. Not only, that is, do we fail to witness her "surrender," being left to deduce it from subsequent irrefutable evidence, but we never learn just how she is "induced" to do so. In fact, Charlotte does not so much surrender her chastity—in the sense of giving up under duress something she values—as lose track of it altogether, along with every other aspect of her being. Thus, whereas to be seduced is to put "private and individual needs ahead of others" (by giving in to one's reciprocal lust), Charlotte loses her virginity only when she loses the ability to experience need altogether.[8] As the story develops, she becomes increasingly incapable of knowing what it is she feels, and she does what she feels she ought not, it turns out, not through an excessive respect for her desires, but rather through an increasing distrust of them. With "her ideas . . . confused," she is soon allowing herself to be "directed" not only by La Rue, but by her "betrayer" Montraville, rather than by her own self-appraisal, according to which she longs to remain loyal to her "forsaken parents" (p. 48). In sum, it is in relaxing her sensitivity to her own impulses, not in giving in to them, that Charlotte loses her virginity and then her life.

Unlike her sister protagonist Eliza Wharton, who begins the novel *The Coquette* in constant appreciation of the effect she has on men, Charlotte rarely refers to her own ability to obtain power, or pleasure, from erotically charged social interactions.[9] But she does spend a great deal of time in contemplation of another aspect of her being, namely, its terrifying absence of self-direction. Just before collapsing into her lover's arms, Charlotte asks of her "torn heart": "How shall I act?" without receiving an answer (p. 48). It may be possible to explain her habit of prostrating herself as a manifestation of something other than sexual desire, for while fainting and napping share with more licentious behavior the tendency to take place lying down, they also possess another quality in common that is more important to understanding Charlotte than lust. They both entail the loss of consciousness and with it any capacity for self-direction. Asleep or passed out, Charlotte has virtually no say over how her life unfolds. Awake, she fares almost no better. *Charlotte Temple,* despite appearances to the contrary and decades of critical assumption, is *not* really a novel of seduction, in the sense of being a document that provides sexual titillation under cover of pedagogic censure. Instead, far from depicting Charlotte's overweening desire, the novel portrays the fatal consequences of a woman's inability to want anything enough to motivate decisive action. Charlotte falls into compromising positions not so much because she yearns to as because she does not, in the words of her evil counsel La Rue, "know [her] own mind two minutes at a time," and what she loses when she "falls" (p. 44) is not, or at least not importantly, her virginity, but rather her independent agency.

Disorientation, therefore, rather than passion, leads Charlotte from her British boarding school to her lover's arms and from there to a transatlantic crossing, the outskirts of New York, pregnancy, childbirth among strangers, temporary madness, and death in the redeeming presence of her father. This reading helps make sense of the observation that since Anglo-American women, far from being ostracized for having had premarital intercourse, were marrying after conception in record numbers by the late eighteenth century, the novel's extraordinary popular appeal in the new United States cannot be explained by its veracity as historical transcript.[10] As recent studies make clear, postrevolutionary Philadelphia, where the novel's first two American editions were published in 1794 shortly after the author's arrival from England the previous year, had a "sexual climate . . . remarkable for its lack of restraint. Casual sex, unmarried relationships, and adulterous affairs were commonplace," and although such activity highlighted the predicament of extramarital pregnancy for young women, it also featured a frank acknowledgment in popular print media of the sexuality of women outside the elite. Her contemporary urban readers may have found Charlotte's struggle to maintain her chastity most important not as a reflection on her ability to regulate sexual desire but rather class status. For while women outside the elite were often depicted as explicitly and even joyfully carnal, those who wished to claim the status of a lady needed to subdue lustful urges in order to lay claim to the virtue that was theirs to safeguard in the new republic. Attitudes toward sexuality were thus key indicators of social standing. As the daughter of a rural commoner and a father who had married beneath him, Charlotte bore a class status that was as indeterminate as that of many of her readers, and her control over her virginity would determine, for a fascinated young American urban female reader in a similarly volatile class hierarchy, whether the heroine descended into Philadelphia's "naturally lustful and licentious" lower class or qualified as an "exemplar[] of moral integrity." Furthermore, that she managed to reclaim her virtue, in the guise of her father's forgiveness, even after being seduced, suggested a way out for those who found the requirements of female gentility trying, while the high cost of reclamation (namely, imminent death) reminded them of the risks involved.[11]

The pressure to "assume responsibility for sexual propriety" in a culture dedicated to sexual transgression provides but one example of the myriad difficulties facing a young woman of the early national period hoping to "possess her soul in serenity," to borrow Judith Sargent Murray's polemic of a decade earlier on "Desultory Thoughts."[12] For even as certain valorized traits came to be associated with post-revolutionary womanhood, ranging from a duty-bound notion of rights to a public, but no longer politically useful, conception of virtue, women's behavioral options were increasingly limited. Female rights, while not ignored, were conceived of according to Scottish common sense notions of societal obligation, while men alone, following the alternate trajectory of Lockean natural rights philosophy, possessed liberty, the ability "to choose one's destiny." At the same time, virtue in the previously male-oriented sense of active self-denial for the good of the polis was feminized in early national period precisely because, as a holdover from classical republicanism, it no longer served a nascent liberal political sphere premised on competition.[13]

The savage irony of a notion of female rights developing after the Revolution only to foster an increased sense of duty to outmoded notions of sexual virtue is made even more severe when one compares it with the ideology of perpetual opportunity facing young men of the period. Jay Fliegelman has written about the late eighteenth-century Anglo-American "adaptation and secularization of the Puritan narrative of the fortunate fall" by which "God had 'allowed' Adam and Eve to fall to permit them eventually to return to an even more intimate relationship with their Father than that they

had originally lost." This dawning cultural emphasis on man's capacity to learn, and hence to benefit, from his mistakes is nowhere more evident than in the ultimate report of a prodigal son returned, Benjamin Franklin's Autobiography. By substituting the term "errata" for sin, Franklin turns moral trespasses into printer's errors that can, in the words of the epitaph Franklin wrote for himself, be "Corrected and amended." As Fliegelman suggests, the Autobiography exemplifies the belief that a prodigal son who has perfected himself is more valuable as a testament to self-improvement than would be one who had never failed.[14]

Franklin hardly mentions women in the Autobiography, and elsewhere he uses them mostly to illustrate lessons for men. This is because pregnancy gives the lie to Franklin's philosophy. Illicit sexual activity may, for a man, be simply another printer's mistake. A man who impregnates a woman bears no tangible mark of the experience, except possibly venereal disease (no slight possibility in postwar Philadelphia). But an impregnated woman bears a mark that can only be erased at great physical and emotional cost, either through abortion or miscarriage. Pregnancy is a uniquely tangible sign of past activity, and it cannot be "corrected" without leaving record of itself. Unsanctioned pregnancy thus threatened the optimism of a newly developing moral and cultural system that emphasized man's capacity for self-determination. Prodigal daughters such as Charlotte were not offered the welcome their brothers received because it was impossible to reconcile their condition with the ideology of self-correctability that was reinforced by welcoming home a prodigal son. As exemplars of national virtue, women, like men, needed to learn, and learning required experimentation, but women's experiments were uniquely terrifying, since they did not possess the corollary privilege of having their mistakes expunged from the record. In such a climate, the secret wish to abdicate all decision-making must have had its appeal, even though, as Charlotte's story shows, it provided no real escape.[15]

The terrible consequences attendant on Charlotte's tendency to fall rather than step into events—her tragic indecisiveness, which made her a complete product of her surroundings, prey to nothing but circumstance—appealed to a female populace with increasingly limited capacity to experience themselves as independent, coherent beings in a post-revolutionary culture that made them the centerpiece of national identity even as it circumscribed their roles ever more closely. In her failure to become an agent, as opposed to an instrument of her destiny, Charlotte thematized, for the young American women who made her novel a household name, their difficulty in making contemporary theories of self-enfranchisement function in accord with equally powerful ideologies of womanhood that were an at best unwieldy fit with the mechanisms of agency in the new republic. Essentially, then, *Charlotte Temple* asks its American readers how women are to derive an integrated model of the self from the tortured cultural lexicon provided them.

In Charlotte, Rowson shows a woman who seems to fail at this task, only to commit, at the last minute of her life, a single decisive act: the handing over of her infant daughter to her father. This highly charged gesture suggests two contrary impulses. On the one hand, Charlotte literally makes her daughter the substance of her first autonomous act, investing her with a symbolic decisiveness unknown to her mother before this moment. On the other, that act is accompanied by a request for "protection" from the family patriarch, as if her daughter were to pick up right where Charlotte left off, leaving her fate to others to determine. "'Protect her,' said she, 'and bless your dying . . . .'" (p. 127). With this unfinished sentence, the reader is left hanging on the sounds of a wordless infant girl to find out how Charlotte would last have named herself. Will her daughter embody Charlotte's final courage and decisiveness or the meandering not-knowingness that led to her conception? Not until thirty-four years later would readers find out, in a posthumously published and similarly eponymous sequel, *Lucy Temple.* By that point, the young female readers asking this question of the early editions of *Charlotte Temple* would already have had to answer it for themselves, making the latter novel an exercise in nostalgia, whereas the original played a crucial role in the self-formation of a culture.

Whatever her legacy, Charlotte's final "ability to act" does suggest some "new knowledge": as La Rue would say, Charlotte does at last know her own mind, and as a result, she experiences agency, the "fortitude to put it in execution" (p. 47).[16] Of what exactly is the awareness that finally lets Charlotte take action composed? What kind of agency was available to a woman who had previously only seen herself as others saw her, or saw for her? And through what catalytic event could she come to experience it? Immediately before awaking to find her father at her side, Charlotte descends into a "phrenzy" that owes much to the evangelical tradition whose prioritization of affect as a means to understanding makes it an important precursor to American sentimentalism. Charlotte is no evangelical. Like Ellen in *The Wide, Wide World,* she loves her mother more than God, and her isolation is resolutely social, as opposed to spiritual, in nature. But she does proceed through something like conversion: the anxiety and alienation of a self distanced from its wished-for object drives her to a state Charles Chauncy would have been glad to label "enthusiasm," and her final return to her senses has all the earmarks of a work of grace, in that it seems impossible to explain without recourse to an intervening agent. Given the well-established historical links between evangelical and sentimentalist discourse and the

almost uncanny way Charlotte's experience echoes accounts by female converts such as Sarah Pierpont, it seems useful to draw on one of the finest recent works on female conversion to come to an understanding of Charlotte's transformation. According to Susan Juster, published female evangelical conversion narratives from the late eighteenth-century United States reflected women's tendency to apprehend the world in terms of personal attachments, as opposed to men's relationship to an abstract order. For women, the challenge of conversion was to "disengage themselves from overdependence on friends and family" enough to experience "individuation." Passing through the isolation of spiritual struggle, female converts emerged newly "empowered by recovering their sense of self through the assertion of independence from others." Certainly, Charlotte's progression from misplaced reliance on others, to being left "a prey to her own melancholy reflexions," to "the total deprivation of her reason," and to her final awakening makes sense in this frame, with the exception that most of the people Charlotte deemed friends turned out not to have her best interests at heart (pp. 103, 120). Moreover, in that the novel ends with Charlotte dictating terms to her father, however gently, it supports Juster's idea that evangelical women undergoing religious conversion obtained autonomy by passing through a period of alienation from those through whom they had formerly experienced life's significance. Torn from her country, her family, her schoolmates, her lover, and penultimately, any sense of her own reality (after giving birth, Charlotte "was totally insensible of everything. . . . She was not conscious of being a mother, nor took the least notice of her child except to ask whose it was, and why it was not carried to its parents"), Charlotte returns to familiar faces able for the first time to set the terms, albeit not of her own, but of her daughter's, future course (p. 122).[17]

But does the clarity of purpose this act portends, while obtained through isolation, necessarily derive from the forced rending of attachments that has characterized Charlotte's entire course in the novel? It would seem more likely that the new ability she demonstrates when she hands her daughter to her father is how to acknowledge her need for others. Before this decisive act, Charlotte turned away from love both licit and illicit, neither awaiting her grandfather's imminent arrival at her school nor actively defying her family in a spirited if socially disastrous adventure with her beseeching lieutenant. Far from experiencing herself as more distinct from others than she did before her period of "incoherence," Charlotte's final act may suggest that she has made her previously tenuous grasps at connection with them a fundamental aspect of her autonomy. In that case, she, like Franklin, has learned from her mistakes.[18]

To suggest that Charlotte would have been better off had she acted on any form of preference, even sexual desire, than she was as a mere reflection of others' wishes for her is to see sexuality not only as a figure for agency but also as a potentially fundamental aspect of it.[19] For Charlotte to move from being unable to act on any predilection, including that of a barely registered sexual yearning, to determining her daughter's guardian in the last moments of her life, suggests that the desire she once neither heeded nor subjugated underwent some form of transmutation in order to serve as the basis for a sophisticated moral agency. There is a tension in the novel, then, between understanding female desire as an impediment to autonomy (such that the seduction novel must warn against it in a fledgling democracy) and seeing desire as in some sense primary to autonomy (as I am suggesting Charlotte's final gesture should be read). The intensity of this struggle to understand the relationship between desire and independent action in the late eighteenth century can be seen in the first definition of "will" to appear in the fourth edition of Dr. Johnson's *Dictionary,* published in 1773, which does not appear in the first, published in 1755. Whereas previously Johnson was content to start off by calling will "choice," in the later edition he began by calling will "That power by which we desire, and purpose; velleity." "Velleity," in turn, is precisely what is left of will in the absence of subsequent action or choice; it is the "quality of merely willing, wishing, or desiring, without any effort or advance towards action or realization." Johnson's insertion of a definition of will that isolated desire from its execution demonstrates that he considered desire to be both will's fundamental impulse and insufficient to its exercise.[20]

This paradox, in turn, points to the difficulty of conceptualizing the self in a liberal polity. Locke defined the experience of selfhood as "perceiving that he does perceive," admitting the potentially infinitely regressive nature of self-awareness, given that each act of self-perception entails a new perceiving entity itself in need of witness for self-understanding to be complete.[21] But because women were appointed guardians of features that threatened an ideology of male self-determination, post-revolutionary America had little use for what has been called "the constitutive disjunction of the self" into the perceiving *"I"* and the *"I"* as another object, perceived. Instead, self-possession was all: as the latter-day French *philosophe* Destutt de Tracy would exult, in a translation supervised by Thomas Jefferson for use in the United States, "individuality" is our "inalienable property."[22] Learning from one's mistakes was well and good, but the important thing was that one rest assured in the enabling fiction that one did in fact own oneself—that one existed in a fixed and commanding position over one's myriad psychic impulses. Self-formation thus entailed subjugating those aspects of mental experience that did not mesh with a forward-looking, self-promoting, property-obtaining citizenry. Authors such as Rowson and readers such as those who made *Char-*

lotte Temple a hit in its first years of American publication were toying with a notion of the self that found little favor in other cultural channels, one in which human errata, rather than needing to be corrected to fit a pre-existing order, could serve as constituent components of a changed order, much as Charlotte's daughter becomes part of her father's world after Charlotte herself is gone. In this environment, female error suggests not a fault on the part of the agent so much as an insufficiency in her surroundings, and female desire does not portend disaster, but rather independent action, a quality in short supply as young women learned elsewhere how not to want.

If one understands Charlotte's failure to direct her own life in its relation to the behavior of other characters in the novel, one sees these divergent modes of negotiating between impulse and action embodied in distinct characters. Lest there be any doubt that this is a book about the making of choices, its first words have to do with whether a character prefers to walk or drive. The central terms in the novel's discussion of agency are two, and they are used again and again in the text: "inclination" and "resolution." Both are considered modes of willing during the period (Johnson's definitions of the verb "to will" include "to be inclined or resolved to have"). Where they differ, not surprisingly, is in their relationship to desire. To be inclined is to experience "incipient desire" or "disposition of mind," while to be resolved is to possess "fixed determination." The latter category, though it does not deny desire outright, is differentiated from the former by a more explicit focus on subsequent action and, correspondingly, by an emphasis on the regulation of potentially inconsistent impulses to make such action possible as well as beneficial. In short, resolution directs will from "velleity" to "choice," from the passions to the understanding, and from proclivity to explicit action, with the latter's implications for self-mastery. The struggle between the two terms in the novel extends from the protagonist's coming to terms with her own propensities, to the interactions between characters, to the narrative mode itself, in which appeals to the reader's sympathetic identification based on benevolent inclination alternate with calls to disciplined detachment based on steely resolve.

Characters in *Charlotte Temple* tend to one of three ways of resolving these two terms, only one of which brings satisfaction. The most successful individuals, who end the book alive, well, and free from lasting inner torment, tend to experience simultaneity of inclination and resolve. Charlotte's father, Mr. Temple, wants Lucy Eldridge for his wife. He discerns that despite his father's objections and the resultant decline he can expect in his annual income, Lucy will bring him earthly felicity otherwise unattainable, and he pursues her without hesitation. Similarly, much later on, Lucy, now Mrs. Temple, wants to give her daughter a birthday party, and she knows to go to some lengths to persuade her reluctant husband to allow her to do so, because the party will make everybody happy (if only everyone, including her daughter, would attend). These are cases where inclinations based on affect (loving the woman, yearning to please the daughter) and resolutions directing understanding to satisfy inclination (defying the father, persuading the husband) go hand-in-hand. There is no real tension, no danger, no potential negative consequence, to giving into impulse. Moreover, on the rare occasions where resolution and inclination are in conflict, these individuals are also capable of self-regulation; when, for instance, Mrs. Temple learns of her daughter's elopement, she insists that "I will wear a smile on my face, though the thorn rankles in my heart," in order to make her husband feel better, and she proceeds immediately to "the execution of so laudable a resolution" (p. 59). Having somehow managed to cultivate a passion for duty, these characters embody what one critic considers the novel's mission to "instruct young ladies . . . in being content with one's lot in life," and while they lead peaceful lives, they make for extremely boring novels.[23]

Never fear, however, because these exemplars are inevitably paired with less benevolent twins who, while similarly inclined to follow their impulses, arrive at no such happy results for themselves or others. Their deleterious effects derive from two sources, rashness or sheer sadism—or both. Like Mr. and Mrs. Temple, Lieutenant Montraville knows what he wants and acts on his wishes, but in his case, the effects on those he meets are disastrous. Thus "generous in his disposition, liberal in his opinions, and good-natured almost to a fault," Montraville is nevertheless "eager and impetuous in the pursuit of a favorite object," and "he staid not to reflect on the consequence which might follow the attainment of his wishes" (p. 36), even though he realizes that Charlotte is too poor to marry. Montraville learns too late the difference between "momentary passion" (p. 88) and lasting love; for him, inclination is all.

Finally, there are persons, such as La Rue and Belcour, who glory in the suffering of others. Ironically, these are beings capable of great resolve, happy to put off the satisfaction of a ruinous impulse as long as the ruination will be all the more dramatic. Thus La Rue can feign indifference as to whether Charlotte accompanies her on her nocturnal visit to the local regiment, and Belcour can (literally) lie in wait for Montraville's arrival, rather than accost Charlotte on the spot. Both know how to manipulate momentary impulse in the service of a greater end. It is significant, however, that Charlotte is finally undone not by these caricatures but by Montraville himself, who lifts her into the carriage at Chichester and leaves her alone among skeptical strangers outside New York. For pure evil, like pure good, is easy to recognize. It is those with good intentions but no capacity to regulate their outcome—those in whom inclination and resolve are at odds—that the novel trains its readers to detect, both outside and within themselves.

The problem is that even when, like Charlotte, the reader knows not to act on every impulse, disaster cannot necessarily be averted. Smart enough to doubt her inclinations but not strong enough either to defy or to indulge them, Charlotte ends up unable to form a resolution, and it is her fundamental inaction, rather than any particular inclination, that proves her undoing. Ironically, her strongest wish, had she merely obeyed it, was to rejoin her parents. Had she trusted to impulse, as Mr. and Mrs. Temple did before her, she would have been fine. Thus the novel presents contrary, and gendered, models of deportment. For young women such as Charlotte, it seems to suggest a surer grasp on benevolent impulse, a quickness to action that can prevent the reader from falling into vacuous indecision. For young men such as Montraville the call to action is tempered by another to reflection, because impulse itself in such cases seems less certainly altruistic. In a book addressed to "the young and thoughtless of the fair sex," Charlotte's indecisiveness takes precedence over Rowson's less detailed representation of the male subject.

Charlotte has several methods for forestalling choice. Unable to figure out her own preference, she tends to act according to whether she thinks her actions will make others think well of her. For this reason, La Rue, ever alert to the best ways to manipulate others to her own ends, can mock Charlotte's reticence to meet Montraville by pointing out that the whole school will laugh at her: "You will bear the odium of having formed the resolution of eloping, and every girl of spirit will laugh at your want of fortitude to put it in execution" (p. 47). Second, Charlotte possesses a fatal optimism regarding the possibility of remediable action: a faith most tragically misplaced in her misunderstanding of the nature of chastity, but nicely anticipated in her observation early in the novel that, because the wafer on a letter from Montraville is not dry (she has unknowingly wet it with her tears), she might "read it, and return it afterwards" (p. 30). In the context of her attempt to decide whether to see the lieutenant again, Charlotte's opening a letter from him with the idea that she can make the letter look as though it hasn't been read (since the wafer is wet, she won't have to break a seal) serves as a metonym for the event to which the letter invites her—the loss of her virginity—whose consequence, she also fails to anticipate, is ineradicable. Both these habits of mind get Charlotte into trouble. But by far her greatest failing is her over-great faith in her own "stability," as demonstrated in such passages as "Charlotte had, when she went out to meet Montraville, flattered herself that her resolution was not to be shaken, and that . . . she would never repeat the indiscretion" (p. 37) and "in her heart every meeting was resolved to be the last" (p. 42). At one point, she even exults: "How shall I rejoice . . . in this triumph of reason over inclination" (p. 47). Charlotte is good at resolving, or at least planning to resolve, but "resolutions will not execute themselves," and she is incapable of granting any single impetus to action enough sway to direct her once and for all.[24] Charlotte is not impetuous; she does not give in to inclinations once she senses that they might hurt her, but having come to the point of knowing not to do something, she is nonetheless incapable of doing something else, and this inability to come to any decision haunts her. At moments of great dramatic import, she is inflicted by a desire to be doing the opposite of whatever she is engaged in, such that "even in the moment when . . . I fled from you . . . even then I loved you most" (pp. 83-84), as she explains to her mother.

In a nation where individuality was seen as the ability to take action consistent with one's intent, for Charlotte not to know what she wants—or not to be able to act accordingly when she does know—is for her not to know who she is. And the novel brings the reader to a similar relationship to its words that Charlotte experiences in relation to her own fluctuating psychic processes. To the degree that incompatibilities between "inclination" and "resolve" operate in the book as a mode as well as a topic, with appeals to appetite and stern correctives occurring simultaneously on the page, the reader becomes an unwilling participant in the processes he or she might hope to have contemplated from a distance. Characteristic of the late eighteenth-century American sentimental novel as represented by its best-selling volume is not only its much-denigrated appeal to convention, its seemingly manipulative and paradoxically quite cold machinery for evoking emotion in its spectators both inside and outside the text, but another, more genuinely performative kind of energy.[25]

Many critics deny such a possibility in their assumption that Rowson's narrative persona is seamlessly controlling.[26] Such readings mistake a need for control with its achievement. That is, the very ostentation of the Rowsonian narrator's comforting asides might just as easily suggest an anticipation of loss such as that proposed by Julia Stern in her analysis of "the absent mother who occupies and directs the narrative frame."[27] This alternative is supported by an oscillation in the novel's narrative mode, which shifts between the self-monitoring impulse characteristic of the sentimental novel's didactic strand and a self-losing, almost ecstatic impulse of submission to forces outside the self.

The narrative is rent by opposing impulses and seems unable to decide on its own course of action. Instead, it swerves without seeming rhyme or reason between appeals to disciplined detachment and appeals to sympathetic identification. At the very moment, for instance, that Belcour is abandoning the dying Charlotte—a moment readers might be expected to empathize with her sad state—the description takes place at further and further removes:

> His visits became less frequent; he forgot the solemn charge given him by Montraville; he even forgot the money entrusted to his care; and, *the burning blush of indignation and shame tinges my cheek while I write it,* this disgrace to humanity and manhood at length forgot even the injured Charlotte; and, attracted by the blooming health of a farmer's daughter . . . left the unhappy girl to sink unnoticed to the grave.
>
> [pp. 106-07, emphasis added]

Why does the narrator feel compelled to interject her own cheek at this moment? By doing so, she inserts another link in the perceptual chain separating victim from reader, as we now must witness the narrator watching Belcour watching (or failing to watch) Charlotte. She thereby exacerbates the scene's already voyeuristic aspect, creating a spectacle now "dependent not only on the implied spectatorship of the reader/viewer," nor even "on the express spectatorship of internal witnesses" alone, but on a third, explicitly embodied narrative presence.[28] Her comment thus distances us even further from the events at hand and reinforces a sense of the remoteness of the events taking place that is at odds with any sympathetic identification with Charlotte. At the same time, the narrator provides the reader with an extremely uncharacteristic reference to her own body. As such, it mimics Charlotte's blush of shame and encourages the reader to reflect on what she, too, might have to "blush" for, thereby creating a sense of shared vulnerability with the protagonist. The Rowsonian narrator is thus at her most confessional at the very moment she puts us at the furthest remove from the details of her story. She appeals to our sympathetic and our censorious tendencies simultaneously and leaves us, like Charlotte, like the narrator herself, unable to do anything effective. Instead, we dwell in the kind of anxious self-doubt that Charlotte found so painful.[29]

A similar entanglement occurs in the last paragraph of the novel, when the dead Charlotte's father takes in the woman who could be said to have murdered his daughter:

> Greatly as Mr. Temple had reason to detest Mrs. Crayton, he could not behold her in this distress without some emotions of pity. He gave her shelter that night beneath his hospitable roof, and the next day got her admission into an hospital; where having lingered a few weeks, she died, *a striking example, that vice, however prosperous in the beginning, in the end leads only to misery and shame.* FINIS.
>
> [p. 132, emphasis added]

Here the reader is treated to one last surrender to benevolent inclination ("he could not") over steely resolve ("had reason to"), only to be asked to relish it from a distance—to look not on Mr. Temple's kindness but on Mrs. Crayton's just desserts. The warmth of forgiveness is elicited, only to be trumped by the far more readily indulged satisfaction at the death of an enemy.

That American readers welcomed the opportunity to make Charlotte's struggle their own is indicated by the memorial they established for her in New York's Trinity Churchyard.[30] Susanna Rowson could have asked for no surer testament that her "novel" had been received, at least in the United States, according to the plan laid out for it in her preface, as a template for the "conduct" of its readers, as opposed to a guilty pleasure meant to be forgotten as soon as finished (p. 1). It may have been the first American novel to take on antebellum sentimentalism's signature task: making imaginary engagement (reading) result in specific subsequent action (such as ending slavery). (In the most famous articulation of this ethos, President Lincoln is said to have credited Harriet Beecher Stowe with writing the book—*Uncle Tom's Cabin*—that started the Civil War.) In this sense at least, Rowson helped initiate American sentimentalism's most astounding accomplishment: causing the aesthetic to be re-conceived in implicitly political terms.[31] Peering down at a presumably empty grave—or at least, we can assume, one that did not contain any fictional characters—also speaks to the ambivalence that lingers alongside Rowson's call to female action. Through its dissonant appeals to contrary readerly responses, the novel provides an instantiation, as well as an allegory, of the paradoxical nature of female subjectivity during a period in which women were expected to submit to codes limiting both pleasure and agency, and yet to conceive of their position as one they chose and from which they derived satisfaction.

Notes

1. Susanna Rowson, *Charlotte Temple and Lucy Temple,* ed. and intro. Ann Douglas (New York, 1991), 74, 48, 74, 91. References to this text are in parentheses in the body of the article.

2. William C. Spengemann, *The Adventurous Muse: The Poetics of American Fiction, 1789-1900* (New Haven, 1977), 88; Herbert Ross Brown, *The Sentimental Novel in America, 1789-1860* (Durham, N. C., 1940), 44; John Seelye, "Charles Brockden Brown and Early American Fiction," in Emory Elliott, gen. ed., *Columbia Literary History of the United States* (New York, 1988), 168-86, 170; Cathy N. Davidson, "The Life and Times of *Charlotte Temple*: The Biography of a Book," in Davidson, ed., *Reading in America: Literature and Social History* (Baltimore, 1989), 170; Joseph Fichtelberg, "Early American Prose Fiction and the Anxieties of Affluence," in Carla Mulford, ed., *Teaching the Literatures of Early America* (New York, 1999), 200-12, 206; Maureen L. Woodard,

"Female Captivity and the Deployment of Race in Three Early American Texts," *Papers on Language and Literature,* 32 (1996), 115-46, 127.

3. Many scholars have embraced the position problematized here, arguing that the novel is, whether sensational or didactic, really about Charlotte's "insufficiently disciplined inclination"—in other words, that it describes a woman undone by passion. Generally, critics who take this approach consider the novel mostly for its similarities to contemporaries such as *The Coquette* and *The Power of Sympathy,* as when Gareth Evans, "Rakes, Coquettes, and Republican Patriarchs: Class, Gender, and Nation in Early American Sentimental Fiction," *Canadian Review of American Studies,* 25 (Fall 1995), 51, 42, considers it one of several novels promoting "a form of 'self-governance' by which [the new model woman] checks both sexual desire and the desire for social eminence." Elizabeth Barnes, *States of Sympathy: Seduction and Democracy in the American Novel* (New York, 1997), 45, notes that the above novels all "foreground situations wherein the characters' own emotions or senses lead them astray" and presents two possible ways of understanding the significance of this digression. "Read along the lines of conventional education, these characters suffer the consequences of their own weaknesses," she argues; "read in the spirit of seductive subversion, they die from the strength of their passions."

Another body of scholarly work concerns itself more, like this article, with what Charlotte lacks than what she possesses and suggests that we stop reading the novel "as a didactic fable warning against the dangers of seduction"; Julia A. Stern, *The Plight of Feeling: Sympathy and Dissent in the Early American Novel* (Chicago, 1997), 41. For these critics, Charlotte lacks many things, including voice and "individuation," but most important for this argument, she lacks agency; Blythe Forcey, "Charlotte Temple and the End of Epistolarity," *American Literature,* 63 (1991), 225-41, esp. 237; Douglas, Introduction, *Charlotte Temple and Lucy Temple,* xxiii. It is the purpose of this article to explore how this lack functions in the novel in the way that "passion" does for the former readings: it serves as both the primary explanatory force behind Charlotte's behavior and as the single quality of her being against which the novel cautions its female readers. See also Mona Scheuermann, "The American Novel of Seduction: An Explanation of the Omission of the Sex Act in *The Scarlet Letter," The Nathaniel Hawthorne Journal 1978,* ed. C. E. Frazer Clark, Jr. (Detroit, 1978) 105-18; Eva Cherniavsky, "Charlotte Temple's Remains," in Christoph K. Lohmann, ed., *Discovering Difference: Contemporary*

Essays in American Culture (Bloomington, Ind., 1993) 35-47, esp. 40; and Kay Ferguson Ryals, "America, Romance, and the Fate of the Wandering Woman: The Case of *Charlotte Temple*," in *Women, America, and Movement: Narratives of Relocation,* ed. Susan L. Roberson (Columbia, Mo., 1998), 81-105, esp. 90.

4. Rowson, *Slaves in Algiers, or, A Struggle for Freedom; A Play, Interspersed with Songs, in Three Acts* (Philadelphia, 1794), in *Plays by Early American Women, 1775-1850,* ed. Amelia Howe Kritzer (Ann Arbor, 1995), 59, 79; Rowson, "America, Commerce, and Freedom," music by Mr. Reinagle (Philadelphia, 1794). On early American attitudes toward sexuality in marriage, see John D'Emilio and Estelle B. Freedman, *Intimate Matters: A History of Sexuality in America* (New York, 1988), esp. chap. 2; Ellen K. Rothman, *Hands and Hearts: A History of Courtship in America* (New York, 1984); and Richard Godbeer, *Sexual Revolution in Early America* (Baltimore, 2002). Analysis of *Slaves in Algiers* occurs in Susan Branson, *These Fiery Frenchified Dames: Women and Political Culture in Early National Philadelphia* (Philadelphia, 2001), and Kritzer, "Playing with Republican Motherhood: Self-Representation in Plays by Susanna Haswell Rowson and Judith Sargent Murray," *Early American Literature,* 31 (1996), 150-66.

5. Book-length studies of Rowson include Ellen B. Brandt, *Susanna Haswell Rowson, America's First Best-Selling Novelist* (Chicago, 1975); Patricia L. Parker, *Susanna Rowson* (Boston, 1986); and Dorothy Weil, *In Defense of Women: Susanna Rowson (1762-1824)* (University Park, Pa., 1976). In *Revolution and the Word: The Rise of the Novel in America* (New York, 1986), Davidson depicts the social climate of early American female authorship and readership.

6. Scheuermann, "American Novel of Seduction," 108.

7. *The Compact Edition of the Oxford English Dictionary* (Oxford, 1971).

8. Michael T. Gilmore, "The Literature of the Revolutionary and Early National Periods," in *The Cambridge History of American Literature,* gen. ed. Sacvan Bercovitch, vol. 1: *1590-1820* (Cambridge, 1994), 539-694, 587.

9. *Charlotte Temple* may be unique among early American sentimental novels in its avoidance of sexually charged language. William Hill Brown's *The Power of Sympathy* (1798) capitalizes the word "seduction" in the dedication to its 1789 edition. Another popular novel from the 1790s,

Hannah Foster's *The Coquette* (1797), also invokes Elizabeth Whitman's seduction, abandonment, and death, as first reported in the *Salem Mercury* in 1788. The *Coquette* goes even further than the *Power of Sympathy* in making passion its primary theme. "Sensation" appears twice in its first sentence and "pleasure" twice in its second, giving the astute reader notice that Eliza's destruction will be accompanied by plenty of sensual indulgence along the way. Eliza thrills in her "conquests" and admits to a pleasant "perturbation" at being so much "the taste of the other sex"; "letter 5" in Hannah W. Foster, *The Coquette* (New York, 1986), 8, 12; Brown, *The Power of Sympathy,* ed. William S. Kable (Columbus, Ohio, 1969).

10. Larzer Ziff, *Writing in the New Nation: Prose, Print, and Politics in the Early United States* (New Haven, 1991), 56. D'Emilio and Freedman, *Intimate Matters,* 43, provide the historical ground for Ziff's observation, noting that premarital pregnancy rates rose sharply in late 18th-century America, to as many as ⅓ of all brides in parts of New England. Summarizing the work of Joan Hoff Wilson, they claim this rise indicates "a breakdown of the traditional familial and community regulation of sexuality," as witnessed in "'a revolt of the young' against familial controls over marriage and sexuality." A rise in premarital pregnancy rates suggests increasing leniency toward the issue of women having sex out of wedlock, since increasingly, they were able to gain the social sanction accorded by marriage even in the face of irrefutable evidence of having had exactly that. *Charlotte Temple* thus dramatizes the fate that more and more of its readers seemed to be avoiding: a young woman is impregnated by a man who then abandons her. See also Rothman, *Hands and Hearts,* 46.

On the history of *Charlotte Temple*'s American reception, see Davidson, "Life and Times of *Charlotte Temple*," 157-59. Following a moderate reception in England on its publication in 1791, *Charlotte Temple* went through more than 200 American editions after Mathew Carey first published it there in 1794, to become "one of his, and America's, all-time bestsellers."

11. Godbeer, *Sexual Revolution in Early America,* 300, 306-07. On erotica in early America, see Peter Wagner, *Eros Revived: Erotica of the Enlightenment in England and America* (London, 1988). For an excellent summation of scholarly attitudes toward the history of sexuality in the 18th century, see Lynn Hunt and Margaret Jacob, "The Affective Revolution in 1790s Britain," *Eighteenth-Century Studies,* 34 (2001), esp. 496-97. Michel Foucault, *The History of Sexuality,* vol. 1: *An In-*

troduction, trans. Robert Hurley (New York, 1978), 15, 17, recounts "the repressive hypothesis" by which "an age of repression" intensified through the 19th century, only to turn the story on its head by performing a sort of word count. The more people condemned sex, he points out, the more certainly they inscribed it on their world in "a veritable discursive explosion"—the more certainly, that is, they produced it. Here, I reverse Foucault's gesture by noting how an apparent thematic presence (Charlotte's desire) is in fact more noteworthy as a discursive absence. On the relationship between the pursuit of gentility and the reading of sentimental novels, see Richard Bushman, *The Refinement of America: Persons, Houses, Cities* (New York, 1992), chap. 9.

12. Godbeer, *Sexual Revolution in Early America,* 306; Murray, "Desultory Thoughts . . ." (1784), in Sharon M. Harris, ed., *Selected Writings of Judith Sargent Murray* (New York, 1995), 47.

13. Rosemary Zagarri, "The Rights of Man and Woman in Post-Revolutionary America," *William and Mary Quarterly,* 3d Ser., 55 (1998), 203-30, 219; Ruth H. Bloch, "The Gendered Meanings of Virtue in Revolutionary America," *Signs,* 13 (1987), 37-58. For recent appraisals of the tensions between republican ideologies of "property and liberty" and liberal self-interest in the early U. S., see Philip Gould, *Covenant and Republic: Historical Romance and the Politics of Puritanism* (Cambridge, 1996), esp. 25-26, and Nancy Isenberg, *Sex and Citizenship in Antebellum America* (Chapel Hill, 1998). Both authors delineate how early American republican ideology depended on self-denial. Gould also distinguishes this republican worldview from a potentially encroaching liberalism in which self-mastery—the limitation, as opposed to renunciation, of selfish pleasures—loomed large. Summarizing two decades of scholarship, he asks: "Was the nation, in other words, founded on an anticapitalist ideology or on a materialist one?"

14. Fliegelman, *Prodigals and Pilgrims: The American Revolution against Patriarchal Authority* (Cambridge, 1982), 13, 83 (quotation), III; Franklin, *Autobiography and Other Writings,* ed. Ormond Seavey (Oxford, 1993), esp. 227-28.

15. For an example of Franklin's textual use of women to illustrate lessons for men, see, for instance, his "Advice to a Friend on Choosing a Mistress," 1745, http://www.bibliomania.com/2/9/77/124/21473/1/frameset.html. Harris, "Hannah Webster Foster's *The Coquette*: Critiquing Franklin's America," in *Redefining the Political Novel: American Women Writers, 1797-1901* (Knoxville, 1995), 1-22, 18, argues that another early American novel, Foster's *Coquette,* suggests "that the rectification of errata could become possible for young women."

16. Susan Juster, "'In a Different Voice': Male and Female Narratives of Religious Conversion in Post-Revolutionary America," *American Quarterly,* 41 (1989), 53. See also Juster, *Disorderly Women: Sexual Politics and Evangelicalism in Revolutionary New England* (Ithaca, 1994). In viewing Charlotte's descent into madness through the lens of evangelical conversion, this essay expands on a field of inquiry linking 19th-century American sentimentalism to 18th-century evangelicalism initiated by Jane Tompkins, David S. Reynolds, Amanda Porterfield, Sandra Gustafson, and others. Tompkins, *Sensational Designs: The Cultural Work of American Fiction, 1790-1860* (New York, 1985), 149, claims that "sentimental fiction was perhaps the most influential expression of the beliefs that animated the revival movement." Reynolds, *Faith in Fiction: The Emergence of Religious Literature in America* (Cambridge, Mass., 1981); Porterfield, *Feminine Spirituality in America: From Sarah Edwards to Martha Graham* (Philadelphia, 1980); Gustafson, "Jonathan Edwards and the Reconstruction of 'Feminine' Speech," *American Literary History,* 6 (1994), 185-212.

17. Juster, "In a Different Voice," 51, 53. Susan Warner, *The Wide, Wide World* (New York, 1987; orig. pub. 1851); Chauncy, "Enthusiasm Described and Caution'd Against," in Alan Heimert and Perry Miller, eds., *The Great Awakening: Documents Illustrating the Crisis and Its Consequences* (Indianapolis, 1967), 228-56. Sarah Pierpont Edwards's conversion narrative in Sereno Edwards Dwight, ed., *The Works of President Edwards: With a Memoir of His Life . . . ,* 10 vols. (New York, 1830), 1:171-86. For a more punitive interpretation of Charlotte's delirium, according to which Rowson "reserves fits of insanity to identify and punish those guilty of sexual misbehavior," see Karen A. Weyler, "'The Fruit of Unlawful Embraces': Sexual Transgression and Madness in Early American Sentimental Fiction," in Merril D. Smith, ed., *Sex and Sexuality in Early America* (New York, 1998), 299.

18. In a study of 19th-century sentimental literature, Marianne Noble, *The Masochistic Pleasures of Sentimental Literature* (Princeton, 2000), 7, 9, argues that desire "is itself constitutive of subjectivity" and suggests moreover that even its seemingly self-destructive masochistic elaborations "can represent forms of agency as well as pleasure." Fliegelman, *Declaring Independence: Jefferson, Natural Language, and the Culture of Per-*

formance (Stanford, 1993), 36, notes the early republic's "antirationalist preoccupation with ruling passions, desire, and an involuntary moral sense, all of which are more effectively excited by powerful delivery than by rational argumentation."

19. Samuel Johnson, *A Dictionary of the English Language on CD-ROM,* ed. Anne McDermott (Cambridge, 1996); *Compact OED.* Johnson granted the novel a role in divesting will of its power, worrying that the desire inspired by fiction could "produce effects almost without the intervention of the will." As Patricia Meyer Spacks, *Desire and Truth: Functions of Plot in Eighteenth-Century English Novels* (Chicago, 1990), 22, glosses the passage: "Johnson's sentence rings with anxiety about the ways that forces other than the will may dominate the mind and the imagination. The violence with which fictional examples operate on the memory corresponds to desire's violence."

20. Locke, *An Essay Concerning Human Understanding* (1690), ed. A. D. Woozley (Glasgow, 1980), 211.

21. Paul Downes, "The Secrets of the Republic: From Annapolis to Norwalk," paper given at the first annual conference of the Institute for Early American History and Culture, University of Michigan, Ann Arbor, June 2-4, 1995, cited with permission of author.

22. [Comte Antoine Louis Claude] Destutt de Tracy, "A Treatise on Political Economy" (1817), in *Psychology of Political Science,* ed. John M. Dorsey, trans. Jefferson (Detroit, 1973), 41-42, 47.

23. Patricia Parker, cited in Devon White, "Contemporary Criticism of Five Early American Sentimental Novels, 1970-1994: An Annotated Bibliography," *Bulletin of Bibliography,* 52 (1995), 294.

24. Johnson, *The Rambler,* 1752, cited in *Compact OED.*

25. In reference to British novels of the same period, J. S. Tompkins, *The Popular Novel in England, 1770-1800* (Lincoln, Neb., 1961 [1932]), 107, describes the joining of mechanism to extravagance beautifully in the phrase "conventionalized extravagance of bearing."

26. Forcey, "Charlotte Temple and the End of Epistolarity," 231, 236, writes, "Rowson's narrative incursions provide an authoritative unifying voice which gives structure and guidance to the reader." She characterizes the novel's "narrative voice" as "unselfish, affectionate, gently admonitory, helpful, teacherly, and attentive," functioning primarily to "inform, improve and enrich the lives of [Rowson's] readers." Her premise, that *Charlotte Temple* represents "the end of epistolarity" because readers were coming to need more "intervention" than allowed for by epistolary discourse, is rendered dubious by the fact that Rowson's next novel, *Trials of the Human Heart* (Philadelphia, 1795), is in an epistolary format, although the latter work's minimal commercial and critical success might indicate that readers did need something Rowson was not there providing. See also Donna R. Bontatibus, *The Seduction Novel of the Early Nation: A Call for Socio-Political Reform* (East Lansing, Mich., 1999), esp. chap. 1 and conclusion, for emphasis on Rowson's pedagogical skills and reformative intent.

27. Stern, *Plight of Feeling,* 35.

28. Karen Halttunen, "Humanitarianism and the Pornography of Pain in Anglo-American Culture," *American Historical Review,* 100 (1995), 317.

29. What Spacks, *Desire and Truth,* 121, calls the "incongruity between the benevolent human being's utter separation from the object of benevolence" and "the impulse toward merging implicit in the idea of 'sympathy'" has been central to discussions of 18th- and 19th-century sentimentalism for some time now. Halttunen, "Humanitarianism and the Pornography of Pain in Anglo-American Culture," 308, notes that "the convention of spectatorial sympathy . . . was deeply ambivalent in its treatment of the pain and suffering of other sentient beings. Sentimental sympathy was said to be . . . an emotional experience that liberally mingled pleasure with vicarious pain." The most incisive commentary on spectacle and sentimentalism in the American novel remains James Baldwin's attack on Harriet Beecher Stowe's *Uncle Tom's Cabin* and Richard Wright's *Native Son:* "Sentimentality, the ostentatious parading of excessive and spurious emotion, is the mark of dishonesty, the inability to feel; the wet eyes of the sentimentalist betray his aversion to experience, his fear of life, his arid heart; and it is always, therefore, the signal of secret and violent inhumanity, the mask of cruelty"; Baldwin, "Everybody's Protest Novel," *Notes of a Native Son* (Boston, 1984 [1955]), 14.

Scheuermann, "American Novel of Seduction," 106, distinguishes early American fiction from its British counterpart according to a transition from "social games" to "psychological effects." Another way of phrasing this distinction might be as an internalization of the phenomenon of sentimental spectacle. Thus questions about what legitimizes the inherently voyeuristic witness of suffering are in an American context transformed into questions involving the inherently spectacular nature of identity as suggested by Locke's above-cited definition of the self as "perceiving that he does perceive" or Adam Smith's definition of sympathy as "conceiving what we ourselves should feel." How is one to reconcile the myriad entities that make up a single perceptual being in order to derive an agent capable of choice and action? What means do sentimental texts use to stabilize identity enough to allow their protagonists to develop in meaningful ways? Locke, "Essay Concerning Human Understanding," 211; Smith, *The Theory of Moral Sentiments* (1759), ed. Knud Haakonssen (Amherst, N. Y., 2000), 11. For an indication of how sympathy operated similarly in the late 18th-century American political realm to the way it did in the aesthetic, see Jack N. Rakove, *Original Meanings: Politics and Ideas in the Making of the Constitution* (New York, 1997), esp. chap. 8.

30. Barnes, *States of Sympathy,* 61, argues that this event attests to the novel's emblematicity as a sentimental text: "At its most effective, sentimental representation obscures the distinctions between fiction and reality, heroine and reader, so that readers feel personally invested in the story's events." Charlotte's grave is also discussed in Davidson, "Life and Times of *Charlotte Temple,*" 168.

31. Tompkins, *Sensational Designs,* 4, and Philip Fisher, *Hard Facts: Setting and Form in the American Novel* (New York, 1985), 4, state this thesis powerfully. Behavior can include what Fisher calls "habits of moral perception," which presumably influence the "hard facts" of a culture (such as institutional slavery, for instance) by causing people to reconsider actions and situations previously deemed acceptable. Stowe, *Uncle Tom's Cabin,* ed. Elizabeth Ammons (New York, 1994). The legend that Lincoln told Stowe "So you're the little woman who wrote the book that started this Great War!" is at http://www.harrietbeecherstowecenter.org/life/#war.

FURTHER READING

Criticism

Castiglia, Christopher. "Susanna Rowson's *Reuben and Rachel*: Captivity, Colonization, and the Domestication of Columbus." In *Redefining the Political Novel: American Women Writers, 1797-1901,* edited by Sharon M. Harris, pp. 23-42. Knoxville: University of Tennessee Press, 1995.

Asserts that Rowson's *Reuben and Rachel* is an indictment of colonization.

Davidson, Cathy N. "Ideology and Genre: The Rise of the Novel in America." *Proceedings of the American Antiquarian Society* 96, no. 2 (October 1986): 295-321.

Discusses *Charlotte Temple* and its distinction as one of America's first "best sellers."

Epley, Steven. "Alienated, Betrayed, and Powerless: A Possible Connection between *Charlotte Temple* and the Legend of Inkle and Yarico." *Papers on Language and Literature* 38, no. 2 (spring 2002): 200-22.

Compares the plot and themes of *Charlotte Temple* and a popular folk legend.

Additional coverage of Rowson's life and career is contained in the following sources published by Thomson Gale: *American Writers Supplement,* Vol. 15; *Dictionary of Literary Biography,* Vols. 37, 200; *Literature Resource Center*; *Nineteenth-Century Literature Criticism,* Vols. 5, 69; and *Reference Guide to American Literature,* Ed. 4.

How to Use This Index

The main references

Calvino, Italo
    1923-1985 .... CLC 5, 8, 11, 22, 33, 39,
                                    73; SSC 3, 48

list all author entries in the following Thomson Gale Literary Criticism series:

AAL = *Asian American Literature*
BG = *The Beat Generation: A Gale Critical Companion*
BLC = *Black Literature Criticism*
BLCS = *Black Literature Criticism Supplement*
CLC = *Contemporary Literary Criticism*
CLR = *Children's Literature Review*
CMLC = *Classical and Medieval Literature Criticism*
DC = *Drama Criticism*
FL = *Feminism in Literature: A Gale Critical Companion*
GL = *Gothic Literature: A Gale Critical Companion*
HLC = *Hispanic Literature Criticism*
HLCS = *Hispanic Literature Criticism Supplement*
HR = *Harlem Renaissance: A Gale Critical Companion*
LC = *Literature Criticism from 1400 to 1800*
NCLC = *Nineteenth-Century Literature Criticism*
NNAL = *Native North American Literature*
PC = *Poetry Criticism*
SSC = *Short Story Criticism*
TCLC = *Twentieth-Century Literary Criticism*
WLC = *World Literature Criticism, 1500 to the Present*
WLCS = *World Literature Criticism Supplement*

The cross-references

See also CA 85-88, 116; CANR 23, 61;
DAM NOV; DLB 196; EW 13; MTCW 1, 2;
RGSF 2; RGWL 2; SFW 4; SSFS 12

list all author entries in the following Thomson Gale biographical and literary sources:

AAYA = *Authors & Artists for Young Adults*
AFAW = *African American Writers*
AFW = *African Writers*
AITN = *Authors in the News*
AMW = *American Writers*
AMWR = *American Writers Retrospective Supplement*
AMWS = *American Writers Supplement*
ANW = *American Nature Writers*
AW = *Ancient Writers*
BEST = *Bestsellers*
BPFB = *Beacham's Encyclopedia of Popular Fiction: Biography and Resources*
BRW = *British Writers*
BRWS = *British Writers Supplement*
BW = *Black Writers*
BYA = *Beacham's Guide to Literature for Young Adults*
CA = *Contemporary Authors*
CAAS = *Contemporary Authors Autobiography Series*
CABS = *Contemporary Authors Bibliographical Series*
CAD = *Contemporary American Dramatists*
CANR = *Contemporary Authors New Revision Series*
CAP = *Contemporary Authors Permanent Series*
CBD = *Contemporary British Dramatists*
CCA = *Contemporary Canadian Authors*
CD = *Contemporary Dramatists*
CDALB = *Concise Dictionary of American Literary Biography*

CDALBS = *Concise Dictionary of American Literary Biography Supplement*
CDBLB = *Concise Dictionary of British Literary Biography*
CMW = *St. James Guide to Crime & Mystery Writers*
CN = *Contemporary Novelists*
CP = *Contemporary Poets*
CPW = *Contemporary Popular Writers*
CSW = *Contemporary Southern Writers*
CWD = *Contemporary Women Dramatists*
CWP = *Contemporary Women Poets*
CWRI = *St. James Guide to Children's Writers*
CWW = *Contemporary World Writers*
DA = *DISCovering Authors*
DA3 = *DISCovering Authors 3.0*
DAB = *DISCovering Authors: British Edition*
DAC = *DISCovering Authors: Canadian Edition*
DAM = *DISCovering Authors: Modules*
   DRAM: *Dramatists Module;* **MST:** *Most-studied Authors Module;*
   MULT: *Multicultural Authors Module;* **NOV:** *Novelists Module;*
   POET: *Poets Module;* **POP:** *Popular Fiction and Genre Authors Module*
DFS = *Drama for Students*
DLB = *Dictionary of Literary Biography*
DLBD = *Dictionary of Literary Biography Documentary Series*
DLBY = *Dictionary of Literary Biography Yearbook*
DNFS = *Literature of Developing Nations for Students*
EFS = *Epics for Students*
EXPN = *Exploring Novels*
EXPP = *Exploring Poetry*
EXPS = *Exploring Short Stories*
EW = *European Writers*
FANT = *St. James Guide to Fantasy Writers*
FW = *Feminist Writers*
GFL = *Guide to French Literature,* Beginnings to 1789, 1798 to the Present
GLL = *Gay and Lesbian Literature*
HGG = *St. James Guide to Horror, Ghost & Gothic Writers*
HW = *Hispanic Writers*
IDFW = *International Dictionary of Films and Filmmakers: Writers and Production Artists*
IDTP = *International Dictionary of Theatre: Playwrights*
LAIT = *Literature and Its Times*
LAW = *Latin American Writers*
JRDA = *Junior DISCovering Authors*
MAICYA = *Major Authors and Illustrators for Children and Young Adults*
MAICYAS = *Major Authors and Illustrators for Children and Young Adults Supplement*
MAWW = *Modern American Women Writers*
MJW = *Modern Japanese Writers*
MTCW = *Major 20th-Century Writers*
NCFS = *Nonfiction Classics for Students*
NFS = *Novels for Students*
PAB = *Poets: American and British*
PFS = *Poetry for Students*
RGAL = *Reference Guide to American Literature*
RGEL = *Reference Guide to English Literature*
RGSF = *Reference Guide to Short Fiction*
RGWL = *Reference Guide to World Literature*
RHW = *Twentieth-Century Romance and Historical Writers*
SAAS = *Something about the Author Autobiography Series*
SATA = *Something about the Author*
SFW = *St. James Guide to Science Fiction Writers*
SSFS = *Short Stories for Students*
TCWW = *Twentieth-Century Western Writers*
WLIT = *World Literature and Its Times*
WP = *World Poets*
YABC = *Yesterday's Authors of Books for Children*
YAW = *St. James Guide to Young Adult Writers*

Literary Criticism Series
Cumulative Author Index

Aeschylus 525(?)B.C.-456(?)B.C. .. **CMLC 11, 51; DC 8; WLCS**
See also AW 1; CDWLB 1; DA; DAB; DAC; DAM DRAM, MST; DFS 5, 10; DLB 176; LMFS 1; RGWL 2, 3; TWA; WLIT 8

Aesop 620(?)B.C.-560(?)B.C. .... **CMLC 24**
See also CLR 14; MAICYA 1, 2; SATA 64

Affable Hawk
See MacCarthy, Sir (Charles Otto) Desmond

Africa, Ben
See Bosman, Herman Charles

Afton, Effie
See Harper, Frances Ellen Watkins

Agapida, Fray Antonio
See Irving, Washington

Agee, James (Rufus) 1909-1955 ...... **TCLC 1, 19, 180**
See also AAYA 44; AITN 1; AMW; CA 148; CAAE 108; CANR 131; CDALB 1941-1968; DAM NOV; DLB 2, 26, 152; DLBY 1989; EWL 3; LAIT 3; LATS 1:2; MAL 5; MTCW 2; MTFW 2005; NFS 22; RGAL 4; TUS

A Gentlewoman in New England
See Bradstreet, Anne

A Gentlewoman in Those Parts
See Bradstreet, Anne

Aghill, Gordon
See Silverberg, Robert

Agnon, S(hmuel) Y(osef Halevi) 1888-1970 .... **CLC 4, 8, 14; SSC 30; TCLC 151**
See also CA 17-18; CAAS 25-28R; CANR 60, 102; CAP 2; DLB 329; EWL 3; MTCW 1, 2; RGHL; RGSF 2; RGWL 2, 3; WLIT 6

Agrippa von Nettesheim, Henry Cornelius 1486-1535 .... **LC 27**

Aguilera Malta, Demetrio 1909-1981 .... **HLCS 1**
See also CA 124; CAAE 111; CANR 87; DAM MULT, NOV; DLB 145; EWL 3; HW 1; RGWL 3

Agustini, Delmira 1886-1914 .... **HLCS 1**
See also CA 166; DLB 290; HW 1, 2; LAW

Aherne, Owen
See Cassill, R(onald) V(erlin)

Ai 1947- .... **CLC 4, 14, 69; PC 72**
See also CA 85-88; 13; CANR 70; CP 6, 7; DLB 120; PFS 16

Aickman, Robert (Fordyce) 1914-1981 .... **CLC 57**
See also CA 5-8R; CANR 3, 72, 100; DLB 261; HGG; SUFW 1, 2

Aidoo, (Christina) Ama Ata 1942- .... **BLCS; CLC 177**
See also AFW; BW 1; CA 101; CANR 62, 144; CD 5, 6; CDWLB 3; CN 6, 7; CWD; CWP; DLB 117; DNFS 1, 2; EWL 3; FW; WLIT 2

Aiken, Conrad (Potter) 1889-1973 .... **CLC 1, 3, 5, 10, 52; PC 26; SSC 9**
See also AMW; CA 5-8R; CAAS 45-48; CANR 4, 60; CDALB 1929-1941; CN 1; CP 1; DAM NOV, POET; DLB 9, 45, 102; EWL 3; EXPS; HGG; MAL 5; MTCW 1, 2; MTFW 2005; PFS 24; RGAL 4; RGSF 2; SATA 3, 30; SSFS 8; TUS

Aiken, Joan (Delano) 1924-2004 ...... **CLC 35**
See also AAYA 1, 25; CA 182; 9-12R, 182; CAAS 223; CANR 4, 23, 34, 64, 121; CLR 1, 19, 90; DLB 161; FANT; HGG; JRDA; MAICYA 1, 2; MTCW 1; RHW; SAAS 1, 2, 30, 73; SATA-Essay 109; SATA-Obit 152; SUFW 2; WYA; YAW

Ainsworth, William Harrison 1805-1882 .... **NCLC 13**
See also DLB 21; HGG; RGEL 2; SATA 24; SUFW 1

Aitmatov, Chingiz (Torekulovich) 1928- .... **CLC 71**
See Aytmatov, Chingiz
See also CA 103; CANR 38; CWW 2; DLB 302; MTCW 1; RGSF 2; SATA 56

Akers, Floyd
See Baum, L(yman) Frank

Akhmadulina, Bella Akhatovna 1937- .... **CLC 53; PC 43**
See also CA 65-68; CWP; CWW 2; DAM POET; EWL 3

Akhmatova, Anna 1888-1966 ..... **CLC 11, 25, 64, 126; PC 2, 55**
See also CA 19-20; CAAS 25-28R; CANR 35; CAP 1; DA3; DAM POET; DLB 295; EW 10; EWL 3; FL 1:5; MTCW 1, 2; PFS 18; RGWL 2, 3

Aksakov, Sergei Timofeevich 1791-1859 .... **NCLC 2, 181**
See also DLB 198

Aksenov, Vasilii (Pavlovich)
See Aksyonov, Vassily (Pavlovich)
See also CWW 2

Aksenov, Vassily
See Aksyonov, Vassily (Pavlovich)

Akst, Daniel 1956- .... **CLC 109**
See also CA 161; CANR 110

Aksyonov, Vassily (Pavlovich) 1932- .... **CLC 22, 37, 101**
See Aksenov, Vasilii (Pavlovich)
See also CA 53-56; CANR 12, 48, 77; DLB 302; EWL 3

Akutagawa Ryunosuke 1892-1927 ... **SSC 44; TCLC 16**
See also CA 154; CAAE 117; DLB 180; EWL 3; MJW; RGSF 2; RGWL 2, 3

Alabaster, William 1568-1640 .... **LC 90**
See also DLB 132; RGEL 2

Alain 1868-1951 .... **TCLC 41**
See also CA 163; EWL 3; GFL 1789 to the Present

Alain de Lille c. 1116-c. 1203 .... **CMLC 53**
See also DLB 208

Alain-Fournier TCLC 6
See Fournier, Henri-Alban
See also DLB 65; EWL 3; GFL 1789 to the Present; RGWL 2, 3

Al-Amin, Jamil Abdullah 1943- .... **BLC 1**
See also BW 1, 3; CA 125; CAAE 112; CANR 82; DAM MULT

Alanus de Insluis
See Alain de Lille

Alarcon, Pedro Antonio de 1833-1891 .... **NCLC 1; SSC 64**

Alas (y Urena), Leopoldo (Enrique Garcia) 1852-1901 .... **TCLC 29**
See also CA 131; CAAE 113; HW 1; RGSF 2

Albee, Edward (III) 1928- ..... **CLC 1, 2, 3, 5, 9, 11, 13, 25, 53, 86, 113; DC 11; WLC 1**
See also AAYA 51; AITN 1; AMW; CA 5-8R; CABS 3; CAD; CANR 8, 54, 74, 124; CD 5, 6; CDALB 1941-1968; DA; DA3; DAB; DAC; DAM DRAM, MST; DFS 2, 3, 8, 10, 13, 14; DLB 7, 266; EWL 3; INT CANR-8; LAIT 4; LMFS 2; MAL 5; MTCW 1, 2; MTFW 2005; RGAL 4; TUS

Alberti (Merello), Rafael
See Alberti, Rafael
See also CWW 2

Alberti, Rafael 1902-1999 .... **CLC 7**
See Alberti (Merello), Rafael
See also CA 85-88; CAAS 185; CANR 81; DLB 108; EWL 3; HW 2; RGWL 2, 3

Albert the Great 1193(?)-1280 ...... **CMLC 16**
See also DLB 115

Alcaeus c. 620B.C.- .... **CMLC 65**
See also DLB 176

Alcala-Galiano, Juan Valera y
See Valera y Alcala-Galiano, Juan

Alcayaga, Lucila Godoy
See Godoy Alcayaga, Lucila

Alciato, Andrea 1492-1550 .... **LC 116**

Alcott, Amos Bronson 1799-1888 ... **NCLC 1, 167**
See also DLB 1, 223

Alcott, Louisa May 1832-1888 . **NCLC 6, 58, 83; SSC 27, 98; WLC 1**
See also AAYA 20; AMWS 1; BPFB 1; BYA 2; CDALB 1865-1917; CLR 1, 38, 109; DA; DA3; DAB; DAC; DAM MST, NOV; DLB 1, 42, 79, 223, 239, 242; DLBD 14; FL 1:2; FW; JRDA; LAIT 2; MAICYA 1, 2; NFS 12; RGAL 4; SATA 100; TUS; WCH; WYA; YABC 1; YAW

Alcuin c. 730-804 .... **CMLC 69**
See also DLB 148

Aldanov, M. A.
See Aldanov, Mark (Alexandrovich)

Aldanov, Mark (Alexandrovich) 1886-1957 .... **TCLC 23**
See also CA 181; CAAE 118; DLB 317

Aldhelm c. 639-709 .... **CMLC 90**

Aldington, Richard 1892-1962 .... **CLC 49**
See also CA 85-88; CANR 45; DLB 20, 36, 100, 149; LMFS 2; RGEL 2

Aldiss, Brian W. 1925- .. **CLC 5, 14, 40; SSC 36**
See also AAYA 42; CA 190; 5-8R, 190; 2; CANR 5, 28, 64, 121; CN 1, 2, 3, 4, 5, 6, 7; DAM NOV; DLB 14, 261, 271; MTCW 1, 2; MTFW 2005; SATA 34; SCFW 1, 2; SFW 4

Aldrich, Bess Streeter 1881-1954 .... **TCLC 125**
See also CLR 70; TCWW 2

Alegria, Claribel
See Alegria, Claribel
See also CWW 2; DLB 145, 283

Alegria, Claribel 1924- .... **CLC 75; HLCS 1; PC 26**
See Alegria, Claribel
See also CA 131; 15; CANR 66, 94, 134; DAM MULT; EWL 3; HW 1; MTCW 2; MTFW 2005; PFS 21

Alegria, Fernando 1918-2005 .... **CLC 57**
See also CA 9-12R; CANR 5, 32, 72; EWL 3; HW 1, 2

Aleixandre, Vicente 1898-1984 .... **HLCS 1; TCLC 113**
See also CANR 81; DLB 108, 329; EWL 3; HW 2; MTCW 1, 2; RGWL 2, 3

Alekseev, Konstantin Sergeivich
See Stanislavsky, Constantin

Alekseyer, Konstantin Sergeyevich
See Stanislavsky, Constantin

Aleman, Mateo 1547-1615(?) .... **LC 81**

Alencar, Jose de 1829-1877 .... **NCLC 157**
See also DLB 307; LAW; WLIT 1

Alencon, Marguerite d'
See de Navarre, Marguerite

Alepoudelis, Odysseus
See Elytis, Odysseus
See also CWW 2

Aleshkovsky, Joseph 1929-
See Aleshkovsky, Yuz
See also CA 128; CAAE 121

Aleshkovsky, Yuz CLC 44
See Aleshkovsky, Joseph
See also DLB 317

Alexander, Lloyd (Chudley) 1924- ... **CLC 35**
See also AAYA 1, 27; BPFB 1; BYA 5, 6, 7, 9, 10, 11; CA 1-4R; CANR 1, 24, 38, 55, 113; CLR 1, 5, 48; CWRI 5; DLB 52; FANT; JRDA; MAICYA 1, 2; MAICYAS 1; MTCW 1; SAAS 19; SATA 3, 49, 81, 129, 135; SUFW; TUS; WYA; YAW

Alexander, Meena 1951- .... **CLC 121**
See also CA 115; CANR 38, 70, 146; CP 5, 6, 7; CWP; DLB 323; FW

Alexander, Samuel 1859-1938 .... **TCLC 77**

Alexeiev, Konstantin
See Stanislavsky, Constantin

Alexeyev, Constantin Sergeivich
See Stanislavsky, Constantin

Alexeyev, Konstantin Sergeyevich
See Stanislavsky, Constantin

Alexie, Sherman 1966- .... **CLC 96, 154; NNAL; PC 53**
See also AAYA 28; BYA 15; CA 138; CANR 65, 95, 133; CN 7; DA3; DAM MULT; DLB 175, 206, 278; LATS 1:2; MTCW 2; MTFW 2005; NFS 17; SSFS 18

al-Farabi 870(?)-950 .... **CMLC 58**
See also DLB 115

Alfau, Felipe 1902-1999 .... **CLC 66**
See also CA 137

Alfieri, Vittorio 1749-1803 .... **NCLC 101**
See also EW 4; RGWL 2, 3; WLIT 7

Alfonso X 1221-1284 .... **CMLC 78**

Alfred, Jean Gaston
See Ponge, Francis

Alger, Horatio, Jr. 1832-1899 .... **NCLC 8, 83**
See also CLR 87; DLB 42; LAIT 2; RGAL 4; SATA 16; TUS

Al-Ghazali, Muhammad ibn Muhammad 1058-1111 .... **CMLC 50**
See also DLB 115

Algren, Nelson 1909-1981 ..... **CLC 4, 10, 33; SSC 33**
See also AMWS 9; BPFB 1; CA 13-16R; CAAS 103; CANR 20, 61; CDALB 1941-1968; CN 1, 2; DLB 9; DLBY 1981, 1982, 2000; EWL 3; MAL 5; MTCW 1, 2; MTFW 2005; RGAL 4; RGSF 2

al-Hariri, al-Qasim ibn 'Ali Abu Muhammad al-Basri 1054-1122 .... **CMLC 63**
See also RGWL 3

Ali, Ahmed 1908-1998 .... **CLC 69**
See also CA 25-28R; CANR 15, 34; CN 1, 2, 3, 4, 5; DLB 323; EWL 3

Ali, Tariq 1943- .... **CLC 173**
See also CA 25-28R; CANR 10, 99, 161

Alighieri, Dante
See Dante
See also WLIT 7

al-Kindi, Abu Yusuf Ya'qub ibn Ishaq c. 801-c. 873 .... **CMLC 80**

Allan, John B.
See Westlake, Donald E.

Allan, Sidney
See Hartmann, Sadakichi

Allan, Sydney
See Hartmann, Sadakichi

Allard, Janet CLC 59

Allen, Edward 1948- .... **CLC 59**

Allen, Fred 1894-1956 .... **TCLC 87**

Allen, Paula Gunn 1939- .... **CLC 84, 202; NNAL**
See also AMWS 4; CA 143; CAAE 112; CANR 63, 130; CWP; DA3; DAM MULT; DLB 175; FW; MTCW 2; MTFW 2005; RGAL 4; TCWW 2

Allen, Roland
See Ayckbourn, Alan

Allen, Sarah A.
See Hopkins, Pauline Elizabeth

Allen, Sidney H.
See Hartmann, Sadakichi

Allen, Woody 1935- .... **CLC 16, 52, 195**
See also AAYA 10, 51; AMWS 15; CA 33-36R; CANR 27, 38, 63, 128; DAM POP; DLB 44; MTCW 1; SSFS 21

Allende, Isabel 1942- ... **CLC 39, 57, 97, 170; HLC 1; SSC 65; WLCS**
See also AAYA 18, 70; CA 130; CAAE 125; CANR 51, 74, 129; CDWLB 3; CLR 99; CWW 2; DA3; DAM MULT, NOV; DLB 145; DNFS 1; EWL 3; FL 1:5; FW; HW 1, 2; INT CA-130; LAIT 5; LAWS 1; LMFS 2; MTCW 1, 2; MTFW 2005; NCFS 1; NFS 6, 18; RGSF 2; RGWL 3; SATA 163; SSFS 11, 16; WLIT 1

Alleyn, Ellen
See Rossetti, Christina

Alleyne, Carla D. CLC 65

Allingham, Margery (Louise) 1904-1966 .... **CLC 19**
See also CA 5-8R; CAAS 25-28R; CANR 4, 58; CMW 4; DLB 77; MSW; MTCW 1, 2

Allingham, William 1824-1889 ...... **NCLC 25**
See also DLB 35; RGEL 2

Allison, Dorothy E. 1949- .... **CLC 78, 153**
See also AAYA 53; CA 140; CANR 66, 107; CN 7; CSW; DA3; FW; MTCW 2; MTFW 2005; NFS 11; RGAL 4

Alloula, Malek CLC 65

Allston, Washington 1779-1843 .... **NCLC 2**
See also DLB 1, 235

Almedingen, E. M. CLC 12
See Almedingen, Martha Edith von
See also SATA 3

Almedingen, Martha Edith von 1898-1971
See Almedingen, E. M.
See also CA 1-4R; CANR 1

Almodovar, Pedro 1949(?)- .... **CLC 114, 229; HLCS 1**
See also CA 133; CANR 72, 151; HW 2

Almqvist, Carl Jonas Love 1793-1866 .... **NCLC 42**

al-Mutanabbi, Ahmad ibn al-Husayn Abu al-Tayyib al-Jufi al-Kindi 915-965 .... **CMLC 66**
See Mutanabbi, Al-
See also RGWL 3

Alonso, Damaso 1898-1990 .... **CLC 14**
See also CA 131; CAAE 110; CAAS 130; CANR 72; DLB 108; EWL 3; HW 1, 2

Alov
See Gogol, Nikolai (Vasilyevich)

al'Sadaawi, Nawal
See El Saadawi, Nawal
See also FW

al-Shaykh, Hanan 1945- .... **CLC 218**
See Shaykh, al- Hanan
See also CA 135; CANR 111; WLIT 6

Al Siddik
See Rolfe, Frederick (William Serafino Austin Lewis Mary)
See also GLL 1; RGEL 2

Alta 1942- .... **CLC 19**
See also CA 57-60

Alter, Robert B. 1935- .... **CLC 34**
See also CA 49-52; CANR 1, 47, 100, 160

Alter, Robert Bernard
See Alter, Robert B.

Alther, Lisa 1944- .... **CLC 7, 41**
See also BPFB 1; CA 65-68; 30; CANR 12, 30, 51; CN 4, 5, 6, 7; CSW; GLL 2; MTCW 1

Althusser, L.
See Althusser, Louis

Althusser, Louis 1918-1990 .... **CLC 106**
See also CA 131; CAAS 132; CANR 102; DLB 242

Altman, Robert 1925-2006 .... **CLC 16, 116**
See also CA 73-76; CAAS 254; CANR 43

Alurista HLCS 1; PC 34
See Urista (Heredia), Alberto (Baltazar)
See also CA 45-48R; DLB 82; LLW

Alvarez, A. 1929- .... **CLC 5, 13**
See also CA 1-4R; CANR 3, 33, 63, 101, 134; CN 3, 4, 5, 6; CP 1, 2, 3, 4, 5, 6, 7; DLB 14, 40; MTFW 2005

Alvarez, Alejandro Rodriguez 1903-1965
See Casona, Alejandro
See also CA 131; CAAS 93-96; HW 1

Alvarez, Julia 1950- .... **CLC 93; HLCS 1**
See also AAYA 25; AMWS 7; CA 147; CANR 69, 101, 133; DA3; DLB 282; LATS 1:2; LLW; MTCW 2; MTFW 2005; NFS 5, 9; SATA 129; WLIT 1

Alvaro, Corrado 1896-1956 .... **TCLC 60**
See also CA 163; DLB 264; EWL 3

Amado, Jorge 1912-2001 ... **CLC 13, 40, 106, 232; HLC 1**
See also CA 77-80; CAAS 201; CANR 35, 74, 135; CWW 2; DAM MULT, NOV; DLB 113, 307; EWL 3; HW 2; LAW; LAWS 1; MTCW 1, 2; MTFW 2005; RGWL 2, 3; TWA; WLIT 1

Ambler, Eric 1909-1998 .... **CLC 4, 6, 9**
See also BRWS 4; CA 9-12R; CAAS 171; CANR 7, 38, 74; CMW 4; CN 1, 2, 3, 4, 5, 6; DLB 77; MSW; MTCW 1, 2; TEA

Ambrose, Stephen E. 1936-2002 ..... **CLC 145**
See also AAYA 44; CA 1-4R; CAAS 209; CANR 3, 43, 57, 83, 105; MTFW 2005; NCFS 2; SATA 40, 138

Amichai, Yehuda 1924-2000 .. **CLC 9, 22, 57, 116; PC 38**
See also CA 85-88; CAAS 189; CANR 46, 60, 99, 132; CWW 2; EWL 3; MTCW 1, 2; MTFW 2005; PFS 24; RGHL; WLIT 6

Amichai, Yehudah
See Amichai, Yehuda

Amiel, Henri Frederic 1821-1881 .... **NCLC 4**
See also DLB 217

Amis, Kingsley 1922-1995 . **CLC 1, 2, 3, 5, 8, 13, 40, 44, 129**
See also AITN 2; BPFB 1; BRWS 2; CA 9-12R; CAAS 150; CANR 8, 28, 54; CD-BLB 1945-1960; CN 1, 2, 3, 4, 5, 6; CP 1, 2, 3, 4; DA; DA3; DAB; DAC; DAM MST, NOV; DLB 15, 27, 100, 139, 326; DLBY 1996; EWL 3; HGG; INT CANR-8; MTCW 1, 2; MTFW 2005; RGEL 2; RGSF 2; SFW 4

Amis, Martin 1949- ... **CLC 4, 9, 38, 62, 101, 213**
See also BEST 90:3; BRWS 4; CA 65-68; CANR 8, 27, 54, 73, 95, 132; CN 5, 6, 7; DA3; DLB 14, 194; EWL 3; INT CANR-27; MTCW 2; MTFW 2005

Ammianus Marcellinus c. 330-c. 395 .... **CMLC 60**
See also AW 2; DLB 211

Ammons, A.R. 1926-2001 .. **CLC 2, 3, 5, 8, 9, 25, 57, 108; PC 16**
See also AITN 1; AMWS 7; CA 9-12R; CAAS 193; CANR 6, 36, 51, 73, 107, 156; CP 1, 2, 3, 4, 5, 6, 7; CSW; DAM POET; DLB 5, 165; EWL 3; MAL 5; MTCW 1, 2; PFS 19; RGAL 4; TCLE 1:1

Ammons, Archie Randolph
See Ammons, A.R.

Amo, Tauraatua i
See Adams, Henry (Brooks)

Amory, Thomas 1691(?)-1788 .... **LC 48**
See also DLB 39

Aragon, Louis 1897-1982 .... **CLC 3, 22;**
TCLC 123
See also CA 69-72; CAAS 108; CANR 28,
71; DAM NOV, POET; DLB 72, 258; EW
11; EWL 3; GFL 1789 to the Present;
GLL 2; LMFS 2; MTCW 1, 2; RGWL 2,
3
Arany, Janos 1817-1882 .... **NCLC 34**
Aranyos, Kakay 1847-1910
See Mikszath, Kalman
Aratus of Soli c. 315B.C.-c.
240B.C. .... **CMLC 64**
See also DLB 176
Arbuthnot, John 1667-1735 .... **LC 1**
See also DLB 101
Archer, Herbert Winslow
See Mencken, H(enry) L(ouis)
Archer, Jeffrey 1940- .... **CLC 28**
See also AAYA 16; BEST 89:3; BPFB 1;
CA 77-80; CANR 22, 52, 95, 136; CPW;
DA3; DAM POP; INT CANR-22; MTFW
2005
Archer, Jeffrey Howard
See Archer, Jeffrey
Archer, Jules 1915- .... **CLC 12**
See also CA 9-12R; CANR 6, 69; SAAS 5;
SATA 4, 85
Archer, Lee
See Ellison, Harlan
Archilochus c. 7th cent. B.C.- .... **CMLC 44**
See also DLB 176
Arden, John 1930- .... **CLC 6, 13, 15**
See also BRWS 2; CA 13-16R; 4; CANR
31, 65, 67, 124; CBD; CD 5, 6; DAM
DRAM; DFS 9; DLB 13, 245; EWL 3;
MTCW 1
Arenas, Reinaldo 1943-1990 .. **CLC 41; HLC**
1
See also CA 128; CAAE 124; CAAS 133;
CANR 73, 106; DAM MULT; DLB 145;
EWL 3; GLL 2; HW 1; LAW; LAWS 1;
MTCW 2; MTFW 2005; RGSF 2; RGWL
3; WLIT 1
Arendt, Hannah 1906-1975 .... **CLC 66, 98**
See also CA 17-20R; CAAS 61-64; CANR
26, 60; DLB 242; MTCW 1, 2
Aretino, Pietro 1492-1556 .... **LC 12**
See also RGWL 2, 3
Arghezi, Tudor CLC 80
See Theodorescu, Ion N.
See also CA 167; CDWLB 4; DLB 220;
EWL 3
Arguedas, Jose Maria 1911-1969 .... **CLC 10,**
18; HLCS 1; TCLC 147
See also CA 89-92; CANR 73; DLB 113;
EWL 3; HW 1; LAW; RGWL 2, 3; WLIT
1
Argueta, Manlio 1936- .... **CLC 31**
See also CA 131; CANR 73; CWW 2; DLB
145; EWL 3; HW 1; RGWL 3
Arias, Ron 1941- .... **HLC 1**
See also CA 131; CANR 81, 136; DAM
MULT; DLB 82; HW 1, 2; MTCW 2;
MTFW 2005
Ariosto, Lodovico
See Ariosto, Ludovico
See also WLIT 7
Ariosto, Ludovico 1474-1533 ... **LC 6, 87; PC**
42
See Ariosto, Lodovico
See also EW 2; RGWL 2, 3
Aristides
See Epstein, Joseph
Aristophanes 450B.C.-385B.C. .... **CMLC 4,**
51; DC 2; WLCS
See also AW 1; CDWLB 1; DA; DA3;
DAB; DAC; DAM DRAM, MST; DFS
10; DLB 176; LMFS 1; RGWL 2, 3;
TWA; WLIT 8

Aristotle 384B.C.-322B.C. .... **CMLC 31;**
WLCS
See also AW 1; CDWLB 1; DA; DA3;
DAB; DAC; DAM MST; DLB 176;
RGWL 2, 3; TWA; WLIT 8
Arlt, Roberto (Godofredo Christophersen)
1900-1942 .... **HLC 1; TCLC 29**
See also CA 131; CAAE 123; CANR 67;
DAM MULT; DLB 305; EWL 3; HW 1,
2; IDTP; LAW
Armah, Ayi Kwei 1939- . **BLC 1; CLC 5, 33,**
136
See also AFW; BRWS 10; BW 1; CA 61-
64; CANR 21, 64; CDWLB 3; CN 1, 2,
3, 4, 5, 6, 7; DAM MULT, POET; DLB
117; EWL 3; MTCW 1; WLIT 2
Armatrading, Joan 1950- .... **CLC 17**
See also CA 186; CAAE 114
Armin, Robert 1568(?)-1615(?) .... **LC 120**
Armitage, Frank
See Carpenter, John (Howard)
Armstrong, Jeannette (C.) 1948- .... **NNAL**
See also CA 149; CCA 1; CN 6, 7; DAC;
SATA 102
Arnette, Robert
See Silverberg, Robert
Arnim, Achim von (Ludwig Joachim von
Arnim) 1781-1831 .. **NCLC 5, 159; SSC**
29
See also DLB 90
Arnim, Bettina von 1785-1859 ...... **NCLC 38,**
123
See also DLB 90; RGWL 2, 3
Arnold, Matthew 1822-1888 ..... **NCLC 6, 29,**
89, 126; PC 5; WLC 1
See also BRW 5; CDBLB 1832-1890; DA;
DAB; DAC; DAM MST, POET; DLB 32,
57; EXPP; PAB; PFS 2; TEA; WP
Arnold, Thomas 1795-1842 .... **NCLC 18**
See also DLB 55
Arnow, Harriette (Louisa) Simpson
1908-1986 .... **CLC 2, 7, 18**
See also BPFB 1; CA 9-12R; CAAS 118;
CANR 14; CN 2, 3, 4; DLB 6; FW;
MTCW 1, 2; RHW; SATA 42; SATA-Obit
47
Arouet, Francois-Marie
See Voltaire
Arp, Hans
See Arp, Jean
Arp, Jean 1887-1966 .... **CLC 5; TCLC 115**
See also CA 81-84; CAAS 25-28R; CANR
42, 77; EW 10
Arrabal
See Arrabal, Fernando
Arrabal (Teran), Fernando
See Arrabal, Fernando
See also CWW 2
Arrabal, Fernando 1932- ... **CLC 2, 9, 18, 58**
See Arrabal (Teran), Fernando
See also CA 9-12R; CANR 15; DLB 321;
EWL 3; LMFS 2
Arreola, Juan Jose 1918-2001 .... **CLC 147;**
HLC 1; SSC 38
See also CA 131; CAAE 113; CAAS 200;
CANR 81; CWW 2; DAM MULT; DLB
113; DNFS 2; EWL 3; HW 1, 2; LAW;
RGSF 2
Arrian c. 89(?)-c. 155(?) .... **CMLC 43**
See also DLB 176
Arrick, Fran CLC 30
See Gaberman, Judie Angell
See also BYA 6
Arrley, Richmond
See Delany, Samuel R., Jr.

Artaud, Antonin (Marie Joseph)
1896-1948 .... **DC 14; TCLC 3, 36**
See also CA 149; CAAE 104; DA3; DAM
DRAM; DFS 22; DLB 258, 321; EW 11;
EWL 3; GFL 1789 to the Present; MTCW
2; MTFW 2005; RGWL 2, 3
Arthur, Ruth M(abel) 1905-1979 ..... **CLC 12**
See also CA 9-12R; CAAS 85-88; CANR
4; CWRI 5; SATA 7, 26
Artsybashev, Mikhail (Petrovich)
1878-1927 .... **TCLC 31**
See also CA 170; DLB 295
Arundel, Honor (Morfydd)
1919-1973 .... **CLC 17**
See also CA 21-22; CAAS 41-44R; CAP 2;
CLR 35; CWRI 5; SATA 4; SATA-Obit
24
Arzner, Dorothy 1900-1979 .... **CLC 98**
Asch, Sholem 1880-1957 .... **TCLC 3**
See also CAAE 105; DLB 333; EWL 3;
GLL 2; RGHL
Ascham, Roger 1516(?)-1568 .... **LC 101**
See also DLB 236
Ash, Shalom
See Asch, Sholem
Ashbery, John 1927- ... **CLC 2, 3, 4, 6, 9, 13,**
15, 25, 41, 77, 125, 221; PC 26
See Berry, Jonas
See also AMWS 3; CA 5-8R; CANR 9, 37,
66, 102, 132; CP 1, 2, 3, 4, 5, 6, 7; DA3;
DAM POET; DLB 5, 165; DLBY 1981;
EWL 3; INT CANR-9; MAL 5; MTCW
1, 2; MTFW 2005; PAB; PFS 11; RGAL
4; TCLE 1:1; WP
Ashdown, Clifford
See Freeman, R(ichard) Austin
Ashe, Gordon
See Creasey, John
Ashton-Warner, Sylvia (Constance)
1908-1984 .... **CLC 19**
See also CA 69-72; CAAS 112; CANR 29;
CN 1, 2, 3; MTCW 1, 2
Asimov, Isaac 1920-1992 ..... **CLC 1, 3, 9, 19,**
26, 76, 92
See also AAYA 13; BEST 90:2; BPFB 1;
BYA 4, 6, 7, 9; CA 1-4R; CAAS 137;
CANR 2, 19, 36, 60, 125; CLR 12, 79;
CMW 4; CN 1, 2, 3, 4, 5; CPW; DA3;
DAM POP; DLB 8; DLBY 1992; INT
CANR-19; JRDA; LAIT 5; LMFS 2;
MAICYA 1, 2; MAL 5; MTCW 1, 2;
MTFW 2005; RGAL 4; SATA 1, 26, 74;
SCFW 1, 2; SFW 4; SSFS 17; TUS; YAW
Askew, Anne 1521(?)-1546 .... **LC 81**
See also DLB 136
Assis, Joaquim Maria Machado de
See Machado de Assis, Joaquim Maria
Astell, Mary 1666-1731 .... **LC 68**
See also DLB 252; FW
Astley, Thea (Beatrice May)
1925-2004 .... **CLC 41**
See also CA 65-68; CAAS 229; CANR 11,
43, 78; CN 1, 2, 3, 4, 5, 6, 7; DLB 289;
EWL 3
Astley, William 1855-1911
See Warung, Price
Aston, James
See White, T(erence) H(anbury)
Asturias, Miguel Angel 1899-1974 .... **CLC 3,**
8, 13; HLC 1; TCLC 184
See also CA 25-28; CAAS 49-52; CANR
32; CAP 2; CDWLB 3; DA3; DAM
MULT, NOV; DLB 113, 290, 329; EWL
3; HW 1; LAW; LMFS 2; MTCW 1, 2;
RGWL 2, 3; WLIT 1
Atares, Carlos Saura
See Saura (Atares), Carlos
Athanasius c. 295-c. 373 .... **CMLC 48**

Bagryana, Elisaveta CLC 10
See Belcheva, Elisaveta Lyubomirova
See also CA 178; CDWLB 4; DLB 147; EWL 3

Bailey, Paul 1937- .... **CLC 45**
See also CA 21-24R; CANR 16, 62, 124; CN 1, 2, 3, 4, 5, 6, 7; DLB 14, 271; GLL 2

Baillie, Joanna 1762-1851 ...... **NCLC 71, 151**
See also DLB 93; GL 2; RGEL 2

Bainbridge, Beryl 1934- ...... **CLC 4, 5, 8, 10, 14, 18, 22, 62, 130**
See also BRWS 6; CA 21-24R; CANR 24, 55, 75, 88, 128; CN 2, 3, 4, 5, 6, 7; DAM NOV; DLB 14, 231; EWL 3; MTCW 1, 2; MTFW 2005

Baker, Carlos (Heard)
1909-1987 .... **TCLC 119**
See also CA 5-8R; CAAS 122; CANR 3, 63; DLB 103

Baker, Elliott 1922-2007 .... **CLC 8**
See also CA 45-48; CANR 2, 63; CN 1, 2, 3, 4, 5, 6, 7

Baker, Jean H. TCLC 3, 10
See Russell, George William

Baker, Nicholson 1957- .... **CLC 61, 165**
See also AMWS 13; CA 135; CANR 63, 120, 138; CN 6; CPW; DA3; DAM POP; DLB 227; MTFW 2005

Baker, Ray Stannard 1870-1946 .... **TCLC 47**
See also CAAE 118

Baker, Russell 1925- .... **CLC 31**
See also BEST 89:4; CA 57-60; CANR 11, 41, 59, 137; MTCW 1, 2; MTFW 2005

Bakhtin, M.
See Bakhtin, Mikhail Mikhailovich

Bakhtin, M. M.
See Bakhtin, Mikhail Mikhailovich

Bakhtin, Mikhail
See Bakhtin, Mikhail Mikhailovich

Bakhtin, Mikhail Mikhailovich
1895-1975 .... **CLC 83; TCLC 160**
See also CA 128; CAAS 113; DLB 242; EWL 3

Bakshi, Ralph 1938(?)- .... **CLC 26**
See also CA 138; CAAE 112; IDFW 3

Bakunin, Mikhail (Alexandrovich)
1814-1876 ....**NCLC 25, 58**
See also DLB 277

Baldwin, James 1924-1987 ... **BLC 1; CLC 1, 2, 3, 4, 5, 8, 13, 15, 17, 42, 50, 67, 90, 127; DC 1; SSC 10, 33, 98; WLC 1**
See also AAYA 4, 34; AFAW 1, 2; AMWR 2; AMWS 1; BPFB 1; BW 1; CA 1-4R; CAAS 124; CABS 1; CAD; CANR 3, 24; CDALB 1941-1968; CN 1, 2, 3, 4; CPW; DA; DA3; DAB; DAC; DAM MST, MULT, NOV, POP; DFS 11, 15; DLB 2, 7, 33, 249, 278; DLBY 1987; EWL 3; EXPS; LAIT 5; MAL 5; MTCW 1, 2; MTFW 2005; NCFS 4; NFS 4; RGAL 4; RGSF 2; SATA 9; SATA-Obit 54; SSFS 2, 18; TUS

Baldwin, William c. 1515-1563 .... **LC 113**
See also DLB 132

Bale, John 1495-1563 .... **LC 62**
See also DLB 132; RGEL 2; TEA

Ball, Hugo 1886-1927 .... **TCLC 104**

Ballard, J.G. 1930- .... **CLC 3, 6, 14, 36, 137; SSC 1, 53**
See also AAYA 3, 52; BRWS 5; CA 5-8R; CANR 15, 39, 65, 107, 133; CN 1, 2, 3, 4, 5, 6, 7; DA3; DAM NOV, POP; DLB 14, 207, 261, 319; EWL 3; HGG; MTCW 1, 2; MTFW 2005; NFS 8; RGEL 2; RGSF 2; SATA 93; SCFW 1, 2; SFW 4

Balmont, Konstantin (Dmitriyevich)
1867-1943 .... **TCLC 11**
See also CA 155; CAAE 109; DLB 295; EWL 3

Baltausis, Vincas 1847-1910
See Mikszath, Kalman

Balzac, Honore de 1799-1850 ... **NCLC 5, 35, 53, 153; SSC 5, 59; WLC 1**
See also DA; DA3; DAB; DAC; DAM MST, NOV; DLB 119; EW 5; GFL 1789 to the Present; LMFS 1; RGSF 2; RGWL 2, 3; SSFS 10; SUFW; TWA

Bambara, Toni Cade 1939-1995 .... **BLC 1; CLC 19, 88; SSC 35; TCLC 116; WLCS**
See also AAYA 5, 49; AFAW 2; AMWS 11; BW 2, 3; BYA 12, 14; CA 29-32R; CAAS 150; CANR 24, 49, 81; CDALBS; DA; DA3; DAC; DAM MST, MULT; DLB 38, 218; EXPS; MAL 5; MTCW 1, 2; MTFW 2005; RGAL 4; RGSF 2; SATA 112; SSFS 4, 7, 12, 21

Bamdad, A.
See Shamlu, Ahmad

Bamdad, Alef
See Shamlu, Ahmad

Banat, D. R.
See Bradbury, Ray

Bancroft, Laura
See Baum, L(yman) Frank

Banim, John 1798-1842 .... **NCLC 13**
See also DLB 116, 158, 159; RGEL 2

Banim, Michael 1796-1874 .... **NCLC 13**
See also DLB 158, 159

Banjo, The
See Paterson, A(ndrew) B(arton)

Banks, Iain
See Banks, Iain M.
See also BRWS 11

Banks, Iain M. 1954- .... **CLC 34**
See Banks, Iain
See also CA 128; CAAE 123; CANR 61, 106; DLB 194, 261; EWL 3; HGG; INT CA-128; MTFW 2005; SFW 4

Banks, Iain Menzies
See Banks, Iain M.

Banks, Lynne Reid CLC 23
See Reid Banks, Lynne
See also AAYA 6; BYA 7; CLR 86; CN 4, 5, 6

Banks, Russell 1940- . **CLC 37, 72, 187; SSC 42**
See also AAYA 45; AMWS 5; CA 65-68; 15; CANR 19, 52, 73, 118; CN 4, 5, 6, 7; DLB 130, 278; EWL 3; MAL 5; MTCW 2; MTFW 2005; NFS 13

Banville, John 1945- .... **CLC 46, 118, 224**
See also CA 128; CAAE 117; CANR 104, 150; CN 4, 5, 6, 7; DLB 14, 271, 326; INT CA-128

Banville, Theodore (Faullain) de
1832-1891 .... **NCLC 9**
See also DLB 217; GFL 1789 to the Present

Baraka, Amiri 1934- .... **BLC 1; CLC 1, 2, 3, 5, 10, 14, 33, 115, 213; DC 6; PC 4; WLCS**
See Jones, LeRoi
See also AAYA 63; AFAW 1, 2; AMWS 2; BW 2, 3; CA 21-24R; CABS 3; CAD; CANR 27, 38, 61, 133; CD 3, 5, 6; CDALB 1941-1968; CP 4, 5, 6, 7; CPW; DA; DA3; DAC; DAM MST, MULT, POET, POP; DFS 3, 11, 16; DLB 5, 7, 16, 38; DLBD 8; EWL 3; MAL 5; MTCW 1, 2; MTFW 2005; PFS 9; RGAL 4; TCLE 1:1; TUS; WP

Baratynsky, Evgenii Abramovich
1800-1844 .... **NCLC 103**
See also DLB 205

Barbauld, Anna Laetitia
1743-1825 .... **NCLC 50**
See also DLB 107, 109, 142, 158; RGEL 2

Barbellion, W. N. P. TCLC 24
See Cummings, Bruce F(rederick)

Barber, Benjamin R. 1939- .... **CLC 141**
See also CA 29-32R; CANR 12, 32, 64, 119

Barbera, Jack (Vincent) 1945- .... **CLC 44**
See also CA 110; CANR 45

Barbey d'Aurevilly, Jules-Amedee
1808-1889 .... **NCLC 1; SSC 17**
See also DLB 119; GFL 1789 to the Present

Barbour, John c. 1316-1395 .... **CMLC 33**
See also DLB 146

Barbusse, Henri 1873-1935 .... **TCLC 5**
See also CA 154; CAAE 105; DLB 65; EWL 3; RGWL 2, 3

Barclay, Alexander c. 1475-1552 .... **LC 109**
See also DLB 132

Barclay, Bill
See Moorcock, Michael

Barclay, William Ewert
See Moorcock, Michael

Barea, Arturo 1897-1957 .... **TCLC 14**
See also CA 201; CAAE 111

Barfoot, Joan 1946- .... **CLC 18**
See also CA 105; CANR 141

Barham, Richard Harris
1788-1845 .... **NCLC 77**
See also DLB 159

Baring, Maurice 1874-1945 .... **TCLC 8**
See also CA 168; CAAE 105; DLB 34; HGG

Baring-Gould, Sabine 1834-1924 ... **TCLC 88**
See also DLB 156, 190

Barker, Clive 1952- .... **CLC 52, 205; SSC 53**
See also AAYA 10, 54; BEST 90:3; BPFB 1; CA 129; CAAE 121; CANR 71, 111, 133; CPW; DA3; DAM POP; DLB 261; HGG; INT CA-129; MTCW 1, 2; MTFW 2005; SUFW 2

Barker, George Granville
1913-1991 .... **CLC 8, 48; PC 77**
See also CA 9-12R; CAAS 135; CANR 7, 38; CP 1, 2, 3, 4, 5; DAM POET; DLB 20; EWL 3; MTCW 1

Barker, Harley Granville
See Granville-Barker, Harley
See also DLB 10

Barker, Howard 1946- .... **CLC 37**
See also CA 102; CBD; CD 5, 6; DLB 13, 233

Barker, Jane 1652-1732 .... **LC 42, 82**
See also DLB 39, 131

Barker, Pat 1943- .... **CLC 32, 94, 146**
See also BRWS 4; CA 122; CAAE 117; CANR 50, 101, 148; CN 6, 7; DLB 271, 326; INT CA-122

Barker, Patricia
See Barker, Pat

Barlach, Ernst (Heinrich)
1870-1938 .... **TCLC 84**
See also CA 178; DLB 56, 118; EWL 3

Barlow, Joel 1754-1812 .... **NCLC 23**
See also AMWS 2; DLB 37; RGAL 4

Barnard, Mary (Ethel) 1909- .... **CLC 48**
See also CA 21-22; CAP 2; CP 1

Barnes, Djuna 1892-1982 .... **CLC 3, 4, 8, 11, 29, 127; SSC 3**
See Steptoe, Lydia
See also AMWS 3; CA 9-12R; CAAS 107; CAD; CANR 16, 55; CN 1, 2, 3; CWD; DLB 4, 9, 45; EWL 3; GLL 1; MAL 5; MTCW 1, 2; MTFW 2005; RGAL 4; TCLE 1:1; TUS

Barnes, Jim 1933- .... **NNAL**
See also CA 175; 108, 175; 28; DLB 175

Barnes, Julian 1946- .... **CLC 42, 141**
See also BRWS 4; CA 102; CANR 19, 54, 115, 137; CN 4, 5, 6, 7; DAB; DLB 194; DLBY 1993; EWL 3; MTCW 2; MTFW 2005; SSFS 24
Barnes, Julian Patrick
See Barnes, Julian
Barnes, Peter 1931-2004 .... **CLC 5, 56**
See also CA 65-68; 12; CAAS 230; CANR 33, 34, 64, 113; CBD; CD 5, 6; DFS 6; DLB 13, 233; MTCW 1
Barnes, William 1801-1886 .... **NCLC 75**
See also DLB 32
Baroja, Pio 1872-1956 .... **HLC 1; TCLC 8**
See also CA 247; CAAE 104; EW 9
Baroja y Nessi, Pio
See Baroja, Pio
Baron, David
See Pinter, Harold
Baron Corvo
See Rolfe, Frederick (William Serafino Austin Lewis Mary)
Barondess, Sue K(aufman)
1926-1977 .... **CLC 8**
See Kaufman, Sue
See also CA 1-4R; CAAS 69-72; CANR 1
Baron de Teive
See Pessoa, Fernando (Antonio Nogueira)
Baroness Von S.
See Zangwill, Israel
Barres, (Auguste-)Maurice
1862-1923 .... **TCLC 47**
See also CA 164; DLB 123; GFL 1789 to the Present
Barreto, Afonso Henrique de Lima
See Lima Barreto, Afonso Henrique de
Barrett, Andrea 1954- .... **CLC 150**
See also CA 156; CANR 92; CN 7; SSFS 24
Barrett, Michele CLC 65
Barrett, (Roger) Syd 1946-2006 .... **CLC 35**
Barrett, William (Christopher)
1913-1992 .... **CLC 27**
See also CA 13-16R; CAAS 139; CANR 11, 67; INT CANR-11
Barrett Browning, Elizabeth
1806-1861 ...... **NCLC 1, 16, 61, 66, 170; PC 6, 62; WLC 1**
See also AAYA 63; BRW 4; CDBLB 1832-1890; DA; DA3; DAB; DAC; DAM MST, POET; DLB 32, 199; EXPP; FL 1:2; PAB; PFS 2, 16, 23; TEA; WLIT 4; WP
Barrie, J(ames) M(atthew)
1860-1937 .... **TCLC 2, 164**
See also BRWS 3; BYA 4, 5; CA 136; CAAE 104; CANR 77; CDBLB 1890-1914; CLR 16; CWRI 5; DA3; DAB; DAM DRAM; DFS 7; DLB 10, 141, 156; EWL 3; FANT; MAICYA 1, 2; MTCW 2; MTFW 2005; SATA 100; SUFW; WCH; WLIT 4; YABC 1
Barrington, Michael
See Moorcock, Michael
Barrol, Grady
See Bograd, Larry
Barry, Mike
See Malzberg, Barry N(athaniel)
Barry, Philip 1896-1949 .... **TCLC 11**
See also CA 199; CAAE 109; DFS 9; DLB 7, 228; MAL 5; RGAL 4
Bart, Andre Schwarz
See Schwarz-Bart, Andre
Barth, John (Simmons) 1930- ... **CLC 1, 2, 3, 5, 7, 9, 10, 14, 27, 51, 89, 214; SSC 10, 89**
See also AITN 1, 2; AMW; BPFB 1; CA 1-4R; CABS 1; CANR 5, 23, 49, 64, 113; CN 1, 2, 3, 4, 5, 6, 7; DAM NOV; DLB 2, 227; EWL 3; FANT; MAL 5; MTCW 1; RGAL 4; RGSF 2; RHW; SSFS 6; TUS

Barthelme, Donald 1931-1989 ... **CLC 1, 2, 3, 5, 6, 8, 13, 23, 46, 59, 115; SSC 2, 55**
See also AMWS 4; BPFB 1; CA 21-24R; CAAS 129; CANR 20, 58; CN 1, 2, 3, 4; DA3; DAM NOV; DLB 2, 234; DLBY 1980, 1989; EWL 3; FANT; LMFS 2; MAL 5; MTCW 1, 2; MTFW 2005; RGAL 4; RGSF 2; SATA 7; SATA-Obit 62; SSFS 17
Barthelme, Frederick 1943- ...... **CLC 36, 117**
See also AMWS 11; CA 122; CAAE 114; CANR 77; CN 4, 5, 6, 7; CSW; DLB 244; DLBY 1985; EWL 3; INT CA-122
Barthes, Roland (Gerard)
1915-1980 .... **CLC 24, 83; TCLC 135**
See also CA 130; CAAS 97-100; CANR 66; DLB 296; EW 13; EWL 3; GFL 1789 to the Present; MTCW 1, 2; TWA
Bartram, William 1739-1823 .... **NCLC 145**
See also ANW; DLB 37
Barzun, Jacques (Martin) 1907- ..... **CLC 51, 145**
See also CA 61-64; CANR 22, 95
Bashevis, Isaac
See Singer, Isaac Bashevis
Bashevis, Yitskhok
See Singer, Isaac Bashevis
Bashkirtseff, Marie 1859-1884 .... **NCLC 27**
Basho, Matsuo
See Matsuo Basho
See also RGWL 2, 3; WP
Basil of Caesaria c. 330-379 .... **CMLC 35**
Basket, Raney
See Edgerton, Clyde (Carlyle)
Bass, Kingsley B., Jr.
See Bullins, Ed
Bass, Rick 1958- .... **CLC 79, 143; SSC 60**
See also AMWS 16; ANW; CA 126; CANR 53, 93, 145; CSW; DLB 212, 275
Bassani, Giorgio 1916-2000 .... **CLC 9**
See also CA 65-68; CAAS 190; CANR 33; CWW 2; DLB 128, 177, 299; EWL 3; MTCW 1; RGHL; RGWL 2, 3
Bastian, Ann CLC 70
Bastos, Augusto Roa
See Roa Bastos, Augusto
Bataille, Georges 1897-1962 .... **CLC 29; TCLC 155**
See also CA 101; CAAS 89-92; EWL 3
Bates, H(erbert) E(rnest)
1905-1974 .... **CLC 46; SSC 10**
See also CA 93-96; CAAS 45-48; CANR 34; CN 1; DA3; DAB; DAM POP; DLB 162, 191; EWL 3; EXPS; MTCW 1, 2; RGSF 2; SSFS 7
Bauchart
See Camus, Albert
Baudelaire, Charles 1821-1867 . **NCLC 6, 29, 55, 155; PC 1; SSC 18; WLC 1**
See also DA; DA3; DAB; DAC; DAM MST, POET; DLB 217; EW 7; GFL 1789 to the Present; LMFS 2; PFS 21; RGWL 2, 3; TWA
Baudouin, Marcel
See Peguy, Charles (Pierre)
Baudouin, Pierre
See Peguy, Charles (Pierre)
Baudrillard, Jean 1929- .... **CLC 60**
See also CA 252; DLB 296
Baum, L(yman) Frank 1856-1919 .. **TCLC 7, 132**
See also AAYA 46; BYA 16; CA 133; CAAE 108; CLR 15, 107; CWRI 5; DLB 22; FANT; JRDA; MAICYA 1, 2; MTCW 1, 2; NFS 13; RGAL 4; SATA 18, 100; WCH
Baum, Louis F.
See Baum, L(yman) Frank

Baumbach, Jonathan 1933- .... **CLC 6, 23**
See also CA 13-16R; 5; CANR 12, 66, 140; CN 3, 4, 5, 6, 7; DLBY 1980; INT CANR-12; MTCW 1
Bausch, Richard (Carl) 1945- .... **CLC 51**
See also AMWS 7; CA 101; 14; CANR 43, 61, 87; CN 7; CSW; DLB 130; MAL 5
Baxter, Charles 1947- .... **CLC 45, 78**
See also CA 57-60; CANR 40, 64, 104, 133; CPW; DAM POP; DLB 130; MAL 5; MTCW 2; MTFW 2005; TCLE 1:1
Baxter, George Owen
See Faust, Frederick (Schiller)
Baxter, James K(eir) 1926-1972 .... **CLC 14**
See also CA 77-80; CP 1; EWL 3
Baxter, John
See Hunt, E. Howard
Bayer, Sylvia
See Glassco, John
Bayle, Pierre 1647-1706 .... **LC 126**
See also DLB 268, 313; GFL Beginnings to 1789
Baynton, Barbara 1857-1929 .... **TCLC 57**
See also DLB 230; RGSF 2
Beagle, Peter S. 1939- .... **CLC 7, 104**
See also AAYA 47; BPFB 1; BYA 9, 10, 16; CA 9-12R; CANR 4, 51, 73, 110; DA3; DLBY 1980; FANT; INT CANR-4; MTCW 2; MTFW 2005; SATA 60, 130; SUFW 1, 2; YAW
Beagle, Peter Soyer
See Beagle, Peter S.
Bean, Normal
See Burroughs, Edgar Rice
Beard, Charles A(ustin)
1874-1948 .... **TCLC 15**
See also CA 189; CAAE 115; DLB 17; SATA 18
Beardsley, Aubrey 1872-1898 .... **NCLC 6**
Beattie, Ann 1947- ..... **CLC 8, 13, 18, 40, 63, 146; SSC 11**
See also AMWS 5; BEST 90:2; BPFB 1; CA 81-84; CANR 53, 73, 128; CN 4, 5, 6, 7; CPW; DA3; DAM NOV, POP; DLB 218, 278; DLBY 1982; EWL 3; MAL 5; MTCW 1, 2; MTFW 2005; RGAL 4; RGSF 2; SSFS 9; TUS
Beattie, James 1735-1803 .... **NCLC 25**
See also DLB 109
Beauchamp, Kathleen Mansfield 1888-1923
See Mansfield, Katherine
See also CA 134; CAAE 104; DA; DA3; DAC; DAM MST; MTCW 2; TEA
Beaumarchais, Pierre-Augustin Caron de
1732-1799 .... **DC 4; LC 61**
See also DAM DRAM; DFS 14, 16; DLB 313; EW 4; GFL Beginnings to 1789; RGWL 2, 3
Beaumont, Francis 1584(?)-1616 .. **DC 6; LC 33**
See also BRW 2; CDBLB Before 1660; DLB 58; TEA
Beauvoir, Simone de 1908-1986 .... **CLC 1, 2, 4, 8, 14, 31, 44, 50, 71, 124; SSC 35; WLC 1**
See also BPFB 1; CA 9-12R; CAAS 118; CANR 28, 61; DA; DA3; DAB; DAC; DAM MST, NOV; DLB 72; DLBY 1986; EW 12; EWL 3; FL 1:5; FW; GFL 1789 to the Present; LMFS 2; MTCW 1, 2; MTFW 2005; RGSF 2; RGWL 2, 3; TWA
Beauvoir, Simone Lucie Ernestine Marie Bertrand de
See Beauvoir, Simone de
Becker, Carl (Lotus) 1873-1945 ..... **TCLC 63**
See also CA 157; DLB 17

Bengtsson, Frans (Gunnar)
1894-1954 .... **TCLC 48**
See also CA 170; EWL 3
Benjamin, David
See Slavitt, David R(ytman)
Benjamin, Lois
See Gould, Lois
Benjamin, Walter 1892-1940 .... **TCLC 39**
See also CA 164; DLB 242; EW 11; EWL 3
Ben Jelloun, Tahar 1944-
See Jelloun, Tahar ben
See also CA 135; CWW 2; EWL 3; RGWL 3; WLIT 2
Benn, Gottfried 1886-1956 .. **PC 35; TCLC 3**
See also CA 153; CAAE 106; DLB 56; EWL 3; RGWL 2, 3
Bennett, Alan 1934- .... **CLC 45, 77**
See also BRWS 8; CA 103; CANR 35, 55, 106, 157; CBD; CD 5, 6; DAB; DAM MST; DLB 310; MTCW 1, 2; MTFW 2005
Bennett, (Enoch) Arnold
1867-1931 .... **TCLC 5, 20**
See also BRW 6; CA 155; CAAE 106; CD-BLB 1890-1914; DLB 10, 34, 98, 135; EWL 3; MTCW 2
Bennett, Elizabeth
See Mitchell, Margaret (Munnerlyn)
Bennett, George Harold 1930-
See Bennett, Hal
See also BW 1; CA 97-100; CANR 87
Bennett, Gwendolyn B. 1902-1981 .... **HR 1:2**
See also BW 1; CA 125; DLB 51; WP
Bennett, Hal CLC 5
See Bennett, George Harold
See also CA 13; DLB 33
Bennett, Jay 1912- .... **CLC 35**
See also AAYA 10, 73; CA 69-72; CANR 11, 42, 79; JRDA; SAAS 4; SATA 41, 87; SATA-Brief 27; WYA; YAW
Bennett, Louise 1919-2006 .. **BLC 1; CLC 28**
See also BW 2, 3; CA 151; CAAS 252; CD-WLB 3; CP 1, 2, 3, 4, 5, 6, 7; DAM MULT; DLB 117; EWL 3
Bennett, Louise Simone
See Bennett, Louise
Bennett-Coverley, Louise
See Bennett, Louise
Benoit de Sainte-Maure fl. 12th cent.
- .... **CMLC 90**
Benson, A. C. 1862-1925 .... **TCLC 123**
See also DLB 98
Benson, E(dward) F(rederic)
1867-1940 .... **TCLC 27**
See also CA 157; CAAE 114; DLB 135, 153; HGG; SUFW 1
Benson, Jackson J. 1930- .... **CLC 34**
See also CA 25-28R; DLB 111
Benson, Sally 1900-1972 .... **CLC 17**
See also CA 19-20; CAAS 37-40R; CAP 1; SATA 1, 35; SATA-Obit 27
Benson, Stella 1892-1933 .... **TCLC 17**
See also CA 154, 155; CAAE 117; DLB 36, 162; FANT; TEA
Bentham, Jeremy 1748-1832 .... **NCLC 38**
See also DLB 107, 158, 252
Bentley, E(dmund) C(lerihew)
1875-1956 .... **TCLC 12**
See also CA 232; CAAE 108; DLB 70; MSW
Bentley, Eric 1916- .... **CLC 24**
See also CA 5-8R; CAD; CANR 6, 67; CBD; CD 5, 6; INT CANR-6
Bentley, Eric Russell
See Bentley, Eric
ben Uzair, Salem
See Horne, Richard Henry Hengist

Beranger, Pierre Jean de
1780-1857 .... **NCLC 34**
Berdyaev, Nicolas
See Berdyaev, Nikolai (Aleksandrovich)
Berdyaev, Nikolai (Aleksandrovich)
1874-1948 .... **TCLC 67**
See also CA 157; CAAE 120
Berdyayev, Nikolai (Aleksandrovich)
See Berdyaev, Nikolai (Aleksandrovich)
Berendt, John 1939- .... **CLC 86**
See also CA 146; CANR 75, 83, 151
Berendt, John Lawrence
See Berendt, John
Beresford, J(ohn) D(avys)
1873-1947 .... **TCLC 81**
See also CA 155; CAAE 112; DLB 162, 178, 197; SFW 4; SUFW 1
Bergelson, David (Rafailovich)
1884-1952 .... **TCLC 81**
See Bergelson, Dovid
See also CA 220; DLB 333
Bergelson, Dovid
See Bergelson, David (Rafailovich)
See also EWL 3
Berger, Colonel
See Malraux, (Georges-)Andre
Berger, John (Peter) 1926- .... **CLC 2, 19**
See also BRWS 4; CA 81-84; CANR 51, 78, 117; CN 1, 2, 3, 4, 5, 6, 7; DLB 14, 207, 319, 326
Berger, Melvin H. 1927- .... **CLC 12**
See also CA 5-8R; CANR 4, 142; CLR 32; SAAS 2; SATA 5, 88, 158; SATA-Essay 124
Berger, Thomas 1924- .... **CLC 3, 5, 8, 11, 18, 38**
See also BPFB 1; CA 1-4R; CANR 5, 28, 51, 128; CN 1, 2, 3, 4, 5, 6, 7; DAM NOV; DLB 2; DLBY 1980; EWL 3; FANT; INT CANR-28; MAL 5; MTCW 1, 2; MTFW 2005; RHW; TCLE 1:1; TCWW 1, 2
Bergman, (Ernst) Ingmar 1918- ...... **CLC 16, 72, 210**
See also AAYA 61; CA 81-84; CANR 33, 70; CWW 2; DLB 257; MTCW 2; MTFW 2005
Bergson, Henri(-Louis) 1859-1941 . **TCLC 32**
See also CA 164; DLB 329; EW 8; EWL 3; GFL 1789 to the Present
Bergstein, Eleanor 1938- .... **CLC 4**
See also CA 53-56; CANR 5
Berkeley, George 1685-1753 .... **LC 65**
See also DLB 31, 101, 252
Berkoff, Steven 1937- .... **CLC 56**
See also CA 104; CANR 72; CBD; CD 5, 6
Berlin, Isaiah 1909-1997 .... **TCLC 105**
See also CA 85-88; CAAS 162
Bermant, Chaim (Icyk) 1929-1998 ... **CLC 40**
See also CA 57-60; CANR 6, 31, 57, 105; CN 2, 3, 4, 5, 6
Bern, Victoria
See Fisher, M(ary) F(rances) K(ennedy)
Bernanos, (Paul Louis) Georges
1888-1948 .... **TCLC 3**
See also CA 130; CAAE 104; CANR 94; DLB 72; EWL 3; GFL 1789 to the Present; RGWL 2, 3
Bernard, April 1956- .... **CLC 59**
See also CA 131; CANR 144
Bernard, Mary Ann
See Soderbergh, Steven
Bernard of Clairvaux 1090-1153 .. **CMLC 71**
See also DLB 208
Bernard Silvestris fl. c. 1130-fl. c. 1160 .... **CMLC 87**
See also DLB 208
Berne, Victoria
See Fisher, M(ary) F(rances) K(ennedy)

Bernhard, Thomas 1931-1989 ..... **CLC 3, 32, 61; DC 14; TCLC 165**
See also CA 85-88; CAAS 127; CANR 32, 57; CDWLB 2; DLB 85, 124; EWL 3; MTCW 1; RGHL; RGWL 2, 3
Bernhardt, Sarah (Henriette Rosine)
1844-1923 .... **TCLC 75**
See also CA 157
Bernstein, Charles 1950- .... **CLC 142**
See also CA 129; 24; CANR 90; CP 4, 5, 6, 7; DLB 169
Bernstein, Ingrid
See Kirsch, Sarah
Beroul fl. c. 12th cent. - .... **CMLC 75**
Berriault, Gina 1926-1999 .... **CLC 54, 109; SSC 30**
See also CA 129; CAAE 116; CAAS 185; CANR 66; DLB 130; SSFS 7,11
Berrigan, Daniel 1921- .... **CLC 4**
See also CA 187; 33-36R, 187; 1; CANR 11, 43, 78; CP 1, 2, 3, 4, 5, 6, 7; DLB 5
Berrigan, Edmund Joseph Michael, Jr.
1934-1983
See Berrigan, Ted
See also CA 61-64; CAAS 110; CANR 14, 102
Berrigan, Ted CLC 37
See Berrigan, Edmund Joseph Michael, Jr.
See also CP 1, 2, 3; DLB 5, 169; WP
Berry, Charles Edward Anderson 1931-
See Berry, Chuck
See also CA 115
Berry, Chuck CLC 17
See Berry, Charles Edward Anderson
Berry, Jonas
See Ashbery, John
See also GLL 1
Berry, Wendell 1934- .... **CLC 4, 6, 8, 27, 46; PC 28**
See also AITN 1; AMWS 10; ANW; CA 73-76; CANR 50, 73, 101, 132; CP 1, 2, 3, 4, 5, 6, 7; CSW; DAM POET; DLB 5, 6, 234, 275; MTCW 2; MTFW 2005; TCLE 1:1
Berryman, John 1914-1972 ... **CLC 1, 2, 3, 4, 6, 8, 10, 13, 25, 62; PC 64**
See also AMW; CA 13-16; CAAS 33-36R; CABS 2; CANR 35; CAP 1; CDALB 1941-1968; CP 1; DAM POET; DLB 48; EWL 3; MAL 5; MTCW 1, 2; MTFW 2005; PAB; RGAL 4; WP
Bertolucci, Bernardo 1940- ...... **CLC 16, 157**
See also CA 106; CANR 125
Berton, Pierre (Francis de Marigny)
1920-2004 .... **CLC 104**
See also CA 1-4R; CAAS 233; CANR 2, 56, 144; CPW; DLB 68; SATA 99; SATA-Obit 158
Bertrand, Aloysius 1807-1841 .... **NCLC 31**
See Bertrand, Louis oAloysiusc
Bertrand, Louis oAloysiusc
See Bertrand, Aloysius
See also DLB 217
Bertran de Born c. 1140-1215 .... **CMLC 5**
Besant, Annie (Wood) 1847-1933 ..... **TCLC 9**
See also CA 185; CAAE 105
Bessie, Alvah 1904-1985 .... **CLC 23**
See also CA 5-8R; CAAS 116; CANR 2, 80; DLB 26
Bestuzhev, Aleksandr Aleksandrovich
1797-1837 .... **NCLC 131**
See also DLB 198
Bethlen, T. D.
See Silverberg, Robert
Beti, Mongo BLC 1; CLC 27
See Biyidi, Alexandre
See also AFW; CANR 79; DAM MULT; EWL 3; WLIT 2

Bulwer-Lytton, Edward (George Earle Lytton) 1803-1873 .... NCLC 1, 45
See also DLB 21; RGEL 2; SFW 4; SUFW 1; TEA

Bunin, Ivan
See Bunin, Ivan Alexeyevich

Bunin, Ivan Alekseevich
See Bunin, Ivan Alexeyevich

Bunin, Ivan Alexeyevich 1870-1953 ... SSC 5; TCLC 6
See also CAAE 104; DLB 317, 329; EWL 3; RGSF 2; RGWL 2, 3; TWA

Bunting, Basil 1900-1985 ...... CLC 10, 39, 47
See also BRWS 7; CA 53-56; CAAS 115; CANR 7; CP 1, 2, 3, 4; DAM POET; DLB 20; EWL 3; RGEL 2

Bunuel, Luis 1900-1983 ... CLC 16, 80; HLC 1
See also CA 101; CAAS 110; CANR 32, 77; DAM MULT; HW 1

Bunyan, John 1628-1688 .. LC 4, 69; WLC 1
See also BRW 2; BYA 5; CDBLB 1660-1789; DA; DAB; DAC; DAM MST; DLB 39; RGEL 2; TEA; WCH; WLIT 3

Buravsky, Alexandr CLC 59

Burckhardt, Jacob (Christoph) 1818-1897 .... NCLC 49
See also EW 6

Burford, Eleanor
See Hibbert, Eleanor Alice Burford

Burgess, Anthony CLC 1, 2, 4, 5, 8, 10, 13, 15, 22, 40, 62, 81, 94
See Wilson, John (Anthony) Burgess
See also AAYA 25; AITN 1; BRWS 1; CD-BLB 1960 to Present; CN 1, 2, 3, 4, 5; DAB; DLB 14, 194, 261; DLBY 1998; EWL 3; RGEL 2; RHW; SFW 4; YAW

Burke, Edmund 1729(?)-1797 .... LC 7, 36; WLC 1
See also BRW 3; DA; DA3; DAB; DAC; DAM MST; DLB 104, 252; RGEL 2; TEA

Burke, Kenneth (Duva) 1897-1993 ... CLC 2, 24
See also AMW; CA 5-8R; CAAS 143; CANR 39, 74, 136; CN 1, 2; CP 1, 2, 3, 4, 5; DLB 45, 63; EWL 3; MAL 5; MTCW 1, 2; MTFW 2005; RGAL 4

Burke, Leda
See Garnett, David

Burke, Ralph
See Silverberg, Robert

Burke, Thomas 1886-1945 .... TCLC 63
See also CA 155; CAAE 113; CMW 4; DLB 197

Burney, Fanny 1752-1840 .... NCLC 12, 54, 107
See also BRWS 3; DLB 39; FL 1:2; NFS 16; RGEL 2; TEA

Burney, Frances
See Burney, Fanny

Burns, Robert 1759-1796 ... LC 3, 29, 40; PC 6; WLC 1
See also AAYA 51; BRW 3; CDBLB 1789-1832; DA; DA3; DAB; DAC; DAM MST, POET; DLB 109; EXPP; PAB; RGEL 2; TEA; WP

Burns, Tex
See L'Amour, Louis

Burnshaw, Stanley 1906-2005 ..... CLC 3, 13, 44
See also CA 9-12R; CAAS 243; CP 1, 2, 3, 4, 5, 6, 7; DLB 48; DLBY 1997

Burr, Anne 1937- .... CLC 6
See also CA 25-28R

Burroughs, Edgar Rice 1875-1950 . TCLC 2, 32
See also AAYA 11; BPFB 1; BYA 4, 9; CA 132; CAAE 104; CANR 131; DA3; DAM NOV; DLB 8; FANT; MTCW 1, 2; MTFW 2005; RGAL 4; SATA 41; SCFW 1, 2; SFW 4; TCWW 1, 2; TUS; YAW

Burroughs, William S. 1914-1997 . CLC 1, 2, 5, 15, 22, 42, 75, 109; TCLC 121; WLC 1
See Lee, William; Lee, Willy
See also AAYA 60; AITN 2; AMWS 3; BG 1:2; BPFB 1; CA 9-12R; CAAS 160; CANR 20, 52, 104; CN 1, 2, 3, 4, 5, 6; CPW; DA; DA3; DAB; DAC; DAM MST, NOV, POP; DLB 2, 8, 16, 152, 237; DLBY 1981, 1997; EWL 3; HGG; LMFS 2; MAL 5; MTCW 1, 2; MTFW 2005; RGAL 4; SFW 4

Burroughs, William Seward
See Burroughs, William S.

Burton, Sir Richard F(rancis) 1821-1890 .... NCLC 42
See also DLB 55, 166, 184; SSFS 21

Burton, Robert 1577-1640 .... LC 74
See also DLB 151; RGEL 2

Buruma, Ian 1951- .... CLC 163
See also CA 128; CANR 65, 141

Busch, Frederick 1941-2006 .. CLC 7, 10, 18, 47, 166
See also CA 33-36R; 1; CAAS 248; CANR 45, 73, 92, 157; CN 1, 2, 3, 4, 5, 6, 7; DLB 6, 218

Busch, Frederick Matthew
See Busch, Frederick

Bush, Barney (Furman) 1946- .... NNAL
See also CA 145

Bush, Ronald 1946- .... CLC 34
See also CA 136

Bustos, F(rancisco)
See Borges, Jorge Luis

Bustos Domecq, H(onorio)
See Bioy Casares, Adolfo; Borges, Jorge Luis

Butler, Octavia E. 1947-2006 .... BLCS; CLC 38, 121, 230
See also AAYA 18, 48; AFAW 2; AMWS 13; BPFB 1; BW 2, 3; CA 73-76; CAAS 248; CANR 12, 24, 38, 73, 145; CLR 65; CN 7; CPW; DA3; DAM MULT, POP; DLB 33; LATS 1:2; MTCW 1, 2; MTFW 2005; NFS 8, 21; SATA 84; SCFW 2; SFW 4; SSFS 6; TCLE 1:1; YAW

Butler, Octavia Estelle
See Butler, Octavia E.

Butler, Robert Olen, (Jr.) 1945- ...... CLC 81, 162
See also AMWS 12; BPFB 1; CA 112; CANR 66, 138; CN 7; CSW; DAM POP; DLB 173; INT CA-112; MAL 5; MTCW 2; MTFW 2005; SSFS 11, 22

Butler, Samuel 1612-1680 .... LC 16, 43
See also DLB 101, 126; RGEL 2

Butler, Samuel 1835-1902 .... TCLC 1, 33; WLC 1
See also BRWS 2; CA 143; CDBLB 1890-1914; DA; DA3; DAB; DAC; DAM MST, NOV; DLB 18, 57, 174; RGEL 2; SFW 4; TEA

Butler, Walter C.
See Faust, Frederick (Schiller)

Butor, Michel (Marie Francois) 1926- .... CLC 1, 3, 8, 11, 15, 161
See also CA 9-12R; CANR 33, 66; CWW 2; DLB 83; EW 13; EWL 3; GFL 1789 to the Present; MTCW 1, 2; MTFW 2005

Butts, Mary 1890(?)-1937 .... TCLC 77
See also CA 148; DLB 240

Buxton, Ralph
See Silverstein, Alvin; Silverstein, Virginia B(arbara Opshelor)

Buzo, Alex
See Buzo, Alexander (John)
See also DLB 289

Buzo, Alexander (John) 1944- .... CLC 61
See also CA 97-100; CANR 17, 39, 69; CD 5, 6

Buzzati, Dino 1906-1972 .... CLC 36
See also CA 160; CAAS 33-36R; DLB 177; RGWL 2, 3; SFW 4

Byars, Betsy 1928- .... CLC 35
See also AAYA 19; BYA 3; CA 183; 33-36R, 183; CANR 18, 36, 57, 102, 148; CLR 1, 16, 72; DLB 52; INT CANR-18; JRDA; MAICYA 1, 2; MAICYAS 1; MTCW 1; SAAS 1; SATA 4, 46, 80, 163; SATA-Essay 108; WYA; YAW

Byars, Betsy Cromer
See Byars, Betsy

Byatt, Antonia Susan Drabble
See Byatt, A.S.

Byatt, A.S. 1936- .... CLC 19, 65, 136, 223; SSC 91
See also BPFB 1; BRWC 2; BRWS 4; CA 13-16R; CANR 13, 33, 50, 75, 96, 133; CN 1, 2, 3, 4, 5, 6; DA3; DAM NOV, POP; DLB 14, 194, 319, 326; EWL 3; MTCW 1, 2; MTFW 2005; RGSF 2; RHW; TEA

Byrd, William II 1674-1744 .... LC 112
See also DLB 24, 140; RGAL 4

Byrne, David 1952- .... CLC 26
See also CA 127

Byrne, John Keyes 1926-
See Leonard, Hugh
See also CA 102; CANR 78, 140; INT CA-102

Byron, George Gordon (Noel) 1788-1824 ..... DC 24; NCLC 2, 12, 109, 149; PC 16; WLC 1
See also AAYA 64; BRW 4; BRWC 2; CD-BLB 1789-1832; DA; DA3; DAB; DAC; DAM MST, POET; DLB 96, 110; EXPP; LMFS 1; PAB; PFS 1, 14; RGEL 2; TEA; WLIT 3; WP

Byron, Robert 1905-1941 .... TCLC 67
See also CA 160; DLB 195

C. 3. 3.
See Wilde, Oscar (Fingal O'Flahertie Wills)

Caballero, Fernan 1796-1877 .... NCLC 10

Cabell, Branch
See Cabell, James Branch

Cabell, James Branch 1879-1958 .... TCLC 6
See also CA 152; CAAE 105; DLB 9, 78; FANT; MAL 5; MTCW 2; RGAL 4; SUFW 1

Cabeza de Vaca, Alvar Nunez 1490-1557(?) .... LC 61

Cable, George Washington 1844-1925 .... SSC 4; TCLC 4
See also CA 155; CAAE 104; DLB 12, 74; DLBD 13; RGAL 4; TUS

Cabral de Melo Neto, Joao 1920-1999 .... CLC 76
See Melo Neto, Joao Cabral de
See also CA 151; DAM MULT; DLB 307; LAW; LAWS 1

Cabrera Infante, G. 1929-2005 ... CLC 5, 25, 45, 120; HLC 1; SSC 39
See also CA 85-88; CAAS 236; CANR 29, 65, 110; CDWLB 3; CWW 2; DA3; DAM MULT; DLB 113; EWL 3; HW 1, 2; LAW; MTCW 1, 2; MTFW 2005; RGSF 2; WLIT 1

Cabrera Infante, Guillermo
See Cabrera Infante, G.

Cade, Toni
See Bambara, Toni Cade

Cadmus and Harmonia
See Buchan, John

Caedmon fl. 658-680 .... **CMLC 7**
See also DLB 146

Caeiro, Alberto
See Pessoa, Fernando (Antonio Nogueira)

Caesar, Julius CMLC 47
See Julius Caesar
See also AW 1; RGWL 2, 3; WLIT 8

Cage, John (Milton), (Jr.)
1912-1992 .... **CLC 41; PC 58**
See also CA 13-16R; CAAS 169; CANR 9,
78; DLB 193; INT CANR-9; TCLE 1:1

Cahan, Abraham 1860-1951 .... **TCLC 71**
See also CA 154; CAAE 108; DLB 9, 25,
28; MAL 5; RGAL 4

Cain, G.
See Cabrera Infante, G.

Cain, Guillermo
See Cabrera Infante, G.

Cain, James M(allahan) 1892-1977 .. **CLC 3,
11, 28**
See also AITN 1; BPFB 1; CA 17-20R;
CANR 8, 34, 61; CMW 4;
CN 1, 2; DLB 226; EWL 3; MAL 5;
MSW; MTCW 1; RGAL 4

Caine, Hall 1853-1931 .... **TCLC 97**
See also RHW

Caine, Mark
See Raphael, Frederic (Michael)

Calasso, Roberto 1941- .... **CLC 81**
See also CA 143; CANR 89

Calderon de la Barca, Pedro
1600-1681 . **DC 3; HLCS 1; LC 23, 136**
See also DFS 23; EW 2; RGWL 2, 3; TWA

Caldwell, Erskine 1903-1987 ... **CLC 1, 8, 14,
50, 60; SSC 19; TCLC 117**
See also AITN 1; AMW; BPFB 1; CA 1-4R;
1; CAAS 121; CANR 2, 33; CN 1, 2, 3,
4; DA3; DAM NOV; DLB 9, 86; EWL 3;
MAL 5; MTCW 1, 2; MTFW 2005;
RGAL 4; RGSF 2; TUS

Caldwell, (Janet Miriam) Taylor (Holland)
1900-1985 .... **CLC 2, 28, 39**
See also BPFB 1; CA 5-8R; CAAS 116;
CANR 5; DA3; DAM NOV, POP; DLBD
17; MTCW 2; RHW

Calhoun, John Caldwell
1782-1850 .... **NCLC 15**
See also DLB 3, 248

Calisher, Hortense 1911- ..... **CLC 2, 4, 8, 38,
134; SSC 15**
See also CA 1-4R; CANR 1, 22, 117; CN
1, 2, 3, 4, 5, 6, 7; DA3; DAM NOV; DLB
2, 218; INT CANR-22; MAL 5; MTCW
1, 2; MTFW 2005; RGAL 4; RGSF 2

Callaghan, Morley Edward
1903-1990 ..... **CLC 3, 14, 41, 65; TCLC
145**
See also CA 9-12R; CAAS 132; CANR 33,
73; CN 1, 2, 3, 4; DAC; DAM MST; DLB
68; EWL 3; MTCW 1, 2; MTFW 2005;
RGEL 2; RGSF 2; SSFS 19

Callimachus c. 305B.C.-c.
240B.C. .... **CMLC 18**
See also AW 1; DLB 176; RGWL 2, 3

Calvin, Jean
See Calvin, John
See also DLB 327; GFL Beginnings to 1789

Calvin, John 1509-1564 .... **LC 37**
See Calvin, Jean

Calvino, Italo 1923-1985 .... **CLC 5, 8, 11, 22,
33, 39, 73; SSC 3, 48; TCLC 183**
See also AAYA 58; CA 85-88; CAAS 116;
CANR 23, 61, 132; DAM NOV; DLB
196; EW 13; EWL 3; MTCW 1, 2; MTFW
2005; RGHL; RGSF 2; RGWL 2, 3; SFW
4; SSFS 12; WLIT 7

Camara Laye
See Laye, Camara
See also EWL 3

Camden, William 1551-1623 .... **LC 77**
See also DLB 172

Cameron, Carey 1952- .... **CLC 59**
See also CA 135

Cameron, Peter 1959- .... **CLC 44**
See also AMWS 12; CA 125; CANR 50,
117; DLB 234; GLL 2

Camoens, Luis Vaz de 1524(?)-1580
See Camoes, Luis de
See also EW 2

Camoes, Luis de 1524(?)-1580 . **HLCS 1; LC
62; PC 31**
See Camoens, Luis Vaz de
See also DLB 287; RGWL 2, 3

Campana, Dino 1885-1932 .... **TCLC 20**
See also CA 246; CAAE 117; DLB 114;
EWL 3

Campanella, Tommaso 1568-1639 .... **LC 32**
See also RGWL 2, 3

Campbell, John W(ood, Jr.)
1910-1971 .... **CLC 32**
See also CA 21-22; CAAS 29-32R; CANR
34; CAP 2; DLB 8; MTCW 1; SCFW 1,
2; SFW 4

Campbell, Joseph 1904-1987 .... **CLC 69;
TCLC 140**
See also AAYA 3, 66; BEST 89:2; CA 1-4R;
CAAS 124; CANR 3, 28, 61, 107; DA3;
MTCW 1, 2

Campbell, Maria 1940- .... **CLC 85; NNAL**
See also CA 102; CANR 54; CCA 1; DAC

Campbell, (John) Ramsey 1946- ..... **CLC 42;
SSC 19**
See also AAYA 51; CA 228; 57-60, 228;
CANR 7, 102; DLB 261; HGG; INT
CANR-7; SUFW 1, 2

Campbell, (Ignatius) Roy (Dunnachie)
1901-1957 .... **TCLC 5**
See also AFW; CA 155; CAAE 104; DLB
20, 225; EWL 3; MTCW 2; RGEL 2

Campbell, Thomas 1777-1844 .... **NCLC 19**
See also DLB 93, 144; RGEL 2

Campbell, Wilfred TCLC 9
See Campbell, William

Campbell, William 1858(?)-1918
See Campbell, Wilfred
See also CAAE 106; DLB 92

Campbell, William Edward March
1893-1954
See March, William
See also CAAE 108

Campion, Jane 1954- .... **CLC 95, 229**
See also AAYA 33; CA 138; CANR 87

Campion, Thomas 1567-1620 .... **LC 78**
See also CDBLB Before 1660; DAM POET;
DLB 58, 172; RGEL 2

Camus, Albert 1913-1960 ...... **CLC 1, 2, 4, 9,
11, 14, 32, 63, 69, 124; DC 2; SSC 9,
76; WLC 1**
See also AAYA 36; AFW; BPFB 1; CA 89-
92; CANR 131; DA; DA3; DAB; DAC;
DAM DRAM, MST, NOV; DLB 72, 321,
329; EW 13; EWL 3; EXPN; EXPS; GFL
1789 to the Present; LATS 1:2; LMFS 2;
MTCW 1, 2; MTFW 2005; NFS 6, 16;
RGHL; RGSF 2; RGWL 2, 3; SSFS 4;
TWA

Canby, Vincent 1924-2000 .... **CLC 13**
See also CA 81-84; CAAS 191

Cancale
See Desnos, Robert

Canetti, Elias 1905-1994 .. **CLC 3, 14, 25, 75,
86; TCLC 157**
See also CA 21-24R; CAAS 146; CANR
23, 61, 79; CDWLB 2; CWW 2; DA3;
DLB 85, 124, 329; EW 12; EWL 3;
MTCW 1, 2; MTFW 2005; RGWL 2, 3;
TWA

Canfield, Dorothea F.
See Fisher, Dorothy (Frances) Canfield

Canfield, Dorothea Frances
See Fisher, Dorothy (Frances) Canfield

Canfield, Dorothy
See Fisher, Dorothy (Frances) Canfield

Canin, Ethan 1960- .... **CLC 55; SSC 70**
See also CA 135; CAAE 131; MAL 5

Cankar, Ivan 1876-1918 .... **TCLC 105**
See also CDWLB 4; DLB 147; EWL 3

Cannon, Curt
See Hunter, Evan

Cao, Lan 1961- .... **CLC 109**
See also CA 165

Cape, Judith
See Page, P(atricia) K(athleen)
See also CCA 1

Capek, Karel 1890-1938 .... **DC 1; SSC 36;
TCLC 6, 37; WLC 1**
See also CA 140; CAAE 104; CDWLB 4;
DA; DA3; DAB; DAC; DAM DRAM,
MST, NOV; DFS 7, 11; DLB 215; EW
10; EWL 3; MTCW 2; MTFW 2005;
RGSF 2; RGWL 2, 3; SCFW 1, 2; SFW 4

Capella, Martianus fl. 4th cent. - .. **CMLC 84**

Capote, Truman 1924-1984 . **CLC 1, 3, 8, 13,
19, 34, 38, 58; SSC 2, 47, 93; TCLC
164; WLC 1**
See also AAYA 61; AMWS 3; BPFB 1; CA
5-8R; CAAS 113; CANR 18, 62; CDALB
1941-1968; CN 1, 2, 3; CPW; DA; DA3;
DAB; DAC; DAM MST, NOV, POP;
DLB 2, 185, 227; DLBY 1980, 1984;
EWL 3; EXPS; GLL 1; LAIT 3; MAL 5;
MTCW 1, 2; MTFW 2005; NCFS 2;
RGAL 4; RGSF 2; SATA 91; SSFS 2;
TUS

Capra, Frank 1897-1991 .... **CLC 16**
See also AAYA 52; CA 61-64; CAAS 135

Caputo, Philip 1941- .... **CLC 32**
See also AAYA 60; CA 73-76; CANR 40,
135; YAW

Caragiale, Ion Luca 1852-1912 ...... **TCLC 76**
See also CA 157

Card, Orson Scott 1951- .... **CLC 44, 47, 50**
See also AAYA 11, 42; BPFB 1; BYA 5, 8;
CA 102; CANR 27, 47, 73, 102, 106, 133;
CLR 116; CPW; DA3; DAM POP; FANT;
INT CANR-27; MTCW 1, 2; MTFW
2005; NFS 5; SATA 83, 127; SCFW 2;
SFW 4; SUFW 2; YAW

Cardenal, Ernesto 1925- .... **CLC 31, 161;
HLC 1; PC 22**
See also CA 49-52; CANR 2, 32, 66, 138;
CWW 2; DAM MULT, POET; DLB 290;
EWL 3; HW 1, 2; LAWS 1; MTCW 1, 2;
MTFW 2005; RGWL 2, 3

Cardinal, Marie 1929-2001 .... **CLC 189**
See also CA 177; CWW 2; DLB 83; FW

Cardozo, Benjamin N(athan)
1870-1938 .... **TCLC 65**
See also CA 164; CAAE 117

Carducci, Giosue (Alessandro Giuseppe)
1835-1907 .... **PC 46; TCLC 32**
See also CA 163; DLB 329; EW 7; RGWL
2, 3

Carew, Thomas 1595(?)-1640 . **LC 13; PC 29**
See also BRW 2; DLB 126; PAB; RGEL 2

Carey, Ernestine Gilbreth
1908-2006 .... **CLC 17**
See also CA 5-8R; CAAS 254; CANR 71;
SATA 2

Carey, Peter 1943- .... **CLC 40, 55, 96, 183**
See also BRWS 12; CA 127; CAAE 123;
CANR 53, 76, 117, 157; CN 4, 5, 6, 7;
DLB 289, 326; EWL 3; INT CA-127;
MTCW 1, 2; MTFW 2005; RGSF 2;
SATA 94

Ciardi, John (Anthony) 1916-1986 . **CLC 10, 40, 44, 129; PC 69**
See also CA 5-8R; 2; CAAS 118; CANR 5, 33; CLR 19; CP 1, 2, 3, 4; CWRI 5; DAM POET; DLB 5; DLBY 1986; INT CANR-5; MAICYA 1, 2; MAL 5; MTCW 1, 2; MTFW 2005; RGAL 4; SAAS 26; SATA 1, 65; SATA-Obit 46

Cibber, Colley 1671-1757 .... **LC 66**
See also DLB 84; RGEL 2

Cicero, Marcus Tullius
106B.C.-43B.C. .... **CMLC 3, 81**
See also AW 1; CDWLB 1; DLB 211; RGWL 2, 3; WLIT 8

Cimino, Michael 1943- .... **CLC 16**
See also CA 105

Cioran, E(mil) M. 1911-1995 .... **CLC 64**
See also CA 25-28R; CAAS 149; CANR 91; DLB 220; EWL 3

Cisneros, Sandra 1954- .... **CLC 69, 118, 193; HLC 1; PC 52; SSC 32, 72**
See also AAYA 9, 53; AMWS 7; CA 131; CANR 64, 118; CN 7; CWP; DA3; DAM MULT; DLB 122, 152; EWL 3; EXPN; FL 1:5; FW; HW 1, 2; LAIT 5; LATS 1:2; LLW; MAICYA 2; MAL 5; MTCW 2; MTFW 2005; NFS 2; PFS 19; RGAL 4; RGSF 2; SSFS 3, 13; WLIT 1; YAW

Cixous, Helene 1937- .... **CLC 92**
See also CA 126; CANR 55, 123; CWW 2; DLB 83, 242; EWL 3; FL 1:5; FW; GLL 2; MTCW 1, 2; MTFW 2005; TWA

Clair, Rene CLC 20
See Chomette, Rene Lucien

Clampitt, Amy 1920-1994 .... **CLC 32; PC 19**
See also AMWS 9; CA 110; CAAS 146; CANR 29, 79; CP 4, 5; DLB 105; MAL 5

Clancy, Thomas L., Jr. 1947-
See Clancy, Tom
See also CA 131; CAAE 125; CANR 62, 105; DA3; INT CA-131; MTCW 1, 2; MTFW 2005

Clancy, Tom CLC 45, 112
See Clancy, Thomas L., Jr.
See also AAYA 9, 51; BEST 89:1, 90:1; BPFB 1; BYA 10, 11; CANR 132; CMW 4; CPW; DAM NOV, POP; DLB 227

Clare, John 1793-1864 .. **NCLC 9, 86; PC 23**
See also BRWS 11; DAB; DAM POET; DLB 55, 96; RGEL 2

Clarin
See Alas (y Urena), Leopoldo (Enrique Garcia)

Clark, Al C.
See Goines, Donald

Clark, Brian (Robert)
See Clark, (Robert) Brian
See also CD 6

Clark, (Robert) Brian 1932- .... **CLC 29**
See Clark, Brian (Robert)
See also CA 41-44R; CANR 67; CBD; CD 5

Clark, Curt
See Westlake, Donald E.

Clark, Eleanor 1913-1996 .... **CLC 5, 19**
See also CA 9-12R; CAAS 151; CANR 41; CN 1, 2, 3, 4, 5, 6; DLB 6

Clark, J. P.
See Clark Bekederemo, J.P.
See also CDWLB 3; DLB 117

Clark, John Pepper
See Clark Bekederemo, J.P.
See also AFW; CD 5; CP 1, 2, 3, 4, 5, 6, 7; RGEL 2

Clark, Kenneth (Mackenzie)
1903-1983 .... **TCLC 147**
See also CA 93-96; CAAS 109; CANR 36; MTCW 1, 2; MTFW 2005

Clark, M. R.
See Clark, Mavis Thorpe

Clark, Mavis Thorpe 1909-1999 ...... **CLC 12**
See also CA 57-60; CANR 8, 37, 107; CLR 30; CWRI 5; MAICYA 1, 2; SAAS 5; SATA 8, 74

Clark, Walter Van Tilburg
1909-1971 .... **CLC 28**
See also CA 9-12R; CAAS 33-36R; CANR 63, 113; CN 1; DLB 9, 206; LAIT 2; MAL 5; RGAL 4; SATA 8; TCWW 1, 2

Clark Bekederemo, J.P. 1935- . **BLC 1; CLC 38; DC 5**
See Bekederemo, J. P. Clark; Clark, J. P.; Clark, John Pepper
See also BW 1; CA 65-68; CANR 16, 72; DAM DRAM, MULT; DFS 13; EWL 3; MTCW 2; MTFW 2005

Clarke, Arthur C. 1917- .... **CLC 1, 4, 13, 18, 35, 136; SSC 3**
See also AAYA 4, 33; BPFB 1; BYA 13; CA 1-4R; CANR 2, 28, 55, 74, 130; CLR 119; CN 1, 2, 3, 4, 5, 6, 7; CPW; DA3; DAM POP; DLB 261; JRDA; LAIT 5; MAICYA 1, 2; MTCW 1, 2; MTFW 2005; SATA 13, 70, 115; SCFW 1, 2; SFW 4; SSFS 4, 18; TCLE 1:1; YAW

Clarke, Austin 1896-1974 .... **CLC 6, 9**
See also CA 29-32; CAAS 49-52; CAP 2; CP 1, 2; DAM POET; DLB 10, 20; EWL 3; RGEL 2

Clarke, Austin C. 1934- . **BLC 1; CLC 8, 53; SSC 45**
See also BW 1; CA 25-28R; 16; CANR 14, 32, 68, 140; CN 1, 2, 3, 4, 5, 6, 7; DAC; DAM MULT; DLB 53, 125; DNFS 2; MTCW 2; MTFW 2005; RGSF 2

Clarke, Gillian 1937- .... **CLC 61**
See also CA 106; CP 3, 4, 5, 6, 7; CWP; DLB 40

Clarke, Marcus (Andrew Hislop)
1846-1881 .... **NCLC 19; SSC 94**
See also DLB 230; RGEL 2; RGSF 2

Clarke, Shirley 1925-1997 .... **CLC 16**
See also CA 189

Clash, The
See Headon, (Nicky) Topper; Jones, Mick; Simonon, Paul; Strummer, Joe

Claudel, Paul (Louis Charles Marie)
1868-1955 .... **TCLC 2, 10**
See also CA 165; CAAE 104; DLB 192, 258, 321; EW 8; EWL 3; GFL 1789 to the Present; RGWL 2, 3; TWA

Claudian 370(?)-404(?) .... **CMLC 46**
See also RGWL 2, 3

Claudius, Matthias 1740-1815 .... **NCLC 75**
See also DLB 97

Clavell, James 1925-1994 .... **CLC 6, 25, 87**
See also BPFB 1; CA 25-28R; CAAS 146; CANR 26, 48; CN 5; CPW; DA3; DAM NOV, POP; MTCW 1, 2; MTFW 2005; NFS 10; RHW

Clayman, Gregory CLC 65

Cleaver, (Leroy) Eldridge
1935-1998 .... **BLC 1; CLC 30, 119**
See also BW 1, 3; CA 21-24R; CAAS 167; CANR 16, 75; DA3; DAM MULT; MTCW 2; YAW

Cleese, John (Marwood) 1939- .... **CLC 21**
See Monty Python
See also CA 116; CAAE 112; CANR 35; MTCW 1

Cleishbotham, Jebediah
See Scott, Sir Walter

Cleland, John 1710-1789 .... **LC 2, 48**
See also DLB 39; RGEL 2

Clemens, Samuel Langhorne 1835-1910
See Twain, Mark
See also CA 135; CAAE 104; CDALB 1865-1917; DA; DA3; DAB; DAC; DAM MST, NOV; DLB 12, 23, 64, 74, 186, 189; JRDA; LMFS 1; MAICYA 1, 2; NCFS 4; NFS 20; SATA 100; YABC 2

Clement of Alexandria
150(?)-215(?) .... **CMLC 41**

Cleophil
See Congreve, William

Clerihew, E.
See Bentley, E(dmund) C(lerihew)

Clerk, N. W.
See Lewis, C.S.

Cleveland, John 1613-1658 .... **LC 106**
See also DLB 126; RGEL 2

Cliff, Jimmy CLC 21
See Chambers, James
See also CA 193

Cliff, Michelle 1946- .... **BLCS; CLC 120**
See also BW 2; CA 116; CANR 39, 72; CD-WLB 3; DLB 157; FW; GLL 2

Clifford, Lady Anne 1590-1676 .... **LC 76**
See also DLB 151

Clifton, Lucille 1936- ... **BLC 1; CLC 19, 66, 162; PC 17**
See also AFAW 2; BW 2, 3; CA 49-52; CANR 2, 24, 42, 76, 97, 138; CLR 5; CP 2, 3, 4, 5, 6, 7; CSW; CWP; CWRI 5; DA3; DAM MULT, POET; DLB 5, 41; EXPP; MAICYA 1, 2; MTCW 1, 2; MTFW 2005; PFS 1, 14; SATA 20, 69, 128; WP

Clinton, Dirk
See Silverberg, Robert

Clough, Arthur Hugh 1819-1861 .. **NCLC 27, 163**
See also BRW 5; DLB 32; RGEL 2

Clutha, Janet Paterson Frame 1924-2004
See Frame, Janet
See also CA 1-4R; CAAS 224; CANR 2, 36, 76, 135; MTCW 1, 2; SATA 119

Clyne, Terence
See Blatty, William Peter

Cobalt, Martin
See Mayne, William (James Carter)

Cobb, Irvin S(hrewsbury)
1876-1944 .... **TCLC 77**
See also CA 175; DLB 11, 25, 86

Cobbett, William 1763-1835 .... **NCLC 49**
See also DLB 43, 107, 158; RGEL 2

Coburn, D(onald) L(ee) 1938- .... **CLC 10**
See also CA 89-92; DFS 23

Cocteau, Jean 1889-1963 ... **CLC 1, 8, 15, 16, 43; DC 17; TCLC 119; WLC 2**
See also AAYA 74; CA 25-28; CANR 40; CAP 2; DA; DA3; DAB; DAC; DAM DRAM, MST, NOV; DLB 65, 258, 321; EW 10; EWL 3; GFL 1789 to the Present; MTCW 1, 2; RGWL 2, 3; TWA

Cocteau, Jean Maurice Eugene Clement
See Cocteau, Jean

Codrescu, Andrei 1946- .... **CLC 46, 121**
See also CA 33-36R; 19; CANR 13, 34, 53, 76, 125; CN 7; DA3; DAM POET; MAL 5; MTCW 2; MTFW 2005

Coe, Max
See Bourne, Randolph S(illiman)

Coe, Tucker
See Westlake, Donald E.

Coen, Ethan 1958- .... **CLC 108**
See also AAYA 54; CA 126; CANR 85

Coen, Joel 1955- .... **CLC 108**
See also AAYA 54; CA 126; CANR 119

The Coen Brothers
See Coen, Ethan; Coen, Joel

Cook, Robin 1940- .... CLC 14
    See also AAYA 32; BEST 90:2; BPFB 1;
    CA 111; CAAE 108; CANR 41, 90, 109;
    CPW; DA3; DAM POP; HGG; INT CA-
    111

Cook, Roy
    See Silverberg, Robert

Cooke, Elizabeth 1948- .... CLC 55
    See also CA 129

Cooke, John Esten 1830-1886 .... NCLC 5
    See also DLB 3, 248; RGAL 4

Cooke, John Estes
    See Baum, L(yman) Frank

Cooke, M. E.
    See Creasey, John

Cooke, Margaret
    See Creasey, John

Cooke, Rose Terry 1827-1892 ...... NCLC 110
    See also DLB 12, 74

Cook-Lynn, Elizabeth 1930- .... CLC 93;
    NNAL
    See also CA 133; DAM MULT; DLB 175

Cooney, Ray CLC 62
    See also CBD

Cooper, Anthony Ashley 1671-1713 .. LC 107
    See also DLB 101

Cooper, Dennis 1953- .... CLC 203
    See also CA 133; CANR 72, 86; GLL 1;
    HGG

Cooper, Douglas 1960- .... CLC 86

Cooper, Henry St. John
    See Creasey, John

Cooper, J. California (?)- .... CLC 56
    See also AAYA 12; BW 1; CA 125; CANR
    55; DAM MULT; DLB 212

Cooper, James Fenimore
    1789-1851 .... NCLC 1, 27, 54
    See also AAYA 22; AMW; BPFB 1;
    CDALB 1640-1865; CLR 105; DA3;
    DLB 3, 183, 250, 254; LAIT 1; NFS 9;
    RGAL 4; SATA 19; TUS; WCH

Cooper, Susan Fenimore
    1813-1894 .... NCLC 129
    See also ANW; DLB 239, 254

Coover, Robert 1932- .. CLC 3, 7, 15, 32, 46,
    87, 161; SSC 15
    See also AMWS 5; BPFB 1; CA 45-48;
    CANR 3, 37, 58, 115; CN 1, 2, 3, 4, 5, 6,
    7; DAM NOV; DLB 2, 227; DLBY 1981;
    EWL 3; MAL 5; MTCW 1, 2; MTFW
    2005; RGAL 4; RGSF 2

Copeland, Stewart (Armstrong)
    1952- .... CLC 26

Copernicus, Nicolaus 1473-1543 .... LC 45

Coppard, A(lfred) E(dgar)
    1878-1957 .... SSC 21; TCLC 5
    See also BRWS 8; CA 167; CAAE 114;
    DLB 162; EWL 3; HGG; RGEL 2; RGSF
    2; SUFW 1; YABC 1

Coppee, Francois 1842-1908 .... TCLC 25
    See also CA 170; DLB 217

Coppola, Francis Ford 1939- ... CLC 16, 126
    See also AAYA 39; CA 77-80; CANR 40,
    78; DLB 44

Copway, George 1818-1869 .... NNAL
    See also DAM MULT; DLB 175, 183

Corbiere, Tristan 1845-1875 .... NCLC 43
    See also DLB 217; GFL 1789 to the Present

Corcoran, Barbara (Asenath)
    1911- .... CLC 17
    See also AAYA 14; CA 191; 21-24R, 191;
    2; CANR 11, 28, 48; CLR 50; DLB 52;
    JRDA; MAICYA 2; MAICYAS 1; RHW;
    SAAS 20; SATA 3, 77; SATA-Essay 125

Cordelier, Maurice
    See Giraudoux, Jean(-Hippolyte)

Corelli, Marie TCLC 51
    See Mackay, Mary
    See also DLB 34, 156; RGEL 2; SUFW 1

Corinna c. 225B.C.-c. 305B.C. ...... CMLC 72

Corman, Cid CLC 9
    See Corman, Sidney
    See also CA 2; CP 1, 2, 3, 4, 5, 6, 7; DLB
    5, 193

Corman, Sidney 1924-2004
    See Corman, Cid
    See also CA 85-88; CAAS 225; CANR 44;
    DAM POET

Cormier, Robert 1925-2000 .... CLC 12, 30
    See also AAYA 3, 19; BYA 1, 2, 6, 8, 9;
    CA 1-4R; CANR 5, 23, 76, 93; CDALB
    1968-1988; CLR 12, 55; DA; DAB; DAC;
    DAM MST, NOV; DLB 52; EXPN; INT
    CANR-23; JRDA; LAIT 5; MAICYA 1,
    2; MTCW 1, 2; MTFW 2005; NFS 2, 18;
    SATA 10, 45, 83; SATA-Obit 122; WYA;
    YAW

Corn, Alfred (DeWitt III) 1943- .... CLC 33
    See also CA 179; 179; 25; CANR 44; CP 3,
    4, 5, 6, 7; CSW; DLB 120, 282; DLBY
    1980

Corneille, Pierre 1606-1684 .. DC 21; LC 28,
    135
    See also DAB; DAM MST; DFS 21; DLB
    268; EW 3; GFL Beginnings to 1789;
    RGWL 2, 3; TWA

Cornwell, David
    See le Carre, John

Cornwell, Patricia 1956- .... CLC 155
    See also AAYA 16, 56; BPFB 1; CA 134;
    CANR 53, 131; CMW 4; CPW; CSW;
    DAM POP; DLB 306; MSW; MTCW 2;
    MTFW 2005

Cornwell, Patricia Daniels
    See Cornwell, Patricia

Corso, Gregory 1930-2001 .... CLC 1, 11; PC
    33
    See also AMWS 12; BG 1:2; CA 5-8R;
    CAAS 193; CANR 41, 76, 132; CP 1, 2,
    3, 4, 5, 6, 7; DA3; DLB 5, 16, 237; LMFS
    2; MAL 5; MTCW 1, 2; MTFW 2005; WP

Cortazar, Julio 1914-1984 ... CLC 2, 3, 5, 10,
    13, 15, 33, 34, 92; HLC 1; SSC 7, 76
    See also BPFB 1; CA 21-24R; CANR 12,
    32, 81; CDWLB 3; DA3; DAM MULT,
    NOV; DLB 113; EWL 3; EXPS; HW 1,
    2; LAW; MTCW 1, 2; MTFW 2005;
    RGSF 2; RGWL 2, 3; SSFS 3, 20; TWA;
    WLIT 1

Cortes, Hernan 1485-1547 .... LC 31

Corvinus, Jakob
    See Raabe, Wilhelm (Karl)

Corwin, Cecil
    See Kornbluth, C(yril) M.

Cosic, Dobrica 1921- .... CLC 14
    See also CA 138; CAAE 122; CDWLB 4;
    CWW 2; DLB 181; EWL 3

Costain, Thomas B(ertram)
    1885-1965 .... CLC 30
    See also BYA 3; CA 5-8R; CAAS 25-28R;
    DLB 9; RHW

Costantini, Humberto 1924(?)-1987 . CLC 49
    See also CA 131; CAAS 122; EWL 3; HW
    1

Costello, Elvis 1954- .... CLC 21
    See also CA 204

Costenoble, Philostene
    See Ghelderode, Michel de

Cotes, Cecil V.
    See Duncan, Sara Jeannette

Cotter, Joseph Seamon Sr.
    1861-1949 .... BLC 1; TCLC 28
    See also BW 1; CA 124; DAM MULT; DLB
    50

Couch, Arthur Thomas Quiller
    See Quiller-Couch, Sir Arthur (Thomas)

Coulton, James
    See Hansen, Joseph

Couperus, Louis (Marie Anne)
    1863-1923 .... TCLC 15
    See also CAAE 115; EWL 3; RGWL 2, 3

Coupland, Douglas 1961- .... CLC 85, 133
    See also AAYA 34; CA 142; CANR 57, 90,
    130; CCA 1; CN 7; CPW; DAC; DAM
    POP

Court, Wesli
    See Turco, Lewis (Putnam)

Courtenay, Bryce 1933- .... CLC 59
    See also CA 138; CPW

Courtney, Robert
    See Ellison, Harlan

Cousteau, Jacques-Yves 1910-1997 .. CLC 30
    See also CA 65-68; CAAS 159; CANR 15,
    67; MTCW 1; SATA 38, 98

Coventry, Francis 1725-1754 .... LC 46

Coverdale, Miles c. 1487-1569 .... LC 77
    See also DLB 167

Cowan, Peter (Walkinshaw)
    1914-2002 .... SSC 28
    See also CA 21-24R; CANR 9, 25, 50, 83;
    CN 1, 2, 3, 4, 5, 6, 7; DLB 260; RGSF 2

Coward, Noel (Peirce) 1899-1973 . CLC 1, 9,
    29, 51
    See also AITN 1; BRWS 2; CA 17-18;
    CAAS 41-44R; CANR 35, 132; CAP 2;
    CBD; CDBLB 1914-1945; DA3; DAM
    DRAM; DFS 3, 6; DLB 10, 245; EWL 3;
    IDFW 3, 4; MTCW 1, 2; MTFW 2005;
    RGEL 2; TEA

Cowley, Abraham 1618-1667 .... LC 43
    See also BRW 2; DLB 131, 151; PAB;
    RGEL 2

Cowley, Malcolm 1898-1989 .... CLC 39
    See also AMWS 2; CA 5-8R; CAAS 128;
    CANR 3, 55; CP 1, 2, 3, 4; DLB 4, 48;
    DLBY 1981, 1989; EWL 3; MAL 5;
    MTCW 1, 2; MTFW 2005

Cowper, William 1731-1800 ..... NCLC 8, 94;
    PC 40
    See also BRW 3; DA3; DAM POET; DLB
    104, 109; RGEL 2

Cox, William Trevor 1928-
    See Trevor, William
    See also CA 9-12R; CANR 4, 37, 55, 76,
    102, 139; DAM NOV; INT CANR-37;
    MTCW 1, 2; MTFW 2005; TEA

Coyne, P. J.
    See Masters, Hilary

Cozzens, James Gould 1903-1978 . CLC 1, 4,
    11, 92
    See also AMW; BPFB 1; CA 9-12R; CAAS
    81-84; CANR 19; CDALB 1941-1968;
    CN 1, 2; DLB 9, 294; DLBD 2; DLBY
    1984, 1997; EWL 3; MAL 5; MTCW 1,
    2; MTFW 2005; RGAL 4

Crabbe, George 1754-1832 .... NCLC 26, 121
    See also BRW 3; DLB 93; RGEL 2

Crace, Jim 1946- .... CLC 157; SSC 61
    See also CA 135; CAAE 128; CANR 55,
    70, 123; CN 5, 6, 7; DLB 231; INT CA-
    135

Craddock, Charles Egbert
    See Murfree, Mary Noailles

Craig, A. A.
    See Anderson, Poul

Craik, Mrs.
    See Craik, Dinah Maria (Mulock)
    See also RGEL 2

Craik, Dinah Maria (Mulock)
    1826-1887 .... NCLC 38
    See Craik, Mrs.; Mulock, Dinah Maria
    See also DLB 35, 163; MAICYA 1, 2;
    SATA 34

Cram, Ralph Adams 1863-1942 ..... TCLC 45
    See also CA 160

Cranch, Christopher Pearse
1813-1892 .... NCLC 115
See also DLB 1, 42, 243

Crane, (Harold) Hart 1899-1932 .... PC 3;
TCLC 2, 5, 80; WLC 2
See also AMW; AMWR 2; CA 127; CAAE
104; CDALB 1917-1929; DA; DA3;
DAB; DAC; DAM MST, POET; DLB 4,
48; EWL 3; MAL 5; MTCW 1, 2; MTFW
2005; RGAL 4; TUS

Crane, R(onald) S(almon)
1886-1967 .... CLC 27
See also CA 85-88; DLB 63

Crane, Stephen (Townley)
1871-1900 ...... SSC 7, 56, 70; TCLC 11,
17, 32; WLC 2
See also AAYA 21; AMW; AMWC 1; BPFB
1; BYA 3; CA 140; CAAE 109; CANR
84; CDALB 1865-1917; DA; DA3; DAB;
DAC; DAM MST, NOV, POET; DLB 12,
54, 78; EXPN; EXPS; LAIT 2; LMFS 2;
MAL 5; NFS 4, 20; PFS 9; RGAL 4;
RGSF 2; SSFS 4; TUS; WYA; YABC 2

Cranmer, Thomas 1489-1556 .... LC 95
See also DLB 132, 213

Cranshaw, Stanley
See Fisher, Dorothy (Frances) Canfield

Crase, Douglas 1944- .... CLC 58
See also CA 106

Crashaw, Richard 1612(?)-1649 .... LC 24
See also BRW 2; DLB 126; PAB; RGEL 2

Cratinus c. 519B.C.-c. 422B.C. ..... CMLC 54
See also LMFS 1

Craven, Margaret 1901-1980 .... CLC 17
See also BYA 2; CA 103; CCA 1; DAC;
LAIT 5

Crawford, F(rancis) Marion
1854-1909 .... TCLC 10
See also CA 168; CAAE 107; DLB 71;
HGG; RGAL 4; SUFW 1

Crawford, Isabella Valancy
1850-1887 .... NCLC 12, 127
See also DLB 92; RGEL 2

Crayon, Geoffrey
See Irving, Washington

Creasey, John 1908-1973 .... CLC 11
See Marric, J. J.
See also CA 5-8R; CAAS 41-44R; CANR
8, 59; CMW 4; DLB 77; MTCW 1

Crebillon, Claude Prosper Jolyot de (fils)
1707-1777 .... LC 1, 28
See also DLB 313; GFL Beginnings to 1789

Credo
See Creasey, John

Credo, Alvaro J. de
See Prado (Calvo), Pedro

Creeley, Robert 1926-2005 .... CLC 1, 2, 4, 8,
11, 15, 36, 78; PC 73
See also AMWS 4; CA 1-4R; 10; CAAS
237; CANR 23, 43, 89, 137; CP 1, 2, 3,
4, 5, 6, 7; DA3; DAM POET; DLB 5, 16,
169; DLBD 17; EWL 3; MAL 5; MTCW
1, 2; MTFW 2005; PFS 21; RGAL 4; WP

Creeley, Robert White
See Creeley, Robert

Crenne, Helisenne de 1510-1560 .... LC 113
See also DLB 327

Crevecoeur, Hector St. John de
See Crevecoeur, Michel Guillaume Jean de
See also ANW

Crevecoeur, Michel Guillaume Jean de
1735-1813 .... NCLC 105
See Crevecoeur, Hector St. John de
See also AMWS 1; DLB 37

Crevel, Rene 1900-1935 .... TCLC 112
See also GLL 2

Crews, Harry 1935- .... CLC 6, 23, 49
See also AITN 1; AMWS 11; BPFB 1; CA
25-28R; CANR 20, 57; CN 3, 4, 5, 6, 7;
CSW; DA3; DLB 6, 143, 185; MTCW 1,
2; MTFW 2005; RGAL 4

Crichton, Michael 1942- ..... CLC 2, 6, 54, 90
See also AAYA 10, 49; AITN 2; BPFB 1;
CA 25-28R; CANR 13, 40, 54, 76, 127;
CMW 4; CN 2, 3, 6, 7; CPW; DA3; DAM
NOV, POP; DLB 292; DLBY 1981; INT
CANR-13; JRDA; MTCW 1, 2; MTFW
2005; SATA 9, 88; SFW 4; YAW

Crispin, Edmund CLC 22
See Montgomery, (Robert) Bruce
See also DLB 87; MSW

Cristina of Sweden 1626-1689 .... LC 124

Cristofer, Michael 1945(?)- .... CLC 28
See also CA 152; CAAE 110; CAD; CANR
150; CD 5, 6; DAM DRAM; DFS 15;
DLB 7

Cristofer, Michael Ivan
See Cristofer, Michael

Criton
See Alain

Croce, Benedetto 1866-1952 .... TCLC 37
See also CA 155; CAAE 120; EW 8; EWL
3; WLIT 7

Crockett, David 1786-1836 .... NCLC 8
See also DLB 3, 11, 183, 248

Crockett, Davy
See Crockett, David

Crofts, Freeman Wills 1879-1957 .. TCLC 55
See also CA 195; CAAE 115; CMW 4;
DLB 77; MSW

Croker, John Wilson 1780-1857 .... NCLC 10
See also DLB 110

Crommelynck, Fernand 1885-1970 .. CLC 75
See also CA 189; CAAS 89-92; EWL 3

Cromwell, Oliver 1599-1658 .... LC 43

Cronenberg, David 1943- .... CLC 143
See also CA 138; CCA 1

Cronin, A(rchibald) J(oseph)
1896-1981 .... CLC 32
See also BPFB 1; CA 1-4R; CAAS 102;
CANR 5; CN 2; DLB 191; SATA 47;
SATA-Obit 25

Cross, Amanda
See Heilbrun, Carolyn G(old)
See also BPFB 1; CMW; CPW; DLB 306;
MSW

Crothers, Rachel 1878-1958 .... TCLC 19
See also CA 194; CAAE 113; CAD; CWD;
DLB 7, 266; RGAL 4

Croves, Hal
See Traven, B.

Crow Dog, Mary (?)- .... CLC 93
See Brave Bird, Mary
See also CA 154

Crowfield, Christopher
See Stowe, Harriet (Elizabeth) Beecher

Crowley, Aleister TCLC 7
See Crowley, Edward Alexander
See also GLL 1

Crowley, Edward Alexander 1875-1947
See Crowley, Aleister
See also CAAE 104; HGG

Crowley, John 1942- .... CLC 57
See also AAYA 57; BPFB 1; CA 61-64;
CANR 43, 98, 138; DLBY 1982; FANT;
MTFW 2005; SATA 65, 140; SFW 4;
SUFW 2

Crowne, John 1641-1712 .... LC 104
See also DLB 80; RGEL 2

Crud
See Crumb, R.

Crumarums
See Crumb, R.

Crumb, R. 1943- .... CLC 17
See also CA 106; CANR 107, 150

Crumb, Robert
See Crumb, R.

Crumbum
See Crumb, R.

Crumski
See Crumb, R.

Crum the Bum
See Crumb, R.

Crunk
See Crumb, R.

Crustt
See Crumb, R.

Crutchfield, Les
See Trumbo, Dalton

Cruz, Victor Hernandez 1949- ... HLC 1; PC
37
See also BW 2; CA 65-68; 17; CANR 14,
32, 74, 132; CP 1, 2, 3, 4, 5, 6, 7; DAM
MULT, POET; DLB 41; DNFS 1; EXPP;
HW 1, 2; LLW; MTCW 2; MTFW 2005;
PFS 16; WP

Cryer, Gretchen (Kiger) 1935- .... CLC 21
See also CA 123; CAAE 114

Csath, Geza TCLC 13
See Brenner, Jozef
See also CAAE 111

Cudlip, David R(ockwell) 1933- .... CLC 34
See also CA 177

Cullen, Countee 1903-1946 . BLC 1; HR 1:2;
PC 20; TCLC 4, 37; WLCS
See also AFAW 2; AMWS 4; BW 1; CA
124; CAAE 108; CDALB 1917-1929;
DA; DA3; DAC; DAM MST, MULT,
POET; DLB 4, 48, 51; EWL 3; EXPP;
LMFS 2; MAL 5; MTCW 1, 2; MTFW
2005; PFS 3; RGAL 4; SATA 18; WP

Culleton, Beatrice 1949- .... NNAL
See also CA 120; CANR 83; DAC

Cum, R.
See Crumb, R.

Cumberland, Richard
1732-1811 .... NCLC 167
See also DLB 89; RGEL 2

Cummings, Bruce F(rederick) 1889-1919
See Barbellion, W. N. P.
See also CAAE 123

Cummings, E(dward) E(stlin)
1894-1962 .. CLC 1, 3, 8, 12, 15, 68; PC
5; TCLC 137; WLC 2
See also AAYA 41; AMW; CA 73-76;
CANR 31; CDALB 1929-1941; DA;
DA3; DAB; DAC; DAM MST, POET;
DLB 4, 48; EWL 3; EXPP; MAL 5;
MTCW 1, 2; MTFW 2005; PAB; PFS 1,
3, 12, 13, 19; RGAL 4; TUS; WP

Cummins, Maria Susanna
1827-1866 .... NCLC 139
See also DLB 42; YABC 1

Cunha, Euclides (Rodrigues Pimenta) da
1866-1909 .... TCLC 24
See also CA 219; CAAE 123; DLB 307;
LAW; WLIT 1

Cunningham, E. V.
See Fast, Howard

Cunningham, J(ames) V(incent)
1911-1985 .... CLC 3, 31
See also CA 1-4R; CAAS 115; CANR 1,
72; CP 1, 2, 3, 4; DLB 5

Cunningham, Julia (Woolfolk)
1916- .... CLC 12
See also CA 9-12R; CANR 4, 19, 36; CWRI
5; JRDA; MAICYA 1, 2; SAAS 2; SATA
1, 26, 132

Cunningham, Michael 1952- .... CLC 34
See also AMWS 15; CA 136; CANR 96,
160; CN 7; DLB 292; GLL 2; MTFW
2005; NFS 23

Davis, B. Lynch
See Bioy Casares, Adolfo; Borges, Jorge Luis

Davis, Frank Marshall 1905-1987 ...... **BLC 1**
See also BW 2, 3; CA 125; CAAS 123; CANR 42, 80; DAM MULT; DLB 51

Davis, Gordon
See Hunt, E. Howard

Davis, H(arold) L(enoir) 1896-1960 . **CLC 49**
See also ANW; CA 178; CAAS 89-92; DLB 9, 206; SATA 114; TCWW 1, 2

Davis, Hart
See Poniatowska, Elena

Davis, Natalie Zemon 1928- .... **CLC 204**
See also CA 53-56; CANR 58, 100

Davis, Rebecca (Blaine) Harding
1831-1910 .... **SSC 38; TCLC 6**
See also AMWS 16; CA 179; CAAE 104; DLB 74, 239; FW; NFS 14; RGAL 4; TUS

Davis, Richard Harding
1864-1916 .... **TCLC 24**
See also CA 179; CAAE 114; DLB 12, 23, 78, 79, 189; DLBD 13; RGAL 4

Davison, Frank Dalby 1893-1970 ..... **CLC 15**
See also CA 217; CAAS 116; DLB 260

Davison, Lawrence H.
See Lawrence, D(avid) H(erbert Richards)

Davison, Peter (Hubert) 1928-2004 . **CLC 28**
See also CA 9-12R; CAAS 234; CANR 3, 43, 84; CP 1, 2, 3, 4, 5, 6, 7; DLB 5

Davys, Mary 1674-1732 .... **LC 1, 46**
See also DLB 39

Dawson, (Guy) Fielding (Lewis)
1930-2002 .... **CLC 6**
See also CA 85-88; CAAS 202; CANR 108; DLB 130; DLBY 2002

Dawson, Peter
See Faust, Frederick (Schiller)
See also TCWW 1, 2

Day, Clarence (Shepard, Jr.)
1874-1935 .... **TCLC 25**
See also CA 199; CAAE 108; DLB 11

Day, John 1574(?)-1640(?) .... **LC 70**
See also DLB 62, 170; RGEL 2

Day, Thomas 1748-1789 .... **LC 1**
See also DLB 39; YABC 1

Day Lewis, C(ecil) 1904-1972 . **CLC 1, 6, 10; PC 11**
See Blake, Nicholas; Lewis, C. Day
See also BRWS 3; CA 13-16; CAAS 33-36R; CANR 34; CAP 1; CP 1; CWRI 5; DAM POET; DLB 15, 20; EWL 3; MTCW 1, 2; RGEL 2

Dazai Osamu SSC 41; TCLC 11
See Tsushima, Shuji
See also CA 164; DLB 182; EWL 3; MJW; RGSF 2; RGWL 2, 3; TWA

de Andrade, Carlos Drummond
See Drummond de Andrade, Carlos

de Andrade, Mario 1892(?)-1945
See Andrade, Mario de
See also CA 178; HW 2

Deane, Norman
See Creasey, John

Deane, Seamus (Francis) 1940- ...... **CLC 122**
See also CA 118; CANR 42

de Beauvoir, Simone
See Beauvoir, Simone de

de Beer, P.
See Bosman, Herman Charles

De Botton, Alain 1969- .... **CLC 203**
See also CA 159; CANR 96

de Brissac, Malcolm
See Dickinson, Peter (Malcolm de Brissac)

de Campos, Alvaro
See Pessoa, Fernando (Antonio Nogueira)

de Chardin, Pierre Teilhard
See Teilhard de Chardin, (Marie Joseph) Pierre

de Crenne, Helisenne c. 1510-c.
1560 .... **LC 113**

Dee, John 1527-1608 .... **LC 20**
See also DLB 136, 213

Deer, Sandra 1940- .... **CLC 45**
See also CA 186

De Ferrari, Gabriella 1941- .... **CLC 65**
See also CA 146

de Filippo, Eduardo 1900-1984 ... **TCLC 127**
See also CA 132; CAAS 114; EWL 3; MTCW 1; RGWL 2, 3

Defoe, Daniel 1660(?)-1731 .... **LC 1, 42, 108; WLC 2**
See also AAYA 27; BRW 3; BRWR 1; BYA 4; CDBLB 1660-1789; CLR 61; DA; DA3; DAB; DAC; DAM MST, NOV; DLB 39, 95, 101; JRDA; LAIT 1; LMFS 1; MAICYA 1, 2; NFS 9, 13; RGEL 2; SATA 22; TEA; WCH; WLIT 3

de Gouges, Olympe
See de Gouges, Olympe

de Gouges, Olympe 1748-1793 .... **LC 127**
See also DLB 313

de Gourmont, Remy(-Marie-Charles)
See Gourmont, Remy(-Marie-Charles) de

de Gournay, Marie le Jars
1566-1645 .... **LC 98**
See also DLB 327; FW

de Hartog, Jan 1914-2002 .... **CLC 19**
See also CA 1-4R; CAAS 210; CANR 1; DFS 12

de Hostos, E. M.
See Hostos (y Bonilla), Eugenio Maria de

de Hostos, Eugenio M.
See Hostos (y Bonilla), Eugenio Maria de

Deighton, Len CLC 4, 7, 22, 46
See Deighton, Leonard Cyril
See also AAYA 6; BEST 89:2; BPFB 1; CDBLB 1960 to Present; CMW 4; CN 1, 2, 3, 4, 5, 6, 7; CPW; DLB 87

Deighton, Leonard Cyril 1929-
See Deighton, Len
See also AAYA 57; CA 9-12R; CANR 19, 33, 68; DA3; DAM NOV, POP; MTCW 1, 2; MTFW 2005

Dekker, Thomas 1572(?)-1632 ..... **DC 12; LC 22**
See also CDBLB Before 1660; DAM DRAM; DLB 62, 172; LMFS 1; RGEL 2

de Laclos, Pierre Ambroise Franois
See Laclos, Pierre-Ambroise Francois

Delacroix, (Ferdinand-Victor-)Eugene
1798-1863 .... **NCLC 133**
See also EW 5

Delafield, E. M. TCLC 61
See Dashwood, Edmee Elizabeth Monica de la Pasture
See also DLB 34; RHW

de la Mare, Walter (John)
1873-1956 ..... **PC 77; SSC 14; TCLC 4, 53; WLC 2**
See also CA 163; CDBLB 1914-1945; CLR 23; CWRI 5; DA3; DAB; DAC; DAM MST, POET; DLB 19, 153, 162, 255, 284; EWL 3; EXPP; HGG; MAICYA 1, 2; MTCW 2; MTFW 2005; RGEL 2; RGSF 2; SATA 16; SUFW 1; TEA; WCH

de Lamartine, Alphonse (Marie Louis Prat)
See Lamartine, Alphonse (Marie Louis Prat) de

Delaney, Franey
See O'Hara, John (Henry)

Delaney, Shelagh 1939- .... **CLC 29**
See also CA 17-20R; CANR 30, 67; CBD; CD 5, 6; CDBLB 1960 to Present; CWD; DAM DRAM; DFS 7; DLB 13; MTCW 1

Delany, Martin Robison
1812-1885 .... **NCLC 93**
See also DLB 50; RGAL 4

Delany, Mary (Granville Pendarves)
1700-1788 .... **LC 12**

Delany, Samuel R., Jr. 1942- ... **BLC 1; CLC 8, 14, 38, 141**
See also AAYA 24; AFAW 2; BPFB 1; BW 2, 3; CA 81-84; CANR 27, 43, 116; CN 2, 3, 4, 5, 6, 7; DAM MULT; DLB 8, 33; FANT; MAL 5; MTCW 1, 2; RGAL 4; SATA 92; SCFW 1, 2; SFW 4; SUFW 2

de la Parra, (Ana) Teresa (Sonojo)
1890(?)-1936 .... **TCLC 185**
See Parra Sanojo, Ana Teresa de la
See also CA 178; HW 2

De La Ramee, Marie Louise 1839-1908
See Ouida
See also CA 204; SATA 20

de la Roche, Mazo 1879-1961 .... **CLC 14**
See also CA 85-88; CANR 30; DLB 68; RGEL 2; RHW; SATA 64

De La Salle, Innocent
See Hartmann, Sadakichi

de Laureamont, Comte
See Lautreamont

Delbanco, Nicholas 1942- ..... **CLC 6, 13, 167**
See also CA 189; 17-20R, 189; 2; CANR 29, 55, 116, 150; CN 7; DLB 6, 234

Delbanco, Nicholas Franklin
See Delbanco, Nicholas

del Castillo, Michel 1933- .... **CLC 38**
See also CA 109; CANR 77

Deledda, Grazia (Cosima)
1875(?)-1936 .... **TCLC 23**
See also CA 205; CAAE 123; DLB 264, 329; EWL 3; RGWL 2, 3; WLIT 7

Deleuze, Gilles 1925-1995 .... **TCLC 116**
See also DLB 296

Delgado, Abelardo (Lalo) B(arrientos)
1930-2004 .... **HLC 1**
See also CA 131; 15; CAAS 230; CANR 90; DAM MST, MULT; DLB 82; HW 1, 2

Delibes, Miguel CLC 8, 18
See Delibes Setien, Miguel
See also DLB 322; EWL 3

Delibes Setien, Miguel 1920-
See Delibes, Miguel
See also CA 45-48; CANR 1, 32; CWW 2; HW 1; MTCW 1

DeLillo, Don 1936- ..... **CLC 8, 10, 13, 27, 39, 54, 76, 143, 210, 213**
See also AMWC 2; AMWS 6; BEST 89:1; BPFB 1; CA 81-84; CANR 21, 76, 92, 133; CN 3, 4, 5, 6, 7; CPW; DA3; DAM NOV, POP; DLB 6, 173; EWL 3; MAL 5; MTCW 1, 2; MTFW 2005; RGAL 4; TUS

de Lisser, H. G.
See De Lisser, H(erbert) G(eorge)
See also DLB 117

De Lisser, H(erbert) G(eorge)
1878-1944 .... **TCLC 12**
See de Lisser, H. G.
See also BW 2; CA 152; CAAE 109

Deloire, Pierre
See Peguy, Charles (Pierre)

Deloney, Thomas 1543(?)-1600 .... **LC 41**
See also DLB 167; RGEL 2

Deloria, Ella (Cara) 1889-1971(?) ..... **NNAL**
See also CA 152; DAM MULT; DLB 175

Deloria, Vine, Jr. 1933-2005 .... **CLC 21, 122; NNAL**
See also CA 53-56; CAAS 245; CANR 5, 20, 48, 98; DAM MULT; DLB 175; MTCW 1; SATA 21; SATA-Obit 171

Deloria, Vine Victor, Jr.
See Deloria, Vine, Jr.

del Valle-Inclan, Ramon (Maria)
See Valle-Inclan, Ramon (Maria) del
See also DLB 322

Del Vecchio, John M(ichael) 1947- .. **CLC 29**
See also CA 110; DLBD 9

de Man, Paul (Adolph Michel)
1919-1983 .... **CLC 55**
See also CA 128; CAAS 111; CANR 61;
DLB 67; MTCW 1, 2

DeMarinis, Rick 1934- .... **CLC 54**
See also CA 184; 57-60, 184; 24; CANR 9,
25, 50, 160; DLB 218; TCWW 2

de Maupassant, (Henri Rene Albert) Guy
See Maupassant, (Henri Rene Albert) Guy
de

Dembry, R. Emmet
See Murfree, Mary Noailles

Demby, William 1922- .... **BLC 1; CLC 53**
See also BW 1, 3; CA 81-84; CANR 81;
DAM MULT; DLB 33

de Menton, Francisco
See Chin, Frank (Chew, Jr.)

Demetrius of Phalerum c.
307B.C.- .... **CMLC 34**

Demijohn, Thom
See Disch, Thomas M.

De Mille, James 1833-1880 .... **NCLC 123**
See also DLB 99, 251

Deming, Richard 1915-1983
See Queen, Ellery
See also CA 9-12R; CANR 3, 94; SATA 24

Democritus c. 460B.C.-c. 370B.C. .. **CMLC 47**

de Montaigne, Michel (Eyquem)
See Montaigne, Michel (Eyquem) de

de Montherlant, Henry (Milon)
See Montherlant, Henry (Milon) de

Demosthenes 384B.C.-322B.C. ...... **CMLC 13**
See also AW 1; DLB 176; RGWL 2, 3;
WLIT 8

de Musset, (Louis Charles) Alfred
See Musset, Alfred de

de Natale, Francine
See Malzberg, Barry N(athaniel)

de Navarre, Marguerite 1492-1549 ... **LC 61;**
SSC 85
See Marguerite d'Angouleme; Marguerite
de Navarre
See also DLB 327

Denby, Edwin (Orr) 1903-1983 .... **CLC 48**
See also CA 138; CAAS 110; CP 1

de Nerval, Gerard
See Nerval, Gerard de

Denham, John 1615-1669 .... **LC 73**
See also DLB 58, 126; RGEL 2

Denis, Julio
See Cortazar, Julio

Denmark, Harrison
See Zelazny, Roger

Dennis, John 1658-1734 .... **LC 11**
See also DLB 101; RGEL 2

Dennis, Nigel (Forbes) 1912-1989 ...... **CLC 8**
See also CA 25-28R; CAAS 129; CN 1, 2,
3, 4; DLB 13, 15, 233; EWL 3; MTCW 1

Dent, Lester 1904-1959 .... **TCLC 72**
See also CA 161; CAAE 112; CMW 4;
DLB 306; SFW 4

De Palma, Brian 1940- .... **CLC 20**
See also CA 109

De Palma, Brian Russell
See De Palma, Brian

de Pizan, Christine
See Christine de Pizan
See also FL 1:1

De Quincey, Thomas 1785-1859 ..... **NCLC 4,**
87
See also BRW 4; CDBLB 1789-1832; DLB
110, 144; RGEL 2

Deren, Eleanora 1908(?)-1961
See Deren, Maya
See also CA 192; CAAS 111

Deren, Maya **CLC 16, 102**
See Deren, Eleanora

Derleth, August (William)
1909-1971 .... **CLC 31**
See also BPFB 1; BYA 9, 10; CA 1-4R;
CAAS 29-32R; CANR 4; CMW 4; CN 1;
DLB 9; DLBD 17; HGG; SATA 5; SUFW
1

Der Nister 1884-1950 .... **TCLC 56**
See Nister, Der

de Routisie, Albert
See Aragon, Louis

Derrida, Jacques 1930-2004 ...... **CLC 24, 87,**
225
See also CA 127; CAAE 124; CAAS 232;
CANR 76, 98, 133; DLB 242; EWL 3;
LMFS 2; MTCW 2; TWA

Derry Down Derry
See Lear, Edward

Dersonnes, Jacques
See Simenon, Georges (Jacques Christian)

Der Stricker c. 1190-c. 1250 .... **CMLC 75**
See also DLB 138

Desai, Anita 1937- .... **CLC 19, 37, 97, 175**
See also BRWS 5; CA 81-84; CANR 33,
53, 95, 133; CN 1, 2, 3, 4, 5, 6, 7; CWRI
5; DA3; DAB; DAM NOV; DLB 271,
323; DNFS 2; EWL 3; FW; MTCW 1, 2;
MTFW 2005; SATA 63, 126

Desai, Kiran 1971- .... **CLC 119**
See also BYA 16; CA 171; CANR 127

de Saint-Luc, Jean
See Glassco, John

de Saint Roman, Arnaud
See Aragon, Louis

Desbordes-Valmore, Marceline
1786-1859 .... **NCLC 97**
See also DLB 217

Descartes, Rene 1596-1650 .... **LC 20, 35**
See also DLB 268; EW 3; GFL Beginnings
to 1789

Deschamps, Eustache 1340(?)-1404 .. **LC 103**
See also DLB 208

De Sica, Vittorio 1901(?)-1974 .... **CLC 20**
See also CAAS 117

Desnos, Robert 1900-1945 .... **TCLC 22**
See also CA 151; CAAE 121; CANR 107;
DLB 258; EWL 3; LMFS 2

Destouches, Louis-Ferdinand
1894-1961 .... **CLC 9, 15**
See Celine, Louis-Ferdinand
See also CA 85-88; CANR 28; MTCW 1

de Tolignac, Gaston
See Griffith, D(avid Lewelyn) W(ark)

Deutsch, Babette 1895-1982 .... **CLC 18**
See also BYA 3; CA 1-4R; CAAS 108;
CANR 4, 79; CP 1, 2, 3; DLB 45; SATA
1; SATA-Obit 33

Devenant, William 1606-1649 .... **LC 13**

Devkota, Laxmiprasad 1909-1959 . **TCLC 23**
See also CAAE 123

De Voto, Bernard (Augustine)
1897-1955 .... **TCLC 29**
See also CA 160; CAAE 113; DLB 9, 256;
MAL 5; TCWW 1, 2

De Vries, Peter 1910-1993 ..... **CLC 1, 2, 3, 7,**
10, 28, 46
See also CA 17-20R; CAAS 142; CANR
41; CN 1, 2, 3, 4, 5; DAM NOV; DLB 6;
DLBY 1982; MAL 5; MTCW 1, 2;
MTFW 2005

Dewey, John 1859-1952 .... **TCLC 95**
See also CA 170; CAAE 114; CANR 144;
DLB 246, 270; RGAL 4

Dexter, John
See Bradley, Marion Zimmer
See also GLL 1

Dexter, Martin
See Faust, Frederick (Schiller)

Dexter, Pete 1943- .... **CLC 34, 55**
See also BEST 89:2; CA 131; CAAE 127;
CANR 129; CPW; DAM POP; INT CA-
131; MAL 5; MTCW 1; MTFW 2005

Diamano, Silmang
See Senghor, Leopold Sedar

Diamond, Neil 1941- .... **CLC 30**
See also CA 108

Diaz del Castillo, Bernal c.
1496-1584 .... **HLCS 1; LC 31**
See also DLB 318; LAW

di Bassetto, Corno
See Shaw, George Bernard

Dick, Philip K. 1928-1982 ... **CLC 10, 30, 72;**
SSC 57
See also AAYA 24; BPFB 1; BYA 11; CA
49-52; CAAS 106; CANR 2, 16, 132; CN
2, 3; CPW; DA3; DAM NOV, POP; DLB
8; MTCW 1, 2; MTFW 2005; NFS 5;
SCFW 1, 2; SFW 4

Dick, Philip Kindred
See Dick, Philip K.

Dickens, Charles (John Huffam)
1812-1870 .... **NCLC 3, 8, 18, 26, 37, 50,**
86, 105, 113, 161; SSC 17, 49, 88; WLC
2
See also AAYA 23; BRW 5; BRWC 1, 2;
BYA 1, 2, 3, 13, 14; CDBLB 1832-1890;
CLR 95; CMW 4; DA; DA3; DAB; DAC;
DAM MST, NOV; DLB 21, 55, 70, 159,
166; EXPN; GL 2; HGG; JRDA; LAIT 1,
2; LATS 1:1; LMFS 1; MAICYA 1, 2;
NFS 4, 5, 10, 14, 20; RGEL 2; RGSF 2;
SATA 15; SUFW 1; TEA; WCH; WLIT
4; WYA

Dickey, James (Lafayette)
1923-1997 .... **CLC 1, 2, 4, 7, 10, 15, 47,**
109; PC 40; TCLC 151
See also AAYA 50; AITN 1, 2; AMWS 4;
BPFB 1; CA 9-12R; CAAS 156; CABS
2; CANR 10, 48, 61, 105; CDALB 1968-
1988; CP 1, 2, 3, 4, 5, 6; CPW; CSW;
DA3; DAM NOV, POET, POP; DLB 5,
193; DLBD 7; DLBY 1982, 1993, 1996,
1997, 1998; EWL 3; INT CANR-10;
MAL 5; MTCW 1, 2; NFS 9; PFS 6, 11;
RGAL 4; TUS

Dickey, William 1928-1994 .... **CLC 3, 28**
See also CA 9-12R; CAAS 145; CANR 24,
79; CP 1, 2, 3, 4; DLB 5

Dickinson, Charles 1951- .... **CLC 49**
See also CA 128; CANR 141

Dickinson, Emily (Elizabeth)
1830-1886 ..... **NCLC 21, 77, 171; PC 1;**
WLC 2
See also AAYA 22; AMW; AMWR 1;
CDALB 1865-1917; DA; DA3; DAB;
DAC; DAM MST, POET; DLB 1, 243;
EXPP; FL 1:3; MBL; PAB; PFS 1, 2, 3,
4, 5, 6, 8, 10, 11, 13, 16; RGAL 4; SATA
29; TUS; WP; WYA

Dickinson, Mrs. Herbert Ward
See Phelps, Elizabeth Stuart

Dickinson, Peter (Malcolm de Brissac)
1927- .... **CLC 12, 35**
See also AAYA 9, 49; BYA 5; CA 41-44R;
CANR 31, 58, 88, 134; CLR 29; CMW 4;
DLB 87, 161, 276; JRDA; MAICYA 1, 2;
SATA 5, 62, 95, 150; SFW 4; WYA; YAW

Dickson, Carr
See Carr, John Dickson

Dickson, Carter
See Carr, John Dickson

Doty, Mark 1953(?)- .... **CLC 176; PC 53**
See also AMWS 11; CA 183; 161, 183;
CANR 110; CP 7

Doty, Mark A.
See Doty, Mark

Doty, Mark Alan
See Doty, Mark

Doughty, Charles M(ontagu)
1843-1926 .... **TCLC 27**
See also CA 178; CAAE 115; DLB 19, 57,
174

Douglas, Ellen **CLC 73**
See Haxton, Josephine Ayres; Williamson,
Ellen Douglas
See also CN 5, 6, 7; CSW; DLB 292

Douglas, Gavin 1475(?)-1522 .... **LC 20**
See also DLB 132; RGEL 2

Douglas, George
See Brown, George Douglas
See also RGEL 2

Douglas, Keith (Castellain)
1920-1944 .... **TCLC 40**
See also BRW 7; CA 160; DLB 27; EWL
3; PAB; RGEL 2

Douglas, Leonard
See Bradbury, Ray

Douglas, Michael
See Crichton, Michael

Douglas, (George) Norman
1868-1952 .... **TCLC 68**
See also BRW 6; CA 157; CAAE 119; DLB
34, 195; RGEL 2

Douglas, William
See Brown, George Douglas

Douglass, Frederick 1817(?)-1895 ..... **BLC 1;
NCLC 7, 55, 141; WLC 2**
See also AAYA 48; AFAW 1, 2; AMWC 1;
AMWS 3; CDALB 1640-1865; DA; DA3;
DAC; DAM MST, MULT; DLB 1, 43, 50,
79, 243; FW; LAIT 2; NCFS 2; RGAL 4;
SATA 29

Dourado, (Waldomiro Freitas) Autran
1926- .... **CLC 23, 60**
See also CA 25-28R, 179; CANR 34, 81;
DLB 145, 307; HW 2

Dourado, Waldomiro Freitas Autran
See Dourado, (Waldomiro Freitas) Autran

Dove, Rita 1952- .. **BLCS; CLC 50, 81; PC 6**
See also AAYA 46; AMWS 4; BW 2; CA
109; 19; CANR 27, 42, 68, 76, 97, 132;
CDALBS; CP 5, 6, 7; CSW; CWP; DA3;
DAM MULT, POET; DLB 120; EWL 3;
EXPP; MAL 5; MTCW 2; MTFW 2005;
PFS 1, 15; RGAL 4

Dove, Rita Frances
See Dove, Rita

Doveglion
See Villa, Jose Garcia

Dowell, Coleman 1925-1985 .... **CLC 60**
See also CA 25-28R; CAAS 117; CANR
10; DLB 130; GLL 2

Dowson, Ernest (Christopher)
1867-1900 .... **TCLC 4**
See also CA 150; CAAE 105; DLB 19, 135;
RGEL 2

Doyle, A. Conan
See Doyle, Sir Arthur Conan

Doyle, Sir Arthur Conan
1859-1930 ..... **SSC 12, 83, 95; TCLC 7;
WLC 2**
See Conan Doyle, Arthur
See also AAYA 14; BRWS 2; CA 122;
CAAE 104; CANR 131; CDBLB 1890-
1914; CLR 106; CMW 4; DA; DA3;
DAB; DAC; DAM MST, NOV; DLB 18,
70, 156, 178; EXPS; HGG; LAIT 2;

MSW; MTCW 1, 2; MTFW 2005; RGEL
2; RGSF 2; RHW; SATA 24; SCFW 1, 2;
SFW 4; SSFS 2; TEA; WCH; WLIT 4;
WYA; YAW

Doyle, Conan
See Doyle, Sir Arthur Conan

Doyle, John
See Graves, Robert

Doyle, Roddy 1958- .... **CLC 81, 178**
See also AAYA 14; BRWS 5; CA 143;
CANR 73, 128; CN 6, 7; DA3; DLB 194,
326; MTCW 2; MTFW 2005

Doyle, Sir A. Conan
See Doyle, Sir Arthur Conan

Dr. A
See Asimov, Isaac; Silverstein, Alvin; Silverstein, Virginia B(arbara Opshelor)

Drabble, Margaret 1939- ...... **CLC 2, 3, 5, 8,
10, 22, 53, 129**
See also BRWS 4; CA 13-16R; CANR 18,
35, 63, 112, 131; CDBLB 1960 to Present;
CN 1, 2, 3, 4, 5, 6, 7; CPW; DA3; DAB;
DAC; DAM MST, NOV, POP; DLB 14,
155, 231; EWL 3; FW; MTCW 1, 2;
MTFW 2005; RGEL 2; SATA 48; TEA

Drakulic, Slavenka 1949- .... **CLC 173**
See also CA 144; CANR 92

Drakulic-Ilic, Slavenka
See Drakulic, Slavenka

Drapier, M. B.
See Swift, Jonathan

Drayham, James
See Mencken, H(enry) L(ouis)

Drayton, Michael 1563-1631 .... **LC 8**
See also DAM POET; DLB 121; RGEL 2

Dreadstone, Carl
See Campbell, (John) Ramsey

Dreiser, Theodore 1871-1945 .... **SSC 30;
TCLC 10, 18, 35, 83; WLC 2**
See also AMW; AMWC 2; AMWR 2; BYA
15, 16; CA 132; CAAE 106; CDALB
1865-1917; DA; DA3; DAC; DAM MST,
NOV; DLB 9, 12, 102, 137; DLBD 1;
EWL 3; LAIT 2; LMFS 2; MAL 5;
MTCW 1, 2; MTFW 2005; NFS 8, 17;
RGAL 4; TUS

Dreiser, Theodore Herman Albert
See Dreiser, Theodore

Drexler, Rosalyn 1926- .... **CLC 2, 6**
See also CA 81-84; CAD; CANR 68, 124;
CD 5, 6; CWD; MAL 5

Dreyer, Carl Theodor 1889-1968 ...... **CLC 16**
See also CAAS 116

Drieu la Rochelle, Pierre
1893-1945 .... **TCLC 21**
See also CA 250; CAAE 117; DLB 72;
EWL 3; GFL 1789 to the Present

Drieu la Rochelle, Pierre-Eugene 1893-1945
See Drieu la Rochelle, Pierre

Drinkwater, John 1882-1937 .... **TCLC 57**
See also CA 149; CAAE 109; DLB 10, 19,
149; RGEL 2

Drop Shot
See Cable, George Washington

Droste-Hulshoff, Annette Freiin von
1797-1848 .... **NCLC 3, 133**
See also CDWLB 2; DLB 133; RGSF 2;
RGWL 2, 3

Drummond, Walter
See Silverberg, Robert

Drummond, William Henry
1854-1907 .... **TCLC 25**
See also CA 160; DLB 92

Drummond de Andrade, Carlos
1902-1987 .... **CLC 18; TCLC 139**
See Andrade, Carlos Drummond de
See also CA 132; CAAS 123; DLB 307;
LAW

du Gard, Roger Martin
See Martin du Gard, Roger

Drummond of Hawthornden, William
1585-1649 .... **LC 83**
See also DLB 121, 213; RGEL 2

Drury, Allen (Stuart) 1918-1998 .... **CLC 37**
See also CA 57-60; CAAS 170; CANR 18,
52; CN 1, 2, 3, 4, 5, 6; INT CANR-18

Druse, Eleanor
See King, Stephen

Dryden, John 1631-1700 ..... **DC 3; LC 3, 21,
115; PC 25; WLC 2**
See also CDBLB 1660-1789; DA;
DAB; DAC; DAM DRAM, MST, POET;
DLB 80, 101, 131; EXPP; IDTP; LMFS
1; RGEL 2; TEA; WLIT 3

du Bellay, Joachim 1524-1560 .... **LC 92**
See also DLB 327; GFL Beginnings to
1789; RGWL 2, 3

Duberman, Martin (Bauml) 1930- ..... **CLC 8**
See also CA 1-4R; CAD; CANR 2, 63, 137;
CD 5, 6

Dubie, Norman (Evans) 1945- .... **CLC 36**
See also CA 69-72; CANR 12, 115; CP 3,
4, 5, 6, 7; DLB 120; PFS 12

Du Bois, W(illiam) E(dward) B(urghardt)
1868-1963 ..... **BLC 1; CLC 1, 2, 13, 64,
96; HR 1:2; TCLC 169; WLC 2**
See also AAYA 40; AFAW 1, 2; AMWC 1;
AMWS 2; BW 1, 3; CA 85-88; CANR
34, 82, 132; CDALB 1865-1917; DA;
DA3; DAC; DAM MST, MULT, NOV;
DLB 47, 50, 91, 246, 284; EWL 3; EXPP;
LAIT 2; LMFS 2; MAL 5; MTCW 1, 2;
MTFW 2005; NCFS 1; PFS 13; RGAL 4;
SATA 42

Dubus, Andre 1936-1999 ..... **CLC 13, 36, 97;
SSC 15**
See also AMWS 7; CA 21-24R; CAAS 177;
CANR 17; CN 5, 6; CSW; DLB 130; INT
CANR-17; RGAL 4; SSFS 10; TCLE 1:1

Duca Minimo
See D'Annunzio, Gabriele

Ducharme, Rejean 1941- .... **CLC 74**
See also CAAS 165; DLB 60

du Chatelet, Emilie 1706-1749 .... **LC 96**
See Chatelet, Gabrielle-Emilie Du

Duchen, Claire **CLC 65**

Duclos, Charles Pinot- 1704-1772 .... **LC 1**
See also GFL Beginnings to 1789

Ducornet, Erica 1943-
See Ducornet, Rikki
See also CA 37-40R; CANR 14, 34, 54, 82;
SATA 7

Ducornet, Rikki **CLC 232**
See Ducornet, Erica

Dudek, Louis 1918-2001 .... **CLC 11, 19**
See also CA 45-48; 14; CAAS 215; CANR
1; CP 1, 2, 3, 4, 5, 6, 7; DLB 88

Duerrenmatt, Friedrich 1921-1990 ... **CLC 1,
4, 8, 11, 15, 43, 102**
See Durrenmatt, Friedrich
See also CA 17-20R; CANR 33; CMW 4;
DAM DRAM; DLB 69, 124; MTCW 1, 2

Duffy, Bruce 1953(?)- .... **CLC 50**
See also CA 172

Duffy, Maureen (Patricia) 1933- ...... **CLC 37**
See also CA 25-28R; CANR 33, 68; CBD;
CN 1, 2, 3, 4, 5, 6, 7; CP 5, 6, 7; CWD;
CWP; DFS 15; DLB 14, 310; FW; MTCW
1

Du Fu
See Tu Fu
See also RGWL 2, 3

Dugan, Alan 1923-2003 .... **CLC 2, 6**
See also CA 81-84; CAAS 220; CANR 119;
CP 1, 2, 3, 4, 5, 6, 7; DLB 5; MAL 5;
PFS 10

du Gard, Roger Martin
See Martin du Gard, Roger

Ellison, Ralph 1914-1994 . **BLC 1; CLC 1, 3, 11, 54, 86, 114; SSC 26, 79; WLC 2**
See also AAYA 19; AFAW 1, 2; AMWC 2; AMWR 2; AMWS 2; BPFB 1; BW 1, 3; BYA 2; CA 9-12R; CAAS 145; CANR 24, 53; CDALB 1941-1968; CN 1, 2, 3, 4, 5; CSW; DA; DA3; DAB; DAC; DAM MST, MULT, NOV; DLB 2, 76, 227; DLBY 1994; EWL 3; EXPN; EXPS; LAIT 4; MAL 5; MTCW 1, 2; MTFW 2005; NCFS 3; NFS 2, 21; RGAL 4; RGSF 2; SSFS 1, 11; YAW

Ellmann, Lucy 1956- .... **CLC 61**
See also CA 128; CANR 154

Ellmann, Lucy Elizabeth
See Ellmann, Lucy

Ellmann, Richard (David)
1918-1987 .... **CLC 50**
See also BEST 89:2; CA 1-4R; CAAS 122; CANR 2, 28, 61; DLB 103; DLBY 1987; MTCW 1, 2; MTFW 2005

Elman, Richard (Martin)
1934-1997 .... **CLC 19**
See also CA 17-20R; 3; CAAS 163; CANR 47; TCLE 1:1

Elron
See Hubbard, L. Ron

El Saadawi, Nawal 1931- .... **CLC 196**
See also al'Sadaawi, Nawal; Sa'adawi, al-Nawal; Saadawi, Nawal El; Sa'dawi, Nawal al-
See also CA 118; 11; CANR 44, 92

Eluard, Paul PC 38; TCLC 7, 41
See Grindel, Eugene
See also EWL 3; GFL 1789 to the Present; RGWL 2, 3

Elyot, Thomas 1490(?)-1546 .... **LC 11**
See also DLB 136; RGEL 2

Elytis, Odysseus 1911-1996 .... **CLC 15, 49, 100; PC 21**
See Alepoudelis, Odysseus
See also CA 102; CAAS 151; CANR 94; CWW 2; DAM POET; DLB 329; EW 13; EWL 3; MTCW 1, 2; RGWL 2, 3

Emecheta, Buchi 1944- .... **BLC 2; CLC 14, 48, 128, 214**
See also AAYA 67; AFW; BW 2, 3; CA 81-84; CANR 27, 81, 126; CDWLB 3; CN 4, 5, 6, 7; CWRI 5; DA3; DAM MULT; DLB 117; EWL 3; FL 1:5; FW; MTCW 1, 2; MTFW 2005; NFS 12, 14; SATA 66; WLIT 2

Emerson, Mary Moody
1774-1863 .... **NCLC 66**

Emerson, Ralph Waldo 1803-1882 . **NCLC 1, 38, 98; PC 18; WLC 2**
See also AAYA 60; AMW; ANW; CDALB 1640-1865; DA; DA3; DAB; DAC; DAM MST, POET; DLB 1, 59, 73, 183, 223, 270; EXPP; LAIT 2; LMFS 1; NCFS 3; PFS 4, 17; RGAL 4; TUS; WP

Eminem 1972- .... **CLC 226**
See also CA 245

Eminescu, Mihail 1850-1889 .. **NCLC 33, 131**

Empedocles 5th cent. B.C.- .... **CMLC 50**
See also DLB 176

Empson, William 1906-1984 ... **CLC 3, 8, 19, 33, 34**
See also BRWS 2; CA 17-20R; CAAS 112; CANR 31, 61; CP 1, 2, 3; DLB 20; EWL 3; MTCW 1, 2; RGEL 2

Enchi, Fumiko (Ueda) 1905-1986 ..... **CLC 31**
See Enchi Fumiko
See also CA 129; CAAS 121; FW; MJW

Enchi Fumiko
See Enchi, Fumiko (Ueda)
See also DLB 182; EWL 3

Ende, Michael (Andreas Helmuth)
1929-1995 .... **CLC 31**
See also BYA 5; CA 124; CAAE 118; CAAS 149; CANR 36, 110; CLR 14; DLB 75; MAICYA 1, 2; MAICYAS 1; SATA 61, 130; SATA-Brief 42; SATA-Obit 86

Endo, Shusaku 1923-1996 ..... **CLC 7, 14, 19, 54, 99; SSC 48; TCLC 152**
See Endo Shusaku
See also CA 29-32R; CAAS 153; CANR 21, 54, 131; DA3; DAM NOV; MTCW 1, 2; MTFW 2005; RGSF 2; RGWL 2, 3

Endo Shusaku
See Endo, Shusaku
See also CWW 2; DLB 182; EWL 3

Engel, Marian 1933-1985 .... **CLC 36; TCLC 137**
See also CA 25-28R; CANR 12; CN 2, 3; DLB 53; FW; INT CANR-12

Engelhardt, Frederick
See Hubbard, L. Ron

Engels, Friedrich 1820-1895 .. **NCLC 85, 114**
See also DLB 129; LATS 1:1

Enright, D(ennis) J(oseph)
1920-2002 .... **CLC 4, 8, 31**
See also CA 1-4R; CAAS 211; CANR 1, 42, 83; CN 1, 2; CP 1, 2, 3, 4, 5, 6, 7; DLB 27; EWL 3; SATA 25; SATA-Obit 140

Ensler, Eve 1953- .... **CLC 212**
See also CA 172; CANR 126; DFS 23

Enzensberger, Hans Magnus
1929- .... **CLC 43; PC 28**
See also CA 119; CAAE 116; CANR 103; CWW 2; EWL 3

Ephron, Nora 1941- .... **CLC 17, 31**
See also AAYA 35; AITN 2; CA 65-68; CANR 12, 39, 83, 161; DFS 22

Epicurus 341B.C.-270B.C. .... **CMLC 21**
See also DLB 176

Epsilon
See Betjeman, John

Epstein, Daniel Mark 1948- .... **CLC 7**
See also CA 49-52; CANR 2, 53, 90

Epstein, Jacob 1956- .... **CLC 19**
See also CA 114

Epstein, Jean 1897-1953 .... **TCLC 92**

Epstein, Joseph 1937- .... **CLC 39, 204**
See also AMWS 14; CA 119; CAAE 112; CANR 50, 65, 117

Epstein, Leslie 1938- .... **CLC 27**
See also AMWS 12; CA 215; 73-76, 215; 12; CANR 23, 69; DLB 299; RGHL

Equiano, Olaudah 1745(?)-1797 . **BLC 2; LC 16**
See also AFAW 1, 2; CDWLB 3; DAM MULT; DLB 37, 50; WLIT 2

Erasmus, Desiderius 1469(?)-1536 ..... **LC 16, 93**
See also DLB 136; EW 2; LMFS 1; RGWL 2, 3; TWA

Erdman, Paul E(mil) 1932- .... **CLC 25**
See also AITN 1; CA 61-64; CANR 13, 43, 84

Erdrich, Karen Louise
See Erdrich, Louise

Erdrich, Louise 1954- .... **CLC 39, 54, 120, 176; NNAL; PC 52**
See also AAYA 10, 47; AMWS 4; BEST 89:1; BPFB 1; CA 114; CANR 41, 62, 118, 138; CDALBS; CN 5, 6, 7; CP 6, 7; CPW; CWP; DA3; DAM MULT, NOV, POP; DLB 152, 175, 206; EWL 3; EXPP; FL 1:5; LAIT 5; LATS 1:2; MAL 5; MTCW 1, 2; MTFW 2005; NFS 5; PFS 14; RGAL 4; SATA 94, 141; SSFS 14, 22; TCWW 2

Erenburg, Ilya (Grigoryevich)
See Ehrenburg, Ilya (Grigoryevich)

Erickson, Stephen Michael
See Erickson, Steve

Erickson, Steve 1950- .... **CLC 64**
See also CA 129; CANR 60, 68, 136; MTFW 2005; SFW 4; SUFW 2

Erickson, Walter
See Fast, Howard

Ericson, Walter
See Fast, Howard

Eriksson, Buntel
See Bergman, (Ernst) Ingmar

Eriugena, John Scottus c.
810-877 .... **CMLC 65**
See also DLB 115

Ernaux, Annie 1940- .... **CLC 88, 184**
See also CA 147; CANR 93; MTFW 2005; NCFS 3, 5

Erskine, John 1879-1951 .... **TCLC 84**
See also CA 159; CAAE 112; DLB 9, 102; FANT

Eschenbach, Wolfram von
See von Eschenbach, Wolfram
See also RGWL 3

Eseki, Bruno
See Mphahlele, Ezekiel

Esenin, S.A.
See Esenin, Sergei
See also EWL 3

Esenin, Sergei 1895-1925 .... **TCLC 4**
See Esenin, S.A.
See also CAAE 104; RGWL 2, 3

Esenin, Sergei Aleksandrovich
See Esenin, Sergei

Eshleman, Clayton 1935- .... **CLC 7**
See also CA 212; 33-36R, 212; 6; CANR 93; CP 1, 2, 3, 4, 5, 6, 7; DLB 5

Espada, Martin 1957- .... **PC 74**
See also CA 159; CANR 80; CP 7; EXPP; LLW; MAL 5; PFS 13, 16

Espriella, Don Manuel Alvarez
See Southey, Robert

Espriu, Salvador 1913-1985 .... **CLC 9**
See also CA 154; CAAS 115; DLB 134; EWL 3

Espronceda, Jose de 1808-1842 ..... **NCLC 39**

Esquivel, Laura 1950(?)- ... **CLC 141; HLCS 1**
See also AAYA 29; CA 143; CANR 68, 113, 161; DA3; DNFS 2; LAIT 3; LMFS 2; MTCW 2; MTFW 2005; NFS 5; WLIT 1

Esse, James
See Stephens, James

Esterbrook, Tom
See Hubbard, L. Ron

Estleman, Loren D. 1952- .... **CLC 48**
See also AAYA 27; CA 85-88; CANR 27, 74, 139; CMW 4; CPW; DA3; DAM NOV, POP; DLB 226; INT CANR-27; MTCW 1, 2; MTFW 2005; TCWW 1, 2

Etherege, Sir George 1636-1692 . **DC 23; LC 78**
See also BRW 2; DAM DRAM; DLB 80; PAB; RGEL 2

Euclid 306B.C.-283B.C. .... **CMLC 25**

Eugenides, Jeffrey 1960(?)- .... **CLC 81, 212**
See also AAYA 51; CA 144; CANR 120; MTFW 2005; NFS 24

Euripides c. 484B.C.-406B.C. .... **CMLC 23, 51; DC 4; WLCS**
See also AW 1; CDWLB 1; DA; DA3; DAB; DAC; DAM DRAM, MST; DFS 1, 4, 6; DLB 176; LAIT 1; LMFS 1; RGWL 2, 3; WLIT 8

Evan, Evin
See Faust, Frederick (Schiller)

Evans, Caradoc 1878-1945 ... **SSC 43; TCLC 85**
See also DLB 162

Evans, Evan
See Faust, Frederick (Schiller)

Evans, Marian
See Eliot, George

Evans, Mary Ann
See Eliot, George
See also NFS 20

Evarts, Esther
See Benson, Sally

Everett, Percival
See Everett, Percival L.
See also CSW

Everett, Percival L. 1956- .... **CLC 57**
See Everett, Percival
See also BW 2; CA 129; CANR 94, 134;
CN 7; MTFW 2005

Everson, R(onald) G(ilmour)
1903-1992 .... **CLC 27**
See also CA 17-20R; CP 1, 2, 3, 4; DLB 88

Everson, William (Oliver)
1912-1994 .... **CLC 1, 5, 14**
See Antoninus, Brother
See also BG 1:2; CA 9-12R; CAAS 145;
CANR 20; CP 2, 3, 4, 5; DLB 5, 16, 212;
MTCW 1

Evtushenko, Evgenii Aleksandrovich
See Yevtushenko, Yevgeny (Alexandrovich)
See also CWW 2; RGWL 2, 3

Ewart, Gavin (Buchanan)
1916-1995 .... **CLC 13, 46**
See also BRWS 7; CA 89-92; CAAS 150;
CANR 17, 46; CP 1, 2, 3, 4, 5, 6; DLB
40; MTCW 1

Ewers, Hanns Heinz 1871-1943 ..... **TCLC 12**
See also CA 149; CAAE 109

Ewing, Frederick R.
See Sturgeon, Theodore (Hamilton)

Exley, Frederick (Earl) 1929-1992 .... **CLC 6, 11**
See also AITN 2; BPFB 1; CA 81-84;
CAAS 138; CANR 117; DLB 143; DLBY
1981

Eynhardt, Guillermo
See Quiroga, Horacio (Sylvestre)

Ezekiel, Nissim (Moses) 1924-2004 .. **CLC 61**
See also CA 61-64; CAAS 223; CP 1, 2, 3,
4, 5, 6, 7; DLB 323; EWL 3

Ezekiel, Tish O'Dowd 1943- .... **CLC 34**
See also CA 129

Fadeev, Aleksandr Aleksandrovich
See Bulgya, Alexander Alexandrovich
See also DLB 272

Fadeev, Alexandr Alexandrovich
See Bulgya, Alexander Alexandrovich
See also EWL 3

Fadeyev, A.
See Bulgya, Alexander Alexandrovich

Fadeyev, Alexander TCLC 53
See Bulgya, Alexander Alexandrovich

Fagen, Donald 1948- .... **CLC 26**

Fainzil'berg, Il'ia Arnol'dovich
See Fainzilberg, Ilya Arnoldovich

Fainzilberg, Ilya Arnoldovich
1897-1937 .... **TCLC 21**
See Il'f, Il'ia
See also CA 165; CAAE 120; EWL 3

Fair, Ronald L. 1932- .... **CLC 18**
See also BW 1; CA 69-72; CANR 25; DLB
33

Fairbairn, Roger
See Carr, John Dickson

Fairbairns, Zoe (Ann) 1948- .... **CLC 32**
See also CA 103; CANR 21, 85; CN 4, 5,
6, 7

Fairfield, Flora
See Alcott, Louisa May

Fairman, Paul W. 1916-1977
See Queen, Ellery
See also CAAS 114; SFW 4

Falco, Gian
See Papini, Giovanni

Falconer, James
See Kirkup, James

Falconer, Kenneth
See Kornbluth, C(yril) M.

Falkland, Samuel
See Heijermans, Herman

Fallaci, Oriana 1930-2006 .... **CLC 11, 110**
See also CA 77-80; CAAS 253; CANR 15,
58, 134; FW; MTCW 1

Faludi, Susan 1959- .... **CLC 140**
See also CA 138; CANR 126; FW; MTCW
2; MTFW 2005; NCFS 3

Faludy, George 1913- .... **CLC 42**
See also CA 21-24R

Faludy, Gyoergy
See Faludy, George

Fanon, Frantz 1925-1961 ... **BLC 2; CLC 74; TCLC 188**
See also BW 1; CA 116; CAAS 89-92;
DAM MULT; DLB 296; LMFS 2; WLIT 2

Fanshawe, Ann 1625-1680 .... **LC 11**

Fante, John (Thomas) 1911-1983 .... **CLC 60; SSC 65**
See also AMWS 11; CA 69-72; CAAS 109;
CANR 23, 104; DLB 130; DLBY 1983

Far, Sui Sin SSC 62
See Eaton, Edith Maude
See also SSFS 4

Farah, Nuruddin 1945- ...... **BLC 2; CLC 53, 137**
See also AFW; BW 2, 3; CA 106; CANR
81, 148; CDWLB 3; CN 4, 5, 6, 7; DAM
MULT; DLB 125; EWL 3; WLIT 2

Fargue, Leon-Paul 1876(?)-1947 .... **TCLC 11**
See also CAAE 109; CANR 107; DLB 258;
EWL 3

Farigoule, Louis
See Romains, Jules

Farina, Richard 1936(?)-1966 .... **CLC 9**
See also CA 81-84; CAAS 25-28R

Farley, Walter (Lorimer)
1915-1989 .... **CLC 17**
See also AAYA 58; BYA 14; CA 17-20R;
CANR 8, 29, 84; DLB 22; JRDA; MAI-
CYA 1, 2; SATA 2, 43, 132; YAW

Farmer, Philip Jose 1918- .... **CLC 1, 19**
See also AAYA 28; BPFB 1; CA 1-4R;
CANR 4, 35, 111; DLB 8; MTCW 1;
SATA 93; SCFW 1, 2; SFW 4

Farquhar, George 1677-1707 .... **LC 21**
See also BRW 2; DAM DRAM; DLB 84;
RGEL 2

Farrell, J(ames) G(ordon)
1935-1979 .... **CLC 6**
See also CA 73-76; CAAS 89-92; CANR
36; CN 1, 2; DLB 14, 271, 326; MTCW
1; RGEL 2; RHW; WLIT 4

Farrell, James T(homas) 1904-1979 . **CLC 1, 4, 8, 11, 66; SSC 28**
See also AMW; BPFB 1; CA 5-8R; CAAS
89-92; CANR 9, 61; CN 1, 2; DLB 4, 9,
86; DLBD 2; EWL 3; MAL 5; MTCW 1,
2; MTFW 2005; RGAL 4

Farrell, Warren (Thomas) 1943- ...... **CLC 70**
See also CA 146; CANR 120

Farren, Richard J.
See Betjeman, John

Farren, Richard M.
See Betjeman, John

Fassbinder, Rainer Werner
1946-1982 .... **CLC 20**
See also CA 93-96; CAAS 106; CANR 31

Fast, Howard 1914-2003 .... **CLC 23, 131**
See also AAYA 16; BPFB 1; CA 181; 1-4R;
181; 18; CAAS 214; CANR 1, 33, 54, 75,
98, 140; CMW 4; CN 1, 2, 3, 4, 5, 6, 7;
CPW; DAM NOV; DLB 9; INT CANR-
33; LATS 1:1; MAL 5; MTCW 2; MTFW
2005; RHW; SATA 7; SATA-Essay 107;
TCWW 1, 2; YAW

Faulcon, Robert
See Holdstock, Robert

Faulkner, William (Cuthbert)
1897-1962 .... **CLC 1, 3, 6, 8, 9, 11, 14, 18, 28, 52, 68; SSC 1, 35, 42, 92, 97; TCLC 141; WLC 2**
See also AAYA 7; AMW; AMWR 1; BPFB
1; BYA 5, 15; CA 81-84; CANR 33;
CDALB 1929-1941; DA; DA3; DAB;
DAC; DAM MST, NOV; DLB 9, 11, 44,
102, 316, 330; DLBD 2; DLBY 1986,
1997; EWL 3; EXPN; EXPS; GL 2; LAIT
2; LATS 1:1; LMFS 2; MAL 5; MTCW
1, 2; MTFW 2005; NFS 4, 8, 13, 24;
RGAL 4; RGSF 2; SSFS 2, 5, 6, 12; TUS

Fauset, Jessie Redmon
1882(?)-1961 .. **BLC 2; CLC 19, 54; HR 1:2**
See also AFAW 2; BW 1; CA 109; CANR
83; DAM MULT; DLB 51; FW; LMFS 2;
MAL 5; MBL

Faust, Frederick (Schiller)
1892-1944 .... **TCLC 49**
See Brand, Max; Dawson, Peter; Frederick,
John
See also CA 152; CAAE 108; CANR 143;
DAM POP; DLB 256; TUS

Faust, Irvin 1924- .... **CLC 8**
See also CA 33-36R; CANR 28, 67; CN 1,
2, 3, 4, 5, 6, 7; DLB 2, 28, 218, 278;
DLBY 1980

Fawkes, Guy
See Benchley, Robert (Charles)

Fearing, Kenneth (Flexner)
1902-1961 .... **CLC 51**
See also CA 93-96; CANR 59; CMW 4;
DLB 9; MAL 5; RGAL 4

Fecamps, Elise
See Creasey, John

Federman, Raymond 1928- .... **CLC 6, 47**
See also CA 208; 17-20R, 208; 8; CANR
10, 43, 83, 108; CN 3, 4, 5, 6; DLBY
1980

Federspiel, J.F. 1931- .... **CLC 42**
See also CA 146

Federspiel, Juerg F.
See Federspiel, J.F.

Feiffer, Jules 1929- .... **CLC 2, 8, 64**
See also AAYA 3, 62; CA 17-20R; CAD;
CANR 30, 59, 129, 161; CD 5, 6; DAM
DRAM; DLB 7, 44; INT CANR-30;
MTCW 1; SATA 8, 61, 111, 157

Feiffer, Jules Ralph
See Feiffer, Jules

Feige, Hermann Albert Otto Maximilian
See Traven, B.

Feinberg, David B. 1956-1994 .... **CLC 59**
See also CA 135; CAAS 147

Feinstein, Elaine 1930- .... **CLC 36**
See also CA 69-72; 1; CANR 31, 68, 121;
CN 3, 4, 5, 6, 7; CP 2, 3, 4, 5, 6, 7; CWP;
DLB 14, 40; MTCW 1

Feke, Gilbert David CLC 65

Feldman, Irving (Mordecai) 1928- ..... **CLC 7**
See also CA 1-4R; CANR 1; CP 1, 2, 3, 4,
5, 6, 7; DLB 169; TCLE 1:1

Felix-Tchicaya, Gerald
See Tchicaya, Gerald Felix

Fellini, Federico 1920-1993 .... **CLC 16, 85**
See also CA 65-68; CAAS 143; CANR 33

GFL 1789 to the Present; LAIT 2; LMFS
1; NFS 14; RGSF 2; RGWL 2, 3; SSFS
6; TWA

Flavius Josephus
See Josephus, Flavius

Flecker, Herman Elroy
See Flecker, (Herman) James Elroy

Flecker, (Herman) James Elroy
1884-1915 .... **TCLC 43**
See also CA 150; CAAE 109; DLB 10, 19;
RGEL 2

Fleming, Ian 1908-1964 .... **CLC 3, 30**
See also AAYA 26; BPFB 1; CA 5-8R;
CANR 59; CDBLB 1945-1960; CMW 4;
CPW; DA3; DAM POP; DLB 87, 201;
MSW; MTCW 1, 2; MTFW 2005; RGEL
2; SATA 9; TEA; YAW

Fleming, Ian Lancaster
See Fleming, Ian

Fleming, Thomas 1927- .... **CLC 37**
See also CA 5-8R; CANR 10, 102, 155;
INT CANR-10; SATA 8

Fleming, Thomas James
See Fleming, Thomas

Fletcher, John 1579-1625 .... **DC 6; LC 33**
See also BRW 2; CDBLB Before 1660;
DLB 58; RGEL 2; TEA

Fletcher, John Gould 1886-1950 .... **TCLC 35**
See also CA 167; CAAE 107; DLB 4, 45;
LMFS 2; MAL 5; RGAL 4

Fleur, Paul
See Pohl, Frederik

Flieg, Helmut
See Heym, Stefan

Flooglebuckle, Al
See Spiegelman, Art

Flora, Fletcher 1914-1969
See Queen, Ellery
See also CA 1-4R; CANR 3, 85

Flying Officer X
See Bates, H(erbert) E(rnest)

Fo, Dario 1926- .... **CLC 32, 109, 227; DC 10**
See also CA 128; CAAE 116; CANR 68,
114, 134; CWW 2; DA3; DAM DRAM;
DFS 23; DLB 330; DLBY 1997; EWL 3;
MTCW 1, 2; MTFW 2005; WLIT 7

Foden, Giles 1967- .... **CLC 231**
See also CA 240; DLB 267; NFS 15

Fogarty, Jonathan Titulescu Esq.
See Farrell, James T(homas)

Follett, Ken 1949- .... **CLC 18**
See also AAYA 6, 50; BEST 89:4; BPFB 1;
CA 81-84; CANR 13, 33, 54, 102, 156;
CMW 4; CPW; DA3; DAM NOV, POP;
DLB 87; DLBY 1981; INT CANR-33;
MTCW 1

Follett, Kenneth Martin
See Follett, Ken

Fondane, Benjamin 1898-1944 ..... **TCLC 159**

Fontane, Theodor 1819-1898 . **NCLC 26, 163**
See also CDWLB 2; DLB 129; EW 6;
RGWL 2, 3; TWA

Fonte, Moderata 1555-1592 .... **LC 118**

Fontenot, Chester CLC 65

Fonvizin, Denis Ivanovich
1744(?)-1792 .... **LC 81**
See also DLB 150; RGWL 2, 3

Foote, Horton 1916- .... **CLC 51, 91**
See also CA 73-76; CAD; CANR 34, 51,
110; CD 5, 6; CSW; DA3; DAM DRAM;
DFS 20; DLB 26, 266; EWL 3; INT
CANR-34; MTFW 2005

Foote, Mary Hallock 1847-1938 .. **TCLC 108**
See also DLB 186, 188, 202, 221; TCWW
2

Foote, Samuel 1721-1777 .... **LC 106**
See also DLB 89; RGEL 2

Foote, Shelby 1916-2005 .... **CLC 75, 224**
See also AAYA 40; CA 5-8R; CAAS 240;
CANR 3, 45, 74, 131; CN 1, 2, 3, 4, 5, 6,
7; CPW; CSW; DA3; DAM NOV, POP;
DLB 2, 17; MAL 5; MTCW 1; MTFW
2005; RHW

Forbes, Cosmo
See Lewton, Val

Forbes, Esther 1891-1967 .... **CLC 12**
See also AAYA 17; BYA 2; CA 13-14;
CAAS 25-28R; CAP 1; CLR 27; DLB 22;
JRDA; MAICYA 1, 2; RHW; SATA 2,
100; YAW

Forché, Carolyn 1950- .. **CLC 25, 83, 86; PC
10**
See also CA 117; CAAE 109; CANR 50,
74, 138; CP 4, 5, 6, 7; CWP; DA3; DAM
POET; DLB 5, 193; INT CA-117; MAL
5; MTCW 2; MTFW 2005; PFS 18;
RGAL 4

Forché, Carolyn Louise
See Forché, Carolyn

Ford, Elbur
See Hibbert, Eleanor Alice Burford

Ford, Ford Madox 1873-1939 ... **TCLC 1, 15,
39, 57, 172**
See Chaucer, Daniel
See also BRW 6; CA 132; CAAE 104;
CANR 74; CDBLB 1914-1945; DA3;
DAM NOV; DLB 34, 98, 162; EWL 3;
MTCW 1, 2; RGEL 2; TEA

Ford, Henry 1863-1947 .... **TCLC 73**
See also CA 148; CAAE 115

Ford, Jack
See Ford, John

Ford, John 1586-1639 .... **DC 8; LC 68**
See also BRW 2; CDBLB Before 1660;
DA3; DAM DRAM; DFS 7; DLB 58;
IDTP; RGEL 2

Ford, John 1895-1973 .... **CLC 16**
See also AAYA 75; CA 187; CAAS 45-48

Ford, Richard 1944- .... **CLC 46, 99, 205**
See also AMWS 5; CA 69-72; CANR 11,
47, 86, 128; CN 5, 6, 7; CSW; DLB 227;
EWL 3; MAL 5; MTCW 2; MTFW 2005;
RGAL 4; RGSF 2

Ford, Webster
See Masters, Edgar Lee

Foreman, Richard 1937- .... **CLC 50**
See also CA 65-68; CAD; CANR 32, 63,
143; CD 5, 6

Forester, C(ecil) S(cott) 1899-1966 . **CLC 35;
TCLC 152**
See also CA 73-76; CAAS 25-28R; CANR
83; DLB 191; RGEL 2; RHW; SATA 13

Forez
See Mauriac, François (Charles)

Forman, James
See Forman, James D(ouglas)

Forman, James D(ouglas) 1932- .... **CLC 21**
See also AAYA 17; CA 9-12R; CANR 4,
19, 42; JRDA; MAICYA 1, 2; SATA 8,
70; YAW

Forman, Milos 1932- .... **CLC 164**
See also AAYA 63; CA 109

Fornes, Maria Irene 1930- .... **CLC 39, 61,
187; DC 10; HLCS 1**
See also CA 25-28R; CAD; CANR 28, 81;
CD 5, 6; CWD; DLB 7; HW 1, 2; INT
CANR-28; LLW; MAL 5; MTCW 1;
RGAL 4

Forrest, Leon (Richard)
1937-1997 .... **BLCS; CLC 4**
See also AFAW 2; BW 2; CA 89-92; 7;
CAAS 162; CANR 25, 52, 87; CN 4, 5,
6; DLB 33

Forster, E(dward) M(organ)
1879-1970 ...... **CLC 1, 2, 3, 4, 9, 10, 13,
15, 22, 45, 77; SSC 27, 96; TCLC 125;
WLC 2**
See also AAYA 2, 37; BRW 6; BRWR 2;
BYA 12; CA 13-14; CAAS 25-28R;
CANR 45; CAP 1; CDBLB 1914-1945;
DA; DA3; DAB; DAC; DAM MST, NOV;
DLB 34, 98, 162, 178, 195; DLBD 10;
EWL 3; EXPN; LAIT 3; LMFS 1; MTCW
1, 2; MTFW 2005; NCFS 1; NFS 3, 10,
11; RGEL 2; RGSF 2; SATA 57; SUFW
1; TEA; WLIT 4

Forster, John 1812-1876 .... **NCLC 11**
See also DLB 144, 184

Forster, Margaret 1938- .... **CLC 149**
See also CA 133; CANR 62, 115; CN 4, 5,
6, 7; DLB 155, 271

Forsyth, Frederick 1938- .... **CLC 2, 5, 36**
See also BEST 89:4; CA 85-88; CANR 38,
62, 115, 137; CMW 4; CN 3, 4, 5, 6, 7;
CPW; DAM NOV, POP; DLB 87; MTCW
1, 2; MTFW 2005

Forten, Charlotte L. 1837-1914 .... **BLC 2;
TCLC 16**
See Grimké, Charlotte L(ottie) Forten
See also DLB 50, 239

Fortinbras
See Grieg, (Johan) Nordahl (Brun)

Foscolo, Ugo 1778-1827 .... **NCLC 8, 97**
See also EW 5; WLIT 7

Fosse, Bob 1927-1987
See Fosse, Robert L.
See also CAAE 110; CAAS 123

Fosse, Robert L. CLC 20
See Fosse, Bob

Foster, Hannah Webster
1758-1840 .... **NCLC 99**
See also DLB 37, 200; RGAL 4

Foster, Stephen Collins
1826-1864 .... **NCLC 26**
See also RGAL 4

Foucault, Michel 1926-1984 . **CLC 31, 34, 69**
See also CA 105; CAAS 113; CANR 34;
DLB 242; EW 13; EWL 3; GFL 1789 to
the Present; GLL 1; LMFS 2; MTCW 1,
2; TWA

**Fouqué, Friedrich (Heinrich Karl) de la
Motte** 1777-1843 .... **NCLC 2**
See also DLB 90; RGWL 2, 3; SUFW 1

Fourier, Charles 1772-1837 .... **NCLC 51**

Fournier, Henri-Alban 1886-1914
See Alain-Fournier
See also CA 179; CAAE 104

Fournier, Pierre 1916-1997 .... **CLC 11**
See Gascar, Pierre
See also CA 89-92; CANR 16, 40

Fowles, John 1926-2005 .... **CLC 1, 2, 3, 4, 6,
9, 10, 15, 33, 87; SSC 33**
See also BPFB 1; BRWS 1; CA 5-8R;
CAAS 245; CANR 25, 71, 103; CDBLB
1960 to Present; CN 1, 2, 3, 4, 5, 6, 7;
DA3; DAB; DAC; DAM MST; DLB 14,
139, 207; EWL 3; HGG; MTCW 1, 2;
MTFW 2005; NFS 21; RGEL 2; RHW;
SATA 22; SATA-Obit 171; TEA; WLIT 4

Fowles, John Robert
See Fowles, John

Fox, Paula 1923- .... **CLC 2, 8, 121**
See also AAYA 3, 37; BYA 3, 8; CA 73-76;
CANR 20, 36, 62, 105; CLR 1, 44, 96;
DLB 52; JRDA; MAICYA 1, 2; MTCW
1; NFS 12; SATA 17, 60, 120, 167; WYA;
YAW

Fox, William Price (Jr.) 1926- .... **CLC 22**
See also CA 17-20R; 19; CANR 11, 142;
CSW; DLB 2; DLBY 1981

Foxe, John 1517(?)-1587 .... **LC 14**
See also DLB 132

Frame, Janet CLC 2, 3, 6, 22, 66, 96; SSC 29
See Clutha, Janet Paterson Frame
See also CN 1, 2, 3, 4, 5, 6, 7; CP 2, 3, 4;
CWP; EWL 3; RGEL 2; RGSF 2; TWA

France, Anatole TCLC 9
See Thibault, Jacques Anatole Francois
See also DLB 123, 330; EWL 3; GFL 1789
to the Present; RGWL 2, 3; SUFW 1

Francis, Claude CLC 50
See also CA 192

Francis, Dick
See Francis, Richard Stanley
See also CN 2, 3, 4, 5, 6

**Francis, Richard Stanley 1920- ... CLC 2, 22,
42, 102**
See Francis, Dick
See also AAYA 5, 21; BEST 89:3; BPFB 1;
CA 5-8R; CANR 9, 42, 68, 100, 141; CD-
BLB 1960 to Present; CMW 4; CN 7;
DA3; DAM POP; DLB 87; INT CANR-9;
MSW; MTCW 1, 2; MTFW 2005

Francis, Robert (Churchill)
1901-1987 .... CLC 15; PC 34
See also AMWS 9; CA 1-4R; CAAS 123;
CANR 1; CP 1, 2, 3, 4; EXPP; PFS 12;
TCLE 1:1

Francis, Lord Jeffrey
See Jeffrey, Francis
See also DLB 107

Frank, Anne(lies Marie)
1929-1945 .... TCLC 17; WLC 2
See also AAYA 12; BYA 1; CA 133; CAAE
113; CANR 68; CLR 101; DA; DA3;
DAB; DAC; DAM MST; LAIT 4; MAI-
CYA 2; MAICYAS 1; MTCW 1, 2;
MTFW 2005; NCFS 2; RGHL; SATA 87;
SATA-Brief 42; WYA; YAW

Frank, Bruno 1887-1945 .... TCLC 81
See also CA 189; DLB 118; EWL 3

Frank, Elizabeth 1945- .... CLC 39
See also CA 126; CAAE 121; CANR 78,
150; INT CA-126

Frankl, Viktor E(mil) 1905-1997 ...... CLC 93
See also CA 65-68; CAAS 161; RGHL

Franklin, Benjamin
See Hasek, Jaroslav (Matej Frantisek)

**Franklin, Benjamin 1706-1790 .. LC 25, 134;
WLCS**
See also AMW; CDALB 1640-1865; DA;
DA3; DAB; DAC; DAM MST; DLB 24,
43, 73, 183; LAIT 1; RGAL 4; TUS

**Franklin, (Stella Maria Sarah) Miles
(Lampe) 1879-1954 .... TCLC 7**
See also CA 164; CAAE 104; DLB 230;
FW; MTCW 2; RGEL 2; TWA

Franzen, Jonathan 1959- .... CLC 202
See also AAYA 65; CA 129; CANR 105

Fraser, Antonia 1932- .... CLC 32, 107
See also AAYA 57; CA 85-88; CANR 44,
65, 119; CMW; DLB 276; MTCW 1, 2;
MTFW 2005; SATA-Brief 32

Fraser, George MacDonald 1925- ...... CLC 7
See also AAYA 48; CA 180; 45-48, 180;
CANR 2, 48, 74; MTCW 2; RHW

Fraser, Sylvia 1935- .... CLC 64
See also CA 45-48; CANR 1, 16, 60; CCA
1

**Frayn, Michael 1933- .... CLC 3, 7, 31, 47,
176; DC 27**
See also AAYA 69; BRWC 2; BRWS 7; CA
5-8R; CANR 30, 69, 114, 133; CBD; CD
5, 6; CN 1, 2, 3, 4, 5, 6, 7; DAM DRAM,
NOV; DFS 22; DLB 13, 14, 194, 245;
FANT; MTCW 1, 2; MTFW 2005; SFW
4

Fraze, Candida (Merrill) 1945- .... CLC 50
See also CA 126

Frazer, Andrew
See Marlowe, Stephen

Frazer, J(ames) G(eorge)
1854-1941 .... TCLC 32
See also BRWS 3; CAAE 118; NCFS 5

Frazer, Robert Caine
See Creasey, John

Frazer, Sir James George
See Frazer, J(ames) G(eorge)

Frazier, Charles 1950- .... CLC 109, 224
See also AAYA 34; CA 161; CANR 126;
CSW; DLB 292; MTFW 2005

Frazier, Ian 1951- .... CLC 46
See also CA 130; CANR 54, 93

Frederic, Harold 1856-1898 ... NCLC 10, 175
See also AMW; DLB 12, 23; DLBD 13;
MAL 5; NFS 22; RGAL 4

Frederick, John
See Faust, Frederick (Schiller)
See also TCWW 2

Frederick the Great 1712-1786 .... LC 14

Fredro, Aleksander 1793-1876 .... NCLC 8

Freeling, Nicolas 1927-2003 .... CLC 38
See also CA 49-52; 12; CAAS 218; CANR
1, 17, 50, 84; CMW 4; CN 1, 2, 3, 4, 5,
6; DLB 87

Freeman, Douglas Southall
1886-1953 .... TCLC 11
See also CA 195; CAAE 109; DLB 17;
DLBD 17

Freeman, Judith 1946- .... CLC 55
See also CA 148; CANR 120; DLB 256

Freeman, Mary E(leanor) Wilkins
1852-1930 .... SSC 1, 47; TCLC 9
See also CA 177; CAAE 106; DLB 12, 78,
221; EXPS; FW; HGG; MBL; RGAL 4;
RGSF 2; SSFS 4, 8; SUFW 1; TUS

Freeman, R(ichard) Austin
1862-1943 .... TCLC 21
See also CAAE 113; CANR 84; CMW 4;
DLB 70

French, Albert 1943- .... CLC 86
See also BW 3; CA 167

French, Antonia
See Kureishi, Hanif

French, Marilyn 1929- .. CLC 10, 18, 60, 177
See also BPFB 1; CA 69-72; CANR 3, 31,
134; CN 5, 6, 7; CPW; DAM DRAM,
NOV, POP; FL 1:5; FW; INT CANR-31;
MTCW 1, 2; MTFW 2005

French, Paul
See Asimov, Isaac

**Freneau, Philip Morin 1752-1832 .. NCLC 1,
111**
See also AMWS 2; DLB 37, 43; RGAL 4

Freud, Sigmund 1856-1939 .... TCLC 52
See also CA 133; CAAE 115; CANR 69;
DLB 296; EW 8; EWL 3; LATS 1:1;
MTCW 1, 2; MTFW 2005; NCFS 3; TWA

Freytag, Gustav 1816-1895 .... NCLC 109
See also DLB 129

Friedan, Betty 1921-2006 .... CLC 74
See also CA 65-68; CAAS 248; CANR 18,
45, 74; DLB 246; FW; MTCW 1, 2;
MTFW 2005; NCFS 5

Friedan, Betty Naomi
See Friedan, Betty

Friedlander, Saul 1932- .... CLC 90
See also CA 130; CAAE 117; CANR 72;
RGHL

Friedman, B(ernard) H(arper)
1926- .... CLC 7
See also CA 1-4R; CANR 3, 48

Friedman, Bruce Jay 1930- ...... CLC 3, 5, 56
See also CA 9-12R; CAD; CANR 25, 52,
101; CD 5, 6; CN 1, 2, 3, 4, 5, 6, 7; DLB
2, 28, 244; INT CANR-25; MAL 5; SSFS
18

**Friel, Brian 1929- .... CLC 5, 42, 59, 115; DC
8; SSC 76**
See also BRWS 5; CA 21-24R; CANR 33,
69, 131; CBD; CD 5, 6; DFS 11; DLB
13, 319; EWL 3; MTCW 1; RGEL 2; TEA

Friis-Baastad, Babbis Ellinor
1921-1970 .... CLC 12
See also CA 17-20R; CAAS 134; SATA 7

**Frisch, Max 1911-1991 ...... CLC 3, 9, 14, 18,
32, 44; TCLC 121**
See also CA 85-88; CAAS 134; CANR 32,
74; CDWLB 2; DAM DRAM, NOV; DLB
69, 124; EW 13; EWL 3; MTCW 1, 2;
MTFW 2005; RGHL; RGWL 2, 3

Fromentin, Eugene (Samuel Auguste)
1820-1876 .... NCLC 10, 125
See also DLB 123; GFL 1789 to the Present

Frost, Frederick
See Faust, Frederick (Schiller)

**Frost, Robert 1874-1963 . CLC 1, 3, 4, 9, 10,
13, 15, 26, 34, 44; PC 1, 39, 71; WLC 2**
See also AAYA 21; AMW; AMWR 1; CA
89-92; CANR 33; CDALB 1917-1929;
CLR 67; DA; DA3; DAB; DAC; DAM
MST, POET; DLB 54, 284; DLBD 7;
EWL 3; EXPP; MAL 5; MTCW 1, 2;
MTFW 2005; PAB; PFS 1, 2, 3, 4, 5, 6,
7, 10, 13; RGAL 4; SATA 14; TUS; WP;
WYA

Frost, Robert Lee
See Frost, Robert

Froude, James Anthony
1818-1894 .... NCLC 43
See also DLB 18, 57, 144

Froy, Herald
See Waterhouse, Keith (Spencer)

Fry, Christopher 1907-2005 ... CLC 2, 10, 14
See also BRWS 3; CA 17-20R; 23; CAAS
240; CANR 9, 30, 74, 132; CBD; CD 5,
6; CP 1, 2, 3, 4, 5, 6, 7; DAM DRAM;
DLB 13; EWL 3; MTCW 1, 2; MTFW
2005; RGEL 2; SATA 66; TEA

Frye, (Herman) Northrop
1912-1991 .... CLC 24, 70; TCLC 165
See also CA 5-8R; CAAS 133; CANR 8,
37; DLB 67, 68, 246; EWL 3; MTCW 1,
2; MTFW 2005; RGAL 4; TWA

Fuchs, Daniel 1909-1993 .... CLC 8, 22
See also CA 81-84; 5; CAAS 142; CANR
40; CN 1, 2, 3, 4, 5; DLB 9, 26, 28;
DLBY 1993; MAL 5

Fuchs, Daniel 1934- .... CLC 34
See also CA 37-40R; CANR 14, 48

**Fuentes, Carlos 1928- .. CLC 3, 8, 10, 13, 22,
41, 60, 113; HLC 1; SSC 24; WLC 2**
See also AAYA 4, 45; AITN 2; BPFB 1;
CA 69-72; CANR 10, 32, 68, 104, 138;
CDWLB 3; CWW 2; DA; DA3; DAB;
DAC; DAM MST, MULT, NOV; DLB
113; DNFS 2; EWL 3; HW 1, 2; LAIT 3;
LATS 1:2; LAW; LAWS 1; LMFS 2;
MTCW 1, 2; MTFW 2005; NFS 8; RGSF
2; RGWL 2, 3; TWA; WLIT 1

Fuentes, Gregorio Lopez y
See Lopez y Fuentes, Gregorio

Fuertes, Gloria 1918-1998 .... PC 27
See also CA 178, 180; DLB 108; HW 2;
SATA 115

**Fugard, (Harold) Athol 1932- . CLC 5, 9, 14,
25, 40, 80, 211; DC 3**
See also AAYA 17; AFW; CA 85-88; CANR
32, 54, 118; CD 5, 6; DAM DRAM; DFS
3, 6, 10; DLB 225; DNFS 1, 2; EWL 3;
LATS 1:2; MTCW 1; MTFW 2005; RGEL
2; WLIT 2

Fugard, Sheila 1932- .... CLC 48
See also CA 125

Fujiwara no Teika 1162-1241 .... CMLC 73
See also DLB 203

Fukuyama, Francis 1952- .... **CLC 131**
See also CA 140; CANR 72, 125
Fuller, Charles (H.), (Jr.) 1939- .... **BLC 2;
CLC 25; DC 1**
See also BW 2; CA 112; CAAE 108; CAD;
CANR 87; CD 5, 6; DAM DRAM,
MULT; DFS 8; DLB 38, 266; EWL 3;
INT CA-112; MAL 5; MTCW 1
Fuller, Henry Blake 1857-1929 .... **TCLC 103**
See also CA 177; CAAE 108; DLB 12;
RGAL 4
Fuller, John (Leopold) 1937- .... **CLC 62**
See also CA 21-24R; CANR 9, 44; CP 1, 2,
3, 4, 5, 6, 7; DLB 40
Fuller, Margaret
See Ossoli, Sarah Margaret (Fuller)
See also AMWS 2; DLB 183, 223, 239; FL
1:3
Fuller, Roy (Broadbent) 1912-1991 ... **CLC 4,
28**
See also BRWS 7; CA 5-8R; 10; CAAS
135; CANR 53, 83; CN 1, 2, 3, 4, 5; CP
1, 2, 3, 4, 5; CWRI 5; DLB 15, 20; EWL
3; RGEL 2; SATA 87
Fuller, Sarah Margaret
See Ossoli, Sarah Margaret (Fuller)
Fuller, Sarah Margaret
See Ossoli, Sarah Margaret (Fuller)
See also DLB 1, 59, 73
Fuller, Thomas 1608-1661 .... **LC 111**
See also DLB 151
Fulton, Alice 1952- .... **CLC 52**
See also CA 116; CANR 57, 88; CP 5, 6, 7;
CWP; DLB 193; PFS 25
Furphy, Joseph 1843-1912 .... **TCLC 25**
See Collins, Tom
See also CA 163; DLB 230; EWL 3; RGEL
2
Fuson, Robert H(enderson) 1927- .... **CLC 70**
See also CA 89-92; CANR 103
Fussell, Paul 1924- .... **CLC 74**
See also BEST 90:1; CA 17-20R; CANR 8,
21, 35, 69, 135; INT CANR-21; MTCW
1, 2; MTFW 2005
Futabatei, Shimei 1864-1909 .... **TCLC 44**
See Futabatei Shimei
See also CA 162; MJW
Futabatei Shimei
See Futabatei, Shimei
See also DLB 180; EWL 3
Futrelle, Jacques 1875-1912 .... **TCLC 19**
See also CA 155; CAAE 113; CMW 4
Gaboriau, Emile 1835-1873 .... **NCLC 14**
See also CMW 4; MSW
Gadda, Carlo Emilio 1893-1973 ...... **CLC 11;
TCLC 144**
See also CA 89-92; DLB 177; EWL 3;
WLIT 7
Gaddis, William 1922-1998 ... **CLC 1, 3, 6, 8,
10, 19, 43, 86**
See also AMWS 4; BPFB 1; CA 17-20R;
CAAS 172; CANR 21, 48, 148; CN 1, 2,
3, 4, 5, 6; DLB 2, 278; EWL 3; MAL 5;
MTCW 1, 2; MTFW 2005; RGAL 4
Gage, Walter
See Inge, William (Motter)
Gaiman, Neil 1960- .... **CLC 195**
See also AAYA 19, 42; CA 133; CANR 81,
129; CLR 109; DLB 261; HGG; MTFW
2005; SATA 85, 146; SFW 4; SUFW 2
Gaiman, Neil Richard
See Gaiman, Neil
Gaines, Ernest J. 1933- .. **BLC 2; CLC 3, 11,
18, 86, 181; SSC 68**
See also AAYA 18; AFAW 1, 2; AITN 1;
BPFB 2; BW 2, 3; BYA 6; CA 9-12R;
CANR 6, 24, 42, 75, 126; CDALB 1968-
1988; CLR 62; CN 1, 2, 3, 4, 5, 6, 7;
CSW; DA3; DAM MULT; DLB 2, 33,

152; DLBY 1980; EWL 3; EXPN; LAIT
5; LATS 1:2; MAL 5; MTCW 1, 2;
MTFW 2005; NFS 5, 7, 16; RGAL 4;
RGSF 2; RHW; SATA 86; SSFS 5; YAW
Gaitskill, Mary 1954- .... **CLC 69**
See also CA 128; CANR 61, 152; DLB 244;
TCLE 1:1
Gaitskill, Mary Lawrence
See Gaitskill, Mary
Gaius Suetonius Tranquillus
See Suetonius
Galdos, Benito Perez
See Perez Galdos, Benito
See also EW 7
Gale, Zona 1874-1938 .... **TCLC 7**
See also CA 153; CAAE 105; CANR 84;
DAM DRAM; DFS 17; DLB 9, 78, 228;
RGAL 4
Galeano, Eduardo (Hughes) 1940- . **CLC 72;
HLCS 1**
See also CA 29-32R; CANR 13, 32, 100;
HW 1
Galiano, Juan Valera y Alcala
See Valera y Alcala-Galiano, Juan
Galilei, Galileo 1564-1642 .... **LC 45**
Gallagher, Tess 1943- .... **CLC 18, 63; PC 9**
See also CA 106; CP 3, 4, 5, 6, 7; CWP;
DAM POET; DLB 120, 212, 244; PFS 16
Gallant, Mavis 1922- ..... **CLC 7, 18, 38, 172;
SSC 5, 78**
See also CA 69-72; CANR 29, 69, 117;
CCA 1; CN 1, 2, 3, 4, 5, 6, 7; DAC; DAM
MST; DLB 53; EWL 3; MTCW 1, 2;
MTFW 2005; RGEL 2; RGSF 2
Gallant, Roy A(rthur) 1924- .... **CLC 17**
See also CA 5-8R; CANR 4, 29, 54, 117;
CLR 30; MAICYA 1, 2; SATA 4, 68, 110
Gallico, Paul (William) 1897-1976 ..... **CLC 2**
See also AITN 1; CA 5-8R; CAAS 69-72;
CANR 23; CN 1, 2; DLB 9, 171; FANT;
MAICYA 1, 2; SATA 13
Gallo, Max Louis 1932- .... **CLC 95**
See also CA 85-88
Gallois, Lucien
See Desnos, Robert
Gallup, Ralph
See Whitemore, Hugh (John)
Galsworthy, John 1867-1933 .... **SSC 22;
TCLC 1, 45; WLC 2**
See also BRW 6; CA 141; CAAE 104;
CANR 75; CDBLB 1890-1914; DA; DA3;
DAB; DAC; DAM DRAM, MST, NOV;
DLB 10, 34, 98, 162, 330; DLBD 16;
EWL 3; MTCW 2; RGEL 2; SSFS 3; TEA
Galt, John 1779-1839 .... **NCLC 1, 110**
See also DLB 99, 116, 159; RGEL 2; RGSF
2
Galvin, James 1951- .... **CLC 38**
See also CA 108; CANR 26
Gamboa, Federico 1864-1939 .... **TCLC 36**
See also CA 167; HW 2; LAW
Gandhi, M. K.
See Gandhi, Mohandas Karamchand
Gandhi, Mahatma
See Gandhi, Mohandas Karamchand
Gandhi, Mohandas Karamchand
1869-1948 .... **TCLC 59**
See also CA 132; CAAE 121; DA3; DAM
MULT; DLB 323; MTCW 1, 2
Gann, Ernest Kellogg 1910-1991 ..... **CLC 23**
See also AITN 1; BPFB 2; CA 1-4R; CAAS
136; CANR 1, 83; RHW
Gao Xingjian 1940- .... **CLC 167**
See Xingjian, Gao
See also MTFW 2005
Garber, Eric 1943(?)-
See Holleran, Andrew
See also CANR 89

Garcia, Cristina 1958- .... **CLC 76**
See also AMWS 11; CA 141; CANR 73,
130; CN 7; DLB 292; DNFS 1; EWL 3;
HW 2; LLW; MTFW 2005
Garcia Lorca, Federico 1898-1936 ...... **DC 2;
HLC 2; PC 3; TCLC 1, 7, 49, 181;
WLC 2**
See Lorca, Federico Garcia
See also AAYA 46; CA 131; CAAE 104;
CANR 81; DA; DA3; DAB; DAC; DAM
DRAM, MST, MULT, POET; DFS 4, 10;
DLB 108; EWL 3; HW 1, 2; LATS 1:2;
MTCW 1, 2; MTFW 2005; TWA
Garcia Marquez, Gabriel 1928- .... **CLC 2, 3,
8, 10, 15, 27, 47, 55, 68, 170; HLC 1;
SSC 8, 83; WLC 3**
See also AAYA 3, 33; BEST 89:1, 90:4;
BPFB 2; BYA 12, 16; CA 33-36R; CANR
10, 28, 50, 75, 82, 128; CDWLB 3; CPW;
CWW 2; DA; DA3; DAB; DAC; DAM
MST, MULT, NOV, POP; DLB 113, 330;
DNFS 1, 2; EWL 3; EXPN; EXPS; HW
1, 2; LAIT 2; LATS 1:2; LAW; LAWS 1;
LMFS 2; MTCW 1, 2; MTFW 2005;
NCFS 3; NFS 1, 5, 10; RGSF 2; RGWL
2, 3; SSFS 1, 6, 16, 21; TWA; WLIT 1
Garcia Marquez, Gabriel Jose
See Garcia Marquez, Gabriel
Garcilaso de la Vega, El Inca
1539-1616 .... **HLCS 1; LC 127**
See also DLB 318; LAW
Gard, Janice
See Latham, Jean Lee
Gard, Roger Martin du
See Martin du Gard, Roger
Gardam, Jane (Mary) 1928- .... **CLC 43**
See also CA 49-52; CANR 2, 18, 33, 54,
106; CLR 12; DLB 14, 161, 231; MAI-
CYA 1, 2; MTCW 1; SAAS 9; SATA 39,
76, 130; SATA-Brief 28; YAW
Gardner, Herb(ert George)
1934-2003 .... **CLC 44**
See also CA 149; CAAS 220; CAD; CANR
119; CD 5, 6; DFS 18, 20
Gardner, John, Jr. 1933-1982 ... **CLC 2, 3, 5,
7, 8, 10, 18, 28, 34; SSC 7**
See also AAYA 45; AITN 1; AMWS 6;
BPFB 2; CA 65-68; CAAS 107; CANR
33, 73; CDALBS; CN 2, 3; CPW; DA3;
DAM NOV, POP; DLB 2; DLBY 1982;
EWL 3; FANT; LATS 1:2; MAL 5;
MTCW 1, 2; MTFW 2005; NFS 3; RGAL
4; RGSF 2; SATA 40; SATA-Obit 31;
SSFS 8
Gardner, John (Edmund) 1926- .... **CLC 30**
See also CA 103; CANR 15, 69, 127; CMW
4; CPW; DAM POP; MTCW 1
Gardner, Miriam
See Bradley, Marion Zimmer
See also GLL 1
Gardner, Noel
See Kuttner, Henry
Gardons, S. S.
See Snodgrass, W.D.
Garfield, Leon 1921-1996 .... **CLC 12**
See also AAYA 8, 69; BYA 1, 3; CA 17-
20R; CAAS 152; CANR 38, 41, 78; CLR
21; DLB 161; JRDA; MAICYA 1, 2;
MAICYAS 1; SATA 1, 32, 76; SATA-Obit
90; TEA; WYA; YAW
Garland, (Hannibal) Hamlin
1860-1940 .... **SSC 18; TCLC 3**
See also CAAE 104; DLB 12, 71, 78, 186;
MAL 5; RGAL 4; RGSF 2; TCWW 1, 2
Garneau, (Hector de) Saint-Denys
1912-1943 .... **TCLC 13**
See also CAAE 111; DLB 88

Garner, Alan 1934- .... **CLC 17**
See also AAYA 18; BYA 3, 5; CA 178; 73-
76, 178; CANR 15, 64, 134; CLR 20;
CPW; DAB; DAM POP; DLB 161, 261;
FANT; MAICYA 1, 2; MTCW 1, 2;
MTFW 2005; SATA 18, 69; SATA-Essay
108; SUFW 1, 2; YAW

Garner, Hugh 1913-1979 .... **CLC 13**
See Warwick, Jarvis
See also CA 69-72; CANR 31; CCA 1; CN
1, 2; DLB 68

Garnett, David 1892-1981 .... **CLC 3**
See also CA 5-8R; CAAS 103; CANR 17,
79; CN 1, 2; DLB 34; FANT; MTCW 2;
RGEL 2; SFW 4; SUFW 1

Garnier, Robert c. 1545-1590 .... **LC 119**
See also DLB 327; GFL Beginnings to 1789

Garrett, George (Palmer, Jr.) 1929- . **CLC 3,
11, 51; SSC 30**
See also AMWS 7; BPFB 2; CA 202; 1-4R,
202; 5; CANR 1, 42, 67, 109; CN 1, 2, 3,
4, 5, 6, 7; CP 1, 2, 3, 4, 5, 6, 7; CSW;
DLB 2, 5, 130, 152; DLBY 1983

Garrick, David 1717-1779 .... **LC 15**
See also DAM DRAM; DLB 84, 213;
RGEL 2

Garrigue, Jean 1914-1972 .... **CLC 2, 8**
See also CA 5-8R; CAAS 37-40R; CANR
20; CP 1; MAL 5

Garrison, Frederick
See Sinclair, Upton

Garrison, William Lloyd
1805-1879 .... **NCLC 149**
See also CDALB 1640-1865; DLB 1, 43,
235

Garro, Elena 1920(?)-1998 .. **HLCS 1; TCLC
153**
See also CA 131; CAAS 169; CWW 2;
DLB 145; EWL 3; HW 1; LAWS 1; WLIT
1

Garth, Will
See Hamilton, Edmond; Kuttner, Henry

Garvey, Marcus (Moziah, Jr.)
1887-1940 ... **BLC 2; HR 1:2; TCLC 41**
See also BW 1; CA 124; CAAE 120; CANR
79; DAM MULT

Gary, Romain **CLC 25**
See Kacew, Romain
See also DLB 83, 299; RGHL

Gascar, Pierre **CLC 11**
See Fournier, Pierre
See also EWL 3; RGHL

Gascoigne, George 1539-1577 .... **LC 108**
See also DLB 136; RGEL 2

Gascoyne, David (Emery)
1916-2001 .... **CLC 45**
See also CA 65-68; CAAS 200; CANR 10,
28, 54; CP 1, 2, 3, 4, 5, 6, 7; DLB 20;
MTCW 1; RGEL 2

Gaskell, Elizabeth Cleghorn
1810-1865 .... **NCLC 5, 70, 97, 137; SSC
25, 97**
See also BRW 5; CDBLB 1832-1890; DAB;
DAM MST; DLB 21, 144, 159; RGEL 2;
RGSF 2; TEA

Gass, William H. 1924- . **CLC 1, 2, 8, 11, 15,
39, 132; SSC 12**
See also AMWS 6; CA 17-20R; CANR 30,
71, 100; CN 1, 2, 3, 4, 5, 6, 7; DLB 2,
227; EWL 3; MAL 5; MTCW 1, 2;
MTFW 2005; RGAL 4

Gassendi, Pierre 1592-1655 .... **LC 54**
See also GFL Beginnings to 1789

Gasset, Jose Ortega y
See Ortega y Gasset, Jose

Gates, Henry Louis, Jr. 1950- ... **BLCS; CLC
65**
See also BW 2, 3; CA 109; CANR 25, 53,
75, 125; CSW; DA3; DAM MULT; DLB
67; EWL 3; MAL 5; MTCW 2; MTFW
2005; RGAL 4

Gatos, Stephanie
See Katz, Steve

Gautier, Theophile 1811-1872 .. **NCLC 1, 59;
PC 18; SSC 20**
See also DAM POET; DLB 119; EW 6;
GFL 1789 to the Present; RGWL 2, 3;
SUFW; TWA

Gay, John 1685-1732 .... **LC 49**
See also BRW 3; DAM DRAM; DLB 84,
95; RGEL 2; WLIT 3

Gay, Oliver
See Gogarty, Oliver St. John

Gay, Peter 1923- .... **CLC 158**
See also CA 13-16R; CANR 18, 41, 77,
147; INT CANR-18; RGHL

Gay, Peter Jack
See Gay, Peter

Gaye, Marvin (Pentz, Jr.)
1939-1984 .... **CLC 26**
See also CA 195; CAAS 112

Gebler, Carlo 1954- .... **CLC 39**
See also CA 133; CAAE 119; CANR 96;
DLB 271

Gee, Maggie 1948- .... **CLC 57**
See also CA 130; CANR 125; CN 4, 5, 6,
7; DLB 207; MTFW 2005

Gee, Maurice 1931- .... **CLC 29**
See also AAYA 42; CA 97-100; CANR 67,
123; CLR 56; CN 2, 3, 4, 5, 6, 7; CWRI
5; EWL 3; MAICYA 2; RGSF 2; SATA
46, 101

Gee, Maurice Gough
See Gee, Maurice

Geiogamah, Hanay 1945- .... **NNAL**
See also CA 153; DAM MULT; DLB 175

Gelbart, Larry
See Gelbart, Larry (Simon)
See also CAD; CD 5, 6

Gelbart, Larry (Simon) 1928- .... **CLC 21, 61**
See Gelbart, Larry
See also CA 73-76; CANR 45, 94

Gelber, Jack 1932-2003 ...... **CLC 1, 6, 14, 79**
See also CA 1-4R; CAAS 216; CAD;
CANR 2; DLB 7, 228; MAL 5

Gellhorn, Martha (Ellis)
1908-1998 .... **CLC 14, 60**
See also CA 77-80; CAAS 164; CANR 44;
CN 1, 2, 3, 4, 5, 6 7; DLBY 1982, 1998

Genet, Jean 1910-1986 .. **CLC 1, 2, 5, 10, 14,
44, 46; DC 25; TCLC 128**
See also CA 13-16R; CANR 18; DA3;
DAM DRAM; DFS 10; DLB 72, 321;
DLBY 1986; EW 13; EWL 3; GFL 1789
to the Present; GLL 1; LMFS 2; MTCW
1, 2; MTFW 2005; RGWL 2, 3; TWA

Genlis, Stephanie-Felicite Ducrest
1746-1830 .... **NCLC 166**
See also DLB 313

Gent, Peter 1942- .... **CLC 29**
See also AITN 1; CA 89-92; DLBY 1982

Gentile, Giovanni 1875-1944 .... **TCLC 96**
See also CAAE 119

Geoffrey of Monmouth c.
1100-1155 .... **CMLC 44**
See also DLB 146; TEA

George, Jean
See George, Jean Craighead

George, Jean Craighead 1919- .... **CLC 35**
See also AAYA 8, 69; BYA 2, 4; CA 5-8R;
CANR 25; CLR 1; 80; DLB 52; JRDA;
MAICYA 1, 2; SATA 2, 68, 124, 170;
WYA; YAW

George, Stefan (Anton) 1868-1933 . **TCLC 2,
14**
See also CA 193; CAAE 104; EW 8; EWL
3

Georges, Georges Martin
See Simenon, Georges (Jacques Christian)

Gerald of Wales c. 1146-c. 1223 ... **CMLC 60**

Gerhardi, William Alexander
See Gerhardie, William Alexander

Gerhardie, William Alexander
1895-1977 .... **CLC 5**
See also CA 25-28R; CAAS 73-76; CANR
18; CN 1, 2; DLB 36; RGEL 2

Gerson, Jean 1363-1429 .... **LC 77**
See also DLB 208

Gersonides 1288-1344 .... **CMLC 49**
See also DLB 115

Gerstler, Amy 1956- .... **CLC 70**
See also CA 146; CANR 99

Gertler, T. **CLC 34**
See also CA 121; CAAE 116

Gertsen, Aleksandr Ivanovich
See Herzen, Aleksandr Ivanovich

Ghalib **NCLC 39, 78**
See Ghalib, Asadullah Khan

Ghalib, Asadullah Khan 1797-1869
See Ghalib
See also DAM POET; RGWL 2, 3

Ghelderode, Michel de 1898-1962 ..... **CLC 6,
11; DC 15; TCLC 187**
See also CA 85-88; CANR 40, 77; DAM
DRAM; DLB 321; EW 11; EWL 3; TWA

Ghiselin, Brewster 1903-2001 .... **CLC 23**
See also CA 13-16R; 10; CANR 13; CP 1,
2, 3, 4, 5, 6, 7

Ghose, Aurabinda 1872-1950 .... **TCLC 63**
See Ghose, Aurobindo
See also CA 163

Ghose, Aurobindo
See Ghose, Aurabinda
See also EWL 3

Ghose, Zulfikar 1935- .... **CLC 42, 200**
See also CA 65-68; CANR 67; CN 1, 2, 3,
4, 5, 6, 7; CP 1, 2, 3, 4, 5, 6, 7; DLB 323;
EWL 3

Ghosh, Amitav 1956- .... **CLC 44, 153**
See also CA 147; CANR 80, 158; CN 6, 7;
DLB 323; WWE 1

Giacosa, Giuseppe 1847-1906 .... **TCLC 7**
See also CAAE 104

Gibb, Lee
See Waterhouse, Keith (Spencer)

Gibbon, Edward 1737-1794 .... **LC 97**
See also BRW 3; DLB 104; RGEL 2

Gibbon, Lewis Grassic **TCLC 4**
See Mitchell, James Leslie
See also RGEL 2

Gibbons, Kaye 1960- .... **CLC 50, 88, 145**
See also AAYA 34; AMWS 10; CA 151;
CANR 75, 127; CN 7; CSW; DA3; DAM
POP; DLB 292; MTCW 2; MTFW 2005;
NFS 3; RGAL 4; SATA 117

Gibran, Kahlil 1883-1931 . **PC 9; TCLC 1, 9**
See also CA 150; CAAE 104; DA3; DAM
POET, POP; EWL 3; MTCW 2; WLIT 6

Gibran, Khalil
See Gibran, Kahlil

Gibson, Mel 1956- .... **CLC 215**

Gibson, William 1914- .... **CLC 23**
See also CA 9-12R; CAD; CANR 9, 42, 75,
125; CD 5, 6; DA; DAB; DAC; DAM
DRAM, MST; DFS 2; DLB 7; LAIT 2;
MAL 5; MTCW 2; MTFW 2005; SATA
66; YAW

Gibson, William 1948- .... **CLC 39, 63, 186,
192; SSC 52**
See also AAYA 12, 59; AMWS 16; BPFB
2; CA 133; CAAE 126; CANR 52, 90,
106; CN 6, 7; CPW; DA3; DAM POP;
DLB 251; MTCW 2; MTFW 2005; SCFW
2; SFW 4

Gibson, William Ford
See Gibson, William

Gogarty, Oliver St. John
1878-1957 .... **TCLC 15**
See also CA 150; CAAE 109; DLB 15, 19;
RGEL 2

Gogol, Nikolai (Vasilyevich)
1809-1852 .... **DC 1; NCLC 5, 15, 31,**
162; SSC 4, 29, 52; WLC 3
See also DA; DAB; DAC; DAM DRAM,
MST; DFS 12; DLB 198; EW 6; EXPS;
RGSF 2; RGWL 2, 3; SSFS 7; TWA

Goines, Donald 1937(?)-1974 ... **BLC 2; CLC**
80
See also AITN 1; BW 1, 3; CA 124; CAAS
114; CANR 82; CMW 4; DA3; DAM
MULT, POP; DLB 33

Gold, Herbert 1924- ... **CLC 4, 7, 14, 42, 152**
See also CA 9-12R; CANR 17, 45, 125; CN
1, 2, 3, 4, 5, 6, 7; DLB 2; DLBY 1981;
MAL 5

Goldbarth, Albert 1948- .... **CLC 5, 38**
See also AMWS 12; CA 53-56; CANR 6,
40; CP 3, 4, 5, 6, 7; DLB 120

Goldberg, Anatol 1910-1982 .... **CLC 34**
See also CA 131; CAAS 117

Goldemberg, Isaac 1945- .... **CLC 52**
See also CA 69-72; 12; CANR 11, 32; EWL
3; HW 1; WLIT 1

Golding, Arthur 1536-1606 .... **LC 101**
See also DLB 136

Golding, William 1911-1993 . **CLC 1, 2, 3, 8,**
10, 17, 27, 58, 81; WLC 3
See also AAYA 5, 44; BPFB 2; BRWR 1;
BRWS 1; BYA 2; CA 5-8R; CAAS 141;
CANR 13, 33, 54; CDBLB 1945-
1960; CLR 94; CN 1, 2, 3, 4; DA; DA3;
DAB; DAC; DAM MST, NOV; DLB 15,
100, 255, 326, 330; EWL 3; EXPN; HGG;
LAIT 4; MTCW 1, 2; MTFW 2005; NFS
2; RGEL 2; RIIW; SFW 4; TEA; WLIT
4; YAW

Golding, William Gerald
See Golding, William

Goldman, Emma 1869-1940 .... **TCLC 13**
See also CA 150; CAAE 110; DLB 221;
FW; RGAL 4; TUS

Goldman, Francisco 1954- .... **CLC 76**
See also CA 162

Goldman, William 1931- .... **CLC 1, 48**
See also BPFB 2; CA 9-12R; CANR 29,
69, 106; CN 1, 2, 3, 4, 5, 6, 7; DLB 44;
FANT; IDFW 3, 4

Goldman, William W.
See Goldman, William

Goldmann, Lucien 1913-1970 .... **CLC 24**
See also CA 25-28; CAP 2

Goldoni, Carlo 1707-1793 .... **LC 4**
See also DAM DRAM; EW 4; RGWL 2, 3;
WLIT 7

Goldsberry, Steven 1949- .... **CLC 34**
See also CA 131

Goldsmith, Oliver 1730(?)-1774 .... **DC 8; LC**
2, 48, 122; PC 77; WLC 3
See also BRW 3; CDBLB 1660-1789; DA;
DAB; DAC; DAM DRAM, MST, NOV,
POET; DFS 1; DLB 39, 89, 104, 109, 142;
IDTP; RGEL 2; SATA 26; TEA; WLIT 3

Goldsmith, Peter
See Priestley, J(ohn) B(oynton)

Gombrowicz, Witold 1904-1969 .... **CLC 4, 7,**
11, 49
See also CA 19-20; CAAS 25-28R; CANR
105; CAP 2; CDWLB 4; DAM DRAM;
DLB 215; EW 12; EWL 3; RGWL 2, 3;
TWA

Gomez de Avellaneda, Gertrudis
1814-1873 .... **NCLC 111**
See also LAW

Gomez de la Serna, Ramon
1888-1963 .... **CLC 9**
See also CA 153; CAAS 116; CANR 79;
EWL 3; HW 1, 2

Goncharov, Ivan Alexandrovich
1812-1891 .... **NCLC 1, 63**
See also DLB 238; EW 6; RGWL 2, 3

Goncourt, Edmond (Louis Antoine Huot) de
1822-1896 .... **NCLC 7**
See also DLB 123; EW 7; GFL 1789 to the
Present; RGWL 2, 3

Goncourt, Jules (Alfred Huot) de
1830-1870 .... **NCLC 7**
See also DLB 123; EW 7; GFL 1789 to the
Present; RGWL 2, 3

Gongora (y Argote), Luis de
1561-1627 .... **LC 72**
See also RGWL 2, 3

Gontier, Fernande 19(?)- .... **CLC 50**

Gonzalez Martinez, Enrique
See Gonzalez Martinez, Enrique
See also DLB 290

Gonzalez Martincz, Enrique
1871-1952 .... **TCLC 72**
See Gonzalez Martinez, Enrique
See also CA 166; CANR 81; EWL 3; HW
1, 2

Goodison, Lorna 1947- .... **PC 36**
See also CA 142; CANR 88; CP 5, 6, 7;
CWP; DLB 157; EWL 3; PFS 25

Goodman, Paul 1911-1972 ..... **CLC 1, 2, 4, 7**
See also CA 19-20; CAAS 37-40R; CAD;
CANR 34; CAP 2; CN 1; DLB 130, 246;
MAL 5; MTCW 1; RGAL 4

GoodWeather, Harley
See King, Thomas

Googe, Barnabe 1540-1594 .... **LC 94**
See also DLB 132; RGEL 2

Gordimer, Nadine 1923- ...... **CLC 3, 5, 7, 10,**
18, 33, 51, 70, 123, 160, 161; SSC 17,
80; WLCS
See also AAYA 39; AFW; BRWS 2; CA
5-8R; CANR 3, 28, 56, 88, 131; CN 1, 2,
3, 4, 5, 6, 7; DA; DA3; DAB; DAC; DAM
MST, NOV; DLB 225, 326, 330; EWL 3;
EXPS; INT CANR-28; LATS 1:2; MTCW
1, 2; MTFW 2005; NFS 4; RGEL 2;
RGSF 2; SSFS 2, 14, 19; TWA; WLIT 2;
YAW

Gordon, Adam Lindsay
1833-1870 .... **NCLC 21**
See also DLB 230

Gordon, Caroline 1895-1981 . **CLC 6, 13, 29,**
83; SSC 15
See also AMW; CA 11-12; CAAS 103;
CANR 36; CAP 1; CN 1, 2; DLB 4, 9,
102; DLBD 17; DLBY 1981; EWL 3;
MAL 5; MTCW 1, 2; MTFW 2005;
RGAL 4; RGSF 2

Gordon, Charles William 1860-1937
See Connor, Ralph
See also CAAE 109

Gordon, Mary 1949- .. **CLC 13, 22, 128, 216;**
SSC 59
See also AMWS 4; BPFB 2; CA 102;
CANR 44, 92, 154; CN 4, 5, 6, 7; DLB 6;
DLBY 1981; FW; INT CA-102; MAL 5;
MTCW 1

Gordon, Mary Catherine
See Gordon, Mary

Gordon, N. J.
See Bosman, Herman Charles

Gordon, Sol 1923- .... **CLC 26**
See also CA 53-56; CANR 4; SATA 11

Gordone, Charles 1925-1995 .. **CLC 1, 4; DC**
8
See also BW 1, 3; CA 180; 93-96, 180;
CAAS 150; CAD; CANR 55; DAM
DRAM; DLB 7; INT CA-93-96; MTCW
1

Gore, Catherine 1800-1861 .... **NCLC 65**
See also DLB 116; RGEL 2

Gorenko, Anna Andreevna
See Akhmatova, Anna

Gorky, Maxim SSC 28; TCLC 8; WLC 3
See Peshkov, Alexei Maximovich
See also DAB; DFS 9; DLB 295; EW 8;
EWL 3; TWA

Goryan, Sirak
See Saroyan, William

Gosse, Edmund (William)
1849-1928 .... **TCLC 28**
See also CAAE 117; DLB 57, 144, 184;
RGEL 2

Gotlieb, Phyllis (Fay Bloom) 1926- .. **CLC 18**
See also CA 13-16R; CANR 7, 135; CN 7;
CP 1, 2, 3, 4; DLB 88, 251; SFW 4

Gottesman, S. D.
See Kornbluth, C(yril) M.; Pohl, Frederik

Gottfried von Strassburg fl. c.
1170-1215 .... **CMLC 10**
See also CDWLB 2; DLB 138; EW 1;
RGWL 2, 3

Gotthelf, Jeremias 1797-1854 .... **NCLC 117**
See also DLB 133; RGWL 2, 3

Gottschalk, Laura Riding
See Jackson, Laura (Riding)

Gould, Lois 1932(?)-2002 .... **CLC 4, 10**
See also CA 77-80; CAAS 208; CANR 29;
MTCW 1

Gould, Stephen Jay 1941-2002 .... **CLC 163**
See also AAYA 26; BEST 90:2; CA 77-80;
CAAS 205; CANR 10, 27, 56, 75, 125;
CPW; INT CANR-27; MTCW 1, 2;
MTFW 2005

Gourmont, Remy(-Marie-Charles) de
1858-1915 .... **TCLC 17**
See also CA 150; CAAE 109; GFL 1789 to
the Present; MTCW 2

Gournay, Marie le Jars de
See de Gournay, Marie le Jars

Govier, Katherine 1948- .... **CLC 51**
See also CA 101; CANR 18, 40, 128; CCA
1

Gower, John c. 1330-1408 .... **LC 76; PC 59**
See also BRW 1; DLB 146; RGEL 2

Goyen, (Charles) William
1915-1983 .... **CLC 5, 8, 14, 40**
See also AITN 2; CA 5-8R; CAAS 110;
CANR 6, 71; CN 1, 2, 3; DLB 2, 218;
DLBY 1983; EWL 3; INT CANR-6; MAL
5

Goytisolo, Juan 1931- .... **CLC 5, 10, 23, 133;**
HLC 1
See also CA 85-88; CANR 32, 61, 131;
CWW 2; DAM MULT; DLB 322; EWL
3; GLL 2; HW 1, 2; MTCW 1, 2; MTFW
2005

Gozzano, Guido 1883-1916 .... **PC 10**
See also CA 154; DLB 114; EWL 3

Gozzi, (Conte) Carlo 1720-1806 .... **NCLC 23**

Grabbe, Christian Dietrich
1801-1836 .... **NCLC 2**
See also DLB 133; RGWL 2, 3

Grace, Patricia Frances 1937- .... **CLC 56**
See also CA 176; CANR 118; CN 4, 5, 6,
7; EWL 3; RGSF 2

Gracian y Morales, Baltasar
1601-1658 .... **LC 15**

Gracq, Julien CLC 11, 48
See Poirier, Louis
See also CWW 2; DLB 83; GFL 1789 to
the Present

Grade, Chaim 1910-1982 .... **CLC 10**
See also CA 93-96; CAAS 107; DLB 333;
EWL 3; RGHL

Grade, Khayim
See Grade, Chaim

Graduate of Oxford, A
See Ruskin, John

Grafton, Garth
See Duncan, Sara Jeannette

Grafton, Sue 1940- .... **CLC 163**
See also AAYA 11, 49; BEST 90:3; CA 108;
CANR 31, 55, 111, 134; CMW 4; CPW;
CSW; DA3; DAM POP; DLB 226; FW;
MSW; MTFW 2005

Graham, John
See Phillips, David Graham

Graham, Jorie 1950- .... **CLC 48, 118; PC 59**
See also AAYA 67; CA 111; CANR 63, 118;
CP 4, 5, 6, 7; CWP; DLB 120; EWL 3;
MTFW 2005; PFS 10, 17; TCLE 1:1

Graham, R(obert) B(ontine) Cunninghame
See Cunninghame Graham, Robert
(Gallnigad) Bontine
See also DLB 98, 135, 174; RGEL 2; RGSF
2

Graham, Robert
See Haldeman, Joe

Graham, Tom
See Lewis, (Harry) Sinclair

Graham, W(illiam) S(ydney)
1918-1986 .... **CLC 29**
See also BRWS 7; CA 73-76; CAAS 118;
CP 1, 2, 3, 4; DLB 20; RGEL 2

Graham, Winston (Mawdsley)
1910-2003 .... **CLC 23**
See also CA 49-52; CAAS 218; CANR 2,
22, 45, 66; CMW 4; CN 1, 2, 3, 4, 5, 6,
7; DLB 77; RHW

Grahame, Kenneth 1859-1932 ...... **TCLC 64,**
136
See also BYA 5; CA 136; CAAE 108;
CANR 80; CLR 5; CWRI 5; DA3; DAB;
DLB 34, 141, 178; FANT; MAICYA 1, 2;
MTCW 2; NFS 20; RGEL 2; SATA 100;
TEA; WCH; YABC 1

Granger, Darius John
See Marlowe, Stephen

Granin, Daniil 1918- .... **CLC 59**
See also DLB 302

Granovsky, Timofei Nikolaevich
1813-1855 .... **NCLC 75**
See also DLB 198

Grant, Skeeter
See Spiegelman, Art

Granville-Barker, Harley
1877-1946 .... **TCLC 2**
See Barker, Harley Granville
See also CA 204; CAAE 104; DAM
DRAM; RGEL 2

Granzotto, Gianni
See Granzotto, Giovanni Battista

Granzotto, Giovanni Battista
1914-1985 .... **CLC 70**
See also CA 166

Grass, Guenter
See Grass, Gunter
See also CWW 2; DLB 330; RGHL

Grass, Gunter 1927- .. **CLC 1, 2, 4, 6, 11, 15,**
22, 32, 49, 88, 207; WLC 3
See Grass, Guenter
See also BPFB 2; CA 13-16R; CANR 20,
75, 93, 133; CDWLB 2; DA; DA3; DAB;
DAC; DAM MST, NOV; DLB 75, 124;
EW 13; EWL 3; MTCW 1, 2; MTFW
2005; RGWL 2, 3; TWA

Grass, Gunter Wilhelm
See Grass, Gunter

Gratton, Thomas
See Hulme, T(homas) E(rnest)

Grau, Shirley Ann 1929- .... **CLC 4, 9, 146;**
SSC 15
See also CA 89-92; CANR 22, 69; CN 1, 2,
3, 4, 5, 6, 7; CSW; DLB 2, 218; INT CA-
89-92; CANR-22; MTCW 1

Gravel, Fern
See Hall, James Norman

Graver, Elizabeth 1964- .... **CLC 70**
See also CA 135; CANR 71, 129

Graves, Richard Perceval
1895-1985 .... **CLC 44**
See also CA 65-68; CANR 9, 26, 51

Graves, Robert 1895-1985 ... **CLC 1, 2, 6, 11,**
39, 44, 45; PC 6
See also BPFB 2; BRW 7; BYA 4; CA 5-8R;
CAAS 117; CANR 5, 36; CDBLB 1914-
1945; CN 1, 2, 3; CP 1, 2, 3, 4; DA3;
DAB; DAC; DAM MST, POET; DLB 20,
100, 191; DLBD 18; DLBY 1985; EWL
3; LATS 1:1; MTCW 1, 2; MTFW 2005;
NCFS 2; NFS 21; RGEL 2; RHW; SATA
45; TEA

Graves, Valerie
See Bradley, Marion Zimmer

Gray, Alasdair 1934- .... **CLC 41**
See also BRWS 9; CA 126; CANR 47, 69,
106, 140; CN 4, 5, 6, 7; DLB 194, 261,
319; HGG; INT CA-126; MTCW 1, 2;
MTFW 2005; RGSF 2; SUFW 2

Gray, Amlin 1946- .... **CLC 29**
See also CA 138

Gray, Francine du Plessix 1930- ..... **CLC 22,**
153
See also BEST 90:3; CA 61-64; 2; CANR
11, 33, 75, 81; DAM NOV; INT CANR-
11; MTCW 1, 2; MTFW 2005

Gray, John (Henry) 1866-1934 ...... **TCLC 19**
See also CA 162; CAAE 119; RGEL 2

Gray, John Lee
See Jakes, John

Gray, Simon (James Holliday)
1936- .... **CLC 9, 14, 36**
See also AITN 1; CA 21-24R; 3; CANR 32,
69; CBD; CD 5, 6; CN 1, 2, 3; DLB 13;
EWL 3; MTCW 1; RGEL 2

Gray, Spalding 1941-2004 .... **CLC 49, 112;**
DC 7
See also AAYA 62; CA 128; CAAS 225;
CAD; CANR 74, 138; CD 5, 6; CPW;
DAM POP; MTCW 2; MTFW 2005

Gray, Thomas 1716-1771 .... **LC 4, 40; PC 2;**
WLC 3
See also BRW 3; CDBLB 1660-1789; DA;
DA3; DAB; DAC; DAM MST; DLB 109;
EXPP; PAB; PFS 9; RGEL 2; TEA; WP

Grayson, David
See Baker, Ray Stannard

Grayson, Richard (A.) 1951- .... **CLC 38**
See also CA 210; 85-88, 210; CANR 14,
31, 57; DLB 234

Greeley, Andrew M. 1928- .... **CLC 28**
See also BPFB 2; CA 5-8R; 7; CANR 7,
43, 69, 104, 136; CMW 4; CPW; DA3;
DAM POP; MTCW 1, 2; MTFW 2005

Green, Anna Katharine
1846-1935 .... **TCLC 63**
See also CA 159; CAAE 112; CMW 4;
DLB 202, 221; MSW

Green, Brian
See Card, Orson Scott

Green, Hannah
See Greenberg, Joanne (Goldenberg)

Green, Hannah 1927(?)-1996 .... **CLC 3**
See also CA 73-76; CANR 59, 93; NFS 10

Green, Henry CLC 2, 13, 97
See Yorke, Henry Vincent
See also BRWS 2; CA 175; DLB 15; EWL
3; RGEL 2

Green, Julian CLC 3, 11, 77
See Green, Julien (Hartridge)
See also EWL 3; GFL 1789 to the Present;
MTCW 2

Green, Julien (Hartridge) 1900-1998
See Green, Julian
See also CA 21-24R; CAAS 169; CANR
33, 87; CWW 2; DLB 4, 72; MTCW 1, 2;
MTFW 2005

Green, Paul (Eliot) 1894-1981 .... **CLC 25**
See also AITN 1; CA 5-8R; CAAS 103;
CAD; CANR 3; DAM DRAM; DLB 7, 9,
249; DLBY 1981; MAL 5; RGAL 4

Greenaway, Peter 1942- .... **CLC 159**
See also CA 127

Greenberg, Ivan 1908-1973
See Rahv, Philip
See also CA 85-88

Greenberg, Joanne (Goldenberg)
1932- .... **CLC 7, 30**
See also AAYA 12, 67; CA 5-8R; CANR
14, 32, 69; CN 6, 7; NFS 23; SATA 25;
YAW

Greenberg, Richard 1959(?)- .... **CLC 57**
See also CA 138; CAD; CD 5, 6

Greenblatt, Stephen J(ay) 1943- ...... **CLC 70**
See also CA 49-52; CANR 115

Greene, Bette 1934- .... **CLC 30**
See also AAYA 7, 69; BYA 3; CA 53-56;
CANR 4, 146; CLR 2; CWRI 5; JRDA;
LAIT 4; MAICYA 1, 2; NFS 10; SAAS
16; SATA 8, 102, 161; WYA; YAW

Greene, Gael CLC 8
See also CA 13-16R; CANR 10

Greene, Graham 1904-1991 .. **CLC 1, 3, 6, 9,**
14, 18, 27, 37, 70, 72, 125; SSC 29;
WLC 3
See also AAYA 61; AITN 2; BPFB 2;
BRWR 2; BRWS 1; BYA 3; CA 13-16R;
CAAS 133; CANR 35, 61, 131; CBD;
CDBLB 1945-1960; CMW 4; CN 1, 2, 3,
4; DA; DA3; DAB; DAC; DAM MST,
NOV; DLB 13, 15, 77, 100, 162, 201,
204; DLBY 1991; EWL 3; MSW; MTCW
1, 2; MTFW 2005; NFS 16; RGEL 2;
SATA 20; SSFS 14; TEA; WLIT 4

Greene, Robert 1558-1592 .... **LC 41**
See also BRWS 8; DLB 62, 167; IDTP;
RGEL 2; TEA

Greer, Germaine 1939- .... **CLC 131**
See also AITN 1; CA 81-84; CANR 33, 70,
115, 133; FW; MTCW 1, 2; MTFW 2005

Greer, Richard
See Silverberg, Robert

Gregor, Arthur 1923- .... **CLC 9**
See also CA 25-28R; 10; CANR 11; CP 1,
2, 3, 4, 5, 6, 7; SATA 36

Gregor, Lee
See Pohl, Frederik

Gregory, Lady Isabella Augusta (Persse)
1852-1932 .... **TCLC 1, 176**
See also BRW 6; CA 184; CAAE 104; DLB
10; IDTP; RGEL 2

Gregory, J. Dennis
See Williams, John A(lfred)

Gregory of Nazianzus, St.
329-389 .... **CMLC 82**

Grekova, I. CLC 59
See Ventsel, Elena Sergeevna
See also CWW 2

Grendon, Stephen
See Derleth, August (William)

Grenville, Kate 1950- .... **CLC 61**
See also CA 118; CANR 53, 93, 156; CN
7; DLB 325

Grenville, Pelham
See Wodehouse, P(elham) G(renville)

Greve, Felix Paul (Berthold Friedrich)
1879-1948
See Grove, Frederick Philip
See also CA 141, 175; CAAE 104; CANR
79; DAC; DAM MST

Greville, Fulke 1554-1628 .... **LC 79**
See also BRWS 11; DLB 62, 172; RGEL 2

Grey, Lady Jane 1537-1554 .... **LC 93**
See also DLB 132

Grey, Zane 1872-1939 .... **TCLC 6**
See also BPFB 2; CA 132; CAAE 104;
DA3; DAM POP; DLB 9, 212; MTCW 1,
2; MTFW 2005; RGAL 4; TCWW 1, 2;
TUS

Griboedov, Aleksandr Sergeevich
1795(?)-1829 .... **NCLC 129**
See also DLB 205; RGWL 2, 3

Grieg, (Johan) Nordahl (Brun)
1902-1943 .... **TCLC 10**
See also CA 189; CAAE 107; EWL 3

Grieve, C(hristopher) M(urray)
1892-1978 .... **CLC 11, 19**
See MacDiarmid, Hugh; Pteleon
See also CA 5-8R; CAAS 85-88; CANR
33, 107; DAM POET; MTCW 1; RGEL 2

Griffin, Gerald 1803-1840 .... **NCLC 7**
See also DLB 159; RGEL 2

Griffin, John Howard 1920-1980 ..... **CLC 68**
See also AITN 1; CA 1-4R; CAAS 101;
CANR 2

Griffin, Peter 1942- .... **CLC 39**
See also CA 136

Griffith, D(avid Lewelyn) W(ark)
1875(?)-1948 .... **TCLC 68**
See also CA 150; CAAE 119; CANR 80

Griffith, Lawrence
See Griffith, D(avid Lewelyn) W(ark)

Griffiths, Trevor 1935- .... **CLC 13, 52**
See also CA 97-100; CANR 45; CBD; CD
5, 6; DLB 13, 245

Griggs, Sutton (Elbert)
1872-1930 .... **TCLC 77**
See also CA 186; CAAE 123; DLB 50

Grigson, Geoffrey (Edward Harvey)
1905-1985 .... **CLC 7, 39**
See also CA 25-28R; CAAS 118; CANR
20, 33; CP 1, 2, 3, 4; DLB 27; MTCW 1,
2

Grile, Dod
See Bierce, Ambrose (Gwinett)

Grillparzer, Franz 1791-1872 .... **DC 14;**
NCLC 1, 102; SSC 37
See also CDWLB 2; DLB 133; EW 5;
RGWL 2, 3; TWA

Grimble, Reverend Charles James
See Eliot, T(homas) S(tearns)

Grimke, Angelina (Emily) Weld
1880-1958 .... **HR 1:2**
See Weld, Angelina (Emily) Grimke
See also BW 1; CA 124; DAM POET; DLB
50, 54

Grimke, Charlotte L(ottie) Forten
1837(?)-1914
See Forten, Charlotte L.
See also BW 1; CA 124; CAAE 117; DAM
MULT, POET

Grimm, Jacob Ludwig Karl
1785-1863 .... **NCLC 3, 77; SSC 36**
See Grimm Brothers
See also CLR 112; DLB 90; MAICYA 1, 2;
RGSF 2; RGWL 2, 3; SATA 22; WCH

Grimm, Wilhelm Karl 1786-1859 .. **NCLC 3,**
77; SSC 36
See Grimm Brothers
See also CDWLB 2; CLR 112; DLB 90;
MAICYA 1, 2; RGSF 2; RGWL 2, 3;
SATA 22; WCH

Grimm and Grim
See Grimm, Jacob Ludwig Karl; Grimm,
Wilhelm Karl

Grimm Brothers SSC 88
See Grimm, Jacob Ludwig Karl; Grimm,
Wilhelm Karl
See also CLR 112

Grimmelshausen, Hans Jakob Christoffel
von
See Grimmelshausen, Johann Jakob Christoffel von
See also RGWL 2, 3

Grimmelshausen, Johann Jakob Christoffel
von 1621-1676 .... **LC 6**
See Grimmelshausen, Hans Jakob Christof-
fel von
See also CDWLB 2; DLB 168

Grindel, Eugene 1895-1952
See Eluard, Paul
See also CA 193; CAAE 104; LMFS 2

Grisham, John 1955- .... **CLC 84**
See also AAYA 14, 47; BPFB 2; CA 138;
CANR 47, 69, 114, 133; CMW 4; CN 6,
7; CPW; CSW; DA3; DAM POP; MSW;
MTCW 2; MTFW 2005

Grosseteste, Robert 1175(?)-1253 . **CMLC 62**
See also DLB 115

Grossman, David 1954- .... **CLC 67, 231**
See also CA 138; CANR 114; CWW 2;
DLB 299; EWL 3; RGHL; WLIT 6

Grossman, Vasilii Semenovich
See Grossman, Vasily (Semenovich)
See also DLB 272

Grossman, Vasily (Semenovich)
1905-1964 .... **CLC 41**
See Grossman, Vasilii Semenovich
See also CA 130; CAAE 124; MTCW 1;
RGHL

Grove, Frederick Philip TCLC 4
See Greve, Felix Paul (Berthold Friedrich)
See also DLB 92; RGEL 2; TCWW 1, 2

Grubb
See Crumb, R.

Grumbach, Doris 1918- .... **CLC 13, 22, 64**
See also CA 5-8R; 2; CANR 9, 42, 70, 127;
CN 6, 7; INT CANR-9; MTCW 2; MTFW
2005

Grundtvig, Nikolai Frederik Severin
1783-1872 .... **NCLC 1, 158**
See also DLB 300

Grunge
See Crumb, R.

Grunwald, Lisa 1959- .... **CLC 44**
See also CA 120; CANR 148

Gryphius, Andreas 1616-1664 .... **LC 89**
See also CDWLB 2; DLB 164; RGWL 2, 3

Guare, John 1938- .... **CLC 8, 14, 29, 67; DC**
20
See also CA 73-76; CAD; CANR 21, 69,
118; CD 5, 6; DAM DRAM; DFS 8, 13;
DLB 7, 249; EWL 3; MAL 5; MTCW 1,
2; RGAL 4

Guarini, Battista 1537-1612 .... **LC 102**

Gubar, Susan (David) 1944- .... **CLC 145**
See also CA 108; CANR 45, 70, 139; FW;
MTCW 1; RGAL 4

Gudjonsson, Halldor Kiljan 1902-1998
See Halldor Laxness
See also CA 103; CAAS 164

Guenter, Erich
See Eich, Gunter

Guest, Barbara 1920-2006 ... **CLC 34; PC 55**
See also BG 1:2; CA 25-28R; CAAS 248;
CANR 11, 44, 84; CP 1, 2, 3, 4, 5, 6, 7;
CWP; DLB 5, 193

Guest, Edgar A(lbert) 1881-1959 ... **TCLC 95**
See also CA 168; CAAE 112

Guest, Judith 1936- .... **CLC 8, 30**
See also AAYA 7, 66; CA 77-80; CANR
15, 75, 138; DA3; DAM NOV, POP;
EXPN; INT CANR-15; LAIT 5; MTCW
1, 2; MTFW 2005; NFS 1

Guevara, Che CLC 87; HLC 1
See Guevara (Serna), Ernesto

Guevara (Serna), Ernesto
1928-1967 .... **CLC 87; HLC 1**
See Guevara, Che
See also CA 127; CAAS 111; CANR 56;
DAM MULT; HW 1

Guicciardini, Francesco 1483-1540 ..... **LC 49**

Guido delle Colonne c. 1215-c.
1290 .... **CMLC 90**

Guild, Nicholas M. 1944- .... **CLC 33**
See also CA 93-96

Guillemin, Jacques
See Sartre, Jean-Paul

Guillen, Jorge 1893-1984 . **CLC 11; HLCS 1;**
PC 35
See also CA 89-92; CAAS 112; DAM
MULT, POET; DLB 108; EWL 3; HW 1;
RGWL 2, 3

Guillen, Nicolas (Cristobal)
1902-1989 .... **BLC 2; CLC 48, 79; HLC**
1; PC 23
See also BW 2; CA 125; CAAE 116; CAAS
129; CANR 84; DAM MST, MULT,
POET; DLB 283; EWL 3; HW 1; LAW;
RGWL 2, 3; WP

Guillen y Alvarez, Jorge
See Guillen, Jorge

Guillevic, (Eugene) 1907-1997 .... **CLC 33**
See also CA 93-96; CWW 2

Guillois
See Desnos, Robert

Guillois, Valentin
See Desnos, Robert

Guimaraes Rosa, Joao 1908-1967 .... **HLCS 2**
See Rosa, Joao Guimaraes
See also CA 175; LAW; RGSF 2; RGWL 2,
3

Guiney, Louise Imogen
1861-1920 .... **TCLC 41**
See also CA 160; DLB 54; RGAL 4

Guinizelli, Guido c. 1230-1276 ...... **CMLC 49**
See Guinizzelli, Guido

Guinizzelli, Guido
See Guinizelli, Guido
See also WLIT 7

Guiraldes, Ricardo (Guillermo)
1886-1927 .... **TCLC 39**
See also CA 131; EWL 3; HW 1; LAW;
MTCW 1

Gumilev, Nikolai (Stepanovich)
1886-1921 .... **TCLC 60**
See Gumilyov, Nikolay Stepanovich
See also CA 165; DLB 295

Gumilyov, Nikolay Stepanovich
See Gumilev, Nikolai (Stepanovich)
See also EWL 3

Gump, P. Q.
See Card, Orson Scott

Gunesekera, Romesh 1954- .... **CLC 91**
See also BRWS 10; CA 159; CANR 140;
CN 6, 7; DLB 267, 323

Gunn, Bill CLC 5
See Gunn, William Harrison
See also DLB 38

Gunn, Thom(son William)
1929-2004 . **CLC 3, 6, 18, 32, 81; PC 26**
See also BRWS 4; CA 17-20R; CAAS 227;
CANR 9, 33, 116; CDBLB 1960 to
Present; CP 1, 2, 3, 4, 5, 6, 7; DAM
POET; DLB 27; INT CANR-33; MTCW
1; PFS 9; RGEL 2

Gunn, William Harrison 1934(?)-1989
See Gunn, Bill
See also AITN 1; BW 1, 3; CA 13-16R;
CAAS 128; CANR 12, 25, 76

Gunn Allen, Paula
See Allen, Paula Gunn

Gunnars, Kristjana 1948- .... **CLC 69**
See also CA 113; CCA 1; CP 6, 7; CWP;
DLB 60

Gunter, Erich
See Eich, Gunter
Gurdjieff, G(eorgei) I(vanovich)
1877(?)-1949 .... **TCLC 71**
See also CA 157
Gurganus, Allan 1947- .... **CLC 70**
See also BEST 90:1; CA 135; CANR 114;
CN 6, 7; CPW; CSW; DAM POP; GLL 1
Gurney, A. R.
See Gurney, A(lbert) R(amsdell), Jr.
See also DLB 266
Gurney, A(lbert) R(amsdell), Jr.
1930- .... **CLC 32, 50, 54**
See Gurney, A. R.
See also AMWS 5; CA 77-80; CAD; CANR
32, 64, 121; CD 5, 6; DAM DRAM; EWL
3
Gurney, Ivor (Bertie) 1890-1937 ... **TCLC 33**
See also BRW 6; CA 167; DLBY 2002;
PAB; RGEL 2
Gurney, Peter
See Gurney, A(lbert) R(amsdell), Jr.
Guro, Elena (Genrikhovna)
1877-1913 .... **TCLC 56**
See also DLB 295
Gustafson, James M(oody) 1925- ... **CLC 100**
See also CA 25-28R; CANR 37
Gustafson, Ralph (Barker)
1909-1995 .... **CLC 36**
See also CA 21-24R; CANR 8, 45, 84; CP
1, 2, 3, 4, 5, 6; DLB 88; RGEL 2
Gut, Gom
See Simenon, Georges (Jacques Christian)
Guterson, David 1956- .... **CLC 91**
See also CA 132; CANR 73, 126; CN 7;
DLB 292; MTCW 2; MTFW 2005; NFS
13
Guthrie, A(lfred) B(ertram), Jr.
1901-1991 .... **CLC 23**
See also CA 57-60; CAAS 134; CANR 24;
CN 1, 2, 3; DLB 6, 212; MAL 5; SATA
62; SATA-Obit 67; TCWW 1, 2
Guthrie, Isobel
See Grieve, C(hristopher) M(urray)
Guthrie, Woodrow Wilson 1912-1967
See Guthrie, Woody
See also CA 113; CAAS 93-96
Guthrie, Woody CLC 35
See Guthrie, Woodrow Wilson
See also DLB 303; LAIT 3
Gutierrez Najera, Manuel
1859-1895 .... **HLCS 2; NCLC 133**
See also DLB 290; LAW
Guy, Rosa (Cuthbert) 1925- .... **CLC 26**
See also AAYA 4, 37; BW 2; CA 17-20R;
CANR 14, 34, 83; CLR 13; DLB 33;
DNFS 1; JRDA; MAICYA 1, 2; SATA 14,
62, 122; YAW
Gwendolyn
See Bennett, (Enoch) Arnold
H. D. CLC 3, 8, 14, 31, 34, 73; PC 5
See Doolittle, Hilda
See also FL 1:5
H. de V.
See Buchan, John
Haavikko, Paavo Juhani 1931- .. **CLC 18, 34**
See also CA 106; CWW 2; EWL 3
Habbema, Koos
See Heijermans, Herman
Habermas, Juergen 1929- .... **CLC 104**
See also CA 109; CANR 85; DLB 242
Habermas, Jurgen
See Habermas, Juergen
Hacker, Marilyn 1942- ...... **CLC 5, 9, 23, 72,**
91; PC 47
See also CA 77-80; CANR 68, 129; CP 3,
4, 5, 6, 7; CWP; DAM POET; DLB 120,
282; FW; GLL 2; MAL 5; PFS 19

Hadewijch of Antwerp fl. 1250- ... **CMLC 61**
See also RGWL 3
Hadrian 76-138 .... **CMLC 52**
Haeckel, Ernst Heinrich (Philipp August)
1834-1919 .... **TCLC 83**
See also CA 157
Hafiz c. 1326-1389(?) .... **CMLC 34**
See also RGWL 2, 3; WLIT 6
Hagedorn, Jessica T(arahata)
1949- .... **CLC 185**
See also CA 139; CANR 69; CWP; DLB
312; RGAL 4
Haggard, H(enry) Rider
1856-1925 .... **TCLC 11**
See also BRWS 3; BYA 4, 5; CA 148;
CAAE 108; CANR 112; DLB 70, 156,
174, 178; FANT; LMFS 1; MTCW 2;
RGEL 2; RHW; SATA 16; SCFW 1, 2;
SFW 4; SUFW 1; WLIT 4
Hagiosy, L.
See Larbaud, Valery (Nicolas)
Hagiwara, Sakutaro 1886-1942 .... **PC 18;**
TCLC 60
See Hagiwara Sakutaro
See also CA 154; RGWL 3
Hagiwara Sakutaro
See Hagiwara, Sakutaro
See also EWL 3
Haig, Fenil
See Ford, Ford Madox
Haig-Brown, Roderick (Langmere)
1908-1976 .... **CLC 21**
See also CA 5-8R; CAAS 69-72; CANR 4,
38, 83; CLR 31; CWRI 5; DLB 88; MAI-
CYA 1, 2; SATA 12; TCWW 2
Haight, Rip
See Carpenter, John (Howard)
Haij, Vera
See Jansson, Tove (Marika)
Hailey, Arthur 1920-2004 .... **CLC 5**
See also AITN 2; BEST 90:3; BPFB 2; CA
1-4R; CAAS 233; CANR 2, 36, 75; CCA
1; CN 1, 2, 3, 4, 5, 6, 7; CPW; DAM
NOV, POP; DLB 88; DLBY 1982; MTCW
1, 2; MTFW 2005
Hailey, Elizabeth Forsythe 1938- ..... **CLC 40**
See also CA 188; 93-96, 188; 1; CANR 15,
48; INT CANR-15
Haines, John (Meade) 1924- .... **CLC 58**
See also AMWS 12; CA 17-20R; CANR
13, 34; CP 1, 2, 3, 4, 5; CSW; DLB 5,
212; TCLE 1:1
Ha Jin 1956- .... **CLC 109**
See Jin, Xuefei
See also CA 152; CANR 91, 130; DLB 244,
292; MTFW 2005; SSFS 17
Hakluyt, Richard 1552-1616 .... **LC 31**
See also DLB 136; RGEL 2
Haldeman, Joe 1943- .... **CLC 61**
See Graham, Robert
See also AAYA 38; CA 179; 53-56, 179;
25; CANR 6, 70, 72, 130; DLB 8; INT
CANR-6; SCFW 2; SFW 4
Haldeman, Joe William
See Haldeman, Joe
Hale, Janet Campbell 1947- .... **NNAL**
See also CA 49-52; CANR 45, 75; DAM
MULT; DLB 175; MTCW 2; MTFW 2005
Hale, Sarah Josepha (Buell)
1788-1879 .... **NCLC 75**
See also DLB 1, 42, 73, 243
Halevy, Elie 1870-1937 .... **TCLC 104**
Haley, Alex(ander Murray Palmer)
1921-1992 .... **BLC 2; CLC 8, 12, 76;**
TCLC 147
See also AAYA 26; BPFB 2; BW 2, 3; CA
77-80; CAAS 136; CANR 61; CDALBS;
CPW; CSW; DA; DA3; DAB; DAC;
DAM MST, MULT, POP; DLB 38; LAIT
5; MTCW 1, 2; NFS 9

Haliburton, Thomas Chandler
1796-1865 .... **NCLC 15, 149**
See also DLB 11, 99; RGEL 2; RGSF 2
Hall, Donald 1928- .. **CLC 1, 13, 37, 59, 151;**
PC 70
See also AAYA 63; CA 5-8R; 7; CANR 2,
44, 64, 106, 133; CP 1, 2, 3, 4, 5, 6, 7;
DAM POET; DLB 5; MAL 5; MTCW 2;
MTFW 2005; RGAL 4; SATA 23, 97
Hall, Donald Andrew, Jr.
See Hall, Donald
Hall, Frederic Sauser
See Sauser-Hall, Frederic
Hall, James
See Kuttner, Henry
Hall, James Norman 1887-1951 ..... **TCLC 23**
See also CA 173; CAAE 123; LAIT 1;
RHW 1; SATA 21
Hall, Joseph 1574-1656 .... **LC 91**
See also DLB 121, 151; RGEL 2
Hall, Marguerite Radclyffe
See Hall, Radclyffe
Hall, Radclyffe 1880-1943 .... **TCLC 12**
See also BRWS 6; CA 150; CAAE 110;
CANR 83; DLB 191; MTCW 2; MTFW
2005; RGEL 2; RHW
Hall, Rodney 1935- .... **CLC 51**
See also CA 109; CANR 69; CN 6, 7; CP
1, 2, 3, 4, 5, 6, 7; DLB 289
Hallam, Arthur Henry
1811-1833 .... **NCLC 110**
See also DLB 32
Halldor Laxness CLC 25
See Gudjonsson, Halldor Kiljan
See also DLB 293; EW 12; EWL 3; RGWL
2, 3
Halleck, Fitz-Greene 1790-1867 .... **NCLC 47**
See also DLB 3, 250; RGAL 4
Halliday, Michael
See Creasey, John
Halpern, Daniel 1945- .... **CLC 14**
See also CA 33-36R; CANR 93; CP 3, 4, 5,
6, 7
Hamburger, Michael (Peter Leopold)
1924- .... **CLC 5, 14**
See also CA 196; 5-8R, 196; 4; CANR 2,
47; CP 1, 2, 3, 4, 5, 6, 7; DLB 27
Hamill, Pete 1935- .... **CLC 10**
See also CA 25-28R; CANR 18, 71, 127
Hamilton, Alexander
1755(?)-1804 .... **NCLC 49**
See also DLB 37
Hamilton, Clive
See Lewis, C.S.
Hamilton, Edmond 1904-1977 .... **CLC 1**
See also CA 1-4R; CANR 3, 84; DLB 8;
SATA 118; SFW 4
Hamilton, Elizabeth 1758-1816 ... **NCLC 153**
See also DLB 116, 158
Hamilton, Eugene (Jacob) Lee
See Lee-Hamilton, Eugene (Jacob)
Hamilton, Franklin
See Silverberg, Robert
Hamilton, Gail
See Corcoran, Barbara (Asenath)
Hamilton, (Robert) Ian 1938-2001 . **CLC 191**
See also CA 106; CAAS 203; CANR 41,
67; CP 1, 2, 3, 4, 5, 6, 7; DLB 40, 155
Hamilton, Jane 1957- .... **CLC 179**
See also CA 147; CANR 85, 128; CN 7;
MTFW 2005
Hamilton, Mollie
See Kaye, M.M.
Hamilton, (Anthony Walter) Patrick
1904-1962 .... **CLC 51**
See also CA 176; CAAS 113; DLB 10, 191

Hamilton, Virginia 1936-2002 .... **CLC 26**
　　See also AAYA 2, 21; BW 2, 3; BYA 1, 2,
　　8; CA 25-28R; CAAS 206; CANR 20, 37,
　　73, 126; CLR 1, 11, 40; DAM MULT;
　　DLB 33, 52; DLBY 2001; INT CANR-
　　20; LAIT 5; MAICYA 1, 2; MAI-
　　CYAS 1; MTCW 1, 2; MTFW 2005;
　　SATA 4, 56, 79, 123; SATA-Obit 132;
　　WYA; YAW
Hammett, (Samuel) Dashiell
　　1894-1961 .... **CLC 3, 5, 10, 19, 47; SSC**
　　17; TCLC 187
　　See also AAYA 59; AITN 1; AMWS 4;
　　BPFB 2; CA 81-84; CANR 42; CDALB
　　1929-1941; CMW 4; DA3; DLB 226, 280;
　　DLBD 6; DLBY 1996; EWL 3; LAIT 3;
　　MAL 5; MSW; MTCW 1, 2; MTFW
　　2005; NFS 21; RGAL 4; RGSF 2; TUS
Hammon, Jupiter 1720(?)-1800(?) .... **BLC 2;**
　　NCLC 5; PC 16
　　See also DAM MULT, POET; DLB 31, 50
Hammond, Keith
　　See Kuttner, Henry
Hamner, Earl (Henry), Jr. 1923- ...... **CLC 12**
　　See also AITN 2; CA 73-76; DLB 6
Hampton, Christopher 1946- .... **CLC 4**
　　See also CA 25-28R; CD 5, 6; DLB 13;
　　MTCW 1
Hampton, Christopher James
　　See Hampton, Christopher
Hamsun, Knut .... **TCLC 2, 14, 49, 151**
　　See Pedersen, Knut
　　See also DLB 297, 330; EW 8; EWL 3;
　　RGWL 2, 3
Handke, Peter 1942- .... **CLC 5, 8, 10, 15, 38,**
　　134; DC 17
　　See also CA 77-80; CANR 33, 75, 104, 133;
　　CWW 2; DAM DRAM, NOV; DLB 85,
　　124; EWL 3; MTCW 1, 2; MTFW 2005;
　　TWA
Handy, W(illiam) C(hristopher)
　　1873-1958 .... **TCLC 97**
　　See also BW 3; CA 167; CAAE 121
Hanley, James 1901-1985 ..... **CLC 3, 5, 8, 13**
　　See also CA 73-76; CAAS 117; CANR 36;
　　CBD; CN 1, 2, 3; DLB 191; EWL 3;
　　MTCW 1; RGEL 2
Hannah, Barry 1942- .. **CLC 23, 38, 90; SSC**
　　94
　　See also BPFB 2; CA 110; CAAE 108;
　　CANR 43, 68, 113; CN 4, 5, 6, 7; CSW;
　　DLB 6, 234; INT CA-110; MTCW 1;
　　RGSF 2
Hannon, Ezra
　　See Hunter, Evan
Hansberry, Lorraine (Vivian)
　　1930-1965 ... **BLC 2; CLC 17, 62; DC 2**
　　See also AAYA 25; AFAW 1, 2; AMWS 4;
　　BW 1, 3; CA 109; CAAS 25-28R; CABS
　　3; CAD; CANR 58; CDALB 1941-1968;
　　CWD; DA; DA3; DAB; DAC; DAM
　　DRAM, MST, MULT; DFS 2; DLB 7, 38;
　　EWL 3; FL 1:6; FW; LAIT 4; MAL 5;
　　MTCW 1, 2; MTFW 2005; RGAL 4; TUS
Hansen, Joseph 1923-2004 .... **CLC 38**
　　See Brock, Rose; Colton, James
　　See also BPFB 2; CA 29-32R; 17; CAAS
　　233; CANR 16, 44, 66, 125; CMW 4;
　　DLB 226; GLL 1; INT CANR-16
Hansen, Karen V. 1955- .... **CLC 65**
　　See also CA 149; CANR 102
Hansen, Martin A(lfred)
　　1909-1955 .... **TCLC 32**
　　See also CA 167; DLB 214; EWL 3
Hanson, Kenneth O(stlin) 1922- .... **CLC 13**
　　See also CA 53-56; CANR 7; CP 1, 2, 3, 4, 5

Hardwick, Elizabeth 1916- .... **CLC 13**
　　See also AMWS 3; CA 5-8R; CANR 3, 32,
　　70, 100, 139; CN 4, 5, 6; CSW; DA3;
　　DAM NOV; DLB 6; MBL; MTCW 1, 2;
　　MTFW 2005; TCLE 1:1
Hardy, Thomas 1840-1928 .... **PC 8; SSC 2,**
　　60; TCLC 4, 10, 18, 32, 48, 53, 72, 143,
　　153; WLC 3
　　See also AAYA 69; BRW 6; BRWC 1, 2;
　　BRWR 1; CA 123; CAAE 104; CDBLB
　　1890-1914; DA; DA3; DAB; DAC; DAM
　　MST, NOV, POET; DLB 18, 19, 135, 284;
　　EWL 3; EXPN; EXPP; LAIT 2; MTCW
　　1, 2; MTFW 2005; NFS 3, 11, 15, 19; PFS
　　3, 4, 18; RGEL 2; RGSF 2; TEA; WLIT
　　4
Hare, David 1947- . **CLC 29, 58, 136; DC 26**
　　See also BRWS 4; CA 97-100; CANR 39,
　　91; CBD; CD 5, 6; DFS 4, 7, 16; DLB
　　13, 310; MTCW 1; TEA
Harewood, John
　　See Van Druten, John (William)
Harford, Henry
　　See Hudson, W(illiam) H(enry)
Hargrave, Leonie
　　See Disch, Thomas M.
Hariri, Al- al-Qasim ibn 'Ali Abu
　　Muhammad al-Basri
　　See al-Hariri, al-Qasim ibn 'Ali Abu Mu-
　　hammad al-Basri
Harjo, Joy 1951- ..... **CLC 83; NNAL; PC 27**
　　See also AMWS 12; CA 114; CANR 35,
　　67, 91, 129; CP 6, 7; CWP; DAM MULT;
　　DLB 120, 175; EWL 3; MTCW 2; MTFW
　　2005; PFS 15; RGAL 4
Harlan, Louis R(udolph) 1922- .... **CLC 34**
　　See also CA 21-24R; CANR 25, 55, 80
Harling, Robert 1951(?)- .... **CLC 53**
　　See also CA 147
Harmon, William (Ruth) 1938- .... **CLC 38**
　　See also CA 33-36R; CANR 14, 32, 35;
　　SATA 65
Harper, F. E. W.
　　See Harper, Frances Ellen Watkins
Harper, Frances E. W.
　　See Harper, Frances Ellen Watkins
Harper, Frances E. Watkins
　　See Harper, Frances Ellen Watkins
Harper, Frances Ellen
　　See Harper, Frances Ellen Watkins
Harper, Frances Ellen Watkins
　　1825-1911 ..... **BLC 2; PC 21; TCLC 14**
　　See also AFAW 1, 2; BW 1, 3; CA 125;
　　CAAE 111; CANR 79; DAM MULT,
　　POET; DLB 50, 221; MBL; RGAL 4
Harper, Michael S(teven) 1938- ... **CLC 7, 22**
　　See also AFAW 2; BW 1; CA 224; 33-36R,
　　224; CANR 24, 108; CP 2, 3, 4, 5, 6, 7;
　　DLB 41; RGAL 4; TCLE 1:1
Harper, Mrs. F. E. W.
　　See Harper, Frances Ellen Watkins
Harpur, Charles 1813-1868 .... **NCLC 114**
　　See also DLB 230; RGEL 2
Harris, Christie
　　See Harris, Christie (Lucy) Irwin
Harris, Christie (Lucy) Irwin
　　1907-2002 .... **CLC 12**
　　See also CA 5-8R; CANR 6, 83; CLR 47;
　　DLB 88; JRDA; MAICYA 1, 2; SAAS 10;
　　SATA 6, 74; SATA-Essay 116
Harris, Frank 1856-1931 .... **TCLC 24**
　　See also CA 150; CAAE 109; CANR 80;
　　DLB 156, 197; RGEL 2
Harris, George Washington
　　1814-1869 .... **NCLC 23, 165**
　　See also DLB 3, 11, 248; RGAL 4

Harris, Joel Chandler 1848-1908 ..... **SSC 19;**
　　TCLC 2
　　See also CA 137; CAAE 104; CANR 80;
　　CLR 49; DLB 11, 23, 42, 78, 91; LAIT 2;
　　MAICYA 1, 2; RGSF 2; SATA 100; WCH;
　　YABC 1
Harris, John (Wyndham Parkes Lucas)
　　Beynon 1903-1969
　　See Wyndham, John
　　See also CA 102; CAAS 89-92; CANR 84;
　　SATA 118; SFW 4
Harris, MacDonald .... **CLC 9**
　　See Heiney, Donald (William)
Harris, Mark 1922- .... **CLC 19**
　　See also CA 5-8R; 3; CANR 2, 55, 83; CN
　　1, 2, 3, 4, 5, 6, 7; DLB 2; DLBY 1980
Harris, Norman .... **CLC 65**
Harris, (Theodore) Wilson 1921- .... **CLC 25,**
　　159
　　See also BRWS 5; BW 2, 3; CA 65-68; 16;
　　CANR 11, 27, 69, 114; CDWLB 3; CN 1,
　　2, 3, 4, 5, 6, 7; CP 1, 2, 3, 4, 5, 6, 7; DLB
　　117; EWL 3; MTCW 1; RGEL 2
Harrison, Barbara Grizzuti
　　1934-2002 .... **CLC 144**
　　See also CA 77-80; CAAS 205; CANR 15,
　　48; INT CANR-15
Harrison, Elizabeth (Allen) Cavanna
　　1909-2001
　　See Cavanna, Betty
　　See also CA 9-12R; CAAS 200; CANR 6,
　　27, 85, 104, 121; MAICYA 2; SATA 142;
　　YAW
Harrison, Harry (Max) 1925- .... **CLC 42**
　　See also CA 1-4R; CANR 5, 21, 84; DLB
　　8; SATA 4; SCFW; SFW 4
Harrison, James
　　See Harrison, Jim
Harrison, James Thomas
　　See Harrison, Jim
Harrison, Jim 1937- .... **CLC 6, 14, 33, 66,**
　　143; SSC 19
　　See also AMWS 8; CA 13-16R; CANR 8,
　　51, 79, 142; CN 5, 6; CP 1, 2, 3, 4, 5, 6;
　　DLBY 1982; INT CANR-8; RGAL 4;
　　TCWW 2; TUS
Harrison, Kathryn 1961- .... **CLC 70, 151**
　　See also CA 144; CANR 68, 122
Harrison, Tony 1937- .... **CLC 43, 129**
　　See also BRWS 5; CA 65-68; CANR 44,
　　98; CBD; CD 5, 6; CP 2, 3, 4, 5, 6, 7;
　　DLB 40, 245; MTCW 1; RGEL 2
Harriss, Will(ard Irvin) 1922- .... **CLC 34**
　　See also CA 111
Hart, Ellis
　　See Ellison, Harlan
Hart, Josephine 1942(?)- .... **CLC 70**
　　See also CA 138; CANR 70, 149; CPW;
　　DAM POP
Hart, Moss 1904-1961 .... **CLC 66**
　　See also CA 109; CAAS 89-92; CANR 84;
　　DAM DRAM; DFS 1; DLB 7, 266; RGAL
　　4
Harte, (Francis) Bret(t)
　　1836(?)-1902 ... **SSC 8, 59; TCLC 1, 25;**
　　WLC 3
　　See also AMWS 2; CA 140; CAAE 104;
　　CANR 80; CDALB 1865-1917; DA;
　　DA3; DAC; DAM MST; DLB 12, 64, 74,
　　79, 186; EXPS; LAIT 2; RGAL 4; RGSF
　　2; SATA 26; SSFS 3; TUS
Hartley, L(eslie) P(oles) 1895-1972 ... **CLC 2,**
　　22
　　See also BRWS 7; CA 45-48; CAAS 37-
　　40R; CANR 33; CN 1; DLB 15, 139;
　　EWL 3; HGG; MTCW 1, 2; MTFW 2005;
　　RGEL 2; RGSF 2; SUFW 1
Hartman, Geoffrey H. 1929- .... **CLC 27**
　　See also CA 125; CAAE 117; CANR 79;
　　DLB 67

Hartmann, Sadakichi 1869-1944 ... **TCLC 73**
See also CA 157; DLB 54

Hartmann von Aue c. 1170-c. 1210 .... **CMLC 15**
See also CDWLB 2; DLB 138; RGWL 2, 3

Hartog, Jan de
See de Hartog, Jan

Haruf, Kent 1943- .... **CLC 34**
See also AAYA 44; CA 149; CANR 91, 131

Harvey, Caroline
See Trollope, Joanna

Harvey, Gabriel 1550(?)-1631 .... **LC 88**
See also DLB 167, 213, 281

Harwood, Ronald 1934- .... **CLC 32**
See also CA 1-4R; CANR 4, 55, 150; CBD; CD 5, 6; DAM DRAM, MST; DLB 13

Hasegawa Tatsunosuke
See Futabatei, Shimei

Hasek, Jaroslav (Matej Frantisek) 1883-1923 .... **SSC 69; TCLC 4**
See also CA 129; CAAE 104; CDWLB 4; DLB 215; EW 9; EWL 3; MTCW 1, 2; RGSF 2; RGWL 2, 3

Hass, Robert 1941- ... **CLC 18, 39, 99; PC 16**
See also AMWS 6; CA 111; CANR 30, 50, 71; CP 3, 4, 5, 6, 7; DLB 105, 206; EWL 3; MAL 5; MTFW 2005; RGAL 4; SATA 94; TCLE 1:1

Hastings, Hudson
See Kuttner, Henry

Hastings, Selina CLC 44

Hathorne, John 1641-1717 .... **LC 38**

Hatteras, Amelia
See Mencken, H(enry) L(ouis)

Hatteras, Owen TCLC 18
See Mencken, H(enry) L(ouis); Nathan, George Jean

Hauptmann, Gerhart (Johann Robert) 1862-1946 .... **SSC 37; TCLC 4**
See also CA 153; CAAE 104; CDWLB 2; DAM DRAM; DLB 66, 118, 330; EW 8; EWL 3; RGSF 2; RGWL 2, 3; TWA

Havel, Vaclav 1936- ..... **CLC 25, 58, 65, 123; DC 6**
See also CA 104; CANR 36, 63, 124; CDWLB 4; CWW 2; DA3; DAM DRAM; DFS 10; DLB 232; EWL 3; LMFS 2; MTCW 1, 2; MTFW 2005; RGWL 3

Haviaras, Stratis CLC 33
See Chaviaras, Strates

Hawes, Stephen 1475(?)-1529(?) .... **LC 17**
See also DLB 132; RGEL 2

Hawkes, John 1925-1998 .. **CLC 1, 2, 3, 4, 7, 9, 14, 15, 27, 49**
See also BPFB 2; CA 1-4R; CAAS 167; CANR 2, 47, 64; CN 1, 2, 3, 4, 5, 6; DLB 2, 7, 227; DLBY 1980, 1998; EWL 3; MAL 5; MTCW 1, 2; MTFW 2005; RGAL 4

Hawking, S. W.
See Hawking, Stephen W.

Hawking, Stephen W. 1942- ..... **CLC 63, 105**
See also AAYA 13; BEST 89:1; CA 129; CAAE 126; CANR 48, 115; CPW; DA3; MTCW 2; MTFW 2005

Hawkins, Anthony Hope
See Hope, Anthony

Hawthorne, Julian 1846-1934 .... **TCLC 25**
See also CA 165; HGG

Hawthorne, Nathaniel 1804-1864 ... **NCLC 2, 10, 17, 23, 39, 79, 95, 158, 171; SSC 3, 29, 39, 89; WLC 3**
See also AAYA 18; AMW; AMWC 1; AMWR 1; BPFB 2; BYA 3; CDALB 1640-1865; CLR 103; DA; DA3; DAB; DAC; DAM MST, NOV; DLB 1, 74, 183,

223, 269; EXPN; EXPS; GL 2; HGG; LAIT 1; NFS 1, 20; RGAL 4; RGSF 2; SSFS 1, 7, 11, 15; SUFW 1; TUS; WCH; YABC 2

Hawthorne, Sophia Peabody 1809-1871 .... **NCLC 150**
See also DLB 183, 239

Haxton, Josephine Ayres 1921-
See Douglas, Ellen
See also CA 115; CANR 41, 83

Hayaseca y Eizaguirre, Jorge
See Echegaray (y Eizaguirre), Jose (Maria Waldo)

Hayashi, Fumiko 1904-1951 .... **TCLC 27**
See Hayashi Fumiko
See also CA 161

Hayashi Fumiko
See Hayashi, Fumiko
See also DLB 180; EWL 3

Haycraft, Anna 1932-2005
See Ellis, Alice Thomas
See also CA 122; CAAS 237; CANR 90, 141; MTCW 2; MTFW 2005

Hayden, Robert E(arl) 1913-1980 ..... **BLC 2; CLC 5, 9, 14, 37; PC 6**
See also AFAW 1, 2; AMWS 2; BW 1, 3; CA 69-72; CAAS 97-100; CABS 2; CANR 24, 75, 82; CDALB 1941-1968; CP 1, 2, 3; DA; DAC; DAM MST, POET; DLB 5, 76; EWL 3; EXPP; MAL 5; MTCW 1, 2; PFS 1; RGAL 4; SATA 19; SATA-Obit 26; WP

Haydon, Benjamin Robert 1786-1846 .... **NCLC 146**
See also DLB 110

Hayek, F(riedrich) A(ugust von) 1899-1992 .... **TCLC 109**
See also CA 93-96; CAAS 137; CANR 20; MTCW 1, 2

Hayford, J(oseph) E(phraim) Casely
See Casely-Hayford, J(oseph) E(phraim)

Hayman, Ronald 1932- .... **CLC 44**
See also CA 25-28R; CANR 18, 50, 88; CD 5, 6; DLB 155

Hayne, Paul Hamilton 1830-1886 . **NCLC 94**
See also DLB 3, 64, 79, 248; RGAL 4

Hays, Mary 1760-1843 .... **NCLC 114**
See also DLB 142, 158; RGEL 2

Haywood, Eliza (Fowler) 1693(?)-1756 .... **LC 1, 44**
See also BRWS 12; DLB 39; RGEL 2

Hazlitt, William 1778-1830 ...... **NCLC 29, 82**
See also BRW 4; DLB 110, 158; RGEL 2; TEA

Hazzard, Shirley 1931- .... **CLC 18, 218**
See also CA 9-12R; CANR 4, 70, 127; CN 1, 2, 3, 4, 5, 6, 7; DLB 289; DLBY 1982; MTCW 1

Head, Bessie 1937-1986 ...... **BLC 2; CLC 25, 67; SSC 52**
See also AFW; BW 2, 3; CA 29-32R; CAAS 119; CANR 25, 82; CDWLB 3; CN 1, 2, 3, 4; DA3; DAM MULT; DLB 117, 225; EWL 3; EXPS; FL 1:6; FW; MTCW 1, 2; MTFW 2005; RGSF 2; SSFS 5, 13; WLIT 2; WWE 1

Headon, (Nicky) Topper 1956(?)- ... **CLC 30**

Heaney, Seamus 1939- . **CLC 5, 7, 14, 25, 37, 74, 91, 171, 225; PC 18; WLCS**
See also AAYA 61; BRWR 1; BRWS 2; CA 85-88; CANR 25, 48, 75, 91, 128; CD-BLB 1960 to Present; CP 1, 2, 3, 4, 5, 6, 7; DA3; DAB; DAM POET; DLB 40, 330; DLBY 1995; EWL 3; EXPP; MTCW 1, 2; MTFW 2005; PAB; PFS 2, 5, 8, 17; RGEL 2; TEA; WLIT 4

Hearn, (Patricio) Lafcadio (Tessima Carlos) 1850-1904 .... **TCLC 9**
See also CA 166; CAAE 105; DLB 12, 78, 189; HGG; MAL 5; RGAL 4

Hearne, Samuel 1745-1792 .... **LC 95**
See also DLB 99

Hearne, Vicki 1946-2001 .... **CLC 56**
See also CA 139; CAAS 201

Hearon, Shelby 1931- .... **CLC 63**
See also AITN 2; AMWS 8; CA 25-28R; 11; CANR 18, 48, 103, 146; CSW

Heat-Moon, William Least CLC 29
See Trogdon, William (Lewis)
See also AAYA 9

Hebbel, Friedrich 1813-1863 . **DC 21; NCLC 43**
See also CDWLB 2; DAM DRAM; DLB 129; EW 6; RGWL 2, 3

Hebert, Anne 1916-2000 .... **CLC 4, 13, 29**
See also CA 85-88; CAAS 187; CANR 69, 126; CCA 1; CWP; CWW 2; DA3; DAC; DAM MST, POET; DLB 68; EWL 3; GFL 1789 to the Present; MTCW 1, 2; MTFW 2005; PFS 20

Hecht, Anthony (Evan) 1923-2004 .... **CLC 8, 13, 19; PC 70**
See also AMWS 10; CA 9-12R; CAAS 232; CANR 6, 108; CP 1, 2, 3, 4, 5, 6, 7; DAM POET; DLB 5, 169; EWL 3; PFS 6; WP

Hecht, Ben 1894-1964 ..... **CLC 8; TCLC 101**
See also CA 85-88; DFS 9; DLB 7, 9, 25, 26, 28, 86; FANT; IDFW 3, 4; RGAL 4

Hedayat, Sadeq 1903-1951 .... **TCLC 21**
See also CAAE 120; EWL 3; RGSF 2

Hegel, Georg Wilhelm Friedrich 1770-1831 .... **NCLC 46, 151**
See also DLB 90; TWA

Heidegger, Martin 1889-1976 .... **CLC 24**
See also CA 81-84; CAAS 65-68; CANR 34; DLB 296; MTCW 1, 2; MTFW 2005

Heidenstam, (Carl Gustaf) Verner von 1859-1940 .... **TCLC 5**
See also CAAE 104; DLB 330

Heidi Louise
See Erdrich, Louise

Heifner, Jack 1946- .... **CLC 11**
See also CA 105; CANR 47

Heijermans, Herman 1864-1924 .... **TCLC 24**
See also CAAE 123; EWL 3

Heilbrun, Carolyn G(old) 1926-2003 .... **CLC 25, 173**
See Cross, Amanda
See also CA 45-48; CAAS 220; CANR 1, 28, 58, 94; FW

Hein, Christoph 1944- .... **CLC 154**
See also CA 158; CANR 108; CDWLB 2; CWW 2; DLB 124

Heine, Heinrich 1797-1856 .... **NCLC 4, 54, 147; PC 25**
See also CDWLB 2; DLB 90; EW 5; RGWL 2, 3; TWA

Heinemann, Larry 1944- .... **CLC 50**
See also CA 110; 21; CANR 31, 81, 156; DLBD 9; INT CANR-31

Heinemann, Larry Curtiss
See Heinemann, Larry

Heiney, Donald (William) 1921-1993
See Harris, MacDonald
See also CA 1-4R; CAAS 142; CANR 3, 58; FANT

Heinlein, Robert A. 1907-1988 .. **CLC 1, 3, 8, 14, 26, 55; SSC 55**
See also AAYA 17; BPFB 2; BYA 4, 13; CA 1-4R; CAAS 125; CANR 1, 20, 53; CLR 75; CN 1, 2, 3, 4; CPW; DA3; DAM POP; DLB 8; EXPS; JRDA; LAIT 5; LMFS 2; MAICYA 1, 2; MTCW 1, 2; MTFW 2005; RGAL 4; SATA 9, 69; SATA-Obit 56; SCFW 1, 2; SFW 4; SSFS 7; YAW

Helforth, John
See Doolittle, Hilda

Heliodorus fl. 3rd cent. - .... **CMLC 52**
See also WLIT 8

Hellenhofferu, Vojtech Kapristian z
See Hasek, Jaroslav (Matej Frantisek)

Heller, Joseph 1923-1999 . **CLC 1, 3, 5, 8, 11, 36, 63; TCLC 131, 151; WLC 3**
See also AAYA 24; AITN 1; AMWS 4; BPFB 2; BYA 1; CA 5-8R; CAAS 187; CABS 1; CANR 8, 42, 66, 126; CN 1, 2, 3, 4, 5, 6; CPW; DA; DA3; DAB; DAC; DAM MST, NOV, POP; DLB 2, 28, 227; DLBY 1980, 2002; EWL 3; EXPN; INT CANR-8; LAIT 4; MAL 5; MTCW 1, 2; MTFW 2005; NFS 1; RGAL 4; TUS; YAW

Hellman, Lillian 1906-1984 . **CLC 2, 4, 8, 14, 18, 34, 44, 52; DC 1; TCLC 119**
See also AAYA 47; AITN 1, 2; AMWS 1; CA 13-16R; CAAS 112; CAD; CANR 33; CWD; DA3; DAM DRAM; DFS 1, 3, 14; DLB 7, 228; DLBY 1984; EWL 3; FL 1:6; FW; LAIT 3; MAL 5; MBL; MTCW 1, 2; MTFW 2005; RGAL 4; TUS

Helprin, Mark 1947- .... **CLC 7, 10, 22, 32**
See also CA 81-84; CANR 47, 64, 124; CDALBS; CN 7; CPW; DA3; DAM NOV, POP; DLBY 1985; FANT; MAL 5; MTCW 1, 2; MTFW 2005; SUFW 2

Helvetius, Claude-Adrien 1715-1771 .. **LC 26**
See also DLB 313

Helyar, Jane Penelope Josephine 1933-
See Poole, Josephine
See also CA 21-24R; CANR 10, 26; CWRI 5; SATA 82, 138; SATA-Essay 138

Hemans, Felicia 1793-1835 ...... **NCLC 29, 71**
See also DLB 96; RGEL 2

Hemingway, Ernest (Miller)
1899-1961 .... **CLC 1, 3, 6, 8, 10, 13, 19, 30, 34, 39, 41, 44, 50, 61, 80; SSC 1, 25, 36, 40, 63; TCLC 115; WLC 3**
See also AAYA 19; AMW; AMWC 1; AMWR 1; BPFB 2; BYA 2, 3, 13, 15; CA 77-80; CANR 34; CDALB 1917-1929; DA; DA3; DAB; DAC; DAM MST, NOV; DLB 4, 9, 102, 210, 308, 316, 330; DLBD 1, 15, 16; DLBY 1981, 1987, 1996, 1998; EWL 3; EXPN; EXPS; LAIT 3, 4; LATS 1:1; MAL 5; MTCW 1, 2; MTFW 2005; NFS 1, 5, 6, 14; RGAL 4; RGSF 2; SSFS 17; TUS; WYA

Hempel, Amy 1951- .... **CLC 39**
See also CA 137; CAAE 118; CANR 70; DA3; DLB 218; EXPS; MTCW 2; MTFW 2005; SSFS 2

Henderson, F. C.
See Mencken, H(enry) L(ouis)

Henderson, Sylvia
See Ashton-Warner, Sylvia (Constance)

Henderson, Zenna (Chlarson)
1917-1983 .... **SSC 29**
See also CA 1-4R; CAAS 133; CANR 1, 84; DLB 8; SATA 5; SFW 4

Henkin, Joshua CLC 119
See also CA 161

Henley, Beth CLC 23; DC 6, 14
See Henley, Elizabeth Becker
See also AAYA 70; CABS 3; CAD; CD 5, 6; CSW; CWD; DFS 2, 21; DLBY 1986; FW

Henley, Elizabeth Becker 1952-
See Henley, Beth
See also CA 107; CANR 32, 73, 140; DA3; DAM DRAM, MST; MTCW 1, 2; MTFW 2005

Henley, William Ernest 1849-1903 .. **TCLC 8**
See also CA 234; CAAE 105; DLB 19; RGEL 2

Hennissart, Martha 1929-
See Lathen, Emma
See also CA 85-88; CANR 64

Henry VIII 1491-1547 .... **LC 10**
See also DLB 132

Henry, O. SSC 5, 49; TCLC 1, 19; WLC 3
See Porter, William Sydney
See also AAYA 41; AMWS 2; EXPS; MAL 5; RGAL 4; RGSF 2; SSFS 2, 18; TCWW 1, 2

Henry, Patrick 1736-1799 .... **LC 25**
See also LAIT 1

Henryson, Robert 1430(?)-1506(?) ..... **LC 20, 110; PC 65**
See also BRWS 7; DLB 146; RGEL 2

Henschke, Alfred
See Klabund

Henson, Lance 1944- .... **NNAL**
See also CA 146; DLB 175

Hentoff, Nat(han Irving) 1925- .... **CLC 26**
See also AAYA 4, 42; BYA 6; CA 1-4R; 6; CANR 5, 25, 77, 114; CLR 1, 52; INT CANR-25; JRDA; MAICYA 1, 2; SATA 42, 69, 133; SATA-Brief 27; WYA; YAW

Heppenstall, (John) Rayner
1911-1981 .... **CLC 10**
See also CA 1-4R; CAAS 103; CANR 29; CN 1, 2; CP 1, 2, 3; EWL 3

Heraclitus c. 540B.C.-c. 450B.C. ... **CMLC 22**
See also DLB 176

Herbert, Frank 1920-1986 ... **CLC 12, 23, 35, 44, 85**
See also AAYA 21; BPFB 2; BYA 4, 14; CA 53-56; CAAS 118; CANR 5, 43; CDALBS; CPW; DAM POP; DLB 8; INT CANR-5; LAIT 5; MTCW 1, 2; MTFW 2005; NFS 17; SATA 9, 37; SATA-Obit 47; SCFW 1, 2; SFW 4; YAW

Herbert, George 1593-1633 . **LC 24, 121; PC 4**
See also BRW 2; BRWR 2; CDBLB Before 1660; DAB; DAM POET; DLB 126; EXPP; PFS 25; RGEL 2; TEA; WP

Herbert, Zbigniew 1924-1998 ..... **CLC 9, 43; PC 50; TCLC 168**
See also CA 89-92; CAAS 169; CANR 36, 74; CDWLB 4; CWW 2; DAM POET; DLB 232; EWL 3; MTCW 1; PFS 22

Herbst, Josephine (Frey)
1897-1969 .... **CLC 34**
See also CA 5-8R; CAAS 25-28R; DLB 9

Herder, Johann Gottfried von
1744-1803 .... **NCLC 8**
See also DLB 97; EW 4; TWA

Heredia, Jose Maria 1803-1839 .... **HLCS 2**
See also LAW

Hergesheimer, Joseph 1880-1954 ... **TCLC 11**
See also CA 194; CAAE 109; DLB 102, 9; RGAL 4

Herlihy, James Leo 1927-1993 .... **CLC 6**
See also CA 1-4R; CAAS 143; CAD; CANR 2; CN 1, 2, 3, 4, 5

Herman, William
See Bierce, Ambrose (Gwinett)

Hermogenes fl. c. 175- .... **CMLC 6**

Hernandez, Jose 1834-1886 .... **NCLC 17**
See also LAW; RGWL 2, 3; WLIT 1

Herodotus c. 484B.C.-c. 420B.C. ... **CMLC 17**
See also AW 1; CDWLB 1; DLB 176; RGWL 2, 3; TWA; WLIT 8

Herr, Michael 1940(?)- .... **CLC 231**
See also CA 89-92; CANR 68, 142; DLB 185; MTCW 1

Herrick, Robert 1591-1674 .... **LC 13; PC 9**
See also BRW 2; BRWC 2; DA; DAB; DAC; DAM MST, POP; DLB 126; EXPP; PFS 13; RGAL 4; RGEL 2; TEA; WP

Herring, Guilles
See Somerville, Edith Oenone

Herriot, James 1916-1995 .... **CLC 12**
See Wight, James Alfred
See also AAYA 1, 54; BPFB 2; CAAS 148; CANR 40; CLR 80; CPW; DAM POP; LAIT 3; MAICYA 2; MAICYAS 1; MTCW 2; SATA 86, 135; TEA; YAW

Herris, Violet
See Hunt, Violet

Herrmann, Dorothy 1941- .... **CLC 44**
See also CA 107

Herrmann, Taffy
See Herrmann, Dorothy

Hersey, John 1914-1993 .. **CLC 1, 2, 7, 9, 40, 81, 97**
See also AAYA 29; BPFB 2; CA 17-20R; CAAS 140; CANR 33; CDALBS; CN 1, 2, 3, 4, 5; CPW; DAM POP; DLB 6, 185, 278, 299; MAL 5; MTCW 1, 2; MTFW 2005; RGHL; SATA 25; SATA-Obit 76; TUS

Herzen, Aleksandr Ivanovich
1812-1870 .... **NCLC 10, 61**
See Herzen, Alexander

Herzen, Alexander
See Herzen, Aleksandr Ivanovich
See also DLB 277

Herzl, Theodor 1860-1904 .... **TCLC 36**
See also CA 168

Herzog, Werner 1942- .... **CLC 16**
See also CA 89-92

Hesiod c. 8th cent. B.C.- .... **CMLC 5**
See also AW 1; DLB 176; RGWL 2, 3; WLIT 8

Hesse, Hermann 1877-1962 ... **CLC 1, 2, 3, 6, 11, 17, 25, 69; SSC 9, 49; TCLC 148; WLC 3**
See also AAYA 43; BPFB 2; CA 17-18; CAP 2; CDWLB 2; DA; DA3; DAB; DAC; DAM MST, NOV; DLB 66, 330; EW 9; EWL 3; EXPN; LAIT 1; MTCW 1, 2; MTFW 2005; NFS 6, 15, 24; RGWL 2, 3; SATA 50; TWA

Hewes, Cady
See De Voto, Bernard (Augustine)

Heyen, William 1940- .... **CLC 13, 18**
See also CA 220; 33-36R; 220; 9; CANR 98; CP 3, 4, 5, 6, 7; DLB 5; RGHL

Heyerdahl, Thor 1914-2002 .... **CLC 26**
See also CA 5-8R; CAAS 207; CANR 5, 22, 66, 73; LAIT 4; MTCW 1, 2; MTFW 2005; SATA 2, 52

Heym, Georg (Theodor Franz Arthur)
1887-1912 .... **TCLC 9**
See also CA 181; CAAE 106

Heym, Stefan 1913-2001 .... **CLC 41**
See also CA 9-12R; CAAS 203; CANR 4; CWW 2; DLB 69; EWL 3

Heyse, Paul (Johann Ludwig von)
1830-1914 .... **TCLC 8**
See also CA 209; CAAE 104; DLB 129, 330

Heyward, (Edwin) DuBose
1885-1940 .... **HR 1:2; TCLC 59**
See also CA 157; CAAE 108; DLB 7, 9, 45, 249; MAL 5; SATA 21

Heywood, John 1497(?)-1580(?) .... **LC 65**
See also DLB 136; RGEL 2

Heywood, Thomas 1573(?)-1641 .... **LC 111**
See also DAM DRAM; DLB 62; LMFS 1; RGEL 2; TEA

Hibbert, Eleanor Alice Burford
1906-1993 .... **CLC 7**
See Holt, Victoria
See also BEST 90:4; CA 17-20R; CAAS 140; CANR 9, 28, 59; CMW 4; CPW; DAM POP; MTCW 2; MTFW 2005; RHW; SATA 2; SATA-Obit 74

EWL 3; EXPN; EXPS; FL 1:6; FW; LAIT 3; LATS 1:1; LMFS 2; MAL 5; MBL; MTCW 1, 2; MTFW 2005; NFS 3; RGAL 4; RGSF 2; SSFS 1, 6, 11, 19, 21; TUS; YAW

Husserl, E. G.
See Husserl, Edmund (Gustav Albrecht)

Husserl, Edmund (Gustav Albrecht)
1859-1938 .... **TCLC 100**
See also CA 133; CAAE 116; DLB 296

Huston, John (Marcellus)
1906-1987 .... **CLC 20**
See also CA 73-76; CAAS 123; CANR 34; DLB 26

Hustvedt, Siri 1955- .... **CLC 76**
See also CA 137; CANR 149

Hutten, Ulrich von 1488-1523 .... **LC 16**
See also DLB 179

Huxley, Aldous (Leonard)
1894-1963 .... **CLC 1, 3, 4, 5, 8, 11, 18, 35, 79; SSC 39; WLC 3**
See also AAYA 11; BPFB 2; BRW 7; CA 85-88; CANR 44, 99; CDBLB 1914-1945; DA; DA3; DAB; DAC; DAM MST, NOV; DLB 36, 100, 162, 195, 255; EWL 3; EXPN; LAIT 5; LMFS 2; MTCW 1, 2; MTFW 2005; NFS 6; RGEL 2; SATA 63; SCFW 1, 2; SFW 4; TEA; YAW

Huxley, T(homas) H(enry)
1825-1895 .... **NCLC 67**
See also DLB 57; TEA

Huygens, Constantijn 1596-1687 .... **LC 114**
See also RGWL 2, 3

Huysmans, Joris-Karl 1848-1907 ... **TCLC 7, 69**
See also CA 165; CAAE 104; DLB 123; EW 7; GFL 1789 to the Present; LMFS 2; RGWL 2, 3

Hwang, David Henry 1957- .... **CLC 55, 196; DC 4, 23**
See also CA 132; CAAE 127; CAD; CANR 76, 124; CD 5, 6; DA3; DAM DRAM; DFS 11, 18; DLB 212, 228, 312; INT CA-132; MAL 5; MTCW 2; MTFW 2005; RGAL 4

Hyde, Anthony 1946- .... **CLC 42**
See Chase, Nicholas
See also CA 136; CCA 1

Hyde, Margaret O(ldroyd) 1917- ..... **CLC 21**
See also CA 1-4R; CANR 1, 36, 137; CLR 23; JRDA; MAICYA 1, 2; SAAS 8; SATA 1, 42, 76, 139

Hynes, James 1956(?)- .... **CLC 65**
See also CA 164; CANR 105

Hypatia c. 370-415 .... **CMLC 35**

Ian, Janis 1951- .... **CLC 21**
See also CA 187; CAAE 105

Ibanez, Vicente Blasco
See Blasco Ibanez, Vicente
See also DLB 322

Ibarbourou, Juana de
1895(?)-1979 .... **HLCS 2**
See also DLB 290; HW 1; LAW

Ibarguengoitia, Jorge 1928-1983 ..... **CLC 37; TCLC 148**
See also CA 124; CAAS 113; EWL 3; HW 1

Ibn Battuta, Abu Abdalla
1304-1368(?) .... **CMLC 57**
See also WLIT 2

Ibn Hazm 994-1064 .... **CMLC 64**

Ibn Zaydun 1003-1070 .... **CMLC 89**

Ibsen, Henrik (Johan) 1828-1906 .... **DC 2; TCLC 2, 8, 16, 37, 52; WLC 3**
See also AAYA 46; CA 141; CAAE 104; DA; DA3; DAB; DAC; DAM DRAM, MST; DFS 1, 6, 8, 10, 11, 15, 16; EW 7; LAIT 2; LATS 1:1; MTFW 2005; RGWL 2, 3

Ibuse, Masuji 1898-1993 .... **CLC 22**
See Ibuse Masuji
See also CA 127; CAAS 141; MJW; RGWL 3

Ibuse Masuji
See Ibuse, Masuji
See also CWW 2; DLB 180; EWL 3

Ichikawa, Kon 1915- .... **CLC 20**
See also CA 121

Ichiyo, Higuchi 1872-1896 .... **NCLC 49**
See also MJW

Idle, Eric 1943- .... **CLC 21**
See Monty Python
See also CA 116; CANR 35, 91, 148

Idris, Yusuf 1927-1991 .... **SSC 74**
See also AFW; EWL 3; RGSF 2, 3; RGWL 3; WLIT 2

Ignatow, David 1914-1997 .... **CLC 4, 7, 14, 40; PC 34**
See also CA 9-12R; 3; CAAS 162; CANR 31, 57, 96; CP 1, 2, 3, 4, 5, 6; DLB 5; EWL 3; MAL 5

Ignotus
See Strachey, (Giles) Lytton

Ihimaera, Witi (Tame) 1944- .... **CLC 46**
See also CA 77-80; CANR 130; CN 2, 3, 4, 5, 6, 7; RGSF 2; SATA 148

Il'f, Il'ia
See Fainzilberg, Ilya Arnoldovich
See also DLB 272

Ilf, Ilya
See Fainzilberg, Ilya Arnoldovich

Illyes, Gyula 1902-1983 .... **PC 16**
See also CA 114; CAAS 109; CDWLB 4; DLB 215; EWL 3; RGWL 2, 3

Imalayen, Fatima-Zohra
See Djebar, Assia

Immermann, Karl (Lebrecht)
1796-1840 .... **NCLC 4, 49**
See also DLB 133

Ince, Thomas H. 1882-1924 .... **TCLC 89**
See also IDFW 3, 4

Inchbald, Elizabeth 1753-1821 ...... **NCLC 62**
See also DLB 39, 89; RGEL 2

Inclan, Ramon (Maria) del
See Valle-Inclan, Ramon (Maria) del

Infante, G(uillermo) Cabrera
See Cabrera Infante, G.

Ingalls, Rachel 1940- .... **CLC 42**
See also CA 127; CAAE 123; CANR 154

Ingalls, Rachel Holmes
See Ingalls, Rachel

Ingamells, Reginald Charles
See Ingamells, Rex

Ingamells, Rex 1913-1955 .... **TCLC 35**
See also CA 167; DLB 260

Inge, William (Motter) 1913-1973 ..... **CLC 1, 8, 19**
See also CA 9-12R; CAD; CDALB 1941-1968; DA3; DAM DRAM; DFS 1, 3, 5, 8; DLB 7, 249; EWL 3; MAL 5; MTCW 1, 2; MTFW 2005; RGAL 4; TUS

Ingelow, Jean 1820-1897 .... **NCLC 39, 107**
See also DLB 35, 163; FANT; SATA 33

Ingram, Willis J.
See Harris, Mark

Innaurato, Albert (F.) 1948(?)- ... **CLC 21, 60**
See also CA 122; CAAE 115; CAD; CANR 78; CD 5, 6; INT CA-122

Innes, Michael
See Stewart, J(ohn) I(nnes) M(ackintosh)
See also DLB 276; MSW

Innis, Harold Adams 1894-1952 .... **TCLC 77**
See also CA 181; DLB 88

Insluis, Alanus de
See Alain de Lille

Iola
See Wells-Barnett, Ida B(ell)

Ionesco, Eugene 1912-1994 ... **CLC 1, 4, 6, 9, 11, 15, 41, 86; DC 12; WLC 3**
See also CA 9-12R; CAAS 144; CANR 55, 132; CWW 2; DA; DA3; DAB; DAC; DAM DRAM, MST; DFS 4, 9; DLB 321; EW 13; EWL 3; GFL 1789 to the Present; LMFS 2; MTCW 1, 2; MTFW 2005; RGWL 2, 3; SATA 7; SATA-Obit 79; TWA

Iqbal, Muhammad 1877-1938 .... **TCLC 28**
See also CA 215; EWL 3

Ireland, Patrick
See O'Doherty, Brian

Irenaeus St. 130- .... **CMLC 42**

Irigaray, Luce 1930- .... **CLC 164**
See also CA 154; CANR 121; FW

Iron, Ralph
See Schreiner, Olive (Emilie Albertina)

Irving, John 1942- . **CLC 13, 23, 38, 112, 175**
See also AAYA 8, 62; AMWS 6; BEST 89:3; BPFB 2; CA 25-28R; CANR 28, 73, 112, 133; CN 3, 4, 5, 6, 7; CPW; DA3; DAM NOV, POP; DLB 6, 278; DLBY 1982; EWL 3; MAL 5; MTCW 1, 2; MTFW 2005; NFS 12, 14; RGAL 4; TUS

Irving, John Winslow
See Irving, John

Irving, Washington 1783-1859 . **NCLC 2, 19, 95; SSC 2, 37; WLC 3**
See also AAYA 56; AMW; CDALB 1640-1865; CLR 97; DA; DA3; DAB; DAC; DAM MST; DLB 3, 11, 30, 59, 73, 74, 183, 186, 250, 254; EXPS; GL 2; LAIT 1; RGAL 4; RGSF 2; SSFS 1, 8, 16; SUFW 1; TUS; WCH; YABC 2

Irwin, P. K.
See Page, P(atricia) K(athleen)

Isaacs, Jorge Ricardo 1837-1895 ... **NCLC 70**
See also LAW

Isaacs, Susan 1943- .... **CLC 32**
See also BEST 89:1; BPFB 2; CA 89-92; CANR 20, 41, 65, 112, 134; CPW; DA3; DAM POP; INT CANR-20; MTCW 1, 2; MTFW 2005

Isherwood, Christopher 1904-1986 ... **CLC 1, 9, 11, 14, 44; SSC 56**
See also AMWS 14; BRW 7; CA 13-16R; CAAS 117; CANR 35, 97, 133; CN 1, 2, 3; DA3; DAM DRAM, NOV; DLB 15, 195; DLBY 1986; EWL 3; IDTP; MTCW 1, 2; MTFW 2005; RGAL 4; RGEL 2; TUS; WLIT 4

Ishiguro, Kazuo 1954- . **CLC 27, 56, 59, 110, 119**
See also AAYA 58; BEST 90:2; BPFB 2; BRWS 4; CA 120; CANR 49, 95, 133; CN 5, 6, 7; DA3; DAM NOV; DLB 194, 326; EWL 3; MTCW 1, 2; MTFW 2005; NFS 13; WLIT 4; WWE 1

Ishikawa, Hakuhin
See Ishikawa, Takuboku

Ishikawa, Takuboku 1886(?)-1912 ..... **PC 10; TCLC 15**
See Ishikawa Takuboku
See also CA 153; CAAE 113; DAM POET

Iskander, Fazil (Abdulovich) 1929- .. **CLC 47**
See Iskander, Fazil' Abdulevich
See also CA 102; EWL 3

Iskander, Fazil' Abdulevich
See Iskander, Fazil (Abdulovich)
See also DLB 302

Isler, Alan (David) 1934- .... **CLC 91**
See also CA 156; CANR 105

Ivan IV 1530-1584 .... **LC 17**

Ivanov, V.I.
See Ivanov, Vyacheslav

Ivanov, Vyacheslav 1866-1949 .... **TCLC 33**
See also CAAE 122; EWL 3

Ivanov, Vyacheslav Ivanovich
See Ivanov, Vyacheslav

Ivask, Ivar Vidrik 1927-1992 .... **CLC 14**
See also CA 37-40R; CAAS 139; CANR 24

Ives, Morgan
See Bradley, Marion Zimmer
See also GLL 1

Izumi Shikibu c. 973-c. 1034 .... **CMLC 33**

J. R. S.
See Gogarty, Oliver St. John

Jabran, Kahlil
See Gibran, Kahlil

Jabran, Khalil
See Gibran, Kahlil

Jackson, Daniel
See Wingrove, David

Jackson, Helen Hunt 1830-1885 .... **NCLC 90**
See also DLB 42, 47, 186, 189; RGAL 4

Jackson, Jesse 1908-1983 .... **CLC 12**
See also BW 1; CA 25-28R; CAAS 109; CANR 27; CLR 28; CWRI 5; MAICYA 1, 2; SATA 2, 29; SATA-Obit 48

Jackson, Laura (Riding) 1901-1991 .... **PC 44**
See Riding, Laura
See also CA 65-68; CAAS 135; CANR 28, 89; DLB 48

Jackson, Sam
See Trumbo, Dalton

Jackson, Sara
See Wingrove, David

Jackson, Shirley 1919-1965 . **CLC 11, 60, 87; SSC 9, 39; TCLC 187; WLC 3**
See also AAYA 9; AMWS 9; BPFB 2; CA 1-4R; CAAS 25-28R; CANR 4, 52; CDALB 1941-1968; DA; DA3; DAC; DAM MST; DLB 6, 234; EXPS; HGG; LAIT 4; MAL 5; MTCW 2; MTFW 2005; RGAL 4; RGSF 2; SATA 2; SSFS 1; SUFW 1, 2

Jacob, (Cyprien-)Max 1876-1944 .... **TCLC 6**
See also CA 193; CAAE 104; DLB 258; EWL 3; GFL 1789 to the Present; GLL 2; RGWL 2, 3

Jacobs, Harriet A(nn)
1813(?)-1897 .... **NCLC 67, 162**
See also AFAW 1, 2; DLB 239; FL 1:3; FW; LAIT 2; RGAL 4

Jacobs, Jim 1942- .... **CLC 12**
See also CA 97-100; INT CA-97-100

Jacobs, W(illiam) W(ymark)
1863-1943 .... **SSC 73; TCLC 22**
See also CA 167; CAAE 121; DLB 135; EXPS; HGG; RGEL 2; RGSF 2; SSFS 2; SUFW 1

Jacobsen, Jens Peter 1847-1885 .... **NCLC 34**

Jacobsen, Josephine (Winder)
1908-2003 .... **CLC 48, 102; PC 62**
See also CA 33-36R; 18; CAAS 218; CANR 23, 48; CCA 1; CP 2, 3, 4, 5, 6, 7; DLB 244; PFS 23; TCLE 1:1

Jacobson, Dan 1929- ...... **CLC 4, 14; SSC 91**
See also AFW; CA 1-4R; CANR 2, 25, 66; CN 1, 2, 3, 4, 5, 6, 7; DLB 14, 207, 225, 319; EWL 3; MTCW 1; RGSF 2

Jacqueline
See Carpentier (y Valmont), Alejo

Jacques de Vitry c. 1160-1240 ...... **CMLC 63**
See also DLB 208

Jagger, Michael Philip
See Jagger, Mick

Jagger, Mick 1943- .... **CLC 17**
See also CA 239

Jahiz, al- c. 780-c. 869 .... **CMLC 25**
See also DLB 311

Jakes, John 1932- .... **CLC 29**
See also AAYA 32; BEST 89:4; BPFB 2; CA 214; 57-60, 214; CANR 10, 43, 66, 111, 142; CPW; CSW; DA3; DAM NOV,

POP; DLB 278; DLBY 1983; FANT; INT CANR-10; MTCW 1, 2; MTFW 2005; RHW; SATA 62; SFW 4; TCWW 1, 2

James I 1394-1437 .... **LC 20**
See also RGEL 2

James, Andrew
See Kirkup, James

James, C(yril) L(ionel) R(obert)
1901-1989 .... **BLCS; CLC 33**
See also BW 2; CA 125; CAAE 117; CAAS 128; CANR 62; CN 1, 2, 3, 4; DLB 125; MTCW 1

James, Daniel (Lewis) 1911-1988
See Santiago, Danny
See also CA 174; CAAS 125

James, Dynely
See Mayne, William (James Carter)

James, Henry Sr. 1811-1882 .... **NCLC 53**

James, Henry 1843-1916 .... **SSC 8, 32, 47; TCLC 2, 11, 24, 40, 47, 64, 171; WLC 3**
See also AMW; AMWC 1; AMWR 1; BPFB 2; BRW 6; CA 132; CAAE 104; CDALB 1865-1917; DA; DA3; DAB; DAC; DAM MST, NOV; DLB 12, 71, 74, 189; DLBD 13; EWL 3; EXPS; GL 2; HGG; LAIT 2; MAL 5; MTCW 1, 2; MTFW 2005; NFS 12, 16, 19; RGAL 4; RGEL 2; RGSF 2; SSFS 9; SUFW 1; TUS

James, M. R. SSC 93
See James, Montague (Rhodes)
See also DLB 156, 201

James, Montague (Rhodes)
1862-1936 .... **SSC 16; TCLC 6**
See James, M. R.
See also CA 203; CAAE 104; HGG; RGEL 2; RGSF 2; SUFW 1

James, P. D. CLC 18, 46, 122, 226
See White, Phyllis Dorothy James
See also BEST 90:2; BPFB 2; BRWS 4; CDBLB 1960 to Present; CN 4, 5, 6; DLB 87, 276; DLBD 17; MSW

James, Philip
See Moorcock, Michael

James, Samuel
See Stephens, James

James, Seumas
See Stephens, James

James, Stephen
See Stephens, James

James, William 1842-1910 .... **TCLC 15, 32**
See also AMW; CA 193; CAAE 109; DLB 270, 284; MAL 5; NCFS 5; RGAL 4

Jameson, Anna 1794-1860 .... **NCLC 43**
See also DLB 99, 166

Jameson, Fredric (R.) 1934- .... **CLC 142**
See also CA 196; DLB 67; LMFS 2

James VI of Scotland 1566-1625 .... **LC 109**
See also DLB 151, 172

Jami, Nur al-Din 'Abd al-Rahman
1414-1492 .... **LC 9**

Jammes, Francis 1868-1938 .... **TCLC 75**
See also CA 198; EWL 3; GFL 1789 to the Present

Jandl, Ernst 1925-2000 .... **CLC 34**
See also CA 200; EWL 3

Janowitz, Tama 1957- .... **CLC 43, 145**
See also CA 106; CANR 52, 89, 129; CN 5, 6, 7; CPW; DAM POP; DLB 292; MTFW 2005

Jansson, Tove (Marika) 1914-2001 ... **SSC 96**
See also CA 17-20R; CAAS 196; CANR 38, 118; CLR 2; CWW 2; DLB 257; EWL 3; MAICYA 1, 2; RGSF 2; SATA 3, 41

Japrisot, Sebastien 1931- .... **CLC 90**
See Rossi, Jean-Baptiste
See also CMW 4; NFS 18

Jarrell, Randall 1914-1965 .... **CLC 1, 2, 6, 9, 13, 49; PC 41; TCLC 177**
See also AMW; BYA 5; CA 5-8R; CAAS 25-28R; CABS 2; CANR 6, 34; CDALB 1941-1968; CLR 6, 111; CWRI 5; DAM POET; DLB 48, 52; EWL 3; EXPP; MAICYA 1, 2; MAL 5; MTCW 1, 2; PAB; PFS 2; RGAL 4; SATA 7

Jarry, Alfred 1873-1907 .... **SSC 20; TCLC 2, 14, 147**
See also CA 153; CAAE 104; DA3; DAM DRAM; DFS 8; DLB 192, 258; EW 9; EWL 3; GFL 1789 to the Present; RGWL 2, 3; TWA

Jarvis, E. K.
See Ellison, Harlan

Jawien, Andrzej
See John Paul II, Pope

Jaynes, Roderick
See Coen, Ethan

Jeake, Samuel, Jr.
See Aiken, Conrad (Potter)

Jean Paul 1763-1825 .... **NCLC 7**

Jefferies, (John) Richard
1848-1887 .... **NCLC 47**
See also DLB 98, 141; RGEL 2; SATA 16; SFW 4

Jeffers, (John) Robinson 1887-1962 .. **CLC 2, 3, 11, 15, 54; PC 17; WLC 3**
See also AMWS 2; CA 85-88; CANR 35; CDALB 1917-1929; DA; DAC; DAM MST, POET; DLB 45, 212; EWL 3; MAL 5; MTCW 1, 2; MTFW 2005; PAB; PFS 3, 4; RGAL 4

Jefferson, Janet
See Mencken, H(enry) L(ouis)

Jefferson, Thomas 1743-1826 . **NCLC 11, 103**
See also AAYA 54; ANW; CDALB 1640-1865; DA3; DLB 31, 183; LAIT 1; RGAL 4

Jeffrey, Francis 1773-1850 .... **NCLC 33**
See Francis, Lord Jeffrey

Jelakowitch, Ivan
See Heijermans, Herman

Jelinek, Elfriede 1946- .... **CLC 169**
See also AAYA 68; CA 154; DLB 85, 330; FW

Jellicoe, (Patricia) Ann 1927- .... **CLC 27**
See also CA 85-88; CBD; CD 5, 6; CWD; CWRI 5; DLB 13, 233; FW

Jelloun, Tahar ben 1944- .... **CLC 180**
See Ben Jelloun, Tahar
See also CA 162; CANR 100

Jemyma
See Holley, Marietta

Jen, Gish AAL; CLC 70, 198
See Jen, Lillian
See also AMWC 2; CN 7; DLB 312

Jen, Lillian 1955-
See Jen, Gish
See also CA 135; CANR 89, 130

Jenkins, (John) Robin 1912- .... **CLC 52**
See also CA 1-4R; CANR 1, 135; CN 1, 2, 3, 4, 5, 6, 7; DLB 14, 271

Jennings, Elizabeth (Joan)
1926-2001 .... **CLC 5, 14, 131**
See also BRWS 5; CA 61-64; 5; CAAS 200; CANR 8, 39, 66, 127; CP 1, 2, 3, 4, 5, 6, 7; CWP; DLB 27; EWL 3; MTCW 1; SATA 66

Jennings, Waylon 1937-2002 .... **CLC 21**

Jensen, Johannes V(ilhelm)
1873-1950 .... **TCLC 41**
See also CA 170; DLB 214, 330; EWL 3; RGWL 3

Jensen, Laura (Linnea) 1948- .... **CLC 37**
See also CA 103

Jerome, Saint 345-420 .... **CMLC 30**
See also RGWL 3

Kerrigan, (Thomas) Anthony 1918- .. **CLC 4, 6**
See also CA 49-52; 11; CANR 4

Kerry, Lois
See Duncan, Lois

Kesey, Ken 1935-2001 .... **CLC 1, 3, 6, 11, 46, 64, 184; WLC 3**
See also AAYA 25; BG 1:3; BPFB 2; CA 1-4R; CAAS 204; CANR 22, 38, 66, 124; CDALB 1968-1988; CN 1, 2, 3, 4, 5, 6, 7; CPW; DA; DA3; DAB; DAC; DAM MST, NOV, POP; DLB 2, 16, 206; EWL 3; EXPN; LAIT 4; MAL 5; MTCW 1, 2; MTFW 2005; NFS 2; RGAL 4; SATA 66; SATA-Obit 131; TUS; YAW

Kesselring, Joseph (Otto) 1902-1967 .... **CLC 45**
See also CA 150; DAM DRAM, MST; DFS 20

Kessler, Jascha (Frederick) 1929- ...... **CLC 4**
See also CA 17-20R; CANR 8, 48, 111; CP 1

Kettelkamp, Larry (Dale) 1933- .... **CLC 12**
See also CA 29-32R; CANR 16; SAAS 3; SATA 2

Key, Ellen (Karolina Sofia) 1849-1926 .... **TCLC 65**
See also DLB 259

Keyber, Conny
See Fielding, Henry

Keyes, Daniel 1927- .... **CLC 80**
See also AAYA 23; BYA 11; CA 181; 17-20R, 181; CANR 10, 26, 54, 74; DA; DA3; DAC; DAM MST, NOV; EXPN; LAIT 4; MTCW 2; MTFW 2005; NFS 2; SATA 37; SFW 4

Keynes, John Maynard 1883-1946 .... **TCLC 64**
See also CA 162, 163; CAAE 114; DLBD 10; MTCW 2; MTFW 2005

Khanshendel, Chiron
See Rose, Wendy

Khayyam, Omar 1048-1131 ... **CMLC 11; PC 8**
See Omar Khayyam
See also DA3; DAM POET; WLIT 6

Kherdian, David 1931- .... **CLC 6, 9**
See also AAYA 42; CA 192; 21-24R, 192; 2; CANR 39, 78; CLR 24; JRDA; LAIT 3; MAICYA 1, 2; SATA 16, 74; SATA-Essay 125

Khlebnikov, Velimir TCLC 20
See Khlebnikov, Viktor Vladimirovich
See also DLB 295; EW 10; EWL 3; RGWL 2, 3

Khlebnikov, Viktor Vladimirovich 1885-1922
See Khlebnikov, Velimir
See also CA 217; CAAE 117

Khodasevich, V.F.
See Khodasevich, Vladislav

Khodasevich, Vladislav 1886-1939 .... **TCLC 15**
See also CAAE 115; DLB 317; EWL 3

Khodasevich, Vladislav Felitsianovich
See Khodasevich, Vladislav

Kielland, Alexander Lange 1849-1906 .... **TCLC 5**
See also CAAE 104

Kiely, Benedict 1919-2007 . **CLC 23, 43; SSC 58**
See also CA 1-4R; CANR 2, 84; CN 1, 2, 3, 4, 5, 6, 7; DLB 15, 319; TCLE 1:1

Kienzle, William X. 1928-2001 .... **CLC 25**
See also CA 93-96; 1; CAAS 203; CANR 9, 31, 59, 111; CMW 4; DA3; DAM POP; INT CANR-31; MSW; MTCW 1, 2; MTFW 2005

Kierkegaard, Soren 1813-1855 ..... **NCLC 34, 78, 125**
See also DLB 300; EW 6; LMFS 2; RGWL 3; TWA

Kieslowski, Krzysztof 1941-1996 .... **CLC 120**
See also CA 147; CAAS 151

Killens, John Oliver 1916-1987 .... **CLC 10**
See also BW 2; CA 77-80; 2; CAAS 123; CANR 26; CN 1, 2, 3, 4; DLB 33; EWL 3

Killigrew, Anne 1660-1685 .... **LC 4, 73**
See also DLB 131

Killigrew, Thomas 1612-1683 .... **LC 57**
See also DLB 58; RGEL 2

Kim
See Simenon, Georges (Jacques Christian)

Kincaid, Jamaica 1949- ...... **BLC 2; CLC 43, 68, 137, 234; SSC 72**
See also AAYA 13, 56; AFAW 2; AMWS 7; BRWS 7; BW 2, 3; CA 125; CANR 47, 59, 95, 133; CDALBS; CDWLB 3; CLR 63; CN 4, 5, 6, 7; DA3; DAM MULT, NOV; DLB 157, 227; DNFS 1; EWL 3; EXPS; FW; LATS 1:2; LMFS 2; MAL 5; MTCW 2; MTFW 2005; NCFS 1; NFS 3; SSFS 5, 7; TUS; WWE 1; YAW

King, Francis (Henry) 1923- .... **CLC 8, 53, 145**
See also CA 1-4R; CANR 1, 33, 86; CN 1, 2, 3, 4, 5, 6, 7; DAM NOV; DLB 15, 139; MTCW 1

King, Kennedy
See Brown, George Douglas

King, Martin Luther, Jr. 1929-1968 . **BLC 2; CLC 83; WLCS**
See also BW 2, 3; CA 25-28; CANR 27, 44; CAP 2; DA; DA3; DAB; DAC; DAM MST, MULT; LAIT 5; LATS 1:2; MTCW 1, 2; MTFW 2005; SATA 14

King, Stephen 1947- .... **CLC 12, 26, 37, 61, 113, 228; SSC 17, 55**
See also AAYA 1, 17; AMWS 5; BEST 90:1; BPFB 2; CA 61-64; CANR 1, 30, 52, 76, 119, 134; CN 7; CPW; DA3; DAM NOV, POP; DLB 143; DLBY 1980; HGG; JRDA; LAIT 5; MTCW 1, 2; MTFW 2005; RGAL 4; SATA 9, 55, 161; SUFW 1, 2; WYAS 1; YAW

King, Stephen Edwin
See King, Stephen

King, Steve
See King, Stephen

King, Thomas 1943- .... **CLC 89, 171; NNAL**
See also CA 144; CANR 95; CCA 1; CN 6, 7; DAC; DAM MULT; DLB 175; SATA 96

Kingman, Lee CLC 17
See Natti, (Mary) Lee
See also CWRI 5; SAAS 3; SATA 1, 67

Kingsley, Charles 1819-1875 .... **NCLC 35**
See also CLR 77; DLB 21, 32, 163, 178, 190; FANT; MAICYA 2; MAICYAS 1; RGEL 2; WCH; YABC 2

Kingsley, Henry 1830-1876 .... **NCLC 107**
See also DLB 21, 230; RGEL 2

Kingsley, Sidney 1906-1995 .... **CLC 44**
See also CA 85-88; CAAS 147; CAD; DFS 14, 19; DLB 7; MAL 5; RGAL 4

Kingsolver, Barbara 1955- .... **CLC 55, 81, 130, 216**
See also AAYA 15; AMWS 7; CA 134; CAAE 129; CANR 60, 96, 133; CDALBS; CN 7; CPW; CSW; DA3; DAM POP; DLB 206; INT CA-134; LAIT 5; MTCW 2; MTFW 2005; NFS 5, 10, 12, 24; RGAL 4; TCLE 1:1

Kingston, Maxine Hong 1940- .... **AAL; CLC 12, 19, 58, 121; WLCS**
See also AAYA 8, 55; AMWS 5; BPFB 2; CA 69-72; CANR 13, 38, 74, 87, 128; CDALBS; CN 6, 7; DA3; DAM MULT, NOV; DLB 173, 212, 312; DLBY 1980; EWL 3; FL 1:6; FW; INT CANR-13; LAIT 5; MAL 5; MBL; MTCW 1, 2; MTFW 2005; NFS 6; RGAL 4; SATA 53; SSFS 3; TCWW 2

Kinnell, Galway 1927- ..... **CLC 1, 2, 3, 5, 13, 29, 129; PC 26**
See also AMWS 3; CA 9-12R; CANR 10, 34, 66, 116, 138; CP 1, 2, 3, 4, 5, 6, 7; DLB 5; DLBY 1987; EWL 3; INT CANR-34; MAL 5; MTCW 1, 2; MTFW 2005; PAB; PFS 9; RGAL 4; TCLE 1:1; WP

Kinsella, Thomas 1928- .... **CLC 4, 19, 138; PC 69**
See also BRWS 5; CA 17-20R; CANR 15, 122; CP 1, 2, 3, 4, 5, 6, 7; DLB 27; EWL 3; MTCW 1, 2; MTFW 2005; RGEL 2; TEA

Kinsella, W.P. 1935- .... **CLC 27, 43, 166**
See also AAYA 7, 60; BPFB 2; CA 222; 97-100, 222; 7; CANR 21, 35, 66, 75, 129; CN 4, 5, 6, 7; CPW; DAC; DAM NOV, POP; FANT; INT CANR-21; LAIT 5; MTCW 1, 2; MTFW 2005; NFS 15; RGSF 2

Kinsey, Alfred C(harles) 1894-1956 .... **TCLC 91**
See also CA 170; CAAE 115; MTCW 2

Kipling, (Joseph) Rudyard 1865-1936 . **PC 3; SSC 5, 54; TCLC 8, 17, 167; WLC 3**
See also AAYA 32; BRW 6; BRWC 1, 2; BYA 4; CA 120; CAAE 105; CANR 33; CDBLB 1890-1914; CLR 39, 65; CWRI 5; DA; DA3; DAB; DAC; DAM MST, POET; DLB 19, 34, 141, 156, 330; EWL 3; EXPS; FANT; LAIT 3; LMFS 1; MAICYA 1, 2; MTCW 1, 2; MTFW 2005; NFS 21; PFS 22; RGEL 2; RGSF 2; SATA 100; SFW 4; SSFS 8, 21, 22; SUFW 1; TEA; WCH; WLIT 4; YABC 2

Kircher, Athanasius 1602-1680 .... **LC 121**
See also DLB 164

Kirk, Russell (Amos) 1918-1994 .. **TCLC 119**
See also AITN 1; CA 1-4R; 9; CAAS 145; CANR 1, 20, 60; HGG; INT CANR-20; MTCW 1, 2

Kirkham, Dinah
See Card, Orson Scott

Kirkland, Caroline M. 1801-1864 . **NCLC 85**
See also DLB 3, 73, 74, 250, 254; DLBD 13

Kirkup, James 1918- .... **CLC 1**
See also CA 1-4R; 4; CANR 2; CP 1, 2, 3, 4, 5, 6, 7; DLB 27; SATA 12

Kirkwood, James 1930(?)-1989 .... **CLC 9**
See also AITN 2; CA 1-4R; CAAS 128; CANR 6, 40; GLL 2

Kirsch, Sarah 1935- .... **CLC 176**
See also CA 178; CWW 2; DLB 75; EWL 3

Kirshner, Sidney
See Kingsley, Sidney

Kis, Danilo 1935-1989 .... **CLC 57**
See also CA 118; CAAE 109; CAAS 129; CANR 61; CDWLB 4; DLB 181; EWL 3; MTCW 1; RGSF 2; RGWL 2, 3

Kissinger, Henry A(lfred) 1923- ..... **CLC 137**
See also CA 1-4R; CANR 2, 33, 66, 109; MTCW 1

Kittel, Frederick August
See Wilson, August

Kivi, Aleksis 1834-1872 .... **NCLC 30**

Lamming, George (William) 1927- ... **BLC 2; CLC 2, 4, 66, 144**
See also BW 2, 3; CA 85-88; CANR 26, 76; CDWLB 3; CN 1, 2, 3, 4, 5, 6, 7; CP 1; DAM MULT; DLB 125; EWL 3; MTCW 1, 2; MTFW 2005; NFS 15; RGEL 2

L'Amour, Louis 1908-1988 .... **CLC 25, 55**
See also AAYA 16; AITN 2; BEST 89:2; BPFB 2; CA 1-4R; CAAS 125; CANR 3, 25, 40; CPW; DA3; DAM NOV, POP; DLB 206; DLBY 1980; MTCW 1, 2; MTFW 2005; RGAL 4; TCWW 1, 2

Lampedusa, Giuseppe (Tomasi) di TCLC 13
See Tomasi di Lampedusa, Giuseppe
See also CA 164; EW 11; MTCW 2; MTFW 2005; RGWL 2, 3

Lampman, Archibald 1861-1899 ... **NCLC 25**
See also DLB 92; RGEL 2; TWA

Lancaster, Bruce 1896-1963 .... **CLC 36**
See also CA 9-10; CANR 70; CAP 1; SATA 9

Lanchester, John 1962- .... **CLC 99**
See also CA 194; DLB 267

Landau, Mark Alexandrovich
See Aldanov, Mark (Alexandrovich)

Landau-Aldanov, Mark Alexandrovich
See Aldanov, Mark (Alexandrovich)

Landis, Jerry
See Simon, Paul

Landis, John 1950- .... **CLC 26**
See also CA 122; CAAE 112; CANR 128

Landolfi, Tommaso 1908-1979 .... **CLC 11, 49**
See also CA 127; CAAS 117; DLB 177; EWL 3

Landon, Letitia Elizabeth
1802-1838 .... **NCLC 15**
See also DLB 96

Landor, Walter Savage
1775-1864 .... **NCLC 14**
See also BRW 4; DLB 93, 107; RGEL 2

Landwirth, Heinz 1927-2007
See Lind, Jakov
See also CA 9-12R; CANR 7

Lane, Patrick 1939- .... **CLC 25**
See also CA 97-100; CANR 54; CP 3, 4, 5, 6, 7; DAM POET; DLB 53; INT CA-97-100

Lane, Rose Wilder 1887-1968 ...... **TCLC 177**
See also CA 102; CANR 63; SATA 29; SATA-Brief 28; TCWW 2

Lang, Andrew 1844-1912 .... **TCLC 16**
See also CA 137; CAAE 114; CANR 85; CLR 101; DLB 98, 141, 184; FANT; MAICYA 1, 2; RGEL 2; SATA 16; WCH

Lang, Fritz 1890-1976 .... **CLC 20, 103**
See also AAYA 65; CA 77-80; CAAS 69-72; CANR 30

Lange, John
See Crichton, Michael

Langer, Elinor 1939- .... **CLC 34**
See also CA 121

Langland, William 1332(?)-1400(?) .... **LC 19, 120**
See also BRW 1; DA; DAB; DAC; DAM MST, POET; DLB 146; RGEL 2; TEA; WLIT 3

Langstaff, Launcelot
See Irving, Washington

Lanier, Sidney 1842-1881 . **NCLC 6, 118; PC 50**
See also AMWS 1; DAM POET; DLB 64; DLBD 13; EXPP; MAICYA 1; PFS 14; RGAL 4; SATA 18

Lanyer, Aemilia 1569-1645 .... **LC 10, 30, 83; PC 60**
See also DLB 121

Lao-Tzu
See Lao Tzu

Lao Tzu c. 6th cent. B.C.-3rd cent.
B.C. .... **CMLC 7**

Lapine, James (Elliot) 1949- .... **CLC 39**
See also CA 130; CAAE 123; CANR 54, 128; INT CA-130

Larbaud, Valery (Nicolas)
1881-1957 .... **TCLC 9**
See also CA 152; CAAE 106; EWL 3; GFL 1789 to the Present

Larcom, Lucy 1824-1893 .... **NCLC 179**
See also AMWS 13; DLB 221, 243

Lardner, Ring
See Lardner, Ring(gold) W(ilmer)
See also BPFB 2; CDALB 1917-1929; DLB 11, 25, 86, 171; DLBD 16; MAL 5; RGAL 4; RGSF 2

Lardner, Ring W., Jr.
See Lardner, Ring(gold) W(ilmer)

Lardner, Ring(gold) W(ilmer)
1885-1933 .... **SSC 32; TCLC 2, 14**
See Lardner, Ring
See also AMW; CA 131; CAAE 104; MTCW 1, 2; MTFW 2005; TUS

Laredo, Betty
See Codrescu, Andrei

Larkin, Maia
See Wojciechowska, Maia (Teresa)

Larkin, Philip (Arthur) 1922-1985 ... **CLC 3, 5, 8, 9, 13, 18, 33, 39, 64; PC 21**
See also BRWS 1; CA 5-8R; CAAS 117; CANR 24, 62; CDBLB 1960 to Present; CP 1, 2, 3, 4; DA3; DAB; DAM MST, POET; DLB 27; EWL 3; MTCW 1, 2; MTFW 2005; PFS 3, 4, 12; RGEL 2

La Roche, Sophie von
1730-1807 .... **NCLC 121**
See also DLB 94

La Rochefoucauld, Francois
1613-1680 .... **LC 108**

Larra (y Sanchez de Castro), Mariano Jose
de 1809-1837 .... **NCLC 17, 130**

Larsen, Eric 1941- .... **CLC 55**
See also CA 132

Larsen, Nella 1893(?)-1963 .... **BLC 2; CLC 37; HR 1:3**
See also AFAW 1, 2; BW 1; CA 125; CANR 83; DAM MULT; DLB 51; FW; LATS 1:1; LMFS 2

Larson, Charles R(aymond) 1938- ... **CLC 31**
See also CA 53-56; CANR 4, 121

Larson, Jonathan 1960-1996 .... **CLC 99**
See also AAYA 28; CA 156; DFS 23; MTFW 2005

La Sale, Antoine de c. 1386-1460(?) . **LC 104**
See also DLB 208

Las Casas, Bartolome de
1474-1566 .... **HLCS; LC 31**
See Casas, Bartolome de las
See also DLB 318; LAW

Lasch, Christopher 1932-1994 .... **CLC 102**
See also CA 73-76; CAAS 144; CANR 25, 118; DLB 246; MTCW 1, 2; MTFW 2005

Lasker-Schueler, Else 1869-1945 ... **TCLC 57**
See Lasker-Schuler, Else
See also CA 183; DLB 66, 124

Lasker-Schuler, Else
See Lasker-Schueler, Else
See also EWL 3

Laski, Harold J(oseph) 1893-1950 . **TCLC 79**
See also CA 188

Latham, Jean Lee 1902-1995 .... **CLC 12**
See also AITN 1; BYA 1; CA 5-8R; CANR 7, 84; CLR 50; MAICYA 1, 2; SATA 2, 68; YAW

Latham, Mavis
See Clark, Mavis Thorpe

Lathen, Emma CLC 2
See Hennissart, Martha; Latsis, Mary J(ane)
See also BPFB 2; CMW 4; DLB 306

Lathrop, Francis
See Leiber, Fritz (Reuter, Jr.)

Latsis, Mary J(ane) 1927-1997
See Lathen, Emma
See also CA 85-88; CAAS 162; CMW 4

Lattany, Kristin
See Lattany, Kristin (Elaine Eggleston) Hunter

Lattany, Kristin (Elaine Eggleston) Hunter
1931- .... **CLC 35**
See Hunter, Kristin
See also AITN 1; BW 1; BYA 3; CA 13-16R; CANR 13, 108; CLR 3; CN 7; DLB 33; INT CANR-13; MAICYA 1, 2; SAAS 10; SATA 12, 132; YAW

Lattimore, Richmond (Alexander)
1906-1984 .... **CLC 3**
See also CA 1-4R; CAAS 112; CANR 1; CP 1, 2, 3; MAL 5

Laughlin, James 1914-1997 .... **CLC 49**
See also CA 21-24R; 22; CAAS 162; CANR 9, 47; CP 1, 2, 3, 4, 5, 6; DLB 48; DLBY 1996, 1997

Laurence, Margaret 1926-1987 ..... **CLC 3, 6, 13, 50, 62; SSC 7**
See also BYA 13; CA 5-8R; CAAS 121; CANR 33; CN 1, 2, 3, 4; DAC; DAM MST; DLB 53; EWL 3; FW; MTCW 1, 2; MTFW 2005; NFS 11; RGEL 2; RGSF 2; SATA-Obit 50; TCWW 2

Laurent, Antoine 1952- .... **CLC 50**

Lauscher, Hermann
See Hesse, Hermann

Lautreamont 1846-1870 .. **NCLC 12; SSC 14**
See Lautreamont, Isidore Lucien Ducasse
See also GFL 1789 to the Present; RGWL 2, 3

Lautreamont, Isidore Lucien Ducasse
See Lautreamont
See also DLB 217

Lavater, Johann Kaspar
1741-1801 .... **NCLC 142**
See also DLB 97

Laverty, Donald
See Blish, James (Benjamin)

Lavin, Mary 1912-1996 . **CLC 4, 18, 99; SSC 4, 67**
See also CA 9-12R; CAAS 151; CANR 33; CN 1, 2, 3, 4, 5, 6; DLB 15, 319; FW; MTCW 1; RGEL 2; RGSF 2; SSFS 23

Lavond, Paul Dennis
See Kornbluth, C(yril) M.; Pohl, Frederik

Lawes, Henry 1596-1662 .... **LC 113**
See also DLB 126

Lawler, Ray
See Lawler, Raymond Evenor
See also DLB 289

Lawler, Raymond Evenor 1922- .... **CLC 58**
See Lawler, Ray
See also CA 103; CD 5, 6; RGEL 2

Lawrence, D(avid) H(erbert Richards)
1885-1930 .... **PC 54; SSC 4, 19, 73; TCLC 2, 9, 16, 33, 48, 61, 93; WLC 3**
See Chambers, Jessie
See also BPFB 2; BRW 7; BRWR 2; CA 121; CAAE 104; CANR 131; CDBLB 1914-1945; DA; DA3; DAB; DAC; DAM MST, NOV, POET; DLB 10, 19, 36, 98, 162, 195; EWL 3; EXPP; EXPS; LAIT 2, 3; MTCW 1, 2; MTFW 2005; NFS 18; PFS 6; RGEL 2; RGSF 2; SSFS 2, 6; TEA; WLIT 4; WP

Lawrence, T(homas) E(dward)
1888-1935 .... **TCLC 18**
See Dale, Colin
See also BRWS 2; CA 167; CAAE 115; DLB 195

Lawrence of Arabia
See Lawrence, T(homas) E(dward)

Lawson, Henry (Archibald Hertzberg)
1867-1922 .... **SSC 18; TCLC 27**
See also CA 181; CAAE 120; DLB 230;
RGEL 2; RGSF 2

Lawton, Dennis
See Faust, Frederick (Schiller)

Layamon fl. c. 1200- .... **CMLC 10**
See also DLB 146; RGEL 2

Laye, Camara 1928-1980 ..... **BLC 2; CLC 4, 38**
See Camara Laye
See also AFW; BW 1; CA 85-88; CAAS
97-100; CANR 25; DAM MULT; MTCW
1, 2; WLIT 2

Layton, Irving 1912-2006 ..... **CLC 2, 15, 164**
See also CA 1-4R; CAAS 247; CANR 2,
33, 43, 66, 129; CP 1, 2, 3, 4, 5, 6, 7;
DAC; DAM MST, POET; DLB 88; EWL
3; MTCW 1, 2; PFS 12; RGEL 2

Layton, Irving Peter
See Layton, Irving

Lazarus, Emma 1849-1887 ...... **NCLC 8, 109**

Lazarus, Felix
See Cable, George Washington

Lazarus, Henry
See Slavitt, David R(ytman)

Lea, Joan
See Neufeld, John (Arthur)

Leacock, Stephen (Butler)
1869-1944 .... **SSC 39; TCLC 2**
See also CA 141; CAAE 104; CANR 80;
DAC; DAM MST; DLB 92; EWL 3;
MTCW 2; MTFW 2005; RGEL 2; RGSF
2

Lead, Jane Ward 1623-1704 .... **LC 72**
See also DLB 131

Leapor, Mary 1722-1746 .... **LC 80**
See also DLB 109

Lear, Edward 1812-1888 ..... **NCLC 3; PC 65**
See also AAYA 48; BRW 5; CLR 1, 75;
DLB 32, 163, 166; MAICYA 1, 2; RGEL
2; SATA 18, 100; WCH; WP

Lear, Norman (Milton) 1922- .... **CLC 12**
See also CA 73-76

Leautaud, Paul 1872-1956 .... **TCLC 83**
See also CA 203; DLB 65; GFL 1789 to the
Present

Leavis, F(rank) R(aymond)
1895-1978 .... **CLC 24**
See also BRW 7; CA 21-24R; CAAS 77-
80; CANR 44; DLB 242; EWL 3; MTCW
1, 2; RGEL 2

Leavitt, David 1961- .... **CLC 34**
See also CA 122; CAAE 116; CANR 50,
62, 101, 134; CPW; DA3; DAM POP;
DLB 130; GLL 1; INT CA-122; MAL 5;
MTCW 2; MTFW 2005

Leblanc, Maurice (Marie Emile)
1864-1941 .... **TCLC 49**
See also CAAE 110; CMW 4

Lebowitz, Fran(ces Ann) 1951(?)- ... **CLC 11, 36**
See also CA 81-84; CANR 14, 60, 70; INT
CANR-14; MTCW 1

Lebrecht, Peter
See Tieck, (Johann) Ludwig

le Carre, John 1931- .... **CLC 9, 15**
See also AAYA 42; BEST 89:4; BPFB 2;
BRWS 2; CA 5-8R; CANR 13, 33, 59,
107, 132; CDBLB 1960 to Present; CMW
4; CN 1, 2, 3, 4, 5, 6, 7; CPW; DA3;
DAM POP; DLB 87; EWL 3; MSW;
MTCW 1, 2; MTFW 2005; RGEL 2; TEA

Le Clezio, J. M.G. 1940- .... **CLC 31, 155**
See also CA 128; CAAE 116; CANR 147;
CWW 2; DLB 83; EWL 3; GFL 1789 to
the Present; RGSF 2

Le Clezio, Jean Marie Gustave
See Le Clezio, J. M.G.

Leconte de Lisle, Charles-Marie-Rene
1818-1894 .... **NCLC 29**
See also DLB 217; EW 6; GFL 1789 to the
Present

Le Coq, Monsieur
See Simenon, Georges (Jacques Christian)

Leduc, Violette 1907-1972 .... **CLC 22**
See also CA 13-14; CAAS 33-36R; CANR
69; CAP 1; EWL 3; GFL 1789 to the
Present; GLL 1

Ledwidge, Francis 1887(?)-1917 .... **TCLC 23**
See also CA 203; CAAE 123; DLB 20

Lee, Andrea 1953- .... **BLC 2; CLC 36**
See also BW 1, 3; CA 125; CANR 82;
DAM MULT

Lee, Andrew
See Auchincloss, Louis

Lee, Chang-rae 1965- .... **CLC 91**
See also CA 148; CANR 89; CN 7; DLB
312; LATS 1:2

Lee, Don L. CLC 2
See Madhubuti, Haki R.
See also CP 2, 3, 4, 5

Lee, George W(ashington)
1894-1976 .... **BLC 2; CLC 52**
See also BW 1; CA 125; CANR 83; DAM
MULT; DLB 51

Lee, Harper 1926- ... **CLC 12, 60, 194; WLC 4**
See also AAYA 13; AMWS 8; BPFB 2;
BYA 3; CA 13-16R; CANR 51, 128;
CDALB 1941-1968; CSW; DA; DA3;
DAB; DAC; DAM MST, NOV; DLB 6;
EXPN; LAIT 3; MAL 5; MTCW 1, 2;
MTFW 2005; NFS 2; SATA 11; WYA;
YAW

Lee, Helen Elaine 1959(?)- .... **CLC 86**
See also CA 148

Lee, John CLC 70

Lee, Julian
See Latham, Jean Lee

Lee, Larry
See Lee, Lawrence

Lee, Laurie 1914-1997 .... **CLC 90**
See also CA 77-80; CAAS 158; CANR 33,
73; CP 1, 2, 3, 4, 5, 6; CPW; DAB; DAM
POP; DLB 27; MTCW 1; RGEL 2

Lee, Lawrence 1941-1990 .... **CLC 34**
See also CAAS 131; CANR 43

Lee, Li-Young 1957- .... **CLC 164; PC 24**
See also AMWS 15; CA 153; CANR 118;
CP 6, 7; DLB 165, 312; LMFS 2; PFS 11,
15, 17

Lee, Manfred B. 1905-1971 .... **CLC 11**
See Queen, Ellery
See also CA 1-4R; CAAS 29-32R; CANR
2, 150; CMW 4; DLB 137

Lee, Manfred Bennington
See Lee, Manfred B.

Lee, Nathaniel 1645(?)-1692 .... **LC 103**
See also DLB 80; RGEL 2

Lee, Shelton Jackson
See Lee, Spike
See also AAYA 4, 29

Lee, Spike 1957(?)- .... **BLCS; CLC 105**
See Lee, Shelton Jackson
See also BW 2, 3; CA 125; CANR 42;
DAM MULT

Lee, Stan 1922- .... **CLC 17**
See also AAYA 5, 49; CA 111; CAAE 108;
CANR 129; INT CA-111; MTFW 2005

Lee, Tanith 1947- .... **CLC 46**
See also AAYA 15; CA 37-40R; CANR 53,
102, 145; DLB 261; FANT; SATA 8, 88,
134; SFW 4; SUFW 1, 2; YAW

Lee, Vernon SSC 33, 98; TCLC 5
See Paget, Violet
See also DLB 57, 153, 156, 174, 178; GLL
1; SUFW 1

Lee, William
See Burroughs, William S.
See also GLL 1

Lee, Willy
See Burroughs, William S.
See also GLL 1

Lee-Hamilton, Eugene (Jacob)
1845-1907 .... **TCLC 22**
See also CA 234; CAAE 117

Leet, Judith 1935- .... **CLC 11**
See also CA 187

Le Fanu, Joseph Sheridan
1814-1873 .... **NCLC 9, 58; SSC 14, 84**
See also CMW 4; DA3; DAM POP; DLB
21, 70, 159, 178; GL 3; HGG; RGEL 2;
RGSF 2; SUFW 1

Leffland, Ella 1931- .... **CLC 19**
See also CA 29-32R; CANR 35, 78, 82;
DLBY 1984; INT CANR-35; SATA 65;
SSFS 24

Leger, Alexis
See Leger, (Marie-Rene Auguste) Alexis
Saint-Leger

Leger, (Marie-Rene Auguste) Alexis
Saint-Leger 1887-1975 .. **CLC 4, 11, 46;
PC 23**
See Perse, Saint-John; Saint-John Perse
See also CA 13-16R; CAAS 61-64; CANR
43; DAM POET; MTCW 1

Leger, Saintleger
See Leger, (Marie-Rene Auguste) Alexis
Saint-Leger

Le Guin, Ursula K. 1929- ...... **CLC 8, 13, 22,
45, 71, 136; SSC 12, 69**
See also AAYA 9, 27; AITN 1; BPFB 2;
BYA 5, 8, 11, 14; CA 21-24R; CANR 9,
32, 52, 74, 132; CDALB 1968-1988; CLR
3, 28, 91; CN 2, 3, 4, 5, 6, 7; CPW; DA3;
DAB; DAC; DAM MST, POP; DLB 8,
52, 256, 275; EXPS; FANT; FW; INT
CANR-32; JRDA; LAIT 5; MAICYA 1,
2; MAL 5; MTCW 1, 2; MTFW 2005;
NFS 6, 9; SATA 4, 52, 99, 149; SCFW 1,
2; SFW 4; SSFS 2; SUFW 1, 2; WYA;
YAW

Lehmann, Rosamond (Nina)
1901-1990 .... **CLC 5**
See also CA 77-80; CAAS 131; CANR 8,
73; CN 1, 2, 3, 4; DLB 15; MTCW 2;
RGEL 2; RHW

Leiber, Fritz (Reuter, Jr.)
1910-1992 .... **CLC 25**
See also AAYA 65; BPFB 2; CA 45-48;
CAAS 139; CANR 2, 40, 86; CN 2, 3, 4,
5; DLB 8; FANT; HGG; MTCW 1, 2;
MTFW 2005; SATA 45; SATA-Obit 73;
SCFW 1, 2; SFW 4; SUFW 1, 2

Leibniz, Gottfried Wilhelm von
1646-1716 .... **LC 35**
See also DLB 168

Leimbach, Martha 1963-
See Leimbach, Marti
See also CA 130

Leimbach, Marti CLC 65
See Leimbach, Martha

Leino, Eino TCLC 24
See Lonnbohm, Armas Eino Leopold
See also EWL 3

Leiris, Michel (Julien) 1901-1990 ..... **CLC 61**
See also CA 128; CAAE 119; CAAS 132;
EWL 3; GFL 1789 to the Present

Leithauser, Brad 1953- .... **CLC 27**
See also CA 107; CANR 27, 81; CP 5, 6, 7;
DLB 120, 282

le Jars de Gournay, Marie
See de Gournay, Marie le Jars

Lelchuk, Alan 1938- .... **CLC 5**
See also CA 45-48; 20; CANR 1, 70, 152;
CN 3, 4, 5, 6, 7

Lewton, Val 1904-1951 .... **TCLC 76**
　See also CA 199; IDFW 3, 4
Leyner, Mark 1956- .... **CLC 92**
　See also CA 110; CANR 28, 53; DA3; DLB
　292; MTCW 1; MTFW 2005
Lezama Lima, Jose 1910-1976 .... **CLC 4, 10,**
　101; HLCS 2
　See also CA 77-80; CANR 71; DAM
　MULT; DLB 113, 283; EWL 3; HW 1, 2;
　LAW; RGWL 2, 3
L'Heureux, John (Clarke) 1934- ...... **CLC 52**
　See also CA 13-16R; CANR 23, 45, 88; CP
　1, 2, 3, 4; DLB 244
Li Ch'ing-chao 1081(?)-1141(?) .... **CMLC 71**
Liddell, C. H.
　See Kuttner, Henry
Lie, Jonas (Lauritz Idemil)
　1833-1908(?) .... **TCLC 5**
　See also CAAE 115
Lieber, Joel 1937-1971 .... **CLC 6**
　See also CA 73-76; CAAS 29-32R
Lieber, Stanley Martin
　See Lee, Stan
Lieberman, Laurence (James)
　1935- .... **CLC 4, 36**
　See also CA 17-20R; CANR 8, 36, 89; CP
　1, 2, 3, 4, 5, 6, 7
Lieh Tzu fl. 7th cent. B.C.-5th cent.
　B.C. .... **CMLC 27**
Lieksman, Anders
　See Haavikko, Paavo Juhani
Lifton, Robert Jay 1926- .... **CLC 67**
　See also CA 17-20R; CANR 27, 78, 161;
　INT CANR-27; SATA 66
Lightfoot, Gordon 1938- .... **CLC 26**
　See also CA 242; CAAE 109
Lightfoot, Gordon Meredith
　See Lightfoot, Gordon
Lightman, Alan P(aige) 1948- .... **CLC 81**
　See also CA 141; CANR 63, 105, 138;
　MTFW 2005
Ligotti, Thomas (Robert) 1953- ...... **CLC 44;**
　SSC 16
　See also CA 123; CANR 49, 135; HGG;
　SUFW 2
Li Ho 791-817 .... **PC 13**
Li Ju-chen c. 1763-c. 1830 .... **NCLC 137**
Lilar, Francoise
　See Mallet-Joris, Francoise
Liliencron, Detlev
　See Liliencron, Detlev von
Liliencron, Detlev von 1844-1909 .. **TCLC 18**
　See also CAAE 117
Liliencron, Friedrich Adolf Axel Detlev von
　See Liliencron, Detlev von
Liliencron, Friedrich Detlev von
　See Liliencron, Detlev von
Lille, Alain de
　See Alain de Lille
Lillo, George 1691-1739 .... **LC 131**
　See also DLB 84; RGEL 2
Lilly, William 1602-1681 .... **LC 27**
Lima, Jose Lezama
　See Lezama Lima, Jose
Lima Barreto, Afonso Henrique de
　1881-1922 .... **TCLC 23**
　See Lima Barreto, Afonso Henriques de
　See also CA 181; CAAE 117; LAW
Lima Barreto, Afonso Henriques de
　See Lima Barreto, Afonso Henrique de
　See also DLB 307
Limonov, Eduard
　See Limonov, Edward
　See also DLB 317
Limonov, Edward 1944- .... **CLC 67**
　See Limonov, Eduard
　See also CA 137

Lin, Frank
　See Atherton, Gertrude (Franklin Horn)
Lin, Yutang 1895-1976 .... **TCLC 149**
　See also CA 45-48; CAAS 65-68; CANR 2;
　RGAL 4
Lincoln, Abraham 1809-1865 .... **NCLC 18**
　See also LAIT 2
Lind, Jakov CLC 1, 2, 4, 27, 82
　See Landwirth, Heinz
　See also CA 4; DLB 299; EWL 3; RGHL
Lindbergh, Anne Morrow
　1906-2001 .... **CLC 82**
　See also BPFB 2; CA 17-20R; CAAS 193;
　CANR 16, 73; DAM NOV; MTCW 1, 2;
　MTFW 2005; SATA 33; SATA-Obit 125;
　TUS
Lindsay, David 1878(?)-1945 .... **TCLC 15**
　See also CA 187; CAAE 113; DLB 255;
　FANT; SFW 4; SUFW 1
Lindsay, (Nicholas) Vachel
　1879-1931 .... **PC 23; TCLC 17; WLC 4**
　See also AMWS 1; CA 135; CAAE 114;
　CANR 79; CDALB 1865-1917; DA;
　DA3; DAC; DAM MST, POET; DLB 54;
　EWL 3; EXPP; MAL 5; RGAL 4; SATA
　40; WP
Linke-Poot
　See Doeblin, Alfred
Linney, Romulus 1930- .... **CLC 51**
　See also CA 1-4R; CAD; CANR 40, 44,
　79; CD 5, 6; CSW; RGAL 4
Linton, Eliza Lynn 1822-1898 .... **NCLC 41**
　See also DLB 18
Li Po 701-763 .... **CMLC 2, 86; PC 29**
　See also PFS 20; WP
Lipsius, Justus 1547-1606 .... **LC 16**
Lipsyte, Robert 1938- ...., **CLC 21**
　See also AAYA 7, 45; CA 17-20R; CANR
　8, 57, 146; CLR 23, 76; DA; DAC; DAM
　MST, NOV; JRDA; LAIT 5; MAICYA 1,
　2; SATA 5, 68, 113, 161; WYA; YAW
Lipsyte, Robert Michael
　See Lipsyte, Robert
Lish, Gordon 1934- .... **CLC 45; SSC 18**
　See also CA 117; CAAE 113; CANR 79,
　151; DLB 130; INT CA-117
Lish, Gordon Jay
　See Lish, Gordon
Lispector, Clarice 1925(?)-1977 .... **CLC 43;**
　HLCS 2; SSC 34, 96
　See also CA 139; CAAS 116; CANR 71;
　CDWLB 3; DLB 113, 307; DNFS 1; EWL
　3; FW; HW 2; LAW; RGSF 2; RGWL 2,
　3; WLIT 1
Littell, Robert 1935(?)- .... **CLC 42**
　See also CA 112; CAAE 109; CANR 64,
　115; CMW 4
Little, Malcolm 1925-1965
　See Malcolm X
　See also BW 1, 3; CA 125; CAAS 111;
　CANR 82; DA; DA3; DAB; DAC; DAM
　MST, MULT; MTCW 1, 2; MTFW 2005
Littlewit, Humphrey Gent.
　See Lovecraft, H. P.
Litwos
　See Sienkiewicz, Henryk (Adam Alexander
　Pius)
Liu, E. 1857-1909 .... **TCLC 15**
　See also CA 190; CAAE 115; DLB 328
Lively, Penelope 1933- .... **CLC 32, 50**
　See also BPFB 2; CA 41-44R; CANR 29,
　67, 79, 131; CLR 7; CN 5, 6, 7; CWRI 5;
　DAM NOV; DLB 14, 161, 207, 326;
　FANT; JRDA; MAICYA 1, 2; MTCW 1,
　2; MTFW 2005; SATA 7, 60, 101, 164;
　TEA
Lively, Penelope Margaret
　See Lively, Penelope

Livesay, Dorothy (Kathleen)
　1909-1996 .... **CLC 4, 15, 79**
　See also AITN 2; CA 25-28R; 8; CANR 36,
　67; CP 1, 2, 3, 4, 5; DAC; DAM MST,
　POET; DLB 68; FW; MTCW 1; RGEL 2;
　TWA
Livy c. 59B.C.-c. 12 .... **CMLC 11**
　See also AW 2; CDWLB 1; DLB 211;
　RGWL 2, 3; WLIT 8
Lizardi, Jose Joaquin Fernandez de
　1776-1827 .... **NCLC 30**
　See also LAW
Llewellyn, Richard
　See Llewellyn Lloyd, Richard Dafydd Viv-
　ian
　See also DLB 15
Llewellyn Lloyd, Richard Dafydd Vivian
　1906-1983 .... **CLC 7, 80**
　See Llewellyn, Richard
　See also CA 53-56; CAAS 111; CANR 7,
　71; SATA 11; SATA-Obit 37
Llosa, Jorge Mario Pedro Vargas
　See Vargas Llosa, Mario
　See also RGWL 3
Llosa, Mario Vargas
　See Vargas Llosa, Mario
Lloyd, Manda
　See Mander, (Mary) Jane
Lloyd Webber, Andrew 1948-
　See Webber, Andrew Lloyd
　See also AAYA 1, 38; CA 149; CAAE 116;
　DAM DRAM; SATA 56
Llull, Ramon c. 1235-c. 1316 .... **CMLC 12**
Lobb, Ebenezer
　See Upward, Allen
Locke, Alain (Le Roy)
　1886-1954 .... **BLCS; HR 1:3; TCLC 43**
　See also AMWS 14; BW 1, 3; CA 124;
　CAAE 106; CANR 79; DLB 51; LMFS
　2; MAL 5; RGAL 4
Locke, John 1632-1704 .... **LC 7, 35, 135**
　See also DLB 31, 101, 213, 252; RGEL 2;
　WLIT 3
Locke-Elliott, Sumner
　See Elliott, Sumner Locke
Lockhart, John Gibson 1794-1854 .. **NCLC 6**
　See also DLB 110, 116, 144
Lockridge, Ross (Franklin), Jr.
　1914-1948 .... **TCLC 111**
　See also CA 145; CAAE 108; CANR 79;
　DLB 143; DLBY 1980; MAL 5; RGAL
　4; RHW
Lockwood, Robert
　See Johnson, Robert
Lodge, David 1935- .... **CLC 36, 141**
　See also BEST 90:1; BRWS 4; CA 17-20R;
　CANR 19, 53, 92, 139; CN 1, 2, 3, 4, 5,
　6, 7; CPW; DAM POP; DLB 14, 194;
　EWL 3; INT CANR-19; MTCW 1, 2;
　MTFW 2005
Lodge, Thomas 1558-1625 .... **LC 41**
　See also DLB 172; RGEL 2
Loewinsohn, Ron(ald William)
　1937- .... **CLC 52**
　See also CA 25-28R; CANR 71; CP 1, 2, 3,
　4
Logan, Jake
　See Smith, Martin Cruz
Logan, John (Burton) 1923-1987 .... **CLC 5**
　See also CA 77-80; CAAS 124; CANR 45;
　CP 1, 2, 3, 4; DLB 5
Lo Kuan-chung 1330(?)-1400(?) .... **LC 12**
Lombard, Nap
　See Johnson, Pamela Hansford
Lombard, Peter 1100(?)-1160(?) ... **CMLC 72**
Lombino, Salvatore
　See Hunter, Evan

Lurie, Alison 1926- ..... **CLC 4, 5, 18, 39, 175**
See also BPFB 2; CA 1-4R; CANR 2, 17, 50, 88; CN 1, 2, 3, 4, 5, 6, 7; DLB 2; MAL 5; MTCW 1; NFS 24; SATA 46, 112; TCLE 1:1

Lustig, Arnost 1926- .... **CLC 56**
See also AAYA 3; CA 69-72; CANR 47, 102; CWW 2; DLB 232, 299; EWL 3; RGHL; SATA 56

Luther, Martin 1483-1546 .... **LC 9, 37**
See also CDWLB 2; DLB 179; EW 2; RGWL 2, 3

Luxemburg, Rosa 1870(?)-1919 ..... **TCLC 63**
See also CAAE 118

Luzi, Mario (Egidio Vincenzo)
1914-2005 .... **CLC 13**
See also CA 61-64; CAAS 236; CANR 9, 70; CWW 2; DLB 128; EWL 3

L'vov, Arkady **CLC 59**

Lydgate, John c. 1370-1450(?) .... **LC 81**
See also BRW 1; DLB 146; RGEL 2

Lyly, John 1554(?)-1606 .... **DC 7; LC 41**
See also BRW 1; DAM DRAM; DLB 62, 167; RGEL 2

L'Ymagier
See Gourmont, Remy(-Marie-Charles) de

Lynch, B. Suarez
See Borges, Jorge Luis

Lynch, David 1946- .... **CLC 66, 162**
See also AAYA 55; CA 129; CAAE 124; CANR 111

Lynch, David Keith
See Lynch, David

Lynch, James
See Andreyev, Leonid (Nikolaevich)

Lyndsay, Sir David 1485-1555 .... **LC 20**
See also RGEL 2

Lynn, Kenneth S(chuyler)
1923-2001 .... **CLC 50**
See also CA 1-4R; CAAS 196; CANR 3, 27, 65

Lynx
See West, Rebecca

Lyons, Marcus
See Blish, James (Benjamin)

Lyotard, Jean-Francois
1924-1998 .... **TCLC 103**
See also DLB 242; EWL 3

Lyre, Pinchbeck
See Sassoon, Siegfried (Lorraine)

Lytle, Andrew (Nelson) 1902-1995 ... **CLC 22**
See also CA 9-12R; CAAS 150; CANR 70; CN 1, 2, 3, 4, 5, 6; CSW; DLB 6; DLBY 1995; RGAL 4; RHW

Lyttelton, George 1709-1773 .... **LC 10**
See also RGEL 2

Lytton of Knebworth, Baron
See Bulwer-Lytton, Edward (George Earle Lytton)

Maas, Peter 1929-2001 .... **CLC 29**
See also CA 93-96; CAAS 201; INT CA-93-96; MTCW 2; MTFW 2005

Mac A'Ghobhainn, Iain
See Smith, Iain Crichton

Macaulay, Catherine 1731-1791 .... **LC 64**
See also DLB 104

Macaulay, (Emilie) Rose
1881(?)-1958 .... **TCLC 7, 44**
See also CAAE 104; DLB 36; EWL 3; RGEL 2; RHW

Macaulay, Thomas Babington
1800-1859 .... **NCLC 42**
See also BRW 4; CDBLB 1832-1890; DLB 32, 55; RGEL 2

MacBeth, George (Mann)
1932-1992 .... **CLC 2, 5, 9**
See also CA 25-28R; CAAS 136; CANR 61, 66; CP 1, 2, 3, 4, 5; DLB 40; MTCW 1; PFS 8; SATA 4; SATA-Obit 70

MacCaig, Norman (Alexander)
1910-1996 .... **CLC 36**
See also BRWS 6; CA 9-12R; CANR 3, 34; CP 1, 2, 3, 4, 5, 6; DAB; DAM POET; DLB 27; EWL 3; RGEL 2

MacCarthy, Sir (Charles Otto) Desmond
1877-1952 .... **TCLC 36**
See also CA 167

MacDiarmid, Hugh **CLC 2, 4, 11, 19, 63; PC 9**
See Grieve, C(hristopher) M(urray)
See also BRWS 12; CDBLB 1945-1960; CP 1, 2; DLB 20; EWL 3; RGEL 2

MacDonald, Anson
See Heinlein, Robert A.

Macdonald, Cynthia 1928- .... **CLC 13, 19**
See also CA 49-52; CANR 4, 44, 146; DLB 105

MacDonald, George 1824-1905 .... **TCLC 9, 113**
See also AAYA 57; BYA 5; CA 137; CAAE 106; CANR 80; CLR 67; DLB 18, 163, 178; FANT; MAICYA 1, 2; RGEL 2; SATA 33, 100; SFW 4; SUFW; WCH

Macdonald, John
See Millar, Kenneth

MacDonald, John D. 1916-1986 .. **CLC 3, 27, 44**
See also BPFB 2; CA 1-4R; CAAS 121; CANR 1, 19, 60; CMW 4; CPW; DAM NOV, POP; DLB 8, 306; DLBY 1986; MSW; MTCW 1, 2; MTFW 2005; SFW 4

Macdonald, John Ross
See Millar, Kenneth

Macdonald, Ross **CLC 1, 2, 3, 14, 34, 41**
See Millar, Kenneth
See also AMWS 4; BPFB 2; CN 1, 2, 3; DLBD 6; MAL 5; MSW; RGAL 4

MacDougal, John
See Blish, James (Benjamin)

MacDougal, John
See Blish, James (Benjamin)

MacDowell, John
See Parks, Tim(othy Harold)

MacEwen, Gwendolyn (Margaret)
1941-1987 .... **CLC 13, 55**
See also CA 9-12R; CAAS 124; CANR 7, 22; CP 1, 2, 3, 4; DLB 53, 251; SATA 50; SATA-Obit 55

Macha, Karel Hynek 1810-1846 .... **NCLC 46**

Machado (y Ruiz), Antonio
1875-1939 .... **TCLC 3**
See also CA 174; CAAE 104; DLB 108; EW 9; EWL 3; HW 2; PFS 23; RGWL 2, 3

Machado de Assis, Joaquim Maria
1839-1908 .... **BLC 2; HLCS 2; SSC 24; TCLC 10**
See also CA 153; CAAE 107; CANR 91; DLB 307; LAW; RGSF 2; RGWL 2, 3; TWA; WLIT 1

Machaut, Guillaume de c.
1300-1377 .... **CMLC 64**
See also DLB 208

Machen, Arthur **SSC 20; TCLC 4**
See Jones, Arthur Llewellyn
See also CA 179; DLB 156, 178; RGEL 2; SUFW 1

Machiavelli, Niccolo 1469-1527 ... **DC 16; LC 8, 36; WLCS**
See also AAYA 58; DA; DAB; DAC; DAM MST; EW 2; LAIT 1; LMFS 1; NFS 9; RGWL 2, 3; TWA; WLIT 7

MacInnes, Colin 1914-1976 .... **CLC 4, 23**
See also CA 69-72; CAAS 65-68; CANR 21; CN 1, 2; DLB 14; MTCW 1, 2; RGEL 2; RHW

MacInnes, Helen (Clark)
1907-1985 .... **CLC 27, 39**
See also BPFB 2; CA 1-4R; CAAS 117; CANR 1, 28, 58; CMW 4; CN 1, 2; CPW; DAM POP; DLB 87; MSW; MTCW 1, 2; MTFW 2005; SATA 22; SATA-Obit 44

Mackay, Mary 1855-1924
See Corelli, Marie
See also CA 177; CAAE 118; FANT; RHW

Mackay, Shena 1944- .... **CLC 195**
See also CA 104; CANR 88, 139; DLB 231, 319; MTFW 2005

Mackenzie, Compton (Edward Montague)
1883-1972 .... **CLC 18; TCLC 116**
See also CA 21-22; CAAS 37-40R; CAP 2; CN 1; DLB 34, 100; RGEL 2

Mackenzie, Henry 1745-1831 .... **NCLC 41**
See also DLB 39; RGEL 2

Mackey, Nathaniel 1947- .... **PC 49**
See also CA 153; CANR 114; CP 6, 7; DLB 169

Mackey, Nathaniel Ernest
See Mackey, Nathaniel

MacKinnon, Catharine A. 1946- .... **CLC 181**
See also CA 132; CAAE 128; CANR 73, 140; FW; MTCW 2; MTFW 2005

Mackintosh, Elizabeth 1896(?)-1952
See Tey, Josephine
See also CAAE 110; CMW 4

Macklin, Charles 1699-1797 .... **LC 132**
See also DLB 89; RGEL 2

MacLaren, James
See Grieve, C(hristopher) M(urray)

MacLaverty, Bernard 1942- .... **CLC 31**
See also CA 118; CAAE 116; CANR 43, 88; CN 5, 6, 7; DLB 267; INT CA-118; RGSF 2

MacLean, Alistair (Stuart)
1922(?)-1987 .... **CLC 3, 13, 50, 63**
See also CA 57-60; CAAS 121; CANR 28, 61; CMW 4; CP 2, 3, 4, 5, 6, 7; CPW; DAM POP; DLB 276; MTCW 1; SATA 23; SATA-Obit 50; TCWW 2

Maclean, Norman (Fitzroy)
1902-1990 .... **CLC 78; SSC 13**
See also AMWS 14; CA 102; CAAS 132; CANR 49; CPW; DAM POP; DLB 206; TCWW 2

MacLeish, Archibald 1892-1982 ... **CLC 3, 8, 14, 68; PC 47**
See also AMW; CA 9-12R; CAAS 106; CAD; CANR 33, 63; CDALBS; CP 1, 2; DAM POET; DFS 15; DLB 4, 7, 45; DLBY 1982; EWL 3; EXPP; MAL 5; MTCW 1, 2; MTFW 2005; PAB; PFS 5; RGAL 4; TUS

MacLennan, (John) Hugh
1907-1990 .... **CLC 2, 14, 92**
See also CA 5-8R; CAAS 142; CANR 33; CN 1, 2, 3, 4; DAC; DAM MST; DLB 68; EWL 3; MTCW 1, 2; MTFW 2005; RGEL 2; TWA

MacLeod, Alistair 1936- .. **CLC 56, 165; SSC 90**
See also CA 123; CCA 1; DAC; DAM MST; DLB 60; MTCW 2; MTFW 2005; RGSF 2; TCLE 1:2

Macleod, Fiona
See Sharp, William
See also RGEL 2; SUFW

MacNeice, (Frederick) Louis
1907-1963 .... **CLC 1, 4, 10, 53; PC 61**
See also BRW 7; CA 85-88; CANR 61; DAB; DAM POET; DLB 10, 20; EWL 3; MTCW 1, 2; MTFW 2005; RGEL 2

MacNeill, Dand
See Fraser, George MacDonald

Macpherson, James 1736-1796 .... **LC 29**
See Ossian
See also BRWS 8; DLB 109; RGEL 2

Mann, Emily 1952- .... **DC 7**
See also CA 130; CAD; CANR 55; CD 5, 6; CWD; DLB 266
Mann, (Luiz) Heinrich 1871-1950 ... **TCLC 9**
See also CA 164, 181; CAAE 106; DLB 66, 118; EW 8; EWL 3; RGWL 2, 3
Mann, (Paul) Thomas 1875-1955 . **SSC 5, 80, 82; TCLC 2, 8, 14, 21, 35, 44, 60, 168; WLC 4**
See also BPFB 2; CA 128; CAAE 104; CANR 133; CDWLB 2; DA; DA3; DAB; DAC; DAM MST, NOV; DLB 66, 331; EW 9; EWL 3; GLL 1; LATS 1:1; LMFS 1; MTCW 1, 2; MTFW 2005; NFS 17; RGSF 2; RGWL 2, 3; SSFS 4, 9; TWA
Mannheim, Karl 1893-1947 .... **TCLC 65**
See also CA 204
Manning, David
See Faust, Frederick (Schiller)
Manning, Frederic 1882-1935 .... **TCLC 25**
See also CA 216; CAAE 124; DLB 260
Manning, Olivia 1915-1980 .... **CLC 5, 19**
See also CA 5-8R; CAAS 101; CANR 29; CN 1, 2; EWL 3; FW; MTCW 1; RGEL 2
Mannyng, Robert c. 1264-c. 1340 .... **CMLC 83**
See also DLB 146
Mano, D. Keith 1942- .... **CLC 2, 10**
See also CA 25-28R; 6; CANR 26, 57; DLB 6
Mansfield, Katherine SSC 9, 23, 38, 81; TCLC 2, 8, 39, 164; WLC 4
See Beauchamp, Kathleen Mansfield
See also BPFB 2; BRW 7; DAB; DLB 162; EWL 3; EXPS; FW; GLL 1; RGEL 2; RGSF 2; SSFS 2, 8, 10, 11; WWE 1
Manso, Peter 1940- .... **CLC 39**
See also CA 29-32R; CANR 44, 156
Mantecon, Juan Jimenez
See Jimenez (Mantecon), Juan Ramon
Mantel, Hilary 1952- .... **CLC 144**
See also CA 125; CANR 54, 101, 161; CN 5, 6, 7; DLB 271; RHW
Mantel, Hilary Mary
See Mantel, Hilary
Manton, Peter
See Creasey, John
Man Without a Spleen, A
See Chekhov, Anton (Pavlovich)
Manzano, Juan Franciso 1797(?)-1854 .... **NCLC 155**
Manzoni, Alessandro 1785-1873 ... **NCLC 29, 98**
See also EW 5; RGWL 2, 3; TWA; WLIT 7
Map, Walter 1140-1209 .... **CMLC 32**
Mapu, Abraham (ben Jekutiel) 1808-1867 .... **NCLC 18**
Mara, Sally
See Queneau, Raymond
Maracle, Lee 1950- .... **NNAL**
See also CA 149
Marat, Jean Paul 1743-1793 .... **LC 10**
Marcel, Gabriel Honore 1889-1973 . **CLC 15**
See also CA 102; CAAS 45-48; EWL 3; MTCW 1, 2
March, William TCLC 96
See Campbell, William Edward March
See also CA 216; DLB 9, 86, 316; MAL 5
Marchbanks, Samuel
See Davies, Robertson
See also CCA 1
Marchi, Giacomo
See Bassani, Giorgio
Marcus Aurelius
See Aurelius, Marcus
See also AW 2
Marguerite
See de Navarre, Marguerite

Marguerite d'Angouleme
See de Navarre, Marguerite
See also GFL Beginnings to 1789
Marguerite de Navarre
See de Navarre, Marguerite
See also RGWL 2, 3
Margulies, Donald 1954- .... **CLC 76**
See also AAYA 57; CA 200; CD 6; DFS 13; DLB 228
Marie de France c. 12th cent. - ..... **CMLC 8; PC 22**
See also DLB 208; FW; RGWL 2, 3
Marie de l'Incarnation 1599-1672 ...... **LC 10**
Marier, Captain Victor
See Griffith, D(avid Lewelyn) W(ark)
Mariner, Scott
See Pohl, Frederik
Marinetti, Filippo Tommaso 1876-1944 .... **TCLC 10**
See also CAAE 107; DLB 114, 264; EW 9; EWL 3; WLIT 7
Marivaux, Pierre Carlet de Chamblain de 1688-1763 .... **DC 7; LC 4, 123**
See also DLB 314; GFL Beginnings to 1789; RGWL 2, 3; TWA
Markandaya, Kamala CLC 8, 38
See Taylor, Kamala
See also BYA 13; CN 1, 2, 3, 4, 5, 6, 7; DLB 323; EWL 3
Markfield, Wallace (Arthur) 1926-2002 .... **CLC 8**
See also CA 69-72; 3; CAAS 208; CN 1, 2, 3, 4, 5, 6, 7; DLB 2, 28; DLBY 2002
Markham, Edwin 1852-1940 .... **TCLC 47**
See also CA 160; DLB 54, 186; MAL 5; RGAL 4
Markham, Robert
See Amis, Kingsley
Marks, J.
See Highwater, Jamake (Mamake)
Marks-Highwater, J.
See Highwater, Jamake (Mamake)
Markson, David M. 1927- .... **CLC 67**
See also CA 49-52; CANR 1, 91, 158; CN 5, 6
Markson, David Merrill
See Markson, David M.
Marlatt, Daphne (Buckle) 1942- .... **CLC 168**
See also CA 25-28R; CANR 17, 39; CN 6, 7; CP 4, 5, 6, 7; CWP; DLB 60; FW
Marley, Bob CLC 17
See Marley, Robert Nesta
Marley, Robert Nesta 1945-1981
See Marley, Bob
See also CA 107; CAAS 103
Marlowe, Christopher 1564-1593 . **DC 1; LC 22, 47, 117; PC 57; WLC 4**
See also BRW 1; BRWR 1; CDBLB Before 1660; DA; DA3; DAB; DAC; DAM DRAM, MST; DFS 1, 5, 13, 21; DLB 62; EXPP; LMFS 1; PFS 22; RGEL 2; TEA; WLIT 3
Marlowe, Stephen 1928- .... **CLC 70**
See Queen, Ellery
See also CA 13-16R; CANR 6, 55; CMW 4; SFW 4
Marmion, Shakerley 1603-1639 .... **LC 89**
See also DLB 58; RGEL 2
Marmontel, Jean-Francois 1723-1799 .. **LC 2**
See also DLB 314
Maron, Monika 1941- .... **CLC 165**
See also CA 201
Marot, Clement c. 1496-1544 .... **LC 133**
See also DLB 327; GFL Beginnings to 1789
Marquand, John P(hillips) 1893-1960 .... **CLC 2, 10**
See also AMW; BPFB 2; CA 85-88; CANR 73; CMW 4; DLB 9, 102; EWL 3; MAL 5; MTCW 2; RGAL 4

Marques, Rene 1919-1979 .. **CLC 96; HLC 2**
See also CA 97-100; CAAS 85-88; CANR 78; DAM MULT; DLB 305; EWL 3; HW 1, 2; LAW; RGSF 2
Marquez, Gabriel Garcia
See Garcia Marquez, Gabriel
Marquis, Don(ald Robert Perry) 1878-1937 .... **TCLC 7**
See also CA 166; CAAE 104; DLB 11, 25; MAL 5; RGAL 4
Marquis de Sade
See Sade, Donatien Alphonse Francois
Marric, J. J.
See Creasey, John
See also MSW
Marryat, Frederick 1792-1848 .... **NCLC 3**
See also DLB 21, 163; RGEL 2; WCH
Marsden, James
See Creasey, John
Marsh, Edward 1872-1953 .... **TCLC 99**
Marsh, (Edith) Ngaio 1895-1982 .. **CLC 7, 53**
See also CA 9-12R; CANR 6, 58; CMW 4; CN 1, 2, 3; CPW; DAM POP; DLB 77; MSW; MTCW 1, 2; RGEL 2; TEA
Marshall, Allen
See Westlake, Donald E.
Marshall, Garry 1934- .... **CLC 17**
See also AAYA 3; CA 111; SATA 60
Marshall, Paule 1929- .. **BLC 3; CLC 27, 72; SSC 3**
See also AFAW 1, 2; AMWS 11; BPFB 2; BW 2, 3; CA 77-80; CANR 25, 73, 129; CN 1, 2, 3, 4, 5, 6, 7; DA3; DAM MULT; DLB 33, 157, 227; EWL 3; LATS 1:2; MAL 5; MTCW 1, 2; MTFW 2005; RGAL 4; SSFS 15
Marshallik
See Zangwill, Israel
Marsten, Richard
See Hunter, Evan
Marston, John 1576-1634 .... **LC 33**
See also BRW 2; DAM DRAM; DLB 58, 172; RGEL 2
Martel, Yann 1963- .... **CLC 192**
See also AAYA 67; CA 146; CANR 114; DLB 326; MTFW 2005
Martens, Adolphe-Adhemar
See Ghelderode, Michel de
Martha, Henry
See Harris, Mark
Marti, Jose PC 76
See Marti (y Perez), Jose (Julian)
See also DLB 290
Marti (y Perez), Jose (Julian) 1853-1895 .... **HLC 2; NCLC 63**
See Marti, Jose
See also DAM MULT; HW 2; LAW; RGWL 2, 3; WLIT 1
Martial c. 40-c. 104 .... **CMLC 35; PC 10**
See also AW 2; CDWLB 1; DLB 211; RGWL 2, 3
Martin, Ken
See Hubbard, L. Ron
Martin, Richard
See Creasey, John
Martin, Steve 1945- .... **CLC 30, 217**
See also AAYA 53; CA 97-100; CANR 30, 100, 140; DFS 19; MTCW 1; MTFW 2005
Martin, Valerie 1948- .... **CLC 89**
See also BEST 90:2; CA 85-88; CANR 49, 89
Martin, Violet Florence 1862-1915 .. **SSC 56; TCLC 51**
Martin, Webber
See Silverberg, Robert
Martindale, Patrick Victor
See White, Patrick (Victor Martindale)

Mayo, Jim
See L'Amour, Louis
Maysles, Albert 1926- .... **CLC 16**
See also CA 29-32R
Maysles, David 1932-1987 .... **CLC 16**
See also CA 191
Mazer, Norma Fox 1931- .... **CLC 26**
See also AAYA 5, 36; BYA 1, 8; CA 69-72;
CANR 12, 32, 66, 129; CLR 23; JRDA;
MAICYA 1, 2; SAAS 1; SATA 24, 67,
105, 168; WYA; YAW
Mazzini, Guiseppe 1805-1872 .... **NCLC 34**
McAlmon, Robert (Menzies)
1895-1956 .... **TCLC 97**
See also CA 168; CAAE 107; DLB 4, 45;
DLBD 15; GLL 1
McAuley, James Phillip 1917-1976 .. **CLC 45**
See also CA 97-100; CP 1, 2; DLB 260;
RGEL 2
McBain, Ed
See Hunter, Evan
See also MSW
McBrien, William (Augustine)
1930- .... **CLC 44**
See also CA 107; CANR 90
McCabe, Patrick 1955- .... **CLC 133**
See also BRWS 9; CA 130; CANR 50, 90;
CN 6, 7; DLB 194
McCaffrey, Anne 1926- .... **CLC 17**
See also AAYA 6, 34; AITN 2; BEST 89:2;
BPFB 2; BYA 5; CA 227; 25-28R, 227;
CANR 15, 35, 55, 96; CLR 49; CPW;
DA3; DAM NOV, POP; DLB 8; JRDA;
MAICYA 1, 2; MTCW 1, 2; MTFW 2005;
SAAS 11; SATA 8, 70, 116, 152; SATA-
Essay 152; SFW 4; SUFW 2; WYA; YAW
McCaffrey, Anne Inez
See McCaffrey, Anne
McCall, Nathan 1955(?)- .... **CLC 86**
See also AAYA 59; BW 3; CA 146; CANR
88
McCann, Arthur
See Campbell, John W(ood, Jr.)
McCann, Edson
See Pohl, Frederik
McCarthy, Charles, Jr.
See McCarthy, Cormac
McCarthy, Cormac 1933- .... **CLC 4, 57, 101,
204**
See also AAYA 41; AMWS 8; BPFB 2; CA
13-16R; CANR 10, 42, 69, 101, 161; CN
6, 7; CPW; CSW; DA3; DAM POP; DLB
6, 143, 256; EWL 3; LATS 1:2; MAL 5;
MTCW 2; MTFW 2005; TCLE 1:2;
TCWW 2
McCarthy, Mary (Therese)
1912-1989 .. **CLC 1, 3, 5, 14, 24, 39, 59;
SSC 24**
See also AMW; BPFB 2; CA 5-8R; CAAS
129; CANR 16, 50, 64; CN 1, 2, 3, 4;
DA3; DLB 2; DLBY 1981; EWL 3; FW;
INT CANR-16; MAL 5; MBL; MTCW 1,
2; MTFW 2005; RGAL 4; TUS
McCartney, James Paul
See McCartney, Paul
McCartney, Paul 1942- .... **CLC 12, 35**
See also CA 146; CANR 111
McCauley, Stephen (D.) 1955- .... **CLC 50**
See also CA 141
McClaren, Peter CLC 70
McClure, Michael (Thomas) 1932- ... **CLC 6,
10**
See also BG 1:3; CA 21-24R; CAD; CANR
17, 46, 77, 131; CD 5, 6; CP 1, 2, 3, 4, 5,
6, 7; DLB 16; WP
McCorkle, Jill (Collins) 1958- .... **CLC 51**
See also CA 121; CANR 113; CSW; DLB
234; DLBY 1987; SSFS 24

McCourt, Frank 1930- .... **CLC 109**
See also AAYA 61; AMWS 12; CA 157;
CANR 97, 138; MTFW 2005; NCFS 1
McCourt, James 1941- .... **CLC 5**
See also CA 57-60; CANR 98, 152
McCourt, Malachy 1931- .... **CLC 119**
See also SATA 126
McCoy, Horace (Stanley)
1897-1955 .... **TCLC 28**
See also AMWS 13; CA 155; CAAE 108;
CMW 4; DLB 9
McCrae, John 1872-1918 .... **TCLC 12**
See also CAAE 109; DLB 92; PFS 5
McCreigh, James
See Pohl, Frederik
McCullers, (Lula) Carson (Smith)
1917-1967 .... **CLC 1, 4, 10, 12, 48, 100;
SSC 9, 24, 99; TCLC 155; WLC 4**
See also AAYA 21; AMW; AMWC 2; BPFB
2; CA 5-8R; CAAS 25-28R; CABS 1, 3;
CANR 18, 132; CDALB 1941-1968; DA;
DA3; DAB; DAC; DAM MST, NOV;
DFS 5, 18; DLB 2, 7, 173, 228; EWL 3;
EXPS; FW; GLL 1; LAIT 3, 4; MAL 5;
MBL; MTCW 1, 2; MTFW 2005; NFS 6,
13; RGAL 4; RGSF 2; SATA 27; SSFS 5;
TUS; YAW
McCulloch, John Tyler
See Burroughs, Edgar Rice
McCullough, Colleen 1937- .... **CLC 27, 107**
See also AAYA 36; BPFB 2; CA 81-84;
CANR 17, 46, 67, 98, 139; CPW; DA3;
DAM NOV, POP; MTCW 1, 2; MTFW
2005; RHW
McCunn, Ruthanne Lum 1946- .... **AAL**
See also CA 119; CANR 43, 96; DLB 312;
LAIT 2; SATA 63
McDermott, Alice 1953- .... **CLC 90**
See also CA 109; CANR 40, 90, 126; CN
7; DLB 292; MTFW 2005; NFS 23
McElroy, Joseph 1930- .... **CLC 5, 47**
See also CA 17-20R; CANR 149; CN 3, 4,
5, 6, 7
McElroy, Joseph Prince
See McElroy, Joseph
McEwan, Ian 1948- .... **CLC 13, 66, 169**
See also BEST 90:4; BRWS 4; CA 61-64;
CANR 14, 41, 69, 87, 132; CN 3, 4, 5, 6,
7; DAM NOV; DLB 14, 194, 319, 326;
HGG; MTCW 1, 2; MTFW 2005; RGSF
2; SUFW 2; TEA
McFadden, David 1940- .... **CLC 48**
See also CA 104; CP 1, 2, 3, 4, 5, 6, 7; DLB
60; INT CA-104
McFarland, Dennis 1950- .... **CLC 65**
See also CA 165; CANR 110
McGahern, John 1934-2006 .... **CLC 5, 9, 48,
156; SSC 17**
See also CA 17-20R; CAAS 249; CANR
29, 68, 113; CN 1, 2, 3, 4, 5, 6, 7; DLB
14, 231, 319; MTCW 1
McGinley, Patrick (Anthony) 1937- . **CLC 41**
See also CA 127; CAAE 120; CANR 56;
INT CA-127
McGinley, Phyllis 1905-1978 .... **CLC 14**
See also CA 9-12R; CAAS 77-80; CANR
19; CP 1, 2; CWRI 5; DLB 11, 48; MAL
5; PFS 9, 13; SATA 2, 44; SATA-Obit 24
McGinniss, Joe 1942- .... **CLC 32**
See also AITN 2; BEST 89:2; CA 25-28R;
CANR 26, 70, 152; CPW; DLB 185; INT
CANR-26
McGivern, Maureen Daly
See Daly, Maureen
McGivern, Maureen Patricia Daly
See Daly, Maureen
McGrath, Patrick 1950- .... **CLC 55**
See also CA 136; CANR 65, 148; CN 5, 6,
7; DLB 231; HGG; SUFW 2

McGrath, Thomas (Matthew)
1916-1990 .... **CLC 28, 59**
See also AMWS 10; CA 9-12R; CAAS 132;
CANR 6, 33, 95; CP 1, 2, 3, 4, 5; DAM
POET; MAL 5; MTCW 1; SATA 41;
SATA-Obit 66
McGuane, Thomas 1939- .. **CLC 3, 7, 18, 45,
127**
See also AITN 2; BPFB 2; CA 49-52;
CANR 5, 24, 49, 94; CN 2, 3, 4, 5, 6, 7;
DLB 2, 212; DLBY 1980; EWL 3; INT
CANR-24; MAL 5; MTCW 1; MTFW
2005; TCWW 1, 2
McGuckian, Medbh 1950- .... **CLC 48, 174;
PC 27**
See also BRWS 5; CA 143; CP 4, 5, 6, 7;
CWP; DAM POET; DLB 40
McHale, Tom 1942(?)-1982 .... **CLC 3, 5**
See also AITN 1; CA 77-80; CAAS 106;
CN 1, 2, 3
McHugh, Heather 1948- .... **PC 61**
See also CA 69-72; CANR 11, 28, 55, 92;
CP 4, 5, 6, 7; CWP; PFS 24
McIlvanney, William 1936- .... **CLC 42**
See also CA 25-28R; CANR 61; CMW 4;
DLB 14, 207
McIlwraith, Maureen Mollie Hunter
See Hunter, Mollie
See also SATA 2
McInerney, Jay 1955- .... **CLC 34, 112**
See also AAYA 18; BPFB 2; CA 123;
CAAE 116; CANR 45, 68, 116; CN 5, 6,
7; CPW; DA3; DAM POP; DLB 292; INT
CA-123; MAL 5; MTCW 2; MTFW 2005
McIntyre, Vonda N. 1948- .... **CLC 18**
See also CA 81-84; CANR 17, 34, 69;
MTCW 1; SFW 4; YAW
McIntyre, Vonda Neel
See McIntyre, Vonda N.
**McKay, Claude BLC 3; HR 1:3; PC 2;
TCLC 7, 41; WLC 4**
See McKay, Festus Claudius
See also AFAW 1, 2; AMWS 10; DAB;
DLB 4, 45, 51, 117; EWL 3; EXPP; GLL
2; LAIT 3; LMFS 2; MAL 5; PAB; PFS
4; RGAL 4; WP
McKay, Festus Claudius 1889-1948
See McKay, Claude
See also BW 1, 3; CA 124; CAAE 104;
CANR 73; DA; DAC; DAM MST, MULT,
NOV, POET; MTCW 1, 2; MTFW 2005;
TUS
McKuen, Rod 1933- .... **CLC 1, 3**
See also AITN 1; CA 41-44R; CANR 40;
CP 1
McLoughlin, R. B.
See Mencken, H(enry) L(ouis)
McLuhan, (Herbert) Marshall
1911-1980 .... **CLC 37, 83**
See also CA 9-12R; CAAS 102; CANR 12,
34, 61; DLB 88; INT CANR-12; MTCW
1, 2; MTFW 2005
McManus, Declan Patrick Aloysius
See Costello, Elvis
McMillan, Terry 1951- .. **BLCS; CLC 50, 61,
112**
See also AAYA 21; AMWS 13; BPFB 2;
BW 2, 3; CA 140; CANR 60, 104, 131;
CN 7; CPW; DA3; DAM MULT, NOV,
POP; MAL 5; MTCW 2; MTFW 2005;
RGAL 4; YAW
McMurtry, Larry 1936- .... **CLC 2, 3, 7, 11,
27, 44, 127**
See also AAYA 15; AITN 2; AMWS 5;
BEST 89:2; BPFB 2; CA 5-8R; CANR
19, 43, 64, 103; CDALB 1968-1988; CN
2, 3, 4, 5, 6, 7; CPW; CSW; DA3; DAM
NOV, POP; DLB 2, 143, 256; DLBY
1980, 1987; EWL 3; MAL 5; MTCW 1,
2; MTFW 2005; RGAL 4; TCWW 1, 2

McMurtry, Larry Jeff
See McMurtry, Larry

McNally, Terrence 1939- ... **CLC 4, 7, 41, 91; DC 27**
See also AAYA 62; AMWS 13; CA 45-48; CAD; CANR 2, 56, 116; CD 5, 6; DA3; DAM DRAM; DFS 16, 19; DLB 7, 249; EWL 3; GLL 1; MTCW 2; MTFW 2005

McNally, Thomas Michael
See McNally, T.M.

McNally, T.M. 1961- .... **CLC 82**
See also CA 246

McNamer, Deirdre 1950- .... **CLC 70**
See also CA 188

McNeal, Tom CLC 119
See also CA 252

McNeile, Herman Cyril 1888-1937
See Sapper
See also CA 184; CMW 4; DLB 77

McNickle, (William) D'Arcy
1904-1977 .... **CLC 89; NNAL**
See also CA 9-12R; CAAS 85-88; CANR 5, 45; DAM MULT; DLB 175, 212; RGAL 4; SATA-Obit 22; TCWW 1, 2

McPhee, John 1931- .... **CLC 36**
See also AAYA 61; AMWS 3; ANW; BEST 90:1; CA 65-68; CANR 20, 46, 64, 69, 121; CPW; DLB 185, 275; MTCW 1, 2; MTFW 2005; TUS

McPherson, James Alan 1943- . **BLCS; CLC 19, 77; SSC 95**
See also BW 1, 3; CA 25-28R; 17; CANR 24, 74, 140; CN 3, 4, 5, 6; CSW; DLB 38, 244; EWL 3; MTCW 1, 2; MTFW 2005; RGAL 4; RGSF 2; SSFS 23

McPherson, William (Alexander)
1933- .... **CLC 34**
See also CA 69-72; CANR 28; INT CANR-28

McTaggart, J. McT. Ellis
See McTaggart, John McTaggart Ellis

McTaggart, John McTaggart Ellis
1866-1925 .... **TCLC 105**
See also CAAE 120; DLB 262

Mead, George Herbert 1863-1931 . **TCLC 89**
See also CA 212; DLB 270

Mead, Margaret 1901-1978 .... **CLC 37**
See also AITN 1; CA 1-4R; CAAS 81-84; CANR 4; DA3; FW; MTCW 1, 2; SATA-Obit 20

Meaker, Marijane 1927-
See Kerr, M. E.
See also CA 107; CANR 37, 63, 145; INT CA-107; JRDA; MAICYA 1, 2; MAICYAS 1; MTCW 1; SATA 20, 61, 99, 160; SATA-Essay 111; YAW

Medoff, Mark (Howard) 1940- .... **CLC 6, 23**
See also AITN 1; CA 53-56; CAD; CANR 5; CD 5, 6; DAM DRAM; DFS 4; DLB 7; INT CANR-5

Medvedev, P. N.
See Bakhtin, Mikhail Mikhailovich

Meged, Aharon
See Megged, Aharon

Meged, Aron
See Megged, Aharon

Megged, Aharon 1920- .... **CLC 9**
See also CA 49-52; 13; CANR 1, 140; EWL 3; RGHL

Mehta, Deepa 1950- .... **CLC 208**

Mehta, Gita 1943- .... **CLC 179**
See also CA 225; CN 7; DNFS 2

Mehta, Ved 1934- .... **CLC 37**
See also CA 212; 1-4R, 212; CANR 2, 23, 69; DLB 323; MTCW 1; MTFW 2005

Melanchthon, Philipp 1497-1560 .... **LC 90**
See also DLB 179

Melanter
See Blackmore, R(ichard) D(oddridge)

Meleager c. 140B.C.-c. 70B.C. ...... **CMLC 53**

Melies, Georges 1861-1938 .... **TCLC 81**

Melikow, Loris
See Hofmannsthal, Hugo von

Melmoth, Sebastian
See Wilde, Oscar (Fingal O'Flahertie Wills)

Melo Neto, Joao Cabral de
See Cabral de Melo Neto, Joao
See also CWW 2; EWL 3

Meltzer, Milton 1915- .... **CLC 26**
See also AAYA 8, 45; BYA 2, 6; CA 13-16R; CANR 38, 92, 107; CLR 13; DLB 61; JRDA; MAICYA 1, 2; SAAS 1; SATA 1, 50, 80, 128; SATA-Essay 124; WYA; YAW

Melville, Herman 1819-1891 ..... **NCLC 3, 12, 29, 45, 49, 91, 93, 123, 157, 181; SSC 1, 17, 46, 95; WLC 4**
See also AAYA 25; AMW; AMWR 1; CDALB 1640-1865; DA; DA3; DAB; DAC; DAM MST, NOV; DLB 3, 74, 250, 254; EXPN; EXPS; GL 3; LAIT 1, 2; NFS 7, 9; RGAL 4; RGSF 2; SATA 59; SSFS 3; TUS

Members, Mark
See Powell, Anthony

Membreno, Alejandro CLC 59

Menand, Louis 1952- .... **CLC 208**
See also CA 200

Menander c. 342B.C.-c. 293B.C. .... **CMLC 9, 51; DC 3**
See also AW 1; CDWLB 1; DAM DRAM; DLB 176; LMFS 1; RGWL 2, 3

Menchu, Rigoberta 1959- .. **CLC 160; HLCS 2**
See also CA 175; CANR 135; DNFS 1; WLIT 1

Mencken, H(enry) L(ouis)
1880-1956 .... **TCLC 13**
See also AMW; CA 125; CAAE 105; CDALB 1917-1929; DLB 11, 29, 63, 137, 222; EWL 3; MAL 5; MTCW 1, 2; MTFW 2005; NCFS 4; RGAL 4; TUS

Mendelsohn, Jane 1965- .... **CLC 99**
See also CA 154; CANR 94

Mendoza, Inigo Lopez de
See Santillana, Inigo Lopez de Mendoza, Marques de

Menton, Francisco de
See Chin, Frank (Chew, Jr.)

Mercer, David 1928-1980 .... **CLC 5**
See also CA 9-12R; CAAS 102; CANR 23; CBD; DAM DRAM; DLB 13, 310; MTCW 1; RGEL 2

Merchant, Paul
See Ellison, Harlan

Meredith, George 1828-1909 .. **PC 60; TCLC 17, 43**
See also CA 153; CAAE 117; CANR 80; CDBLB 1832-1890; DAM POET; DLB 18, 35, 57, 159; RGEL 2; TEA

Meredith, William (Morris) 1919- .... **CLC 4, 13, 22, 55; PC 28**
See also CA 9-12R; 14; CANR 6, 40, 129; CP 1, 2, 3, 4, 5, 6, 7; DAM POET; DLB 5; MAL 5

Merezhkovsky, Dmitrii Sergeevich
See Merezhkovsky, Dmitry Sergeyevich
See also DLB 295

Merezhkovsky, Dmitry Sergeevich
See Merezhkovsky, Dmitry Sergeyevich
See also EWL 3

Merezhkovsky, Dmitry Sergeyevich
1865-1941 .... **TCLC 29**
See Merezhkovsky, Dmitrii Sergeevich; Merezhkovsky, Dmitry Sergeevich
See also CA 169

Merimee, Prosper 1803-1870 ... **NCLC 6, 65; SSC 7, 77**
See also DLB 119, 192; EW 6; EXPS; GFL 1789 to the Present; RGSF 2; RGWL 2, 3; SSFS 8; SUFW

Merkin, Daphne 1954- .... **CLC 44**
See also CA 123

Merleau-Ponty, Maurice
1908-1961 .... **TCLC 156**
See also CA 114; CAAS 89-92; DLB 296; GFL 1789 to the Present

Merlin, Arthur
See Blish, James (Benjamin)

Mernissi, Fatima 1940- .... **CLC 171**
See also CA 152; FW

Merrill, James 1926-1995 ...... **CLC 2, 3, 6, 8, 13, 18, 34, 91; PC 28; TCLC 173**
See also AMWS 3; CA 13-16R; CAAS 147; CANR 10, 49, 63, 108; CP 1, 2, 3, 4; DA3; DAM POET; DLB 5, 165; DLBY 1985; EWL 3; INT CANR-10; MAL 5; MTCW 1, 2; MTFW 2005; PAB; PFS 23; RGAL 4

Merrill, James Ingram
See Merrill, James

Merriman, Alex
See Silverberg, Robert

Merriman, Brian 1747-1805 .... **NCLC 70**

Merritt, E. B.
See Waddington, Miriam

Merton, Thomas (James)
1915-1968 . **CLC 1, 3, 11, 34, 83; PC 10**
See also AAYA 61; AMWS 8; CA 5-8R; CAAS 25-28R; CANR 22, 53, 111, 131; DA3; DLB 48; DLBY 1981; MAL 5; MTCW 1, 2; MTFW 2005

Merwin, W.S. 1927- ..... **CLC 1, 2, 3, 5, 8, 13, 18, 45, 88; PC 45**
See also AMWS 3; CA 13-16R; CANR 15, 51, 112, 140; CP 1, 2, 3, 4, 5, 6, 7; DA3; DAM POET; DLB 5, 169; EWL 3; INT CANR-15; MAL 5; MTCW 1, 2; MTFW 2005; PAB; PFS 5, 15; RGAL 4

Metastasio, Pietro 1698-1782 .... **LC 115**
See also RGWL 2, 3

Metcalf, John 1938- .... **CLC 37; SSC 43**
See also CA 113; CN 4, 5, 6, 7; DLB 60; RGSF 2; TWA

Metcalf, Suzanne
See Baum, L(yman) Frank

Mew, Charlotte (Mary) 1870-1928 .. **TCLC 8**
See also CA 189; CAAE 105; DLB 19, 135; RGEL 2

Mewshaw, Michael 1943- .... **CLC 9**
See also CA 53-56; CANR 7, 47, 147; DLBY 1980

Meyer, Conrad Ferdinand
1825-1898 .... **NCLC 81; SSC 30**
See also DLB 129; EW; RGWL 2, 3

Meyer, Gustav 1868-1932
See Meyrink, Gustav
See also CA 190; CAAE 117

Meyer, June
See Jordan, June

Meyer, Lynn
See Slavitt, David R(ytman)

Meyers, Jeffrey 1939- .... **CLC 39**
See also CA 186; 73-76, 186; CANR 54, 102, 159; DLB 111

Meynell, Alice (Christina Gertrude Thompson) 1847-1922 .... **TCLC 6**
See also CA 177; CAAE 104; DLB 19, 98; RGEL 2

Meyrink, Gustav TCLC 21
See Meyer, Gustav
See also DLB 81; EWL 3

Naylor, Gloria 1950- ..... **BLC 3; CLC 28, 52, 156; WLCS**
See also AAYA 6, 39; AFAW 1, 2; AMWS 8; BW 2, 3; CA 107; CANR 27, 51, 74, 130; CN 4, 5, 6, 7; CPW; DA; DA3; DAC; DAM MST, MULT, NOV, POP; DLB 173; EWL 3; FW; MAL 5; MTCW 1, 2; MTFW 2005; NFS 4, 7; RGAL 4; TCLE 1:2; TUS

Neal, John 1793-1876 .... **NCLC 161**
See also DLB 1, 59, 243; FW; RGAL 4

Neff, Debra CLC 59

Neihardt, John Gneisenau
1881-1973 .... **CLC 32**
See also CA 13-14; CANR 65; CAP 1; DLB 9, 54, 256; LAIT 2; TCWW 1, 2

Nekrasov, Nikolai Alekseevich
1821-1878 .... **NCLC 11**
See also DLB 277

Nelligan, Emile 1879-1941 .... **TCLC 14**
See also CA 204; CAAE 114; DLB 92; EWL 3

Nelson, Willie 1933- .... **CLC 17**
See also CA 107; CANR 114

Nemerov, Howard 1920-1991 .... **CLC 2, 6, 9, 36; PC 24; TCLC 124**
See also AMW; CA 1-4R; CAAS 134; CABS 2; CANR 1, 27, 53; CN 1, 2, 3; CP 1, 2, 3, 4, 5; DAM POET; DLB 5, 6; DLBY 1983; EWL 3; INT CANR-27; MAL 5; MTCW 1, 2; MTFW 2005; PFS 10, 14; RGAL 4

Nepos, Cornelius c. 99B.C.-c.
24B.C. .... **CMLC 89**
See also DLB 211

Neruda, Pablo 1904-1973 .. **CLC 1, 2, 5, 7, 9, 28, 62; HLC 2; PC 4, 64; WLC 4**
See also CA 19-20; CAAS 45-48; CANR 131; CAP 2; DA; DA3; DAB; DAC; DAM MST, MULT, POET; DLB 283, 331; DNFS 2; EWL 3; HW 1; LAW; MTCW 1, 2; MTFW 2005; PFS 11; RGWL 2, 3; TWA; WLIT 1; WP

Nerval, Gerard de 1808-1855 ... **NCLC 1, 67; PC 13; SSC 18**
See also DLB 217; EW 6; GFL 1789 to the Present; RGSF 2; RGWL 2, 3

Nervo, (Jose) Amado (Ruiz de)
1870-1919 .... **HLCS 2; TCLC 11**
See also CA 131; CAAE 109; DLB 290; EWL 3; HW 1; LAW

Nesbit, Malcolm
See Chester, Alfred

Nessi, Pio Baroja y
See Baroja, Pio

Nestroy, Johann 1801-1862 .... **NCLC 42**
See also DLB 133; RGWL 2, 3

Netterville, Luke
See O'Grady, Standish (James)

Neufeld, John (Arthur) 1938- .... **CLC 17**
See also AAYA 11; CA 25-28R; CANR 11, 37, 56; CLR 52; MAICYA 1, 2; SAAS 3; SATA 6, 81, 131; SATA-Essay 131; YAW

Neumann, Alfred 1895-1952 .... **TCLC 100**
See also CA 183; DLB 56

Neumann, Ferenc
See Molnar, Ferenc

Neville, Emily Cheney 1919- .... **CLC 12**
See also BYA 2; CA 5-8R; CANR 3, 37, 85; JRDA; MAICYA 1, 2; SAAS 2; SATA 1; YAW

Newbound, Bernard Slade 1930-
See Slade, Bernard
See also CA 81-84; CANR 49; CD 5; DAM DRAM

Newby, P(ercy) H(oward)
1918-1997 .... **CLC 2, 13**
See also CA 5-8R; CAAS 161; CANR 32, 67; CN 1, 2, 3, 4, 5, 6; DAM NOV; DLB 15, 326; MTCW 1; RGEL 2

Newcastle
See Cavendish, Margaret Lucas

Newlove, Donald 1928- .... **CLC 6**
See also CA 29-32R; CANR 25

Newlove, John (Herbert) 1938- .... **CLC 14**
See also CA 21-24R; CANR 9, 25; CP 1, 2, 3, 4, 5, 6, 7

Newman, Charles 1938-2006 .... **CLC 2, 8**
See also CA 21-24R; CAAS 249; CANR 84; CN 3, 4, 5, 6

Newman, Charles Hamilton
See Newman, Charles

Newman, Edwin (Harold) 1919- ...... **CLC 14**
See also AITN 1; CA 69-72; CANR 5

Newman, John Henry 1801-1890 . **NCLC 38, 99**
See also BRWS 7; DLB 18, 32, 55; RGEL 2

Newton, (Sir) Isaac 1642-1727 ...... **LC 35, 53**
See also DLB 252

Newton, Suzanne 1936- .... **CLC 35**
See also BYA 7; CA 41-44R; CANR 14; JRDA; SATA 5, 77

New York Dept. of Ed. CLC 70

Nexo, Martin Andersen
1869-1954 .... **TCLC 43**
See also CA 202; DLB 214; EWL 3

Nezval, Vitezslav 1900-1958 .... **TCLC 44**
See also CAAE 123; CDWLB 4; DLB 215; EWL 3

Ng, Fae Myenne 1957(?)- .... **CLC 81**
See also BYA 11; CA 146

Ngema, Mbongeni 1955- .... **CLC 57**
See also BW 2; CA 143; CANR 84; CD 5, 6

Ngugi, James T(hiong'o) CLC 3, 7, 13, 182
See Ngugi wa Thiong'o
See also CN 1, 2

Ngugi wa Thiong'o
See Ngugi wa Thiong'o
See also CD 3, 4, 5, 6, 7; DLB 125; EWL 3

Ngugi wa Thiong'o 1938- ... **BLC 3; CLC 36, 182**
See Ngugi, James T(hiong'o); Ngugi wa Thiong'o
See also AFW; BRWS 8; BW 2; CA 81-84; CANR 27, 58; CDWLB 3; DAM MULT, NOV; DNFS 2; MTCW 1, 2; MTFW 2005; RGEL 2; WWE 1

Niatum, Duane 1938- .... **NNAL**
See also CA 41-44R; CANR 21, 45, 83; DLB 175

Nichol, B(arrie) P(hillip) 1944-1988 . **CLC 18**
See also CA 53-56; CP 1, 2, 3, 4; DLB 53; SATA 66

Nicholas of Cusa 1401-1464 .... **LC 80**
See also DLB 115

Nichols, John 1940- .... **CLC 38**
See also AMWS 13; CA 190; 9-12R, 190; 2; CANR 6, 70, 121; DLBY 1982; LATS 1:2; MTFW 2005; TCWW 1, 2

Nichols, Leigh
See Koontz, Dean R.

Nichols, Peter (Richard) 1927- .... **CLC 5, 36, 65**
See also CA 104; CANR 33, 86; CBD; CD 5, 6; DLB 13, 245; MTCW 1

Nicholson, Linda CLC 65

Ni Chuilleanain, Eilean 1942- .... **PC 34**
See also CA 126; CANR 53, 83; CP 5, 6, 7; CWP; DLB 40

Nicolas, F. R. E.
See Freeling, Nicolas

Niedecker, Lorine 1903-1970 ..... **CLC 10, 42; PC 42**
See also CA 25-28; CAP 2; DAM POET; DLB 48

Nietzsche, Friedrich (Wilhelm)
1844-1900 .... **TCLC 10, 18, 55**
See also CA 121; CAAE 107; CDWLB 2; DLB 129; EW 7; RGWL 2, 3; TWA

Nievo, Ippolito 1831-1861 .... **NCLC 22**

Nightingale, Anne Redmon 1943-
See Redmon, Anne
See also CA 103

Nightingale, Florence 1820-1910 ... **TCLC 85**
See also CA 188; DLB 166

Nijo Yoshimoto 1320-1388 .... **CMLC 49**
See also DLB 203

Nik. T. O.
See Annensky, Innokenty (Fyodorovich)

Nin, Anais 1903-1977 ..... **CLC 1, 4, 8, 11, 14, 60, 127; SSC 10**
See also AITN 2; AMWS 10; BPFB 2; CA 13-16R; CAAS 69-72; CANR 22, 53; CN 1, 2; DAM NOV, POP; DLB 2, 4, 152; EWL 3; GLL 2; MAL 5; MBL; MTCW 1, 2; MTFW 2005; RGAL 4; RGSF 2

Nisbet, Robert A(lexander)
1913-1996 .... **TCLC 117**
See also CA 25-28R; CAAS 153; CANR 17; INT CANR-17

Nishida, Kitaro 1870-1945 .... **TCLC 83**

Nishiwaki, Junzaburo 1894-1982 .... **PC 15**
See Junzaburo, Nishiwaki
See also CA 194; CAAS 107; MJW; RGWL 3

Nissenson, Hugh 1933- .... **CLC 4, 9**
See also CA 17-20R; CANR 27, 108, 151; CN 5, 6; DLB 28

Nister, Der
See Der Nister
See also DLB 333; EWL 3

Niven, Larry 1938-
See Niven, Laurence VanCott
See also CA 207; 21-24R, 207; 12; CANR 14, 44, 66, 113, 155; CPW; DAM POP; MTCW 1, 2; SATA 95, 171; SFW 4

Niven, Laurence VanCott CLC 8
See Niven, Larry
See also AAYA 27; BPFB 2; BYA 10; DLB 8; SCFW 1, 2

Nixon, Agnes Eckhardt 1927- .... **CLC 21**
See also CA 110

Nizan, Paul 1905-1940 .... **TCLC 40**
See also CA 161; DLB 72; EWL 3; GFL 1789 to the Present

Nkosi, Lewis 1936- .... **BLC 3; CLC 45**
See also BW 1, 3; CA 65-68; CANR 27, 81; CBD; CD 5, 6; DAM MULT; DLB 157, 225; WWE 1

Nodier, (Jean) Charles (Emmanuel)
1780-1844 .... **NCLC 19**
See also DLB 119; GFL 1789 to the Present

Noguchi, Yone 1875-1947 .... **TCLC 80**

Nolan, Christopher 1965- .... **CLC 58**
See also CA 111; CANR 88

Noon, Jeff 1957- .... **CLC 91**
See also CA 148; CANR 83; DLB 267; SFW 4

Norden, Charles
See Durrell, Lawrence (George)

Nordhoff, Charles Bernard
1887-1947 .... **TCLC 23**
See also CA 211; CAAE 108; DLB 9; LAIT 1; RHW 1; SATA 23

Norfolk, Lawrence 1963- .... **CLC 76**
See also CA 144; CANR 85; CN 6, 7; DLB 267

Norman, Marsha (Williams) 1947- . **CLC 28, 186; DC 8**
See also CA 105; CABS 3; CAD; CANR 41, 131; CD 5, 6; CSW; CWD; DAM DRAM; DFS 2; DLB 266; DLBY 1984; FW; MAL 5

Parra, Nicanor 1914- ... **CLC 2, 102; HLC 2; PC 39**
  See also CA 85-88; CANR 32; CWW 2; DAM MULT; DLB 283; EWL 3; HW 1; LAW; MTCW 1

Parra Sanojo, Ana Teresa de la 1890-1936 .... **HLCS 2**
  See de la Parra, (Ana) Teresa (Sonojo)
  See also LAW

Parrish, Mary Frances
  See Fisher, M(ary) F(rances) K(ennedy)

Parshchikov, Aleksei 1954- .... **CLC 59**
  See Parshchikov, Aleksei Maksimovich

Parshchikov, Aleksei Maksimovich
  See Parshchikov, Aleksei
  See also DLB 285

Parson, Professor
  See Coleridge, Samuel Taylor

Parson Lot
  See Kingsley, Charles

Parton, Sara Payson Willis 1811-1872 .... **NCLC 86**
  See also DLB 43, 74, 239

Partridge, Anthony
  See Oppenheim, E(dward) Phillips

Pascal, Blaise 1623-1662 .... **LC 35**
  See also DLB 268; EW 3; GFL Beginnings to 1789; RGWL 2, 3; TWA

Pascoli, Giovanni 1855-1912 .... **TCLC 45**
  See also CA 170; EW 7; EWL 3

Pasolini, Pier Paolo 1922-1975 .. **CLC 20, 37, 106; PC 17**
  See also CA 93-96; CAAS 61-64; CANR 63; DLB 128, 177; EWL 3; MTCW 1; RGWL 2, 3

Pasquini
  See Silone, Ignazio

Pastan, Linda (Olenik) 1932- .... **CLC 27**
  See also CA 61-64; CANR 18, 40, 61, 113; CP 3, 4, 5, 6, 7; CSW; CWP; DAM POET; DLB 5; PFS 8, 25

Pasternak, Boris 1890-1960 ... **CLC 7, 10, 18, 63; PC 6; SSC 31; TCLC 188; WLC 4**
  See also BPFB 3; CA 127; CAAS 116; DA; DA3; DAB; DAC; DAM MST, NOV, POET; DLB 302, 331; EW 10; MTCW 1, 2; MTFW 2005; RGSF 2; RGWL 2, 3; TWA; WP

Patchen, Kenneth 1911-1972 .... **CLC 1, 2, 18**
  See also BG 1:3; CA 1-4R; CAAS 33-36R; CANR 3, 35; CN 1; CP 1; DAM POET; DLB 16, 48; EWL 3; MAL 5; MTCW 1; RGAL 4

Pater, Walter (Horatio) 1839-1894 . **NCLC 7, 90, 159**
  See also BRW 5; CDBLB 1832-1890; DLB 57, 156; RGEL 2; TEA

Paterson, A(ndrew) B(arton) 1864-1941 .... **TCLC 32**
  See also CA 155; DLB 230; RGEL 2; SATA 97

Paterson, Banjo
  See Paterson, A(ndrew) B(arton)

Paterson, Katherine 1932- .... **CLC 12, 30**
  See also AAYA 1, 31; BYA 1, 2, 7; CA 21-24R; CANR 28, 59, 111; CLR 7, 50; CWRI 5; DLB 52; JRDA; LAIT 4; MAICYA 1, 2; MAICYAS 1; MTCW 1; SATA 13, 53, 92, 133; WYA; YAW

Paterson, Katherine Womeldorf
  See Paterson, Katherine

Patmore, Coventry Kersey Dighton 1823-1896 .... **NCLC 9; PC 59**
  See also DLB 35, 98; RGEL 2; TEA

Paton, Alan 1903-1988 ..... **CLC 4, 10, 25, 55, 106; TCLC 165; WLC 4**
  See also AAYA 26; AFW; BPFB 3; BRWS 2; BYA 1; CA 13-16; CAAS 125; CANR 22; CAP 1; CN 1, 2, 3, 4; DA; DA3;

DAB; DAC; DAM MST, NOV; DLB 225; DLBD 17; EWL 3; EXPN; LAIT 4; MTCW 1, 2; MTFW 2005; NFS 3, 12; RGEL 2; SATA 11; SATA-Obit 56; TWA; WLIT 2; WWE 1

Paton Walsh, Gillian
  See Paton Walsh, Jill
  See also AAYA 47; BYA 1, 8

Paton Walsh, Jill 1937- .... **CLC 35**
  See Paton Walsh, Gillian; Walsh, Jill Paton
  See also AAYA 11; CANR 38, 83, 158; CLR 2, 65; DLB 161; JRDA; MAICYA 1, 2; SAAS 3; SATA 4, 72, 109; YAW

Patsauq, Markoosie 1942- .... **NNAL**
  See also CA 101; CLR 23; CWRI 5; DAM MULT

Patterson, (Horace) Orlando (Lloyd) 1940- .... **BLCS**
  See also BW 1; CA 65-68; CANR 27, 84; CN 1, 2, 3, 4, 5, 6

Patton, George S(mith), Jr. 1885-1945 .... **TCLC 79**
  See also CA 189

Paulding, James Kirke 1778-1860 ... **NCLC 2**
  See also DLB 3, 59, 74, 250; RGAL 4

Paulin, Thomas Neilson
  See Paulin, Tom

Paulin, Tom 1949- .... **CLC 37, 177**
  See also CA 128; CAAE 123; CANR 98; CP 3, 4, 5, 6, 7; DLB 40

Pausanias c. 1st cent. - .... **CMLC 36**

Paustovsky, Konstantin (Georgievich) 1892-1968 .... **CLC 40**
  See also CA 93-96; CAAS 25-28R; DLB 272; EWL 3

Pavese, Cesare 1908-1950 .... **PC 13; SSC 19; TCLC 3**
  See also CA 169; CAAE 104; DLB 128, 177; EW 12; EWL 3; PFS 20; RGSF 2; RGWL 2, 3; TWA; WLIT 7

Pavic, Milorad 1929- .... **CLC 60**
  See also CA 136; CDWLB 4; CWW 2; DLB 181; EWL 3; RGWL 3

Pavlov, Ivan Petrovich 1849-1936 . **TCLC 91**
  See also CA 180; CAAE 118

Pavlova, Karolina Karlovna 1807-1893 .... **NCLC 138**
  See also DLB 205

Payne, Alan
  See Jakes, John

Payne, Rachel Ann
  See Jakes, John

Paz, Gil
  See Lugones, Leopoldo

Paz, Octavio 1914-1998 . **CLC 3, 4, 6, 10, 19, 51, 65, 119; HLC 2; PC 1, 48; WLC 4**
  See also AAYA 50; CA 73-76; CAAS 165; CANR 32, 65, 104; CWW 2; DA; DA3; DAB; DAC; DAM MST, MULT, POET; DLB 290, 331; DLBY 1990, 1998; DNFS 1; EWL 3; HW 1, 2; LAW; LAWS 1; MTCW 1, 2; MTFW 2005; PFS 18; RGWL 2, 3; SSFS 13; TWA; WLIT 1

p'Bitek, Okot 1931-1982 .... **BLC 3; CLC 96; TCLC 149**
  See also AFW; BW 2, 3; CA 124; CAAS 107; CANR 82; CP 1, 2, 3; DAM MULT; DLB 125; EWL 3; MTCW 1, 2; MTFW 2005; RGEL 2; WLIT 2

Peabody, Elizabeth Palmer 1804-1894 .... **NCLC 169**
  See also DLB 1, 223

Peacham, Henry 1578-1644(?) .... **LC 119**
  See also DLB 151

Peacock, Molly 1947- .... **CLC 60**
  See also CA 103; 21; CANR 52, 84; CP 5, 6, 7; CWP; DLB 120, 282

Peacock, Thomas Love 1785-1866 .... **NCLC 22**
  See also BRW 4; DLB 96, 116; RGEL 2; RGSF 2

Peake, Mervyn 1911-1968 .... **CLC 7, 54**
  See also CA 5-8R; CAAS 25-28R; CANR 3; DLB 15, 160, 255; FANT; MTCW 1; RGEL 2; SATA 23; SFW 4

Pearce, Philippa 1920-2006
  See Christie, Philippa
  See also CA 5-8R; CANR 4, 109; CWRI 5; FANT; MAICYA 2

Pearl, Eric
  See Elman, Richard (Martin)

Pearson, T. R. 1956- .... **CLC 39**
  See also CA 130; CAAE 120; CANR 97, 147; CSW; INT CA-130

Pearson, Thomas Reid
  See Pearson, T. R.

Peck, Dale 1967- .... **CLC 81**
  See also CA 146; CANR 72, 127; GLL 2

Peck, John (Frederick) 1941- .... **CLC 3**
  See also CA 49-52; CANR 3, 100; CP 4, 5, 6, 7

Peck, Richard 1934- .... **CLC 21**
  See also AAYA 1, 24; BYA 1, 6, 8, 11; CA 85-88; CANR 19, 38, 129; CLR 15; INT CANR-19; JRDA; MAICYA 1, 2; SAAS 2; SATA 18, 55, 97, 110, 158; SATA-Essay 110; WYA; YAW

Peck, Richard Wayne
  See Peck, Richard

Peck, Robert Newton 1928- .... **CLC 17**
  See also AAYA 3, 43; BYA 1, 6; CA 182; 81-84, 182; CANR 31, 63, 127; CLR 45; DA; DAC; DAM MST; JRDA; LAIT 3; MAICYA 1, 2; SAAS 1; SATA 21, 62, 111, 156; SATA-Essay 108; WYA; YAW

Peckinpah, David Samuel
  See Peckinpah, Sam

Peckinpah, Sam 1925-1984 .... **CLC 20**
  See also CA 109; CAAS 114; CANR 82

Pedersen, Knut 1859-1952
  See Hamsun, Knut
  See also CA 119; CAAE 104; CANR 63; MTCW 1, 2

Peele, George 1556-1596 .... **DC 27; LC 115**
  See also BRW 1; DLB 62, 167; RGEL 2

Peeslake, Gaffer
  See Durrell, Lawrence (George)

Peguy, Charles (Pierre) 1873-1914 .... **TCLC 10**
  See also CA 193; CAAE 107; DLB 258; EWL 3; GFL 1789 to the Present

Peirce, Charles Sanders 1839-1914 .... **TCLC 81**
  See also CA 194; DLB 270

Pellicer, Carlos 1897(?)-1977 .... **HLCS 2**
  See also CA 153; CAAS 69-72; DLB 290; EWL 3; HW 1

Pena, Ramon del Valle y
  See Valle-Inclan, Ramon (Maria) del

Pendennis, Arthur Esquir
  See Thackeray, William Makepeace

Penn, Arthur
  See Matthews, (James) Brander

Penn, William 1644-1718 .... **LC 25**
  See also DLB 24

PEPECE
  See Prado (Calvo), Pedro

Pepys, Samuel 1633-1703 ... **LC 11, 58; WLC 4**
  See also BRW 2; CDBLB 1660-1789; DA; DA3; DAB; DAC; DAM MST; DLB 101, 213; NCFS 4; RGEL 2; TEA; WLIT 3

Percy, Thomas 1729-1811 .... **NCLC 95**
  See also DLB 104

Percy, Walker 1916-1990 .... **CLC 2, 3, 6, 8, 14, 18, 47, 65**
See also AMWS 3; BPFB 3; CA 1-4R; CAAS 131; CANR 1, 23, 64; CN 1, 2, 3, 4; CPW; CSW; DA3; DAM NOV, POP; DLB 2; DLBY 1980, 1990; EWL 3; MAL 5; MTCW 1, 2; MTFW 2005; RGAL 4; TUS

Percy, William Alexander
1885-1942 .... **TCLC 84**
See also CA 163; MTCW 2

Perec, Georges 1936-1982 .... **CLC 56, 116**
See also CA 141; DLB 83, 299; EWL 3; GFL 1789 to the Present; RGHL; RGWL 3

Pereda (y Sanchez de Porrua), Jose Maria de 1833-1906 .... **TCLC 16**
See also CAAE 117

Pereda y Porrua, Jose Maria de
See Pereda (y Sanchez de Porrua), Jose Maria de

Peregoy, George Weems
See Mencken, H(enry) L(ouis)

Perelman, S(idney) J(oseph)
1904-1979 .. **CLC 3, 5, 9, 15, 23, 44, 49; SSC 32**
See also AITN 1, 2; BPFB 3; CA 73-76; CAAS 89-92; CANR 18; DAM DRAM; DLB 11, 44; MTCW 1, 2; MTFW 2005; RGAL 4

Peret, Benjamin 1899-1959 .... **PC 33; TCLC 20**
See also CA 186; CAAE 117; GFL 1789 to the Present

Peretz, Isaac Leib
See Peretz, Isaac Loeb
See also CA 201; DLB 333

Peretz, Isaac Loeb 1851(?)-1915 ...... **SSC 26; TCLC 16**
See Peretz, Isaac Leib
See also CAAE 109

Peretz, Yitzkhok Leibush
See Peretz, Isaac Loeb

Perez Galdos, Benito 1843-1920 ..... **HLCS 2; TCLC 27**
See Galdos, Benito Perez
See also CA 153; CAAE 125; EWL 3; HW 1; RGWL 2, 3

Peri Rossi, Cristina 1941- .. **CLC 156; HLCS 2**
See also CA 131; CANR 59, 81; CWW 2; DLB 145, 290; EWL 3; HW 1, 2

Perlata
See Peret, Benjamin

Perloff, Marjorie G(abrielle)
1931- .... **CLC 137**
See also CA 57-60; CANR 7, 22, 49, 104

Perrault, Charles 1628-1703 .... **LC 2, 56**
See also BYA 4; CLR 79; DLB 268; GFL Beginnings to 1789; MAICYA 1, 2; RGWL 2, 3; SATA 25; WCH

Perry, Anne 1938- .... **CLC 126**
See also CA 101; CANR 22, 50, 84, 150; CMW 4; CN 6, 7; CPW; DLB 276

Perry, Brighton
See Sherwood, Robert E(mmet)

Perse, St.-John
See Leger, (Marie-Rene Auguste) Alexis Saint-Leger

Perse, Saint-John
See Leger, (Marie-Rene Auguste) Alexis Saint-Leger
See also DLB 258, 331; RGWL 3

Persius 34-62 .... **CMLC 74**
See also AW 2; DLB 211; RGWL 2, 3

Perutz, Leo(pold) 1882-1957 .... **TCLC 60**
See also CA 147; DLB 81

Peseenz, Tulio F.
See Lopez y Fuentes, Gregorio

Pesetsky, Bette 1932- .... **CLC 28**
See also CA 133; DLB 130

Peshkov, Alexei Maximovich 1868-1936
See Gorky, Maxim
See also CA 141; CAAE 105; CANR 83; DA; DAC; DAM DRAM, MST, NOV; MTCW 2; MTFW 2005

Pessoa, Fernando (Antonio Nogueira)
1888-1935 ..... **HLC 2; PC 20; TCLC 27**
See also CA 183; CAAE 125; DAM MULT; DLB 287; EW 10; EWL 3; RGWL 2, 3; WP

Peterkin, Julia Mood 1880-1961 ...... **CLC 31**
See also CA 102; DLB 9

Peters, Joan K(aren) 1945- .... **CLC 39**
See also CA 158; CANR 109

Peters, Robert L(ouis) 1924- .... **CLC 7**
See also CA 13-16R; 8; CP 1, 5, 6, 7; DLB 105

Petofi, Sandor 1823-1849 .... **NCLC 21**
See also RGWL 2, 3

Petrakis, Harry Mark 1923- .... **CLC 3**
See also CA 9-12R; CANR 4, 30, 85, 155; CN 1, 2, 3, 4, 5, 6, 7

Petrarch 1304-1374 .... **CMLC 20; PC 8**
See also DA3; DAM POET; EW 2; LMFS 1; RGWL 2, 3; WLIT 7

Petronius c. 20-66 .... **CMLC 34**
See also AW 2; CDWLB 1; DLB 211; RGWL 2, 3; WLIT 8

Petrov, Evgeny **TCLC 21**
See Kataev, Evgeny Petrovich

Petry, Ann (Lane) 1908-1997 .. **CLC 1, 7, 18; TCLC 112**
See also AFAW 1, 2; BPFB 3; BW 1, 3; BYA 2; CA 5-8R; 6; CAAS 157; CANR 4, 46; CLR 12; CN 1, 2, 3, 4, 5, 6; DLB 76; EWL 3; JRDA; LAIT 1; MAICYA 1, 2; MAICYAS 1; MTCW 1; RGAL 4; SATA 5; SATA-Obit 94; TUS

Petursson, Halligrimur 1614-1674 .... **LC 8**

Peychinovich
See Vazov, Ivan (Minchov)

Phaedrus c. 15B.C.-c. 50 .... **CMLC 25**
See also DLB 211

Phelps (Ward), Elizabeth Stuart
See Phelps, Elizabeth Stuart
See also FW

Phelps, Elizabeth Stuart
1844-1911 .... **TCLC 113**
See Phelps (Ward), Elizabeth Stuart
See also CA 242; DLB 74

Philips, Katherine 1632-1664 . **LC 30; PC 40**
See also DLB 131; RGEL 2

Philipson, Ilene J. 1950- .... **CLC 65**
See also CA 219

Philipson, Morris H. 1926- .... **CLC 53**
See also CA 1-4R; CANR 4

Phillips, Caryl 1958- ..... **BLCS; CLC 96, 224**
See also BRWS 5; BW 2; CA 141; CANR 63, 104, 140; CBD; CD 5, 6; CN 5, 6, 7; DA3; DAM MULT; DLB 157; EWL 3; MTCW 2; MTFW 2005; WLIT 4; WWE 1

Phillips, David Graham
1867-1911 .... **TCLC 44**
See also CA 176; CAAE 108; DLB 9, 12, 303; RGAL 4

Phillips, Jack
See Sandburg, Carl (August)

Phillips, Jayne Anne 1952- .... **CLC 15, 33, 139; SSC 16**
See also AAYA 57; BPFB 3; CA 101; CANR 24, 50, 96; CN 4, 5, 6, 7; CSW; DLBY 1980; INT CANR-24; MTCW 1, 2; MTFW 2005; RGAL 4; RGSF 2; SSFS 4

Phillips, Richard
See Dick, Philip K.

Phillips, Robert (Schaeffer) 1938- .... **CLC 28**
See also CA 17-20R; 13; CANR 8; DLB 105

Phillips, Ward
See Lovecraft, H. P.

Philostratus, Flavius c. 179-c.
244 .... **CMLC 62**

Piccolo, Lucio 1901-1969 .... **CLC 13**
See also CA 97-100; DLB 114; EWL 3

Pickthall, Marjorie L(owry) C(hristie)
1883-1922 .... **TCLC 21**
See also CAAE 107; DLB 92

Pico della Mirandola, Giovanni
1463-1494 .... **LC 15**
See also LMFS 1

Piercy, Marge 1936- .... **CLC 3, 6, 14, 18, 27, 62, 128; PC 29**
See also BPFB 3; CA 187; 21-24R, 187; 1; CANR 13, 43, 66, 111; CN 3, 4, 5, 6, 7; CP 1, 2, 3, 4, 5, 6, 7; CWP; DLB 120, 227; EXPP; FW; MAL 5; MTCW 1, 2; MTFW 2005; PFS 9, 22; SFW 4

Piers, Robert
See Anthony, Piers

Pieyre de Mandiargues, Andre 1909-1991
See Mandiargues, Andre Pieyre de
See also CA 103; CAAS 136; CANR 22, 82; EWL 3; GFL 1789 to the Present

Pilnyak, Boris 1894-1938 . **SSC 48; TCLC 23**
See Vogau, Boris Andreyevich
See also EWL 3

Pinchback, Eugene
See Toomer, Jean

Pincherle, Alberto 1907-1990 ...... **CLC 11, 18**
See Moravia, Alberto
See also CA 25-28R; CAAS 132; CANR 33, 63, 142; DAM NOV; MTCW 1; MTFW 2005

Pinckney, Darryl 1953- .... **CLC 76**
See also BW 2, 3; CA 143; CANR 79

Pindar 518(?)B.C.-438(?)B.C. .... **CMLC 12; PC 19**
See also AW 1; CDWLB 1; DLB 176; RGWL 2

Pineda, Cecile 1942- .... **CLC 39**
See also CA 118; DLB 209

Pinero, Arthur Wing 1855-1934 .... **TCLC 32**
See also CA 153; CAAE 110; DAM DRAM; DLB 10; RGEL 2

Pinero, Miguel (Antonio Gomez)
1946-1988 .... **CLC 4, 55**
See also CA 61-64; CAAS 125; CAD; CANR 29, 90; DLB 266; HW 1; LLW

Pinget, Robert 1919-1997 .... **CLC 7, 13, 37**
See also CA 85-88; CAAS 160; CWW 2; DLB 83; EWL 3; GFL 1789 to the Present

Pink Floyd
See Barrett, (Roger) Syd; Gilmour, David; Mason, Nick; Waters, Roger; Wright, Rick

Pinkney, Edward 1802-1828 .... **NCLC 31**
See also DLB 248

Pinkwater, D. Manus
See Pinkwater, Daniel Manus

Pinkwater, Daniel
See Pinkwater, Daniel Manus

Pinkwater, Daniel M.
See Pinkwater, Daniel Manus

Pinkwater, Daniel Manus 1941- .... **CLC 35**
See also AAYA 1, 46; BYA 9; CA 29-32R; CANR 12, 38, 89, 143; CLR 4; CSW; FANT; JRDA; MAICYA 1, 2; SAAS 3; SATA 8, 46, 76, 114, 158; SFW 4; YAW

Pinkwater, Manus
See Pinkwater, Daniel Manus

Author Index

Rinehart, Mary Roberts
1876-1958 .... **TCLC 52**
See also BPFB 3; CA 166; CAAE 108;
RGAL 4; RHW
Ringmaster, The
See Mencken, H(enry) L(ouis)
Ringwood, Gwen(dolyn Margaret) Pharis
1910-1984 .... **CLC 48**
See also CA 148; CAAS 112; DLB 88
Rio, Michel 1945(?)- .... **CLC 43**
See also CA 201
Rios, Alberto 1952- .... **PC 57**
See also AAYA 66; AMWS 4; CA 113;
CANR 34, 79, 137; CP 6, 7; DLB 122;
HW 2; MTFW 2005; PFS 11
Ritsos, Giannes
See Ritsos, Yannis
Ritsos, Yannis 1909-1990 .... **CLC 6, 13, 31**
See also CA 77-80; CAAS 133; CANR 39,
61; EW 12; EWL 3; MTCW 1; RGWL 2,
3
Ritter, Erika 1948(?)- .... **CLC 52**
See also CD 5, 6; CWD
Rivera, Jose Eustasio 1889-1928 ... **TCLC 35**
See also CA 162; EWL 3; HW 1, 2; LAW
Rivera, Tomas 1935-1984 .... **HLCS 2**
See also CA 49-52; CANR 32; DLB 82;
HW 1; LLW; RGAL 4; SSFS 15; TCWW
2; WLIT 1
Rivers, Conrad Kent 1933-1968 .... **CLC 1**
See also BW 1; CA 85-88; DLB 41
Rivers, Elfrida
See Bradley, Marion Zimmer
See also GLL 1
Riverside, John
See Heinlein, Robert A.
Rizal, Jose 1861-1896 .... **NCLC 27**
Roa Bastos, Augusto 1917-2005 ...... **CLC 45;
HLC 2**
See also CA 131; CAAS 238; CWW 2;
DAM MULT; DLB 113; EWL 3; HW 1;
LAW; RGSF 2; WLIT 1
Roa Bastos, Augusto Jose Antonio
See Roa Bastos, Augusto
Robbe-Grillet, Alain 1922- .... **CLC 1, 2, 4, 6,
8, 10, 14, 43, 128**
See also BPFB 3; CA 9-12R; CANR 33,
65, 115; CWW 2; DLB 83; EW 13; EWL
3; GFL 1789 to the Present; IDFW 3, 4;
MTCW 1, 2; MTFW 2005; RGWL 2, 3;
SSFS 15
Robbins, Harold 1916-1997 .... **CLC 5**
See also BPFB 3; CA 73-76; CAAS 162;
CANR 26, 54, 112, 156; DA3; DAM
NOV; MTCW 1, 2
Robbins, Thomas Eugene 1936-
See Robbins, Tom
See also CA 81-84; CANR 29, 59, 95, 139;
CN 7; CPW; CSW; DA3; DAM NOV;
POP; MTCW 1, 2; MTFW 2005
Robbins, Tom .... **CLC 9, 32, 64**
See Robbins, Thomas Eugene
See also AAYA 32; AMWS 10; BEST 90:3;
BPFB 3; CN 3, 4, 5, 6, 7; DLBY 1980
Robbins, Trina 1938- .... **CLC 21**
See also AAYA 61; CA 128; CANR 152
Roberts, Charles G(eorge) D(ouglas)
1860-1943 .... **SSC 91; TCLC 8**
See also CA 188; CAAE 105; CLR 33;
CWRI 5; DLB 92; RGEL 2; RGSF 2;
SATA 88; SATA-Brief 29
Roberts, Elizabeth Madox
1886-1941 .... **TCLC 68**
See also CA 166; CAAE 111; CLR 100;
CWRI 5; DLB 9, 54, 102; RGAL 4;
RHW; SATA 33; SATA-Brief 27; TCWW
2; WCH
Roberts, Kate 1891-1985 .... **CLC 15**
See also CA 107; CAAS 116; DLB 319

Roberts, Keith (John Kingston)
1935-2000 .... **CLC 14**
See also BRWS 10; CA 25-28R; CANR 46;
DLB 261; SFW 4
Roberts, Kenneth (Lewis)
1885-1957 .... **TCLC 23**
See also CA 199; CAAE 109; DLB 9; MAL
5; RGAL 4; RHW
Roberts, Michele (Brigitte) 1949- .... **CLC 48,
178**
See also CA 115; CANR 58, 120; CN 6, 7;
DLB 231; FW
Robertson, Ellis
See Ellison, Harlan; Silverberg, Robert
Robertson, Thomas William
1829-1871 .... **NCLC 35**
See Robertson, Tom
See also DAM DRAM
Robertson, Tom
See Robertson, Thomas William
See also RGEL 2
Robeson, Kenneth
See Dent, Lester
Robinson, Edwin Arlington
1869-1935 .... **PC 1, 35; TCLC 5, 101**
See also AAYA 72; AMW; CA 133; CAAE
104; CDALB 1865-1917; DA; DAC;
DAM MST, POET; DLB 54; EWL 3;
EXPP; MAL 5; MTCW 1, 2; MTFW
2005; PAB; PFS 4; RGAL 4; WP
Robinson, Henry Crabb
1775-1867 .... **NCLC 15**
See also DLB 107
Robinson, Jill 1936- .... **CLC 10**
See also CA 102; CANR 120; INT CA-102
Robinson, Kim Stanley 1952- .... **CLC 34**
See also AAYA 26; CA 126; CANR 113,
139; CN 6, 7; MTFW 2005; SATA 109;
SCFW 2; SFW 4
Robinson, Lloyd
See Silverberg, Robert
Robinson, Marilynne 1944- ...... **CLC 25, 180**
See also AAYA 69; CA 116; CANR 80, 140;
CN 4, 5, 6, 7; DLB 206; MTFW 2005;
NFS 24
Robinson, Mary 1758-1800 .... **NCLC 142**
See also DLB 158; FW
Robinson, Smokey .... **CLC 21**
See Robinson, William, Jr.
Robinson, William, Jr. 1940-
See Robinson, Smokey
See also CAAE 116
Robison, Mary 1949- .... **CLC 42, 98**
See also CA 116; CAAE 113; CANR 87;
CN 4, 5, 6, 7; DLB 130; INT CA-116;
RGSF 2
Roches, Catherine des 1542-1587 ...... **LC 117**
See also DLB 327
Rochester
See Wilmot, John
See also RGEL 2
Rod, Edouard 1857-1910 .... **TCLC 52**
Roddenberry, Eugene Wesley 1921-1991
See Roddenberry, Gene
See also CA 110; CAAS 135; CANR 37;
SATA 45; SATA-Obit 69
Roddenberry, Gene .... **CLC 17**
See Roddenberry, Eugene Wesley
See also AAYA 5; SATA-Obit 69
Rodgers, Mary 1931- .... **CLC 12**
See also BYA 5; CA 49-52; CANR 8, 55,
90; CLR 20; CWRI 5; INT CANR-8;
JRDA; MAICYA 1, 2; SATA 8, 130
Rodgers, W(illiam) R(obert)
1909-1969 .... **CLC 7**
See also CA 85-88; DLB 20; RGEL 2
Rodman, Eric
See Silverberg, Robert

Rodman, Howard 1920(?)-1985 .... **CLC 65**
See also CAAS 118
Rodman, Maia
See Wojciechowska, Maia (Teresa)
Rodo, Jose Enrique 1871(?)-1917 .... **HLCS 2**
See also CA 178; EWL 3; HW 2; LAW
Rodolph, Utto
See Ouologuem, Yambo
Rodriguez, Claudio 1934-1999 .... **CLC 10**
See also CA 188; DLB 134
Rodriguez, Richard 1944- .... **CLC 155; HLC
2**
See also AMWS 14; CA 110; CANR 66,
116; DAM MULT; DLB 82, 256; HW 1,
2; LAIT 5; LLW; MTFW 2005; NCFS 3;
WLIT 1
Roelvaag, O(le) E(dvart) 1876-1931
See Rolvaag, O(le) E(dvart)
See also AAYA 75; CA 171; CAAE 117
Roethke, Theodore (Huebner)
1908-1963 .... **CLC 1, 3, 8, 11, 19, 46,
101; PC 15**
See also AMW; CA 81-84; CABS 2;
CDALB 1941-1968; DA3; DAM POET;
DLB 5, 206; EWL 3; EXPP; MAL 5;
MTCW 1, 2; PAB; PFS 3; RGAL 4; WP
Rogers, Carl R(ansom)
1902-1987 .... **TCLC 125**
See also CA 1-4R; CAAS 121; CANR 1,
18; MTCW 1
Rogers, Samuel 1763-1855 .... **NCLC 69**
See also DLB 93; RGEL 2
Rogers, Thomas Hunton 1927- .... **CLC 57**
See also CA 89-92; INT CA-89-92
Rogers, Will(iam Penn Adair)
1879-1935 .... **NNAL; TCLC 8, 71**
See also CA 144; CAAE 105; DA3; DAM
MULT; DLB 11; MTCW 2
Rogin, Gilbert 1929- .... **CLC 18**
See also CA 65-68; CANR 15
Rohan, Koda
See Koda Shigeyuki
Rohlfs, Anna Katharine Green
See Green, Anna Katharine
Rohmer, Eric .... **CLC 16**
See Scherer, Jean-Marie Maurice
Rohmer, Sax .... **TCLC 28**
See Ward, Arthur Henry Sarsfield
See also DLB 70; MSW; SUFW
Roiphe, Anne 1935- .... **CLC 3, 9**
See also CA 89-92; CANR 45, 73, 138;
DLBY 1980; INT CA-89-92
Roiphe, Anne Richardson
See Roiphe, Anne
Rojas, Fernando de 1475-1541 ... **HLCS 1, 2;
LC 23**
See also DLB 286; RGWL 2, 3
Rojas, Gonzalo 1917- .... **HLCS 2**
See also CA 178; HW 2; LAWS 1
Roland (de la Platiere), Marie-Jeanne
1754-1793 .... **LC 98**
See also DLB 314
**Rolfe, Frederick (William Serafino Austin
Lewis Mary)** 1860-1913 .... **TCLC 12**
See Al Siddik
See also CA 210; CAAE 107; DLB 34, 156;
RGEL 2
Rolland, Romain 1866-1944 .... **TCLC 23**
See also CA 197; CAAE 118; DLB 65, 284,
332; EWL 3; GFL 1789 to the Present;
RGWL 2, 3
Rolle, Richard c. 1300-c. 1349 ...... **CMLC 21**
See also DLB 146; LMFS 1; RGEL 2
Rolvaag, O(le) E(dvart) .... **TCLC 17**
See Roelvaag, O(le) E(dvart)
See also DLB 9, 212; MAL 5; NFS 5;
RGAL 4
Romain Arnaud, Saint
See Aragon, Louis

Runyon, (Alfred) Damon
1884(?)-1946 .... **TCLC 10**
See also CA 165; CAAE 107; DLB 11, 86,
171; MAL 5; MTCW 2; RGAL 4

Rush, Norman 1933- .... **CLC 44**
See also CA 126; CAAE 121; CANR 130;
INT CA-126

Rushdie, Salman 1947- .... **CLC 23, 31, 55,
100, 191; SSC 83; WLCS**
See also AAYA 65; BEST 89:3; BPFB 3;
BRWS 4; CA 111; CAAE 108; CANR 33,
56, 108, 133; CN 4, 5, 6, 7; CPW 1; DA3;
DAB; DAC; DAM MST, NOV, POP;
DLB 194, 323, 326; EWL 3; FANT; INT
CA-111; LATS 1:2; LMFS 2; MTCW 1,
2; MTFW 2005; NFS 22, 23; RGEL 2;
RGSF 2; TEA; WLIT 4

Rushforth, Peter 1945-2005 .... **CLC 19**
See also CA 101; CAAS 243

Rushforth, Peter Scott
See Rushforth, Peter

Ruskin, John 1819-1900 .... **TCLC 63**
See also BRW 5; BYA 5; CA 129; CAAE
114; CDBLB 1832-1890; DLB 55, 163,
190; RGEL 2; SATA 24; TEA; WCH

Russ, Joanna 1937- .... **CLC 15**
See also BPFB 3; CA 25-28; CANR 11, 31,
65; CN 4, 5, 6, 7; DLB 8; FW; GLL 1;
MTCW 1; SCFW 1, 2; SFW 4

Russ, Richard Patrick
See O'Brian, Patrick

Russell, George William 1867-1935
See A.E.; Baker, Jean H.
See also BRWS 8; CA 153; CAAE 104;
CDBLB 1890-1914; DAM POET; EWL
3; RGEL 2

Russell, Jeffrey Burton 1934- .... **CLC 70**
See also CA 25-28R; CANR 11, 28, 52

Russell, (Henry) Ken(neth Alfred)
1927- .... **CLC 16**
See also CA 105

Russell, William Martin 1947-
See Russell, Willy
See also CA 164; CANR 107

Russell, Willy CLC 60
See Russell, William Martin
See also CBD; CD 5, 6; DLB 233

Russo, Richard 1949- .... **CLC 181**
See also AMWS 12; CA 133; CAAE 127;
CANR 87, 114

Rutherford, Mark TCLC 25
See White, William Hale
See also DLB 18; RGEL 2

Ruysbroeck, Jan van 1293-1381 ... **CMLC 85**

Ruyslinck, Ward CLC 14
See Belser, Reimond Karel Maria de

Ryan, Cornelius (John) 1920-1974 ..... **CLC 7**
See also CA 69-72; CAAS 53-56; CANR
38

Ryan, Michael 1946- .... **CLC 65**
See also CA 49-52; CANR 109; DLBY
1982

Ryan, Tim
See Dent, Lester

Rybakov, Anatoli (Naumovich)
1911-1998 .... **CLC 23, 53**
See Rybakov, Anatolii (Naumovich)
See also CA 135; CAAE 126; CAAS 172;
SATA 79; SATA-Obit 108

Rybakov, Anatolii (Naumovich)
See Rybakov, Anatoli (Naumovich)
See also DLB 302; RGHL

Ryder, Jonathan
See Ludlum, Robert

Ryga, George 1932-1987 .... **CLC 14**
See also CA 101; CAAS 124; CANR 43,
90; CCA 1; DAC; DAM MST; DLB 60

Rymer, Thomas 1643(?)-1713 .... **LC 132**
See also DLB 101

S. H.
See Hartmann, Sadakichi

S. S.
See Sassoon, Siegfried (Lorraine)

Sa'adawi, al- Nawal
See El Saadawi, Nawal
See also AFW; EWL 3

Saadawi, Nawal El
See El Saadawi, Nawal
See also WLIT 2

Saba, Umberto 1883-1957 .... **TCLC 33**
See also CA 144; CANR 79; DLB 114;
EWL 3; RGWL 2, 3

Sabatini, Rafael 1875-1950 .... **TCLC 47**
See also BPFB 3; CA 162; RHW

Sabato, Ernesto 1911- ... **CLC 10, 23; HLC 2**
See also CA 97-100; CANR 32, 65; CD-
WLB 3; CWW 2; DAM MULT; DLB 145;
EWL 3; HW 1, 2; LAW; MTCW 1, 2;
MTFW 2005

Sa-Carneiro, Mario de 1890-1916 . **TCLC 83**
See also DLB 287; EWL 3

Sacastru, Martin
See Bioy Casares, Adolfo
See also CWW 2

Sacher-Masoch, Leopold von
1836(?)-1895 .... **NCLC 31**

Sachs, Hans 1494-1576 .... **LC 95**
See also CDWLB 2; DLB 179; RGWL 2, 3

Sachs, Marilyn 1927- .... **CLC 35**
See also AAYA 2; BYA 6; CA 17-20R;
CANR 13, 47, 150; CLR 2; JRDA; MAI-
CYA 1; SAAS 2; SATA 3, 68, 164;
SATA-Essay 110; WYA; YAW

Sachs, Marilyn Stickle
See Sachs, Marilyn

Sachs, Nelly 1891-1970 .... **CLC 14, 98**
See also CA 17-18; CAAS 25-28R; CANR
87; CAP 2; DLB 332; EWL 3; MTCW 2;
MTFW 2005; PFS 20; RGHL; RGWL 2,
3

Sackler, Howard (Oliver)
1929-1982 .... **CLC 14**
See also CA 61-64; CAAS 108; CAD;
CANR 30; DFS 15; DLB 7

Sacks, Oliver 1933- .... **CLC 67, 202**
See also CA 53-56; CANR 28, 50, 76, 146;
CPW; DA3; INT CANR-28; MTCW 1, 2;
MTFW 2005

Sacks, Oliver Wolf
See Sacks, Oliver

Sackville, Thomas 1536-1608 .... **LC 98**
See also DAM DRAM; DLB 62, 132;
RGEL 2

Sadakichi
See Hartmann, Sadakichi

Sa'dawi, Nawal al-
See El Saadawi, Nawal
See also CWW 2

Sade, Donatien Alphonse Francois
1740-1814 .... **NCLC 3, 47**
See also DLB 314; EW 4; GFL Beginnings
to 1789; RGWL 2, 3

Sade, Marquis de
See Sade, Donatien Alphonse Francois

Sadoff, Ira 1945- .... **CLC 9**
See also CA 53-56; CANR 5, 21, 109; DLB
120

Saetone
See Camus, Albert

Safire, William 1929- .... **CLC 10**
See also CA 17-20R; CANR 31, 54, 91, 148

Sagan, Carl 1934-1996 .... **CLC 30, 112**
See also AAYA 2, 62; CA 25-28R; CAAS
155; CANR 11, 36, 74; CPW; DA3;
MTCW 1, 2; MTFW 2005; SATA 58;
SATA-Obit 94

Sagan, Francoise CLC 3, 6, 9, 17, 36
See Quoirez, Francoise
See also CWW 2; DLB 83; EWL 3; GFL
1789 to the Present; MTCW 2

Sahgal, Nayantara (Pandit) 1927- .... **CLC 41**
See also CA 9-12R; CANR 11, 88; CN 1,
2, 3, 4, 5, 6, 7; DLB 323

Said, Edward W. 1935-2003 .... **CLC 123**
See also CA 21-24R; CAAS 220; CANR
45, 74, 107, 131; DLB 67; MTCW 2;
MTFW 2005

Saint, H(arry) F. 1941- .... **CLC 50**
See also CA 127

St. Aubin de Teran, Lisa 1953-
See Teran, Lisa St. Aubin de
See also CA 126; CAAE 118; CN 6, 7; INT
CA-126

Saint Birgitta of Sweden c.
1303-1373 .... **CMLC 24**

Sainte-Beuve, Charles Augustin
1804-1869 .... **NCLC 5**
See also DLB 217; EW 6; GFL 1789 to the
Present

Saint-Exupery, Antoine de
1900-1944 .... **TCLC 2, 56, 169; WLC**
See also AAYA 63; BPFB 3; BYA 3; CA
132; CAAE 108; CLR 10; DA3; DAM
NOV; DLB 72; EW 12; EWL 3; GFL
1789 to the Present; LAIT 3; MAICYA 1,
2; MTCW 1, 2; MTFW 2005; RGWL 2,
3; SATA 20; TWA

**Saint-Exupery, Antoine Jean Baptiste Marie
Roger de**
See Saint-Exupery, Antoine de

St. John, David
See Hunt, E. Howard

St. John, J. Hector
See Crevecoeur, Michel Guillaume Jean de

Saint-John Perse
See Leger, (Marie-Rene Auguste) Alexis
Saint-Leger
See also EW 10; EWL 3; GFL 1789 to the
Present; RGWL 2

Saintsbury, George (Edward Bateman)
1845-1933 .... **TCLC 31**
See also CA 160; DLB 57, 149

Sait Faik TCLC 23
See Abasiyanik, Sait Faik

Saki SSC 12; TCLC 3; WLC 5
See Munro, H(ector) H(ugh)
See also BRWS 6; BYA 11; LAIT 2; RGEL
2; SSFS 1; SUFW

Sala, George Augustus 1828-1895 . **NCLC 46**

Saladin 1138-1193 .... **CMLC 38**

Salama, Hannu 1936- .... **CLC 18**
See also CA 244; EWL 3

Salamanca, J(ack) R(ichard) 1922- .. **CLC 4,
15**
See also CA 193; 25-28R, 193

Salas, Floyd Francis 1931- .... **HLC 2**
See also CA 119; 27; CANR 44, 75, 93;
DAM MULT; DLB 82; HW 1, 2; MTCW
2; MTFW 2005

Sale, J. Kirkpatrick
See Sale, Kirkpatrick

Sale, John Kirkpatrick
See Sale, Kirkpatrick

Sale, Kirkpatrick 1937- .... **CLC 68**
See also CA 13-16R; CANR 10, 147

Salinas, Luis Omar 1937- ... **CLC 90; HLC 2**
See also AMWS 13; CA 131; CANR 81,
153; DAM MULT; DLB 82; HW 1, 2

Salinas (y Serrano), Pedro
1891(?)-1951 .... **TCLC 17**
See also CAAE 117; DLB 134; EWL 3

Salinger, J.D. 1919- . **CLC 1, 3, 8, 12, 55, 56, 138; SSC 2, 28, 65; WLC 5**
See also AAYA 2, 36; AMW; AMWC 1; BPFB 3; CA 5-8R; CANR 39, 129; CDALB 1941-1968; CLR 18; CN 1, 2, 3, 4, 5, 6, 7; CPW 1; DA; DA3; DAB; DAC; DAM MST, NOV, POP; DLB 2, 102, 173; EWL 3; EXPN; LAIT 4; MAICYA 1, 2; MAL 5; MTCW 1, 2; MTFW 2005; NFS 1; RGAL 4; RGSF 2; SATA 67; SSFS 17; TUS; WYA; YAW

Salisbury, John
See Caute, (John) David

Sallust c. 86B.C.-35B.C. .... **CMLC 68**
See also AW 2; CDWLB 1; DLB 211; RGWL 2, 3

Salter, James 1925- .. **CLC 7, 52, 59; SSC 58**
See also AMWS 9; CA 73-76; CANR 107, 160; DLB 130

Saltus, Edgar (Everton) 1855-1921 . **TCLC 8**
See also CAAE 105; DLB 202; RGAL 4

Saltykov, Mikhail Evgrafovich
1826-1889 .... **NCLC 16**
See also DLB 238:

Saltykov-Shchedrin, N.
See Saltykov, Mikhail Evgrafovich

Samarakis, Andonis
See Samarakis, Antonis
See also EWL 3

Samarakis, Antonis 1919-2003 .... **CLC 5**
See Samarakis, Andonis
See also CA 25-28R; 16; CAAS 224; CANR 36

Sanchez, Florencio 1875-1910 .... **TCLC 37**
See also CA 153; DLB 305; EWL 3; HW 1; LAW

Sanchez, Luis Rafael 1936- .... **CLC 23**
See also CA 128; DLB 305; EWL 3; HW 1; WLIT 1

Sanchez, Sonia 1934- .... **BLC 3; CLC 5, 116, 215; PC 9**
See also BW 2, 3; CA 33-36R; CANR 24, 49, 74, 115; CLR 18; CP 2, 3, 4, 5, 6, 7; CSW; CWP; DA3; DAM MULT; DLB 41; DLBD 8; EWL 3; MAICYA 1, 2; MAL 5; MTCW 1, 2; MTFW 2005; SATA 22, 136; WP

Sancho, Ignatius 1729-1780 .... **LC 84**

Sand, George 1804-1876 ..... **NCLC 2, 42, 57, 174; WLC 5**
See also DA; DA3; DAB; DAC; DAM MST, NOV; DLB 119, 192; EW 6; FL 1:3; FW; GFL 1789 to the Present; RGWL 2, 3; TWA

Sandburg, Carl (August) 1878-1967 . **CLC 1, 4, 10, 15, 35; PC 2, 41; WLC 5**
See also AAYA 24; AMW; BYA 1, 3; CA 5-8R; CAAS 25-28R; CANR 35; CDALB 1865-1917; CLR 67; DA; DA3; DAB; DAC; DAM MST, POET; DLB 17, 54, 284; EWL 3; EXPP; LAIT 2; MAICYA 1, 2; MAL 5; MTCW 1, 2; MTFW 2005; PAB; PFS 3, 6, 12; RGAL 4; SATA 8; TUS; WCH; WP; WYA

Sandburg, Charles
See Sandburg, Carl (August)

Sandburg, Charles A.
See Sandburg, Carl (August)

Sanders, (James) Ed(ward) 1939- .... **CLC 53**
See Sanders, Edward
See also BG 1:3; CA 13-16R; 21; CANR 13, 44, 78; CP 1, 2, 3, 4, 5, 6, 7; DAM POET; DLB 16, 244

Sanders, Edward
See Sanders, (James) Ed(ward)
See also DLB 244

Sanders, Lawrence 1920-1998 .... **CLC 41**
See also BEST 89:4; BPFB 3; CA 81-84; CAAS 165; CANR 33, 62; CMW 4; CPW; DA3; DAM POP; MTCW 1

Sanders, Noah
See Blount, Roy (Alton), Jr.

Sanders, Winston P.
See Anderson, Poul

Sandoz, Mari(e Susette) 1900-1966 .. **CLC 28**
See also CA 1-4R; CAAS 25-28R; CANR 17, 64; DLB 9, 212; LAIT 2; MTCW 1, 2; SATA 5; TCWW 1, 2

Sandys, George 1578-1644 .... **LC 80**
See also DLB 24, 121

Saner, Reg(inald Anthony) 1931- .... **CLC 9**
See also CA 65-68; CP 3, 4, 5, 6, 7

Sankara 788-820 .... **CMLC 32**

Sannazaro, Jacopo 1456(?)-1530 .... **LC 8**
See also RGWL 2, 3; WLIT 7

Sansom, William 1912-1976 . **CLC 2, 6; SSC 21**
See also CA 5-8R; CAAS 65-68; CANR 42; CN 1, 2; DAM NOV; DLB 139; EWL 3; MTCW 1; RGEL 2; RGSF 2

Santayana, George 1863-1952 .... **TCLC 40**
See also AMW; CA 194; CAAE 115; DLB 54, 71, 246, 270; DLBD 13; EWL 3; MAL 5; RGAL 4; TUS

Santiago, Danny CLC 33
See James, Daniel (Lewis)
See also DLB 122

Santillana, Inigo Lopez de Mendoza, Marques de 1398-1458 .... **LC 111**
See also DLB 286

Santmyer, Helen Hooven
1895-1986 .... **CLC 33; TCLC 133**
See also CA 1-4R; CAAS 118; CANR 15, 33; DLBY 1984; MTCW 1; RHW

Santoka, Taneda 1882-1940 .... **TCLC 72**

Santos, Bienvenido N(uqui)
1911-1996 ... **AAL; CLC 22; TCLC 156**
See also CA 101; CAAS 151; CANR 19, 46; CP 1; DAM MULT; DLB 312; EWL; RGAL 4; SSFS 19

Sapir, Edward 1884-1939 .... **TCLC 108**
See also CA 211; DLB 92

Sapper TCLC 44
See McNeile, Herman Cyril

Sapphire
See Sapphire, Brenda

Sapphire, Brenda 1950- .... **CLC 99**

Sappho fl. 6th cent. B.C.- ... **CMLC 3, 67; PC 5**
See also CDWLB 1; DA3; DAM POET; DLB 176; FL 1:1; PFS 20; RGWL 2, 3; WLIT 8; WP

Saramago, Jose 1922- ..... **CLC 119; HLCS 1**
See also CA 153; CANR 96; CWW 2; DLB 287, 332; EWL 3; LATS 1:2; SSFS 23

Sarduy, Severo 1937-1993 .... **CLC 6, 97; HLCS 2; TCLC 167**
See also CA 89-92; CAAS 142; CANR 58, 81; CWW 2; DLB 113; EWL 3; HW 1, 2; LAW

Sargeson, Frank 1903-1982 ..... **CLC 31; SSC 99**
See also CA 25-28R; CAAS 106; CANR 38, 79; CN 1, 2, 3; EWL 3; GLL 2; RGEL 2; RGSF 2; SSFS 20

Sarmiento, Domingo Faustino
1811-1888 .... **HLCS 2; NCLC 123**
See also LAW; WLIT 1

Sarmiento, Felix Ruben Garcia
See Dario, Ruben

Saro-Wiwa, Ken(ule Beeson)
1941-1995 .... **CLC 114**
See also BW 2; CA 142; CAAS 150; CANR 60; DLB 157

Saroyan, William 1908-1981 ... **CLC 1, 8, 10, 29, 34, 56; SSC 21; TCLC 137; WLC 5**
See also AAYA 66; CA 5-8R; CAAS 103; CAD; CANR 30; CDALBS; CN 1, 2; DA; DA3; DAB; DAC; DAM DRAM, MST, NOV; DFS 17; DLB 7, 9, 86; DLBY 1981; EWL 3; LAIT 4; MAL 5; MTCW 1, 2; MTFW 2005; RGAL 4; RGSF 2; SATA 23; SATA-Obit 24; SSFS 14; TUS

Sarraute, Nathalie 1900-1999 .... **CLC 1, 2, 4, 8, 10, 31, 80; TCLC 145**
See also BPFB 3; CA 9-12R; CAAS 187; CANR 23, 66, 134; CWW 2; DLB 83, 321; EW 12; EWL 3; GFL 1789 to the Present; MTCW 1, 2; MTFW 2005; RGWL 2, 3

Sarton, May 1912-1995 ... **CLC 4, 14, 49, 91; PC 39; TCLC 120**
See also AMWS 8; CA 1-4R; CAAS 149; CANR 1, 34, 55, 116; CN 1, 2, 3, 4, 5, 6; CP 1, 2, 3, 4, 5, 6; DAM POET; DLB 48; DLBY 1981; EWL 3; FW; INT CANR-34; MAL 5; MTCW 1, 2; MTFW 2005; RGAL 4; SATA 36; SATA-Obit 86; TUS

Sartre, Jean-Paul 1905-1980 . **CLC 1, 4, 7, 9, 13, 18, 24, 44, 50, 52; DC 3; SSC 32; WLC 5**
See also AAYA 62; CA 9-12R; CAAS 97-100; CANR 21; DA; DA3; DAB; DAC; DAM DRAM, MST, NOV; DFS 5; DLB 72, 296, 321, 332; EW 12; EWL 3; GFL 1789 to the Present; LMFS 2; MTCW 1, 2; MTFW 2005; NFS 21; RGHL; RGSF 2; RGWL 2, 3; SSFS 9; TWA

Sassoon, Siegfried (Lorraine)
1886-1967 .... **CLC 36, 130; PC 12**
See also BRW 6; CA 104; CAAS 25-28R; CANR 36; DAB; DAM MST, NOV, POET; DLB 20, 191; DLBD 18; EWL 3; MTCW 1, 2; MTFW 2005; PAB; RGEL 2; TEA

Satterfield, Charles
See Pohl, Frederik

Satyremont
See Peret, Benjamin

Saul, John (W. III) 1942- .... **CLC 46**
See also AAYA 10, 62; BEST 90:4; CA 81-84; CANR 16, 40, 81; CPW; DAM NOV, POP; HGG; SATA 98

Saunders, Caleb
See Heinlein, Robert A.

Saura (Atares), Carlos 1932-1998 .... **CLC 20**
See also CA 131; CAAE 114; CANR 79; HW 1

Sauser, Frederic Louis
See Sauser-Hall, Frederic

Sauser-Hall, Frederic 1887-1961 ...... **CLC 18**
See Cendrars, Blaise
See also CA 102; CAAS 93-96; CANR 36, 62; MTCW 1

Saussure, Ferdinand de
1857-1913 .... **TCLC 49**
See also DLB 242

Savage, Catharine
See Brosman, Catharine Savage

Savage, Richard 1697(?)-1743 .... **LC 96**
See also DLB 95; RGEL 2

Savage, Thomas 1915-2003 .... **CLC 40**
See also CA 132; 15; CAAE 126; CAAS 218; CN 6, 7; INT CA-132; SATA-Obit 147; TCWW 2

Savan, Glenn 1953-2003 .... **CLC 50**
See also CA 225

Sax, Robert
See Johnson, Robert

Saxo Grammaticus c. 1150-c. 1222 .... **CMLC 58**

Saxton, Robert
See Johnson, Robert

Sayers, Dorothy L(eigh) 1893-1957 . **SSC 71; TCLC 2, 15**
See also BPFB 3; BRWS 3; CA 119; CAAE 104; CANR 60; CDBLB 1914-1945; CMW 4; DAM POP; DLB 10, 36, 77, 100; MSW; MTCW 1, 2; MTFW 2005; RGEL 2; SSFS 12; TEA

Seabrook, John
See Hubbard, L. Ron
Seacole, Mary Jane Grant
1805-1881 .... NCLC 147
See also DLB 166
Sealy, I(rwin) Allan 1951- .... CLC 55
See also CA 136; CN 6, 7
Search, Alexander
See Pessoa, Fernando (Antonio Nogueira)
Sebald, W(infried) G(eorg)
1944-2001 .... CLC 194
See also BRWS 8; CA 159; CAAS 202;
CANR 98; MTFW 2005; RGHL
Sebastian, Lee
See Silverberg, Robert
Sebastian Owl
See Thompson, Hunter S.
Sebestyen, Igen
See Sebestyen, Ouida
Sebestyen, Ouida 1924- .... CLC 30
See also AAYA 8; BYA 7; CA 107; CANR
40, 114; CLR 17; JRDA; MAICYA 1, 2;
SAAS 10; SATA 39, 140; WYA; YAW
Sebold, Alice 1963(?)- .... CLC 193
See also AAYA 56; CA 203; MTFW 2005
Second Duke of Buckingham
See Villiers, George
Secundus, H. Scriblerus
See Fielding, Henry
Sedges, John
See Buck, Pearl S(ydenstricker)
Sedgwick, Catharine Maria
1789-1867 .... NCLC 19, 98
See also DLB 1, 74, 183, 239, 243, 254; FL
1:3; RGAL 4
Sedulius Scottus 9th cent. -c. 874 .. CMLC 86
Seelye, John (Douglas) 1931- .... CLC 7
See also CA 97-100; CANR 70; INT CA-
97-100; TCWW 1, 2
Seferiades, Giorgos Stylianou 1900-1971
See Seferis, George
See also CA 5-8R; CAAS 33-36R; CANR
5, 36; MTCW 1
Seferis, George CLC 5, 11; PC 66
See Seferiades, Giorgos Stylianou
See also DLB 332; EW 12; EWL 3; RGWL
2, 3
Segal, Erich (Wolf) 1937- .... CLC 3, 10
See also BEST 89:1; BPFB 3; CA 25-28R;
CANR 20, 36, 65, 113; CPW; DAM POP;
DLBY 1986; INT CANR-20; MTCW 1
Seger, Bob 1945- .... CLC 35
Seghers, Anna CLC 7
See Radvanyi, Netty
See also CDWLB 2; DLB 69; EWL 3
Seidel, Frederick (Lewis) 1936- .... CLC 18
See also CA 13-16R; CANR 8, 99; CP 1, 2,
3, 4, 5, 6, 7; DLBY 1984
Seifert, Jaroslav 1901-1986 . CLC 34, 44, 93;
PC 47
See also CA 127; CDWLB 4; DLB 215,
332; EWL 3; MTCW 1, 2
Sei Shonagon c. 966-1017(?) ..... CMLC 6, 89
Sejour, Victor 1817-1874 .... DC 10
See also DLB 50
Sejour Marcou et Ferrand, Juan Victor
See Sejour, Victor
Selby, Hubert, Jr. 1928-2004 ..... CLC 1, 2, 4,
8; SSC 20
See also CA 13-16R; CAAS 226; CANR
33, 85; CN 1, 2, 3, 4, 5, 6, 7; DLB 2, 227;
MAL 5
Selzer, Richard 1928- .... CLC 74
See also CA 65-68; CANR 14, 106
Sembene, Ousmane
See Ousmane, Sembene
See also AFW; EWL 3; WLIT 2

Senancour, Etienne Pivert de
1770-1846 .... NCLC 16
See also DLB 119; GFL 1789 to the Present
Sender, Ramon (Jose) 1902-1982 ...... CLC 8;
HLC 2; TCLC 136
See also CA 5-8R; CAAS 105; CANR 8;
DAM MULT; DLB 322; EWL 3; HW 1;
MTCW 1; RGWL 2, 3
Seneca, Lucius Annaeus c. 4B.C.-c.
65 .... CMLC 6; DC 5
See also AW 2; CDWLB 1; DAM DRAM;
DLB 211; RGWL 2, 3; TWA; WLIT 8
Senghor, Leopold Sedar 1906-2001 ... BLC 3;
CLC 54, 130; PC 25
See also AFW; BW 2; CA 125; CAAE 116;
CAAS 203; CANR 47, 74, 134; CWW 2;
DAM MULT, POET; DNFS 2; EWL 3;
GFL 1789 to the Present; MTCW 1, 2;
MTFW 2005; TWA
Senior, Olive (Marjorie) 1941- .... SSC 78
See also BW 3; CA 154; CANR 86, 126;
CN 6; CP 6, 7; CWP; DLB 157; EWL 3;
RGSF 2
Senna, Danzy 1970- .... CLC 119
See also CA 169; CANR 130
Serling, (Edward) Rod(man)
1924-1975 .... CLC 30
See also AAYA 14; AITN 1; CA 162; CAAS
57-60; DLB 26; SFW 4
Serna, Ramon Gomez de la
See Gomez de la Serna, Ramon
Serpieres
See Guillevic, (Eugene)
Service, Robert
See Service, Robert W(illiam)
See also BYA 4; DAB; DLB 92
Service, Robert W(illiam)
1874(?)-1958 ... PC 70; TCLC 15; WLC
5
See Service, Robert
See also CA 140; CAAE 115; CANR 84;
DA; DAC; DAM MST, POET; PFS 10;
RGEL 2; SATA 20
Seth, Vikram 1952- .... CLC 43, 90
See also BRWS 10; CA 127; CAAE 121;
CANR 50, 74, 131; CN 6, 7; CP 5, 6, 7;
DA3; DAM MULT; DLB 120, 271, 282,
323; EWL 3; INT CA-127; MTCW 2;
MTFW 2005; WWE 1
Seton, Cynthia Propper 1926-1982 .. CLC 27
See also CA 5-8R; CAAS 108; CANR 7
Seton, Ernest (Evan) Thompson
1860-1946 .... TCLC 31
See also ANW; BYA 3; CA 204; CAAE
109; CLR 59; DLB 92; DLBD 13; JRDA;
SATA 18
Seton-Thompson, Ernest
See Seton, Ernest (Evan) Thompson
Settle, Mary Lee 1918-2005 .... CLC 19, 61
See also BPFB 3; CA 89-92; 1; CAAS 243;
CANR 44, 87, 126; CN 6, 7; CSW; DLB
6; INT CA-89-92
Seuphor, Michel
See Arp, Jean
Sevigne, Marie (de Rabutin-Chantal)
1626-1696 .... LC 11
See Sevigne, Marie de Rabutin Chantal
See also GFL Beginnings to 1789; TWA
Sevigne, Marie de Rabutin Chantal
See Sevigne, Marie (de Rabutin-Chantal)
See also DLB 268
Sewall, Samuel 1652-1730 .... LC 38
See also DLB 24; RGAL 4
Sexton, Anne (Harvey) 1928-1974 ..... CLC 2,
4, 6, 8, 10, 15, 53, 123; PC 2; WLC 5
See also AMWS 2; CA 1-4R; CAAS 53-56;
CABS 2; CANR 3, 36; CDALB 1941-
1968; CP 1, 2; DA; DA3; DAB; DAC;
DAM MST, POET; DLB 5, 169; EWL 3;

EXPP; FL 1:6; FW; MAL 5; MBL;
MTCW 1, 2; MTFW 2005; PAB; PFS 4,
14; RGAL 4; RGHL; SATA 10; TUS
Shaara, Jeff 1952- .... CLC 119
See also AAYA 70; CA 163; CANR 109;
CN 7; MTFW 2005
Shaara, Michael 1929-1988 .... CLC 15
See also AAYA 71; AITN 1; BPFB 3; CA
102; CAAS 125; CANR 52, 85; DAM
POP; DLBY 1983; MTFW 2005
Shackleton, C. C.
See Aldiss, Brian W.
Shacochis, Bob CLC 39
See Shacochis, Robert G.
Shacochis, Robert G. 1951-
See Shacochis, Bob
See also CA 124; CAAE 119; CANR 100;
INT CA-124
Shadwell, Thomas 1641(?)-1692 .... LC 114
See also DLB 80; IDTP; RGEL 2
Shaffer, Anthony 1926-2001 .... CLC 19
See also CA 116; CAAE 110; CAAS 200;
CBD; CD 5, 6; DAM DRAM; DFS 13;
DLB 13
Shaffer, Anthony Joshua
See Shaffer, Anthony
Shaffer, Peter 1926- ... CLC 5, 14, 18, 37, 60;
DC 7
See also BRWS 1; CA 25-28R; CANR 25,
47, 74, 118; CBD; CD 5, 6; CDBLB 1960
to Present; DA3; DAB; DAM DRAM,
MST; DFS 5, 13; DLB 13, 233; EWL 3;
MTCW 1, 2; MTFW 2005; RGEL 2; TEA
Shakespeare, William 1564-1616 .... WLC 5
See also AAYA 35; BRW 1; CDBLB Be-
fore 1660; DA; DA3; DAB; DAC; DAM
DRAM, MST, POET; DFS 20, 21; DLB
62, 172, 263; EXPP; LAIT 1; LATS 1:1;
LMFS 1; PAB; PFS 1, 2, 3, 4, 5, 8, 9;
RGEL 2; TEA; WLIT 3; WP; WS; WYA
Shakey, Bernard
See Young, Neil
Shalamov, Varlam (Tikhonovich)
1907-1982 .... CLC 18
See also CA 129; CAAS 105; DLB 302;
RGSF 2
Shamloo, Ahmad
See Shamlu, Ahmad
Shamlou, Ahmad
See Shamlu, Ahmad
Shamlu, Ahmad 1925-2000 .... CLC 10
See also CA 216; CWW 2
Shammas, Anton 1951- .... CLC 55
See also CA 199
Shandling, Arline
See Berriault, Gina
Shange, Ntozake 1948- ... BLC 3; CLC 8, 25,
38, 74, 126; DC 3
See also AAYA 9, 66; AFAW 1, 2; BW 2;
CA 85-88; CABS 3; CAD; CANR 27, 48,
74, 131; CD 5, 6; CP 5, 6, 7; CWD; CWP;
DA3; DAM DRAM, MULT; DFS 2, 11;
DLB 38, 249; FW; LAIT 4, 5; MAL 5;
MTCW 1, 2; MTFW 2005; NFS 11;
RGAL 4; SATA 157; YAW
Shanley, John Patrick 1950- .... CLC 75
See also AAYA 74; AMWS 14; CA 133;
CAAE 128; CAD; CANR 83, 154; CD 5,
6; DFS 23
Shapcott, Thomas W(illiam) 1935- .. CLC 38
See also CA 69-72; CANR 49, 83, 103; CP
1, 2, 3, 4, 5, 6, 7; DLB 289
Shapiro, Jane 1942- .... CLC 76
See also CA 196
Shapiro, Karl 1913-2000 ... CLC 4, 8, 15, 53;
PC 25
See also AMWS 2; CA 1-4R; 6; CAAS 188;
CANR 1, 36, 66; CP 1, 2, 3, 4, 5, 6; DLB
48; EWL 3; EXPP; MAL 5; MTCW 1, 2;
MTFW 2005; PFS 3; RGAL 4

Sharp, William 1855-1905 .... **TCLC 39**
See Macleod, Fiona
See also CA 160; DLB 156; RGEL 2

Sharpe, Thomas Ridley 1928-
See Sharpe, Tom
See also CA 122; CAAE 114; CANR 85;
INT CA-122

Sharpe, Tom **CLC 36**
See Sharpe, Thomas Ridley
See also CN 4, 5, 6, 7; DLB 14, 231

Shatrov, Mikhail **CLC 59**

Shaw, Bernard
See Shaw, George Bernard
See also DLB 10, 57, 190

Shaw, G. Bernard
See Shaw, George Bernard

Shaw, George Bernard 1856-1950 ..... **DC 23;**
TCLC 3, 9, 21, 45; WLC 5
See Shaw, Bernard
See also AAYA 61; BRW 6; BRWC 1;
BRWR 2; CA 128; CAAE 104; CDBLB
1914-1945; DA; DA3; DAB; DAC; DAM
DRAM, MST; DFS 1, 3, 6, 11, 19, 22;
DLB 332; EWL 3; LAIT 3; LATS 1:1;
MTCW 1, 2; MTFW 2005; RGEL 2;
TEA; WLIT 4

Shaw, Henry Wheeler 1818-1885 .. **NCLC 15**
See also DLB 11; RGAL 4

Shaw, Irwin 1913-1984 .... **CLC 7, 23, 34**
See also AITN 1; BPFB 3; CA 13-16R;
CAAS 112; CANR 21; CDALB 1941-
1968; CN 1, 2, 3; CPW; DAM DRAM,
POP; DLB 6, 102; DLBY 1984; MAL 5;
MTCW 1, 21; MTFW 2005

Shaw, Robert (Archibald)
1927-1978 .... **CLC 5**
See also AITN 1; CA 1-4R; CAAS 81-84;
CANR 4; CN 1, 2; DLB 13, 14

Shaw, T. E.
See Lawrence, T(homas) E(dward)

Shawn, Wallace 1943- .... **CLC 41**
See also CA 112; CAD; CD 5, 6; DLB 266

Shaykh, al- Hanan
See al-Shaykh, Hanan
See also CWW 2; EWL 3

Shchedrin, N.
See Saltykov, Mikhail Evgrafovich

Shea, Lisa 1953- .... **CLC 86**
See also CA 147

Sheed, Wilfrid (John Joseph) 1930- . **CLC 2,**
4, 10, 53
See also CA 65-68; CANR 30, 66; CN 1,
3, 4, 5, 6, 7; DLB 6; MAL 5; MTCW 1,
2; MTFW 2005

Sheehy, Gail 1937- .... **CLC 171**
See also CA 49-52; CANR 1, 33, 55, 92;
CPW; MTCW 1

Sheldon, Alice Hastings Bradley
1915(?)-1987
See Tiptree, James, Jr.
See also CA 108; CAAS 122; CANR 34;
INT CA-108; MTCW 1

Sheldon, John
See Bloch, Robert (Albert)

Sheldon, Walter J(ames) 1917-1996
See Queen, Ellery
See also AITN 1; CA 25-28R; CANR 10

Shelley, Mary Wollstonecraft (Godwin)
1797-1851 .... **NCLC 14, 59, 103, 170;**
SSC 92; WLC 5
See also AAYA 20; BPFB 3; BRW 3;
BRWC 2; BRWS 3; BYA 5; CDBLB
1789-1832; DA; DA3; DAB; DAC; DAM
MST, NOV; DLB 110, 116, 159, 178;
EXPN; FL 1:3; GL 3; HGG; LAIT 1;
LMFS 1, 2; NFS 1; RGEL 2; SATA 29;
SCFW 1, 2; SFW 4; TEA; WLIT 3

Shelley, Percy Bysshe 1792-1822 .. **NCLC 18,**
93, 143, 175; PC 14, 67; WLC 5
See also AAYA 61; BRW 4; BRWR 1; CD-
BLB 1789-1832; DA; DA3; DAB; DAC;
DAM MST, POET; DLB 96, 110, 158;
EXPP; LMFS 1; PAB; PFS 2; RGEL 2;
TEA; WLIT 3; WP

Shepard, James R.
See Shepard, Jim

Shepard, Jim 1956- .... **CLC 36**
See also AAYA 73; CA 137; CANR 59, 104,
160; SATA 90, 164

Shepard, Lucius 1947- .... **CLC 34**
See also CA 141; CAAE 128; CANR 81,
124; HGG; SCFW 2; SFW 4; SUFW 2

Shepard, Sam 1943- .... **CLC 4, 6, 17, 34, 41,**
44, 169; DC 5
See also AAYA 1, 58; AMWS 3; CA 69-72;
CABS 3; CAD; CANR 22, 120, 140; CD
5, 6; DA3; DAM DRAM; DFS 3, 6, 7,
14; DLB 7, 212; EWL 3; IDFW 3, 4;
MAL 5; MTCW 1, 2; MTFW 2005;
RGAL 4

Shepherd, Jean (Parker)
1921-1999 .... **TCLC 177**
See also AAYA 69; AITN 2; CA 77-80;
CAAS 187

Shepherd, Michael
See Ludlum, Robert

Sherburne, Zoa (Lillian Morin)
1912-1995 .... **CLC 30**
See also AAYA 13; CA 1-4R; CAAS 176;
CANR 3, 37; MAICYA 1, 2; SAAS 18;
SATA 3; YAW

Sheridan, Frances 1724-1766 .... **LC 7**
See also DLB 39, 84

Sheridan, Richard Brinsley
1751-1816 . **DC 1; NCLC 5, 91; WLC 5**
See also BRW 3; CDBLB 1660-1789; DA;
DAB; DAC; DAM DRAM, MST; DFS
15; DLB 89; WLIT 3

Sherman, Jonathan Marc 1968- .... **CLC 55**
See also CA 230

Sherman, Martin 1941(?)- .... **CLC 19**
See also CA 123; CAAE 116; CAD; CANR
86; CD 5, 6; DFS 20; DLB 228; GLL 1;
IDTP; RGHL

Sherwin, Judith Johnson
See Johnson, Judith (Emlyn)
See also CANR 85; CP 2, 3, 4, 5; CWP

Sherwood, Frances 1940- .... **CLC 81**
See also CA 220; 146, 220; CANR 158

Sherwood, Robert E(mmet)
1896-1955 .... **TCLC 3**
See also CA 153; CAAE 104; CANR 86;
DAM DRAM; DFS 11, 15, 17; DLB 7,
26, 249; IDFW 3, 4; MAL 5; RGAL 4

Shestov, Lev 1866-1938 .... **TCLC 56**

Shevchenko, Taras 1814-1861 .... **NCLC 54**

Shiel, M(atthew) P(hipps)
1865-1947 .... **TCLC 8**
See Holmes, Gordon
See also CA 160; CAAE 106; DLB 153;
HGG; MTCW 2; MTFW 2005; SCFW 1,
2; SFW 4; SUFW

Shields, Carol 1935-2003 .. **CLC 91, 113, 193**
See also AMWS 7; CA 81-84; CAAS 218;
CANR 51, 74, 98, 133; CCA 1; CN 6, 7;
CPW; DA3; DAC; MTCW 2; MTFW
2005; NFS 23

Shields, David 1956- .... **CLC 97**
See also CA 124; CANR 48, 99, 112, 157

Shields, David Jonathan
See Shields, David

Shiga, Naoya 1883-1971 .... **CLC 33; SSC 23;**
TCLC 172
See Shiga Naoya
See also CA 101; CAAS 33-36R; MJW;
RGWL 3

Shiga Naoya
See Shiga, Naoya
See also DLB 180; EWL 3; RGWL 3

Shilts, Randy 1951-1994 .... **CLC 85**
See also AAYA 19; CA 127; CAAE 115;
CAAS 144; CANR 45; DA3; GLL 1; INT
CA-127; MTCW 2; MTFW 2005

Shimazaki, Haruki 1872-1943
See Shimazaki Toson
See also CA 134; CAAE 105; CANR 84;
RGWL 3

Shimazaki Toson **TCLC 5**
See Shimazaki, Haruki
See also DLB 180; EWL 3

Shirley, James 1596-1666 .... **DC 25; LC 96**
See also DLB 58; RGEL 2

Sholokhov, Mikhail (Aleksandrovich)
1905-1984 .... **CLC 7, 15**
See also CA 101; CAAS 112; DLB 272,
332; EWL 3; MTCW 1, 2; MTFW 2005;
RGWL 2, 3; SATA-Obit 36

Sholom Aleichem 1859-1916 .... **SSC 33;**
TCLC 1, 35
See Rabinovitch, Sholem
See also DLB 333; TWA

Shone, Patric
See Hanley, James

Showalter, Elaine 1941- .... **CLC 169**
See also CA 57-60; CANR 58, 106; DLB
67; FW; GLL 2

Shreve, Susan
See Shreve, Susan Richards

Shreve, Susan Richards 1939- .... **CLC 23**
See also CA 49-52; 5; CANR 5, 38, 69, 100,
159; MAICYA 1, 2; SATA 46, 95, 152;
SATA-Brief 41

Shue, Larry 1946-1985 .... **CLC 52**
See also CA 145; CAAS 117; DAM DRAM;
DFS 7

Shu-Jen, Chou 1881-1936
See Lu Hsun
See also CAAE 104

Shulman, Alix Kates 1932- .... **CLC 2, 10**
See also CA 29-32R; CANR 43; FW; SATA
7

Shuster, Joe 1914-1992 .... **CLC 21**
See also AAYA 50

Shute, Nevil **CLC 30**
See Norway, Nevil Shute
See also BPFB 3; DLB 255; NFS 9; RHW;
SFW 4

Shuttle, Penelope (Diane) 1947- .... **CLC 7**
See also CA 93-96; CANR 39, 84, 92, 108;
CP 3, 4, 5, 6, 7; CWP; DLB 14, 40

Shvarts, Elena 1948- .... **PC 50**
See also CA 147

Sidhwa, Bapsi 1939-
See Sidhwa, Bapsy (N.)
See also CN 6, 7; DLB 323

Sidhwa, Bapsy (N.) 1938- .... **CLC 168**
See Sidhwa, Bapsi
See also CA 108; CANR 25, 57; FW

Sidney, Mary 1561-1621 .... **LC 19, 39**
See Sidney Herbert, Mary

Sidney, Sir Philip 1554-1586 .... **LC 19, 39,**
131; PC 32
See also BRW 1; BRWR 2; CDBLB Before
1660; DA; DA3; DAB; DAC; DAM MST,
POET; DLB 167; EXPP; PAB; RGEL 2;
TEA; WP

Sidney Herbert, Mary
See Sidney, Mary
See also DLB 167

Siegel, Jerome 1914-1996 .... **CLC 21**
See Siegel, Jerry
See also CA 169; CAAE 116; CAAS 151

Siegel, Jerry
See Siegel, Jerome
See also AAYA 50

Sienkiewicz, Henryk (Adam Alexander Pius)
1846-1916 .... **TCLC 3**
See also CA 134; CAAE 104; CANR 84;
DLB 332; EWL 3; RGSF 2; RGWL 2, 3

Sierra, Gregorio Martinez
See Martinez Sierra, Gregorio

Sierra, Maria de la O'LeJarraga Martinez
See Martinez Sierra, Maria

Sigal, Clancy 1926- .... **CLC 7**
See also CA 1-4R; CANR 85; CN 1, 2, 3,
4, 5, 6, 7

Siger of Brabant 1240(?)-1284(?) . **CMLC 69**
See also DLB 115

Sigourney, Lydia H.
See Sigourney, Lydia Howard (Huntley)
See also DLB 73, 183

Sigourney, Lydia Howard (Huntley)
1791-1865 .... **NCLC 21, 87**
See Sigourney, Lydia H.; Sigourney, Lydia
Huntley
See also DLB 1

Sigourney, Lydia Huntley
See Sigourney, Lydia Howard (Huntley)
See also DLB 42, 239, 243

Siguenza y Gongora, Carlos de
1645-1700 .... **HLCS 2; LC 8**
See also LAW

Sigurjonsson, Johann
See Sigurjonsson, Johann

Sigurjonsson, Johann 1880-1919 ... **TCLC 27**
See also CA 170; DLB 293; EWL 3

Sikelianos, Angelos 1884-1951 .... **PC 29;
TCLC 39**
See also EWL 3; RGWL 2, 3

Silkin, Jon 1930-1997 .... **CLC 2, 6, 43**
See also CA 5-8R; 5; CANR 89; CP 1, 2, 3,
4, 5, 6; DLB 27

Silko, Leslie 1948- ...... **CLC 23, 74, 114, 211;
NNAL; SSC 37, 66; WLCS**
See also AAYA 14; AMWS 4; ANW; BYA
12; CA 122; CAAE 115; CANR 45, 65,
118; CN 4, 5, 6, 7; CP 4, 5, 6, 7; CPW 1;
CWP; DA; DA3; DAC; DAM MST,
MULT, POP; DLB 143, 175, 256, 275;
EWL 3; EXPP; EXPS; LAIT 4; MAL 5;
MTCW 2; MTFW 2005; NFS 4; PFS 9,
16; RGAL 4; RGSF 2; SSFS 4, 8, 10, 11;
TCWW 1, 2

Sillanpaa, Frans Eemil 1888-1964 ... **CLC 19**
See also CA 129; CAAS 93-96; DLB 332;
EWL 3; MTCW 1

Sillitoe, Alan 1928- .. **CLC 1, 3, 6, 10, 19, 57,
148**
See also AITN 1; BRWS 5; CA 191; 9-12R,
191; 2; CANR 8, 26, 55, 139; CDBLB
1960 to Present; CN 1, 2, 3, 4, 5, 6; CP 1,
2, 3, 4, 5; DLB 14, 139; EWL 3; MTCW
1, 2; MTFW 2005; RGEL 2; RGSF 2;
SATA 61

Silone, Ignazio 1900-1978 .... **CLC 4**
See also CA 25-28; CAAS 81-84; CANR
34; CAP 2; DLB 264; EW 12; EWL 3;
MTCW 1; RGSF 2; RGWL 2, 3

Silone, Ignazione
See Silone, Ignazio

Silver, Joan Micklin 1935- .... **CLC 20**
See also CA 121; CAAE 114; INT CA-121

Silver, Nicholas
See Faust, Frederick (Schiller)

Silverberg, Robert 1935- .... **CLC 7, 140**
See also AAYA 24; BPFB 3; BYA 7, 9; CA
186; 1-4R, 186; 3; CANR 1, 20, 36, 85,
140; CLR 59; CN 6, 7; CPW; DAM POP;
DLB 8; INT CANR-20; MAICYA 1, 2;
MTCW 1, 2; MTFW 2005; SATA 13, 91;
SATA-Essay 104; SCFW 1, 2; SFW 4;
SUFW 2

Silverstein, Alvin 1933- .... **CLC 17**
See also CA 49-52; CANR 2; CLR 25;
JRDA; MAICYA 1, 2; SATA 8, 69, 124

Silverstein, Shel 1932-1999 .... **PC 49**
See also AAYA 40; BW 3; CA 107; CAAS
179; CANR 47, 74, 81; CLR 5, 96; CWRI
5; JRDA; MAICYA 1, 2; MTCW 2;
MTFW 2005; SATA 33, 92; SATA-Brief
27; SATA-Obit 116

Silverstein, Virginia B(arbara Opshelor)
1937- .... **CLC 17**
See also CA 49-52; CANR 2; CLR 25;
JRDA; MAICYA 1, 2; SATA 8, 69, 124

Sim, Georges
See Simenon, Georges (Jacques Christian)

Simak, Clifford D(onald) 1904-1988 . **CLC 1,
55**
See also CA 1-4R; CAAS 125; CANR 1,
35; DLB 8; MTCW 1; SATA-Obit 56;
SCFW 1, 2; SFW 4

Simenon, Georges (Jacques Christian)
1903-1989 .... **CLC 1, 2, 3, 8, 18, 47**
See also BPFB 3; CA 85-88; CAAS 129;
CANR 35; CMW 4; DA3; DAM POP;
DLB 72; DLBY 1989; EW 12; EWL 3;
GFL 1789 to the Present; MSW; MTCW
1, 2; MTFW 2005; RGWL 2, 3

Simic, Charles 1938- .... **CLC 6, 9, 22, 49, 68,
130; PC 69**
See also AMWS 8; CA 29-32R; 4; CANR
12, 33, 52, 61, 96, 140; CP 2, 3, 4, 5, 6,
7; DA3; DAM POET; DLB 105; MAL 5;
MTCW 2; MTFW 2005; PFS 7; RGAL 4;
WP

Simmel, Georg 1858-1918 .... **TCLC 64**
See also CA 157; DLB 296

Simmons, Charles (Paul) 1924- .... **CLC 57**
See also CA 89-92; INT CA-89-92

Simmons, Dan 1948- .... **CLC 44**
See also AAYA 16, 54; CA 138; CANR 53,
81, 126; CPW; DAM POP; HGG; SUFW
2

Simmons, James (Stewart Alexander)
1933- .... **CLC 43**
See also CA 105; 21; CP 1, 2, 3, 4, 5, 6, 7;
DLB 40

Simms, William Gilmore
1806-1870 .... **NCLC 3**
See also DLB 3, 30, 59, 73, 248, 254;
RGAL 4

Simon, Carly 1945- .... **CLC 26**
See also CA 105

Simon, Claude 1913-2005 ... **CLC 4, 9, 15, 39**
See also CA 89-92; CAAS 241; CANR 33,
117; CWW 2; DAM NOV; DLB 83, 332;
EW 13; EWL 3; GFL 1789 to the Present;
MTCW 1

Simon, Claude Eugene Henri
See Simon, Claude

Simon, Claude Henri Eugene
See Simon, Claude

Simon, Marvin Neil
See Simon, Neil

Simon, Myles
See Follett, Ken

Simon, Neil 1927- .... **CLC 6, 11, 31, 39, 70,
233; DC 14**
See also AAYA 32; AITN 1; AMWS 4; CA
21-24R; CAD; CANR 26, 54, 87, 126;
CD 5, 6; DA3; DAM DRAM; DFS 2, 6,
12, 18; DLB 7, 266; LAIT 4; MAL 5;
MTCW 1, 2; MTFW 2005; RGAL 4; TUS

Simon, Paul 1941(?)- .... **CLC 17**
See also CA 153; CAAE 116; CANR 152

Simon, Paul Frederick
See Simon, Paul

Simonon, Paul 1956(?)- .... **CLC 30**

Simonson, Rick CLC 70

Simpson, Harriette
See Arnow, Harriette (Louisa) Simpson

Simpson, Louis 1923- ... **CLC 4, 7, 9, 32, 149**
See also AMWS 9; CA 1-4R; 4; CANR 1,
61, 140; CP 1, 2, 3, 4, 5, 6, 7; DAM
POET; DLB 5; MAL 5; MTCW 1, 2;
MTFW 2005; PFS 7, 11, 14; RGAL 4

Simpson, Mona 1957- .... **CLC 44, 146**
See also CA 135; CAAE 122; CANR 68,
103; CN 6, 7; EWL 3

Simpson, Mona Elizabeth
See Simpson, Mona

Simpson, N(orman) F(rederick)
1919- .... **CLC 29**
See also CA 13-16R; CBD; DLB 13; RGEL
2

Sinclair, Andrew (Annandale) 1935- . **CLC 2,
14**
See also CA 9-12R; 5; CANR 14, 38, 91;
CN 1, 2, 3, 4, 5, 6, 7; DLB 14; FANT;
MTCW 1

Sinclair, Emil
See Hesse, Hermann

Sinclair, Iain 1943- .... **CLC 76**
See also CA 132; CANR 81, 157; CP 5, 6,
7; HGG

Sinclair, Iain MacGregor
See Sinclair, Iain

Sinclair, Irene
See Griffith, D(avid Lewelyn) W(ark)

Sinclair, Julian
See Sinclair, May

Sinclair, Mary Amelia St. Clair (?)-
See Sinclair, May

Sinclair, May 1865-1946 .... **TCLC 3, 11**
See also CA 166; CAAE 104; DLB 36, 135;
EWL 3; HGG; RGEL 2; RHW; SUFW

Sinclair, Roy
See Griffith, D(avid Lewelyn) W(ark)

Sinclair, Upton 1878-1968 ...... **CLC 1, 11, 15,
63; TCLC 160; WLC 5**
See also AAYA 63; AMWS 5; BPFB 3;
BYA 2; CA 5-8R; CAAS 25-28R; CANR
7; CDALB 1929-1941; DA; DA3; DAB;
DAC; DAM MST, NOV; DLB 9; EWL 3;
INT CANR-7; LAIT 3; MAL 5; MTCW
1, 2; MTFW 2005; NFS 6; RGAL 4;
SATA 9; TUS; YAW

Sinclair, Upton Beall
See Sinclair, Upton

Singe, (Edmund) J(ohn) M(illington)
1871-1909 .... **WLC**

Singer, Isaac
See Singer, Isaac Bashevis

Singer, Isaac Bashevis 1904-1991 .. **CLC 1, 3,
6, 9, 11, 15, 23, 38, 69, 111; SSC 3, 53,
80; WLC 5**
See also AAYA 32; AITN 1, 2; AMW;
AMWR 2; BPFB 3; BYA 1, 4; CA 1-4R;
CAAS 134; CANR 1, 39, 106; CDALB
1941-1968; CLR 1; CN 1, 2, 3, 4; CWRI
5; DA; DA3; DAB; DAC; DAM MST,
NOV; DLB 6, 28, 52, 278, 332, 333;
DLBY 1991; EWL 3; EXPS; HGG;
JRDA; LAIT 3; MAICYA 1, 2; MAL 5;
MTCW 1, 2; MTFW 2005; RGAL 4;
RGHL; RGSF 2; SATA 3, 27; SATA-Obit
68; SSFS 2, 12, 16; TUS; TWA

Singer, Israel Joshua 1893-1944 .... **TCLC 33**
See Zinger, Yisroel-Yehoyshue
See also CA 169; DLB 333; EWL 3

Singh, Khushwant 1915- .... **CLC 11**
See also CA 9-12R; 9; CANR 6, 84; CN 1,
2, 3, 4, 5, 6, 7; DLB 323; EWL 3; RGEL
2

Singleton, Ann
See Benedict, Ruth

Tanizaki Jun'ichiro
  See Tanizaki, Jun'ichiro
  See also DLB 180; EWL 3
Tannen, Deborah 1945- .... **CLC 206**
  See also CA 118; CANR 95
Tannen, Deborah Frances
  See Tannen, Deborah
Tanner, William
  See Amis, Kingsley
Tante, Dilly
  See Kunitz, Stanley
Tao Lao
  See Storni, Alfonsina
Tapahonso, Luci 1953- .... **NNAL; PC 65**
  See also CA 145; CANR 72, 127; DLB 175
Tarantino, Quentin (Jerome)
  1963- .... **CLC 125, 230**
  See also AAYA 58; CA 171; CANR 125
Tarassoff, Lev
  See Troyat, Henri
Tarbell, Ida M(inerva) 1857-1944 . **TCLC 40**
  See also CA 181; CAAE 122; DLB 47
Tarkington, (Newton) Booth
  1869-1946 .... **TCLC 9**
  See also BPFB 3; BYA 3; CA 143; CAAE
  110; CWRI 5; DLB 9, 102; MAL 5;
  MTCW 2; RGAL 4; SATA 17
Tarkovskii, Andrei Arsen'evich
  See Tarkovsky, Andrei (Arsenyevich)
Tarkovsky, Andrei (Arsenyevich)
  1932-1986 .... **CLC 75**
  See also CA 127
Tartt, Donna 1964(?)- .... **CLC 76**
  See also AAYA 56; CA 142; CANR 135;
  MTFW 2005
Tasso, Torquato 1544-1595 .... **LC 5, 94**
  See also EFS 2; EW 2; RGWL 2, 3; WLIT
  7
Tate, (John Orley) Allen 1899-1979 .. **CLC 2,**
  4, 6, 9, 11, 14, 24; PC 50
  See also AMW; CA 5-8R; CAAS 85-88;
  CANR 32, 108; CN 1, 2; CP 1, 2; DLB 4,
  45, 63; DLBD 17; EWL 3; MAL 5;
  MTCW 1, 2; MTFW 2005; RGAL 4;
  RHW
Tate, Ellalice
  See Hibbert, Eleanor Alice Burford
Tate, James (Vincent) 1943- ..... **CLC 2, 6, 25**
  See also CA 21-24R; CANR 29, 57, 114;
  CP 1, 2, 3, 4, 5, 6, 7; DLB 5, 169; EWL
  3; PFS 10, 15; RGAL 4; WP
Tate, Nahum 1652(?)-1715 .... **LC 109**
  See also DLB 80; RGEL 2
Tauler, Johannes c. 1300-1361 ...... **CMLC 37**
  See also DLB 179; LMFS 1
Tavel, Ronald 1940- .... **CLC 6**
  See also CA 21-24R; CAD; CANR 33; CD
  5, 6
Taviani, Paolo 1931- .... **CLC 70**
  See also CA 153
Taylor, Bayard 1825-1878 .... **NCLC 89**
  See also DLB 3, 189, 250, 254; RGAL 4
Taylor, C(ecil) P(hilip) 1929-1981 .... **CLC 27**
  See also CA 25-28R; CAAS 105; CANR
  47; CBD
Taylor, Edward 1642(?)-1729 . **LC 11; PC 63**
  See also AMW; DA; DAB; DAC; DAM
  MST, POET; DLB 24; EXPP; RGAL 4;
  TUS
Taylor, Eleanor Ross 1920- .... **CLC 5**
  See also CA 81-84; CANR 70
Taylor, Elizabeth 1912-1975 ..... **CLC 2, 4, 29**
  See also CA 13-16R; CANR 9, 70; CN 1,
  2; DLB 139; MTCW 1; RGEL 2; SATA
  13
Taylor, Frederick Winslow
  1856-1915 .... **TCLC 76**
  See also CA 188

Taylor, Henry (Splawn) 1942- .... **CLC 44**
  See also CA 33-36R; 7; CANR 31; CP 6, 7;
  DLB 5; PFS 10
Taylor, Kamala 1924-2004
  See Markandaya, Kamala
  See also CA 77-80; CAAS 227; MTFW
  2005; NFS 13
Taylor, Mildred D. 1943- .... **CLC 21**
  See also AAYA 10, 47; BW 1; BYA 3, 8;
  CA 85-88; CANR 25, 115, 136; CLR 9,
  59, 90; CSW; DLB 52; JRDA; LAIT 3;
  MAICYA 1, 2; MTFW 2005; SAAS 5;
  SATA 135; WYA; YAW
Taylor, Peter (Hillsman) 1917-1994 .. **CLC 1,**
  4, 18, 37, 44, 50, 71; SSC 10, 84
  See also AMWS 5; BPFB 3; CA 13-16R;
  CAAS 147; CANR 9, 50; CN 1, 2, 3, 4,
  5; CSW; DLB 218, 278; DLBY 1981,
  1994; EWL 3; EXPS; INT CANR-9;
  MAL 5; MTCW 1, 2; MTFW 2005; RGSF
  2; SSFS 9; TUS
Taylor, Robert Lewis 1912-1998 .... **CLC 14**
  See also CA 1-4R; CAAS 170; CANR 3,
  64; CN 1, 2; SATA 10; TCWW 1, 2
Tchekhov, Anton
  See Chekhov, Anton (Pavlovich)
Tchicaya, Gerald Felix 1931-1988 .. **CLC 101**
  See Tchicaya U Tam'si
  See also CA 129; CAAS 125; CANR 81
Tchicaya U Tam'si
  See Tchicaya, Gerald Felix
  See also EWL 3
Teasdale, Sara 1884-1933 .... **PC 31; TCLC 4**
  See also CA 163; CAAE 104; DLB 45;
  GLL 1; PFS 14; RGAL 4; SATA 32; TUS
Tecumseh 1768-1813 .... **NNAL**
  See also DAM MULT
Tegner, Esaias 1782-1846 .... **NCLC 2**
Teilhard de Chardin, (Marie Joseph) Pierre
  1881-1955 .... **TCLC 9**
  See also CA 210; CAAE 105; GFL 1789 to
  the Present
Temple, Ann
  See Mortimer, Penelope (Ruth)
Tennant, Emma (Christina) 1937- .. **CLC 13,**
  52
  See also BRWS 9; CA 65-68; 9; CANR 10,
  38, 59, 88; CN 3, 4, 5, 6, 7; DLB 14;
  EWL 3; SFW 4
Tenneshaw, S. M.
  See Silverberg, Robert
Tenney, Tabitha Gilman
  1762-1837 .... **NCLC 122**
  See also DLB 37, 200
Tennyson, Alfred 1809-1892 ... **NCLC 30, 65,**
  115; PC 6; WLC 6
  See also AAYA 50; BRW 4; CDBLB 1832-
  1890; DA; DA3; DAB; DAC; DAM MST,
  POET; DLB 32; EXPP; PAB; PFS 1, 2, 4,
  11, 15, 19; RGEL 2; TEA; WLIT 4; WP
Teran, Lisa St. Aubin de **CLC 36**
  See St. Aubin de Teran, Lisa
Terence c. 184B.C.-c. 159B.C. ...... **CMLC 14;**
  DC 7
  See also AW 1; CDWLB 1; DLB 211;
  RGWL 2, 3; TWA; WLIT 8
Teresa de Jesus, St. 1515-1582 .... **LC 18**
Teresa of Avila, St.
  See Teresa de Jesus, St.
Terkel, Louis **CLC 38**
  See Terkel, Studs
  See also AAYA 32; AITN 1; MTCW 2; TUS
Terkel, Studs 1912-
  See Terkel, Louis
  See also CA 57-60; CANR 18, 45, 67, 132;
  DA3; MTCW 1, 2; MTFW 2005
Terry, C. V.
  See Slaughter, Frank G(ill)

Terry, Megan 1932- .... **CLC 19; DC 13**
  See also CA 77-80; CABS 3; CAD; CANR
  43; CD 5, 6; CWD; DFS 18; DLB 7, 249;
  GLL 2
Tertullian c. 155-c. 245 .... **CMLC 29**
Tertz, Abram
  See Sinyavsky, Andrei (Donatevich)
  See also RGSF 2
Tesich, Steve 1943(?)-1996 .... **CLC 40, 69**
  See also CA 105; CAAS 152; CAD; DLBY
  1983
Tesla, Nikola 1856-1943 .... **TCLC 88**
Teternikov, Fyodor Kuzmich 1863-1927
  See Sologub, Fyodor
  See also CAAE 104
Tevis, Walter 1928-1984 .... **CLC 42**
  See also CA 113; SFW 4
Tey, Josephine **TCLC 14**
  See Mackintosh, Elizabeth
  See also DLB 77; MSW
Thackeray, William Makepeace
  1811-1863 ...... **NCLC 5, 14, 22, 43, 169;**
  WLC 6
  See also BRW 5; BRWC 2; CDBLB 1832-
  1890; DA; DA3; DAB; DAC; DAM MST,
  NOV; DLB 21, 55, 159, 163; NFS 13;
  RGEL 2; SATA 23; TEA; WLIT 3
Thakura, Ravindranatha
  See Tagore, Rabindranath
Thames, C. H.
  See Marlowe, Stephen
Tharoor, Shashi 1956- .... **CLC 70**
  See also CA 141; CANR 91; CN 6, 7
Thelwall, John 1764-1834 .... **NCLC 162**
  See also DLB 93, 158
Thelwell, Michael Miles 1939- .... **CLC 22**
  See also BW 2; CA 101
Theobald, Lewis, Jr.
  See Lovecraft, H. P.
Theocritus c. 310B.C.- .... **CMLC 45**
  See also AW 1; DLB 176; RGWL 2, 3
Theodorescu, Ion N. 1880-1967
  See Arghezi, Tudor
  See also CAAS 116
Theriault, Yves 1915-1983 .... **CLC 79**
  See also CA 102; CANR 150; CCA 1;
  DAC; DAM MST; DLB 88; EWL 3
Theroux, Alexander (Louis) 1939- .... **CLC 2,**
  25
  See also CA 85-88; CANR 20, 63; CN 4, 5,
  6, 7
Theroux, Paul 1941- .... **CLC 5, 8, 11, 15, 28,**
  46, 159
  See also AAYA 28; AMWS 8; BEST 89:4;
  BPFB 3; CA 33-36R; CANR 20, 45, 74,
  133; CDALBS; CN 1, 2, 3, 4, 5, 6, 7; CP
  1; CPW 1; DA3; DAM POP; DLB 2, 218;
  EWL 3; HGG; MAL 5; MTCW 1, 2;
  MTFW 2005; RGAL 4; SATA 44, 109;
  TUS
Thesen, Sharon 1946- .... **CLC 56**
  See also CA 163; CANR 125; CP 5, 6, 7;
  CWP
Thespis fl. 6th cent. B.C.- .... **CMLC 51**
  See also LMFS 1
Thevenin, Denis
  See Duhamel, Georges
Thibault, Jacques Anatole Francois
  1844-1924
  See France, Anatole
  See also CA 127; CAAE 106; DA3; DAM
  NOV; MTCW 1, 2; TWA
Thiele, Colin 1920-2006 .... **CLC 17**
  See also CA 29-32R; CANR 12, 28, 53,
  105; CLR 27; CP 1, 2; DLB 289; MAI-
  CYA 1, 2; SAAS 2; SATA 14, 72, 125;
  YAW
Thistlethwaite, Bel
  See Wetherald, Agnes Ethelwyn

Thomas, Audrey (Callahan) 1935- .... **CLC 7, 13, 37, 107; SSC 20**
See also AITN 2; CA 237; 21-24R, 237; 19; CANR 36, 58; CN 2, 3, 4, 5, 6, 7; DLB 60; MTCW 1; RGSF 2

Thomas, Augustus 1857-1934 .... **TCLC 97**
See also MAL 5

Thomas, D.M. 1935- ..... **CLC 13, 22, 31, 132**
See also BPFB 3; BRWS 4; CA 61-64; 11; CANR 17, 45, 75; CDBLB 1960 to Present; CN 4, 5, 6, 7; CP 1, 2, 3, 4, 5, 6, 7; DA3; DLB 40, 207, 299; HGG; INT CANR-17; MTCW 1, 2; MTFW 2005; RGHL; SFW 4

Thomas, Dylan (Marlais) 1914-1953 .... **PC 2, 52; SSC 3, 44; TCLC 1, 8, 45, 105; WLC 6**
See also AAYA 45; BRWS 1; CA 120; CAAE 104; CDBLB 1945-1960; DA; DA3; DAB; DAC; DAM DRAM, MST, POET; DLB 13, 20, 139; EWL 3; EXPP; LAIT 3; MTCW 1, 2; MTFW 2005; PAB; PFS 1, 3, 8; RGEL 2; RGSF 2; SATA 60; TEA; WLIT 4; WP

Thomas, (Philip) Edward 1878-1917 . **PC 53; TCLC 10**
See also BRW 6; BRWS 3; CA 153; CAAE 106; DAM POET; DLB 19, 98, 156, 216; EWL 3; PAB; RGEL 2

Thomas, Joyce Carol 1938- .... **CLC 35**
See also AAYA 12, 54; BW 2, 3; CA 116; CAAE 113; CANR 48, 114, 135; CLR 19; DLB 33; INT CA-116; JRDA; MAICYA 1, 2; MTCW 1, 2; MTFW 2005; SAAS 7; SATA 40, 78, 123, 137; SATA-Essay 137; WYA; YAW

Thomas, Lewis 1913-1993 .... **CLC 35**
See also ANW; CA 85-88; CAAS 143; CANR 38, 60; DLB 275; MTCW 1, 2

Thomas, M. Carey 1857-1935 .... **TCLC 89**
See also FW

Thomas, Paul
See Mann, (Paul) Thomas

Thomas, Piri 1928- .... **CLC 17; HLCS 2**
See also CA 73-76; HW 1; LLW

Thomas, R(onald) S(tuart) 1913-2000 .... **CLC 6, 13, 48**
See also CA 89-92; 4; CAAS 189; CANR 30; CDBLB 1960 to Present; CP 1, 2, 3, 4, 5, 6, 7; DAB; DAM POET; DLB 27; EWL 3; MTCW 1; RGEL 2

Thomas, Ross (Elmore) 1926-1995 .. **CLC 39**
See also CA 33-36R; CAAS 150; CANR 22, 63; CMW 4

Thompson, Francis (Joseph) 1859-1907 .... **TCLC 4**
See also BRW 5; CA 189; CAAE 104; CD-BLB 1890-1914; DLB 19; RGEL 2; TEA

Thompson, Francis Clegg
See Mencken, H(enry) L(ouis)

Thompson, Hunter S. 1937(?)-2005 .. **CLC 9, 17, 40, 104, 229**
See also AAYA 45; BEST 89:1; BPFB 3; CA 17-20R; CAAS 236; CANR 23, 46, 74, 77, 111, 133; CPW; CSW; DA3; DAM POP; DLB 185; MTCW 1, 2; MTFW 2005; TUS

Thompson, James Myers
See Thompson, Jim (Myers)

Thompson, Jim (Myers) 1906-1977(?) .... **CLC 69**
See also BPFB 3; CA 140; CMW 4; CPW; DLB 226; MSW

Thompson, Judith (Clare Francesca) 1954- .... **CLC 39**
See also CA 143; CD 5, 6; CWD; DFS 22

Thomson, James 1700-1748 .... **LC 16, 29, 40**
See also BRWS 3; DAM POET; DLB 95; RGEL 2

Thomson, James 1834-1882 .... **NCLC 18**
See also DAM POET; DLB 35; RGEL 2

Thoreau, Henry David 1817-1862 .. **NCLC 7, 21, 61, 138; PC 30; WLC 6**
See also AAYA 42; AMW; ANW; BYA 3; CDALB 1640-1865; DA; DA3; DAB; DAC; DAM MST; DLB 1, 183, 223, 270, 298; LAIT 2; LMFS 1; NCFS 3; RGAL 4; TUS

Thorndike, E. L.
See Thorndike, Edward L(ee)

Thorndike, Edward L(ee) 1874-1949 .... **TCLC 107**
See also CAAE 121

Thornton, Hall
See Silverberg, Robert

Thorpe, Adam 1956- .... **CLC 176**
See also CA 129; CANR 92, 160; DLB 231

Thubron, Colin 1939- .... **CLC 163**
See also CA 25-28R; CANR 12, 29, 59, 95; CN 5, 6, 7; DLB 204, 231

Thubron, Colin Gerald Dryden
See Thubron, Colin

Thucydides c. 455B.C.-c. 395B.C. . **CMLC 17**
See also AW 1; DLB 176; RGWL 2, 3; WLIT 8

Thumboo, Edwin Nadason 1933- .... **PC 30**
See also CA 194; CP 1

Thurber, James (Grover) 1894-1961 .. **CLC 5, 11, 25, 125; SSC 1, 47**
See also AAYA 56; AMWS 1; BPFB 3; BYA 5; CA 73-76; CANR 17, 39; CDALB 1929-1941; CWRI 5; DA; DA3; DAB; DAC; DAM DRAM, MST, NOV; DLB 4, 11, 22, 102; EWL 3; EXPS; FANT; LAIT 3; MAICYA 1, 2; MAL 5; MTCW 1, 2; MTFW 2005; RGAL 4; RGSF 2; SATA 13; SSFS 1, 10, 19; SUFW; TUS

Thurman, Wallace (Henry) 1902-1934 ..... **BLC 3; HR 1:3; TCLC 6**
See also BW 1, 3; CA 124; CAAE 104; CANR 81; DAM MULT; DLB 51

Tibullus c. 54B.C.-c. 18B.C. .... **CMLC 36**
See also AW 2; DLB 211; RGWL 2, 3; WLIT 8

Ticheburn, Cheviot
See Ainsworth, William Harrison

Tieck, (Johann) Ludwig 1773-1853 .... **NCLC 5, 46; SSC 31**
See also CDWLB 2; DLB 90; EW 5; IDTP; RGSF 2; RGWL 2, 3; SUFW

Tiger, Derry
See Ellison, Harlan

Tilghman, Christopher 1946- .... **CLC 65**
See also CA 159; CANR 135, 151; CSW; DLB 244

Tillich, Paul (Johannes) 1886-1965 .... **CLC 131**
See also CA 5-8R; CAAS 25-28R; CANR 33; MTCW 1, 2

Tillinghast, Richard (Williford) 1940- .... **CLC 29**
See also CA 29-32R; 23; CANR 26, 51, 96; CP 2, 3, 4, 5, 6, 7; CSW

Timrod, Henry 1828-1867 .... **NCLC 25**
See also DLB 3, 248; RGAL 4

Tindall, Gillian (Elizabeth) 1938- ...... **CLC 7**
See also CA 21-24R; CANR 11, 65, 107; CN 1, 2, 3, 4, 5, 6, 7

Tiptree, James, Jr. **CLC 48, 50**
See Sheldon, Alice Hastings Bradley
See also DLB 8; SCFW 1, 2; SFW 4

Tirone Smith, Mary-Ann 1944- .... **CLC 39**
See also CA 136; CAAE 118; CANR 113; SATA 143

Tirso de Molina 1580(?)-1648 .... **DC 13; HLCS 2; LC 73**
See also RGWL 2, 3

Titmarsh, Michael Angelo
See Thackeray, William Makepeace

Tocqueville, Alexis (Charles Henri Maurice Clerel Comte) de 1805-1859 .. **NCLC 7, 63**
See also EW 6; GFL 1789 to the Present; TWA

Toer, Pramoedya Ananta 1925-2006 .... **CLC 186**
See also CA 197; CAAS 251; RGWL 3

Toffler, Alvin 1928- .... **CLC 168**
See also CA 13-16R; CANR 15, 46, 67; CPW; DAM POP; MTCW 1, 2

Toibin, Colm 1955- .... **CLC 162**
See also CA 142; CANR 81, 149; CN 7; DLB 271

Tolkien, J(ohn) R(onald) R(euel) 1892-1973 .... **CLC 1, 2, 3, 8, 12, 38; TCLC 137; WLC 6**
See also AAYA 10; AITN 1; BPFB 3; BRWC 2; BRWS 2; CA 17-18; CAAS 45-48; CANR 36, 134; CAP 2; CDBLB 1914-1945; CLR 56; CN 1; CPW 1; CWRI 5; DA; DA3; DAB; DAC; DAM MST, NOV, POP; DLB 15, 160, 255; EFS 2; EWL 3; FANT; JRDA; LAIT 1; LATS 1:2; LMFS 2; MAICYA 1, 2; MTCW 1, 2; MTFW 2005; NFS 8; RGEL 2; SATA 2, 32, 100; SATA-Obit 24; SFW 4; SUFW; TEA; WCH; WYA; YAW

Toller, Ernst 1893-1939 .... **TCLC 10**
See also CA 186; CAAE 107; DLB 124; EWL 3; RGWL 2, 3

Tolson, M. B.
See Tolson, Melvin B(eaunorus)

Tolson, Melvin B(eaunorus) 1898(?)-1966 .... **BLC 3; CLC 36, 105**
See also AFAW 1, 2; BW 1, 3; CA 124; CAAS 89-92; CANR 80; DAM MULT, POET; DLB 48, 76; MAL 5; RGAL 4

Tolstoi, Aleksei Nikolaevich
See Tolstoy, Alexey Nikolaevich

Tolstoi, Lev
See Tolstoy, Leo (Nikolaevich)
See also RGSF 2; RGWL 2, 3

Tolstoy, Aleksei Nikolaevich
See Tolstoy, Alexey Nikolaevich
See also DLB 272

Tolstoy, Alexey Nikolaevich 1882-1945 .... **TCLC 18**
See Tolstoy, Aleksei Nikolaevich
See also CA 158; CAAE 107; EWL 3; SFW 4

Tolstoy, Leo (Nikolaevich) 1828-1910 . **SSC 9, 30, 45, 54; TCLC 4, 11, 17, 28, 44, 79, 173; WLC 6**
See Tolstoi, Lev
See also AAYA 56; CA 123; CAAE 104; DA; DA3; DAB; DAC; DAM MST, NOV; DLB 238; EFS 2; EW 7; EXPS; IDTP; LAIT 2; LATS 1:1; LMFS 1; NFS 10; SATA 26; SSFS 5; TWA

Tolstoy, Count Leo
See Tolstoy, Leo (Nikolaevich)

Tomalin, Claire 1933- .... **CLC 166**
See also CA 89-92; CANR 52, 88; DLB 155

Tomasi di Lampedusa, Giuseppe 1896-1957
See Lampedusa, Giuseppe (Tomasi) di
See also CAAE 111; DLB 177; EWL 3; WLIT 7

Tomlin, Lily 1939(?)-
See Tomlin, Mary Jean
See also CAAE 117

Tomlin, Mary Jean **CLC 17**
See Tomlin, Lily

Tomline, F. Latour
See Gilbert, W(illiam) S(chwenck)

Tomlinson, (Alfred) Charles 1927- .... **CLC 2, 4, 6, 13, 45; PC 17**
See also CA 5-8R; CANR 33; CP 1, 2, 3, 4, 5, 6, 7; DAM POET; DLB 40; TCLE 1:2

Tomlinson, H(enry) M(ajor) 1873-1958 .... **TCLC 71**
See also CA 161; CAAE 118; DLB 36, 100, 195

Tonna, Charlotte Elizabeth 1790-1846 .... **NCLC 135**
See also DLB 163

Tonson, Jacob fl. 1655(?)-1736 .... **LC 86**
See also DLB 170

Toole, John Kennedy 1937-1969 ..... **CLC 19, 64**
See also BPFB 3; CA 104; DLBY 1981; MTCW 2; MTFW 2005

Toomer, Eugene
See Toomer, Jean

Toomer, Eugene Pinchback
See Toomer, Jean

Toomer, Jean 1894-1967 .. **BLC 3; CLC 1, 4, 13, 22; HR 1:3; PC 7; SSC 1, 45; TCLC 172; WLCS**
See also AFAW 1, 2; AMWS 3, 9; BW 1; CA 85-88; CDALB 1917-1929; DA3; DAM MULT; DLB 45, 51; EWL 3; EXPP; EXPS; LMFS 2; MAL 5; MTCW 1, 2; MTFW 2005; NFS 11; RGAL 4; RGSF 2; SSFS 5

Toomer, Nathan Jean
See Toomer, Jean

Toomer, Nathan Pinchback
See Toomer, Jean

Torley, Luke
See Blish, James (Benjamin)

Tornimparte, Alessandra
See Ginzburg, Natalia

Torre, Raoul della
See Mencken, H(enry) L(ouis)

Torrence, Ridgely 1874-1950 .... **TCLC 97**
See also DLB 54, 249; MAL 5

Torrey, E. Fuller 1937- .... **CLC 34**
See also CA 119; CANR 71, 158

Torrey, Edwin Fuller
See Torrey, E. Fuller

Torsvan, Ben Traven
See Traven, B.

Torsvan, Benno Traven
See Traven, B.

Torsvan, Berick Traven
See Traven, B.

Torsvan, Berwick Traven
See Traven, B.

Torsvan, Bruno Traven
See Traven, B.

Torsvan, Traven
See Traven, B.

Tourneur, Cyril 1575(?)-1626 .... **LC 66**
See also BRW 2; DAM DRAM; DLB 58; RGEL 2

Tournier, Michel 1924- .... **CLC 6, 23, 36, 95; SSC 88**
See also CA 49-52; CANR 3, 36, 74, 149; CWW 2; DLB 83; EWL 3; GFL 1789 to the Present; MTCW 1, 2; SATA 23

Tournier, Michel Edouard
See Tournier, Michel

Tournimparte, Alessandra
See Ginzburg, Natalia

Towers, Ivar
See Kornbluth, C(yril) M.

Towne, Robert (Burton) 1936(?)- ..... **CLC 87**
See also CA 108; DLB 44; IDFW 3, 4

Townsend, Sue **CLC 61**
See Townsend, Susan Lilian
See also AAYA 28; CA 127; CAAE 119; CANR 65, 107; CBD; CD 5, 6; CPW; CWD; DAB; DAC; DAM MST; DLB 271; INT CA-127; SATA 55, 93; SATA-Brief 48; YAW

Townsend, Susan Lilian 1946-
See Townsend, Sue

Townshend, Pete
See Townshend, Peter (Dennis Blandford)

Townshend, Peter (Dennis Blandford) 1945- .... **CLC 17, 42**
See also CA 107

Tozzi, Federigo 1883-1920 .... **TCLC 31**
See also CA 160; CANR 110; DLB 264; EWL 3; WLIT 7

Tracy, Don(ald Fiske) 1905-1970(?)
See Queen, Ellery
See also CA 1-4R; CAAS 176; CANR 2

Trafford, F. G.
See Riddell, Charlotte

Traherne, Thomas 1637(?)-1674 .. **LC 99; PC 70**
See also BRW 2; BRWS 11; DLB 131; PAB; RGEL 2

Traill, Catharine Parr 1802-1899 .. **NCLC 31**
See also DLB 99

Trakl, Georg 1887-1914 .... **PC 20; TCLC 5**
See also CA 165; CAAE 104; EW 10; EWL 3; LMFS 2; MTCW 2; RGWL 2, 3

Trambley, Estela Portillo **TCLC 163**
See Portillo Trambley, Estela
See also CA 77-80; RGAL 4

Tranquilli, Secondino
See Silone, Ignazio

Transtroemer, Tomas Gosta
See Transtromer, Tomas (Goesta)

Transtromer, Tomas (Gosta)
See Transtromer, Tomas (Goesta)
See also CWW 2

Transtromer, Tomas (Goesta) 1931- .... **CLC 52, 65**
See Transtromer, Tomas (Gosta)
See also CA 129; 17; CAAE 117; CANR 115; DAM POET; DLB 257; EWL 3; PFS 21

Transtromer, Tomas Gosta
See Transtromer, Tomas (Goesta)

Traven, B. 1882(?)-1969 .... **CLC 8, 11**
See also CA 19-20; CAAS 25-28R; CAP 2; DLB 9, 56; EWL 3; MTCW 1; RGAL 4

Trediakovsky, Vasilii Kirillovich 1703-1769 .... **LC 68**
See also DLB 150

Treitel, Jonathan 1959- .... **CLC 70**
See also CA 210; DLB 267

Trelawny, Edward John 1792-1881 .... **NCLC 85**
See also DLB 110, 116, 144

Tremain, Rose 1943- .... **CLC 42**
See also CA 97-100; CANR 44, 95; CN 4, 5, 6, 7; DLB 14, 271; RGSF 2; RHW

Tremblay, Michel 1942- .... **CLC 29, 102, 225**
See also CA 128; CAAE 116; CCA 1; CWW 2; DAC; DAM MST; DLB 60; EWL 3; GLL 1; MTCW 1, 2; MTFW 2005

Trevanian **CLC 29**
See Whitaker, Rod

Trevor, Glen
See Hilton, James

Trevor, William **CLC 7, 9, 14, 25, 71, 116; SSC 21, 58**
See Cox, William Trevor
See also BRWS 4; CBD; CD 5, 6; CN 1, 2, 3, 4, 5, 6, 7; DLB 14, 139; EWL 3; LATS 1:2; RGEL 2; RGSF 2; SSFS 10; TCLE 1:2

Trifonov, Iurii (Valentinovich)
See Trifonov, Yuri (Valentinovich)
See also DLB 302; RGWL 2, 3

Trifonov, Yuri (Valentinovich) 1925-1981 .... **CLC 45**
See Trifonov, Iurii (Valentinovich); Trifonov, Yury Valentinovich
See also CA 126; CAAS 103; MTCW 1

Trifonov, Yury Valentinovich
See Trifonov, Yuri (Valentinovich)
See also EWL 3

Trilling, Diana (Rubin) 1905-1996 . **CLC 129**
See also CA 5-8R; CAAS 154; CANR 10, 46; INT CANR-10; MTCW 1, 2

Trilling, Lionel 1905-1975 ..... **CLC 9, 11, 24; SSC 75**
See also AMWS 3; CA 9-12R; CAAS 61-64; CANR 10, 105; CN 1, 2; DLB 28, 63; EWL 3; INT CANR-10; MAL 5; MTCW 1, 2; RGAL 4; TUS

Trimball, W. H.
See Mencken, H(enry) L(ouis)

Tristan
See Gomez de la Serna, Ramon

Tristram
See Housman, A(lfred) E(dward)

Trogdon, William (Lewis) 1939-
See Heat-Moon, William Least
See also AAYA 66; CA 119; CAAE 115; CANR 47, 89; CPW; INT CA-119

Trollope, Anthony 1815-1882 .... **NCLC 6, 33, 101; SSC 28; WLC 6**
See also BRW 5; CDBLB 1832-1890; DA; DA3; DAB; DAC; DAM MST, NOV; DLB 21, 57, 159; RGEL 2; RGSF 2; SATA 22

Trollope, Frances 1779-1863 .... **NCLC 30**
See also DLB 21, 166

Trollope, Joanna 1943- .... **CLC 186**
See also CA 101; CANR 58, 95, 149; CN 7; CPW; DLB 207; RHW

Trotsky, Leon 1879-1940 .... **TCLC 22**
See also CA 167; CAAE 118

Trotter (Cockburn), Catharine 1679-1749 .... **LC 8**
See also DLB 84, 252

Trotter, Wilfred 1872-1939 .... **TCLC 97**

Trout, Kilgore
See Farmer, Philip Jose

Trow, George W.S. 1943-2006 .... **CLC 52**
See also CA 126; CANR 91

Troyat, Henri 1911-2007 .... **CLC 23**
See also CA 45-48; CANR 2, 33, 67, 117; GFL 1789 to the Present; MTCW 1

Trudeau, Garry B. **CLC 12**
See Trudeau, G.B.
See also AAYA 10; AITN 2

Trudeau, G.B. 1948-
See Trudeau, Garry B.
See also AAYA 60; CA 81-84; CANR 31; SATA 35, 168

Truffaut, Francois 1932-1984 ... **CLC 20, 101**
See also CA 81-84; CAAS 113; CANR 34

Trumbo, Dalton 1905-1976 .... **CLC 19**
See also CA 21-24R; CAAS 69-72; CANR 10; CN 1, 2; DLB 26; IDFW 3, 4; YAW

Trumbull, John 1750-1831 .... **NCLC 30**
See also DLB 31; RGAL 4

Trundlett, Helen B.
See Eliot, T(homas) S(tearns)

Truth, Sojourner 1797(?)-1883 ...... **NCLC 94**
See also DLB 239; FW; LAIT 2

Tryon, Thomas 1926-1991 .... **CLC 3, 11**
See also AITN 1; BPFB 3; CA 29-32R; CAAS 135; CANR 32, 77; CPW; DA3; DAM POP; HGG; MTCW 1

Tryon, Tom
See Tryon, Thomas

Ts'ao Hsueh-ch'in 1715(?)-1763 .... **LC 1**

Valle-Inclan, Ramon (Maria) del
1866-1936 .... **HLC 2; TCLC 5**
See del Valle-Inclan, Ramon (Maria)
See also CA 153; CAAE 106; CANR 80;
DAM MULT; DLB 134; EW 8; EWL 3;
HW 2; RGSF 2; RGWL 2, 3
Vallejo, Antonio Buero
See Buero Vallejo, Antonio
Vallejo, Cesar (Abraham)
1892-1938 .... **HLC 2; TCLC 3, 56**
See also CA 153; CAAE 105; DAM MULT;
DLB 290; EWL 3; HW 1; LAW; RGWL
2, 3
Valles, Jules 1832-1885 .... **NCLC 71**
See also DLB 123; GFL 1789 to the Present
Vallette, Marguerite Eymery
1860-1953 .... **TCLC 67**
See Rachilde
See also CA 182; DLB 123, 192
Valle Y Pena, Ramon del
See Valle-Inclan, Ramon (Maria) del
Van Ash, Cay 1918-1994 .... **CLC 34**
See also CA 220
Vanbrugh, Sir John 1664-1726 .... **LC 21**
See also BRW 2; DAM DRAM; DLB 80;
IDTP; RGEL 2
Van Campen, Karl
See Campbell, John W(ood, Jr.)
Vance, Gerald
See Silverberg, Robert
Vance, Jack 1916-
See Queen, Ellery; Vance, John Holbrook
See also CA 29-32R; CANR 17, 65, 154;
CMW 4; MTCW 1
Vance, John Holbrook CLC 35
See Vance, Jack
See also DLB 8; FANT; SCFW 1, 2; SFW
4; SUFW 1, 2
**Van Den Bogarde, Derek Jules Gaspard
Ulric Niven** 1921-1999 .... **CLC 14**
See Bogarde, Dirk
See also CA 77-80; CAAS 179
Vandenburgh, Jane CLC 59
See also CA 168
Vanderhaeghe, Guy 1951- .... **CLC 41**
See also BPFB 3; CA 113; CANR 72, 145;
CN 7
van der Post, Laurens (Jan)
1906-1996 .... **CLC 5**
See also AFW; CA 5-8R; CAAS 155;
CANR 35; CN 1, 2, 3, 4, 5, 6; DLB 204;
RGEL 2
van de Wetering, Janwillem 1931- ... **CLC 47**
See also CA 49-52; CANR 4, 62, 90; CMW
4
Van Dine, S. S. TCLC 23
See Wright, Willard Huntington
See also DLB 306; MSW
Van Doren, Carl (Clinton)
1885-1950 .... **TCLC 18**
See also CA 168; CAAE 111
Van Doren, Mark 1894-1972 .... **CLC 6, 10**
See also CA 1-4R; CAAS 37-40R; CANR
3; CN 1; CP 1; DLB 45, 284; MAL 5;
MTCW 1, 2; RGAL 4
Van Druten, John (William)
1901-1957 .... **TCLC 2**
See also CA 161; CAAE 104; DLB 10;
MAL 5; RGAL 4
Van Duyn, Mona 1921-2004 .... **CLC 3, 7, 63,
116**
See also CA 9-12R; CAAS 234; CANR 7,
38, 60, 116; CP 1, 2, 3, 4, 5, 6, 7; CWP;
DAM POET; DLB 5; MAL 5; MTFW
2005; PFS 20
Van Dyne, Edith
See Baum, L(yman) Frank

van Itallie, Jean-Claude 1936- .... **CLC 3**
See also CA 45-48; 2; CAD; CANR 1, 48;
CD 5, 6; DLB 7
Van Loot, Cornelius Obenchain
See Roberts, Kenneth (Lewis)
van Ostaijen, Paul 1896-1928 .... **TCLC 33**
See also CA 163
Van Peebles, Melvin 1932- .... **CLC 2, 20**
See also BW 2, 3; CA 85-88; CANR 27,
67, 82; DAM MULT
van Schendel, Arthur(-Francois-Emile)
1874-1946 .... **TCLC 56**
See also EWL 3
Vansittart, Peter 1920- .... **CLC 42**
See also CA 1-4R; CANR 3, 49, 90; CN 4,
5, 6, 7; RHW
Van Vechten, Carl 1880-1964 ... **CLC 33; HR
1:3**
See also AMWS 2; CA 183; CAAS 89-92;
DLB 4, 9, 51; RGAL 4
van Vogt, A(lfred) E(lton) 1912-2000 . **CLC 1**
See also BPFB 3; BYA 13, 14; CA 21-24R;
CAAS 190; CANR 28; DLB 8, 251;
SATA 14; SATA-Obit 124; SCFW 1, 2;
SFW 4
Vara, Madeleine
See Jackson, Laura (Riding)
Varda, Agnes 1928- .... **CLC 16**
See also CA 122; CAAE 116
Vargas Llosa, Jorge Mario Pedro
See Vargas Llosa, Mario
Vargas Llosa, Mario 1936- .. **CLC 3, 6, 9, 10,
15, 31, 42, 85, 181; HLC 2**
See Llosa, Jorge Mario Pedro Vargas
See also BPFB 3; CA 73-76; CANR 18, 32,
42, 67, 116, 140; CDWLB 3; CWW 2;
DA; DA3; DAB; DAC; DAM MST,
MULT, NOV; DLB 145; DNFS 2; EWL
3; HW 1, 2; LAIT 5; LATS 1:2; LAW;
LAWS 1; MTCW 1, 2; MTFW 2005;
RGWL 2; SSFS 14; TWA; WLIT 1
Varnhagen von Ense, Rahel
1771-1833 .... **NCLC 130**
See also DLB 90
Vasari, Giorgio 1511-1574 .... **LC 114**
Vasilikos, Vasiles
See Vassilikos, Vassilis
Vasiliu, George
See Bacovia, George
Vasiliu, Gheorghe
See Bacovia, George
See also CA 189; CAAE 123
Vassa, Gustavus
See Equiano, Olaudah
Vassilikos, Vassilis 1933- .... **CLC 4, 8**
See also CA 81-84; CANR 75, 149; EWL 3
Vaughan, Henry 1621-1695 .... **LC 27**
See also BRW 2; DLB 131; PAB; RGEL 2
Vaughn, Stephanie CLC 62
Vazov, Ivan (Minchov) 1850-1921 . **TCLC 25**
See also CA 167; CAAE 121; CDWLB 4;
DLB 147
Veblen, Thorstein B(unde)
1857-1929 .... **TCLC 31**
See also AMWS 1; CA 165; CAAE 115;
DLB 246; MAL 5
Vega, Lope de 1562-1635 ... **HLCS 2; LC 23,
119**
See also EW 2; RGWL 2, 3
Veldeke, Heinrich von c. 1145-c.
1190 .... **CMLC 85**
Vendler, Helen (Hennessy) 1933- ... **CLC 138**
See also CA 41-44R; CANR 25, 72, 136;
MTCW 1, 2; MTFW 2005
Venison, Alfred
See Pound, Ezra (Weston Loomis)
Ventsel, Elena Sergeevna 1907-2002
See Grekova, I.
See also CA 154

Verdi, Marie de
See Mencken, H(enry) L(ouis)
Verdu, Matilde
See Cela, Camilo Jose
Verga, Giovanni (Carmelo)
1840-1922 .... **SSC 21, 87; TCLC 3**
See also CA 123; CAAE 104; CANR 101;
EW 7; EWL 3; RGSF 2; RGWL 2, 3;
WLIT 7
Vergil 70B.C.-19B.C. ... **CMLC 9, 40; PC 12;
WLCS**
See Virgil
See also AW 2; DA; DA3; DAB; DAC;
DAM MST, POET; EFS 1; LMFS 1
Vergil, Polydore c. 1470-1555 .... **LC 108**
See also DLB 132
Verhaeren, Emile (Adolphe Gustave)
1855-1916 .... **TCLC 12**
See also CAAE 109; EWL 3; GFL 1789 to
the Present
Verlaine, Paul (Marie) 1844-1896 .. **NCLC 2,
51; PC 2, 32**
See also DAM POET; DLB 217; EW 7;
GFL 1789 to the Present; LMFS 2; RGWL
2, 3; TWA
Verne, Jules (Gabriel) 1828-1905 ... **TCLC 6,
52**
See also AAYA 16; BYA 4; CA 131; CAAE
110; CLR 88; DA3; DLB 123; GFL 1789
to the Present; JRDA; LAIT 2; LMFS 2;
MAICYA 1, 2; MTFW 2005; RGWL 2, 3;
SATA 21; SCFW 1, 2; SFW 4; TWA;
WCH
Verus, Marcus Annius
See Aurelius, Marcus
Very, Jones 1813-1880 .... **NCLC 9**
See also DLB 1, 243; RGAL 4
Vesaas, Tarjei 1897-1970 .... **CLC 48**
See also CA 190; CAAS 29-32R; DLB 297;
EW 11; EWL 3; RGWL 3
Vialis, Gaston
See Simenon, Georges (Jacques Christian)
Vian, Boris 1920-1959(?) .... **TCLC 9**
See also CA 164; CAAE 106; CANR 111;
DLB 72, 321; EWL 3; GFL 1789 to the
Present; MTCW 2; RGWL 2, 3
Viaud, (Louis Marie) Julien 1850-1923
See Loti, Pierre
See also CAAE 107
Vicar, Henry
See Felsen, Henry Gregor
Vicente, Gil 1465-c. 1536 .... **LC 99**
See also DLB 318; IDTP; RGWL 2, 3
Vicker, Angus
See Felsen, Henry Gregor
Vidal, Eugene Luther Gore
See Vidal, Gore
Vidal, Gore 1925- ...... **CLC 2, 4, 6, 8, 10, 22,
33, 72, 142**
See Box, Edgar
See also AAYA 64; AITN 1; AMWS 4;
BEST 90:2; BPFB 3; CA 5-8R; CAD;
CANR 13, 45, 65, 100, 132; CD 5, 6;
CDALBS; CN 1, 2, 3, 4, 5, 6, 7; CPW;
DA3; DAM NOV, POP; DFS 2; DLB 6,
152; EWL 3; INT CANR-13; MAL 5;
MTCW 1, 2; MTFW 2005; RGAL 4;
RHW; TUS
Viereck, Peter 1916-2006 .... **CLC 4; PC 27**
See also CA 1-4R; CAAS 250; CANR 1,
47; CP 1, 2, 3, 4, 5, 6, 7; DLB 5; MAL 5;
PFS 9, 14
Viereck, Peter Robert Edwin
See Viereck, Peter
Vigny, Alfred (Victor) de
1797-1863 .... **NCLC 7, 102; PC 26**
See also DAM POET; DLB 119, 192, 217;
EW 5; GFL 1789 to the Present; RGWL
2, 3

West, Dorothy 1907-1998 ...... **HR 1:3; TCLC 108**
　See also BW 2; CA 143; CAAS 169; DLB 76

West, (Mary) Jessamyn 1902-1984 ... **CLC 7, 17**
　See also CA 9-12R; CAAS 112; CANR 27; CN 1, 2, 3; DLB 6; DLBY 1984; MTCW 1, 2; RGAL 4; RHW; SATA-Obit 37; TCWW 2; TUS; YAW

West, Morris L(anglo) 1916-1999 ..... **CLC 6, 33**
　See also BPFB 3; CA 5-8R; CAAS 187; CANR 24, 49, 64; CN 1, 2, 3, 4, 5, 6; CPW; DLB 289; MTCW 1, 2; MTFW 2005

West, Nathanael 1903-1940 .. **SSC 16; TCLC 1, 14, 44**
　See also AMW; AMWR 2; BPFB 3; CA 125; CAAE 104; CDALB 1929-1941; DA3; DLB 4, 9, 28; EWL 3; MAL 5; MTCW 1, 2; MTFW 2005; NFS 16; RGAL 4; TUS

West, Owen
　See Koontz, Dean R.

West, Paul 1930- .... **CLC 7, 14, 96, 226**
　See also CA 13-16R; 7; CANR 22, 53, 76, 89, 136; CN 1, 2, 3, 4, 5, 6, 7; DLB 14; INT CANR-22; MTCW 2; MTFW 2005

West, Rebecca 1892-1983 ... **CLC 7, 9, 31, 50**
　See also BPFB 3; BRWS 3; CA 5-8R; CAAS 109; CANR 19; CN 1, 2, 3; DLB 36; DLBY 1983; EWL 3; FW; MTCW 1, 2; MTFW 2005; NCFS 4; RGEL 2; TEA

Westall, Robert (Atkinson) 1929-1993 .... **CLC 17**
　See also AAYA 12; BYA 2, 6, 7, 8, 9, 15; CA 69-72; CAAS 141; CANR 18, 68; CLR 13; FANT; JRDA; MAICYA 1, 2; MAICYAS 1; SAAS 2; SATA 23, 69; SATA-Obit 75; WYA; YAW

Westermarck, Edward 1862-1939 . **TCLC 87**

Westlake, Donald E. 1933- .... **CLC 7, 33**
　See also BPFB 3; CA 17-20R; 13; CANR 16, 44, 65, 94, 137; CMW 4; CPW; DAM POP; INT CANR-16; MSW; MTCW 2; MTFW 2005

Westlake, Donald Edwin
　See Westlake, Donald E.

Westmacott, Mary
　See Christie, Agatha (Mary Clarissa)

Weston, Allen
　See Norton, Andre

Wetcheek, J. L.
　See Feuchtwanger, Lion

Wetering, Janwillem van de
　See van de Wetering, Janwillem

Wetherald, Agnes Ethelwyn 1857-1940 .... **TCLC 81**
　See also CA 202; DLB 99

Wetherell, Elizabeth
　See Warner, Susan (Bogert)

Whale, James 1889-1957 .... **TCLC 63**
　See also AAYA 75

Whalen, Philip (Glenn) 1923-2002 .... **CLC 6, 29**
　See also BG 1:3; CA 9-12R; CAAS 209; CANR 5, 39; CP 1, 2, 3, 4, 5, 6, 7; DLB 16; WP

Wharton, Edith (Newbold Jones) 1862-1937 ... **SSC 6, 84; TCLC 3, 9, 27, 53, 129, 149; WLC 6**
　See also AAYA 25; AMW; AMWC 2; AMWR 1; BPFB 3; CA 132; CAAE 104; CDALB 1865-1917; DA; DA3; DAB; DAC; DAM MST, NOV; DLB 4, 9, 12, 78, 189; DLBD 13; EWL 3; EXPS; FL 1:6; GL 3; HGG; LAIT 2, 3; LATS 1:1;

MAL 5; MBL; MTCW 1, 2; MTFW 2005; NFS 5, 11, 15, 20; RGAL 4; RGSF 2; RHW; SSFS 6, 7; SUFW; TUS

Wharton, James
　See Mencken, H(enry) L(ouis)

Wharton, William (a pseudonym) 1925- .... **CLC 18, 37**
　See also CA 93-96; CN 4, 5, 6, 7; DLBY 1980; INT CA-93-96

Wheatley (Peters), Phillis 1753(?)-1784 ... **BLC 3; LC 3, 50; PC 3; WLC 6**
　See also AFAW 1, 2; CDALB 1640-1865; DA; DA3; DAC; DAM MST, MULT, POET; DLB 31, 50; EXPP; FL 1:1; PFS 13; RGAL 4

Wheelock, John Hall 1886-1978 .... **CLC 14**
　See also CA 13-16R; CAAS 77-80; CANR 14; CP 1, 2; DLB 45; MAL 5

Whim-Wham
　See Curnow, (Thomas) Allen (Monro)

Whisp, Kennilworthy
　See Rowling, J.K.

Whitaker, Rod 1931-2005
　See Trevanian
　See also CA 29-32R; CAAS 246; CANR 45, 153; CMW 4

White, Babington
　See Braddon, Mary Elizabeth

White, E. B. 1899-1985 .... **CLC 10, 34, 39**
　See also AAYA 62; AITN 2; AMWS 1; CA 13-16R; CAAS 116; CANR 16, 37; CDALBS; CLR 1, 21, 107; CPW; DA3; DAM POP; DLB 11, 22; EWL 3; FANT; MAICYA 1, 2; MAL 5; MTCW 1, 2; MTFW 2005; NCFS 5; RGAL 4; SATA 2, 29, 100; SATA-Obit 44; TUS

White, Edmund 1940- .... **CLC 27, 110**
　See also AAYA 7; CA 45-48; CANR 3, 19, 36, 62, 107, 133; CN 5, 6, 7; DA3; DAM POP; DLB 227; MTCW 1, 2; MTFW 2005

White, Elwyn Brooks
　See White, E. B.

White, Hayden V. 1928- .... **CLC 148**
　See also CA 128; CANR 135; DLB 246

White, Patrick (Victor Martindale) 1912-1990 ...... **CLC 3, 4, 5, 7, 9, 18, 65, 69; SSC 39; TCLC 176**
　See also BRWS 1; CA 81-84; CAAS 132; CANR 43; CN 1, 2, 3, 4; DLB 260, 332; EWL 3; MTCW 1; RGEL 2; RGSF 2; RHW; TWA; WWE 1

White, Phyllis Dorothy James 1920-
　See James, P. D.
　See also CA 21-24R; CANR 17, 43, 65, 112; CMW 4; CN 7; CPW; DA3; DAM POP; MTCW 1, 2; MTFW 2005; TEA

White, T(erence) H(anbury) 1906-1964 .... **CLC 30**
　See also AAYA 22; BPFB 3; BYA 4, 5; CA 73-76; CANR 37; DLB 160; FANT; JRDA; LAIT 1; MAICYA 1, 2; RGEL 2; SATA 12; SUFW 1; YAW

White, Terence de Vere 1912-1994 ... **CLC 49**
　See also CA 49-52; CAAS 145; CANR 3

White, Walter
　See White, Walter F(rancis)

White, Walter F(rancis) 1893-1955 ... **BLC 3; HR 1:3; TCLC 15**
　See also BW 1; CA 124; CAAE 115; DAM MULT; DLB 51

White, William Hale 1831-1913
　See Rutherford, Mark
　See also CA 189; CAAE 121

Whitehead, Alfred North 1861-1947 .... **TCLC 97**
　See also CA 165; CAAE 117; DLB 100, 262

Whitehead, Colson 1970- .... **CLC 232**
　See also CA 202

Whitehead, E(dward) A(nthony) 1933- .... **CLC 5**
　See Whitehead, Ted
　See also CA 65-68; CANR 58, 118; CBD; CD 5; DLB 310

Whitehead, Ted
　See Whitehead, E(dward) A(nthony)
　See also CD 6

Whiteman, Roberta J. Hill 1947- ...... **NNAL**
　See also CA 146

Whitemore, Hugh (John) 1936- .... **CLC 37**
　See also CA 132; CANR 77; CBD; CD 5, 6; INT CA-132

Whitman, Sarah Helen (Power) 1803-1878 .... **NCLC 19**
　See also DLB 1, 243

Whitman, Walt(er) 1819-1892 .. **NCLC 4, 31, 81; PC 3; WLC 6**
　See also AAYA 42; AMW; AMWR 1; CDALB 1640-1865; DA; DA3; DAB; DAC; DAM MST, POET; DLB 3, 64, 224, 250; EXPP; LAIT 2; LMFS 1; PAB; PFS 2, 3, 13, 22; RGAL 4; SATA 20; TUS; WP; WYAS 1

Whitney, Isabella fl. 1565-fl. 1575 ..... **LC 130**
　See also DLB 136

Whitney, Phyllis A(yame) 1903- .... **CLC 42**
　See also AAYA 36; AITN 2; BEST 90:3; CA 1-4R; CANR 3, 25, 38, 60; CLR 59; CMW 4; CPW; DA3; DAM POP; JRDA; MAICYA 1, 2; MTCW 2; RHW; SATA 1, 30; YAW

Whittemore, (Edward) Reed, Jr. 1919- .... **CLC 4**
　See also CA 219; 9-12R, 219; 8; CANR 4, 119; CP 1, 2, 3, 4, 5, 6, 7; DLB 5; MAL 5

Whittier, John Greenleaf 1807-1892 .... **NCLC 8, 59**
　See also AMWS 1; DLB 1, 243; RGAL 4

Whittlebot, Hernia
　See Coward, Noel (Peirce)

Wicker, Thomas Grey 1926-
　See Wicker, Tom
　See also CA 65-68; CANR 21, 46, 141

Wicker, Tom **CLC 7**
　See Wicker, Thomas Grey

Wideman, John Edgar 1941- ... **BLC 3; CLC 5, 34, 36, 67, 122; SSC 62**
　See also AFAW 1, 2; AMWS 10; BPFB 4; BW 2, 3; CA 85-88; CANR 14, 42, 67, 109, 140; CN 4, 5, 6, 7; DAM MULT; DLB 33, 143; MAL 5; MTCW 2; MTFW 2005; RGAL 4; RGSF 2; SSFS 6, 12, 24; TCLE 1:2

Wiebe, Rudy 1934- .... **CLC 6, 11, 14, 138**
　See also CA 37-40R; CANR 42, 67, 123; CN 1, 2, 3, 4, 5, 6, 7; DAC; DAM MST; DLB 60; RHW; SATA 156

Wiebe, Rudy Henry
　See Wiebe, Rudy

Wieland, Christoph Martin 1733-1813 .... **NCLC 17, 177**
　See also DLB 97; EW 4; LMFS 1; RGWL 2, 3

Wiene, Robert 1881-1938 .... **TCLC 56**

Wieners, John 1934- .... **CLC 7**
　See also BG 1:3; CA 13-16R; CP 1, 2, 3, 4, 5, 6, 7; DLB 16; WP

Wiesel, Elie 1928- ...... **CLC 3, 5, 11, 37, 165; WLCS**
　See also AAYA 7, 54; AITN 1; CA 5-8R; 4; CANR 8, 40, 65, 125; CDALBS; CWW 2; DA; DA3; DAB; DAC; DAM MST, NOV; DLB 83, 299; DLBY 1987; EWL 3; INT CANR-8; LAIT 4; MTCW 1, 2; MTFW 2005; NCFS 4; NFS 4; RGHL; RGWL 3; SATA 56; YAW

Wilson, Harriet
    See Wilson, Harriet E. Adams
    See also DLB 239
Wilson, Harriet E.
    See Wilson, Harriet E. Adams
    See also DLB 243
Wilson, Harriet E. Adams
    1827(?)-1863(?) .... **BLC 3; NCLC 78**
    See Wilson, Harriet; Wilson, Harriet E.
    See also DAM MULT; DLB 50
Wilson, John 1785-1854 .... **NCLC 5**
Wilson, John (Anthony) Burgess 1917-1993
    See Burgess, Anthony
    See also CA 1-4R; CAAS 143; CANR 2,
    46; DA3; DAC; DAM NOV; MTCW 1,
    2; MTFW 2005; NFS 15; TEA
Wilson, Katharina CLC 65
Wilson, Lanford 1937- .. **CLC 7, 14, 36, 197;
    DC 19**
    See also CA 17-20R; CABS 3; CAD; CANR
    45, 96; CD 5, 6; DAM DRAM; DFS 4, 9,
    12, 16, 20; DLB 7; EWL 3; MAL 5; TUS
Wilson, Robert M. 1941- .... **CLC 7, 9**
    See also CA 49-52; CAD; CANR 2, 41; CD
    5, 6; MTCW 1
Wilson, Robert McLiam 1964- .... **CLC 59**
    See also CA 132; DLB 267
Wilson, Sloan 1920-2003 .... **CLC 32**
    See also CA 1-4R; CAAS 216; CANR 1,
    44; CN 1, 2, 3, 4, 5, 6
Wilson, Snoo 1948- .... **CLC 33**
    See also CA 69-72; CBD; CD 5, 6
Wilson, William S(mith) 1932- .... **CLC 49**
    See also CA 81-84
Wilson, (Thomas) Woodrow
    1856-1924 .... **TCLC 79**
    See also CA 166; DLB 47
Winchilsea, Anne (Kingsmill) Finch
    1661-1720
    See Finch, Anne
    See also RGEL 2
Winckelmann, Johann Joachim
    1717-1768 .... **LC 129**
    See also DLB 97
Windham, Basil
    See Wodehouse, P(elham) G(renville)
Wingrove, David 1954- .... **CLC 68**
    See also CA 133; SFW 4
Winnemucca, Sarah 1844-1891 .... **NCLC 79;
    NNAL**
    See also DAM MULT; DLB 175; RGAL 4
Winstanley, Gerrard 1609-1676 .... **LC 52**
Wintergreen, Jane
    See Duncan, Sara Jeannette
Winters, Arthur Yvor
    See Winters, Yvor
Winters, Janet Lewis CLC 41
    See Lewis, Janet
    See also DLBY 1987
Winters, Yvor 1900-1968 .... **CLC 4, 8, 32**
    See also AMWS 2; CA 11-12; CAAS 25-
    28R; CAP 1; DLB 48; EWL 3; MAL 5;
    MTCW 1; RGAL 4
Winterson, Jeanette 1959- .... **CLC 64, 158**
    See also BRWS 4; CA 136; CANR 58, 116;
    CN 5, 6, 7; CPW; DA3; DAM POP; DLB
    207, 261; FANT; FW; GLL 1; MTCW 2;
    MTFW 2005; RHW
Winthrop, John 1588-1649 .... **LC 31, 107**
    See also DLB 24, 30
Wirth, Louis 1897-1952 .... **TCLC 92**
    See also CA 210
Wiseman, Frederick 1930- .... **CLC 20**
    See also CA 159
Wister, Owen 1860-1938 .... **TCLC 21**
    See also BPFB 3; CA 162; CAAE 108;
    DLB 9, 78, 186; RGAL 4; SATA 62;
    TCWW 1, 2

Wither, George 1588-1667 .... **LC 96**
    See also DLB 121; RGEL 2
Witkacy
    See Witkiewicz, Stanislaw Ignacy
Witkiewicz, Stanislaw Ignacy
    1885-1939 .... **TCLC 8**
    See also CA 162; CAAE 105; CDWLB 4;
    DLB 215; EW 10; EWL 3; RGWL 2, 3;
    SFW 4
Wittgenstein, Ludwig (Josef Johann)
    1889-1951 .... **TCLC 59**
    See also CA 164; CAAE 113; DLB 262;
    MTCW 2
Wittig, Monique 1935-2003 .... **CLC 22**
    See also CA 135; CAAE 116; CAAS 212;
    CANR 143; CWW 2; DLB 83; EWL 3;
    FW; GLL 1
Wittlin, Jozef 1896-1976 .... **CLC 25**
    See also CA 49-52; CAAS 65-68; CANR 3;
    EWL 3
Wodehouse, P(elham) G(renville)
    1881-1975 . **CLC 1, 2, 5, 10, 22; SSC 2;
    TCLC 108**
    See also AAYA 65; AITN 2; BRWS 3; CA
    45-48; CAAS 57-60; CANR 3, 33; CD-
    BLB 1914-1945; CN 1, 2; CPW 1; DA3;
    DAB; DAC; DAM NOV; DLB 34, 162;
    EWL 3; MTCW 1, 2; MTFW 2005; RGEL
    2; RGSF 2; SATA 22; SSFS 10
Woiwode, L.
    See Woiwode, Larry (Alfred)
Woiwode, Larry (Alfred) 1941- ... **CLC 6, 10**
    See also CA 73-76; CANR 16, 94; CN 3, 4,
    5, 6, 7; DLB 6; INT CANR-16
Wojciechowska, Maia (Teresa)
    1927-2002 .... **CLC 26**
    See also AAYA 8, 46; BYA 3; CA 183;
    9-12R, 183; CAAS 209; CANR 4, 41;
    CLR 1; JRDA; MAICYA 1, 2; SAAS 1;
    SATA 1, 28, 83; SATA-Essay 104; SATA-
    Obit 134; YAW
Wojtyla, Karol (Jozef)
    See John Paul II, Pope
Wojtyla, Karol (Josef)
    See John Paul II, Pope
Wolf, Christa 1929- .... **CLC 14, 29, 58, 150**
    See also CA 85-88; CANR 45, 123; CD-
    WLB 2; CWW 2; DLB 75; EWL 3; FW;
    MTCW 1; RGWL 2, 3; SSFS 14
Wolf, Naomi 1962- .... **CLC 157**
    See also CA 141; CANR 110; FW; MTFW
    2005
Wolfe, Gene 1931- .... **CLC 25**
    See also AAYA 35; CA 57-60; 9; CANR 6,
    32, 60, 152; CPW; DAM POP; DLB 8;
    FANT; MTCW 2; MTFW 2005; SATA
    118, 165; SCFW 2; SFW 4; SUFW 2
Wolfe, Gene Rodman
    See Wolfe, Gene
Wolfe, George C. 1954- .... **BLCS; CLC 49**
    See also CA 149; CAD; CD 5, 6
Wolfe, Thomas (Clayton)
    1900-1938 ...... **SSC 33; TCLC 4, 13, 29,
    61; WLC 6**
    See also AMW; BPFB 3; CA 132; CAAE
    104; CANR 102; CDALB 1929-1941;
    DA; DA3; DAB; DAC; DAM MST, NOV;
    DLB 9, 102, 229; DLBD 2, 16; DLBY
    1985, 1997; EWL 3; MAL 5; MTCW 1,
    2; NFS 18; RGAL 4; SSFS 18; TUS
Wolfe, Thomas Kennerly, Jr.
    1931- .... **CLC 147**
    See Wolfe, Tom
    See also CA 13-16R; CANR 9, 33, 70, 104;
    DA3; DAM POP; DLB 185; EWL 3; INT
    CANR-9; MTCW 1, 2; MTFW 2005; TUS

Wolfe, Tom CLC **1, 2, 9, 15, 35, 51**
    See Wolfe, Thomas Kennerly, Jr.
    See also AAYA 8, 67; AITN 2; AMWS 3;
    BEST 89:1; BPFB 3; CN 5, 6, 7; CPW;
    CSW; DLB 152; LAIT 5; RGAL 4
Wolff, Geoffrey 1937- .... **CLC 41**
    See also CA 29-32R; CANR 29, 43, 78, 154
Wolff, Geoffrey Ansell
    See Wolff, Geoffrey
Wolff, Sonia
    See Levitin, Sonia (Wolff)
Wolff, Tobias 1945- .... **CLC 39, 64, 172; SSC
    63**
    See also AAYA 16; AMWS 7; BEST 90:2;
    BYA 12; CA 117; 22; CAAE 114; CANR
    54, 76, 96; CN 5, 6, 7; CSW; DA3; DLB
    130; EWL 3; INT CA-117; MTCW 2;
    MTFW 2005; RGAL 4; RGSF 2; SSFS 4,
    11
Wolitzer, Hilma 1930- .... **CLC 17**
    See also CA 65-68; CANR 18, 40; INT
    CANR-18; SATA 31; YAW
Wollstonecraft, Mary 1759-1797 .... **LC 5, 50,
    90**
    See also BRWS 3; CDBLB 1789-1832;
    DLB 39, 104, 158, 252; FL 1:1; FW;
    LAIT 1; RGEL 2; TEA; WLIT 3
Wonder, Stevie 1950- .... **CLC 12**
    See also CAAE 111
Wong, Jade Snow 1922-2006 .... **CLC 17**
    See also CA 109; CAAS 249; CANR 91;
    SATA 112; SATA-Obit 175
Wood, Mrs. Henry 1814-1887 ...... **NCLC 178**
    See also CMW 4; DLB 18; SUFW
Woodberry, George Edward
    1855-1930 .... **TCLC 73**
    See also CA 165; DLB 71, 103
Woodcott, Keith
    See Brunner, John (Kilian Houston)
Woodruff, Robert W.
    See Mencken, H(enry) L(ouis)
Woolf, (Adeline) Virginia 1882-1941 .. **SSC 7,
    79; TCLC 1, 5, 20, 43, 56, 101, 123,
    128; WLC 6**
    See also AAYA 44; BPFB 3; BRW 7;
    BRWC 2; BRWR 1; CA 130; CAAE 104;
    CANR 64, 132; CDBLB 1914-1945; DA;
    DA3; DAB; DAC; DAM MST, NOV;
    DLB 36, 100, 162; DLBD 10; EWL 3;
    EXPS; FL 1:6; FW; LAIT 3; LATS 1:1;
    LMFS 2; MTCW 1, 2; MTFW 2005;
    NCFS 2; NFS 8, 12; RGEL 2; RGSF 2;
    SSFS 4, 12; TEA; WLIT 4
Woollcott, Alexander (Humphreys)
    1887-1943 .... **TCLC 5**
    See also CA 161; CAAE 105; DLB 29
Woolrich, Cornell CLC 77
    See Hopley-Woolrich, Cornell George
    See also MSW
Woolson, Constance Fenimore
    1840-1894 .... **NCLC 82; SSC 90**
    See also DLB 12, 74, 189, 221; RGAL 4
Wordsworth, Dorothy 1771-1855 . **NCLC 25,
    138**
    See also DLB 107
Wordsworth, William 1770-1850 .. **NCLC 12,
    38, 111, 166; PC 4, 67; WLC 6**
    See also AAYA 70; BRW 4; BRWC 1; CD-
    BLB 1789-1832; DA; DA3; DAB; DAC;
    DAM MST, POET; DLB 93, 107; EXPP;
    LATS 1:1; LMFS 1; PAB; PFS 2; RGEL
    2; TEA; WLIT 3; WP
Wotton, Sir Henry 1568-1639 .... **LC 68**
    See also DLB 121; RGEL 2
Wouk, Herman 1915- .... **CLC 1, 9, 38**
    See also BPFB 2, 3; CA 5-8R; CANR 6,
    33, 67, 146; CDALBS; CN 1, 2, 3, 4, 5,
    6; CPW; DA3; DAM NOV, POP; DLBY
    1982; INT CANR-6; LAIT 4; MAL 5;
    MTCW 1, 2; MTFW 2005; NFS 7; TUS

Literary Criticism Series
Cumulative Topic Index

This index lists all topic entries in Thompson Gale's *Children's Literature Review* (CLR), *Classical and Medieval Literature Criticism* (CMLC), *Contemporary Literary Criticism* (CLC), *Drama Criticism* (DC), *Literature Criticism from 1400 to 1800* (LC), *Nineteenth-Century Literature Criticism* (NCLC), *Short Story Criticism* (SSC), and *Twentieth-Century Literary Criticism* (TCLC). The index also lists topic entries in the Gale Critical Companion Collection, which includes the following publications: *The Beat Generation* (BG), *Feminism in Literature* (FL), *Gothic Literature* (GL), and *Harlem Renaissance* (HR).

Topic Index

NCLC Cumulative Nationality Index

Fouqué, Friedrich (Heinrich Karl) de la Motte **2**
Freytag, Gustav **109**
Goethe, Johann Wolfgang von **4, 22, 34, 90, 154**
Grabbe, Christian Dietrich **2**
Grimm, Jacob Ludwig Karl **3, 77**
Grimm, Wilhelm Karl **3, 77**
Hebbel, Friedrich **43**
Hegel, Georg Wilhelm Friedrich **46, 151**
Heine, Heinrich **4, 54, 147**
Herder, Johann Gottfried von **8**
Hoffmann, E(rnst) T(heodor) A(madeus) **2**
Hölderlin, (Johann Christian) Friedrich **16**
Humboldt, Alexander von **170**
Humboldt, Wilhelm von **134**
Immermann, Karl (Lebrecht) **4, 49**
Jean Paul **7**
Kant, Immanuel **27, 67**
Kleist, Heinrich von **2, 37**
Klinger, Friedrich Maximilian von **1**
Klopstock, Friedrich Gottlieb **11**
Kotzebue, August (Friedrich Ferdinand) von **25**
La Roche, Sophie von **121**
Ludwig, Otto **4**
Marx, Karl (Heinrich) **17, 114**
Mörike, Eduard (Friedrich) **10**
Novalis **13, 178**
Schelling, Friedrich Wilhelm Joseph von **30**
Schiller, Friedrich von **39, 69, 166**
Schlegel, August Wilhelm von **15, 142**
Schlegel, Friedrich **45**
Schleiermacher, Friedrich **107**
Schopenhauer, Arthur **51, 157**
Schumann, Robert **143**
Storm, (Hans) Theodor (Woldsen) **1**
Tieck, (Johann) Ludwig **5, 46**
Varnhagen, Rahel **130**
Wagner, Richard **9, 119**
Wieland, Christoph Martin **17, 177**

GREEK

Foscolo, Ugo **8, 97**
Solomos, Dionysios **15**

HUNGARIAN

Arany, Janos **34**
Madach, Imre **19**
Petofi, Sándor **21**

INDIAN

Chatterji, Bankim Chandra **19**
Dutt, Michael Madhusudan **118**
Dutt, Toru **29**

IRISH

Allingham, William **25**
Banim, John **13**
Banim, Michael **13**
Boucicault, Dion **41**
Carleton, William **3**
Croker, John Wilson **10**
Darley, George **2**
Edgeworth, Maria **1, 51, 158**
Ferguson, Samuel **33**
Griffin, Gerald **7**
Jameson, Anna **43**
Le Fanu, Joseph Sheridan **9, 58**
Lever, Charles (James) **23**

Maginn, William **8**
Mangan, James Clarence **27**
Maturin, Charles Robert **6, 169**
Merriman, Brian **70**
Moore, Thomas **6, 110**
Morgan, Lady **29**
O'Brien, Fitz-James **21**
Sheridan, Richard Brinsley **5, 91**

ITALIAN

Alfieri, Vittorio **101**
Collodi, Carlo **54**
Foscolo, Ugo **8, 97**
Gozzi, (Conte) Carlo **23**
Leopardi, Giacomo **22, 129**
Manzoni, Alessandro **29, 98**
Mazzini, Guiseppe **34**
Nievo, Ippolito **22**

JAMAICAN

Seacole, Mary Jane Grant **147**

JAPANESE

Akinari, Ueda **131**
Ichiyō, Higuchi **49**
Motoori, Norinaga **45**

LITHUANIAN

Mapu, Abraham (ben Jekutiel) **18**

MEXICAN

Lizardi, Jose Joaquin Fernandez de **30**
Najera, Manuel Gutierrez **133**

NORWEGIAN

Collett, (Jacobine) Camilla (Wergeland) **22**
Wergeland, Henrik Arnold **5**

POLISH

Fredro, Aleksander **8**
Krasicki, Ignacy **8**
Krasiński, Zygmunt **4**
Mickiewicz, Adam **3, 101**
Norwid, Cyprian Kamil **17**
Slowacki, Juliusz **15**

ROMANIAN

Eminescu, Mihail **33, 131**

RUSSIAN

Aksakov, Sergei Timofeevich **2, 181**
Bakunin, Mikhail (Alexandrovich) **25, 58**
Baratynsky, Evgenii Abramovich **103**
Bashkirtseff, Marie **27**
Belinski, Vissarion Grigoryevich **5**
Bestuzhev, Aleksandr Aleksandrovich **131**
Chernyshevsky, Nikolay Gavrilovich **1**
Dobrolyubov, Nikolai Alexandrovich **5**
Dostoevsky, Fedor Mikhailovich **2, 7, 21, 33, 43, 119, 167**
Gogol, Nikolai (Vasilyevich) **5, 15, 31, 162**
Goncharov, Ivan Alexandrovich **1, 63**
Granovsky, Timofei Nikolaevich **75**
Griboedov, Aleksandr Sergeevich **129**
Herzen, Aleksandr Ivanovich **10, 61**
Karamzin, Nikolai Mikhailovich **3, 173**
Krylov, Ivan Andreevich **1**
Lermontov, Mikhail Yuryevich **5, 47, 126**

Leskov, Nikolai (Semyonovich) **25, 174**
Nekrasov, Nikolai Alekseevich **11**
Ostrovsky, Alexander **30, 57**
Pavlova, Karolina Karlovna **138**
Pisarev, Dmitry Ivanovich **25**
Pushkin, Alexander (Sergeyevich) **3, 27, 83**
Saltykov, Mikhail Evgrafovich **16**
Smolenskin, Peretz **30**
Turgenev, Ivan **21, 37, 122**
Tyutchev, Fyodor **34**
Zhukovsky, Vasily (Andreevich) **35**

SCOTTISH

Baillie, Joanna **2, 151**
Beattie, James **25**
Blair, Hugh **75**
Campbell, Thomas **19**
Carlyle, Thomas **22, 70**
Ferrier, Susan (Edmonstone) **8**
Galt, John **1, 110**
Hogg, James **4, 109**
Jeffrey, Francis **33**
Lockhart, John Gibson **6**
Mackenzie, Henry **41**
Miller, Hugh **143**
Oliphant, Margaret (Oliphant Wilson) **11, 61**
Scott, Walter **15, 69, 110**
Stevenson, Robert Louis (Balfour) **5, 14, 63**
Thomson, James **18**
Wilson, John **5**
Wright, Frances **74**

SERBIAN

Karadžić, Vuk Stefanović **115**

SLOVENIAN

Kopitar, Jernej **117**
Prešeren, Francè **127**

SPANISH

Alarcon, Pedro Antonio de **1**
Bécquer, Gustavo Adolfo **106**
Caballero, Fernan **10**
Castro, Rosalia de **3, 78**
Espronceda, Jose de **39**
Larra (y Sanchez de Castro), Mariano Jose de **17, 130**
Martínez de la Rosa, Francisco de Paula **102**
Tamayo y Baus, Manuel **1**
Zorrilla y Moral, Jose **6**

SWEDISH

Almqvist, Carl Jonas Love **42**
Bremer, Fredrika **11**
Stagnelius, Eric Johan **61**
Tegner, Esaias **2**

SWISS

Amiel, Henri Frederic **4**
Burckhardt, Jacob (Christoph) **49**
Charriere, Isabelle de **66**
Gotthelf, Jeremias **117**
Keller, Gottfried **2**
Lavater, Johann Kaspar **142**
Meyer, Conrad Ferdinand **81**
Wyss, Johann David Von **10**

UKRAINIAN

Shevchenko, Taras **54**

VENEZUELAN

Bello, Andrés **131**

Nationality Index

NCLC-182 Title Index

ISBN-13: 978-0-7876-9853-9
ISBN-10: 0-7876-9853-9

90000